A Comic Vision of Sacred Kinship

For Julie, Peter, and Michael,
with love

MASCOT BOOKS
an imprint of Amplify Publishing Group

www.mascotbooks.com

A Comic Vision of Sacred Kinship: Poetry about the Crowning of a Living (Loving) Soul: Readings of C. S. Lewis, Roger Scruton, Shakespeare, Goethe, and Plato

For more information, please contact:
Mascot Books, an imprint of Amplify Publishing Group
620 Herndon Parkway, Suite 320
Herndon, VA 20170
info@mascotbooks.com

Library of Congress Control Number: 2022921265

CPSIA Code: PRS0223A
ISBN-13: 978-1-63755-260-5

Printed in the United States

A Comic Vision of Sacred Kinship

Poetry about the Crowning of a Living (Loving) Soul

Readings of C. S. Lewis, Roger Scruton, Shakespeare, Goethe, and Plato

Alan Griesinger

CONTENTS

Follow the Breath (In)

Breathe,
Oh,
Breathe
To be a living soul . . .

It
Is
The
Gift beyond compare

Of
An
Unbroken
Line of ancestry.

Again
We
Wake
With breath that lifts the breast,

(Each
A
Perfect
End unto itself)

That
Would
Be
Given again to the source

Of
Breath
And life
And all and everything.

I wrote the first stanza of this poem at the beginning of my inquiry. The poem grew to its present shape over the years. Like a lighthouse and a North Star, it warned me about getting off track and guided me home.

As I reread and edited the work near the end of the process, I noticed that the phrase "all and everything" kept showing up throughout the text like a refrain in a song. Since it has taken upon itself this kind of importance, I need to acknowledge that I've borrowed the phrase from Neville Coghill's translation of Chaucer's "The Knight's Tale." It appears in the speech in which Theseus delivers his "sentence" to the court on the events that have unfolded (for the reader as well as his subjects) over the course of the narrative. Since the narrative involves the death of a young knight, his sentence (the meaning) must include the sentence of death that hangs over all human life, like the sword of Damocles. Theseus has much to say, but I've abbreviated it to these six lines:

There is no help for it, all take the track,
For all must die and there is none comes back.
Who orders this but Jupiter the King,
The Prince and Cause of all and everything,
Converting all things back into the source
From which they were derived, to which they course?

In the last four lines, Theseus appears to be asking a question: "Who orders this?" But at the same time, he is answering the question by affirming that "this" is ordered by a sacred king. I argue in my book that the conversion he describes is like a hinge on which all and everything turns to reveal what it means to be a living soul.

Introduction

On Poetry That Rescues the Soul for Health and Happiness

As I did in the preface of my first book, it's only fair to advise the reader that the readings in this book are much closer to poetry than scholarship for a simple reason: I'm not a scholar. I'm an interested party, a layman in these matters that have concerned human beings for as long as we have been human beings. By virtue of being a language-using member of that species, I have been granted access to their thoughts, which have been expressed in texts and artifacts handed down from previous generations, and I can't help thinking about them. So here I am with my thoughts.

Since I taught English to junior high and high school students in a small public school for twenty-eight years in the Finger Lakes region of Upstate New York, my thoughts are closely related to that community of dairy farms, vineyards, Widmer's winery, and the small businesses along Main Street. Like a writer who experiments with content, form, and style, I had the opportunity over those years to limit and refine my subject in order to effectively communicate. I quickly discovered that my students needed to know at the deepest level why I had been authorized to teach them. For thousands of years, students have tested a teacher's knowledge, judgment, and good sense. My trial by fire, while difficult, helped me to learn from year to year how to serve the children of that community.

As it was in my first book, it's still the case that I approach the subject of *this* book—the crowning of a living, loving soul—with a great longing to understand the world and myself. In my first book, I did readings of Chaucer and Shakespeare to body forth a comic vision of Wisdom. In this book, I conduct readings of C. S. Lewis, Roger Scruton, and Plato to consider what the crowning of a living soul might entail. As I advised the reader in the preface of my first book, I'm still like my friend Jonathan playing Bach at an Eastman Music School recital, who brought to life for himself and for us the composer's musical legacy. The performance may have involved intense study—of other pieces by Bach, of music history, of music theory, and so on, but all this is subsumed finally in the act of bringing the music to life. Why does Bach attract such interest? What poetry better than his to hear thousands of physical notes composing themselves into a beautiful, otherworldly whole.

What is the act that brings this life to life? I will be arguing that we need poetry to help us answer the question. When I was a child, we would say the Lord's Prayer in church. The whole congregation recited it at the prescribed place in the service. At the school I attended from grades six to twelve, the day began with a brief service, which included a recitation of the Lord's Prayer. This is how I learned it by heart. As the Lord's Prayer has it, if I can forgive the trespasses of others, maybe my own will be forgiven. These are the acts with which I'm concerned, for my own trespasses weigh on me. I hold the Lord's Prayer to be poetry of a high order, as it informs a body so full of years with the spiritual truth of poetry. Note how this central passage in the prayer relies on the metaphor of trespassing, which employs a well-understood physical (and illegal) act in this world to describe acts that have meaning. We "trespass," the poetry suggests, when we don't treat another as we would want to be treated.

Not only is this book closer to poetry in that it's an expressive vehicle of its author but it also tends, as it strives toward that expression, to be about poetry. Since I was an English teacher, it was part of my job to read and think about the subject. After years of reading and thinking about the poetry of Homer, Chaucer, and Shakespeare, I'm inclined to believe that the self-awareness of their work as poetry has made me more aware of my own nature as a human subject who lives in two worlds—one that's earthly (or material, if you prefer) and the other that's heavenly (or immaterial, if you prefer). Maybe it was easier to generate that awareness in poetry where human beings shared the stage with ghostly figures, which is the case with all three of these authors. Homer's epics about human beings are full of gods; the gods are fully involved with the action in Chaucer's "The Knight's Tale"; and in the middle acts of *A Midsummer Night's Dream*, the king and queen of fairies have much to do with the matching, unmatching, and mating of human beings.

In 2016, long after I retired from teaching, my teaching life readied me for reading *The Soul of the World* by Roger Scruton. It helped me realize that a love of poetry is closely involved with an unspoken (and perhaps repressed) interest in the soul. I wrote this book to look into the question. I know very well that it only "scratches the surface." Scruton's book in turn led me to *The Allegory of Love* by C. S. Lewis. I sensed that both authors wrote their books to revive the thought of a soul in readers like myself who, thanks to our modern secular culture, left it for dead. In gratitude for their efforts, I have sought to render for others what moved me in their work.

I couldn't have written this book without poetry. At important points in this narrative, I rely on metaphors to frame with a material object the immaterial subject I'll be discussing. For example, in Book One, I use Andrew Wyeth's little sailboat in *Below Dover* (see page 65) as a vehicle to express, as Wyeth does, the way a human subject lives in two worlds and embodies them both. Wyeth's little boat prepares the reader for the way C. S. Lewis develops this idea in his exposition of love and allegory, which is the subject of my Book Two. To assist with the transition from Book Two to Book Three, I imagine for the reader a bridge arching over the gap between the work of C. S. Lewis and Roger Scruton. The two writers are addressing the same subject, the presence of the soul (the sacred) in this life, but they have decidedly different "takes" on the subject (more about this later). To assist with the transition from Book Three to Book Four, I imagine for the reader that we can ride the centaur Chiron, as Goethe's Faust did, from a world characterized by division and alienation to a sacred wonderland (see page 373).

Here, at the beginning, to assist the reader's transition into the book itself, I invoke that scene in *Macbeth* at the beginning of act 4, where the three witches are throwing gross bits into a boiling cauldron:

FIRST WITCH: Round about the cauldron go;
In the poisoned entrails throw.
Toad, that under cold stone
Days and nights has thirty-one
Sweltered venom sleeping got,
Boil thou first i' th' charmèd pot.

(The witches circle the cauldron)

ALL: Double, double toil and trouble;
Fire burn, and cauldron bubble.

SECOND WITCH: Fillet of a fenny snake
In the cauldron boil and bake.
Eye of newt and toe of frog,
Wool of bat and tongue of dog,
Adder's fork and blindworm's sting,
Lizard's leg and howlet's wing,
For a charm of powerful trouble,
Like a hell-broth boil and bubble.

ALL: Double, double toil and trouble;
Fire burn, and cauldron bubble.

They go on in this vein for twenty more lines, mixing in more ugly bits to make a venomous medium for viewing the future. To fulfill the purpose of my introduction, I'd like the reader to hold in mind this image of a pot into which certain ingredients are thrown. The witches are making a brew, a soup, a substance that stands for the life of Macbeth, and which gives the witches a view of it. These three would corrupt Macbeth's soul with the fatal story of his Fate.

In contrast with the witches of *Macbeth* and this image of his soul, Shakespeare has also given us the fairies of *A Midsummer Night's Dream* and the image of a wood around the city of Athens. In my first book, I compared this wood to an alembic in alchemy, and I do so again in this one. Into it all the ingredients of the play are thrown, and here they are transformed by the alchemy of poetry into the liquid gold of timeless love. Like the bubbling cauldron in *Macbeth*, the wood is a fictional representation of a soul, only in this play it's a soul made whole by love and restored to its true nature. As we participate in the play along with the actors, we experience what it means to be a living soul. Shakespeare, I'm convinced, believed that we are a soul and that like creation itself it is good because it expresses the love of its creator. We learn from these plays and others that some ingredients can poison the whole, and some ingredients can rescue the whole for health and happiness.

With that, I'd like to introduce other simples that have gone into the making of this book. It's my hope that the meaning that emerges from these pages will have the restorative effect on the reader that it has had on its author.

The Format of a Sermon

Since the summer of 2016, I've been reading and thinking about the soul in Scruton's title (I'm writing this in 2020). After sixty years of not thinking about it, I was out of practice. When we were children, every Sunday we went to Saint Christopher's, and Reverend Patty would give a sermon on an Old or New Testament text. He would read the text and then tell us what it meant. I didn't enjoy them or him very much. As an adult, once a year for twenty years, I attended a seven-day silent retreat at the Springwater Center for Meditative Inquiry. Every day of the retreat, the teacher would give a talk to encourage us, the effect of her voice magnified by the hours of silence prior to it. In the first few years, the talks were commentaries on koans. Just as in the minister's sermon, the teacher would recite the koan and then say what came to mind about it, what it meant to her at the moment of speaking. In Christianity, the subject is God; in Buddhism and Zen, it is Mind. It seems to me that Scruton, the Anglican philosopher, has room for both East and West in his thought. For example, his references to the figures of Brahman and Atman in *The Soul of the World* come at important moments and help him make his argument about two approaches to the sacred: the cosmological-intellectual-objective approach and the psychological-emotional-subjective approach. C. S. Lewis, another modern Anglican philosopher, calls our guarantor of true values the Tao in *The Abolition of Man*. He, too, makes room for the religious vocabularies of East and West. The Tao, Lewis tells us, informs both cultures with a life affirming spirit, and human beings have been aware of this Way for millennia.

For my inquiry, I have borrowed the format of Reverend Patty's sermons and of those talks at the Springwater Center. I've taken as my text the words from Genesis: "And the Lord God formed man of the dust of the ground, and breathed into his nostrils the breath of life; and man became a living soul" (Genesis 2:7).

The rest of my "talk" addresses the question: "What does it mean to be a living soul?" I've borrowed the format of a sermon, but I've not been ordained to give one. I'm just an interested party.

At some point, I think it was in 2017, a title occurred to me that would justify yet another commentary on Scruton's work. I would call it "The Poetry of Roger Scruton," for poetry, not philosophy, is the field with which I'm more acquainted. In May 2019, I began writing in earnest, and in the spring of 2020, I completed a rough draft of the text. After a pause of several months, as I explain in my postscript, I added a commentary on Plato's *Republic.*

Book One describes a significant transition in my thinking and outlook. It meanders through some brief readings and finishes with the personal experience described in the next section of my introduction. In Book Two, I do a reading of the first two chapters of *The Allegory of Love* by C. S. Lewis, which I've called "The Poetry of C. S. Lewis," and then in Book Three I do a reading of the first chapter of *The Soul of the World,* "Believing in God," which I knew would be called "The Poetry of Roger Scruton" long before I began writing it. Book Four, titled "The Survival Value of Sacred Wonderlands," is an extended commentary on the way an ordinary person, like myself, as opposed to an Abraham or a Buddha, can approach the sacred. Scruton introduces the idea of survival value in his first chapter, and Lewis refers to the allegories in his book as wonderlands. The two come together in the title of my Book Four. In my postscript, I find parallels in the form and content of Plato's and Scruton's arguments that helped me to interpret both texts.

Near the end of my book, I quote a passage from *The Soul of the World,* in which Scruton compares a human subject's consciousness to an archaeological dig that has layers. Consciousness, Lewis and Scruton maintain, is one. It can't be divided, I imagine, for that way madness lies. Nevertheless, we tell stories that reveal the layers of consciousness, Scruton points out, "as though each layer is somehow 'earlier' than the one that rests on it." My book is much like this image of a tell with layers. Book One, as I've mentioned, is the earliest. Just as philosophy in the West begins with the myths of Homer, my inquiry begins with the mythic poetry of Genesis, medieval allegory, and Shakespeare. From there it progresses (as early Western poetry did) into the thoughts of great philosophers. In my book, they are the thoughts of C. S. Lewis, Roger Scruton, and Plato. I confess that Book One is the most subjective layer of my inquiry. I've included my intuitions about the matter, even though they manifest as something struggling to be born, because my life as a questioning human subject began with readings in literature, the field of inquiry with which I'm most familiar.

If I extend the analogy with an archeological dig a little further, it suggests a different way for the reader to dig into my inquiry, this "tell" of consciousness. For those readers interested in Plato, they might like to begin with the topmost layer, my postscript on the *Republic*. Book Four can easily be read as a stand-alone piece, and its review of Books Three and Two will serve as an introduction to those readings. If the book is read in this way, the subjectivity of Book One comes last, even though it came first. That said, there are advantages to reading the book in the usual order as the text builds on examples and ideas already discussed.

Pilgrimages

Part 1: Sanctuaries Our Greatest Poet Has Made for Us

My wife and I had our first date in the fall of 1968, and we took our first road trip together over the summer of 1969. A friend of ours from the Cleveland Institute of Music got a summer job in the orchestra of the Marlborough Music Festival, so we went there to hear him and Pablo Casals play. Our main objective, though, was the Stratford Shakespeare Festival in Stratford, Ontario. We had been English majors in college, and we shared a love of Shakespeare. In both our destinations, we pitched a tent in a public campground. The one at Stratford, called the Fairgrounds, had recently been occupied by a herd of cows, so their continuing presence added a little local color to our nights. We have been going to Stratford ever since. We missed some years when the kids were little, but it has been our annual pilgrimage after they flew the nest. We were determined to see every play in the canon. Stratford supplied most of them, but we finished the lot in 2010, when we saw Michael Hayden play Richard II in Washington, DC.

In addition to these pilgrimages and familiarity with the canon as a whole, I read *Much Ado About Nothing* every year from 1988 to 2002 with juniors in my AP English class, and I read *A Midsummer Night's Dream*, *Hamlet*, and a handful of sonnets every year from 1984 to 2002 with seniors in my AP English class. For me, this, too, was like an annual pilgrimage to sanctuaries that our greatest poet has made for us. Thanks to the richness of this exposure with hundreds of students, the words, the music, the situations, and the themes are deeply impressed on my imagination.

Part 2: The Sanctuary Where We Are at Home

On First Looking into Chapman's Homer

Much have I travell'd in the realms of gold,
And many goodly states and kingdoms seen;
Round many western islands have I been
Which bards in fealty to Apollo hold.
Oft of one wide expanse had I been told
That deep-brow'd Homer ruled as his demesne;
Yet did I never breathe its pure serene
Till I heard Chapman speak out loud and bold:
Then felt I like some watcher of the skies
When a new planet swims into his ken;
Or like stout Cortez when with eagle eyes
He star'd at the Pacific—and all his men
Look'd at each other with a wild surmise—
Silent, upon a peak in Darien.

John Keats, 1816

In the summer of 2016, I read that Prince Charles had knighted an English philosopher whose name I had not heard before. I went online and found a video of him being interviewed by a former student as they walked through the green fields of his farm in Wiltshire. It was my first look into the world of Roger Scruton. Looking back, I now know why it was so inviting. Here's a transcription of what was said in a three-minute segment of a tour that went on for about an hour. The reader has to imagine the natural pauses and the speaker's somewhat labored breathing as he finds his way on the path. The thought, though, isn't labored at all. It moves effortlessly from beginning to end:

> *It's hard to find a transcendental source for moral values given the skepticism about religion so we have to look for other sources. It's been very much part of the consciousness of Western civilization since the enlightenment that there are other sources. One must open one's eyes to nature and to the human world and see, as it were, the immanence of value. When things speak to you, shine at you, when the light that is present in everything shines through—that's essentially what we mean by aesthetic values, or what we ought to mean by it. Beauty isn't this casual thing that you might choose to be interested in or not, just as someone might choose to be interested in chocolate or something. It's, if you like, it's the thing that attaches us to the world in the first place. That is the thing that is telling us, "You belong here," and you in response saying, "Yes, I do belong here because you are here."*

I'm pausing the transcription a moment to note what he has just imagined for his companion. He imagines that the beauty of the world (or Beauty-of-the-World if Scruton has personified her in a kind of allegory) can speak to us. An otherworldly presence affirms that we have come home. Not only that but we can also reply to and affirm the presence of the one who has spoken, "Yes, I'm at home now because of you." From the images of them together in a green field, from the sound of his voice, which was somewhat labored but steady, and from what he was saying, I had an impression of a man who was indeed at home—on his beautiful farm and in his thoughts.

In the pause that follows, his companion remarks:
So only we can recognize beautiful things.

And he replies:

Only human beings. It's part of our self-consciousness, our understanding, that we are in the world in a questioning relationship with it. I think everybody is open to the experience of beauty and to what I have been saying, and in moments will perceive the truth of them. But people turn away from it because the truth is difficult and can be uncomfortable. And people turn away from it and go back to consuming, to excitements, you know, distractions. And that's reasonable. I'm not saying they shouldn't do that, but they're missing out on something. Maybe missing out on everything that matters.

His companion asks:

And what does matter in life?

And he replies:

Well, there's no one thing that matters. You matter, your life matters, and what you make of it, but also you can only make anything of your life if you recognize that others matter more. It's a relationship with others, which is where mattering begins. And not just human others, the otherness of the world, the world that stands out there inviting your attention, and the other who invites not just your attention but love and compassion and all the other positive things we feel for each other.

"You matter." He said this in response to his companion's question. Her presence and participation prompted him to put together a thought, in two words, that holds a worldview. Scruton is a philosopher, and he's perfectly aware of the freight that the words "matter" and "mattering" carry. In philosophy, Matter is the physical something, the gross unshaped stuff, that's the opposite of Mind. This impression of matter completely changes in the context here, where he suggests that people who willfully ignore beauty may be missing out on everything that "matters" in life. This is common usage. It's not a particularly interesting thought, but the word *matter* here no longer refers to physical matter. It denotes meaning. He is saying that people who willfully ignore beauty are missing out on those things that have profound meaning for us.

His companion asks him to be more specific. What *does* "matter?" What makes this life meaningful, intelligible, purposeful? And he answers, "You matter." You belong here. You are important in the grand scheme of things. You mean something. You, as you have already said, can recognize beautiful things.

"Matter" has transcended that mute, unintelligent stuff and now has a spiritual quality, for meaning is a spiritual matter. There's magic in the mutuality of an otherworldly "You" (otherworldly because it stands for the metaphysical reality of a self-conscious subject who is being addressed) combined with otherworldly "mattering" (otherworldly because the word here denotes meaning), for the word *matter* still refers to the material stuff out of which things are made. "You matter" holds a worldview in which his companion's life is intrinsically physical and meaningful. But beauty and meaning don't reveal themselves in isolation, he warns. As in this case, relationship with others is where mattering and meaning begins.

I would argue that during the course of this dialogue Scruton makes the experience of Beauty a real experience. We aren't just imagining Beauty; it exists as surely as the world itself exists. As they speak back and forth, reflecting, imagining, and speaking for themselves, the other in the dialogue confirms the presence of an objective reality, and Beauty is at the heart of it.

Part 3: A Pilgrimage to Scrutopia Lost and Regained

I read a number of Scruton's books through the summer, fall, and winter of 2016. I was especially interested in *The Soul of the World*. In early 2017, I applied and was accepted to participate in a weeklong seminar, his first annual Scrutopia Summer School, conducted in and around his farm in Wiltshire. As it turned out, I wasn't able to attend due to family obligations. In my place, I sent him both of my books, along with a cover letter that documented those ideas in our writings I thought we shared. Lo and behold, I received a lovely email from him. He thanked me for the books and agreed that we had a similar outlook, for he had looked through my texts.

"You matter" for me now was not just a thought that I had heard spoken by an image on my computer. Consider the kindness of this very busy man. It would have been the easiest thing in the world to have ignored the letter and the books I sent him. I have no standing in the world of letters to speak of other than what I've written in my books and what I wrote to him. What he said to his companion in the video, someone he knew well, in essence was said to me in his letter. He had devoted some time to tell me "You matter."

Part 4: Revisiting the Site (Sight) of a Childhood Experience

In the summer of 2017, my wife and I joined our eldest son and his family on their vacation in Nantucket. For me, it was also a kind of pilgrimage because I wanted to revisit, after sixty years, the hotel where I had a remarkable experience as a child during a family dinner. I arranged for the family to have dinner at that hotel on the second of our three nights. It's no longer called the Gordon Folger, and the layout had been changed from what it was in the 1950s, so it didn't match what I remembered. We ate in a new dining room that had been added when they remodeled the place. The manager showed me around, and luckily the room where my family took meals sixty years ago was still there. It was being used, however, for a different purpose. Of course, I didn't relive the experience. It can't be done. The pilgrimage was not a failure though. Once home, I was moved to write what is now chapter 2 of Book One about my childhood experience. So the writing began, and this first fruit could now be tossed into the alembic of my inquiry.

A Window into Shakespeare's Soul Finally Opened

Sometime in 2017 I found a book on my bookshelf that I had bought years before at the Stratford Festival but had never opened. It was *Shakespeare's*

Window into the Soul by Martin Lings. This discovery came at the perfect time, and I quickly read it. The view through Lings's window was one more "simple" tossed into the mental soup that was starting to bubble over the course of that year. Like Scruton, Lings would recover the sacred, which he thought was being phased out of Western culture since the time of the Renaissance. With his focus on the sacred, he interprets a number of Shakespeare's plays as allegories about characters who (like Everyman in the medieval play called *Everyman*) go a journey to find their souls. Over and over it's the same story. Just as the soul is One, it has one story. It is always about one going a journey to find one's soul. Reading that book convinced me that I could profitably read Shakespeare's works allegorically. (Note well: I freely admit his works can be read any number of ways.) It also convinced me that the canon could be profitably read as one long story, one long confession, as Goethe said of his own work. Lings's interest in *All's Well That Ends Well* prompted me to study it for myself to test this new interpretive frame. Later in the fall, I wrote "And Man Became a Living Soul" to outline in general terms the shape of my project. Before I could continue, though, I knew I had to do a great deal of reading, so I stopped writing and studied for two years. That need to study brought me to *The Allegory of Love*, Spenser's *The Faerie Queene*, and Goethe's major works—like *Faust*, *The Sorrows of Young Werther*, and *Wilhelm Meister's Apprenticeship*. The latter includes a novella titled *Confessions of a Beautiful Soul*. Due to space considerations, I didn't include a reading of it in this book. Perhaps another time, for it fits perfectly into this inquiry as the whole of *Wilhelm Meister* does.

The Pairing of Lewis and Scruton

Part 1: A Common Objective

When I read *The Soul of the World*, it awakened an interest in the soul. Allegory, I thought from familiarity with the mystery play called *Everyman*, was a literary form about the soul so this led me to Lewis's book. It turned out to be a perfect fit with my inquiry, as I hope to show. Lewis's text helped quite directly with the question: "What does it mean to be a living soul?" In his reading of *De Mundi Universitate sive Megacosmus et Microcosmus* by Bernardus Sylvestris, Lewis includes the following quote from the beginning of the work when the allegorical figure of Nature initiates creation by complaining in her own voice to the allegorical figure of Mind:

> *Lo! Matter, eldest of all things, would fain*
> *Be limited by shape and born again.*

Lewis informs us that:

> *I have quoted these words from the speech of Nature with which the book opens. The goddess is addressing Noys [Mind] . . . and pleading the cause of matter; the remainder of the book relates in detail the answering of her prayer. (*The Allegory of Love, *pages 113–114)*

The allegorical figure of Nature prays—just as human beings do—for the stuff of life (even ourselves) to be a well-wrought thing in itself and not just a lump in a mishmash; for the love of a larger intelligence; for the strength of purpose endowed by a larger intelligence; in short, for rebirth as a living soul (in terms that resonate with the story of Christ's passion). Nature's prayer, I believe, expresses the spirit of Lewis's enterprise. He prays that the world he imagines, with help from classical and medieval poets, makes the world he imagines more possible.

Throughout the book, Lewis suggests a tension between two ontologies: Dante's interest in the soul as the primary unitary substance of life and a modern scientist's interest in physical matter as the primary substance of life. (Of course, the word *substance* has a range of meanings. The online *Stanford Encyclopedia of Philosophy* informs us that, translated from its roots, it means "something that stands under or grounds things." It's like the foundation of a house or the bottom of a ship. From that foundation of meaning in its roots, the *Stanford Encyclopedia* also tells us that "the substances in a given philosophical system are those that, according to the system, are the foundational or fundamental entities of reality." When I consider "an accident in a substance," the Aristotelean concept that plays a crucial role in Lewis's book, I'm therefore tempted to picture substance as that without which there is nothing. As such, it's loaded with ontological meaning. Whether substance is material or immaterial is a question for inquiry, one of many in this inquiry about what it means to be a living soul. In the end, I found Scruton's definition of substance in *Kant: A Very Short Introduction* to be helpful. Scruton writes: "A substance is that which is able to exist independently and which supports the properties that depend upon it" (see pages 36–37). It may be helpful to keep this definition in mind when we try to understand the role that the soul of the world, anima mundi, plays in Scruton's *The Soul of the World*. Lewis is aware that the world can be known either allegorically or scientifically, but the world science knows is only a shadow presence in his narrative. Instead, he presents allegorical wonderlands that reknit what was divided by a dualistic worldview without formally and directly confronting it as a scientific worldview. Perhaps Lewis leaves the scientific position as a shadow presence because he understands that Dante's interest and a scientist's interest are incommensurable. Because he wasn't prepared to fully engage with a scientist's interest in this book, he concentrates on recovering the wonderlands of allegory. (Ten years later, Lewis wrote *The Abolition of Man*, which directly confronts the effects on human beings of our modern worldview.)

Writing seventy years after *The Allegory of Love*, Roger Scruton engages the issue of the two interests. In the end, however, both writers share a common objective: *they would persuade their readers that there's an opening to the sacred in this world.* Lewis finds it in allegorical stories. Scruton finds it, for the most part, in philosophical reasoning, but his poetry appeals to our sentiments as well. We are attracted, for example, to the beauty of his writing. I have already mentioned earlier in this introduction that my Book One describes a significant transition in my thinking and outlook. The zeitgeist had carried me along for many years in a strong secular current, but then an eddy in the middle of it threw me against the rock of Scruton's philosophy. I borrow the New Testament metaphor of a rock to convey the impression of a solid, ontological, epistemological, ethical, and aesthetic foundation for the conduct of a life that emerged from Scruton's writings, but he doesn't advocate for a specific religion. He's interested, I would say, in the bedrock of human thought and culture. He shares this interest with C. S. Lewis, the bedrock being the fusing of sensibles and insensibles in beautiful forms that promote human flourishing—like poetry, philosophy, architecture, music, painting, and scripture. Lewis helps us to grasp this foundation by telling a story about the way an expressive form of poetry called allegory developed over centuries. In *The Soul of the World*, Scruton constructs for us a philosophic foundation by proposing "a kind of cognitive dualism." From this first principle, he builds an argument that reopens for human subjects an approach to the sacred.

In *The Allegory of Love*, Lewis only suggests that the world can be interpreted either allegorically or scientifically. Scruton, on the other hand, argues in chapter 2 of *The Soul of the World* from well-established philosophic precedent that "the world can be understood in two incommensurate ways, the way of science and the way of interpersonal understanding." He writes:

> *Spinoza was perhaps the first to argue that the world is one thing, seen in two (at least two) distinct ways. Thought and extension were, for Spinoza, two attributes of a single unified reality. Both delivered a complete form of knowledge: we could know the world as extension, through the study of physics. And through this study we would know, eventually, all that there is to be known. But the resulting science would make no mention of ideas, or of the mind as their vehicle. Likewise, through the study of ideas, we could know the world as thought, and through this study too we would come to know all that is to be known. But the two studies would be incommensurable.*

Scruton adds that Kant had a similar approach:

> *Our world, he argues, can be seen from the point of view of the understanding, in which case we know it as a web of causal connections*

> *laid out in space and time and subject to universal and necessary laws. But certain items within that world can be seen, indeed must be seen, in another way, from the perspective of practical reason. That which, from the point of view of the understanding, is subject to biological laws that determine its behavior is, from the point of view of practical reason, a free agent, obedient to the laws of reason. These two points of view are incommensurable. (These two quotes are from* The Soul of the World, *pages 35–36.)*

Scruton openly acknowledges the split between the world of science and the world of interpersonal understanding, and with great skill he advocates for the Lebenswelt —the lifeworld shared by language-using, symbol-interpreting, self-conscious human beings—as the world wherein human subjects still have access to the sacred. It's a world that *emerges* from the material world studied by science. Despite the dominance of science in our culture, human subjects still live in the Lebenswelt, whether they are aware of it or not, because this is where the sensible and insensible worlds are fused and have meaning. Like Lewis, Scruton would restore poetry in all its forms to a place of respect in our culture, for human subjects who consciously or unconsciously ignore or reject the poetry of this lifeworld will be divided from their own nature. This leads to a rootless, unsettled life.

Part 2: The Train That Moves but Never Leaves the Station

As I reported at the beginning of this section, my reading of *The Allegory of Love* has helped me quite directly with the question: "What does it mean to be a living soul?" Lewis establishes in our minds—by recovering for us the form of allegory as understood by classical and medieval poets—the sense of oneness that is the essential characteristic of allegory and of the soul. He establishes this oneness in our minds with fictions that assume the oneness of mind. To that end, he removes, with metaphoric sleight of hand at the beginning of his book, the temporal foundation on which science rests. He has us imagine humanity as a train. We are passengers on a train that moves from station to station, just as the reader of Lewis's book will move from chapter to chapter. Lewis's train, however, never leaves any of the stations. Like the reader of his book, we are free to revisit previous stations or to jump ahead to the last chapter. Wherever we are, the mind of humanity is actually and always one. I would argue that with this image of the train, which moves but which never leaves the station, Lewis formally disarms the notion that literature or philosophy proceeds the way an ordinary train progresses along a route to get to a distant destination, our destiny. His train is one mind and contains all the stations. On this train, we can go back as well as forward. We aren't required to leave Plato, Aristotle, Aquinas, and their ideas about transcendent values forever behind. We aren't necessarily destined to progress to a postmodern station where men have no chests (Lewis's description of heartless human automatons in *The Abolition of Man*). In C. S. Lewis's allegorical world, there is no time, and there is nothing missing that we require for our happiness. We take in Lewis's whole argument when we glimpse the wholeness of his train.

Part 3: The Sacred, the Human Subject, and the Soul

Scruton has helped me quite directly in *The Soul of the World* with the question: "What does it mean to be a human subject?" I think it's much the same question as "What does it mean to be a living soul?" Scruton has a slightly different focus in order to make a new argument and to engage a new generation of skeptical readers. In his introductory chapter, "Believing in God," he builds a case for how we can approach the sacred (the soul of the world) even though he acknowledges that the sacred is and must always be a mystery:

> *That God is present among us and communicating directly with us is a central claim of the Old Testament. This "real presence" or shekhinah is, however, a mystery. God reveals himself by concealing himself, as he concealed himself from Moses in the burning bush, and as he conceals himself from his worshippers in the Tabernacle (mishkhan) and the Holy of Holies. (*The Soul of the World, *page 10)*

How do we approach the real presence of God (the soul of the world) if he reveals himself by concealing himself? This is the problem Scruton sets before us. After wrestling with the question throughout the first chapter, he goes back and forth at the end of it concerning the "veracity" of the sacred—whether there's anything there to believe. He credits the skeptical view of it even as he invites the reader with his argument to believe that people can and have experienced the sacred in this life. And not just a famous figure like Moses. After all, Moses was but a lonely herdsman and a fugitive on the backside of the desert when God found him and spoke to him through the burning bush.

Scruton writes in chapter 3 that the concept of the human subject is "the defining feature of the human condition, and the feature to which the mystery of the world is owed." He describes the human subject in this way, I suspect, to prepare us for the next paragraph, where he introduces the idea of the soul. The mystery of the sacred, he argues, is closely related to the mystery that's always present in a human subject's relationships with other human subjects:

> *In all our responses to each other, whether love or hate, affection or disaffection, approval or disapproval, anger or desire, we look into the other, in search of that unattainable horizon from which he or she addresses us. We are animals swimming in the currents of causality, who relate to each other in that way. Each human object is also a subject, addressing us in looks gestures, and words, from the transcendental horizon of the "I." Our responses to others aim toward that horizon, passing on beyond the body to the being it incarnates. It is this feature of our interpersonal responses that gives such compelling force to the myth of the soul, of the true but hidden self that is veiled by the flesh.* (The Soul of the World, *page 74)*

We are not just objects swimming in the currents of causality, he insists. If we were just objects, then a secular science could explain us the way it explains and can predict the trajectory of a rocket. Within this veil of flesh, we are subjects who engage in relationships with other subjects. From these encounters, we sense the mystery of a self (our own and that of another) veiled by the flesh, and this, he argues, gives rise to the idea of a soul. Because this self is free in a way that a rocket is not free, it is not limited or constrained by the order of nature the way a rocket is limited and constrained. In the penultimate sentence of the first chapter, Scruton makes a crucial argument concerning a human subject's "search of that unattainable horizon," where we sense the presence of the sacred in the world, in others, and in ourselves:

> *This "reaching beyond" of the religious moment is not different, I shall suggest, from the transcendental urge of reason itself. (*The Soul of the World, *page 26)*

Reason, he argues, is not constrained by the natural order that science studies. It is urged by its own internal logic to "reach beyond" in its search for knowledge.

Is the soul a myth? Scruton calls it a myth, but before he leaves chapter 3, he explains why some regard it as a myth or a fiction. This sense of a soul, he writes:

> *is not an unalterable given; it can be educated, turned in new directions, disciplined through virtues, and corrupted through vice. In some cases of extreme autism it may even be lacking, as it is lacking in animals. But learning to direct your attitudes to the horizon of another's being, from which he in turn directs his gaze—this requires a discipline that goes further than mere respect. In all that touches what is deepest and most lasting in our lives—religious faith, erotic love, friendship, family ties, and the enjoyment of art, music and literature—we address the horizon from which the other's gaze is seeking us. Moral education involves the maintenance of this overreaching intentionality, so as to make possible, in the hardest circumstances, to look the other person in the I. That is what people mean by spiritual discipline, and it is what Plato calls "the care of the soul." (*The Soul of the World, *page 75)*

Scruton tells a story here that's like an allegory or a myth about a hero or a heroine fighting an evil dragon. Scruton's allegory or myth, however, describes the triumph of virtue in everyday interpersonal relationships. We discipline ourselves even "in the hardest circumstances" to see another as a human subject like ourselves. Borrowing Plato's expression of it, he calls this discipline "the care of the soul." I believe Scruton would have us infer from his allegory or myth that those not engaged in the care of the soul are not likely to think that such a thing or such a practice exists.

In chapter 5, "Facing Each Other," Scruton adds context to "the myth of the soul" by developing the concept of a "myth of origins" with his reading of the Fall in Genesis. In a chapter titled "In Defense of Poetry," I conclude my book with this and two other examples of the concept (see pages 495–512). Like the story he tells about the myth of the soul, a myth of origin is "a fiction which tells a true story." The ones he tells in my last chapter perform for us the magic of an art which turns an airy nothing into a word (like *soul* or *Creation*). Thanks to the language that we have been learning since birth, we have the words, and the words move us to imagine the thing to which they refer, even if it's not a thing in space and time. Scruton addresses the mystery of these words with the stories he tells; like a detective, he is much moved to look into it.

Part 4: A Relationship with *The Soul of the World*

How do we approach the real presence of God (the soul of the world)? In my reading of his argument, Scruton implies an intimate relationship between the soul of the world (the substance of things "out there") and his own soul (the substance of a human subject). When the divine beauty of the world "shines through," it lights up the divine beauty of that which perceives it. Because my interest in Scruton's thoughts has given me this thought, I need to consider the "window," the poetry, which has conveyed it. For that, let's return to the walk Scruton had with his companion through the green fields of his farm, where he imagines the Beauty of the world telling him, "You belong here," and he imagines replying to the Beauty of the world, "Yes, I do belong here because you are here." Scruton engages his companion with the sort of allegory that Lewis describes in his book. There's a compelling rhythm and dynamic in this little allegorical dialogue, and it moves me to add an additional thought having to do with Scruton's inquiry into the sacred. I imagine this time *the soul of the world* saying to him and to us, "You belong here," and our own souls reply, "Yes, we do belong here because you are here." A sense of the soul emerges in relationship with another subject. This relationship is our window. In the case at hand, as we read through the chapter titled "Believing in God" in my Book Three, it's a relationship with the mind, the reasoning, the soul of Roger Scruton, who has framed this window on the soul of the world.

A Crown of Sacred Kingship

In his book on Shakespeare, Martin Lings praised Simon Martini's *Annunciation* as an example of sacred art. I found it online and knew immediately that it would be the figurehead and the frontispiece for my inquiry and for the book I hoped to write. The painting celebrates that moment when, for believing Christians, the spiritual form of the world was made flesh and crowned creation with a golden radiance. (Speaking of which, all the paintings I've collected are available online. They deserve to be rescued from a black-and-white limbo for their full effect. The gold of Martini's *Annunciation* helps to tell the story as do the colors of the other works.) The good news of the Gospels repeatedly reminded Christians of a greater, more splendid kingdom than that of Caesar. In that moment of annunciation, the home of a carpenter's wife was transformed into a celestial throne room, where each of the four figures we can see in the painting is crowned with the spiritual power of a living soul. The author of it all, the soul of the world, remains hidden. The soul of the world, though, has his angels, and they serve as mediums to the sacred. Martini makes it clear in his painting, as Scruton does, that the presence of the sacred in this world is realized in relationship, in the face-to-face, eye to eye (I to I) contact between Gabriel and Mary, which takes the form of the golden words "Ave [Maria] gratia plena Dominus tecum."

In addition to this painting, I have to confess that the Netflix series about the life of Elizabeth Regina, *The Crown*, sparked my interest in a crown as a concrete manifestation of sacred kingship. The opening sequence of each episode mesmerizes the viewer with pictures and music that give the crown a mystical power, and the stories that follow develop for the audience how this particular queen answers the question: What does it mean to be the soul of a nation?

As part of my research for much of 2018, I read the works by Goethe outlined above. I also read a very good book about him by John Armstrong, which mentioned that Goethe liked to think about his ideal reader. When he was in Rome, he saw a painting of Saint Catherine and wrote of it in a letter:

> *I found a female Saint, an exquisite picture; Raphael has made her healthy, secure, youthful; but she's not frigid or unsophisticated. I'm going to read my Iphigenia to her.* (Love, Life, Goethe, *page 164)*

Iphigenia was a work Goethe had written earlier, but which he was transcribing into verse during his time in Rome. That's where he got to see Raphael's paintings in the flesh. Goethe had a knack for making the best of a situation, and his characters bear this out. Just as Raphael could bring Saint Catherine back to life to serve as Goethe's ideal reader, Goethe liked to conjure up mythical figures, like Helen of Troy and Chiron the centaur, to serve as inspirational ideals and teachers. It's the magic of art.

I think it's fair to say the work I have been doing ever since I embarked on the project is like a very long letter to the mind of Roger Scruton. He was my ideal reader. In addition, I hoped that some other summer I would be able to attend his summer school. That hope or fantasy ended, however, on the night of January 12, 2020, when I read the news that Roger Scruton had died.

Writing now many months later, this is what I can say about that moment. Over the previous autumn and winter, day after day, I had been immersed in his thoughts, and this after almost four years of reading a number of his books. My immersion during those many months was a relationship, a give-and-take of ideas and insights. He would speak, and I would respond; this went on week after week. Throughout this process, I pictured him as I had seen him online, an active man in mind and body. Word of his death negated that image. It felt like the rug had been pulled out from under the entire project, even though my relationship with the man himself was so slight. As naturally as I breathe to live, though, the work continued. Just as we still have life, we still have his gift, the poetry of his thought (an eternal summer) about the soul of the world. It's the magic of art. This relationship with a text is the theme I develop in Book Four and again in the postscript.

Martini's figures aren't the only ones crowned with a sacred light in my book. I have gathered for my presentation of what it means to be a living soul a word-painting filled with other pilgrim souls who project a sacred light of wholeness and health into the world. We see a crown of love (in our imaginations) over the heads of Arcite and Palamon at the end of "The Knight's Tale." We see it over the heads of the four Athenian lovers in *A Midsummer Night's Dream*, when they wake from a dreamless sleep that has made their "eyeballs roll with wonted sight." In the last scene of Goethe's *Faust*, we see that Goethe has given him a spectacular crown, with all kinds of spiritual figures embedded in it; in place of radiant light that a painting would provide, they sing words of praise over the living soul of Faust as it rises into heavenly spheres. Having been thoroughly tested with trials of worldliness, Helena humbly wears the crown at the end of *All's Well That Ends Well*. If I were producing the play *Everyman*, I would have him wearing a crown of renewed faith at the end as he goes to his reckoning. In my reading of the play, I imagine Hamlet wearing the crown of sacred kingship as he selflessly settles the question of succession with his last breath.

Artists have depicted radiant crowns, like the ones we see in Martini's painting on the cover of this book, for thousands of years. They suggest the light and warmth that the sun possesses radiating into the world. Notice the similarity between this description of a crown and Scruton's words to his companion as they walked through the green fields of his farm:

> *When things speak to you, shine at you, when the light that is present in everything shines through—that's essentially what we mean by aesthetic values, or what we ought to mean by it.*

Dear reader, I hope that my reading of the many texts and paintings in this book conveys the light and warmth shining at us from a crown of poetry and philosophy.

Book One

A Sacred Space and Time

Chapter 1

And Man Became a Living Soul

Marc Chagall's

Moses with the Burning Bush

A Pilgrimage to a Sacred Place

And the Lord God formed man of the dust of the ground, and breathed into his nostrils the breath of life; and man became a living soul.

Genesis 2:7

Poor soul, the center of my sinful earth . . .

William Shakespeare, "Sonnet 146"

So much depends
upon

a red wheel
barrow

glazed with rain
water

beside the white
chickens.

William Carlos Williams, "The Red Wheelbarrow"

And as imagination bodies forth
The forms of things unknown, the poet's pen
Turns them to shapes and gives to airy nothing
A local habitation and a name.

A Midsummer Night's Dream, act 5, scene 1

In *The Canterbury Tales*, Chaucer's characters embark on a pilgrimage to a sacred place, the great cathedral where Thomas à Becket was martyred. This is something that people have done and still do in the real world. Because a pilgrimage has to do with a spiritual goal, however, it has the character of a metaphor: the movement from London to Canterbury is like a change of heart and mind. My first book, *A Comic Vision of Great Constancy: Stories about Unlocking the Wisdom of Everyman*, interprets "The Knight's Tale" as a kind of parable about a spiritual shift from one form of love to another. The main character's "heart" must go a journey from the love of an object (*cupiditas* in the Latin of the medieval church) to love of the whole from which the object derives (*caritas* in Latin). Like the church in Canterbury that refers us to the martyrdom of Becket, *caritas* as a concept refers to the presence of divine love. I argue in the book that "The Knight's Tale" and Shakespeare's retelling of it, *A Midsummer Night's Dream*, are designed to represent that presence, not as a concept, but as the experience represented in the poem and the play. We each judge for ourselves the accuracy of that representation, I suppose, according to the degree we are moved by it.

Something there is, though, that has spoken out of Chaucer's tales and Shakespeare's plays, for they have moved millions with the power of a creator's love for his creation. A narrative may be required since we learn in them that the presence of divine love reveals itself in several acts, featuring first the form of love called *cupiditas* and then the other called *caritas*. The two forms appear to be as different as day and night or a hand grasping and a hand letting go, but they are in fact the darkness and the light of one day, the grasping and letting go of one hand, the two sides of the same coin, two waves of the same ocean, and the potency of a woman and a man in one child. Each one of us is one like this and potent with desire, imagination, and a strong will to create a home that's fit for ourselves and our families. To achieve this home, the old stories tell us, we need to go a journey to restore our health.

I can say this because Chaucer tells us, in the prologue to *The Canterbury Tales*, that the men and women of his day made a pilgrimage to a sacred place like Canterbury to regain their health (their haleness, holiness, or wholeness) "when that they were sick" (all quotes of "The Knight's Tale" are from the Neville Coghill translation). This is the purpose that frames the tales that follow, and Shakespeare follows in Chaucer's footsteps. The tales and the plays address us as pilgrims who aim to end in a better place (Why else would we join in their entertainments?), and they would heal specifically those illnesses that lay us low because we are divided in ourselves and from the world. Our authors have a point. Like the characters we walk with on this pilgrimage, we passionately want what we don't have, and disappointment may darken the way we look at the world. Like the characters we walk with, though, we can learn from their mistakes and our own the true source of discontent and division. As Titania tells Oberon in *A Midsummer Night's Dream*, concerning the rains that have flooded the lands around Athens:

> *And this same progeny of evils comes*
> *From our debate, from our dissension;*
> *We are their parents and originals.*

Over the course of their midsummer night, all the lovers wake from their dissensions to find themselves "new in amity." As we walk with them (in their shoes, if you will), we wake with them as one who wants (lacks) nothing, and the content radiates to all in one's compass. In *A Comic Vision of Great Constancy*, I describe how these experiences of disappointment unlock the Wisdom of Everyman. There's a pattern of behavior that can be recognized. In this book, I have reframed the argument slightly to revive a concept long left for dead in our secular age and in my own understanding. In this book on sacred kingship, I argue that these fictional characters and we who walk with them wake to the power and freedom of a living soul.

So much depends upon the red wheelbarrow, the actual and the metaphorical heart that carries us through every second of our lives (with apologies to Dr. William Carlos Williams for transplanting his image). We live by it, and we live for what we love. In addition to being a physical organ, the heart is a desperate longing stuck in a muddle of organs, entrails, glands, and the entire nervous system. In contrast with the heart's darkness, it's easy to love the wisdom that's sleek and portable, like a silver bullet. Information, our modern form of Wisdom, can go around the world three times in the twinkling of an eye and land on anyone's screen as pristine as a god sprung from the forehead of Zeus. But the heart is different. It's personal. The soul is like the heart in this. I have to say of it, as Shakespeare does, that it's the center of *my* sinful earth, nobody else's.

After a long life of my heart's countless heartbeats, I now realize the extent to which I've ignored the importance of this tireless servant in my life even though I owe my life to it, and I feel this way about many things I take for granted, even though I owe my life to them. As I write this, I imagine that hearts all over the world are stopping, and yet here I am, alive and breathing the sweet air. But if *my* heart stops, well, that's a different matter. So I wonder about my life and why it continues. I know that no scientist ever will determine why I was born and why I continue to live. We see every day just by driving to the grocery store that at any moment whether we live or die is a matter of inches. So I wonder about the center of my sinful earth and the life I've made out of everything I've ever said or done or thought.

That's why, for as long as I have a heart that lives for what it loves, in those hours wrested from material obligations of an earthly life, I read poets and sacred texts to learn what they have to say about love. This inquiry has prompted a question about the soul that hovers around the subject of love in our literature. It's strikes me with some force that, like the heart, the soul is something else I've taken for granted. A presumption of knowledge set the idea of a soul on the shelf where it sat as a cold case. I have my excuse. The zeitgeist made me do it! When life is reduced to natural causes and effects, men and women will shed the soul as naturally as a snake sheds its skin. Nevertheless, something is asking with great seriousness "What does it mean to be a living soul?" It's as if my sinful earth were in the balance to be weighed, as if my life depended on an answer.

Despite a zeitgeist that refuses to acknowledge it, the question beats on the door of the self in time with the heart telling the heart-stopping tale of my life. Knock. Knock. "Who's there?" (the question with which *Hamlet* begins). And who is asking whom? The knocking stirs things up. The feeling of it shadows habitual behaviors accumulated over a life lived with little regard for what it might mean to be a living soul. What's happening? Who *is* there? What to do? To triage the question, it seems best for the time being to do no harm to others or myself. That will take some doing, but (if possible) it may clear a decent space for the inquiry.

Even though the question involves what could be called an "airy nothing," there must be something to examine. It can't be nothing. I follow, therefore, the airy nothing that gives me life—the breath of life. Fish gotta swim, and they evolved, we're told, into birds that gotta fly. As for me, as a species of person who has lived by reading and teaching literature, I have to conclude that I'm fated to swim and fly in the great sea and sky of timeless poetry. And so I set off, immersed in that which projects from time to time a hologram of a living soul.

Metaphors and Meaning

You have a reputation of being alive, but you are dead. Wake up!

Revelation 3:2–3

I counsel you to buy from me gold refined in the fire, so you can become rich; and white clothes to wear, so you can cover your shameful nakedness; and salve to put on your eyes, so you can see.

Revelation 3:18

I've mused on these lifelines over a lifetime of reading, made them my own, and from them made my own. They take the form of narratives, allegories, similes, symbols, and other figures of speech that give to airy nothing a shape and a name. They are vehicles imagined by the poet to convey us to the tenor, the sanctuary of meaning. This last, the image of a vehicle, is a traditional metaphor about metaphors. The poet's vision takes the shape of images—rather than the logic of numbers, for example, and the human mind has a special love for images. In my case, I study these visions to learn what it means to be a living soul.

Metaphors don't measure or make up a fact. Instead, they can wake us out of a presumption of knowledge. Chaucer's characters (presumably) don't embark on a pilgrimage just to see the sights in Canterbury. They would wake themselves and us from the dream of worldliness that ends in death. Metaphors of sickness and health carry the same message; they convey how we look to a remedy, like the salve in the book of Revelation and *A Midsummer Night's Dream*. Puck applies it to the eyes of Lysander, who sleeps on the ground at the end of his midsummer antics, to make his eyeballs "roll with wonted sight." That done, Puck intones over the four Athenian lovers the prayer of countrymen who live close to the ground:

> *And the country proverb known*
> *That everyman should take his own*
> *In your waking shall be shown:*
> *Jack shall have Jill;*
> *Naught shall go ill;*
> *The man shall have his mare again, and all shall be well.*
>
> *A Midsummer Night's Dream*, act 3, scene 2

The play's theme, suggested in the title and here in the country proverb, rests on imagery of dreaming and waking. Robin's countrymen (his Everymen) have added in their proverb the imagery of sickness and health, of something lost and something found, and of a frustrated Jack and a satisfied Jack.

Bemused throughout the play by the fact that foolish human beings sleep and dream a goodly portion of every day even when they're awake, Puck nevertheless prays the lovers will wake to discover they have the something they ardently sought. This having of what they lacked, however, is swallowed up quite suddenly by the word *naught* in the next line. It suggests that the lack of nothing is a kind of nothing; nothing now can be lost or go ill. By closely juxtaposing the longed-for-something with the naught-that-goes-ill, Shakespeare suggests a shape for the end of our pilgrimage. Clearly, it's not a Saturday or a Sunday in town or country; rather, it's a thing that's nothing. Shakespeare has put his metaphor on the horizon between a physical world and a metaphysical world, and that's where we find it. That's where we learn something about a living soul. There's a light, which isn't a light, that comes to life in the gap between the two parts of it, the something and the nothing. As a thing that's nothing (a body and a mind, a thing that lives and a thing that dies), we are the light, the shock, the awareness, and the meaning that emerges. Thanks to the poetry of Shakespeare and others, we are a self-conscious human being and the light of a living soul.

A Metaphor That Engenders a Will to Live

Early in Shakespeare's career as a dramatist, he wrote a play he called *All's Well That Ends Well*. With these five words, he proclaims a comic vision, and they settle together to be a foundation for all he wrote. The works erected on that foundation have weathered four centuries and continue to serve as a sanctuary for countless human beings haunted by their past and fearful of their future. In other words, he made his poetry for Everyman. *All's Well That Ends Well* has become proverbial, if it wasn't already a proverb, and as a foundational statement about human life and as a sanctuary for human hope, it, too, is a metaphor. He compares the universal "all" that ends well to a play that ends well. *All's Well That Ends Well* is a play about that which awakens a will to live in a king who is dying of a deadly "fistula" and in a wife who has been abandoned by her husband. It's possible that all will be well: Jack will have Jill, naught will go ill, and the woman will have her man again. The title and the text of the play primes the pump of this hope. Anyone who attends the play witnesses how all can end well and is encouraged to see-life-through to the end. Why not say a renewed will to live marks the presence of a living soul?

The Breath Means Life

Why not compare the sanctuary we seek to the breath of life? We swim in this immense ocean that floods the entire globe with a well-spring of life wherein we breathe and move freely. What would we be without it? We can't imagine. If life is the goal of life, then we're here. We've arrived. The breath is not an idea, a philosophy, or a religion. It is what it is, a thing that appears to be nothing, and yet for us alive in this world it's the source of all and everything.

This vision of the breath recalls the famous lines in Genesis about it. To do the lines justice, I need to put them in the context that has been carefully prepared for them. Genesis chapter 1 describes the creation of the world, and chapter 2 begins with the work of the previous six days resting in an interim state filled with potential yet unrealized:

> *These are the generations of the heavens and of the earth when they were created, in the day that the Lord God made the earth and the heavens, And every plant of the field before it was in the earth, and every herb of the field before it grew: for the Lord God had not caused it to rain upon the earth, and there was not a man to till the ground.*

Sometimes, at the beginning of a play, the director will have the actors frozen in place for a time as the light comes up, or at the beginning of a movie the director will freeze-frame an image while the credits unroll. Then, in an instant, everything springs to life.

As the Lord rests on the seventh day, the universe of these verses, along with the reader, pauses as if to take stock of what has been done. It's all there, but the things He has made are strangely unplanted. We observe the plants before they are in the earth and the herbs before they grow. They exist but lack that which makes them live as we can see from what happens next:

But there went up a mist from the earth, and watered the whole face of the ground. And the Lord God formed man of the dust of the ground, and breathed into his nostrils the breath of life; and man became a living soul.

Here there's no "And God said." This time God says nothing. The mist went up of its own accord and watered everything with the liquor of life, and what comes out of the earth is not a plant but a man.

The ground watered with the liquor of life and a man animated with the breath of life are joined in a final verse:

And the Lord God planted a garden eastward in Eden; and there he put the man whom he had formed.

With a habitable earth to feed him and provide him with a stage for action, man is ready to go about his business, and it's his business, we were already told, "to till the ground" and give life to the plants as they give life to him. On day six of Genesis chapter 1, God creates mankind in his own image, and Genesis chapter 2 completes the story. God informs mankind with the breath of life, which is His own breath, and mankind now informs the ground with the presence of a living soul.

These verses from Genesis address the alienation that so many experience in any time and place with a story that describes how mankind in the beginning was one with the world. Adam and Eve changed all that, though, when they ate the forbidden fruit, and God cursed the ground. Nowadays we know so many facts about the ground, its molecular depths and deep space galaxies, but facts only increase the alienation. A fact stands alone, and the human being who observes it (objectively) stands alone. The alienation is built into the modern method. Clearly, though, we are not the first human beings to stand on a desert with numberless stars overhead and feel like a blip adrift in a multitude of things. This is the wound that people go on pilgrimage to heal, and this is the wound addressed by the breath of life and the waking of a living soul. Or so it seems to me, for this describes my own pilgrimage.

The Metaphor of Another Who Supplies the Breath of Life

The image of divine CPR in Genesis figures for us a foundational, interpersonal relationship. It's not enough just to hope that all can end well. The hope is realized in relationship with another who supplies the breath of life. The story in Genesis about the breath is not just a story; it's a powerful metaphor. Because air is so plentiful and because breathing goes on automatically, the significance of a breath can fade into the background as a given. When we're drowning, though, like the remnants from the wreck in *The Tempest*, and what's been given has been taken away, then we long for it. "Drowning" is the vehicle in the metaphor that frames that play. When we're "drowning" in any of the many forms of self-pity, including aggression, and alienation from others that afflicts human beings (and we see plenty of that on stage in the cast of *The Tempest*, but especially in the alienation of Caliban), we're out of air and in despair. The play itself, as it resolves the conflict between brother and brother, plays the part of a divine breath, which revives in them a living soul.

Shakespeare writes his dialogues with the air of a man who has found that the breath of life in everyday speech can have a life-saving function. This will always be the case. The breath of life in everyday speech is as vital now as in Shakespeare's day. In these faithless times, we still find that we must speak to others and others must speak to us. We still speak and act out our love with intense single-mindedness, and when children come, they still serve as a sanctuary of selfless purpose for parents who sustain their children's lives with an instinct like self-preservation. Along with these primeval passions, like creatures in nature excited by excitement, the usual turbulence and temptations of the times work on human hearts one way or another. In these tempestuous seas, parents depend on true speech for the family's survival. We are individuals, and true speech is the breath that steadies and unites us. We may not like to admit it, but others (our parents, siblings, spouses, children, and colleagues) very likely know us better than we know ourselves. Their speech can function like a breath of life.

The Ark of Our Lives

The sacred words of Genesis tell us that we are individuals with names like Adam and Eve, Isaac and Rebecca, and Jacob and Rachel, but we are made out of others—our father and mother and those who have gone before them in our lineage. The immediate family as well as the family of man reaching back to our first parents remind us of the timeless breadth and depth of our interdependence. Like the main characters in Genesis, from *Titus Andronicus* through to *The Tempest*, Shakespeare's main characters come to life within the context of a family. It's a context or a setting that insures close contact with others. Then, too, family members, friends of long standing, and spouses are the most immediate reminders (for better or for worse) of the life we have made out of everything we've ever said or done or thought. No wonder our relationships with them prompt such fierce passions.

Dependent children are living proof of our interdependence, but in time the child must cease to be a child and leave the parents. In the end, we all are left to our own devices. No one else can live our life for us. No one else can die for us as Alcestis did for her husband, the fearful and cowardly King Admetus. No longer children, we leave our parents to find a place where all will end well. We come from parents who, for better or for worse, found each other. And, for better or worse, many of us end up like them. If we consult with Shakespeare as we're desperately searching for that place, though, we have to notice that for his characters (and for us) again and again he holds up a mirror to faces in headlong pursuit of a sanctuary "out there" somewhere. This sanctuary can be many things. For Helena, in *All's Well That Ends Well*, it's her husband Bertram, but we frankly wonder whether he's worth all the trouble of securing him. For Falstaff, it's the tavern where he can eat, drink, and entertain the company. For men in the history plays and the tragedies, it's the crown of England or some other worldly authority.

Even though these things loom so large in our imaginations, they are never enough to catch and hold a restless soul. To end well, his fables tell us, we must discover and settle on our true self like a lost continent. (This is an image suggested by the brave new world that's discovered in *The Tempest.*)

In the ups and downs of the play's plotline, Shakespeare's mirror can take the shape of events in the world. This reminds us that even a seemingly small request or misstep has a place in the arc of our life and can't be discounted or forgotten. For example, to please her husband Iago, Emelia shows him the handkerchief, the one in which Iago had expressed a keen interest, that she picked up when Desdemona dropped it. This little thing that's casually dropped takes on the ultimate meaning a thing in this world can have when it's picked up, for it leads in the end to the deaths of Desdemona, Othello, Iago, and Emelia herself. In dramatic scenes, the mirror consists of others, people who know the main character better than he knows himself. For example, after Prince Hal was crowned King Henry V, he refuses to recognize Falstaff when they meet in the street, but when Falstaff persists, Henry takes some pains to explain why:

> *I know thee not, old man, fall to thy prayers.*
> *How ill white hairs becomes a fool and jester.*
> *I have long dreamt of such a kind of man,*
> *So surfeit-swell'd, so old, and so profane;*
> *But being awak'd, I do despise my dream.*
> *Make less thy body hence and more thy grace,*
> *Leave gormandizing, know the grave doth gape*
> *For thee thrice wider than for other men.*
>
> *Henry IV, Part 2*, act 5, scene 5

Shakespeare's mirror often consists of poetry that revives our sense of a physical, sensible body at the center of all and everything. So much depends upon being born, on our existence, and this consciousness of a body at the center renews the wonder of it all. It's the wonder that emerges when we consider what it is to be in light of what it is not to be.

As we participate in the play of these things, the play of these things serves as our own consciousness. It becomes the ark of our life within which we move and breathe. In our witness of it, the play becomes the mass and moral weight of a living soul, Shakespeare's soul, but which, for the time being, is our own soul. It's the magic of art.

The Calling of a Living Soul

> *And the angel of the Lord appeared unto him in a flame of fire out of the midst of a bush: and he looked, and, behold, the bush burned with fire, and the bush was not consumed. And Moses said, I will now turn aside, and see this great sight, why the bush is not burnt. And when the Lord saw that he turned aside to see, God called unto him out of the midst of the bush, and said, Moses, Moses. And he said, Here am I. And he said, Draw not nigh hither: put off thy shoes from off thy feet, for the place whereon thou standest is holy ground.*
>
> Exodus 3:2–5

> *And Moses said unto God, Behold, when I come unto the children of Israel, and shall say unto them, The God of your fathers hath sent me unto you; and they shall say to me, What is his name? what shall I say unto them? And God said unto Moses, I Am That I Am: and he said, Thus shalt thou say unto the children of Israel, I Am hath sent me unto you.*
>
> Exodus 3:13–14

Shakespeare's narratives have in mind the divine Other who says to Abram, "Do not be afraid, Abram. I am your shield, your very great reward" (Genesis 15:1). His narratives remember the experience of a lonely herdsman in the backside of a desert who encounters a bush burning with self-substantial fuel and who calls himself *I Am That I Am*. Because of these meetings, Abram and Moses were changed, for the Lord knew them, called them by name, and laid the salvation of His people on them. At great cost to themselves—that is, to the life they had led up to this point—the power of divine love impressed and crowned them with a sacred purpose. These stories and others Shakespeare has made in their likenesses outline the calling of a living soul.

We hear the call in these lines from *The Tempest*. Ariel sings it (as a suggestion on the wind) to give Ferdinand news of his father, whom Ferdinand believes has drowned in the tempest at the beginning of the play:

Ariel: Full fathom five thy father lies;
Of his bones are coral made;
Those are pearls that were his eyes:
Nothing of him that doth fade,
But doth suffer a sea-change
Into something rich and strange.
Sea-nymphs hourly ring his knell:
Spirits: (within) Ding-dong.
Ariel: Hark! Now I hear them.
Spirits: (within) Ding-dong, bell.

The Tempest, act 1, scene 2

Ariel has good news of Ferdinand's father; the sea of life is fundamentally changing him. The old duke (who usurped the dukedom of his brother) is dying. Long live the new duke!

The Tempest begins with a raging storm that destroys the ark carrying many of the characters who will play prominent roles in the rest of the play. The beginning of the play looks like the ending of their lives, but they are reborn instead on Prospero's Island. In this, they are much like Everyman in the morality play about him, for his play begins when Death comes to him in great haste "From God out of his majesty." Everyman and his play don't end there though. Instead, he goes an allegorical journey to discover the "immanence of value" in death and in life.

When I consider the greatness of Shakespeare's achievement as a writer, I'm inclined to believe that something happened to him (within) that answered the bell of the Spirits (Hark! Now I hear them) in Ariel's song. He, too, experienced the power and responsibility of *I Am*, suffered a sea change, and heard the sea nymphs sing the bell of his passing. Just as Ariel informs Ferdinand of his father's change, the poet has informed us of *his* change in a deluge of words. It poured forth from him and drowned his people with the waters of life, words with a power to renew creation. He's the deluge and the ark. Having discovered himself, his being in the world, to be the ark that holds and preserves all that lives against a waste of not-being, he devoted his writing to the sanctuary of a life made whole in the love of *I Am That I Am*.

He would love the world the way a loving parent and creator would, but the children and the trials of this world prove, as they did before the flood in Genesis, to be difficult to love. He may have found himself difficult to love. If the persona he employs in the sonnets speaks for him, then he is no saint. What would his wife Anne have to say about him, her absentee husband? Perhaps he would confess, as Hamlet confesses to Ophelia:

> *I could accuse me of such things that it were better my mother had not borne me: I am very proud, revengeful, ambitious, with more offenses at my beck than I have thoughts to put them in, imagination to give them shape, or time to act them in.*
>
> *Hamlet*, act 3, scene 1

Like Hamlet, Shakespeare must have felt the pressures and the fissures of an earthly life. For all that, he loves the world and his true self as a sanctuary of being, and so he embarks in his craft to explore the nature of love and his own nature, which love commands, within the vast shape-shifting theater of present experience.

Two Famous Allegorical Interims

I am Alpha and Omega, the beginning and the ending, saith the Lord, which is, and which was, which is to come, the Almighty.

Revelation 1:8

A horse, a horse, my kingdom for a horse!

Richard III, act 5, scene 4

It will be short: the interim is mine;
And a man's life's no more than to say "One."

Hamlet, act 5, scene 2

To body forth the nature of the soul, Shakespeare has at hand the themes and devices of mystery and morality plays. As the wagons of the mystery cycles did, he can gather the stages in time and space on which the story of mankind is acted out. As in the play of *Everyman*, which begins when Death comes to Everyman, he can tell the story of Everyman's soul in the form of an allegory. Like the paradox of a something that's a nothing or a nothing that's a something, Everyman's play begins where Everyman ends, for, as I pointed out in the last section, it begins with God sending Death to find Everyman. After the meeting with Death, it goes on to relate Everyman's encounter with the whole of his life, for allegory can express a vision of time and space that's compassed in a compact three letter word—the "all" that would end well, the "all" that's redeemed as a living soul.

Shakespeare's allegorical vision, which can pack a man's life into a one-syllable word, can also see a man's life as a coming-of-age narrative, and he makes room in it for us to fit even the tragedy of *Hamlet,* his longest play. To succeed in this mighty task, he calls on the powers of allegory and imagination to move Hamlet's narrative out of its accustomed matrices of time and space into another dimension. He rolls the whole of Hamlet's life into the end point that gives it a compact shape and meaning. Hamlet himself prepares us for his end (the purpose of his life) in these lines with Horatio:

> *HAMLET: Does it not, think's thee, stand me now upon—*
> *He that hath kill'd my king and whored my mother,*
> *Popped in between the election and my hopes,*
> *Thrown out his angle for my proper life,*
> *And with such cozenage—is't not perfect conscience,*
> *To quit him with this arm? And is't not to be damn'd,*
> *To let this canker of our nature come*
> *In further evil?*
> *HORATIO: It must be shortly known to him from England*
> *What is the issue of the business there.*
> *HAMLET: It will be short: the interim is mine;*
> *And a man's life's no more than to say "One."*
>
> *Hamlet*, act 5, scene 2

We find in Hamlet's thinking, to which he invites the thinking of Horatio ("Does it not, thinks thee"), two very different visions of time. In the first passage, time is the meaningless hole between learning of his father's murder and avenging it. This gap of fruitless hours, days, and months without end holds Hamlet like the keep of a castle as he arms himself with justifications for murder. It hems in an angry, questing, restless, uncertain, spirit so that he resembles nothing so much as the ghost of his father, Hamlet. The dreadful, desperate want of vengeance has turned both Hamlets into ghosts.

Horatio then draws young Hamlet's attention to the fact of which the new king—his greedy, usurping, uncle—is unaware. Rosencrantz and Guildenstern are dead; Hamlet cleverly arranged to have the king of England kill them instead of himself. His uncle doesn't know that, but he soon will when

England sends him word. That word, Hamlet knows, will be the death of Hamlet. Now he resembles nothing so much as Everyman at the beginning of his play, for the word is Death. Nevertheless, just as it did for Everyman, Death opens up an "interim," a vision that lifts his life and everything in it into a timeless present. The interim is mine, he says. It's the time it takes to say "one" and time enough to accomplish all. Hamlet now lives as Damocles did. With the "word" from England poised to strike at any moment, time can only be the time it takes to say "one." The time that it takes to say one, though short, now holds a life made whole by the word that will come from England.

In the end, the jolting from a time that's out of joint has an effect on Hamlet for which a physical science has no explanation. It jars a passage open and breathes life finally into Hamlet's enterprise, which is to take his place as his father's rightful heir. Once the passage opens, Hamlet acts to kill the false king. If we view the story as an allegory, Hamlet must kill the false king, the grasping self or ego, to become a living soul. Like a prince invested with a sacred kingship by the crown of his father, in this allegorical interim, he inherits the breath of life passed down from Adam and Noah.

It comes to pass in Hamlet's final speech:

> *Oh, I die, Horatio—*
> *The potent poison quite o'crows my spirit.*
> *I cannot live to hear the news from England,*
> *But I do prophesy th'election lights*
> *On Fortinbras—he has my dying voice.*
> *So tell him, with th'occurents more and less*
> *Which have solicited—the rest is silence.*

In the end, once Claudius is dead, Hamlet is king for the time it takes to designate one to be a successor. The news from England has been changed from the deaths of Rosencrantz and Guildenstern to the affirmation that Fortinbras, thanks to Hamlet's vote, will succeed him. Hamlet acts—as he just did in avenging his father and mother—decisively without all the second guessing that previously clouded his bounded and cursed self like a plague. By confiding in Horatio throughout, he has left a true record of his actions for the world to see and judge. Everything in his life has prepared him for the moment he would be king, and, though the time is short (due to the poison on Laertes's sword) as he foresaw, he wears the crown of sacred kingship in an action that preserves his realm. Why is it a sacred kingship? Because there's absolutely no self-interest in it. "Oh, I die," he tells Horatio, in virtually the same breath that dictates the will of a sacred king.

Because the soul, the center of our story, is not a material thing, the story about it can't be realistic in the modern sense. It has to be an allegory. Shakespeare gives his King Richard III one of the most famous lines ever spoken on stage: "A horse, a horse, my kingdom for a horse," he cries after he has been unhorsed in battle. This, too, is an allegorical interim with great meaning. Given his desperation to live, we might judge that the king's exchange makes commercial sense. His offer makes more sense, however, when it's understood within the context of an allegory. This is what King Richard intuitively begins to understand when, as a messenger from God, Death comes to find him. King Richard's words are perfectly clear, but to fit them into this stage of my inquiry I'll add a brief interpretation.

Now that he has been unhorsed, Richard has to confront what he is without the horse. Putting myself in his place, I find I'm on the cusp of existence where we can view this world in one direction and a divine order in the other direction. Looking into this world, we can see that we have to credit the greatness of our physical bodies. Without the horse—all the things of this world that sustain us, including our own bodies—we lose the kingdom, our worldly home. King Richard must first be born into this world for him to be King Richard. The body must breathe from moment to moment, or the world goes away. Looking into the divine order (as this world goes away), we see that our kingdom is not *a thing* in time and space; it's the soul of the world. Without the soul of the world, we lose the true horse, a living soul that's one with the soul of the world (as in that moment of divine CPR in

Genesis). We have to credit the greatness of the soul. If we don't, it corrupts, as worldly things do, and goes dark, for then it's ruled by a usurping tyrant king, our grasping insular selves. (See also Scruton's thoughts on how the soul can be corrupted, pages 23–24.)

As it was for Hamlet and as it was for Richard, the rotten kingdom of a usurping tyrant king is a threat to all the things of this world we love. This is what allegory teaches.

The Birth and the Burden of a Living Soul

The Lord saw how great the wickedness of the human race had become on the earth, and that every inclination of the thoughts of the human heart was only evil all the time.

Genesis 6:5

But Noah found favor in the eyes of the Lord.

Genesis 6:8

The word of the Lord came to Jonah son of Amittai: "Go to the great city of Nineveh and preach against it, because its wickedness has come up before me." But Jonah ran away from the Lord and headed for Tarshish. He went down to Joppa, where he found a ship bound for that port. After paying the fare, he went aboard and sailed for Tarshish to flee from the Lord.

Jonah 1:1–3

Midway in our life's journey, I went astray
from the straight road and woke to find myself
alone in a dark wood. How shall I say
what wood that was! I never saw so drear,
so rank, so arduous a wilderness!
Its very memory gives a shape to fear!
Death could scarce be more bitter than that place!
But since it came to good, I will recount
all that I found revealed there by God's grace.

The Inferno, Ciardi translation, canto 1, 1–9

And as I fell to my soul's ruin, a presence
gathered before me on the discolored air,
the figure of one who seemed hoarse from long silence.
At sight of him in that friendless waste I cried:
"Have pity on me, whatever thing you are,
whether shade or living man."

The Inferno, Ciardi translation, canto 1, 61–66

Despite the wickedness of the human race, the Lord found a man to bear His will—Noah, from whom we inherit the breath of life. Because Noah found favor in the eyes of the Lord, He commands him to bear the burden of an immense task. Noah must contain and preserve in his vessel all sentient beings. Over the course of God's story in the Bible, the Lord finds others who must bear His will, and the burden is the same.

As the biblical narrative unfolds, the Lord makes do with imperfect men. Moses fled to the backside of the desert because he killed an overseer belonging to Pharaoh, but God found him there anyway and spoke to him out of the burning bush. God found Jonah and told him to bear His will to the people of Nineveh, but Jonah didn't want to be found and ran away. Because there is no time or space in creation that isn't His, the Lord found Jonah anyway and delivered him up, reborn, in Nineveh. David loved another man's wife and sent that man to certain death in battle. This in spite of the fact that Samuel once took "the horn of oil, and anointed him in the midst of his brethren: and the Spirit of the Lord came upon David from that day forward" (1 Samuel 16:13).

Midway through his life's journey, Dante fell into an allegorical sleep and woke to find himself in an allegorical dark wood. He had arrived at that point where his own ideas and appetites could take him no further. He was lost, but a holy spirit found him. Dante's cry, "Have pity on me," comes from a heart that's both full (of worldly disappointment) and empty (from the loss of everything). His heart, his whole body, is a cup full of holy bitterness and ready to receive Virgil's guidance; his cry marks the birth of a living soul.

But this is just the beginning of a much longer story. Dante must now train and temper that heart by going a journey through all three stages of the *Commedia*.

Constellations in the Sky of Timeless Poetry

Fair Helena; who more engilds the night
Than all yon fiery oes and eyes of light.

A Midsummer Night's Dream, act 3, scene 2

In the conclusion of "A Pilgrimage to a Sacred Place," I imagined for the reader lines of poetry that project a hologram of a living soul. Perhaps this image was suggested to me by the constellations that emerge from the "oes and eyes of light" in a night sky. In the lines of the epigraph above, Lysander asks us to look up and see the fiery beauty of the night's oes and eyes. The stars are beautiful in themselves, and it's beautiful how they coalesce into timeless mythical figures. At the same time, though, Lysander is asking us to imagine—as in imagining a constellation—how the sun of fair Helena's eyes gives far greater value to the things of this world. We can't see her sun, but it shines forth in these two lines of poetry.

The poet who wrote them for Lysander (who is embroiled in an argument over Helena with his rival Demetrius) would have us consider our own myth making powers. After all, the play consists of words and sentences that light up our minds with the constellations of Oberon, Titania, Lysander, Theseus, Robin, Helena, and so on. So much depends on the human subject who observes the night sky and finds in those oes and eyes of light beauty and meaning, and, in the same way, so much depends on us, the reader or listener. We put the constellations together out of these points of light, but the points of light—the words and the lines that represent these characters—have a life of their own. Even as the characters speak their minds about their life in this world, they can become messengers of an otherworldly intelligence. I would argue that the effect (the beauty) of these lines signals the presence of a living soul—the soul of the one who wrote them and the soul of the world that inspired them. As the soul of the world was for the poet, the beauty of these lines is "catching" so that the soul of the one who wrote them gives life to the soul of the one who hears them.

Shakespeare calls on Lysander several times to convey the beauty of this intelligence. For example, after they have heard the duke's judgment that Hermia must marry Demetrius or die, Lysander and Hermia commiserate their loss, and Lysander muses that love is:

> *. . . momentany as a sound*
> *Swift as a shadow, short as any dream,*
> *Brief as the lightning in the collied night,*
> *That, in a spleen, unfolds both heaven and earth,*
> *And ere a man hath power to say "Behold!"*
> *The jaws of darkness do devour it up:*
> *So quick bright things come to confusion.*

He is speaking to Hermia about their immediate situation, but he appears to have fallen into a kind of trance to transmit these reflections on a moving, splenetic universe. For those of us who overhear their conversation, the words and actions presented through the rest of the play (as lovers fall in and out of love) remind us that love is like lightning. It lights up the world with sudden power, but the giant darkness just as quickly devours it as if it had never been. How can something so real be lost so quickly, we wonder, and this question leads quite naturally to others: How can life itself be so real and yet be lost so quickly? Why is it lost? Why is this something also a nothing? Lysander speaks these words, but he doesn't own them. In the end, they belong to the universe of timeless poetry. This universe is the timeless, spaceless setting for allegory and for addressing the question "Why?"

When Helena says to Hermia, "Oh, teach me how you look," because Hermia's "look" has won Demetrius's love and Helena's has not, she may have intended one thing, but the words themselves speak of a longing that literature for thousands of years aims to satisfy. We who love poetry would look with the eyes of these masters, and so we read and imagine the world they have made for us to give us what we lack. Helena's line addressed to Hermia leads to another that's the climatic idea in Helena's soliloquy after Hermia and Lysander exit. Because this speech of a beautiful, self-conscious soul is so important to my inquiry, I'll add it to the record:

> *How happy some o're other some can be!*
> *Through Athens I am thought as fair as she.*
> *But what of that? Demetrius thinks not so,*
> *He will not know what all but he do know.*
> *And as he errs, doting on Hermia's eyes,*
> *So I, admiring of his qualities.*
> *Things base and vile, holding no quantity,*
> *Love can transpose to form and dignity.*
> *Love looks not with the eyes, but with the mind;*
> *And therefore is winged Cupid painted blind.*

Nor hath Love's mind of any judgment taste;
Wings and no eyes, figure unheedy haste.
And therefore is Love said to be a child,
Because in choice he is so oft beguiled.
As waggish boys in game themselves forswear,
So the boy Love is perjured everywhere:
For ere Demetrius looked on Hermia's eyne,
He hailed down oaths that he was only mine;
And when this hail some heat from Hermia felt,
So he dissolved, and showers of oaths did melt.

To explain why Demetrius doesn't love her, Helena declares, "Love looks, not with the eyes, but with the mind," and my reading of the play is based on this judgment. Helena complains that the man she loves (like a blind Cupid) cannot or will not "see" her. Her complaint carries within it an insight that used to be enshrined, studied, and revered in our literature as wisdom. Her sentence on Demetrius invites—urges—us all to "see" the beauty of this world, which has been clouded over by obsessive thoughts. Love here is a love of parts (*cupiditas*) rather than a love of the whole (*caritas*). She speaks, I believe, for Shakespeare, as this is the goal of his allegorical poetry.

When Nick Bottom the weaver tells Titania, the beautiful fairy queen, in their first little tête-à-tête that "reason and love keep little company together nowadays. The more the pity that some honest neighbors will not make them friends," it's hard to attribute the wisdom of what he says to him. Prior to his transformation into a real ass (as opposed to the human variety) when he behaves as a perfect gentleman, Bottom was a grandiose, self-centered braggart. The words come out of his now gentle mouth, but they belong to the ages. He got lucky, we think (which is what he thinks as well, "Nay, I can gleek, upon occasion," with an explanation that neighs and squeaks like a donkey), just as he's about to get lucky with Titania! Transformations and transcendental wisdom like this are possible in the wonderlands of an allegory.

When Theseus wakes the four Athenian lovers after their midsummer night, Demetrius tries to account for why they are lying side by side in the wood. Over the course of his explanation, he declares to the duke his love for Helena, whom he once loved but then abandoned. Helena, half asleep, hears the words with a mind eager to claim his love but still full of sleep and doubt:

And I have found Demetrius like a jewel,
Mine own, and not mine own.

Her words express what it is to love and be loved in this world. It's like a priceless jewel, but it's a jewel that—like the gift of life itself—we may enjoy for a while but never "own."

We have to wonder, then: To what can we lay claim in this life when all is so uncertain, transitory, and ruled by chance—like random bolts of lightning? This is the great question that an allegory like *Everyman* addresses, and it informs Shakespeare's poetry as well.

I Have Now Found Thee

Prince: This oily rascal is known as well as Paul's. Go, call him forth.
Peto: Falstaff!—Fast asleep behind the arras, and snorting like a horse.

Henry IV, Part 1, act 2, scene 5

Nay, sure, he's not in hell: he's in Arthur's bosom, if ever man went to Arthur's bosom. 'A made a finer end, and went away an it had been any christom child. 'A parted e'en just between twelve and one, e'en at the turning of the tide. For after I saw him fumble with the sheets, and play with flowers, and smile upon his fingers' ends, I knew there was but one way. For his nose was as sharp as a pen, and 'a babbled of green fields. "How now, Sir John?" quoth I. "What, man! Be o'good cheer." So 'a cried out, "God, God, God," three or four times. Now I, to comfort him, bid him 'a should not think of God; I hoped there was no need to trouble himself with any such thoughts yet. So 'a bade me lay more clothes on his feet. I put my hand into the bed and felt them, and they were as cold as any stone. Then I felt to his knees, and so upward and upward, and all was cold as any stone.

Henry V, act 2, scene 3

I have now found thee; when I lose thee again, I care not. Yet art thou good for nothing but taking up, and that thou'rt scarce worth.

All's Well That Ends Well, act 2, scene 3

Part 1: Falstaff as Everyman and Old Adam

The poets I study in this book encourage us to believe that we can wake to discover our true self, which is a living soul. This is the end of our pilgrimage, a kingdom of ends and beginnings. The argument has to begin somewhere. I have chosen to begin with the verse in Genesis, in which God breathes into the man's nostrils, and he becomes a living soul. The rest of the book describes what becoming a living soul entails. It takes some doing since our true self is a paradoxical something and nothing.

I conclude this collection of lifelines that suggest the shape of a living soul with "I have now found thee," a line from *All's Well That Ends Well.* Lord Lafew says this to Parolles, a man much like Falstaff in character and vocation. Within the context of the play, the words are perfectly apt; once freed from that local constraint, though, the entire play reverberates with them. Before I get to this implacable, great man in the life of the play, I return to my argument about reading Shakespeare's work as allegory.

From personal experience, I've learned that a modern wit instinctively puts up a wall of separation between himself and a medieval allegory. For a modern wit, *Everyman* is absurd. Death is personified and can talk; even though Death finds Everyman, Everyman still has "time" in a cursory review of his life to redeem his soul before a reckoning with God. God, by the way, addresses the audience in a prologue at the beginning of the play. Death personified, salvation, God—for a modern secular audience, these things are beyond the pale of reason. A modern wit thinks a play like *Everyman* belongs (at best) in a literary museum. People visit a museum; they don't live there. This can't explain, however, why the opening lines leapt off the page as living speech when I read them after fifty years of not reading them.

In the play of *Everyman*, the end we are born for, like the beginning, is to be a living soul. Over the course of a life, that's long enough to feed strong appetites and ambitions, though, our poor soul, the center of our sinful earth, can suffocate under the weight of gross worldliness and fall asleep or, more ominously, fall into a perilous dis-ease. Dante tells this story at the beginning of his *Commedia*, and Shakespeare tells it through the character of Falstaff. After the high jinks at Gad's Hill and the tall tales in Mistress Quickly's tavern, we find him behind the arras "snorting like a horse." Just as Moses would hide in the desert from the murder of a man and Jonah would hide his faint heart by boarding a ship to Tarshish, Falstaff hides his bloated worldliness and beastliness (from himself) by falling into a constrained, fitful, liquor-infused unconsciousness behind the arras. We see his state well enough and may be inclined to pass judgment, but surely his desperate striving for breath touches the heart's core of any creature who breathes the sweet air to live. It's a subtle, sobering reminder of the lifeline, the open airway, we share with all living creatures. The body that lies, first snorting like a horse behind the arras and later breathing his last on Mistress Quickly's bed, is Everyman, and we are Everyman.

Falstaff is the life of the party and the soul of wit, but the great mask of his persona can't conceal in the end his evasions, cowardice, and bad faith. Once he's unconscious, we hear a desperate striving for breath, for life. By the end of his life on stage, including his reincarnation in *The Merry Wives*, we have found him to be Old Adam, the crooked stock from which humanity springs, the timber of a man who wittily approves the dictates of worldly appetites and worldly knowledge. Modern readers don't like the notion that Shakespeare's plays have a didactic point, but it's hard not to conclude, even if it's only when Death comes in great haste from God out of his majesty, that a man can only be the ghost or the shadow of a man (Shadow being one of Falstaff's companions) if he relies on the false staff of Falstaff's wit. For all that, it's never too late to transcend it. According to the Hostess, who relates his final minutes, even Falstaff himself—with his body cold as stone—has breath enough to call on God three or four times. Was it enough? Did it wake a living soul?

Some centuries ago, our ancestors passed the baton of a skeptical, worldly wit to those who would be scientists, along with others who followed their lead. They have created the modern world as modern man knows it. Much as Christians tried to root the pagan gods out of their sacred stories, prayers, and festivals, and much as Falstaff mocked the sacred cows of church and state in his day, scientists and others have tried to drain all traces of metaphysics out of their conclusions about reality. The mysteries of faith have been cordoned off in museums or generally made anathema, and the mystery of death has been tidied up as a statistic in official records—the time of death, tabulations about the cause of death, the price of a funeral for death, and the payout for a death in actuarial tables. These are facts about a death, but only a fool with no imagination at all would find them commensurate with the end of a life.

Like the fairies who represent an unseen but lively metaphysical realm working in a helter-skelter way to benefit mankind, *A Midsummer Night's Dream* is lighter fare for the Athenian lovers and for the audience; it's a comedy. The escape from Athens to fairyland prepares the lovers for marriage, and all ends well. Unlike the fairies, Falstaff is heavier fare for one who would be king; in *Henry V*, Sir John (as Old Adam) prepares King Henry for death prior to the battles he will fight in France. Sir John's bulk lies in Mistress Quickly's bed to show one and all that the preparation involves the mass of one's entire life.

Fast-forward four hundred years. Excluded and repressed, the metaphysical power of Love and Death still seeps into Everyman's consciousness and disrupts the peace that Reason would make with waking hours. Popping up everywhere on devices of all sizes like an antic impresario pitching his wares from deep cyber space, popular culture shadows the Athenian sunlight of our days with enticing images of all kinds—with political opinion, business advice, drugs to cure sickness, beer and soda pop to effervesce our get-togethers, and so on and on. But especially there are those images of the love god at play and the war god at work, livestreamed wherever and whenever we like. In particular, there's the modern sweet spot for imagination, the sleepy twilight for relaxing before bedtime. As in an after-dinner dream, night after night, we read or watch on quicksilver screens the stories of intrepid detectives who hunt down the mystery of love and death as if they could get to the bottom of it.

I would make the case that *Everyman*, a model for Shakespeare's poetic universe, is more commensurate with the end (the purpose) of a life than all the statistics and calculations of science. In the play of *Everyman*, Death is not the end; he's a messenger from God. Within that moment of meeting, the time it takes to say "one," Everyman is not in Kansas anymore nor is he the sole owner of himself. Death has come to tell him he must go a journey and give the "reckoning" God must have. Because he's a messenger of divine mercy, though, Death allows Everyman to prove his friends to see who will help him on this pilgrimage. The drama plays out in a succession of scenes as Everyman tries to get Good Fellowship, Kindred, and Worldly Goods to go with him in judgment, but they all refuse. In each of these relationships Everyman had developed an image of himself to which he was passionately attached. After a lifetime of landing on the durability and goodness of these images as a hedge against Death, Everyman is forced in the end to land on that which is his own and not his own. Death initiates him into what it means to be a living soul.

Part 2: Saving Captain Parolles

All's Well That Ends Well deploys the firepower of a full-length play to dramatize this story in modern dress. In particular, Lafew's words to Parolles—"I have now found you"—invoke that moment when Everyman is forced in the end to find himself and reckon his true substance. The character of Parolles is so flamboyantly absurd that he's a standing invitation to find him out, and many do. Lafew's whole speech to him bears quoting:

> *I did think thee, for two ordinaries [meals], to be a pretty wise fellow; thou didst make tolerable vent of thy travel; it might pass. Yet the scarfs and bannerets about thee did manifoldly dissuade me from believing thee a vessel of too great burden. I have now found thee; when I lose thee again, I care not. Yet thou art good for nothing but the taking up, and that thou'rt scare worth.*

Just as Death finds Everyman to make him an honest man, Lafew has found Parolles. Because Lafew is honest, he says to Parolles face-to-face, "You seem to be something, but I find you next to nothing." Parolles is but a word or words, like his name. To bring his argument home, Lafew points to the absurd scarfs and bannerets that Parolles wears to dress his naked nothingness. Parolles's scarfs and his tales of world travel don't make the man. These things express rather a palpable fear that he is a man—which makes him Everyman. He's a soldier in that he knows (at some level) he is at war with forces that would kill him, but his "bravery" is an empty show. He wears the scarfs and tells the tales to cover up what Lafew says of him, that he's good for nothing but the taking up in death, which makes him nothing.

To be kind, Lafew has to be cruel. Parolles wears the scarfs because he credits them with more substance than his poor, naked self. This self, the one that attaches itself to the things of this world for status and protection (the way Parolles attaches himself to his master, the Count of Roussillon)—this is the self that Lafew rates as good for nothing but the taking up. It's the self to which he refers when he tells Parolles, "I have now found thee."

The finding of a petty, small, grasping self, however, may wake us, as from a dream, to our true self—a lost continent newly discovered (again, Shakespeare's idea of the new world that's the setting for *The Tempest*). All the main characters in the play—the king, Parolles, Bertram, and Helena—are pilgrims who undergo this initiation. The discovery of a true self begins when Death comes to them in great haste "From God out of his majesty" to tell them "I have now found thee," but the self Death finds is both the husk of worldliness and that which would be quickened (when the husk is cracked) to become a living soul. When a man like Lafew, standing in for Death, informs a man like Parolles, "I have now found thee," this is but a preparation for when later in the play that same man, Parolles, after he goes a journey to give a reckoning for his life, can say to Lord Lafew, "I thank God for thee." Does he mean it? For the time being, Shakespeare might say, it's enough that he has good reasons to say it.

By putting the king of France at the head of these pilgrims, they all gather under the sacred crown he wears. Likewise, we, the readers of *All's Well That Ends Well*, are gathered under the crown that sanctifies our reading of the play.

Chapter 2
The Human Subject

Andrew Wyeth's
Below Dover

Throughout my adult life, I've trailed in my little boat the traces and bubbles that Shakespeare's ark leaves as it passes through our oceans of time and space. Lately, though, after so much study, it seems like I've walked the gangway into the ark itself. An image like this may have come to mind thanks to a vivid and life changing experience when I was ten or eleven years old. Because I suspect the incident has informed the better parts of my life—the study of literature in college and university, a career teaching literature to high school kids, and marriage to a woman who loves Shakespeare as much as I do—and informs the readings of Shakespeare I'm proposing, I'll add it to the record as a part of the evidence.

Back in the 1950s, for several years our family vacationed on Nantucket at the Gordon Folger Hotel. One evening my family and I were sitting at dinner in the dining room, as we did every night. In the middle of this ordinary meal, though, my perception and habitual perspective, the placement of people and things in an orderly space, "out there" in the world, suddenly collapsed, as if it had been swallowed up by something. Space was a substance, a living flood of feeling, and it vibrated forcefully with the family's motions and with the sound of voices. The habitual shell of things had burst, and this new substance drowned everything. It was a fearful wonder. And why didn't the others notice the tremendous change? How could they behave as if nothing was happening? Has life always been like this? Or is this watery, boisterous, extravagant show being put on for me alone? And then I knew. They were there, eating and talking—they existed—because of me, because I was there to see and hear them. I was producing the scene. Without me, nothing. With me, nothing separate, no distance between or beyond. Just life, pressing on eyes and ears.

I went up to my room, dumbstruck, and the force of the vision lasted for some days. Before now, I have not written about it. I supposed that everyone at some point has had an experience like this; it was an innate coming-of-age rite initiating me into adolescent self-consciousness. So much time has passed. Yet something of its immediacy endures, and so I wonder to what extent it effected a sea change in my life. It's curious that the Folger family in New England is closely associated with Shakespeare, whose thought has taken up so much space in my professional life and who has helped me year after year to more fully realize the significance of that which took place in the Gordon Folger Hotel.

Looking back at what I've written, I see that I'm pulled as a writer to frame my experience as a child with imagery that draws on the flood in Genesis and the Leviathan in the book of Jonah. These weren't conscious choices; they came to me instinctively. Now the choices have been made, I notice, too, that they have a strong connection with an island famous for its encounters with the sea and its Leviathans.

Why does anyone go to sea? Nantucketers went for the oil that made light in darkness and put money in their pockets. People generally don't argue with money, so it gave them a good excuse to go to sea and sail all over the mighty Pacific. Back in the 1950s, we went for a vacation, and we, too, felt the pull of the sea, the pull of greatness. Because of it we drove east from Ohio, as far as the continent could take us, to land's end in Woods Hole. In the harbor, as we waited for the ferry, the scent of the salt sea and the cry of the seagulls tugged at us like the tide going out. Once embarked, and as the land slowly fell away, we were all that was in a waste of water. By drowning the distractions of a million things, the sea simplified the world and without a word the sea laid it out so we all could see the greatness of the globe and the sky. Topside, the horizon surrounded us in a perfect circle, and the sky arched overhead in a perfect dome. We were the center. No wonder Ptolemy imagined a model of the universe like this; it's a system with a shape that's true and beautiful.

We rode the ferry on a Nantucket sleigh ride to Nantucket itself, pulled to a small island where men once were called to go to sea and where, once at sea, Nantucket called them back again. Life on an island supplies the metaphor that our life, like our vacation, is an island rounded with an ocean. An ocean of what and governed by what or whom? To answer that, we're called upon to hunt for the greatest words that have ever been said about it, to the Bible and to the texts of Homer and Shakespeare. We embark because we must, even if we will never answer the question asked by the Voice out of the Whirlwind:

Who shut up the sea behind doors
when it burst forth from the womb,
when I made the clouds its garment
and wrapped it in thick darkness,
when I fixed limits for it
and set its doors and bars in place,
when I said, 'This far you may come and no farther;
here is where your proud waves halt'?

Job 38:9–11

We cannot say, and yet we find ourselves for as long as we're alive in a place where the sea is shut up behind doors. It's a space for breathing, for life, and for wondering about the sea on the other side of the doors. On this side, feeling the tenuousness and the strangeness of this breathing space, why wouldn't we feel that we're supposed to wonder about what's on the other side; why wouldn't we feel that this life is intimately connected to what is pressing against the door on the other side; why wouldn't we wonder about the role we play in reenacting the whole drama of a flood and the creation of a habitable space, the firmament.

I've selected Wyeth's painting to illustrate this chapter for several reasons. His pictures simplify a scene the way going to sea on a ship does, and *Below Dover* is no exception. There's the sky above, the land below, and the little boat, sunk below the horizon (but which the arrow of the mast and rigging pierces.) The frame of the picture severely crops the earth and sky on the left and right, but through this limiting device we sense, we imagine, the greatness of earth and sky all around.

The frame contains the story of the little boat. At first glance the painting appears to be a static tableau, like a still life (*nature morte*, as the French say), but then it comes alive. The boat doesn't lie lifelessly in a field; it floats as in a dream several feet above the earth. Not only does it float; it moves by the force of a ghostly wind that swells invisible sails and lists the little boat to the starboard. The ghostly wind and the movement of the boat blow back the lines on the boom, and the lines off the stern trail behind. When we look closer, we see that the horizon is something more than a line; it's the sea battering, even, one could say, biting the land. It comes to life in the near distance on the left but then abstracts itself as if it would sail away to infinity beyond the frame. The land holds the sea at bay, but our little boat appears to be sailing without any sails effortlessly toward its home beyond the verge. After all, it was made for this.

Wyeth paints perfectly recognizable everyday objects, but the picture only makes sense as the dreamlike perspective of the person who made the image. We wonder about him. His boat looks like a boat. It looks like an empty shell made of wood left in a field, but as it moves, for no discernible reason, it takes on a life of its own. Wyeth has wryly hinted at the boat's subjectivity by painting a dark little porthole, like an eye (an "I") on the side of the cabin, positioned like the eye of a whale. And so our little boat moves, as in a dream, even though it's awake, through the field of this world. On the horizon to the left, the land seems to be saying to the sea, "This far you may come and no farther; here is where your proud waves halt." The sea appears to object as it batters the land. We, the people viewing the painting, are content to breathe the sweet air behind that barrier, but the little boat is different. Like a fish out of water, it wants the sea.

As such, it's like the personification mankind, with whom C. S. Lewis makes our acquaintance in *The Allegory of Love,* for mankind, we learn, has a foot in both worlds. It's also like the sacred objects Roger Scruton will be describing in *The Soul of the World*, which serve as a passage in this world to the soul of the world. The eye ("I") of the little boat suggests a human subject who is sometimes called to be that passage.

Book Two

The Poetry of C. S. Lewis

Chapter 1
Courtly Love in *The Allegory of Love*

Henry Justice Ford's
Guinevere

Shapes for the Airy Nothings of Love and the Soul

For thousands of years, poets have made the wonder of creation their subject—in scripture, in epic poems, in lyrics, and in allegories. To better understand how allegories express the wonder of creation, I studied *The Allegory of Love* by C. S. Lewis. Modern readers may no longer concern themselves with the classical and medieval forms of allegory, but it doesn't follow that a poet like Shakespeare ignored them. On the contrary, the existence of *The Faerie Queene* proves that this legacy could inspire great poetry at a time when Shakespeare was writing his plays and poems. Lewis's book is a learned (and sympathetic) survey of allegory, and his depiction of it establishes grounds for arguing that Shakespeare's poetry can be profitably read allegorically.

I have called Book Two "The Poetry of C. S. Lewis." Even though Lewis didn't write the poetry quoted in his book, he has translated some of it. Also, he is the one who found these lifelines of a nearly lost tradition, valued their vision of life, and published them to the world in an admirable work of scholarship, imagination, and literary skill. Without his diligence, for example, I would know nothing about the twelfth-century School of Chartres. I had never heard of it. Lewis committed himself to the work because the tradition addresses a deep longing that human beings have always experienced, which is poignantly expressed in a passage by Johannes de Altavilla, a poet-philosopher of that school. His Architrenius, the archmourner, has despaired at the wickedness within him and around him; he would go on a journey to find his true nature and be healed:

This must I do—go exiled through the world
And seek for Nature till far hence I find
Her secret dwelling place; there drag to light
The hidden cause of quarrel, and reknit,
Haply reknit, the long-divided Love.

The Allegory of Love, page 138

In this, he is like any person, now a reader, who would discover the hidden cause of alienation. In allegory we find not so much a cause as a remedy. For example, Bernardus Sylvestris, founder of Altavilla's school, has the Supreme Mind describe the role that mankind will play in Creation:

He shall be heavenly, earthly; by his care
Shall rule the earth, and reach the heaven by prayer,
For as the diverse sources whence he drew
His being, so himself will still be two . . .

Man is both heavenly and earthly. Through prayer, he comes to life in the union of sensible and insensible worlds. He is the meaning that emerges.

As such, man will have power denied other creatures:

He shall drag forth to light the causes hid
In secret gloom, though Nature long forbid . . .
To him, unbounded, in all lands, I give
High crown and priesthood over all that live.

The Allegory of Love, page 120

By being both earthly and heavenly, man occupies a unique station in creation. Like mankind in Bernard's poem, Altavilla's archmourner would realize his true nature. He's not alone, for C. S. Lewis shows us that the Supreme Mind's high crown is the subject and the goal of the other allegories he studies. I suspect Lewis would revive the tradition because he believed that allegories may more successfully describe mind than science ever will. I will be arguing throughout my book that the crown has been preserved, handed down, and made available to us in the form of great poetry. Why is it so important? Without it, Lewis might say, we lose the wonder of creation and lose the love of its creator.

As the title of his book indicates, Lewis finds that allegory and love are intimately related, and for centuries poets have shown us how love and the soul are intimately related. Dante is the supreme example; by composing *La*

Vita Nuova and *Commedia*, he represents in his allegorical poetry how his love for Beatrice draws him (his soul) step by step through the divine order of Creation. In "And Man Became a Living Soul," I included the following quote from *A Midsummer Night's Dream* as an epigraph for the section titled "A Pilgrimage to a Sacred Place":

> *And as imagination bodies forth*
> *The forms of things unknown, the poet's pen*
> *Turns them to shapes and gives to airy nothing*
> *A local habitation and a name.*

Shakespeare's famous lines capture the raison d'être for allegory; they describe for the reader how the airy nothings of love and the soul take shape in the world. It's a marriage of imaginative forms and unshaped matter. Shakespeare's lines are a wonder of creation, and without the poet's pen they would be lost to mankind. Therefore, just as Shakespeare did, Lewis took up his pen to document, in over four hundred pages of scholarship, why he values the genre of allegory. Because I found him to be a credible, persuasive source about the subject, I have ventured to summarize the first two chapters of his work, as briefly as I can, in order to "body forth" my own argument.

As I've indicated, Lewis includes many passages of poetry, but these parts are all tied together in his prose by a kind of logic. This logic is an immaterial bond—like that between the married pairs of a subject and predicate in a sentence and like that between the married pairs of a vehicle and a tenor in a metaphor. His work as a whole makes sense, has meaning, has a soul. It illuminates his immaterial subject—for example, love or the oneness of our life—with the lights of poetry in a language. Language itself *in all its aspects* is a figure for the forms of things unknown *prior to the speech that gives them life*. That's why we love language. It gives love and oneness a shape and a name. Poets write love songs to their love, exercise their love of language, and strengthen their sense of what it means to be a living soul.

A Realm Out of Time

Lewis begins the work with a significant statement of purpose. He fears that we have "grown away" from the tradition that brought forth *The Romance of the Rose*. He tells us he doesn't want to galvanize a corpse (of course, we picture Frankenstein). He would persuade us that the tradition still lives:

> *Humanity does not pass through phases as a train passes through stations: being alive, it has the privilege of always moving yet never leaving anything behind. Whatever we have been, in some sort we are still. Neither the form nor the sentiment of this old poetry has passed away without leaving indelible traces on our minds. We shall understand our present, and perhaps even our future, the better if we can succeed, by an effort of historical imagination, in reconstructing that long-lost state of mind for which the allegorical love poem was a natural mode of expression.*

To describe humanity, all human subjects gathered into a single word, Lewis compares us to a train, but it's not like any train we know in this world. Lewis's train moves but remains in the station. He puts us on notice that he would describe a world that can't be studied the way a scientist studies the natural order, which exists in time. Through the medium of allegorical love poems, he studies timeless, immaterial objects—like love, the soul, and humanity. He will show us how allegories like *The Romance of the Rose* make these things available to the imagination.

There's a wholeness about these things, like the wholeness of Lewis's train. Wholeness is our goal as we make our pilgrimage through *The Allegory of Love*, but Lewis warns us that achieving the goal will take effort. We can't succeed "unless we begin by carrying our attention back to a period long before that poetry [like *The Romance of the Rose*] was born." He proposes first to trace "the rise of the sentiment called 'Courtly Love' and of the allegorical method" in separate chapters. He apologizes for delaying his readings of texts—for example, of *The Romance of the Rose*, *Troilus and Criseyde*, and *The Faerie Queene*—that are his main acts, but he assures us that the first two chapters are quite necessary. To argue that the poetry of the Troubadours is not a "mere episode in literary history," Lewis must situate humanity and the culture that sustains it in a timeless realm, and this wonderland is what his survey gradually reveals.

An Origin in Time

We may not realize it, but there's a continuity, Lewis writes, which "connects the Provencal love song with the love poetry of the later Middle Ages, and thence, through Petrarch and many others, with that of the present day [Lewis is writing in the 1930s]." That said, Lewis takes off his philosopher's hat (with which he makes ontological arguments about wholeness and timelessness) and puts on his literary historian hat to argue that this poetry is an episode in literary history that has a beginning in history. Because romantic love is such a dominant feature of our culture, "we mistake it for something natural and universal and therefore do not inquire into its origins." This insight leads to an important thesis of his book: "There can be no mistake about the novelty of romantic love." He then supports that argument with a brief survey of love as Catullus, Propertius, Plato, and Ovid characterized it. There's nothing like romantic love, he argues, to be found in their writings.

Nevertheless, it makes an appearance in the poetry of Provençal after the fall of classical civilization. Lewis discounts the influence of the Germanic temperament (their awe of women as uncanny beings) as well as the cult of Mary in Christianity. (The church didn't encourage reverence for women, and it consistently regarded sexual passion as a sin.) The people of that time "preferred to hear how a holy man went to heaven or how a brave man went to battle." They didn't tell stories "of how a man married, or failed to marry, a woman."

On Developing Our Confidence in Poetic Visions

In short, Lewis can't explain the cause of this "new thing." He *can* explain the particular form it took in the four "marks" of humility, courtesy, adultery, and the religion of love. Humility derives from the relation in feudal society between vassal and lord. This was a passionate relationship, the blood brotherhood of warriors, and served as "a mould into which romantic passion would almost certainly be poured." In a relationship with a feudal superior, humility, Lewis argues, "becomes entirely natural and inevitable." Courtesy follows from the same relationship. The lady of the seigneur shares her lord's authority and power within the court. She's the "arbitress of manners and the scourge of villainy even before she is loved."

As to the "association of love with adultery," Lewis gives two explanations. First, he holds that in feudal societies "marriages had nothing to do with love." Instead, it was "the dull background against which that love [courtly love, a newcomer on the scene] stood out in all the contrast of its new tenderness and delicacy." The second explanation, concerning "the sexology of the Medieval Church," takes him five pages to unravel. After surveying what Gregory, Hugo of Saint Victor, Peter Lombard, Albertus Magnus, and Thomas Aquinas thought about the sexual act and the desire that is its efficient cause (the agent that acts on a thing), Lewis concludes that the official teachers of the church regarded all love, but especially the passion and exalted devotion in courtly love, as wicked. This bred a rebellion in those who practiced it: "Thus if the Church tells them that the ardent lover even of his own wife is in mortal sin, they presently reply with the rule that true love is impossible in marriage." The church's view of sexuality created a "cleavage" between court and church. The division between the two is important for his argument and mine because it leads us to an important question: How can this duality be resolved into wholeness, the goal of our pilgrimage? How can a person be a lover and a Christian?

The fourth mark of courtly love, the love religion of the love god Amor, marks the divide between romantic love and Christianity as adultery did. Lewis quotes passages from "a twelfth-century jeu-d'esprit called the *Concilium in Monte Romarici*" to show how Ovid's mock devotion to the love god Amor (and mock devotion to women) could be developed into an "impudent parody" and a "humorous blasphemy" of Christian practices. The love religion, Lewis insists, "often begins as a parody of the real religion," but this parody, he adds, can become "something more serious than a parody." Dante's love of Beatrice, for example, produces "a noble fusion of sexual and religious experience." The author of the *Concilium* is not serious, whereas "Dante is as serious as a man can be." The tradition of the love god's religion is wide and complex; we should be prepared, he warns us, "for a certain ambiguity."

At this point Lewis proposes a resolution of duality and ambiguity in a paragraph I'll quote at length, given its importance to his and my theme. The love religion, he tells us:

> *. . . can become more serious without becoming reconciled to the real religion. Where it is not a parody of the Church it may be, in a sense, her rival—a temporary escape, a truancy from the ardours of a religion that was believed into the delights of a religion that was merely imagined. To describe it as the revenge of Paganism on her conquerer would be to exaggerate; but to think of it as a direct coloring of human passions by religious emotion would be a far graver error. It is as if some lover's metaphor when he said "Here is my heaven" in a moment of passionate abandonment were taken up and expanded into a system. Even while he speaks he knows that "here" is not his real heaven; and yet it is a delightful audacity to develop the idea a little further . . . If you picture the lover praying, sinning, repenting, and finally admitted to bliss, you will find yourself in the precarious dream-world of medieval poetry.*

Lewis's (imagined) lover has found his heaven—thanks to what he is experiencing in this world. Here he lacks nothing. As if he never left, he has come home. As Lewis suggests in the opening paragraph of the book, when we imagine a train that moves but never leaves the station, the lover experiences his life as one even though he knows he lives and moves in time. Nevertheless, as the book progresses, Lewis will argue that the lover's "here is my heaven" can be more than just a metaphor that expresses the lover's sensation of pleasure. It points to an experience in this world that unites secular and sacred love. He has already referred to Dante in this regard.

For whom is the dream world of medieval love poetry "precarious"? If it's a medieval reader who loses himself in the story, then perhaps he risks damnation by flouting the church's teaching about physical love. If it's a modern reader who aspires to live in this dream world, he risks scorn and ridicule by flouting the dictates of material science about what is real and what is not. As we move through Lewis's narrative, *he would develop our confidence in poetic visions* because he's convinced man does not live on bread alone.

Chretien's Allegory, though a Fiction, Points to Something Real

Just as the Federal Reserve has two mandates—the regulation of inflation and unemployment—C. S. Lewis has given himself two mandates: the explication of love and allegory. Having presented the "marks" of courtly love (humility, courtesy, adultery, and the religion of love) in general terms, in the next section Lewis shows how these marks can be seen in the romances of Chretien de Troyes, which were composed in the second half of the twelfth century. For example, in his *Lancelot*, the main character has all four marks clearly imprinted on him. Lancelot must rescue Guinevere who is held captive in the land of Gorre. He quickly loses his horse, though, and after a moment's hesitation, rides to the castle of her captivity in a tumbril, the cart of shame for criminals. In other words, he arrives humiliated. Guinevere increases his lowliness by refusing to acknowledge him and by ordering him to lose in the lists of a tournament. Observing the laws of courtesy, Lancelot submits to her haughty and whimsical demands. Of course, Guinevere is married to Arthur, so the love of Lancelot and Guinevere is marked with adultery. As to the mark of religion, Lewis writes: “The submission which Lancelot shows in his actions is accompanied, on the subjective side, by a feeling that deliberately apes religious devotion.”

The poem also employs allegory, the subject of the second mandate. Lewis explains the significance of this device for his narrative about allegory and love:

> *Chretien de Troyes, judged by modern standards, is on the whole an objective poet. The adventures still occupy the greater part of his stories. By the standard of his own times, on the other hand, he must have appeared strikingly subjective. The space devoted to action that goes forward only in the souls of his characters was probably beyond all medieval precedent. He was one of the first explorers of the human heart, and is therefore rightly to be numbered among the fathers of the novel of sentiment. But these psychological passages have usually one characteristic which throws special light on the subject of this book. Chretien can hardly turn to the inner world without, at the same time, turning to allegory . . . It is as if the insensible could not yet knock at the doors of the poetic consciousness without transforming itself into the likeness of the sensible: as if men could not easily grasp the reality of moods and emotions without turning them into shadowy persons. Allegory, besides being many other things, is the subjectivism of an objective age. When Lancelot hesitates before mounting the cart, Chretien represents his indecision as a debate between Reason which forbids, and Love which urges him on. A later poet would have told us directly—though not, after all without metaphor—what Lancelot was feeling: an earlier poet would not have attempted such a scene at all.*

Lewis here continues his argument about “the reality of moods and emotions” begun in the last section with his imaginary lover who exclaims, “Here is my heaven.” As a poet, our imaginary lover employed the reality of Christian doctrine to express the reality of what he felt in present experience.

After describing Chretien’s use of allegory in the quote above, Lewis warns us not to assume “as to what can, and what cannot be the expression of a real imaginative experience.” An allegory may strike a modern reader as an arcane literary device, but Lewis encourages us to believe that it points to something real, the inner world (even the soul) of a person.

Andreas and the Rift between Courtly and Divine Love

In Chretien, Lewis tells us, "we see the developed theory of love put into action in the course of stories." Andreas Capellanus puts the theory of courtly love into a didactic, theoretical work called *De Arte Honeste Amandi*. In it, Andreas the Chaplin teaches his pupils all the explicit and implicit rules in the honest art of courtly love. He quotes chapter and verse and gives case histories. There's a tradition of precedent as in common law. The rules stipulate that a courtly lover must be a true gentleman, and Lewis quotes and comments on Andreas's overall judgment about this religion of Amor:

> *With such a conception of the lover's qualifications, it is not surprising that Andreas should return again and again to the power of love for good. "It is agreed among all men that there is no good thing in the world, and no courtesy, which is not derived from love as from its fountain." It is "the fountain and origin of all good things"; without it "all usages of courtesy would be unknown to man." The lady is allowed free choice in her acceptance or rejection of a lover in order that she may reward the merit of the best: she must not abuse this power in order to gratify her own fancies. Only women who are "enlisted in the soldiery of love" are praised among men. Even a young unmarried woman should have a lover. It is true that her husband, when she marries, is bound to discover it, but if he is a wise man he will know that a woman who had not followed the "commands of love" would necessarily have less probitas.*

Unlike the author of the of the *Concilium*, Andreas is not writing a work of mock devotion or an impudent parody. Andreas, Lewis claims, "is most serious in those places where he dwells upon the power of love to call forth all knightly and courtly excellences . . . If this is not a religion, it is, at any rate, a system of ethics."

Lewis closes his reading, however, with a conclusion that eclipses the praise Andreas expressed earlier for Amor and his religion. In the end, Andreas finds that the rift between the two worlds of courtly love and divine love is "irremediable." He meant what he said:

> *. . . when he told us that love was the source of everything in saeculo bonum, and it is our fault if we are apt to forget the limitation—in saeculo . . . He means the really good things, in a human sense, as contrasted with the really bad things: courage and courtesy and generosity, as against baseness. But, rising like a sheer cliff above and behind this humane or secular scale of values, he has another which is not to be reconciled with it, another by whose standard there is very little to choose between the worldly good and the worldly bad . . . When courtly love succeeds in fusing with religion, as in Dante, unity is restored to the mind, and love can be treated with a solemnity that is whole-hearted. But where it is not so fused, it can never, under the shadow of its tremendous rival, be more than a temporary truancy.*

The light of the difference between a worldly good and a worldly bad pales in comparison with the bright, shining light of sacred truth. For this reason, Lewis points out, Andreas repents what he has written at the end of his book, just as Chaucer retracts what he has written at the end of *The Canterbury Tales* and *Troilus*. Despite the rift Lewis has found in these writings, he still holds out for Dante's wholehearted love of Beatrice. In Dante, he tells us, "the quarrel between Christianity and the love religion was made up." This may be true for Dante, but his relationship with Beatrice was sexual only in a very limited sense. Dante loved her beauty as a girl and as a woman, but they were never lovers. Lewis's narrative about love aims at the wholeness of married love, which he finds in Spenser's *The Faerie Queene*.

A Preview of Married Love in Chaucer and Shakespeare

About eighty years after Dante died, Chaucer wrote "The Knight's Tale." It takes the form of what we nowadays call a romantic comedy. After certain trials of courtship, the knight concludes his tale with a wedding:

Palamon was espoused to Emily,
And God that all this wide, wide world has wrought,
Send them his love, for it was dearly bought!
Now Palamon's in joy, amid a wealth
Of bliss and splendor, happiness and wealth.
He's tenderly beloved of Emily
And serves her with a gentle constancy,
And never a jealous word between them spoken
Or other sorrow in a love unbroken.
Thus ended Palamon and Emily,
And God save all this happy company!

The requirement in courtly love that it take the form of adultery has now been overlooked. Shakespeare's romantic comedies all end in marriages, like the three that conclude *A Midsummer Night's Dream*. These are marriages in the fullest sense. The most important couple, though, is not included in that number. Oberon and Titania, the king and queen of fairyland, don't need to be married, because they already are married and have been since time began. True, they first appear as combatants in a full-fledged battle of the sexes, but the play ends with them "new in amity." The alembic of their midsummer night transforms them into loving partners. It's an alchemical phenomenon for which a science of nature has no explanation. Shakespeare's play and the prominent role he gives the court of Oberon and Titania expresses "a real imaginative experience" (see the quote on page 80 about Lewis's warning), in which we participate in a process that sustains and enriches married love.

Chapter 2

Sensibles and Insensibles in Symbolism and Allegory

Henry Holiday's

Dante Meets Beatrice at Ponte Santa Trinita

The Married Pairs

In his role as a literary historian, Lewis informs the reader that a certain kind of poetry came into being around the beginning of the twelfth century; this is the phenomenon he studies. It's a body of work that developed over centuries and its influence, he argues, can still be found in the literature and popular culture of the present. I have already shown, however, that he also approaches his subject as a philosopher. His study of the tradition exemplified by *The Romance of the Rose* leads him (and now us) into the ontological question, "What is real?" In the opening paragraph of the book, he questions our picture of time as a series of discreet moments one after another where each moment, once passed, is forever lost. Humanity, he tells us, "does not pass through phases as a train passes through stations: being alive, it has the privilege of always moving yet never leaving anything behind." The tradition of courtly love, in this analogy, is like one of those stations, but humanity—as he conceives of us—has been granted a privilege that allows us to move even as we are allowed to stay, for Lewis here imagines time as a whole, not a discreet series of parts. He begins his book with this assertion because a false picture of time distorts our picture of humanity and of ourselves as instances of it. Allegories of love, he'll argue, provide a different and more realistic picture.

Where the opening paragraph on courtly love questions our sense of reality as it is governed by our sense of time, section 1 of the chapter on allegory questions our sense of reality as it is governed by our sense of space. Space is extension (time is also extension, but in a different dimension); space is the world and all the objects we encounter in it. To set the stage for his treatment of allegory, Lewis engages us in precise definitions of *allegory* and *symbolism*, and these definitions bear tidings concerning the substance of reality. As in his previous assertion about the wholeness of time, an allegory presents our substance as a whole.

Section 1 deserves to be quoted in full. Lewis writes with feeling and insight into matters of great importance for his theme of human wholeness, growth, and happiness. Nevertheless, I will summarize and quote as best I can. Having given us a brief history of courtly love and having briefly discussed the use of allegory in Chretien, Lewis writes that it "now remains to consider independently the history of the allegorical method." A complete history, however, can't be done because:

> *Allegory, in some sense, belongs not to medieval man but to man, or even to mind, in general. It is of the very nature of thought and language to represent what is immaterial in picturable terms. What is good or happy has always been high like heavens and bright like the sun.*

I have been making an argument like this about the nature of thought and metaphoric language repeatedly thus far in my own text. The origin of allegory is as much a mystery as the origin of language itself.

Lewis then offers a tantalizing observation: "To ask how these married pairs of sensibles and insensibles first came together would be great folly; the real question is how they ever came apart, and to answer that question is beyond the province of the mere historian." I find his disclaimer somewhat arch, for he is not a "mere historian," as I suspect he well knows. I include his observation, even though it digresses from the immediate subject, because it describes sensibles and insensibles as a "married pair." As he conceives of them, the two play a primal role, like that of Adam and Eve, in the history of human thought. Returning to his theme, he plans to inquire "how something latent in human speech [the marrying of sensibles and insensibles] becomes . . . explicit in the structure of whole poems; and how poems of that [allegorical] kind come to enjoy an unusual popularity in the Middle Ages."

The Two Ways the Mind Can Marry Sensibles and Insensibles

Lewis then explains how these married pairs are joined by the mind in two different literary figures:

> *This fundamental equivalence between the immaterial and the material may be used by the mind in two ways, and we need here be concerned with only one of them. On the one hand you can start with an immaterial fact such as the passions which you actually experience, and can then invent visibilia to express them. If you are hesitating between an angry retort and a soft answer, you can express your state of mind by inventing a person called Ira with a torch and letting her contend with another invented person called Patientia. This is allegory, and it is this alone that we have to deal. But there is another way of using the equivalence, which is almost the opposite of allegory, and which I would call sacramentalism or symbolism. If our passions, being immaterial, can be copied by material inventions, then it is possible that our material world in its turn is the copy of an invisible world. As the god Amor and his figurative garden are to the actual passions of men, so perhaps we ourselves and our "real" world are to something else. The attempt to read that something else through its sensible imitations, to see the archetype in the copy, is what I mean by symbolism or sacramentalism . . . The difference between the two can hardly be exaggerated. The allegorist leaves the given—his own passions—to talk of that which is confessedly less real, which is a fiction. The symbolist leaves the given to find that which is more real. To put the difference in another way, for the symbolist it is we who are the allegory. We are the frigid personifications* [like Amor and Patientia in the examples above]; *the heavens above us are the "shadowy abstractions"* [the Platonic forms, mathematical perfection]; *the world which we mistake for reality is the flat outline of that which elsewhere veritably is in all the round of its unimaginable dimensions.*

Lewis tells us that we need be concerned only with the way an allegorist leaves the given to talk of a fiction, but he makes us aware of the way a symbolist "leaves the given to find that which is more real." To my ear, this sounds like the ontological debate between Aristotle and Plato as to whether we concern ourselves with the things of this world or whether we concern ourselves with transcendent forms. Like Aristotle, the allegorist takes the given world as the real world, and this world is informed by an "immaterial fact," like the passion of love, which is expressed in a fiction like *The Romance of the Rose*. When allegory and symbolism are described in this way, though, we can see why someone would want to read what the symbolist has to say, for the symbolist is concerned with what is real, not a fiction. The reality we find, however, is an abstraction, not something alive, even if it is "in all the round of its unimaginable dimensions."

In the next paragraph, he gives us a brief history of symbolism, starting with the dialogues of Plato—where "The Sun is a copy of the Good," through Neoplatonism, Augustine, Boethius, and Hugo of Saint Victor in the Middle Ages. I would guess that Lewis equates symbolism with sacramentalism because a sacrament is a powerful symbol of the faith for believing Catholics and Anglicans. As Hugo explains, it is a physical thing, like the water in baptism, but it is also a sacred thing, the immaterial grace of the Holy Ghost. In the sacrament, the material and the immaterial are joined in a mystical union. We experience the archetype in the copy. No wonder sacraments have such a powerful effect on our minds. Lewis, however, doesn't leave the question of symbolism there. He closes out the paragraph with an observation about the "literary side" of symbolism. "But of course the poetry of symbolism does not find its greatest expression in the Middle ages at all, but rather in the time of the Romantics; and this, again, is significant of the *profound difference* that separates it from allegory."

I wish Lewis had taken more time with symbolism as sacramentalism. Because he didn't, I have to infer why he adds sacramentalism to the discussion. Since Lewis was a devout Anglican, the way a sacrament married the material and the immaterial must have been important to him. The Romantics Lewis has in mind, however, lived in a skeptical time when science and Enlightenment thought made it harder for many to believe that a sacrament could marry the material and the immaterial as the church believed. Instead, Romantics resisted or ignored the symbolic forms of the church and made symbols of their own to ignite their personal, transcendental flights. These images are meaningful, but I suspect that for Lewis they lack the power of a sacred object to bind members in a community. It may be that for Lewis Romantic symbolism is *faux* sacramentalism. Its root is too shallow to grow into the great tree, axis mundi, the real, tangible center of the world. For a believing Christian, this center became flesh when Jesus was conceived in Mary. I believe Lewis is distinguishing allegory from *Romantic symbolism*, and he confirms this reading of a "profound difference" in what follows his assertion of it.

Substance in Dante's Allegories

Lewis develops his argument about this profound difference in three paragraphs on Dante that complete section 1. Romantic symbolism, he tells us, had become the dominant form of poetic expression and interpretation in the time he was writing. Because of this, modern readers "prefer symbol to allegory; and when an allegory pleases them, they are therefore anxious to pretend that it is not allegory but symbol." He describes the way modern readers would like to understand Dante as an example of this error:

> *It seems chilling to be told that Amor in the Vita Nuova is only a personification; we would willingly believe that Dante, like a modern romantic, feels himself to be reaching after some transcendental reality which the forms of discursive thought cannot contain. It is quite certain, however, that Dante feels nothing of the kind.*

Having asserted this in sentences of his own, in the next paragraph Lewis quotes from the *Vita Nuova* so that Dante can speak for himself on this point:

> *"You may be surprised," says Dante, "that I speak of love as if it were a thing that could exist by itself; and not only as if it were an intelligent substance, but even as if it were a corporeal substance. Now this, according to the truth, is false. For love has not, like a substance, an existence of its own, but is only an accident occurring in a substance."*

Lewis then comments that:

> *However the personification is to be defended, it is clear that Dante has no*

> *thought of pretending that it is more than a personification. It is as he says himself a moment later . . . a piece of technique, a weapon in the armory . . . As such it is naturally defended by an appeal to literary precedent.*

Dante finds that precedent in classical Latin poetry. Even though he is writing in the Italian vernacular, Lewis tells us that Dante claims:

> *. . . all those licenses which were already conceded to the versifier. He must not, however, use them arbitrarily; he must have a reason, and it must even be "the sort of reason that could be explained in prose." "It would be a great disgrace," Dante adds, "to a man, if he should rime matters under figure and rhetorical coloring, and then, when he was asked, could not strip off the vesture and show the true sense."*

And this is what Dante does throughout *La Vita Nuova*, as he alternates between prose and poetry. He would show the true sense of his poetry.

In the final paragraph of the section, Lewis makes a critical distinction between allegory and symbolism:

> *The great allegorist's firm thinking leaves no room for misunderstanding. There is nothing "mystical" or mysterious about medieval allegory; the poets know quite clearly what they are about and are well aware that the figures which they present to us are fictions. Symbolism is a mode of thought, allegory is a mode of expression. It belongs to the form of poetry, more than to its content, and it is learned from the practice of the ancients.*

I found the last two sentences to be difficult, so I've written the following interpretation. A symbol entails a thought about reality—for example, Plato's symbol of the cave, which conveys the thought that the true form of Beauty exists objectively apart from the beauty of appearances. An allegory, on the other hand, entails the reality of Dante himself expressing himself in poetry. Allegory "belongs" to forms of expressive poetry, not to a philosophy or a science, which "belongs" to an objective reality (a content). In Dante's poetic world, an "accident" like Love exists in the substance of his poetry. It has no existence apart from the poem.

In short, Dante follows Aristotle into a space that consists of the distinct objects we encounter in this world. Those objects become one, though, in his poetry. Symbolists follow Plato in a quest for "shadowy abstractions" (see the quote on pages 87–88) of which we and the things of the world are mere copies. For Aristotle and Dante, the things of this world are not a random collection of atoms nor are they mystical, otherworldly. They occupy, as it were, a middle ground between the two; they have an intelligible shape. In Aristotle's model of reality, form is immanent in matter. In Dante's model of reality, his poetry is immanent in all his experiences. His poetry is where these experiences come meaningfully together like words in a meaningful sentence.

Dante speaks of accidents in the substance of an allegory, but the substance of an allegory points inevitably to the substance of the one writing the allegory. Even though Dante is famous as the poet who gave us vivid pictures of hell, purgatory, and heaven, his theory of allegory suggests these are but fictions of the real substance, which is Dante himself. His poetry allows him to express his encounters in *this world,* the given world—with people, with the circumstances of his life, and most importantly, for a real poet like Dante, with the great and very real imaginative works of poetry that take up so much space in Dante's thought. In the poetic space of *La Vita Nuova* and the *Commedia*, the accidents of his life, his thoughts and feelings from encounters in the world, live as one substance. Likewise, in the poetic space of *The Allegory of Love,* the accidents of Lewis's encounters in the world live as one substance.

How can I say that they live? This, I suppose, must be regarded as a fiction, a metaphor. The poetry of Dante and the poetry of C. S. Lewis come to life in the reader's imagination. So much depends, in my inquiry, on the reader.

Melville's Symbol of Hate

Lewis tells us that we need not be concerned with the other way of marrying the sensible with the insensible, but Melville's *Moby Dick* may help us grasp the profound difference between allegory and the Romantic symbolism to which Lewis refers. For Ahab, the white whale is a symbol of his existence; it's a symbol of the life that disfigured him in mortal combat with it. Ahab seeks to give his life meaning by taking vengeance on his existence, but that act and that meaning is veiled by mile after mile and fathoms upon fathoms of wastewater. To win the combat, to thrust through the veil and kill the mystical heart of what he hates, he "leaves the given" in a fruitless quest that ends in the destruction of his ship, his crew, and himself. (In an aside, this description of Ahab, I believe, anticipates the mass murderers of our own day, who wreak vengeance-for-being-born on scores of innocents.)

Ahab is an egoist, an idealist, who makes a grave mistake in his thinking. As Starbuck tries to warn him, the white whale can only be a creature, not a symbol. In contrast with *The Allegory of Love*, we could call Melville's story about Ahab *The Symbol of Hate*. Wholeness characterizes Dante's allegory; division characterizes Ahab's symbolism. A veil of separation always falls between Ahab and his ideal of vengeance. Try as you might, you can't kill a symbol. In contrast with the symbolist, who loves abstractions (otherworldly forms), the allegorist loves Creation. In an allegory, like the one in the book of Jonah, the whale is the whole of Jonah's substance, which transports him to a life that's worthy of the gift. Jonah's whale is the All of "All's well."

Moby Dick is an imaginative work of the highest order. Ishmael, the narrator, survives. He has seen it all, and as Horatio does for Hamlet's story, Ishmael faithfully records the tragedy of Ahab and his crew. By pitching the whole story into Ishmael's point of view, Melville preserves the wholeness of his poetic vision from Ahab's illusory and fatally divisive ideal. Ishmael has the last word and speaks to us, the living, of this *accident,* the Rage (worthy of Mars in an allegory) in the substance of Ahab that, admittedly, takes up so much space in Ishmael's life.

Chapter 3

The Drift Toward Allegory in Statius

Gustave Doré's

Dante in the Gloomy Wood

The Crown

In addition to presenting material from the next "station" in Lewis's book, I offer once more a review of my overall argument. It is one train of thought, but it moves through many stations.

In section 2 of his chapter on allegory, Lewis describes "the drift toward allegory" in the *Thebaid*, a Latin poem from first century AD by Statius. Just as Lewis's choice of this poem about two brothers from Thebes occupies a central place in his explication of allegory, Chaucer's "The Knight's Tale" about two cousins from Thebes occupies a central place in my explication of a comic vision in my first book, *A Comic Vision of Great Constancy*. There are similarities and differences between the narratives of Statius and Chaucer, who reworked Boccaccio's *Teseida*. In the *Thebaid*, the two brothers fight to possess for themselves the crown of Thebes, which they both own by virtue of inheritance from their father, Oedipus. In Chaucer's tale, the two cousins from Thebes fight to possess the crown of love, which they think they own by virtue of seeing and claiming the image of a woman, unfortunately the same woman. Who will wear the crown of kingship? The brothers in the *Thebaid* fought for the crown of worldly power that will go to the strongest man. The cousins in "The Knight's Tale" fought for the crown of love that will go to the truest lover.

The shift from a worldly crown in Statius's poem to a crown of love in Boccaccio's and Chaucer's versions of it mirrors the shift that characters in the works of Chaucer and Shakespeare experience during the course of the narrative. They undergo a rite of initiation in which the worldly love of an object is transformed into a spiritual love of the whole from which the object derives. This shift, as I mentioned in the opening pages of Book One, frames my reading of "The Knight's Tale" and *A Midsummer Night's Dream*.

Years later, while reading *Henry IV, Part 2*, it occurred to me with some force that this shift serves as a thematic frame more generally for the rest of Shakespeare's canon and that a crown is the center around which his narratives turn. The crown becomes the focus of the play in the scene in which

Prince Hal, thinking the king had died, prematurely picks it up, puts it on his head, and leaves the room to grieve for his father. When he first sees the crown next to his father in bed, though, he considers what it means:

> *Why doth the crown lie there upon his pillow,*
> *Being so troublesome a bedfellow?*
> *O polished perturbation! Golden care!*
> *That keep's the ports of slumber open wide*
> *To many a watchful night!*
>
> *Henry IV, Part 2*, act 4, scene 5

The crown is a troublesome bedfellow because it represents what it means to be a living soul. Whether you are a glove maker or a king, the burden is the same.

What is that burden? I addressed this question in the introduction and Book One but summed it up in the paragraph at the beginning of that section about "The Birth and the Burden of a Living Soul" (see pages 51–53): "Despite the wickedness of the human race the Lord found a man to bear His will—Noah, from whom we inherit the breath of life. Because Noah found favor in the eyes of the Lord, He commands him to bear the burden of an immense task. Noah must contain and preserve in his vessel all sentient beings. Over the course of God's story in the Bible, the Lord finds others who must bear His will, and the burden is the same." A living soul, I maintain throughout these readings, is governed by the golden rule, and this is a wakeful, troublesome matter for Everyman. How can a fallible human being live up to it? This is the question that the crown puts to the prince. In the "golden care" of the crown before him, Prince Hal glimpses the difficulty of framing *his* rule so that it meets the standard of that golden rule.

So many of Shakespeare's plays revolve around a crown of worldly power—whether that of a king, a duke, an ensign (like Iago), a husband (like Mr. Ford in *The Merry Wives*), or a majordomo (like Falstaff or Parolles). The histories of English kings fit this theme perfectly (like well-made gloves in

Shakespeare's first profession) for a writer just getting started and for an audience that loved seeing their history acted out on the stage. People love worldly power, and they crave stories about the people who would wield it. Shakespeare could easily see how the theme played out in the histories available to him, and he could see it for himself as an active member of Elizabeth's court.

The crown, though, can also signal an otherworldly presence. Within Shakespeare's Christian culture, there are countless pictures, like Simone Martini's vision in the *Annunciation,* of figures who are blessed with a crown of spiritual power. As I have pointed out in the introduction, the painting also celebrates that moment when, for believing Christians, the spiritual form of the world was made flesh and crowned creation with a golden radiance. The good news of the Gospels repeatedly reminded Christians of a greater, more splendid kingdom than that of Caesar. In the material world, a crown is a material *symbol* that represents the reality of concrete authority. When the one who wears the crown commands, the people obey. If they don't, then the one who wears the crown is not the real king.

A phenomenon like this, I believe, prompted Shakespeare to inquire into the nature of true power, and it led him (inevitably, I believe) to inquire into the nature of the soul. True government is self-government, and self-government derives from insight into the nature and the reality of the soul. The power of a living soul is self-evident and requires no symbols, special oils, titles, accessories, or perks to impress others. In the play of *Everyman,* Death initiates the journey Everyman must take to learn the nature of his soul, and Shakespeare happily borrowed the dramatic form of this lesson for his plays. *All's Well That Ends Well* is a case in point. Like other Shakespearean heroines, the main character, Helena, has the gift of life. Thanks to her father, who was a famous physician, she possesses a secret power of healing. She reveals that power to the world when she saves the king of France from a disease that otherwise would have ended in death. The king wears the crown, but Helena is the one who invests it with spiritual power. Because the play never reveals exactly what the disease is (it's referred to as a "fistula," an image that suggests a knockout blow), we have to imagine it.

For all we know, it might be, as it was for Ahab, a deeply rooted resentment that he had been born into a life that must end in death. Life is diseased in this way. For saving his life, the king asks Helena what she would have in return, and she asks to be married to Bertram, the son of her guardian. At a time when feudal kings arranged their vassals' marriages, the king of France commands Bertram to marry Helena, but he rebels. He thinks she is below his station.

To satisfy the king's will, Bertram marries Helena but immediately abandons her. The court (and the audience), observing his breach in the social order, has to wonder wherein lies the locus of power. Does it lie with the king, or does it lie with Bertram? To gratify his self-image, Bertram runs away to fight as a mercenary in a foreign land. He proves in Italy that he's a skilled horseman and warrior, and this inflates his sense of self-sufficiency even further. He's his own master; he can do what he wants. Bertram, however, has foolishly overestimated his powers. He doesn't know that Helena has followed him to Italy, where she enlists the help of her landlady and the landlady's daughter to win back her husband. In Italy, Bertram fights successfully against men to secure his sense of entitlement, but in Italy the three women successfully lure him into a trap that completely undoes his fortress of self-love.

All's Well is not a popular play, and I think there's a simple reason. Helena's love for Bertram makes no sense. He's a snob who loves his status, and yet he rejects his place in the social order by refusing to participate in it. There's nothing to like about Bertram, and yet Helena goes to absurd lengths to make him her husband. In other romantic comedies, like *Much Ado About Nothing*, *The Taming of the Shrew*, or *As You Like It*, we sense a strong "chemistry" between the man and the woman that's completely lacking in *All's Well*. The play makes sense, however, if we read it as an allegory. For example, it has a plotline similar to that of canto 1 in *The Faerie Queene*. Here's a brief summary. The Redcrosse Knight and his soul (mate) Una are separated, and he rides instead with the false Duessa, who would destroy his goodness. Una faithfully seeks him out and restores him to health after his bout with evil. Just as the king of France helps Helena in her quest to recover her husband at the end of Shakespeare's play, Arthur helps Una in Spenser's poem. Good kings, the ones who wear the crown of golden care, play this restorative role in the lives of their subjects.

If we interpret the play as an allegory like *Everyman*, Bertram (as Everyman) is forced in the final scene to "go a journey" in order to discover his true nature as a subject and a living soul. The three women have sweetly lulled him into an unexpected trial, where he has to stand in judgment before the court. There, they produce clear evidence that he is a liar and a seducer. Like Death finding Everyman, Death finds Bertram's inflated and corrupt opinion of himself. He is roundly scourged in full view of the king and the court so he can be reborn as a proper subject. For a time, he was "high on his horse" with the material power a sword and a powerful animal could give him, but his fall from grace will force him to consider what it means to lack the spirit of a living, loving soul. A modern reader may fault the play's lack of "realism," but I believe it maintains its integrity as an allegory. After all, my book is dedicated to the proposition that allegory is telling, in its own way, a true story. Once I read it in that spirit, I find wonderful poetry consistent with the theme I've outlined.

What are Bertram's and Helena's prospects in marriage? For an answer I look to Chaucer, Shakespeare's master in these matters. There's very little in the way of chemistry between Emily and the knights who contend for her love in "The Knight's Tale," and yet Chaucer ends his story with a vision of their happiness in the passage I've already quoted for another reason (see pages 82–83):

Palamon was espoused to Emily,
And God that all this wide, wide world has wrought,
Send them his love, for it was dearly bought!
Now Palamon's in joy, amid a wealth
Of bliss and splendor, happiness and wealth.
He's tenderly beloved of Emily

And serves her with a gentle constancy,
And never a jealous word between them spoken
Or other sorrow in a love unbroken.
Thus ended Palamon and Emily,
And God save all this happy company!

In place of "chemistry"—feelings produced by the chemistry of the body—Chaucer inserts another reason for a "love unbroken." Their love is and will be whole because it is God's love and because God's love has been "dearly bought." Palamon's cousin and alter ego Arcite, his rival to Emily's love, suffered a mortal injury to his heart minutes after winning the right to marry the woman he and Palamon had sought for many years, but before he died, he blessed the marriage of Palamon and Emily. A marriage, a lasting relationship, isn't just about a feeling that arises quite naturally in the chemistry of the body. It has to involve an awareness about life itself as a gift and a pearl beyond price. Because Palamon constantly lives with Emily by his side, he lives constantly with an awareness of Arcite's loss, and this sorrow gives the gift of Emily a joyful, gentle glow. This effect derives, not from the chemistry of the body, but from intellectual insight. The effect is like a crown of light, and a crown, we remember, is for the head.

Shakespeare leaves the marriage of Bertram and Helena as a completely open question. If I read the story as an allegory, however, it fits within the thematic framework of "The Knight's Tale." Bertram's self-image dies of shame before the whole court. But the king forgives his trespass as does Helena. Respect for the sacred power of the crown, respect for Helena's faithfulness, and gratitude for a second chance at life may open the way for Bertram to the happiness that Palamon and Emily knew.

Just as Shakespeare frames his stories around a shift from a material to an immaterial crown, C. S. Lewis begins his study of allegory with a meditation on the married pairs of sensibles and insensibles—like the body of a brute safely married to the soul that will teach it manners and spiritual insight. *The Allegory of Love* has been a great help to my inquiry about these matters. The texts Lewis has selected to treat, the passages he quotes, and his commentary have given my inquiry a proper foundation. It seems to me only fitting to acknowledge that my readings of Shakespeare would not exist without the literary practices we have inherited from the ancients, and from those like Dante, Chaucer, Goethe, and Lewis, who studied them carefully. Shakespeare's plays and poems are a treasure house for understanding the relationship between these married pairs. The crown is a symbol of real power, but Shakespeare frames the journey a man takes to win that crown as an allegory. It's a journey Everyman must take, king and commoner alike.

A Spectrum of Poetic Figures

Lewis doesn't retell much of Statius's story. Instead, he narrates the story of allegory's development. Personification is his main character, and we follow along as it grows into a different sort of thing. The setting for Lewis's story is a spectrum of poetic figures. On one end of the spectrum, he puts those personifications, which, according to Samuel Johnson, can only "perch and hover." This may have been true in eighteenth-century England, but in Roman times, Lewis informs us, they had more freedom. This freedom is related to the fact that Romans throughout their history worshipped abstractions like Fides and Concordia. These figures are universals, but they could also be living spirits.

To place them more clearly, Lewis establishes the other end of the spectrum where we find mythological figures like Mars and Juno. In the *Thebaid*, Lewis tells us:

> *. . . there is a double process at work. On the one hand, the gods are becoming more and more like mere personifications; on the other, the personifications are beginning to trespass farther and farther beyond the boundaries which Johnson assigns them. The first process can be seen in the treatment of Mars. Statius has a good deal to say about Mars [in a story about war], but the place which he finds for him in the story is not a genuinely mythological place—such, for example, as Juno's place in the Aeneid. Juno has a mythological reason for disliking the Trojans.*

> *[Paris gave the famous apple to Venus]. She has personal motives for her conduct, and those motives can be explained by the earlier history which is presupposed in the poem. If Mars were to be introduced in the Theban war in the same mythological fashion, we should expect to find him interfering on one side or the other for some intelligible personal motive . . . In the Thebaid, however, he has no such motive. Indeed he does not act independently at all. He is simply summoned by Jupiter; and it is equally significant that Jupiter commands him, not to interfere in the war, but simply and solely to stir it up . . . His business is not to influence wars, but to inspire them; he is in fact "an accident occurring in a substance," the martial or pugnacious spirit as it exists in the mind now of one nation, and now of another, at the bidding of Fate . . . "War" or "Bellicosity" is not itself Fate: it is one of the instruments of Fate, to be called up in the minds of men when Fate requires.*

This passage clearly foreshadows what's coming; we are about to witness the birth of a literary form which will explore "the minds of men" in a novel, more dramatic way.

When Jupiter sends for Mars, and he appears for the first time in the story, he is "discovered raging" without any reason to rage. Lewis tells us this is natural, for "It is his *esse* to rage." The same is true in Statius's portrayal of Bacchus. He is merely "Drunkenness personified," an accident, a character's state of mind. Lewis then looks at the gods' new position from both ends of the spectrum. "But the twilight of the gods is the mid-morning of the personifications." In a memorable form, Lewis prepares the place between personification and mythology that allegory will occupy.

Things That Live and Die in the Inner World of the Soul

But we are not there yet. Lewis argues that allegory makes its appearance for the first time in Western literature at a specific place in Statius's poem. Before we get there, he gives examples of personifications that have become living spirits and not "frigid" abstractions (as in the quote on page 88). Statius has Virtus—and not Pallas, Mercury, or Apollo—tell a young warrior that a heroic destiny awaits him; he can save the city by sacrificing himself. Lewis explains the reason she can play this important role:

> *Virtus too had her temples, and if Statius employs her rather than the Olympians as the machine for one of the gravest and most affecting passages in his poem, this is because she is to him a deity more serious and, in a sense, more real than all the Graeco-Roman pantheon.*

When Statius speaks of Clementia, Lewis tells us "we find something like real religious emotion," and this time he gives us the quote:

> *An altar midst the city rose*
> *Which none of all the mightier gods can claim,*
> *Mild Mercy's seat, hallow'd continually*
> *By suppliant sorrow, never thence repulsed—*
> *To ask is to obtain.*

Lewis's commentary that follows is important to my argument about the nature of the soul:

> *Yet with all this—and the point is crucial—there is no pretense that Clementia is other than a state of mind; "the mind and heart of man her chosen haunt," says Statius; and the same might be said of all his gods. They are all things that live and die in the inner world of the soul, all "accidents occurring in a substance."*

To support my argument, I thought it was important to learn from literary precedent—as understood by Lewis, Dante, and the ancients—about the link in literature between the "inner world" and the soul. For a modern reader this may seem more like a tautology than an insight. In this and subsequent parts of the chapter on allegory, Lewis develops—as a literary historian—his argument that ancient and classical writers had not up to this point depicted "the inner world" of their characters. The drift toward allegory, he argues in *this* section, is what allowed a writer like Statius to discover it. In addition, the passage supports my argument in previous commentary that Lewis is inclined to regard the soul as the substance wherein the accidents of life "occur" (see the italicized quote above). Not only are we drifting toward allegory but we are also drifting toward understanding that the soul is the substance of this life, the substance wherein even the gods live and die. Lewis is arguing as a philosopher for an ontology incommensurate with that of science.

So Much Depends upon What We Mean by the Soul

Once again, I would take the view from Olympus to review my argument.

So much depends upon what we mean by the soul. As it's commonly understood, and as I have described in "And Man Became a Living Soul," the soul of a person belongs to that person alone. This is true, but the statement needs some clarification if we think the word refers to an inner life to which we and no one else has private access. My wife and I recently saw a production of *Private Lives* by Noël Coward in which a man and a woman act out their intention to disengage from public life in order to live and love in their private lives. The experiment, shall we say, has its ups and downs. Mr. Coward may or may not agree, but long experience generally proves that people make a serious mistake when they associate their souls solely with their private lives. Instead, great writers question the notion of a private life. For example, Shakespeare's Claudius probably thought that if no one saw him pour the poison into his brother Hamlet's ear this would remain a private and not a public act. Instead, his brother's ghost tells the story to his son and proves that:

Foul deeds will rise
Though all the earth o'erwhelm them to men's eyes.

After months of reading Goethe, I found a quote in John Armstrong's *Love, Life, Goethe,* in which Goethe addresses in a letter to a lady the interchangeability of inner and outer:

> *In the last months in Frankfort prior to his departure for Weimar, writing to Augusta von Stolberg, Goethe described the state of his soul. It is, he says, "like a sock that is being turned inside out: the outer becoming inner; the inner outer."*
>
> *Love, Life, Goethe*, page 99

Goethe is writing at a turning point in his life. Prior to this, he had been engaged in the concerns of a private citizen. He did some routine legal work, he traveled, he wrote poetry, and, notably, he wrote the blockbuster novel *The Sorrows of Young Werther*. Goethe has Werther tell his story in the form of letters that he wrote to a friend prior to his suicide; as such, it's a form that gives his presentation an intensely subjective character. The letter to Augusta marks a turning point because in Weimar Goethe would serve as a member of the duke's government responsible for public rather than personal matters. He expresses his thought as a private matter in a letter to a lady; we have an impression of something briefly glimpsed and quickly expressed. Still, we can't miss Goethe's great gift for condensing a world of insight in a simple image. He's looking ahead to being turned inside out. The soul, he tells her, takes in everything in our life—the things "out there" in the world as well as our mental states. Inner and outer inform each other as they interact; they are one substance. We see this as easily as we can see that a sock can be turned inside out.

The relationship of inner and outer, of the individual soul and the soul of the world, is an important issue in *The Soul of the World* as well. Does the notion of our "inner life" infer the existence of a private world to which only we have access? Is this what we mean by a self? Scruton briefly summarizes how or why the notion arises on pages 41–43. He writes: "The idea of the inner 'whatness' or *quale* gains purchase only from the case of self-consciousness—the consciousness of creatures who, like me, can say what they are feeling and who have an immediate and criterionless awareness of their own mental state. It is true that each person has privileged knowledge of his own present state of mind and is immediately aware of a whole range of mental states that he can attribute to himself on no basis. The illusion persists that therefore *there is some special fact about those mental states*, an inner glow, as it were, revealed only to him, which he is able to record because it is immediately present to his consciousness in a way that no physical object or event could be present." With an assist from Kant, Scruton tells us that Wittgenstein "demolished" this view that "there is some special fact about those mental states" in the private language argument. Saving the reader from further details for now, I'll add simply that Wittgenstein gives Goethe's insight a basis in philosophy rather than poetry. I return to this theme in a section titled "In Allegory, the Self Disappears" on pages 124–128. For the record, Scruton has written a very helpful chapter in *Modern Philosophy* on the private language argument, pages 45–57.

Dante's substance in which all the accidents occur, like this image of Goethe's sock, suggests the wholeness that's the goal of our pilgrimage in reading and in life. Since all things live and die in the substance of our being, we are like Ishmael; we have the last word. We alone can report what life looks like from our unique perspective. More importantly, though, we alone are *accountable* for it all, but we are not alone in this. We share this accountability with every other person, and this is the basis for our moral education. As speakers and readers of a language with a long tradition of stories and thoughts about the human condition, we can still find ourselves—like a Paroles, an abstraction (a word) *pretending* to be a man, who is "found" by Lafew—in the company of others, a company that can include great writers and poets. The discovery of our accountability to others, who quite possibly know us better than we know ourselves, may be what finally loosens our grip on that Pretender.

This is the story Dante tells at the beginning of his *Commedia*. He awakened to find himself lost in a dark wood. The light on the shoulder of a small hill (the Mount of Joy) gives him hope and direction, but three allegorical beasts get in his way—the leopard of Lust, the lion of Pride, and the she-wolf of Greed. Initially, he was just lost. Now he's utterly defeated by these accidents of his own soul. This defeat, though, marks a turning point, when:

> *. . . as I fell to my soul's ruin, a presence*
> *gathered before me on the discolored air,*
> *the figure of one who seemed hoarse from long silence.*
>
> *At sight of him in that friendless waste I cried:*
> *"Have pity on me, whatever thing you are,*
> *whether shade or living man."*

Dante's cry, which follows his frank (allegorical) confession of those things that obstruct him, reveals without any veil of ego the state of his soul, the substance wherein the accidents of his life live and die, and it invites the speech of Virgil. As we follow in Dante's footsteps line by line, we learn through him, our alter ego, that we can't ignore the accidents, any thing or person or event that comes to life in the great globe of our life, any more than we can ignore the breath of life, even if these things bring us to despair; they are all accidents of a living soul. Virgil's speech is the accident that turns out to be a saving grace.

We are free to discover the wholeness, but we are also free to fall, as Ahab does, into an obsession (an accident) that divides us from the roots of life. Prior to his cry, Dante's life had been reduced to a tableau wherein the goal of a sunlit little hill was obstructed by the darkness of allegorical beasts. It's a mental state of division and disappointment, and the division opened him up to despair. He had arrived at a turning point. Since the despair is a mental state, he must own it. It's up to him whether his substance grows light and lively or whether division continues to darken it. But it's not only a mental state. His cry calls up the speech of another who knows him better than he knows himself. Virgil's presence spurs him on to discover that which reconciles the accidents of his life and renews the whole. Dante demonstrates this in the three parts of the *Commedia*: to rise to the light on that hill, he first must go a pilgrimage through all the different forms the darkness can take *in this life*. Though the pilgrimage is an allegory that's set in metaphysical places, it's more true to life than many works of fiction where a "realistic" setting serves merely to lull the reader into an agreeable sentiment (like puppy love) or a mind set (like vengeance).

The Birth of Allegory in Statius

Part 1: After Brothers Kill Each Other, the Sorrow of Pietas

As we get closer to that moment when Statius's personifications come to life in a psychological drama, Lewis introduces us to Pietas and Natura before raising the curtain on the scene that drifts into allegory. His presentation, however, begins with a scene that takes place *after* the sons of Oedipus have killed each other in their battle for the crown. Lewis continues to demonstrate the importance and respect Statius accorded his personifications:

> *If there is anything in the whole poem which is serious, which is struck out from the author's real sense of life, it is surely the words with which Pietas begins her speech:*
>
> > *Why didst thou make me, Sovran Nature? Why*
> > *Create me to oppose the cruel will*
> > *Of mortals, and oft-times immortals too?*
>
> *—words in which one can almost see the faded gods of mythology being shouldered aside between those potent abstractions Pietas and Natura—Pite and Kind as they are called in the centuries that follow.*

Pietas (the personification of compassion) poses a great question: She wonders how a compassionate state of mind all by itself can oppose a cruel will, which appears to come naturally to human beings *and the gods*.

Part 2: Chaucer's Respect for Natura and Pietas

Chaucer learned from the ancients a respect for figures like Natura and Pietas. His characters' obsessive love of an object, a natural phenomenon that Chaucer refers to as *cupiditas*, trips them up, and they are compelled to wake as from a dream. Pietas represents this mixture of loss and gain. The loss of an obsessive attachment is painful, but the wonder of a brave new world (without the obsession) is present too. Shakespeare's narratives follow the same pattern. Since we identify with Chaucer's and Shakespeare's characters, they take us through natural experiences of disappointment, and, if the magic of the story works as designed, the experience teaches our heart that it, too, can be transformed from an obsessive selfish love to a love of the whole. Chaucer's word for Pietas was *Caritas*, but both words refer to the same phenomenon. The personifications of Pietas and Wisdom are voices, like that of Virgil in Dante's *Commedia*, which guide us through painful experiences of disappointment and rebirth.

Chaucer's Pardoner may be a venial cheat, but his sermon has the ring of truth. Cupiditas (Dante's she-wolf), he warns us, is a corruptor, the root of all evil, and every tale in *The Canterbury Tales* supports this judgment. We learn to love the whole, Chaucer tells us over and over, only through the disappointment that inevitably follows in the train of cupiditas. Through these experiences, for they never end, we learn to love the darkness of cupiditas as well as the light of caritas. Life as we know it is a workout; Love exercises itself through disappointment and grows stronger. From the way I describe all this here, I have to conclude that life as we know it in this way has nothing to do with the world that science investigates. This observation takes nothing away from the world that science knows. It still can save our lives with knowledge of disease, healing medicines, and lifesaving surgeries; it still can purify water and deliver it to millions in a metropolis; it still can help us to grow food and warm our houses; and it still can blow us all to smithereens.

Part 3: The Holy War between the Furies and Pietas

Having heard the disappointment in the speech of Pietas, we are ready for the introduction of allegory into Western literature as a vehicle for expressing the inner life, which is born in disappointment. To set the stage, Lewis rewinds Statius's story to a time right before the fatal battle between the two brothers:

> *A few hundred lines before the speech of Pietas [in the quote above], Tisiphone and Megaera—themselves scarcely less allegorical than she—have met to consummate the horrors of the Theban war by promoting a single combat between the brothers Polynices and Eteocles. "It shall be done," cry the Furies.*
>
> *Though Piety, though gentle Faith forbid,*
> *They shall be conquer'd.*
>
> *If this stood alone it might pass for ordinary rhetoric, and the reader who felt himself, in this suggested conflict of the fiends and the virtues, reminded of the theme of the Psychomachia [the war in the conscience between good and evil], might be suspected of whimsicality.*

It might pass for ordinary rhetoric because the Furies are merely giving a speech in which they *imagine* Piety and Faith forbidding war. The passage is significant for Lewis, however, because Statius has Pietas herself make an appearance.

The reader doesn't have to be whimsically reminded of a Psychomachia ("reminded" because a modern reader would know about this form of allegory); it actually takes place. The inner imagined world is turned inside out:

> *But what the Furies prophesy actually comes to pass; Pietas is introduced for no other purpose than that she should descend to the field of battle, not primarily to influence the brothers—though she does that too—but to meet Megaera and Tisiphone face to face. She is indeed defeated, and flies at a blow from the torch and serpents of her adversaries; but in that moment, while the human (and Olympian) action of the poem stays suspended and the personified good and evil of the human soul contend, not through their human representatives, but, face to face, with each other, lies the germ of*

all the allegorical poetry. Here already in the pagan poet we have in no ambiguous form the favorite theme of the Middle ages—the battle of the virtues and the vices, the Pyschomachia, the bellum intestium, the Holy War.

The defeat of Pietas explains her passionate complaint quoted earlier. Why, she asks Nature, did you make me if you allow me to suffer like this? She expresses a very human sentiment, one that Ahab felt as well. Then, too, the allegory makes sense. For the war to be prosecuted, a love of the whole must be defeated.

Part 4: Theseus Quickly Ends the Abominations

After this confrontation, Lewis tells us, the story ends quickly. Duke Theseus comes from Athens and in short order cuts away "all the tangled foulness of Thebes":

> *This is told rapidly, as it ought to be . . . because it is essential that we should have the impression, not of new wars following upon the old, but of waking from nightmare, of sudden quiet after storm, of a single sword-stroke ending for ever the abominations. But brief as he is, Statius finds time to put the significance of his Theseus beyond mistake. His war is a holy war: his victory wipes out the momentary defeat of Pietas. For Theseus, like Pietas herself, claims Natura as his patron, and sees the struggle as a Psychomachia:*
>
> *Comrades, defenders of the laws of Earth*
> *And universal covenant, be your minds*
> *Worthy the task! on whose cause gods and men*
> *Smile, and our captain Nature, and the realms*
> *Of mute Avernus. On the other side*
> *For Thebes the snaky-headed sisters raise*
> *Their standard and the Spirits of Vengeance come.*

It turns out that Natura and Pietas are allies. Natura supports (patronizes) Pietas (compassion) as a state of being, and Theseus fights to *defend* them both. If we believe it's completely natural to have a compassionate relationship with the things of this world, both animate and inanimate, then we're a long way from a Darwinian Nature, red in tooth and claw. Human beings, this allegory implies, live in a different world than that of animals.

Before ending this section, let's remember that Lewis fought in the hellish trench battles of World War I. A mortar shell wounded him badly, and it killed his good friend and commander next to him. Many of his comrades died in the fighting; these experiences turned him against religion for a time. When Lewis writes of war, he does so as a veteran, not an academic.

Part 5: Chaucer's Theseus Defends Nature's Law

In "The Knight's Tale," Chaucer's Theseus "defends" Nature and restores our human nature. He corrects the mistake of Creon who became king of Thebes once the two brothers killed each other. Creon had decreed that the bodies of the dead could not be buried (see the play of *Antigone* by Sophocles for the Greek version of that story), but Theseus cuts away this foulness by killing Creon in single combat on the battlefield. As in Statius, Chaucer's Theseus represents the creative force of Nature's Law and Nature's love of Creation. It goes against Nature to leave the bodies of the dead unburied where they are exposed to the sun and to animals that devour them. The dead, like the darkness they now represent, deserve respect. This holds even if they were your enemy.

My reading of Chaucer also agrees with Lewis's sense of a single swordstroke and of waking from a dream as similes for the sudden end of conflict. Division, the stories imply, comes from an inner world, and we can wake to the wholeness of inner and outer as suddenly as one can wake from a dream. Shakespeare saw this as well, which is why he rewrote "The Knight's Tale" as *A Midsummer Night's Dream*. Following Chaucer's example, Shakespeare has his characters experience the wake-up call that emerges from a comic fall. Melville follows them both: his Ahab dies, but Ahab dying is perfectly balanced with Ishmael waking up.

The Interchangeability of Inner and Outer

Whether in hell or purgatory, every step of Dante's *Commedia* moves us forward toward the wholeness of paradise. There's one incident in particular that would wake us to the interchangeability of inner and outer, and it involves Statius. In canto 21 of *Purgatorio*, Dante and Virgil meet Statius, and he accompanies the two of them through the rest of the book. The story of their meeting contains an incident that captures with subtle narrative power what Dante has learned about the accidents of a substance in allegory. At the end of the previous canto, Dante and Virgil experienced a shock (like that of a wake-up call) when the mountain quaked "as if it tottered" (Ciardi, canto 20, line 128). The experience left Dante with a burning thirst to understand the meaning of all the suffering he was seeing and the meaning of the shaking. Just as Virgil came to him at the beginning in his time of need, a shade appears and greets them kindly. He explains that the mountain shook when a soul was free to ascend to the next level on the Mount of Purgatory. He was that soul, newly released.

Virgil asks who he is, and Statius gives them a brief sketch of his life including his name. The main event has to do with his soul's salvation, which explains why he is on the Mount of purgatory and not in hell, as Virgil himself was since he lived before the time of Christ. Statius tells them of his great debt to the poetry of the *Aeneid*, for reading it converted him to Christianity. By making Statius ignorant that he speaks these words to Virgil himself, Dante sets up a tableau that will explore like a parable the interchangeability of inner and outer. Statius's Ignorance on this matter is a state of mind, an accident of his substance. Dante's Knowledge on this matter, that Statius is conversing with the man who saved him, is a state of mind, an accident of Dante's substance. Even though Virgil, "Shot me a glance / that said in silence, 'Silence'" (Ciardi, canto 21, lines 103–104), Dante could not help smiling briefly at the gap in their inner worlds between his Knowledge and Statius's Ignorance. But that's not the end of the story, as it would be in a modern comedian's notion that comedy consists solely in an ironic contrast. Statius notices the smile, the outward sign of an inward thought or emotion, inquires about it, and Virgil quickly agrees to have his identity revealed; inner is turned inside out in an instant. Dante's substance, his inner life, naturally expressed itself in his face. Because his face has this transparency, the three are then made whole in mutual confessions of identity. Dante's substance now is the whole newly created.

Chapter 4

Nature, the Soul, the Quest for Wholeness, the Unity of a Self-Conscious Subject, and the Confession of Augustine's "I"

Vittore Carpaccio's
Saint Augustine in His Study

The One, Nature, and the Soul

At the beginning of section 3 (my chapter 4), Lewis puts on his literary historian hat to continue his story about the fading of mythological gods and the apotheosis of the abstractions (the personifications.) First, he weeds out several explanations for this "double movement." It wasn't caused by a decline of literary power. There are great passages of poetry in Statius. It wasn't caused by Christianity; the movement had begun long before the birth of Christ. At this point he puts on his philosopher hat to develop an ontology of wholeness in the heavens. The movement represents, he tells us:

> *. . . the modus vivendi between monotheism and mythology. Monotheism should not be regarded as the rival of polytheism, but rather as its maturity. Where you find polytheism, combined with any speculative power and leisure for speculation, monotheism will sooner or later arise as a natural development. The principle, I understand, is well illustrated in the history of Indian religion. Behind the gods arises the One, and the gods as well as the men are only his dreams. European thought did not follow the same path, but it was faced with the same problem. The best minds embrace monotheism. What is to be done with the gods of the popular religion? The answer . . . was given by the Stoics . . . The gods are to be aspects, manifestations, temporary or partial embodiments of the single power. They are, in fact, personifications of the abstracted attributes of the One.*

Lewis's depiction of the modus vivendi between mythology and monotheism is similar to Dante's delineation of accidents in the substance of *La Vita Nuova*. Love, Dante writes, is a fiction, a personification in the substance of his poetry. In my reading of this passage (see pages 90–92), I added that both Love and Dante's poetry are accidents of his own substance. Lewis's modus vivendi and Dante's poetry are models of wholeness. We don't have to wonder why people adopted the modus vivendi of monotheism or why Dante employed allegory (in the way he defined it), for the best minds, Lewis explains, embrace wholeness.

Lewis's modus vivendi also explains the importance of Princeps Natura for Statius and for the place on Lewis's spectrum that he has prepared for her. Lewis writes of Statius that:

> *It is his mythological treatment of Bacchus which is purely literary and derivative; it is his allegorical treatment of Bacchus and of Mars which is alive. The same clue enables us to understand his Princeps Natura; for this "Nature," to whom Pietas can appeal over the heads of men and gods* [see page 109], *is no other than that One in whose light the Olympians are beginning to look pale. She is the Whole (or God, or Nature, or Cosmus) of the Stoics . . . the Natura of Seneca; the ancestress of Alanus' Natura and Chaucer's Kinde.*

Lewis raises in our minds an ontology of wholeness because this is the goal of our pilgrimage as we read through his book. He would have us embrace a wholistic ontology rather than the dualistic ontology of science, which is constructed on the divisions inherent in dualisms of cause and effect, mind and body, and the world "in here" and the world "out there."

Lewis, though, does not explicitly rely on a virgin birth and a savior to affect this oneness. He would ground This Life, I believe, in what he calls "the given world," all the things he encounters in This Life, which he interprets to be the accidents of his substance. In this, he is like Dante, who writes about the people he knew in Florence and historical figures he knew from his reading. It should be noted that under the umbrella of "the given world" we might also find the allegorical figure of Love and the only begotten son of God. The real Dante encountered them in his reading, and, in the case of the latter, maybe even as a real presence in his life through the real presence of Beatrice. The real Dante is an accident of Lewis's substance, and the two are now an accident of my substance. They exist; they have a real presence there. And this substance that I have called the given world, what more can I say about it? I could refer to it as my consciousness, but I'm inclined to call it my soul as well, since this reading of *The Allegory of Love* is steadily moving me in that direction.

Once More, the View from Olympus

I have read the whole of *The Allegory of Love*, so I'm privileged to have an Olympian view of it. I'm happy to say it ends well, but first we'll look back at the problem his book proposes to resolve. By the end of Lewis's chapter on courtly love, we learned that Love was divided in two. Lovers like Chaucer had to choose. One could love and serve God, or one could love and serve a woman. The reader is left to wonder how Love can be whole. In section 3 of Lewis's narrative about allegory, he would persuade us that allegorical stories about our inner life are stories about the wholeness of life. By personifying the One as Nature, the stories may persuade us that wholeness can be found in Nature, the given world.

Looking ahead to the survey in section 6 of allegorical literature leading up to *The Romance of the Rose*, I see from my Olympian perch how Nature takes a lead role in late medieval poems. Lewis will show that the School of Chartres resolves the dualism of church and courtly love in the figure of Natura, who prizes all aspects of her creation, including those "tools" having to do with reproduction. For example, Alanus de Lille (1128–1202), Lewis writes, "acknowledges no breach" between the church and courtly life:

> *. . . for the naturalism of Chartres has given him a tertium quid [third way] that can moderate both the rigors of theology and the wantonness of the court. Goodness does not mean asceticism; knighthood does not mean adultery. Both are brought together under the law of Natura who is the vicar of God and essentially good. It is not a question of grace redeeming Nature: it is a question of sin departing from Nature. The position is summed up in the advice given by Honest to the perfect man:*
>
> *Let him love Nature who would flee from vice,*
> *Eschew what guilt or naughty will brought forth*
> *And to his breast clasp all that Nature made.*

It is in this that the true value of Alanus consists. I do not say he has effected a real reconciliation between the two ideals of the Middle Ages. The rift went deeper than he thought. He assumes, rather than makes, a peace. But he is at least trying to be a whole man, and however the elements of his synthesis may hereafter fall apart, they will retain some mark of their brief union.

Lewis's scholarship and dedication have allowed him to discover this comic view of love made whole and at peace. Meanwhile, though, we return to the holy war that, along with the One, is also the subject of section 3.

The Inner Life as Holy War and as Allegory

In the first line of Sonnet 146, Shakespeare addresses the problem of sin. "Poor soul," he writes, "the center of my sinful earth . . ." Our sinful earth, it's fair to say, is Nature, and for better or worse it's our nature to be a soul at the center of a sinful earth. (Jumping from Sonnet 146 to *Hamlet*, I derive this notion of a sinful earth in part from my reading of the scene near the end of act 1, where Hamlet insists that Marcellus and Horatio must swear on his sword to keep Hamlet's meeting with the ghost a secret. The ghost apparently agrees, for from the ground underfoot he prompts them to "Swear!" Three times he prompts them, and three times the three scramble to find ground that isn't haunted by the ghost's insistence. The vow, they assume, must be sworn on solid ground to avoid corruption. It's a hopeless conundrum, for after the fall of Adam and Eve the Lord cursed the ground. And so, we wonder, "What will make this rottenness whole again?" We embark on the play of *Hamlet* to find out.) Shakespeare's view confirms what Lewis writes about Alanus's synthesis in the passage above. Sin has not departed from Nature. Soul and earth are one, and as one they represent the "stage" on which the drama of our life plays out. I say "for better or worse" in the second sentence above because Shakespeare's soul, he tells us, is acquainted with the darkness of earth (since we are made of earth) of which the soul is the center. The soul, we think, inherits the gifts of our heavenly Father, along with the breath of life, but, Shakespeare tells us, his is poor. In two words, "poor soul," he sums up the moral tension in his life.

I bring in Shakespeare's line from the sonnet to introduce the ethical theme Lewis develops through the rest of section 3. Before I pick up that ethical thread, once more I'll indulge in a digression, this time a short one. A soul that can be good or bad reminds me of a nursery rhyme. It claims, quite innocently, that we can be both:

> *There once was a little girl who had a little curl*
> *Right in the middle of her forehead.*
> *When she was good she was very very good,*
> *And when she was bad she was horrid.*

This remarkable poem addresses the theme with a lightness of touch that may keep a child (which is all of us at whatever age) from wallowing in self-pity for the way nature made us. By approaching the subject with such playfulness, humor, and truth, the child in us may discover in time's fullness that the soul is larger than the badness, that the badness is but an accident of our soul-substance. This may encourage a child (at whatever age) not to give up the soul, which is the whole of life, to that which is unworthy of it.

Our literary historian-philosopher also would lift our kind from despairing over the way Nature made us, but he has a much longer and more difficult story to tell. Lewis describes the movement toward oneness in allegory as a "a change of moral experience rather than of thought." Just as Lewis declines to find a specific cause for the rise of courtly love in chapter 1, here again he has "foresworn any attempt to explain" the causes of this change. Instead, he would give us a "ready way of indicating its nature." He indicates simply that human beings now experience their moral life as a holy war.

To establish that there was in fact a change, Lewis posits the modern view that for most people:

> *. . . the moral life seems to lie in the antithesis between duty and inclination . . . All our serious imaginative work, when it touches morals, paints a conflict: all practical moralists sing to battle or give hints about the appropriate strategy. Take away the concept of "temptation" and nearly all that we say or think about good and evil would vanish into thin air.*

He then contrasts this with what we find when we read Aristotle's ethics:

> *But when we first opened our Aristotle, we found to our astonishment that this inner conflict was for him so little of the essence of the moral life, that he tended to thrust it into a corner and treat it almost as a special case . . . The really good man, in Aristotle's view, is not tempted . . . Aristotle coolly remarks that the man who is temperate at a cost is profligate: the really temperate man abstains because he likes abstaining.*

All this changes, Lewis argues, for moralists in the Roman Empire. Every moralist thought it was hard to be good. He finds examples in Saint Paul, Epictetus, and Seneca who advises us to be soldiers and to conquer all things.

The moral change from Aristotle to Saint Paul, Lewis asserts, brings us closer to understanding the use of personifications in the poetry of Statius and other poets of his time:

> *. . . if they had not discovered the moral conflict, [they] had at least discovered in it a new importance. They were vividly aware, as the Greeks had not been, of the divided will, the bellum intestinum . . . It is plain that to fight against temptation is also to explore the inner world; and it is scarcely less plain that to do so is to be already on the verge of allegory. We cannot speak, perhaps we can hardly think, of an inner conflict without a metaphor; and every metaphor is an allegory in little.*

A metaphor is an allegory, I suppose, because it personalizes or humanizes creation. For example, a metaphor or simile like "O, my love is like a red, red rose" humanizes the rose for the writer and the reader. It projects the poet's inner life into the rose so we now can clearly see the beauty of his experience. It also breaks down the dualism of subject and object. The poet's love and the rose are one. This in itself is surely part of the metaphor's beauty.

Even though Lewis declines to investigate why there was this change of moral experience, we may guess at the connection between "the divided will" in the inner world and *the quest for wholeness in the inner world that's the subject of allegory*. As people explored a will divided between good and evil, they also sought a means to express and resolve that moral tension. Why did they seek to resolve a divided will? The best minds, Lewis tells us, instinctively embrace wholeness, and when they embrace it, they come to life, just as Statius's poetry came to life in allegory (see the quote on page 118).

In Allegory, the Self Disappears

Lewis next initiates his own holy war against those who would consign allegory to the dust bin of history:

> *It would be a misunderstanding to suggest that there is another and better way of representing that inner world, and that we have found it in the novel and the drama. The gaze turned inward with a moral purpose does not discover character. No man is a character to himself, and least of all while he thinks of good and evil. Character is what he [Everyman] has to produce; within he finds only the raw material, the passions and emotions which contend for mastery. That unitary "soul" or "personality" which interests the novelist is for him merely the arena in which the combatants meet: it is to the combatants—those "accidents in a substance"—that he must attend.*

Just as a novelist builds his story around a character's character, people build the story of their lives around their "image," the way they see themselves. By maintaining an identity (as a doctor, teacher, businessman, husband, father, good person, etc.) we gain a certain heft in our dealings, for these things function like armor. Shielded in this way, we go on adventures like knights of yore. Only by wrestling with the raw material unmediated by our image of a self, Lewis tells us, will a person develop character. In allegory, he believes, the encounter is more direct and real. Lewis's critique here has important implications for the self, for in allegory the self disappears. An allegory like *Everyman* teaches that the soul is not the self; the soul is "the arena" within which the accidents of our life contribute to the wholeness and health of our substance. Or not, as the case may be.

Once more, if we look ahead for a moment, this insight explains why *The Romance of the Rose* is so important to the literary history he is studying. In the initial part of the poem by Guillaume de Lorris, the lady can't be found anywhere. She appears only in the various moods that the young lover encounters as he tries to win the Rose. She is Fair Welcome, Danger, Shame, Fear, and so on. There is no "end" to the person he is wooing, no firm "character" (see page 130, where Augustine addresses this issue as well). She is what she is as he finds her at the time, and then she's something else as he finds her another time. In this way, Lewis critiques our modern sense of the self. Contrary to popular opinion, the self (as we conceive of it in ordinary usage) is not our substance.

Lewis's image of "the arena in which the combatants meet" deserves special attention. The quote from *La Vita Nuova* about "accidents in a substance" has initiated a train of thought that has wound itself all through my text. The quote led me to infer that Dante regarded his soul as the substance of his life. I have interpreted the sections that follow in this light. As Lewis has developed the allegory of Love, he now compares the soul to an arena, and I find it to be an intriguing figure.

An arena is a place, a setting, and yet, if we imagine ourselves as the unmoving center of the turning world, our world seethes and moves with life as we move without moving through it. Viewed this way, the setting comes alive, and it's filled with all forms of life, like a mighty, swelling Pacific. This Pacific has swallowed us up like a whale, and it still holds us fast. Then again, we are this mighty Pacific. Outer is inner. We view the world, we experience it, from our own unique perspective. From this perspective, it's but a short step to conclude that, in order to have our unique perspective, we have to be born into the universe. What was it before that? What were we? We, as eyewitnesses, cannot say. What will the universe be when we are gone? We, as living, breathing creatures, cannot say. What will we be when it is gone? Again, we cannot say.

Anything we do think or say about this world depends on our consciousness, which springs to life over time in childhood to give us our unique perspective. Our consciousness develops into self-consciousness thanks to the fact that we are language-using, symbol-interpreting creatures. Our language has given us the personal pronoun "I," the point of view from which Dante tells the story of *La Vita Nuova* and *Commedia*. Our consciousness is real, we think, just as we are a real creature. This is common sense reasoning. Without our consciousness, we have to admit, the universe *as we know it* would not exist, so it makes sense to say our consciousness of this world, which seethes and moves with life, is our substance. But where in this consciousness is the self? I've looked, and I cannot say. If we identify our consciousness with the body, we still have to ask, "Where in the body is the self?" Scientists have studied this question, and to my knowledge they haven't answered it.

If the self is simply the arena of all and everything, then it's tempting to agree with Lewis that it has no separate identity over and above the arena. If we agree with Lewis that modern depictions of the self miss the mark, perhaps we are more ready to go for satisfaction to the story in Genesis, when God breathed into the nostrils of man the breath of life, when man became a living soul, and when God placed him in the garden eastward of Eden to inform the ground. This arena is our identity. It's who we are with every breath we take.

Because I enjoy the view from Olympus over my whole inquiry, and because my train of thought includes simultaneously all the stations along the way, however, I can add here that Scruton addresses this difficult question of personal identity at various points in *The Soul of the World*. From his study of Kant and from his own experience, Scruton can say:

> *I know that I am a single and unified subject of experience. This present thought, this pain, this hope, and this memory are features of one thing, and that thing is what I am. I know this on no basis, without having to carry out*

> *any kind of check, and, indeed, without the use of criteria of any kind—this is what is (or what ought to be) meant by the term "transcendental." The unity of the self-conscious subject is not the conclusion of any inquiry, but the presupposition of all inquiries. The unity of consciousness "transcends" all argument since it is the premise without which argument makes no sense. (*The Soul of the World*, page 72)*

All this is implied, Scruton argues from his study of Kant, in a person's use of the personal pronoun "I." If the use of "I" in our consciousness and speech reflects the unity of a self-conscious subject, then I'd say it implies the arena to which Lewis refers.

Lewis's modus vivendi and Dante's poetry are models of wholeness. We don't have to wonder why people adopted the modus vivendi of monotheism or why Dante employed allegory—in the way he defined it—as the best minds, Lewis explains, embrace wholeness. In that spirit, my reading of *The Soul of the World* adds another layer to the following series of accidents in a substance. Love, Dante tells us, is an accident of the poem's substance. My reading of *The Allegory of Love* concludes that *La Vita Nuova* is an accident of Dante's soul-substance, and I'm inclined to believe that Scruton, from his reading of Kant and Hegel, suggests in *The Soul of the World* that Dante's, or anyone's, soul is an accident of the soul of the world.

Because we are dealing with difficult metaphysical matters, there is no easy path to this conclusion. Kant himself makes it difficult. Our sense of a soul-substance, Kant argued, is an illusion, for a subject cannot also be an object. If we accept Kant's reasoning, Scruton writes in his book on Kant, then the "I" we use to refer to ourselves "is the expression of my perspective, but denotes no item within it" (quoted from *Kant: A Very Short Introduction*, pages 70–72).

In the section of Book One titled "I have now found thee," I argue that *All's Well That Ends Well* takes the character of Paroles through a process in which he is challenged by Lord Lafew to find his "true self." In Book Two, I quoted what Goethe wrote to a lady about the state of his soul as he looked forward to being an official in the government of Weimar. It is, he says,

"Like a sock that is being turned inside out: the outer becoming inner; the inner outer."

When I put these two things together, I find I can still say a true self is not an illusion nor is the search for it impossible as long as we understand that our true self can't be an "item" within consciousness. Our true self—our soul, Goethe writes—is a seamless union of inner and outer. With this in mind, it's apparent that the inclusion of anima mundi, the soul of the world, into the inquiry must have a significant effect on what it means to be a living soul. This thought goes a long way toward explaining why Scruton calls his book *The Soul of the World* even though he doesn't refer to the soul of the world until the final five words of it.

Augustine's Pilgrimage "Step by Step" through Mind

Lewis admits that the movement toward allegory he has been cataloging in section 2 (my chapter 3) and section 3 (my chapter 4) may have other "subsidiary" causes. For example, both pagans and Christians interpreted ancient texts with allegorical constructions. "Saturn eating his children could be harmlessly interpreted as Time 'bearing all his sons away.'" Philo Judaeus interpreted the Hebrew scriptures allegorically, and Christians like Hilary and Ambrose followed his example. But Lewis discounts the importance of influences like these, for he argues that much deeper causes produced the need for allegory:

> *The root of this need as we have seen is twofold; on the one hand, the gods sink into personifications; on the other, a widespread moral revolution forces men to personify their passions.*

From this root grows "the emergence of mental facts into allegory."

Lewis has characterized metaphor as a form of allegory, and he underscores at this point "how naturally such experience [of the inner life] expressed itself in metaphors—and in just those metaphors borrowed from the battlefield and the arena." Writers found other metaphors as well—like a lawsuit that ties us up forever, appetites that attack us "like thieves in Egypt," and a journey that wears us out or puts us in fear of a great danger. Some metaphors, he will argue, are more true to life than others. Even though a battlefield is a popular metaphor, Lewis will argue in section 4 (my next chapter) that the allegory of a pilgrimage is more true to life.

Lewis concludes section 3 with the one whose journey into his inner life came to be prized by readers all over the Western world: "But perhaps there is no writer who admits us so intimately into the heart of that age as Augustine." His confession serves as a window for him and his reader to view his inner life. Lewis begins his commentary with a story from *Confessions* about Augustine's teacher Ambrose. Augustine observed Ambrose reading and:

> *. . . comments on the fact—to him, apparently, remarkable—that Ambrose, when reading to himself, read silently. You could see his eyes moving, but you could hear nothing. In such a passage one has the solemn privilege of being present at the birth of a new world. Behind us is that almost unimaginable period, so relentlessly objective that in it even "reading" (in our sense) did not yet exist. The book was still . . . speech; thinking was still . . . talking. Before us is our own world, the world of the printed page, and of the solitary reader who is accustomed to pass hours in the silent society of mental images evoked by written characters. This is a new light [the light that reveals the newness of reading in this way] and a better one than we have yet had, on that turning inward which I have tried to describe.*

Often, Lewis writes, Augustine reveals:

> *. . . a vivid sense of the delighted and horrified wonder with which he is consciously exploring the new inner world—"I myself comprehend not all the thing I am." Every new path in this country excited his curiosity and his awe. Why did he rob the pear tree? Why does tragedy please? He worries such problems as a dog worries a bone. He wanders hither and thither in his own mind and speaks the very language of a traveller. "Climbing up, therefore, step by step to Him that made me, I will pass beyond this faculty of my nature and come to the fields and wide pavilions of the Memory."*

Did his climb "step by step to Him that made me" suggest the metaphor that structures Dante's *Commedia*? To stress the importance of Augustine's journey into his own mind, Lewis quotes a passage about memory at length. Even in translation, we can feel the wonder Augustine felt in his own being. A wonder had been present all along, like a heart steadily beating, and yet he hadn't known it. The passage seems to come from the heart, just as Dante's cry, "Have pity on me," spoken to the shape that comes to him out of darkness, comes from the heart:

> *Great is the power of Memory, Lord; an astonishment, a deep and boundless manifold. Yet this also is mind and I am this. What am I, Lord? What is my kind? Even a life that changes and hath many modes and cannot in any wise be measured. The fields, the caves, the dens of Memory cannot be counted; their fulness cannot be counted nor the kinds of things counted that fill them . . . I force my way in amidst them, even as far as my power reaches, and nowhere find an end.*

"What is my kind?" He might as well be asking, "What is my human nature? What is my substance?" The question still resonates.

Lewis gives us this passage to illustrate an experience "of the age in which allegory was born . . ." Augustine describes here the "arena," his own mind, for Memory is Mind, which is the setting for allegory. Lewis has made this point several times before: "Allegory, in some sense, belongs not to medieval man but to man, *or even to mind*, in general" (page 87); "War . . . is one of the instruments of Fate, to be called up *in the minds of men* when Fate requires" (pages 102–103); "there is no pretense that Clementia is other than *a state of mind*; '*the mind* and heart of man her chosen haunt,' says Statius" (page 104).

In the next passage from *Confessions*, Augustine employs allegorical figures of "mistresses" so that the arena of his inner life comes alive with dramatic action:

> *Trifles of trifles, and very vanities which I had made my mistresses now held me back and plucked me by my carnal robe, whispering me, "Will*

you turn us away? Shall the moment come when you must part from us for ever? Shall the moment come when this—and this—will be forbidden you for ever?" And now I harkened to them with less than half myself. No longer did they gainsay me openly nor look me in the face, but came as it were behind me whispering and plucking at my robe as I went away; holding me back while I yet delayed to tear myself from them, to shake them off, to leap whither I was called—tyrannous custom asking me the while, "Is it possible, think you, to live without them."

Lewis ends the section about the discovery of an inner life here. Once more, I need to look briefly back and forward to consider this discovery and why I'm considering it. I am reminded in this regard of the dolphins that pass through the canal bordering the property where we stay in Florida. They rise to breathe and then glide out of sight to feed and to move on to the next breath. Like the dolphins, I live in two worlds, my life when reading or writing and my life when not reading or writing. Just as the dolphin does, I find that I need them both to live. I'm considering the discovery of the inner world because I'm reading about it in *The Allegory of Love*, but truly it must be said that without the breath of life, which gave me and continues to maintain my substance as a human being, I wouldn't be reading the book. What I read is an accident of my substance, the substance that will be lost if I don't regularly take a breath. So I breathe, whether consciously or not, as if to say inwardly to the body, "I have now found thee."

From immersion in the work of great poets, I also can say inwardly of my substance: "I have now found thee." It seems to me that I need the poetry as much as I need the breath. The breath and the poetry work together to move me along step by step in the path of those who have gone before me. I notice that I am in this much like mankind in Bernard's poem; I have a foot in two worlds. The text exists as an objective object, the work of Augustine or Lewis, but it comes to life in me as an immaterial, subjective experience of meaning. This meaning in turn helps me to live in the world. The breath also exists as an objective fact or element "out there" in the world, but it comes to life in me as the spiritual without-which-nothing of my consciousness. I wouldn't live at all without it. Through the breath, I notice that I am in fact like Goethe's sock, where the outer becomes the inner; the inner, outer.

The sentence "I have now found thee" implies that what is found can also be lost. The quote from Augustine that begins with "great is the power of memory" hints at the problem. A person can get lost in his inner life as easily as he can get lost in an actual forest or at sea as Ahab did. We can search and search for an "end" and find it "nowhere." This is where Dante finds himself when he tells us at the beginning of the *Commedia*:

> *Midway in our life's journey, I went astray*
> *from the straight road and woke to find myself*
> *alone in a dark wood. How shall I say*
> *what a wood that was! I never saw so drear,*
> *so rank, so arduous a wilderness!*
> *Its very memory gives a shape to fear.*
>
> Ciardi, canto 1, lines 1–6

A person undergoing psychotherapy can get lost in dreams and fantasies—and many have. A scientist who studies the objective world can get lost in assumptions, methodology, and data—and many do. The discovery of an inner life is not the end of Lewis's story nor is it the exploration of an objective world. Since we are human beings, we can only know the world as a human being experiences it. This book follows in the footsteps of those who understand that to bear the crown of sacred kingship, a grave responsibility, we must be one who lacks nothing. Here we are at home with all and everything. When our world is complete, it stands to reason that we will follow the golden rule quite naturally. When our world is complete, it stands to reason that we will lose even the need to "abstain" (see Lewis's quote on abstaining, page 123).

I've illustrated this chapter with Carpaccio's delightful painting of Augustine in his study. What a cheerful room it is, full of light from windows that line the wall, and this light clearly illuminates everything in the study. The room itself is classical, for Augustine, like any educated man of that time, had a classical education. The focal point at the back of the room looks like an altar, with a statue of Christ holding a symbol of the cross, but the pose of the savior is a graceful curve, similar to young men in Greek statuary. Within that sanctuary, we also see the symbols of Augustine's power, the bishop's staff and miter, but these are things Augustine the man has set aside as he sits at his desk near the natural light. It's a library, and the books are causally placed around his writing desk and around the room. The cupboard at the back on the left looks like an ark for holding God's Word, but the globe on the shelf above him and other pieces on the shelf across the room suggest an interest in science and art.

The painting depicts—quite objectively—an interior, the inner life if you will, of Augustine. I believe it captures the delight he describes as he explores that inner world in the quotes above, which is why I've selected it for the chapter. It also depicts Augustine himself at the center of this world. He has looked up from his writing to look out the window. Like the light that streams into his study, his eye beams stream toward the source of all and everything "out there" in the world. One last thing: Why has the artist included the little lap dog gazing at his master so intently? As always, and rather curiously, the dog's interest and love humanize the man. The way Augustine looks out the window with such interest echoes the interest and love of his pet. Does it humanize Augustine's master the way his pet humanizes him?

Chapter 5

The Road to Fairyland Runs through Allegory

Rembrandt's

Faust

The Link That's Missing: A Living, Loving Soul

To grasp the significance of section 4 (Lewis doesn't use titles), I resort once more to a view from Olympus from which we can observe at large the scene before us. The road to understanding Lewis's intent begins with the title of his book, *The Allegory of Love*. Because the chapter on allegory is quite long and complex, we may lose sight of the fact that his true subject is love. Allegory is a technique in the poet's "armory" for expressing the play of Love in the poet's life. Allegory suspends our usual sense of time and space and puts us instead in an arena that encompasses the "All" in *All's Well that Ends Well*. An allegory is a new Creation, and in a story like *The Romance of the Rose*, we find the allegorical figure of Love there armed with his arrows. Section 4 connects the subjects of Lewis's first two chapters—chapter 1 about courtly love and chapter 2 about allegory. Just as section 2 (my chapter 3) narrates the drift towards allegory in the poetry of Statius, section 4 narrates the drift toward a romantic fairyland in allegories written during the twilight of the Roman Empire. Lewis brings these different parts of his narrative together in the substance, the soul, of this fairyland. Poets discovered it, Lewis tells us, almost by an accident of the imagination's creative powers. The poets who developed this tradition, he suggests, loved the fairyland they created. They created the beautiful gardens, they created the figure of Love to inhabit them, and the whole comes to life in the love of its creator.

Love is our subject, and love, we think, is real. Passion is real even if it's intangible, and we employ figurative language to express it. Lewis argues that figurative language is built into the DNA of language use (this last is my own figure of speech). Figures of speech, however, come in different sizes and shapes, and they have different effects, as the figures of human beings do. Thus, in the beginning of the chapter on allegory, Lewis makes a critical distinction between the way allegory and symbolism marry sensibles and insensibles. He explains that the allegorist "leaves the given—his own passions—to talk of that which is confessedly less real, a fiction." An allegorist like Dante confesses that the allegorical story is a fiction, but it serves to express a real passion, his love for something "out there" in the world. Dante is not Beatrice. He loved a real person in the world, not a fantasy. Both his passion and the expression of his passion stay rooted in the given world, for the fiction comes from the imagination of a real allegorist. The expression of his passion is the action of his passion in the world, the action of a lover that expresses and wins his Love, the Rose of the world. In Dante's case, he would win her love even though she had already died. His poetry proves, though, that she is present in his love for her.

The symbolist, on the other hand, "leaves the given to find that which is more real," that which Lewis describes in the same sentence as having "unimaginable dimensions" (see page 88). In sum, if I'm a pilgrim-allegorist, I may reach my goal of expressing and receiving love, for I never abandon the given world. If I'm a pilgrim-symbolist, I can't reach my goal of expressing and receiving love, for the object exists in an unimaginable dimension. The expression goes out into a void, and the void can't send it back confirmed and enhanced. Ahab symbolizes his love (of avenging the pain of existence), but the device gets him nowhere. He wants what is unimaginable and mistakes it for killing a whale. As sure as night follows the day, the whale fights back, and the void has Ahab instead. He isn't the first or last; millions are deeply invested in this kind of quest. Ahab is another Narcissus. He loves the image on the surface of the pool—which is an illusion of light, a ghost, a nothing, and the pool has him in the end.

Before I resume a reading of Lewis, though, I would like to add that I'm grateful for that which brought Ahab and Moby Dick into the world. Even though Ahab regarded the white whale as a symbol, Melville, I believe, doesn't discourage a reader from interpreting them as figures in an allegory concerning the nature of a soul. A living soul, his story tells us, is not a nothing. It may be as difficult to raise as the white whale proved to be, but it exists. Just as the whale wants to live, a living soul will rise to breathe the sweet air of this life. In the end, the white whale carries Ahab—lashed to it by the harpoon and the cords he himself has flung at Creation in order to kill it—into the deep and out of sight. His love of vengeance on his existence turned out to be a hopeless knot to untangle. In one respect, though, Ahab now is Everyman; he's a man who came into the world and who returns from whence he came. What happens next to the soul of Ahab? The author of it all has arranged it so that the question rises in the substance of the living, in Ishmael and in us. Ahab now lives in us.

I'm also grateful that Goethe was able to complete his allegory of *Faust*. The arc of Ahab's quest is like the arc in *Faust, Part One*. In that segment of his epic pilgrimage, Faust signs the death warrant of his soul in a contract with Mephistopheles and then suffers the consequences. Those first scenes of Faust in his study reveal, however, that he had abandoned his soul long before he signed it away to the devil. He was an academic who had foregone all contact with the living air and springs of life outside his little study and who had effectively killed that which might stir in him a love of life. He was lost and desperate to save his image of himself in the robe of a scholar and a sage. Mephistopheles knew this very well about Faust "from going to and fro in the earth, and from walking up and down in it" (Job 1:7).

In an illuminating interlude, Mephistopheles pretends to be a scholar by putting on the robe of Faust, and he then tells a prospective student:

> *When scholars study a thing, they strive*
> *To kill it first, if it's alive;*
> *Then they have the parts and they've lost the whole,*
> *For the link that's missing is the living soul.*
>
> *Faust*, lines 1936–1939

Mephistopheles can safely describe the activity of a scholar in this way without endangering the young man's prospects, for the young man is hopelessly in love with the image of himself in that robe. Oh, to wear that which has respect, honor, and even fame sewed into it. The reality, which Mephistopheles describes so clearly, makes no impression.

I've illustrated this chapter with Rembrandt's etching of Faust. As in Carpaccio's painting of Augustine (see page 117), we see Faust in his study, but it appears to be more like a cell than a room. Augustine's room is filled with the light of the blessed sun which streams through many windows. All that light gives his study and the things in it a wondrous transparency. Faust's cell, on the other hand, is a much darker place, an impression which is increased by the fact that it's an etching in black and white. As in Carpaccio's recreation of a moment when Augustine looks up from his work, Faust has his attention suddenly drawn toward the light. Rembrandt has arranged it, though, so that the light is not that of the blessed sun out there in the world. The light of the blessed sun has been interrupted and effectively blocked by abstract symbols that coalesce and shine forth with a spectral brilliance. This is what has caught Faust's attention, but the little cell itself is still dark. We sense that Augustine looks through the window to be refreshed in his work by the light outside. We sense that Faust is being tempted by an illusion to forsake what Lewis refers to as "the given world." Since the contrast between the two works is so significant, I wonder if Rembrandt was familiar with Carpaccio's painting.

Along with these remarkable four lines, we need the whole of massive allegories, like the stories of Moby Dick and Faust, to find the link that's missing—a living, loving soul. We need that immersion for the soul substance to be absorbed, drop by drop from the mass of these masterworks. This is why we do well to be thankful for the love, the effort, and the discipline that went into creating them. Goethe labored for over fifty years to finish the second part of *Faust,* wherein Faust becomes a living soul, completing it just months before he died. As for Ahab, we don't know what transpired when Death came to him as a messenger. Did Ahab, like Everyman, go a journey before the reckoning? More to Melville's point and to the point of *Everyman*, will we, the living, go a journey to "reckon" whether we're living a life worthy of the gift?

The question may result in a hypothesis that needs to be tried to be proved: If we love the gift, we are more likely to live in a way that's worthy of the gift.

In the Twilight of the Gods, the Poets Discover Fairyland

Part 1: Prudentius

Lewis begins section 4 with his critique of "the fully-fledged allegorical poem, the *Psychomachia* of Prudentius." In this work from the late fourth century, the inner life, the soul, is the setting for a battle between good and evil. Lewis credits Prudentius with some insight into the inner life. For example, he has Avarice hide among the virtues disguised as Frugality, "and we must remember how rarely we find in classical literature any adequate recognition of the great fact of self-deception." For this reason, Lewis judges the *Psychomachia* to be an "admirable pioneer work" by an allegorist.

In an earlier passage, though, Lewis explains his objections to a psychomachia or holy war as an expression of our inner life, and this critique puts us on the road to fairyland:

> *While it is true that the bellum intestinum is the root of allegory, it no less true that only the crudest allegory will represent it by a pitched battle. The abstractions owe their life to the inner conflict; but when once they have come to life, the poet must fetch a compass and dispose his fiction more artfully if he is to succeed. Seneca, with his imagery of life as a journey, was nearer to the mark than Prudentius; for Seneca outlined the theme of the Pilgrim's Progress, and the Pilgrim's Progress is a better book than the Holy War. It is not hard to see why this should be so. The journey has its ups and downs, its pleasant resting-places enjoyed for a night and then abandoned, its unexpected meetings, its rumors of dangers ahead, and above all, the sense of its goal, at first far distant and dimly heard of, but growing nearer at every turn of the road. Now this represents far more truly than any combat . . . the perennial strangeness, the adventurousness, and the sinuous forward movement of the inner life.*

Lewis credits Prudentius (AD 348–413) with inventing a genre which became "no small part of the history of medieval literature." To help us grasp the structure of his presentation, Lewis himself offers the view from Olympus on this station about allegory. He points out that these first eight pages of section 4 (devoted to Prudentius) develop half of the double movement discussed in sections 2 and 3—namely, the drift of personifications into allegory. In Prudentius, personifications have fully matured into lively figures that act out the drama of our inner life. For the next fourteen pages, Lewis will describe the other half, "the ever deepening twilight of the gods," in works by Claudian (AD 370–404), Sidonius Apollinaris (AD 430–489), Ennodius (AD 473–521), and Martianus Capella (AD 360–428).

As an aside, I'd ask the reader to remember Lewis's "strenuous forward movement of the inner life" when we come to Scruton's "transcendental urge of reason" at the end of his chapter on "Believing in God."

Part 2: Claudian

Prudentius was a Christian, whereas Claudian was the court poet of the pagan emperor Honorius. The psychomachia, though, belongs to both cultures: "For Claudian, just as for the religious poet, allegorical conflict is the natural method of dealing with psychology." Claudian agrees with Prudentius that a good man "can only be good as the result of a successful psychomachy." Lewis is more interested, though, in two passages, "which are full of the promise of the Middle Ages":

> *The first comes in the Counsulship of Stilicho [a Roman General]. We have been long immersed in the virtues and the vices of the hero, and in the rhetoric of the personified nations; then suddenly, at the end of the book, the scene changes. We are shown the cavern of all the years . . . scarcely approachable by God or man. On the floor the serpent of eternity lies sleeping with his tail in his mouth. Before the entrance sits Nature . . . and the souls of the unborn flit round her; by her side is an old man who writes her decrees in a book. To the threshold of this cave comes Sol; as he alights, Nature rises to greet him.*

It is an allegory about Creation. There's the source of All, the oneness of eternity. From this cavern issue the souls of the unborn, where Nature decrees what they will be. After the setting has been established, Sol and Nature act out Claudian's reason for writing his poem: he must praise his patron. The two enter the cave and retrieve from the ages of gold, silver, and brass the gold that will "grace" the General's consulship. We notice how Claudian mixes the Roman personification of Nature with the sun, a god from traditional mythology. They come alive at the apotheosis of the personifications and the twilight of the gods that Lewis has been describing as the vital center of his presentation. In Claudian's treatment of this allegorical center, Lewis finds the kind of writing that eventually grows into "the pleasant-resting places" of fairyland:

> *The poet's aim is decoration. But for that very reason, because he is merely decorating, he is free to rest from the serious purpose of the poem, and to luxuriate in description. The drowsy cavern and the silent figures meeting at the threshold exist, for a moment, in their own right. The allegory is only the pretext.*

An epithalamium, which is sung to praise a bride and groom on their wedding day, is one of the oldest forms of poetry in the Western tradition. It celebrates the work of Venus and Love in this world and the springtime of new life. In *Epithalamium for Honorius*, Lewis writes that Claudian creates another scene that exists in its own right to luxuriate in description:

> *Turning his back on the nominal subject of his poem, he carries us away to a mountain in Cyprus which the frosts never whiten and the winds never beat. On the mountain head is a meadow guarded by a hedge of gold, and all within it blooms unsown . . . Only the sweetest songbirds live in its copses, where:*
>
> > *Each happy tree*
> > *Woos and is wooed. Palms nodding from above*
> > *Exchange their notes and poplar sighs for love*
> > *Of poplar, plane for plane, and whispers low*
> > *Of love along the alder thickets go.*

Eight hundred years before Guillaume de Lorris wrote *The Romance of the Rose*, Claudian imagines a garden where trees whisper of love and where a young lover might go to find love.

Before leaving these examples from Claudian, Lewis adds a critical observation regarding their inclusion in his narrative about the road to fairyland running through allegory. He did not cite the preceding passage, he tells us, just to show the connection with *The Romance of the Rose:*

> *I have cited . . . this passage . . . because I would willingly begin to show as soon as possible that the decline of the gods, from deity to hypostasis and then from hypostasis to decoration, was not, for them nor for us, a history of sheer loss. For decoration may let romance in. The poet is free to invent, beyond the limits of the possible, regions of strangeness and beauty for their own sake . . . Under the pretext of allegory something else has slipped in . . . something which, under many names, lurks at the back of most romantic poetry. I mean the "other world" not of religion, but of imagination; the land of longing, the Earthly Paradise, the garden east of the sun and west of the moon. Just as the gods—and their homes—are fading into mere decoration, in the mythological poets of this age, we catch a glimpse of the new life and the new dwellings that poetry will find for them.*

By "them," I would guess, he means both the gods and the poets. The gods may have ceased to be gods and they may have devolved, first to a personification like Nature—the hypostasis or substance of reality—and then to mere decoration in a poem which has another purpose (the honoring of the poet's patron), but Lewis's story has a different point. There's new life in that "other world" of imagination for the gods and the poets.

Part 3: Epithalamiums in Sidonius and Ennodius

As in the example from Claudian, Lewis tells us, Sidonius Apollinaris expended his best work "on the trappings of the allegory, on the effect of light on water in the *Epithalamium Ruricio et Iberia.*" The Christian bishop Ennodius, Lewis tells us, also wrote an epithalamium that follows the example of Claudian and Sidonius:

> *He goes, however, beyond his masters, and allegorizes with a boldness and gusto that are somewhat surprising [for a bishop]. He begins by striking the genuine May morning note of the later poets:*
>
> *When young blades shoot and Nature in her bower,*
> *Sits at her work, the world grows warm the while,*
> *And when the sun paints earth with many a flower,*
> *Love, beauty, bravery, all are in his smile.*
>
> *From this we pass to the picture of Venus playing among the flowers . . . and her naked beauty . . . is described. Cupid approaches her with a complaint. "We have lost our old empire. Cold virginity possesses the world. Arise! Shake off your sleep."*

As in Claudian, we have Nature and the Sun working together to produce the gold of love, beauty, and bravery. These are the things that adorn a good marriage and good government.

Lewis then ties this passage to the idea he has been developing throughout sections 2, 3, and 4:

> *No comment can add anything to the starling significance of this little poem. If the gods had not died into allegory, the Bishop would not have dared to use them; conversely, if he had not had allegorical gods for his mouthpiece, he could scarcely have put the "case" of Venus against asceticism so strongly. He had probably in his allegory no purpose but to decorate an occasional copy of verses according to the best models. Yet in doing so he stumbles upon freedom. He is free to wander in fairyland, and he is also free to anticipate the eleventh-century reaction against asceticism.*

In the verse quoted above, in which Cupid complains to Venus, "We have lost our old empire," Ennodius anticipates the use of allegory in the poems of courtly love. Five hundred years after Ennodius, Venus and Cupid strive once more to regain their sovereignty in the courts of southern France after being suppressed for so many centuries by the church fathers' censure of physical love.

Part 4: Martianus Capella

Lewis concludes his survey of works depicting the twilight of the gods with *De Nuptis Philologiae et Mercurii*, the marriage of Eloquence and Learning, by Martianus Capella. As in the other examples, love and wholeness are the focus. Here's a brief summary: Mercury and Virtue meet Apollo in a melodious grove (note once again the alliance of Greek mythological figures with a Roman personification). Together they fly to heaven where they observe "the globe in which the gods behold depicted the whole universe." Next, they return to earth to find the bride Philology, and she undergoes a purge of sorts, which allows her then to drink from the cup of immortality. They all go to heaven again, and at her journey's end:

> *. . . the bride leaps from her floating couch, and sees 'the immense plains of light and the springtime of the ethereal peace'; but knowing that the true God is beyond all these and far even from the knowledge of the gods—words which may bear a Neoplatonic as well as a Christian interpretation—she prays in silence to the dweller in that intelligible world . . .*

Philology—once she's supported by Mercury, Virtue, and Apollo—can "see" this wonderland, but then her vision fails her. Nevertheless, she can "sense" the true God, for He and His world are "intelligible" (available in some form to the mind). This is why she can pray.

It's not known whether Martianus was a Christian or a pagan; either way, his book was popular in the Middle Ages. Lewis finds much with which to fault him as an artist, but in the end, he concludes:

> *Martianus may have been a bad fairy; but I think he had the fairy blood in him . . . At every moment we are reminded of something in the far past or something still to come. What is at hand may be dull [Martianus was an indefatigable pedant]; but we never lose faith in the richness of the collection as a whole. Anything may come next. We are "pleased like travelers, with seeing more," and we are not always disappointed. Among all these figurative woods and streams, these wheeling poles and pedantic rituals, these solemn processions and councils of the gods—gods that seem*

> *no bigger than marionettes . . . among all these, some at any rate suffer us to forget their doctrinal purpose, and breathe the air of wonderland.*

Since all this reading and thinking about Martianus transpires in the substance of C. S. Lewis, can't we say that he, along with the gods and things he lists, has breathed the air of wonderland in the work.

Part 5: The Three Worlds

Having shown through these examples from late Roman poets how the drift of personifications and the twilight of the gods meet in the center of his spectrum, Lewis can sum up their importance for his narrative:

> *In all of them alike, as I hinted above, we see the beginnings of that free creation of the marvelous which first slips in under the cloak of allegory. It is difficult for the modern man of letters to value this quiet revolution as it deserves. We are apt to take it for granted that a poet has at his command, besides the actual world and the world of his own religion, a third world of myth and fancy. The probable, the marvelous-taken-as-fact, the marvelous-known-to-be-fiction—such is the triple equipment of the post-Renaissance poet. Such were the three worlds which Spenser, Shakespeare, and Milton were born to. London and Warwick, Heaven and Hell, Fairyland and Prospero's Island—each has its own laws and its appropriate poetry. But this triple heritage is a late conquest. Go back to the beginnings of any literature and you will not find it. At the beginning the only marvels are the marvels which are taken for fact. The poet has only two of these three worlds. In the fullness of time the third world crept in, but only by a sort of accident. The old gods, when they ceased to be taken as gods, might so easily have been suppressed as devils . . . Only their allegorical use, prepared by slow developments within paganism itself, saved them, as in a temporary tomb, for the day when they could wake again in the beauty of acknowledged myth and thus provide modern Europe with its "third world" of romantic imagining. And when they rose they were changed [as in Ariel's song, page 45] and gave to poetry that which poetry had scarcely had before. The gods . . . were not to paganism what they are to us. In classical poetry we hear plenty of them as objects of worship, of fear, of hatred; even as comic characters. But pure aesthetic*

contemplation of their eternity, their remoteness, and their peace, for its own sake, is curiously rare.

It's a long quote but well worth the reading. What care Lewis has taken in building his argument and what time and effort in reading and thinking led him to conceive of it. Thanks to the learning and gifted speech of C. S. Lewis, maybe we won't be so "apt" to take this third world for granted. If we don't take it for granted, if we begin to grasp why this fairyland came to life, then we may be more apt to appreciate its value as a form of knowledge and "a gift of grace" (this is how Scruton describes the real presence of the sacred on page 329). If we compare our reading of Lewis's argument about Love and allegory to climbing Mount Everest, then we have arrived at a stage or station where we can imagine that it's possible to reach the summit. Some questions about the way forward remain, though, which are discussed in the next section and in chapter 6.

For Gods Must Die to Live

Lewis closes this stage of his argument about the third world of myth and fancy by suggesting why the classical poets (the ones before the discovery of fairyland) didn't see the beauty of the gods. He takes the hint from Lucretius, who warned that it is a grave mistake to picture the gods as "aboil with billows of rolling wrath," for then we won't "enter their temples with peace at heart" (translation by Frank O. Copley of *On the Nature of Things, Book Six*, lines 74–75). Religion, Lewis argues, is what hides their beauty:

> *No religion, so long as it is believed, can have that kind of beauty which we find in the gods of Titian, of Botticelli, or of our own romantic poets . . . The gods must be, as it were, disinfected of belief; the last taint of the sacrifice, and of the urgent practical interest, the selfish prayer, must be washed away from them, before that other divinity [the Beauty of poetry] can come to light in the imagination. For poetry to spread its wings fully, there must be, besides the believed religion, a marvelous that knows itself*

as myth. For this to come about, the old marvelous, which once was taken as fact, must be stored up somewhere, not wholly dead, but in a winter sleep, waiting its time. If it is not so stored up, if it is allowed to perish, then the imagination is impoverished. Such a sleeping place was provided for the gods by allegory. Allegory may seem, at first, to have killed them; but it killed only as the sower kills, for gods, like other creatures, must die to live.

By "romantic poets," I believe Lewis is referring to the poets who wrote medieval romances and a poet like Shakespeare who wrote romantic comedies like *Pericles*, *Cymbeline*, *The Winter's Tale*, and *The Tempest*. It's another remarkable passage, full of potent suggestion. For example, if the gods or even God must die to live, then perhaps Lewis considers that the loss of faith in his and our own time can still be a blessing. Lewis's idea suggests this loss may yet initiate in some a true calling of faith and service, for the inner life—as the defeat of Pietas in Statius's poem suggests—comes to life in disappointment. Lewis's own faith, we recall, experienced a death and a rebirth.

The passage raises another weighty issue, one touched on earlier as to whether sin has departed from nature, as Alanus claimed, or whether we are endowed with a "poor soul" like Shakespeare's and subject to the darkness of earth (see pages 121–122). We also have to wrestle with what Lewis means by "the taint of sacrifice." A sacrifice implies a need for it so it would appear that Lewis implicates the selfishness that necessitates propitiation and absolution. A taint or infection must be "washed away," he tells us, *for the gods to rise reborn from the deep in poetry* (an image that's expressed in Raphael's painting on page 151 and in the text on pages 154–155), but he leaves much in question. Why and where does the taint exist? Are the gods tainted because they are greedy for sacrifice (the view of Lucretius), or are we tainted because our flesh is weak and needy? Can the stain only be washed in conjunction with religious belief, or can the stain be washed in the marvelous that knows itself as myth?

Given questions like this that I can't answer, I'll summarize what I can say about this passage with the assistance of that wonderful word *if* and a modal verb. If we follow the advice of Lecretius to live freely without fear of

God, of the gods, or of death and as the stain (wherever it exists) is washed away, then the beauty of poetry can rise as in Botticelli's *The Birth of Venus* and Raphael's *The Triumph of Galatea*.

Chapter 6

On the Death and Rebirth of Metaphysics

Raphael's

The Triumph of Galatea

Goethe's Faust, unlike Marlowe's, Dies to Live

As to the washing of the stain on ourselves, it's a safe bet to suppose that the washing is our responsibility for the most part. We understand perfectly well what it is to get dirty and to need a bath. We often do get dirty and need a bath. Some stains, though, run deep. How do human beings wash away the practical interest, the selfish prayer? Centuries of human history pile up proofs that systematic and shallow forms of Reason consistently fail to get the job done. The stain of self-interest can't be rationalized away.

Goethe wrote his epic about Faust, a brilliant professor, to imagine the process wherein the suffering that ensues from the shortfalls of Reason gives rise to a living soul. Faust doesn't go to hell, as he does in Marlowe's play, *Doctor Faustus*. We may think that Goethe's Faust deserves to be damned, for he sold his soul to Mephistopheles and employed that devil to corrupt an innocent girl. Nevertheless, he is saved, as Dante was, *by the woman he loved in this world*. Faust loved Gretchen's innocence, the thing his love corrupted. This is a trap for which his mouse of a mind had no answer. Desperate, he sought her out in prison (despite the wish of Mephistopheles), encountered her suffering, and saw himself in her as in a mirror. If she was in prison for the murder of their child, then so was he. She never would have had a child out of wedlock but for him. Once he abandoned her, she was wedded to despair. There was no escape for both parents; the child's death is an irrevocable accident in the substance of her life and his. He wanted to escape, wanted her to escape with him, but she wouldn't. The die was cast. It stained the whole. He was accountable—for his own actions, for her life and death, and for the life and death of their child. With that, the Faust of *Part One* dies. He "vanishes" with Mephistopheles, but Gretchen's cries of "Heinrich! Heinrich!" (which end *Part One*) wash over him and into the time and space of what's to come. She loves him still, the way, we might imagine, a soul that's been abandoned loves the body of which the soul is the center.

Thus, we are given in the prologue of *Part Two* a healing flood of poetry in which Faust is reborn. The Chorus, like God saying, "Let there be light," proclaims a new Creation over Faust's insensate body. The scene recalls the one in *A Midsummer Night's Dream*, in which Robin intones his prayer over the four insensate lovers from Athens:

And the country proverb known
That everyman should take his own
In your waking shall be shown:
Jack shall have Jill;
Naught shall go ill;
The man shall have his mare again, and all shall be well.

All four lie together on the ground, dead to the world, but unaware that they now lie perfectly matched, two and two. This is what they wake to discover.

Even in translation, the beauty of Goethe's poetry washes over us like the gentle rolling and lapping of a great sea:

When a fragrance has descended
All about the green-girt plain,
Richer air with mist-clouds blended
Evening dusk comes down again;
Lulls to infant-sweet reposing,
Rocks the heart with whispering sighs,
And this wanderer feels it closing
On his daylight-weary eyes.
Now to night the world surrenders,
Sacred love joins star to star;
Little sparkles, greater splendours,
Glitter near and gleam from far.
Glitter in the lake reflecting,
Gleam against the clear night sky;

Deepest seals of rest protecting
Glows the full moon strong and high.
Soon the hours have slipped away,
Pain and happiness are past;
Trust the light of the new day,
Feel your sickness will not last!
Green the valleys, hillsides swelling,
Bushing thick to restful shade,
And the fields, their wealth foretelling,
Rippling ripe and silver-swayed!
Have you wishes without number?
Watch the promise of the dawn!
Lightly you are wrapped in slumber:
Shed this husk and be reborn!
Venture boldly; hesitation
Is for lesser men—when deeds
Are a noble mind's creation,
All his enterprise succeeds.

These words—spoken by otherworldly spirits, such as Robin in *A Midsummer Night's Dream* and Ariel in *The Tempest—wash* him in preparation for rebirth. As in Shakespeare's plays, the author's imagination gives them voices. They speak to us in this world of that which still lives within a lifeless husk; they speak of becoming—after one's idea of the self dies—a soul that's healthy and brave.

I employed the image of gods reborn and rising from the depths at the end of the last section (see the italicized words on page 148). The conclusion of act 2 in *Faust, Part Two* suggested the image to me. Goethe has Galatea rise reborn from the deep so that the Homunculus [a little man, a spiritual embryo who, like the word in the opening lines of John's gospel, would become flesh] can meet his destiny by merging with her. Goethe retells in dramatic form the story Raphael has depicted in "The Triumph of Galatea."

As in Goethe's story about the Homunculus, Galatea rises from the waters of life, along with other lusty life-forms, and conquers all who see her. In her presence, our old, abstracted life dies, and we become human, even if our humanity only takes the form of desire. The moment suggests Dante's first sight of Beatrice, but Galetea's nakedness adds what Dante omitted. We have to assume that Raphael has consciously made a painting that attracts a physical viewer to the physical body of Galatea. (This theme in Goethe's work is also discussed on pages 372–373.)

The example from *Faust* matches perfectly with Lewis's argument. He could have said Titian, Botticelli, *and Raphael* show that the practical interest and the selfish prayer have been washed away and that the beauty of the gods can now rise from the deep to men's eyes. Raphael's painting tells us that Beauty, like that of Galatea, can appear, but he doesn't tell us how the depths do the washing. Goethe has taken upon himself to answer the question through the fall of Faust into Gretchen's prison cell, Melville documents it through the drowning of Ahab in his vengeance, Chaucer represents it through the crushing of Arcite's heart in "The Knight's Tale," and Shakespeare represents it through the crushing, hateful words with which the lovers in *A Midsummer Night's Dream* address each other in act 3. Love (Himself, as in an allegory) must be crushed in disappointment to be reborn and love in a new way. Even the gods (or God) must die to live.

Love Is and Is Not Problematic

On Chaucer's authority, we learn in "The Knight's Tale" that love is problematic. Palamon and Arcite love the same woman, and this leads to years of conflict. On Lewis's authority, we learn in chapter 1 that Love is problematic. We come to that conclusion when we consider Love's classical reputation as a disruptor of social order as well as the tensions in courtly love that Lewis documents. If it is adulterous love, then it must divorce the husband from the fruits of a loving, faithful companionship. If it is married love, the church fathers still found carnal desire to be, variously, a punishment for the Fall, a weakening of the rational faculty, an animal intoxication, and a necessary evil. "It is better to marry than to burn," Saint Paul told the Corinthians. Lovers in the West have wondered for centuries how carnal love can be saved from the opinion of church fathers. On Dante's authority, we learn that love is problematic. Dante loved Beatrice, and she saved him when he was lost in a dark wood, as he eventually discovers. Nevertheless, on the first stage of his journey he meets hundreds of human beings who, like Ahab, loved their own destruction. How can Love be both a destroyer and a savior?

Love as desire may involve human beings in a problematic duality, but it is also one. To comprehend its wholeness we need poetry, like the first eighteen lines of *The Canterbury Tales*:

When in April the sweet showers fall
And pierce the drought of March to the root, and all
The veins are bathed in liquor of such power
As brings about the engendering of the flower,
When also Zephyrus with his sweet breath
Exhales an air in every grove and heath
Upon the tender shoots, and the young sun
His half-course in the sign of the Ram has run,
And the small fowl are making melody
That sleep away the night with open eye
(So nature pricks them and their heart engages)
Then people long to go on pilgrimages
And palmers long to seek the stranger strands
Of far off saints, hallowed in sundry lands,
And specially, from every shires end
Of England, down to Canterbury they wend
To seek the holy blissful martyr, quick
To give them help when they were sick.

Despite the drought of March, the fact of suffering, the root is ripe for renewal in a springtime of rain and wind and sun, along with all the other influences of the season. These lines plant an image in our minds that prepares us for the flourishing of life that we read about throughout the tales. Just as Chaucer's root can engender a flower, a grasping love can engender a selfless, sunlit love of Creation. Chaucer's root is also like his poetry; it expresses a longing for springtime, adventure, love, and the balm of the sacred—a longing to be wholly alive.

The poetry begins underground in darkness absorbing all the natural influences there, like a child in the womb, but it rises to breathe the air by which we all live and to bask in the heat of the sun. The poetry ripens as it opens to take in all the things of this world including the death of a man and his rebirth as a saint. These opening lines serve as the universal stage on which the pilgrims and the characters in their tales will act.

Love, as Chaucer describes it here, is like Lewis's train that moves and never leaves the station. It moves through many stations—root, branch, stem, and blossom—while remaining in one place, for love lives, as the soul does, at the center of the turning world.

Physics and Metaphysics

Part 1: On Chemistry and Purity

To encourage us when competing forces contend within (picture Augustine walking away as the vanities pluck at his carnal robe), Lewis has written his book to show how Love, along with everything else, is made whole in allegory. To perform this herculean task, he would resurrect metaphysics from the tomb where Science thought it was safely stowed.

Courtly love, Lewis argued in his first chapter, came into existence as "a temporary escape, a truancy from the ardours of a religion that was believed into the delights of a religion that was merely imagined" (see page 78). Specifically, courtly lovers attempted an escape from the belief that sexual passion was wicked. Lewis then fast-forwards seven hundred years to contrast the scholastic idea of passion with the doctrine of nineteenth-century Romantics. Passion for the scholastics meant "an animal intoxication," whereas these Romantics saw it as "*a passion that purifies.*" For these Romantics (as opposed to medieval and Renaissance writers of romances), this passion "*works a chemical change upon appetite and affection and turns them into a thing different from either*" (quoted from *The Allegory of Love*, pages 20–21). How well I remember discovering the books of D. H. Lawrence for the first time in college. This undergraduate was quick to identify with lovers who escaped the strictures of the Dark Ages on physical love.

Lewis advises us that Thomas Aquinas would have nothing to say about nineteenth-century Romantic passion "as he has nothing to say about the steam engine. He had not heard of it." In the passages quoted above, which I've italicized, Lewis's description of Romantic passion has an otherworldly air about it, thanks to its association with purification, but at the same time he makes it sound like a drug we can take to dissolve the stain on sex. Since we are all just chemistry, chemistry can change us. For the record, Romantics from the nineteenth century through to the twenty-first century have experimented extensively with mind-altering drugs. We might notice, too, that modern media sells passion at a premium. It's their product, and there's a huge demand for it, just as there's a huge demand for "spirits" that change our chemistry. For someone who wants something stronger, opioids can briefly induce an altered state that obliterates the pain of passionate wanting.

Lewis inserts chemistry into his commentary on passion in the chapter on courtly love not only to contrast medieval and nineteenth-century Romantic views on the subject of passion. He is suggesting the tension between two ontologies: Dante's interest in spiritual "substances" (like a soul) and a modern scientist's interest in the chemical makeup of physical matter. It's fair to say Lewis is a skeptic about the claims of nineteenth-century Romantic symbolists. From his description of their doctrine, these Romantics, despite putting on transcendental airs, have adopted the view of science that reality consists of chemicals and their constituent parts.

Relations between people begin and begin again in the chemistry of the body. So be it, but these Romantics, Lewis implies, have overreached; they claim the process can purify, make us better. For Lewis, I suspect, the chemistry of the body (the passion it produces) can't purify anything. Chemicals in combination with other chemicals will change into a different thing. They can't change into purity, though, for purity belongs to a different realm—to human standards of measurement, to fairyland, or to the sacred.

Part 2: On Prejudging Soulful Presocratic Primary Substances

In the first paragraph of *The Allegory of Love*, Lewis asserts, "Humanity does not pass through phases as a train passes through stations: being alive, it has the privilege of always moving yet never leaving anything behind. Whatever we have been, in some sort we are still." He asserts this to persuade us that we have not left the station of courtly love, even though the poems about courtly love were written a thousand years ago. I see no reason why the same can't be said about humanity and stations in the history of philosophy. In which case, we are still alive to seriously consider the Presocratic argument that nature is composed of a primary substance that is both physical and metaphysical. Richard Tarnas narrates a history of Presocratic primary substances in *The Passion of the Western Mind* that resonates with the ontological theme—that mankind is a composed of a body and a heavenly soul—which Lewis develops through these different stations to convey the significance of allegory.

Tarnas writes well, so I'm quoting him at length. He begins with some speculation as to what might have "impelled" these early philosophers to think about the nature of reality in a new way:

> *Yet whatever their immediate inspiration, these prototypical scientists made the remarkable assumption that an underlying rational unity and order existed within the flux and variety of the world, and established for themselves the task of discovering a simple fundamental principle, or arche, that both governed nature and composed its basic substance.*

In so doing, they began to complement their traditional mythological understanding with more impersonal and conceptual explanations based on their observations of natural phenomena.

At this pivotal stage, there was a distinct overlap of the mythic and scientific modes, visible in the principle statement attributed to Thales in which he affirmed both a single unifying primary substance and a divine omnipresence: "All is water, and the world is full of gods." Thales and his successors proposed that nature arose from a self-animated substance that continued to move and change itself into various forms. Because it was author of its own ordered motions and transmutations, and because it was everlasting, this primary substance was considered to be not only material but also alive and divine. Much like Homer, these earliest philosophers perceived nature and divinity as yet intertwined . . .

In their search for simplicity in explaining nature, the Ionian philosophers [like Thales] had stated that the world was one thing, but had become many. But in Parmenides's early struggle with language and logic, "to be" something made it impossible for it to change into something it is not, for what "is not" cannot be said to exist at all. Similarly, he argued that "what is" can never have come into being or pass away, since something cannot come from nothing if nothing cannot exist at all. Things cannot be as they appear to the senses: the familiar world of change, motion, and multiplicity must be mere opinion, for the true reality by logical necessity is changeless and unitary . . .

These two advancing trends of naturalism and rationalism impelled the development of a series of increasingly sophisticated theories to explain the natural world. Obliged to reconcile the conflicting demands of sensory observation with the new logical rigor, Empedocles, Anaxagoras, and finally the atomists attempted to explain the world's apparent change and multiplicity by reinterpreting and modifying Parmenides's absolute monism—reality as one, motionless, and changeless—in terms of more pluralistic systems . . . Empedocles posited four ultimate root elements—earth, water, air, and fire—which were eternal, and which were moved together and apart by the primary forces of Love and Strife. Anaxagoras proposed that the universe was constituted by an infinite number of minute, qualitatively different seeds. But instead of explaining matter's movement in terms of blind, semimythic forces (such as Love and Strife), he postulated a transcendent primordial Mind (Nous), which set the material universe into motion and gave it form and order.

But the most comprehensive system in this development was that of atomism. In an attempt to fulfill the Ionians' search for an elementary substance constituting the material world, while also overcoming the Parmenidean argument against change and multiplicity, Leucippus and his successor Democritus constructed a complex explanation of all phenomena in purely materialistic terms: The world was composed exclusively of uncaused and immutable material atoms—a unitary changeless substance, as Parmenides required, though of infinite number. The invisibly minute and indivisible particles perpetually moved about in a boundless void and by their random collisions and varying combinations produced the phenomena of the visible world. (These passages were quoted from The Passion of the Western Mind, *pages 20–22.)*

Both Socrates and Plato were attracted by Anaxagoras's first principle [Nous or Mind], with its suggestion of a rational teleology as the basis of the universe's existence [a mind implies meaning and purpose]. They were disappointed, however, as was Aristotle later, that Anaxogoras had not developed the principle further in his own philosophy (which was predominantly materialistic, like that of the atomists), and particularly that he had not made explicit the intentional goodness of the universal mind. But about a half-century before Anaxagoras, the poet-philosopher Xenophanes, having criticized the anthropomorphic deities of naive popular tradition, had posited instead a single supreme God, a universal divinity who influenced the world through pure intellection, and who was in essence identified with the world itself. Shortly afterward, another Presocratic philosopher, the solitary and enigmatic Heraclitus, introduced a similarly immanent conception of the divine intelligence with his use of the term logos (originally meaning word, speech, or thought) to signify the rational principle governing the cosmos. All things are in constant flux, and yet are fundamentally related and ordered through the universal Logos, which is also manifest in the human being's power of reason. Heraclitus associated the Logos with the element of fire, which like the Heraclitean world as a whole, is born of strife, ever-consuming, and in constant movement. It is the law of the universal Logos that everything is defined by, tends toward, and is ultimately balanced by its opposite, so that all opposites ultimately constitute a unity. The finest harmony is composed of elements that are in tension with each other. (This passage was quoted from The Passion of the Western Mind, *pages 45–46.)*

Like Dante, Thales affirms that nature consists of a single, unifying, self-animated substance, whereas, like modern scientists, Democritus affirms that nature consists only of material atoms moving and colliding in a boundless void. Heraclitus appears to combine the two models; he posits a material universe ordered through the universal Logos. I'm inclined to agree with Lewis about humanity and the "stations" of our development: because we have yet to leave the Presocratics' station, we would do well to examine it with interest and an open mind. Their investigations, I believe, have much to do with Dante's substance, which he associates with the soul.

The Presocratics give the airy nothing of Lewis's subject and the airy nothing of these essays a shape, a name, and a place of respect as we study the passions of the Western mind. The Presocratics give me confidence to move ahead in my own inquiry; these matters have been investigated from that moment when man came to self-consciousness and wondered about the reality of his experience. The history of Western civilization teaches that this business of what is real has its twists and turns and ups and downs. At least since the time of Homer, a great poet has understood that even a great king and strategist like Odysseus can make a serious mistake about the reality of a situation. Odysseus blithely led his men into the cave of the Cyclops, the one-eyed giant, expecting that the host would respect the laws of hospitality decreed and enforced by Zeus himself. Odysseus didn't know that the host, a son of Zeus, would consider his visitors his dinner rather than his dinner guests. If the great Odysseus can make a mistake about the reality of a situation, an ordinary man, no matter his profession, can make one too.

I'm painfully aware I have made big and little mistakes in my life, and I have observed how great institutions make serious mistakes. For example, Kodak, the largest employer in our city, failed to comprehend until it was too late how the revolution in digital technology would shortly rule the imaging business, and that technology, when it did rule the business, in short order ate up Kodak's share of it. The people of the Soviet Union failed to see, until it was too late, that the communist model of government would quite naturally produce scarcity and corruption rather than all the good things the government had promised them. Instead, the government, a one-party state, devoured the people (their "guests") in order to survive. Once embarked on their experiment, the state couldn't and wouldn't correct the mistake. In death throes that lasted as for as long as the state existed, it ate up the people in brutal famines, dislocations, and war. It even devoured those most loyal to it in show trials designed to increase the terror. No one was safe. The Mind ruling the nation was out of its mind, except where it concerned itself. Since no sane person was safe, it was best not to think at all.

Part 3: A Gordian Knot to Untangle

It may be that ontological questions aren't as settled as a physicist, a sociologist, or a political scientist might claim. Writers like Goethe and Lewis had lived long enough in a world ordered around scientific explanations to conclude that they don't explain everything; there are some things that science can't explain at all, especially about human beings. Goethe and Lewis stake out the position that we need metaphysics and poetry to understand ourselves and our place in the order of nature; we need them to overcome the alienation that plagues human beings in modern life; we need them to live bravely and well. Why is this? To answer, I propose a small thought experiment: What if the alienation begins in metaphysics? What if Heraclitus has it about right: we are one, but oneness simultaneously creates the shadow presence of its opposite (alienation) and lights the fire of desire—of wanting oneness. If there's flooding in Athens, you wouldn't go to Boston to fix it. If the disease begins in metaphysics, we must go to metaphysics to heal it.

For thousands of years, people have embarked on pilgrimages to resolve this tension: we want to be whole, but the wanting is alienation—burning disappointment. The pilgrimage may cover a thousand miles or more, but we hear stories of those who complete it in a single step or less. For the tension exists in the mind, and the mind must resolve it. The mind must come to terms with the appearance of a Gordian knot: the Not of wanting (not-having)—the desire that feeds on desire, like a dragon perpetually devouring its own tail. For centuries, poets have studied desire through their fictions like that dragon. It may be this is the only way it can be studied. If desire is not physical, how can science study it? At the present writing, for that matter, the human mind has no place in empirical science. Science (personified) has yet to locate the physical location of Mind in the body so, as with desire, it can't be strictly observed and measured.

Part 4: The Pivot

Allegory, on the other hand, is about that substance with different names like the "self," "mind," or "soul." Just as Lewis has explained that the gods must die to live, we learn from an allegory like *Everyman* that the grasping self must die for Everyman to save his soul, his true self. Since allegories involve figures that personify a state of mind, Everyman at the beginning of his allegory personifies a grasping self, one that would "own" the things of this world. This Everyman consists of his attachments—to Fellowship, Kindred, and material Goods. He loves these things. They make him laugh; they secure a place in a family; and they ensure, like money in the bank, the future. When Death comes and Everyman must go a journey for a reckoning, however, these attachments dissolve. Everyman finds himself like Dante at the beginning of his pilgrimage—a naked soul humbled and infinitely exposed.

The outcome rests on a pivot Everyman must make; he must turn from that form of love—from love as attachment to things and from love of that allegorical figure, the Self of Everyman. It's the pivot that Shakespeare captures in Hamlet's final scene, which I've already described in Book One. Because (in my opinion) it bears repeating, here it is. After fencing with Laertes, Hamlet finally turns from his sport—the game he plays to avoid the regicide, which will expose and end his own life, the game he plays because he loves his life even though he thinks about ending it—and kills the usurping uncle. After killing the king, he lives, and yet he can truly say, "Oh, I am dead, Horatio," for Laertes has confessed the treachery at the tip of his sword. While Hamlet is both alive and dead from the wound of a deadly poison, in the moment that *he* is king (virtually the time it takes to say "one"), he orders in his last breath a plan of succession to ensure the health and safety of the kingdom. On the horizon between life and death, Hamlet becomes a living soul and declares in his last breath what he wills for his people. As such, he lives on in Horatio's and Shakespeare's timeless report of him.

If *Hamlet* is an allegory about the grasping self, as I believe it is, then Hamlet must kill that usurper—the alienated one, the one that wants and wants and wants—to exercise real power. If we understand the story as an allegory, we can also read it as a parable: a crown of sacred kingship is *given, not taken* and only to one who has killed the usurping, grasping self. Since it's a spiritual crown, Hamlet doesn't need the trappings of investiture—the oil and all that. The uncle got all that at his investiture and still wasn't the real king, for he lacked truth. Material facts on the ground made the usurper king, but the ghost of Hamlet's father exposed the truth. The father's son, young Hamlet, finally did what needed to be done. That's real power, not a symbol. The mainstream of Lewis's intent moves me to make the following observation and to briefly elaborate on it. By inserting a ghost into the story, Shakespeare makes the story about metaphysics. The ghost in Shakespeare's play exercises real power, for the health and safety of the realm depends on the metaphysical word of a ghost. Then again, it might be said that all words are metaphysical, which puts even science, despite its claims, on a metaphysical basis.

Like Hamlet, Everyman, in the play named after him, must die to become a living soul; it's a story that Science cannot and does not want to tell. Its ontology rests on the chemicals of the body and brain, and chemicals simply act and react. Chemicals don't self-consciously choose to examine consciousness. Science has trouble explaining sacrifice because natural selection strongly inveighs against it. Metaphysics, on the other hand, has always pointed to that universe of which the soul is the center, where:

Sacred love joins star to star;
Little sparkles, greater splendours,
Glitter near and gleam from far.
Glitter in the lake reflecting,
Gleam against the clear night sky;

Deepest seals of rest protecting
Glows the full moon strong and high.

This vision of things draws us unto itself. All three texts—*Hamlet*, *Everyman*, and *Faust*—suggest that it is possible to be whole; to join star to star in a constellation that involves everything in the universe, to be that full moon, to love beauty, and to be restful and secure in our being. It doesn't just happen. The self, the wanting, and the divisions don't just wither away in time or in a chemical soup. For that we need metaphysics, a comic vision of a sacrificial act. We need to be brave, and this is what these plays dramatize. To aid us in the work, philosophy must cease to act as the handmaiden of science. She must take her true place once more as a credible and compassionate judge of the human condition.

An Alchemic Alembic in *A Midsummer Night's Dream*

Thales posited a primary substance that's both physical and metaphysical, and our poets do much the same when they employ figurative language. "What is good or happy," Lewis maintains, "has always been high like heavens and bright like the sun." When *Hamlet*, *Everyman*, and *Faust* are read as allegory, and when we consider them as a whole, they become the *arena* where man becomes a living soul. In *A Midsummer Night's Dream*, the change occurs in the wood outside Athens where the fairies rule. It takes place, therefore, in the imagined world of the poem. The text suggests that the wood (and the poem as a whole) is like an alembic into which all the elements of the play are poured. There they interact at a primal level and liquify into a stream of gold that spills from the wood and floods the land like morning sun. Shakespeare conjures the power of this place, which isn't a place necessarily but a state of mind, through poetry of breathtaking beauty. To make my case, I've collected three samples and added commentary adapted from *A Comic Vision of Great Constancy*.

Shakespeare has set his play during a season, Titania tells us, when the land around Athens is under water. In the end, after all the words and sentences, we realize it was a flood fed by his mighty stream of consciousness (see pages 44–46). In the first sample, Oberon raises an image from the past as he recalls for Robin Goodfellow a moment when the power of poetry and music transformed the "rude sea" of the natural world:

> *My gentle Puck, come hither. Thou remem'b'rest*
> *Since once I sat upon a promontory*
> *And heard a mermaid, on a dophin's back,*
> *Uttering such dulcet and harmonious breath*
> *That the rude sea grew civil at the song,*
> *And certain stars shot madly from their spheres*
> *to hear the sea-maid's music.*

To fully take in the image, along with the mermaid on her dolphin we must include Oberon and Robin on the promontory, enraptured by the beauty they share once more. Perhaps even we who hear of it through the poetry will, like the rude sea, grow civil in its presence. We need to picture the two together—for the civility of the sea is enhanced by presence of an enduring friendship, and we need to picture them on that promontory (which probs into the vastness of sea and sky) to convey the enduring friendship they enjoy with the world.

"I remember," replies Puck, as who would not.

Oberon raises the second image to describe the grove where Robin will find the Fairy Queen. It's not exactly a memory; it's a place that exists, but at some remove:

> *I know a bank where the wild thyme blows,*
> *Where oxlips and the nodding violet grows,*
> *Quite overcanopied with luscious woodbine,*
> *With sweet musk-roses, and with eglantine.*

There sleeps Titania sometime of the night,
Lulled in these flowers with dances and delight;
And there the snake throws her enameled skin,
Weed wide enough to wrap a fairy in.

The beauty of this place, Shakespeare's fairyland, comes to life in lush, luxurious sounds, as intricate and varied as anything in a garden or on the floor of a forest. Here, even the snake, so important in the mythology of the West, "throws" the armor that emboldened it in Genesis, the power of speech to play with truth and illusion. What role does the serpent play now, we wonder, without it? The armor, though, remains. Instead of enameling the snake, it's transformed into the House of Fairyland.

Robin and Oberon are featured in the third sample as well. I argue in my book about the play that they present the two forces involved in a comic resolution. One belongs to the Puckish Robin who loves nothing better than the confusion that ensues when someone's pretensions take a fall; his pranks and misrule expose the self-love that left unchecked will move a person to self-destruct. The other belongs to Oberon who, once he recognizes the harm in his own pretensions (his prolonged war with Titania for sovereignty), acts in a timely way to create a space where warlike passions can safely bottom out. In keeping with his new resolve to be more involved in the government of the wood, Oberon gives commands that limit the disorder. Robin points out, though, that he doesn't have much time to complete the work:

My fairy lord, this must be done with haste,
For night's swift dragons cut the clouds full fast,
And yonder shines Aurora's harbinger;
At whose approach ghosts, wand'ring here and there,
Troop home to churchyards . . . damned spirits all,
That in crossways and floods have burial,
Already to their wormy beds are gone.
For fear lest day should look their shames upon,

They wilfully themselves exile from light,
And must for aye consort with black-brow'd night.

Like these ghosts and spirits, Oberon and Robin are active at night. It's a time for fantasy and dreams that act out the desires of mortals. Even as spirits, they hide their desires from the light since they are selfish and shameful. In a tragedy, desire can end in suicide, which is why those spirits are damned. Robin is reminding Oberon (and us) there's no time to waste.

Since this play is a comedy, our lovers' desires safely play themselves out and find a bottom in the dreamless sleep that concludes their midsummer night, for Oberon commands the powers of healing. In one more burst of poetic gold, he celebrates a new day of love. It is true that he and Robin are largely nocturnal:

But we are spirits of another sort.
I with the Morning's love have oft made sport;
And, like a forester, the groves may tread
Even till the eastern gate, all fiery red,
Opening on Neptune, with fair blessed beams
Turns into yellow gold his salt green streams.

Make no mistake, Oberon is a lover. He is a man of action who, before and after lovemaking, treads the woods at dawn refreshed and awake, and he's a poet who can imagine the sun penetrating the green wood as if its beams were transmuting salt green streams of ocean into yellow gold. In his vision, he walks toward the east, where the light brings a great change to those who move resolutely in its direction. Oberon treads with confidence and purpose, for he is acquainted with a life-giving power that can transform the bitter and turbulent salt of experience into the yellow gold of wisdom and well-being.

Once Oberon determines he must act to restore order in his realm, he enlivens the dukedom with a creative energy that binds human beings and fairies alike. They love and are loved. The love of Oberon's creator, the author of all, makes it so. Everything about this experience is real. We are real people; the text or the dramatic performance is real; our mind—illuminated by the words and actions of the poem—is real. And yet this is an experience about which pure science can only scoff and deny. Of course, there have been skeptics since Xenophanes and probably before that; skeptics are nothing new. We need to consider our actual situation, not historical imperatives. When Love floods the city of Athens at the end of act 5, maybe it washes over those of us attending the play as well. It must. How else to explain why millions continue to attend performances of his work.

The House of a Living Soul

In Lewis's exposition, the center of his literary spectrum—where the drift of personifications and the twilight of the gods come together from different directions to make allegory a vital form of expression—is like the alembic of alchemy and the wood outside Athens. It transforms personifications like Nature and the gods of myth into something new, the figures of fairyland. Lewis mentions Spenser, Shakespeare, and Milton earlier in connection with the triple world of London, Christianity, and fairyland. In their fictions, the problems of desire are transformed into something new, something beautiful, and something of great constancy in the lives of human beings. It's an arena, like the heavenly globe that Martianus imagined; it's the content of that which is perfectly understood, as when Philology drinks from the cup of immortality; it's the theater of life, as in Genesis when everything comes to life in the mist and the breath. It is the inner state of a person, the setting for allegory; as such, it might as well be called a living soul. Lest we forget, though, a great allegorist confessed the state of his soul in a letter to friend. It is "like a sock that is being turned inside out: the outer becoming the inner; the inner, outer." Inner and outer, subjective and objective, are interchangeable.

In an allegory, the pilgrim soul often ends up in a house or enclosure of some kind—the House of Fame, the House of Alma, the Bower of Bliss, the

House of Holiness, and so on. This "House" is the world of our experience. Like the soul, it is a perspective unique to each individual. It comes to life, it breathes, as it were, when we do. If we would be as God intended man to be in Genesis, we would be the House of a Living Soul, wherein everything is animated and made whole by the love of its creator. But there are other houses. There the soul falls asleep, like Falstaff behind the arras in Mistress Quickly's tavern, or it is drugged and turns into something less than human, like the pigs in Circe's lair.

Lewis wrote his book—about the twilight of the gods in the twilight of the Roman Empire—in the 1930s. An earlier quote from his text describes this twilight. Since it's beautifully put, here it is again:

> *For poetry to spread its wings fully, there must be, besides the believed religion, a marvelous that knows itself as myth. For this to come about, the old marvelous, which once was taken as fact, must be stored up somewhere, not wholly dead, but in a winter sleep, waiting its time. If it is not so stored up, if it is allowed to perish, then the imagination is impoverished. Such a sleeping place was provided for the gods by allegory. Allegory may seem, at first, to have killed them; but it killed only as the sower kills, for gods, like other creatures, must die to live.*

If I borrow Lewis's metaphor in this passage, I say that he is writing when it seemed to many that metaphysics had been killed as a subject worthy of consideration, not by allegory but by those who live in the House of Science. How many millions in the twenty-first century share this impression? From the image of a "sower" at the end of the passage, I picture him sowing a seed of doubt, which is actually a seed of hope, a comic vision, as to whether metaphysics is dead or whether it's waiting its time in a winter sleep.

It's doubtful our culture will experience a Great Awakening, like the one in the eighteenth century, when George Whitefield could move even a scientist like Ben Franklin. Too many millions are too invested in skepticism about metaphysics for the time being. Too many people are not just skeptical about religion; they actively hate and resist it—despite the popularity of New Age spiritualism. Nevertheless, in section 4, Lewis builds a bridge from holy war in the conscience to fairyland in the imagination. He gave us a preview of this movement in the chapter on courtly love, in which he writes of the new religion of love that:

> *Where it is not a parody of the Church it may be, in a sense, her rival—a temporary escape, a truancy from the ardours of a religion that was believed into the delights of a religion that was merely imagined.*

It may be that he viewed fairyland in our own age as a "sleeping place" between the faith in numbers of a skeptic—who has purified his thinking by banishing any taint of metaphysics—and the Judeo-Christian faith in a divine Creator and Savior.

Allegory played an important role in the new religion of love, which came into being in the late eleventh century; in Lewis's narrative, it rose from the deep to express something the people wanted. In his own time and place, Lewis sensed a deep need in himself and in the culture. He wrote his book to bring us back to the given world: to a world of substances, not abstractions; to the reality of our own substance; to the reality of a Mother, a sacred source, from whom we emerged, like a miracle, into life; and to the recognition of another, the Rose of our love, who has our heart and with whom we can exchange hearts. It's a world to which we respond, and which responds to us. Maybe we need not worry about a Great Awakening. Maybe it just takes one to make the vision live again.

All Is Parable

Goethe, I believe, made it his life's work to describe the progress and burden of love and of becoming a living soul, and to that end he wrote an allegory about a man named Faust having to account for his life, just as Everyman did in his play. It also has the effect of a parable, a narrative that teaches us something important about the human condition. The work marries the real substance of a human being, Goethe, with a fiction, a story that illuminates his substance and makes it more real.

Death comes to Everyman; however, instead of dying then and there, Everyman goes through a lengthy process that opens up his entire life for the "reckoning" he must give as in the parable of the talents:

> *After a long time the lord of those servants cometh,*
> *and reckoneth with them.*
>
> Matthew 25:19

At the end of Goethe's play, Death also comes to Faust. This mirrors those first scenes of the play when Mephistopheles comes to Faust to seal the fate of his soul. Despite this spiritual death early in the play, Faust lives on to free his soul from a bad bargain. It takes Goethe over 12,000 lines of poetry to tell this story. In the end, Faust is saved by angelic powers and becomes a living soul. First, though, in "Burial Rites" Angels descend to rescue his soul before Mephistopheles can snatch it and take it through the gaping jaws of hell. It turns out that the Devil, the great tempter, can be tempted and distracted from his true purpose. By its very nature, a contract with the Father of Lies can't be true anymore than he can be true. Then in "Mountain Gorges," a whole host of heavenly powers lifts Faust's soul in a rising tide. They sing songs of praise for the good things of this world and for the goal Faust has finally achieved. He is raised by this flood to "sense" his love, the penitent Gretchen, as she, too, rises "into higher spheres."

Goethe has given us this dramatization of transcendence as a safe house for our imaginations. It has many rooms for Faust and for us. We follow him over the threshold and into the hall; we climb the stairs with him and turn on the landing to climb some more. In the corridor at the top, we walk a bit and turn into the study. By this time, through the magic of these stories and the power of imagination, we have become one with Faust. What happens to him happens to us. We are the living soul of Faust. Without a living soul, there is no Faust. If Faust is functioning as I think Goethe intends, then the converse is also true. Without Faust, there is no living soul. There's magic in Goethe's tale. We bring it to life, and it returns the favor. Each room—the entryway, the hall, the stairway, and the corridor—comes alive as we walk through. Life walks with us. We are at the center, and each room blooms into life as we enter and disappears when we leave for another room. Goethe is what we call the living soul that holds Faust as an accident of itself, but we are now the living soul that holds him too. And not just Faust but every room in our Father's mansion.

The poem concludes with an affirmation that our life in the world and our inner life, the sensible and the insensible, are one. They are facets of the same thing:

All that must disappear
Is but a parable.

All the things of this world, along with Faust himself, must disappear, but at the same time they are absorbed into the word *all*—the all that is, always has been, and always will be but a parable. As such, *all* lives on in the "play" of Faust. Something disappears, and something appears (it "is"), but the change is so seamlessly rendered it feels like nothing has changed. Life has been changed, without being changed, into a parable about a wonderland. If we are reading these lines, it's not too late to be changed by the parable and to find ourselves in it. Is this what it means to be a living soul?

The same thing gets said in a different way in the next two lines:

What lay beyond us, here
All is made visible . . .
(All four lines come from *Faust, Part Two*, David Luke's translation, page 239.)

Notice how the past tense in *lay* is laid to rest in "is." What is it that (once, but no longer) "lay beyond us?" Was it something "out there" beyond the horizon of what we can sense? Was it a poor soul at the center of our sinful earth, that great intangible thing? Was it the inner life of another—another's infinity of thoughts, memories, and feelings, another undiscovered country?

It's all of these and more, I suppose, than we can imagine. Once again, Goethe's letter to Augusta von Stolberg helps me to interpret the passage. In it, Goethe described the state of his soul prior to taking up his new position in Weimar. It is, he says, "like a sock that is being turned inside out: the outer becoming inner; the inner outer." It's a change where what was hidden (his true self, for example) comes to light as it reveals itself in the visible world.

This is just a guess. In addition, we notice how the words catch us up with a kind of wonderment. We love the magic of it. Would it be fair to say Goethe saw the place (here) where "all is made visible" as the magic of a living soul that's fully realized inside and out?

Chapter 7

Substance as the Infinite Self-Subsistent Ground of All Being

Benozzo Gozzoli's
The Triumph of Saint Aquinas

Plate Armor and Aristotelianism: The Philosopher of Divisions

As a literary historian, Lewis has been preparing the reader for his readings of works by Guillaume de Lorris, Jean de Meun, Chaucer, Gower, Lydgate, Douglas, and Spenser. They represent "the great age of allegory." At the last station, he shows us how Claudian, Ennodius, and Capella discovered almost by accident a "third world of romantic imagining" while writing traditional allegories. But we're a long way—over eight hundred years—from a medieval allegory like *The Romance of the Rose*. As he finishes section 5 (what follows is the only thing I've included in my text from section 5) and approaches section 6, the last station before we get to those readings of Guillaume *et al.*, Lewis informs us that "the poets of courtly love [late eleventh-century troubadours] were not the pioneers of the medieval allegory." This form of literature, he will argue in section 6, came to writers like Gulliaume (1200–1240) "already revivified" by the philosophical poets of the twelfth-century School of Chartres.

With that, in section 6, Lewis once more puts on his philosophical hat to describe the ideas of this school. He covers a great deal of ground in a difficult opening paragraph, the subject of this and the following chapter, which I quote below and to which I'll add context once again with passages from *The Passion of the Western Mind* by Richard Tarnas. The paragraph is difficult because it touches on a large and difficult subject—the tension that existed in the Middle Ages between the ontologies of Plato and Aristotle. Lewis writes:

> *In dealing with the Middle Ages we are often tricked by our imagination. We think of plate armor and Aristotelianism. But the end of the Middle Ages is already in sight when these attractive things appear. And just as the lobster shell of steel gave to the warrior, along with the security, something of the inertia, of the crustacean, so it is possible, without disrespect to the great philosophical panoply in which Dante and Aquinas walked complete, to hint that those who wore it necessarily lost some of the grace*

and freedom of their forebears. The recovery of Aristotle's text dates from the second half of the twelfth century: the dominance of his doctrine soon followed.

Unfortunately, Lewis doesn't tell us exactly what makes us think of plate armor and Aristotelianism. He must be thinking of the knights in medieval romances, or he wouldn't have given us the plate armor. I would guess that Scholastics in the final centuries of the Middle Ages also made him think of Aristotelianism. I think it makes sense to say that, for Lewis, the Scholastics lost some of the grace and freedom of their forbears.

What makes plate armor and Aristotelianism "attractive?" With their focus on love, romances were a popular literary form, and the Scholastics were warriors who combatted ignorance with a profound faith in human reason. It's easy to see how plate armor would slow a warrior down. But what were the disadvantages of Aristotle's "plate armor?" Perhaps Aristotle's role as a founder of the physical sciences and the Scholastics's obsessive concern with logic and hairsplitting reminded Lewis of the straitjacket positive science had put on philosophy in his own time. He wrote his book, I have been arguing, to combat a loss of grace that continues into our own day. At any rate, we can only guess about his lobsters since he doesn't tell us. We don't have to guess, however, that Aquinas (1225–1274) and Dante (1265–1321) are the forbears who walked with complete grace and freedom within Aristotle's great philosophical panoply, which had been available to writers in the West for about a hundred years when Aquinas went to Naples in 1239 to study at the university there.

Lewis continues his critique of knights in Aristotelian plate armor and links them to Descartes, the philosopher who sought certainty in a material, mechanical world:

> *Aristotle is, before all, the philosopher of divisions. His effect on his greatest disciple [Aquinas] . . . was to dig new chasms between God and the world, between human knowledge and reality, between faith and reason. Heaven began, under this dispensation, to seem further off. The danger of Pantheism grew less: the danger of mechanical Deism came a step nearer.*

It is almost as if the first, faint shadow of Descartes, or even of "our present discontents" had fallen across the scene.

Like a doctor or a biologist, Aristotle reasoned about the observable things of this world. Perhaps this accounts for why Lewis asserts here that he helped Aquinas to dig new chasms between God (in his heaven) and the world.

If the world is identical with God, as Spinoza taught, then I would guess He loses his mystery as a person. It's my understanding that, even though Spinoza may have been a God-intoxicated man, his philosophy removed the idea that a person could have a personal relationship with God. The chasm between God and the world, which Lewis attributes to Aristotle, reduces the danger of Pantheism. It doesn't reduce, however, the danger from mechanical deism. According to Deists, God created the world, but since then he left it alone. The world works according to natural laws, and God gave man natural reason to know those laws. By "our present discontents," Lewis must be referring to the materialism of modern culture. His acknowledgment of the discontents (certainly his own discontents) supports what I argue above about combating a loss of "grace" in the modern era.

Perhaps Lewis calls Aristotle the philosopher of division because he was a master at distinguishing the different parts of a subject. For example, he famously divides his explanation of a material change in the world into four causes: the material, the formal, the efficient, and the final. I had difficulty with Lewis's characterization, however, because he has given such prominence to Dante's poetic doctrine of accidents in a substance, an Aristotelian concept. I wondered, therefore, how Aristotle could be the philosopher of division and the shadow of Cartesian dualism as well as the philosopher who supplies the concept of accidents in a substance that serves as a conceptual foundation for Lewis's narrative about the wholeness of allegory.

Aquinas and Aristotle

I cannot fully account for Lewis's characterization of Aristotle as the philosopher of division. I find I can add additional context around this question by understanding the achievement of Aquinas and by providing a more detailed picture of the relationship between the ideas of Plato and Aristotle in Aquinas's philosophy. The painting by Benozzo Gozzoli illustrates the theme of this chapter and the one that follows, for Gozzoli put Aquinas in between Plato on his left and Aristotle on his right. Completed in 1471, it celebrates the wholeness of Aquinas's thought as the middle way between the two. As a spiritual medium between these two great philosophers, the painting also shows us that he's the medium through which we have a glimpse of the sacred son-sun who created the world and gave it meaning. (This concept of a medium has an important role to play in my Books Three and Four.)

Around the beginning of the new millennium, living conditions in Europe began to improve. There was less war from migrations, there were innovations that made work easier, trade increased wealth, which gave rise to comfortable houses and towns, people organized in the towns to improve their civic life, and some had time and opportunity to learn about the art and literature of classical civilizations. As life became more pleasant, it might have been more difficult to agree with Augustine that man was a fallen creature living in a fallen world. Aquinas and his teacher Albertus were Dominicans. Dominic and Francis of Assisi awakened in their followers a new appreciation for the natural world and the world of man. Francis taught them to see the beauty of the world, and Dominic encouraged them to study and use their God given reason to understand God's creation. Aquinas was born only four years after the death of Dominic, so the movement was still alive with the spirit of its founder.

To supply a more detailed picture of the relationship between the ideas of Plato and Aristotle in the philosophy of Thomas Aquinas, I'm including here passages from the chapter on Aquinas in *The Passion of the Western Mind*. Tarnas writes that:

> *Aquinas's appreciation for human nature extended to the human body, an appreciation that affected his distinctive epistemological orientation. In contrast to Plato's antiphysical stance, reflected in much of the tenor of traditional Augustinian theology, Aquinas incorporated Aristotelian concepts to assert a new attitude. In man, spirit and nature were distinguishable, but they were also aspects of a homogeneous whole: the soul was the form of man, the body was the matter. Man's body was thus intrinsically necessary to his existence.*

The lesson couldn't have been clearer. Aristotle showed Aquinas how to resolve the dualism in Platonism between this world and transcendent forms.

Aquinas informed the substances of this world with the "eternal types" of Augustine and Plato. Because we are infused with an active intelligence with which to grasp the things of this world, the world is intelligible, as Tarnas explains:

> *In epistemological terms, it was to man's benefit that his soul was united with a body, for it was only man's physical observations that could activate his potential understanding of things. Aquinas repeatedly quoted from Paul's Letter to the Romans, "the invisible things of God are clearly seen . . . by the things that are made." The divine invisibles, among which Aquinas included the "eternal types" of Augustine and Plato, could be approached only through the empirical, the observation of the visible and particular. Therefore both sense experience and intellect were necessary for cognition, each informing the other. In contrast to Plato's implication, sense and intellect for Aquinas were not opponents in the quest for knowledge, but partners.*

Tarnas includes Paul's quote from Romans in this context, I believe, to recall for the reader a chapter in *The Passion of the Western Mind* devoted to "Exultant Christianity." The title refers to the faith of early Christians that Christ had redeemed through his sacrifice not only humanity but all of creation, all "the things that are made." This interpretation of His coming, however, faded as the Second Coming, the *Parousia*, failed to materialize, and Augustine's writings effectively ended that early understanding. The quote from

Romans suggests that Aquinas would renew a faith in exultant Christianity. *By the things that are made*, we can see the invisible things of God. According to Tarnas, Aquinas held that "both sense experience and intellect were necessary for cognition." Because I can survey the whole of my inquiry from my Olympian point of view, I discovered much later Kant's view of the same subject. Here's how Scruton puts it in *Kant: A Very Short Introduction*:

> *Neither experience nor reason is alone able to provide knowledge. The first provides content without form, the second form without content. Only in their synthesis is knowledge possible; hence there is no knowledge that does not bear the marks of reason and of experience. (See page 364 for this quote's place in my reading of "Believing in God.")*

The Substantiality and the Wonder of This World's Existence

Tarnas argues that Aquinas's model for reliable knowledge of the world also affirms the existence of the world. The *existence* of the world is the rock on which Aquinas constructed his philosophy:

> *Just as Aquinas's epistemology more deeply stressed the value and even necessity of this-world experience for human knowledge, so did his ontology assert the essential worth and substantiality of this world's existence. Sensible things did not exist merely as relatively unreal images, as shadowy replications of the Platonic Ideas; rather, they had a substantial reality of their own, as Aristotle had maintained. The forms were genuinely embedded in matter, united with matter to produce a composite whole.*

Tarnas here relates Aquinas's argument for the substantiality of things in the world and of the world itself, and he relates Aquinas's view that spirit and nature are "aspects of a homogeneous whole." That said, Tarnas acknowledges the chasm in Aristotle's model "between God and the world," which may be the main reason Lewis describes him as the philosopher of division. Tarnas goes on to explain, however, how Aquinas resolved this division, for:

> *Aquinas went beyond the Aristotelians' tendency to view nature as existing apart from God, arguing that a deeper philosophical understanding of the meaning of existence would fully connect the created world with God. To accomplish this, Aquinas reintroduced the Platonic notion of "participation" [for example, something is beautiful because it participates in the form of beauty] in this new context: Created things have true substantial reality because they participate in Existence, which is from God, the infinite self-subsistent ground of all being. For God's essence was precisely his existence, his infinite act of being which underlay the finite existence of all created things, each with its own particular essence. (I have quoted the four passages in this chapter from pages 182–183 of* The Passion of the Western Mind.*)*

I have to conclude that Aristotle's view of nature "as existing apart from God" was a problem for both Aquinas and for Lewis. Once again, I return to the argument that Lewis wrote *The Allegory of Love* to confront the central problem human beings face in the modern world: we suffer from alienation. We think we are solitary individuals who exist apart: from other people, who might kill us for any number of reasons; from nature, which might kill us in a flood or a tornado; from our bodies, which might grow a cancer and kill us; from our minds, which may despair and urge suicide; from other circumstances, which may involve us in a fatal accident; and certainly we exist apart from God if God doesn't exist. I write this after a weekend of mass shootings, rampages perpetrated by alienated young men. People sense that the body politic is sick with little cells that have gone crazy, that the craziness can easily spread, that it may kill the body that gave it life.

Lewis wrote about allegory and about love to revive a kind of poetry that can still "spread its wings fully" to acquaint us with "a marvelous that knows itself as myth." In my opinion, he is also describing a mind—like Aristotle's or Aquinas's mind—that holds all the accidents of life and makes them not only intelligible but wonderful. It's a marvelous, living substance. The "old marvelous" (like the son of God dying on the cross to save mankind and creation from the fall), he has suggested, once was taken as fact, but something killed it as a living presence in the minds of men. Nevertheless, it has been stored up, "not wholly dead, but in a winter sleep, waiting its time." As Dante did in his time, Lewis invites us to become a living soul, to "find" ourselves alive in allegory's arena, the infinite self-subsistent ground of all being.

I must confess: I write about these matters with great interest. They are attractive things, even if studying them is weighty and difficult.

Chapter 8

The Example of Socrates

Jacques-Louis David's
The Death of Socrates

Leaving Aristotle and the shadow of Descartes, which fell across the scene in the previous chapter, Lewis's long paragraph now introduces his readers to the School of Chartres and the influence of that other famous Greek philosopher. Previously, Lewis described "knights" whose plate armor stole their grace:

> *Certainly, something fresh and adventurous, which belonged to the earlier movement, had disappeared. Of that earlier movement the school of Chartres, in the first half of the twelfth century, may perhaps be regarded as the culminating point. The school of Chartres is Platonic, as Platonism was understood in those days, when Chalcidius's translation of the Timaeus, and the pseudo-Dionysius, were the important texts. It was humane, in both senses of the word. It was a school of naturalism, and this again in the double sense of studying and reverencing nature. Thus Thierry of Chartres—like some of his Platonic descendants at the Renaissance—will reconcile Genesis and the Timaeus; while in the poets of the school Nature appears, not to be corrected by Grace, but as the goddess and the vicaria of God, herself correcting the unnatural. It goes without saying that in such a school, on the theological side, immanence is more stressed than transcendence; and I have read that by two of its philosophers—Therry and William of Conches—the Holy Ghost is identified with the Anima Mundi of the Platonists.*

This long paragraph (now concluded and which begins in my text on page 178) continues to invite interpretation on a number of points. First, Lewis does not say to what he's referring as "that earlier movement." The freshness and adventurousness of it and the proximity in Lewis's text of the movement described in the last section make me think that it must be represented by those poets who discovered fairyland—Claudian, Sidonius, Ennodius, and Capella. Second, he invites us to consider the reconciliation of creation in Genesis and Timaeus without going into it himself, so here's a short reading of it that relates to the humanism of the school. Creation has to be linked to a creator: the Bible tells us how God created the world, and in *Timaeus*, Plato has a divine craftsman do the work. By imagining the creator as a craftsman, Plato employs a metaphor that draws on the human world. The divine world and the human world come together in the image of a creator or craftsman. Third, Lewis describes the school as humane in two senses. From the first sense, we understand that it focuses on the world as experienced by a human being. For example, we will learn that Bernard tells the story of creation from the point of view of man, the creature. Lewis develops the significance of this later in the section. From the second sense, we understand that the school taught human beings to have a compassionate relationship with creation. We must treat creation the way we would like to be treated, for we are creation (the center of our sinful earth, Shakespeare tells us). Fourth, Lewis has included the School of Chartres in a book about allegory since the school enlarged the importance of Nature as an allegorical figure, and this has significance, not only for literature but for philosophy and a new orientation toward the natural world borne out by Dominic and Francis.

Fifth, even though Plato is strongly identified with transcendence, "on the theological side," Platonism, as it was understood in the School of Chartres, stressed immanence more than transcendence. Since it's a Christian school, this may refer to the Christian belief that Christ, the transcendent God, was incarnated to save us from the fall. Like the merging of form and matter in Aristotle's thought, He came and infused this world with a living soul. In the dialogue *Timaeus,* Plato has Timaeus describe the immanence of anima mundi, the world soul of the Platonists:

> *And so the likely account must say that this world came to be in very truth through god's forethought, a living being with soul and intelligence. (Timaeus, 30b–c)*

Anima Mundi infuses "this world" with a living soul. For Plato this was a philosophical truth. It's a representation that points to a world that is one. Just as the individual objects and experiences belonging to the life of a human subject, like Dante, are accidents of one substance, individuals like Dante and ourselves all are accidents belonging to a "living being" endowed with an intelligent soul, which is referred to as anima mundi, the soul of the world.

Having presented Lewis's paragraph in full, I would like to draw a more general conclusion after first reviewing two salient facts about it. Lewis identifies Aristotle as the philosopher of division, despite Aristotle's ontology, which integrates form and matter, and Lewis tells us that Platonism in the School of Chartres stressed immanence more than transcendence, despite Plato's theory of the forms as transcendent. These facts suggest to me the following observation: Aristotle and Plato do not stake out positions carved in stone, even though it may appear that they do. They, and those who come after them, are engaged in a passionate, ongoing, all-consuming inquiry, and they go where the inquiry leads them.

I feel safe in concluding that their positions are not carved in stone for another important reason. Plato and Aristotle have deep roots in the principal figure who impressed them with the stamp of his world-historical example, and Socrates wrote nothing down. Instead, his mind, the living speech that issued forth from his mind, arrested the citizens of Athens and held them in a way they had never been held before. I turn once more to Richard Tarnas for his portrait of Socrates:

> *It is evident from these [reports of Socrates in works by Plato, Xenophon, Aristophanes, Aristotle, and others] that Socrates was a man of singular character and intelligence, who was imbued with a passion for intellectual honesty and moral integrity rare of his or any other age. He insistently sought answers to questions that had not before been asked, attempted to undermine conventional assumptions and beliefs to provoke more careful thinking about ethical matters, and tirelessly compelled both himself and those with whom he conversed to seek a deeper understanding of what constituted a good life. His words and deeds embodied an abiding conviction that the act of rational self-criticism could free the human mind from the bondage of false opinion. Because of his dedication to the task of discovering wisdom and drawing it forth from others, Socrates neglected his private affairs, spending all his time instead in earnest discussion with his fellow citizens. Unlike the Sophists, he did not charge for his instruction. Although intimate with the elite of Athens, he was altogether indifferent to material wealth and conventional standards of success. Socrates gave the impression of being a man unusually at one with himself, though his*

personal character was full of paradoxical contrasts. Disarmingly humble yet presumptuously confident, puckishly witty yet morally urgent, engaging and gregarious yet solitary and contemplative, Socrates was above all a man consumed by a passion for truth.

This portrait of Socrates and Eros, the passion for truth that Tarnas finds in Socrates, makes Socrates the founder of a monumental train of thought, the one that Tarnas describes in his book as *The Passion of the Western Mind*. Shakespeare's portrait of Oberon expresses the same spirit. Oberon is a lover. After making love to the dawn, he rises to walk resolutely toward the sun as it "turns into yellow gold" the salt green streams of earth and ocean. If we follow the example of Socrates, Oberon, and the sun, we need the temperament of a lover for this work. These portraits help to explain why the thing we seek, the truth, is so hard to describe. It's not a thing; it's a passion. And it's not a passion for a thing, for we cannot say what truth is exactly, any more than we can say what mind is. Just as we use mirrors to look at ourselves, we throw out ideas to see if they reflect a true image of ourselves. But do we end up merely in a hall of mirrors and endless illusion?

In the next passage, Tarnas gathers up these issues and puts them in the place that Lewis compares to the arena we refer to with that difficult word, the soul:

In Socrates's view, any attempt to foster true success and excellence in human life had to take account of the innermost reality of a human being, his soul or psyche. Perhaps on the basis of his own highly developed sense of individual selfhood and self-control, Socrates brought to the Greek mind a new awareness of the central significance of the soul, establishing it for the first time as the seat of the individual waking consciousness and of the moral and intellectual character. He affirmed the Delphic motto "Know thyself," for he believed that it was only through self-knowledge, through an understanding of one's own psyche and its proper condition, that one could find genuine happiness. All human beings seek happiness by their very nature, and happiness, Socrates taught, is achieved through living the kind of life that best serves the nature of the soul. [In my introduction, Scruton described this teaching as "the care of the soul" (see pages 23–24).]

Happiness is the consequence not of physical or external circumstances, of wealth or power or reputation, but of living a life that is good for the soul.

In other words, moral truth completely saturates and animates what we seek and our passion for seeking it. Moral truth is the ballast that keeps our ship of state steady in tempestuous seas. Nature (the things that are made), as an instrument of moral truth and as the School of Chartres teaches, "corrects" (see "corrected" and "correcting" in the quote on page 188) unnatural impressions whether we like it or not. This touches on an important theme in Lewis's text, as when he brings up "the passion that purifies" in eighteenth- and nineteenth-century Romantic thought. Lewis would clarify for a modern audience—as Chaucer, Shakespeare, and others have done over two millennia—the difference between a passion for a thing, like the nakedness of the human form, and a passion for the moral truth that we all exist in the gift of existence itself. It's a gift, the sacred gift of life, which we also call the soul, and we have the care of it. As a sacred gift, it's a sacrilege to abuse it. In our relationships, we have the care of the one we desire as well, for he or she is a soul just as we are. The person we desire is not separate from ourselves, and we must nurture and guard that person as we would nurture and guard ourselves. The golden rule is not just a rule; it describes the nature of the soul.

A final passage from Tarnas helps me to make the case that the ballast we seek is immanent in the world and in us, not transcendent. Just as Christians find the immanence of moral truth in Christ's incarnation and pilgrimage on earth, for centuries before and for centuries after the birth and death of Christ, many found that ballast in the more secular figure of Socrates. Tarnas gives us a sense of why that is so:

The friends and disciples who gathered around Socrates in his last days were drawn to a man who, to a singular degree, had embodied his own ideal. With its unique synthesis of eros and logos—of passion and mind, friendship and argument, desire and truth—Socrates's philosophy appears to have been a direct expression of his personality. Each Socratic idea and its articulation bore the mark of, and seemed to have been born of, the

> *very core of his personal character. Indeed, as he was portrayed in the full course of Plato's dialogues, it was this very fact—that Socrates spoke and thought with an intellectual and moral confidence based on profound self-knowledge, rooted as it were in the depths of his psyche—that gave him the capacity to express a truth that was in some sense universal, grounded in divine truth itself. (I have quoted the last three passages from pages 31–36 of* The Passion of the Western Mind.*)*

If Tarnas's assessment is correct, and if we agree with what it says about Socrates, then we are encouraged by them to believe that Everyman carries this ballast of moral truth, which is grounded in divine truth, as a birthright by virtue of being born into this world. By virtue of being born, we are grounded in divine truth. We are encouraged to believe that the psychomachia of allegory, the battle of good and evil in our souls, arises for a good and true reason. The battle arises in the soul because we are free to acknowledge or deny that our life in the world is governed by a moral truth, and we are free then to recognize or ignore the signs that we have run afoul of its laws. Socrates drew people to him because he recognized that freedom and didn't flinch, didn't give in to complacency or conformity even if it meant the end of his life. He loved his freedom as he loved the moral law that assumed his freedom. Right to the end, he was free to choose on moral grounds how he would live.

Because the inner life inevitably involves the issue of subjectivity, I find it necessary to refute a possible objection to the way I have described the vision of Socrates. Someone might object that a terrorist may also be entirely convinced that he carries within a birthright of moral truth and that this moral truth tells him to kill as many unbelievers as he can. To refute the argument, I look to the example of Socrates—as Plato and Tarnas do. Socrates is no terrorist. He doesn't kill people on behalf of his moral truth. The terrorists, the people who insist on conformity, do the killing. Socrates stands alone for what we seek. His students, his friends if you will, are free to agree or disagree with him. Over and over, Plato makes this clear; after their conversations and symposiums, Socrates lets his friends alone and goes his own way.

Before leaving Socrates, I return to the passage in which Lewis makes a critical distinction between allegory and symbolism in his commentary on Dante:

> *The great allegorist's firm thinking leaves no room for misunderstanding. There is nothing "mystical" or mysterious about medieval allegory; the poets know quite clearly what they are about and are well aware that the figures which they present to us are fictions. Symbolism is a mode of thought, allegory is a mode of expression. It belongs to the form of poetry, more than to its content, and it is learned from the practice of the ancients.*

I found the last two sentences to be somewhat cryptic, so I wrote the following interpretation: "A symbol entails a thought about reality—for example, Plato's symbol of the cave, which conveys the thought that the true form of Beauty exists objectively apart from the beauty of appearances; an allegory entails the reality of Dante himself expressing himself in poetry. Allegory 'belongs' to forms of expressive poetry, not to a philosophy or a science, which 'belongs' to an objective reality (a content). In Dante's poetic world, an 'accident' like Love exists in the substance of his poetry. It has no existence apart from the poem" (originally appeared on page 91.)

Even though Plato's works have objective reality as their subject, in a work like the *Symposium*, he doesn't put his thoughts down in the form of a lecture or an essay. He explicitly writes a kind of fiction with characters who get together in a very specific spot at a very specific time and who then engage in a conversation. Some of his most famous works (like the *Republic*, the subject of my postscript) take the form of expressive poetry (even though Plato argues against poetry), and within that form he has given us Socrates, one of the most famous characters in Western literature. He's as famous as Achilles or Odysseus. The poets of that "earlier movement" (my chapter 5, pages 135–149) and those in the School of Chartres follow Plato, "as Plato was understood in those days," in that their allegories belong to "a mode of expression." Their expression of an inner life, which has been Lewis's subject and the subject of these essays, anticipates the poems of Petrarch and the great flourishing of poetry that spills in a flood out of Italy, streams across the channel, and fills the courts and theaters of London with models for the greatest poets in English literature: Chaucer and Shakespeare.

Chapter 9

Nature and Mind in the School of Chartres

National Roman Museum's statue of *Demeter*

Nature and Mind Make a World Soul in *De Mundi Universitate*

Part 1: Creation Told from the Point of View of the Created

With that introduction to the School of Chartres, Lewis looks at its founding text. Composed in the years 1147 and 1148, *De Mundi Universitate sive Megacosmus et Microcosmus* by Bernardus Sylvestris has as its subject the creation of the world (the macrocosm) and man (the microcosm). Lewis's reading of it has important ontological implications:

> *It is the story of creation told from the point of view of the created: the female longing of matter to receive the form, not the creative impulse of the Deity, is the moving passion of the work, which thus becomes a curious pendant to the Miltonic handling of the same theme.*

In the Bible's version of creation, God is the actor: "And God said, 'Let there be light: and there was light.'" His story is told objectively, from the third-person point of view. In Bernard's version, the allegorical figure of Nature is the actor. She initiates creation in the first two lines of the work by complaining in her own voice to the allegorical figure of Mind on behalf of her daughter Matter.

Before quoting Nature's words, which initiate Creation, however, Lewis provides a critique and a defense of Bernard's point of view:

> *In adopting such a standpoint it is clear that the author incurs certain dangers. Of necessity he comes perilously near to representing non-existents as petitioners for their own existence. Yet, as a philosopher, he may reply that he is dealing with processes that are not in time at all, and that such a presentation is therefore not more inadequate than another: from the purely literary point of view we may plead in his defense that we, after all, belong to the created ourselves and that the response of the*

work to the workman [the response, for example, of a son to a father] is precisely that aspect of creation which comes, by remote analogy, within our experience and is therefore a proper object for the imagination.

Speaking for Bernard ("he may reply"), Lewis justifies the forwardness of nonexistents petitioning for their own existence by shifting from an ontological question about substance (the reality of nonexistents) to an ontological argument about time, which vitiates any need for a human being to be concerned whether the egg or the chicken came first. Whatever we have been, Lewis writes in the first paragraph of the book, in some sort we are still. If this is true, why wouldn't it also be the case that, at any moment, we are in some sort uncreated, mute, unshaped matter as well as what we would be—a living soul. We are what we are; we are one throughout the "process." A wave has a distinctive shape that continually moves and changes, but it is one substance throughout. According to Lewis, this view of our substance gives us license to tell our story the way we do. (In the last chapter of the book, I discuss Roger Scruton's concept of a myth of origin, in which he makes a similar argument. See pages 495–512.)

Since we are made in God's image, we identify with our Creator. We, the work, exist as a physical body in the world, and we need a body, Aquinas's argument goes, for knowledge of anything. Lewis's argument—telling creation from the creature's point of view—suggests we come to know God as Creator through "a remote analogy." Like the Creator, we create that which intelligently supports our existence: our homes, our children, our clothes, the food we eat, and the records we keep of what works to support our life and what tends to lead us into temptation and death. Just as a workman combines the materials of a physical world, like wood and stone, with an intellectual blueprint for how all the materials will fit together to make the needful house, as workmen we have some sense that we ourselves are not just a random collection of parts. A form of some kind informs us, and so the argument takes one more step toward our creator as it follows this analogy.

Lewis continues to explain the analogy in this passage that picks up from where the last quote left off:

> *Nor would such an analogy be foreign to the mind of the author [the Christian philosopher Bernard]; for the very words in which he describes the longing of matter to be "born again" by the reception of form, must have suggested, then as now, an individual, and specifically Christian experience:*
>
> *Lo! Matter, eldest of all things, would fain*
> *Be limited by shape and born again.*
>
> *I have quoted these words from the speech of Nature with which the book opens. The goddess is addressing Noys [Mind] . . . and pleading the cause of matter; the remainder of the book relates in detail the answering of her prayer.*

I've already argued in Book One (see pages 16–17) that, like Nature's prayer, which begins Bernard's poem, Lewis's book on allegory and love is a kind of prayer. He prays "that the world he imagines, with help from classical and medieval poets, makes the world he imagines more possible." This passage of play in Lewis's history is just the thing "to develop our confidence in poetic visions" (see the end of the paragraph on page 79). It helps to persuade us that there's great survival value in being a well-wrought thing in itself. As a lively and reasonable whole (a limited shape), we're less likely to be "unmade" (see "unmake" in the one quote of part 2). Bernard humanizes creation by making it an allegory. One human figure, an allegorical mother, expresses to another, an allegorical Mind, the longing of her eldest. We experience the situation from her point of view. The scene resonates with any parent whose child is ill or impaired in some way. Mind is the one who will save the child. To illustrate the theme of this chapter, I have selected a Roman statue of Demeter—the Great Mother who longed for her daughter in the winter months. She expresses the female longing of Nature and Matter in these lines. No narrative effect distracts us from her very physical presence; she's the whole story as she reaches out to the invisible Mind of the viewer.

As to whether the chicken came first or the egg, perhaps Homer's *Odyssey* set a classical precedent that permitted Bernard to begin his story of creation in medias res, for Homer begins his narrative in the tenth year of Odysseus's ten-year quest for home. When Odysseus finally lands on the island of the Phaeacians, Homer also has Odysseus tell the story of his adventures to his hosts *from his own point of view*. In a significant shift, he becomes his own bard. Virgil followed Homer's example and began the *Aeneid* in medias res long after the fall of Troy, and he has Aeneas tell the story of his adventures up to that point *from his own point of view* to Dido and her court. Bernard opens his narrative with the ontological issue Lewis has been developing from the beginning of his history. He tells the story from the creature's point of view, just as Dante tells the story of *La Vita Nuova* and the *Commedia* from his point of view. By sharing Dante's point of view, the reader absorbs his "sense" that the soul of a human subject is the substance in which the accidents of our life, including our reading of these works, transpire.

Part 2: The Macrocosm Is a Lively and Reasonable Animal with a Soul

In Bernard's version of Creation, Mind acts to transform matter in stages. She informs it with appearances, which are copies of the eternal ideas, separates the elements, and:

> *. . . proceeds to generate soul: for the Macrocosm, here as in Plato, is a lively and reasonable animal, whose indwelling spirit comforts and protects it against the elemental catastrophes which would otherwise speedily unmake it again.*

I have already shown that this is how Plato describes anima mundi in *Timaeus* (see pages 189–190). In the Bible, God acts to create the world. In *De Mundi Universitate,* Nature and Mind act to create the world. Thanks to Mind, the world becomes a soul, a soul that's "a reasonable animal." Because the second part of *De Mundi* has to do with the creation of man as a reasonable animal, we are encouraged to conclude that there's a strong link between the two, the intelligent World Soul and the intelligent soul of Man. This must be what Lewis means when he tells us that the School of Chartres is "humane" (see pages 188–189).

To sum up this section on the creation of the macrocosm, the writers of the school look at creation from the point of view of a human being. In telling the story of creation in this way, we are not representing nonexistents as petitioners for their own existence. As Christians, Bernard might say, we can tell the story of creation from our own point of view because creation is a proper object for the imaginations of human beings, especially since God's only begotten son was born in Bethlehem as a human being. He came into the world to save both mankind and the world from the fall; He came into the world to plant the seed of a redeemed soul in us and in the world itself. He is the seed of holiness. In Him, the world is reborn with a humane shape. Yes, we are limited in our "shape" and understanding. But this is a good thing. After all, as Nature informs Mind, this limiting into an individual shape is what (at a primal level) we long for. Nature's passion is what moves Mind to give us a form and rebirth as a living soul.

Bernard and Haydn Rejoice in Creation

Once mind and matter have become anima mundi, the soul of the world, Lewis writes, Bernard "shakes off his metaphysics, and rejoices for some five hundred elegiac verses in the visible and tangible":

> *A land of streams and flowers, by man possessed*
> *So short a time it scarce could call him Guest.*

The poet rejoices in creation, but he is circumspect about our relationship with it. As individuals we live for so short a time that, even though we possess this land of streams and flowers by virtue of being born into it, we are hardly even a guest here, much less an owner. We longed to be a limited shape, which entails being limited in time as well as space. This theme of an end or a limit to life is the point of *Everyman*, for his story begins when Death finds him with a message from God.

Rather than a pride of ownership, Lewis tells us that the poet strikes "a note of fresh and delighted applause" at the wonder of creation and its creatures, each one "a new tour de force of Deity" as in these lines about the lynx:

Forth comes the lynx to test the streams of light
That flow in him, his miracle of sight.

I, too, take delight in these lines, but my delight derives from my whole enterprise, the inquiry with which I'm engaged. When I first was reading Lewis's book, my wife and I attended a concert featuring Haydn's *Creation*. Haydn gives the baritone Raphael a recitative that presents the creatures of this world in the same spirit as that of Bernard:

Cheerful, roaring, stands the tawny lion . . .

Haydn matches the thought in a dignified musical line that settles on the word *stands* and then resolves itself on C in the key of C.

With sudden leap the flexible tiger appears . . .

This musical line jumps up and down in sudden starts.

The nimble stag bears up his branching head . . .

Here the music rises before settling gently back down on the word *head*.

In long dimension creeps, with sinuous trace, the worm.

To express the sluggishness and lowliness of this creature, the line slows down to a crawl, and its "sinuous trace" falls very low in the baritone's register.

I find the similarity of Bernard's text with that of Haydn to be delightful. Of all classical composers Haydn is a perfect match with the theme and the spirit of *De Mundi*. His music reflects a witty, inventive, good humored, worldly man, and one capable of great seriousness, as the orchestral opening of *Creation* bears witness. I hear in those fifty-eight bars the wonder of something that begins as a kind of nothing, like gross matter, but which grows into the intelligible form we now recognize as music. It's the musical equivalent of Chaucer's root engendering a flower in the opening lines of *The Canterbury Tales*.

In a related thought, the similarity in Barnard's and Haydn's texts reminds me of a moment in his *Creation* that expresses very directly the experience of becoming a living soul. This part of *Creation* is more a wonderment laced with terror than delightful, for it concerns the fall when, after the transgression of Adam and Eve, God pulls the rug out from underneath their perfect life in the Garden.

Prior to that moment, the two praise God in a heartfelt duet, for He, they tell us:

> *fillest all with good:*
> *On thee, On thee each living soul awaits;*
> *From thee, O Lord, all seek their food;*
> *Thou openest thy hand,*
> *And fillest all all with good*

But then everything changes, and the point of view shifts to the angel Raphael, who observes:

> *But when thy face, O Lord, is hid,*
> *With sudden terror they are struck;*
> *Thou takst their breath away,*
> *They vanish into dust,*
> *Thou takst their breath away,*
> *They vanish into dust.*

In the performance we heard, the conductor brought the tempo down in the last two lines to a point where the music stopped for a moment after the final "dust." The orchestra ceased to breathe.

But since this is a comedy, it suddenly breathes again with new life as three angels sing:

Thou sendest forth thy breath again,
And life with vigor fresh returns;
Revived earth unfolds
New strengths and new delights . . .

In Haydn's musical vision, Adam and Eve die briefly to know the magnitude of what they stand to lose. I think of Falstaff behind the arras struggling to breathe in his sleep. I think, too, of someone very dear to me who lived for a year with Lou Gehrig's disease. Since the disease collapses the body's ability to breathe, month after month she walked in the valley of the shadow of those minideaths.

As the verse in Genesis teaches, we begin with the breath to learn what it means to be a living soul.

Three Powers Unite to Make Man in *De Mundi Universitate*

Mind begins the second book of *De Mundi* with a speech about creating "the little world of man." To accomplish the task, Natura must visit the heaven-spirit Urania, for she will ensure that man participates in the divine order. At Natura's approach, Urania rises and "prophesies the high destiny of Man":

With me through all the expanse of heaven must go
Man's soul, and I will make her know
The laws of Fate allowing no repeal
And Fortune's alterable wheel . . .
Her godlike essence when her body dies
Will seek again those kindred skies.

In the beginning, therefore, the soul of man learns of her high destiny as a heavenly substance and learns, at the same time, about laws of Fate, which cannot be changed. As Urania's subject on this pilgrimage through the expanse of heaven, the soul absorbs a strength that derives from obedience to divine law.

So far so good. To finish the task, though, Nature and Urania must descend to earth to meet with Physis to ensure that man participates in the material order. Lewis devotes some space in the text to explain why Natura in the first book is now divided in two in the second book. "Natura, in fact, is a personification of the general order of things." She is akin to Fate, for people in Bernard's time thought that "the course of history is written in the stars." Physis, on the other hand, "is almost 'organic nature,' the object of biology: she is the reservoir of vital possibilities on which the general ordering of Nature draws: she lives on earth, and in visiting her fruitful garden Natura really descends to 'the Mothers.'" There's more than one because Physis has two daughters called Theory and Practice.

The two daughters represent, Lewis writes, "the theoretical and therapeutic sides of the Physicus's profession," and with that he continues with the narrative. Natura and Urania:

> *. . . find Physis in her garden meditating upon the origins and powers of the several "natures," and also on the remedies for diseases. Such, then, is one of the new powers [the power of healing, of making the body whole] invoked for the making of man. In order to fabricate the organism inhabitable by human mind, the ordering spirit of Nature must invoke those yet unexhausted possibilities of the vital force, which are symbolized as Physis, the earth dweller.*

Earth is not heaven, but it has a power of its own, the "yet unexhausted possibilities of the vital force." Every spring we get to witness this amazing power, which gladdens the heart of Demeter. Nature, heaven, and earth are finally in place to create man:

> *But the supreme Mind, though it delegates, is not absent, and works itself in its lower agents: "such privilege hath omnipresence." Suddenly,*

therefore, Noys is visible among them in the garden, and her voice is heard propounding the nature of Man, in lines which give lofty expression to the humanism of Chartres, and which, if they were written in English blank verse, would be universally hailed as typical of the Renaissance.

> *He shall be heavenly, earthly; by his care*
> *Shall rule the earth, and reach the heaven by prayer,*
> *For as the diverse sources whence he drew*
> *His being, so himself will still be two . . .*

Man is both heavenly and earthly. He comes to life in the union of insensible and sensible worlds. Man is like the meaning of a metaphor—he's the link, the medium between the two worlds.

As such, man will have power denied other creatures:

> *He shall drag forth to light the causes hid*
> *In secret gloom, though Nature long forbid . . .*
> *To him, unbounded, in all lands, I give*
> *High crown and priesthood over all that live.*

From being both earthly and heavenly, man occupies a unique station in creation. With that, "the three powers fall to the work." And with that, I close this section on Bernard.

To complete his survey of writers in the School of Chartres, Lewis will summarize and comment on three more works, two by Alanus ab Insulis and one by Johannes de Altavilla. Before presenting that material, I'll draw the reader's attention to the high crown and priesthood Mind gives to man "over all that live" and to the power the poet gives to Mind that does the crowning. Lewis, I'm sure, was delighted to find it and was delighted to draw our attention to it. A crown, we all know, represents material power in this world. No wonder so many are greedy for it. In my inquiry, I have made the case that the crown, as here in *De Mundi*, also represents the presence in our life of a living soul. I maintain as well that Lewis wrote his book because he thought that those who sought the crown of material power in his own day actively sought to usurp the crown of spiritual power. This power struggle has existed for thousands of years, and the struggle continues into our own time. "Render unto Caesar the things that are Caesar's, and unto God the things that are God's," Jesus advises in Matthew 22. To render the advice more palatable in our secular age, we can change it to read "Render unto physics the things that have to do with physics, and unto metaphysics the things that have to do with metaphysics." As a philosopher dealing with competing ontologies, Lewis is giving us this good advice.

Nature and Her Sisters Make the Perfect Man

Lewis holds that *Anticlaudianus* by Alanus ab Insulis (1128–1202) has no literary merit. Nevertheless, he thinks it may be even more important than *De Mundi*, for "it conferred new prestige on the allegorical method" and celebrated a "third way between the courtly and the religious conceptions of the good life." Of course, Lewis must explain what Claudian has to do with this work by Alanus. Claudian wrote *In Rufinum* to praise the good government of his patron Theodosius. The emperor deserves the praise, the allegory explains, because he defeated the powers of evil. The fury Allecto begins the poem with the complaint that Theodosius has diminished her empire. She calls a counsel, and the powers of evil make Rufinus their champion. This is all that Lewis summarizes of Claudian's story.

Instead of creating an evil man, Alanus has Nature create a perfect man as a champion against Allecto. He is the anti-Claudian. Lewis goes on to summarize Alanus's narrative:

> *Natura, the story says, once resolved to sum up in a single crowning work all the goodness that lay scattered among her creatures. But her old anvil was worn away and the task beyond her powers. Therefore she called her sisters to council, in her secret place . . . To these Natura opened her heart. In all her works she saw nothing that was wholly blessed. The old stain*

could not be removed; but still it might be possible to make one work which could redeem the whole, and be the mirror of themselves.

Nature's allegorical sisters—Concord, Youth, Laughter, Reason, Honesty, Prudence, Good Faith, Virtue, and Nobility—work together to make this new creation. Word of him goes down to hell, and Allecto gathers an army of infernal peers to oppose him. The story "concludes with the psychomachy, and the victory of the perfect man ushers in the golden age."

The poem, Lewis tells us, also documents "the humanism of Chartres." Alanus depicts "not so much a perfect man by the standards of the Church" but rather "a noble and virtuous gentleman according to the standards of chivalry." In Lewis's opinion, Alanus is to be numbered "less among the followers of Prudentius [writers describing a holy war of good against evil] than among the predecessors of Castiglione, of Elyot, and of Spenser," writers who celebrate the courtly virtues of Largesse, Nobility, Fidelity, and Moderation (as opposed to abstinence). Lewis argues that if Castiglione can be both a Platonic philosopher and a dancing master, then Alanus can describe the perfect gentleman in the highest ethical terms and give lessons how a gentleman should dress his hair.

Having identified Alanus as one who shares the values of courtesy described in the chapter on courtly love, Lewis tackles the major question that chapter raises: How can the tension between the church's view of physical love and the court's view of it be resolved?

But while Alanus thus stands side by side with Castiglione, and indeed fills up the concept of virtue with purely secular and courtly excellences, it is of the essence of his work that he does so with not the slightest sense of rebellion or defiance. The courtesy of the Troubadours, of Andreas, of Chretien, was a truancy. Behind the courtly scale of values rose the unappeasable claims of a totally different and irreconcilable world: it was to this truancy and insecurity that the courtly life owed half its willful beauty and pathos.

Lewis has not forgotten that love is his subject, and in my reading of his book he is concerned with how physical love can be rescued from the judgment by church fathers that it is wicked, even in marriage. Page after page of the chapter on allegory has been devoted to the theme of wholeness, and now this longing for wholeness is being directed at a basic human function, the desire to mate. How can man be whole if a vital part of him has been so censured? The troubadours, Andreas and Chretien, left the issue unresolved; they merely ran away from it.

Alanus, Lewis tells us, offers a different perspective in a passage I quoted earlier (see pages 120–121):

> *But Alanus is equally serious in his theological passages and in his notes on deportment. He acknowledges no breach; for the naturalism of Chartres has given him a tertium quid [a third way] that can moderate both the rigors of theology and the wantonness of the court. Goodness does not mean asceticism; knighthood does not mean adultery. Both are brought together under the law of Natura who is the vicar of God and essentially good. It is not a question of grace redeeming Nature: it is a question of sin departing from Nature. The position is summed up in the advice given by Honest to the perfect man:*
>
> *Let him love Nature who would flee from vice*
> *Eschew what guilt or naughty will brought forth*
> *And to his breast clasp all that Nature made.*
>
> *It is in this that the true value of Alanus consists. I do not say he has effected a real reconciliation between the two ideals of the Middle Ages. The rift went deeper than he thought. He assumes, rather than makes, a peace. But at least he is trying to be a whole man, and however the elements of his synthesis may hereafter fall apart, they will retain some mark of their brief union. The courtly ideal is becoming, as Arnold would have said, "more possible," and for that reason more potent: if you will, more insidious. Its long hold upon the vernacular poetry, its adaptability to some future compromise, are now assured.*

If it's not a question of grace redeeming Nature but of sin departing from Nature, it would appear that Alanus has moved away from Augustine's view that nature had been irremediably tainted by original sin. In courtly love, physical love is sanctified ("Here is my heaven!"). For whom would the courtly ideal be insidious? It must be for those who are still convinced that physical love is wicked. When did his synthesis fall apart? As an adolescent in the 1950s, eight hundred years after Alanus assumed a peace between the church and Natura, I can witness for younger readers that the issue of sex still had a dark and potent cloud of guilt and sin around it when adults gave their children "the talk" about it. Intellectuals who read and wrote Latin may have longed for the church fathers' view, but the people who spoke the vernacular, Lewis implies, learned from vernacular poetry to regard physical love as a natural part of life. This was also my experience, for older boys gave me a completely different view of it in a language I could understand.

A Lover of Nature and Lovers of the Hunt

Alanus' *De Planctu Naturae* (*The Complaint of Kind*) and its significance, Lewis writes, can be quickly summarized:

> *Nature appears to the author and laments the unnatural vices of humanity; the Virtues come to share their grievance with hers; and Genius is ordered to pronounce an anathema against the offenders. That is the whole matter. The importance of the theme, for our purpose, clearly lies in the advantage to which Nature appears in such a setting; and with Nature, natural love.*

Lewis goes on to criticize Alanus, as he has criticized Martianus Capella, as a "disinterested" stylist, but he judges that "hidden in the rhetorician, there was, after all, a real, though wayward, lover of nature." There's a wantonness and a "wilderness of sweets" in a passage Lewis himself translates, which "may be compared with one of those old tapestries where richness of the material suggests indoor luxury, but the forms, nearer viewed, reveal, however faintly, the stir and morning airs of a hunting scene."

Act 4 of *A Midsummer Night's Dream* opens with a hunting scene like that tapestry in which indoor luxury is turned inside out. Theseus and Hippolyta have risen early on the day of their wedding and leave the court with a large party of men and dogs. Later in the day, they will die as individuals and will be reborn as a married couple. The death that's the goal of the hunt allows them to explore, as a dream does, the way hate and love are bound to each other and the way a comedy can come close to a tragedy and vice versa. After all, the two of them were mortal enemies before they were lovers.

Theseus would have them climb the mountain where they can hear the sound of the hounds echoing in the western valley. The duke and his queen confess to each other that they love to hear the different voices that fill the space with "so musical a discord, such sweet thunder." This setting, so full of passionate voices, reminds us of the theater, which holds the action of the play along with its spectators and recalls the voices we have heard over the previous three acts—of lovers in fits of passionate wanting. It suggests as well the potent contrarieties out of which the duke and his Amazon queen must compose a married life. Therefore, there's another theater present in the scene, that of marriage itself. Just as the valley composes the voices (both high and low) into music of great power, just as a theater gathers people together to school us in emotions of great power, the form of marriage has composed the relationships of millions over thousands of years, with rules of the road and guardrails that can prevent deadly accidents.

As Lewis progresses in his narrative about love to a reading of Spenser's *The Faerie Queene* at the end of the book, he makes the case that the tension between church and court in the matter of physical love is resolved in married love. Shakespeare was writing his romantic comedies at roughly the same time, and his female heroines managed their affairs of the heart with great skill. They resolve the problem with their active minds, warm hearts, and natural goodness. These ladies are fully engaged in the business of marriage, and if they are, how can the man not be. This is only natural.

Reknitting the Long-Divided Love

Lewis makes quick work of *Architrenius*, which Johannes de Altavilla composed around 1184. Having introduced *The Allegory of Love* with it, I now conclude my reading of the first two chapters with Lewis's retelling of Altavilla's poem:

> *This long narrative . . . tells the story of the "Arch-mourner," the youthful Architrenius, who, in mere despair at the wickedness within him and about him, sets out to seek his mother Nature and be healed. His journeys lead him through many places, including the university of Paris and the island of Thule [a cold, far-distant place in the north like Iceland], thus offering the author the opportunity to lavish satiric description, before the wanderer finally meets Nature . . . The work as a whole has little relevance for our special study except in so far as it illustrates the popularity of the personification Natura and gives us an early example of the allegory in the form of a journey—that is, in its best form. But what really matters in the poem is the unusual energy with which the wanderer's motive is presented . . . In his picture of Architrenius at his setting out he far excels any of his fellow workers in this kind. Suddenly . . . a living voice begins to speak . . . A universal human longing is expressed, and, but for the language, the lines might have been written in any age:*
>
> *This must I do—go exiled through the world*
> *And seek for Nature till far hence I find*
> *Her secret dwelling place; there drag to light*
> *The hidden cause of quarrel, and reknit,*
> *Haply reknit, the long-divided Love.*

Lewis has landed on the perfect quote with which to sum up what he has learned about the allegory of love from "the practice of the ancients." Allegory itself represents an exile from the world, the one that's defined by a matrix of time and space. For example, in the story of *Everyman*, space and time dissolve in the presence of Death so the soul can go a journey of discovery prior to a reckoning. Within the allegory, time is one, and space is one. This oneness comes to life naturally in the "I" point of view. The

Archmourner speaks to us directly from this perspective, "This must I do—go exiled through the world" to seek for Nature's secret dwelling place.

Through a kind of spiritual transference, I now participate in his point of view, even though the allegorical figure exists in a text over eight hundred years old. I am the archmourner. I would end alienation by reknitting the long-divided Love. Just as I have merged with the substance of the allegory, which is one, I discover that I, too, am one in the quest. I am that I am, and with every breath this "I" burns with self-substantial fuel in a timeless realm. How can I say this? Because this consciousness (rendered by the "I") is and can only be one. There's no way to measure it or time it objectively nor can we divide it. Like Lewis's train, it moves even though it never leaves the station. It moves intelligently to not be "unmade."

Now that I've studied Lewis's book, this is the story I'd like to tell. It appears I must go a journey, like Everyman's, to be a living soul. The "I" must undergo an alchemical, allegorical process wherein its attachments dissolve, and it "doth suffer a sea change / Into something rich and strange." Chagall renders the process pictorially as a ghostly Moses moves from right to left—through the experience of the bush burning with self-substantial fuel—to realize his true self, a living self-substantial soul, but the story is more accurately told as a colorized image online (see page 31). As such, I live with an awareness that something has preserved me from the moment of birth through all the accidents of life and even now preserves me from the flood. It's a miracle. No longer estranged from the world "out there," I have come home, for I never actually left. This is the homecoming—the miracle—that allegory imagines. A skeptic may scoff and reject it as a fairy tale, but while fairy tales, myths, and allegories are clearly fictions, they may in the end be telling a true story.

It's not hard to see that this miracle is married to the breath of life, which every human being has inherited from our first ancestor. This story of the breath is a true story, and yet it barely registers in our consciousness as we have become so accustomed to it and complacent about it. I wonder at the length of this ancestral chain that connects us to that first breath of life. I wonder at how the breath here and now is still the beginning and the end of all we long for—a living, loving soul.

Book Three

The Poetry of Roger Scruton

Chapter 1
The Eye of Vermeer

Vermeer's
The Allegory of Painting

On Bridges, Poetry, and Making a Transition

I have called Book Three "The Poetry of Roger Scruton" to link it with "The Poetry of C. S. Lewis" in Book Two. Let me illustrate the importance of poetry to my inquiry with a little story that serves as a metaphor. A year ago, men and machines from the highway department of our state started building a bridge near where we live. It will replace the old causeway, which has a drawbridge in the middle. The new one will soar over the water high enough to let tall ships pass without the occasional inconvenience of a raised or lowered bridge for parties on the road or on the water. I have never witnessed anything like the growth of this massive, epic undertaking. The point I wish to make has to do with the foundation for the piers, which in turn will be the foundation for the beams that hold the roadway. The work began on land. For each pier, four concrete pillars, like gigantic two-hundred-foot-long nails, were set by tall cranes into frames that held them in a tight pattern, and then they were pounded inch by inch into the earth by a sky-scraping pile driver. Bang. Bang. Bang. A bang every second and a half, and this over several days for each one. Once the pillars were sunk, one by one, into the earth, the piers sprang up from the ground and now from the water, like concrete trees with spreading concrete branches and deep concrete roots.

I tell this story as a kind of confession. I am well aware that an inquiry into what it means to be a living soul could easily sink of its own weight into the quicksand of pure subjectivity. I would give the inquiry a proper foundation with the poetry and philosophy of C. S. Lewis and Roger Scruton. As to the business of poetry, you can see from this metaphor of bridge-building that I have much to say in favor of it. I've already pointed out in the introduction that I could not write this book at all without the language of poetry. As to the philosopher Roger Scruton, I have also already acknowledged with gratitude that this long train of thought, which engages me from day to day to this day, would not exist without the long stop I made at the "station" of his philosophy. Like the "bridge" that I'm building here, these are sentences I could not write without the devices of poetry and philosophy.

Transitions are difficult. Baptisms, coming-of-age initiations, marriages, and funerals mark an attempt to resolve the difficulty of these transitions by ritualizing them. I have chosen, therefore, to ritualize the transition from Lewis to Scruton with one of the most beautiful works of art ever painted, Vermeer's *The Allegory of Painting*. On Lewis's side of my bridge, we have personifications—in this case, Nature, Mind, and Death—that act out the meaning of the allegory. On the other side, we have Scruton's argument in *The Soul of the World* concerning the "I" of a human subject—in this case, the "I" (the eye) of Vermeer, and we have Scruton's argument concerning the emergence of meaning—in this case, from the "colored patches" on Vermeer's canvas.

The Allegory of Painting

If we agree with C. S. Lewis's argument that the exploration of an inner world developed through the stations he describes in his book, then Vermeer's painting represents—along with works by Titian, Botticelli, and Raphael—a timeless stop along the way. Again and again, Vermeer painted people in the interior of a home. Of course, artists had been doing this for centuries. Vittoro Carpaccio's painting of Saint Augustine in his study is a case in point, along with Simone Martini's *Annunciation Altarpiece*, which depicts the archangel Gabriel approaching the Virgin Mary in her home. Vermeer, however, frames his interiors in such a way that he places me, the viewer, quite concretely in the entryway of the room, in an adjacent room, or in a hallway leading into the room. He sets it up so that I "participate" in the scene.

In *The Allegory of Painting*, I see an artist sitting at an easel intent on his work, the transformation of reality into an allegory. But this painter is not the real artist. He's a figure in an allegory that the real artist has created for the same reason that the author of *Everyman* created his play. It serves as a wake-up call. What wakes me up? The real artist keeps poking me as I take in the different images he has painted. For starters, the allegorical artist puts me in mind of a Mind completely occupied with the wonder of Creation. He is our model. Why bother to be an artist if not to celebrate creation. For that matter, why bother to be any kind of human being if not to celebrate creation. The real artist pokes me and points as if to say, "Imitate him as I do."

Just as the allegorical artist would recreate the wonder of life before his eyes and the real artist would do the same, I wake to find that I am sitting where the real artist sits. Fully conscious now that I have been deliberately placed there, I realize I am in fact recreating the scene. Without me, no picture at all. I am the eye of Vermeer. He has put me on his seat, and we both occupy it *for real*. So I say again with a slightly different emphasis, Vermeer has set it up so "I" participate in the existence of this world. As I am doing now, I'm invited to tell the story of this allegory from my own point of view. What's the effect when Vermeer invites me to share his seat? Thanks to Lewis's study of allegory, I have learned how oneness comes to life naturally in the "I" point of view.

The wake-up call also involves the curtain on the left. It's cropped in such a way that we can't see why, by what, or by whom it has been pulled back to begin the show, to reveal the intensely personal interior scene behind it, but for real it has been pulled back. Prior to this, our vision may had been blocked by a patterned but indeterminate dullness. After this, our vision may be blocked once more. How sensitive we are to the light streaming from an unseen source behind the curtain, for we sit in a darker place. Vermeer has put us in the dark to better appreciate the light of the interior room.

Now we clearly see the artist absorbed in his work and the young woman who is his subject—her eyes (almost?) closed in concentration on her pose—as absorbed in *her* work as the artist. What is her work? It's *to be*, nothing more or less—specifically to be a woman, source of human life, standing in for the whole of Nature with her crown of laurel. Though she can't see the man who is so interested in everything about her, for her gaze is turned inward, a smile radiates outward from what she feels. How sensitive she is to the light of his attention, and this, too, may awaken us, like the curtain drawn suddenly back, to the light of an inner life. Her face, her smile, gives us a sense that the young woman and young man we can see painting her are strongly linked to each other.

Since the painting as a whole is an allegory, to my mind the light we sense in the young woman's face illuminates the whole. She is not just a beautiful young woman; she's a beautiful soul. No wonder the artist would paint her; no wonder we, too, delight in a glimpse of her. If we look over the allegorical artist's shoulder, we see he has begun with the laurel wreath, the crown of nature, Apollo, and poetry. By itself, there on the canvas, it is but a symbol, and it may recall Daphne's transformation into Nature. The young woman in blue, however, is no symbol. She is the poetry of nature, the soul of the world, and she wears the crown of a sacred queen.

She recalls not only Daphne but also the Virgin Mary in Simone Martini's *Annunciation Altarpiece*. Martini's Mary, in her blue mantle, has been crowned with spiritual gold, for she is now the vessel for what will grow within, the soul of the world. As it happens, she was an initial inspiration for my inquiry. We're so lucky that we can bring up from nothing with a few clicks this gorgeous work of art glowing on the screen. I notice that the gold, and there's so much gold, reflects the light, but the deep blue of her mantle completely absorbs it. What does she make of this sudden burst of gold? Her face expresses surprise and wonder, a wordless "What's the meaning of this?" Like the blue drawing in the light, the painting and her question draws me in as well.

Why do we come to Vermeer's young woman from a darker place? For one thing, we are not angels. The oversized and appalling death mask on the table also suggests an answer. If the curtain didn't so severely crop our view, would we see the rest of an enormous corpse lying there? Like Death itself, the mask of death teases the imagination. It calls to mind the opening scene of *Everyman* when Death shows up to tell Everyman he must go a journey. The presence of Death in the play of these objects suggests as well the tradition of a still life, what the French call "nature *morte*." The presence of the death mask pales, however, before the beauty of the young woman. She brings the scene to life. It's not a still life; it's an allegory. The death mask is right in her line of sight, but our beautiful soul, true subject of the allegory, is wholly engaged with the wonder of her life.

As we sit with Vermeer, we have a different perspective and experience. Just as Death comes to Everyman as a messenger from God in the play of *Everyman*, it may be that, in Vermeer's allegory, this Mask of Death initiates the journey we must take to wake a soul from a still life, nature *morte*. In Vermeer's allegory, the journey takes us not to the grave but to the scene behind the curtain that has suddenly revealed itself. For the soul can't and won't be awakened by fear and force. Like the smile on the young woman's face, love of life and a living soul come to life when we feel the love of another. In my reading of Lewis's book, an allegory represents a world that's no less real for being imagined. Vermeer understood that he needed the language of an allegory, an elaborate metaphor with a long history in art, to express, to realize, his love of life, and this is what he has given to us as we sit with him. The love comes around as it goes around. From his seat, the allegorical artist can clearly see that a beautiful soul loves him as much as he loves her. As the love goes round, Vermeer and I are looped in.

What we imagine is what we see in the painting, an allegorical interior space that mirrors a perfectly recognizable exterior space. Whether inner or outer, we are its substance; we are the creators of it all. For us, the living, a light still streams through an unseen window. If the allegory does its work, it awakens in us a love for that which animates the whole—the Creator of the whole and the breath and the light of a living soul. All this is as real as the light we see in the young girl's face (or any face, for that matter, when smiling), as real as the breath that even now sustains our life.

Vermeer's painting celebrates the eye of a painter that goes, thanks to the figures of the allegory, full circle to hold past, present, future, and the whole of the Netherlands—the Netherlands we imagine in an allegory—all within the frame of one work, like the map on the wall. The artist in his seat sees the history of painting and the whole of the Netherlands in the carefully staged objects of a still life. These are the subjects and techniques he has incorporated, thanks to a lifetime devoted to a study of them, into his work. But one of his objects in particular is (allegorically) alive, his model of a beautiful soul. She faces the actual artist and us, the viewer. She doesn't see us, though, for how could she. She faces us, and in her smile, we imagine a whole world opening up. Like the young woman lit up from within by the painter's intention, we come to life, we find ourselves, in the eye of Vermeer.

Creation Told from the Point of View of the Created: A Proper Object for the Imagination

In my (highly) imaginative reading of *The Allegory of Painting*, a great artist has shared with us the way he looks at the world. If I approach the work from Lewis's side of my bridge, Vermeer's vision (in my telling of it) reminds me of the allegories written by the School of Chartres nature poets and Dante's thoughts on the nature of allegory. Specifically, Lewis has told us that *De Mundi Universitate* "is the story of creation told from the point of view of the created." Here is how Lewis frames the issue:

> *In adopting such a standpoint it is clear that the author incurs certain dangers. Of necessity he comes perilously near to representing non-existents as petitioners for their own existence. Yet, as a philosopher, he may reply that he is dealing with processes that are not in time at all, and that such a presentation is therefore not more inadequate than another: from the purely literary point of view we may plead in his defense that we, after all, belong to the created ourselves and that the response of the work to the workman is precisely that aspect of creation which comes, by remote analogy, within our experience and is therefore a proper object for the imagination.* (This was originally quoted on pages 198–199.)

Like Bernard's focus on Nature and Mind, Vermeer has painted a picture of a young woman, the natural source of human life, and an artist for whom creation is a proper subject for his imagination. Each one is both the work and the workman, a part of creation and a creator. The young woman and the artist, who stands in for Vermeer himself, effectively play the roles of Nature and Mind in Bernard's narrative when they work together to make the soul of the world (see pages 198–202). Perhaps I exaggerate to view them as primal parents, but I'm wondering and trying to answer why this painting has such a hold on imaginations all over the world. Vermeer's young woman and the artist also remind me of Beatrice and Dante. When Dante sees Beatrice, he credits her with giving birth *in his poetry* to a new life (*La Vita Nuova*), and the young woman in blue (the color of Mary) gives birth to a new life for the artist and those who participate *in Vermeer's painting*. The poetry and the painting are clearly fictions, but they express a real human being's vision of a love that's commensurate with the gift of life.

I think it's fair to say Lewis admires Bernard's approach. Bernard humanizes creation. Just as human beings for millennia have turned deadwood into something useful or beautiful, like a log in a fire on a cold day or a statue of the Buddha, a human being can imagine that we have been shaped to serve creation in some way—to keep someone warm or to inspire someone with an image that awakens us to the presence of a living soul. Unlike science, Lewis is not concerned with origins. Like Bernard, he is concerned with the longing of matter for a form that gives it meaning. Every breath we take expresses this longing to stay in the game, to meet the challenge our limited shape presents. It's involuntary and forward looking.

Chapter 2
The Human Subject

Leonardo da Vinci's
Mona Lisa

The "I" of the Writer

Part 1: The "I" and the Inner Life

As we cross over from Lewis's to Scruton's side of the bridge, I must emphasize that we don't actually see a beautiful soul. A soul is immaterial, so it's impossible to see it. It is possible, however, for the viewer to be aware of its presence. Thanks to the front-row seat Vermeer has given us, we are present to imagine, according to my reading of it, a soul emerging not only in the face of the young woman but also from the effect of the whole painting. I don't apologize for my extended reading; the silence of this beautiful work prompts me to give it speech. Because I love it, I wonder about it. Or perhaps I should say: Because I wonder about it, I love it. I wonder what it is saying, and so I do as I have done. I speak for it. Anyone who has lived with and loved a dog, as I have, knows the feeling. Something about our silent partner prompts us to speak to her and to speak for her (like at the vet when she's not eating and listless) despite the surprising fact that she has never spoken a word.

A writer has different means for sharing the way he looks at the world. As my own reading of the painting demonstrates, we have at hand all the shapes, colors, timbers, tastes, and sensations evoked by the words, figures, phrases, clauses, syntax, and rhythms of a language. In particular, when speaking or writing, our interior, our inner life, comes to life in the personal pronoun "I," the great gift in all languages (in different forms) for marking our place—for suggesting the interior of our home, if you will—in public and private speech. My first-person reading of *The Allegory of Painting* and the little snapshot of my Cavalier King Charles Spaniel invite the reader into the interior of my home. My writing, which leans on first-person narration, is one long confession, as Goethe has confessed about his work.

I might as well add before moving on that the English language provides such an easy transition from the eye of an artist to the "I" of the human subject in speaking and writing.

Part 2: The Origin and Reality of the "I"

Who invented, who gave us the word *I*? Even as scientists probe ever deeper into the macrocosm and the microcosm for the origin of the world and all the things in the world, they have yet to describe scientifically the origin of language. Nor, in what may well be a related matter, can they say how a conscious animal became a self-conscious human being. The "I," of course, marks the change. From studying the nature of language in *The Allegory of Love* and from studying works like *The Soul of the World*, I propose here the reason I have inferred from Lewis and Scruton for this gap in scientific knowledge. Science does very well in describing the laws that govern the motions of objects, the chemistry of the universe, but it has to stop short when confronted with a metaphysical reality. As speech, language has a physical reality. It consists of real sounds, vibrations as real as a wave moving through water, but the sounds of a language don't make it a language. For a language to be a language, the sounds have to have meaning, and we will never find meaning in the physical world. Meaning is metaphysical. Meaning *emerges*, like a beautiful soul from Vermeer's pigments, from the sounds, but it is not a physical reality. The "I" that we use with such abandon makes perfect sense, but as a word in a language it is as metaphysical as the meaning of a sentence.

Part 3: The "I" of a Human Subject versus Data in Science

Scruton illustrates the concept of emergence and cognitive dualism in chapter 2 of *The Soul of the World* by outlining two ways of describing and knowing a painting like *Mona Lisa*. I introduced his concepts of cognitive dualism and emergence in my introduction (see pages 19–20). A scientist, if true to the mandate of science, can only describe the physical reality, the blobs of paint on a two-dimensional surface. With a machine like a camera, a scientist can reproduce the colors and shapes, but the camera cannot tell us what the shapes and colors mean. I, on the other hand, can see the face that emerges "from pigments on the canvas," for I'm a human subject who sees the face and wonders about it. Scruton points out that the imaginative, subjective mind of a human subject is the one thing a scientist must exclude from his observations. If that mind is excised, then meaning is excised as well. Of course, cameras and the machines that support them are being used all over the world to recognize faces, but this is a simple matter of physical characteristics and likenesses informed by a database. Will a machine ever know the "otherness" of Da Vinci's Lisa, the person who holds his heart in safekeeping, which moved him to paint her? Some very smart people are working hard to prove that it will, but as far as I know they haven't yet succeeded.

Part 4: The Married Pairs and the "I"

The material world and a language that is essentially immaterial: these two remind me of the married pairs with which Lewis begins his chapter on allegory. He writes:

> *Allegory, in some sense, belongs not to medieval man but to man, or even to mind, in general. It is of the very nature of thought and language to represent what is immaterial in picturable terms. What is good or happy has always been high like heavens and bright like the sun. Evil and misery were deep and dark from the first. To ask how these married pairs of sensibles and insensibles first came together would be great folly; the real question is how they ever came apart, and to answer that question is beyond the province of the mere historian. Our task is less ambitious. We have to inquire how something always latent in human speech becomes, in addition, explicit in the structure of whole poems; and how poems of that kind come to enjoy an unusual popularity in the Middle Ages.*

The "I" in particular combines a physical and metaphysical reality: it refers to that which is both a body and a mind. For Scruton, the use of the personal pronoun "I" plays a critical role in the all-important drama of personal identity (see "In Allegory, the Self Disappears," pages 124–128).

Part 5: If I Marry Sensibles and Insensibles, I Am Writing Poetry

Because these married pairs are a latent presence in all language, I called Book Two "The Poetry of C. S. Lewis," even though I'm interpreting over 150 pages of his prose. I argued that poets "write love songs to their love, and in so doing they exercise their love of language" (see the last sentence on page 74). Lewis is a lover and a poet like this. Like Lewis, I write about love in prose, and I know as well as I know anything that I'm exercising my love of language. As I write, my prose helps me to imagine and share with others what I think it means to be a living, loving soul. As Lewis did, I find that to express myself I resort to the married pairs within figures of speech. When I engage them, I play the role of a poet, for the joining of sensibles and insensibles, to my mind, is the essential function of poetry. If we agree with Lewis, it follows then that anyone who speaks or writes is a poet, for "It is of the very nature of thought and language to represent what is immaterial in picturable terms." We are all lovers now.

Humanity

In the opening paragraph of *The Allegory of Love*, Lewis encourages the reader to study a medieval allegory, like *The Romance of the Rose*. He argues:

> *Humanity does not pass through phases as a train passes through stations: being alive, it has the privilege of always moving yet never leaving anything behind. Whatever we have been, in some sort we are still. Neither the form nor the sentiment of this old poetry has passed away without leaving indelible traces on our minds. We shall understand our present, and perhaps even our future, the better if we can succeed, by an effort of historical imagination, in reconstructing that long-lost state of mind for which the allegorical love poem was a natural mode of expression.*

Earlier I quoted this passage to introduce "A Realm Out of Time," which is such an important characteristic of allegory in Lewis's reading of it. This time I quote it to consider what underlies this realm—namely, the human subject who is the individual instance of "humanity."

I find a strong connection in Lewis's quote with Scruton's writings on this subject of the human subject. Both writers see humanity, our collective mind coming to consciousness in the language we speak, as the bridge between sensible and insensible worlds. This is the mind that's always moving but never leaving anything behind. This is the mind, even our own mind, that learns to refer to itself as "I." If I approach these matters from the perspective of a human subject, which is an explicit feature of Scruton's philosophy, I'm persuaded to conclude that Lewis can write about "humanity" because he is a language using, self-conscious human subject. I can read what he has to say about "humanity" because I am a language user. Thanks to the language I learned without even knowing I was learning it, I learned, among many other things, to refer to myself with the personal pronoun "I," just as I do here. Lewis, Scruton, and I represent a very small sampling of "humanity," but with all humility, I think it's fair to say the word *humanity*, in essence, refers to beings like ourselves, who are self-conscious language users in possession of the personal pronoun "I." This is a theme that Scruton also develops in *On Human Nature*.

What follows from this definition? If, as a kind of creature, we are essentially language users (Would we even be considering the matter if we weren't?), then to my mind it follows that our "humanity" can only be grasped in the metaphysical realm of a language-using human subject's consciousness. Scruton points out that a neuroscientist like Patricia Churchland must frame her inquiry and report her results using highly sophisticated linguistic concepts. I would add that she shares this ground with an allegorist. (For Scruton's observations on neuroscience, see chapter 3, "Looking at the Brain," pages 51–75 in *The Soul of the World*.)

In this view, metaphysics plays a role in how we know ourselves and the world. That's why an accurate understanding that marries sensibles and insensibles is not a pointless exercise in folk psychology or sophistry. It's eminently practical, for language has been used for thousands of years as a tool to insure the survival and enrichment of human life. With it we can conduct thought experiments about the world at a great savings of time, expense, and even loss of life, but after studying *The Allegory of Love*, I'm quite sure the utilitarian aspect of language is not Lewis's concern nor is it Scruton's concern in *The Soul of the World*. They regard the quest to understand our true nature and our place in the world as an end in itself, for man does not live on bread alone. A purely physical description of reality can't explain everything, not by a long shot.

Unfortunately, there's a dark side to language use. It has contributed to our exile, the painful alienation that pilgrims go on pilgrimage to heal. An "alienation" from others and from the world can only take shape in our minds thanks to the language that gives us the word as well as words strung together, which have an alienating effect. Along with social interactions in that language, a complex system of thought can produce it. For example, Descartes, for all his brilliance as a thinker and writer, vigorously promoted at a high level of literacy and the best of intentions a dualistic ontology of body and mind that alienates mankind from the world.

Language can be used to deceive. The serpent in the garden, the Bible tells us, was a language user. With the power of words, he ensnared the minds of our primeval parents and brought death into the world. It's just a story, but who can deny the truth of it? Because we are intelligent language users, we have the word *death*, and we live in the valley of the shadow of death. It's difficult to imagine my Cavalier getting depressed about her mortality. For all our vaunted intellect and use of language, we are often fearful, irrational creatures because we live in this valley. We are fearful, irrational creatures whether we know the story in Genesis or not. I choose to think that the story exists, though, not to excuse or blame but to shed light on our nature as language using human subjects. The story exists within the whole of a sacred text to wake human beings from alienation. This opinion reflects the redemptive side of language use.

We know from history and from personal experience that often enough we hold in our language-using, language-created minds a fixed opinion about the world "out there" that is false. We think the world is flat; we think the sun moves in the sky from east to west; we think this person is an enemy; we think the world consists only of objects in motion that move without purpose to no end; and so on and on. I present these examples to draw attention to a remarkable feature of the human mind. To grasp this feature, human beings have employed a figure of speech that marries the sensible and the insensible.

We learn from experience in the sensible world that at the end of a long day and much labor we can lie down in a soft place, draw up a covering to stay warm, close our eyes, and go to sleep. We also know from experience what it means to wake from sleep after a night of rest. While asleep, we may dream, and when we wake, we see the real world, not a dream. For time out of mind, human beings have used this experience to describe the mind "waking," when in fact it is already awake. This is an idea that only a language could convey. We "wake" to the fact: that the earth is a sphere, not flat; that the earth moves, not the sun; that the man we mistrusted is a friend; and, crucially for our study of love and allegory, that our alienation from the things of this world, including other human beings, is a product of thinking. We and the world are one; we can wake from the spell of "alienation." For thousands of years human beings have been telling stories about waking in this way.

In "And Man Became a Living Soul," I quoted those lines from *A Midsummer Night's Dream* in which Robin prays over the four insensate lovers at the end of their midsummer night. His speech has as its focus the image of "waking" with which Robin addresses the alienation that's a primal concern of humanity (see pages 36–38). We find this waking of a living soul in the poetry of Genesis, when God breathed the breath of life into Man's nostrils, and I would argue that this story is another way of referring to the waking of a fully self-aware human subject.

I would guess that Lewis wrote his book because he feared that, in the eye of science, Physics (personified) has marshaled certain forces it can acquire from a language to divorce its mate, Metaphysics (personified), and since the divorce, Lewis might say, the children have suffered. This story is part of an allegory where the dark side of language for a time triumphs over humanity. To combat the dark side, Lewis wrote stories for children that rekindle the imagination and reknit the long-divided worlds outside and inside the wardrobe. He conveyed his concern as a literary historian, a philosopher, and a writer of fiction for adults. In a text like *The Soul of the World*, Scruton conveys his concern by critiquing the dualistic philosophy on which modern science is founded (Descartes was its godfather) and by proposing arguments that restore the wholeness and health of the human subject.

I have illustrated this chapter with Leonardo's *Mona Lisa*, I suppose, primarily because, like Vermeer's *Allegory of Painting*, it's a beautiful work. (Scruton does refer to her, as I mentioned earlier, in his explication of emergence later in chapter 2 of *The Soul of the World*.) I also think it's fair to say Leonardo intends *Mona Lisa* to be about the inner life of a person, which is the subject of my Book Two, and this is as much to say that it's about the human subject, which is the subject of my Book Three. It's a much simpler work than Vermeer's allegory since Lisa is the only subject. Still, if we know her as *Mona Lisa* (as most do), then Leonardo has put himself into the work, but less concretely than Vermeer has placed himself in the interior of a Dutch home. He has painted "my" Lisa, the one he loves. We are inclined to suppose this because how else can we explain the way she draws us in to wonder about the inner life that presents itself outwardly—in her composure but especially in her face? I've been to the Louvre to see her and marveled at how she draws people in like a powerful magnet.

As Dante tells us in *La Vita Nuova*, people who love lose their hearts to the person they love. Leonardo would paint the heart of his Lisa. In essaying to paint hers, therefore, he would paint his own. She's his mirror, and they look at each other. Standing in Leonard's shoes, we look, too, to see if we see our own hearts reflected there.

The Presence of a Soul in Scruton's Argument

I observed at the beginning of this chapter that we are present to imagine, according to my reading of it, a soul emerging from the visual objects in Vermeer's *The Allegory of Painting*. Among other objectives, an allegorical reading of Vermeer's painting helps me to suggest the way the soul comes to light in Scruton's argument over the many chapters of my Book Three. Like one who sits on Vermeer's bench with him to view the scene that the withdrawn curtain has revealed, we are present to imagine an immaterial, sacred soul emerging from the dabs and strokes of insight and assertion in Scruton's argument.

Chapter 3

The Threshold between Mundane and Sacred Worlds

A meteorolcgical illustration known as

The Flammarion Engraving, 1888

An Analogy

The form of our front porch suggests a transition into another world, even if it has lost that meaning in everyday use. It imitates a small, truncated Greek temple. There's a raised platform approached by two steps, a roof held up by two fluted Doric columns, and a door enclosed by sidelight windows and a sunburst frieze radiating over it. The whole structure highlights and celebrates the threshold, the line dividing outside from inside. For Greeks, the interior of the temple housed the goods and even the person of a god. Since one must approach a temple from the outside, the porch and its columns—with space in between for a human being to pass through—ordered the transition from the mundane into a sacred world. If we take Homer's word for it, human beings often interacted with the gods. They weren't locked up in a temple though. At critical times, Athena sought out Odysseus where *he* was.

Early in his career, Scruton wrote a book titled *The Aesthetics of Architecture*, which documents the importance and meaning of the classical orders. His interest in this kind of architecture gave me the idea for the following analogy. Just as my porch suggests a transition from a secular to a sacred world, "Believing in God," the first chapter of *The Soul of the World*, functions in a similar way. As I understand it, this chapter is designed, as in fact the whole book is designed, to bring a reader through the columns to the threshold where the secular ends and the sacred begins.

The View of Fashionable Commentators

Scruton's narrative about believing in God opens with an observation involving 9/11:

> *The currently fashionable discussions of religious belief arose partly in response to the confrontation between Christianity and modern science,*

and partly in response to the attacks of 9/11, which drew attention to another confrontation, between Islam and the modern world.

The title of the book and the title of the first chapter put us in mind of the sacred matters that are housed within the temple of the book and the chapter: the soul of the world and believing in God. The first sentence, however, places us "outside" in the fashionable, secular world of commentaries on current events. Scruton concludes the first paragraph with what looks like a conclusion:

In both confrontations, as popularly understood, reason points one way, and faith the other. And if faith justifies murder, faith is not an option.

Scruton tells us that 9/11 has added a new witness in the debate between science and religion. In this sentence, it would appear he is stating the popular opinion of commentators that Islamic "suicide bombers," like the perpetrators of 9/11, pose a challenge, not just for Islam but for all faith traditions. Now that the suicide bombers have revealed the true character of religion, reasonable people have to conclude that belief in God is not just a proposition that in public opinion loses an Oxford debate but it's a mortal danger to public health.

Reclaiming the True Ground of Religion

Any good general makes sure he commands the high ground prior to hostilities. It would appear from the first paragraph that, by their lights—the lights of science and secular society—the commentators thought *they* were occupying the high ground. Make no mistake though: Scruton is engaged in a battle for hearts and minds about believing in God, and the second paragraph makes it clear the commentators do not convince him:

> *However, the two confrontations have entirely different origins. One is intellectual, the other emotional. One concerns the nature of reality; the other concerns how we should live. Public intellectuals who have espoused the atheist cause often give the impression that religion is defined by a comprehensive explanation of the world, one that incidentally brings comfort and hope, but which, like every explanation, can be refuted by the evidence. But the religion of the Islamists is not like that. It is not primarily an attempt to explain the world, or to show the place of creation in the course of nature. It originates in a need for sacrifice and obedience. No doubt Islamists entertain many metaphysical beliefs, including the belief that the world was created by Allah. But they also believe that they are subject to Allah's commands, that they are called to sacrifice themselves on Allah's behalf, and that their lives will acquire a meaning when thrown away for Allah's sake. Those beliefs are more important to them than the metaphysics, and will survive any niggling attempt to refute the basic tenets of theology. They express an emotional need that precedes rational argument and which shapes the conclusions of theology in advance.*

In the commentators' eagerness to excise the sacred from public discourse, they have ignored that religion can be understood in these two very different ways. Scruton also intuits that if the argument about belief in God is grounded in "the nature of reality" as an intellectual matter, secular intellectuals will carry the day with the public. In his second paragraph, therefore, he shifts the ground on which the battle is being fought.

Like good detectives, the commentators begin with material facts: almost three thousand people have died; they were killed by people from the Middle East. When they look further into the question—"What is the cause of these deaths?"—they conclude from the evidence that religion ultimately is the cause. Their explanation may go like this: We have here people who believe that God's Providence, as laid out in an ancient book, is a comprehensive explanation of the world. If God has commanded the murder of unbelievers (you can find this in the Bible as well as the Koran), then God commanded the murders on 9/11. Obviously, the commentators must reject this worldview. The murder of innocents can't be justified.

With that great word *however* at the beginning of the paragraph,

Scruton sets forth to disarm their reasoning with his own reasoning. The commentators assume that religion is defined as an intellectual worldview concerning "the nature of reality" like the one science provides. Rather than assuming this, Scruton pursues the definition the way Socrates might have; after all, he's a philosopher. He works from the evidence at hand—namely, the events of 9/11. Ironically, the Islamists—who in the eyes of the commentators expose why belief in God should be thrown on the ash heap of history—embody that which shifts the ground of the argument. Instead of a "comprehensive explanation"—the view from Olympus, Scruton offers the point of view of men who sacrifice themselves to preserve the life of their community. The Islamists demonstrate, he tells us, that religion originates, not in an intellectual search for explanations, but in the need human beings have "for sacrifice and obedience."

Having noted this emotional need, which "precedes rational argument," Scruton moves the argument about belief in God from an objective to a subjective point of view. The focus of the inquiry has shifted from the "Workman," the cosmic whatever that made the world and makes it tick, to the Work, even ourselves, the center of our sinful earth. When Scruton observes that the Islamists "believe that they are subject to Allah's commands, that they are called to sacrifice themselves on Allah's behalf, and that their lives will acquire a meaning when thrown away for Allah's sake," we go imaginatively into the mind of a human subject, a man prepared to die for the belief that he owes something, even his life, to others in his community.

Scruton doesn't excuse what the Islamists did—far from it. He argues that their obedience and sacrifice define religion more accurately than the intellectual explanations of the commentators. The commentators want to explain the facts on the ground objectively. God told the Islamists to kill infidels, and they did. If the explanation follows the mandate of an objective view, however, it cannot rest on the mental states of the Islamists. As I have argued throughout the book, science—the objective view—can't admit mental states into its calculations, for a mental state is not a material fact.

Motive is not a material fact. Many a prosecutor would agree that motive is devilishly hard to prove.

Religion has been accused of murder, and Scruton has set out to prove that it has been falsely accused. The commentators, who pride themselves on their intellectual prowess, have misunderstood what believing in God means to people who believe in God—an unsurprising outcome for people who don't believe in God and who have no experience of what it means to practice a faith. After these two paragraphs, the skeptical reader may realize the author has blocked the approach to religion approved by public intellectuals and may choose to stop reading. If the author's argument is reasonable, however, a fair-minded reader may be tempted to explore along with the author the mental state that believes in God.

Science and Poetry

The image of a threshold is critical, I believe, for Scruton's whole enterprise, which is why I introduced it at the outset of my commentary. The line of a threshold serves my purpose in commentary on these introductory paragraphs, but Scruton himself later employs the image of a horizon as the line that divides secular and sacred worlds. I'll have more to say about that image when we come to it in the text, but for now I'd like to emphasize the role both images play as expressive vehicles. They are poetic devices, and the image of a horizon exemplifies the poetry of Roger Scruton.

The way he sorts out the two pairs of contrasting realities (of intellect and emotion, reason and faith) in the second paragraph strongly reminds me of the way Lewis sorts out the difference between symbol and allegory in his commentary on *La Vita Nuova*. Here's the quote that appeared originally on page 91 and then again on page 194:

> *The great allegorist's firm thinking leaves no room for misunderstanding. There is nothing "mystical" or mysterious about medieval allegory; the poets know quite clearly what they are about and are well aware that*

> *the figures which they present to us are fictions. Symbolism is a mode of thought; allegory is a mode of expression. It belongs to the form of poetry, more than to its content, and it is learned from the practice of the ancients.*

Just as symbols in an equation are a mode of thought (for example, in the famous equation $E=mc^2$, where E is a symbol for energy, m is the symbol for mass, c^2 is the symbol for the speed of light squared, and = is the symbol for "equals"), the work of science entails a thought about reality. Just as an allegory expresses the meaning of the poet's experience, the work of a religious faith expresses the meaning of a believer's life. The one is objective; E=mc(squared) describes a law of nature. The other is subjective; "O, my luv is like a red, red rose" expresses a human subject's experience of meaning. The poet tells the reader that his love (both the person he loves and his wholehearted response to that person) is beautiful. The beauty of love, his metaphor implies, gives his life meaning.

As Dante does in his poetry, Scruton strives to define and describe an immaterial concept like the sacred with a kind of fiction, a comparison with some *thing* we know in the world. As we read his book, an image like a threshold or a horizon asks us to consider the experience of living in the material world and at the same time sensing "the real presence" of the sacred on the other side of the threshold. ("The real presence" is how he describes the sacred later in the chapter.) Scruton writes that a sense of the sacred is like an awareness of another's "presence," that intangible "something" about another person. He will argue that a sense of a person's "presence" is real, not merely imagined. And so we have the poetry of Roger Scruton; like Dante, he learned about figurative language from the practice of the ancients. Like Dante, he writes about that which takes shape in the substance of his poetry and which expresses the real presence of his own substance.

The Connection between Sacrifice and Meaning

The third paragraph completes Scruton's introduction to "Believing in God" and his introduction to the argument of the whole book. He argues that the emotional need for sacrifice and obedience "can be widely observed" and "is rooted deep in all of us." Because members of secular communities also sacrifice themselves in time of war, he quotes for us Durkheim's definition of *the core religious experience,* even if the experience doesn't directly involve a religion. It is:

> *. . . the experience of myself as a member of something, called upon to renounce my interests for those of the group and to celebrate my membership of the group in acts of devotion which might have no other justification than that they are commanded.*

This definition allows Scruton to move ahead into the question of meaning, the ineffable something that emerges from sentences, metaphors, allegories, blobs of paint on a canvas, and from actions in the world:

> *Others have emphasized the connection between sacrifice and meaning. Patocka, for example, argues that the meaning of life, even of life in the godless twentieth century, resides in the thing for which life—one's own life—can be sacrificed . . . This is the secular residue of the core religious thought—the thought that the sacred and the sacrificial coincide.*

Before concluding his introduction to the way he will approach the sacred, Scruton makes it clear what he means by a true sacrifice:

> *Of course, there is the greatest difference in the world between religions that demand self-sacrifice, and those, (like that of the Aztecs) that demand the sacrifice of others. If there is anything that could be called progress in the religious history of mankind, it resides in the gradual preference for the self over the other as the primary sacrificial victim. It is precisely in this that the Christian religion rests its moral claim.*

Scruton will be making the argument that people throughout human history have experienced "the real presence" at the threshold between secular and sacred worlds. In paragraph three, we approach the threshold, but Scruton needs all the arguments in the rest of the chapter to make his case for the sacred on the other side. He has strictly qualified his use of the Islamists as exemplars, but the fact that he puts them forward to initiate his argument is characteristic of a man who welcomes the challenge of a fair fight. The commentators saw 9/11 as an opportunity to condemn religion. Scruton saw their commentary as an opportunity to rescue religion from its present status as the preferred straw man of secular intellectuals. "Straw man" may be too mild an epithet for the fierce passions that religion evokes in those who oppose it. "Whipping boy" is better and goes nicely with the scourging of Jesus.

Chapter 4

An Age of Debunking

Adolph Weinman's

Winged Liberty

The Changing of the Guard in Heaven

To get into the spirit of "Religion and Evolutionary Psychology," the first section in the chapter with a title, let's consider what stories from mythology, philosophy, and religion say about heaven and the changing of the guard there. For the Greeks, the dynasty begins with Uranus, Father Sky, father of the gods, and the first to rule the whole world. Kronos, youngest of the Titans, violently overthrew Uranus and ruled tyrannically in his place. To keep himself safe from what he did to his father, he swallowed each child as soon as it was born, but Rhea, the mother of those children, saved Zeus from this fate. When the time was ripe, Zeus rose up against his father and imprisoned him in Tartarus, a deep chasm like the Christian idea of hell.

We don't know when these stories were first told. We do know that the poetry of Homer can be dated to around 800 BC and that he predates Socrates by, give or take, five hundred years. In Homer's time, Zeus and his family ruled in heaven, and they maintained their rule for many centuries after that. Socrates and Plato built their philosophies on the world of thought that Homer brought into being. Unlike those previous changes of the guard, though, the gods of Homer coexisted with the forms in Plato's dialogues. In Book Two, my chapter titled "The Example of Socrates" describes the change Socrates wrought in spiritual matters, and it includes this quote from Richard Tarnas:

> *In Socrates's view, any attempt to foster true success and excellence in human life had to take account of the inner most reality of a human being, his soul or psyche. Perhaps on the basis of his own highly developed sense of individual selfhood and self-control, Socrates brought to the Greek mind a new awareness of the central significance of the soul, establishing it for the first time as the seat of the individual waking consciousness and of the moral and intellectual character.*

For the purpose of my argument, Tarnas encourages me to believe that

Socrates discovered a kind of heaven in his own soul. This soul does not preclude, in Plato's speculations, the existence of a world soul, as we find in *Timaeus*, nor was Socrates at war with the gods.

The Greeks, of course, weren't the only ones who looked to the sky for stories and guidance. In the East, Yahweh (originally a storm god some scholars think) took a small nomadic tribe under his protection if they agreed to have no other gods before him. The rest, as they say, is monotheistic history. Christians, though, worshipped the mystic Trinity of the Father, Son, and Holy Ghost. Almost eight hundred years after the birth of Socrates, Christianity overthrew pagan gods, mystery religions, and the cult of the emperor to become the ruling power in Rome. Despite the clash of cultures and their representative deities, church fathers like Augustine, theologians like Aquinas, and Roman poets like Virgil and Statius inspired Dante to unite in his *Commedia* the poetry of the Bible with the philosophies of Plato and Aristotle.

The final chapter of this little story has nothing to say about heaven. For about five hundred years now, Science (personified) has sought to overthrow the preoccupation with an immaterial heaven and an immaterial soul in Western thought. Scruton's first sentence of "Religion and Evolutionary Psychology" made me think of these transitions in the ruling order of heaven. He writes:

> *We live in an age of debunking explanations, and the once popular debunkings of the sociologists are now in turn debunked by evolutionary psychology.*

Castrating, defenestrating, being aware of the soul as of a piece with heaven, the Lord God creating and ruling the world with no other gods before Him, the Lord God mystically dividing into a Trinity, the Lord God becoming strictly One again in Arabia, and now in the age of science a debunking of the whole show. Out with the old, and in with the new. Poetry, philosophy, Christianity, Islam, and now science have each had their shot at describing a ruling order in heaven. Scruton aims at a rapprochement with science, but first he has to point out the mistakes scientists and others are making when they argue about religion and the sacred. "Religion and Evolutionary Psychology" is about debunking. In Scruton's lifetime (and mine), sociologists and evolutionary psychologists have taken turns at debunking religion, but Scruton himself, in the spirit of the age, aims at debunking the claims of those who would overrule a human subject's sense of the sacred.

What Does It Mean to Be a Human Subject?

Since my train of thought moves but never leaves the station, it still hasn't left the original question posed in my introduction and Book One: "What does it mean to be a living soul?" The lifelines of poetry that I have interpreted in them suggest to me a common theme: to be a living soul means to be one with the world. The soul is one. Lewis's *The Allegory of Love* gives us the history of a literary form that develops this characterization of it. With his image of a train that moves but never leaves the station, Lewis asks us to imagine that which develops, just as allegory developed, through different stages into its full expression. Our time at each stage is a part of a process, but the process itself is one. Like the development of allegory, the soul in an allegory is one from beginning to end. In addition to this ontological oneness, its substance is informed by a simple, ethical rule, which tells us to do unto others as we would have them do unto us. This is easier for us to understand and to do when our sense of life as a living soul gathers another as one with ourselves.

As I point out in the introduction, Scruton has called his book *The Soul of the World*, but he rarely mentions the word *soul*, even though it's in the title. To fit his work into my own inquiry, I thought it best to reframe slightly my original question. I follow Scruton's lead, therefore, and ask, "What does it mean to be a human subject?" Scruton's book will argue that, like Lewis's portrait of a soul, a human subject is, by definition, whole, and is wholly concerned (whether the subject likes it or not) with ethical accountability. If this is the case, why is it human beings so often act unethically? From my own experience, I would guess people act unethically because they have forgotten or have never known what it means to be a human subject. If we have forgotten or never knew, perhaps we will find the answer to that question in our encounter with *The Soul of the World*.

In this section of the first chapter, Scruton introduces the argument that human subjects are by definition free. There is no personification of freedom in Lewis's history of allegory. Perhaps Scruton has to make the argument for freedom in *his* book because the sociologists and the evolutionary psychologists of our own day have laid siege to the freedom of a human subject.

Sociologists and the Debunking of Agency

During the seventies, eighties, and nineties, when I was teaching public school, the concept of conditioning was a hot topic. Social scientists argued that people behaved the way they did because they were conditioned to do so. This theory had a large impact, and still does, in our criminal justice system. The lyrics of "Gee, Officer Krupke" in *West Side Story* describe the theory in a comic vein:

Dear kindly Sergeant Krupke,
You gotta understand,
It's just our bringin' up-ke
That gets us out of hand.
Our mothers all are junkies,
Our fathers all are drunks.
Golly Moses, natcherly we're punks!
Gee, Officer Krupke, we're very upset;
We never had the love that ev'ry child oughta get.

We ain't no delinquents,
We're misunderstood.
Deep down inside us there is good!
There is good!

The theory does explain a great deal of human behavior, and so it captured the imagination of many well-meaning people. It doesn't explain everything though. It can't because people are not automatons. In Scruton's philosophy, freedom is a given, a thought he borrows from Kant. Scruton develops Kant's argument about "the self-identifying subject" in the chapter titled "Looking for People," which follows this one. As the lyrics show, a kid can figure out that freedom is a given without any help from Kant. They "act out" because they are free to do so. These high-spirited young men (demonstrated by the lively choreography around Krupke) clearly are not automatons. Automatons couldn't have this much fun with Krupke, for automatons don't have a sense of humor. The boys laugh at Krupke because their well-meaning social workers have given them a fool-proofed get-out-of-jail card.

Nevertheless, the theory of social conditioning debunks the idea that human beings have "agency," and the boys ape this idea in the song. The well-meaning social workers would liberate their clients from the false consciousness Society has impressed on them that they are free agents who do bad things. They must learn that it's not their fault. Lucky for the boys, they have social workers on the job to fix the problem. Society has given the boys the wrong idea, and social workers will save them from it. It's a picture of human life like that of a rat in maze. The maze determines what we think and do. We need social scientists to build a maze that gets us to where we can happily eat, sleep, and entertain ourselves. We need social scientists to fix *the negative thoughts* with treats and facile affirmations.

Evolutionary Psychologists and the Debunking of Agency

I have spent time on sociologists (more time than Scruton does) because it allows me to introduce the theme of agency (and the debunking of it) through experiences in my own life and work. Also, I wanted to emphasize that social scientists and their social workers are still engaged with *the thoughts* of the people they would help. The boys have a relationship with Krupke and their social workers, even if they "act out."

Scruton therefore is more concerned about the siege on human freedom by the debunkings of evolutionary psychologists. The effect of these debunkings *can't be as easily observed or addressed* as a kid saved from crime by the ministrations of cops and social workers. He writes:

> *There is a widespread sense that social facts that were previously understood as part of "culture" are now to be explained as adaptations, and that when we have so explained them, we have removed their aura, so to speak, deprived them of any independent hold on our beliefs and emotions, and reduced them to aspects of our biology.*

He doesn't say to what social facts is he referring. Since this statement follows the discussion about religion in the three-paragraph introduction, he must have this in mind, along with institutions like marriage, family life, and civic institutions that can play important roles in the life of a human subject. What happens to social facts that have their "aura" removed? By excising their "aura," the evolutionary explainers disenchant these social facts and render them ineffective or inoperative. This new attack on human freedom isn't as obvious as an earnest and well-meaning cop or social worker; to borrow a military metaphor, it flies under the radar. Evolutionary psychologists, he says, have removed the aura of social facts, but he might have added that this new explanation has removed from them the aura given to them by the mind or soul of a human subject. How else can we account for an aura in the first place?

Scruton's observation about social facts here is in line with the critique maintained throughout my book that Science (personified) cannot be concerned with the world as it is interpreted by a subjective human subject. Science came into being to avoid this. (Obviously, elite scientists are excepted from the rule because their discipline certifies them as objective observers.) The theory of evolution allows an evolutionary psychologist to skirt the problems posed by mental states in a science of the physical world and to argue that we are automatons directed, not by social conditioning, which involves a thought process even if it's a socially conditioned thought process, or by an individual's free choice, but by a selfish gene. Social facts merely reflect the behaviors that have been "selected for" over thousands of years.

Since the selfish gene is focused entirely on survival, how do we explain the fact that human beings sometimes sacrifice themselves to save the life of another? Scruton shows how an evolutionary psychologist answers this question. Religions that encourage self-sacrifice, it could be argued, have been selected for by the evolutionary process "because they further the reproductive 'strategies' of our genes." With this kind of reasoning, Scruton observes:

> *. . . we arrive at a picture of religious belief that seems entirely to discount its rational credentials, as both illusory in themselves and irrelevant to the form and force of religious feeling.*

According to an evolutionary psychologist, people may have strong religious feelings and they may act in accordance with those feelings, but all this is an illusion. People are genetically programmed to act in certain ways. The religious urge:

> *. . . is an adaptation like any other, and if it seems to be rooted so deeply within us as to be beyond the reach of rational argument, this is entirely to be expected, since that is how adaptations are passed on.*

It's hard to argue about what you can't argue about. It seems to me that evolutionary psychologists would close the door on interpretation or explanation the way (as Scruton later points out) Sunni Muslims closed the door on interpretation of the Koran many centuries ago. Now there's a thought!

At this point Scruton advises the reader that he intends to argue that "functional explanations of the evolutionary kind have no bearing on the content of our religious beliefs and emotions." He has laid down his marker. Now he has to persuade us.

Aboutness

Scruton proposes to give two reasons for debunking evolutionary explanations of religious belief:

> *The first is this: explanations of the kind popularized in the contemporary literature overlook the aspect of our mental states that is most important to us, and through which we understand and act upon each other's motives, namely, their intentionality or "aboutness."*

The aboutness of our mental states, Scruton argues, is self-evident. Consciousness can only exist as consciousness of something. This second formal move on the chessboard of his argument builds on the previous move, where he shifted the ground of the argument from the objective point of view of an outside observer to the subjective point of view of a free human subject. He makes the argument specifically about subjective mental states, just the thing that evolutionary psychologists must "overlook" if they are to be scientific.

"How can you overlook," he seems to say to them (and to the reader), "the fact that you are a human subject? You are not an automaton. You have freely chosen to study a question 'about' people's mental states to prove that they are really adaptations and not applications of reason by a free human subject, and you pursue this question with a passionate interest. But this is just one example of how a human subject can have an interest. If you are in love, you have a passionate interest in the person you love. You find over time, though, that you don't know everything 'about' her. She says or does something that comes 'out of the blue,' maybe something you don't like. It probably happens more than once because she, like every human subject, has a unique perspective on the world. You wonder 'about' what she says or does. What does it say 'about' her mental state? If what she said was critical of you, what does it say 'about' you? This is the stuff of relationship that you ignore to your peril, if you value the relationship."

"How," he goes on in my imagined dressing down, "can you ignore the core function of your own mind, which attaches itself to thoughts 'about' the world and to thoughts 'about' yourself in relation to others? In your own work, the intentionality of the mind, its aboutness, is the aspect of your mental state that is most important to you. You obviously love your work. Because you are attached to your theory of a selfish gene, do you get annoyed or angry when someone like me doesn't agree with your explanation? If you do, congratulations. You are not an automaton. You are a free human subject who thinks about things, loves them, judges them, and fears your own limitations."

Scruton then contrasts Freud's explanation of incest with that of an evolutionary psychologist. Freud does not give "a true causal explanation of the incest taboo, but rather a redescription of it as part of a rational strategy, though one pursued by the unconscious." Freud wants to explain:

> *. . . not only why incest is forbidden, but why the thought of [about] it affects us in the deepest reaches of our being. The disgust we feel, and which led Oedipus to stab out his eyes and Jocasta to hang herself, has a peculiar intentionality or directness. It focuses on the idea that this is my sister, mother, brother, or father, and it tells me that any sexual contact would be a kind of pollution, a spoiling of something that will never afterward be the same. Incest is therefore seen as an existential crime, one that changes what we are, both to ourselves and to others.*

For the evolutionary psychologist:

> *. . . it would be sufficient that incest should arouse disgust, in the way rotten flesh or feces arouse disgust. The thought processes add nothing to the reproductive function.*

This contrast in itself does not resolve the argument as to whether the disgust of incest is more accurately explained as a thought about something or an adaptation, so Scruton goes on to point out a hole in the evolutionary theory that effectively deflates it. The thought processes, described by the theory as instinctual:

> *. . . add nothing to the reproductive function. On the contrary, they compromise it, by winding it into the peculiar intentionality of our personal relations, causing us to lift this reproductive error out of the dark realm of biology into the light of moral reflection, and so to find not only reasons against incest, but reasons for it too—of the kind familiar to the Egyptian pharaohs, or the kind that impressed themselves on Siegmund and Sieglinde in their sole moment of joy [in* Die Walküre *by Wagner].*

Intentional thought processes, he points out, can change a "true" belief about incest (that incest represents a reproductive error) into a "false" belief about incest (that incest represents a reproductive gain). The incest taboo compromises the evolutionary explanation because that explanation does not account for *the aboutness of* (*an interest in*) incest whereby it:

> *. . . enters into our thinking and is in turn transformed by that thinking into something that may be wanted as well as forbidden.*

If a scientist is interested in material facts, he can't easily ignore a practice that was not limited to Egyptians and Germans. Also, he could check out the lineage of the Greek gods where incest is quite prominent.

These initial moves are characteristic of Scruton's arguments. This above all: he must ground the argument as we are grounded—in the world as it is observed and understood by a human subject. We are conscious, language-using, self-identifying human beings who think *about* the world. The thought of incest "affects us in the deepest reaches of our being," and this prepares the reader for the argument to follow that the thought of the sacred also affects us in the deepest reaches of our being. The mind of a human subject is the lynchpin to any inquiry having to do with human happiness, and for what other reason would we pursue an inquiry into our life as a human subject. Before closing this section, I also would like to note the good humor with which he proceeds. He likes to surprise his reader with the sudden insight that emerges from telling little ironies so that even as perilous a subject as incest has a humorous twist in store for us.

Thinking beyond Our Genetic Needs

Like the previous two arguments, Scruton's second reason for disregarding evolutionary explanations remains securely grounded in the world as a human subject experiences it. He observes that evolutionary explanations:

> *. . . cannot take note of the internal order of our states of mind. Evolution explains the connection between our thoughts and the world, and between our desires and their fulfillment, in pragmatic terms. We think and feel in ways that promote the goal of reproduction. But our mental states have no such goal. We pursue the true, the good and the beautiful, even though the false, the nasty and the messy might have been just as useful to our genes.*

For example, mathematics developed far beyond the "conundrums of a hunter gatherer":

> *So what is it that explains the crucial fact: that our thinking "latches on" to a realm of necessary truth, reaching infinitely beyond the puzzles that we need to solve? Once over the hump, from an innumerate to a numerate creature, the human species was able to run forward into this new pasture, enjoying its wonderful fruit of futile knowledge, building theories and proofs, and in general transforming its vision without any benefits to its reproductive potential—or without benefits that come too late to exert any evolutionary pressure in favor of the research that produces them.*

This is what I mean by the poetry and wit of Roger Scruton. As we are carried along by the sudden grace of this numerate creature running free in a wonderland, we may jump over the word *research* near the end of the passage. A human subject, though, may also pause to wonder about it, and when we do, we realize it must (humorously) refer to the mindless work of countless genes forever on the "lookout" for a reproductive advantage. The "benefits" of their "research" come too late to exert any evolutionary pressure because the genes have run "over the hump" into a pasture of "futile knowledge." That part of his second sentence after the dash, which concludes the passage, is not just humorous. It throws evolutionary theory into a bottomless pit of meaning.

Math is not the only pasture where this creature gains "understanding of the world by interpreting signs and symbols." These interpretations:

> *... unfold another vision of the world than that contained in the theory of evolution. Language is the most striking example of this. We don't know how it arose. But we do know that language enables us to understand the world as no dumb animal could possibly understand it. Language enables us to distinguish truth and falsehood; past, present, and future; possible, actual, and necessary, and so on. It is fair to say that we live in another world from non-linguistic creatures. They live in nature; we stand forever at its edge.*

Again, for this work (of understanding and meaning) we have language and poetry. We stand forever at the "edge" of two worlds—the natural world and a human world (Scruton later refers to the human world as the Lebenswelt, the lifeworld) that language enables us to interpret. We know what it's like to be at the edge of a cliff and to wonder what it would be like to fall, or to be at the threshold of a house and to wonder who lives inside. Knowing this helps us to imagine our place at Scruton's "edge" and to differentiate ourselves from mindless genes incapable of wonder.

Having grounded his argument in the world of a language-using human subject, Scruton ventures next to explore an important feature of that world: the mind of a human subject that's capable of sacrifice. His image of a creature running free in its new pasture recalls Augustine's wonder as he explores his inner life:

> *The fields, the caves, the dens of Memory cannot be counted; their fulness cannot be counted nor the kinds of things counted that fill them . . . I force my way in amidst them, even as far as my power reaches, and nowhere find an end.*

Scruton's argument can now run on into the field of Mind, including the memories that prompt human emotions and motivations. Specifically, though, he focuses on the thoughts and emotions that lie behind altruism, for his argument concerning religion begins with Durkheim's definition of *the core religious experience*: membership in a group and the sacrifice of oneself for the greater good of others.

> *Since emotions and motives are founded on thoughts, our emotional life and our motives to act will be of an entirely different kind from those of other animals. This is surely why we should question those theories of altruism as an "evolutionary stable strategy" . . . For altruism in people is not just an instinctive thing, even if it has an instinctive component. It is also a considered response, based sometimes on agape or neighbor love, sometimes on complex interpersonal emotions like pride and shame, which are in turn founded on the recognition of the other as another like me. In all cases altruism in people involves the judgment that what is bad for the other is something that I have a motive to remedy. And the existence of that thought is precisely what is not explained by the theory that tells us that altruism is also a dominant strategy in the game of reproduction.*

The theory of evolution can't explain the existence of "that thought" (the recognition of another like me), which is a different way of expressing the golden rule, because it's a thought that can only occur in a relationship between two human subjects, just the thing that science must overlook.

In my reading of *The Allegory of Love* earlier in the chapter, I described another route to the golden rule—the road to the wholeness of the soul as it is represented in an allegory: "Like the development of allegory, the soul in an allegory is one from beginning to end. In addition to this ontological oneness, its substance is informed by a simple, ethical rule, which tells us to do unto others as we would have them do unto us. This is easier for us to understand and to do when our sense of life as a living soul gathers another as one with ourselves" (originally appeared on page 248). The truth of the golden rule may appear to some as a vision or a revelation, like an Athena fully formed out of the forehead of Zeus. Scruton, on the other hand, is describing how difficult, interpersonal relationships lead a person over time to recognize the other as another like me. It's a process, which involves pride and shame, whereby two combatants—like Palamon and Arcite in "The Knight's Tale" and Oberon and Titania in *A Midsummer Night's Dream*—realize the truth of it gradually and grudgingly through months of combat.

Now that this language-using, symbol-interpreting creature has run into the pasture of interpersonal relationships, Scruton can point to ethics as a "realm of necessary truth," like mathematics, which helps us to solve "puzzles" in the world of values. For that matter, science is a realm of necessary truth, which helps us to explain the natural world. This last argument, which gives us a certain perspective on the work of science, suggests the terms Scruton would be willing to accept in a rapprochement with science. Mathematics, philosophy, and great poetry (like that we find in Genesis, Homer, Dante, Chaucer, Shakespeare, and Goethe) imagine a realm of necessary truth, which connects our thoughts to the world in a way that speeds our flourishing in a world of natural forces and a lifeworld of interpersonal relations. Both realms—science and the humanities—deserve respect for the good they do.

The Step from Useful Instinct to Directed Thought

Part 1: Government by Sheer Chance or Teleological Laws

Before moving on to the next stage of his argument, Scruton sums up the last two moves (his reasons for debunking evolutionary explanations of religious belief) in a single sentence:

> *We think about the world, and this means thinking beyond our genetic needs, to the world of which we are a part.*

The next sentence moves his argument further into the mechanical defenses of a scientific worldview:

> *From the evolutionary point of view it is a sheer chance that we made this step, from useful instinct to directed thought.*

In addition to the poetry, like the humorous grace of a numerate creature running "over the hump" into his pasture, Scruton's prose summary of our progress "from useful instinct to directed thought" packs into six words the meaning that emerges from countless centuries of human development. The simplicity, ease, and compactness of his prose are characteristics of great poetry. Since it's a characteristic of Goethe's prose as well as his poetry, I wonder if Scruton was inspired by Goethe's writing in both forms.

Scruton breaches the idea that human beings evolved by *sheer chance*, however, by offering an opposing view:

> *One philosopher, Thomas Nagel, has argued that such a thing cannot be a mere chance, suggesting the universe must therefore be governed by teleological laws. On Nagel's view it is a law of nature that our scientific thinking tends toward the good, and maybe (though he doesn't go this far) our tastes toward the beautiful.*

Scruton tables this question for a later chapter, but he seizes the advantage he has gained by putting Nagel's teleological alternative to "sheer chance" into play on his chessboard. He is ready to assert:

> *Whatever we think of it, we must acknowledge that evolutionary psychology cannot give a complete picture either of our states of mind, or of the universe that is represented in them.*

For example, it can't account for Thomas Nagel's mental state, the thing that's most important to him, which presents the thought of a teleological universe as a credible and desirable possibility.

Part 2: The Outside View Is a Kind of Fiction

To defend his own position, Scruton looks back to the defenses he has set up in his argument. The theory of evolution, he reminds us, "is itself a scientific theory." By this he means that it is an example of thinking that goes beyond our genetic needs:

> *We have reason to believe it only because we trust that the directness of our thinking is not an accidental byproduct of the evolutionary process but an independent guide to the way things are, whose credentials go beyond its adaptive benefits.*

To interpret this passage, it helps to recall the passage earlier in the text where he points out that math is not the only pasture where this creature gains "understanding of the world by interpreting signs and symbols." For example, the interpretations of language, Scruton told us, "unfold another vision of the world than that contained in the theory of evolution," for "language enables us to distinguish truth and falsehood; past, present, and future; possible, actual, and necessary, and so on" (see page 257). When looked at from this perspective, we see that the outside view of a scientific theory, the view that claims to be "objective," is a kind of fiction. It's *a vision* of "an independent guide." This fiction can only derive from a human consciousness, which in turn derives from language, from the values embedded in a language, and from the need human beings have to make choices based on that consciousness and those values.

Scruton then sums up the problem with an outside view by concluding:

> *The theory of evolution may seem to offer an outside view of science. But it is written in the language of science.*

And language, Scruton has argued, is not a material object. It has to be a mental state, for that's the only place we'll find it. As such, it can't be studied or credentialed by science. Nevertheless, science claims to be an outside view of the way things are even though it derives from subjective mental states that go beyond their adaptive benefits.

Part 3: Judge Not by a Much-Loved Theory but by Survival Value

Scruton has one more move to disarm the claim that the scientific theory of evolution is the only explanation for how our species relates to the world:

> *If the theory really did offer an outside view, then it could conceivably have led to the conclusion that false beliefs have a better survival value than true ones, and therefore that all our beliefs are likely to be false.*

A scientist explains something through contingent, empirical evidence. In other words, the explanation could be false. This argument is like the one he made earlier, when he observed that:

> *We think and feel in ways that promote the goal of reproduction. But our mental states have no such goal. We pursue the true, the good and the beautiful, even though the false, the nasty and the messy might have been just as useful to our genes.*

Because we think beyond our genetic needs, we are free to pursue the things we love rather than the things we abhor, even if the things we abhor may be better at fulfilling our genetic needs. (Something like this issue is debated in Plato's *Republic*. Thrasymachus finds justice in the ugliness of a city where a ruthless strongman rules, whereas Socrates finds justice in the beauty of a city where everyone minds their own business.)

In the first quote, Scruton points to the possibility that a "false belief" has a better survival value than an "outside" view of the matter (an objective, third-person, scientific view). What now can we (objectively) conclude about an outside view?

> *Even if it's true [because it's scientific], it is likely to be false. In other words, if we attempt to reach the high ground of naturalism by this route, we encounter a version of the liar paradox: an obstacle to which there is only one response—turn back.*

Scruton has imagined a version of the liar paradox (a Cretan declaring, "All Cretans are liars") to debunk the truth value and survival value of evolution. His little joke about scientific "naturalism" requires some unpacking. To see what he may mean, I'll fill in some gaps that the original statement omitted:

> *If the theory [of evolution] really did offer an outside view [a view of the truth], then it could conceivably have led us to conclude that false beliefs [beliefs in God and God's providence] have a better survival value than true ones [beliefs in scientific theories about the development of a species, which have a basis in material reality], and therefore that all our [scientific] beliefs [about why human beings behave the way they do] are likely to be false.*

It may well be that what a scientist regards as a false belief, like believing in God, has a better survival value for human beings than believing in sheer chance. This explains why Scruton begins the argument about outside views with Nagel's thought that the universe must be governed by teleological laws. Science has a theory, and Nagel has a theory.

Have evolutionary scientists thoroughly investigated this question of survival value? Isn't it possible that human subjects (and human societies) who put their faith in a transcendent God will have a better survival value than human subjects (and human societies) who put their faith in a selfish gene that has been "translated" (by the miracle of natural selection) into a selfless gene? Is it possible evolutionary scientists refuse to study this or ignore evidence so they can preserve their theory? Can any fair-minded person in our own time ignore the evidence provided by the twentieth century of human subjects (and human societies that adamantly denied the existence of a transcendent God) hell-bent on self-destruction. Scruton has run over the hump into this wonderful pasture of philosophy, which allows him to pose these questions. What he suggests here is entirely possible, but it's only possible if the person inquiring into the question is prepared to entertain a view of the truth as opposed to the view of a much-loved theory.

If we wonder how a Cretan can make a statement that isn't a lie, we also might wonder how a subjective human being can make an objective statement about the way the world works. Scruton gets us out of the box, however, by suggesting that statements (or beliefs) in this case can be judged by their "survival value." Evolutionary psychologists believe they hold the high ground over this business of survival value because their view is grounded in the objective reality that science studies, but Scruton undercuts their position as he builds his argument in this chapter and beyond.

The Mind of Winged Liberty

How does this chapter move forward an inquiry about the soul? To build his argument about the sacred soul of the world, Scruton must first debunk scientific explanations that negate human freedom. For science to work within its mandate, Scruton argues, it must overlook the aspect of our mental states that is most important to us. Because our thinking is free to latch on "to a realm of necessary truth" (see page 259), human subjects think about puzzles in the world of values as well as mathematical puzzles. This realm frees us from acting merely on instinct.

I've already pointed out how Scruton's image of a creature running free in a new pasture recalls Augustine's wonder as he explores his inner life:

> *The fields, the caves, the dens of Memory cannot be counted; their fulness cannot be counted nor the kinds of things counted that fill them . . . I force my way in amidst them, even as far as my power reaches, and nowhere find an end.*

I previously employed this quote to show how the aboutness of our thinking goes beyond our genetic needs (see pages 256–259). Here, at the end of this section on debunking, I would point out that for both Augustine and Scruton this is not an exploration of random objects and unrelated experiences. They are accidents of one substance, just as our body is one substance consisting of many parts. With Augustine in mind, I write of Scruton that his: ". . . argument can now run on into the field of Mind, including the memories that prompt human emotions and motivations. Specifically, though, he focuses on the thoughts and emotions that lie behind altruism, for his argument concerning religion begins with Durkheim's definition of *the core religious experience*: membership in a group and the sacrifice of oneself for the greater good of others."

I have illustrated this chapter with the Winged Liberty Dime, the coin that covered the cost of a comic book in the 1950s. After choir practice, Mr. Hurst, the director, paid us with one of those dimes. Liberated at last, we ran from Saint Christopher's over the trestle bridge to the tavern across the river to buy a Coke with it. Some will contend that this behavior was socially determined. We were conditioned by our environment to run there and buy that product. Thus opines the outside observer, but that's not how *we* saw it. Once choir practice was done, we chose to run across the river in a communal act of our own. We were free to run and spend as we would. There was another principle involved beside the one favored by modern social scientists. We had worked, and the dime was our reward for work. The dime was the freedom that came from work.

Scruton argues throughout his presentation in the book that we are endowed with the mind of Winged Liberty, as the coin shows us. The war, when so many signed up to fight for liberty against totalitarian enemies, was still fresh in the national memory during the 1950s. *Life* magazine published *A Picture History of World War II*, which showed in graphic detail the many ways men died fighting for their country, including Americans. My brothers and I found it one day in our library. What a power those pictures had over our imaginations.

Just as Scruton grounds his argument in the human subject, he grounds his argument in the freedom of a human subject. He gives the mind wings in the form of these initial debunkings. Having debunked the claim that the religious thought is an instinct driven by a selfish gene, he prepares us to study the thought on its own terms.

Chapter 5
The Epistemology of Religious Thoughts

Claude Lorrain's

Ulysses Returns Chryseis to Her Father

An Analogy with Dreams

Now that we have made that step "from useful instinct to directed thought," Scruton would establish an epistemology of the religious thought. One could say this exercise is an example of intentionality running over the hump into a philosophic pasture. He began his inquiry by grounding it in the lifeworld of a human subject. It must be conceded that a human subject has a unique perspective on the world; we view it from our own body and its place in the world. It also must be conceded that human subjects are unlike other creatures in that we are self-conscious, language-using, symbol-interpreters who inhabit a culture. Unlike animals who live in the natural world, we live on the edge of it. There we receive intimations about the world unavailable to creatures that aren't equipped to receive them. This gives us a freedom they don't have, for they live by instinct.

Once he has made it clear that the subject inquiring into this question is a language-using symbol-interpreter who has thoughts *about* the world that go beyond his genetic needs, Scruton can turn his attention to his subject's thoughts about religion. He has now shown why he can argue that:

> *To explain religion in terms of its reproductive function is to leave unexplained and indeed unperceived the central core of the phenomenon, which is the religious thought—the aboutness of the urge to sacrifice, of the need to worship and obey, of the trepidation of the one who approaches holy and forbidden things and who prays for their permission.*

Because we are free to run over the hump into new worlds of thought, human subjects can have the religious thought, like the ones Durkheim and others have had. Since his argument, however, has turned on the grounding of his inquiry in a human subject:

> *. . . it does not follow that the explanation of this thought is to be found elsewhere than in the biological and social circumstances of the person in whom it occurs.*

He knows that he is writing for a modern, skeptical reader who requires rational persuasion about these matters. For grizzled skeptics, miracles and revelations are illusions, and blind faith in transcendence is not an option. He must build his case with common sense reasoning. So what is the epistemology of the religious thought? What do we know about this thought?

Scruton begins with a hypothesis:

> *Religious thoughts might be like dream thoughts, which we trace not to the objects represented in them, but to things going on in the nervous system during sleep.*

He is hardly the first to suggest this. Chaucer's "The Nun's Priest's Tale" has a passage that makes this argument. Chanticleer the cock roared and screamed on account of a dream, and he woke up his goodwife, gracious Lady Pertelote. Chanticleer explains:

> *I dreamt that roaming up and down a while*
> *Within our yard I saw a kind of beast,*
> *A sort of hound that tried or seemed at least*
> *To try and seize me . . . would have killed me dead!*
> *His color was a blend of yellow and red,*
> *His ears and tail were tipped with sable fur*
> *Unlike the rest; he was a russet cur.*
> *Small was his snout, his eyes were glowing bright.*
> *It was enough to make one die of fright.*
> *That was no doubt what made me groan and swoon.*

Lady Pertelote roundly upbraids him:

> *Alas, what cowardice! By God above,*
> *You've forfeited my heart and lost my love.*
> *I cannot love a coward, come what may.*
> *For certainly, whatever we may say,*

All women long—and O that it might be!—
For husbands tough dependable and free,
Secret, discreet, no niggard, not a fool
That boasts and then will find his courage cool
At every trifling thing.

Chanticleer has lost her love because he has mistaken a dream for reality and has shown fear in the face of it. To cure him of his fantasies, she interprets the event the way a scientist or a positivist would. She confines the event to the material world:

No doubt the redness in your dream to-night
Comes from the superfluity and force
Of the red choler in your blood. Of course.
That is what puts a dreamer in the dread
Of crimson arrows, fires flaming red,
Of great red monsters making as to fight him,
And big red whelps and little ones to bite him.

Pertelote denies that dreams have anything to do with intimations from another world. Since the problem arises from the chemistry of his own gut, he can cure the problem with a laxative and a purge.

Now that he's fully awake, Chanticleer vigorously defends himself with four pages of learned examples to prove that:

Dreams have quite often been significations
As well of triumphs as of tribulations
That people undergo in this life.
This needs no argument at all, dear wife,
The proof is all too manifest indeed.

In the end, his examples have the effect of persuading himself, if not Lady Pertelote. Emboldened by the way he has won the day with his goodwife, he forgets the warning present in his own theory about dreams, leaves the safety of his perch, and spends the day in the yard.

Scruton acknowledges a critique like Pertelote's in the quote above about "things going on in the nervous system during sleep," but he acknowledges Chanticleer's position as well by observing that:

> *. . . there are cultures in which dreams are regarded as the principal vehicle through which the gods and their doings make themselves known. For that very reason, however, they do not share our theories concerning the bodily origin of dreams. Rather, they think of dreams as giving access to another realm and the beings that haunt it.*

Chaucer presents the same idea in his narrative, for the rest of the tale would seem to contradict Pertelote's reading of the dream. A fox comes into the yard later that day and seizes Chanticleer. Confronted with the actual beast, though, Chanticleer acquits himself well; he escapes the jaws of the beast with a clever appeal to the fox's self-love. (Perhaps his experience has taught him something about the vulnerabilities of self-love.) It's a victory for directed thought over an instinctual response to flattery.

Both Chaucer and Scruton are asking the epistemological question about a dream, "What do we know about it?" Does it exist entirely within the closed system of our physical body, or is it a message from a transcendent world? The question also applies to religious thoughts. Do they emerge from the closed system of a human body? Do we merely project the gods onto the screen of our imaginations—which is Feuerbach's view of them, as Scruton points out in the next chapter? We can pose the question, but at this point he doesn't answer it. Scruton concludes from his analogy with dreams simply "that there is a real problem with the epistemology of religious thoughts."

An Argument against Naturalizing the Epistemology of Religious Thoughts

Part 1: A Brief History of the Epistemology

He then develops the question "What do we know about the religious thought?" with a brief history:

> *The theological tradition to which we are heirs—which begins with Plato and Aristotle, and which achieves its high point of sophistication in medieval times, with Avicenna, Averroes, Maimonides, and Aquinas—tends to the view that there is one and only one God, who is the creator and sustainer of the physical world, but who is also transcendental, outside space and time, and therefore not part of the physical world. Fast forwarding to Kant's* Critique of Pure Reason, *and then a bit further to Einstein's theory of relativity, we move to the conclusion that such a God cannot be part of the system of causes, since the space-time continuum is the matrix in which causes occur. If there is such a thing as (in Eliot's words) "the point of intersection of the timeless with time," it is not discoverable to physics. In which case there can be no causal connection between God and our thoughts of him.*

The worldview of science has changed the study of knowledge. For example, if something is not discoverable by physics, Scruton writes, a modern philosopher like W. V. O. Quine would excise it as a subject for philosophic inquiry; he would "naturalize" epistemology. According to Quine, we should "look on epistemological questions from outside, as questions concerning the relation between an organism and its environment." True beliefs about this relation "link the organism to its environment in the right way, so as to give reliable information about their causes." True beliefs would eliminate "deviant causal chains" precipitated by illusions and false beliefs. This ontology:

> *. . . does not contain the creatures of our dreams or the characters in fiction; nor does it contain the gods and spirits that haunt our lives, however dear to us these are, and however impossible it may be to free ourselves from the belief in their existence.*

These thinkers are positivists, like Pertelote. Their knowledge is strictly limited to the physical world.

Part 2: An Epistemological Stalemate

Scruton's next move in his argument is a feint in Quine's direction. If we accept that:

> *. . . God is a transcendental being, who lies outside the space-time continuum, then it is a deep, perhaps even a necessary, truth that God has no causal role to play in the beliefs that target him—or in any other event in space and time.*

A modern secular reader most likely would agree with this statement. Having drawn the reader in, Scruton springs the trap:

> *If this is sufficient to exclude God from our ontology, then many other things too must be excluded. We also have beliefs about numbers, sets, and other mathematical objects. And these too are outside space and time, or at any rate have no causal role in the physical world . . . Suffice it to say that there have been advances in sophistication, but no advances in consensus, concerning the issue of mathematical truth. And this means that the issue of theological truth cannot be closed so simply as the atheists wish.*

If there is no connection between God and our thoughts of Him because He is transcendental, then believers cannot give a causal explanation for their belief. But if the belief must be explained as a biological, social, or cultural process, these explanations cannot show the belief to be false. God evades any thought for or against Him. In addition, Scruton has called into question the truth value of mathematics; like the sacred, math is "outside space and time." This move on the chessboard of his argument undercuts the whole scientific project, which to a large extent is grounded in mathematical reasoning.

To move his argument beyond this stalemate, Scruton introduces into it the real presence of the sacred.

The Real Presence

Part 1: A Focus on the Content of the Thought

He opens the next section, which is titled "The Real Presence," by commenting on his argument that the issue of theological truth cannot be closed so simply as the atheists wish:

> *That is not an argument for the truth of religious belief, but only a suggestion that will shift the onus away from the believer.*

A thought about God, in other words, is like someone brought to trial in our system of justice. It is innocent until proven to be otherwise, which, in this case, it can never be.

Now that the onus lies with the prosecutor and not the defendant, this shift:

> *. . . is tantamount to the demand that the atheist find arguments directed at the content of the belief, rather than arguments directed at its origins.*

Part 2: The Problem of God's Presence

Scruton has redirected his argument, but he quickly moves on, for:

> *. . . a new problem now arises, and it is one that has been familiar to Jewish, Christian, and Muslim theology from the early Middle Ages, and this is the problem of God's presence. This problem will be my starting*

point, and so I need to set it out carefully.

Here we are, ten pages into closely argued ideas, and we have just reached the starting point, the threshold of the real presence. Given the importance of the place, we would do well to consider it as carefully as he has set it out.

The problem has to do with God's nature as it has been presented in the Bible and with our nature as limited, subjective human subjects:

> *That God is present among us and communicating directly with us is a central claim of the Old Testament. This "real presence" or shekhinah is, however, a mystery. God reveals himself by concealing himself, as he concealed himself from Moses in the burning bush, and as he conceals himself from his worshippers in the Tabernacle (mishkhan) and the Holy of Holies.*

It's God's nature to reveal Himself by concealing Himself. This looks like another stalemate, but our author now helps us to wrestle with it as best a limited, subjective human subject can.

Part 3: How We Settle in the Lifeworld

By examining the biblical words and their root meanings, Scruton establishes that the real presence is closely linked to the idea of settlement:

> *The nouns shekhinah and mishkhan are both from the verb shakhan, to dwell or settle: sakana in Arabic, from which is derived the noun shekhinah, used here and there in the Koran . . . to describe the peace or comfort that comes from God. Dwelling and settling are the underlying themes of the Torah, which tells the story of the Promised Land, and of the people who finally settle there, to build in Jerusalem the temple whose design and rituals were given to Moses, and which will be a dwelling place for God. As the narrative makes clear, it is not the chosen people only who are in search of a place to settle: it is God too, who can dwell among them only by being ritually concealed from them. As God says to Moses, no man shall look upon my face and live.*

The way we settle in the world invites the real presence. I think in this respect of Abraham who would not "settle" his faith in the worship of idols. In response to this man's great conviction, the Lord God spoke to him and promised a land worthy of settlement.

In my reading of Scruton's argument, I equate the human subject's desire for a settled home with the human subject's desire for meaning in the world. In this interpretation, God gives the lifeworld meaning. Even if He has concealed himself, we still can sense a presence that settles us in a meaningful life. Without the real presence, the lifeworld would lose its center, the purpose and meaning that leads to human flourishing. Without that focus, human beings suffer a flood of meanings and goals fatal to life. Water, the double-edged sword! We need it to survive, but we can also drown in it. To survive, we need the ark that God showed Noah how to build; we need those concrete pillars driven through the water, the sand, and the clay down to bedrock to be a foundation for the House of God; we need the House of God to be the axis around which our homes are built.

The focus in the quote on dwelling and settling develops the theme my text has already introduced through musings on Bernard in Book Two and in the commentary on Vermeer. God is like us in some respects; we are creators, builders of houses and cities. Like us, God seeks "a dwelling place" to settle, for like us God would live in a house. He made us in his image to build a house for Him. Just as we visit each other in our homes to develop relationships, the real presence reveals itself in interpersonal relationships, specifically here a relationship with the real presence itself.

This is how we "settle" in the lifeworld; we invite the Real Presence into it with a house that's worthy of Him. In addition to making us aware of the real presence as a possibility, even if it's a mystery, the content of a religion teaches us how to go about building that house. God's instructions to Noah were so specific; his commandments are no less so.

I have selected Lorrain's painting for this chapter because over and over in various settings he expresses this idea of settlement in his work. In addition to peaceful landscapes, he did many paintings of a safe harbor at sunset, which is the goal of a voyage. The title ties the picture to an incident in the *Iliad*, but any number of titles could be attributed to it. Odysseus, as the ambassador of the Greeks, returns Chryseis back to her father after she had been awarded to Agamemnon as a trophy of war. In this context, the painting represents the return of a moral order to a world rocked by its absence. Immediately we recognize a vision of civil peace. The sea is calm and expansive; like the harbor, it invites opportunities for commerce and the enrichment of the town. The people gather at the place where sea-paths and land-paths meet. From the shapes of the buildings, the waterfront, and from the ease of the people, we sense the presence of wisdom built into the place.

If you look for Odysseus in the painting, however, you won't find him. The title has given us a purpose for looking at the picture, but at the same time it frustrates that purpose. Nevertheless, our original impression of a great peace settling over the sea, the sky, and the people in the foreground of the town still holds. In the space where we set out to see Odysseus, we're struck instead with the light, which infuses the buildings (especially the columns), the trees, the people, and the animals with a blessed, unstrained uprightness. The orderliness and firmness of these things is softened by the light even as it acts to reveal them, and we realize this is what we have been seeking. Furthermore, we're not alone. We're looking through the eyes of Claude Lorrain at something that matters a great deal to us. He has acted to represent the light and all that it reveals, and so can we. For me, the painting and the title serve as a kind of parable. Without the title, we wouldn't look for Odysseus in the picture; similarly, without the possibility that a moral order exists in the world, we wouldn't go looking for it.

Part 4: Knowledge of His Presence and a Terrible Truth

The word *shekhinah* (the sacred) is lit from within by our need in the life-world for "settlement" in relationships. We understand a relationship with the sacred through this metaphor of settlement, but the "mystery" of it (see the quote in part 2) removes it from the way we experience relationships in the space-time continuum. This is what Scruton wrestles with through the rest of the paragraph:

> *And the whole tormented story of the relation between God and the chosen people brings home to us the terrible truth, which is that God cannot show himself in this world, except by hiding from those whom he traps into trusting him, as he trapped the Jews. The knowledge of his presence comes with the failure to find him.*

The next paragraph dramatizes the difficulty inherent in an encounter with "an eternal, transcendental being":

> *A direct personal encounter with God, when God is understood in the philosophical way of Avicenna or Aquinas, is no more possible than a direct personal encounter with the number 2. Now you see through a glass darkly, wrote St. Paul, but then face-to-face. However, by "then" he meant "beyond the here and now" in the transcendental realm where God resides. Saint Paul may seem to be denying the hidden nature of God; in fact he is affirming it.*

The rest of Scruton's book will wrestle with the problem he calls his starting point and a terrible truth: that the knowledge of God "comes with the failure to find him."

Part 5: The Real Phenomena of Faith

This starting point, though, is also a turning point. Scruton admits the difficulty around the thought of God:

> *And yet the experience of the "real presence" is at the heart of revealed religion, and foundational to the liturgy and ritual both of the synagogue and of the main Christian churches. It is important to grasp this point.*

This starting point is a turning point if we can wholeheartedly commit to a quest that moves us out of our modern comfort zone—common knowledge as scientific disciplines define it. Skeptics, he writes, compare religious beliefs with scientific beliefs, which can be proven or disproven through observation and experiment in the physical world:

> *Many of those who currently write against religion (and specifically against the Christian religion) seem to think that faith is simply a matter of entertaining beliefs of a cosmological kind, concerning the creation of the world and the hope of eternal life. And these beliefs are imagined to be in some ways rivals to the theories of physics, and exposed to refutation by all that we know of the evolution of the universe.*

Skeptics insist, in other words, on maintaining the view of an objective third-person observer. Scruton reminds us, though, that he has moved the inquiry out of a third-person perspective and into the first-person perspective of someone actively engaged with, as Durkheim defines it, "the experience of myself as a member of something, called upon to renounce my interests for those of the group and to celebrate my membership of the group in acts of devotion that might have no other justification than that they are commanded."

To that definition, Scruton now adds his own description:

> *But the real phenomena of faith are nothing like that [entertaining beliefs of a cosmological kind]. They include prayer and the life of prayer; the love of God and the sense of his presence in the life of the faithful; obedience and submission in the face of temptation and the things of this world; the experience of certain times, places, objects and words as "sacred," which is to say, in Durkheim's phrase, as "set aside and forbidden," reserved to uses that can be understood only on the assumption that these experiences mediate between this world and another that is not otherwise revealed to us.*

Once again, he addresses the religious thought as the thought of a human subject "that is most important to us" (see page 253) and not a fact that's confirmed by an "outside view" (which Quine insists upon, pages 272–273). For example, if I have the thought, "Why was I born and why must I die?" a thought—or a question, rather—of great importance to me, Quine's insistence on an outside view disables the question as there is no outside view on the subject. Throughout his first chapter and the rest of the book, Scruton is continually working the ground of his argument—an image suggested by the fact that Scruton actively worked the ground of his farm in Wiltshire—as he moves us along on our pilgrimage to a sacred place. In the above passage on the phenomena of faith, Scruton returns to the position he takes in the opening paragraphs of the book, where he contrasts the commentators' view of religion with the Islamists' view of it. We're back where we started. When it comes to the thought of religion, given its difficulty, I think we will always be coming back to where we started.

Part 6: Nobody and the Real Presence

Having described the real phenomena of faith, he is ready to move on:

> *Two immensely difficult questions arise from those thoughts. They are not questions for ordinary believers. But they are fundamental to understanding what is at stake in the religious worldview.*

I have argued and will continue to argue that Scruton has written a book that functions like training wheels for skeptics who might be tempted to ride the thought about religion; those familiar with a life of prayer don't need them. After the fanfare of these three sentences, anyone still reading surely would like to learn what the two questions are:

> *The first is metaphysical, namely, how is it possible for the transcendental to manifest itself in the empirical—for the eternal God to be a real presence in the life of his earthly worshippers? The second is conceptual, namely, what is the thought that animates the encounter with sacred things: what concepts, beliefs, and perceptions define the intentionality of faith?*

How carefully he has proceeded. He has already discussed intentionality as a mental state that's "most important" for human subjects. Intentionality, he told us there, is a given—a priori. This explains an authorial decision:

The first of those questions is one that I shall postpone, since I don't believe it can be answered until we have become clear about the second question.

Because the intentionality of the religious thought is (a priori) solid ground, it's the path on which his argument can proceed.

Even though the metaphysical question can't be addressed until we are clear about the intentionality of the religious thought, before closing this section he writes preemptively to defend an experience of the real presence from skeptics:

We rightly think that there is something mysterious and perhaps inexplicable about the "real presence." But nobody who has the experience of that thing is likely to think it to be simply an illusion: it comes to us with a self-verifying character that silences skepticism, even as it calls out for interpretation.

He addresses us as human subjects who are limited by shape and understanding. Because of our limitation in body and mind, we rightly think these matters are mysterious and inexplicable.

Because of this limited shape, we don't know everything, but along with this thought, Scruton puts down a marker that a skeptic can't refute. The wording, I believe, is important to him: "But nobody who has the experience of that thing is likely to think it to be simply an illusion." He might as well be saying, "But somebody who has not had the experience is not in a position to think it is an illusion." I suspect the "nobody" is important because, according to a theme this book has been developing, the experience of the real presence is only available to a Nobody. A Somebody still has too much business with his image. A Nobody, like Dante lost in a dark wood—with a heart that's both full (of worldly disappointment) and empty (from the loss of everything), is ripe for experiencing it.

Part 7: Pascal's Total Certainty

To finish the section on the real presence, Scruton gives a famous example:

> *Such was the nuit de feu of Pascal: the night of 23 November 1654 when, for two hours, he experienced the total certainty that he was in the presence of God—"the God of Abraham, of Isaac and of Jacob, not the God of the philosophers and the wise men," in other words a personal God, intimately revealed, not conjured by by abstract argument. Pere juste, le monde ne t'a point connu, mais moi, je t'ai connu, he wrote then, on the scrap of paper on which he recoded the experience: astonishing words, which only total conviction could have engendered. [Righteous Father, the world doesn't know you at all, but I, I know you.]*

How can a skeptic—who to be a skeptic must confess he doesn't know everything, who doesn't pretend to know what can't be known, who surely must admit he is not God and a perfect mind reader—how can he say Pascal is just making this up and still call himself a skeptic?

Chapter 6
Religion, Magic, and Intersubjectivity

Rembrandt's

Jacob Wrestling with the Angel

What Defines the Intentionality of Religious Faith?

Scruton now turns his attention for the next eleven pages on the conceptual, as opposed to the metaphysical, question: "What is the thought that animates the encounter with sacred things?" I confess I had a chicken or the egg question of my own about the way he has worded this question. Does the encounter somehow depend on the thought to make it live? By telling the story from the creature's point of view, are we animating not only the thought of the sacred but the sacred itself? Luckily, Scruton then rephrases the question: "What concepts, beliefs, and perceptions define the intentionality of faith?" This question allowed me to table those questions and move ahead.

He begins by contrasting religion and magic. Just as the real presence has a history, which Scruton briefly told in the last section, the question "What defines the intentionality of faith?" has a history in anthropology:

> *When anthropologists first addressed the issue of the religious frame of mind, they very quickly discovered patterns of thinking that were both widespread among human beings, and also difficult or impossible to assimilate to the aims and methods of scientific inquiry.*

In *The Golden Bough*, Sir James Frazier "writes as though magical ways of thinking begin life as an attempt at science," but they are in fact quite different. For it's clear that *science represents a world that's "wholly independent of the will of the one who is seeking to understand it* and also that magic aims less to predict results than to command them." The italicized part of the sentence is one of the most important statements in the book. As we inquire into these matters, we must have clarity: science "represents" the world as an object. The scientist is here, and the object is out there. They are in two different places. Unlike a magician, a scientist cannot command an object with words.

Scruton then deploys a thought about magic, which introduces a thought about religion that's at the heart of his argument:

> *Even if the magician needs to summon occult powers, to enlist the cooperation of gods and spirits, he is not trying to discover how nature works, or to use the laws of nature in order to produce some desired effect. He is trying to bypass prediction entirely, so as to address nature as a subject like himself—as something that can submit to his commands and be moved by his beseeching.*

As he has throughout this chapter, "Believing in God," Scruton grounds his argument in the human subject, a magician, but here he enlarges the ground concerning religion to cover an experience most of us have everyday even if we are not magicians—those many moments day or night when we address another subject, a person like ourselves. Since we know what this encounter is like (and since we know from experience that sometimes our words *can move* another subject), we can consider what Scruton has to say about the magician. With his words (his spell), Scruton explains, a magician addresses nature in a subject-to-subject relationship. Frazier had it quite wrong. Magic is an attempt at religion rather than an attempt at science. Its intersubjectivity will help Scruton to define the intentionality of the religious thought. It's a thought about another *subject*.

To make his argument about religious thought, Scruton has to remind his secular readers about that which defines the faith of his religious readers, who don't need to have the thought explained. Most people would dismiss the magician's attempt to produce an effect in nature with a spell as "superstition or idolatry":

> *But even if we put magical thinking behind us, there remains in the religious frame of mind the core thought of another subject, the god toward whom one's thoughts and feelings are directed. The real presence is not that of a mysterious nonentity, a flitting ghost, or a vision. It is the presence of a subject, a first-person singular who can be addressed, implored, reasoned with, and loved. Religious people may not entirely and completely believe that they are addressing another subject in their prayers—for their faith may be weak and vacillating, or they may enter the sacred moment with*

a measure of aesthetic distance, or in one way or another they may fail entirely to give themselves up to the immediate experience. Nevertheless their state of mind is "subject directed." It has the particular intentionality that informs all our interpersonal attitudes, and which adheres to them because they are forms of address from one person to another: a readiness to give and accept reasons, to make demands, and also to respond to demands, a recognition of mutual freedom and all the benefits and dangers that are implied by it. A readiness, as we might put it, remembering the Old Testament story of Jacob and the angel, to "wrestle with God"—the idea contained in the name Isra-el.

I quote at length because, like the quote from Frazier's *The Golden Bough* italicized above (about a world that's "wholly independent"), this is one of the most important passages in the book. To underscore its importance, I've illustrated Scruton's argument in this chapter with Rembrandt's representation of the same subject. To emphasize the importance of this *readiness*, to which he refers in the final two sentences of the quote above, I return to it several more times in the text before it has pride of place near the end, on pages 505–507.

People looking for God are "subject directed." They aren't looking for proof of God's existence, like the cosmological argument, "but for a subject-to-subject encounter, which occurs in this life, but which also in some way reaches beyond this life." Historical figures, like Saint Teresa of Avila, Margery Kempe, Saint John of the Cross, Rumi, and Pascal, Scruton writes:

. . . surely persuade us that one part, at least, of the encounter with God lies in the irruption into consciousness of an intersubjective state of mind, but one that connects with no merely human subject. And included within that state of mind is the sense of reciprocity: the sense of being targeted by the Other, I to I.

This is not, however, the end of the story Scruton has to tell about the religious thought. An individual like Jacob in Rembrandt's painting may experience a subject-to-subject encounter that reaches beyond this life. That experience, though, is intimately tied to his estrangement from Esau, his brother, for Jacob stole Esau's birthright. This aspect of the story tallies with Scruton's next observation about the human subject:

> *It has been evident at least since Durkheim that religion is a social phenomenon, and the individual search for God answers to a deep need of the species. Human beings desire to "throw in their lot" with something, to cease to be cast out, rejected, gewarfen, mere individuals, and to belong, even if the price of doing so is submission or islam. People join together in many different ways, and some, like hermits, seek to be alone with their God. But the normal tendency of the religious urge is toward membership, by which I mean a network of relations that are neither contractual nor negotiated, but which are received as a destiny and a gift.*

Scruton argues here and in his chapter 4, "The First-Person Plural," that "relations of this kind . . . precede political choice and make it possible." These relations, he tells us in this chapter:

> *. . . are the core of all true communities, and are recognized by their transcendent character—that is to say, their character as arising from outside the arena of individual choice.*

Just as Jacob didn't choose to be Esau's brother, he did not seek out an otherworldly "man" with whom he could wrestle. He had enough trouble preparing for the impending war with Esau. The man found him, though, and they wrestled all night. It ended when the man realized Jacob would not let him go. For his persistence, Jacob ended the night with a hip out of joint, a new name, and the blessing of God.

After that encounter, Jacob and Esau reconcile, and, given that encounter, we have to conclude that the reconciliation arose from outside individual choice, that the relationship of the brothers has a transcendent character. Like Moses in Chagall's picture passing through a ring of fire to become fully human (see page 31), Jacob passes through something like an alchemical process, in which he sheds his old identity. He did not choose to have this meeting. Because he had this meeting, though, he becomes a homeland and becomes also the people who live there.

Intersubjectivity and Allegory

I'll pause for a moment in this narrative of Scruton's argument to briefly consider the common ground occupied by the concepts of intersubjectivity and allegory. As we can see from Lewis's study of it, allegory is a literary form that humanizes creation. In Bernard's *De Mundi*, creation is told from the point of view of the work (human beings), not the workman (God) or an invisible third party. Allegory often takes the form of a dream, as in *The Romance of the Rose*. The world we read about in the poem is the creation of the dreamer, and we receive the work through the first-person point of view, the "I" of the poet-narrator.

In *La Vita Nuova*, Dante speaks to us from that point of view. Here are the first four lines of the first sonnet:

> *To every captive soul and gentle lover*
> *Into whose sight this present rhyme may chance,*
> *That, writing back, each may expound its sense,*
> *Greetings in Love, who is their Lord, I offer.*

In the words "I offer," we hear the voice of the poet himself offering us his rhyme. He is present to do the offering, and we are present to receive it. We, the readers, are given direct access to the man who greets us thus. Not only that but we are also invited into a relationship. Dante hopes we will write back and tell him what we think the poem means. (Surely Dante imagined people like me "writing back" to him long after he died.) *La Vita Nuova*, one of the most important poems in our literature, begins explicitly with intersubjectivity. In addition, we learn from Lewis's commentary on *La Vita Nuova* about the concept of "accidents in a substance." On consideration of this substance, I have inferred from it that the poet is one in the "I" point of view, the poem is one as an expression of the "I," and the reader is one with the poem in the experience of reading it.

Along with the "I" point of view, personifications humanize creation.

For example, Statius personifies Pietas (Compassion) and gives her, Lewis tells us, one of the most serious passages in the poem:

> *Why didst thou make me, Sovran Nature? Why*
> *Create me to oppose the cruel will*
> *Of mortals, and oft-times immortals too?*

It's a question posed from the first-person point of view with which the human subject who reads it can easily identify. At the beginning of *De Mundi*, the personification of Nature complains to the personification of Mind:

> *Lo! Matter, eldest of all things, would fain*
> *Be limited by shape and born again.*

These words, given and received, initiate creation. But for the human subject who reads them, Nature sounds like a human mother concerned for her child, her eldest. Nature doesn't use "I" or "me" to emphasize a first-person point of view. Instead, we have her longing, which is expressed directly in the exclamation "Lo!" In the human world of interpersonal communication, a whole range of feelings may prompt this "Lo!" Here, as always, it's a person's urgent appeal for another's attention. Claudian imagines a garden where trees whisper sweet nothings:

> *Each happy tree*
> *Woos and is wooed. Palms nodding from above*
> *Exchange their notes and poplar sighs for love*
> *Of poplar, plane for plane, and whispers low*
> *Of love along the alder thickets go.*

The reader hears in the love talk of trees the happy give-and-take of sentiments. Tom Snout personifies Wall in *A Midsummer Night's Dream*. It's a wall, but in the play of things it's Tom Snout. Since I know how my own reading of Scruton's chapter ends, I know that Tom plays an important part in my reading of Scruton's text near the end of Book Three.

In these allegories, collected and presented by Lewis, along with my example from *A Midsummer Night's Dream*, the world is no longer an object—it's a subject. When the story of my book is told in this way, Lewis has teed up the theme that Scruton hits down the fairway.

Chapter 7
On Defining the Thought of the Sacred

Andrew Wyeth's
Christina's World

A Passage between the Immediate and the Transcendental

Scruton has defined the thought of religion thus far as "an intersubjective state of mind, but one that connects with no merely human subject" (see the quote on page 286) and has linked this state of mind to the "deep need" in all human beings for membership in a community. I say "linked" because I don't find a causal relationship stated or implied in his presentation of these two things. They are both part of the "story" (Scruton's word) he is telling. An intersubjective state of mind, it's fair to say, is the that-without-which-nothing of a community, and an intersubjective state of mind can only develop in a community. Scruton's inquiry isn't interested in their causal relationship, or which came first. Just as we don't know the origin of language or the personal pronoun "I," we don't know the origin of communities or intersubjectivity. He would examine *the content* of religious belief, not its origins. Since membership in a group is a part of his story, he asks, "But what distinguishes religious membership from, say, kinship, nationhood, tribal loyalties, and the sense of territory and customs as 'ours'?" To answer that question, he must define *the thought of the sacred* as opposed to the thoughts behind the other groups, and this is what he now sets out to do.

As he did in the opening pages of the book, Scruton begins his inquiry into the sacred with a quote from Durkheim:

> *Durkheim writes that "a religion is a unified system of beliefs and practices relative to sacred things, that is to say, things set apart and forbidden—beliefs and practices which unite into a single moral community, called a 'church,' all those who adhere to them." But his definition simply shifts the problem onto the concepts invoked into it, the concept of the sacred and the church.*

The great social scientist defines religion as beliefs and practices relative to sacred things, but he leaves the sacred undefined.

Durkheim's characterization of the sacred, Scruton writes, "as 'set apart and forbidden' is suggestive, but far from satisfying. We want to know in what way sacred things are set apart, and how forbidden." The old theories of magic from nineteenth-century anthropologists, Scruton argues, "do not explain the sacred." As he develops his argument, he approaches that threshold with which I began my interpretation of his text:

> *There is a prosaic quality about magic, a here-and-now character, and a practicality too, which have little or nothing in common with the awe-inspiring otherworldliness of sacred things. Consider the examples familiar to us: the Eucharist, and the instruments associated with it; the prayers with which we address God; the Cross, the scroll of the Torah, the pages of the Koran. The faithful approach these things with awe, not because of their magic power, but because they seem to be both in our world, and also out of it—a passage between the immediate and the transcendental. They are both present and absent, like the mishkan and what it hides from us.*

Just as the porch of my home sets up a passage at the threshold between inside and outside, the image of a passage sets up Scruton's definition of *the sacred*:

> *That indeed seems to be a feature of the sacred in all religions. Sacred objects, words, animals, ceremonies, places, all seem to stand at the horizon of the world looking out to that which is not of this world, because it belongs in the sphere of the divine, and looking also into our world, so as to meet us face-to-face. Through sacred things we can influence and be influenced by the transcendental. If there is to be a real presence of the divine in this world, it must be in the form of some sacred event, moment, place, or encounter: so at least we humans have believed.*

In this passage (these two sentences), he has put together the metaphors that frame his thought about the sacred; it's a *passage* (between the immediate and the transcendental) on the *horizon*. Sacred objects and events are the passage, and they stand at the horizon. Like Janus, they are a medium that looks in both directions: at us in this world and into the transcendent world from which they derive.

Wyeth's *Christina's World* and the Sacred on Scruton's Horizon

A horizon, a threshold, and an edge all involve a boundary. The image of a horizon is perhaps most apt in this case because it has a spiritual quality. It exists, but it doesn't really exist. It's simply that point beyond which we cannot see, and it moves as we move. It's proof of our limitation and inspires us to look beyond it. It suggests, perhaps, why the sacred, the *mishkan*, can be both present and absent. Just as a horizon exists and doesn't exist, a sacred object isn't an ordinary object, like the booth on the border where I have to stop and show my passport.

To illustrate this chapter, I have called once more on Andrew Wyeth. What is *Christina's World*? The title indirectly asks the question, and we are called upon to answer it. The picture and the title put us in a relationship with Christina, even though she has her back turned to us. This is a characteristic of intersubjectivity. We can be right next to someone, talking, laughing, arguing, intimately interacting, but we still can only infer "the world" of that person. Christina's world, her perspective on the world as a human subject, is unique to her. To put a decisive point or period on this statement, Christina's unique perspective will die when she dies.

Nevertheless, the creator of Christina's world wants to show how much we have in common with her. Her pose suggests she has a physical limitation (everyone does), and the viewer must imagine what it is. This is the nature of interpersonal relationships. Even when we have the physical person right there in front of us expressing herself, we have to imagine the whole of the life she has led that has brought her to this moment. It's even harder when her face is turned away, and she is saying nothing.

Wyeth has painted Christina in such a way, though, that her body and the place he has put her express her inner life as vividly as a face might if we were looking eye-to-eye. It looks as if gravity, the earth, has claimed her for its own, but it can only claim half of her. The other half resists, and she rises up on her arms. In Christina's world, there are physical facts, but she is also composed of a longing that's tangible, even though a longing is in fact intangible. We can see that this has raised her up, but we still don't know the object of her longing. That's our limitation. We wonder what she wants. This wonder, too, is an immaterial something, and yet it can have great force in relationships. Our constraint, however, is not final, for there's more in the picture.

She looks to the horizon, where there's a house, several outbuildings, and another building, perhaps a barn. The buildings appear to be held or contained by a graceful oval shape in a field of brown. Perhaps it's something like a lawn, for the grass is shorter and lighter. The area defined by this shape is her home, but Christina presently is not at home. While we're on the subject of thresholds, edges, and boundaries, I think Wyeth has a thought about the horizon similar to Scruton's. Like the horizon in *Below Dover,* this one in *Christina's World* is made of earth and sky (just as we are made of earth and sky). If we look more closely, we see that the barn to the left of the house (I might as well call it a barn) has sunk slightly into the earth. Dust to dust; ashes to ashes. Perspective, human intelligence, explains the phenomenon: the barn has not sunk into the earth; it's placed on the other side of the line that serves as the horizon, the top of the hill.

The building on the right, we guess, is her house, where she very likely cooks the food, sits at table to eat and converse, and opens the door to her room to sleep at night. The other building, probably a barn for the animals and for storage of their feed, sits on the other side of the horizon. It looks as if Christina raises herself as she looks—between the building for her kind and the building beyond for the animals—for something, something beyond or between what she might, in casual conversation, have referred to as her home. It must be a hope for something, someplace, or someone, or she wouldn't long for it. In this reading of it, the painting as a whole is a medium for looking through a material body (the painting) to view a transcendent meaning. We can see Christina clearly enough, and we would see (but can't see) what she wants. There's mystery, but the painting clearly has a meaning. We recognize in it that Christina has a unique perspective, and the painting shares that perspective. Compelled by her intention, we look in the same direction. Perhaps, then, it comes to us: even though we know only a little about Christina, we share her perspective. This is a basis for relationship. Christina's world in the painting is, for a moment or two, our world, and this is a hopeful insight.

Her back is turned is turned to us, but her vulnerability may make us aware that our own back is turned to everything behind it. We may then sense that someone is looking at us looking at her—the immaterial creator of it all, Andrew Wythe. The painting makes us wonder about Christina's world, and maybe the painting returns the favor as Wythe's ghostly eyes wonder about us. We experience this, Scruton is arguing, in any intersubjective relation.

This Sacred Medium

Shall I compare thee to a summer's day?
Thou art more lovely and more temperate.
Rough winds do shake the darling buds of May,
And summer's lease hath all too short a date.
Sometime too hot the eye of heaven shines,
And often is his gold complexion dimmed;
And every fair from fair sometime declines,
By chance, or nature's changing course, untrimmed:
But thy eternal summer shall not fade
Nor lose possession of that fair thou ow'st,
Nor shall Death brag thou wand'rest in his shade
When in eternal lines to time thou grow'st.
So long as men can breathe or eyes can see,
So long lives this, and this gives life to thee.

Sonnet 18

Over the years that I studied Shakespeare's sonnets with students, I learned about the disciplined employment of a metaphoric frame. For example, in "Shall I Compare Thee," all the images relate to a summer's day; a summer's day frames everything he has to say about his love for another. The images convey the emotions associated with these images, including emotions—despite a summer's day's association with warmth, brightness, and beauty—that accompany change and loss. In the same way, I find that the image of a passage at the horizon frames what Scruton has to say about the thought of the sacred as he proceeds through the book.

Shakespeare's summer's day contains within it a wide spectrum of feeling. Ordinary face-to-face encounters with someone we love produce emotions of all kinds. When Scruton asks us to consider the thought of the sacred, we are being asked to imagine our emotions when the one we love is divine, and our language and literature strain at the limits of their capacity to oblige. For example, when Moses said to the Lord, "Please show me your glory," in Exodus 33, the Lord put him in the cleft of a rock and covered him with His hand as He passed by. Moses only saw His back. And why? The Lord had warned him, "You cannot see my face, for no man shall see me and live." The image of a passage on the horizon, however, is not a cleft in a rock, a hand in our face, or a threat of death. It invites us into this encounter in a kindly way—like the porch of a Greek temple, an invitation into a summer's day, or a glimpse into Christina's world. But before ending the chapter on "Believing in God," rough winds will shake our curiosity.

Shakespeare's song of praise is the passage, the sacred object on the horizon. It's a medium that looks in both directions. Looking into our world, it sees the darling buds of May shaken by rough winds. Looking into the sphere of the divine, it sees a lovely, temperate, eternal summer. Unlike Semele's fatal encounter with Zeus in all his glory, so long as men can breathe we can safely read Shakespeare's poem where the two worlds are represented (with incomparable artistry) as accidents of one substance.

Standing on the Edge and the Breath of Life

Scruton introduced the metaphor of an edge earlier as part of his argument that language is the most striking example of how "our thinking 'latches on' to a realm of necessary truth, reaching infinitely beyond the puzzles that we need to solve":

> *We don't know how it arose. But we do know that language enables us to understand the world as no dumb animal could possible understand it. Language enables us to distinguish truth and falsehood; past, present, and future; possible, actual, and necessary, and so on. It is fair to say that we live in another world from non-linguistic creatures. They live in nature; we stand forever at its edge.*

To be effective, the image of an edge has to be grounded in real world experiences. We know what it's like to stand on the edge of a cliff. This is a place in the real world, but this place moves us unlike most others. Do we briefly experience in our soul (before we grow more accustomed and emboldened) Death sent to us as a messenger from God? On the edge of things, at night in the silence, when everyone else and everything seems to be sleeping, in the knock-knock of my heart I'm roused to consider how "so much depends upon" that battered, indomitable red wheelbarrow in the secret dark of my chest—apparently self-sustaining except when it's not—which carries me through all the seconds, minutes, hours, days, and years of my life. We don't have to be a dare devil to live on the edge; we do it everywhere in the wide-open plains of everyday.

In Scruton's treatment of the metaphor, it isn't just an edge, a door on the threshold, or the horizon; it's a passage. As to a passage, images in the Bible come to mind, especially the walls of water on either side of the passage that God made for the Israelites through the Red Sea. This image at the heart of the Torah also calls to mind the words in the Twenty-Third Psalm about walking through the valley of the shadow of death. The Red Sea passage and the valley, in the end, bring me back to the breath, the open air way that sustains every moment of our life.

And a man's life's no more than to say "One," Hamlet tells Horatio, the time it takes to take a breath. The breath is that passage through the Sea heaped up on either side and a space for life. The voice out of the whirlwind confronts Job about this passage with a question that reverberates like doors slamming shut against a flood:

> *Who shut up the sea behind doors*
> *when it burst forth from the womb,*
> *when I made the clouds its garment*
> *and wrapped it in thick darkness,*
> *when I fixed limits for it*
> *and set its doors and bars in place,*
> *when I said, 'This far you may come and no farther;*
> *here is where your proud waves halt'?*
>
> Job 38:9–11

The breath functions like that which shuts up the sea behind doors, but it lacks the physicality of a door. Though real, it becomes for us a mystery—an invisible, indispensable part of life. The voice from the whirlwind tells Job directly that he doesn't know why this passage came to be and still saves him for life. All other questions that Job might have had about his life resolve into one: Why? Why do I breathe the breath of life?

For someone who would find an answer, the breath is a passage into another world and a sacred object, and I'm reminded what the verse in Genesis says about it:

> *and God breathed into his nostrils the breath of life*
> *and man became a living soul.*

If that's the case, then through the passage of breath the whole of life is sanctified.

The Forbidden Quality of Sacred Things

Part 1: The Need for a Special Explanation

Scruton agrees with Durkheim that sacred things are "in some way forbidden." This thought allows him to augment his argument about sacred things as mediums on the horizon of our world. What is forbidden, he writes:

> *. . . is to treat a sacred thing as though it belonged in the ordinary frame of nature: as though it had no mediating role. Treating a sacred thing in this day-to-day way is a profanation. One stage beyond profanation is desecration, in which a sacred object is deliberately wrenched from its apartness and trampled on or in some way reduced to its opposite, so as to become mean and disgusting.*

For example, in Judaic tradition, the temple is an example of the sacred, and the history of the temple shows how it was desecrated, first by the Babylonians and later by the Romans. These events had profound implications for Jews, for they thought that if God permitted the desecration, it meant that he had left the temple and left them unprotected. The temple fits Durkheim's definition of something that is set apart and forbidden, but Scruton's argument doesn't rest with this example. The forbidden quality of sacred things, he tells us:

> *. . . is such a strange feature, and puts such intense social and psychological demands on those who receive it, that it must have a special explanation.*

Part 2: The Witness of Incest

As he inquires further into the forbidden quality of sacred things, Scruton relies once more on social science for a way into the question. Anthropologists like Frazier, he writes, "were highly impressed by the Polynesian concept of taboo." Taboo, he points out, goes "hand in hand with the complementary notion of mana, which is the spiritual strength residing in things and radiating from them, by virtue of which they can effect changes in the human environment." Scruton wonders if we should seek to understand the sacred through these terms, proposing that "a thing becomes sacred when ordinary ways of using it are taboo, and when, in a certain special use, it possesses a mana of its own." Then he asks the reader, "Is that an advance?"

He doesn't answer the question right away. Instead, he presents a reading of Freud's *Totem and Taboo*, which picks up a thread he laid down earlier in the book. Scruton calls incest once more to the witness stand. The first time he used it to show that the taboo on incest couldn't be explained as an adaptation. In this instance, he employs the taboo on incest to help him define the sacred. To this end, he gives a short summary of *Totem and Taboo* that's tailored to his argument:

> *A taboo, Freud believed, exists in order to forbid something that is intensely desired. It is the collective response to individual temptation.*

Freud comes to this conclusion from a study of Polynesian totems that he describes in chapter 1 of *Totem and Taboo*. He learned from this study that every clan has a totem. Because the totem is passed down through the mother, Freud concluded that it informed marriageable males whom they could marry. Because it was thought that a man would commit incest if he married any woman from his mother's clan, totems prevented this existential crime. Scruton doesn't include this in his summary, but I find it helpful.

Part 3: The Thought of the Sacred and Its Place in the Psyche

Just as Scruton locates his arguments in the human subject, Freud locates his argument about religion in the intense desires of human beings. With that, Scruton takes the next step:

> *The principal arena of temptation [desire] is sex, and the principal taboo is that forbidding incest, in particular incest between son and mother—the taboo issued by the primeval father to his sons. In* Totem and Taboo, *therefore, Freud gives a theory of primitive religion on the same lines as the theory of the Oedipus complex.*

In this reading of it, a taboo has the aura of something forbidden by an unseen but all-powerful force, a primeval father. This godlike figure regulates with taboos the passions that would destroy the social fabric of the clan. The other three chapters in *Totem and Taboo* have to do with a boy's ambivalent relationship with a father. (Freud clearly identified with this ambivalence.) Just as a young man in the modern world learns to manage a love-hate relationship with his father as he matures (something, I would guess, Freud had to learn for himself and something he observed in his work with patients), cultures over the centuries somehow managed to neutralize the danger to fathers and sons by means of totems, taboos, and tablets of law. Again, Scruton doesn't go into this because he is interested in *the intense desire* aroused by thoughts about sex, and the emotions evoked by the thought of incest, rather than Freud's theory about the origin of religion. Nevertheless, I had to work this out for myself.

As I have indicated, Scruton has already written about the thought of incest in connection with intentionality or "aboutness" (see pages 253–256). Scruton informs us in that station of his argument that he doesn't agree with Freud's invention of the unconscious, which he calls a pseudoexplanation:

> *Nevertheless, we might feel a measure of sympathy for Freud. For he wants to explain not only why incest is forbidden, but also why the thought of it affects us in the deepest reaches of our being. The disgust we feel, and which led Oedipus to stab out his eyes and Jocasta to hang herself, has a peculiar intentionality or directedness. It focuses on the idea that this is my sister, mother, brother, or father, and it tells me that any sexual contact would be a kind of pollution, a spoiling of something that will never afterward be the same. Incest is therefore seen as an existential crime, one that changes what we are, both to ourselves and to others.*

It's important for Scruton's argument here to review his argument there. His focus there was on *the thought* of incest, and his focus here is on *the thought* of the sacred. He is still working within the overall argument that the thought of religion or the sacred cannot be explained as a Darwinian adaptation. We have to understand it as a mental state—as Mind, a medieval allegorist might say. Just as Freud regards the incest taboo as a thought, part of a rational strategy on the part of human beings, Scruton here is defining the sacred as a thought, not an adaptation that has been selected for and mindlessly institutionalized.

Scruton has incest doing double duty, for in this part of the argument Freud's theory helps him to locate the thought of the sacred in the human psyche. Picking up from the quote on page 302, which ends with the theory of the Oedipus complex, he continues:

> *And the theory has an interesting corollary, which is that religious awe and the sense of the sacred belong in the same psychic area as sexual desire and its associated ethic of purity and pollution. Freud arrives at this conclusion by way of the contentious, and indeed discredited theory of the Oedipus complex. But it is a connection that has been made in different ways down the centuries—for example, in Dante's account of Beatrice, forbidden object of his erotic longing, who reveals to him the mysteries of Paradise.*

Earlier he proposed that a thing becomes sacred when ordinary ways of using it are taboo, and asks the reader, "Is that an advance?" He now has answered the question. The theory he proposed there is too clinical, too removed from flesh and blood to account for the power of the sacred. As in Plato's thoughts on fundamental questions about Love, Truth, and Beauty, we need Eros; we need the passion of sex to grasp it.

Henry Holiday's painting (see page 85) illustrates Scruton's thought about Dante. Holiday depicts a scene from *La Vita Nuova*. To hide his love for Beatrice, Dante has pretended to love another. Because his feint in this person's direction became the subject of gossip, Beatrice heard about it and didn't acknowledge him when they met at the Santa Trinita Bridge. This was in stark contrast with a previous meeting when she had greeted him warmly.

In the painting, we see Beatrice walking with her friend Monna; Beatrice's maid servant follows slightly behind the two friends. Monna's pose and dress invite a sexual response, but Beatrice, Monna's Doppelganger, proceeds with the grace and discretion of a woman who lacks nothing and who therefore has no need to flaunt herself at the world, as Monna does. Nevertheless, she and Monna are intimates.

Part 4: The Sacred Goes Dark

Scruton then sums up his reason for including *Totem and Taboo* in a definition of the sacred, which includes the passage I quoted earlier to set up my commentary:

> *Many people today would say that Freud's account of taboo is fanciful . . . But there is an interesting thought behind the theory, which is this: the forbidden quality of sacred things is such a strange feature, and puts such intense social and psychological demands on those who receive it, that it must have a special explanation. There must be a way in which this strange idea enters into a human community, changing it from a loose assemblage of people in competition with each other, into a social unit bound together by its sense of the transcendental significance of the rituals that its members share.* Totem and Taboo *is therefore a theory of "hominization," of the transition from the simian tribe to the human community. According to the theory, this transition is effected by the original sin of parricide, as a result of which the entire community becomes bound by prohibitions and subdued by the unconscious burden of collective guilt.*

The thought of the sacred now points to the intersubjectivity (in the form of collective guilt) that defines religion (see pages 284–286) and points to that which forms a human community (see pages 286–288). Durkheim got Scruton started on this narrative, and *Totem and Taboo* has helped him to reach this point. The narrative of the sacred, however, has gone dark. Instead of enjoying a brilliant and beautiful summer's day with the one we love, we have been exiled for a terrible crime. We're like Oedipus or Faust, not an innocent young lover, like Romeo (before he killed Tybalt).

Chapter 8

The Sacred, Violence, Everyday Life, and the Intentionality of the Religious State of Mind

Pieter Bruegel's
The Harvesters

The Sacred and Violence

In his narrative about the sacred, Scruton stopped for a time at the station having to do with Freud's argument in *Totem and Taboo* to argue that the sacred occupies the same psychic space as the taboos around incest and patricide. With that, we go to the next station where Scruton will discuss *The Violence of the Sacred* by the anthropologist and philosopher Renee Girard. It's a natural stop to make because Girard develops there a theory about the sacred, which builds on Freud's thoughts in *Totem and Taboo*. To appreciate the importance of Girard for Scruton's narrative, though, we must go back to the first station and 9/11, where commentators judge religion to be the cause of violence.

Girard notes that God in the Bible is "deeply implicated in violence." In particular, God demands that Abraham sacrifice his son Isaac. For some, Scruton writes, it's "the ultimate test of faith" as a father concedes that everything "belongs to God," even a beloved son. For others, it's "a provocation, an invitation to condemn religion." And with that, Scruton turns to Girard:

> *For Girard, however, the story has another significance entirely. It illustrates the true role of religion, not as the cause of violence, but as the solution to it, even if the solution must take the form, as here [with Isaac], of a sacrificial offering. The violence itself comes from another source, and there is no society without it since it is engendered by the very attempt of human beings to live together as individuals, rather than as members of a pack or herd. The same can be said too of the obsession with sexuality: religion is not the cause of this, but an attempt to resolve it. In both these thoughts Girard is close to Freud, and indeed* Totem and Taboo *is one of the most frequently cited works in his discussion.*

Scruton has once more called the social sciences to the witness stand. Previously, he agreed with Durkheim that the core religious experience involves being a member of something and being called upon "to renounce my interests for those of the group and to celebrate my membership of the group in acts of devotion which might have no other justification than that they are commanded" (see pages 242–243). In addition, we now learn from the anthropologist Girard that the violence of human beings trying "to live together as individuals" comes from "memetic desire" or envy "as rivals struggle to match each other's social and material acquisitions." To purge the community of this violence, they find a scapegoat:

> *. . . marked by fate as "outside" the community and therefore not entitled to vengeance against it, who can be the target of the accumulated bloodlust, and who can bring the chain of retribution to an end.*

Even though Scruton agrees with Girard that the sacred grows out of "the human world," or Lebenswelt of language using human beings, he doesn't agree with Girard that the sacrifice of a scapegoat is a solution to the violence, for it places violence "in the heart of things." Here, too, at this critical moment in his argument, we have to go back to the first station, the suicide bombers of 9/11 who sacrificed thousands of "outsiders" to restore the psychic health of their Muslim community. As we think about the sacred, is that an advance?

Girard may have noticed the problem, for he suggests in one of his arguments:

> *. . . that Jesus was the first scapegoat to understand the need for his own death and to forgive those who inflicted it. And in submitting to this, Girard argues, Jesus gave the best evidence, and perhaps the only evidence, of his divine nature.*

Scruton judges that Girard's narrative may have merits "as a Christian apologetic" (the violence of the Old Testament God washed away by the blood of the Lamb of God), and he will return to "a movement toward sacrifice" when he finally defines the thought of religion in his summation at the end of the chapter.

A Foundation for the Thought of the Sacred

For now, though, Scruton continues with his critique of this theory. Not only does he have doubts about placing violence at the heart of things:

> *Girard's narrative fails to explain what it is to regard a thing as sacred. Girard draws on the fact that the sacrificial animal is regarded as sacred by those who slaughter it. But why? Does the theory answer the question or does it rather suppose that it is already answered?*

Like the evolutionary explanation for self-sacrifice, which makes it an instinct, Gerard's explanation omits "the thought on which our conceptions of the sacred are *built*."

To discover a "foundation" for the sacred (an image suggested by the metaphor of "building" in the preceding quote), Scruton examines:

> *. . . other areas in which we are inclined to speak of sacred things. The ideas of the sacred and the sacramental attach themselves to birth, to sexual union and marriage, and also to the ordinary death of ordinary people—these are all things that are set apart, regarded with awe, in which God is directly concerned, and which can be desecrated. Why are not these just as important as the more explicitly sacrificial aspects of the religious way of life? Rites of passage are surely more basic than ritual sacrifices—sometimes, perhaps, the occasion for ritual sacrifices, but in themselves far more necessary to the psychic health and togetherness of the community than the sacrifice of the occasional scapegoat. The sense of the sacred surely precedes ritual sacrifice, is more primitive, more basic, more fundamental to the human condition than any of the phenomena normally invoked to explain it.*

This, too, is one of the most important passages in the book. The foundation Scruton would build for the sacred has to do with that which is "fundamental to the human condition." The psychic health and togetherness of a community, he argues, settle more securely on the rites of passage in an ordinary life. These rites give new life to a sense of community, even if the rite they attend is a funeral. Death is common—the strongest commonality.

I Interrupt This Narrative to Briefly Speculate and Editorialize

Even though Scruton disagrees with Girard's theory about the scapegoat, he agrees that envy and ritual sacrifice are *social* phenomena. Girard looks at the human condition from within the human world, the only world we will ever know because we are language-using, symbol-interpreting, social animals. The problem for Scruton, I'm tempted to believe, is that Girard has put on the robe of a language-using, symbol-interpreting scientist, just as Freud did. They both want to explain *the cause* of violence within human society as moment in human history, even though this moment may have occurred in human prehistory. Scruton is not interested in *the origins* of religious belief, about which social scientists can endlessly speculate. He would describe *the content* of the thought.

The sacred, he has written, "lies outside the space-time continuum," so Girard's search for its origin in time and space is impossible. Why would he try to do it? I'm tempted to believe from reading Scruton's books that our modern culture encourages this kind of exercise. People tend to think in terms of the causes and effects of *a thing* in time and space, even when the thing they are studying is the mental state of an individual or the mental state of a community—a thing which, according to the rules of science, is not a thing. I suspect Scruton views these theories about violence—like those laid out by Hobbes, Girard, Marx, and so on—as exercises that serve to excuse the violence. If we blame it on "the state of nature," as Hobbes does, "the primeval condition of society," as Girard does, on those who ruthlessly control "the means of production," as Marx does, on God as the commentators do, or on existence itself as Ahab does, then an individual's violence against the cause can be justified.

Everyday Life

Scruton has made it clear in his writings that Edmund Burke is an important influence. I find that Scruton's argument about origins is similar to Burke's arguments in *Reflections on the Revolution in France*. In addition to works that Burke himself wrote, I read *The Great Debate* by Yuval Levin, who spent a year studying Burke and Thomas Paine in order to contrast their views on the French Revolution. I included Levin's thoughts on their debate in *A Comic Vision of Self-Government: Essays About Political Ideas Shaped and Illuminated by Wisdom Literature*, a companion piece to my first book. It so happens that, in a chapter titled "Everyday Life," I addressed the issue that Scruton has addressed in his critique of Girard. Because Levin's reading of Burke's argument is so important for my reading of Scruton's argument in this book, I'm reproducing the first three paragraphs of that chapter.

"There's a two-paragraph passage in Levin's chapter, 'Choice and Obligation,' which has provided 'Everyday Life' as the title of this essay (see *The Great Debate*, page 108). Thomas Paine relies on his theory of origins to declare that the social contract is an agreement (a matter that involves a conscious choice) between individuals. Unlike Enlightenment-liberal social theorists, Edmund Burke didn't think the nature of society could be discovered in an exercise like this. Levin's paragraphs explain Burke's objections. Instead of proclaiming a universal law like the social contract, Burke would describe (in Levin's words) 'the essential character of social life.' Burke observes that theorists like Paine, who base their social contract on speculations about origins, tend (in Levin's words), to 'apply their contract only to extreme situations, grounding it in the moment of founding and drawing from it rules for when revolution may be appropriate.

"To borrow an analogy from modern aviation, it would appear that Paine's theory is mostly concerned with the takeoff and the landing, usually the most fearful passages of any flight. This approach, Burke writes, 'is not very laudable or safe because in general it is not right to turn our duties into doubts.' The phrase 'duties into doubts' can be understood in two ways.

From Paine's point of view, the duty to guarantee everyone's sovereign right to choose this or that should lead to doubts that everyone has that freedom; properly considered, the doubts will then grow to dissatisfaction and even revolution. (Without much trouble the reader can see this pattern in present day American politics.) From Burke's point of view, an abstract, universal law will undermine with doubts our duty to uphold the binding relations in our families and civic institutions, for the universal law regarding individual choice will supersede those relations. This gravely unsettles the social order, something Burke would avoid. (Here, too, without much trouble, the reader can see this pattern as the modern state whittles away the power of traditional institutions in American life—like families, churches, and the rule of law—and gives it to the state.) Either way, it's an approach that invites second guessing and unrest, and in his own time Burke offers the French Revolution for proof. Opinions about our society and its rules, he writes, 'ought not to be in a state of fluctuation, but steady, sure, and resolved.' Unlike Paine's social contract, which revolves around rights and writes revolution into it as a guarantor of them, Burke's social contract, Levin writes, 'describes the everyday life of society.' Paine would fundamentally transform society with his theory, whereas Burke tries to understand and describe what binds it together in a way that promotes civic health and happiness.

"Bruegel's painting, *The Harvesters*, illustrates Burke's approach. It depicts the people of a town working to harvest the grain, and the picture shows that the work as a whole, a process that grows into the binding of the sheaves, is what binds them to each other. In Bruegel's art and in comedy, everyday life—which because it's so ordinary can seem to be merely a collection of arbitrary or pointless routines—is transformed by means of a comic alchemy into that which has a substantial and timeless value. Some years ago, our family went through a difficult period of transition, and we relied for months on several sources of comfort and wisdom to keep up our spirts. My wife cooked creative and delicious meals every night; our golden retriever kept us centered (around him) with his natural vitality, puckish sense of humor, massive presence, and love of life; and not least, the BBC's tapes of *Jeeves and Wooster* brought us together before bedtime for a happy hour of wonderful wit and farce. Altogether, it was back to the basics in the arts that keep the home fires burning. When daunted with uncertainty, we found a way forward through the natural rhythms and energies of family life" (*A Comic Vision of Self-Government*, pages 62–63).

I tell the personal story in the third paragraph with a feeling of intense gratitude. It was a defining moment of our life when we discovered something almost by accident. This experiment in family life had to be lived from day to day. The meaning of it emerged in the months and years that followed.

Defining the Thought of Religion

Having rooted a sense of the sacred in the less violent rhythms of everyday life, Scruton can proceed to his conclusion. He finds value in Girard's work, but it falls short in that it doesn't explain the thing it set out to explain—namely, an experience of the real presence (the sacred):

> *Still, we can now say something a little more definite about the intentionality of the religious frame of mind. It is a reaching out from subject to subject; it searches for a relation that is close, intimate, and personal, with a being who is present in this world though not of this world; and in this reaching out there is a movement toward sacrifice, in which both self and other might give themselves completely and thereby achieve a reconciliation that lies beyond the reach of ordinary human dialogue.*

Scruton has wrestled with this question about the intentionality of the religious thought over these many pages, and now he has summed it up for us. And going back to the first station, where the suicide bombers of 9/11 initiated the inquiry, Scruton concedes that this "movement toward sacrifice" may be connected to primitive forms of violence, for:

> *. . . there are roots to this state of mind that are far darker than we can, in our daily lives, easily acknowledge. But the essential character of the*

religious frame of mind is that of an intersubjective awareness in which the readiness for sacrifice is in some way contained.

Scruton makes this concession, but it only goes so far:

> *And in judging religions, we are acutely aware of the extent to which the sacrifices they ask for are sacrifices of others or sacrifices of self. It is surely that, above all else, that has entered our awareness through the actions of the Islamist "martyrs."*

Other stations have prepared us for this climactic stage of my inquiry. We stopped briefly to observe how Chaucer's characters made a pilgrimage to the place where a man voluntarily sacrificed his own life and became a saint. C. S. Lewis has shown us how the self in an allegory like *The Romance of the Rose* becomes instead an accident in the substance of the whole. I have argued that as Shakespeare's characters passionately seek the place where "Naught shall go ill," they undergo a process wherein they agree, in the end, to be enough of a naught that a marriage with another can succeed. Now Scruton has gone a journey in his thought to describe an intersubjective awareness, which contains a readiness for sacrifice. All roads in this inquiry have led to this place of sacrifice, the act of which Scruton describes so beautifully in the quote above:

> *. . . and in this reaching out there is a movement toward sacrifice, in which both self and other might give themselves completely and thereby achieve a reconciliation that lies beyond the reach of ordinary human dialogue.*

Scruton's prose here may not look like poetry, but it is doing the work of poetry. It's a medium (he is the medium) that looks at us in this world, using the language we understand, to describe situations we have experienced that hint at this relation of self and other, but it also looks the other way into that which lies beyond the reach of ordinary speech.

Chapter 9

The Ground of the Sacred

Van Gogh's

Green Wheat Fields, Auvers

Steps Taken Prior to Addressing the Ontological Question

As we near the end of "Believing in God," in a section he titled "The Epistemology of the Sacred," Scruton re-presents the question he tabled in "The Real Presence." Before I move ahead, once more I have to look back.

In "The Real Presence" (see pages 274–282), Scruton employed examples from the Bible to point out a "terrible truth, which is that God cannot show himself in this world, except by hiding from those whom he traps into trusting him, as he trapped the Jews. The knowledge of his presence comes with the failure to find him" (see page 278). From these thoughts, which are "fundamental to understanding what is at stake in the religious worldview," he told us, two great questions arise. He has now answered the second one—namely, "What concepts, beliefs, and perceptions define the intentionality of faith?" And he's ready to address the first question, "How is it possible for the transcendent to manifest itself in the empirical?" This question had to wait until the second question was answered.

At a station prior to the one on the real presence, Scruton introduced a question about the epistemology of dream thoughts in order to address "the real problem about the epistemology of religious thoughts." Chaucer, I argued, told his story about Chanticleer and Pertelote to raise the same question. They both are asking whether (paraphrasing Scruton) we can trace religious thoughts to the objects represented in them (to the sacred) or whether we can only trace them to things going on in our nervous system. Scruton asserts there that:

> *. . . if God is a transcendental being, who lies outside the space time continuum, then it is a deep, perhaps even a necessary, truth that God has no causal role to play in the beliefs that target him—or in any other event in space and time.*

If this is true, it sets up his argument that follows from it (in my rewording of it): If it's impossible to prove that religious thoughts can be traced to real objects, it must also be impossible to prove that religious thoughts can't be traced to real objects. This argument allows Scruton to shift the onus of proof away from the believer. It frees him to focus on "the content" of the belief, leaving the ontological concern for later.

Now that he has presented the content of the belief, Scruton returns to the argument begun in "The Real Presence" that it *is* possible for the transcendent to manifest in the empirical. As we learn in the stations that follow the onus of proof argument, which places the sacred "*outside* the space time continuum," he would complement that image with one that places the sacred *on the horizon*, where it functions as a medium between material and transcendent worlds.

The Ground of the Argument

Before he argues the question, "How is it possible for the transcendent to manifest itself in the empirical?" in this section, he has a pregnant, prerequisite condition:

> *We must not think of this merely as a theological or metaphysical question. For it is a question that inhabits the religious sentiment itself.*

Scruton reminds us that he has changed the ground of the argument, as he did in those initial paragraphs about the commentators. He has shifted it from an "outside" view, a pronouncement about the world and the way the world works, to the perspective of a human subject. He has shifted it from an intellectual to an emotional basis, as he put it there. This station called "The Epistemology of the Sacred," is asking and seeks to answer the question, "Can we know the sacred?" By putting the question within a "sentiment," Scruton removes it from a field of objective inquiry (as defined by science and other disciplines) and puts it in the field of a human subject's experience as defined by poetry, philosophy, and paintings like Van Gogh's vision of wheat fields in Auvers.

Once we are reminded that the human subject is the ground on which the question will be argued, we understand why he waited on this question and answered the other first—the one which asks, "What is the intentionality of the religious thought?" and which he has now answered that "it is an intersubjective awareness in which the readiness for sacrifice is in some way contained." The human subject comes into self-consciousness, we know ourselves to be self-conscious subjects, because we live with other language-using, symbol-interpreting human subjects. This is the ground out of which intersubjective awareness grows, and this practice in intersubjective awareness is what prepares the ground for an experience of the real presence, "the ground" being a metaphor for that which has the experience. As we inquire whether it's possible for the transcendent to manifest itself in the empirical, we have to explore the nature of that which has the experience as well.

Doubt

If the question about the reality of the sacred "inhabits the religious sentiment itself," it exists not as a problem in the world of numbers, which can be addressed by a computer, but in the flesh and blood and being of a human subject. It's a question for *a person* who lives and dies in this world and who responds to this world with "sentiments," the feelings or emotions informed by this person's opinions or attitudes. Love, for example, is a sentiment. Doubt is a sentiment. How can these mental states be ruled out as we inquire into the reality of the sacred, as they must be in an "outside" view?

The question may be answered with total certainty, as it was for Pascal, but it might produce instead religious doubt and the challenge to faith. Doubt is a thought (we doubt some idea with some other idea), but it's also a sentiment. As a thought and a sentiment, it represents a certain orientation to the world. It's fair to say religious doubt is different from doubting whether the Yankees will win the pennant this year, even though in a bar after many drinks that issue may rise to the level of religious doubt. Alienation from the sacred is a theme that Scruton shares with Lewis, Altavilla's *Architrenius*, the book of Job, and countless others. For thousands of years, people have experienced religious doubts and challenges to faith; this is nothing new. Religious doubt, however, has driven many, like Pascal, to a *nuit de feu* that resolves the question. During the reign of science, though, which has relegated religious doubt to the ash heap of history, this is less likely to happen, for people in our secular culture no longer think seriously about religion. (Why bother? We have drugs for pain.) Religion is less likely to enter, in any meaningful way, into the conversation, except when it does. For example, in the case of 9/11, religion has entered the conversation as the villain of the story.

I can't resist adding parenthetically the following interpretation of 9/11, which develops this story line. Having described Girard's theory, Scruton could point out that if we look at 9/11 and the commentary about it from Girard's point of view Religion would then be the outsider, the convenient scapegoat. As the victim of a ritual sacrifice, which releases rivalries within our secular community in the West, Religion personified would become both sacrificed and sacred. But, of course, he didn't point this out. This is just my idea, which he gave me. I notice, though, that, even as fashionable commentators proclaim the certainties of a scientific worldview, they can't help looking back at what they have left behind. It's a shadow presence, the ghost of what they no longer believe. Could we say this shadow that haunts their commentary lives on as a form of doubt and a challenge to their faith in material science? Is it ridiculous to imagine that Secular Society (personified) feels compelled to preserve its own often fractious community by ritually killing this ghost? Gerard's theory proves that it's possible to have a thought like this.

The Challenge to Faith

The nature of the sacred itself, Scruton writes, can contribute to the doubt, for, as he has shown, alienation is a built-in feature of it:

> *Often, when a faith-community settles on some particular object, or rite, or words as sacred, it loses the presence of the thing in question, which retreats into the eternal as did the God of Moses and Abraham when his temple was destroyed. The same retreat into the eternal occurred, at a certain stage, with the God of the Koran. If the Koran is really a revelation from God, spoken by the Eternal, the scholars asked, then how can it exist in time, as a mere text among others, to be interpreted and applied through the arguments of ordinary mortals? This question particularly troubled the Asharite school of theology, and the conclusion its scholars drew was that the Koran must be eternal, outside time and change, and therefore not open to interpretation or amendment. From that moment the gate of ijtihad (creative interpretation) was closed. To put it from a Christian perspective, the Koran ceased to be a record of God's presence among us, and became the proof of his absence—the trace left behind as he departed forever from our midst.*

Surely, Scruton has written a description of the sacred in Islam that sounds like a description of God in the Christian West—all those magnificent cathedrals, like Notre Dame in Paris, which mark the traces God left behind as he departed forever from our midst. The thought that God has departed forever from our midst is the challenge to faith.

Scruton's thought then briefly takes a more hopeful turn:

> *The Sufis did not accept this, and the prayers and invocations of Rumi, Hafiz, and Omar Khayyam call upon God once again as the Friend, who moves among us, who meets us in this world, yet freely and unforeseeably, like the sakinah of the Koran.*

He gives us this brief glimpse of the sacred, but then that possibility is foreclosed in other sects:

But as for Sunni Orthodoxy, which tells us that God revealed himself, but only in a book that exists outside space and time, this leaves the question of God's presence in our world exactly as it was—a question without an answer.

We can find the same pattern in Christianity. Scruton makes it clear that some Christians in our own day continue to understand their faith as an active relationship with God. His arguments, though, are primarily addressed to readers who are skeptics. From the beginning, he would encourage these readers not to view religion from the "outside," the way science looks at things. When religion is studied in this way, people think that:

. . . faith is simply of a cosmological kind, concerning the creation of the world and the hope of eternal life. And these beliefs are imagined to be in some ways rivals to the theories of physics, and exposed to refutation by all that we know of the evolution of the universe. But the real phenomena of faith are nothing like that. They included prayer and the life of prayer; the love of God and the sense of his presence in the life of the faithful; obedience and submission in the face of temptation and the things of this world; the experience of certain times, places, objects, and words, as "sacred," which is to say, in Durkheim's phrase, as "set aside and forbidden," reserved for uses that can be understood only on the assumption that these experiences mediate between this world and another that is not otherwise revealed to us. *(originally quoted on page 279)*

As we increasingly identify with phones, computers, and TVs, however, our faith in these machines grows. It's a rich environment for thinking that knowledge of faith, along with knowledge of everything else, is simply of a cosmological kind. Out of habit, and in conformity with the norms dictated by technology, we are locked into an objective point of view. We think the image on the screen is reality, that these machines are windows that present instantaneously and continuously an objective, cosmological point of view. (I say "we" because I fall easily into this error.) It's easy to think from our easy chair that the world is someone else's problem. It's also easy to think that with my godlike objectivity I can fix the world's problems. It's easy to lose in this habit of a third-person point of view the sense that we are a soul, the center of our troubled earth, and the sole proprietor (I use the term loosely) of it. A cosmological (objective) point of view makes the active life of faith that's described in the quote above less and less likely.

Just as Scruton contrasts Sufis who call upon God as a Friend with Sunnis who close the gate of creative interpretation, he also contrasts Christians, who practice "the real phenomena of faith" as described in the quote above, with leaders in Christian thought who encourage congregations to ignore the sacred and focus their faith instead on material concerns—for example, on the latest political concepts of social justice:

> *Perhaps something like this is true of the Protestant tradition too. Paul Ricoeur has argued that the task of religion (and he means the Christian religion) in our time is to complete the expulsion of the sacred from the practice of faith—so that we confront God as he is, not confined in this or that moment or this or that corner of the world.*

The last part of this passage, the thoughts that come after the dash, are difficult. A God who is confined in this or that moment or this or that corner of the world sounds like a person, someone like us, for we are confined in this way. Just as a friend or someone we love can be present or absent, this kind of God can be present or absent, and this is the kind of God Scruton has been describing. Yes, sometimes he's not there, but sometimes he is. So what does Ricoeur mean by confronting "God as he is?" I sense something like Pantheism in this thought, the belief that this world is identical with God. Or maybe it's a form of deism, the belief that God made the world and then left it to its own devices ("God as he is" is elsewhere.) There are no mediums to the sacred in these faiths; man must rely on empirical science and natural reason for knowledge of anything.

The Soil of the Sacred

Part 1: On Excising the Sacred

With that, Scruton delivers, with the assistance of "the ground" as a metaphor, an observation that explains why he has written his book on the soul of the world and this introduction to it called "Believing in God":

> *Yet we know that this excision of the sacred does not encourage faith but merely deprives it of the soil in which it grows.*

How does Scruton know this about the ground for growing faith in the sacred? He doesn't say here, so I have to extrapolate from the evidence he has presented. His book begins with the Islamic "martyrs" on 9/11. They represent a faith that has excised the sacred; these Sunnis no longer call on God as "the Friend." These poor souls have only abstractions, the words of Allah and the words of certain approved Orthodox Sunni scholars, to guide them, not a living presence; it's a good guess that Scruton is offering them up as proof of what he says here.

The suicide bombers, though, are not the only ones deprived of that which nourishes belief in a living God and a living soul. Scruton includes, I have to guess, the commentators with whom he begins the book. Given the dominance of science as the arbiter of knowledge in the modern world, the commentators have sided with its high priests, scientists and intellectuals, who rely on empirical science for their conclusions about the moving parts of the world, moving parts like the Islamists. Following the dictates of science, the commentators have to conclude that human behavior has a physical cause. For example, they assume that the Islamists killed three thousand infidels on orders from the Koran. In this explanation, there's a causal relationship, but this explanation ignores the freedom that for Scruton defines a human subject. The commentators may be tempted to ignore the freedom of the human subject in their explanation because Science (personified) has also taught them to believe that human beings have no agency. The commentators have been taught to believe that human beings are socially conditioned and ruled ultimately by a selfish gene. Even the push to sacrifice has been "selected for." Here's a question that has occurred to me in this regard: If one believes there's a strict causal relationship between a person reading the Koran and then killing an infidel, how does one account for the fact that millions have read and still read the Koran who have not and will not kill infidels? This fact, it would appear, makes it difficult to accuse Islam, as opposed to certain Islamists, of murder. Religion has been accused of murder, Scruton points out in the opening paragraphs of the book. Is this argument enough to establish reasonable doubt?

Then there's the scientists and academics themselves. Throughout the West and the rest of the world now, they have made excising the sacred from their work the litmus test for the credentialing of their work. In this enlightened period of human history, scientists and intellectuals believe they can perfect through reason the means for channeling age-old instincts without the insight of spurious revelations. They are also confident that they can finally solve—by any means necessary, as twentieth-century experiments in social engineering have so graphically demonstrated—the problems posed by those thought to be antisocial members of their communities. I could ask the reader, as Scruton did earlier in another context, "Do those experiments represent an advance in creating and preserving a civil society?" But I already know, as Scruton did, that they do not.

Part 2: The Place Where Earth and Sky Are Joined

What is the soil where faith in the sacred can grow? Once again, he doesn't say in the passage, so once more I have to extrapolate. This, though, is not difficult since the commentary throughout my reading of *The Soul of the World* points to the answer. All his arguments persuade us that the living, breathing human subject is the ground in which faith must grow. I provided an entrance to this thought in the beginning, in the verse from Genesis with which I began my inquiry:

> *But there went up a mist from the earth, and watered the whole face of the ground. And the Lord God formed man of the dust of the ground, and breathed into his nostrils the breath of life; and man became a living soul. And the Lord God planted a garden eastward in Eden; and there he put the man whom he had formed.*

We are made from the dust of the earth; we are the ground. Even natural science would have to agree with this. In the biblical version, or vision of our life, however, this clump of earth becomes something more. God breathed into our nostrils the breath of life, and we became a living soul. God then put man in the garden he planted eastward in Eden. The earth of the garden and the man are mutually sustaining, but we are not plants. We have been given the breath of life and a living soul. This informs us in a way that a plant or a groundhog will never be informed. A plant is entirely constrained by its genetic makeup. Unlike the groundhog, we have a special intelligence and the freedom that goes with it, for we are made in God's image. Like him, we are free to create, and not just the next generation.

We are the ground of faith in the sacred, but to grasp Scruton's vision of this it helps once more to consider the image of a horizon. A horizon, I have argued, is not a physical object. It is both real and an illusion. If we look at Andrew Wyeth's two paintings, we see that the horizon consists of earth and that invisible thing we call the sky. In this respect, the horizon is like us, for we consist both of earth and that invisible something we call self-consciousness. In *Christina's World*, the pull of earth seems to have the upper hand, but her upper body still rises up. We imagine that her eyes look to the horizon where the body of earth meets an invisible something. I would guess that she longs for something like the place where Jack will have Jill, naught will go ill, and the man will have his mare again. (In these gender-fluid times these can be regarded as metaphors, not strict conditions, for human happiness.) *Below Dover* tells much the same story, only with a little boat as its subject, a boat whose eye (a conscious "I?") looks unlikely to be much help. A whale, though, does just fine with eyes on the side instead of the front. The boat need not rely solely on that little porthole. It knows the way to the place it was made for beyond the verge.

For Wyeth, I'm suggesting, Christina and the little boat are mediums on the horizon of material and immaterial worlds. When we experience them as Wyeth did, when we find ourselves planted in Scruton's soil—which is the substance of a human subject and a living soul, we have liftoff from the gravity of earth (see how the little boat sails through the field, how Christina rises up) and become our own medium to a larger intelligence.

The Sovereignty of the Human Subject

Part 1: A Restoration Project

Having so scrupulously prepared the ground for what he now can propose, Scruton challenges commentators of all stripes with a new project:

> *The real question for religion in our time is not how to excise the sacred, but how to rediscover it, so that the moment of pure intersubjectivity, in which nothing concrete appears, but in which everything hangs on the here and now, can exist in pure and God-directed form. Only when we are sure that this moment of the real presence exists in the human being who experiences it, can we then ask the question whether it is or is not a true revelation—a moment not just of faith but of knowledge, and a gift of grace.*

These two sentences follow the form of argument he has used from the start. To support this statement, I need once more to review the ground we have covered.

Part 2: Wrestling with the Question of Veracity

The initial stations in the chapter moved the argument to the point where he could define the intentionality of the religious thought. At the station before this one, we have his answer. To buttress the notion that we never leave any of the stations, here it is again

> *It is a reaching out from subject to subject; it searches for a relation that is close, intimate, and personal, with a being who is present in this world though not of this world; and in this reaching out there is a movement toward sacrifice, in which both self and other might give themselves completely and thereby achieve a reconciliation that lies beyond the reach of ordinary human dialogue.*

Having arrived at a definition, Scruton then must wrestle with the ontological question. As he wrestles, the question takes different forms (as Proteus did when he and Odysseus wrestled). He first explores it when discussing the epistemology of dreams:

> *Religious thoughts might be like dream thoughts, which we trace not to the objects represented in them, but to things going on in the nervous system during sleep.*

Nevertheless, some cultures believe that dreams can be "traced" to objects and events "out there" in the world, so religious thoughts might be like these dream images. Dream images, in this view, "reach beyond" to the sacred (see the first quote of this section for Scruton's metaphor of "reaching").

When he introduces the ontological question in the station called "The Real Presence," he asks first, "How is it possible for the transcendental to manifest itself in the empirical?" and then immediately restates the question, "[How is it possible]—for the eternal God to be a real presence in the life of earthly worshippers?" The first question states the case clearly enough, but to my ear words like *transcendental* and *empirical* are probably too abstract for the thing Scruton would describe. The rephrasing of the question corrects this. Scruton places it now, as he has been doing throughout, as the question a human subject might ask at a life and death moment, not a question that's asked in an Oxford debate.

When he comes back to the question in this station, the one called "The

Epistemology of the Sacred," he refers to it as "the question of veracity," and then rewords it as a question: "Is there anything that answers to this search for the sacred?" Now that we grasp the intentionality of the religious thought as a reaching out from subject to subject, we see that this last sentence conforms with the definition. It suggests the questioning and answering of two subjects. Right after that question, though, he follows up with, "Can the eternal be present among us in the way that rewards our search for it?" This form of it emphasizes the answering of the question as the goal of a narrative, the grail that's the reward of a knightly quest. In other words, he has turned answering the question into a romance, like the one Spenser wrote about the Red Cross Knight. This form of it lands us in the wonderland of allegory.

Part 3: Pascal's *Nuit De Feu*

Both questions, about the definition of the thought and the reality of the thought, arose in Scruton's narrative when the real presence entered into the argument, and to grasp the project he has laid out for us—namely, discovering and cultivating the soil of the sacred, we need to review the story of Pascal's *nuit de feu* on November 23, 1654:

> *. . . when for two hours, he experienced the total certainty that he was in the presence of God—"the God of Abraham, of Isaac and of Jacob, not the God of the philosophers and the wise men," in other words a personal God, intimately revealed, not conjured by abstract argument. "Pere juste, le monde ne t'a point connu, mais moi, je t'ai connu." He wrote then, on the scrap of paper on which he recorded the experience: astonishing words, which only total conviction could have engendered. [Righteous Father, the world doesn't know you, but I, I know you.]*

Scruton, I believe, included Pascal's *nuit de feu* in the text to prepare the reader, the way a good gardener prepares the soil, for this moment—his call to action.

Now that I've provided context, let me quote once more the two sentences that present Scruton's challenge to his readers, this time closer to my commentary on it. In any case, it does not suffer from rereading:

> *The real question for religion in our time is not how to excise the sacred, but how to rediscover it, so that the moment of pure intersubjectivity, in which nothing concrete appears, but in which everything hangs on the here and now, can exist in pure and God-directed form. Only when we are sure that this moment of the real presence exists in the human being who experiences it, can we then ask the question whether it is or is not a true revelation—a moment not just of faith but of knowledge, and a gift of grace.*

The first sentence of the project includes both a statement of the project's objective (to rediscover the sacred) and a review of the thought (that the sacred involves a moment of pure intersubjectivity). In the second sentence, Scruton functions like a bouncer at the door of a bar; he is there to make sure you are qualified to drink. Scruton stands at the door, and he tells those who would engage with the question (as to whether the real presence exists) that you can only enter into the question if you are prepared to agree with Pascal, who had the experience and who was convinced of its reality. Scruton, the bouncer, stands up for Pascal's sovereignty over determining the veracity of his *nuit de feu*.

Part 4: The Gift of Life and the Gift of Poetry

Why does Scruton take this position? What gives him or Pascal the authority? What gives any author the authority to write anything? We write from our own experience, which includes the experiences of others, which we learn directly from watching them, from conversations, or indirectly through their work products. Whether we draw on the experiences of others like Pascal, Shakespeare, Lewis, or Scruton, however, we are still writing from our own experience. We can do no other. It's up to the reader to determine whether the writing rings true, and how can this be done unless we give ourselves to the writer, suspending disbelief while at the same time reading accurately and critically. Of course, a reader enters into this kind of relationship only with authors who compel that kind of commitment.

Why would we make a commitment and suspend disbelief as we read

Pascal's, Shakespeare's, Goethe's, or Scruton's words? To answer this, I return to Scruton's definition in the first sentence. We have to notice that he doesn't define the experience simply as a "moment of pure intersubjectivity," which may be easy enough to write. That definition loses itself in the overall movement of a human subject on a quest to rediscover the sacred:

> *. . . so that the moment of pure intersubjectivity, in which nothing concrete appears, but in which everything hangs on the here and now, can exist in pure and God-directed form.*

How, I wonder, can he write such a thing? I wonder the same thing about Shakespeare and Goethe when I read their texts. This writing, in which nothing concrete appears, nevertheless hangs on the here and now, and we receive the beauty of this poetry, the truth of it, because the writing exists. He couldn't have written it if he hadn't experienced in some measure the moment he describes. I would add, in an analogy of my own, that the moment exists in the same way that the breath exists. A breath exists, but as we observe (or "follow") the breath, nothing concrete appears. Nevertheless, it's as real as our consciousness of it. It's the gift of this moment, which Scruton's words describe. Can anyone explain, scientifically, why this breath exists, why we breathe and continue to breathe? Can anyone explain, scientifically, why or how he wrote that sentence? Rather than asking for an explanation as a causal chain of events, I'm moved by all the lifelines of poetry I've included in my book to say he can write such a thing because he's aware that he has been given the breath of life, and he has given in reply, like the release of breath, the poetry we now read.

Scruton's writing is poetry, as I have defined it, of a high order. His project would restore once more the sovereignty of the human subject to affirm and glorify the breath of life, but this human subject does not wear a crown of worldly power. Like Hamlet, this subject doesn't need the oil and the investiture and all that to realize the power of a living soul, the power that exists in pure and God directed form. Also, let's be clear: This is not the sovereignty of a man who thinks he is Napoleon or of the shooter high above the crowd in Las Vegas. This is the sovereignty of a Socrates or a Buddha. These were men, not Gods, who realized in their life a sovereign soul. Scruton's project, which he has been describing from the first sentence, persuades me at the end of this long train of thought that a living, loving soul is empowered by a moment, not just of faith but of knowledge (see the quote on page 328). He has brought us, through the medium of his thoughts—his beautifully ordered train of thoughts—to the horizon of which he speaks.

I have illustrated this chapter with a work by Van Gogh, another painting that features a horizon. Who better than he to describe the emotional "ground" of our life as a moment of pure intersubjectivity with the soul of the world? Van Gogh did many portraits of his friends and of himself. His wheat fields strike me as portraits of the sacred in action. In these works, Van Gogh paints on the horizon a medium for glimpsing Eros at play. He's fully present, we just can't see him, as he runs to embrace and paint with love the billowing earth and billowing sky.

Chapter 10

The Sense of a Goal

Adriaen Isenbrandt's

The Rest on the Flight into Egypt

The View from Boo Radley's Porch

I used to read *To Kill A Mockingbird* with my students back in the day. The thought of Boo Radley's porch is fresh because I recently saw a dramatic staging of the story at the Shakespeare Festival in Stratford, Ontario. Since its publication in 1960, critics have not had much to say about Harper Lee's novel, even though it's one of the most popular works ever written by an American. Nevertheless, it was performed on the main stage at Stratford, the one reserved for important productions of Shakespeare's plays. The powers that be at the festival know their business; something there is about the story that people still love and will pay good money to see.

I mention the novel here because of the way Boo Radley captures the imaginations of the three children—Scout, her brother Jem, and their neighbor Dill. Boo is a mystery, much like God in Scruton's narrative. The children have never seen him, because he never shows his face, but they can see the Radley place, which looks abandoned and haunted, haunted by a Boo. The house and Boo haunt their imaginations too. Initially, they imagine him as a monster. This changes, though, when they find little gifts, which could only be from him, in the knothole of a tree. This knot (not!) has a message for them: *I am not a monster, and I am not dead*. Because he exists and seems to take an interest in them, they take even more of an interest in him, to the point where they trespass on his property to get a look. Is it just a coincidence that the story about Boo is so similar to the story about the sacred (where God "reveals himself by concealing himself") that Scruton has been telling? Am I just imagining that a message of love in a tree resonates strongly with the Christian story?

When Scout gets into a scrape at school with young Walter Cunningham, her father, Atticus, talks to her about it. He tells her a little about Walter's life at home (he once represented Walter's father in court), which might help her to understand young Walter's unkempt appearance and his behavior at school. Atticus suggests she can't really know someone like Walter until she has walked in his shoes and seen the world the way he sees it. Harper Lee then builds the conclusion of her novel around Atticus's lawyerly advice.

When the villain of the story, Bob Ewell, tries to kill Scout and Jem on their way home from school after a Halloween pageant (the Night of All Saints, along with other spirits), Boo rescues them, kills the villain, and carries the wounded Jem (a pearl beyond price) to their father's house. Scout doesn't know what has happened, doesn't yet know that her costume saved her life, and doesn't know who is carrying her brother. Once she's inside her home, she encounters the mystery, face-to-face. There, in the lamplight, she sees with amazement the object of so much speculation, and yet she greets him informally as if he were a playmate and a friend. "Hey, Boo," she says. Some playmate, some friend, and yet these two words suit the moment perfectly.

Knowing how shy Boo is, Atticus asks Scout to walk with him back to his house, which will remove him from the public gaze. The two walk together through the dark, climb the steps of his porch, and Boo disappears inside. When Scout turns around, though, she pauses for a moment on Boo Radley's porch and takes in a world that has been transformed. Atticus's words have been made flesh. She now looks at the world (with wonder after Jem's and her own brush with death) from Boo's point of view. Jem is alive. She is alive. The world comes alive in a way that it never has before, thanks to Boo, there on his porch, but Boo once again has retreated into his house, which prying eyes will never penetrate. Boo is gone, but Scout has participated with him in an experience that will forever change her perception of the world. Harper Lee wrote her novel, I believe, to capture this moment. Some experience like this of her own, I would guess, gave her a sense of the story she wanted to tell.

The Winding Road to a Wonderland

My rendering of *To Kill a Mockingbird* helps me to make an entrance into Scruton's conclusion of "Believing in God." I suspect, but can't prove, that

Harper Lee isn't just asking Scout to imagine walking in Walter Cunningham's, Tom Robinson's, or Boo Radley's shoes. She would have us wonder about walking in a saint's shoes and viewing the world from there. I don't think it has to be labeled a religious thought. A secular person could wonder about it as easily as a person of faith.

Scruton has been preparing us, after we have followed so carefully the winding road of his argument, for this sort of goal. His conclusion comes at the end of a philosophical argument, but this image of a pilgrimage to the Saint's "house" to restore our health complements Scruton's final reworking of the first question, which frames it as a quest:

> *Can the eternal be present among us in the way that rewards our search for it?*

A journey, Lewis argued in *The Allegory of Love*, is the best metaphor for describing the inner life:

> *The journey has its ups and downs, its pleasant resting-places enjoyed for a night and then abandoned, its unexpected meetings, its rumors of dangers ahead, and above all, the sense of its goal, at first far distant and dimly heard of, but growing nearer at every turn of the road. Now this represents far more truly than any combat . . . the perennial strangeness, the adventurousness, and the sinuous forward movement of the inner life.* *(first quoted on page 140)*

By embarking on a reading of *The Soul of the World*, we go a journey that makes considerable demands on us, but we persist because we have at some point experienced a "sense of its goal." The title itself is the gossip that conveys a rumor about This Life, a well-known celebrity: "Can you believe it? This Life has a soul!" And so we make a pilgrimage until we arrive at that place where we either confirm or discredit the rumor. We have been reading, and now we're almost to the end of Scruton's first chapter. Are we convinced? Is the author himself convinced?

I have illustrated this chapter with Isenbrant's painting because the dirt path at the Madonna's feet and the title suggest she's on a journey. Like the journey in Lewis's quote, this painting is full of wonders. For example, the dirt path appears to have been transformed into a stream of living water as it descends to the Madonna's right. It meanders behind her into the background through the land where people live, around the violent eruption of rock (which rivals the Madonna for our attention), and into a lake. This is only natural. It's what water does, but there's also something very strange about this river. It's not a prosaic, predictable stream of water; it appears and disappears without explanation.

We wonder, too, why the man on the cliff appears to be expostulating with a tree (but a Christian of Isenbrandt's time might make a guess), and the scene behind the Madonna as a whole has been painted as a wonderland. When we look more closely, we notice that the violent eruption of rock has been transformed into something like a hand, and it's holding a house in its palm. The village where the people are peacefully settled has been placed between this imposing rock and a castle-like manor house. Finally, the sense of a journey is implicated in the title and hints of a winding path of light, but I wonder if the painter hasn't magically reversed the "flow" of things into the background. We thought the goal was down there, but maybe the goal for us, who live in the safe harbor below, is the place in the foreground, where the Madonna and her baby absorb our attention. Perhaps we made a journey upstream to the source, and what we see is the soul of the world being held by his mother, Mary.

The Shadow Presence of Divine Wisdom

Harper Lee wasn't writing in a vacuum. She inherited the themes and practices of a literary tradition that informed the work of Chaucer and Shakespeare. My reading of "The Knight's Tale" in *A Comic Vision of Great Constancy* also addresses this goal of an encounter with an otherworldly intelligence. I argued in my interpretation that a sense of the whole, the goal of a pilgrimage, is built into the structure of the poem as three different framing devices. To show how Chaucer imagines the encounter, I've adapted the section that leads off my interpretation of "The Knight's Tale."

Part 1: The Freedom That Shadows a Constraint

Chaucer has used the medieval devotional practice of a pilgrimage to frame his picture of the human comedy. The verb "frame" holds within it the possibility of two meanings. In *A Midsummer Night's Dream*, Shakespeare has Bottom (in the character of Pyramus) lament the supposed death of his Thisbe by saying:

> *O wherefore, nature, didst thou lions frame,*
> *Since lion vile hath here deflowered my dear?*

William Blake emphasizes the same word in his poem "The Tyger":

> *Tyger! Tyger! Burning bright*
> *In the forests of the night,*
> *What immortal hand or eye*
> *Dare frame thy fearful symmetry?*

In these examples, the word *frame* means "create," as when builders frame a structural shell in the making of a house. But the word can also mean "limit." When an artist frames his picture, for example, the frame signals where the picture ends. Chaucer frames or limits his picture to the going to and the coming from Canterbury of these pilgrims. Their past and their future, except as they are suggested in the prologue or in their tale, are not recorded. This limits the scope of the picture, but at the same time makes it possible for him to create the picture. As I am interpreting it here, the word *frame* holds within it the paradox of *a constraint that can resolve into freedom*, and this characterization of the word links it to comedy as a way of framing or picturing human experience.

Bottom's question quoted above points to the most basic constraint of human life: if not a lion or a tiger then eventually something will limit, like a picture frame, the life we hold so dear. Comedy would put this idea into a larger context, which lightens the burden of the "frame." In the case of Pyramus, the audience has just been shown, but Pyramus has not, that his dear ran away before the lion could kill her. Due to his limited point of view—that he shares with Everyman, by the way—Pyramus mistakes, for Thisbe lives.

Despite the loss of life in the Pyramus and Thisbe story (which is Shakespeare's model for *Romeo and Juliet* and ends in a double suicide), we can draw from it a comic conclusion: because human beings don't know everything, they need to respect these limits and act prudently. Pyramus dies, but he's just a fictional character. His example may yet save a life, for Wisdom, who was with God from the beginning, speaks to us through the story. Because the story exists, Wisdom lives in us, and frees us from the constraint of a false conclusion, even so far as a conclusion about death itself.

Part 2: The Third Man Who Walks with Us

Chaucer also frames his picture with the consciousness of a single, limited point of view. The reader can only access the tales through the mind of Chaucer's persona, a rather simple rhymester. This persona joins a cross section of English society at a London inn, where they all decide to travel to Canterbury together and amuse themselves on the way by telling tales. I call this consciousness Chaucer the Pilgrim to distinguish him from Chaucer the Author. A comic worldview looks at the world in a way that's different, for example, from a tragic or a nihilistic worldview. The device of a first-person narrator communicates this concept of a worldview as a point of view without having to explain itself at all. The use of the first-person pronoun "I" gives the reader direct access only to what the persona is thinking and therefore limits what the reader knows to this window on the world.

Like the old vaudeville routine of a pedestrian who is reading a newspaper as he walks, and who is therefore unaware of the banana peel in his path, that limited point of view often leaves out important matters. We come to awareness about this phenomenon because we in the audience have the larger view of things. An awareness about the phenomenon requires an objective observer. How can this happen, though, when we're stuck in the point of view of a first-person narrator?

Chaucer's first-person narration represents or imitates the limited perception of Everyman. Despite the fact that as readers we depend entirely on the persona's point of view, a master of the device, like Chaucer, can make the reader aware when there is a significant blind spot in his persona's thinking. Because he's a limited point of view, Chaucer the Pilgrim sometimes misjudges his fellow travelers, seeing them as they would like to see themselves (or be seen) rather than as they are. For example, he calls the Pardoner "a noble ecclesiast," and it would appear that he means what he says. But there's plenty of evidence, unwittingly supplied by Chaucer the pilgrim, to prove beyond a shadow of a doubt that the Pardoner is a fraud and a blight on the church.

These clues represent the point of view of a godlike, objective observer. The reader is stuck with the limited point of view of Chaucer the Pilgrim, but the godlike, objective observer is still there as a shadow presence. In Chaucer's hands, a limited point of view expresses an essential insight of comedy—no one individual can know everything. It also expresses the other essential insight of comedy: the limited point of view implies a larger point of view, a larger intelligence. Our reading of characters like the Pardoner gives us practice in the art of recognizing the narrator's blind spots. In real life, the narrator is us.

The continual presence of a larger intelligence, the shadow presence or the "third man" who walks with us (in *The Canterbury Tales* it is Chaucer the author), assists with that. Eliot's lines from "The Wasteland" have also helped me with this interpretation:

Who is the third who walks always beside you?
When I count, there are only you and I together
But when I look ahead up the white road

There is always another one walking beside you
Gliding wrapt in a brown mantle, hooded
I do not know whether a man or a woman
—But who is that on the other side of you?

The story in Luke 24, about the disciples on the road to Emmaus, gave Eliot this vision of the third man:

And it came to pass, that, while they communed together and reasoned, Jesus himself drew near, and went with them. But their eyes were holden that they should not know him.

The third man reminds us of that which is hidden from us; I call him a shadow presence. This shadow reminds us to doubt what we think we know. If I personify Doubt as the shadow or the third man, we have in these stories an allegory about *Doubt*, and his story may be as significant and as true to life as the allegory about Death in *Everyman*. We need a story like this, for we need to be constantly reminded that we don't know everything. Doubt, the shadow, is our friend, for communing and reasoning can take us only so far in the way of Wisdom. Doubt, though, is not always a friend. Taken too far, it can change into a killer (the experience of poor, duped Othello). In the middle, between an attachment to an opinion and crippling skeptical, cynical doubt, we can look at things with circumspection and wonder about them.

By the way, I don't think it's unreasonable to speculate that Adam Smith founded his theory of moral sentiments on this third man who always walks beside us, but he called it the Impartial Spectator.

Part 3: A Longing for Health, the Unseen Prime Mover

Finally, the pilgrimage serves to frame the pilgrims' quest with a purpose. Their physical goal is Canterbury Cathedral, but they have unspoken, spiritual goals as well. Chaucer's lines about this are true for seekers of any time or place who are moved by juices in the ground, in plants, in animals, and in themselves to come to life once more in the spring:

> *Then people long to go on pilgrimages*
> *And palmers long to seek the stranger strands*
> *Of far-off saints, hallowed in sundry lands,*
> *And specially, from every shire's end*
> *Of England, down to Canterbury they wend*
> *To seek the holy blissful martyr, quick*
> *To give his help to them when they were sick.*

We don't have to be a medieval Christian to identify with the purpose of a pilgrimage. Everyone seeks to be whole, both physically and mentally. A pilgrimage to make us whole is like the quest for home in the *Odyssey*. We're at home and happy when we're healthy. Some look for health in far-off places like Jerusalem, and others seek it in a nearby town like Canterbury. Some may look in a score of city centers and rural retreats before they find it has been sleeping in the same bed with them in all the places they have ever been.

As in Lewis's argument that allegory envisions a world that is whole, Chaucer's pilgrims would reknit bodies and minds divided by disease; they would be whole. That's the purpose of a pilgrimage. In the examples of this section, I have argued that a sense of the whole exists in minds that usually attach to parts. The examples, you'll notice, have a common theme: Pyramus thinks he has lost his Thisbe; the disciples think they have lost their teacher; a sick person goes on a pilgrimage because he thinks he is about to lose his life. In each case, the characters have only partial knowledge of the situation. An attachment to that partial knowledge can prolong suffering, but Chaucer's devices would persuade us that our health still exists as a shadow presence. And so we are moved to seek it.

Chapter 11
Windows on the Transcendental

Jean-Honoré Fragonard's

Stolen Kiss

Walking in the Shoes of a Skeptic

Part 1: Two Approaches to the Sacred

Scruton titled this final section "Confronting the Skeptic," but before confronting the skeptic, he would walk in the shoes of a skeptic. To clear the stage for this thought experiment, he briefly sets aside questions about the definition and the reality of the sacred, and he looks instead at how human beings have approached these questions. Scruton writes: "There are, it seems to me, two ways into the topic of theology: the cosmological and the psychological." This recalls his position in the opening paragraphs of the book concerning the confrontations between Christianity and science and between Islam and the modern world. As he describes them there in the second paragraph (see "Reclaiming the True Ground of Religion," pages 237–240), the first confrontation involves a cosmological argument about the nature of reality, and the second involves a psychological or emotional argument about how we should live.

Here, at the end of the chapter, the cosmological and psychological arguments have become cosmological and psychological approaches. The change reflects, I would guess, the way he frames for his reader this final stage of his argument. After we have successfully defined the religious thought, we would learn how to approach the sacred. As I conceive of where we are in the process, I picture myself as one of Chaucer's pilgrims walking step by step to Canterbury. We can get to Canterbury by two different routes. Scruton tells us in this section that those on the cosmological route "speculate about the nature and origin of the world, in search of the Being upon whom the natural order depends." Those on the psychological route "speculate about the experience of holiness, in which individuals encounter another order of things, an intrusion into the natural world from a sphere 'beyond' it." As he writes in the third sentence of the book, the first approach has an intellectual origin, and the second has an emotional origin. He affirms that both approaches are paths to the sacred, even though he has preferred the second or psychological path prior to this. It's the argument that goes through the "I" of a human subject and has gotten him this far in his narrative.

Both approaches, he tells us, "*point* toward the supernatural," but he then explains why the cosmological approach must fail:

> *There could not be an explanation of the world as a whole in natural terms since the explanation must reach beyond the realm of nature to its transcendental ground.*

An explanation of the world as a whole in natural terms, he points out, is beyond the reach of a natural science. This recalls his earlier argument, the one that shifts the "onus" of proving the existence of the sacred "away from the believer" since the transcendental ground can't be proved or disproved (see "An Epistemological Stalemate," pages 273–274). Both approaches may "point" toward the supernatural, but we have to conclude that the cosmological approach can only point.

Scruton then addresses the roadblock in the way of the pilgrim who has taken the psychological approach:

> *There could not be an account of holiness—of the "numinous"—that did not relate the experience to a transcendental subject.*

Notice, though, that there is no roadblock in this statement if we can affirm an experience with a transcendental subject, as Pascal relates when he wrote on a scrap of paper during the course of the encounter: "*Pere juste, le monde ne t'a point connu, mais moi, je t'ai connu.*" Since Scruton has shifted "the onus" onto the skeptic and has established that the skeptic cannot prove Pascal didn't have the experience, he has shown that there is no roadblock in the psychological approach (see "A Focus on the Content of the Thought," page 274).

As he has throughout his arguments, Scruton finds a way forward by grounding an approach to the sacred in a human subject. Chaucer frames *The Canterbury Tales* with this insight. His pilgrimage functions like a church. It brings together diverse individuals in a common purpose, the going to and the returning from a sacred place, and along the way they interact with each other through stories and occasional comments about the story or the storyteller. According to Scruton, this Lebenswelt is the necessary environment for an encounter with the sacred. In our case, we have embarked on a pilgrimage with Roger Scruton, an English philosopher. If we engage with him as I have attempted to do here, it is a conversation of sorts and thus an interpersonal relationship.

Relying on a witness like Pascal, with whom Scruton has a relationship like mine with him, Scruton appears to argue that human subjects—who are schooled in relationships from experiences in family life, reading, business, and other social interactions—have the requisite training and experience to pass through the roadblock, for:

> *The experience of sacred things is, I have suggested, a kind of interpersonal encounter.*

We encounter sacred things, therefore, in much the same way that we encounter other human subjects. We are perfectly familiar with this setting for the encounter; it's the Lebenswelt of language using, symbol interpreters.

We may be familiar with the setting, but the divine Other is unlike any other:

> *It is as though you address, and are addressed by, another I, but one that has no embodiment in the natural order. Your experience "reaches beyond" the empirical realm, to a place on its horizon. The idea is vividly conveyed in the Upanishads, in which Brahman, the creative principle, is represented as transcendental, universal, and also as atman, the self in which all our separate selves aspire to be absorbed and united.*

Scruton makes a distinction between the two approaches (the cosmological and the psychological), and for the purpose of his argument in the book he has chosen the latter approach. As he describes this approach in *this* passage, however, by the end of it, the distinction between the two fades away. The two become one. He unites them as they are united in the Upanishads as Brahman and Atman. Brahman, the "transcendental ground" that is the goal of the cosmological quest, and Atman, the "transcendental subject" of the psychological quest, are two sides of the same coin.

Just as Dante's argument about substance in *La Vita Nuova* helped Lewis to establish the ground for his argument about wholeness in *The Allegory of Love*, the *Commedia* helps me to illustrate Scruton's argument about the wholeness of the two approaches. At the beginning of the *Commedia,* Dante found himself in a dark wood:

> *But at the far end of that valley of evil*
> *whose maze had sapped my very heart with fear!*
> *I found myself before a little hill*
> *and lifted up my eyes. Its shoulders glowed*
> *already with the sweet rays of that planet*
> *whose virtue leads men straight on every road,*
> *and the shining strengthened me against the fright*
> *whose agony had wracked the lake of my heart*
> *through all the terror of that piteous night.*
>
> *The Inferno*, translated by John Ciardi, canto 1, lines 13–21

He looked toward the glowing of the sunlit hill, but looking wasn't enough. To achieve it, he had to go himself, in his own person, the long way around. He achieved it by experiencing just about everything that would temper and prepare a soul to step foot finally on the sunlit hill of the transcendental ground, and we have to notice that these experiences consist for the most part of encounters with other souls. His conversations with the souls of Virgil and Beatrice, in particular, help him to bear the great weight of his many questions on his way to the goal.

Dante affirms, as Scruton does, that a human subject must undertake the quest—a subject who doesn't protect his subjectivity with the armor of an image or a method, and Dante notes for us, as Scruton does, that the process is initiated when Dante *senses* the sunlit hill for the first time. From that moment, now that he's fully conscious of it, the power of the transcendental ground attracts him like a cosmic magnet. Brahman, the transcendental ground that is life itself, and Atman, the divine Self of Dante's poem, which holds all his relationships over the course of the pilgrimage, are one. They work in tandem to one end.

Part 2: The Skeptic Response

Having described the two approaches to the sacred, Scruton now looks at them from the point of view of a skeptic, the point of view that he assumes is shared by many of his readers:

> *The skeptical response to those observations is to say that they are both illusions. It is an illusion that the natural world has some other explanation than itself... It is an illusion that there are sacred things, sacred moments, holy mysteries. For we explain such things as we explain everything else, by showing their place in the order of nature.*

He writes that "we" explain phenomena this way because he's looking at the question from the point of view of most modern secular readers. He then finishes the paragraph with the modern secular explanation of "such things":

> *These experiences arise from the pressure of social life, which causes us to read intention, reason, and desire into all that surrounds us so that, finding no human cause for those things that most deeply affect us, we imagine a divine cause instead.*

Because I have the view from Olympus on this section, I know Scruton is playing the part of a skeptic here. He is presenting the skeptical view to show the reader that he is willing to seriously consider it, but his skepticism about the skeptic point of view leaks out in the sentence just quoted. It explains why human beings "imagine" God, but it leaves intact as a fact of human experience two important observations that undercut the skeptic position. The modern skeptic has to concede that, despite the great reach and precision of scientific knowledge, the scientific method still cannot find a "human cause" (a cause that human science can verify) for many things that impact the lives of human beings. This fact has the additional significance that these are things "that most deeply affect us."

I imagine Scruton has in mind "those things" or those experiences that arrest and hold our attention for days or months or even years because we sense that This Life has an intent to communicate something to us. Perhaps we experience this when we cross an ethical line, irrevocably break the bonds of love or friendship through our own misguided behaviors, or fall on our faces because we weren't paying attention. People have these experiences (I have had them), and science can find no material cause for the "sense" that the soul of the world is talking to us, warning us that This Life is not just governed by physical laws or the laws of the state. Scruton has already explained why Science (personified) can't explain the sense that emerges from these life changing experiences; their significance exists on *the horizon* of the world that Science knows. For Science (personified), the horizon doesn't exist; it's just a metaphor.

"Those things" may also refer to smaller everyday matters. For example, Science can't explain why a mind attending This Life with clarity and concentration loses itself in a daydream. Why is it so easy to be a scatterbrain? This is something that deeply affects anyone trying to learn a difficult subject. Science has yet to locate mind or the power of attention in the physical body so how can Science begin to study them as something in time and space. Even if Science can identify a chemical that makes us more attentive, that chemical is still a chemical and not attention itself, which is spiritual in nature.

To back up the skeptic's case, even as he undermines it, Scruton now unlimbers the big guns wielded by Kant and Hume:

> *If we are to take seriously the argument of Kant in the* Critique of Pure Reason, *and that of Hume in the* Dialogues Concerning Natural Religion, *then surely we have no choice but to accept that the two ways*

to the transcendental—the cosmological and the psychological—are both effectively blocked. We cannot, for reasons made clear by Kant, reason beyond the limits of our own point of view, which is circumscribed by the law of causality, and by the forms of space and time. We have no access to the transcendental perspective from which the question of the ultimate ground of reality can be meaningfully asked, let alone answered.

I pause to consider the statement that we have no access to the transcendental perspective from which we can consider the ultimate ground of reality, what Kant called the noumenon. This is what we must believe (surely, we have no choice) if we find Kant's argument to be credible. But what are we to think if we also find Lewis's third world of myth and fancy (where the ground of reality is one) to be a credible picture of This Life? Surely, we all have had experiences when an otherworldly clarity and concentration of mind overwhelms our usual sense of a self-separate from objects "out there" in the world, when, instead, all is one in selfless speech and action. Surely, we think, there's a hint here of a transcendental perspective. And what are we to think if we find Scruton's arguments—about the sacred's place "on the horizon" and the testimony of a man like Pascal—to be credible? In the final argument of "Believing in God," Scruton will document how Kant himself reaches beyond his own idea that we have no access to the transcendental perspective (see pages 361–365).

Returning to the present argument that (supposedly) favors the skeptic view, Scruton supports the skeptic case with Hume's big gun. The last sentence in this passage, you'll notice, has given me the title for this chapter, "Windows on the Transcendental":

And we cannot, for reasons made clear by Hume, deduce from our religious experiences that they are not illusions. To understand religious experiences, we should not look at them from the first-person point of view, but from outside—as though they were experiences of others. And we should look for the natural explanation, the one that would appeal to us, were we trying to understand, as an anthropologist might, the customs of a foreign tribe. We might arrive at the conclusion that the experience of the sacred is a vital adaptation, like the horror of incest. But this does nothing to justify the perspective of the religious believer, for whom this experience is a window onto the transcendental and an encounter with the hidden God.

Scruton's first sentence expresses Hume's conclusion that our religious experiences are illusions. You have to love how Scruton manages something so full of doubt so indirectly. Since there's no objective proof that God exists, God can play no role in the explanation of an experience like Pascal's. Instead of relying on Pascal's first-person report, Hume would have a neutral third party explain it. The objective observer might conclude that the person being observed was born with a brain and body that tends to hold a belief like this thanks to his genetic makeup. He might find other causes. Perhaps the person took a hallucinogenic drug or had an epileptic seizure.

Scruton puts the skeptic's case before us, but I notice that he ends this passage with that "window" onto the transcendental through which a man like Pascal communicated with the God of Abraham. Speaking for Hume, Scruton warns the reader that this experience does not "justify" belief in a transcendental perspective. Scruton's presentation of the thought, though, makes it absurd. According to Hume, the fact that it happened doesn't prove that it happened. Perhaps our genetic makeup is just making it up. This may be true. If it is true, however, how will we ever know when our genetic makeup is *not* just making something up? Isn't this the end of science and knowledge altogether? (Of course, this is the conclusion Kant addresses in the *Critique of Pure Reason*. The problem posed here is also similar to the problem posed by Descartes's demon of doubt.)

Against this prospect, Scruton offers the perspective of the human subject "for whom this experience is a window onto the transcendental and an encounter with the hidden God." Once this image of a window onto the transcendental is introduced at the end of the paragraph, the window has the last word, and the possibility it represents remains open. With the introduction of this image, we are reminded once more that we are reading the poetry of Roger Scruton. Because it's such an important metaphor, I devote some time and space to developing its significance in the next two sections.

Metaphors

Before looking at that particular image, let's consider once again the nature of a metaphor. In Book One, I began my inquiry with lines of poetry that, taken together along with my commentary, I grandly compared to a hologram of a living soul. The passage from *A Midsummer Night's Dream*, in which Robin intones a prayer over the insensate lovers from Athens, has much to say about metaphors and human subjects. I've requoted them before, but here they are again to refresh your memory:

And the country proverb known
That everyman should take his own
In your waking shall be shown:
Jack shall have Jill;
Naught shall go ill;
The man shall have his mare again, and all shall be well.

His metaphor juxtaposes a something—the marriage of Jack and Jill—with a naught, the nothing of metaphysics. Their marriage, the verse suggests, has translated them into the "naught" of spirit. Naught now can go ill, for nothing more is needed. They have come home for good.

Metaphors are the product of a mind on a quest for meaning. They would relate intangible values and meanings with concrete objects and experiences, and, like a marriage, metaphors aim at completion. Jack, the verse suggests, will be whole and happy when he has his Jill and his mare again. To borrow the language of my inquiry, this image of complete good health—which unites Jack, Jill, and his mare—is what it means to be a living soul. To a mind on a quest for meaning, a metaphor is a small beginning, but it's still a beginning. It's only a beginning, though, for one who understands that the point of a metaphor is to marry the different worlds of physics and metaphysics, of a something and a nothing, of things in the world and the immanent values of the Lebenswelt.

Lewis begins his chapter on allegory with his thoughts on the nature of metaphors. Unlike physical objects like a rose or a beautiful human being, the things the mind seeks in allegory—like the wholeness of life, the love of God, or happiness—are "naught" because they are, to use Lewis's word, "insensible." Nevertheless, people seek to know these "things" as if they exist in the world:

> *Allegory, in some sense, belongs not to medieval man but to man, or even to mind, in general. It is of the very nature of thought and language to represent what is immaterial in picturable terms. What is good or happy has always been high like heavens and bright like the sun. Evil and misery were deep and dark from the first. To ask how these married pairs of sensibles and insensibles first came together would be great folly; the real question is how they ever came apart, and to answer that question is beyond the province of the mere historian.*

Lewis describes an essential function of a language. It represents insensible things like brightness in picturable terms. This is why, I've said before, we love language and why we love the culture, made possible by language, that produces a play like *A Midsummer Night's Dream*. To round out this thought, I have related in Book Two how Thomas Aquinas helped me to understand that we are drawn to the insensible thing we seek because the likeness exists. "The invisible things of God . . . are clearly seen by the things that are made" (see page 182). The likeness, Aquinas argues, *participates* in the brightness. Like the sunlit hill did for Dante, something beautiful in this world gives us a goal, and the goal in turn helps us to learn the right way to live in this world as we strive for beauty. For something ugly on a quest for beauty would stick out like a sore thumb.

Lewis employs a metaphor of his own to describe a metaphor. He compares the pairing of sensibles and insensibles to "married pairs" of men and women. This metaphor suggests they are still a married, not a divorced, pair. Since Scruton has emphasized that contact with the sacred comes in the form of an interpersonal relationship, he might applaud Lewis's image of a married pair that, in their union, gives birth to meaning, but Scruton has developed another metaphor to describe the place and the nature of that which joins two worlds:

> *Sacred objects, words, animals, ceremonies, places, all seem to stand at the horizon of the world looking out to that which is not of this world, because it belongs in the sphere of the divine, and looking also into our world, so as to meet us face-to-face. Through sacred things we can influence and be influenced by the transcendental. If there is to be a real presence of the divine in this world, it must be in the form of some sacred event, moment, place, or encounter: so at least we humans have believed. (originally quoted on page 293)*

The sacred is like those marble images of Janus, who can look in both directions. The sacred is the medium through which "we can influence and be influenced by the transcendental." From this thought, it's an easy step to write that the sacred is a window onto the transcendental, where we see and are seen.

Windows

Part 1: Sonnet 3

Look in thy glass, and tell the face thou viewest
Now is the time that face should form another,
Whose fresh repair if now thou not renewest,
Thou dost beguile the world, unbless some mother.
For where is she so fair whose uneared womb
Disdains the tillage of thy husbandry?
Or who is he so fond will be the tomb
Of his self-love, to stop posterity?
Thou art thy mother's glass, and she in thee
Calls back the lovely April of her prime;

So thou through windows of thine age shalt see,
Despite of wrinkles, this thy golden time.
But if thou live remembered not to be,
Die single, and thine image dies with thee.

Scholars have wondered for centuries about the identity of the person being addressed in the sonnets. It's a cottage industry. I have studied different commentaries on "Look in Thy Glass," and it would appear that for these critics the meaning of it is less controversial. The poet is advising a young man—whom he addresses with the words *thee, thou,* and *thy*—to get married and have children. When you are old, he tells him, you'll see your golden time once more in your child. If you never have a child, you lose the pleasure of seeing the youth and beauty of your child. In other words, you lose everything, and everything loses you.

This reading makes sense, but I now propose another one. In this alternative reading, the couplet imagines a completely different state of mind. The previous quatrains have reflected for the reader—as in a mirror—domestic scenes that add up to a sort of comedy. There's the young man looking in his "glass" in preparation for a social event, there's the suggestion of a young woman blessed with new life in her womb, and there's a mother who sees in her child the lovely April of her prime. "Die single" in the couplet, however, dramatically changes the tone and tenor of what has gone before. Here the poet doesn't paint pleasant scenarios for our comic hero; he commands. He sentences him to death.

Instead of this hazy, mazy business of mirrors—in which the poet initiates the business by encouraging a Narcissus to lose himself in his own image, where his wife then loses herself in the image of her child just as his own mother did, and where the now married Narcissus loses himself in the image of his son—the poet suddenly sees that he should be a window, a *transparent* glass. The poet's perspective and mental state have been utterly transformed. Instead of reflecting images that tempt his Narcissus to act a certain way, the poet would be what he now realizes he has always been—a window on the absolute value of creation. His advice, his little hall of mirrors, is a dead end, as the mirror image was for Narcissus. Now the poet sees himself seeing; he sees himself as the creator of the whole tableau brought to life in the poem. *He* is the window on the golden time he has just imagined for the other. The other's problem as well as the other's golden time has become, and has always been, his own problem and his own golden time. This is certainly the case, but it's also true that his relationship with the young man (whatever that might be), which prompted him to write the poem, has opened this window on creation.

Instead of speaking to another about a conventional way to project and perpetuate one's image in the world, he seems now to speak to himself—or to the other as an alter ego—with great urgency about the prospect of this golden time. Maybe, he says to himself—and the reader—it's time to relinquish all that you have invested in your "image" and in being "remembered" a certain way by others. The point is not to be remembered. The point is *to be*. (The clause "But if you live remembered not to be" is a rich vein of golden words for one who would interpret it.) The time has come, the poet tells himself, to slip into the pool like Narcissus did and die single. Why does he feel compelled to impress others with facile advice? Live without attachment, die single, he urges, as if willing himself to do so, and let's see if the transparency of a true self reveals a golden time.

Before closing, I'd like to emphasize that this reading does not advocate for monkish celibacy or a life of monkish isolation in a cell. It's about an obsessive attachment to an image, which is a mental state that can occur even in a room full of people. As in the original story about him, the Narcissus of "Look in thy Glass" drowns, but he's reborn, in this case as a work of art. It exists in the world to beautify and celebrate creation, and in doing so it celebrates those of us who study it. Thanks to the poem, it might be we come to life in a way that we couldn't have without it. The poet poured himself into the poem, and now he lives in us.

Part 2: The Play's the Window and the Window in "The Knight's Tale"

Shakespeare employs a different kind of window as the comic centerpiece of his Pyramus and Thisbe play at the end of *A Midsummer Night's Dream*. Here it's a chink in the wall between the apartments of two families through which the whispers of two lovers may pass. Tom Snout, a tinker, plays Wall in the play, and before his scene begins, he explains himself to the audience:

> *In this same interlude it doth befall*
> *That I, one Snout by name, present a Wall;*
> *And such a Wall, as I would have you think,*
> *That had in it a crannied hole or chink;*
> *Through which the lovers, Pyramus and Thisbe,*
> *Did whisper often, very secretly.*
> *This loam, this roughcast, and this stone doth show*
> *That I am that same wall. The truth is so.*
> *And this the cranny is, right and sinister,*
> *Through which the fearful lovers are to whisper.*

For eighteen years, students in my AP English class acted out the Pyramus and Thisbe play. This scene—in which Tom presents a wall, sticks out his arm, and spreads index and middle fingers to present the chink for the subsequent dialogue between the two lovers—never failed to transform my student actors into practiced comedians. The lovers' conversation that follows, lips almost touching but kept from touching by the cranny of two fingers, is comic gold. As if inspired by that meeting, the rest of Peter Quince's little play unfolds in the same spirit until Thisbe discovers her Pyramus (like Juliet finding Romeo) lying on the ground all bloody.

In addition to being about the relationships between human subjects who fall in and out of love, *A Midsummer Night's Dream* is about the relationships between human subjects and the transcendental world of fairy-land—the world that's the subject of Lewis's book. The play itself is that chink or cranny between the two worlds. Like Janus, like Scruton's description of a sacred object as a medium, it looks in both directions. It looks into fairyland and looks (with sympathy) at the foolishness of human beings. Robin presents fairyland's point of view with words that may live for all time when he exclaims, "Lord, what fools these mortals be."

Peter Quince's little play also highlights another medium, the person of the tinker Tom Snout. Without him, we have no wall, and we have no opening in the wall. Like Peter Quince's play itself, he is the medium without which there is nothing, for he and his chink get the love story going. As such, Tom Snout is standing in for the play, which is standing in for our author; he's our passage on the horizon. Through Tom, the play, Peter Quince, and finally Shakespeare himself we glimpse the transcendental goal of our pilgrimage. Through this window, we can see, despite all our fears about mortality, the golden time of a comic vision, for Peter Quince's little play manages to turn tragedy into comedy. Shakespeare deftly turns the prospect of a double suicide into comic farce, and yet at the last moment he preserves the pathos of it with the magic of Thisbe's poetry at the end. As if to underscore the comic intent, Pyramus and Thisbe rise from the dead to join the entire cast in a dance for their courtly audience—a lively Bergomask, no less. It's a miracle!

It's the miracle of live theater. About the same time that I began teaching *A Midsummer Night's Dream* to seniors, PBS brought out a video of a live performance filmed at the Shakespeare Festival in Central Park. I credit the director Joseph Papp for engaging hundreds of my students with wonderful farce, the speed and energy of fairyland, and the force of great poetry. Papp's direction of Peter Quince's play at the end reveals why I can call it comic gold. It would be impossible to see that gold when it's buried in a printed text; it takes a master director and live theater. (*A Comic Vision of Great Constancy*, pages 409–435, presents a more detailed reading of Peter Quince's play. It includes a discussion of Thisbe's poem, which ends the play.)

Of course, there's comic gold throughout the canon. The plays are chockablock with scenes in which a character does not have all the facts, but other characters and the audience do. In *A Midsummer Night's Dream*, poor Helena doesn't know why Lysander suddenly loves her, when a few hours earlier he had been doting on Hermia. The audience, though, has heard Oberon explain to Puck the power of the love juice he possesses, and it has seen Puck pour the juice on the eyes of Lysander. Scenes that contrast the limited view of a character with a larger view are a staple of Shakespeare's dramaturgy. These scenes function like a sacred medium for the audience; we identify with the ignorance of the character whose perception is limited (we look into our human nature), but the play, the sacred object, gives us a window into the whole of the situation.

I argue in my book that Shakespeare borrowed much from Chaucer for his version of "The Knight's Tale." In Chaucer's story, Theseus has imprisoned two knights at the top of his keep in a cell that has one window. Everything in the tale turns around those moments when first one knight and then the other glimpses a beautiful young woman in the garden below. They fall in love severally and then fight over the woman, but the rest of the story reveals the stages of an alchemical process whereby Love is made whole. Like the meanings of the word *frame*, it's a story about a constraint, one woman and two men who love her, that resolves into freedom. Just as *A Midsummer Night's Dream* does in Peter Quince's play, it mixes tragic and comic elements to tell the story.

Chaucer's window is structurally like the chink in Shakespeare's wall; it's a long hole in the stone through which love is communicated. It's like the view we get from a telescope. What the knights see is strictly limited. They will never have a 360-degree view of things, like the view from Olympus. They are effectively imprisoned by their limited point of view. Nevertheless, experience in the world teaches us that there is a 360-degree perspective. We know it exists, even if we can't have it *right now* due to strict limitations of our perception. This describes a feature of perception that Chaucer reinforces through the use of first-person narration as I pointed out earlier. Chaucer's window and the use of a limited point of view function like sacred objects as Scruton defines them. They make us aware of ourselves as a limited point of view. The awareness of an end, however, gives our point of view a value that it could never have without the limitation. We find ourselves, as it were, at night in a vast wilderness with only a small fire burning. Life then is a great mystery, and what little we see of it dances in the firelight. Shakespeare's poems and plays often leave me with this impression. Can this vision of life in this world be gainsaid, do you think?

Part 3: The Face Is a Window

Light from the window in Vermeer's painting brings the scene to life in the viewer's eyes, but the window itself is "insensible." We have to imagine it. This window and the light are closely linked, I believe, to the light of a smile in the young woman's face. Just as we might ask where the light streaming in from the left is coming from, we also might ask where the light in the young woman's face is coming from. Like that other light, we have to imagine its ultimate source. In my reading of the painting, I argue that Vermeer intends it to be the light of a living soul. It's something that has been called up from within This Life; I could also call it love. The window we can't see and the light shining through it are part of a metaphor. They help Vermeer to express his love of the inner light that shines in the young woman's face.

Scruton wrote a book titled *The Face of God*, which develops his view that the face is a window on the soul. It looks out at us, and it invites us to look for the mystery within. He describes in the book how this interpretation impacts interpersonal relationships, relationships with the earth in our human settlements of it, and finally our relationships with God. *The Soul of the World*, which he wrote after *The Face of God*, includes insights developed in the earlier book. In Scruton's view of it, the face is a medium—like Chaucer's window in "The Knight's Tale," Shakespeare's chink in *A Midsummer Night's Dream*, the body of Tom Snout, the "face" of *A Midsummer Night's Dream* as a whole (the hidden face of its author), and Vermeer's "window" in *The Allegory of Painting*.

Where a skeptic like Hume sees the face as a feature of our bodies, which, like the masks of tragedy and comedy, can express feelings of sadness and amusement, Vermeer and Scruton see in the face a mystery, a subject that appears to us through the medium of the face as an insensible something, the "I" of the other. We speak to this something with our own "I" (I love you). We may try to kiss this something when we kiss the face, but it remains, ultimately, hidden from us. Still, the mystery has shown its face and tempts us to know it. With great mastery of his craft, Fragonard's *The Stolen Kiss* presents the greatness of this mystery in the metaphoric language of a visual art. It's a mystery, Fragonard suggests, that's even more beautiful than the dress that swells with a satin sheen out of the darkness center stage.

On Striving to Grasp the World as a Whole

Three paragraphs remain to discuss; I'll devote a section to each one. Scruton is moving "step by step" toward completing his house with a window onto the transcendental. He shares Kant's and Hume's skepticism about the cosmological and the psychological approaches, he tells us, "up to a point":

> *But it does not satisfy me, and I shall briefly state the reason here. Kant is right in his claim that scientific knowledge shows the world from our point of view—the point of view of "possible experience"—and as bounded by space, time, and causality.*

Before explaining why it doesn't satisfy, Scruton restates Kant's view. I think it's helpful to briefly summarize what I have learned about that view from other readings, which includes a reading of Scruton's *Kant: A Very Short Introduction*. Most of what I write is common knowledge for readers interested in these matters, so I won't be citing other sources for it.

Human beings, Kant argued in the *Critique of Pure Reason*, can only know the phenomenal world. It's the world of appearances that we see from our own point of view. In other words, it's a subjective point of view. In this, Kant agrees with Hume. Kant's theory of knowledge, however, refutes

Hume's argument that objective knowledge of the phenomenal world is not possible. In Kant's theory, objective knowledge of the world is presupposed in our experience, for experience has already been shaped by a priori concepts of space, time, and causality. Kant argues that this theory (called "transcendental idealism") satisfies the requirement for objectivity that defines a scientific observation, but he concedes that we can never know the noumenal world—things-as-they-are. A "perspectiveless" stance or "a God's-eye view of reality," Scruton writes, is the one to which a rationalist like Leibniz aspires (see pages 21 and 23 in *Kant: A Very Short Introduction*, in which he describes Leibniz's theory in these terms). Unlike Hume's point of view, which is subjective, I think it's fair to say Leibniz's view of the whole aspires to be objective, but according to Kant's theory it fails. Scruton sums up Kant's reasoning as follows: "Neither experience nor reason is alone able to provide knowledge. The first provides content without form, the second form without content. Only in their synthesis is knowledge possible; hence there is no knowledge that does not bear the marks of reason and of experience" (*Kant: A Very Brief Introduction*, page 27).

Now that (thanks to Kant's theory) what can be reliably known is firmly located in the world of appearances as they present to a human subject, Scruton gives Kant's concept of "possible experience" a second look. Kant is also right, Scruton explains (once again I'm quoting from *The Soul of the World*):

> *. . . that reason is tempted to reach beyond these boundaries, striving to grasp the world as a whole and from a transcendental perspective. Kant believed that this temptation leads to contradictions, some of which he exposed in the "Antinomies" chapter of the* Critique of Pure Reason.

The concept of "possible experience" is significantly expanded by the temptation inherent in reason. "The effort of transcendence is, Kant argues, inevitable," but this effort leads to illusion. Our reason can't know the world through an idea like an "unconditioned totality" or a "perfect creator who exists of necessity," for these ideas "inevitably end in fallacy and contradiction." Despite this fact, Scruton writes, Kant held that "there is no way in which we can avoid the temptation towards this vain journey into the transcendental. Our very possession of a point of view on the world creates the 'idea' of a world seen from no point of view. Thus we strive always 'to find for the conditioned knowledge of the understanding, the unconditioned, whereby its unity might be brought to completion.'" (See *Kant: A Very Short Introduction*, pages 60–61, for the passages quoted in this paragraph. The quotes within the quotes from Scruton are from Kant.) Kant's argument, once grasped as a whole, Scruton argues, gives reasonable grounds for the soundness of his theory, which has the effect of a transcendental perspective, despite its many ambiguities.

Kant's argument about this perspective begins with the premise on which his entire argument rests. He assumes that a human subject who uses the personal pronoun "I" *by definition* is whole. We learn later in *The Soul of the World* about this concept, which Kant called the "transcendental unity of apperception." (*Apperception* is Kant's and Leibniz's word for self-consciousness.) How, I wonder, if we look at this life from the point of view of a human subject, do we discern it to be not whole? Can consciousness be divided?

To my mind, this effort to view the world as a whole and this unity of self-consciousness must be related. They may even be self-evident to people like myself, who aren't philosophers. I have found hints of these insights in other readings. For example, I wrote about Chaucer's Theseus and the play of *A Midsummer Night's Dream* "striving to grasp the world as a whole" without knowing Kant's or Scruton's views on the subject, and I've documented how Chaucer went about it in the section of this book titled "The Shadow Presence of Divine Wisdom" (see pages 337–342). This striving, I conclude, must be "in the air" of these important works, or I couldn't have written what I did. In addition to examples from Chaucer and Shakespeare, in Book Two of this book, I have pointed out that by telling stories in *La Vita Nuova* and the *Commedia* from the first-person point of view Dante makes his own consciousness the arena for all and everything.

Scruton next introduces Hegel's argument about the antinomies to move his argument forward. Kant's greatest successor, Scruton writes:

> *. . . denied that those contradictions set limits to rational inquiry. Reason, for Hegel, is constantly transcending its own partial viewpoints, on its journey toward the "Absolute Idea." Reason aims of its nature toward a kind of final narrative of how things are, in which all the contradictions (which are contradictions only from a partial perspective) are overcome.*

Reason's journey, as Hegel understood it, reminds me of Lewis's claim that the best minds embrace the oneness of monotheism (see page 118). Just as the figures of Brahman, the transcendental ground that's the goal of the cosmological approach, and Atman, the true Self that's the goal of the psychological approach, assisted Scruton earlier with the thought that the cosmological and the psychological approaches are one, we see this thought from Hegel reaching, despite our "partial" viewpoints, for wholeness.

With that, Scruton is ready once more to shift the argument beyond the objective, perspectiveless stance from which a rationalist like Leibniz and Science (personified) view this life:

> *If Hegel is right, then the cosmological path points beyond the edge of the world as science describes it, to a place where another kind of question can be asked, a question that cannot be answered with a cause, but only with a reason: the question "why?" asked of the world as a whole—the question addressed to Brahman. We can answer such a question only by giving a teleological, rather than a causal, account of things. That account will make no difference to, and have no contact with, cosmological science.*

What is this "place" where the question can be asked? Only a human subject in relationship with another subject can ask the question "Why?" Intersubjectivity is the soil, he has said, in which the sacred can grow. The question "Why?" and any answer that comes of it is off the grid and off the radar (to use approximate metaphors) of cosmological science.

The "if" (in "If Hegel is right") is in keeping with Scruton's inquiry from the beginning. His argument concerns what Kant has called "possible experience" and what I have referred to in my commentaries as a "sense" of the sacred. This quote about the place where the question "Why?" can be asked prepares the reader for the argument that follows in the next chapter, in which Scruton introduces what he calls a "cognitive dualism." As I relate in my introduction, he proposes there two different ways of knowing the world: the way of science and the way of interpersonal understanding. I find in Scruton's presentation of the two the hint of a humorous paradox. The one claims to be objective because it's based on material realities, but this insistence, after five hundred years of use in this world by fallible human beings, has begun to look like a bias that gives the way of science a subjective cast. The other admits to being subjective, focused as it is on the human subject, but this admission reflects a reasoned judgment about our kind that gives the way of interpersonal understanding an objective cast.

The Approach Determines the Reality

Scruton's introductory chapter to *The Soul of the World* has been addressing two important issues that Western philosophers have been writing about since before the time of Plato and Aristotle: the ontological question—"What is real?"—and the epistemological question—"How do we know what is real?" Scruton acknowledges these two issues in the section he titled "The Epistemology of the Sacred," the one in which he returns to the question of veracity: "Is there anything that answers to this search for the sacred?" In these last three paragraphs, having posed the questions—"What is real and how do we know it?"—he outlines the cosmological and the psychological approaches to answering them. From the opening pages of the book, he has been arguing that the epistemological approach he refers to as the psychological approach is how we answer the ontological question.

The teleological "account" that he writes about in the passage quoted above describes a different way of knowing reality than that of the sciences.

Instead of looking for the initial push or the big bang of motion in the physical universe, Scruton asks the questions any human subject wonders about, even if the questions get lost in the busyness of worldly affairs: "Why was I born? What's the meaning of my life? Why must I die?" These questions can't be answered by a gas or a black hole or any other physical phenomenon; we must address them, Scruton writes, to a subject like ourselves.

Before climbing to the final stages of his argument, I'd like to present an observation he may be implying. The physical sciences take a causal approach, and this way of looking at the world reveals the causal laws of physical reality. The approach determines the reality. Scruton takes the teleological approach, and this way of looking at the world reveals a reality that includes the sacred.

A Restatement of the Skeptical Point of View

Scruton's inquiry has led him to the realm of "possible experience," but in the next paragraph he returns once more to the observation that "from the scientific point of view, religious beliefs and practices are not to be explained as the pious would wish." Two centuries of modern thought "must alert us to the evident truth that religion is a natural phenomenon like any other, to be explained first in terms of its social and evolutionary function and second in terms of things going on in the brain of the believer." He points out that religious narratives can have a powerful effect by endowing our life with a goal and a meaning, but he ends the paragraph by calling these narratives "fictions" and asserting that:

> *. . . the fictions neither explain the experience [of sacred things] nor justify its intrinsic claim to veracity.*

This sentence is perfectly balanced between two positions we can hold regarding the sacred. There's the assertion that the fictions can't explain the experience of sacred things nor justify its claim to veracity, but there's also the assertion that experiences of the sacred have an *intrinsic* claim to veracity. For people like Pascal, who have experienced the sacred, the truth of the experience is self-evident. Lewis, I believe, would agree that allegorical fictions like the ones he studied have an intrinsic claim to veracity. Like our beating heart, allegories about the wholeness of life are essential to life. Nevertheless, Scruton here seems to come down on the skeptic side.

Reaching Beyond

Given the tensions built into the last sentence, it's no wonder Scruton begins the next and last paragraph of the chapter with another hedge as to possible experiences. "Yet here too there is more to be said." He's right, and it takes him another 176 pages to say it. In the last paragraph of "Believing in God," he refuses to surrender the field to skeptics.

For readers with a philosophical bent, he has built an attractive, classically proportioned house that may entice a skeptical reader to enter into his argument. It's a structure that artfully combines walls and windows. Before we get to his "window" at the end of the chapter, like Tom Snout he presents walls of skeptical thought beginning with the well-groomed commentators, the skeptical anthropologists, the skeptical evolutionary psychologists, and the skepticism of Kant and Hume. Freud makes a surprising cameo, given that he saw himself as a scientist and an agnostic, for Scruton gives him credit for focusing on *the thought* of the sacred. Freud's approach puts the inquiry where it belongs, as a matter for human subjects who have thoughts and feelings about incest and the sacred that arise in the mind. Pascal's *nuit de feu* serves as the first significant chink in a skeptic's wall for excising the sacred. Once that crack has opened up, Scruton inserts arguments to give it a more rational, architectural shape. Nevertheless, here at the end he has left his window somewhat in limbo. It has been papered over with philosophical doubt.

But this, too, is part of Scruton's architecture. The tension in his presentation mirrors the tension we necessarily find in a wall and a window. A window needs a wall to be a window. We need that wall of skepticism, it would seem, to affect surprise when light suddenly streams through it and infuses a ruck of mundane objects with living colors, with the warmth of a body that's alive and breathing. The two, the wall and the window, work in tandem to one end. To reach the goal, we need the kind of help that Dante got on his pilgrimage. We need to meet and question people who have failed in the quest because they somehow mistook it. We need to meet and question great poets, philosophers, artists, musicians, and mystics like Pascal, for in their work they provide a view of what we love: a life that's whole, beautiful, and intrinsically free.

In the spirit of one who can be both a wall and a window, like Tom Snout, in his final paragraph, Scruton concedes:

> *. . . there are idolatrous religions and religions that muddle the natural and the supernatural in ways that make nonsense of both. But there are also religions that turn their backs on idolatrous practices, that invite us to address the specific moments of ritual involvement with an alertness that reaches precisely beyond what is present to the senses, toward the perspective lying on the edge of things, which addresses us I to I. The narrative of a religion is like a commentary on these moments, a prop to be discarded when the experience, the sakinah, has been fully grasped. This "reaching beyond" of the religious moment is not different, I shall suggest, from the transcendental urge of reason itself. Ultimately the cosmological and the psychological paths are paths toward the same destination, and that destination lies on the far horizon of our world.*

Dear reader, if you have read through my recreation of Scruton's argument on believing in God, I hope you feel the light and warmth that shines out at us from Scruton's crown of poetry and philosophy. In this last paragraph, I find he is describing the way my own inquiry has evolved. It begins with Lewis's allegories, which prime the pump of our interest in a life that is whole and animated with moral truth. Lewis encourages us to believe there's a germ of truth in these fictions. Like Archetrenius, we go in search of it, for we would reknit the divided love. The transcendental urge of Scruton's reasoning, on the other hand, moves us to stand before creation without fictional "props." It persuades us we can experience the real presence of the sacred as "a moment not just of faith but of knowledge, and a gift of grace" (see the quote on page 329). The light and heat of the sacred are not just parts of a metaphor. They are the light and heat of the sacred itself—like the sun all those light-years away, which still can burn your skin on a hot summer's day. Isn't it amazing, up there, blazing away in the endless darkness? Yes, as you can see, I'm still leaning on my props, my metaphors. Apparently, I'm unready at this point to discard them. Book Four and my postscript have more to say about this station on the way to grasping the *sakinah*. Given this last paragraph, though, I can say with some confidence that the sun in my metaphor and in the metaphor that anchors Plato's argument in the *Republic* represents the "alertness," which is the living, beating heart of this final passage. When it shines forth, Scruton argues, the world (as Ariel sings in *The Tempest*):

> *doth suffer a sea-change*
> *Into something rich and strange*

Why do we "suffer" this change? This is something Book Three addresses by paying attention to "the core religious thought—the thought that the sacred and the sacrificial coincide (see page 242)," and it's a question that chapter 4 of Book Four, "The Ghostly Sight That's Dearly Bought," addresses with a number of examples.

Book Four

The Survival Value of Sacred Wonderlands

Chapter 1

On Hunting for the Soul of the World

John Singer Sargent's

Chiron and Achilles

Chiron

For this chapter, I've called on Sargent's *Chiron and Achilles* to illustrate several themes that have emerged from these readings. For example, Lewis has Bernard describe how man is a creature who lives in two worlds:

> *He shall be heavenly, earthly; by his care*
> *Shall rule the earth, and reach the heaven by prayer,*
> *For as the diverse sources whence he drew*
> *His being, so himself will still be two . . .*

We are two (we are a body and a mind), but the allegories Lewis studies also insist that we are one, just as the centaur Chiron unites in himself a beast and a human being. Scruton, I believe, makes a similar argument. The science of evolution teaches us that we belong to the order of nature; we are animals who evolved from animals. To regain a human subject's freedom to act and to be accountable for actions, though, Scruton insists that our species at some point took the step "from useful instinct to directed thought." Very likely, this "step" is connected with the development of human speech. In the lifeworld of human speech, Scruton argues, we experience a reality that can include the sacred.

Just as Chiron transports Achilles in a search for heavenly game in Sargent's image, Chiron transports Faust in a scene from part two called "Classical Walpurgis Night." Chiron is a figure from myth, and yet in the play of *Faust* he is carrying a real man, Goethe (in the shape of his alter ego Faust), further into the wonderland from which Chiron emerged. The real man Goethe wrestled in his life with a very real dilemma. He lived in the land, now called Germany, which was steeped in Gothic Christianity and repressed remnants of pagan magic. Given the darkness of his native culture, he dreamed of Italy and Greece where there was light and color. He loved the light and color of Renaissance Italian art, and especially, he loved the freedom with which gods and men expressed their sexuality in those fictional settings. For Goethe, this freedom was wonderful.

In other words, Goethe was wrestling with the problem Lewis writes about in his chapter on courtly love: In the Christian culture of the West, physical love was thought to be a sin. Goethe has Chiron, with help from others like Mephistopheles and the Homunculus, transport Faust to where he could find a cure. Millions of readers have been attracted to Goethe's venture into this wonderland because the truth and beauty of the poetry is self-evident and wonderful. In this wonderland, Eros can be freely addressed and given a place of respect. Like Goethe, we (his readers) are pilgrims who seek our health, the wholeness of body and mind. To achieve this goal, Goethe concluded that the creative principle deeply embedded in the body itself, the lower half of Chiron, had to be acknowledged and made one in a man who is hunting heavenly game.

What can Chiron do for me? I confess to being not a little out of my element as well as my depth in philosophy. I'm more at home in the wonderlands of literature, and that's where I'd have my Chiron take me. Still, the time spent with C. S. Lewis, when he's wearing his philosopher's hat, and Roger Scruton has been well spent, as I still hope to show.

I would transition from philosophy to the promised land we can read about in the Bible, the pure land in Buddhist literature, and the wonderlands Lewis calls the third world of myth and fancy. We can't deny that these lands exist, for people have been reading about them in our literature—the literature of all human beings—for thousands of years. Having been deeply impressed on the minds of those who have encountered them in the lifeworld of human culture, these wonderlands have deeply impressed themselves in every aspect of our civic life—but especially in institutions like marriage. The rituals of family life serve as a training ground and an arena where we learn to respect the moral order that comes to light in intersubjective relationships.

I begin by reviewing the ground of "Believing in God" in a more compact form. That done, I'll introduce the notion I have gathered from studying Lewis and Scruton that literature, art, music, and architecture all originally served a primal function; they prime the pump for the sacred with the sacred. Both writers, I believe, would revive that function by means of the wonderlands that are revealed in these forms. If modern works are not up to the job, then we must look to the ones that have served in the past. After spending some time on the phenomenon of wonder itself, I'll conclude the chapter with an interpretive framework suggested by Scruton's thoughts on the paths to the sacred. Since I've taken up residence in the House of Scruton, I can view the texts about Abraham and Siddhartha through its windows.

Priming the Pump for the Sacred with the Sacred

With reasoned circumspection, Scruton suggests at the end of "Believing in God" that reaching through to the sacred "is not different . . . from the transcendental urge of reason itself." Looking back to see how we got there, I find that my recreation of his narrative about religious belief has a beginning, a number of significant episodes in the middle, and the back and forth about the sacred at the end. He begins with skeptics like the commentators and the evolutionary psychologists. He demonstrates, though, that a scientist's own closely held beliefs about God and the material world disables any proof that God doesn't exist. Scruton wins that argument, but we then encounter what he calls a "terrible truth." Scripture teaches us that knowledge of God's presence comes with the failure to find him.

Pascal's *nuit de feu* offers an account of the real presence, but Scruton realizes that Pascal's account by itself is not enough to make a serious case for religion in an age of debunking. He sets out, therefore, to resolve the "real problem about the epistemology of religious thoughts" by establishing what thoughts define the intentionality of faith. Once we understand that the religious frame of mind is "a reaching out from subject to subject," the skeptical reader can relate it to something we often experience, for interaction with another subject is common among us.

Having established that the thought of religion is grounded in a subject-to-subject relationship, he's ready to present an epistemology of the sacred. An experience of the sacred is what distinguishes a religion from other interpersonal experiences like sports and politics. He would address whether the sacred "can be present among us in a way that rewards our search for it." He begins by comparing the religious thought with magic. He argues that magic spells, while similar to religious prayers, cannot explain the sacred, for the business of magic is too "prosaic" and "practical" to account for "the awe-inspiring otherworldliness of sacred things." The faithful, he tells us, approach sacred objects with awe because "they seem to be both in our world, and also out of it." This is why he places sacred objects on "the horizon of our world." Like the burning bush that spoke to Moses or Pascal's *nuit de feu*, they serve as mediums. They connect an otherworldly subject with a human subject in this world. He dismisses Girard's theory that a sense of the sacred derives from the death of a human scapegoat who becomes sacred through a ritual sacrifice. Scruton finds the sacred instead in rites of passage around birth, initiations into adulthood, marriage, and ordinary deaths.

His narrative reaches a turning point in my chapter 9 of Book Three (pages 315–330). To move ahead, he has to look back at the terrible truth he introduced earlier, that knowledge of God's presence comes with the failure to find him. Because this failure is a real problem, many people experience religious doubt. Some have said that alienation is a primary characteristic of the modern age, suggesting it's something unique to our time, but literature going back to Homer's time includes characters who suffer from alienation in different forms—from family, from community life, from life, and from God. For example, the *Odyssey* begins with Odysseus in despair. He is the captive of the nymph Calypso, who loves him and who provides every possible physical comfort. Odysseus, however, longs only for his home in Ithaca and has given up hope of ever reaching it. He thinks Athena, his guardian spirit, has abandoned him.

Scruton points out in this station of his narrative that some religions endorse a position that encourages alienation from the sacred. For example, he describes the practice of Sunnis who forbid creative interpretation of the Koran because God dictated and then abandoned it. Also, he cites Protestants like Paul Ricoeur who base their faith on natural reason, not revelation. It's at this critical stage that Scruton makes a decisive ruling on questions about the sacred. In my title for chapter 9, "The Ground of the Sacred," I employed a metaphor that Scruton himself uses to express in a single sentence the argument directed at the religious doctrine that God has departed forever from our midst:

> *Yet we know that this excision of the sacred does not encourage faith but merely deprives it of the soil in which it grows.*

It's the argument he has been making more generally with secular skeptics. To borrow an old expression, to have the sacred in our lives we have to "prime the pump" for the sacred with the sacred. We need to explore the thought of the sacred, as he has been doing, to make a fair assessment. Scruton began his argument by presenting the skeptic positions of the commentators, the sociologists, and the evolutionary psychologists. In each case, he turned away their thrusts at the sacred with insight, logic, and poetry. His intelligence, grace, and good humor are attractive. I find a useful lesson here; this is how a good man primes the pump.

In addition, he makes a consistent case for the ground of the sacred. From the opening pages, he asserts that the thought of the sacred and any argument about it must be grounded in the human subject. The human subject alone is capable of insight, logic, poetry, and relationships with other subjects. The human subject is the soil in which faith and the presence of the sacred itself must grow. He aims in the early skirmishes of his campaign to expose a critical weakness in his opponents' position: the natural sciences would deny the freedom of the human subject, the freedom Scruton knows he possesses. Why does he know this? It's self-evident or, as Kant would say, presupposed. It comes with being a language-using human being. The natural sciences, it appears, would refashion the human subject as a human animal that lives close to its reproductive strategies. In this, they are doing

Nature's work. In this way, Nature can reclaim the human species. Is this an advance? Scruton clearly doesn't think it is.

This view of human nature is the Achilles' heel or the soft underbelly of his opponents' position because it overlooks "the aspect of our mental states that is most important to us, and through which we understand and act upon each other's motives, namely, their intentionality or 'aboutness'" (pages 253–256). It denies our freedom to run over the hump of "useful instinct" into the pasture—the wonderland—of "directed thought" (see pages 259–264), and it denies the intersubjectivity that is the without-which-nothing of the Lebenswelt, the human world. This is the soil in which love, compassion, and sacrifice can grow; this is the soil in which the sacred grows. By making the human subject the without-which-nothing of the Lebenswelt, Scruton primes the pump of the sacred with a human subject's world-historical responsibility of freedom and spiritual kingship in the realm of which a human subject is the center.

Quite naturally, then, in addition to excising the human subject, the natural sciences would excise the sacred from the way the world is understood, but Scruton takes us chapter by chapter through *The Soul of the World* to build his case that this is a mistake. In a section I titled "The Sovereignty of the Human Subject," he writes about the real presence of the sacred in terms that a dyed-in-the-wool skeptic may find difficult to understand or accept, and he points out the initial critical error that skeptics make in judging religious thoughts:

> *The real question for religion in our time is not how to excise the sacred, but how to rediscover it, so that the moment of pure intersubjectivity, in which nothing concrete appears, but in which everything hangs on the here and now, can exist in pure and God-directed form. Only when we are sure that this moment of the real presence exists in the human being who experiences it, can we then ask the question whether it is or is not a true revelation—a moment not just of faith but of knowledge, and a gift of grace.*

The first sentence is intended for those who aren't dyed-in-the-wool skeptics, who may find in it something that catches the imagination, something that wonders, "How can he say such a thing?" In the second sentence Scruton takes up the first order in the business of rediscovering the sacred. He establishes, in no uncertain terms, who can judge as to whether the experience of the real presence is or is not a true revelation. A skeptic, he tells us, cannot judge, and that's that. Who can be sure that this moment of the real presence exists in the human being who experiences it? It has to be someone who has experienced some form, some hint, of the real presence. For example, Scruton may at one time have been a skeptic, but something changed him. Let me put it in the first person as Scruton does in the quote. If I was a skeptic but am no longer because I've experienced the real presence in some form, I now must doubt the skeptics. Turnabout is fair play. Once "we" are sure that the real presence exists, then "we" can question whether or not the experience is a true revelation and knowledge about this life.

Why are "we" able to judge? Scruton asserts the sovereignty of an individual's experience of the sacred, but, of course, his assertion doesn't prove anything. What does prove it? The proof is in the pudding, they say. "We" are able to judge because, like our freedom, an experience of the sacred is self-evident. I can't think of a better place to use "self-evident" as the capstone of an argument. Scruton himself weighs in on this thought in the following passage (see page 281):

> *We rightly think that there is something mysterious and perhaps inexplicable about the "real presence." But nobody who has the experience of that thing is likely to think it to be simply an illusion: it comes to us with a self-verifying character that silences skepticism, even as it calls out for interpretation.*

I'm convinced this is true for the person who has experienced the real presence. What about those of us who have not experienced the real presence? This chapter, "On Hunting for the Soul of the World," addresses that question directly, but the whole of my Book Three has been addressing it. To bridge that gap between myself, who has not experienced the real presence, and my teacher who has I would make the case that the "presence" of that person, the one who had the experience, also comes to us in his person or in his work with a self-verifying character. The transformative power of the real presence radiates an "aura" out into the world (see pages 251–253 for Scruton's introduction of an "aura" into his argument by pointing out how scientists would remove the aura around social facts). It communicates directly with or without speech. The person who has had the experience is a medium through which we sense the presence (a pre-sense) of something great.

Scruton cannot prove that the real presence exists. He can, however, prime the mind of his reader with his interest and insight. He's a gifted teacher, and he works within a long tradition of gifted teachers. Along with Lewis and Scruton, these others serve this great need in our lives: they prime the pump for the sacred with the sacred. In their work, we sense the presence of something great. What is it about this person, this work? we wonder. That's a start. That's a priming of the pump.

Ways to Wonder

Part 1: Lewis and Scruton as Mediums

It is our great good fortune that these mediums, most of them dead for hundreds even thousands of years, have left us the wonderlands of our literature as a legacy. The wonderlands are the about-which-nothing for someone who would explore the thought of the real presence. C. S. Lewis and Roger Scruton inherited this legacy and have passed it along to us in their interpretations of it.

Lewis describes how the wonderlands of allegory developed through the centuries as a literary form. As he does so, he helps us to understand the nature and function of allegory. He begins his history with Dante's thoughts on the subject, for they give the subject a bottom, a floor, or a foundation on which Lewis can build the rest. These are metaphors I employ to describe the substance of Dante's *La Vita Nuova* as well as Dante's own substance. From my reading of Lewis's text and the others that form the basis of my inquiry, I concluded that I might as well call this substance a living soul.

According to Dante and Lewis, allegory pictures our inner life as one, and Lewis also argues that allegory emerged from a widespread ethical revolution in Europe as the Roman Empire slowly died. Judging from experiences in my own lifetime, I imagine that the people of that time had to internalize the government of their lives. Lewis's narrative suggests that an awareness took root among them that a living soul, our substance, is enlivened by a basic principle that is best expressed as the golden rule: Do unto others as you would have them do unto you. Out of this awareness the notion of an internal holy war grows, the all-consuming effort to fight those impulses that break the golden rule. To sum up, allegory portrays with imaginative figures and plotlines how a living soul, our substance, strives to live in accord with its true nature. (Like an allegory, this sentence about Lewis and his book tells a story, a fiction, about a living soul.)

Just as Lewis's allegories are stories about the soul, the title of Scruton's book alerts the reader that he is writing about the soul of the world. Scruton communicates with philosophical ideas, but he also resorts to poetry in order to express himself. We are invited to look through the "window" on the sacred he has framed for us. Even though he rarely mentions the soul in almost two hundred pages of text, his title makes it the focus of his book. As Scruton seeks to define the sacred and to test for himself whether it's real, he leaves us with the impression that he encounters the soul of the world in the transcendental urge of his own soul.

These are wonderful works. They have primed the pump. They lift up my thoughts like Chiron lifting up Achilles in Sargent's painting.

Part 2: Wonder

Before moving ahead, let's briefly consider the experience of wonder itself. We can experience it anywhere. In addition to wondering at the effect of goodness and wholeness in the poetry of Shakespeare, I wonder at the presence of mind in the speech and actions of people I have known. I wonder about a sound late at night that I can't explain. I'm tempted to conclude that the effect of wonder—which is whole, unforced, unpremeditated—gives the real presence its character of self-evidence. A magnetic attraction accompanies wonder; we attend and are drawn to that which produced it. Lewis was attracted to the way allegories guided a pilgrim reader like himself to a place where life is whole and good, so he wrote *The Allegory of Love* to share that place with others. The attraction for that place is self-evident. I read Lewis's narrative carefully because I, too, wanted to go there. Shakespeare fashioned *A Midsummer Night's Dream* and *The Tempest* around a wonderland of fairies and magic, and in my opinion, these plays contain some of the greatest poetry ever written in English. The truth and beauty of these poems are self-evident. No wonder they are two of his most popular plays.

Why do we wonder about life itself? To borrow a thought from Scruton's conclusion of "Believing in God," we wonder about it because we can't explain it, and so we go to Brahman with the question "Why?" We can't explain *why* we live in a universe of infinite space like this one or *why* we were born into a species whose mental states evolved from useful instinct to directed thought. While we're at it, we would ask Brahman, the transcendental ground, why we were born so we know what to do about it. Great magicians make a good living because their tricks are wonderful. Why do we admire a magician's power of illusion? Because we can't see how he did it, we wonder how he pulled it off. A skeptic would remove the magic and explain the trick. For some, though, the wonder is the point, for wonder is a whole, unforced, unpremeditated response to life, an end unto itself. We could do worse than to conceive that we were born as human beings to be amazed by creation. There's plenty of room in a human subject for that along with the transactional matters required to maintain a decent life.

I think it's safe to say we experience wonder by different routes and in different places. For example, Scruton's philosophical arguments are wonderful. They please our intellectual sense with how precise and true to life they are. At the same time, and sometimes in the same place, his prose, I have pointed out, can please our aesthetic sense when it communicates not only a thought but the pleasure of being in the presence of something beautiful. The aesthetic sense is certainly the route to wonder on which Faust embarked. He loved, as Goethe undoubtedly did, to be in the presence of a beautiful woman. There are wonders everywhere in the natural world. When I look past the stars and the moon at night, I wonder at infinite space and time. This evening, standing outside on the terrace, I felt a slight breeze on my face. Like an invisible lover, it lit up a sense of my skin and, by implication, the shell of my being and, by implication, of Being. This morning at first light the dogs and I took our first walk of the day in a wonderland. I moved half asleep through a murky space full of the silence that had gathered in it all through the night. Along the way, a small bird on the fence just a few feet from us burst into piercing song. We stopped, of course, the whole world stopped, to take it in. Such passion from one so slight!

An Interpretive Framework

Just as we experience wonder in different ways, Scruton has argued that we experience the sacred in different ways. Since his thoughts on this subject have given me an interpretive framework for my readings of the sacred wonderlands in the next two chapters, I'll review them here.

As he was winding up his chapter on "Believing in God," Scruton has the reader consider the ways human beings have thought about the sacred:

> *There are, it seems to me, two ways into the topic of theology: the cosmological and the psychological. We can speculate about the nature and origin of the world, in search of the Being upon which the natural order depends. And we can speculate about the experience of holiness, in which individuals encounter another order of things, an intrusion into the natural world from a sphere "beyond" it.*

The first, he told us in the second paragraph of the book, is intellectual; the second is emotional. He suggests later that the two involve a different point of view. The first looks at things from the third-person point of view of an outside observer, like an anthropologist observing "from outside" the behaviors of a tribe. The second looks at things from the first-person point of view. The first concerns the nature of reality; the second concerns how we should live.

Which path has Scruton taken?

Unlike the way I frequently insert myself into the commentary, I notice he does not—except as the author of the script, as the set designer, as the stage manager of the cues, and as the one who does the lighting. I notice in particular that he doesn't explicitly claim to have experienced the real presence himself. Since he's a philosopher, he carefully builds on those concrete objects available to all readers of philosophy, the published thoughts of other philosophers; it's a point of view and an approach that aims, it would seem, at objectivity. I have argued throughout, however, that he has followed the psychological approach. It's the one that allows him to define the intentionality of faith as "a reaching out from subject to subject." This definition follows a careful philosophical argument. It is "sound" in that way, philosophically objective, but at the same time it's grounded in the human subject. The objective point of view and the subjective point of view both play a role in the argument. Even though his argument is rooted in the human subject, the philosophical form of it allows him to write at the end of the chapter that reaching through to the sacred "is not different . . . from the transcendental urge of reason itself." The reader has to agree because we have witnessed how reason has urged him along.

Scruton concludes his observations about the two approaches by identifying them with figures from Hindu mythology:

> *The experience of sacred things is, I have suggested, a kind of interpersonal encounter. It is as though you address, and are addressed by, another I, but one that has no embodiment in the natural order. Your experience "reaches beyond" the empirical realm, to a place on its horizon. The idea is vividly conveyed in the Upanishads, in which Brahman, the creative principle, is represented as transcendental, universal, and also as atman, the self in which all our separate selves aspire to be absorbed and united.*

Brahman—the creative principle—and Atman—the self of all selves—are a married pair, to borrow the way Lewis describes the primal structure of language as a joining of the insensible with the sensible.

They are like Rama and Sita, and they are like all those who come together to be a married pair in Shakespeare's comedies. The creative principle is "out there" in the world. In *A Midsummer Night's Dream,* Shakespeare imagines it as Oberon and Titania in fairyland, and in *The Tempest* he imagines it as Prospero and Ariel on their magic island. Just as the creative principle impacts the characters in the world of the play that it oversees, the creative principle of his play as a whole affects us in the audience. For me, the experience of a play as live theater (if it's competently executed) lifts up my spirit the way, I imagine, an experience of holiness does.

I recall as well that time in my life some five years ago—as I cast about for a way to frame my inquiry—the creative principle led me to the text in Genesis, when God breathed into our nostrils, and we became a living soul. I find something like this in Martini's *Annunciation Altarpiece*, where the golden trace of the angel's words and his invisible eye beam do the work of the breath as they *settle* the soul of the world within Mary. The married pair is a central concern throughout my inquiry, and my readings of the texts on Abraham and Siddhartha in the next chapters reveal how these stories marry the objective and subjective halves of a life that's whole and meaningful.

More importantly, this married pair describes my relationship with the wonderlands I would study. The text is Brahman, and the reader is Atman. As I read, the soul of the world addresses the substance (I might as well call it a living, loving soul) that unites all the accidents of my life. This is a wonder. It primes the pump for the sacred with the sacred. It's a process whereby the soul of the world breathes life into a living, loving soul, and (for all intents and purposes) a living, loving soul becomes the soul of the world. Scruton's book has suggested to me this reading of the verse in Genesis.

The experience of encountering a sacred text fits Scruton's description of an experience that "reaches beyond" rather well. As Scruton has argued and as I have maintained throughout my own commentaries, the meaning of a language has no embodiment in the natural order. A book has a physical body, but the story or the idea in the book does not. The story and the idea belong to the lifeworld created in the interpersonal relationships of language using human subjects. The authors of sacred texts are long dead. If we have a sense of an "I" speaking to us through the story or the idea, the "I" that's addressing us "has no embodiment in the natural order" any more than the meaning of the text does.

It goes without saying that few texts in existence can produce an experience that "reaches beyond." I follow Scruton in making the argument that some do.

Chapter 2

Abraham

Rembrandt's

Abraham Serving the Three Angels

Abraham in Genesis Rabbah

For my portrait of Abraham, I draw on three different texts. The first tells stories about Abraham when he was still living with Terah, his father. This text is taken from Genesis Rabbah, chapter 38, a *midrash* from around 300 CE. It is based on the verse in Genesis 11:28: "And Haran [Abraham's brother] died in the presence of his father Terah in the land of his nativity, in Ur of the Chaldees." Here's the first incident in the story:

> *Terah was an idol manufacturer who once went away and left Abraham in charge of the store. A man walked in and wished to buy an idol. Abraham asked him how old he was and the man responded "50 years old." Abraham then said, "You are 50 years old and would worship a day old statue!" At this point the man left, ashamed.*

Since Abraham works in his father's shop, he knows the value of the idols they sell. They make them cheap, in a day or less, and sell them dear. He knows that the idols are impostors, but he doesn't yet know the One God. He can only imagine Him. At this point the story is describing a psychological route to the sacred. Abraham challenges the fifty-year-old buyer, not with the One God, but with the knowledge and infinite worth of his fifty-year-old body and mind.

Even though the One God of Abraham's faith is not mentioned (for He has not yet revealed himself to the boy), the incident establishes the human subject as the ground for what will become the worship of the One God. The incident takes place within the Lebenswelt of ordinary interpersonal relationships. Abraham speaks to the man directly in the language they share. By means of their language, Abraham would wake him up to his own nature: "You are alive. That thing is dead. You already have the intelligence to see the difference—it's a priceless gift. The idol adds nothing. Why waste anything on it?" The man's shame is a sign of his intelligence; he has seen the difference. The story continues:

> *Later, a woman walked into the store and wanted to make an offering to the idols. So Abraham took a stick, smashed the idols and placed the stick in the hand of the largest idol. When Terah returned, he asked Abraham what happened to all the idols. Abraham told him that a woman came in to make an offering to the idols. The idols argued about which one should eat the offering first, then the largest idol took the stick and smashed all the other idols. Terah responded by saying that they are only statues and have no knowledge. Whereupon Abraham responded by saying that you deny their knowledge, yet you worship them! At this point, Terah took Abraham to Nimrod.*

As a human subject who can imagine a story and then tell the story to his father, Abraham imagines that the idols he and his father have made are like us. They have life and knowledge, and they are greedy and ambitious as we are. Terah takes the bait and points out the obvious: the idols are dead things with no knowledge or ambition, which leads to Abraham's rejoinder. It's clear the idols are no match for a human subject with an imagination and an arm to smash them (not to mention the One God, whom we can't mention because he hasn't yet revealed Himself). Terah also realizes he is no match for his son, so he takes his brilliant, wayward boy to the king. At this point we are still on the psychological route to the real presence.

The next incident describes that meeting with the king:

> *Nimrod proclaims to Abraham that we should worship fire. Abraham responds that water puts out fire. So Nimrod declares they worship water. Abraham responds that clouds hold water. So Nimrod declares they worship clouds. Abraham responds that wind pushes clouds. So Nimrod declares they worship wind. Abraham responds that people withstand wind.*

Yes, but it helps if that person is a fully realized human subject like Abraham.

This story is like a folktale that leads to the same conclusion as the previous stories. No thing, no spirit, not even a king can resist being "held" by a human subject or, by implication, by the One God. Terah holds the idols in his mind and his hand when he designs and shapes the images. The fifty-year-old man holds in his hand the idol he would buy. For this interpretation, I have selected the verb "held" over the other two ("puts out" and "pushes") as the metaphor that most clearly expresses the thought. I would link Abraham's thought here with Dante's thought in *La Vita Nuova* that a human subject is one substance, and for a fully awake subject like Abraham a king is but an accident of that substance. Nimrod, on the other hand, reveals that he has no sense of his own substance and its innate power to hold everything in it. To be kingly, he puts on the power of fire only to realize, thanks to Abraham, that fire is held by water. The pattern repeats with water, clouds, and wind as he seeks the one that holds them all, but the others prove to be but an accident of some other substance. At the end of the exercise, he is empty; he lacks the power to resist the intelligence of a boy.

There isn't anything overtly cosmological in these incidents. The story is told from the third-person point of view, but it's the view that a courtier might have of Terah's son. We know Abraham from what he does and what he says, which is how anyone ever reads another person. Nevertheless, what he does and what he says reveals a wonderful intelligence about something. This is self-evident, even if we don't know and haven't experienced that intelligence ourselves.

The next incident moves the narrative out of the psychological route, and introduces God as a cosmological fact:

> *Nimrod becomes angry with Abraham and declares that Abraham shall be cast into the fire, and if Abraham is correct, i.e. that there is a God, then that God will save him. Abraham is cast into the fire and is saved by God. Abraham's brother Haran sees what happened and says that he believes in the God of Abraham. Haran is thrown into the fire, and is not saved by God. Hence the verse in Genesis 11:28, "And Haran died in the presence of his father Terah in the land of his nativity, in Ur of the Chaldees."*

Would that this story about biblical brothers were better known. The language human subjects use to communicate with each other creates the lifeworld, the human world we inhabit, but our language and the world it creates is "held" by the One God. Haran can say he believes in the Lord, but the words mean nothing except when they are "held" by one who knows the One God. For the Lord is the alpha and omega of meaning. Haran reminds me of the suitors in the *Odyssey*. Like Haran, they usurp the symbols of power, and they die when the symbols—of feasting and drinking in the king's palace—can't save them from the wrath of the true king.

In this incident, Abraham does and says nothing. His psychology is no longer the focus. Instead, the One God, the creative principle, acts to save Abraham from the fire, for Abraham has proved his faith. The One God then reveals to Nimrod and all in his court that he "holds" the fire in himself, where it can either burn or not burn.

Abraham in Genesis

In addition to explaining the passage in Torah about Haran dying in the presence of his father, the stories in Genesis Rabbah help us to understand why the Lord would reveal himself, for the first time in history, to a human being. The second text, Genesis 12:1–3, records the beginning of this relationship:

> *The Lord had said to Abram, "Go from your country, your people and your father's household to the land I will show you*

The Lord is the sole speaker and actor. We view this encounter, first from a third-person objective point of view and then from the point of view, the words, of the One God Himself, the creative principle "out there" that governs all and everything. He commands Abraham to make a complete break from the life he had been living up to that moment. Who would obey? Only a man who knew he was "held" by the One God. The Lord now teaches Abraham the lesson Abraham taught Nimrod.

In the verses that follow, however, the voice softens from One who commands to One who loves. The Lord no longer instructs Abraham into "the nature of reality" (a cosmological encounter). He addresses him as a subject like Himself (a psychological encounter):

> *"I will make you into a great nation,*
> *and I will bless you;*
> *I will make your name great,*
> *and you will be a blessing.*
> *I will bless those who bless you,*
> *and whoever curses you I will curse;*
> *and all peoples on earth*
> *will be blessed through you."*

It's impossible to say exactly when these words were written. It's not hard to say that for this narrative about the thought of religion these words have great meaning. In addressing Abraham the way he does, the Lord establishes the ground of the relationship. It consists of a subject using the first-person form of the word *I* to address another subject in the second-person form as the word *you*. The poetry of these verses springs out of this form of relationship. At this point, though, Abram has yet to reply.

Even though the Lord does the speaking, his form of address opens the reader of this text to the point of view of the man having the experience. The Lord opens up Abram to Him, the One God, through his use of the word *you*. It's like the window I described near the end of Book Three (see pages 356–363). Through this sacred window or passage, he pours Himself: "I will make you . . ."; "I will bless you . . ."; "I will make your name great"; "you will be a blessing"; and on to the grand finale, "and all peoples on earth will be blessed through you." If I write those last two words, "through you," a little differently as "through [the word] 'you,'" the word *you* is revealed as a medium between the two. Viewed in this way, language and specifically these forms of address are a sacred medium on the horizon between this world and a divine order. Can we, do we identify with Abraham? Why not.

"You" is such a common, simple word. We're quite used to being addressed in that way. Because we are so sensitive to language and the world it creates, it wouldn't be hard to imagine being told, "You will be a blessing . . . and all peoples on earth will be blessed through you." These verses invite us into this wonderland.

In the third text, Genesis 17:1–21, the Lord proposes over the first fourteen verses the terms of the covenant he would make with Abraham. It's a contract between two sovereign individuals, but of course the Lord is the mightier of the two. Still, he recognizes Abram's freedom to enter into the agreement. On his side Abram must walk before the Lord faithfully and blamelessly. More specifically, this means that every male must be circumcised; this is the sign of the covenant. Abram also must change his name; he is now to be known as Abraham. In return for obedience, the Lord will make of Abraham a great nation, and He gives him the whole land of Canaan as an everlasting possession.

After instructing Abram into "the nature of reality" (in this case, the nature of the covenant), in verses 15–21, the story comes to life as a drama between two sovereign individuals. The shift occurs when the Lord turns his attention to Sarai and her role in what is promised:

> *God also said to Abraham, "As for Sarai your wife, you are no longer to call her Sarai; her name will be Sarah. I will bless her and will surely give you a son by her. I will bless her so that she will be the mother of nations; kings of peoples will come from her."*

At age ninety, she will bear Abraham a son. The Lord reveals himself to be the creative principle in this, for Sarai has been barren all her married life. She introduced Hagar, her Egyptian handmaiden, into the family for this reason, but this is also why Hagar's son Ishmael complicates the Lord's promise to make Abraham the father of a mighty nation:

> *Abraham fell facedown; he laughed and said to himself, "Will a son be born to a man a hundred years old? Will*

Sarah bear a child at the age of ninety?" And Abraham said to God, "If only Ishmael might live under your blessing!" Then God said, "Yes, but your wife Sarah will bear you a son, and you will call him Isaac. I will establish my covenant with him as an everlasting covenant for his descendants after him. And as for Ishmael, I have heard you: I will surely bless him; I will make him fruitful and will greatly increase his numbers. He will be the father of twelve rulers, and I will make him into a great nation.

Abraham, even as he has just become one whom the Lord has chosen and renamed, doubts in himself what the Lord is promising. This is a wonderful, beautiful moment. It captures something everyone experiences in relationships. The person with whom we are speaking says something—maybe it's a promise to do something, maybe it's an opinion, and we doubt that the thing will be done, or we doubt the opinion. This is not the end of relationship. It marks the true beginning of one, for doubting and testing what is said is the underlying function of relationship. It's how we learn about the opinions of others, about our own opinions, and about the nature of reality.

This moment is wonderful and beautiful because of the way Abraham addresses the question and because of the way the Lord answers it. Abraham has doubts, but he moves ahead with the possibility that Sarah will bear a son. Holding in his mind that possibility, he then worries aloud to the Lord about the fate of Ishmael once Sarah's son precedes Ishmael in the line of succession. The Lord assures Abraham, "I have heard you." These are wonderful, beautiful words. They are the words that keep a relationship alive, and the Lord then follows up with his assurances about Ishmael's life. The Lord heard Abraham's concern about Ishmael, but he also heard Abraham's unspoken doubt that he and Sarah would have a son born unto them. In response to that unspoken doubt, the Lord assures him that "Sarah will bear a son."

In the first fourteen lines of this passage, Abram encounters the Lord.

In Scruton's terms, this is the goal of the cosmological approach. The Lord is the transcendental ground—"the nature and the origin of the world." In that capacity, the Lord lays out the terms of his covenant with Abram. This, he tells him, is the way it is. In verses 15–21, however, the encounter becomes a relationship. Abram (now Abraham) comes alive, as he did in his father's shop. He's not a piece of wood or a clump of clay like the images there; he's a human subject. He's a man with a certain perspective on things. He's a singular man in those times, for his perspective is radically different from that of his father, Terah. He's a man who can even have doubts about what the Lord Himself has promised. Let's stand for a moment in Abraham's shoes. He has two wives. If each one has given him a son, from his perspective as a man of the world, this situation can only mean trouble.

As a free human subject considering whether to enter into a contract, Abraham very carefully puts a condition on the Lord's creativity. "If only Ishmael might live under your blessing!" he tells the Lord. Is it a wish, or is he drawing a line in the sand? This is the beauty of biblical poetry. His words are so specific, and yet they suggest an unspoken universe, the inner life of Abraham. The Lord's reply reveals the scope and depth of the creative principle. In the Lord, there's no inner and outer—there's just Him. His providence hears the unspoken doubt and declares that Sarah will bear a son. There's a connection between the creative principle and the transparency of their relationship, thanks to his Providence. Abraham cannot hide from the Lord any more than Adam and Eve could after they transgressed. This puts their relationship on a solid footing. It models what is needed as the foundation for those relationships that will make Abraham a mighty nation.

Those taking the psychological approach, Scruton tells us, "speculate about the experience of holiness." In verses 15–21, we experience this momentous event in world history through the eyes of Abraham, a human subject. He's our medium, the sacred object through which we, too, encounter the sacred, and so we reach the goal of the psychological approach, even if it's just a story that we read in a book. The psychological path has a more secular feel to it. It smacks of this lifeworld where we encounter the interests of others and express our own, in a language we both understand. The passage moves from Abraham's encounter with the first cause and creator of all and everything—the cosmological approach, to a conversation like one he might have with his wife when they discuss the covenant—the psychological approach. Both are stories that prime the pump for the sacred with the sacred. When he has this conversation with Sarah, as he undoubtedly must, the third party of these discussions about the covenant is the Lord Himself even if he is no longer demonstrably present. In Him, we now know, there's no inner and outer, inside the house and outside in the world. There's just Him. This transparency is how a married pair survives and prospers in the world He has made, the one we learn about in this sacred text.

What's the survival value of stories like these vignettes of Abraham's life if I find in them a light that illuminates our universe? If I wanted to buy them, what would they cost? Luckily, I don't have to buy them. They are part of the Lebenswelt, the commonwealth of Everyman, but to gain full possession of their meaning is another matter. That's the subject for a final chapter.

Chapter 3
SIDDHARTHA

A representation from the Tang dynasty
of *Tejaprabha Buddha and the Five Planets*

Siddhartha in *Old Paths White Clouds*

Why is the Buddha still a world historical figure? From the literature about him we learn that he's a man whose enlightenment of mind was self-evident. Thich Nhat Hanh added to that literature when he wrote a contemporary biography of the Buddha called *Old Paths White Clouds*. Nhat Hanh is not an academic. He's a Vietnamese Buddhist monk who, in writing about the Buddha's path, is writing about his own life experiences for a Western audience. The passages in his book about the Buddha's enlightenment complement the readings I have done in this book. They embody the themes of wholeness and compassion that are central to Lewis's interpretation of allegory, and they support Scruton's argument about the two approaches to the sacred.

The Buddha experienced enlightenment after years of searching. For what? He couldn't say exactly when he began because he hadn't experienced it. He started out with a sense that he was called to search for answers to the question "Why?" put to Brahman: "Why was I born? What am I meant to achieve in this life? Can I find a way to end suffering?" Siddhartha was born the prince and heir of a king. He enjoyed every comfort and great beauty in his palace and the palace grounds. He married a beautiful woman who was devoted to him, and they had a son to whom Siddhartha was devoted. The prince was greatly loved by his father the king, and the people loved him too. In time, he would be a worthy successor to his father. For Siddhartha, though, something too important to ignore was missing. Just as Abraham had to leave everything he had ever known in order to start a new life in the direction the Lord had pointed, Siddhartha left everything he had ever known to become a monk in the forest. Abraham knew nothing about the land he had been promised, and Siddhartha didn't know what he would find in his search or how to go about it.

Due to a strong "sense" of his goal, he persisted, trying this and that spiritual practice. In Nhat Hanh's portrait, Siddhartha Gautama, his name before he became the Buddha, knew his search would bear fruit without knowing exactly what would be revealed, and he knew it would relieve his own and others' suffering. His mind, his whole being, was primed with what he devoted himself to find.

With that, Nhat Hanh recreates for us the unfolding of his Great Awakening:

> *The village children came to visit him only in the early afternoons. One day Sujata [a girl from the nearby village] brought him an offering of rice porridge cooked with milk and honey, and Savasti [her brother] brought him a fresh armful of kusa grass. After Savasti left to lead the buffaloes home, Gautama was seized with a deep feeling that he would attain the Great Awakening that very night. Only the previous night he had had several unusual dreams. In one he saw himself lying on his side, his knees brushing against the Himalayas, his left hand touching the shores of the Eastern Sea, his right hand touching the shores of the Western Sea, and his two feet resting against the shores of the Southern Sea. In another dream, a great lotus as large as a carriage wheel grew from his navel and floated up to touch the highest clouds. In a third dream, birds of all colors, too many to be counted, flew towards him from all directions. These dreams seem to announce that his Great Awakening was at hand.*

Siddhartha was fortunate in his dreams, and with the confidence he already possessed he interpreted the dreams in the way he did. They announced a great awakening. Scruton, you recall, discussed dreams in relation to the sacred. It's the issue Chaucer raises in "The Nun's Priest's Tale": Can a dream be a form of knowledge? Is it real in that it tells us something about the world "out there?" In the same way, Scruton questions whether a thought of the sacred can be a form of knowledge or real in that sense. Even if a dream cannot predict the future, Freud and others thought it could tell us a great deal about our past, which impacts our present and future. Scruton includes Freud in his argument about the sacred because a dream is very much like a thought, and I have shown that a large part of Scruton's first chapter is about the thought of the sacred. We want to know whether the thought of the sacred tells us something about the world "out there."

By means of this passage by Nhat Hahn, which follows the idea I have introduced as priming the pump for the sacred with the sacred, I'm proposing that Siddhartha's dreams function in this way. They are like an architect's blueprints for a building. They are not an actual building; they are his dream of a building that he knows can become real. Every competent architect goes to work with this confidence. He lives by it. Scruton's "dream," if you will, is his argument about the nature and reality of holiness. He has given us a thought, a blueprint. That's all any writer can do. Is it a true thought? Scruton argues that it is, but the reader must determine the truth of it for himself. The reader has been given a blueprint. He can build from it if he likes.

What sort of world has Siddhartha dreamed? As in Scruton's depiction of Brahman and Atman, it is one just as Siddhartha's body is one with the north, the east, the west, and the south. This vision of his true self extends not only to this world but to the heavens as well. All the accidents of Creation, like the birds of all colors, come to roost in his substance. I hasten to add that not only is it one, but it is also good. It sustains and comforts a man, as Sujata and Savasti sustain and comfort Siddhartha. Nhat Hanh continues:

> *Early that evening, Gautama did walking meditation along the banks of the river. He waded into the water and bathed. When twilight descended, he returned to sit beneath his familiar pippala tree. He smiled as he looked at the newly spread kusa grass at the foot of the tree. Beneath this tree he had made so many important discoveries in his meditation. Now the moment he had long awaited was approaching. The door to Enlightenment was about to open.*

Obviously, we are not the Buddha nor are we Thich Nhat Hanh. We cannot dispute the experiences they have had in their spiritual practice. We *can* examine our own experience, which curiously is always one. Scruton refers to Kant in this matter, who called it "the transcendental unity of apperception." A sense of oneness, they argue, emerges around the personal pronoun "I" in speech with others. Our perception is always one, and we experience it as one through time. I am one with what I was ten years ago, or seventy, even though I may look and feel different.

In time, our consciousness can develop as Chaucer's root did—which absorbs in the earth the elements of water and minerals, which grows out of the earth and absorbs the elements of air and the power of the sun, and which in the final act engenders the flower. Wholeness and growth. These are Goethe's two great themes, and these are the themes with which Nhat Hanh begins the story of the Buddha's enlightenment. The thing he is about to experience, call it enlightenment in the case of the Buddha, is present in the run up to it. This is also the way Lewis approaches his subject, the representation of a soul in allegory. To grasp his subject, he takes us through the different "stations" of its development. We appear to be moving in time, but in fact the train never leaves the first station, nor the one after that, nor the one after that, and so on. These stations are accidents in the literature of the West, which is one because the reader's substance is one. Scruton has a vision of this oneness as well, which is the thought behind our use of the personal pronoun "I" (as well as the thought behind a "myth of origins," which is the subject of my last chapter).

Nhat Hanh's narrative continues through the three watches of the night. The first watch begins with the evening star, and the third watch ends with the morning star. (We give them different names, but they are in fact one star.) The first paragraph sets the stage:

> *Slowly, Siddhartha sat down in the lotus position. He looked at the river flowing quietly in the distance as soft breezes rustled the grasses along the banks. The night forest was tranquil yet very much alive. Around him chirped a thousand different insects. He turned his awareness to his breath and lightly closed his eyes. The evening star appeared in the sky.*

Nhat Hanh is not constructing a symbol that points to a transcendental world of meaning. The star is not a symbol; it's a star. He puts Siddhartha at the center of *this world*, the one we all experience. At the same time, I think Nhat Hanh would agree with Dante that the things he describes in this scene, the things of this world that we know from our own experience, are in reality fictions. He is creating this scene of the Buddha's enlightenment out of his own imagination. Nevertheless, the things he describes are real, just as Nhat Hanh is a real person. We know the sounds and sights of rivers, breezes, grasses, forests, and insects from our experience in the world. We are real people reading these real words put together by their author. From Nhat Hanh's perspective, they are accidents of his substance that help him to express the reality of his substance, even if they are a story about the Buddha.

From our third-person point of view, Nhat Hanh's interpretation of the Buddha's enlightenment has to be subjective; he's approaching holiness from his own point of view even though it appears to be the Buddha's point of view. The evening star "out there" in the world, however, is not a fiction. It exists. I saw it the other night. It's Venus glowing in the night sky. Nhat Hanh has seen the same star that the Buddha saw. So the evening begins with this mixing of the fictional, subjective, inner life of Siddhartha and an objective world that exists "out there" and that we share with others. It's the world Siddhartha shares with Sujata, Savasti, Nhat Hanh, and me. Siddhartha *lightly* closes his eyes and observes both the breath and the star, inner and outer, subjective and objective.

Nhat Hanh would prime his and his reader's mind by imagining in his own words a Buddha. His approach, however, is grounded in the reality of this world, for this is the only way a human subject can approach either the Buddha Mind or the sacred. (Thomas Aquinas shared this approach, for he often cited Paul's sentence in Romans that "the invisible things of God are clearly seen . . . by the things that are made.") The evening star is not a symbol; it's a star in this world. It is also beautiful, a point of light, behind which opens up an endless and seemingly unknowable universe. The two together, the star and the universe that holds it, are a source for endless wonder. So is the breath. We breathe in, and it enlivens that which we can never see, hear, taste, smell, or touch—namely, the inner life of the body that maintains the life of all and everything from moment to moment. The breath and the magic of a live body creates or holds for the time being our awareness of a vast, inscrutable universe. The breath and the star: These wonders draw Siddhartha's attention inward and outward, into the microcosm and into the macrocosm. Both the psychological and the cosmological approaches are represented and ready.

Once Siddhartha has taken his seat and can turn his awareness in both directions, Nhat Hanh describes what he experienced during the first watch of the night:

> *Through mindfulness, Siddhartha's mind, body, and breath were perfectly at one. His practice of mindfulness had enabled him to build great powers of concentration which he could now use to shine awareness on his mind and body. After deeply entering meditation, he began to discern the presence of countless other beings in his own body right in the present moment. Organic and inorganic beings, minerals, mosses and grasses, insects, animals, and people were all within him. He saw that other beings were himself right in the present moment. He saw his own past lives, all his births and deaths. He saw the creation and destruction of thousands of worlds and thousands of stars. He felt all the joys and sorrows or every living being—those born of mothers, those born of eggs, and those born of fission, who divided themselves into new creatures. He saw that every cell of his body contained all of Heaven and Earth, and spanned the three times—past, present, and future. It was the hour of the first watch of the night.*

He realizes himself as the without-which-nothing of creation. He is Noah's ark. Like Abraham's encounter with the One God, he encounters the transcendental ground.

Nhat Hanh then describes the second watch of the night, where he has insight into all defilements (as in Dante's pilgrimage through hell and purgatory on his way to paradise), and the third watch of the night, when he realizes the way to heal the suffering that comes from alienation.

In the end, when Siddhartha looked up and saw the morning star, the reality and the significance of his experience were self-evident:

> *Siddhartha knew he had found the Great Way. He had attained his goal,*

> *and now his heart experienced perfect peace and ease . . . Along the grassy riverbank, colorful flowers blossomed in the early morning sunlight. Sun danced on leaves and sparkled on the water. His pain was gone. All the wonders of life revealed themselves. Everything appeared strangely new. How wondrous were the blue skies and drifting white clouds! He felt as though he and all the universe had been newly created.*

Siddhartha refers to his experience as the Great Way. The description suggests a passage into life that's as astonishing as creation itself, but the passage is also great in the sense that's it's a superhighway for anyone. It's not a narrow, niggling passage that fits only a special kind of person. Every human subject in the world is the without-which-nothing of creation in exactly the same way he is.

Through this great way, we also experience the wonder of interpersonal relations. To emphasize the point that this experience belongs to every individual, according to each individual's circumstances, Nhat Hanh reintroduces the boy who had made the kusa grass seat for Siddhartha's meditations:

> *Just then, Svasti appeared. When Siddhartha saw the young buffalo boy come running towards him, he smiled. Suddenly Svasti stopped in his tracks and stared at Siddhartha, his mouth wide open. Siddhartha called, "Savasti!"*
>
> *The boy came to his senses and answered, "Teacher!"*
>
> *Savasti joined his palms and bowed. He took a few steps forward but then stopped and gazed again at Siddhartha in awe. Embarrassed by his own behavior, he spoke haltingly, "Teacher, you look so different today."*

The Buddha's enlightenment is no secret. It expresses itself through his whole body. Inner has been turned inside out:

> *Siddhartha motioned for the boy to approach. He took him in his arms and asked, "How do I look different today?"*
>
> *Gazing up at Siddhartha, Savasti answered, "It's hard to say. It's just you look so different. It's like you were a star."*

With that, we come to the great theme that Lewis's introduces in the first page of his chapter on allegory. All language is metaphorical, but sometimes it has to be explicitly metaphoric. Siddartha and Savasti are talking with each other. They share the same language, and so the language may be able to convey the difference he sees in Siddartha. Even a beginner, this small boy, reaches for the thing in this world that will describe the thing out-of-this-world (but still-suggestively-in-it) that he senses in the Buddha.

> *Siddhartha patted the boy on the head and said, "Is that so? What else do I look like?"*

Siddhartha here isn't looking for a complement. He's encouraging Savasti to look at him again and see what comes to mind. Savasti's mind is the object of his interest, and Siddhartha's interest may lead Savasti to an interest in his own mind:

> *"You look like a lotus that's just blossomed. And like, like the moon over the Gayasisa Peak."*

The question about what he looks like involves a complex web of meaning. Savasti is called upon to look at this man before him and then to imagine something that's like what he sees when he looks at the man. What he sees is an immaterial grace, and the Buddha is asking him to find that grace in the world that he inhabits every day. Savasti does so. He's like a lotus, but not just any lotus. A lotus at a particular moment in its development. He's like the moon, but not just any moon. It has to be the moon over the Gayasisa Peak. The exercise joins the breathtaking beauty Savasti sees in the Buddha with the beauty we can find in the special times and special places of this world.

> *Siddhartha looked into Savasti's eyes and said, "Why, you're a poet, Svasti! Now tell me, why are you here so early today? And where are your buffaloes?"*

The Buddha here shows that he's not a mystic or a gnostic longing for another, better world. He's satisfied that Savasti can be a poet, when the occasion demands. Meanwhile, he's still responsible for his buffaloes, and, this other business having been completed, the two of them turn to the business of the buffaloes.

Like the evening and the morning star, Siddhartha's experience begins and ends with Savasti, the young buffalo boy. He completes the circle of Siddhartha's experience. Not only was the experience self-evident to Siddhartha but it was also self-evident to Savasti. Siddhartha has reached the goal of his pilgrimage, but the end of his pilgrimage instantaneously becomes the beginning of another. He sees himself in Savasti and sees Savasti in himself. The embrace expresses his insight. It's not a symbol; it's an expression of his love for the life he has been given, which is the life Savasti has been given as well. They are one in the gift.

The experience teaches this, but Siddhartha knows from his long and difficult pilgrimage that Savasti, while one with Siddhartha, is not Siddhartha. He is himself, Savasti, and Savasti is just a boy. Savasti's relationship with Siddhartha is like our relationship with any great teacher as we read their texts or the texts about them. The reader is Savasti. Through Nhat Hanh's window about the Great Awakening, the reader views wonders, things available only to the imagination, thoughts that come together due to the attraction of an invisible moral sense at the center of this world.

We are Savasti looking at the wonder we see in Siddhartha. The wonder stops him in his tracks. It's self-evident that Siddhartha has been changed, but Savasti has only the outside view of it. After Savasti stops in his tracks, Siddhartha initiates a dialogue. He calls him by name, "Savasti!" and Savasti replies "Teacher!" They acknowledge each other. Behind the name, each one knows there's a human subject. When Siddhartha addressed him by name, Savasti understood the intent within that one word, "Savasti!" Siddhartha had noticed a sudden change *in him*. They are equals in this; they both have noticed a change in the other. From this mutual recognition, the rest of the dialogue flows beautifully to its conclusion. In their meeting, Nhat Hanh creates a subject-to-subject relationship. He's inviting his reader to have this relationship with his text.

Savasti expresses what is self-evident; Siddhartha has changed. Siddhartha, the teacher, turns the issue of his change into his first act as a teacher. It's a beautiful, wonderful, meaningful moment. In Savasti's eyes, Siddhartha is a wonder. Siddhartha, now the Buddha, has seeded that wonder in the boy, and he encourages its growth with an embrace and intelligent speech. This conclusion of the enlightenment experience defines our relationship with the text.

The *Tejaprabha Buddha and the Five Planets*

I have illustrated this chapter with a painting from the Tang period (AD 618–907). It pictures the Buddha in a cart, which is unusual. His eyes aren't lowered in meditation; he's awake and on the move. He's not just any Buddha; he's the Buddha of blazing light, as the painting shows. The five planets form a graceful semicircle around the left side and front of the cart. Clockwise from the bottom: Mars has four arms; Venus plays a lute; Saturn leads a bull; Jupiter, a benign government official, holds flowers; and Mercury conveys information with a brush and paper. Four hundred years before the Tang period, teachers of Buddhism came to China, and they brought with them cultural and astrological ideas from India, Greece, and Rome. In China, before this period, the planets had not been represented in human form. The planets are now personifications. The universe has been transcribed into a human world of people who support the commonweal of the universe in their different capacities.

I chose this painting for the chapter because it has the characteristics of a Western allegory. It conveys a sense of wholeness as everything revolves around the Buddha. The personifications are all aspects or accidents of his substance. I don't think the Chinese thought in terms of a heliocentric system. The painting depicts something more like the philosophy of

Neoplatonism, a system that assumes a supreme, transcendent one as the source of all and everything. The things of this world, which we know as objects in a physical world, nevertheless are still informed and magnetically attracted to the one. Neoplatonists, without any knowledge of the heliocentric planetary system, equated the one with the Sun's physical properties of light, warmth, and renewal. The one is like the sun, and in this painting the Buddha is like the sun.

In allegory, Mind, the soul of the world, can speak, and in this painting the wisdom of the Buddha's mind radiates out into the world. The enlightened man *comprehends* the universe and becomes its representative to human beings. If the universe does speak through the insights of a Buddha about the nature of things and the conduct of our life, what do we learn? The painting doesn't say exactly. It reassures the viewer that the questions can be answered. It's priming the pump that will produce an answer.

What's the survival value of this painting for me if I imagine that it illuminates our universe? If I wanted to buy it, what would it cost? Luckily, I don't have to buy it. It's part of the Lebenswelt, the commonwealth of Everyman, but to gain full possession of its meaning is another matter. That's the subject for a final chapter.

Chapter 4
The Ghostly Sight That's Dearly Bought

Odilon Redon's
Dante and Beatrice

A Recapitulation of Themes Near the End

Haydn, Mozart, and Beethoven developed new forms to give their long musical scores greater unity. For example, near the end of a symphony they recapitulated themes from the previous movements. As repeated rhythms and melodies do within an individual movement, these ghosts of rhythm and melody from the different movements are reborn as one movement. I fancy that it's a musical idea similar to C. S. Lewis's train, which moves but never leaves any of its stations.

My book has imitated this innovation in symphonic form with restatements of important texts, and there are a number of recapitulations in the final movement of Book Four. Originally, this chapter was going to be the conclusion of the book, but the urge to make the inquiry in the first place moved me to add the postscript. In "The Ghostly Sight That's Dearly Bought," I have recalled passages and examples from the first three books of my *Comic Vision*, along with some new material to address the gravest question posed by the human condition.

For those with excellent memories, just skip to the end of the quoted passage. I don't have an excellent memory and never did. That's why I have to read some texts two, three, four, or more times to be reasonably sure I understand them.

The Way Home Runs through the Land of the Dead

Part 1: For Answers, We Must Go to Where the Question Can Be Asked

What's the act that brings this life to life? I asked this question at the beginning of my introduction. It was suggested to me by the text in Genesis when:

> *... the Lord God formed man of the dust of the ground, and breathed into his nostrils the breath of life; and man became a living soul.*

This is where my inquiry began, and it has moved me in these last few chapters to express my gratitude for the wonderlands, like the one depicted in this verse from the Bible, that are the crown jewels of our culture. To gain full measure of their meaning, however, we have to pass through a final chapter. Scruton earlier described certain philosophical roadblocks in the way of both the cosmological and the psychological approaches, and we read with great interest how the transcendental urge of his argument removes them. The final chapter of our reading or of anything else, though, is death, and death is the subject of this chapter. How do we unroll that rock?

We can't, obviously.

Nevertheless, Lewis gives voice to a literary form that wrestled, like Jacob wrestling an angel, with the alienating dualisms that haunt this life—between home and exile, good and evil, life and death, and the self versus the world "out there." In Book One, I speculated about what moved him to undertake all the research and writing that went into making *The Allegory of Love* a reality:

"Lewis committed himself to the work because the tradition of allegory addresses a deep longing that human beings have always experienced, which is poignantly expressed in a passage by Johannes de Altavilla, a poet-philosopher of that school [the School of Chartres]. His Architrenius, the archmourner, has despaired at the wickedness within him and around him; he would go on a journey to find his true nature and be healed:

> *This must I do—go exiled through the world*
> *And seek for Nature till far hence I find*
> *Her secret dwelling place; there drag to light*
> *The hidden cause of quarrel, and reknit,*
> *Haply reknit, the long-divided Love.*

"In this, he is like any person, now a reader, who would discover the hidden cause of alienation. In allegory, we find not so much a cause as a remedy. For example, Bernardus Sylvestris, founder of Altavilla's school, has the Supreme Mind describe the role that mankind, the microcosm, will play in Creation:

He shall be heavenly, earthly; by his care
Shall rule the earth, and reach the heaven by prayer,
For as the diverse sources whence he drew
His being, so himself will still be two . . .

"Man is both heavenly and earthly. Through prayer, he comes to life in the union of sensible and insensible worlds. He is the meaning that emerges.

As such, man will have power denied other creatures:
He shall drag forth to light the causes hid
In secret gloom, though Nature long forbid . . .
To him, unbounded, in all lands, I give
High crown and priesthood over all that live.

"By being both earthly and heavenly, man occupies a unique station in creation. Like mankind in Bernard's poem, Altavilla's archmourner would realize his true nature as one with the Supreme Mind. He's not alone, for C. S. Lewis shows us that this Mind is the subject and the goal of the allegories he studies. I suspect Lewis would revive the tradition because he believed that allegories may more successfully describe Mind than science ever will. I will be arguing throughout my book that that this 'high crown' has been preserved, handed down, and made available to us in the form of great poetry. Why is it so important? Without it, Lewis might say, we lose the wonder of creation and lose the love of its creator" (originally appeared on pages 72–73).

Before we give up on life altogether because it appears to end so badly, we are invited by the authors in my book to see if we can begin again with what poetry celebrates—the wonder of creation and the wonder of our own being, which is both earthly and heavenly.

Scruton's onus of proof argument in "Believing in God" (see pages 273–274) turns the tables on Science in our debate about religion. I concluded from it that "a thought about God . . . is like someone brought to trial in our system of justice. It is innocent until proven to be otherwise, which, in this case, it can never be." Instead of Science (personified) asking Pascal for proof that he met with God (proof, in other words, that he's not lying to the court), Scruton puts Science in the dock. He asks Science, in effect, "Can you prove that this man did not experience the real presence?" in order to create reasonable doubt. If Science cannot, then we might as well go to Brahman to ask the many questions that begin with "Why?" If we want answers, we must go where the question can be asked.

Part 2: A Pilgrimage to Earth and the Land of the Dead

At the beginning of Book Four, I tell the story of Faust riding Chiron further into the wonderlands of myth and magic. In like manner, I imagined him carrying me (and any reader who is still with me) through the wonderland of Scruton's argument once more, through the wonderland in which God speaks to Abraham, and through the wonderland that presented itself to the Buddha in his enlightenment. Here, at the end of the chapter, I would have Chiron take us to witness how the gods of ancient Greece helped Odysseus navigate the many dangers of this world so he could safely return to his place as husband of Penelope, father of Telemachus, and king of his people. Specifically, I'd have Chiron take us through the episode in which Odysseus, much like Everyman, encounters Death in a pilgrimage to the land of the dead.

In Sargent's painting, we see Chiron hunting heavenly game. This is what we have done thus far in Book Four with the chapters on Abraham and Siddhartha, but we are earthly as well as heavenly. It's time now to go to Earth. We must go the journey to Earth that Nature and Urania undertook when, in the process of making Man, they met with Physis to ensure that man participates in the material order (see pages 206–207). Lewis explains that:

In order to fabricate the organism inhabitable by human mind, the ordering spirit of Nature must invoke those yet unexhausted possibilities of the vital force, which are symbolized as Physis, the earth dweller.

Homer has Odysseus go a journey like this. It begins when he and his men land on Circe's island to rest from the trials of their exile. (In this exile, they are like Architrenius.) His men eagerly drink her potions, but by this act they are turned into pigs, which then root in the earth of Circe's sty. The things of earth can provide a certain comfort, but they can also enchant and enslave. Hermes helped Odysseus to avoid this fate. Because he doesn't abandon himself to her charms, Circe loves him and becomes a willing ally and healer. She frees his men from the spell she put on them, and for a year the Greeks enjoy all the luxurious comforts of her estate. Odysseus, though, never forgets his reason for being: he is bound to Ithaca. Circe takes this fact of life well, resupplies their ships with provisions, and gives Odysseus helpful advice about the journey home. He must go, she tells him, to the land of the dead and speak with the blind seer Teiresias. He will have more to say about the journey. To that end she explains how he can approach the dead and get them to speak. If he digs a circular trench in a certain place and fills it with blood, the dead will want to drink the blood, but he should fight them off until Teiresias himself appears. He then can drink, and the blood will give him speech.

And so it came to pass. Circe didn't prepare him, however, for the way hundreds of dead souls swarm around him greedily to drink the blood; they are desperate to briefly live again, to tell their stories, and to be remembered. Odysseus panics at the strangeness of the place and the sudden rush of these spirits, but he holds his ground, fights them off, and waits for Teiresias.

Even though this story is about death and fear of death, it is a wonder of storytelling. It perfectly fits the theme I'm developing here; Odysseus must go to the land of the dead where he'll be reborn with the ghostly sight given to him by the blind seer Teiresias. There's that, but there's also much more. There's that swarm of souls desperate to come alive for a moment and tell their stories. The reader will pardon me, but this part of the story reminds me of what I can see every day on TV. It seems to me that being on TV has the same attraction as the blood that Odysseus pours into the trench. I think of the line from Eliot's *The Wasteland*, which he borrowed from canto 3 of *The Inferno*:

> *A crowd flowed over London Bridge, so many,*
> *I had not thought death had undone so many.*

Like the souls in Homer's tale, so many (that death has undone) are so desperate to be on TV, as if life can only mean coming to life on this machine. This is as true for TV professionals as it is for shows and spots in the news that feature members of "the public."

Odysseus conquers his fear, refuses to let any drink the blood before Teiresias can, and wins from Teiresias the ghostly sight he needs to return home. The story celebrates, as my Book Four does, the relationship that primes the pump of ghostly sight. Wisdom, the soul of world, exists in this world, but a human subject has to bring the warm lifeblood of a living body to that place where the ghostly sight of a living soul can be realized. I find that place in the wonderlands that have been the subject of my book. The text is there in the land of the dead. It could be said that we both are living a soulless existence till we come together. Once together, I drink of it, and it drinks of me. Homer comes to life, and so do I. Together we awaken a living soul within and without. (Of course, this is a story I am telling. For it not to be just a fiction, it requires just a dash of the real presence.) Shakespeare also describes this relationship in the famous couplet of Sonnet 18:

> *So long as men can breathe or eyes can see,*
> *So long lives this, and this gives life to thee.*

I think Homer and Shakespeare wrote what they did because they believed that a reader could then ride their magnificent poems, like Odysseus riding in the stern of the Phaeacians's ship, which moves with the speed of thought, safely home. Their confidence conveys to this reader the heart, mind, and soul of one who knows the way.

Now that I've set the scene, on the way to the end (where all is silence) I propose to review other stories where (for me) the soul of the world comes to life and endows the reader with ghostly sight of the sacred in this world. Many of them I've already visited. My survey follows the narrative of my book with one exception. It begins with Shakespeare and the play of *Everyman*, which were a focus of Book One, but I've moved my reading of *The Harvesters*, which appears in Book Three, so it can support my reading of *Everyman*. We pass through Lewis's thoughts on love and allegory in Book Two, and we revisit Scruton's thoughts about the sacred. The narrative loops around at the end to finish near the beginning of Book Two with the questions stirred up about physical love by the eleventh-century movement called courtly love.

Dying to Live in Shakespeare, *Everyman*, and Bruegel

Part 1: The Policy behind the Knot (Not!)

I begin by visiting act 1, scene 1 of *Henry V*, in which the archbishop of Canterbury speaks to the bishop of Ely about the young King, Henry V, who has just ascended to the throne:

> *Turn him to any cause of policy,*
> *The Gordian Knot of it he will unloose,*
> *Familiar as his garter.*

Indulging in the privilege enjoyed by authors, I venture to opine parenthetically that Shakespeare could have said this about himself, if he were given to boasting. As if I were standing in the shoes of a king, like the one the archbishop describes or in the shoes of Shakespeare himself, I would address in this final chapter the knot (Not!) of death that we have encountered during the course of my inquiry. The wonderlands that I study are treasured for their survival value, but the life we seek, the stories tell us, involves a death. What's the "policy" behind the author of such a world? How can we, too, become as "familiar" with the question as we are with a belt we wear around our waist?

This isn't the first time I've introduced the image of a knot. (On pages 137–138, you'll find the knot that ties Ahab to the white whale. On pages 163–164, there's the knot of desire that feeds on desire. And on pages 334–335, there's the knot in a tree filled with Boo Radley's messages of love, which paradoxically unlooses or undoes the notion Boo doesn't exist.) Like death, this "knot," or "not," which sound the same as spoken words, poses an impossible problem that we have to solve. It rings a resonant bell for personal reasons. When I became a member of the Zen Center here in our city (this was almost fifty years ago), the teacher assigned me, as he assigned all his beginning students, the koan Mu, in which a student asks a teacher, "Does a dog have Buddha nature?" and the teacher replies, "Mu!" which means "not" in Japanese. I worked on that koan for years. This "knot" or "not" also reminds me of the nothingness with which Lord Lafew confronts Parolles when he tells Parolles, "I have now found thee." Lord Lafew has found him to be nothing, despite his scarves and bannerets. There may be a surprising upside for Parolles in the discovery, however. As the song says (and more than one song says it):

> *If you ain't got nothing,*
> *You ain't got nothing to lose.*

One more thing: In the last chapter of *The Soul of the World*, Scruton discusses with approval Sartre's book *Being and Nothingness*, which argues that "nothingness lies coiled in the heart of being, like a worm." These details about the knot-not insisted on being included in my survey about the dying-to-live theme (Sartre's quote appears on page 177 in *The Soul of the World*).

Part 2: If Time Is One, There's Always Time to Be a Living Soul

How did Shakespeare himself become familiar with the idea that we must die to live? Who knows? But to move my narrative along, I fancy that the play of *Everyman* may have contributed to his understanding, and this is where I also found the notion of ghostly sight. Therefore, I'll present here lines from the opening of the play so a reader unfamiliar with them may come to value them as I do.

The allegory of *Everyman* teaches that Everyman must die, but the encounter with death initiates the renewal of his soul. In the prologue, the author writes that his "treatise" is presented "in the manner of a moral play." What does that mean? The first character to speak, named Messenger, tells us that the play will show:

> *How transitory we be all day.*
> *This matter is wondrous precious,*
> *But the intent of it is more gracious,*
> *And sweet to bear away.*
> *The story saith,—Man, in the beginning,*
> *Look well, and take good heed to the ending . . .*

If the beginning and ending are so close together, then it's indeed a very transitory life. Nevertheless, the Messenger tells us, this matter is precious and gracious. Maybe when Hamlet tells Horatio, "And a man's life's no more than to say, 'One,'" he had these lines from *Everyman* in mind. The "play," the field, the life of Everyman occupies the time it takes to say, "One." As Lewis has shown us, allegory is a literary genre that represents a life in this way. In allegory, Life is one. As such, it can be redeemed as a whole in an instant. This makes the moment precious and gracious.

Everyman's substance or soul has absorbed the many accidents of his life, and now:

our heaven king
Calleth Everyman to a general reckoning.

The worth of the whole can and must be weighed. The prologue done, God Himself then speaks to the audience:

I perceive here in my majesty
How that all creatures be to me unkind,
Living without dread in worldly prosperity:
Of Ghostly sight the people be so blind,
Drowned in sin, they know me not for their God . . .

For modern audiences, the idea of sin has gone out of fashion. It went out when God Himself went out of fashion. If we change "sin" to "self-destructive behaviors" these remarkable lines make the argument that Lewis and Scruton have made in *The Allegory of Love* and *The Soul of the World*. Thanks to a worldview that has staked out the material world as the basis for all knowledge, people have lost their "ghostly sight." They no longer can conceive of a life as one, and they are blind to the real presence of the sacred. The soul at the center of their earth is no longer "poor." It doesn't exist.

Shakespeare may have seen this blindness and extinction developing in his own time when science was about to become a worldview. Hamlet went to college in Wittenberg to study this new way of knowing the world, but Shakespeare also gave him that ghostly sight of his murdered father with which the play opens. Since the play is a tragedy, Hamlet's ghostly sight initiates him into a harrowing night of the soul and physical death, but in my allegorical reading of the play, he dies as a dispossessed prince and is reborn—for one more breath, the time it takes to say, "One"—as a sacred king.

If time is always and only one for Everyman, then for you and me, for as long as we live, there's time to be reborn with ghostly sight of a living soul.

Part 3: An Interesting Paradox or Knot in God's Reasoning

With ghostly sight, God in the play of *Everyman* has witnessed the effects of Everyman's blindness:

> *Everyman liveth so after his own pleasure,*
> *And yet of their life they are nothing sure.*

Long before the rise of science as a worldview, human beings have striven mightily to rationalize life into something predictable and safe, and a great complacency and self-satisfaction may set in that convinces them they have done so. From another perspective, however, it's quite true to say of them, "And yet of their life they are nothing sure." A global pandemic, for example, can expose glaring weaknesses in systems that are supposed to insulate the people from reasons to fear.

As if mesmerized by this insecurity, there's something intractable and dim-witted about Everyman:

> *My law I shewed, when I for them died,*
> *They forget clean, and shedding of my blood red;*
> *I hanged between two, it cannot be denied;*
> *To get them life I suffered to be dead.*

This is a law and a love that passes all understanding, which may be why they have been forgotten.

His law may be the one that governs the world He has made, but apparently only those with ghostly sight can see it, even when his law is understood, less violently, as the golden rule. God, on the other hand, can see perfectly well the way people behave:

> *I see the more that I them forbear*
> *The worse they be from year to year;*

All that liveth appaireth [degenerates] fast,
Therefore I will in all the haste
Have a reckoning of Everyman's person
For and [if] I leave the people thus alone
In their life and wicked tempests,
Verily they will become much worse than beasts;
For now one would by envy another up eat;
Charity they all do clean forget.

No wonder Everyman is insecure, even if the eating is just a metaphor. People have many faults, but God singles out Envy.

There's an interesting paradox or knot in God's reasoning. People are dim-witted and intractable, but we all can see for ourselves how "all that liveth appaireth." We know that we must die, and this surely has something to do with the beastly behavior described at the end of the quote. Death, therefore, is very likely a large part of the problem, but, according to God's observations here, Death is also what's required to solve the problem. Death arranges (or initiates) the "reckoning" that gives us ghostly sight of the One who judges. The play of *Everyman* does just that. It's an imaginative work in which God comes to life on the stage and explains all this, and then Death prepares Everyman for the reckoning. If we know from personal experience that the prospect of a reckoning tends to sober us up in the conduct of everyday affairs, then surely a reckoning for the whole of our life must have the same effect. For this reason, I would argue that a story like *Everyman* has great survival value for the community entertained by it. (See pages 262–264 for the place where Scruton introduces the concept of survival value into his argument.)

Part 4: A Source of Wonder and Renewal

Envy may describe a behavior that is worse than that of beasts, but it doesn't answer the question underlying God's complaint when he reminds his audience how he died for them. He is asking, "Why didn't my sacrifice suffice?"

It's an interesting question for one who is all-knowing and all powerful. Perhaps it's an acknowledgment (in sadness) of the freedom mankind inherently possesses. On our side, mankind might have a question too. We might ask why the parousia, the promised end of days, has been delayed. This is a question that Christians wrestled with for centuries until the development of an orthodox Christianity more or less laid them to rest after Augustine. Augustine saw the need posed by these related facts: people are envious and eat each other up; they have forgotten the selflessness of God's example; and God has not come again to resolve the issue once and for all. Augustine saw with ghostly sight that the church must fill the need presented by these facts.

This view of the church, as I understand it, supports Scruton's insight that we need to cultivate the soil of the sacred for the sacred to be present in our lives. We need to prime the pump of the sacred with the sacred. For centuries, the church did this with the liturgy, the sacraments, the cathedrals, the music, the stained-glass windows, the Holy Weeks of Christmas and Easter, and the pomp and circumstance of festivals and processions through the towns and cities of Christendom. Now that these things have gone out of fashion, Scruton stepped in to see what he could do about it. Admittedly, though, it's a rearguard action against armies of secular positivists.

The allegory of *Everyman* reflects this need for ghostly sight of the sacred even in a time when the church was triumphant. God's speech to a medieval audience confirms it. Human beings, he tells us, lack ghostly sight. At the same time, the play attempts to satisfy the need. It was written to be performed on holidays and at festivals, and people from the community may have acted in it. There was a tradition of community theater. In *A Midsummer Night's Dream*, for example, Bottom was on fire to play Ercules, but Peter Quince had already chosen the romance of Pyramus and Thisbe. God wasn't a celebrity on the silver screen, someone as distant as the deity; he might have been played by a neighbor.

If we are in the audience watching the play, we know the universe is governed by God and his law because there he is explaining it to us. He's alive and well, even if he's upset with us. God makes it clear that he's an active judge. He takes an interest in the people's welfare. The everyday properties of the play—the stage, the costumes, the instruments of music and special effects, and of course live actors from the community—emphasize the fact that *the sacred is present among us every day even if we're not in church.* God is a neighbor, not a priest. The play is being performed in the street. Here personifications of Good Deeds (Charity), Strength, Knowledge, Beauty, and God himself have come to town and have come alive on the stage. It's the magic of theater. It's a wonderland, Lewis's third world of myth and fancy, that gives free play to the imagination. It's an allegory and an exercise in ghostly sight. It's not the Second Coming, but it's something. It's a source of wonder and renewal, and I suspect it was one more thing that fired the imagination of our greatest poet.

The imagination, Shakespeare knew, is a form of ghostly sight. Like all the gifts of creation, though, he also saw that it could be used for good or ill. He gave us characters like Iago, Macbeth, and Claudius to make that point. As I argued in Book One, I'm convinced that he had an experience, maybe like the one Pascal had, which seeded his imagination with a comic, not a tragic, vision. I wrote: "When I consider the greatness of Shakespeare's achievement as a writer, I'm inclined to believe that something happened to him (within) that answered the bell of the Spirits (Hark! Now I hear them) in Ariel's song. He, too, experienced the power and responsibility of *I Am*, suffered a sea change, and heard the sea nymphs sing the bell of his passing. Like Ariel, he now informs us of it in a deluge of words. The deluge poured forth from him and drowned his people with the waters of life, words with a power to renew creation. Having discovered himself, his being in the world, to be the ark that holds and preserves all that lives against a waste of not-being, he devoted his writing to the sanctuary of a life made whole in the love of *I Am That I Am*" (originally appeared on page 44).

Part 5: Fellow Feeling

I've been considering why these communities moved God's story out of scripture and put it into a play about Everyman that's the focus of a festive occasion. *The Harvesters* illustrates how the sacred emerges in this kind of communal gathering. I remarked in Book Three that: "Bruegel's painting . . . depicts the people of a town working to harvest the grain, and the picture shows that the work as a whole, a process that grows into the binding of the sheaves, is what binds them to each other. In Bruegel's art and in comedy, everyday life—which because it's so ordinary can seem to be merely a collection of arbitrary or pointless routines—is transformed by means of a comic alchemy into that which has a substantial and timeless value" (originally appeared in this book on page 311).

Bruegel has given us different stages in the harvesting of the grain and different stages in the rhythm of the day as work, refreshment, and rest. It's an important day in the life of the village; it means something to everyone. That man sprawled at the foot of the tree, however, gives us pause. Is he resting or is he dead? It must be he's resting because no one seems at all concerned. Still, in the midst of life . . . The doubt it generates is just that, a shadow in the life of everyday, and life goes on. Suppose he did die, as he must. When we see how everyone has silently agreed (Do we see anyone talking in the picture?) that the gift of the grain must be harvested, the work may help them to accept that the gift of a body must also be harvested. The man resting gave himself to the work, and the village will survive because he had a part in it. If he did die, he did so peacefully pillowed on the root of the tree.

To live at all, we all need a beating heart that circulates the blood to every cell in the body, just as souls need the blood in the trench Odysseus dug to live again and to speak. We need to breathe in and breathe out the air that circulates within and which passes its goodness through the blood to every cell of the body, and we need the nutrients of the grain that circulates within and passes their goodness to every cell in the body. When Death comes to tell us that we must go on a journey—which in effect happens, whether consciously or unconsciously, anytime this personification of Death comes to us in the word *death*—Death is pointing out the obvious, which tends to be lost in the busyness of our everyday affairs: we are a physical body completely at the mercy of these three needs. In the case of the first two, we will die immediately without them. In the case of the third, death comes slowly but inexorably, like an old moon waning. No wonder, then, that a story like Noah and the flood resonates so strongly down through the ages. We float every moment, it could be said, on a mighty ocean of uncertainty, insecurity, and fear.

I've borrowed this image of a moon waning from Theseus's speech, which opens the play of *A Midsummer Night's Dream* and sets it all in motion:

> *Now, fair Hippolyta, our nuptial hour*
> *Draws on apace; four happy days bring in*
> *Another moon. But oh, methinks how slow*
> *This old moon wanes! She lingers my desires,*
> *Like to a stepdame, or a dowager,*
> *Long withering out a young man's revenue.*

It must be that the two sovereigns decided the marriage must take place when there's no moon in the sky, perhaps so Diana will not witness the loss of her pristine Amazon queen. Theseus waits impatiently for the moon to die so their love can be consummated. There's a feeling behind his thought, though, that's much stronger than impatience. Theseus prides himself as a mighty warrior and survivor, but Time, which withers all things, will defeat him in the end, just as Time will frustrate his desire over the next four days. In addition to impatience, there's helplessness.

I would argue that in his painting of *The Harvesters* Bruegel has given us ghostly sight of this ocean of uncertainty and fear, but he has placed it on the horizon of the picture (see page 305). The people of the town work and live—in the field and in the town below—on terra firma, where they find a workable foundation for life. Here those three things are amply present, and the body is sustained by the good things of this life. The people are outdoors, where there's plenty of air to breathe, the field has yielded plenty of grain for the bread the people must eat, and there's plenty of work outdoors, which keeps the body fit and the heart strong.

Along with these necessities, there's the ghostly, unspoken fellow feeling of all who work there. These are grown-ups. They aren't the fools and the blind leading the-blind that Bruegel depicts in other paintings. They have seen with ghostly sight that they are mortal; they have learned that they all share the same basic needs; and they accept that they must work together to stave off the uncertainty, insecurity, and fear of that ocean in the distance. With ghostly sight Bruegel has imagined a church. Within this church, the people actively live out their faith that the body they have been given is a worthy vessel and that the community they have been given is a worthy vessel. With ghostly sight, Bruegel includes in his painting our ghostly Savior who comforts us through that season when we are harvested.

It seems to me that as they work the people of the town silently give thanks for the ground, the air, and the fellowship that sustain the life of their bodies and the comity of their town.

The Theme of Dying to Live in Book Two

Part 1: A Temporary Tomb for the Gods and Rebirth as Poetry

I presented a lengthy discussion about dying to live in the station of Lewis's narrative I called "The Road to Fairyland Runs through Allegory" (see pages 135–149). Having shown with examples from late Roman poets how the drift of personifications and the twilight of the gods meet in the center of his spectrum, Lewis sums up their importance for his narrative:

> *In all of them alike, as I hinted above, we see the beginnings of that free creation of the marvelous which first slips in under the cloak of allegory. It is difficult for the modern man of letters to value this quiet revolution*

as it deserves. We are apt to take it for granted that a poet has at his command, besides the actual world and the world of his own religion, a third world of myth and fancy. The probable, the marvelous-taken-as-fact, the marvelous-known-to-be-fiction—such is the triple equipment of the post-Renaissance poet. Such were the three worlds which Spenser, Shakespeare, and Milton were born to. London and Warwick, Heaven and Hell, Fairyland and Prospero's Island—each has its own laws and its appropriate poetry. But this triple heritage is a late conquest. Go back to the beginnings of any literature and you will not find it. At the beginning the only marvels are the marvels which are taken for fact. The poet has only two of these three worlds. In the fullness of time the third world crept in, but only by a sort of accident. The old gods, when they ceased to be taken as gods, might so easily have been suppressed as devils . . . Only their allegorical use, prepared by slow developments within paganism itself, saved them, as in a temporary tomb, for the day when they could wake again in the beauty of acknowledged myth and thus provide modern Europe with its "third world" of romantic imagining. And when they rose they were changed [as in Ariel's song, pages 44–46] and gave to poetry that which poetry had scarcely had before. The gods . . . were not to paganism what they are to us. In classical poetry we hear plenty of them as objects of worship, of fear, of hatred; even as comic characters. But pure aesthetic contemplation of their eternity, their remoteness, and their peace, for its own sake, is curiously rare.

The gods of Greece and Rome spent some time in a temporary tomb but rose again "in the beauty of acknowledged myth."

Lewis then describes how the gods endure a kind of initiation or ritual cleansing in the "tomb" of allegory:

No religion, so long as it is believed, can have that kind of beauty which we find in the gods of Titian, of Botticelli, or of our own romantic poets . . . The gods must be, as it were, disinfected of belief; the last taint of the sacrifice, and of the urgent practical interest, the selfish prayer, must be washed away from them, before that other divinity [the Beauty of Poetry] can come to light in the imagination. For poetry to spread its wings fully, there must be, besides the believed religion, a marvelous that knows itself as myth. For this to come about, the old marvelous, which once was taken as fact, must be stored up somewhere, not wholly dead, but in a winter sleep, waiting its time. If it is not so stored up, if it is allowed to perish, then the imagination is impoverished. Such a sleeping place was provided for the gods by allegory. Allegory may seem, at first, to have killed them; but it killed only as the sower kills, for gods, like other creatures, must die to live.

His history of allegory now reveals itself as a night of the soul for gods, a passage and a transition that readies them for rebirth. Lewis suggests that, along with the gods, the world is reborn through this process as the Beauty of Poetry.

Part 2: The Ghostly Sight of Arcite and Rosalind

In "On the Death and Rebirth of Metaphysics" (see pages 151–175), I describe how Goethe's Faust and Chaucer's Arcite, like the gods in Lewis's history of them, die to live. The acquisitive self, the one that would possess a Gretchen or an Emily, finds that it can do nothing of the sort. The project ends in bitter disappointment. The things of this world in the end are not objects that can be possessed, and the self that would possess these things is but an idea or an illusion.

After obsessing over Emily's image for decades and after finally winning her in the tournament—which pitted him against his cousin and rival, Palamon—Arcite suffers a fatal injury during the course of his victory lap. Three days later he pours out his disappointment to Emily in his last breaths:

Alas the woe! Alas the pain so strong,
That I have suffered for you, and so long!
Alas, O Death! Alas my Emily!
Alas the parting of our company!
Alas, my heart's own queen, alas my wife,
O lady of my heart that ends my life!
What does man ask to have?
Now with his love, now in his cold, cold grave,
Alone, alone, with none for company!
Farewell, my sweetest foe, my Emily!

But even as these words cover the entire world with a dark and bitter flood, the equation of Death with Emily holds within it another effect. The emptying out of "Emily" empties out fear and jealousy as well. His empty heart now fills with a different kind of love, and he continues:

O softly take me in your arms, I pray,
For love of God, and harken what I say.
I have here with my cousin Palamon,
Had strife and rancor many a day now gone,
For love of you, and for my jealousy.
And may Jove's wisdom touch the soul in me,
To speak of love and what its service means
Through all the circumstances and the scenes
Of life, namely good faith and knightly deed,
Wisdom, humility and noble breed,
Honor and truth and openness of heart,
For, as I hope my soul may have its part
With Jove, in all the world I know of none
So worthy to be loved as Palamon,
Who serves you and will serve you all his life.
And should you ever choose to be a wife,
Forget not Palamon, that great-hearted man.

This scene in "The Knight's Tale," which depicts Arcite breathing his last breath in the arms of Emily, is much like the scene at the end of *Hamlet*, which depicts Hamlet breathing his last breath in the arms of Horatio. Much as Hamlet, half dead and endowed with ghostly sight, settles his kingdom on a worthy successor, Arcita now sees with ghostly sight a world that settles in peace on timeless virtues, on noble actions, and especially on the constancy of partners in a marriage.

Shakespeare's characters inevitably experience disappointment, even the best of them. For example, Rosalind in *As You Like It* is disinherited and banished by her uncle, the false duke. Lewis's narrative about the gods in allegory helps to interpret what happens next. To win her love, Rosalind dies and lives in the temporary tomb of Ganymede, the identity she takes as a young man. Her womanhood is now invisible. She's like a ghost that's free to move in the world of men. In that state, she gains ghostly sight of her love, Orlando. In the final scene, though, she's reborn once more, this time as the bride of her love and daughter of Duke Senior, who has been restored to his rightful place.

Since we have gone through the experience step by step with Rosalind and Ganymede, we feel with her how tenuous an identity can be. One minute we're the daughter of a duke, and the next we're a nobody. Rosalind's story is Hamlet's story, but one with an explicitly comic ending. An experience like this can be a good thing. The time is out of joint; it jars loose an image of the self, which leaves space for questioning. An experience like this can be the accident that wakes a soul that's healthy and brave.

The Theme of Dying to Live in Book Three

Part 1: The Sacred, Sacrifice, and Meaning

Scruton introduces the theme of sacrifice on the first two pages of the book by making the events of 9/11 the starting point of his argument. He points out that for the attackers on 9/11 the religion of Islam "originates in a need for sacrifice and obedience." The attackers believed that "their lives will acquire a meaning when thrown away for Allah's sake." He then presents Durkheim's definition of *the core religious experience* as "the experience of myself as a member of something, called upon to renounce my interests for the sake of the group and to celebrate my membership of the group in *acts of devotion*, which might have no other justification than that they are commanded." Durkheim's definition takes in acts of sacrifice in secular communities during a time of war, acts of renunciation in a religious community, and the work of everyday that supports a family and a community. Finally, Scruton cites Jan Patocka's thought that "the meaning of life, even in the godless twentieth century, resides in the thing for which life—one's own life—can be sacrificed." Patocka probably has in mind activists who fought Soviet communism in satellite countries like Czechoslovakia. Scruton himself participated in that resistance, which may explain why he is familiar with Patocka's thought. By the end of the paragraph, he makes it clear that it's one thing to sacrifice one's own life for Allah and quite another to sacrifice the lives of three thousand so-called infidels.

Scruton makes the connection between sacrifice and meaning early on to establish the psychology of the human subject as the focus of his study about the sacred, and it establishes the psychological approach as the path to the sacred his argument will take. He will argue that human beings make these sacrifices as *free* human subjects. We are not insects acting on genetic impulse. A human subject's action of sacrifice derives not from instinct but from directed thought. What's the origin of this thought about sacrifice? Scruton maintains that the order of nature, the realm that science studies, cannot answer this question. The science of evolution depends for its success as a theory on the selfish gene. It must explain everything. This gene is like a virus, and a virus wants to survive. Full stop. To account for sacrifice, Scruton argues, we have to rely not on science but on *the wonderlands* of directed thought. We are part of a language-speaking community, and we take our meaning from it.

Part 2: A Movement toward Sacrifice in Relationships

God in *Everyman* tells us that envy blinds human beings in a community. It's obviously a powerful force. The French anthropologist Rene Girard proposed a theory that the sacred is rooted in the violence of "mimetic desire," an anthropological term for envy that avoids any association with religious virtues or vices. Scruton introduced Girard into his argument on the sacred in order to explain why he rejects Girard's theory. It's Scruton's final move before he defines "the intentionality of the religious frame of mind." Girard argued that primitive societies resolved the enmity of envy in the ritual death of a scapegoat. Because the scapegoat purged the community of the "accumulated bloodlust," it became a sacred object.

Scruton, on the other hand, would identify the things that bind human beings in a community without violence. He writes that there are:

> *. . . other areas in which we are inclined to speak of sacred things. The ideas of the sacred and the sacramental attach themselves to birth, to sexual union and marriage, and also to the ordinary death of ordinary people—these are all things that are set apart, regarded with awe, in which God is directly concerned, and which can be desecrated. Why are not these just as important as the more explicitly sacrificial aspects of the religious way of life? Rites of passage are surely more basic than ritual sacrifices—sometimes, perhaps, the occasion for ritual sacrifices, but in themselves far more necessary to the psychic health and togetherness of the community than the sacrifice of the occasional scapegoat. The sense of the sacred surely precedes ritual sacrifice, is more primitive, more basic, more fundamental to the human condition than any of the phenomena normally invoked to explain it.*

With that, Scruton is ready to present the beating heart and the life-sustaining breath of his argument. Here's how I described this climactic moment in Book Three: "Having rooted a sense of the sacred in the less violent rhythms of everyday life, Scruton can proceed to his conclusion. He finds value in Girard's work, but it falls short in that it doesn't explain the thing it set out to explain:

> *Still, we can now say something a little more definite about the intentionality of the religious frame of mind. It is a reaching out from subject to subject; it searches for a relation that is close, intimate, and personal, with a being who is present in this world though not of this world; and in this reaching out there is a movement toward sacrifice, in which both self and other might give themselves completely and thereby achieve a reconciliation that lies beyond the reach of ordinary human dialogue.*

"Scruton has wrestled with this question about the intentionality of the religious thought over these many pages, and now he has summed it up for us. And going back to the first station, where the suicide bombers of 9/11 initiated the inquiry, Scruton concedes that this 'movement toward sacrifice' may be connected to primitive forms of violence, for:

> *. . . there are roots to this state of mind that are far darker than we can, in our daily lives, easily acknowledge. But the essential character of the religious frame of mind is that of an intersubjective awareness in which the readiness for sacrifice is in some way contained.*

"He makes this concession, but it only goes so far:

> *And in judging religions, we are acutely aware of the extent to which to sacrifices they ask for are sacrifices of others or sacrifices of self. It is surely that, above all else, that has entered our awareness through the actions of the Islamist 'martyrs.'*

"Other stations have prepared us for this climactic stage of my inquiry. We stopped briefly to observe how Chaucer's characters made a pilgrimage to the place where a man voluntarily sacrificed his own life and became a saint. C. S. Lewis has shown us how the self in the allegories he studies dissolves as an accident in the substance of a living soul. I have argued that as Shakespeare's characters passionately seek the place where 'Naught shall go ill,' they undergo a process wherein they agree, in the end, to be enough of a naught that a marriage with another can succeed. Now Scruton has gone a journey in his thought to describe an intersubjective awareness, which contains a readiness for sacrifice. All roads in this inquiry have led to this place of sacrifice, the act of which Scruton describes so beautifully in the quote above:

> *. . . and in this reaching out there is a movement toward sacrifice, in which both self and other might give themselves completely and thereby achieve a reconciliation that lies beyond the reach of ordinary human dialogue.*

"Scruton's prose here may not look like poetry, but it is doing the work of poetry. It's a medium (he is the medium) that looks at us in this world, using the language we understand, to describe situations we have experienced that hint at this relation of self and other, but it also looks the other way into that which lies beyond the reach of ordinary speech" (originally appeared on pages 312–313).

I value Scruton's beautiful passages on intellectual and aesthetic grounds. Thanks to the insight, artistry, and infinite care of their author, they give a shape to my inquiry about what it means to be a living soul. Scruton places the experience of dying to live in everyday relationships—with family, friends, acquaintances, store clerks, policemen, including someone you may think is an enemy. In every meeting, we have the opportunity to acknowledge a sovereign power like ourselves. We are sovereign powers that are married, like Oberon and Titania, and creation is the ball we share in a game of catch. The ball unites us. Maybe the throw is a little off or one of us flubs the catch. No matter. The ball is still in the game. It's objective, and it's our common ground. That's why we give ourselves completely to keep it in play. The game brings us face-to-face with another, where she is a medium for me, I am a medium for her, and with ghostly sight we may sense the real presence of the sacred. This was Dante's experience, and this is what Redon's painting suggests.

Not every "meeting" is like this though. A friend of ours was recently mugged at a service station. While she pumped gas, a robber tried to take her purse, which was on the passenger-side seat. Our friend saved her purse but was brutally attacked for resisting. This was an invasion, not a meeting under a white flag of truce, and certainly not a game of catch.

Part 3: Ghostly Sight of a Love That Comes Out of Nowhere

Harper Lee takes her protagonist Scout through a dying-to-live experience. This is the goal of the whole novel. Lee would have Scout reborn on Boo Radley's porch so she can see the world through his ghostly point of view.

He's "Boo," the spirit word that comes out of nowhere to wake us from a dream, but on the night of All Saints' Day he's more like an archangel. When Scout turns around to see the neighborhood from his point of view, she experiences the real presence of an interest in her that came out of nowhere to save her life.

Part 4: Scruton Puts on and Takes off His Skeptic Hat

In a spirit of healthy skepticism, Scruton plays a skeptic in the final pages of the chapter; he slips in and out of the role. When he puts on his skeptic hat for the last time, though, he ends the chapter by doubting the skeptic point of view on the sacred. It does not satisfy him, so the skeptic view dies. Instead, he suggests we can be moved by the transcendental urge of reason itself to sense with ghostly sight the real presence of the sacred. With that, we move forward on our pilgrimage into the rest of the book.

Part 5: The Ghostly Sight That Lends a Gentle Glow to Life

The dying-to-live theme is certainly present in Scruton's "movement toward sacrifice," and the movement results in a ghostly relationship with another that is "beyond the reach of ordinary human dialogue." The intimacy of this "reconciliation" can lead, I would argue, to another instance of ghostly sight at a later phase of the relationship. Dante is my witness, for he made this phenomenon the focus of *La Vita Nuova* and the *Commedia*. From the moment he first saw Beatrice, Dante understood their meeting to be a movement in which he gave himself to her goodness completely, and she, because she already radiated compassion to everyone and everything in existence as an expression of her spirit, responded in kind. Both *La Vita Nuova* and the *Commedia* have to do with that moment, but Dante's narratives move the implication of it forward. Beatrice dies, and Dante lives on to wonder about that moment of pure intersubjectivity.

I would add here near the conclusion of these reflections on ghostly sight some thoughts on the ghostly sight that attends the one who still lives after another dies. Chaucer traveled to Italy on a diplomatic mission, and he undoubtedly brought back to England books by Boccaccio. If he didn't bring back works by Dante, he most certainly knew about the most important Italian poet of that century. They were brothers in the new movement to write poetry in the vernacular. I mention this because I find that the story of Palamon and Arcite in "The Knight's Tale" captures quite poignantly the effect on Palamon when Arcite, his intimate alter ego, dies. To restore the longed-for peace between Athens and Thebes, Theseus proposes after a time that Emily should marry Palamon in Arcite's ghostly place. Chaucer describes the effect of Arcite's death on their marriage in lines that deserve to be quoted a third time in my book:

Palamon was espoused to Emily,
And God that all this wide, wide world has wrought,
Send them his love, for it was dearly bought!
Now Palamon's in joy, amid a wealth
Of bliss and splendor, happiness and wealth.
He's tenderly beloved of Emily
And serves her with a gentle constancy,
And never a jealous word between them spoken
Or other sorrow in a love unbroken.
Thus ended Palamon and Emily,
And God save all this happy company!

My second commentary on this quote inferred the reason these two now experience "a love unbroken." I explained there that "their love is and will be whole because it is God's love and because God's love has been 'dearly bought.' Palamon's cousin Arcite, his rival to Emily's love, suffered a mortal injury to his heart minutes after winning the right to marry the woman he and Palamon had sought for many years, but before he died, he blessed the marriage of Palamon and Emily. A marriage, a lasting relationship, isn't just about a feeling that arises quite naturally in the chemistry of the body. It has to involve an awareness about life itself as a gift and a pearl beyond price. Because Palamon constantly lives with Emily by his side, he lives constantly with an awareness of Arcite's loss, and this sorrow gives the gift of Emily a joyful, gentle glow. This effect derives, not from the chemistry of the body, but from intellectual insight. The effect is like a crown of light, and a crown, we remember, is for the head" (originally quoted on pages 100–101).

I have experienced the ghostly sight of this gentle glow. Everyone of a certain age has, I'm sure. When someone we love dies, the light of every day, despite the pain of loss, has a different quality or meaning. For some reason, we are still present to see the light of day and sunsets and the dusk of evening. Perhaps this light is infused with the question we ask of Brahman or God or whomever—the question "Why?" In which case, it's the beginning of a relationship with This Life, the celebrity I've mentioned before. The question, Scruton suggests, is a good thing. For him, I would say, it's an opening to the sacred.

The Experience of Divine CPR

Turn him to any cause of policy,
The Gordian Knot of it he will unloose,
Familiar as his garter.

To close the circle of this chapter, I've returned to the quote with which it began. Familiarity means intimacy, like that in a family. What could be more intimate than the relationship described in Genesis:

> *But there went up a mist from the earth, and watered the whole face of the ground. And the Lord God formed man of the dust of the ground, and breathed into his nostrils the breath of life; and man became a living soul.*

From these famous, familiar lines, my inquiry about what it means to be a living soul emerged, and the following three passages from Book One suggest how these verses address the Gordian knot of a life that includes a death.

"The image of divine CPR in Genesis figures for us a foundational, interpersonal relationship. It's not enough just to hope that all can end well. The hope is realized in relationship with another who supplies the breath of life. The story in Genesis about the breath is not just a story; it's a powerful metaphor. Because air is so plentiful and because breathing goes on automatically, the significance of a breath can fade into the background as a given. When we're drowning, though, like the remnants from the wreck in *The Tempest*, and what's been given has been taken away, then we long for it. 'Drowning' is the vehicle in the metaphor that frames that play. When we're 'drowning' in any of the many forms of self-pity, including aggression, and alienation from others that afflicts human beings (and we see plenty of that on stage in the human characters of *The Tempest*, but especially in the character of Caliban), we're out of air and in despair. The play itself, as it resolves the alienation between brother and brother, plays the role of a divine breath, which revives in them a living soul.

"Shakespeare writes his dialogues with the air of a man who has found that the breath of life in everyday speech can have a life-saving function. The breath of life in everyday speech is as vital now as in Shakespeare's day. In these faithless times, we still find that we must speak to others and others must speak to us. We still speak and act out our love with intense single-mindedness, and when children come, they still serve as a sanctuary of selfless purpose for parents who sustain their children's lives with an instinct like self-preservation. Along with these primeval passions, like creatures in nature excited by excitement, the usual turbulence and temptations of the times work on human hearts one way or another. In these tempestuous seas, parents depend on true speech for the family's survival. We are individuals, and true speech is the breath that steadies and unites us. It's the most effective nonlethal instrument in a critical network of checks and balances. We may not like to admit it, but the other very likely knows us better than we know ourselves.

"The sacred words of Genesis tell us that we are individuals with names like Adam and Eve, Isaac and Rebecca, and Jacob and Rachel, but we are made out of others—our father and mother and those who have gone before them in our lineage. The immediate family as well as the family of man reaching back to our first parents remind us of the timeless breadth and depth of our interdependence. Like the main characters in Genesis, from *Titus Andronicus* through to *The Tempest*, Shakespeare's main characters come to life within the context of a family; it's a context or a setting that insures close contact with others. Then, too, family members and friends of long standing are the most immediate reminders (for better or for worse) of the life we have made out of everything we've ever said or done or thought. No wonder our relationships with them prompt such fierce passions" (originally appeared on pages 41–42).

Scruton argues that within these relationships we learn "step by step" how to "unloose" the knot (Not!) that constrains us—our alienation from others and from creation. If that's the case, then it's possible that a human subject could relive in everyday speech that experience of divine CPR in Genesis. Scruton reminds us that we are a species defined by the presence in our life of a language and the thoughts we have in that language. Because of it, the intentionality or directedness of our minds can run "over the hump" into a "pasture," which includes the sacred. This pasture is an essential part of our species life. Within these relationships, we become familiar with the sacred "policy" of this life that a human subject experiences the real presence of This Life as another subject. Is this true? It's an idea that needs to be tried to be proved. Having seen the possibility, the sunlit hill, we can take the idea for a test drive in the relationships of everyday. As we become more familiar with it, the practice may prove to be an end unto itself, which doesn't need to be justified.

On Dying to Live in Courtly Love

Having read Scruton's chapter on believing in God, I find it of interest to look once more at Lewis's study of courtly love, the place where he began his inquiry into love and the soul as they are represented in allegory. Lewis clearly believed that the rise of courtly love in the south of France had great significance for Western culture. We can't say for sure, because it took place about a thousand years ago, but it appears that the ideas of courtly love gave the lady of a feudal lord an authority usually reserved only for the lord. To give the practice a context, Lewis has us imagine the setting for its nativity:

> *We must picture a castle which is a little island of comparative leisure and luxury, and therefore at least of possible refinement, in a barbarous country-side. There are many men in it, and very few women—the lady and her damsels. Around these throng the whole male meiny, the inferior nobles, the landless knights, the squires, and the pages—haughty creatures enough in relation to the peasantry beyond the walls, but feudally inferior to the lady as to her lord—her "men" as feudal language had it. Whatever courtesy is in the place flows from her: all female charm from her and her damsels. All these circumstances together come very near to being a "cause" [which explains the birth of courtly love]; but they do not explain why very similar conditions elsewhere had to wait for Provencal example before they produced like results. Some part of the mystery remains inviolate.*

What's the mystery? To fit the question within the theme of my chapter on dying to live, Lewis wonders how it ever happened that a whole social code came into existence, which dictated that the will of a man must die before he can be reborn in the arms of his lady. Lewis illustrates this, as I have shown, in Chretien de Troyes's romance about Lancelot—"the flower of the courtly tradition in France" (see pages 79–80), and Chaucer illustrates it in his scene depicting Arcite's death in the arms of his Emily, which visually is so like Michelangelo's *Pieta* (see pages 428–430).

We may never know why courtly love came to be, but we do know quite a bit about its effect. Lewis argues that it has changed the relationship between men and women throughout the West down to our own time. When a man has an interest in a woman, the woman determines the level of intimacy. She can't be forced. If we view the code of courtly love through the window that Scruton has given us about the sacred, we can appreciate why courtly love was such an important development. It's perfectly natural for a man to have a passionate interest in a woman. Courtly love recognizes that it's perfectly natural for a woman to resist its imposition on her. She's not a thing, a robot; she's a human subject, just as her passionate admirer is. Then again, if the man behaves like a beast, the lady has to conclude that he is *not yet* a human subject. The trials she devises will prove it one way or another.

From the man's point of view, her coldness, in conjunction with the code of courtly love, informs him that he has to "count to ten," that old device for anger management. The woman's adamancy acts like a polished mirror that reflects his passion back on himself. The pain of it may do what pain is supposed to do. He may be forced to wonder, "What's wrong? Why does this hurt?" Instead of forcing himself on the woman, he is forced to look at himself as a passionate human subject. Reciprocally, this ghostly sight of himself may give him ghostly sight of her as a passionate human subject (as opposed to an object). Pain and disappointment act like a formal invitation to meet with Wisdom—who was with God, she tells us in Proverbs 8, from the beginning. The lady plays Wisdom's part in courtly love.

Envoi

What's the survival value of an inquiry about what it means to be a living soul? For myself, I have to say it has given wonderful days and nights of engagement with the question. Countless times I have run forward "over the hump" into a pasture full of surprises when words and ideas come from out of nowhere and leave me eager to continue the search. I might as well be asking what's the survival value of happiness.

What's the survival value of stories like the one I just told about courtly love—where a lover dies and is reborn in the arms of his love? Scruton has grounded the idea of dying to live in everyday relationships, for it's possible in any relationship to "reach beyond" in the way he has described. I might as well be asking what's the survival value of happiness in relationships.

Postscript

The Republic and *The Soul of the World*

Chapter 1
The Form of Dialectic

Josef Abel's

Socrates Teaching His Disciples

Introduction

For several months, I thought I had come to the end of my inquiry, but I found it difficult to ignore how little I knew about the subject. Years ago I had read parts of Plato's *Republic*, and I remembered that his definition of justice involved the soul of a city and the soul of an individual. To see what Plato had to say about those souls, I purchased translations of the *Republic* by Allan Bloom and Benjamin Jowett. From a review of these texts, I found similarities with Scruton's account in both the form and the content of Plato's representations.

This postscript is an unplanned addition to the family. The work, it appears, has a life of its own, and it is compelling me to finish what I started, no matter the labor. I imagine this means there will be much to do after this reading of the *Republic* is added to my train of thought.

Scruton's Mousetrap for Sovereign Souls

As to form, Plato has Socrates engage a group of young men in the form of inquiry called dialectic. The discussion takes place in the home of Cephalus, an elderly and wealthy businessman. Instead of giving a straightforward lecture, Socrates converses with another person, and at some point a question arises, like "What is justice?" The question belongs to both participants in the dialogue, although it must be said that Socrates is clearly the dominant speaker. Nevertheless, the ideas he presents must pass through the mind and understanding of the other. The other may agree with Socrates (as he does, most of the time), he may ask for clarification, or he may add to the discussion with a statement of his own. Since dialectic involves at least two people and takes the form of *an exchange* of thoughts, it emphasizes and makes us aware that every human being is a sovereign soul with a unique perspective on the world. We can only know the world from our own perspective, which is intrinsically limited. Socrates made his mark as a philosopher by publicly acknowledging that limitation. According to his interpretation of the oracle at Delphi, he was the wisest man in Athens because he understood that he knew nothing. Each day represented an opportunity to discover whether this was still true, and so he engaged others in the marketplace to test his hypothesis.

It's hard not to notice that "dialectic" and "intersubjectivity" are closely related. They both denote the ground on which Scruton builds his definition of *religion* as well as the ground on which he proves that an experience of the sacred is possible. With a reading of the *Republic* fresh in mind, it seemed to me that Scruton imitates the form of an interpersonal interaction even though he is writing expository prose, but I admit that it requires a little imagination to see it that way. Instead of creating a fictional conversation between two characters in a narrative as Plato does, Scruton, I imagine, has imagined his readers as characters like the young men in the *Republic*. We are a shadow presence in a dialogue. He has imagined that we are intellectual Everymen in the modern mode, which means we are skeptics about religion just as the young men in the *Republic* are skeptical that a just man will be happier than an unjust man. Scruton, the man in full, is also a shadow presence. Even though he comes to us in a disembodied voice, which reveals no specifics about his personal life, he makes us aware that he's the master of ceremonies with a certain character. He makes little jokes. He leads his skeptical readers effortlessly into a position where, as master of ceremonies, he can easily win a point in his favor—just as Socrates did with his students. Because he has devoted his life to these issues, we realize after several pages that he commands the high ground in the argument. Some readers, I imagine, stop reading when they realize what their skepticism is up against.

Even though Scruton has aimed his argument at those who don't believe in God and who don't believe they are a soul or that the world is a soul, if we continue to read through the first chapter, we may be persuaded to recognize that something—in us and in a culture where a book like *The Soul of the World* can still be imagined, written, published, and discussed in intellectual circles—has moved us to purchase his book and to read page after page of the first chapter. Something has moved us to entertain an interest in metaphysical things, something that's a little more than idle curiosity. I know the character of these readers well, for I am one of them. I bought the book and read the first chapter. I was the mouse that walked into Scruton's mousetrap. Like others who value his work and now mourn his passing, his dialectical inquiry into the nature of religion held my attention until it was too late to stop. Why stop when something beautiful shown forth from the wit and wisdom of the text.

It would appear that my experience in reading *The Soul of the World* is much like the young men's experience in their discussion with Socrates.

Aporia, Mystery, and the Philosopher-As-Midwife

By the end of Book One of the *Republic*, Socrates has isolated "What is justice?" as the subject of the dialogue, but he has managed only to explode the ideas that Cephalus, Polemarchus, and Thrasymachus had about it. The young men are left in aporia (Cephalus didn't stay for long), a state of not-knowing. The initial pain and confusion when successive definitions of justice fail, however, can quite naturally resolve into an attractive mystery around the question: "What *is* justice?" Since people love solving mysteries, the question motivates the young men to continue searching. The attraction of that mystery moves them through the next nine books of the *Republic*. The presence of Socrates effects the changes from complacent certainty to aporia and from aporia to a mystery we want to solve. He's the lover of wisdom, magi, and midwife who has experience in these matters, as the boys remind him when it looks like he's about to leave them. He has to finish what he started. Once Socrates established himself as the leader of their little community, his presence gives them confidence that the answer can come to life in this world.

As I have explained in my introduction, initially I wondered why Scruton called his book *The Soul of the World*, when the word *soul* rarely appears in the text. The question Scruton poses with his title, I would argue, motivates the reader to find how this mystery, the soul of the world, emerges from the text. Since Scruton can only speak to his readers through the medium of his writing, he can't impose on us with his physical presence nor can he physically engage us in a dialogue. Nevertheless, much like the arc of a Socratic dialogue, he proceeds step by step in an argument that, if credited, will transport his readers out of their comfort zone—which by deliberate choice or habit excluded metaphysical notions about God or a soul—and will leave them in some doubt about the nonexistence of God and the soul. He proceeds with the methodical, inexorable, and willful drip, drip, drip of his thought on our foreheads. Just as Socrates isolates the questions "What is justice?" and "Is justice possible?" as a focus for the discussion with his students, Scruton isolates the questions "What is religion?" and "Is it possible for the eternal God to be a real presence in the life of his earthly worshippers?" as the focus of his dialogue with his reader. Every sentence of his argument moves us a little closer toward doubting the nonexistence of the sacred and the soul.

He warned us about his intention. No mystery there. We are reading a chapter about believing in God, which serves as the introduction to a book about the soul of the world. We willingly put ourselves in a position where his argument, for the time being, becomes the most important thing in our lives. There may be danger for the skeptic, but something there is in some of us that doesn't stop reading. The something, now that we have bought the book and are reading it, is a like-mindedness with the mind of Roger Scruton; it grabs our attention whether we follow what he is saying or not. Reading him, we want *to know* because we sense what he knows will be worth knowing. This is the effect, I suggest, that Socrates had on the ambitious young men of Athens.

Thus, I argue that the form of dialectic informs the form of Scruton's presentation. In a subtle but important way, he reminds us that we are engaged in an intersubjective dialogue with another subject, like those in the *Republic* between Socrates and his students.

The Skeptic Who Now Must Doubt His Doubting

At an early stage of the argument, Scruton patiently removes the primary obstacle to belief in God: that part in the theory of evolution that takes agency away from the self-consciousness and moral freedom of a human subject and gives it to a selfish gene. Once a human subject realizes that freedom and the accountability that goes with it, an approach to the sacred opens up. In the great battle for freedom and accountability, the selfish gene is the Wicked Witch of the West; she must be squashed for us to walk the yellow brick road. Scruton titled the last section of the first chapter "Confronting the Skeptic." I think there's a subtle joke in the title. It may refer to the skeptic who continues to not believe in God, the soul, or the sacred despite Scruton's argument. This skeptic, true to his rational nature, still doubts. Thanks to Scruton's reading of Kant and Hegel, however, the chapter ends on the possibility that Reason itself is moved by a "transcendental urge" to reach beyond what empirical science can know. Reason itself now has reason to doubt the nonexistence of God and the soul. In this case, it's not Scruton who is confronting the skeptic. The skeptic himself now must doubt his doubting, for Reason has changed sides. This is real doubt, doubt about everything, and this is Scruton's goal in the intersubjective dialectic I imagine he is having with his skeptical reader. For Scruton's purposes, the skeptic's aporia (a state that, to some extent, Scruton himself acts out) at the end of the first chapter is a state of being in which believing in God is more possible.

A Passion for Truth

Part 1: Introduction

Socrates thought that a true philosopher must have a passion for truth, and he embodied that passion for his students. For some readers, the passion for truth of a great philosopher is self-evident, and they aspire to it. Because people as a general rule are complacent and incurious about their opinions, however, Socrates sometimes stirred up their passions with a provocation. Talking with Socrates, people said, was like getting stung by a gadfly. Just as Plato begins the dialogues of the *Republic* with a provocation, Scruton begins *The Soul of the World* with one. I'll describe how he does this at the end of this section on a passion for truth.

Part 2: Socrates Challenges the Report of Cephalus

When Socrates agrees to have dinner with the young men who have "arrested" him, Cephalus, the elderly and wealthy host, greets him in a friendly manner and invites him to be a frequent guest. Socrates tells his host that he would enjoy being at home with Cephalus. He likes talking to older men, for he wonders whether the way they travel (into old age) is easy or hard. "What report do you give of it?" he asks.

I would quote the whole of Cephalus's response, for it is wonderful, but in short, he reports that old age doesn't bother him, because he has "a calm and happy nature." Socrates, though, has doubts about the report. "I listened in admiration," he tells his students:

> *. . . and wanting to draw him out, that he might go on—Yes, Cephalus, I said: but I rather suspect that the people in general are not convinced by you when you speak thus; they think that old age sits lightly upon you, not because of your happy disposition, but because you are rich, and wealth is well known to be a great comforter (Jowett translation, 329e).*

Like a surgeon deftly opening up the body with a scalpel, Socrates opens up the character of Cephalus for more serious scrutiny. "How can you be satisfied with that answer," Socrates is asking, "when it's quite possible you are ignoring the real reason for your happy disposition?"

If you look once more at the sentence I have quoted, you can see that it is beautifully restrained and brutally direct at the same time. A calm and happy nature "sits lightly" on it while a bag of gold gives it weight. What would you pick as the foundation for your retirement? Also, the sentence as a whole conveys the real burden of living in a social order, which incorporates both the rich and the not-so-rich. It's a weighty matter that the art of politics addresses, and this is the art that Socrates is midwifing into life over the course of the ten books.

To his credit, Cephalus is not put off by the aggressive challenge from Socrates. He answers Socrates the way Themistocles answered the Seriphian who said that Themistocles was famous "not for his own merits but because he was an Athenian." Themistocles replies (in my own paraphrase of a difficult passage) that one's character develops in one's native city in a way that suits both, but one's native city doesn't *determine* one's character. Your character is still your character, and you become famous or not due to your character, not to your city. Cephalus then applies this idea to whether a person lives in a poor or a rich part of a city. If you are poor and impatient, Cephalus tells us, old age will be especially difficult. If you are poor and patient, old age "cannot be a light burden." To conclude the argument, Cephalus asserts that "a bad rich man will never have peace with himself." Cephalus admits that "people in general" ("the many" or in Greek the *hoi polloi*) think that wealth by its nature confers happiness, but, despite the opinion of "the many" that Socrates has put to him, Cephalus still believes that character matters more, whether you are rich or poor.

Socrates's sudden and somewhat rude challenge derives from his passion for truth, and this one passionate sentence gives life to the argument that struggles to be born through all the subsequent passages of the book. This sentence asks Cephalus to take a second look at the foundation of his comfort, and he is then moved to answer with a complex elaboration of his idea. To move that elaboration along further, Socrates prompts Cephalus to tell him about the origin of his money and about the greatest blessing he has received from it. In my opinion, Cephalus's reply to these questions is also wonderful, so much so that I quote it in full.

The greatest blessing of wealth, he tells Socrates, is one that most people might not expect (possibly, I would guess, because it's not a physical pleasure like eating and drinking):

> *For let me tell you, Socrates, that when a man thinks himself to be near death, fears and cares enter into his mind which he never had before; the tales of a world below and the punishment which is exacted there of deeds done here were once a laughing matter to him, but now he is tormented with the thought that they may be true: either from the weakness of age, or because he is now drawing nearer to that place, he has a clearer view of these things; suspicions and alarms crowd thinly upon him, and he begins to reflect and consider what wrongs he has done to others. And when he finds that the sum of his transgressions is great he will many a time like a child start up in his sleep for fear, and he is filled with dark forebodings. But to him who is conscious of no sin, sweet hope, as Pindar charmingly says, is the kind nurse of his age:*
>
> > *"Hope," he says, "cherishes the soul of him who lives in justice and holiness;—hope which is mightiest to sway the restless soul of man."*
>
> *How admirable are his words! And the great blessing riches, I do not say to every man, but to a good man, is, that he has had no occasion to deceive or to defraud others, whether intentionally or unintentionally; and when he departs to the world below he is not in any apprehension about offerings due to the gods or debts which he owes to men. Now to this peace of mind the possession of wealth greatly contributes; and therefore I say, that, setting one thing against another, of the great advantages which wealth has to give, to a man of sense this is in my opinion the greatest. (Jowett translation, 330d–331b)*

We see here in this passage how the passion for truth, which initiates a dialogue with Cephalus, brings us in fits and starts to "the soul of him who lives in justice and holiness." We see how the dialectical process, which begins with the origins and comforts of money, ends with the goal of life, which is justice and holiness (wholeness). In this way, Cephalus has given the goal of their conversation a shape and a name. We would know "the soul of him who lives in justice and holinesss."

Before moving on, though, I have to note how accurately Cephalus describes an elderly person concerned about transgressions—you know, the one who wrote about *The Lord's Prayer* in the introduction and the one who wrote the opening pages of "And Man Became a Living Soul"—that person being myself.

Part 3: The Passion of Polemarchus

The dialogue with Cephalus continues as Socrates summarizes from what Cephalus has said that justice means speaking the truth and paying your debts, but then Socrates gives an example of when paying your debt (returning a sword to a man who went crazy after he loaned it) is not justice. Polemarchus, Cephalus's son, jumps in at that point to defend his father's idea with a slightly different definition but one that's in keeping with his family's position in the city: Justice is giving goods to friends and harm to enemies, he tells Socrates. Polemarchus must feel that the honor of his family and class (they are wealthy Metics, nonresident aliens) is at stake. Cephalus is not much moved by the challenge of his calm and happy nature, nor is he much moved by the challenge to his definition of *justice*. He simply retires from the conversation, leaving it in the hands of his heir, Polemarchus. Polemarchus *is* moved by the intellectual and emotional currents swirling around the dialogue with Socrates, so he eagerly continues the dialectic about justice begun by his father.

The young men gathered in the home of Cephalus to question Socrates have observed that a wealthy man in Athens gets more respect than a poor man. Wealth gives a man power over others in his private affairs, and it gives him political power to insure the city's policies work to his advantage. In his debate with Polemarchus, Socrates proves that justice is not giving goods to friends and harm to enemies because (among other reasons) people can easily mistake who is a friend and who is an enemy. Socrates eventually takes Polemarchus through a logical process whereby he "proves" that a just person would never deliberately harm anyone's character, whether he's a friend or a foe. Socrates has not yet provided a definition of *justice*, but he converts Polemarchus to this description of a just man.

Part 4: The Passion That Loves Wisdom

Thrasymachus, a sophist, takes over the discussion from Polemarchus and presents his opinion that justice is the advantage of the stronger. For perfect happiness, he argues, a man must have not only wealth but a ruthless nature that seeks its own advantage in every situation. Since he is a master of rhetoric, Thraymachus speaks with great power and confidence, but Socrates in the end makes him a friend to his point of view—that injustice is never more profitable than justice. Socrates defeats the passionate self-interest of Thrasymachus with his passion for truth.

Socrates demonstrates that passion, but his argument falls short. It wasn't enough to persuade an ambitious young man like Glaucon that he shouldn't seek to become wealthy and powerful. (Socrates recognizes that Glaucon is intelligent and spirited enough to succeed in any enterprise to which he sets his mind, and he is determined to save such a man for the virtue and harmony of the city.) Playing the devil's advocate, Glaucon asserts that justice is not desirable for its own sake as Socrates says it is. It's more advantageous *to pretend* to be just while secretly being unjust. Both Glaucon and his brother Adeimantus doubt Socrates's conclusion that the just man is happier than the unjust man because they can easily picture a scenario where he is not. They like how Socrates defeated Thraymachus, but they aren't convinced. They want to know how to live their lives, and so they urge Socrates to continue with the discussion. A passion to know now drives it, but since Socrates is still master of the situation that passion will be ruled by reason, by the best argument. This is what it means to love wisdom.

Part 5: Passion Wakes Up and Goes to School

In addition to strategic, stinging comments, Socrates stimulates passion in the others by engaging them one on one. Can you imagine speaking eye to eye with Socrates? Who wouldn't fear looking like a fool in a dialogue with him? There's fear in shame and uncertainty, but fear is mixed up with a passion for life. Most people want to live, not just any life but a good life. That passion for the honor of a good life (a life that's just because ruled by reason) is what Socrates calls spiritedness. We need this spiritedness or courage or passion to act justly in the face of fear. Spiritedness or courage, Socrates believed, had to be learned, for people are not naturally brave. They have to be trained to know in any situation *what things are to be feared*. For example, abandoning your position in a battle line should be feared, whereas facing the enemy and holding the line should not be feared. We learn later in the *Republic* that this kind of training may take thirty or forty years.

Part 6: Scruton Challenges the Report of the 9/11 Commentators

Just as Socrates provoked Cephalus with an observation that initiates a search for a definition of justice, Scruton provokes the reader of "Believing in God" with an observation that challenges the popular view of religion. He relates how public intellectuals in the West interpreted the events of 9/11. Because they see religion as an explanation of reality, like physics, they judge religion to be the cause of the violence: the Koran, in black and white, instructs the faithful to kill infidels; the Islamists read the Koran; because they read the book and believe it to be the Word of God, they launched the attacks of 9/11. Scruton explains, however, that these commentators have misunderstood the nature of religion. It doesn't explain, like science does, the cause of a phenomenon; it concerns "how we should live." While not condoning the violence, Scruton proposes that the commentators could gain from the Islamists a more accurate understanding of what a religion means to those who actually practice one. Observers who study religion from an objective, third-person point of view cannot know what it means to practice the day-to-day rhythm of a religious discipline like prayer. They don't know how faith in God may lead to "acts of devotion which might have no other justification than that they are commanded."

I fancy that Scruton's challenge is like a red cape in front of bullish secularists eager to defend their faith in science and reason. He informs those readers who agree with the commentators, who pride themselves on the power of their intellects and their reasoning, that they are ignorant about something of great importance to human beings. He argues that these primitive, despised Islamists have a better answer to the question "What is religion?" than the commentators do. In making his challenge, he shifts the ground for his argument about religion out of an objective third-person point of view and into a subjective first-person point of view, for that's where religion lives. If readers identify with the commentators and their passion for an objective, scientific, utilitarian point of view, perhaps they will be stung by Scruton's condescension and will come at him with their passionate hatred of ancient prejudice.

Perhaps, though, there is good reason for looking at religion from a subjective point of view. Let's imagine that we are not inquiring into the nature of religion but rather into the nature of death, which, after all, is a subject with which religion is much concerned. What does an outside view of death tell the observer? The answer is definitive and quite simple: absolutely nothing. About a dead object an observer can say many things relating to the physical properties we can observe—along with cause of death, time of death, cost of death, and so on. None of this has anything to say about a human subject's experience of death. That belongs to the person who died, who is silent. A live consciousness can only perceive or know what lies within the boundaries of its own live consciousness.

Religion, Scruton argues through the first chapter, begins with God speaking to a man like Abraham or Moses and commanding a new direction for his life. We learn from the Torah in the subsequent history of them and their people the effect of this initial encounter. Abraham's experience of God must have persuaded him that He is real, we think, but we are merely outside observers of the phenomenon. What does an outside view of another's experience of God tell the observer? Like the facts around a death, there are things we notice, but the experience itself eludes us (until maybe one day, like death itself, it doesn't). So I conclude, and I believe Scruton would have us conclude, that in the matter of death and religion we must be content with the limitations of a subjective point of view. There cannot be an objective point of view of them. With that, we move ahead to see what we can see.

Since the commentators have called for a crusade against ancient prejudice, what about the ancient prejudice against religion, which has existed at least from the time of Protagoras? Both Scruton and the commentators might agree that a passion in defense of an illusion or a misconception is a terrible waste of our vital force. They might even agree that intellectual complacency is a vice in one who would be known as a public intellectual. Scruton and Socrates before him would rouse a passion in their interlocutors, and then they would redirect it. With this challenge to popular prejudice against religion, the first few pages of Scruton's book readies us to follow the searching argument of one who has a passion for truth.

Chapter 2

The Content That Emerges from the Dialectic

Rembrandt's
Old Woman Reading

A Passage to the Sacred Still Exists

So long as men can breathe or eyes can see,
So long lives this, and this gives life to thee.

Sonnet 18

As to content, the title of Scruton's book, *The Soul of the World*, acquaints a reader with the subject of the book, and the first chapter, "Believing in God," argues it's possible a passage to the sacred still exists in this world, despite concerted efforts by modern thinkers to debunk the notion. In chapter 2, "Looking for Persons," Scruton asserts that religion has an all-important function: it maintains "the life of the person." Reciprocally, the human subject is the without-which-nothing of religion. Alone of all other species, we look on the world as an occasion "for thought, action, and emotion." We are directed toward what Scruton refers to as "the Lebenswelt, the world of life, a world that is open to action, and organized by the concepts that shape our deeds." Through us—as symbol-interpreting language users who employ in everyday use words like *I* and *you* and other concepts that shape "our mutual dealings"—the meaning of things emerges. Scruton will argue through the rest of the book that this urge for meaning leads us into a search for the sacred because, as already stated, this is what maintains the life of the person. In chapter 3, "Looking at the Brain," he revisits his argument in "Believing in God" that the concept of the person can't be translated "into the idiom of neuroscience." Rather, we come to self-consciousness, we become persons, through "the deep grammar of self-reference" in interpersonal relationships. Kant persuaded him to this view.

Having established these three—the human subject, the Lebenswelt of language and culture, and interpersonal relationships—as the ground of his argument, Scruton looks at specific facets of the Lebenswelt that function as a passage to the sacred. In chapter 4, "The First-Person Plural," he looks at ways that human beings have instituted principles of fair play in their interactions with each other. He argues that there's a passage to the sacred in the "transcendent bonds" of vows, in pieties like honoring parents, and in nontransferable attachments of love. Human beings who live in a society organized around a contract, however, are ruled by "the forces of selfish desire." The order of a contract, Scruton believes, must be "overreached" by the obligations of love. Without that, "we humans are not truly at home." In subsequent chapters, he finds other passages to the sacred. I've already mentioned that he finds it in the face of a human subject. He claims the passage also can be found in sacred architecture where even a stone has a soul. The same can be said for certain streets where houses, which have faces like people do, stand side by side and lean against each other. We find it in the overall architecture of a city, which radiates outward from the sacred center where the temple was consecrated. We find it in music, which exists in an otherworldly one-dimensional space. Finally, to close out the book, we find it in the search for God. These two paragraphs briefly summarize the content of the book.

Scruton employs different rhetorical figures to convey the content of his first chapter to the reader. For example, he divides his argument into two distinct stages, each of which has its own goal. They have different goals, but the content of each stage has the same foundation; they are both grounded in intersubjectivity. The first stage takes the reader through a process that ends when he formulates a definition of religion based on the evidence he has provided. I presented it in a chapter titled "The Sacred and Everyday Life," in which Scruton writes:

> *Still, we can now say something a little more definite about the intentionality of the religious frame of mind. It is a reaching out from subject to subject; it searches for a relation that is close, intimate, and personal, with a being who is present in this world though not of this world; and in this reaching out there is a movement toward sacrifice, in which both self and other might give themselves completely and thereby achieve a reconciliation that lies beyond the reach of ordinary human dialogue.*

Scruton's definition of *religion* involves a "reaching out from subject to subject." Because we receive this definition by reading his book, the act of reading complements the definition with a concrete demonstration of what he means. In this case, we find the definition of religion "tumbling out at our feet" as we read the book, for the definition describes the act of reading an important poetic, philosophical, or religious text. (In Book Four of the *Republic*, Socrates finds a definition of justice "tumbling out at their feet." The quote is from Jowett, 432d.) The reader listens carefully to what the author is saying, and, if the reader understands, he may say, in effect, to the author, "I see what you mean. In this movement to understand you, to which I give my whole attention, we are one for the time being."

The definition of religion, which is rooted in intersubjectivity, allows Scruton then to move ahead into the second stage, "the question of veracity"—whether it is possible for human beings to experience the sacred in this world. To move his argument ahead, Scruton defines the sacred as a medium like Janus that looks one way into our world and the other way into a divine order from which it derives. The existence of his book makes the existence of the sacred self-evident. Scruton's chapter on believing in God, as I have shown, ends with a measured, reasoned confidence that it *is* possible to experience the sacred in this world. In religious stories and in religious practices, the reaching out from subject to subject occurs between an individual soul and the real presence. Scruton's title moves us a long way in that direction if it's true that the other subject (as we read) is the soul of the world. So the title itself is like a Socratic provocation. The author has arranged matters so that reading the book is a passage to the sacred.

Even though the argument of the first chapter appears to be structured around its two parts—the definition of the religious frame of mind and the question of veracity—a proper reading of the argument must include the reader as the without-which-nothing of the whole exercise. So much depends upon the reader! We piece the words together into meaningful sentences. We put the two stages of his argument together to find the gift of the good its author intends us to have. This awareness of ourselves, as creators of the whole, is the gift. We are a medium, maybe even a passage to the sacred. The book gives life to this possibility, gives new life to us.

Within the chapter, he gives us other reasons to believe. Perhaps the stories about Moses and Pascal persuade us that it's possible to experience the sacred in this life. Since Scruton defines the sacred as a reaching out from subject to subject, all our interpersonal relations in this world carry within them something like a hint or a seed of the sacred. This link to everyday life brings the sacred closer to us as a possibility, and the mystery of the sacred may reanimate the mystery of everyday relationships. His argument also rests on the "transcendental urge" of reason itself. Thanks to philosophy, our confidence need not depend on faith alone. Scruton mentions Kant and Hegel in this respect, but my postscript is adding Plato as another influence.

Thanks, too, to poetry like Shakespeare's, our confidence grows. We continue to read him—as I suspect readers will read *The Soul of the World* for generations to come—because we find in his poetry a passage to wholeness and beauty. The final couplet quoted above is especially important to my vision of sacred kingship, for our visions both look to the simple passage of breath in and out of the body as a medium between material and spiritual worlds. (For thoughts on Sonnet 18 and the breath of life as a passage, see the section titled "Standing on the Edge and the Breath of Life," pages 298–299.)

The "Sun" as a Medium

Scruton and Plato argue that the sacred (as Scruton would say) or the good (as Plato would say) can be at times as present as the sun and can communicate at times as directly as the sun (see Scruton's quote, pages 274–275, about what the Old Testament claims). This "sun" is a medium that unites an individual soul with the soul of the world. As we read about it in *The Soul of the World* and the *Republic*, it comes to life for us in the world of human speech, the Lebenswelt. This world of speech is a medium full of possibilities. In Book Six, Plato has Socrates call the sun "a child of the good and most similar to it" (Bloom, 506e). It's another remarkable image in which we are invited to experience the real presence of the good through the "son" who derives from the real presence. The child's close relationship to the real presence illuminates a world that's intelligible and whole (without our being burnt to a crisp by the real presence itself as Semele's fate warns us). For

Plato, the good illuminates "that which really is" (Bloom, 507b).

Gozzoli's *The Triumph of Saint Aquinas* depicts Christ the savior as the sun of light as well as the son of God, who mediates our relationship with the Father, and the book Saint Thomas holds also radiates light and performs a similar function for its readers. For Scruton, too, a sacred object is like a divine light illuminating a world that is whole and good. If you recall, he uses imagery of light in the dialogue with his former student to make his point about the sacred. "It's hard to find a transcendental source for moral values given the skepticism about religion," he tells her. Nevertheless, that source exists in the world. Like the sun, which illuminates the things of this world, the beauty of this "source" brings out "the immanence of value." When the sacred, when the real presence, when "things speak to you, shine at you, when the light that is present in everything shines through," then our individual souls and the things of this world come to life as one in the light of the sacred. The light of the sacred "shines through" and unites subject and object; they are and always have been one. (This dialogue originally appeared on pages 11–14.)

In the section titled "Death and Transcendence," which concludes the book, Scruton quotes a poem by Richard Crashaw, who prays for an encounter with this source:

> *Come love! Come Lord! and that long day*
> *For which I languish, come away.*
> *When this dry soul those eyes shall see,*
> *And drink the unseal'd source of thee.*
> *When Glory's sun faith's shades shall chase,*
> *And for thy veil give me thy face.*

Crashaw's poem is a sacred medium (a prayer) about a sacred medium (those eyes) between his dry soul and "Glory's sun." It's quite possible that Crashaw had in mind Plato's "child of the good" when he wrote these lines. As Scruton does, Crashaw describes an experience of the real presence as a face-to-face ("I" to "I" encounter) between two subjects. Surely, though, Crashaw is familiar with the passage in Exodus 33, when Moses wished to see God in his glory, and the Lord replied, "You cannot see my face for no man can see me and live."

Scruton has already addressed this issue in his chapter on "Believing in God":

> *A direct personal encounter with God, when God is understood in the philosophical way of Avicenna or Aquinas, is no more possible than a direct personal encounter with the number 2. Now you see through a glass darkly, wrote St. Paul, but then face-to-face. However, by "then" he meant "beyond the here and now" in the transcendental realm where God resides. Saint Paul may seem to be denying the hidden nature of God; in fact he is affirming it. (originally quoted on pages 277–278)*

If this is the case, then Crashaw must be languishing for that long day with God in another world. The rest of this chapter discusses how Scruton continues to work on these images and thoughts—about a divine light that makes the world intelligible, about a passage to the sacred, about the face of God, about a life of longing for God, and about the soul of the world.

It's Up to Us

Shortly after the quote from Crashaw, the last sentence of the book also affirms Scruton's image of a passage on the horizon, which serves as a medium to the sacred. He writes:

> *The life of prayer rescues us from the fall, and prepares us for a death that we can meaningfully see as a redemption, since it unites us with the soul of the world.*

Here Scruton pronounces his sentence—his judgment on the whole of his inquiry—on a life of prayer and a life that ends in death. When I first read it, I thought he was saying that "the life of prayer" unites the soul of an individual with the soul of the world. When I reread it, though, I saw that Scruton has left the antecedent of the pronoun "it" unclear, "death" being the other candidate. It's tempting to believe that this is the intended meaning since "death" is closer to the verb than "the life of prayer." It's also the subject of this final section in the book. Nevertheless, by beginning the sentence with a life of prayer that rescues us from the fall (of death) and by separating "and prepares us for a death that we can meaningfully see as a redemption" from the rest of the sentence with commas, it looks like he intends to say that the life of prayer unites us with the soul of the world. According to this view, the discipline and wholeheartedness of a religious practice can have the same effect as an experience of the real presence. In a book that has made a living human subject its hero, this reading of the sentence makes sense.

But I can't rule out the other one. In the morality play of *Everyman*, for example, Death comes to him as "a messenger from God." He's the catalyst for Everyman's redemption. As a play for the living, though, those in the audience identify completely with Everyman. They live through the stations of his pilgrimage, and yet they return to their homes after the play ends to resume what's left of their lives. There's support for this reading if we go back to what Scruton has to say about those lines by Crashaw. The encounter with Death that Scruton describes in his commentary strongly reminds me of Everyman's meeting with Death and of the journey on which Everyman must embark prior to his final "reckoning":

> *Here [in Crashaw's poem], it seems to me, is a way in which faith verges on hope. We can shun death as an annihilation, or greet it as a transition. We can see it as a loss of something precious, or as the gain of another way of being. It is, in a sense, up to us. When we live in full awareness and acceptance of our mortality, we see the world as making a place for us. We open ourselves to death, and accept death as our completion . . . To approach death in such a way is therefore to draw near to God: we become, through our works of love and sacrifice, a part of the eternal order; we "pass over" into that other place, so that death is no longer a threat to us. (The poem and this passage are quoted from pages 197–198 in* The Soul of the World.*)*

This is the "approach" described in the play of *Everyman*. This is the approach, I would argue, that Bruegel has depicted in *The Harvesters*. In Bruegel's presentation of the theme, the work of harvesting the grain, which sustains their lives, has become a meditation on Creation, which includes that moment when they are harvested. The whole scene plays out in perfect silence and acceptance.

This thought in Bruegel's painting also recalls for me the scene in *A Midsummer Night's Dream* when Helena, still groggy from the dreamless sleep with which Puck enchanted the four lovers, tells her companions:

> *And I have found Demetrius like a jewel,*
> *Mine own, and not mine own.*

The previous day Helena heard Demetrius plead with the Duke for Hermia in marriage, but here this morning she heard him declare his love for her—for Helena. She has found him, a gift out of nowhere, but her experience with him has taught her that she doesn't "own" the gift. He is only like a jewel, which is a manner of speaking. He isn't a jewel. He's a human subject, and that, as we have seen, makes all the difference in the world.

Demetrius must have heard what she has said, along with the other two. *She* is his own, and not his own. This thought about the one we love carries a thought about "owning" our own life. When we are forced to consider the end of our life, as Everyman was forced in the play about him, it's up to us, Scruton writes, whether we gain "another way of being" or not. Life is a gift, an inheritance. Since it's not mine own, because life is just passing through, I'm called on not to waste it, as if it were mine own to waste. It needs to be respectfully held for a bit and passed on. It's up to us to learn, he tells us, how we can do that. (See page 57 for the original treatment of "mine own, and not mine own"; of course, there are many passages in the book where the brief intake and release of a breath helps a person to grasp this thought from moment to moment.)

Why did Scruton wait until the final four words of the final sentence before mentioning the soul of the world in his text? The mystery about Scruton's title, my self that's not "mine own," the presence of death, our sense of a soul, and the real presence of the soul of the world—I throw these things into the bubbling alembic of my inquiry, and I wonder about one more thing: In this life, if we are united with the soul of the world, as Scruton suggests, through prayer or through an experience of the real presence, are we for the time being the soul of the world? Does a question like that matter? So again, why did Scruton wait until the final four words of the final sentence before mentioning the soul of the world in his text? He breathes the words, and the rest is silence.

His silence makes us aware of a silence as vast as the world itself of which we are the center. The rest, he knows, is up to us, his readers, to discover for ourselves.

A Mirror Image in the Structure of Plato's Argument

In *The Soul of the World*, Scruton tells a story about defining the thought of religion and about whether it's possible to experience the real presence of the sacred in this world. In the *Republic*, Socrates leads a discussion about defining justice and about determining whether it's possible to find justice (tumbling out at our feet) in this world. He looks for a definition first in the soul of the city, and that gives him a pattern for defining it in the soul of an individual. By the end of Book Four, he has defined justice in the city and in the individual (We find justice when each class of the city or each part of the soul minds its own business), and halfway through Book Five he has answered his students' questions about the communal lifestyles of the guardians. At this point Glaucon initiates the second phase of the overall argument. He agrees that the model city-in-speech they have founded would be a just city, but he is still not satisfied. He wants to know:

> *Is such an order of things possible, and how, if at all.*
>
> Jowett, 471c

The discussions through the rest of Book Five and in all of Books Six and Seven answer Glaucon's question. I think it's clear that the pattern in Scruton's argument about religion is a mirror image of Plato's argument about justice.

The Question of Ontological Priority

To mitigate the dominance of the scientific worldview in our self-understanding, Scruton advocates for what he calls a cognitive dualism where the humanities share the ontological and epistemological stage with science. When he presents the concept in chapter 2, he judiciously gives the world studied by science ontological priority. The Lebenswelt, the world studied by the humanities, he writes, *emerges* from the world studied by science the way a face emerges from the pigments of a painting. The material world, he concedes, has ontological priority.

Fresh from a reading of *The Soul of the World*, I found Scruton's concept of emergence helped me to understand relationships between the parts of Plato's argument about justice. From the classes that make up the city—the guardians, the auxiliaries, and the producers—and from the virtues that maintain the health of a city—wisdom, courage, and temperance—justice emerges. To prepare us for the idea that the three classes of the city *can be unified*, Socrates shows us that temperance is common to all three, for every class must recognize the need for moderation. He now can more convincingly argue that justice, the object of their search, is also common to all three. Like a face emerging from the pigments of paint on a canvas, justice emerges from this painting of the three classes as the principle that unites them.

The principle has been present from the beginning, when they founded a primitive city around the idea that one person should do one job and learn to do it well. This principle of specialization has now grown into the unifying principle of justice: that each class must mind its own business in order to maintain the health of the city. When each class does its job, the producers make products of good quality, the auxiliaries guard the temper of the producers, and the guardians guard the temper of the auxiliaries. Justice emerges from the individual soul in the same way: When each part of the psyche does its job, the appetitive soul makes sure the body's needs are met, the spirited soul maintains a healthy balance in the appetites, and the rational soul guides the spirited soul. In both cases, justice emerges from the intellectual objects out of which Socrates has made an ideal city-in-speech and an ideal soul-in-speech.

It's obvious why Socrates would begin with the city. The city consists of real people, and his students would recognize these classes from real experiences in the city. The correct ordering of the three classes ensures the city's health and prosperity, but "health" and "prosperity" are harder to see and more difficult to find. They are intangible. Because the three classes are composed of real people who are doing real jobs, though, the students can more easily picture the relations that Socrates imagines for them. All this work with the physical materials of a city helps us to see what can't be so easily seen, the three classes or parts of a human soul. Socrates uses the city as a model to show how justice emerges from the soul of an individual. Another question can now be asked: Does the principle of justice that Socrates outlines for us begin in the city or in the individual?

Socrates proposes that they look for justice in the city before looking for it in an individual. Because of this, it may appear that the physicality of the city gives it a natural priority. Nevertheless, before Socrates begins his discussion about the soul of an individual, he makes it clear which part of his metaphor is the tenor (his main concern) and which the vehicle (the object a poet uses to express his main concern):

> *Must we not acknowledge, I said, that in each of us there are the same principles and habits which there are in the State; and that from the individual they pass into the State?—how else can they come there? Take the quality of passion or spirit;—it would be ridiculous to imagine that this quality, when found in States, is not derived from the individuals who are supposed to possess it, e.g. the Thracians, Scythians, and in general*

the northern nations; and the same may be said of the love of knowledge, which is the special characteristic of our part of the world, nor of the love of money, which may, with equal truth, be attributed to the Phoenicians and Egyptians. (Jowett translation, 435d–e)

No doubt, Socrates has a great interest in politics. But in the *Republic*, he is more interested, I believe, in the role the soul of an individual must play in the founding of a just state. (So much depends on us, the readers!) The character of an individual, he tells us here, determines the character of a city. (This reading, by the way, is similar to the point Cephalus makes at the very beginning of the discussion.) Individual souls have the priority. This ordering of things agrees with the oracle at Delphi, which advises those who seek knowledge about anything to "know thyself."

A few pages later, in Book Four, the question as to which has ontological priority, the city or the individual, comes up again right before the topic shifts from justice in cities and individuals to injustice in cities and individuals. Socrates asks Glaucon if he hopes to find a better definition of *justice*, and Glaucon replies:

Not I, indeed.
Then our dream has been realized; and the suspicion which we entertained at the beginning of our work of construction, that some divine power must have conducted us to a primary form of justice, has now been verified.
Yes, certainly.
And the division of labour which required the carpenter and the shoemaker and the rest of the citizens to be doing each his own business, and not another's, was a shadow of justice, and for that reason it was of use.
Clearly.
But in reality justice was such as we were describing, being concerned however, not with the outward man, but with the inward, which is the true self and concernment of man: for the just man does not permit the several elements within him to interfere with one another, or any of them to do the work of others,—he sets in order his own inner life, and is his own master and his own law, and at peace with himself; and when he has

bound together the three principles within him, which may be compared to the higher, lower, and middle notes of the scale, and the intermediate intervals—when he has bound all these together, and is no longer many but has become one entirely temperate and perfectly adjusted nature, then he proceeds to act, if he has to act, whether in a matter of property, or in the treatment of the body, or in some affair of politics or private business; always thinking and calling that which preserves and cooperates with this harmonious condition, just and good action, and the knowledge which presides over it, wisdom, and that which at any time impairs this condition, he will call unjust action, and the opinion which presides over it ignorance. (Jowett translation, 443b–e)

It's a beautiful passage for my purpose here. He describes here *a person* capable of founding a just city. The business about the city, he tells Glaucon, reveals but a "shadow of justice." It's through that shadow, though, that we are made aware of "a primary form of justice," the proper ordering of appetite, spirit, and wisdom within our own souls. *We are primary*; knowledge and wisdom begin with us. Unfortunately, though, opinion presided over by ignorance also begins with us.

To sum up, consider the verse by Robert Burns:

O, my Luv is like a red, red rose
That's newly sprung in June . . .

Burns seizes on the rose as an objective correlative for what he is experiencing in his own being. He wants to express his love. If we agree with Socrates that the individual soul is the tenor (the main focus) and the city is the vehicle (the objective correlative) in his analogy, then within the world of the *Republic* the philosopher-poet's own being is ontologically and epistemologically prior.

These passages from the *Republic* and the glance at the poem by Burns raise an interesting question in regard to Scruton's cognitive dualism. The pigments of Da Vinci's *Mona Lisa*, he explains, are "real" in that they materially exist, whereas the face must emerge from the pigments in the imagination of the viewer. Still, I have the distinct impression from reading Scruton that, because the Lebenswelt has priority for the self-understanding of a human subject, the question of priority may be rendered moot. The priority of one or the other is a great question for those interested in the human condition. The next section presents some final thoughts on this subject.

The Philosopher King

Part 1: Introduction

For the second time in my book, therefore, I have turned to the example of Socrates to help me explicate a difficult question. In the chapter titled "The Example of Socrates," I discussed whether the forms are separate from the things-of-this-world, the view attributed to Plato, or whether they are immanent in the things-of-this-world, the view attributed to Aristotle. I attempted there to resolve the tension between them. I addressed that issue in the three paragraphs that follow.

"Even though Plato is strongly identified with transcendence, 'on the theological side,' Platonism as it was understood in the School of Chartres stressed immanence more than transcendence. Since it's a Christian school, this may refer to the Christian belief that Christ, the transcendent god, was incarnated to save us from the fall. Like the merging of form and matter in Aristotle's thought, He came and infused this world with a living soul. In the dialogue called *Timaeus*, one of the few dialogues available to medieval scholars, Plato has Timaeus describe the immanence of anima mundi, the world soul of the Platonists:

> *And so the likely account must say that this world came to be in very truth through god's forethought, a living being with soul and intelligence. (Timaeus, 30b)*

For Plato, it was a philosophical truth that anima mundi infuses this world with a living soul. It's a representation that points to a world that is one. Just as the individual objects and experiences belonging to the life of a human subject, like Dante, are accidents of one substance, individuals like Dante and ourselves are accidents of a living being endowed with an intelligent soul, which is referred to as anima mundi, the soul of the world.

"Having presented Lewis's long paragraph on Aristotle and Plato that I needed two chapters to interpret, I would like to draw a more general conclusion after first reviewing two salient facts about it. Lewis identifies Aristotle as the philosopher of division, despite Aristotle's ontology, which integrates form and matter, and Lewis tells us that Platonism in the School of Chartres stressed immanence more than transcendence, despite Plato's theory that the forms are transcendent. These facts suggest to me the following observation: Aristotle and Plato do not necessarily stake out positions carved in stone, even though it may appear that they do. They (and those who come after them) are engaged in a passionate, ongoing, all-consuming inquiry, and they go where the inquiry leads them.

"I feel safe in concluding that their positions are not carved in stone for another important reason. Plato and Aristotle have deep roots in the principal figure who impressed them with the stamp of his world-historical example, and Socrates wrote nothing down. Instead, his mind, the living speech that issued forth from his mind, arrested the citizens of Athens and held them in a way they had never been held before" (originally appeared on pages 189–190).

Now that I've studied the *Republic*, I see that scholars in the West, once the *Republic* was available to them in the Renaissance, might easily have recognized something like the Christian story in the story Socrates tells about the emergence of a philosopher king, for the philosopher, as Socrates imagines him, is the without-which-nothing of justice and goodness in this world. The philosopher is like anima mundi, the soul of the world, for he is indeed a living being endowed with a soul and intelligence.

Part 2: A Divine Power and the Example of Socrates

In Book Two, Socrates establishes that their ideal city has three parts. The work of founding the republic then continues well into Book Four. Because everyone in the city must recognize the need for moderation to maintain its health, temperance emerges as a virtue common to all the classes. The moderation of the producers is enforced by the spiritedness of the auxiliaries, and the spiritedness of the auxiliaries is governed by the wisdom of the guardians. But who or what guards the guardians if there is no class above them in authority? Who watches the watchers to make sure they are minding their own business? Almost by necessity, we must move to the other half of the analogy, the soul of an individual, to find the answer.

We find that justice emerges from the appetitive, spirited, and rational parts of our souls in the same way that it emerges from the soul of the city. A sense of honor governs the need we have for sensual pleasures. Most people want to preserve a good reputation in the city, so they moderate their behaviors. Our rational part ensures we don't restrain or punish our worldly appetites too severely, like Scrooge in *A Christmas Carol*, and like Puritanical killjoys in general. The system of education that Socrates has devised for the guardians ensures they will be courageous because they know what to fear, they'll be moderate in their appetites because they have always lived like soldiers entirely focused on their training and mission in life, and they'll be wise from "the commands of reason" (Jowett translation, 442b). Because a person like this is moderate, courageous, and wise, he is also just. Socrates then asks Glaucon:

> *And is justice dimmer in the individual, and is her form different, or is she the same which we found her to be in the State?*
> *There is no difference in my opinion, he said:*
> *Would such a man steal a deposit of gold or silver, Socrates asks. Would he commit treason, or break an oath? Would he commit adultery or "dishonor his mother or father?"*

Glaucon answers that he would do none of these things.

Socrates finds the definition of *justice* at the bottom of these affirmations. He asks Glaucon:

> *And the reason is that each part of him is doing its own business, whether in ruling or being ruled?*
>
> *Exactly so.*
>
> *Are you satisfied then that the quality which makes such men and such states is justice, or do you hope to discover some other?*
>
> *Not I, indeed. (Jowett translation 442d–443b)*

And with that we arrive at the passage I quoted earlier (see pages 470–471), which celebrates the fact they have at last found a definition of *justice*:

> *Then our dream has been realized; and the suspicion which we entertained at the beginning of our work of construction, that some divine power must have conducted us to a primary form of justice, has now been verified?*
>
> *Yes, certainly.*

The suspicion he entertained at the beginning refers to what he said about Glaucon and Adeimantus when, at the beginning of Book Two, they restated the immoralist position of Thrasymachus with powerful arguments and examples. Here's the quote:

> *Sons of an illustrious father, that was not a bad beginning of the Elegiac verses which the admirer of Glaucon made in honor of you after you had distinguished yourselves at the battle of Megara:—*
>
> *"Sons of Ariston," he sang, "divine offspring of an illustrious hero."*
>
> *The epithet is very appropriate, for there is something truly divine in being able to argue as you have done for the superiority of injustice, and remaining unconvinced by your own arguments. (Jowett translation, 367e–368)*

In my reading of the quote, which begins, "Then our dream has been realized," I believe Socrates addresses the fatal weakness I have spotted in his government of the city and the self-government of an individual: In the city, who or what guards the guardians? In the individual, what power guides our reason to what is true and just? Socrates infers that, just as a divine power has conducted them to a primary form of justice in their deliberations, "some divine power" draws those who should rule unto itself so that truth and justice win the day for the individual and for the city. Glaucon and Adeimantus, Socrates declares, are guided by that power both in battle and in the search for the definition of *justice*.

I think it's possible to argue that this is a significant example of Plato's influence on Scruton's thought in *The Soul of the World*. In the *Republic*, we are encouraged to believe that a divine power has guided its participants to a successful conclusion, and in *The Soul of the World* we are encouraged by the title to consider that the soul of the world accounts for the transcendental (teleological) urge that has moved Scruton's argument to its conclusion.

Within the little world of the *Republic*, Socrates recognizes the role a divine power must play in the search for justice. With great humility, but at the same time empowered by a recognition of this power in himself, he assumes for the time being the role of a mediator between secular and divine worlds. For his students, Socrates imagines cities made prosperous and at peace "by kings or princes who are by nature philosophers." Who, then, he asks, would want to destroy them?

> *"Who indeed!" Glaucon replies.*
>
> *But, said I, one is enough; let there be one man who has a city obedient to his will, and he might bring into existence the ideal polity about which the world is so incredulous.*
>
> *"Yes, one is enough." (Jowett translation, 501e–502)*

There must be at least one person in the world who can guard the guardians in this way for justice to be possible. That person in turn is guarded and guided by "some divine power."

Part 3: Preparing the Old Garden for Something New

In chapter 1 of Book Three, I describe how Vermeer effectively invites the viewer onto the seat where he's painting "The Allegory of Painting." He places us there, quite effortlessly, by rendering the place where he is sitting so concretely. We have been in houses and rooms like this, with walls and doors and passageways, so it's easy to imagine ourselves there, but we have never seen anything quite like what he is seeing. In my recreation of the scene, I tried to capture the wonder of it. This is the effect I get when Plato puts me (the reader) in the house of Cephalus, where Socrates sits and debates with the young men (soon-to-be leaders) of Athens. This is the effect when Scruton takes me (the reader) on a tour of his property, sometimes outside in green fields and sometimes in his study where he keeps a piano. For a time, we see the world through the eyes of these remarkable philosophers. As in the painting by Vermeer, though, the effect only works because the setting is represented so concretely. This is the world we have known, but it is changing before our eyes into something rich and strange. This is the effect of any effective metaphor.

After five and a half books of preparing, with meticulous spadework, the ground of this life with which we are so familiar, Socrates is finally ready to plant the seed of an idea that will infuse this world with something new, a king sanctified not by custom or blood or physical strength but by knowledge of absolute being. For Socrates (in Plato's portrait of him), this king is the link that's missing in a city that lacks justice. Within the little world of my inquiry, he's the link to which Mephistopheles refers in Goethe's *Faust*:

When scholars study a thing, they strive
To kill it first, if it's alive;
Then they have the parts and they've lost the whole,
For the link that's missing is the living soul.

Part 4: Socrates and the Dragon

A. Introduction

As I've reported in my introduction to the book, *The Soul of the World* initiated my inquiry into the soul, and that experience led to the essays in Book One on poetry from the Bible, Shakespeare, and the medieval allegory of *Everyman*. For good measure, I added a childhood experience that introduced me to the poetry and mystery of life itself. The inquiry then led me to *The Allegory of Love* by C. S. Lewis. From his essays, I gained a greater appreciation for allegory as a special form of literature. Scruton's definition of the sacred helped me to understand why it's special. Like the sacred, an allegory exists on the horizon between this world and a divine order (if we believe that "some divine power" must have conducted the author in creating it). Through this medium, we have access to a divine order, and it has access to us. Like the world in *Timaeus*, the world in allegory is endowed "with soul and intelligence." This is not so farfetched a notion if we consider the allegorical fiction to be the soul and intelligence of its author. An allegory serves to remind us that, despite popular opinion to the contrary, life is whole. It can't be otherwise. When we see the world as it is, as one substance, it's quite natural to do unto others as we would have them do unto us. The ethical implication of oneness is the other great theme in Lewis's study of allegory and Scruton's book on the soul of the world.

The *Republic* also functions as a medium in which ordinary people like the students of Socrates (and ourselves) are moved by the transcendental urge of Plato's argument to glimpse a divine order. In the last few pages of Book Six, Socrates describes for his students the form of Goodness itself in his vision of the sun and the divided line, and in Book Seven he illuminates those metaphysical wonders with his allegory of the cave. This allegory is so well known that I don't need to rehearse it here. Instead, I'll present the last few pages of Book Five and the first half of Book Six as a kind of narrative.

To simplify the progress of the argument, I've given it a beginning, a middle, and an end. In the beginning, the city-in-speech they have created gives birth to the idea of a philosopher king. Once they have the idea, their discussion breathes life into it by discovering the philosopher's credentials for kingship: he knows absolute being. In the end, the philosopher comes to life in stories where he actively represents justice in the city against the enemies of it. It doesn't take much imagination to realize Plato intends the hero of these stories to be the actual historical Socrates, Plato's teacher. Because the story Plato has in mind is about good ultimately triumphing over evil, it has much in common with epics like the *Odyssey* and the *Aeneid*. Just as mythic heroes like Odysseus and Aeneas must journey to the underworld in order to find a way home or to find a home (in the case of Aeneas), Socrates drinks the hemlock to preserve the integrity of his soul (represented as the voice that guided him in difficult situations), and his death is not the end of the story. Plato and Aristotle carry it forward.

B. Out of Disbelief and Mockery, the Idea of a Philosopher King Emerges

The students want to know that the city they have founded is possible. Socrates dodges their demand for a bit by comparing himself to an artist who paints a picture of an ideal human being. Isn't the picture itself enough proof that an ideal human being (or city) is possible? Finally, he gives in to their demand for a concrete plan of action even though he knows they will laugh at his idea:

> *I said: "Until philosophers are kings, or the kings and princes of this world have the spirit and power of philosophy, and political greatness and wisdom meet in one, and those commoner natures who pursue either to the exclusion of the other are compelled to stand aside, cities will never have rest from their evils,—nor the human race, as I believe,—and then only will this our State have a possibility of life, and behold the light of day." Such was the thought, my dear Glaucon, which I would fain have uttered if it had not seemed too extravagant; for to be convinced that in no*

other State can there be happiness private or public is indeed a hard thing. (Jowett translation, 473c–d)

How beautifully Socrates has framed his idea. He knows that to most people his idea is absurd, but the actual thought, the one in quotes, is simply magnificent. For those of us who have lived in the world long enough to know that governments in this world tend to corruption and disorder, Socrates offers an alternative.

If the alternative is as beautiful as the sentence that proposes it, then we have some hope for good government. Great writing, like the passages I've identified in *The Soul of the World*, gives us that hope. Having raised the idea, though, Socrates quickly retreats back into the skeptical, mocking world from which his idea emerged. Still, the seed has been planted, and in the following sections we see how Socrates nourishes its growth. It's such a weak and absurd little thing, as any seedling is. The wonder of a seed like this is that it sometimes grows, even into a mighty tree around which the world revolves. People call it the Tree of Life or a Bodhi tree, and the ground around it is sacred.

C. The Philosopher Who Knows versus the Many Who Hold an Opinion

To nourish the idea of a philosopher king and to persuade his students that he should be king, Socrates now must create a philosopher by defining him. We started with just a word; the savior of the just city is a "philosopher." To give him the weight and purpose of a human being, Socrates begins where all life begins, with Eros. We must define and describe what a lover is. A lover of wine, they all agree, loves the whole of that class. He loves all wines. A lover of youth (like Glaucon) loves all those "in the spring-time of youth" despite any prominent features (like a hook nose) that may protrude somewhat. From these examples of those who love wine and the beauty of youth, Socrates defines the philosopher as a lover of all knowledge. This rules out those who specialize in "minor arts"; Socrates calls them "imitators." He also compares them to dreamers "who put the copy in place of *the real object*." A lover of art or music is a lover of sights and sounds. A true philosopher, Socrates tells them, loves "the vision of truth."

This still leaves a great deal to be explained. The distinction between a dreamer and one who is awake moves the discussion into another field of inquiry. To know what a philosopher is, we have to know not only what a lover is but also what knowledge is. The material "stuff" of the human body naturally desires certain things. Unlike other creatures, though, a human body is leavened with knowledge, and knowledge, like the material stuff we are made of, is the primal stuff of our identities.

Just as light breaks out into different colors when refracted, we find that knowledge breaks out into three different powers when refracted in the imagination of Socrates. Socrates begins by asking Glaucon:

> *Does he who has knowledge know something or nothing? (You must answer for him.)*
> *I answer that he knows something.*
> *Something that is or is not?*
> *Something that is; for how can that which is not ever be known?*
> *And are we assured, after looking at the matter from many points of view, that absolute being is or may be absolutely known, but that the utterly non-existent is utterly unknown?*
> *Nothing can be more certain (Jowett translation, 476e–477)*

I love this all-or-nothing question about absolute being. I suspect this is the crux of the whole argument. Once it's agreed that absolute being can be absolutely known, we can define a philosopher: a philosopher is one who knows absolute being. Absolute being is "the real object" (see the italicized words on page 481) of which the sights and sounds of the minor arts are mere copies. In addition to having defined a philosopher, we're well on our way, I would say, to understanding what it means for a person to be a living soul; that person knows absolute being.

Having established absolute knowing and complete ignorance, Socrates establishes the third and final power, the one that will be the philosopher's archrival in the allegories that follow this three-part definition of *knowledge*:

> *Good. But if there be anything which is of such a nature as to be and not to be, that will have a place intermediate between pure being and absolute negation of being?*
> *Yes, between them . . .*
> *Do we admit the existence of opinion?*
> *Undoubtedly.*
> *As being the same with knowledge, or another faculty [another word for "power"]?*
> *Another faculty.*
> *Then opinion and knowledge have to do with different kinds of matter corresponding to this difference of faculties?*
> *Yes . . .*
> *Then knowledge and opinion having distinct powers have also distinct spheres or subject-matters?*
> *That is certain.*
> *Being is the sphere or subject-matter of knowledge, and knowledge is to know the nature of being?*
> *Yes.*
> *And opinion is to have an opinion?*
> *Yes . . .*
> *He who has an opinion has an opinion about some one thing?*
> *Yes.*
> *And not-being is not one thing but, properly speaking, nothing?*
> *True.*
> *Of not-being, ignorance was assumed to be the necessary correlative; of being, knowledge?*
> *True, he said.*
> *Then opinion is not concerned either with being or with not-being?*
> *Not with either.*

And can therefore neither be ignorance nor knowledge [because it doesn't know absolute being]?

That seems to be true . . .

Then you would infer that opinion is intermediate?

No question. (Selected passages from Jowett translation, 477–478d)

Once they see that opinion is the sort of power that lies between being and nonbeing, they see that the sights and sounds of the minor arts are the subject of opinion. These observations bring Socrates to a climatic observation:

> *This being premised, I would ask the gentleman who is of opinion that there is no absolute or unchangeable idea of beauty—in whose opinion the beautiful is the manifold—he, I say, your lover of beautiful sights, who cannot bear to be told that the beautiful is one, and the just is one, or that anything is one—to him I would appeal, saying, Will you be so very kind, sir, as to tell us whether, of all these beautiful things, there is one which will not be found ugly; or of the just, which will not be found unjust; or of the holy, which will not also be unholy? (Jowett translation, 478e–479)*

It can't be denied that a beautiful flower quickly loses its beauty. Robert Frost put it this way:

Nature's first green is gold
Her hardest hue to hold.
Her early leaf's a flower;
But only so an hour.
Then leaf subsides to leaf.
So Eden sank to grief,
So dawn goes down to day.
Nothing gold can stay.

This is true of all beautiful things. The same sort of thing can be said of justice. Since the law will always be a limited instrument, it can sometimes produce an unjust verdict. (The reader is invited here to supply an example.) Within great religious institutions, secret predators sometimes lurk. (Here again, the reader is invited to supply an example.)

Socrates wants to distinguish the sights and sounds of the world—"the intermediate flux which is caught and detained by the intermediate faculty" of opinion—from absolute being, which is caught by the faculty of knowledge. Even though most people are caught and detained by the intermediate faculty of opinion, Socrates argues that it's possible to know absolute being. If knowledge of absolute being is possible, then a philosopher is possible. If a philosopher is possible, then a just city is possible. Most people are like "the gentleman" in the passage above who holds the opinion that it's impossible to know absolute being. Most people, therefore, are lovers of sights and sounds, and they are guided by opinions. Because opinions exist in a twilight zone between being and not-being, we have to imagine that the people who hold them and guide their life by them also exist in a kind of twilight zone between being and not-being.

As a reader of the *Republic* and *The Soul of the World*, I'm tempted to see Scruton's cognitive dualism in light of the Socratic spectrum of knowledge, ignorance, and opinion. *Science*, by definition, studies the material world of objects in motion, the world of sights and sounds. According to Socrates, then, these objects are held by the power of opinion. A great philosopher like Descartes clearly understood the problem that Socrates sees with sights and sounds so he grounded his philosophy in the divine order of mathematics (along with with his clear and present idea that God exists). Mathematics, though, for all its otherworldliness and precision, has been unable, despite many attempts like Einstein's search for a "unified theory," to crack the code of absolute being. Until science can grasp the whole, we have to say of these individual objects, as Glaucon does in the *Republic*, that you can't "fix them in your mind, either as being or not-being, or both, or neither."

Even if I am not a philosopher who knows absolute being, I might be persuaded by the Socratic spectrum of knowledge, ignorance, and opinion to believe that knowledge of absolute being must have priority over opinions, since this knowledge surely would enable someone to better live a good life. Still, the world of sights and sounds surely has a role to play in our search for knowledge. From a wholistic perspective, perhaps a theory about a selfish gene must be present in that great mix of all and everything for absolute being to emerge. I'm quite sure that Scruton, a great philosopher, knew Socrates's argument in the *Republic* that a philosopher knows absolute being. Even if Scruton himself didn't know absolute being (he makes no claim for himself in the book), perhaps Socrates's argument encouraged him to insist on the sovereignty of human subjects like Moses and Pascal to determine the validity of their experience with the real presence.

D. The Allegory of the Pilot

Once Socrates has created this likeness of a philosopher, along with the likeness of those who love sights and sounds, he makes the philosopher a principal figure in several narratives. Adeimantus resists the picture Socrates has painted of philosophers. He admits they are clever masters of debate but observes that "most of them become strange monsters, not to say utter rogues, and that those who may be considered the best of them are made useless to the world by the very study you extol." Socrates agrees with him. Some who claim to be philosophers answer that description, but he still insists that the true philosopher should be king.

To contrast the philosopher who has knowledge with a lover of sights and sounds who has opinions and to explain why the philosopher is "made useless," Socrates tells the following story, which he calls a parable, but which I would also liken to an allegory, like the Red Cross Knight enduring the trials of evil in *The Faerie Queene*. Of course, Spenser wants us to know why the Red Cross Knight is the hero, but he also wants us to know the nature of those who oppose him. In fact, the forces of evil often tend to "steal the show" as Lucifer did in *Paradise Lost*. They are great dramatic actors:

> *Imagine then a fleet or a ship in which there is a captain who is taller and stronger than any of the crew, but he is a little deaf and has a similar*

infirmity in sight, and his knowledge of navigation is not much better. The sailors are quarreling with one another about the steering—everyone is of the opinion that he has the right to steer, though he has never learned the art of navigation and cannot tell who taught him when he learned, and will further assert that it cannot be taught, and they are ready to cut in pieces any one who says the contrary. They throng about the captain, begging and praying him to commit the helm to them; and if at any time they do not prevail, but others are preferred to them, they kill the others or throw them overboard, and having first chained up the noble captain's senses with drink or some narcotic drug, they mutiny and take possession of the ship and make free with the stores; thus eating and drinking, they proceed on their voyage in such manner as might be expected of them. Him who is their partisan and cleverly aids them in their plot for getting the ship out of the captain's hands into their own whether by force or persuasion, they compliment with the name of sailor, pilot, able seaman, and abuse the other sort of man [the true pilot], whom they call a good-for-nothing; but that the true pilot must pay attention to the year and seasons and sky and stars and winds, and whatever else belongs to his art, if he intends to be really qualified for the command of a ship, and that he must and will be the steerer, whether other people like or not—the possibility of this union of authority with the steerer's art has never seriously entered into their thoughts or been made part of their calling. Now in vessels which are in a state of mutiny and by sailors who are mutineers, how will the true pilot be regarded? Will he not be called by them a prater, a star-gazer, a good-for-nothing?

Of course, said Adeimantus. (Jowett translation, 488–488e)

The sailors who mutiny are those leaders who speak for the people of democratic Athens. They are the voice of public opinion. The true pilot is "despised and rejected of men" (Isaiah 53:3), as Socrates himself was despised and rejected by the citizens of Athens in his trial and execution. In the *Republic*, Plato gives Socrates the opportunity to set the record straight. Since Socrates is telling the story, we understand it from his (the philosopher's) point of view. We now understand why the sailors reject the one man with knowledge and put themselves in charge. They act the way they do because they know the world the way they do. They mutiny because they are "*of the opinion* that they have a right to steer." We sense that they are motivated to mutiny by a love of personal advantage and power for its own sake that's grounded in a love of sights and sounds—for once they have control of the ship, they make free with the food and drink that the ship supplies. Their actions reflect a narrow self-interest, not an interest in the health of the ship or city as a whole. It's a parable of government that's as true today as it was when Plato wrote it over two thousand years ago.

The oligarchs and tyrants of any day believe, as Thrasymachus taught, that justice is the advantage of the stronger. When oligarchs and tyrants see their opportunity, they are quick to prove the truth of that definition. In the parable of the ship, those with opinions based on sights and sounds win the day. These sailors may have a very high opinion of themselves because they are experts in a particular field—like ropes, metalwork, cooking, fighting, or caulking—but Socrates allows us to see that their expertise and vaunted sense of self don't matter in this case. If they don't know how the whole ship will respond in any sort of weather, if they don't know how to guide the ship in any sort of weather, then their opinions are "useless," which is what they say about the true pilot. The irony in this case is not funny; it's tragic. The true pilot, we might guess, is one of those killed. And yet, as a story told within the context of the *Republic*, the pilot wins in the end, and he is now the hero of it.

E. The Greatest of All Sophists versus the Power of God

It's important to properly identify the enemy. Socrates has shown us that the enemy is not a person *per se*; it's a form of knowing. The sailors have been captured by opinions. The more widespread these opinions the more dangerous they are.

Socrates could have blamed the Sophists for corrupting the city's government, but he does not. He argues that talented young men like Thrasymachus have been corrupted by the education the whole city provides:

> *And may we not say, Adeimantus, that the most gifted minds, when they*

are ill-educated, become pre-eminently bad? Do not great crimes and the spirit of pure evil spring out of a fulness of nature ruined by education rather than from any inferiority, whereas weak natures are scarcely capable of any very great good or very great evil?

There I think you are right.

And our philosopher follows the same analogy—he is like a plant which, having proper nurture, must necessarily grow and mature into all virtue, but, if sown and planted in an alien soil, becomes the most noxious of all weeds, unless he be preserved by some divine power. Do you really think, as people so often say, that our youth are corrupted by Sophists, or that private teachers of the art corrupt them in any degree worth speaking of? Are not the public who say these things the greatest of all Sophists? And do they not educate to perfection young and old, men and women alike, and fashion them after their own hearts.

When is this accomplished? he said.

When they meet together, and the world sits down at an assembly, or in a court of law, a theater, or in any popular resort, and there is a great uproar, and they praise some things which are being said or done, and blame other things, equally exaggerating both, shouting and clapping their hands, and the echo of the rocks and the place in which they are assembled redoubles the sound of the praise and blame—at such a time will not a young man's heart, as they say leap with him? Will any private training enable him to stand firm against the overwhelming flood of popular opinion? or will he be carried away by the stream? Will he not have the notions of good and evil which the public in general have—he will do as they do, and as they are, such will he be?

Yes, Socrates; necessity will compel him. (Jowett translation, 491d–492c)

No sophist, Socrates believes, has any influence in such an unequal contest. Public opinion is a force of nature, like the lightning strike of love at first sight or like a river that overflows its banks in a flood and carries everything before it. He concludes this part of his argument by asserting that:

. . . even to make the attempt is a great piece of folly; there neither is, nor has been, nor is ever likely to be, any different type of character which has had no other training in virtue but that which is supplied by public opinion . . .

But then he makes an important distinction:

I speak, my friend, of human virtue only; what is more than human, as the proverb says, is not included: for I would not have you ignorant that, in the present evil state of governments, whatever is saved and comes to good is saved by the power of God, as we say. (Jowett translation, 492d-e)

Unlike the sailors who are ruled by popular opinion, a philosopher knows absolute being. Socrates's argument here, I would say, describes this knowledge and the power of it in much the way a Christian might describe divine grace. Still, this power to rise above popular opinion and rule oneself and a city with justice must be founded in an individual soul for it to work in the world.

F. We Are Not Obliged to Oblige the Necessity of Diomede

This sounds like the last word on the subject, but Socrates tells them that he would like to make a further observation.

What are you going to say?

And this addition takes the shape of another parable or allegory:

Why, that all those mercenary individuals, whom the many call Sophists and whom they deem to be their adversaries, do, in fact, teach nothing but the opinion of the many, that is to say, the opinions of their assemblies; and this is their wisdom.

When Plato has Socrates speak of "the many," he has in mind, of course, the voters in democratic Athens. They viewed Socrates as a Sophist who corrupted the youth of Athens by undermining the traditional values of the city. If the many want to know their adversaries, Socrates declares, they should look in the mirror. He continues:

> *I might compare them [the Sophists] to a man who should study the tempers and desires of a mighty strong beast who is fed by him—he would learn how to approach and handle him, also at what times and from what causes he is dangerous or the reverse, and what is the meaning of his several cries, and by what sounds, when another utters them, he is soothed or infuriated; and you may suppose further, that when, by continually attending upon him, he has become perfect in all this, he calls his knowledge wisdom, and makes of it a system or art, which he proceeds to teach, although he has no real notion of what he means by the principles or passions of which he is speaking, but calls this honorable and that dishonorable, or good or evil, or just or unjust, all in accordance with the tastes and tempers of the great brute. Good he pronounces to be that in which the beast delights and evil to be that which he dislikes; and he can give no other account of them except that the just and noble are the necessary, having never himself seen, and having no power of explaining to others the nature of either, or the difference between them, which is immense. By heaven, would not such an one be a rare educator. (Jowett translation, 492e–493b)*

The beast is the true educator, but someone who feeds and studies the beast for his own advantage is also a "rare educator." Since Plato has in mind the death of Socrates at the hands of this beast and these educators, we can understand why he resorts to bitter, ironic praise here.

This is beautiful, insightful writing with a powerful judgment at the end. These minders of the beast can only give an account of good and evil from what they observe in the beast—which is Popular Opinion in allegorical form—because they have no real knowledge of either good or evil. Because they lack knowledge of absolute being, they can only hold *an opinion* of good and evil. While we are so close to this important thought, let's look at the light it shines on the critical claim that Scruton, the bouncer who determines who can judge the question of veracity, makes in *The Soul of the World*. Just as this judgment defends someone who has knowledge, which is based on an experience of absolute being, from the depredations of someone who has an opinion, which is based on sights and sounds, Scruton defends the knowledge and the sovereignty of the human subject who has experienced the real presence from the opinions of skeptics.

Socrates doesn't blame these educators for thinking that "discernment of the tastes and tempers of the motley multitude" is a kind of knowledge, but he is strongly encouraging his students not to imitate them. Now that we have learned about the three kinds of knowledge from the previous discussion, we know that what a person learns from the sights and sounds of this beast can only lead *to opinions* about the things they make for the city, about the actions they take with their fellow citizens, and about their conduct within their own families:

> *For when a man consorts with the many, and exhibits to them his poem or other work of art or the service which he has done the State, making them his judges when he is not obliged, the so called necessity of Diomede will oblige him to produce whatever they praise. (Jowett translation, 493c)*

According to Bloom, Diomede forced the strangers "who came to him" to have intercourse with his daughters, who were prostitutes. Then he killed them. Socrates is arguing that these "strangers," talented individuals like Glaucon and Adeimantus, are *not obliged* to come to this Diomede, who personifies the beast Socrates has been describing. They don't need his hospitality, his daughters, or his judgment on them. They are free, as Socrates was when he freely chose to drink the hemlock rather than submit to "the necessity of Diomede."

G. We Conclude That the World Cannot Be a Philosopher

When Adeimantus agrees that they should not produce whatever the beast praises, Socrates continues:

> *You recognize the truth of what I have been saying? Then let me ask you*

to consider further whether the world will ever be induced to believe in the existence of absolute beauty rather than of the many beautiful, or of the absolute in each kind rather than the many of each kind?

With this question, my presentation of arguments from the *Republic* comes to a tipping point. Will "the world," allegorized as the beast of public opinion, ever know absolute beauty? Will "the world" ever know anything beyond mere opinion? Adeimantus replies:

Certainly not.

This looks like a discouraging, dark conclusion. The beast, which wallows in opinion, appears to have won the day, just as the city won the trial against Socrates. It can go on wallowing forever. The "certainly not" spoken by Adeimantus appears to have ended all hope for the world, but Socrates's next question puts "the world" in a different context:

Then the world cannot possibly be a philosopher?
Impossible. (Jowett translation, 493d–e)

The original question had to do whether "the world" would ever be induced to believe in absolute beauty. The answer is no. "The world" is the beast of public opinion. It's a selfish gene and lives by instinct and appetites. There's no wisdom or philosophy in it for knowing absolute being. For that we need a human subject who serves as a medium in this world to a divine order, for "whatever is saved and comes to good is saved by the power of God, as we say" (see the second quote on page 490). We need a philosopher king. All things considered, it turns out the *Republic* is a compelling addition to my vision of sacred kingship.

The city (the beast) didn't really win the day at the trial of Socrates, for Socrates lives on and on as the living soul of Plato's *Republic*. So much depends on the reader, on the transmission of the Good, which is Socrates's and Plato's priceless inheritance. Once Socrates emerges in the living soul of another—a reader who senses in the words of Socrates a plausible like-mindedness, a conviction may also emerge there that it's possible to know absolute being. We are not *obliged* to pass the night in Diomede's house. Like Dante at the beginning of his *Commedia*, we can set our sights on the sunlit hill, even if we have to go the long way around to set foot on it. Even though the words are different, I'm inclined to think that what it means to know absolute being must be very like what it means to be a living soul.

H. Living Proof That a Philosopher Is Possible

It's possible that Plato's portrait of Socrates contributed to Scruton's argument in the book he called *The Soul of the World*. I know for a certainty that *The Soul of the World* contributed to the urge I felt to write this book. So it goes. Before closing this chapter of my inquiry, let's return one more time to the question of ontological and epistemological priority that Scruton raises in chapter 2 of *The Soul of the World*. In chapter 2, Scruton gives the material world "out there" ontological priority. The human world, he tells us there, *emerges* from the world of physical objects in a language-using, self-conscious human subject; the world that science studies, therefore, has ontological priority. Nevertheless, I'm inclined to believe that Scruton agrees with Socrates that "the world cannot possibly be a philosopher" and that cities not ruled by a philosopher (who has knowledge of absolute being by divine grace) will never have rest from the evils of the world. After all, with the advent of nuclear technology we're well on our way to being burnt to a crisp in the grand finale of the scientific project.

Thanks to the gift of language—and how the gift came to be no historian or scientist can tell us—and the self-consciousness that's the gift of language, the human subject, Scruton argues, adds something to creation that no other creature can. When life is viewed from the point of view of a self-conscious human subject, it's only natural for that point of view to have priority. It's also only natural, I suppose, for that sense of priority "to go to our heads" in projects like the tower of Babel and like the dreams countless warlords (and now technocrats) have had of world domination. Human beings, I argued in my first book, have always aspired to the view from Olympus. We imagined a place like the Mount Olympus of myth because we aspire to see the world from a superior vantage point; we would be as omniscient as the gods. Later in our history, after the murderous religious wars of the sixteenth and seventeenth centuries, people aspired to the objectivity and the omniscience that a material science gave them. It has to be said that twenty-first-century technology is working hard to make those goals a virtual reality.

The Soul of the World, I believe, is dedicated to showing that the scientific project to completely objectify "the world" is, in the end, a wish on a par, perhaps, with wishing to see God in his glory, as Moses wished in Exodus 33. The Lord had to warn Moses that "you cannot see my face, for no man shall see me and live." For the purposes of Scruton's argument, right from the opening paragraphs of "Believing in God" he gave the human subject priority over the spurious objectivity of the commentators on the events of 9/11. Shortly after that, he debunked the spurious objectivity of those who have an unreasoning faith in a selfish gene as the explanation for all human behaviors. The human subject Scruton has in mind is not hamstrung by scientific dogma—that, for example, excludes metaphysics from its portfolio, or by religious dogma—that, for example, demands the sacrifice of other human beings. Thanks to the gift of language, thanks to the gift of wisdom built into a language by countless millions of individuals who have lived and died on this earth, thanks to the many literary masterpieces that embody this wisdom, and thanks to a passion for the truth it's possible that the human subject, the hero of Scruton's book, could be a medium to that which is whole, healthy, and at peace. I imagine he is inviting his readers to wonder, as I do, "Is it possible for anyone to be a medium to the sacred?"

If Socrates is living proof that a philosopher is possible, then it's possible for an individual soul to be a medium that reveals that This Life has a soul. Like the breath passed down through the generations that gives life to a living soul, the example of Socrates and those like him is passed down through the medium of the texts I've included in my book. Of course, there are others, like the *Bhagavad Gita*, but that's another story.

Chapter 3
In Defense of Poetry

Masaccio's
Expulsion from the Garden of Eden

On Myths and Metaphors

The writers whose texts I have quoted and interpreted in this book all took pen to paper to increase our confidence in poetic visions. As I have documented throughout the book, they present a vision of this life as a timeless whole. In addition to the window on the sacred Scruton has created for us in "Believing in God" that I've already discussed, he represents this vision in a concept he calls "the myth of origins."

Myths in ancient times tended to be about or in some way to involve the gods. A story or a myth about the gods is like a man with a foot in two worlds, as in Bernard's verses about mankind:

He shall be heavenly, earthly; by his care
Shall rule the earth, and reach the heaven by prayer,
For as the diverse sources whence he drew
His being, so himself will still be two . . .

The story has one foot in this world (or we couldn't understand it), and it has one foot in a divine order (if it is indeed about the gods).

Looked at in this way, a story or a myth about the gods is like a metaphor that joins material and immaterial realities to convey what the poet's experience means. For example, Sonnet 18 conveys the poet's thoughts about the beauty of his friend:

Shall I compare thee to a summer's day?
Thou art more lovely and more temperate.
Rough winds do shake the darling buds of May,
And summer's lease hath all too short a date.

So long as we have these lines to time, there's hope for poetry. They project a timeless vision of poetry in action and of the human condition. The poet would employ the vehicle of a summer's day (a material reality) to express the beauty of his friend (an immaterial reality). The poet also considers the vehicle of a lease we sign with a landlord to live in his summer house (more material realities) to remind himself (and the reader) that leases end, summers end, and life itself ends in death. It appears that if he relies on a summer's day as the vehicle of his metaphor, then he has to bring death into the equation as well.

In the first line, the poet opens a window so we can look into *him*; we see him at work creating the poem. In the second line, we see him looking into his subject; he clearly loves (implied in the word *lovely*) what he's seeing, and he attempts to recreate in the poem his friend's beauty. The first two lines put us in a green field where we enjoy the beauty of nature and the beauty of their friendship, but the next two lines change the scene entirely. In my imagination, we're now in the arena of a prizefight where the poet is of two minds about his friend. Darling Buds takes on Rough Winds. Darling Buds may have scored an early lead in the first two lines, but Rough Winds appears to have delivered knockout punches in the third and fourth lines. How, we wonder, can the poet recapture the ease and simplicity of the first two lines?

The next quatrain compounds the problems that occur to him when he compares the beauty of his friend with a summer's day:

> *Sometime too hot the eye of heaven shines,*
> *And often is his gold complexion dimmed;*
> *And every fair from fair sometime declines,*
> *By chance, or nature's changing course, untrimmed:*

The sun, which plays the starring role in the comparison with a summer's day, can sometimes be overbearing. Sometimes its face may be clouded with discontent or anger. Not only does the weather change but the friend's beauty, we all know, will most likely be marred by a thousand natural shocks just as the darling buds will most likely be shaken by rough winds, and the lease of summer will certainly run out.

As the poet wrestles with these thoughts, he finds the answer in his poetry:

But thy eternal summer shall not fade
Nor lose possession of that fair thou ow'st,
Nor shall Death brag thou wand'rest in his shade
When in eternal lines to time thou grow'st.

The timeless beauty of my poem, he tells his friend, will represent your timeless beauty to the world. Problem solved? Not really. The timeless beauty of the poem may be small comfort for his friend, who still will lose possession of the fair he owns. For he doesn't "own" it. He "owes" it. If the poem becomes famous as the eternal summer the poet has imagined for it, doesn't the poet have more to gain than the friend? The poet must propose, therefore, an additional thought, the one I developed in my reading of "Look in Thy Glass," which precedes this one in the sequence.

He ends the poem with a couplet that contains a life affirming prophecy:

So long as men can breathe or eyes can see,
So long lives this, and this gives life to thee.

So much depends upon "this." To what does "this" refer? The easiest answer is that it refers to the poem that celebrates the beauty of his friend. To accurately express the perfection of his friend, therefore, the poet first must find it in himself. We see this as we see the poet wrestling with how to express his love. So "this" can refer to his friend's timeless beauty, to the poet's love for his beauty, and to the poem, which gives life to the friend's beauty and the poet's love.

As the poet wrestles with a desire to express his love, though, he lands—as he did in "Look in Thy Glass"—on one more layer of meaning for "this," and I would argue that this discovery is what informs the couplet. As he wrestles with the problem—and who knows how long that long night was—of things that dim, decline, and die in time, he finds himself face-to-face with the answer: our eternal summer is present consciousness of being itself. It exists. It holds all and everything. It is and can only be a wondrous whole. It's the gift of an unbroken line of ancestry. It rides on the breath of life as the poetry of Genesis teaches. The breath is what *gives life* to his friend, to himself, and to every living soul because it gives life to consciousness—eyes that see.

With Shakespeare's affirmation of poetry in mind, we can now explore the poetry that Scruton calls a myth of origins. They are fictions, he writes, which tell a true story about the timeless, spaceless veil of the Lebenswelt.

The Fall as a Myth of Origins

After Scruton introduces the idea of a "myth of the soul" in chapter 3, which explains how the notion of a soul may have taken shape in the minds of human subjects as they interact with others (see pages 21–24), in chapter 5—right in the middle of the book—he defines and illustrates his concept of a myth of origins by retelling and interpreting the story of the fall in the book of Genesis. Here's his version:

> *There is an important insight contained in the book of Genesis, concerning the place of shame in our understanding of sex. Adam and Eve have partaken of the forbidden fruit, and obtained the "knowledge of good and evil"—in other words the ability to invent for themselves the code that governs their behavior. God walks in the garden and they hide, conscious for the first time of their bodies as objects of shame. The "shame of the body" is an extraordinary feeling, and one that only a self-conscious animal could have. It is a recognition of the body as both intimately me and in some way not me—a thing that has wandered into the world of objects as though of its own accord, to become the victim of uninvited glances. Adam and Eve have become conscious that they are not only face-to-face, but joined in another way, as bodies, and, in Milton's incomparable version, the objectifying gaze of lust now poisons their once-innocent desire. By means of the fig leaf Adam and Eve are able to rescue each other from the worst: to ensure, however tentatively, that they can still be face-to-face,*

> *even if the erotic has now been privatized and and attached to the private parts. In his well-known fresco of the expulsion from Paradise, Masaccio shows the distinction between the two shames—that of the body, which causes Eve to hide her sexual parts, and that of the soul, which causes Adam to hide his face. Adam hides the self; Eve shows the self in all its confused grief, but still protects the body—for that she now knows, can be tainted by others' eyes.*
>
> *The tree of knowledge that caused the fall of man is surely wrongly described as giving us the knowledge of good and evil. Rather, it gave us knowledge of ourselves as objects—we fell from the realm of subjectivity into the world of things. We learned to look on each other as objects, and to sweep away the face and all that the face stands for. We lost what was most precious to us, which is the untorn veil of the Lebenswelt, stretching from horizon to horizon across the dark matter from which all things, we included, are composed. (quoted from pages 105–106 of* The Soul of the World*)*

In the last sentence, Scruton imagines for us the veil made whole again by imagining what it was before the fall. Even though this sentence appears in a passage of prose and is itself prose, in my opinion it is poetry of a high order. This untorn veil of the Lebenswelt stretched "from horizon to horizon across the dark matter from which all things, we included, are composed" imagines for the reader how dark matter can be transformed into a home by human language and culture. It's an image that's instantly recognizable. Without the veil, dark matter is hopelessly alienating; it can't be domesticated. It inspires only dissolution, revolution, and madness. With the veil, the world is humanized; we see ourselves in it. It's now a mystery, instead of a bald fact, which invites an imaginative, creative response. (My thanks to Mark Dooley and his fourth lecture on Scruton's *Fools, Frauds, and Firebrands*, which is available online, in which he informs his audience that Scruton referred to himself as a "seamstress of the lebenswelt" who "repairs the rents in Maya.")

I've mentioned before that Scruton makes no claim for himself in the book. He doesn't have to, because his writing does it for him. If this were all he had to say about the fall of Adam and Eve, then it looks like a sundering—Adam now divided from Eve, Eve from Adam, the two of them divided from Eden, their own being split in two as an object and a subject, and the Lebenswelt torn asunder to expose the pointless motion of dark matter.

By speaking so clearly about something so important to human beings, though, Scruton's story doesn't alienate me; on the contrary, it attracts me with its truth. His retelling of the fall recalls one of my earliest memories, when I was about three years old. One morning I came down to breakfast and was greeted with laughter from those already at the table. Someone informed me that I had forgotten to put on my shirt. To hide my nakedness from them, I crawled under the table. Isn't it remarkable that, after some seventy years, I still remember this? I find Scruton's interpretation here persuasive because I have experienced, even as a child, the self-consciousness and shame of the body. I imagine everyone has. Scruton persuades me because he seems to be writing from a common ground of understanding. Even though shame is a subjective mental state and even though we consider the story of the fall to be merely a fiction, his reading of the fall, if we identify with this experience, speaks to us with a comforting authority and objectivity about the human condition.

In addition to the comfort this recognition provides, which may seem like small comfort since we lost what was most precious to us (the untorn veil of the Lebenswelt), Scruton retells this story of the human condition with a vision that depicts the mind of a human subject as fundamentally whole even if the mind can imagine a story where it has been divided into a subject and object by that critical fall. To tell that story, he employs a metaphor of a whole, which has layers:

> *The story of man's fall is a "myth of origins." Such myths, which are a vital part of religion, display the layers of consciousness in archaeological terms, as though each layer is somehow "earlier" than the one that rests on it. In the religious frame of mind we read our nature "back to origins," in order to understand as a narrative what is in fact the truth about the present moment, in which we are forever trapped.*

Like a tell that holds two thousand years of city life, Time is One, and space is One in present consciousness, even if an "archaeological" dig into it reveals different layers.

How do we feel about being "forever trapped" in the present moment? To move us out of an association with being physically trapped and to fully realize the freedom to which the myth of origin is pointing, we must sense once again how Scruton has shifted the ground of his argument—from a world that's explained by studying the causes and effects of physical things to the timeless, spaceless realm of the Lebenswelt (the lifeworld) as it's experienced by a human subject. To that end, he encourages us to see a myth of origins as a sacred medium and a window on a divine order, for, he continues:

> *The story of the Fall, as I have just recounted it, records a deep truth about the human psyche. It tells us that we are tempted to conceive our most intimate relations in objectifying terms, as an affair of bodies in which the other is no longer present as a subject in his face. But it represents this truth through a story of the "Fall," the particular transgression occurring at a particular moment, before which we enjoyed the purity that was thereafter lost to us. This story is a fiction, although a fiction that illustrates a truth. All religions involve this kind of reversal, setting out the basic truths of self-conscious being in the form of a narrative of origins. The story of creation is itself such a narrative—which is not to deny that the world is dependent upon God and an expression of his free creative power, but rather to insist that there is no "moment" of creation, no moment before which there was nothing, and after which time began to unfold. (quoted from page 107 of* The Soul of the World*)*

We are strongly conditioned to think of time as divided into past, present, and future, and we're conditioned to think of things in space as separate from ourselves. We are not only conditioned to think in this way; it may be that our minds are preset to think and perceive in this way. The concepts of time and space are built in, presupposed. Nevertheless, Scruton here encourages us with his poetry around the poetry of the fall to imagine "the basic truths of self-conscious being" and to imagine the timeless, spaceless sphere of our lifeworld. Like an infant learning to walk (I've just seen a video this morning of a granddaughter walking for the first time), it's possible to learn, he suggests, what it's like *to be*. His poetry not only encourages us; it urges that we try. Why else has he gone to all this trouble with the book.

As I consider the world that Scruton depicts in this word painting of the fall and creation, it strikes me that, like Plato before him, Scruton aims at describing the difference between knowledge (of absolute being) and opinions (about sights and sounds). If we are on Lewis's train, which moves but never leaves the station, being is one; there can be no sundering, no before and after. We can see this even within the story about falling into a world of objects. As bodies, Adam and Eve are physically one when they conceive a child, and they are one in the child that's born of their bodies. As souls, they are one as they learn to see themselves (objectively) in each other's eyes. The story of the fall looks like a sundering, but it's also an account that unites us as both a subject and an object. If so, then it's a poetic vision in which an objective point of view and a subjective point of view, the cosmological approach, and the psychological approach, emerge at the end of a comic narrative about creation and the fall as a married pair.

Creation as a Myth of Origins

In the quote above from chapter 5, which is in the middle of the book, Scruton refers to the story of creation in Genesis as a myth of origins. Like the story of the fall, the story of creation records a deep truth about the human psyche, and so he revisits it in his final chapter, "Seeking God." Once again, it's best to let Scruton tell the story in his own words:

> *It is not a metaphor to speak of God's will, any more than it is a metaphor to speak of your will when seeking to understand your actions. In neither case does this presuppose some strange metaphysical entity, the will, that acts like a sudden spark to set things in motion. For what we mean by will*

> *is the first-person accountability that I discussed in Chapter 2 [where he establishes the I-you relationship as the without-which-nothing of the life world]. It [the will] is what we are looking for when, in the space of reasons, we ask the question "why?" Those who see God as bringing the world into being at a certain moment by an act that flashes across the primordial nothingness like a thunderbolt from the hand of Zeus, fail to understand the will as it should be understood. The story of creation, as recounted in Genesis, is one of many "myths of origins," which have meaning only because we can rewrite them in the language of reason [which is timeless and spaceless] rather than that of cause. Just as I am accountable to God for what I am and do, so is he accountable to all of us for the world in which we find ourselves. Faith means believing, as Abraham believed, that there is sufficient reason in the mind of God for all that is, and for all that is required of us, death included. Not surprisingly, therefore, faith is hard . . . (quoted from page 191 of* The Soul of the World*)*

You'll notice how, in the first four sentences, Scruton removes the idea that "some strange metaphysical entity," like the concept of a self (which should not be confused with what I have been calling our true self), accounts for "the will." We act, he tells us, not because we are prompted by a "self" but because we are accountable—to others, to our true self, and to God.

Scruton doesn't bother to go into the seven and-God-saids or the two then-God-saids in the biblical story of Creation. When the story is told that way, it would sound too much like the way we describe work in this world: the boss speaks, and the work is done over six days. Instead, Scruton tasks himself with describing a metaphysical whole. The will is not a metaphor for something else. It is. It's the space of reasons. The question "Why?" exists in the space of reasons, not in the world of space and time. "Why did I do that?" When I question myself in this way, I get lost in it. My entire life goes into the question. Accountability, Scruton tells us, is the whole kit and caboodle of Creation. The world, or Creation, is consciousness informed by the question "Why?" Having defined the will in this way, he holds that in the lifeworld of a human subject at any moment "there is sufficient reason in the mind of God for all that is, and for all that is required of us, death included." The readiness (to serve and protect Creation) is all.

Scruton first introduces this readiness into his argument when he describes the intersubjectivity with which he will define the religious thought. A religious person's state of mind, he writes, is subject directed:

> *It has the particular intentionality that informs all our interpersonal attitudes, and which adheres to them because they are forms of address from one person to another: a readiness to give and accept reasons, to make demands, and also to respond to demands, a recognition of mutual freedom and all the benefits and dangers that are implied by it. A readiness, as we might put it, remembering the Old Testament story of Jacob and the angel, to "wrestle with God"—the idea contained in the name Isra-el. (originally quoted on pages 285–286)*

Somewhat later he adds another intentionality (or readiness) that has much to do with his argument about the sacred:

> *. . . there are roots to this state of mind [a reaching out in which there is a movement toward sacrifice] that are far darker than we can, in our daily lives, easily acknowledge. [Scruton has in mind the sacrifice of others rather than the sacrifice of oneself.] But the essential character of the religious frame of mind is that of an intersubjective awareness in which the readiness for sacrifice is in some way contained. (originally quoted on pages 337–338)*

Finally, for "the readiness is all," see *Hamlet*, act 5, scene 2, lines 191–195. These passages help me to understand what Scruton means when he writes that "what we mean by will is the first-person accountability." In this readiness, we are one in wondering how not to "unmake" the soul of the world (see the quote from Timaeus, page 189, and the quote from part 2, pages 201–202).

Scruton continues:

> *The question "why?" is addressed from I to you. It is thrust upon us in those moments in extremis when the order of creation irrupts around us.*

The form of "from I to you" is strange. Why not "from me to you?" Is

Scruton addressing us, his readers? Are we being called to account? The second sentence, though, provides more context for the first sentence. He must be describing what happens in an I-You relationship. The question "Why?" is thrust upon "us," Scruton and his reader alike. "Why did I do what I did?" It also can be read to mean that the question "Why?" is thrust upon us as something we have to ask of another or ask of Creation, "Why did you do this? Why did this happen?" Scruton and his reader are now in the same boat, for creation has irrupted around us, and either we or the other wants to know "Why?" From our perspective we are asking the other to be accountable, but turnabout is fair play. The other can ask the same question of us. Perhaps we have trespassed, and we have to ask of ourselves "Why?" even if the other is silent.

The rest of the quote follows from this reading of the first two sentences:

> *It is then that we cry out to God—who will tell us why we suffer, why we live, and why we die. Within the envelope of nature there are only causes. But for the eye of faith the envelope has a telos, a reason for its being as it is. And to have faith is to believe that the world's teleology will account for my afflictions too. In the faithful frame of mind we are aware that being is not simply a fact but also a gift, and aware that gifts have reasons. And the response of faith is to recognize that we too must give. (The last two passages are quoted from page 191 of* The Soul of the World.*)*

He is clearly addressing his readers now, but he's addressing his own psyche as well. When things fall apart, "we" cry out to God, but maybe we (his readers) felt the power of the question "Why?" when it appeared to be "thrust" at us.

He is asking for all of us. Why do we suffer? Why do we live and die? To understand how he might answer these questions, let's return to the statement with which he begins his second chapter that it's the job of religion to maintain the life of the person. The life of the person, as he has argued throughout *The Soul of the World*, is not the same as the life of the human being. A human being lives within the envelope of nature. A person lives within an envelope with a telos, a reason for being. In any moment and in any situation, a person is accountable, but religion maintains that the soul of the world (the world's teleology) is accountable as well.

The primary function of religion is to preserve our freedom to act, question, and to be accountable. If we accept this freedom and accountability, then it's up to us whether we see the world still "making a place for us" even as the order of creation erupts around us. Scruton quoted Crashaw's poem quite near the end of the book to help us imagine this place. It's where two subjects meet and are accountable to each other, but in the poem it isn't *a place* in this world. It's *a spirit* of openness to another: "Come Love! Come Lord!" To Crashaw's vision, I added that we have the spirit and the place the Lord gave us in Genesis. After he breathed the breath of life into man's nostrils, He placed him in a garden east of Eden. If we describe the work there in Scruton's terms, we can say that man must cultivate the soil for growing faith in the sacred. Because Scruton's commentary on the poem is so important to his project, I'm posting it again:

> *Here [in Crashaw's poem], it seems to me, is a way in which faith verges on hope. We can shun death as an annihilation, or greet it as a transition. We can see it as a loss of something precious, or as the gain of another way of being. It is, in a sense, up to us. When we live in full awareness and acceptance of our mortality, we see the world as making a place for us. We open ourselves to death, and accept death as our completion . . . To approach death in such a way is therefore to draw near to God: we become, through our works of love and sacrifice, a part of the eternal order; we "pass over" into that other place, so that death is no longer a threat to us. (This passage was originally quoted in my text on pages 466–467.)*

He describes here the work, the cultivation of the soil. Faith is hard. Maintaining our personhood in this way is hard. If we don't maintain our personhood, I think Scruton is suggesting, we look to the world (historical necessity, the necessity of Diomedes) as the nurse who provides the painkiller for the pain or as the nurse who doesn't or won't. The suffering is out of our hands and completely pointless.

Scruton encourages us to believe that it's possible, even in times of great stress and suffering, to "see the world as making a place for us." This image reminds me of something very simple and concrete, which I noticed during my many years teaching English in a public high school. Often enough when the bell rang at the end of a class, I joined the students in the corridor to make my way to another place. Even though the corridor was fairly wide, there was little room and no definite pattern of traffic, as there would be on a highway. I often wondered at how, as I encountered many others left and right going the other way, we all made a place for each other in that time and space without a fuss or a collision or any particular effort. It had the effect, I imagined, that the Hebrews leaving Egypt might have experienced as the waters of the Red Sea parted to let them pass. In the ordinary way of things, like the changing of classes in a public high school, each individual soul commands this kind of instinctive respect.

Passover and the Sabbath as Myths of Origins

I'll conclude this survey of myths of origins with two more examples that Scruton presents near the end of the book. They give us additional practice in grasping how the order of nature can be "translated" into the space of reasons, where "there is no before and after."

To make his case, Scruton turns once again to the Hebrew Bible:

> *The old religion of the Israelites arose from intense encounters with the sacred, deeply embedded in the folk memory and in oral tradition, which were steadily incorporated into a new theological vision. According to this vision the God of Israel is the one God, creator of the world, moved in all that he does by stern moral requirements, demanding obedience and granting his chosen people what he has granted to no one else, which is his law—the Torah. This law is not merely a distillation of morality. It is also a summary of those profound experiences of the sacred through which the Israelites had sensed their apartness, and which were subsequently understood as indicating that God was indeed aware of them, watching,*

them, and choosing them.

Hence Orthodox Jews today—those who regard themselves as strictly observant of halakhah (the path ordained by law)—are intensely attached to rituals, which govern their lives in minute particulars, concerning dress, diet, language, ceremonies, mealtimes, and the divisions of the day. Many of these ceremonies repeat episodes in the Bible. The seder, or Passover meal, for example, elaborately recounts the events that surrounded the liberation of the Jews from Egypt. Its beautiful litany asks a sequence of questions, beginning with "why is this night different from all other nights?" And it illustrates three important features of Jewish rituals: first, that they are (for the most part) private affairs, to be performed in the home; second (and connectedly), that they do not involve a priest or anyone taking the role of mediator between man and God—all Jews are directly in God's presence as the sacred words are read and the sacred gestures performed; third, that the ceremony is one of reenactment, as though Passover did not occur at a particular time but eternally and constantly. There is a rabbinical saying that "in the Torah there is no before and after"—in other words, that the events there recounted are not to be seen as ordinary events in time, but as constantly repeated episodes in the relation of God to man. By performing the rites of Passover, the Jew makes himself part of the eternal story, as he does on all other occasions and festivals singled out as sacred. And such is the meaning of every "myth of origins."

Just as the Passover rituals reenact in the present how God saved the Jews—first by passing over their houses during the tenth plague, and then by liberating them from bondage in Egypt—the rituals of the Sabbath Day reenact in the present the one day of creation when God did no work. Here again, it's best to let Scruton speak for himself about my last example of a myth of origins:

Likewise the Sabbath is to be treated as holy, which means as outside the ordinary flow of events. On the eve of the Sabbath man steps out of time into the eternal, and is then at one in the stillness with God. He is also at home with his family, and the Sabbath is simultaneously a consecration of the individual to God and a consecration of the family as the forum in which God's law is observed. All of Judaism is contained in the idea of the Sabbath—the day when man looks on God's creation not as a means to satisfy this or that need or appetite, but as an end unto itself: in other words, the day when man sees the world as God sees it, from outside and as a whole. The Sabbath contains the essence of religion in all its higher forms: an injunction to stop, to be futile, to repeat actions that have no explanation other than themselves, and in all this to recognize that the world is suspended between creation and destruction, and that it is up to you to renew the order of the covenant among those whom you love. At this moment faith and ritual coincide, in the shared experience of God's presence. (These passages on Passover and the Sabbath are quoted from pages 194–196.)

Like Brahman and Atman, Rama and Sita, the cosmological and the psychological approach, insensibles and sensibles in a metaphor, faith and ritual are another married pair. A moment of faith is an item of belief, like the one so carefully documented in *The Soul of the World* that it's possible to experience the sacred in this life. A moment of ritual ties the sacred to the everyday order of a family living in a home. Scruton captures how the two moments of faith and ritual come together in the Seder and the Sabbath.

Thanksgiving for the Act That Brings This Life to Life

It would appear that the story of my inquiry ends with the Sabbath, but it's also true that it begins with the Sabbath, the day of rest after the six days of creation. For it is out of the silence and the fulness of a day of rest that Creation comes to life in these verses from Genesis:

But there went up a mist from the earth, and watered the whole face of the ground. And the Lord God formed man of the dust of the ground, and breathed into his nostrils the breath of life; and man became a living soul.

Like the other examples I have presented in this chapter, this is a myth of origins. After reading *The Soul of the World*, I can see the question "why?"

embedded in it: "Why did we become a living soul?" From this question a person may then wonder, "And what does it mean to be a living soul?" The answer to the second question, which is the subject of my book, helps us to answer the first question.

As we learn in Genesis, after the six other days of Creation, the work stops and "catches its breath," as it were. But then, "there went up a mist from the earth, and watered the whole face of the ground" (Yes, the ground has a face, just as, in the architecture Scruton prefers, a building has a face). Since man is but dust of the ground, he (his face) is watered as well. But in a final touch, the coup de grace of Creation, God breathed into the nostrils of the man he made, "and man became a living soul." This story tells how, in the fulness and silence of the Sabbath, we come to life with the breath of life. Like the Sabbath, the breath is both ordinary and extraordinary. The Sabbath and the breath are a good place to end and begin again. It's a "day," which is but a moment of breath, for us to consider what it means to be a living soul.

Here, at the end of his presentation, before the rest is silence, Scruton would persuade us that Creation is a myth of origin that records a deep truth about the human psyche—the truth that there is no "moment" of creation, no moment before which there was nothing, and after which time began to unfold. What does this sword of truth mean for our psyche? It asks the mind to stop, to be futile, to see a world suspended between creation and destruction (for all of creation hangs by such a slender thread of breath), and to renew the order of the covenant among those whom you love. Here, at the end of my inquiry, I give thanks for his arguments and stories that define what it means to be a living soul. They give us a reason to be.

I give thanks, too, for all the other texts and artworks I've collected in the book. The act of reading a text and of looking at a painting come together quite beautifully, I would say, in Rembrandt's image of *An Old Woman Reading*, which illustrates the chapter before this one. Here, at the end of my inquiry, I imagine this image to be Rembrandt's portrait of a mind that's ready, a concentrated mind—in this case a mind concentrated, I would have to guess, on a sacred text, and so it illustrates the activity of my enterprise. As I have attempted in the writing of this book, it answers the question I asked at the beginning: "What is the act that brings this life to life?" With great understanding and artistry, Rembrandt conveys a concentrated mind in the expression of her face, which is brilliantly lit by a light that seems to radiate from the book she reads. She is old, but her intention is strong and deeply rooted. She would understand what she reads. Rembrandt has emphasized that concentration with her headgear, which, like an act of will (the act of being accountable), seems to direct her into the text. The lack of anything else in the painting increases this effect. As such, Rembrandt's image serves to illustrate this important sentence near the end of *The Soul of the World*:

> *When we live in full awareness and acceptance of our mortality, we see the world as making a place for us.*

With great artistry and wisdom, Rembrandt has created a woman reading a book (most likely a sacred text) "in full awareness." Why is she so intent on it? As we look at her, we realize Rembrandt has created a person whose mind is ripe for this activity. What she reads, however, is a mystery; we have to imagine it. It's immaterial, as Lewis might say, and so Rembrandt's image is like a metaphor in which material and immaterial worlds come together as a married pair. We sense that the one (Is it the something or the nothing?) gives life to the other. We sense, too, how she both loses and finds herself in this activity. Perhaps Rembrandt lost and found himself in this way as he created her. As such, she's a prayer for grace and a prayer of thanksgiving. At the same time, Rembrandt knows very well that she will be seen by others. He's a public as well as a private man. I hazard to guess that he is inviting us to know all this about his reader and to follow her example, even though she and he are silent. It's up to us to make these inferences from their presence in the work. Then it's up to us whether we follow their example or not.

Follow the Breath (Out)

Breathe,
Oh,
Breathe
To be a living soul . . .

It
Is
The
Gift beyond compare

Of
An
Unbroken
Line of ancestry.

Again
We
Wake
With breath that lifts the breast,

(Each
A
Perfect
End unto itself)

That
Would
Be
Given again to the source

Of
Breath
And life
And all and everything.

Bibliography

Adamson, Peter. *Classical Philosophy*. Oxford: Oxford University Press, 2014.

Alighieri, Dante. *La Vita Nuova*. Translated by Barbara Reynolds. Baltimore: Penguin Books, 1969.

————— . *The Inferno*. Translated by John Ciardi. New York: Mentor Books, 1954.

————— . *The Purgatorio*. Translated by John Ciardi. New York: Mentor Books, 1957.

Anonymous. *Everyman and Other Miracle and Morality Plays*. Mineola, NY: Dover Publications, 1995.

Aristotle. *Nicomachean Ethics*. Translated by Joe Sacks: Indianapolis: Hackett Publishing Company, 2002.

Armstrong, John. *Love, Life, Goethe*. New York: Farrar, Straus and Giroux, 2006.

Bloom, Alan. *The Republic of Plato*. Translated and interpreted by Alan Bloom. New York: Basic Books, 1968.

Brown, Peter. *Augustine of Hippo*. Berkeley: University of California Press, 1969.

Burke, Edmund. *Selected Works of Edmund Burke, Volume 1*. Indianapolis: Liberty Fund, 1999.

——————. *Selected Works of Edmund Burke, Volume 2*. Indianapolis: Liberty Fund, 1999.

——————. *Further Reflections on the Revolution in France*. Indianapolis: Liberty Fund, 1992.

——————. *Miscellaneous Writings*. Indianapolis: Liberty Fund, 1999.

Chaucer, Geoffrey. *The Canterbury Tales*. Translated by Neville Coghill. New York: Penguin Books, 2003.

De Lorris, Guillaume and Jean de Meun. *The Romance of the Rose*. Translated by Frances Horgan. Oxford: Oxford University Press, 1994.

Goethe, Johann. *Faust, Part One*. Translated by David Luke. Oxford: Oxford University Press, 1987.

—————————. *Faust, Part Two*. Translated by David Luke. Oxford: Oxford University Press, 1994

—————————. *Elective Affinities*. Translated by David Constantine. Oxford: Oxford University Press, 1994.

—————————. Wilhelm Meister. Translated by H. M. Waidson. Richmond: Alma Classics LTD, 2011.

Griesinger, Alan. *A Comic Vision of Great Constancy*. Herndon, VA: Mascot Books, 2014.

—————————. *A Comic Vision of Self-Government*. Herndon, VA: Mascot Books, 2016.

Kirk, Russel. *Edmund Burke*. Wilmington, DE: Intercollegiate Studies Institute, 1997.

Lewis, C.S. *The Abolition of Man*. New York: Harper Collins, 2001.

————-. *The Allegory of Love*. Cambridge: Cambridge University Press, 2018.

Levin, Yuval. *The Great Debate*. New York: Basic Books, 2014.

Lings, Martin. *Shakespeare's Window into the Soul*. Rochester, VT: Inner Traditions, 2006.

Lucretius (Titus Lucretius Carus). *On the Nature of Things*. Translated by Frank O. Copley. New York: W. W. Norton and Company, 1977.

Mayo, Stephan and Michael S. Russo. *Plato's Republic: A Study Guide*. Translated by Benjamin Jowett. New York: SophiaOmni Press, 2012.

Nhat Hanh, Thich. *Old Path White Clouds*. Translated by Mobi Ho. Berkeley: Parallax Press, 1991.

Plato. *The Symposium*. Translated by Walter Hamilton. New York: Penguin Books, 1951.

Plato. *Timaeus and Critias*. Translated by Desmond Lee. UK: Penguin Classics, 1977.

Scruton, Roger. *Kant: A Very Short Introduction*. Oxford: Oxford University

Press, 2001.
————————. *Modern Philosophy*. New York: Penguin Books, 1994.
———————— . *Modern Culture*. London: Bloomsbury Publishing, 2005.
———————— . *On Human Nature*. Princeton, NJ: Princeton University Press, 2017.
———————— . *The Soul of the World*. Princeton, NJ: Princeton University Press, 2014.
———————— . *The Face of God*. London: Bloomsbury Publishing, 2012.
Shakespeare, William. *A Midsummer Night's Dream*. Waltham, MA: Blaisdell Publishing Company, 1966.
———————— . *All's Well That Ends Well*. New York: Penguin Books, 1964.
———————— . *Henry IV, Part 2*. New York: Signet Classics, 1965.
Tarnas, Richard. *The Passion of the Western Mind*. New York: Ballantine Books, 1993.

Photo Credits

1. Cover: Martini's *Annunciation*. Art Resource.
2. Book One, chapter 1: Chagall's *Moses with the Burning Bush*. Image provided by Art Resource. License provided by Artist Rights Society.
3. Book One, chapter 2: Wyeth's *Below Dover*. Both the image and the license provided by Artists Rights Society.
4. Book Two, chapter 1: Ford's *Guinevere*. Bridgeman Images.
5. Book Two, chapter 2: Holiday's *Dante Meets Beatrice at the Ponte Santa Trinita*. Bridgeman Images.
6. Book Two, chapter 3: Doré's *Dante in the Gloomy Wood*. Art Resource.
7. Book Two, chapter 4: Carpaccio's *Saint Augustine in His Study*. Art Resource.
8. Book Two, chapter 5: Rembrandt's *Faust*. Art Resource.
9. Book Two, chapter 6: Raphael's *The Triumph of Galatea*. Art Resource.
10. Book Two, chapter 7: Gozzoli's *The Triumph of Saint Aquinas*. Art Resource.
11. Book Two, chapter 8: David's *The Death of Socrates*. Art Resource.
12. Book Two, chapter 9: The National Roman Museum's statue of *Demeter*. Art Resource.
13. Book Three, chapter 1: Vermeer's *The Allegory of Painting*. Art Resource.
14. Book Three, chapter 2: Da Vinci's *Mona Lisa*. Art Resource.
15. Book Three, chapter 3: The Flammarion engraving. Art Resource.
16. Book Three, chapter 4: Weinman's *Winged Liberty*. Alamy Images.
17. Book Three, chapter 5: Lorrain's *Ulysses Returns Chryseis to Her Father*. Art Resource.
18. Book Three, chapter 6: Rembrandt's *Jacob Wrestling with the Angel*. Art Resource.
19. Book Three, chapter 7: Wyeth's *Christina's World*. Image provided by

Art Resource. License provided by Artists Rights Society.

20. Book Three, chapter 8: Bruegel's *The Harvesters*. Art Resource.
21. Book Three, chapter 9: Van Gogh's *Wheat Fields, Auvers*. Art Resource.
22. Book Three, chapter 10: Isenbrant's *The Rest on the Flight into Egypt*. Art Resource.
23. Book Three, chapter 11: Fragonard's *Stolen Kiss*. Art Resource.
24. Book Four, chapter 1: Sargent's *Chiron and Achilles*. The Museum of Fine Arts.
25. Book Four, chapter 2: Rembrandt's *Abraham and the Three Angels*. Art Resource.
26. Book Four, chapter 3: From the Tang dynasty, *Tejaprabha Buddha and the Five Planets*. Art Resource.
27. Book Four, chapter 4: Redon's *Dante and Beatrice*. Alamy Images.
28. Postscript, chapter 1: Abel's *Socrates Teaching His Disciples*. Alamy Images.
29. Postscript, chapter 2: Rembrandt's *An Old Woman Reading*. Bridgeman Images.
30. Postscript, chapter 3: Masaccio's *Explusion from the Garden of Eden*. Art Resource.

About the Author

Alan Griesinger graduated from Trinity College in Hartford, Connecticut, and received his master of arts in English from the University of Oregon. Subsequently, he taught junior and senior high school students at Naples Central School in Naples, New York, for twenty-eight years. This is where Mr. Griesinger's true education began—where colleagues, parents, and students gave him a solid grounding in the principles and rituals of community life.

Since retirement, he has written three books. Taken as a whole, they record in a series of related essays a pilgrimage of the spirit. Individually, each work aims at describing a place where people have traditionally found shelter and healing. In the first book, it is wisdom; in the second, it is self-government; and in this third book, it's what the book of Genesis refers to as a "living soul." These three works, like the pilgrimages of Odysseus and Dante in the *Odyssey* and the *Commedia*, tell the story of one whose spirit would come home.

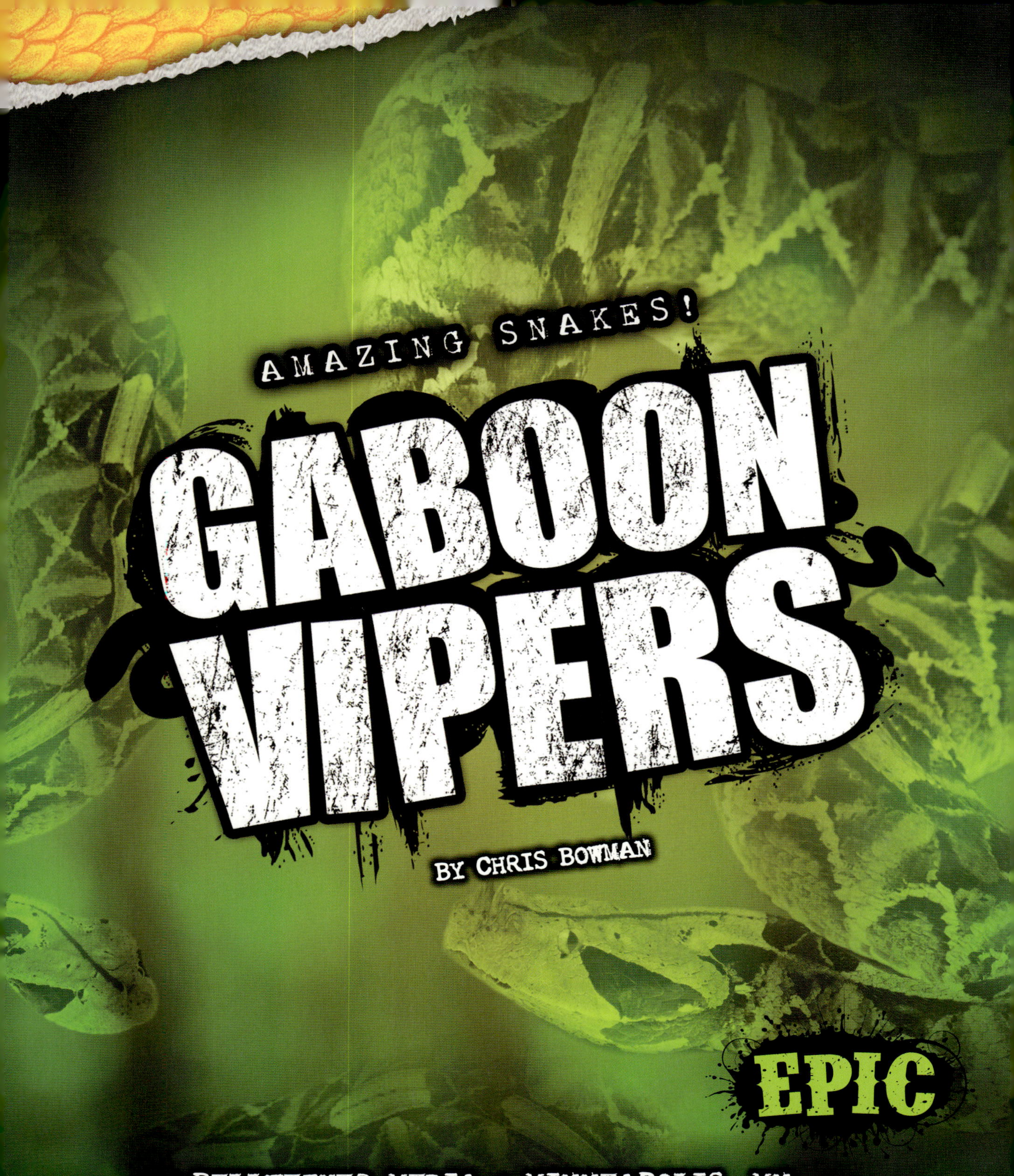

AMAZING SNAKES!

GABOON VIPERS

BY CHRIS BOWMAN

EPIC

BELLWETHER MEDIA • MINNEAPOLIS, MN

EPIC

EPIC BOOKS are no ordinary books. They burst with intense action, high-speed heroics, and shadows of the unknown. Are you ready for an Epic adventure?

This edition first published in 2014 by Bellwether Media, Inc.

Library of Congress Cataloging-in-Publication Data

Bowman, Chris, 1990-
Gaboon Vipers / by Chris Bowman.
pages cm. – (Epic. Amazing Snakes!)
Summary: "Engaging images accompany information about Gaboon vipers. The combination of high-interest subject matter and light text is intended for students in grades 2 through 7"– Provided by publisher.
Audience: Ages 7-12.
Audience: Grades 2 to 7.
Includes bibliographical references and index.
ISBN 978-1-62617-123-7 (hardcover : alk. paper)
1. Gaboon viper–Juvenile literature. I. Title.
QL666.O69B676 2014
597.96'3–dc23

2013050289

Printed in the United States of America, North Mankato, MN.

TABLE OF CONTENTS

WHAT ARE GABOON VIPERS?

Gaboon vipers are **venomous** snakes with small horns on their head. They are the heaviest vipers in the world. These snakes weigh up to 25 pounds (11 kilograms).

WHERE GABOON VIPERS LIVE

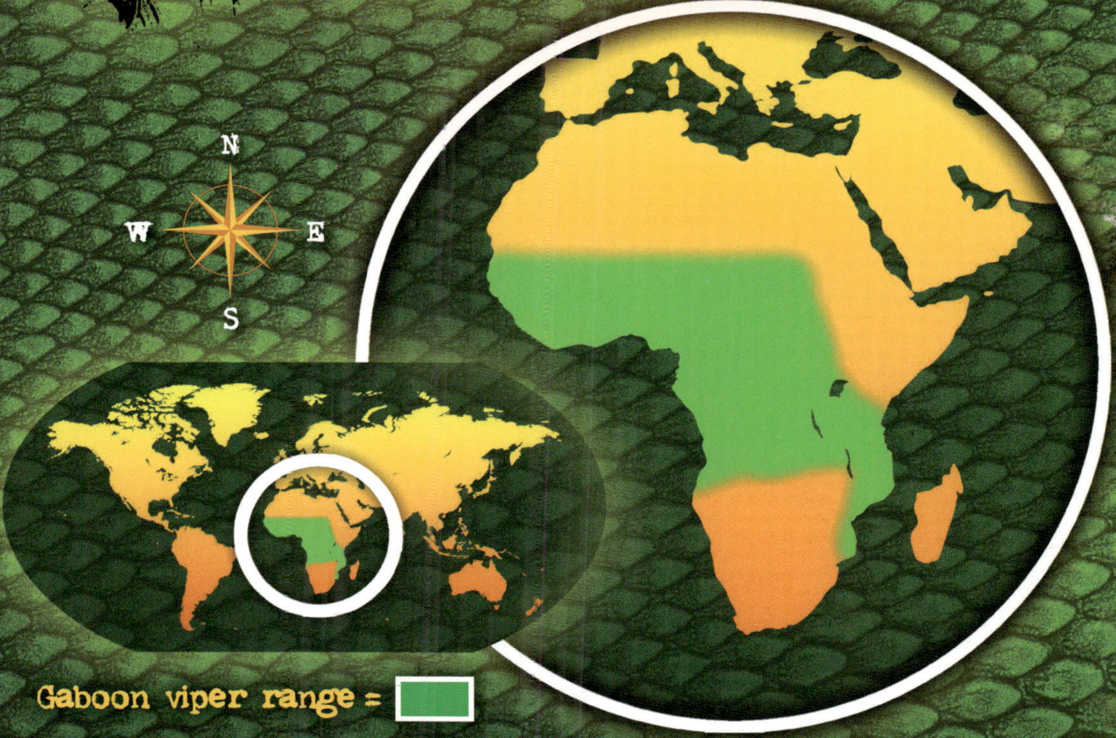

Gaboon vipers live in central Africa. They hide in **savannahs**, forests, and **rain forests**. They make their homes on the ground.

BLENDING IN

Their bodies have brown, purple, white, and yellow **scales**. The colors **camouflage** the snakes. Their scales form patterns that match the leaves on the ground.

secretary bird

Few **predators** spot Gaboon vipers. However, the snakes cannot always hide from secretary birds, badgers, and warthogs. Sometimes other snakes hunt them, too.

Don't Move

Gaboon vipers stay still when they sense danger. They also hiss loudly.

FANGS AND VENOM

Gaboon vipers are **ambush** hunters. They wait for **prey** under leaves near animal trails. They watch for **rodents**, frogs, and lizards. Then they **strike**.

A Bigger Meal

Sometimes they will eat birds, hares, or monkeys!

Gaboon Viper Prey

Gaboon vipers have the longest **fangs** of any snake. Their teeth measure between 1 and 2 inches (2.5 and 5 centimeters) long. These fangs leave **venom** deep in prey.

Out of the Way

Their fangs fold against the roof of their mouth while they rest.

Their venom is not very strong. However, they **inject** the most venom of any snake. This makes the vipers just as deadly as snakes with stronger venom.

The Gaboon viper holds its prey until it dies. It swallows the animal whole. Then it slithers back into hiding.

SPECIES PROFILE

SCIENTIFIC NAME:	*BITIS GABONICA*
NICKNAMES:	BUTTERFLY ADDER, FOREST PUFF ADDER, SWAMPJACK
AVERAGE SIZE:	4-7 FEET (1.2-2.1 METERS)
HABITATS:	FORESTS, RAIN FORESTS, SAVANNAHS
RANGE:	CENTRAL AFRICA
VENOMOUS:	YES
HUNTING METHOD:	AMBUSH, VENOMOUS BITE
COMMON PREY:	RODENTS, BIRDS, FROGS, LIZARDS

GLOSSARY

ambush—to attack by surprise

camouflage—to hide an animal by helping it blend in with the surroundings

fangs—sharp, hollow teeth; venom flows through fangs and into a bite.

inject—to force a liquid into something; venomous snakes inject venom into the bodies of prey.

predators—animals that hunt other animals for food

prey—animals that are hunted by other animals for food

rain forests—hot, rainy areas with tall trees

rodents—small animals that usually gnaw on their food

savannahs—grassy areas with few trees

scales—small plates of skin that cover and protect a snake's body

strike—to bite quickly and with force

venom—a poison created by a snake; snakes use venom to hurt or kill other animals.

venomous—able to create venom in their bodies; Gaboon vipers release venom through their fangs.

TO LEARN MORE

At the Library

Fiedler, Julie. *Vipers*. New York, N.Y.: PowerKids Press, 2008.

Sweazey, Davy. *Bush Vipers*. Minneapolis, Minn.: Bellwether Media, 2014.

Woodward, John. *Everything You Need to Know About Snakes: And Other Scaly Reptiles*. New York, N.Y.: DK Pub., 2013.

On the Web

Learning more about Gaboon vipers is as easy as 1, 2, 3.

1. Go to www.factsurfer.com.

2. Enter "Gaboon vipers" into the search box.

3. Click the "Surf" button and you will see a list of related web sites.

With factsurfer.com, finding more information is just a click away.

INDEX

The images in this book are reproduced through the courtesy of: reptiles4all, front cover, pp. 14-15; Chris Mattison/ FLPA, pp. 4-5; imagebroker/ SuperStock, p. 7; Exactostock/ SuperStock, pp. 8-9; Iv Nikolny, p. 10; Ivan Kuzmin, p. 11; Roger de la Harpe/ SuperStock, pp. 12-13; Heiko Kiera, p. 13 (top); Albie Venter, p. 13 (middle); Mogens Trolle, p. 13 (bottom); Animals Animals, pp. 16-17, 19; Nomad/ SuperStock, p. 18; Michael D. Kern/ Nature Picture Library, pp. 20-21.

läßt sie sich reinigen und über Schwefelsäure trocknen. Sie ist dann ein gelbes, olivenfarbiges Öl ohne Geruch, von scharfem aromatischen Geschmack. Ein wenig davon auf die Zunge gebracht erregt anhaltende Migräne, und Sobrero tötete mit einer geringen Menge davon einen Hund. Beim Erhitzen detoniert diese Substanz. —

Es ist interessant, daß etwa 200 Gramm des ersten von Sobrero erzeugten Nitroglyzerins noch jetzt in der Nobelschen Dynamitfabrik in Avigliana in Italien aufbewahrt und alljährlich geprüft werden; die Fabrikleitung hat dem Verfasser noch neuerdings bestätigt, daß das Präparat noch unverändert erhalten ist und bisher keine Spur freier Säure entwickelt hat; der Stickstoffgehalt dieses Nitroglyzerins wurde in längeren Zwischenräumen geprüft und stets eine Zahl gefunden, die dem Mittel von 18·35 % Stickstoff entspricht. Nebenstehende Abbildung zeigt das in der Fabrik der Dinamite Nobel in Avigliana errichtete Denkmal Sobreros.

Ascanio Sobrero.

Obzwar schon Sobrero das Nitroglyzerin wegen seiner explosiven Eigenschaften für die Sprengtechnik empfohlen hatte, so wurden doch damals die Schwierigkeiten und Gefahren einer fabrikatorischen Herstellung als so groß erachtet, daß die Entdeckung Sobreros fast in Vergessenheit geriet; nur in der Medizin fand der Körper in verdünnten alkoholischen Lösungen unter dem Namen Glonoin einige Verwendung; erst etwa 20 Jahre später wurde durch den schwedischen Ingenieur Alfred Nobel nach Überwindung unsäglicher Schwierigkeiten das Nitroglyzerin dauernd und mit großem Erfolg in die Explosivstofftechnik eingeführt.

Man kann an die Geschichte des Nitroglyzerins und die damit verbundene bahnbrechende Tätigkeit Nobels nicht herantreten, ohne sich — wenigstens in Kürze — mit den wichtigsten persönlichen Daten aus dem Leben dieses kühnen und genialen Erfinders zu befassen.

Das Leben und der Charakter Alfred Nobels, seine unerschütterliche Ausdauer, seine hervorragenden Fähigkeiten und sein vielseitiges Genie sind trefflich von Henry de Mosenthal[1] geschildert; L. Henry[2] beschreibt den äußeren Lebensgang Nobels, sowie die Organisation der Nobelstiftung; Einzelheiten über Nobels Familie hat Werner A. Cronquist[3] gegeben; L. Roux[4] behandelt die Leistungen Nobels auf dem Gebiete der Sprengstoff- und Pulverindustrie; C. Haeussermann[5] speziell die Verdienste Nobels in bezug auf die rauchschwachen Pulver; von besonderem Interesse ist ein Vortrag, den H. de Mosenthal[6] am 1. Mai 1899 in der Society of Chemical Industry in London über die Tätigkeit Alfred Nobels gehalten hat.

Nobels Urgroßvater, Olof Nobilius, war als Zeichenlehrer an der Universität Upsala tätig gewesen; dessen Sohn — Alfreds Großvater —, welcher Militärarzt im finnischen Kriege und später Stadtarzt in Gefle war, gab die lateinische Form des Namens auf und nannte sich Nobel; im Jahre 1801 ward letzterem in Upsala ein Sohn Emanuel geboren.

Emanuel Nobel, Alfreds Vater, verbrachte einige Zeit auf See, um die Konstruktion und Führung von Schiffen zu studieren und kehrte dann nach Schweden zurück, wo er auf einer Schiffswerft angestellt wurde; im Jahre 1824 nahm er eine Stellung als Maschinist bei Mehemed Ali in Ägypten an, vier Jahre später war er wieder in Stockholm als Assistent des bekannten Schiffskonstrukteurs Oberst Blom tätig; bald darauf verheiratete sich Emanuel Nobel mit einer Landsmännin Karoline Henriette Ahlsell, welche ihm vier Söhne schenkte: Robert Hjalmar, Ludwig Emanuel, Alfred Bernard und Oskar

---

[1] Artikel erschien unter dem Titel „The Inventor of Dynamite" in „The Nineteenth Century" im Oktober 1898.

[2] Revue des questions scientifiques, Louvain (M. T. Thirion), t. XIX. p. 541.

[3] Ord och Bild, Stockholm, Februar 1894. — Vgl. auch Vortrag im technischen Institut zu Stockholm am 20. Februar 1897.

[4] Louis Roux: L'œuvre de Nobel in Revue technique. Paris 1897.

[5] „Alfred Nobel und die Erfindung der Nitroglyzerinpulver." Stuttgart 1904.

[6] Journal of the Society of Chemical Industry, Jahrg. 1899; deutsche Übersetzung in Z. f. angew. Chemie 1899, S. 753 u. 782.

Emil; der dritte Sohn, unser Alfred Nobel, wurde am 21. Oktober 1833 in Stockholm geboren.

Emanuel Nobel war selbst erfinderisch tätig, besonders auch auf dem Gebiete der Explosivstoffe; nach einer Explosion, welche in seinem Laboratorium stattfand, verließ derselbe im Jahre 1837 Stockholm und übersiedelte nach St. Petersburg; hier gelang es ihm, die russische Regierung von dem Werte seiner Land- und Seeminen für militärische und submarine Verteidigungszwecke zu überzeugen. Im Jahre 1842 begründete er, gemäß einem mit der russischen Regierung geschlossenen Vertrag, eine kleine Fabrik an der Newa; in erster Linie war diese Fabrik zur Erzeugung von Seeminen bestimmt und solche fanden auch später im Krimkriege Verwendung, um der englischen Flotte das Vordringen gegen Kronstadt zu verwehren. Nach dem Kriege wurden die Regierungsaufträge immer seltener; dabei hatte Emanuel Nobel mit Geldschwierigkeiten zu kämpfen und so gelangte bald die Fabrik in die Hände der Gläubiger. Dies bewog ihn im Jahre 1859 zur Rückkehr nach der Heimat. — Im Jahre 1842, nach Abschluß des Vertrages mit der russischen Regierung, waren ihm Frau und Kinder nach Rußland gefolgt. Alfred besuchte die Schule in St. Petersburg bis zu seinem 16. Lebensjahre, mußte aber infolge einer Schwäche des Rückgrates seine Studien während dieser Zeit häufig unterbrechen. Die finanziellen Verhältnisse in der Familie waren auch nicht immer die besten, und so trat er im Jahre 1849 als Lehrling bei seinem Vater ein, wurde aber schon im nächsten Jahre nach Amerika geschickt, um bei dem schwedischen Landsmann John Ericksson als Maschineningenieur ausgebildet zu werden. Nach vierjährigem Aufenthalte in den Vereinigten Staaten kehrte Alfred im Jahre 1854 nach St. Petersburg zurück und nahm an den Arbeiten seines Vaters teil, beschäftigte sich aber auch selbst mit Erfindungen. Betrachten wir einen Augenblick diesen jungen Mann von 21 Jahren, welcher schwedisch, russisch, deutsch, englisch und französisch sprach, und der nicht nur als Ingenieur ausgebildet war, sondern auch in einer Atmosphäre erfinderischer und schöpferischer Tätigkeit gelebt hatte; er war imstande, die Bücher und Schriften fast aller zivilisierten Nationen zu verstehen, und obgleich seine Fachstudien das Gebiet der Maschinentechnik betrafen, zeigte er eine besondere Vorliebe für chemische Studien. Im Jahre 1857 nahm er sein erstes Patent (englisches Patent Nr. 2705) auf einen Gasometer, zwei Jahre später nahm er Patente (englisches Patent Nr. 177 und Nr. 556) auf einen Apparat zum Messen von Wasser und auf Konstruktionsverbesserungen an Barometern.

Als im Jahre 1859 Emanuel Nobel nach Schweden zurückkehrte, überließ er seinem Sohne Ludwig die Führung der St. Petersburger Fabrik, und es gelang diesem im Laufe der Zeit, daraus ein großes Etablissement der Maschinenindustrie zu entwickeln; im Jahre 1875 begann Ludwig in Gemeinschaft mit seinen Brüdern die Ausbeutung der Naphtaquellen in Baku und erhob das Unternehmen in zehn Jahren zu einer großen Bedeutung. Mit Emanuel Nobel kehrte auch dessen Frau und die jüngeren Söhne Alfred und Emil in die Heimat zurück. In den Jahren 1859/61 beschäftigten sich Alfred Nobel und sein Vater Emanuel hauptsächlich mit dem Studium von Explosivstoffen und sie lenkten besonders ihre Aufmerksamkeit auf das von Sobrero entdeckte Nitroglyzerin. Sie hatten schon früher einige Versuche mit diesem Körper gemacht und waren zur Überzeugung gelangt, daß das Nitroglyzerin der Explosivstoff der Zukunft werden müsse. Sie vervollkommneten die Herstellungsweise dieses Stoffes, welcher zuerst nach Sobrero „Pyroglyzerin", dann „Glonoinöl" später „Nobels Sprengöl" genannt wurde. Im Jahre 1861 unternahm Alfred Nobel eine Reise nach verschiedenen Städten des Kontinents, um sich das nötige Geld zur Errichtung einer Fabrik zu verschaffen; in Paris gelang es ihm, Interesse für seinen neuen Explosivstoff zu erwecken, so daß er genügend Mittel erhielt, um nach seiner Heimkehr in Heleneborg bei Stockholm eine kleine Fabrik zu errichten, woselbst im Jahre 1862 zum ersten Male Nitroglyzerin in größerem Maßstab erzeugt wurde; bei Errichtung der Fabrik unterstützte ihn ein junger Ingenieur, Henrik Liedbeck; er war Alfred Nobels Schulkamerad und bester Freund, beide blieben ihr ganzes Leben lang in innigstem Verkehr; Liedbeck hat auch weiterhin zu den meisten Fabriken Nobels die Pläne entworfen und danach gebaut.

Nobel gibt in seinem bayerischen Patent vom 1. August 1866 sein Fabrikationsverfahren wie folgt an:

1. Bei der Bereitung des Nitroglyzerins. Bisher bereitete man das Nitroglyzerin durch langsames Eintröpfeln des Glyzerins in eine Mischung von Schwefelsäure und rauchende Salpetersäure, wobei die Temperatur nicht 0° übersteigen durfte. Ich bereite es vorzugsweise durch schnelles Zusammenmischen des ganzen Quantums Glyzerin und Säuren, wonach dasselbe in kaltes Wasser ausgegossen wird und das Nitroglyzerin sich dort am Boden ablagert. Läßt man Glyzerin und eine Mischung von Schwefelsäure und Salpetersäure unter starkem Umrühren durch ein Rohr, so erlangt man dadurch eine kontinuierliche Bereitung. Nur bei sehr starker Salpetersäure, wie z. B. von 1·52 spez. Gewicht, ist die oben erwähnte Methode der starken Erhitzung wegen weniger brauchbar. Ich ziehe es dann vor, die Salpeter-

säure der Schwefelsäure in 4 oder 5 Portionen zuzusetzen und jedesmal mit Glyzerin zu sättigen; zwischen jeder Operation lasse ich die Mischung erkalten.

2. Bei der Bereitung der Säuren. Wenn man in $3^1/_2$ Gewichtsteilen Schwefelsäure von 1·83 spez. Gewicht (mehr oder weniger) 1 Gewichtsteil salpetersaures Kali oder Natron auflöst, so kristallisieren beim Erkalten Salze von der chemischen Formel ($KO \cdot 4SO_3 + 6HO$; $NaO \cdot 4SO_3 + 6HO$). Diese Salze sind bei einer Temperatur von 0^0 in der Säure beinahe unlöslich und können davon mittels einer Presse oder durch den Luftdruck leicht getrennt werden; es bleibt dann eine Mischung von Schwefelsäure und Salpetersäure, die sich zur Bereitung des Nitroglyzerins sehr gut eignet. Nimmt man nun so viel Schwefelsäure, daß diese ganz in dem sich ausscheidenden oben erwähnten Salze absorbiert wird, so erhält man ohne Destillation freies Monohydrat von Salpetersäure ($NO_5 \cdot HO$).

Liecke gibt an (Dingl. polyt. Journ. 179, S. 159), daß Nobel zu Salpetersäure vom spez. Gewicht 1·3 und starker Schwefelsäure vermittelst eines Rohres Glyzerin fließen lasse, ohne eine Abkühlung vorzunehmen; auf diese Weise erfolge eine kontinuierliche Darstellung. Nur bei Anwendung einer stärkeren Salpetersäure von 1·5 spez. Gewicht ist diese Methode nicht anwendbar, weil eine zu starke Reaktion erfolgt, welche eine tiefgehende Zersetzung zur Folge hat. Bei einer solchen Säure soll vorzuziehen sein, die Salpetersäure in verschiedenen Portionen zu der Schwefelsäure zu setzen und jedesmal mit Glyzerin zu sättigen, auch für gute Abkühlung zu sorgen.

Besondere Schwierigkeiten verursachte es zunächst, das Nitroglyzerin zuverlässig und vollständig zur Detonation zu bringen.

Während beim Schwarzpulver, dem Gemenge von Salpeter, Schwefel und Kohle, durch direkte Entzündung eine explosionsartige Verbrennung stattfindet, ist dies beim Nitroglyzerin nicht der Fall. Berührung mit glühenden oder flammenden Körpern bringt das Glyzerin höchstens zur Entzündung, wobei das Sprengöl mit einem knisternden und prasselnden Geräusch langsam abbrennt; dagegen reicht eine solche einfache Wärmequelle, z. B. brennende Zündschnur, nicht aus, um an dem Zündpunkt die zur Explosion nötige Wärmemenge anzusammeln. Nobel verwendete daher anfangs das Nitroglyzerin nicht für sich, sondern als Zusatz zu Schwarzpulver, Schießbaumwolle oder anderen Substanzen, um letztere sprengkräftiger zu machen (schwedisches Patent vom 14. Oktober 1863, englisches Patent 2359 vom 24. Februar 1863). Nobel führte die Versuche auf folgende Weise[1] aus:

[1] Dingl. polyt. Journ. Bd. 171, S. 243.

Patronenhülsen von Zinkblech, an einem Ende offen, wurden mit gewöhnlichem Schwarzpulver gefüllt, dazu so viel Nitroglyzerin gegossen, als in den Zwischenräumen des Pulvers Platz hatte; die Hülse wurde hierauf mit einem Korkstopfen genau verschlossen und die Patrone so in das Bohrloch gesteckt, daß der Korkstopfen nach unten kam, d. h. das feste Gestein berührte. Der Zwischenraum zwischen Patrone und Bohrlochwand wurde dann mit Schwarzpulver so ausgefüllt, daß letzteres die Patrone nicht allein ringsum umhüllte, sondern auch von oben bedeckte; diese äußere Hülle von Schwarzpulver wurde dann mittels einer Zündschnur zur Explosion gebracht, welche letztere sich dem mit Sprengöl getränkten Schwarzpulver mitteilte. Die auf diese Weise angestellten Versuche ließen erkennen, daß durch einen Zusatz von Sprengöl die Wirkung des gewöhnlichen Pulvers in hohem Grade verstärkt wird und daß das Sprengöl einstens für den Bergbau von hoher Wichtigkeit werden könne.

Nobel verfolgte nun weiter diesen Gedanken, Schwarzpulver als Zündpulver zu verwenden, und versuchte, ob es möglich wäre, durch Beiladungen von Schwarzpulver das Sprengöl selbst zur Explosion zu bringen, sowie er vorher mit Sprengöl getränktes Schwarzpulver hatte explodieren lassen.

In seinem bayerischen Patente hat sich Nobel eingehend hierüber geäußert und wird nachstehend der betreffende Wortlaut wiedergegeben:[1]

Es gibt eine Unzahl chemischer Stoffe, welche in einem offenen Raum angezündet werden können, ohne zu explodieren, z. B. Nitroglyzerin, Nitromannit, salpetersaurer Harnstoff, die Äthyl- und Methylnitrate usw.; sie erleiden zwar an der Berührungsstelle des Feuers eine Zersetzung, jedoch zu langsam, um eine Explosion hervorzubringen; aus diesem Grunde haben diese Stoffe bisher keine Anwendung als Ersatzmittel des Pulvers gefunden. Einige dieser Körper, z. B. das Nitroglyzerin, detonieren mit großer Heftigkeit durch einen Hammerschlag; die Detonation erfolgt aber nur an der Berührungsstelle; das übrige erleidet weder eine Verpuffung noch eine Anzündung; wenn man eine ebene Fläche, wie z. B. einen Amboß, mit Nitroglyzerin streicht, so kann man damit eine lange Reihe Detonationen darstellen. Der Grund dieser Erscheinung liegt darin, daß das Nitroglyzerin und analoge Stoffe nicht durch Entzündung, sondern durch Erwärmung ihrer Masse auf 180° C explodieren. Es hat nämlich das Nitroglyzerin zwei Zersetzungsgrade — der sehr langsame, wenn die Wärmeleitung als einzige Wärmequelle dient, und die äußerst heftige, wenn die Temperatur der ganzen Masse durch Druck bis auf 180° gesteigert wird; um eine Totalexplosion hervorzubringen, ist

[1] Nach Bayr. Kunst- u. Gewerbebl. 1866, S. 684.

es demnach notwendig, während des kurzen Verlaufs einer Explosion (höchstens etwa $^1/_{300}$ Sekunde) die ganze Masse bis auf 180° zu erwärmen.

Meine Erfindung besteht hauptsächlich in der Lösung dieses Problems, und das Nitroglyzerin ist der Körper, dessen ich mich vorzugsweise bediene. Mein Verfahren ist ein zweifaches:

I. Durch Mischen des Nitroglyzerins mit Schießpulver, Pyroxylin oder analogen Stoffen, wobei die letzteren beim Verbrennen ihre Wärme dem Nitroglyzerin augenblicklich mitteilen. — Das mit Nitroglyzerin gemischte oder sogar in Nitroglyzerin schwimmende Pulver ist für allerlei Sprengarbeiten sehr geeignet; die Explosion des Nitroglyzerins wird hierbei teils durch die Wärmeerzeugung des Pulvers, teils durch die Wärmequelle des Explosionsdruckes bewirkt. — Wird das Nitroglyzerin dagegen in den Poren des Schießpulvers oder analoger Stoffe absorbiert oder damit innig vermengt, so erlangt das letztere eine größere Expansionskraft unter langsamer Verbrennung und eignet sich daher vorzüglich als Schießpulver für Geschütze. Beabsichtigt man nur die Verbrennungsgeschwindigkeit des Schießpulvers zu reduzieren, so läßt man irgend ein nicht explosives Öl in die Poren desselben eindringen.

II. Vermittelst Erwärmung des Nitroglyzerins durch den Druck, welchen eine Lokaldetonation des Nitroglyzerins oder anderer explodierender Stoffe hervorbringt. — Soviel ich weiß, ist diese Wärmequelle noch nie zu einem technischen Zweck angewendet worden. — Hiervon ausgehend ist es nun erforderlich, einen sehr geringen Teil der Masse zur Detonation zu bringen. Wenn das Nitroglyzerin an den Seiten und am Boden Widerstand findet, also nicht entweichen kann; wenn es beispielsweise in einem Bohrloch eingeschlossen ist und die Detonation von der Oberfläche ausgeht, so wirkt der Druck von oben nach unten mit solcher Gewalt auf die ganze Masse, daß sie augenblicklich die Zersetzungstemperatur erlangt und folglich detoniert. Es kann diese lokale Explosion auf verschiedene Art erzeugt werden, z. B.

1. wenn man Nitroglyzerin oder analoge Stoffe in Röhren mit Schießpulver — oder gleichwirkenden, zur Erwärmung beitragenden Stoffen — umgibt oder umgekehrt;

2. wenn man in dem Nitroglyzerin oder analogen Stoffen nur einen kleinen Zünder einsetzt, der mit Pulver oder ähnlichem Stoffe gefüllt ist. Dieser Zünder kann aus einem Glas-, Holz- oder anderem, mit Pulver gefüllten Rohre bestehen; von unten wird es mit einem Kork oder auf andere Weise verschlossen, von oben mit einer Zündschnur verbunden. Da nun dieser Zünder im flüssigen Nitroglyzerin steckt, so dringt bei der Entzündung des Pulvers das heiße Gas desselben im Nitroglyzerin ein und verteilt sich darin in feine Ströme, welche eine Lokaldetonation bewirken, die dann durch den gewaltigen Druck von selbst fortgesetzt wird;

3. durch einen starken elektrischen Funken, dessen Feuer nicht an der Oberfläche des Nitroglyzerins, sondern in die Masse hineindringt;

4. mittels eines Zündhütchens;

5. durch langsame Erwärmung eines geringen Teiles des Nitroglyzerins oder anderer explosiver Stoffe, welche dann die Wirkung durch den Druck fortpflanzen. Die Erwärmung erfolgt durch eine chemische Reaktion, welche die Erwärmung des ersten Teiles Nitroglyzerin bis auf 180° C steigern kann und so langsam geschehen muß, daß sich der Arbeiter vor der Explosion entfernen kann; die Erwärmung geschieht leicht durch Einschließen von einem feinen, mit Nitroglyzerin oder anderem heftig detonierenden Körper gefüllten Röhrchen, in einem größeren, z. B. mit Raketensatz oder auch mit ungelöschtem Kalk und Wasser gefüllten Rohr, welches dann in einem berechneten Zeitraum die gewünschte Erwärmung bewirkt;

6. durch eine einfache Zündschnur. Dieses gelingt, wenn das Nitroglyzerin von allen Seiten eingeschlossen ist und das vergaste Nitroglyzerin nicht entweichen kann, bevor der angesammelte Druck die Totalerwärmung bis auf 180°, oder, was dasselbe ist, die Totalexplosion hervorbringt. Diese letzte Methode ist selten anzuwenden, da bei Benutzung des Nitroglyzerins ein fester Besatz nie den Effekt steigert, leicht aber Gefahr bringen könnte.

Ich gebrauche vorzugsweise die oben im zweiten Punkte erwähnten Pulverzünder.

Da a) das Nitroglyzerin und die analogen Körper (welche in offenem Raume ohne Explosion entzündbar sind) zwar vor Jahren entdeckt, aber in der Praxis keine Anwendung gefunden haben, weil ihre Totalexplosion nicht hervorzubringen war; b) diese Körper nicht nur in offenem, sondern beinahe ganz verschlossenem Raume entzündet werden können, ohne zu explodieren; c) ein Hammerschlag nur eine Lokalexplosion hervorbringt und selbst an dem Hammer nach der Detonation noch flüssiges Nitroglyzerin haftet; d) sogar die Erhitzung der Totalmasse des Nitroglyzerins in einem offenen Geschirr keine Totalexplosion bewirkt; e) ich diese Stoffe aus dem Gebiete der Wissenschaft für die Industrie nutzbar gemacht habe und f) flüssige explosive Körper — wie das Nitroglyzerin — noch nicht zu technischen Zwecken gebraucht worden sind, so beanspruche ich als meine Erfindung:

1. die schnelle Erwärmung des Nitroglyzerins und analoger Körper durch Mischen derselben mit Schießpulver, Pyroxylin oder gleichen Stoffen — und den Gebrauch dieses Pulvers sowohl als Schieß- und Sprengpulver; 2. die plötzliche Erhitzung zum Explosionsgrade des Nitroglyzerins und analoger Körper, oder Mischungen von diesen, durch den heftigen Druck einer lokalen Explosion, welche dann, in der Richtung des Widerstandes wirkend, eine Totalexplosion herbeiführt; 3. den ausschließlichen Gebrauch des Nitroglyzerins und analoger Stoffe, oder Mischungen davon, als Sprengsatz, insoweit dieser Gebrauch sich auf die oben erwähnten Erfindungen zurückführen läßt.

Zum Schluß werden noch Erfindungsansprüche auf Verbesserungen bei Bereitung des Nitroglyzerins und der dazu erforderlichen Säuren geltend gemacht, welche auf Seite 7 angeführt werden.

Der erste Teil des bayerischen Patentes entspricht dem in Schweden und England im Jahre 1863 genommenen, während der weitere Teil durch das schwedische Patent vom 15. Juli 1864, bzw. das englische Patent 1813 vom 20. Juli 1864 geschützt ist. Praktisch versuchte Nobel eine Reihe verschiedener Anordnungen. Zunächst verwandte er einen mit Schwarzpulver gefüllten Holzzünder (Fig. 2). Das Sprengöl wird direkt in das Bohrloch gegossen, eine Zündschnur von angemessener Länge wird in das engere Loch des Patent-Holzzünders fest hineingepaßt; wenn dieses Loch für die Zündschnur zu eng ist, wird solches durch einen Bohrer entsprechend erweitert. Der Patent-Holzzünder wird, nachdem er mit feinem Pulver lose angefüllt worden und am untern Ende durch den Kork verschlossen ist, mit seiner Zündschnur so weit in das Bohrloch hinuntergelassen, daß er etwa zur Hälfte in dem Öle schwimmt; man fühlt solches leicht an dem erhöhten Widerstande beim Hinunterlassen, wenn der Zünder auf das Öl stößt. Wenn der Zünder hinuntergelassen ist, wird die Zündschnur festgehalten, während das Bohrloch mit losem Sand ausgefüllt wird (Fig. 3).

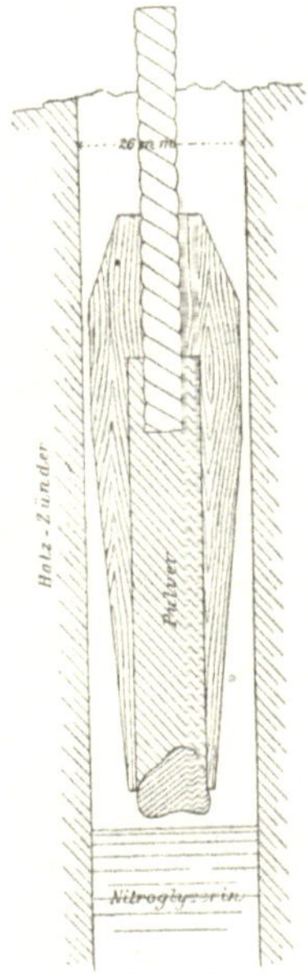

Fig. 2.

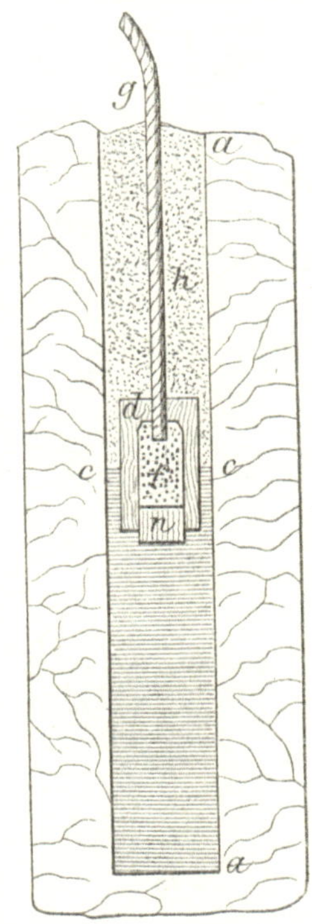

Fig. 3. *a* Bohrloch, *c* Niveau des Sprengöls im Bohrloch, *d* Holzzünder, *f* Pulverkammer, *g* Zündschnur, *h* Besatz, *n* Kork.

Bei horizontalen und schwebenden Bohrlöchern kann man das Nitroglyzerin nicht direkt in das Bohrloch gießen, sondern muß mit Sprengöl gefüllte Patronen anwenden. Der zur Patrone bestimmte Patent-Holzzünder wurde mit feinem Pulver gefüllt, mit angemessen langer Zündschnur versehen und dann in die Patrone sehr fest so weit hineingedrängt, daß das Ende des

Zünders sicher im Öle steckt. Die Patrone wird in das Bohrloch hineingeschoben und Besatz aus losem Sande oder Ton gemacht (Fig. 4).

Nobel konstruierte auch Papp-Patronen mit doppeltem Boden, worin sich unten eine Schicht Pulver befand, welches durch eine Zündschnur zur Explosion gebracht wurde; auf das Pulver kam zunächst über einem durchbohrten Boden noch eine Kreideschicht, oberhalb derselben das Nitroglyzerin (Fig. 5). Auch wandte Nobel ein System von zwei Patronen, bzw. Hülsen an; unten im Bohrloch eine mit Sprengöl gefüllte und mit einem Kork verschlossene Hülse, darüber eine mit Schwarzpulver, in welches eine durch eine Korkscheibe oben festgehaltene Zündschnur eingeführt wurde (Fig. 6).

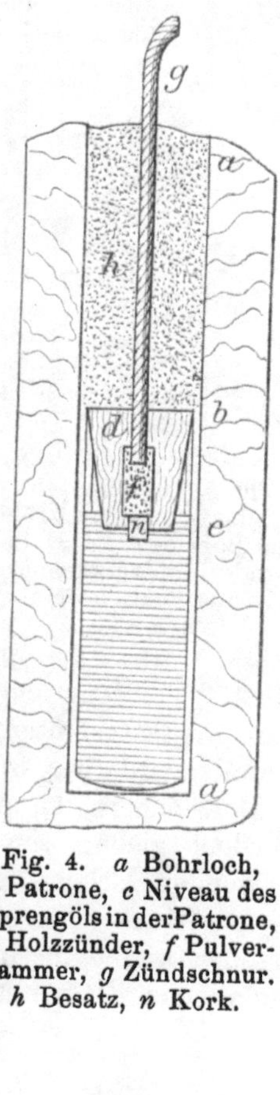

Fig. 4. *a* Bohrloch, *b* Patrone, *c* Niveau des Sprengöls in der Patrone, *d* Holzzünder, *f* Pulverkammer, *g* Zündschnur. *h* Besatz, *n* Kork.

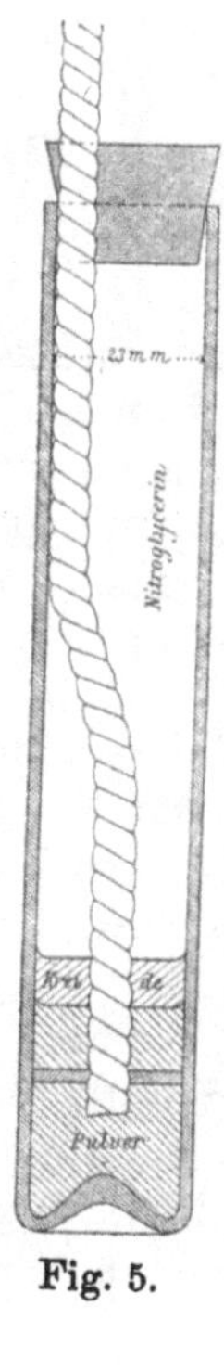

Fig. 5.

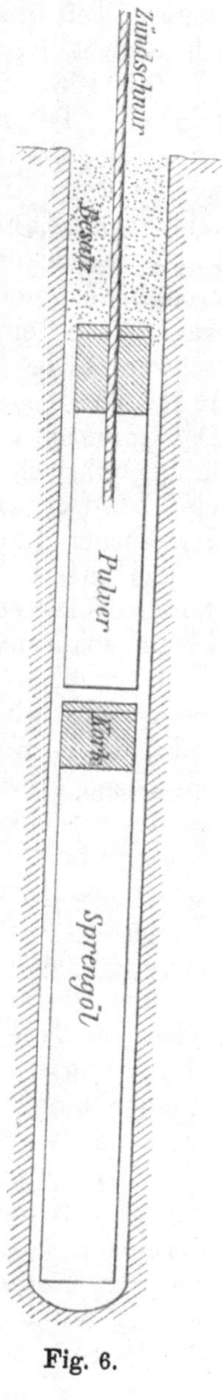

Fig. 6.

Nobel verfuhr ferner so, daß er in eine Hülse unten das Sprengöl und darüber, durch einen Kork getrennt, das Schwarzpulver brachte.

Eine weitere Anordnung ist die, wonach Pulver sich in einer inneren Glasröhre, das Sprengöl sich in einer äußeren Patrone befindet, wie solches in Fig. 7 veranschaulicht ist. Das durch eine Zündschnur zur Explosion gebrachte Schwarzpulver zerschlägt zunächst das innere (Glas-)Rohr und erteilt dann dem äußeren Nitroglyzerin den nötigen Initialimpuls.

Statt Glasröhren verwandte Nobel auch Metallbehälter aus Weißblech, welche in Form einer Düte gerollt und mit Schwarzpulver gefüllt waren, sog. „Nobels Zünder“.

Endlich benutzte Nobel die Knallquecksilber-Zündhütchen, d. s. kleine kupferne Zylinderchen, welche mit dem (im Jahre 1800 von Howard erfundenen) brisantesten Explosivstoff Knallquecksilber gefüllt waren; solche Zündhütchen waren seit 1815 für Handfeuerwaffen eingeführt (durch den englischen Büchsenmacher Josef Egg).

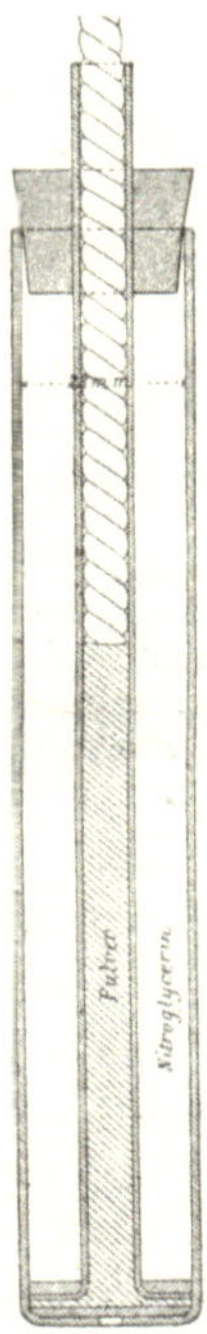

Fig. 7.

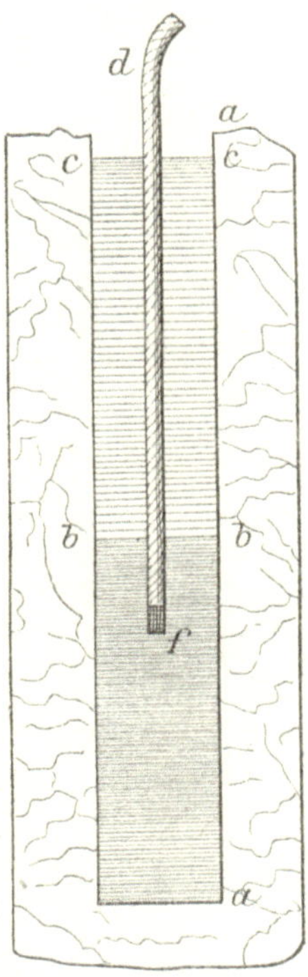

Fig. 8. *a a* Bohrloch, *b* Niveau des Nitroglyzerins, *c* Niveau des Wassers, *d* Zündschnur, *f* Zündhütchen.

Bereits in seinen Patenten vom Jahre 1864 erwähnt Nobel diese Zündhütchen; in einer im Oktober 1865 im Bayr. Kunst- und Gewerbeblatt S. 577 erschienenen Publikation wird als einfachstes Verfahren bei vertikalen und nach unten gerichteten Bohrlöchern folgendes angegeben:

Das Sprengöl wird in das Bohrloch hineingegossen; anstatt Besatz wird der über dem Öl befindliche Raum des Bohrloches mit Wasser angefüllt. An einer Zündschnur von angemessener Länge wird, nachdem dieselbe gerade abgeschnitten ist, ein Patentzündhütchen fest angepaßt; die Zündschnur wird in das Bohrloch so weit heruntergelassen, daß das Patentzündhütchen sicher im Öle steckt, jedoch nicht zu tief, damit der Druck mehr nach unten wirke (Fig. 8). Dazu wird bemerkt: Diese Methode ist noch zu wenig benutzt worden, als daß dieselbe mit Bestimmtheit, trotz ihrer Einfachheit, der zweiten gegenüber in allen Fällen empfohlen werden könnte.

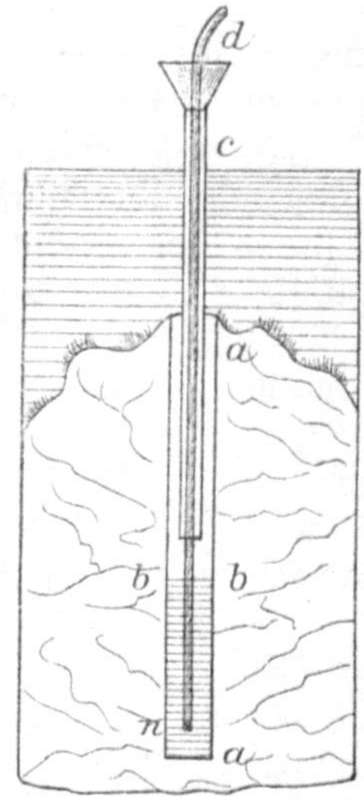

Fig. 10. *a* Bohrloch, *b* Niveau des Sprengöls, *c* Rohr mit Trichter, *d* Zündschnur, *n* Patentzündhütchen.

Auch konnte man das Sprengöl in das Bohrloch gießen; die Zündschnur, an deren unterem Ende ein Patentzündhütchen sich befand, wurde durch einen Kork von dem Durchmesser des Bohrlochs gesteckt und so weit in das letztere hineingeschoben, bis der Kork das Sprengöl berührte (Fig. 9).

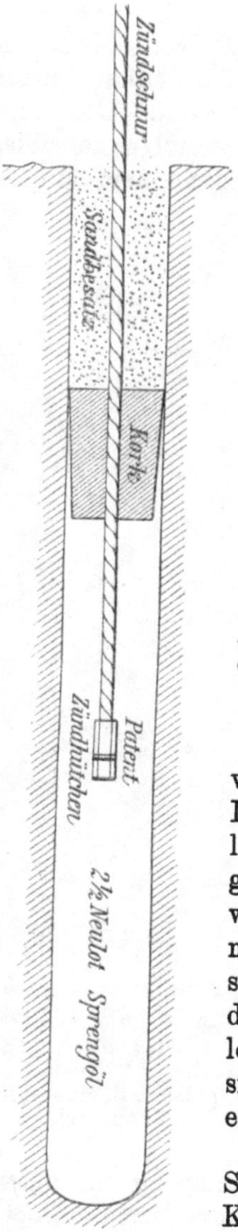

Fig. 9.

Auch bei Unterwasser-Sprengungen verwandte Nobel seine Patentzünder (Fig. 10). Das Blechrohr *c* wird in das Unterwasserbohrloch bis auf den Boden desselben hineingesteckt; durch den Trichter des Rohres, welcher über die Wasserfläche hervorragen muß, wird das Öl hineingegossen; die Zündschnur mit dem Patentzündhütchen wird durch das Blechrohr bis auf die Sohle des Bohrloches hineingeführt und das Blechrohr vorsichtig herausgezogen, womit die Ladung beendet ist.

Nobels Patentzünder enthielten Schwarzpulver, Schwarzpulver und Knallquecksilber, später Knallquecksilber allein. Besonders als Nobel dann im Jahre 1867 statt des reinen Nitroglyzerins Mischungen desselben mit Kieselgur verwandte (das erste Dynamit), hat er zur Erregung der Explosion den stärksten Stoff, das Knallquecksilber, für sich benutzt und unter Weglassung des Schwarzpulvers die noch heute gebräuchlichen Knallqueck-silber-Sprengkapseln zur Herbeiführung der Detonation des Nitroglyzerins angewandt; diese Sprengkapseln enthielten natürlich bedeutend mehr Knallquecksilber als die nur zur Zündung von Treibmitteln bestimmten Gewehrzündhütchen.

Nobel hat also zuerst gezeigt, daß man mit solchem Knallsatz nicht nur zünden, sondern auch den durch einfache Zündung nicht zur Detonation gelangenden Körper jederzeit leicht und sicher zur Explosion bringen kann; er machte somit die höchst interessante und für die Sprengtechnik folgenreiche Entdeckung, daß die Explosion einer verhältnismäßig geringen Menge eines sehr brisanten Knallpräparates genüge, um beliebige Mengen Sprengöl, auch wenn diese sich in ganz leichtem Einschlusse befinden oder selbst zum Teil freiliegend sind, mit voller Sicherheit zur Detonation zu bringen, da die bei der Explosion des Knallquecksilbers entstehenden Explosionswellen synchronisch auf das Sprengöl wirken und so dessen Detonation hervorrufen.[1] Damit war eine höchst einfache Methode erfunden, um Nitroglyzerinladungen zur Explosion zu bringen. Man nennt die Methode, die Detonation von Sprengmitteln durch die Explosion kleiner Mengen starker Knallpräparate zu bewirken: „Zündung durch Detonation“ und die einleitende Explosion selbst: „Initialexplosion“. Nobel hatte, wie schon früher erwähnt, für die Anwendung der Initialexplosion durch Knallpräparate in der Sprengtechnik Metallbehälter aus Weißblech, sogen. Nobels Zünder, später kleine kupferne Hütchen oder Kapseln konstruiert; in seinem englischen Patent 1345 vom 7. Mai 1867[2] sind die Knallquecksilber-Sprengkapseln zum ersten Mal von Nobel beschrieben.

Will[3] sagt in seinem Vortrag über die Entwicklung der Sprengtechnik folgendes: Es ist diese Erkenntnis, daß mit Hilfe von Knallquecksilber als Initialladung die Sprengkraft von Nitroglyzerin wie von Schießwolle und, setzen wir hinzu, einer großen Reihe anderer detonationsfähiger Körper beliebig ausgelöst werden kann, mehrfach als der größte Fortschritt auf dem Gebiete der Sprengtechnik seit Erfindung des Schwarzpulvers bezeichnet worden; sie erst ermöglichte die allgemeine Anwendung der genannten Verbindungen für Sprengzwecke; durch sie erst ist es möglich gewesen,

---

[1] Siehe Contributions to the History of Explosive Agents, by F. A. Abel, Proceedings of the Royal Society 1869, p. 489—516.

[2] Das schwedische Patent ist vom 19. September 1867.

[3] Berl. Ber. 1904, S. 276.

für eine große Zahl anderer wichtiger Sprengstoffe die Sprengstoffnatur zu erkennen und auszuwerten.[1]

Wir sind mit der ausführlichen Beschreibung der Knallquecksilber-Sprengkapseln etwas vorausgeeilt und kehren nun zum Jahre 1864 zurück, zu welcher Zeit Nobel noch seine Pulverzünder benutzte, um sein Sprengöl zur Detonation zu bringen.

Im Hamburger Gewerbeblatt von 1864 (Seite 164) erschien eine Arbeit über Nitroglyzerin, worin die Vorzüge des neuen Sprengmittels beschrieben werden; hierin heißt es:

Die Explosion des Nitroglyzerins bei Sprengungen wird durch einen kleinen Pulverzünder bewerkstelligt, auf dessen Konstruktion und Anbringung das Geheimnis des Erfinders beruht. — Die Kraft, welche durch die Explosion des Sprengöls hervorgebracht wird, ist fünf- bis zehnmal größer als die Kraft des explodierenden Pulvers. Versuche wurden ausgeführt in den Feldspatgruben auf Stora-Roesholmen, in den Granitbrüchen auf Hufwudstadt und Tysbagarebergen (bei Stockholm), sowie an anderen Stellen Schwedens. Auf Stora-Roesholmen wurde mit weniger als $^1/_5$ der Gesamtbohrlänge der Sprenglöcher (also $^1/_5$ der Kosten an Arbeitslohn und Materialverbrauch für die Bohrung) derselbe Effekt erzielt als bei Pulver; manchmal wurde sogar nicht nur das Verhältnis 1 : 5, sondern 1 : 15 erreicht.

Der Artikel schließt mit den Worten:

Der Erfinder, Herr Ingenieur Nobel, hat bereits Patent von der königlich schwedischen Regierung erhalten und sich nach England gewendet, wo ihm bereits Aussicht auf Erlangung des Patentes für dort gegeben wurde. Es wäre schade, wenn nicht auch in Deutschland sich Kapitalisten finden würden, welche diese wichtige Erfindung in die Hand nehmen und für Deutschland ausbeuten.

Durch die erzielten Verbesserungen ermutigt und von der Wichtigkeit des Nitroglyzerins überzeugt, fühlten sich Emmanuel und Alfred Nobel schon nahe dem Ziele, als am 3. September 1864 die kleine Fabrik in Heleneborg durch eine Explosion vollständig zerstört wurde; hierbei fanden Alfreds jüngster Bruder, Oskar Emil, sowie der Chemiker Carl Erik Hertzmann ihren Tod. Emmanuel Nobel wurde durch diese entsetzliche Katastrophe so tief ergriffen, daß er einen Schlaganfall erlitt, von dem er sich bis zu seinem Tode, im Jahre 1872, nicht mehr zu erholen vermochte. — Gegenüber der Verzweiflung und dem Schrecken, welche nach dem Unglück nicht nur in der Nobelschen Familie

[1] Durch das engl. Patent 3115 vom 10. Oktober 1868 (F. A. Abel und E. O. Brown) wurden diese Sprengkapseln dann auch für Schießbaumwolle eingeführt.

herrschten, sondern auch in der ganzen Umgebung sich verbreiteten und die schwedische Regierung veranlaßten, die Fabrikation des Nitroglyzerins in der Nähe von Wohnorten zu verbieten, blieb Alfred Nobel allein unentmutigt; voll Zuversicht, die in dem unheimlichen Körper schlummernden Kräfte doch in gefahrloser Weise auslösen zu können, sann er mit unerschütterlicher Willenskraft und zäher Ausdauer, wie dem Stoff, in den er so große Hoffnungen setzte, Eingang in die Technik zu verschaffen sei; denn trotz allen Mißgeschicks hielt er an dem Gedanken fest, daß die großen, dem Nitroglyzerin innewohnenden Vorzüge dem Körper die Vorherrschaft auf dem Sprengstoffgebiet würden sichern müssen. Alfred Nobel mietete, um allen Unannehmlichkeiten auf dem Lande zu entgehen, ein Schiff, verankerte es im Mälarsee und setzte dort seine Versuche fort. Bald gelang es ihm, auch finanzielle Unterstützung zu finden, und zwar in Hamburg; alsdann errichtete er — zu Anfang des Jahres 1865 — eine Fabrik in Krümmel an der Elbe, welche gegenwärtig zur größten Explosivstoff-Fabrik auf dem Kontinent herangewachsen ist; gleichzeitig gründete er die Firma Alfred Nobel & Cie. in Hamburg, die Vorgängerin der heutigen „Dynamit-Aktiengesellschaft vormals Alfred Nobel & Cie.“ in Hamburg. Ungefähr um dieselbe Zeit wurde eine Fabrik in Wintervicken bei Stockholm errichtet, denn man ging ernstlich dazu über, Nitroglyzerin als Sprengstoff in Schweden und in Deutschland zu benutzen und es auch nach dem Ausland zu exportieren. Im Jahre 1865 verbrauchte man im Bergwerk Bersbo in Schweden schon 314 Pfund Nitroglyzerin; auch in den Bergwerken Persberg, Sjösa und Fangö, sowie in den Hüttenwerken Åtvidaberg, Tunaberg und Falun (hier zum Sprengen großer Eisenmassen) wandte man den neuen Sprengstoff im Jahre 1865 an. In Deutschland wurden die ersten Probesprengungen am 11./12. April 1865 in Meckendorf und bei Eisleben ausgeführt; im gleichen Jahre wurden auf einer Reihe westfälischer Kohlenzechen, insbesondere auf „Constantin der Große“ Versuche mit flüssigem Sprengöl mit befriedigendem Erfolge vorgenommen. Im Oktober 1865 erschien ein größerer Aufsatz im Bayr. Kunst- und Gewerbeblatt (S. 577), dessen wesentlicher Inhalt dann als Prospekt von der Firma Alfred Nobel & Cie. in Hamburg im Februar 1866 herausgegeben wurde, über „Nobels Patentsprengöl“ (Nitroglyzerin) und dessen Verwendung zu Gesteinssprengungen in Gruben und über Tage, zu Metall- und Holzsprengungen, sowie zum Auflockern von Erdarten usw. usw.; hierin wird angegeben, daß die Hauptvorzüge des Sprengöls auf folgendem beruhen:

1. Auf einer großen Arbeitsersparnis beim Bohren der Sprenglöcher.

Das hohe spezifische Gewicht, die vollständige Verbrennung und die außerordentliche Schnelligkeit der Explosion des Patentsprengöles macht dasselbe zum kräftigsten der bisher bekannten Sprengmittel. Die Arbeitskosten für das Bohren sind bei allen Sprengarbeiten vielfach teurer als das Pulver; folglich ist die Ersparnis an Arbeitslohn wichtiger als die Kostenersparnis für das Pulver. Ein Pfund Sprengöl kostet ungefähr so viel wie acht Pfund Sprengpulver, leistet aber wenigstens so viel als zehn Pfund Pulver; den Konsumenten verbleibt demnach die ganze bedeutende Arbeitsersparnis. Die bisherigen Erfahrungen bei den Sprengungen in den Gruben von Clausthal im Harz u. a. haben ergeben, daß ein Arbeiter mit Sprengöl bedeutend mehr leistet, als zwei Arbeiter, welche mit Pulver sprengen, denn es legen die einmännischen Bohrlöcher mit Sprengöl geladen viel mehr als die zweimännischen Bohrlöcher mit Pulver.

2. Auf der Möglichkeit, Sprengarbeiten in kürzerer Zeit zu bewerkstelligen.

Dieser Vorteil ist in den meisten Fällen von äußerster Wichtigkeit, namentlich bei Schachtbauten, Eisenbahnbauten usw. usw. Jede Sprengarbeit läßt sich mit Patentsprengöl mindestens noch einmal so rasch betreiben als mit Sprengpulver und es können somit Arbeitskräfte und Administrationskosten verringert oder die Produktion gesteigert werden. — Herr Eric Unge, welcher für das schwedische Gouvernement den Tunnelbau unter Stockholm leitet, erwähnt in seinem Attest vom 19. Januar 1866, daß seit der Anwendung von Sprengöl die Sprengarbeit 87 % schneller gefördert wird als früher, wo mit Pulver gearbeitet wurde.

3. Auf der Eigenschaft des Patentsprengöls, bei der Explosion keinen Rückstand zu hinterlassen.

Die vollständige Verbrennung ohne Rückstand ist hauptsächlich in Steinsalzbergwerken von großer Wichtigkeit, da nicht, wie beim Pulver, ein großer Teil der gesprengten Masse als Abraumsalz aussortiert zu werden braucht. Es ist bei allen Gesteinsarten von Wichtigkeit, daß das Gestein nicht geschwärzt wird, um die Erze von der Gangart leichter unterscheiden zu können.

4. Auf der großen Explosionsschnelligkeit.

Die Explosionsschnelligkeit des Patentsprengöls ist so bedeutend, daß der Effekt desselben durch Risse im Gestein nicht vermindert wird, was sich auch schon daraus ergibt, daß mittels losen Sandes, ja selbst durch Wasser genügender Besatz für Sprengöl gebildet wird. Da das Pulver viel langsamer verbrennt, so ist es erklärlich, auch praktisch nachgewiesen, daß ein Bohrloch mit Sprengöl in rissigem Gestein mehr leistet als 20 bis 30 Bohrlöcher gleicher Dimension, mit Pulver geladen. Aus derselben Ursache ist das Patentsprengöl auch zum Sprengen von lockerem Kalkstein, Steingerölle, Kreide, Tonerde, Holz usw. usw. zu verwenden, wo das Pulver beinahe ohne Wirkung ist.

5. Auf der geringeren Gefahr beim Transport und bei der Aufbewahrung.

Die große Gefahr beim gewöhnlichen Pulver, durch einen einzigen Funken zu explodieren, existiert beim Sprengöl nicht, dagegen muß es sorgfältig gegen Erhitzung oder starken Stoß im geschlossenen Raume geschützt werden.

6. Auf dem Umstand, die Sprenglöcher ohne festen Besatz laden zu können.

Da das Besetzen der Bohrlöcher nur mit losem Sande oder Wasser geschieht, so ist einesteils jede Gefahr beim Laden unmöglich, andernteils ist es zeitsparender und billiger.

7. Auf der Ersparnis an Schärfen und Verstählen der Bohrer.

In demselben Verhältnis, wie beim Sprengöl weniger Bohrlöcher gebraucht werden als beim Pulver, in demselben Verhältnis werden auch die Kosten für das Schärfen und Verstählen der Bohrer verringert; bei Sprengarbeiten in besonders zähem Gestein ist dies ein Umstand von hervorragender Wichtigkeit.

8. Auf der Ersparnis an Zündschnur.

Der Verbrauch von Zündschnüren (Sicherheitszündern) verringert sich in demselben Verhältnis, als weniger Bohrlöcher mit Sprengöl gegen Bohrlöcher mit Pulver zu laden sind.

9. Auf der Erleichterung des Ladens bei wassersüchtigen Bohrlöchern.

Da das Sprengöl in Wasser unlöslich ist und zufolge seiner größeren spezifischen Schwere sich rasch zu Boden setzt, so können wassersüchtige Bohrlöcher ohne Ausletten oder Patronen einfach durch Hineingießen des Sprengöls in das Bohrloch geladen werden, wogegen bei Anwendung von Pulver das Ausletten schwierig und kostspielig ist.

10. Auf dem einfachen Verfahren, mit demselben Unterwassersprengungen auszuführen.

Die Eigenschaften, welche das Patentsprengöl dem Pulver gegenüber bei wassersüchtigen Bohrlöchern vorteilhaft auszeichnen, treffen noch mehr bei Unterwassersprengungen zu; das Verfahren hierbei ist höchst einfach und von enormer Wirkung.

11. Auf der Möglichkeit, Metallstücke usw. zu zersprengen.

Es lassen sich mit dem Sprengöl Metallstücke aller Art, als Stahlblöcke, Eisenhaue, alte Kanonen usw. in jeder Größe mit verhältnismäßig kleinen Bohrlöchern und geringem Kostenaufwande zerteilen, wo mittels Pulver solches unausführbar ist.

In dem Prospekte werden folgende Vorsichtsmaßregeln bei Benutzung des Nobelschen Patentsprengöles angegeben:

a) bei Aufbewahrung und Transport. Da das Sprengöl durch Erhitzung oder durch gewaltsamen Stoß im geschlossenen Raume explodieren kann, muß es beim Transport und bei der Aufbewahrung vor diesen Gefahren geschützt werden; es darf daher nur in durchaus feuerfesten Räumen, in welchen keine feuergefährlichen Sachen lagern, aufbewahrt werden. In Ermangelung solcher Räume stelle man einfach die Blechflaschen, in den Originalkisten verpackt, in Erdgruben.

b) bei der Verwendung. Das Sprengöl muß nur in den mit Warnungszetteln versehenen Originalflaschen gehalten werden, um Vergiftungen zu vermeiden, welche sonst leicht durch Verwechslung der Flaschen entstehen könnten. Mit den Händen und Lippen darf es nicht in Berührung kommen. Wenn trotzdem die Hände mit Sprengöl beschmiert sind, so entferne man solches durch Abreiben mit trockner Erde, Löschpapier usw. und wasche sich nachher. Das Laden, überhaupt die Verwendung des Sprengöls, ist, solange die Arbeiter mit den Eigenschaften desselben nicht vertraut sind, nur einigen zuverlässigen Leuten, die mit der Behandlungsweise bekannt gemacht worden sind, anzuvertrauen. Es ist das Experimentieren mit dem Sprengöl streng zu untersagen, selbst das Schlagen mit einem Hammer auf einen einzigen Tropfen flüssiges oder gefrorenes Sprengöl gegen einen harten Gegenstand kann gefährlich werden, da der Hammer zerschmettert und die Stücke davon heftig umhergeschleudert werden können. — Es ist streng darauf zu halten, daß beim Laden der Besatz weder durch Schlag noch Stoß angebracht werde; der feste Besatz dient überdem zu nichts. Das gefrorene Sprengöl darf nur durch Einsetzen der Blechflaschen in ein Gefäß mit heißem Wasser aufgetaut werden; im Trichter gefrorenes Sprengöl ist ebenfalls nur durch heißes Wasser aufzutauen; die vielfach übliche Erwärmung des Wassers mittels glühenden Eisens ist entschieden zu verwerfen, da solches möglicherweise in das Wasser ausgelaufenes Sprengöl erhitzen und zur Explosion bringen kann.

Es folgen nun in der Broschüre: Instruktionen über Anwendung des Sprengöls.

Als Utensilien werden hier genannt: 1. Ein gradiertes Maß, ein Pfund Sprengöl fassend, welches für jeden Grad $^1/_{30}$ Pfund Sprengöl angibt. 2. Ein oben trichterförmiges Blechrohr, zur Füllung der Bohrlöcher bei Unterwassersprengungen. 3. Patentzündhütchen für Unterwassersprengungen. 4. Zündschnüre. 5. Papierpatronen.

Das Verfahren beim Laden wird in nachstehender Weise beschrieben:

1. Mit Patronen. Jede Patrone ist in zwei Räume geteilt; der größere ist für Sprengöl, der kleinere für Pulver bestimmt. Nachdem das Sprengöl eingegossen ist (wird kleinere Ladung gewünscht, so schneide man die Patrone um so viel ab), wird der Raum für das Öl durch einen Kork verschlossen. Der kleinere Raum dagegen wird mit Pulver angefüllt, und nachdem die darin hineingesteckte Zündschnur mittels des Bindfadens festgebunden ist, auch dieser kleine Raum durch einen Papierpfropfen, Heede oder dergl. verschlossen. Die so geladene

Patrone wird ins Bohrloch eingeführt und Besatz aus losem Sand oder Letten gegeben. Gut gekorkte Patronen können tagelang geladen aufbewahrt werden. — 2. Ohne Patronen. Will man bei sehr tiefen Bohrlöchern Patronen vermeiden, so ist das Verfahren folgendes: Das Sprengöl wird durch den Trichter ins Bohrloch hineingegossen, sodann ein Papierpfropfen nicht ganz bis aufs Öl hineingeschoben, die Zündschnur bis auf den Papierpfropfen eingeführt, eine Handvoll Pulver aufgeschüttet und Besatz aus losem Sand oder Letten gemacht. — 3. Mit Patentzündhütchen bei Unterwassersprengungen. Bei Unterwassersprengungen gießt man das Sprengöl durch ein langes, trichterförmiges Blechrohr ins Bohrloch, wo es zu Boden sinkt. — Die Guttaperchazündschnur, mit einem unten dicht angepaßten Patentzündhütchen an ein kleines Bleigewicht befestigt, wird durch den Trichter bis auf die Sohle des Bohrloches hineingeführt und das Blechrohr vorsichtig herausgezogen. Wo bei Unterwassersprengungen Patronen vorgezogen werden, wozu auch die Papierpatronen verwendbar sind, muß der Schuß durch Patentzündhütchen entzündet werden.

Schließlich werden noch folgende allgemeine Regeln angegeben:

Es sind nur Bohrlöcher von geringem Durchmesser anzuwenden; bei Sprengungen zu Tage genügen Bohrlöcher von $^3/_4$ bis 1″ Durchmesser; in gedrängten Räumen empfehlen sich solche von so kleinem Durchmesser, als herzustellen möglich ist; mit schwedischen Bessemer Stahlbohrern können Bohrlöcher von $^1/_2$″ geschlagen werden. Beim Laden sind folgende Vorsichtsmaßregeln anzuwenden: 1. Das Sprengöl darf durchaus nicht mit den Händen oder Lippen berührt werden, da es giftig ist. Die Explosionsgase sind durchaus unschädlich, Kopfschmerzen können nur durch Berührung mit dem Öl entstehen. 2. Fester Besatz ist durchaus zu vermeiden, da der Stoß auf das im Bohrloch eingeschlossene Öl das Losgehen des Schusses verursachen kann. 3. Wenn zufolge schlechter Zündschnüre ein Schuß versagt, so kratze man vorsichtig etwa die Hälfte des Besatzes heraus und in dem leeren Teile des Bohrloches bringe man eine neue kleine Sprengölladung an, bei deren Entzündung beide Ladungen explodieren. 4. Es ist schon vorgekommen, daß durch fehlerhaftes Laden der Besatz herausgeworfen, der Schuß aber nicht losgegangen, sondern das Öl durch die Zündschnur angezündet worden ist. In solchen Fällen gebietet es die Vorsicht, daß man in Entfernung bleibe, solange sich Rauch zeigt.

Am 29. März 1866[1] führte Alfred Nobel auf der Rennkoppel bei Horn in Hamburg in Gegenwart von mehr als 120 Personen folgende Versuche mit Sprengöl aus:

I. Zum Nachweis der Ungefährlichkeit beim Transport und bei der Aufbewahrung.

---

[1] Siehe Hamburger Gewerbeblatt 1866, Nr. 13 u. 14. — Bayr. Kunst- u. Gewerbeblatt 1866, S. 289.

a) Ungefährlichkeit durch Schlag und Friktion. 1. Auf einem kleinen Amboß wurden einige Tropfen Sprengöl ausgebreitet. Bei sehr starken Schlägen mit einem Hammer darauf explodierte nur das zwischen Hammer und Amboß befindliche Sprengöl mit gewaltigem Knall, ohne jedoch die Explosion auf das unmittelbar daranfließende Öl fortzupflanzen. 2. Auf ein Brett wurde Sprengöl ausgegossen. Trotz der kräftigsten Schläge mit einem Hammer darauf, trotz des Reibens mit einem Stück Holz und den Stiefelsohlen war das Sprengöl nicht zum Explodieren zu bringen.

Aus diesen Versuchen ist nachgewiesen, wie das Sprengöl wohl schwerlich unter irgendwelchen Verhältnissen beim Transport durch Schlag oder Friktion zum Explodieren gebracht werden könne, sondern daß eine Explosion — wie von Herrn Nobel angegeben — nur dann stattfinden kann, wenn das Sprengöl in einem vollständig und fest eingeschlossenem Raum sich befindet, in welchem die Luft stark zusammengepreßt, somit ein Ausweichen unmöglich ist. Um allen Eventualitäten in dieser Beziehung vorzubeugen, werden die Sprengölflaschen von Eisenblech in starke, mit eisernen Reifen beschlagene Kisten verpackt und der Zwischenraum von 1 Zoll mit dem sehr elastischen Kieselgur ausgefüllt; dabei ist die Vorsicht zu beachten, daß die Flaschen nur zu $^4/_5$ des Inhalts gefüllt werden. Wie in Schweden ausgeführte Versuche dargetan haben, woselbst solche Kisten von bedeutender Höhe auf Felsen herabgestürzt sind, ist das darin befindliche Sprengöl nicht explodiert.

b) Ungefährlichkeit durch Feuer. 1. Ein Quantum Sprengöl wurde in eine Porzellanschale gegossen. Mit brennendem Schwefelholz und mit Papierfidibus wurde das Öl, welches sich an den zündenden Körper anheftete, wohl zur Entzündung gebracht, ohne zu explodieren; das Feuer aber erlosch, sobald der zündende Körper entfernt wurde. 2. Auf ein Brett wurde Sprengöl, auf ein anderes Brennspiritus ausgegossen. Während letzterer durch ein Schwefelhölzchen sich sofort entzündete und, ohne gelöscht werden zu können, bis auf den letzten Tropfen mit gewaltiger Glut verbrannte, erlosch das Sprengöl sofort, als der brennende Fidibus fortgenommen wurde. 3. In einen offenen Glaszylinder war ca. $^1/_2$ Pfund Sprengöl gegossen. Der Zylinder war in die Erde gesteckt und es wurde das Sprengöl durch eine Guttapercha-Pulverzündschnur in Brand gesteckt und darin gelassen; da der Guttaperchazünder mit heller Flamme brannte, so brannte auch das Öl, ohne jedoch zu explodieren. Man konnte deutlich noch auf 30 Fuß Entfernung das Kochen und Wallen des Öles im Glase hören.

Durch diese Versuche hat Herr Nobel deutlich bewiesen, wie wenig Gefahr das Öl darbietet, wenn es einmal in Brand geraten ist. Aus den Packflaschen ausgelaufenes und entzündetes Sprengöl wird nie explodieren; selbst wenn die Flamme in die Blechflaschen hineindringt, wird eine Gefahr nicht entstehen können, denn wo die helle Flamme mit dem Öl in Berührung kommt, kann es wohl brennen, wie wir gesehen haben, aber dadurch nicht auf die Explosionstemperatur (180° C) gebracht werden; bei schon niedrigerer Temperatur, sagen wir 100° C, verbrennt es harmlos. Es können die brennenden Teile des Öles auch die Temperatur der übrigen Teile nicht bis zur Explosionshitze erhöhen, denn lange bevor solche eintritt geht das Öl in Feuer über. Wo aber die Flamme zu dem Öl nicht hinzutreten kann, sondern z. B. von außen ein Gefäß mit Sprengöl umgibt, muß, wenn das Feuer intensiv genug ist, unbedingt die Explosion des Sprengöls erfolgen, denn in solchem Falle steigert sich die Wärme mehr und mehr, bis die ganze Masse 180° Hitze erreicht hat, bei welcher die Explosion stattfindet. Demnach: wo und wann das Sprengöl durch Feuer in Flammen geraten kann, ist es ungefährlich; wo es aber, ohne verbrennen zu können, erhitzt wird, ist Gefahr im Verzuge; aus diesem Grunde muß das Öl in verkorkten Flaschen in feuerfesten Räumen aufbewahrt werden.

II. Zum Nachweis der Kraft im Vergleich zu gewöhnlichem Pulver.

Da Felsen, Eisenstücke usw. nicht zugänglich waren, so mußten die Versuche in Erde und Wasser ausgeführt werden, trotzdem solche nur annähernd den Effekt des Sprengöls nachweisen können.

a) Versuche durch Erdsprengungen. Es wurden Blechhülsen mit Sprengöl gefüllt und dieselben durch einen Holzpfropfen mit einer durchgehenden Zündschnur, an dessen Ende ein Zündhütchen sich befindet, fest verschlossen. Diese Blechhülsen wurden etwa 1 Fuß tief vergraben und die Schüsse entzündet. Die Erde wurde mehrere Fuß im Umfang und in die Tiefe hinein aufgelockert und es flogen die Erdstücke mehr als 100 Fuß hoch in die Luft hinauf. Im Vergleich dazu wurden dann Blechhülsen mit Pulver zur Explosion gebracht, die weit weniger wirkten.

b) Versuche durch Wassersprengungen. Eine starke runde Blechflasche, mit ca. $2^1/_2$ Pfund Sprengöl gefüllt, entlud sich im Wasser mit folgendem Effekt: Eine Wassersäule, ähnlich einer großen Fontaine von 8—10 Fuß im Durchmesser, wurde auf anschlägig 3—400 Fuß Höhe gehoben, von welcher sie stäubend in den Teich zurückfiel; lange Zeit verging, bis das letzte hochgeschleuderte Wasser, als Nebel zerteilt, zurückgefallen war. Rund um den Zentralpunkt der Explosion hob sich das Wasser wellenförmig, um in den gebildeten Krater hineinzustürzen; die Erde erzitterte und der Boden des Teiches schien tief aufgewühlt zu sein.

Zum Schlusse wurden noch Versuche zum Nachweis der Verwendbarkeit des Sprengöls zu Signal- und Notschüssen ausgeführt.

Alfred Nobel verbreitet sich zum Schluß eines Vortrags in der British Association zu Norwich (Dingl. polyt. Journ. 190, S. 124) über die Vorteile des Nitroglyzerins gegenüber dem Schwarzpulver; er hebt hervor, daß bei der Sprengarbeit die Herstellung der Bohrlöcher eine große Rolle spiele; ein Sprengstoff aber, der bei gleichem Volumen eine zehnmal größere

Explosivkraft besitze als gewöhnliches Sprengpulver, gestatte die Anzahl der für eine bestimmte Leistung erforderlichen Bohrlöcher bedeutend zu vermindern, so daß eine Herabsetzung der Generalkosten für die Bohr- und Schießarbeit um wenigstens ein Drittel möglich sei; nach Mitteilungen des Herrn Unge, welcher in Stockholm einen großen Tunnel anlegte, wurden durch die Anwendung von Nitroglyzerin 23 Proz. der Sprengkosten erspart und der Tunnelbau schritt um 87 Proz. rascher vorwärts, als wenn zur Sprengarbeit Pulver gebraucht worden wäre. Ferner ist feuchter Boden bei Schwarzpulver oft störend, bei Sprengöl nicht; letzteres verlangt auch keinen Besatz, der oft zu Unfällen Veranlassung gab. Nobel weist darauf hin, daß Schweden das einzige Land sei, in welchem Nitroglyzerin seit 1865 unausgesetzt angewendet wird; der Absatz der „Stockholmer Nitroglyzerin-Kompagnie“ habe betragen: im Jahre 1865: 32258 Pfund; 1866: 48785 Pfund; 1867: 76575 Pfund und im ersten Halbjahr 1868: 64293 Pfund. — In England sei das Nitroglyzerin, obwohl im allgemeinen ein starkes Vorurteil gegen dasselbe vorherrsche, seit 1866 in den Nord-Waleser Steinbrüchen beständig im Gebrauch und stehe bei den Bergleuten in hoher Gunst.

Nobel verschloß sich selbst nicht der Erkenntnis, daß das flüssige Sprengöl bei der Lagerung und noch mehr beim Transport doch zu Unglücksfällen Veranlassung geben könnte, und sann auf Mittel, diese Gefahr zu beseitigen; zunächst versuchte er es mit der Methylisierung, d. h. der Auflösung in Methylalkohol (Holzgeist); über gebranntem Kalk rektifizierter und wasserfrei gemachter Holzgeist löst Nitroglyzerin vollständig auf; die entstandene Mischung ist unexplosiv, insbesondere gegen Schlag und Stoß ganz unempfindlich und für Transport und Lager als ungefährlich anzusehen, wenn solche in Blechflaschen verschlossen wird, so daß ein Verdunsten des Alkohols und ein Zerbrechen der Gefäße nicht stattfinden kann. — Vor der Verwendung schüttelt man den entsprechenden Teil der Mischung in einem Gefäß, welches oben durch einen Abflußkran verschließbar ist, mit dem 6—8fachen Volumen Wasser leicht durch; das Sprengöl scheidet sich dann rasch ab und wird, nachdem man das Gefäß umgekehrt hat, durch den Hahn abgelassen.

Abgesehen von der Feuergefährlichkeit der Lösung erschien auch die praktische Durchführung des Verfahrens beim Bergbau zu umständlich und Nobel stellte sich die Aufgabe, durch Mischen von Sprengöl mit festen Stoffen einen öligen Teig oder Paste, also eine plastische Masse herzustellen, aus welcher direkt Patronen geformt werden könnten. War er schon zu Anfang von dem Gedanken ausgegangen, Mischungen von Nitroglyzerin mit Schwarzpulver anzuwenden, so lag es jetzt nahe, statt des letzteren andere Aufsaugungsmittel, wie Holzkohlenpulver, Papierbrei und ähnliche Stoffe zu versuchen; ein Zufall führte ihn zu einem besonders geeigneten Mittel. In der Fabrik Krümmel wurde das Sprengöl in Blechkannen verschickt, welche zum Schutze gegen Schlag und Stoß in eine Einhüllung von Infusorienerde (Kieselgur) verpackt wurden, welche Erde nicht weit von Krümmel, bei Unterlüß im Hannöverschen, gewonnen wird. Beim Undichtwerden eines zum Transport bestimmten Nitroglyzeringefäßes sickerte ein Teil des Inhalts in die Gur hinein und Nobel bemerkte bei dieser Gelegenheit das ausgezeichnete Absorptionsvermögen der Kieselerde — einer im trocknen Zustande leicht zerstäubbaren, mehlartigen Substanz — für Nitroglyzerin; er fand, daß man aus 75 % Sprengöl und 25 % Kieselgur eine knetbare Masse von der Konsistenz frischen Glaserkittes darstellen kann, welche einmal gegen Schlag und Stoß bedeutend weniger empfindlich ist als das Nitroglyzerin für sich allein und welche weiterhin ihrer plastischen Beschaffenheit wegen sich vorzüglich zur Formierung von Patronen eignet, die bequem in die Bohrlöcher eingeführt werden können; Nobel nannte die neue Mischung Dynamit und später zum Unterschied von anderen Präparaten Gurdynamit.

Bei einem Vortrage[1] in Norwich äußerte sich der Erfinder hierüber wie folgt:

Der neue Sprengstoff, „Dynamit" genannt, ist nichts anderes als Nitroglyzerin in Verbindung mit sehr poröser Kieselerde, und wenn ich demselben einen neuen Namen gab, so geschah dies wahrlich nicht, um seine Natur zu maskieren; wohl aber treten seine explosiven Eigenschaften in der neuen Form so ganz anders auf, daß eine neue Benennung jedenfalls gerechtfertigt ist. Das Dynamit besteht aus 75 % Nitroglyzerin und 25 % poröser Kieselerde, kann daher nur $^3/_4$ von der Sprengkraft des reinen Nitroglyzerins besitzen; in praktischer Hinsicht gewährt aber die größere Konzentrierung der explosiven Kraft im reinen Nitroglyzerin keinen Vorteil. Letzteres darf nicht direkt in das Bohrloch eingegossen werden, weil es leicht in Spalten und Klüfte des zu sprengenden Gesteins eindringen, in denselben unter den Gezähen des Bergmanns explodieren und somit Unglücksfälle veranlassen kann; es muß demnach in Patronen verpackt angewendet werden, welche bedeutenden Spielraum im Bohrloch übrig lassen. Dynamit dagegen gibt infolge seiner etwas teigigen Beschaffenheit dem schwächsten Drucke leicht nach, so daß er die Seiten des Bohrloches vollständig ausfüllt und durchaus keinen Spielraum läßt; aus diesem Grunde enthält eine Dynamitladung von einer gegebenen Höhe in einem Bohrloche ebenso-

[1] Dinglers polyt. Journ. Bd. 190, S. 124.

viel Nitroglyzerin, als wenn letzteres in seinem reinen flüssigen Zustande angewendet wird.

Die neue Erfindung wurde in England am 7. Mai 1867 (Patent 1345), in Schweden am 19. September 1867, in Bayern am 14. Januar 1868 usw. patentiert; man stellte allenthalben Versuche mit dieser weniger gefährlichen Form des Nitroglyzerins an, mit so günstigem Erfolg, daß kaum ein Jahr später Dynamit schon ein sehr gesuchtes Sprengmittel war, das sich bald Eingang in die Praxis verschaffte; über 1000 Zentner waren schon bis Mitte des Jahres 1868 verkauft, ohne daß alle Bestellungen hätten effektuiert werden können. Es ist verständlich, daß die Detonation des Dynamits schwerer herbeizuführen ist, als die des flüssigen Nitroglyzerins; nur durch die — früher beschriebene — Erfindung der Knallquecksilber-Sprengkapseln war die praktische Anwendung des Dynamits ermöglicht.

Nachdem nunmehr Nobel sich den Weg ziemlich geebnet hatte, ging er mit Energie daran, Gesellschaften und Fabriken zur Ausübung und Verwertung seiner Patente zu gründen. Zu den im Jahre 1865 gebauten Fabriken in Krümmel und in Winterviken war 1866 schon eine Fabrik in Norwegen hinzugekommen; im Jahre 1868 wurde eine Fabrik in Kalifornien errichtet und fast gleichzeitig eine in Zamky bei Prag. Gerade in Österreich-Ungarn [1] sollte Nobel bei den immerhin noch großen Schwierigkeiten, seine Sprengstoffe einzuführen, eine mächtige Förderung durch die Heeresverwaltung erfahren, welche die außergewöhnliche Bedeutung des Dynamits für Sprengungen zu Kriegszwecken auf Grund von eingehenden theoretischen und praktischen Erhebungen und Versuchen zuerst anerkannte und offiziell einführte. Die betreffenden Arbeiten des österreichischen militär-technischen Komitees und der Geniewaffe, bei denen sich im Laufe der Entwicklung die Offiziere Beckerhinn, Hess, Lauer, Schwab, Trauzl und Wuič [2] Namen von europäischem Klang erwarben, waren in jener Zeit von maßgebendstem Einflusse.

Wichtig waren ferner die vergleichenden Versuche, welche der Oberingenieur Pischof beim Bau der Eisenbahnlinie Wien-

---

[1] Siehe Denkschrift der Aktiengesellschaft Dynamit Nobel: Das Dynamit und seine kulturhistorische und technische Bedeutung. 1896.

[2] Vgl. Mitteilungen über Gegenstände der Ingenieur- u. Kriegswissenschaften. Jahrg. 1869. — Mitteilungen über Gegenstände des Artillerie- und Geniewesens 1870 u. folg. — J. Trauzl, Explosive Nitrilverbindungen, insbesondere Dynamit und Schießwolle, deren Eigenschaften und Verwendung in der Sprengtechnik. 2. Aufl. Wien 1870, C. Gerolds Sohn. — Joh. Lauer, Spreng- und Zündversuche mit Dynamit und komprimierter Schießwolle. Wien 1872, Seidel.

Brünn im Syenit des Buchenberger Einschnittes durchführte; hierbei wurde die relative Sprengkraft des Dynamits im Durchschnitt auf das 2·85fache des Pulvers (je nach der Härte des Gesteins zwischen 2·4 bis 3·3 schwankend) ermittelt.[1] — Im Bergbau waren es namentlich die Vergleichsversuche im Rammelsberge bei Goslar, im Reviere von Kladno, in den Eisensteingruben von Zerf, in den Steinkohlengruben am Schneeberge, in den Quecksilbergruben von Neu-Almaden und in den Gruben in Sachsen, Schlesien und bei Saarbrücken, welche die Verwendung des Dynamits förderten. — Erwähnt seien auch die Versuche Abels[2] aus dem Jahre 1869, sowie das ausführliche, auf Veranlassung des Präsidiums des schweizerischen Schulrates von Bolley, Kundt und Pestalozzi abgegebene Gutachten,[3] auf welch letzteres wir noch zurückkommen werden. — Während des Krieges 1870/71 fabrizierten die Ingenieure Champion und Pellet in dem belagerten Paris Nitroglyzerin zu militärischen Zwecken; auch auf deutscher Seite bediente man sich des neuen Sprengmittels.[4]

Verschiedene Chemiker suchten die Fabrikation des Sprengöls zu verbessern. A. E. Rudberg in Stockholm nahm am 30. April 1866 ein schwedisches Patent auf Herstellung von Nitroglyzerin im ununterbrochenen und gefahrlosen Betriebe;[5] E. Kopp arbeitete ein Verfahren aus, um am Sprengorte selbst — in den großen Steinbrüchen des Zorntales im Elsaß, wo seit 1866 mit Nitroglyzerin gesprengt wurde — das Sprengöl herzustellen;[6] G. W. Mowbray in North Adams in Massachussets benutzte zum Umrühren des Säuregemisches während des Nitrierens einen kalten Luftstrom, den er durch teilweise Expansion komprimierter Luft erzeugte; er erkannte auch die große Wichtigkeit der Anwendung chemisch reinen Glyzerins, sowie der Reinigung des gebildeten Nitroglyzerins;[7] die Franzosen Boutmy und Faucher führten ein Verfahren ein, wonach zur Vermeidung von Explo-

---

[1] Vgl. Zeitschr. des österr. Ingenieur- u. Architekten-Vereins, Vortrag Koestlin im November 1869.

[2] Dinglers polyt. Journ. Bd. 195, S. 364.

[3] Dinglers polyt. Journ. Bd. 193, S. 490.

[4] Goetze, Die Tätigkeit der deutschen Ingenieure und techn. Truppen.

[5] Nordenström och Cronquist, Om nitroglyzerinhaltige Sprängämnen, S. 41. — Dinglers polyt. Journ. Bd. 187, S. 207 (1868). — v. Meyer, Explosivkörper, S. 54. — Böckmann, Die explosiven Stoffe, S. 264.

[6] E. Kopp, Sur les applications et la préparation simplifiée de la Nitroglycérine. Paris 1868. — Siehe v. Meyer, S. 53. — Trauzl, Explosive Nitrilverbindungen, S. 21.

[7] Dinglers polyt. Journ. Bd. 192, S. 172 (1869). — v. Meyer, S. 56. Böckmann, S. 265.

sionen das Säuregemisch nicht auf Glyzerin, sondern auf Glyzerindischwefelsäure einwirken solle; auf diese Fabrikationsverschiedenheiten wird in einem späteren Kapitel noch einzugehen sein.

An dieser Stelle seien noch kurz die Bemühungen A. E. Rudbergs[1] erwähnt, das Nitroglyzerin auf eine andere als die von Nobel angegebene Weise zur Detonation zu bringen, indem er durch einen von außen bewirkten genügenden Stoß oder Schlag eine Kompression und Temperaturerhöhung bewirkte, wodurch das Nitroglyzerinpräparat augenblicklich zersetzt und zum Detonieren gebracht wird.

Zu den früher erwähnten fünf Nobelschen Fabriken[2] gesellten sich in den nächsten Jahren noch folgende zehn, von Nobel bzw. seiner Gesellschaft begründete Werke: 1870: in Hangö (Finnland); 1871: in Ardeer bei Glasgow (Schottland) und in Paulilles bei Port Vendre (Frankreich); 1872: in Schlebusch (bei Köln) und in Galdacano bei Bilbao (Spanien); 1873: in Newyork, in Isleten bei Luzern, in Avigliana bei Turin, in Trafalda bei Lissabon, in Preßburg (Ungarn). Leicht war es übrigens nicht für Nobel, sein Dynamit einzuführen; besonders mußte er auch den Widerstand der Bergleute überwinden, die in ihrem ungemein ausgeprägten konservativen Sinne sich sträubten, den neuen Sprengstoff zu gebrauchen, nachdem sie jahrhundertelang nur mit Schwarzpulver geschossen hatten. Andere wieder versprachen sich mehr von der Schießbaumwolle als dem Dynamit; Nobel hat in seinem, in der Society of Arts am 21. Mai 1875 gehaltenem Vortrage über „Moderne Sprengstoffe“ ausgeführt, warum er so zähe am Nitroglyzerin festhielt und von dessen Erfolg überzeugt war; er sagt: „Konzentration der Kraft, Explosionsgeschwindigkeit und Gefahrlosigkeit sind die drei Punkte, von welchen hauptsächlich der Erfolg oder Mißerfolg eines Explosivstoffes abhängt.“ Nitroglyzerin mit einer Dichte von 1·6 enthält aber mehr Energie in demselben Raume, als die weniger dichte Schießbaumwolle; ebenso ist die Explosionsgeschwindigkeit größer. Ferner berücksichtigte Nobel, daß das Nitroglyzerinmolekül alle zu seiner Umwandlung in Kohlensäure und Wasser notwendigen Elemente, sowie noch einen kleinen Überschuß an Sauerstoff enthielt, während Schießwolle einen Überschuß an Kohlenstoff enthält, der

[1] Schwedisches Patent vom 31. Mai 1865. — Dinglers polyt. Journ. Bd. 187, S. 204.

[2] Die damals in diesen Fabriken übliche Herstellung des Nitroglyzerins und des Dynamits hat Ferd. Capitaine in Dinglers polyt. Journ. Bd. 20, S. 34 (1872) näher beschrieben.

zur Entstehung von Kohlenoxyd Veranlassung gibt. — In seinem Vortrage gab Nobel folgende Statistik über die in den Jahren 1867 bis 1874 verkauften Mengen Dynamit; dieselbe betrug sukzessive pro Jahr: 11, 78, 185, 424, 785, 1350, 2050 und (im Jahre 1874) 3120 Tonnen.

Immerhin besaß das Gurdynamit noch zwei erhebliche Nachteile; durch Wasser wird das Nitroglyzerin leicht aus der Kieselgur verdrängt; beim Arbeiten in nassen Bohrlöchern lief man also Gefahr, daß freies Glyzerin aus den Patronen austrat und in die Spalten des Gesteins einsickerte; ferner kam in Betracht, daß Gurdynamit zu 25% aus einem Stoffe bestand, welcher an der Explosion sich nicht nur nicht aktiv beteiligte, sondern auch eine beträchtliche Wärmemenge absorbierte, die so für den Nutzeffekt verloren ging.

In den nächsten Jahren finden wir daher vielseitige Bestrebungen, anstatt der passiven Infusorienerde feste Stoffe als Aufsaugemittel zu nehmen, die kein unnützer Ballast, sondern sprengtechnisch wirksam wären. So wurden Patente genommen: am 19. Juni 1867 von E. A. Björkman in Schweden auf einen Sprengstoff Seranin, bestehend aus 100 Teilen Ammonsalpeter, 12 Tln. Sägespäne, 25 Tln. Nitroglyzerin und 1 Tl. Benzol; — am 5. Dezember 1867 von dem preußischen Artillerieoffizier C. Dittmar in England auf Mischungen von Nitroglyzerin mit poröser, verbrennbarer Substanz, nämlich entweder mit feinverteilter Holzkohle, die mit einer Lösung von Kali- oder Natronsalpeter imprägniert und dann getrocknet wurde, oder mit Nitrozellulose, d. i. fein verteiltem Holzstoff, der mit Salpeterschwefelsäure nitriert wurde, oder mit Holzstoff, der bloß mit Salpeterlösung imprägniert und dann getrocknet wurde; — am 14. August 1868 in England von W. Shaen (J. F. E. Schultze) auf Mischungen von Dynamit mit nitriertem Holz (Dualin); — am 12. Februar 1869 von Alfred Nobel in England auf ein Gemisch von Nitraten (Kalium-, Natrium-, Baryum- oder Bleinitrat) mit Kohle oder kohlenstoffhaltiger Substanz (Stärke, Harz, Zucker) und verhältnismäßig wenig Nitroglyzerin; — am 23. März 1869 von J. Horsley in England auf ein Gemisch von Nitroglyzerin mit pulverisierter Tonerde oder schwefelsaurer Magnesia; — am 19. April 1869 von J. Horsley in England auf ein Gemisch von Galläpfel und chlorsaurem Kali mit Nitroglyzerin; — am 28. August 1872 von A. Beckmann in Schweden auf Sebastin; — am 30. April 1873 von A. Nobel in England auf Gemenge von Natrium- oder Ammoniumnitrat, Holzkohle, Paraffin und Nitroglyzerin; — am 11. September 1873 von W. B. Brain in England auf Mischungen von 40—50% Nitroglyzerin mit Kaliumchlorat, Nitraten, Kohlenwasserstoffen usw.; — am 4. Mai 1874 von der Rheinischen Dynamitfabrik in England auf Kombination von Nitroglyzerin mit Naphtalin.

Trauzl in Österreich, sowie Abel in England bemühten sich, Nitroglyzerin mit gepülpter Schießbaumwolle zu vermischen; diese Schießwolle-Dynamite wurden eine Zeitlang fabriziert.

Gebr. Krebs & Cie. in Deutz bei Köln brachten als Lithofrakteur einen Sprengstoff in den Handel, der aus Nitroglyzerin, Kieselgur, Barytsalpeter, Schwefel, Braunstein und Kohle bestand. Auf der Wiener Weltausstellung im Jahre 1873 wurden von der Firma Nobel Sprengstoffe ausgestellt, welche wenig (5—10%) Kieselgur, daneben als Aufsaugemittel Holzmehl oder nitriertes Holzmehl und Barytsalpeter enthielten (Dynamite Nr. 2, 3 und 4). Auch Zellulosedynamit (70—75% Nitroglyzerin mit fein verteiltem Holzfaserstoff) kam in den Handel.[1]

So bildeten sich zwei Arten von Dynamiten; die einen mit Kieselgur oder einem ähnlichen, bei der Explosion nicht vergasbaren Stoff als Aufsaugemittel, sog. Dynamite mit unwirksamer, inaktiver Basis; die anderen mit einem wirksamen Aufsaugemittel, mit aktiver Basis; als letztere dienten, wie oben erwähnt, kohlenstoffhaltige Stoffe (besonders Holzmehl), die mit dem überschüssigen Sauerstoff des Nitroglyzerins bei der Explosion gasförmige Produkte lieferten; außerdem wurden zur Erhöhung des Gasvolumens Nitrate, auch Chlorate zugefügt.

In den Vereinigten Staaten, Österreich und Frankreich werden diese, durch bloßes Vermischen des Nitroglyzerins mit den Saugstoffen hergestellten Dynamitsorten mit wirksamer Beimischung noch sehr viel fabriziert und werden wir solche in einem späteren Abschnitte näher zu betrachten haben.

Auch Alfred Nobel, der im Jahre 1873 nach Paris übersiedelte, sich ein Haus in der Avenue Malakoff kaufte und in einem speziell errichteten Laboratorium mit seinem Assistenten Fehrenbach weiter arbeitete, hatte, wie schon erwähnt, zwei Patente auf Dynamite mit wirksamer Basis genommen; ein bemerkenswerter Nachteil der Mischungen von Nitroglyzerin mit Holzmehl und Nitraten war aber der, daß letztere das Sprengöl nicht genügend festhielten. Nobel hatte schon in seinem ersten Patente von 1863 sowohl Schwarzpulver als Schießbaumwolle als Aufsaugestoff verwandt; im Laufe der weiteren Versuche ging er

[1] Siehe: „Das Wesen und die Behandlung von brisanten Sprengstoffen". Berlin 1888, Ernst & Korn.

zu dem Gedanken über, sein Sprengöl durch Zusätze von sich auflösenden und verdickend wirkenden Stoffen in einen teigartigen, knetbaren Zustand zu bringen; die mit Schießwolle nach dieser Richtung angestellten Versuche blieben erfolglos, erst bei Anwendung von Kollodiumwolle erreichte er sein Ziel. Man sagt, daß ein Zufall, nämlich eine kleine Wunde, ihn auf Kollodiumlösung (niedrig nitrierte Zellulose in Ätheralkohol) aufmerksam gemacht habe; jedenfalls hatte Nobel den Erfolg, durch Verdunstenlassen eines Gemisches von Nitroglyzerin mit Kollodiumlösung einen plastischen Stoff zu erhalten, den er dann auch direkt aus Nitroglyzerin und (7—10 %) Kollodiumwolle herstellen konnte und Sprenggelatine nannte; letzterer kann seiner Zusammensetzung nach als idealer Sprengstoff bezeichnet werden, da beide Komponenten bei der Detonation völlig vergasen; in kaltem Zustande ist die Sprenggelatine von durchscheinend brauner Farbe und stellt eine zähe, plastische und elastische Gelatine dar, in welcher das Nitroglyzerin so fest gebunden ist, daß Feuchtigkeit nur geringen Einfluß ausübt, so daß man die Sprenggelatine besonders in nassen Gruben und bei Sprengungen unter Wasser verwendet.

Weiterhin stellte Nobel durch Auflösen einer kleineren Menge (3 — 4 %) Kollodiumwolle in Nitroglyzerin sog. gelatiniertes Öl her, eine viskose Masse, welche nicht für sich als Sprengstoff verwendet werden kann, die aber gegenüber dem reinen Nitroglyzerin den Vorzug besitzt, daß sie Beimischungen von salpetersauren Salzen und Holzmehl festhält und ermöglicht, Dynamite mit aktiver Basis herzustellen, bei denen im Wasser oder feuchter Umgebung kein Ausschwitzen des Nitroglyzerins stattfindet. Mischungen aus gelatiniertem Sprengöl und Zumischpulvern, die je nach Nitroglyzeringehalt und Zusammensetzung der Zumischpulver in verschiedenen Stärken hergestellt werden, nennt man Gelatinedynamite; eine typische Zusammensetzung für letztere ist folgende: 62·5 % Sprengöl, 2·5 % Kollodiumwolle, 25·5 % Natronsalpeter, 8·75 % Mehl und 0·75 % Natriumkarbonat.

Auf die neue, bahnbrechende Erfindung nahm Nobel bzw. seine Gesellschaft in allen Staaten Patente, so am 2. Dezember 1875 das englische Patent Nr. 4179, am 8. Juli 1876 ein schwedisches Patent (dessen ausführlicher Text in einem späteren Abschnitt wiedergegeben wird) und am 28. Februar 1878 das deutsche Patent Nr. 4829; letzteres (Verfahren zur Herstellung eines Sprengstoffes aus Nitroglyzerin und löslicher nitrierter Baumwolle unter Zusatz von die Wirkung des Sprengstoffes verstärkenden oder abschwächenden Mitteln) hat folgenden Inhalt:

Die den Nitroglyzerinpulvern (Dynamit usw.) eigene Gefährlichkeit, welche dadurch hervorgerufen ist, daß sich in denselben das Nitroglyzerin in flüssigem Zustande befindet und austretend die große Empfindlichkeit des ungemischten Sprengöls zeigt, hat den Erfinder Alfred Nobel veranlaßt, eine Reihe neuer Sprengstoffe zusammenzusetzen, in welchen das Nitroglyzerin oder das diesem Stoff verwandte Methyl- und Äthylnitrat durch Vermischung mit anderen, in diesen löslichen Körpern (Gelatinierung) aus dem denselben sonst eigentümlichen Aggregatzustande in die feste Form übergeführt ist. Als solchen, die Gelatinierung der vorgenannten Nitroverbindungen herbeiführenden Körper benutzt der Erfinder eine schwach nitrierte Baumwolle, welche durch Einwirkung eines Säuregemisches von gleichen Teilen Salpetersäure (1·44 spez. Gew.) und Schwefelsäure (1·835 spez. Gew.) auf trockene Baumwolle gewonnen wird. Behufs Auflösung der nitrierten Baumwolle in den obengenannten Nitroverbindungen werden letztere im Wasserbad bis auf 70° C erwärmt, bei welcher Temperatur sie bis zu zehn Prozent der ersteren aufzulösen imstande sind; ein geringer Zusatz von Methylalkohol oder eines anderen der unten angegebenen Zusatzstoffe, welche dem Präparat eine geringere Gefährlichkeit erteilen sollen, ist geeignet, diesen Vorgang wesentlich zu beschleunigen. Beim Erkalten erhält man je nach dem stattgefundenen Prozentzusatz an nitrierter Baumwolle eine halbfeste bis druckfeste Gelatine, vom Erfinder „Sprenggelatine" genannt, aus welcher entweder ohne weiteren Zusatz Patronen angefertigt werden, oder unter Beimengung von Stoffen, welche

a) teils die Explosibilität des Präparates bis zur Schußsicherheit vermindern sollen, als Methylalkohol, Essigäther, Aceton, Acetin, Nitrobenzol, Kampfer usw.,
b) teils als Sauerstoffzuträger die Vertrennung der durch die Explosion entstandenen Zersetzungsprodukte zu einer vollkommenen machen sollen, als Natronsalpeter, Kalisalpeter usw.,
c) teils die brisante Wirkung des Sprengstoffes in eine mehr nachwirkende verwandeln sollen, als Minenpulver u. dergl.

Sowohl was Wirkung als Gefahrlosigkeit anbelangt, übertreffen diese Patronen die aus den bisherigen Nitroglyzerinpulvern bestehenden bedeutend.

Der Patentanspruch lautet:

Das Verfahren, das Nytroglyzerin bzw. Methyl- oder Äthylnitrat durch Gelatinierung mit schwach nitrierter Baumwolle in feste Form überzuführen und die Masse durch Zusätze minder gefährlich zu machen.

Sprenggelatine wurde zuerst beim Bau des Gotthardtunnels in größeren Mengen mit ausgezeichnetem Erfolge angewandt; in Österreich bemühten sich besonders Siersch, Roth, Trauzl und Hess, das Präparat für Kriegszwecke verwendbar zu machen;

man inkorporierte der Sprenggelatine bis zu 10 Prozent Kampfer (D.R.P. 5528), um größere Handhabungssicherheit zu erzielen; solche „Kriegssprenggelatine" war einige Zeit in Österreich in Gebrauch.

Am 22. Juli 1879 nahm Alfred Nobel ein schwedisches Patent auf Extradynamit (Ammongelatinedynamite), bei dem er als Zumischpulver Ammonsalpeter anwandte; z. B. 71 Prozent Nitroglyzerin, 4 Prozent Kollodiumwolle, 2 Prozent Kohle, 23 Prozent Ammonsalpeter. Daß Nobel den Ammonsalpeter als mit dem Nitroglyzerin konkurrierendes Explosivmittel erkannte, geht daraus hervor, daß er in dem gleichen Patent auch folgende Zusammensetzung empfahl: 63 Prozent salpetersaures Ammoniak, 24 Prozent Nitroglyzerin, 1 Prozent Kollodiumwolle, 12 Prozent Kohle.

Den Entwicklungsgang der Nitroglyzerinsprengstoffe veranschaulicht folgender Überblick (nach Georgi-Heise):

Sprengöl

Gurdynamit	Dynamite mit wirksamer Beimischung
75 % Sprengöl	25—50 % Sprengöl
25 % Kieselgur	75—50 % Zumischpulver.

Sprengöl + Kollodiumwolle

Sprenggelatine	Gelatiniertes Sprengöl
92 % Sprengöl	97 % Sprengöl
8 % Kollodiumwolle	3 % Kollodiumwolle

Gelatinedynamite	Ammongelatinedynamite
45—65 % gelatin. Öl	Mischungen von gelatiniertem Sprengöl mit Ammonsalpeter.
55—35 % Zumischpulver (Salpeter als Natrium-, Kalium- oder Barytsalpeter)	

Mittlerweile war eine neue Forderung an die Sprengstoffe herangetreten, die vom Kohlenbergbau ausging. Hierüber sagt C. E. Bichel: „Der feine und namentlich in der Tiefe sehr trockene Kohlenstaub wird in den Strecken der Gruben aufgewirbelt und bildet mit der Luft gemischt selbst einen Sprengstoff, ebenso wie das aus den Kohlen entweichende Grubengas, welches sich entweder unmerkbar und langsam aus den Kohlen entwickelt oder aber plötzlich mit gewaltigem Druck als Bläser aus seiner Einschließung hervorbricht, wenn die Hacke des Bergmanns oder ein Sprengschuß eine solche Grubengasansammlung anschlägt. Wehe der unglücklichen Belegschaft, wenn eine unvorsichtig geöffnete

Grubenlampe, ein angezündetes Streichholz, der elektrische Funke oder ein Sprengschuß eine Grubengas- oder Kohlenstaubexplosion herbeiführt. Ein einziges Flammenmeer erfüllt die Gruben, Explosion reiht sich an Explosion, so lange Kohlenstaub und Grubengas vorhanden sind. Alles Lebende verbrennt oder erstickt in den Kohlenoxyd enthaltenden Schwaden." Tatsächlich führte eine große Reihe unheilvoller Explosionen in den Kohlenzechen dazu, in einer Reihe von Staaten diese Frage zu studieren nnd es wurden besondere „Schlagwetter-Kommissionen" eingesetzt (1877 in Frankreich, 1879 in England und Belgien, 1880 in Sachsen und Preußen); doch blieb zunächst gerade die Erörterung des Einflusses der Sprengarbeit auf die Schlagwetterexplosionen sehr lückenhaft (vgl. J. Trauzl, Sprengtechnische Fragen. I. Zur Schlagwetterfrage. Wien 1885, Lehmann & Wentzel); immerhin machte sich mehr und mehr die Notwendigkeit geltend, die Entzündung von explosiven Schlagwettergemischen und Kohlenstaubaufwirbelungen durch die Sprengarbeit zu vermeiden; man stellte daher an die Sprengstoffe die Anforderung, daß sie gegen solche Zündungen und Explosionen Sicherheit gewähren sollten, eine Sicherheit, welche bei Anwendung von Schwarzpulver und den neuen brisanten Sprengstoffen (Schießbaumwolle, Gurdynamit, Sprenggelatine, Gelatinedynamit) nicht zu erreichen war.

Die englische Grubenunfallkommission unter Vorsitz von Sir Fred. Abel versuchte in den Jahren 1880—86 die bei der Explosion von brisanten Sprengmitteln entstehende Flamme dadurch unschädlich zu machen, bzw. auszulöschen, daß man als Besatz eine Wasserpatrone auf die Ladung brachte; Settle vervollkommnete die Form der Wasserpatronen dadurch, daß er die Sprengpatrone ganz und gar in einem weiteren Wassersacke unterbrachte und in diesem gegen seitliche und axiale Verschiebungen sicherte, so daß die Patrone ringsum von Wasser umgeben war; in Herne hat man versucht, bei Abgabe des Schusses einen fein versprühten Wasserstrahl gegen die Strecke zu richten; Galloway wandte einen feuchten Moosbesatz bei der Patrone an; Jicinski schlug vor, die Dynamitpatronen möglichst zentrisch in eine Papierhülse zu stecken und den Raum zwischen den beiden Wandungen mit wasserdurchtränktem Sand oder ebensolcher Kieselgur auszufüllen. Weiterhin ging man dazu über, den Dynamiten selbst kristallwasserhaltige Salze beizumengen; man stellte so z. B. aus Nitroglyzerin, Kieselgur und kristallisierter Soda ($Na_2CO_3 + 10H_2O$) oder Magnesiasulfat ($MgSO_4 + 7H_2O$) Wetterdynamite (franz. Grisoutite) her; auch verwandte man als Beimengung solche Salze, welche durch ihre eigene Vergasung die Explosionstemperatur herabsetzen sollten, wie Ammoniumoxalat, Natriumbikarbonat u. a. — Diese (älteren) Wetterdynamite haben sich indessen weniger bewährt und werden insbesondere in Deutschland nicht mehr viel fabriziert.

Theoretisch gefördert wurde die Frage der wettersicheren Sprengstoffe durch die Arbeiten der französischen, am 12. Februar 1887 eingesetzten Schlagwetter-Kommission, welche — von der Ansicht ausgehend, daß die Entzündung der schlagenden Wetter durch die Flammentemperatur des Schusses verursacht wird — auf rechnerischem Wege die Explosionstemperatur der verschiedenen Sprengstoffe feststellte und verlangte, daß die Anfangstemperatur der Explosionsgase nicht über 2200° liegen dürfe, da hier die Grenze für die Entzündung liege, unter Berücksichtigung der durch die Ausdehnung und Arbeitsleistung der Gase erfolgenden Abkühlung; die französische Bergverwaltung hat dann die rechnungsmäßige Explosionstemperatur als Maßstab der Wettersicherheit festgesetzt und die Grenze bei Verwendung für Kohlenbergwerke auf 1500° fixiert; prinzipiell ist dies deshalb nicht richtig, weil neben der Flammentemperatur die sonstigen Explosionsfaktoren (besonders Detonationsgeschwindigkeit und Kraft) sowie die Ladungsmengen eine Rolle spielen. Eine praktische Folge der neuen Bestimmung war die Fabrikation der Grisoutine, die in Frankreich und Belgien einen großen Aufschwung nahm. Bei diesen Sprengstoffen wird durch starke Beimengung von Ammonsalpeter eine niedrige Explosionstemperatur erzielt. Die Grisoutine haben eine ähnliche Zusammensetzung wie Nobels Extradynamit (Typus II) und bestehen aus 70 bis 80 Prozent Ammonsalpeter und 12 bis 30 Prozent gelatiniertem Sprengöl.

In Deutschland und England verwendet man als wettersichere Nitroglyzerinsprengstoffe besonders die von Chr. Em. Bichel (D.R.P. 39171) eingeführten Karbonite, die sich durch hohe Schlagwettersicherheit auszeichnen; sie bestehen aus 25 bis 30 Prozent Nitroglyzerin und je 25 bis 40 Prozent Mehl und Kali- oder Natronsalpeter.

Man kann bei diesen Karboniten oder (neueren) Wetterdynamiten auch gelatiniertes Sprengöl (Zusatz von Kollodiumwolle) verwenden; solche wettersichere Gelatinedynamite enthalten 30 bis 40 Prozent gelatiniertes Nitroglyzerin und statt Natron- oder Kalisalpeter meist ca. 30 Prozent Ammonsalpeter, die restlichen 30 Prozent sind Mehl, Seife, Kohlenwasserstoffe; ihre gelatinöse Konsistenz läßt aber zu wünschen übrig; nach einem neueren Patent (D.R.P. 182030) der Dynamit-Akt.-Ges. vorm. Nobel erreicht man auch bei den schwächeren, Nitroglyzerin (und Kollodiumwolle) enthaltenden, Sprengstoffen die gewünschte Plastizität dadurch, daß man statt Mehl usw. Kohlehydrate anwendet, die ganz oder teilweise in Wasser löslich sind, besonders Dextrin, Gummi, Stärke; ein derartiger Sprengstoff ist das Nobelit mit 28 Prozent Sprengöl, 0·7 Prozent Kollodiumwolle, 40 Prozent Ammonsalpeter, 11 Prozent Dextrin, 2·5 Prozent Holzmehl, ca. 18 Prozent Chlornatrium; der Zusatz von Kochsalz wirkt günstig auf die Schlagwettersicherheit ein.

Chr. Em. Bichel bedient sich neuerdings zum Gelatinieren einer prinzipiell von dem Nobelschen Verfahren abweichenden Methode, indem er nicht Kollodiumwolle anwendet, sondern eine Lösung von kolloiden Stoffen (z. B. Leim, Gelatine) in Glyzerin (D.R.P. 180685); diese Methode kann bei hohem wie niedrigem Nitroglyzeringehalt angewendet werden, für sich oder in Kombination mit dem Nobelschen Verfahren; so besteht das Gelatinekarbonit aus 25·3 Prozent Sprengöl, 0·7 Prozent Kollodiumwolle, 6·9 Prozent Glyzerinleimgelatine, 41·5 Prozent Ammonsalpeter und 25·6 Prozent Chlornatrium.

Es schien für längere Zeit, als sei der Erfindungsmöglichkeit neuer Nitroglyzerin-Sprengstoffe ein Ziel gesetzt, was die Basis dieser Sprengmittel, das Glyzerintrinitrat oder Nitroglyzerin schlechthin betraf.

Freilich litt das letztere schon von jeher unter einem großen Übelstand: seiner leichten Gefrierbarkeit, die merkwürdigerweise bei größeren Mengen noch schneller eintritt wie bei kleineren[1] und damit nur den Umfang einer gegebenen Falles eintretenden Katastrophe erweitert; nach Kast[1] gefriert Nitroglyzerin bei ca. $+ 13^0$, das Auftauen geht nur ganz allmählich vor sich[2] und verursacht selbst im Sommer noch Unbequemlichkeiten. Nach Volpert[3] wurde im Juni 1905 gelegentlich eines Besuches preußischer Gewerberäte festgestellt, daß nach einer Reihe von heißen Tagen in einem Magazin noch ungeöffnet daliegendes Dynamit gefroren war, obschon das Magazin längst Zimmertemperatur angenommen hatte. Nun fragt man sich: Welche Folgen hat denn das Festwerden des Nitroglyzerins in bezug auf seine Handhabung?

---

[1] Zeitschr. Schieß-Sprengstoffe 1906, S. 225.

[2] Versuche zur Prüfung der Empfindlichkeit gefrorener und halbgefrorener Nitroglyzerinsprengstoffe gegenüber plastischen. Zeitschr. Berg-, Hütten-Salinenwesen.

[3] Zeitschr. Schieß-Sprengstoffe 1906, S. 167.

Jedenfalls sind die Klagen allgemein, daß der Sprengstoff in diesem Zustand weniger brauchbar ist, wenn auch die Wirkungen dieses Zustandes sehr oft ganz verschieden hingestellt werden. Ein Versagen von gefrorenem Dynamit berichtet schon aus der Zeit seiner ersten Anwendung das deutsche Generalstabswerk über den Krieg von 1870/71 aus den Tagen vom 28. Januar und folgenden;[1] eine erhöhte Explosionsneigung schreiben ihm dagegen die meisten statistischen Angaben zu, worunter z. B. aus der englischen Unfallstatistik erhellt, daß 87 Prozent aller Unglücksfälle in der Verwendung von nitroglyzerinhaltigen Sprengstoffen bei der kalten Jahreszeit entstanden sind.[2] So wie diese Beispiele differieren auch die Angaben über die Gefährlichkeit des gefrorenen Dynamits, indem die einen, hauptsächlich die Vertreter der Wissenschaft, nach Laboratoriumsversuchen ihm erheblich verminderte Gefährlichkeit, die Männer der Praxis dagegen nach ihren Erfahrungen im Betrieb eine außerordentlich erhöhte zuschreiben; nach den Prüfungen der Zentralstelle für wissenschaftlich-technische Untersuchungen in Neubabelsberg und den Berichten der k. Bergwerksdirektion zu Saarbrücken[3] sollte man annehmen, daß die gefrorenen Dynamite in ihrer Empfindlichkeit keineswegs über, im Gegenteil in der Regel bedeutend unter derjenigen der plastischen Dynamite stehen. Jedenfalls entstanden aber besonders viele Unglücksfälle beim Wiederauftauen gefrorener Sprengstoffe, wofür die Schuld verschiedentlich gesucht wurde: in der mechanischen Wirkung der einzelnen apatitharten Nitroglyzerinkriställchen auf das flüssige Nitroglyzerin,[4] in der, einen Initialimpuls begünstigenden Druckwirkung der umgebenden Kristallhaut mit Einschlüssen von flüssigem Nitroglyzerin, in der spontanen Entstehung elektrischer Ladungen.[5] Zur Vermeidung der Unglücksfälle konstruierte man besondere Auftau-Apparate, aber es zeigte sich, daß solche oft in den Händen der Arbeiter nicht mit der nötigen Reinlichkeit oder Geduld und Exaktheit behandelt wurden. Ferner bemühte man sich, das Nitroglyzerin schwerer gefrierbar zu machen. Der erste diesbezügliche Versuch dürfte von A. E. Rudberg stammen, welcher dem fertig

[1] Der deutsch-franz. Krieg 1870—71. II. Teil, II. Bd, S. 1160 u. 1164.

[2] Denker, Unfallstatistik der Sprengarbeiten. Vortrag Sektion 3b des internationalen Kongresses 1903.

[3] Versuche zur Prüfung der Empfindlichkeit usw., siehe Fußnote S. 36.

[4] Denker, Die bergmännischen Sprengarbeiten im Lichte der Unfallstatistik. Dissertation. Aachen 1904.

[5] Bredig, Zeitschr. Schieß-Sprengstoffe 1906, S. 228, Fußnote.

gewaschenen Nitroglyzerin einen anderen Stoff, wie Benzol oder Nitrobenzol, beimischt.[1] — Bemühungen Nobels, durch sorgfältiges Trocknen im Vakuum das Nitroglyzerin schwerer gefrierbar zu machen,[2] dürften wohl keinen Erfolg gehabt haben; aussichtsvoller war jedenfalls der spätere Vorschlag Nobels, durch Zusatz von Methyl- und Äthylnitrat, Nitrobenzol, Acetin, Bi- und Triacetin den Gefrierpunkt zu erniedrigen.[3] Am 13. April 1877 nahmen A. W. Wahlenberg und K. J. Sundström ein Patent auf Zusatz von ortho-Nitrotoluol; sie konnten dadurch den Gefrierpunkt des Nitroglyzerins bis unter -20^0 sinken lassen. K. Åmark nahm am 1. März 1878 ein schwedisches Patent auf einen Sprengstoff aus Nitroglyzerin mit Nitrostärke, Nitromannit, Amylnitrat u. a., der auch bei sehr niederen Temperaturen seine Weichheit behalte. Liebert[4] setzt entweder dem Trinitroglyzerin 3 Prozent Isoamylnitrat zu oder nitriert von vornherein ein Gemisch von Glyzerin mit Isoamylalkohol, während Wohl[5] durch Nitrieren von Polyglyzerinen eine Besserung erhoffte.

Sigurd Nauckhoff[6] hat den Gegenstand wissenschaftlich untersucht und gefunden, daß jeder im Nitroglyzerin gelöste Stoff eine Senkung des Gefrierpunktes hervorruft, welche der Konzentration direkt und dem Molekulargewicht des Stoffes umgekehrt proportional ist, vorausgesetzt, daß der betreffende Stoff sich weder dissoziiert noch komplexe Moleküle bildet.

Wenn somit auch die Möglichkeit gegeben war, den Gefrierpunkt des Nitroglyzerins (Glyzerintrinitrats) durch Beimengungen herunterzudrücken und frostbeständige Dynamite herzustellen, so scheint doch dieser Weg in der Praxis nicht viel begangen worden zu sein, auch lag bei dem einen oder anderen Zusatz die Gefahr der Entmischung beim Lagern vor.

Es ist das große Verdienst von Dr. Anton Mikolajczak, durch seine Patentanmeldung vom 15. August 1903 die Nitroglyzerin-Industrie in neue Bahnen gelenkt zu haben. Zum Verständnis

---

[1] Schwed. Patent vom 30. April 1866.

[2] Schwed. Patent vom 1. Oktober 1866.

[3] Schwed. Patent vom 8. Juli 1876. — Obwohl Rudberg wie Nobel bereits frühzeitig den Zusatz von Nitrobenzol empfohlen hatten, wurde derselbe praktisch vor dem Jahre 1885 nicht angewandt; am 16. April 1886 nahm Nobel nochmals ein diesbezügliches Patent in England, auch Oskar Guttmann hatte — unabhängig von Rudberg und Nobel — im Jahre 1885 diesbezügliche Versuche gemacht.

[4] D.R.P. 51022 vom 29. März 1889.

[5] D.R.P. 58957 vom 17. August 1890.

[6] Zeitschr. angew. Chem. 1905, S. 11 u. 53.

der folgenden Ausführungen müssen wir zunächst einige rein chemische Bemerkungen vorausschicken. Das Glyzerin, welches wir nitrieren, ist ein zur Klasse der Alkohole gehöriger Körper, deren einfachster Repräsentant der Äthylalkohol C_2H_5OH ist; wenn wir letzteren mit Salpetersäure (unter Zusatz von Schwefelsäure) behandeln, so führen wir den Äthylalkohol in das Äthylnitrat über

$$\underset{\text{Äthylalkohol}}{C_2H_5OH} + \underset{\text{Salpetersäure}}{HO\cdot NO_2} = \underset{\text{Äthylnitrat}}{C_2H_5O\cdot NO_2} + \underset{\text{Wasser}}{H_2O}.$$

In ganz analoger Weise geht der Prozeß beim Glyzerin vor sich

$$\begin{array}{lcccccc} CH_2OH & & HO\cdot NO_2 & & CH_2O\cdot NO_2 & & \\ | & & & & | & & \\ CHOH & + & HO\cdot NO_2 & = & CHO\cdot NO_2 & + & 3\,H_2O. \\ | & & & & | & & \text{Wasser} \\ CH_2OH & & HO\cdot NO_2 & & CH_2O\cdot NO_2 & & \\ \text{Glyzerin} & & \text{drei Salpetersäure} & & \text{Glyzerintrinitrat oder} & & \\ & & & & \text{Trinitroglyzerin,} & & \\ & & & & \text{Nitroglyzerin genannt} & & \end{array}$$

Da Glyzerin ein dreiwertiger Alkohol ist, d. h. die für Alkohole charakteristische Hydroxylgruppe dreimal enthält, so benötigen wir zur vollständigen Nitrierung, d. i. Überführung in Glyzerintrinitrat $C_3H_5(ONO_2)_3$ 3 Moleküle Salpetersäure auf 1 Molekül Glyzerin. Es ist aber möglich, die Behandlung mit Salpetersäure gelinder zu gestalten, so daß nicht die sämtlichen drei Hydroxylgruppen des Glyzerins esterifiziert werden, sondern nur zwei oder nur eine; so kann man das Glyzerindinitrat $C_3H_5(OH)(ONO_2)_2$ und das Glyzerinmononitrat $C_3H_5(OH)_2(ONO_2)$ gewinnen; über die Existenzmöglichkeit der letzteren beiden Körper war man sich wohl klar, unterließ es jedoch, der Frage näher zu treten, ob diese Verbindungen leicht herstellbar, bzw. in reinem Zustande isolierbar und dann ob dieselben stabil und praktisch verwendbar seien. Im Jahre 1865 hat allerdings Apotheker Liecke in Hannover auf diese Nitrate hingewiesen und ihre Herstellung beschrieben;[1] danach soll sich ein gelbliches Öl von der Zusammensetzung des Dinitroglyzerins abscheiden, wenn man 1 Volumen reines Glyzerin bei 0° unter mäßigem Umrühren in ein Gemenge von 1 Volumen Salpetersäure von 1·4 spezifischem Gewicht und 2 Volumen konzentrierter Schwefelsäure eintropfen läßt und hierauf das Ganze mit Wasser versetzt. Bei späterer Nachprüfung[2] dieser Angabe wurde gefunden, daß die unter den genannten Versuchsbedingungen sich abscheidende ölige Flüssig-

---

[1] Mitteilungen des hannoverschen Gewerbevereins 1865, S. 214.

[2] Nach den Angaben der Zentralstelle Neubabelsberg im D.R.P. 181385.

keit aus Trinitroglyzerin besteht und kein Dinitroglyzerin enthält; der Stickstoffgehalt des Öles schwankte zwischen 18·49 und 18·23 Prozent (für das Trinitrat berechnen sich 18·5, für das Dinitrat 15·4 Prozent N); das allerdings gleichzeitig entstehende Dinitroglyzerin konnte in der sauren Flüssigkeit nachgewiesen werden und blieb, entgegen der Angabe von Liecke, in allen Fällen darin gelöst, einerlei, ob man Eis, Wasser von 0° oder Zimmertemperatur, viel oder wenig Wasser zum Ausfällen des Öles benutzte; die hohe Löslichkeit des Dinitrats in Säure, saurem und neutralem Wasser verhindert dessen Abscheidung. Dinitroglyzerin kann deswegen, in Widerspruch zu der Angabe von Liecke, nicht direkt als sich abscheidendes Öl genommen werden; man muß es dem Reaktionsgemisch vielmehr durch Extraktionsmittel entziehen. — Auch Eissler in seinem 1884 erschienenen Werke „The modern high explosives" erwähnt, daß durch Behandlung von Nitroglyzerin mit Salpetersäure drei Nitroglyzerine entstehen, das Mononitroglyzerin, das Dinitroglyzerin und das Trinitroglyzerin, ebenso Mitting in seinem amerikanischen Patent vom 1. September 1890. Wohl bezeichnet[1] das Mono- und Dinitrat des Glyzerins als schwer zu erhalten und hygroskopisch.

Erst Mikolajczak[2] hat eine Methode zur Herstellung und Reingewinnung des Glyzerindinitrats oder Dinitroglyzerins $C_3H_5(OH)(ONO_2)_2$ ermittelt und beschrieben; er hat nachgewiesen, daß das Dinitroglyzerin nicht nur an sich haltbar, sondern sogar viel stabiler als das Sobrero-Nobelsche Trinitroglyzerin ist und er hat endlich die Vorteile der praktischen Verwendung, insbesondere auch die Ungefrierbarkeit des Dinitroglyzerins festgestellt. — Mikolajczak gibt folgendes Herstellungsverfahren an:

10 Gewichtsteilen Glyzerin vom spez. Gewicht 1·262 werden unter Abkühlung 33 Gewichtsteile Salpetersäure (spez. Gew. 1·50) zugemischt, am besten, indem man die Salpetersäure in das Glyzerin langsam unter umrührender Bewegung einfließen läßt; das hauptsächlich Mononitroglyzerin enthaltende Gemisch läßt man einige Zeit, event. bis zu mehreren Stunden, möglichst bei etwa + 10° C, stehen, wobei sich das Mononitroglyzerin in das Dinitroglyzerin umwandelt. Die ganze Masse wird dann mit ca. 10 Gewichtsteilen kalten Wassers verdünnt und die Salpetersäure durch geeignete Mittel, z. B. kohlensauren Kalk, neutralisiert, bis die Lauge ein spez. Gewicht von 1·58 hat; das Dinitroglyzerin steigt darin auf, läßt sich gut abscheiden und trocknen.

---

[1] in seinem D.R.P. 58957 vom 17. August 1890.

[2] Deutsche Patentanmeldung 25176 vom 15. August 1903.

Etwas später als Mikolajczak hat sich die Zentralstelle Neubabelsberg mit diesem Problem befaßt und am 19. März 1904 ein Verfahren zu Patent angemeldet (D.R.P. 181385), wonach man Dinitroglyzerin in der Weise erhält, daß man Glyzerin bei etwa 18 bis 20° C mit der vier- bis siebenfachen Menge einer Mischsäure nitriert, welche in 100 Gewichtsteilen 8 bis 12 Gewichtsteile Wasser, 60 bis 70 Gewichtsteile Schwefelsäuremonohydrat und 15 bis 32 Gewichtsteile Salpetersäuremonohydrat enthält; aus der Lösung wird das Dinitroglyzerin in üblicher Weise abgeschieden.

Der Leiter der Zentralstelle, Prof. Will, hat weiterhin am 1. Mai 1904 ein Patent eingereicht (D.R.P. 175751) auf ein Verfahren zur Gewinnung von Dinitroglyzerin, darin bestehend, daß man Trinitroglyzerin zwecks Überführung in Dinitroglyzerin mit Schwefelsäure behandelt und aus der so erhaltenen sauren, mit Wasser verdünnten Lösung das Dinitroglyzerin mittels Äther, Chloroform, Benzol usw. extrahiert. — Escales und Novak erhielten bei Verwendung von 1 Tl. Glyzerin und etwas über 2 Tln. Schwefelsäure und Behandeln der intermediär gebileten Glyzerinschwefelsäure mit Salpetersäure das Glyzerindinitrat (deutsche Patentanmeldung E. 12078 vom 10. November 1906).

Für den Praktiker ist ein Gemenge von Di- und Trinitroglyzerin ebensogut, bzw. besser verwendbar als reines Dinitrat. Mikolajczak,[1] ebenso die Dynamit-Akt.-Ges. vorm. Nobel[2] stellen durch Nitrierung mittels erfahrungsmäßig hierfür geeignet befundener Mischsäuren solche Gemenge her. — Escales und Novak (deutsche Patentanmeldung E. 11967 vom 12. September 1906) gehen von der aus 1 Tl. Glyzerin und 4 Tln. Schwefelsäure hergestellten und durch Kalk isolierten Glyzerindischwefelsäure aus und führen solche durch Salpetersäure in Gemenge von Glyzerindi- und -trinitrat über.

Eine Eigenschaft des Dinitroglyzerins scheint allerdings für dessen Einführung in die Praxis störend zu wirken, seine Hygroskopizität. Blochmann[3] fand, daß in einer feuchten Kammer das Trinitroglyzerin 0 Prozent, das Dinitroglyzerin dagegen 3·3 Prozent (in 1 Tag), bzw. 11 Prozent (in 7 Tagen) Wasser aufgenommen habe; Volpert ist übrigens der Ansicht, daß ein

---

[1]) Deutsche Patentanmeldung vom 18. Dezember 1903. — Franz. Patent 349078 vom 8. März 1905. — Amerik. Patent 830909 vom 5. Januar 1905.

[2] Deutsche Patentanmeldung vom 18. März 1904. — Franz. Patent 352486 vom 2. Juni 1905.

[3] Der Bergbau 1905, Nr. 48.

mäßiger Wassergehalt der Dinitroglyzerin-Sprengstoffe auf die Haltbarkeit und praktische Wirkung derselben nicht von schädigendem Einfluß sei.

Es ist typisch für die Geschichte der Erfindungen, daß nach einer langen Stagnation plötzlich auf demselben Gebiet mehrere wichtige Neuerungen auftauchen; so entstanden auch dem Dinitroglyzerin eine Reihe von Konkurrenten.

In erster Linie sei das nitrierte Monochlorhydrin erwähnt. Wenn wir im Glyzerin $C_3H_5(OH)_3$ eine Hydroxylgruppe durch Chlor ersetzen, so kommen wir zum Monochlorhydrin, $C_3H_5(OH)_2Cl$, das — in zwei Modifikationen α und β — schon lange bekannt ist; allerdings war dieser Körper bis vor kurzem nur zu außerordentlich hohen, die technische Verwendung zu Sprengstoffzwecken ausschließenden Preisen zu erhalten; nachdem man jedoch erkannt hat, daß durch Einwirkung von Salpetersäure auf Chlorhydrin wichtige Nitrate erhalten werden, bemühte man sich, eine technisch und wirtschaftlich durchführbare Methode zur Herstellung des Chlorhydrins zu finden und lassen neuere Patente (z. B. D.R.P. 180668, französische Patente 370224 und 370249) die Aufgabe als gelöst betrachten. Das Monochlorhydrin gibt, in üblicher Weise mit Salpeterschwefelsäure behandelt, das Dinitromonochlorhydrin $C_3H_5 \cdot Cl(O \cdot NO_2)_2$, eine schwach gelbliche, leicht bewegliche Flüssigkeit von schwach aromatischem Geruch, die zwar explosive Eigenschaften besitzt und, mit einer Knallquecksilberkapsel initiiert, regelmäßig unter erheblicher Kraftentfaltung detoniert, auch Nitrozellulose gelatiniert, wie das Trinitroglyzerin, die aber diesem gegenüber sich einmal durch große Unempfindlichkeit gegen Stoß, Schlag und Reibung und dann durch ihre Ungefrierbarkeit selbst bei — 25 bis 30° C auszeichnet; mit Trinitroglyzerin in jedem Verhältnis mischbar, setzt es dessen Gefrierbarkeit so herab, daß mit einem Zusatz von 20 Prozent Dinitromonochlorhydrin ungefrierbare Trinitroglyzerin-Sprengstoffe erhalten werden.[1] In der Praxis erzeugt man solche Gemische nicht in der Weise, daß man zunächst Trinitroglyzerin und Dinitromonochlorhydrin getrennt herstellt und die beiden mischt, sondern man nitriert gleich ein Gemisch von Glyzerin und Monochlorhydrin.[2] Dem basischen Dinitrat gegenüber zeichnet sich das chlorierte Produkt dadurch aus, daß es nicht hygroskopisch ist; Belästigungen durch die Bildung

[1] Roewer, Zeitschr. Schieß-Sprengstoffe I, S. 228.

[2] Siehe engl. Patent 4057 (1905); engl. Patent 6361 (1905); engl. Patent 14958 (1905).

von freier Salzsäure bei der Detonation werden dadurch vermieden, daß man den Sprengstoffen Alkalinitrate beifügt, wodurch die Salzsäure als Chlornatrium usw. neutralisiert wird.

Auch das Nitro-dichlor-hydrin $C_3H_5 \cdot Cl_2(O \cdot NO_2)$ wurde neuerdings zum Schutze gegen Gefrieren angewandt (engl. Patent 17891 [1906]).

Schon erheblich früher war Dr. Alfred Wohl (D.R.P. 58957 vom 17. August 1890) auf ein Verfahren gekommen, schwer gefrierbare Nitrate des Glyzerins herzustellen; sein Leitmotiv war in erster Linie nicht, die Gefrierbarkeit des Trinitroglyzerins zu vermeiden, vielmehr war ihm der letztere Körper zu explosionskräftig, auch zu reich an Sauerstoff, so daß er nitrierte Glyzerine suchte, welche weniger als drei Salpetersäurereste im Glyzerinmolekül enthielten; zu diesem Zwecke ging er bei der Nitrierung von Äthern des Glyzerins aus, d. h. Körpern der Formel $C_3H_5(OH)_2 \cdot OR$, worin R entweder $\underset{\text{Methyl—}}{CH_3}$ oder $\underset{\text{Äthyl—}}{C_2H_5}$ oder $\underset{\text{Buthyl—}}{C_4H_9}$ oder $\underset{\text{Glyzeryl—}}{C_3H_5(OH)_2}$ bedeutet; insbesondere mit dem letzteren, dem Glyzeryläther des Glyzerins $C_3H_5(OH)_2 \cdot O \cdot C_3H_5(OH)_2$ oder Diglyzerin beschäftigte er sich; er stellte das Di- oder Polyglyzerin nicht in reinem Zustande, sondern im Gemisch mit Glyzerin her, indem er Glyzerin mit Schwefelsäure auf 130 bis 160° erwärmte; er erhielt so ein zähflüssiges Produkt, in welchem je nach der Dauer des Erhitzens und der verwendeten Säuremenge mehr oder weniger Glyzerin polymerisiert war; das resultierende Gemenge von unverändertem Glyzerin und gebildetem Diglyzerin wurde in üblicher Weise nitriert und lieferte ein Sprengöl, das weniger reich an Sauerstoff war, das aber auch die wertvolle Eigenschaft des Nichtgefrierens besaß. — Statt des Diglyzerins oder Glyzeryläthers des Glyzerins wurden teilweise andere Äther gebildet, wenn vor dem Erhitzen mit Schwefelsäure dem Glyzerin Methyl-, Äthyl- oder Isoamylalkohol zugesetzt wurde.

W. Will (D.R.P. 181754) hat später in Neubabelsberg ein anderes Verfahren ausgearbeitet, um Glyzerin in Di- bzw. Polyglyzerine überzuführen, um dann solche zu nitrieren; er fand, daß durch einfaches Erhitzen von Glyzerin derart, daß nur die höher siedenden Anteile zurückfließen, das abgespaltene Wasser aber abdestilliert, erhebliche Mengen des Glyzerins anhydrisiert werden können, nach der Gleichung

$$2\,C_3H_5(OH)_3 = H_2O + \underbrace{C_3H_5(OH)_2—O—C_3H_5(OH)_2}_{\text{Diglyzerin}}.$$

Wenn man Glyzerin 7 bis 9 Stunden auf 290 bis 295° erhitzt, so bilden sich bis zu 60 Prozent Diglyzerin, daneben je nach der Erhitzung eine etwas größere oder geringere Beimengung von Tri- oder Polyglyzerinen. Wenn man das Kondensationsprodukt durch Zufügen frischen Glyzerins so verdünnt, daß das Gemisch noch 20 bis 25 Prozent Diglyzerin enthält, so kann man durch Nitrieren ein Sprengöl gewinnen, daß bei — 15 bis 20° noch nicht gefriert und ungefähr dieselbe Sprengkraft besitzt wie Trinitroglyzerin. Natürlich kann man aus dem Kondensationsprodukt auch das reine Diglyzerin isolieren und nitrieren; man kommt dann zu reinem Tetranitrodiglyzerin $C_3H_5(ONO_2)_2—O—C_3H_5(ONO_2)_2$, das bei gleicher Sprengkraft wie das Trinitroglyzerin, $C_3H_5(ONO_2)_3$ weniger empfindlich als letzteres ist.

Einen anderen Weg zur Herstellung von Polyglyzerinen hatte bereits erheblich früher Lourenzo angegeben (Lieb. Ann. 119, 218; Compt. rend. 1861, 359), nämlich Erhitzen von mit Salzsäure gesättigtem wässerigen Glyzerin auf 130°; Lourenzo selbst hat sein Kondensationsprodukt nicht nitriert, Will hat später versucht, ein nach Lourenzos Angaben hergestelltes Produkt mit Salpeterschwefelsäure zu behandeln, kam jedoch zu keinem Resultat. Escales und Novak[1] haben das Lourenzosche Verfahren modifiziert und kamen so zu einem Produkt, das neben unverändertem Glyzerin und Mono- bzw. Dichlorhydrin auch Di- und Polyglyzerine bzw. Chlorhydrine derselben enthielt und sich gut nitrieren ließ; das erhaltene Sprengöl, das also nitrierte Chlorhydrine und nitriertes Diglyzerin nebeneinander enthält, genügt den Anforderungen betreffs Nichtgefrierbarkeit.

Neben dem basischen Dinitroglyzerin

$$C_3H_5\begin{cases}OH\\(O\cdot NO_2)_2\end{cases},$$

dem nitrierten Chlorhydrin

$$C_3H_5\begin{cases}Cl\\(O\cdot NO_2)_2\end{cases}$$

und dem nitrierten Diglyzerin

$$C_3H_5(ONO_2)_2—O—C_3H_5(ONO_2)_2$$

hat man auch Ester des Glyzerins mit organischen Säuren, besonders mit Ameisensäure und Essigsäure, nitriert; Vezio

[1] Deutsche Patentanmeldung E. 11704 vom 12. Mai 1906.

Vender[1] führte das Glyzerin-mono-Formin $C_3H_5(OH)_2\cdot(O\cdot CHO)$ und das Glyzerin-mono-Acetin $C_3H_5(OH)_2(O\cdot CH_3\cdot CO)$ in Dinitroformin $C_3H_5(O\cdot NO_2)_2(O\cdot CHO)$ und Dinitroacetin $C_3H_5(ONO_2)_2(O\cdot CH_3\cdot CO)$ über; diese beiden sind Sprengöle von der gleichen Sprengkraft wie Trinitroglyzerin, aber weniger empfindlich, außerdem besitzen sie einen sehr niedrigen Erstarrungspunkt; im Verhältnis von 10 bis 30 Prozent dem Trinitroglyzerin beigemengt ergeben sie Explosivstoffe, deren Erstarrungspunkt bis zu -20^0 C heruntergeht.

Alle bisherigen Nitrate wurden aus dem Glyzerin, dessen Estern oder Äthern erhalten; nun ist es klar, daß man in analoger Weise wie aus dem dreiwertigen Alkohol Glyzerin $CH_2OH-CHOH-CH_2OH$ auch aus einwertigen Alkoholen, z. B. Äthylalkohol C_2N_5OH, Nitrate darstellen kann, welche explosive Eigenschaften besitzen; tatsächlich hat auch Alfred Nobel das Äthylnitrat $C_2H_5ONO_2$, engl. Patent 4179/1875, besonders als Beimengung verwandt; der niedrige Siedepunkt (87^0) sowie große Empfindlichkeit gegen Schlag und Stoß wirken aber störend; deshalb hat Liebert (wie schon erwähnt) in seinem D.R.P. 51022 vom 29. März 1889 als Zusatz zu Trinitroglyzerin das Isoamylnitrat $C_5H_{11}ONO_2$ vorgeschlagen, daß erst bei 148^0 siedet und gegen Schlag und Stoß sehr beständig ist; ein Gehalt von 5 Prozent Isoamylnitrat läßt das gewöhnliche Glyzerintrinitrat auch bei -35^0 C. nicht gefrieren.

Die Köln-Rottweiler Pulverfabriken (Patent Claessen 179879 vom 18. November 1904) verwenden Glykolnitrat; das Glykol CH_2OH-CH_2OH vermag als zweiwertiger Alkohol ein Dinitrat $C_2H_4(O\cdot NO_2)_2$ zu bilden; ein Zusatz von 5 bis 30 Prozent desselben vermag die Gefrierbarkeit des Nitroglyzerins und der daraus hergestellten Sprengstoffe entweder herabzumindern oder ganz aufzuheben.

Eine vollständige Klärung des Kapitels der ungefrierbaren Nitroglyzerinsprengstoffe ist noch nicht erfolgt, da von verschiedenen Seiten hierüber gearbeitet wird und erst die Praxis ergeben kann, welcher Weg der beste ist.

Über die Weltproduktion in Nitroglyzerinstoffen hat Oscar Guttmann für das Jahr 1899 folgende Zusammenstellung gemacht:[2]

[1] Zeitschr. Schieß-Sprengstoffe II. S. 21.
[2] Chem. Zeitschr. I, S. 92.

Deutschland	10300 Tonnen
England.	8100 „
Österreich-Ungarn	2300 „
Frankreich	1500 „
Italien	525 „
Spanien und Portugal.	3500 „
Belgien und Holland	450 „
Schweiz.	600 „
Schweden und Norwegen . . .	600 „
Rußland	500 „
Griechenland	175 „
Transvaal	8000 „
Ver. Staaten von Nordamerika	20000 „
Kanada	5000 „
Australien	600 „
Weltproduktion	62150 Tonnen.

Beim Bau des Simplontunnels wurden 1640000 kg Nitroglyzerinsprengstoffe verwendet; davon waren 1400000 kg Sprenggelatine und 140000 kg Gelatinedynamit; beim Vortrieb des Tunnels wurde die aus 92 Prozent Nitroglyzerin und 8 Prozent Kollodiumwolle hergestellte Sprenggelatine verwendet.

Zweiter Abschnitt.

Die Herstellung des Glyzerintrinitrates (Trinitroglyzerins).

A. Das Glyzerin.

Die zur Fabrikation des Nytroglyzerins benötigten Rohstoffe sind: Glyzerin, Salpetersäure und Schwefelsäure; über die beiden letzteren sind in Band II (Die Schießbaumwolle) nähere Angaben gemacht worden, so daß wir an dieser Stelle uns nur mit dem Glyzerin befassen werden.

Das Glyzerin wurde im Jahre 1779 von dem Apotheker Karl Wilhelm Scheele zu Köping in Schweden bei der — zwecks Erzeugung von Bleipflaster — vorgenommenen Verseifung eines Öles mit Bleioxyd entdeckt und wegen seines süßen Geschmackes „Principium dulce oleorum“ genannt, was mit „Ölsüß“ übersetzt wurde; etwa 40 Jahre später — im Jahre 1817 — folgten dieser ersten Auffindung die bahnbrechenden Arbeitcn der französischen Chemiker Michel Eugène Chevreul und Henry

Braconnot, welche das Glyzerin als die Stammsubstanz fast aller natürlichen Fette und Öle erkannten und — nach dem griechischen Worte γλυκυς (süß) — mit seinem noch heute gebräuchlichen Namen belegten; Pelouze stellte seine Zusammensetzung fest, Berthelot zeigte 1853 die künstlich durchführbare Bildung (Synthese) der Fette aus Glyzerin und Fettsäuren, Berthelot und Wurtz lehrten die Konstitution des Glyzerins kennen. Durch alle diese Arbeiten wurde klargelegt, daß die Fette und Öle Glyzeride, d. h. esterartige Verbindungen des dreiatomigen Alkohols Glyzerin mit höheren Fettsäuren — Palmitinsäure, Stearinsäure, Ölsäure u. a. — sind und gefunden, daß man allgemein bei Einwirkung von esterspaltenden (verseifenden) Mitteln einerseits die genannten Säuren bzw. ihre Salze (Seifen), andererseits Glyzerin erhält. Diese Fettspaltung bzw. Verseifung wird in der Stearinkerzen- und Seifenindustrie in größtem Maßstabe technisch durchgeführt und liefert so viel Glyzerin, daß andere Gewinnungsarten kaum in Betracht kommen; wir erwähnen daher nur ganz kurz das Auftreten des Glyzerins als Nebenprodukt bei der alkoholischen Gärung des Zuckers und Bemühungen, aus den Destillationsrückständen vergorener Flüssigkeiten das Glyzerin zu gewinnen. (D.R.P. 114492, 125788, 129578, 141703.)

Das Ausgangsmaterial für die technische Glyzeringewinnung bilden tierische und pflanzliche Fette (Talg, Schweinefett, Knochenfett, Tran — Palmöl, Palmkernöl, Baumwollsamenöl, Kokosöl, Olivenöl, Sesamöl, Erdnußöl, Rizinusöl, Leinöl). Die Verarbeitung dieser Stoffe zu Seifen ohne Kenntnis der theoretisch-chemischen Grundlagen — auf rein empirischem Wege — ist längst bekannt; die Stearinkerzenindustrie entwickelte sich auf wissenschaftlicher Grundlage seit 1817; die Glyzeringewinnung nahm erst einen Aufschwung, nachdem man — etwa im Jahre 1860 — gelernt hatte, diesen Stoff zu destillieren; wesentlich gefördert wurde die Verwertung der Glyzerinwässer durch die Nachfrage der Dynamitfabriken; seitdem wird fast überall Rücksicht auf das aus den Fetten und Ölen sich abspaltende Glyzerin genommen, während man früher, besonders in den Seifensiedereien, die Unterlaugen einfach weglaufen ließ. Die Verarbeitung der Fette und Öle kann so erfolgen, daß man lediglich Spaltung in freie Säuren und Glyzerin herbeiführt, oder auch in der Weise, daß man direkt verseift, d. h. fettsaures Alkali und Glyzerin erzeugt. In der Seifenfabrikation hat man jahrhundertelang ausschließlich das letztere Verfahren der Verseifung angewandt, indem man das Fett (= fettsaures Glyzerin) durch Ätzkalilauge in fettsaures Kali (Schmierseife) und Glyzerin — oder durch Ätznatronlauge in fettsaures Natron (Kernseife) und Glyzerin überführte. — Von P. Krebitz ist vor einigen Jahren ein Verfahren, das zwar an sich schon früher bekannt, aber nicht betriebsfähig ausgearbeitet war, in die Technik eingeführt worden (D.R.P. 155108), wonach das Fett mittels Ätzkalk zu fettsaurem Kalk (Kalkseife) und Glyzerin verseift und der fettsaure Kalk mittels kohlensaurem Natron in Kernseife umgesetzt wird. — Bei der Fabrikation der Stearinkerzen wird ausschließlich das Fettspaltungsverfahren angewandt, da man hier neben Glyzerin die freien Fettsäuren (nicht deren Alkalisalze, die Seifen) erhalten will; von diesen Säuren sind die Stearinsäure und Palmitinsäure feste Körper, daher für die Kerzenfabrikation — gewöhnlich unter Zusatz von 10 Prozent Paraffin — verwendbar, während die flüssige Ölsäure durch Abpressen entfernt wird. — Die technische Durchführung des Verseifungs- bzw. Spaltungsprozesses der Fette kann hier nur ganz kurz behandelt werden. Bei der gewöhnlichen Verseifung werden 100 Teile Fett mit 13·5 bis 15 Teilen Ätznatron oder 19 bis 21 Teilen Ätzkali in offenen eisernen Siedekesseln gelinde gekocht, dann wird durch Zufügen von Kochsalz (Aussalzen) eine Trennung herbeigeführt, wobei sich oben die als halbgeschmolzene Masse abgeschiedene Seife, unten die das Glyzerin, die Salze und das überschüssige Alkali enthaltende „Unterlauge" abscheidet, aus welch letzterer man ein als Laugenglyzerin bezeichnetes Rohglyzerin erhält. — Bei dem Krebitzverfahren wird Fett mit bestimmten Mengen frischer Kalkmilch (Ätzkalk) versotten, die Kalkseife durch Auswaschen von Glyzerin befreit (Glyzerinwässer nach Krebitz) und dann mit Sodalösung zersetzt. — In der Fettspaltung unterscheidet man grundsätzlich zwei Arten, je nachdem man im geschlossenen Gefäß (Autoklaven) unter Druck oder im offenen Kessel bei gewöhnlichem Atmosphärendruck arbeitet. Im Autoklavenverfahren kann man bei entsprechend hohem Druck (12 bis 15 Atmosphären) schon durch Wasser eine, wenn auch nicht ganz vollständige Spaltung herbeiführen; eine zweckmäßigere Methode fand de Milly im Jahre 1855, wonach bei nur 5 bis 6 Atmosphären Druck gearbeitet und die Reaktion durch Zusatz von wenig gebranntem Kalk, Magnesia, Zinkoxyd oder Zinkstaub eingeleitet wird, um dann von selbst weiter zu gehen. Der Autoklav, gewöhnlich ein aus 22 bis 23 mm starken Kupferplatten hergestelltes zylinderförmiges Gefäß von ca. 1 m Durchmesser und 3 bis 4 m Höhe, wird je nach seiner Größe mit 1000 bis 2000 kg Fett gefüllt, dann werden 2 bis 3 Prozent gebrannter Kalk (oder 1 Prozent Magnesia, bzw. 0·3 bis 0·5 Prozent Zinkoxyd und Zinkstaub) — also viel weniger als nötig wäre, um die im Fett vorhandenen Fettsäuren völlig zu binden — mit etwas Fett angerührt zugegeben, durch einströmenden Dampf eine Spannung von etwa 6 Atmosphären erzeugt und ungefähr 6 Stunden lang unter wiederholtem Durchrühren des Inhalts aufrecht erhalten; nach erfolgter Spaltung wird die ganze Masse automatisch in einen Turm hinübergedrückt und einige Zeit der Ruhe überlassen, worauf das Glyzerinwasser sich abscheidet; hieraus wird später das mit Saponifikationsglyzerin bezeichnete Rohglyzerin gewonnen; die freien Fettsäuren sind mit Bruchteilen von Kalk-(bzw. Magnesia- oder Zink-)Seifen vermengt, welch letztere durch Behandlung mit Schwefelsäure oder auf anderem Wege noch in freie Säuren übergeführt werden müssen. Nach einem Verfahren der Société Generale belge de Deglycerination (D.R.P. 171200) arbeitet man ebenfalls bei 5 bis 6 Atmosphären Druck unter Zusatz von wenig Alkali, Metall oder Metalloxyd, setzt aber außerdem 5 Prozent des Reaktionsproduktes hinzu, welches von der vorausgegangenen Operation her sich nach Abscheidung des Glyzerins im Autoklaven befindet (also wesentlich Fettsäuren); hierdurch soll bei der nächsten Spaltung die Reaktion besser eingeleitet werden. Bei der Spaltung im offenen Kessel, d. h. ohne Druck, arbeitete man früher allgemein mit Schwefelsäure in dem sog. „Sulfurierungsgefäß“, einem zugedeckten, mit Dunstabzugsrohr und Rührvorrichtung versehenen zylindrischen Apparat, in welchem das Fett durch eine Dampfschlange auf 110 bis 120° C erhitzt wird, worauf man unter ständigem Rühren 4 bis 5 Gewichtsprozente Schwefelsäure von 66° Bé zuführt; nach 15 bis 20 Minuten wird die schwarz gewordene Masse in ein bis zu einem Drittel mit kochendem Wasser gefülltes Gefäß gebracht und durch 5- bis 6 stündiges Kochen mit Dampf zersetzt; nach Beendigung schwimmen die freien Fettsäuren oben, das Glyzerin ist in dem Säurewasser gelöst und wird daraus, nach Entfernung der Säuren durch Ausfällen mit Kalk, gewonnen; das hier sich ergebende Rohglyzerin wird (sonderbarerweise) als Destillationsglyzerin bezeichnet, da die bei der Säurespaltung erhaltenen Fettsäuren erst durch Destillation mit Wasserdampf gereinigt werden müssen. — Ernst Twitchell (D.R.P. 114491) verwendet zum Spalten statt der reinen Schwefelsäure Doppelsulfosäuren aromatischer und fetter Körper der Formel $R \cdot HSO_3 \cdot C_{18}H_{35}O_2$ (worin R einen aromatischen Rest bedeutet), welche aus Benzol (oder Phenol oder Naphtalin), Schwefelsäure und Ölsäure hergestellt werden (Twitchells Reagens); das geläuterte Fett wird mit Wasser sowie mit Wasser angerührtem Reagens zunächst 12 bis 24 Stunden, dann mit neuem Wasser noch 12 bis 16 Stunden gekocht und ist dann bis auf etwa 95 Prozent gespalten; die Glyzerinwässer werden nach Trennung von den obenschwimmenden Fettsäuren mittels Baryumkarbonat von Schwefelsäure befreit.

Neben der sauren Verseifung durch Schwefelsäure bzw. Sulfofettsäuren ist neuerdings ein Verfahren ausgebildet worden, die Spaltung ohne Druck in anderer Weise, nämlich durch Enzyme, also nicht organisierte Fermente, vorzunehmen. Diese Methode wurde von W. Connstein, E. Hoyer und H. Wartenberg bzw. den Vereinigten Chemischen Werken in Charlottenburg in der Weise ausgearbeitet, daß feingemahlener Rizinussamen (bzw. Rizinusölextrakt) in ungefährer Menge von 6 Prozent des zu spaltenden Öles dem mit 40 Prozent Wasser und 0·2 Prozent Manganosulfat emulsionierten Öle zugesetzt wird, worauf man 24 Stunden lang unter gelegentlichem Umrühren stehen läßt; die Spaltung ist dann bis etwa 85 bis 95 Prozent gediehen; man leitet nun Wasserdampf ein, erwärmt auf 80°, gibt eine bestimmte Menge Schwefelsäure zu und rührt um, bis die Fettsäure sich abscheidet; nach längerem Stehenlassen hat man oben Fettsäuren, unten Glyzerinwasser, in der Mitte eine schleimige Schicht von Samenteilen,

Fettsäuren und Glyzerinwasser, woraus letzteres durch Auswaschen isoliert wird. — Maurice Nicloux ist es gelungen, durch Zentrifugieren die Gewebeteile und den Aleuronkörper des zerstoßenen Rizinussamens von der Zellsubstanz, dem Cytoplasma, zu trennen und letzteres als Hauptträger des wirksamen Spaltungsprinzips zu eruieren. — Das aus den Glyzerinwässern der Fermentspaltung gewonnene Rohglyzerin wird als Fermentglyzerin bezeichnet. — Über die Verarbeitung der verdünnten Glyzerinwässer auf Rohglyzerin sei folgendes ausgeführt:

Die bei der Autoklavenspaltung erhaltenen Glyzerinwässer mit 6 bis 16 Prozent Glyzerin sind die reinsten; sie werden in offenen Pfannen oder besser in Vakuumapparaten à simple oder double effet (nach C. Heckmann in Berlin D.R.P. 71701 oder V. Hänig & Cie in Dresden) bis zu 80° Bé konzentriert und liefern das wichtige Handelsprodukt „Saponifikationsglyzerin" mit 85 bis 90 Prozent Glyzeringehalt und 0·3 bis 0·5 Prozent Asche; das spezifische Gewicht ist 1·240 bis 1·242, der Geschmack süßlich, die Farbe hell- bis dunkelgelb; es soll mit Bleiacetat nur einen schwachen Niederschlag und mit Salzsäure behandelt kaum eine Trübung geben. Die Bewertung des Rohglyzerins umfaßt die Bestimmung des Aschengehaltes, der organischen Verunreinigungen und des Glyzerins; zur letzteren Bestimmung eignet sich am besten die Acetinmethode oder die Hehnersche Modifikation der Bichromatmethode. — Die Glyzerinwässer nach Krebitz sind ebenfalls recht gut, nur muß man vor dem Eindampfen den Kalkgehalt durch Zusatz von Schwefelsäure entfernen. — Bei der Schwefelsäurespaltung ergeben die Glyzerinwässer nach ihrer Konzentration das sog. Destillationsrohglyzerin mit 84 bis 86 Prozent Glyzerin, 2 bis 3·5 Prozent Asche, einem spezifischen Gewicht von 1·240 bis 1·242; es hat eine helle Farbe, aber einen adstringierenden Geschmack und hinterläßt, zwischen den Händen verrieben, einen unangenehmen Geruch; mit Bleiacetat gibt es einen starken Niederschlag, mit Salzsäure eine starke Trübung; der Glyzeringehalt wird am besten nach dem Acetinverfahren bestimmt. — Um aus den Glyzerinwässern des Twitchell-Verfahrens Rohglyzerin herzustellen, gibt man nach dem Absetzen gerade genug Kalkmilch hinzu, um eben alkalische Reaktion zu erhalten; man entfernt nun den Kalkniederschlag durch Abgießen oder Filtrieren und engt ein; war viel Kalkmilch zur Säureneutralisation angewandt worden, so konzentriert man zweckmäßig die Glyzerinwässer in zwei Phasen; man engt zunächst nur auf 15 oder 20° Bé (ungefähr 45 Prozent Glyzerin) ein, läßt dann das sich noch ausscheidende Calciumsulfat sich ausscheiden und absetzen, zieht die nunmehr klare Flüssigkeit ab und konzentriert dann weiter auf 28° Bé (88 Prozent Glyzerin); Eindampfen in Vakuumapparaten. — Die bei der Seifenfabrikation durch Kochen der Fette und Öle im offenen Kessel mit fixen Alkalien sich ergebenden Seifenunterlaugen enthalten im Durchschnitt 5 bis 10 Prozent Glyzerin, außerdem das zum Aussalzen der Seife benutzte Salz, sowie unverbrauchtes Ätzalkali und kohlensaure Alkalien, ferner Verunreinigungen aller Art, welche teils bei der Gewinnung der Fette durch Pressen,

Auskochen, Extrahieren aus tierischen oder pflanzlichen Organen, teils bei der weiteren Behandlung hinzugekommen sind. Die gelösten Salze haben bei der Konzentration der Flüssigkeit die Neigung, zu Kuchen zusammenzubacken und auf den Heizflächen festzubrennen, die organischen Beimengungen und Verunreinigungen sind wegen ihres kolloidalen Zustandes durch Filtration nicht zu entfernen; somit bietet die Aufarbeitung zum Laugenrohglyzerin Schwierigkeiten. Ähnlich liegen die Verhältnisse bei der Konzentration der Glyzerinwässer der Fermentspaltung zum Fermentrohglyzerin, wobei auch noch Hindernisse durch Aufschäumen eintreten. — Die zur Reinigung vorgeschlagene Dialyse (D.R.P. 13953 und 17547) hat sich nicht bewährt; der Gedanke, das Glyzerin in den verdünnten Wässern durch Erhitzen mit fetten Säuren wieder zu verbinden (D.R.P. 17299), dürfte praktisch auch keine Anwendung finden; ebensowenig das D.R.P. 20275, wonach ein Teil der Lauge konzentriert und damit aus frischer Seifenlauge Glyzerin abgeschieden wird. Thomas und Domeier (engl. Patent 2462 [1881]) säuern zunächst die Laugen an, extrahieren nach dem Neutralisieren und filtrieren die Verunreinigungen durch Lösungsmittel, in welchen das Glyzerin selbst unlöslich ist; Hagemann (engl. Patent 8051 [1885]) setzt zuerst $1^1/_2$ Prozent Kalk hinzu, später Harz und zum Schluß Eisenchlorid; nach dem D.R.P. 50438 werden die in einem Behälter gesammelten rohen alkalischen Unterlaugen mit Ätzkalk versetzt und (bis zur Sättigung der Lauge mit Salz) eingedampft; hierauf wird in einem andern Behälter genau mit Salzsäure neutralisiert; durch Zugabe von Metallchloriden und -sulfaten wird nun der größte Teil der Fett- und Harzkörper infolge doppelter Umsetzung ausgeschieden; die letzten seifenartigen Substanzen werden durch Eisen- oder Chromoxyd in unlösliche und zu entfernende basische Salze übergeführt. Nach dem amerikanischen Patent 774172 wird zuerst die Flüssigkeit mit einer Mineralsäure (H_2SO_4) neutralisiert, die unlöslichen Fettsäuren durch Aluminiumsulfat ausgefällt, die Aluminiumseifen abfiltriert, die Flüssigkeit eingedampft, die Mineralsalze ausgeschieden und Baryumchlorid zugegeben; die entstandenen Baryumseifen und das Baryumsulfat können abfiltriert werden; vor der Destillation im Vakuumdampfapparat wird Natriumkarbonat zugesetzt. J. v. Ruymbecke und F. Jobbins geben in ihrem D.R.P. 86563 folgendes an: Die mit $^1/_3$ bis $^1/_2$ Prozent Kalk behandelte Lauge wird auf freies Alkalihydrat und -karbonat analysiert, wobei das mit Harz, Fettsäure und andern organischen Säuren verbundene Alkali nicht mit in Rechnung gezogen wird; zur Neutralisierung des freien Alkalis wird Ferrisulfat zugesetzt, hierauf filtriert und eingeengt. — Ein in der Praxis benutztes Verfahren ist folgendes: Die Seifenunterlauge wird zunächst in offenen Pfannen eingedampft, um den größten Teil der noch in Lösung befindlichen Seife abzuscheiden; nach dem ersten Eindampfen fügt man wieder Wasser zu und dampft nochmals ein, worauf sich ein weiterer Teil der Seife ausscheidet; nun setzt man gelöschten Kalk oder Chlorcalcium zu, um event. Fettreste zu verseifen, kocht abermals auf und läßt in die Neutralisationskästen abfließen, wo die Laugen mit Schwefelsäure behandelt und schließlich neutralisiert werden; die jetzt kaum noch größere Mengen organischer kolloidaler Stoffe enthaltende Lauge wird bei 70 bis 80° C mit einer 1prozentigen Lösung von schwefelsaurer Tonerde unter Zusatz von etwas Schwefelsäure bis zur deutlich sauren Reaktion versetzt (ein Überschuß von Säure ist notwendig, da sonst der stark auftretende Schaum sich nicht absetzt); nun werden die an der Oberfläche ausgeschiedenen Verunreinigungen abgeschöpft und die Lauge mit Zusatz von 0·5 Prozent kohlensaurem Kalk und 0·1 Prozent kohlensaurer Magnesia aufgekocht; durch die Zusätze wird die überschüssige Säure abgestumpft, die vorhandenen Eisensalze zersetzt und mit den entstandenen Magnesiaseifen in unlösliche Form übergeführt. — Nach einem in der Chem.-Ztg. 1905, S. 84 angegebenen Verfahren werden die Seifenunterlaugen in offenen Pfannen bis zu 30 bis 40 Prozent Glyzeringehalt eingedampft, die dickflüssige Masse mit gepulverter Kreide oder Kieselgur zu kleinen Körnern vermahlen, hieraus mit Weingeist das Glyzerin extrahiert. — Was das Eindampfen der Seifenunterlaugen betrifft, so wären folgende Patente zu erwähnen: D.R.P. 49981 beschreibt einen Apparat zum Einkochen, gekennzeichnet durch die Anordnung einer zur Aufnahme der Glyzerinflüssigkeit bestimmten, mit Seitenfeuerung versehenen Pfanne, deren unterer Teil von den Feuergasen nicht getroffen wird, in Kombination mit einem Ersatzgefäß zur Entfernung der Senkstoffe aus der Glyzerinflüssigkeit. — Das D.R.P. 53500 besagt, daß die einzudampfende Glyzerinflüssigkeit in zwei, durch eine Absperrvorrichtung getrennten Gefäßen teils im kochenden, teils im nichtkochenden Zustand erhalten wird; das kochende Glyzerin wird von den sich ausscheidenden festen Stoffen dadurch befreit, daß letztere in den tiefer liegenden, nicht kochenden Teil hinabsinken. — Nach dem D.R.P. 92803 werden die Laugen im geschlossenen Gefäß durch Dampf unter Druck konzentriert, wobei man bis zu 30° Bé (statt bis zu 28°) gelangen kann. — Das D.R.P. 100881 beschreibt ein Abdampfgefäß mit durchlochtem Zwischenboden zur Aufnahme des sich ausscheidenden Salzes, dadurch gekennzeichnet, daß die Löcher des Zwischenbodens mit konischen Rohraufsätzen versehen sind, durch welche die bis zur Oberkante der Rohraufsätze stehende Lauge hindurchgetrieben wird. — Bei dem D.R.P. 111948 wird die Verdampfung durch rotierende Teller, welche mit Dampf geheizt werden, besorgt, und zwar außerhalb der Flüssigkeitsmasse selbst. — Vielfach verwendet man zum Eindampfen Vakuumapparate, ähnlich den in Zuckerfabriken gelieferten; Bezugsquelle Wegelin & Hübner in Halle, C. E. Rost & Cie. in Dresden. — Das Eindampfen bis zu dem sog. Salzpunkte, d. i. dem Momente, wo sich die Salze auszuscheiden beginnen und die Laugen das spez. Gew. 1·22 bei 15° anzeigen, ist sehr einfach; die Gefäße aber, in welchen die Verdampfung über das spez. Gew. 1·22 bis zum spez. Gew. 1·3 erfolgt, müssen mit geeigneten Rühr- und Kratzapparaten versehen sein, um Verstopfungen der Gefäße durch die sich abscheidenden Salze zu verhindern; zweckentsprechende derartige Vorrichtungen hat Lewkowitsch in den englischen Patenten 28747 und 30616 [1897] angegeben. — Kestner in Lille hat einen Apparat konstruiert, bei welchem die Verdampfung in hohen, vertikalen Röhren mit aufgesetzten Kugeln stattfindet. — Der Vakuumapparat der Firma Heckmann (D.R.P. 106058) hat vertikale Heizröhren und einen konischen, mit sehr weiter Öffnung versehenen Unterteil; daran schließt sich ein auf Rädern ruhendes Gefäß, in welchem sich die während der Verdampfung ausgeschiedenen Salze und Verunreinigungen ablagern und welches vom Apparate getrennt und gesäubert werden kann.

Bis zum Jahre 1890 ließ man die Seifenunterlaugen einfach weglaufen, erst von da ab begann man mit der rationellen Verwertung; die Dynamitfabriken richteten an verschiedenen Orten Verdampfungszentralen ein, wohin die Seifenfabrikanten ihre Laugen abliefern; der Ankauf der letzteren erfolgt nach dem Glyzeringehalt, welcher zu einer lohnenden Gewinnung nicht unter 4 Prozent herabgehen soll. Das auf die eine oder andere Weise erhaltene Rohglyzerin kann man entfärben, klären oder sonst weiter reinigen, doch genügen solche Raffinate für die Fabrikation der Nitrate nicht; zu letzterem Zwecke muß das Glyzerin destilliert werden. Glyzerin ist zwar bei 290° C flüchtig, zersetzt sich jedoch hierbei schon merklich und gibt sehr schlechte Destillationsprodukte; man benutzt daher auch hier das bekannte Verhalten hochsiedender Substanzen, mit Wasserdämpfen schon bei erheblich niedrigeren Temperaturen — besonders im Vakuum — überzudestillieren; Wilson und Payne führten dieses Verfahren zuerst beim Glyzerin ein (1855). Die verdünnten Rohglyzerine vom spez. Gew. 1·1 werden zunächst mit Wasserdampf von 100 bis 110° destilliert, wobei sich die Verunreinigungen ausscheiden; nach allmählicher Steigerung auf 170° reißt der gespannte Wasserdampf die Glyzerindämpfe mit; eine Temperatursteigerung bis 200° muß vermieden werden, um Zersetzungen vorzubeugen. Die Destillate werden in einem System von Röhren kondensiert, welche zu diesem Zwecke mit schlechten Wärmeleitern umgeben sind; im ersten Rohr scheidet sich fast wasserfreies Glyzerin ab, in den folgenden Glyzerinwässer, welche in einer neuen Operation zum Verdünnen des zu destillierenden Rohglyzerins verwandt werden; umstehende Fig. 11 zeigt einen solchen Destillierapparat der Firma C. Heckmann.

In einem neueren Apparat (Fig. 12) der gleichen Firma (D.R.P. 61547) wird das in der Blase *A* enthaltene Rohglyzerin durch 200 bis 300° heißen Dampf auf eine Temperatur von 130 bis 180° gebracht, ohne Erwärmung der Blase durch direkte Feuerung; in dem Destillierapparat ist eventuell eine Vorrichtung zum Niederschlagen des Schaumes angebracht. Aus der Destillierblase *A* treten die glyzerinhaltigen Dämpfe durch ein Rohr *B* in ein Sammelgefäß *C*, welches mit einer Dampfheizungsvorrichtung *D* ausgestattet ist zur Erhaltung einer Temperatur von ca. 90°, damit in dem kondensierten Glyzerin enthaltenes Wasser wieder verdampft; die Dämpfe steigen durch eine Anzahl von Abteilungen *E*, welche über dem Sammelgefäß *C* angeordnet und mit

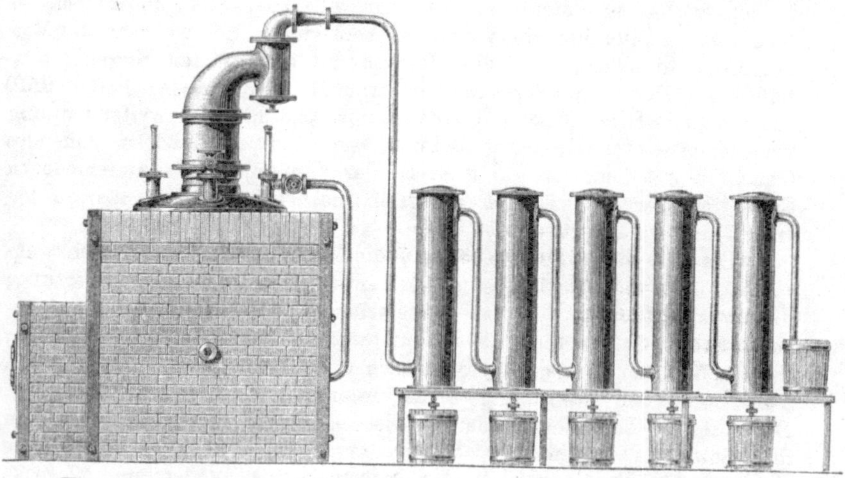

Fig. 11. Glyzerin-Destillierapparat von Heckmann. D.R.P. 61547.

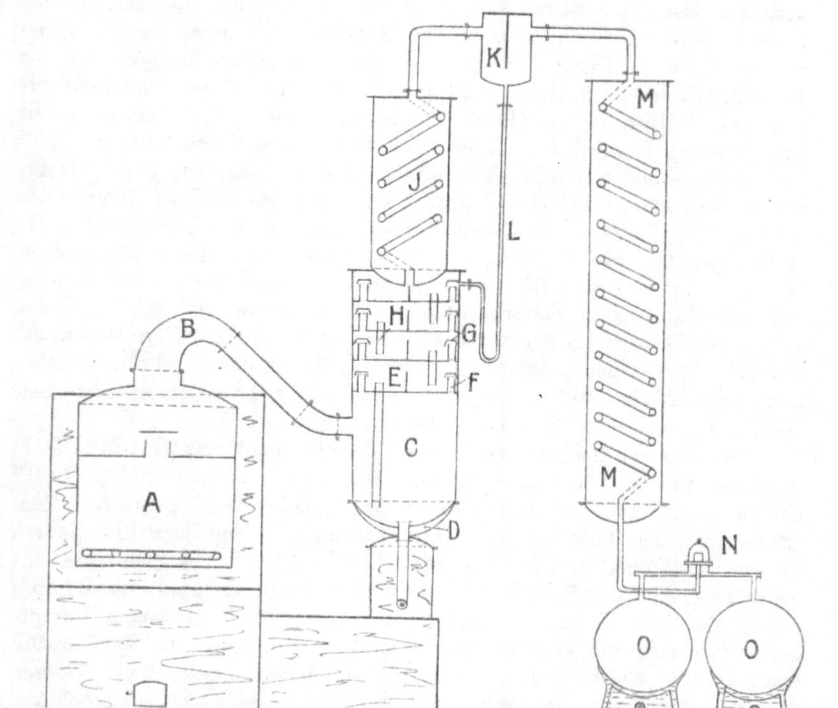

Fig. 12. Glyzerin-Destillierapparat von Heckmann. Durchschnitt.

Dampfdurchtrittsstutzen F, Glocken G und Überlaufrohren H ausgestattet sind und müssen so die sich in den Abteilungen ansammelnde Glyzerinflüssigkeit durchströmen. Hierdurch wird in den einzelnen Abteilungen die kondensierte Flüssigkeit um so reicher an Glyzerin, je näher dieselben nach dem Sammelgefäß hin liegen, so daß die Dämpfe zuerst die glyzerinreichste und weiterhin immer glyzerinärmere Schichten durchdringen und allmählich ihres Glyzeringehaltes beraubt werden, während der Wasserdampf weiter entweicht und in eine darüber liegende Kühlvorrichtung (J) gelangt, welche durch Luft, Gas oder Flüssigkeit bzw. Wasser von einer 80° nicht übersteigenden Temperatur gekühlt wird. Hierdurch wird nur ein verhältnismäßig geringer Teil des Dampfes mit dem letzten Rest von Glyzerin kondensiert und in die darunter befindlichen Abteilungen (E) geführt, wo er die Schichten von Glyzerinflüssigkeit erzeugt, durch welche die Dämpfe hindurchstreichen. Um die Kondensation der letzten etwa im Dampf enthaltenen Glyzerinreste zu befördern, kann man die Kühlvorrichtung noch mit einer zweiten Kondensationsvorrichtung (K) verbinden, aus welcher durch einen Ablauf (L) die etwa noch weiterhin kondensierten Anteile nach den Abteilungen (E) geführt werden. Die nunmehr von Glyzerin vollkommen freien Dämpfe werden in dem Kühler (M) vermittelst Wasserkühlung völlig verdichtet; dieses Kondenswasser gelangt durch eine Probiervorrichtung (N), mittels welcher geprüft werden kann, ob die Destillation richtig geführt wurde, in die Sammelgefäße (O), welche ihrerseits mit einer stark wirkenden Luftpumpe in Verbindung stehen. Durch die im Apparat herrschende Druckverminderung wird es ermöglicht, die Destillation des Glyzerins in der Destillationsblase bei verhältnismäßig niederer Temperatur vor sich gehen zu lassen. Man erzielt dadurch ein Glyzerin von 95 bis 100 Prozent; dabei wird das ganze im Rohmaterial enthaltene Glyzerin auf einen Wurf gereinigt und fast trocken erhalten (spez. Gew. 1·262), so daß besondere Vakuumapparate nicht mehr notwendig sind. Die Verluste bei der Destillation sind dabei sehr geringe und der Gang gut kontrollierbar.

Dieser Apparat wird in Deutschland fast ausschließlich und auch in andern Ländern zum großen Teil für Dynamitglyzerin gebraucht; man kann damit 35 bis 350 kg Destillat pro Stunde gewinnen. Nach Dr. Bela Lach (Chem.-Ztg. 1895) ist es angebracht, vor der Destillation das Rohglyzerin auf ca. 20° Bé zu verdünnen, mit direktem Dampf aufzukochen, etwas frische Kalkmilch zuzusetzen und nun das Ganze 1 bis 2 Stunden tüchtig zu kochen; hierauf läßt man absetzen und filtriert über Spodiumfilter; man entfernt durch diese Operation den größten Anteil an Fettsäuren, Kalkseife und suspendiertem Kalk. Das so behandelte Glyzerin ist nun zur Destillation mit Wasserdampf in eigens konstruiertem Apparate bereit: Das in einem Behälter befindliche Rohglyzerin wird mittels einer geschlossenen Dampfschlange erwärmt und hierauf nach der Destillationsblase abfließen gelassen; ist die Blase gefüllt, so wird durch diese überhitzter Wasserdampf streichen gelassen, bis das Thermometer eine Blasentemperatur von 120° anzeigt; nun wird direkter Wasserdampf eingeleitet, bis die Temperatur auf 200 bis 220° C steigt. Es findet nun eine flotte Destillation statt, die aber nicht zu sehr forciert werden darf. Die ganze Kühlvorrichtung besteht aus Kupferblech und beruht der Hauptsache nach auf Luftkühlung. Ist die Destillation beendet, so kann man durch einen Ablaufstutzen den Glyzeringoudron abziehen; meistens ist aber dieser Rückstand derart zähe, daß man ihn durch das Mannloch herausschaffen muß. In jüngster Zeit hat Dr. Lach seinen Glyzerindestillationsapparat bedeutend vervollkommnet und arbeitet dieser im kontinuierlichen Betriebe. Die Destillation ist durch Anwendung eines Rührwerkes sehr beschleunigt worden; durch das Arbeiten unter Vakuum erhält man das Glyzerin gleich fertig in jeder beliebigen Konzentration, indem die Vorlagen gleichzeitig als Vakuumkonzentrationsapparate dienen. Derartige Apparate baut Krackhardts Nachfolger in Brünn und empfehlen sich dieselben für kleinere Betriebe; für den Großbetrieb eignet sich auch der Apparat von J. v. Ruymbecke und W. F. Jobbins D.R.P. 86829, bei welchem der expandierte Dampf durch indirekte Beheizung mit gesättigtem Dampf von bestimmter Temperatur wieder erhitzt wird. — E. Scott & Sohn in London verwenden einen Multiplexdestillationsapparat, bei welchem ein am Boden angeordneter Hahn die kontinuierliche Abfuhr der ausgeschiedenen Salze gestattet.

Analytische Angaben. Die Bewertung der Glyzerinwässer richtet sich im allgemeinen nach dem Glyzeringehalt, der — um die Verarbeitung auf Rohglyzerin lohnend zu gestalten — nicht unterhalb gewisser, von verschiedenen Momenten abhängiger Grenzen fallen darf; die analytische Bestimmung des Glyzerins wird gewöhnlich nicht direkt in den verdünnten und verunreinigten Glyzerinwässern ausgeführt, sondern man isoliert zunächst möglichst das Glyzerin; Lewkowitsch verfährt wie folgt: 100 ccm der Durchschnittsprobe werden, falls sie sehr sauer, mit Barytwasser neutralisiert, dann mit dem 3- bis 4fachen Volumen absoluten Alkohol und $1\frac{1}{2}$fachen Volumen Äther versetzt und über Nacht stehen gelassen; die abgeschiedenen Substanzen werden dann durch Filtration entfernt und der Rückstand mit frischer Alkoholäthermischung ausgewaschen; Filtrat und Waschflüssigkeit werden in einem Kölbchen auf dem Wasserbad eingeengt, bis kein Alkoholgeruch mehr zu bemerken ist; in dem so erhaltenen Rohglyzerin wird der Glyzeringehalt nach dem Acetinverfahren genau ermittelt und in Prozenten auf die angewandten 100 ccm der Durchschnittsprobe umgerechnet. — O. Heller verfährt bei sämtlichen Glyzerinwässern und Seifenunterlaugen folgendermaßen: 100 ccm der Flüssigkeit (wenn Bodensätze vorliegen, nach vorherigem guten Umschütteln) werden abgemessen, neutralisiert und in ein hohes Becherglas (mindestens 12 cm hoch) filtriert; man stellt dieses Glas in ein Wasserbad und dampft die Flüssigkeit ab; wenn etwa $^2/_3$ abgedampft sind, gibt man etwa 60 ccm Ätheralkohol hinzu und verdampft weiter bis zu einem geringen Rückstand; jetzt werden 150 ccm einer Mischung von $^1/_3$ Äther und $^2/_3$ absolutem Alkohol zugesetzt, gut umgerührt und nach dem Absetzen der Mischung die Flüssigkeit in eine größere tiefe Porzellanschale abfiltriert, wobei das Filter mit Ätheralkohol sehr gut nachzuwaschen ist; der im Becherglase vorhandene Rückstand wird eventuell noch zerrieben und mit Ätheralkohol ausgelaugt. Die Filtrate werden auf dem (nicht kochenden) Wasserbade langsam abgedampft und der Verdampfungsrückstand, welcher gewöhnlich noch einige Sedimente abgeschieden hat, mit etwa 50 ccm Ätheralkohol aufgelöst und in einen genau tarierten Philippsbecher filtriert, letzterer in ein Wasserbad gehängt und sein Inhalt verdampft; ist kein Alkoholgeruch mehr wahrzunehmen, so läßt man erkalten, wägt das erhaltene Rohglyzerin und bestimmt dessen Glyzeringehalt nach dem Acetinverfahren. — In Fabrikbetrieben wird, besonders bei Seifenunterlaugen, nachstehende Methode angewandt: 100 g Lauge werden zum Kochen erhitzt und mit Salzsäure angesäuert; die sich ausscheidenden Fettsäuren usw. werden abfiltriert, das Filtrat neutralisiert und mit Bleiacetat versetzt; nach dem Abfiltrieren des neuen Niederschlages wird die klare Lösung eingedampft, das sich ausscheidende Salz mittels eines Löffels ausgeschöpft und auf der Filterpumpe abgesaugt; dem Salz werden die schließlich resultierenden wenigen Kubikzentimeter Lösung zugefügt und das Ganze dann mit einem Gemisch von drei Teilen Alkohol und einem Teil Äther ausgezogen; aus dem Verdampfungsrückstand des Extraktes wird dann der Glyzeringehalt nach der Acetinmethode ermittelt.

Für Rohglyzerine empfiehlt O. Heller[1] folgende Prüfungsmethode: Man wägt sehr genau ca. 1 g des Glyzerins in ein gewogenes, hochwandiges Wägegläschen (5 cm hoch, 3 cm breit) und trocknet im Trockenschrank bei 105° C bis zum konstanten Gewicht; alsdann läßt man im Exsikkator erkalten, setzt den Glasstöpsel auf und wägt; der Gewichtsverlust ist als Wasser in Rechnung zu stellen. Ferner werden 2 g Glyzerin im Platintiegel über Asbestunterlage langsam verdampft, abgebrannt und mäßig geglüht, bis die Kohle verbrannt ist; der Rückstand, nach dem Erkalten im Exsikkator gewogen, ist die anorganische Asche. Endlich werden 10 g Rohglyzerin, event. nach Zusatz von einem Tropfen Essigsäure, in einem genau gewogenen 100 ccm-Rundkölbchen mit weitem Halse im Vakuum erhitzt, bis alles Wasser und Glyzerin verdampft ist; der Rückstand enthält noch etwas Glyzerin mechanisch eingeschlossen, man unterbricht daher die Destillation, läßt etwas erkalten, gießt ca. 15 ccm Wasser ins Kölbchen und destilliert nochmals im Vakuum (bei der Destillation befindet sich das Kölbchen in einem bis auf 290° erhitzten Luftbad, und zwar in einem Drahtgestell, das unten einen kleinen Drahtboden enthält, auf welchen man über einem Stück Asbestpappe das Kölbchen aufsetzt); es hinterbleibt ein trockener, fast pulveriger Rückstand, der Destillationsrückstand des Glyzerins, welcher nach Abzug der anorganischen Asche den organischen Rückstand des Glyzerins repräsentiert. Die Wiegedifferenz zwischen Kölbchen mit Rohglyzerin und dem Kölbchen mit Rückstand gibt — abzüglich des früher gefundenen Wassers — den Glyzeringehalt.

[1] Seifenindustrie-Kalender 1907, S. 149.

Die gewichtsanalytische Bestimmung des Glyzerins kann nach verschiedenen Methoden erfolgen: a) Acetinverfahren.[1] Glyzerin mit Essigsäureanhydrid zusammen erhitzt gibt Triacetin $C_3H_5(OC_2H_3O)_3$; verseift man letzteres mit einem bekannten Überschusse einer genau titrierten Ätznatronlauge, so wird dieselbe von der im Triacetin gebundenen Essigsäure teilweise neutralisiert; durch Zurücktitrieren des nicht gesättigten Teiles der Lauge ergibt sich, wieviel zur Verseifung des Triacetins verbraucht wurde. — Die Analyse wird wie folgt bewirkt: 1·0 bis 1·5 g Glyzerin, welches mindestens 65prozentig sein muß, werden genau in einen 100 bis 150 ccm fassenden langhalsigen Rundkolben eingewogen, hierzu ca. 3 g wasserfreies Natriumacetat und ca. 8 g Essigsäureanhydrid zugesetzt und dann am Rückflußkühler eine Stunde lang zum gelinden Sieden erwärmt; man entfernt dann die Flamme, läßt abkühlen, spült durch den Rückflußkühler 50 ccm destilliertes Wasser in den Kolben hinein und erwärmt nun gelinde mit der Flamme, ohne den Rückflußkühler zu entfernen, unter zeitweisem Umschwenken des Kolbens; hierbei löst sich das vorher gebildete Triacetin in Wasser auf; man filtriert diese Lösung ohne Verlust in einen Literkolben, wäscht das Filter sehr gut nach, gibt etwas Phenolphtaleinlösung dazu und setzt sofort vorsichtig von einer dünnen, nicht titrierten, etwa 2prozentigen Natronlauge so lange zu, bis die zur Acetylierung nicht verbrauchte, absichtlich im Überschuß zugesetzte Essigsäure gerade neutralisiert ist (minimale Rosafärbung); nun läßt man in den Literkolben genau 25 ccm einer etwa 10prozentigen — aber vorher durch Normalsalzsäure genau titrierten — Natronlauge fließen und bringt diese Mischung zum Kochen, wobei das Triacetin zu essigsaurem Natron und Glyzerin verseift wird, was nach viertelstündigem Kochen geschehen ist; man titriert dann das noch freie, d. h. zur Verseifung des Triacetins nicht verwendete Ätznatron mit Normalsalzsäure zurück. Beispiel. Abgewogen: 1·324 g Glyzerin; die zur Verseifung angewandten 25 ccm Natronlauge entsprachen 60·5 ccm Normalsalzsäure; zum Zurücktitrieren der unverbrauchten Natronlauge nötig 21·5 ccm Normalsalzsäure; zur Verseifung des Triacetins verbraucht 60·5 — 21·5 = 39 ccm Normalsalzsäure. 1 ccm Normalsalzsäure = 1 ccm Normalnatronlauge = 0·092 = 0·03067 g Glyzerin, also 39 ccm = 1·196 g oder 90·3 Prozent des untersuchten Rohglyzerins. — b) Die Permanganatmethode beruht auf der Oxydation des Glyzerins zu Oxalsäure, Kohlensäure und Wasser; 0·2 bis 0·3 g hoch konzentriertes Glyzerin oder eine entsprechende Menge verdünntes Glyzerin werden in einen geräumigen Kolben gebracht, auf 250 ccm mit Wasser verdünnt und mit 10 g festem Ätzkali versetzt; hierauf wird bei gewöhnlicher Temperatur so lange eine 5prozentige Lösung von Kaliumpermanganat zugesetzt, bis die Flüssigkeit nicht mehr grün, sondern blau oder dunkel gefärbt ist; beim Kochen scheidet sich dann Mangansuperoxydhydrat aus und die Flüssigkeit wird rot. Man setzt

---

[1] O. Heller, Seifenindustrie-Kalender 1907, S. 146.

nun tropfenweise eine Lösung von schwefliger Säure oder Natriumsulfit hinzu, bis die Flüssigkeit sich gerade entfärbt, filtriert durch ein großes Filter und wäscht sorgfältig mit heißem Wasser aus, säuert dann mit Essigsäure an, erhitzt zum Sieden und fällt mit 10 ccm einer 10prozentigen Chlorcalciumlösung; der Niederschlag von oxalsaurem Kalk wird in üblicher Weise behandelt und die Oxalsäure auf Glyzerin nach der Reaktionsgleichung $C_3H_8O_3 + 3O_2 = C_2O_4O_2 + CO_2 + 3H_2O$ umgerechnet. — c) Die Bichromatmethode, von Hehner angegeben. Hierzu gebraucht man eine Lösung von 74·86 g $K_2Cr_2O_7$ im Liter, von welcher 1 ccm 0·01 g Glyzerin entspricht; ferner eine Lösung, in der 100 ccm der starken Bichromatlösung auf ein Liter verdünnt sind; endlich eine Lösung von ca. 240 g Ferriammonsulfat im Liter. Zu 25 ccm der glyzerinhaltigen klaren Lösung setzt man 40 ccm konz. Bichromatlösung, fügt dann 25 ccm konz. Schwefelsäure zu, bedeckt das Becherglas mit einem Uhrglas und hält es 2 Stunden lang in siedendem Wasser; der Überschuß des Bichromats wird dann mit einem Überschuß von Ferroammonsulfatlösung reduziert und der Überschuß des letzteren schließlich mit verdünnter Bichromatlösung zurücktitriert, wobei Ferricyankalium als Indikator dient. — d) Bestimmung des Glyzerins als Isopropyljodid nach der Gleichung $C_3H_5(OH)_3 + 5HJ = C_3H_7J + 3H_2O + 2J_2$. Mittels Jodwasserstoffsäure vom spez. Gew. 1·7 bis 1·9 wird Glyzerin in das Isopropyljodid übergeführt, letzteres in alkoholischer Silbernitratlösung in leicht bestimmbares Silberjodid umgesetzt; das gleichzeitig sich ausscheidende Jod wird durch roten Phosphor zurückgehalten. — e) Die Extraktionsmethode von Shukoff und Schestakoff, für Lösungen mit über 40 Prozent Glyzerin verwendbar. Die Lösung wird mit K_2CO_3 schwach alkalisch gemacht (war solche basisch, so wird zuerst schwach angesäuert, filtriert und dann alkalisch gemacht) und dann bis zur sirupösen Konsistenz bei einer 80° nicht übersteigenden Temperatur eingeengt; die so erhaltene Masse, deren Gehalt an Reinglyzerin nicht über 1 g betragen soll, wird mit 20 g ausgeglühtem und gepulvertem Natriumsulfat versetzt und im Soxhletapparat 4 (bzw. 5 bis 6) Stunden mit trockenem, destilliertem Aceton extrahiert; letzteres wird abdestilliert, das zurückbleibende Glyzerin im Extraktionskölbchen bei 75 bis 80° (bzw. 90°) im Luftbad bis zur Konstanz getrocknet. — f) Volumetrische Methode von Schulze, beruhend auf der Verbrennung des Glyzerins mit Bichromat und Schwefelsäure und Messung der entstandenen Kohlensäure über Chlorcalciumlösung. Man ersetzt in dem Schultze-Tiemannschen Nitrometer ein Rohr durch ein doppelt gebogenes gläsernes Hahnrohr und füllt das Eudiometer sowie die Wanne mit einer Chlorcalciumlösung vom spez. Gew. 1·38 bis 1·42; dann bringt man in einen 150 bis 250 ccm fassenden Kochkolben 50 ccm Glyzerinlösung, gibt einige Stückchen Bimsstein zu, setzt den doppelt gebohrten Gummistopfen auf und treibt bei geöffneten Hähnen durch Kochen die Luft aus; hierauf taucht man das Hahnrohr in ein Gefäß mit Bichromatschwefelsäure (50 bis 60 ccm einer Lösung von 60 bis 70 g Bichromat und 150 bis

250 ccm konz. Schwefelsäure in 1 Liter), das Gasentbindungsrohr in die Chlorcalciumlösung und saugt mittels der entstandenen Luftleere die Bichromatlösung ein; selbstverständlich ist darauf zu achten, daß jegliches Eindringen von Luft vermieden wird. Zum Übertreiben sämtlichen Gases ist 2- bis 3maliges Wiederholen der Operation (jedesmal 5 bis 10 ccm Reagens einsaugen) und 2- bis 3maliger Ersatz der Bichromatschwefelsäure erforderlich. Ist die Gasentwicklung beendet (nach etwa 10 Minuten), so bringt man das Eudiometer in den mit Chlorcalciumlösung gefüllten Kühlzylinder und liest nach etwa 10 bis 15 Minuten, wenn der Temperaturausgleich eingetreten ist, Volumen, Temperatur und Barometerstand ab, der auf 0^0 zu reduzieren ist. Wenn g = Glyzerin in Grammen, V = Gasvolumen in Kubikzentimetern, b = den auf 0^0 reduzierten Barometerstand, t = Temperatur der Kühlflüssigkeit, e = Spannkraft des Wasserdampfes bedeutet, so berechnet sich der Prozentgehalt an Glyzerin nach der Formel

$$= \frac{V \cdot (b - e) \cdot 92 \times 0{\cdot}0019772 \times 100}{g \cdot 760\,(1 + \alpha\, t)\, 132}$$

oder einfacher

$$= \frac{V \cdot (b - e) \times 0{\cdot}049545}{g\,(273 + t)}.$$

Diese Methode läßt den Glyzeringehalt bei Seifenunterlaugen etwa um $^1/_2$ Prozent zu niedrig finden. — g) Verbrennungsmethode, beruhend auf der Gewichtsbestimmung der bei der Verbrennung des Glyzerins mit Bichromat und Schwefelsäure entstehenden Kohlensäure. Man wägt 20 bis 30 g verdünnte Unterlauge (oder 10 bis 15 g konz. Unterlauge, bzw. 3 bis 4 g Rohglyzerin) in ein 100 ccm-Meßkölbchen ab; sind größere Mengen Seifenschlamm in der Lauge suspendiert, so kann man zur Glyzerinbestimmung entweder die unfiltrierte Lauge benutzen, indem man durch kräftiges Schütteln den Schlamm gleichmäßig verteilt und dann die Probe nimmt, oder man verwendet die filtrierte Lauge und zieht den nach dem Trocknen gewogenen und auf die Gesamtflüssigkeit in Prozenten berechneten Schlamm bei der Berechnung des Glyzeringehaltes in Berücksichtigung; enthält die Unterlauge größere Mengen Chloride, so ist es ratsam, das Chlor durch etwa 1 g in Wasser geschlemmtes Silberoxyd zu fällen. Zur Ausfällung der Seifen gibt man genügend Bleiacetat hinzu; man füllt dann mit destilliertem Wasser bis zur Marke auf, filtriert und verwendet 10 ccm = $^1/_{10}$ der abgewogenen Unterlauge zur Glyzerinbestimmung; letztere wird in umstehend abgebildetem Apparat (Fig. 13) ausgeführt.

Etwa 5 bis 6 g feingepulverten Kaliumbichromats werden in den Viertelliterkolben A eingeführt, durch dessen zweifach durchbohrten Gummistopfen der Tropftrichter B und das gebogene Rohr des Rückflußkühlers C geht; durch B läßt man die durch eine Pipette abgemessenen 10 ccm der präparierten Lauge, darauf 20 ccm destilliertes Wasser und dann allmählich 20 ccm Schwefelsäure (1 Tl. konz. Schwefelsäure : 2 Tln. Wasser) fließen; dann verbindet man B mit der Kalilauge enthaltenden Waschflasche D und saugt mittels des Aspirators J

einen langsamen Luftstrom durch den Apparat; hierauf erwärmt man den Kolbeninhalt so, daß derselbe in 20 Minuten zum Sieden kommt und weitere 20 Minuten darin verbleibt, entfernt hierauf den Brenner und saugt 20 Minuten Luft durch; die U-Röhren sind mit Chlorcalcium

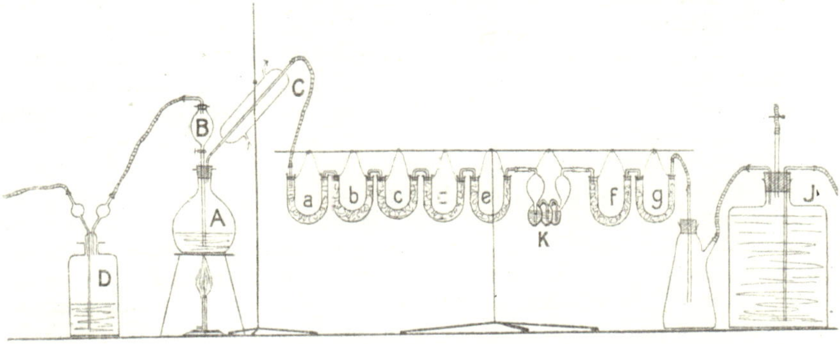

Fig. 13. Apparat für Glyzerinbestimmung.

gefüllt. Die Gewichtszunahme des Kaliapparates $K \times 0{\cdot}6976$ ergibt die in dem zehnten Teil der abgewogenen Probe enthaltene Menge Glyzerin. Die Operation dauert $2^1/_2$ Stunden und soll ausgezeichnete Resultate geben.[1]

Das zur Fabrikation von Glyzerinnitraten bestimmte Glyzerin darf keine Verunreinigungen enthalten, da sonst bei der Fabrikation der Explosivstoffe Gefahren vorhanden sind; gewöhnlich werden daher zwischen Käufer und Verkäufer von Glyzerin die Bedingungen, welchen das Produkt entsprechen muß, kontraktlich festgelegt; es muß ein destilliertes Fabrikat von neutraler Reaktion, frei von Zucker, Glykose u. dergl. sein; es darf nur Spuren von Chlor, Arsen und Eisen enthalten und muß frei sein von Blei, Calcium und anderen anorganischen Verunreinigungen; Fettsäuren und Zersetzungsprodukte des Glyzerins dürfen nicht vorhanden sein; das spezifische Gewicht soll nicht unter 1·262 liegen; die Farbe ist an und für sich kein Maßstab der Qualität, vielmehr kann ein helles Produkt ganz ungeeignet sein, ein dunkles sich gut verarbeiten lassen.

1. Spezifisches Gewicht. Ein hoher Prozentgehalt an Reinglyzerin, der bei der chemischen Analyse gefunden wurde, kann zum Teil auch auf Trimethylenglykol zurückzuführen sein; die spezifische Gewichtsprobe ist daher sehr wichtig. Letztere wird bei 15·5° vorgenommen, wobei dafür zu sorgen ist, daß eine gleichmäßige Temperatur durch

[1] Kurz erwähnt sei hier noch die physikalische Methode zur Bestimmung der Konzentration wäßriger Glyzerinlösungen vermittelst des Zeissschen Eintauch-Refraktometers.

die Masse vorliegt und keine Luftbläschen vorhanden sind; wird das Glyzerin beim Kühlen unvorsichtig gerührt, so nimmt es leicht kleinere Luftbläschen auf, die erst bei längerem Stehen entweichen. Die spezifische Gewichtsbestimmung erfolgt mittels eines Pyknometers; das Gewicht soll keinesfalls unter 1·262 liegen; in letzterer Zeit wird von dem Fabrikanten tatsächlich eine noch höhere Dichte verlangt.

2. Neutralität. Man schüttelt 50 ccm des Musters mit 100 ccm Wasser und einigen Tropfen Phenolphtaleïnlösung; zur Neutralisation sollen höchstens 0·3 ccm normaler Salzsäure oder Natronlauge erforderlich sein.

3. Gesamtrückstand. (Hierzu sei vorbemerkt: Aus den zur Verwendung kommenden Gefäßen geraten häufig kleine Mengen von Blei oder Eisen in das Destillationsglyzerin; Arsen findet man in manchem Glyzerin in erheblicher Menge, es rührt von den benutzten Chemikalien her; man verwende daher zur Fettspaltung arsenfreie Natronlauge, Schwefelsäure usw.; Chlorgehalt kommt von schlecht geleiteter Destillation; Kalksalze schleichen sich auf dieselbe Weise wie Arsen ein oder sie entstammen dem gelegentlich zur Neutralisation dienenden Ätzkalk; Fettsäuren sind in allen Rohglyzerinen in erheblicher Menge enthalten; da sie unter den in der Glyzerindestillation obwaltenden Umständen sich leicht verflüchtigen und obendrein in Glyzerin löslich sind, so verlangt ihre Beseitigung großes Geschick und eine genaue Kenntnis der Zusammensetzung der verschiedenen Destillationsfraktionen; Zersetzungsprodukte entstehen nicht in gut geleiteten Betrieben, wohl aber infolge von Verstößen gegen die der Destillation aller viskosen Flüssigkeiten zugrunde liegenden Prinzipien; Zucker und Glykose sind Verfälschungszusätze.) — Eine genau abgewogene Probe (gewöhnlich 25 g) wird langsam auf 160° erhitzt; schnelles Erhitzen führt zur Bildung von Polyglyzerinen, die dann den Rückstand zu hoch erscheinen lassen. Am besten verfährt man so, daß man von Zeit zu Zeit das Glyzerin in der Platinschale mit einigen Tropfen Wasser befeuchtet und somit das Glyzerin sich mit den Wasserdämpfen verflüchtigen läßt. Der Rückstand wird im Luftbade bei 160° C getrocknet und soll nicht mehr als 0·25 Prozent betragen. — Durch Verglühen und Zurückwägen erhält man den Gehalt an unorganischen Beimengungen (Asche), aus der Differenz den Prozentgehalt an organischen Verunreinigungen.

4. Chlor. Chloride dürfen nur in Spuren vorhanden sein; 1 ccm Glyzerin, mit 2 ccm Wasser verdünnt, darf auf Zusatz von Silbernitrat keine stark milchige Trübung geben; wie Lewkowitsch durch Versuche an zahlreichen Mustern Dynamitglyzerins festgestellt hat, tritt die erwähnte Trübung ein, wenn der Gehalt an Chloriden (als Kochsalz ausgedrückt) zwischen 0·025 und 0·01 Prozent liegt; quantitativ kann man Chlor aus der Asche durch Titrieren mit $^1/_{10}$ normaler Silberlösung, mit neutralem Kalichromat als Indikator, bestimmen; die gefundene Menge soll höchstens 0·005 Prozent Natriumchlorid entsprechen.

5. Arsen. Nur Spuren sind zulässig; das zu untersuchende

Glyzerin wird mit einer sehr geringen Menge Ammoniak gerade alkalisch gemacht (Überschuß von NH_3 vermeiden!) und nun Silbernitrat zugesetzt; eine gelbliche Trübung darf nicht bemerkbar sein.

6. Fettsäuren. Die Gegenwart flüchtiger Fettsäuren, wie Buttersäure, erkennt man an dem beim Erhitzen mit Alkohol und starker Schwefelsäure sich entwickelnden Estergeruch; höhere Fettsäuren, wie Ölsäure, liegen vor, wenn das mit zweifacher Wassermenge verdünnte und mit salpetriger Säure behandelte Glyzerin bei zweistündigem Erhitzen auf dem Wasserbad einen Niederschlag liefert. Wenn man 1 ccm Glyzerin mit 2 ccm Wasser verdünnt und Salzsäure zusetzt, so tritt eine Trübung ein.

7. Verunreinigungen von reduzierender Wirkung. Zu ihrer Entdeckung bedient man sich der zur Bestimmung von Traubenzucker üblichen Fehlingschen Lösung auf folgende Weise: Man mischt das Glyzerin mit dem gleichen Volumen Fehlingscher Lösung und füllt mit dem Gemisch möglichst rasch ein kleines Fläschchen, so daß kein Luftraum zwischen Flüssigkeit und Stopfen bleibt; bei 12stündigem Stehen im Dunkeln soll keine Reduktion eintreten. Wird die Luft nicht gänzlich entfernt, so zeigen auch die besten Sorten eine schwache Reduktionswirkung.

Ein Glyzerin kann vorstehenden Proben gut entsprechen und sich doch in der Praxis schlecht nitrieren lassen; daher bestehen manche Nitroglyzerinfabrikanten darauf, jede Lieferung einem praktischen Nitrierungsversuch mit 500 kg Glyzerin zu unterwerfen, wobei das Verhalten während der Nitrierung, die Trennung des Säuregemisches vom Nitroglyzerin und das Verhalten beim Waschen scharf beobachtet werden; desgleichen wird die Ausbeute an Nitroglyzerin sorgfältig festgestellt. Es genügt jedoch, in kleinem Maßstabe im Laboratorium die Nitrierungsprobe durchzuführen.

Man wägt[1] 20 g des fraglichen Glyzerins in einem kleinen Becher mit Ausguß und läßt es von da tropfenweise in einen größeren Becher fallen, der 150 g Nitriersäure enthält, bestehend aus 1 Gewichtsteil Salpetersäure von 1·5 und 2 Gewichtsteilen Schwefelsäure von 1·845; der Becher mit dem Säuregemisch, das anfangs auf 15° C oder auch noch weiter abgekühlt wird, befindet sich in einer geräumigen Schale kalten Wassers. Während der Glyzerineintragung rührt man die Mischsäure fortwährend mit dem Thermometer um; mit jedem Tropfen Glyzerin steigt die Temperatur, und sobald solche 30° erreicht hat, hört man mit Eintragen auf und wartet, bis sie wieder unter 25° gesunken ist. Man notiert nun zunächst die zum Eintragen des Glyzerins benötigte Zeitdauer; letztere hängt ganz von der Reinheit des Glyzerins ab, da Verunreinigungen mehr Wärme entwickeln und somit ein langsameres Arbeiten bedingen. Nach Beendigung gießt man den

[1] Zeitschr. Schieß-Sprengstoffwesen I, S. 22.

ganzen Becherinhalt in einen Meßzylinder, der vorher sorgfältig zu trocknen oder mit Nitriersäure auszuspülen ist; war das Glyzerin gut, so steigt das ölige Nitroglyzerin rasch nach oben; langsame Trennung deutet auf Verunreinigungen; man notiert daher die zur Trennung nötige Zeit und beschaut dann sorgfältig die Scheidelinie zwischen Öl und Säure; dieselbe soll vollkommen scharf und frei von suspendierten Flocken sein; weder Nitroglyzerin noch Abfallsäure sollen getrübt sein. Die Ausbeute kann man, unter gebührender Berücksichtigung des beim Umgießen des Glyzerins entstehenden Verlustes, annähernd ablesen. Das betriebsmäßige Waschen des Nitroglyzerins läßt sich, der üblichen Proportionen halber, im Laboratorium nicht so gut durchführen; immerhin lehrt die Erfahrung, daß Schwierigkeiten in der Scheidung von solchen beim Waschen begleitet sind und eine schlechte Ausbeute mit sich bringen.

Direktor Schlegel hat einen speziellen Probe-Nitrierapparat für Laboratoriumszwecke konstruiert; eine etwas veränderte Form, wodurch das Waschen des Nitroglyzerins im Apparate selbst ermöglicht wird, hat dann Dr. Novak angegeben; beide Apparate sind von der Firma Ephraim Greiner in Stützerbach zu beziehen.

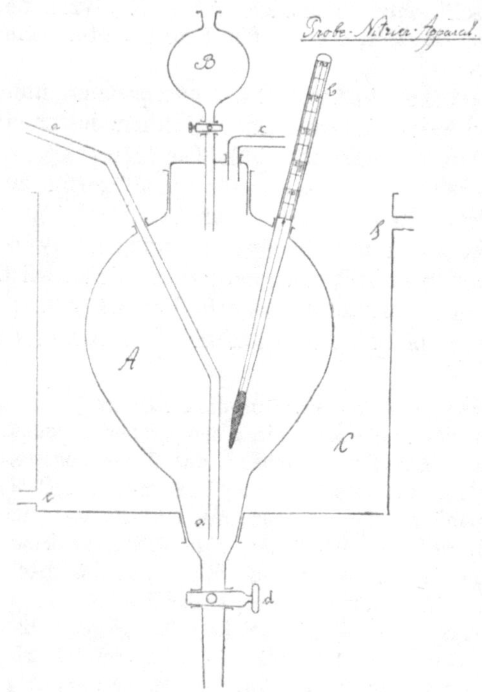

Fig. 14. Schlegel-Probe-Nitrierapparat.

Beim Schlegelschen Apparate (Fig. 14) dient ein größeres Glasgefäß *A*, nach Art eines Scheidetrichters geformt, zur Aufnahme des Säuregemisches; das Gefäß befindet sich in einem Kühlbehälter *C*, welches mit Kühlwasserzufluß- und -ausflußrohr *e* und *f* versehen ist; die jeweilige Temperatur im Innern des Gefäßes *A* wird durch das Thermometer *b* kontrolliert; das bis fast auf den Boden des Gefäßes reichende Glasrohr *a* dient zum Einleiten eines Stromes komprimierter Luft, welcher die Flüssigkeitsmasse in aufwallende Bewegung versetzt; ein Tropftrichter *B* enthält die abgewogene Menge Glyzerin, durch das Glasrohr *c* werden die bei der Operation sich bildenden sauren Dämpfe ins Freie geleitet; alle Teile des Apparates sind mit Glasschliff versehen.

Bei der Nitrierung wird wie folgt vorgegangen: Nachdem man das Säuregemisch in *A* gebracht und durch das Kühlwasser auf 12 bis 15° C abgekühlt hat, versetzt man dasselbe durch Einleiten von Preßluft oder eines Luftstromes (den man auch mittels eines Wassergebläses erzeugen kann) durch das Rohr *a* in eine wallende Bewegung und läßt dann das Glyzerin zufließen, und zwar zunächst in einem möglichst raschem Strahl, bis die Temperatur auf 28° C gestiegen ist. Dann hört man mit der Zugabe auf; die Temperatur steigt von selbst bis auf 30° C. Man wartet, bis die Temperatur gesunken ist und läßt dann von neuem Glyzerin zufließen, wobei man die Temperatur zwischen 28 und 30° C hält. Da das Glyzerin aus der engen Öffnung des Tropftrichters *B* nur sehr langsam austritt, so kann man das Ausfließen durch Anwendung eines geringen Druckes)etwa mittels eines Gummiballons) auf die obere Öffnung des Trichters *B* beschleunigen. Nachdem das Glyzerin tropfenweise eingeflossen ist, spült man den Trichter *B* noch zweimal mit dem in *A* befindlichen Gemische aus und wartet, bis die Temperatur auf 20 bis 25° C gesunken ist; nun stellt man den Luftstrom und das Kühlwasser ab und überläßt das Ganze der Ruhe. Die Nitrierung nimmt etwa zehn Minuten in Anspruch. Während der ganzen Dauer der Operation stellt man unter den Ausflußhahn *d* ein größeres Gefäß mit kaltem Wasser als Notbehälter, um den ganzen Inhalt des Nitrierapparates ablaufen zu lassen, falls bei der Nitration die Temperatur zu hoch steigen sollte. Hat sich das Nitroglyzerin in *A* abgeschieden, so läßt man das darunterstehende Säuregemisch in Wasser abfließen; hierbei geht etwas Nitroglyzerin mit, es scheidet sich aber bald im Wasser aus und kann mit der Hauptmenge vereinigt werden. Das gesamte Nitroglyzerin wird in einem großen Trichter mit Scheidehahn einem Waschprozeß unterworfen. Man wäscht zuerst mit kaltem, dann mit 40 bis 50° warmem Wasser aus, hierauf mit lauwarmer Sodalösung von 10° Bé und zum Schlusse wieder mit kaltem Wasser; dann spült man das gereinigte Nitroglyzerin in eine Meßröhre, um nach 24stündigem Stehen die erhaltene Anzahl Kubikzentimeter abzulesen.

Dr. Novak[1] bemerkt hiezu: Das beim Waschen betätigte Arbeiten in einem offenen Gefäße ist unvorteilhaft, da die Dämpfe des Nitroglyzerins und noch mehr letzteres selbst bei direkter Berührung unangenehme Wirkungen haben; außerdem entspricht es aber weniger den Verhältnissen der Praxis, wenn man nach jeder einzelnen Waschung das Nitroglyzerin aus dem Trichter abläßt. Hierbei entstehen durch die an den Wänden des Gefäßes haften bleibenden Nitroglyzerintröpfchen Verluste, die nach mehrmaliger Wiederholung der Operation ziemlich stark ins Gewicht fallen und dadurch Differenzen zwischen den im Laboratorium und den im Betriebe gewonnenen Resultaten ergeben

[1] Zeitschr. Schieß-Sprengstoffwesen I, S. 191.

können. Novak nimmt daher in einem und demselben Gefäße nicht nur die Nitration des Glyzerins vor, sondern auch die dieser Operation nachfolgenden Waschungen des Nitroglyzerins, die auf diese Weise auch unter äußerer Kühlung vorgenommen werden können. Der Schlegelsche Apparat wird im allgemeinen beibehalten, nur muß das zur Ausführung der üblichen Nitrierung von 50 g Glyzerin dienende Gefäß *A* mit Rücksicht auf die Waschwässer etwas größer genommen werden, und zwar zu einem Liter. Dementsprechend vergrößert sich der äußere Kühlapparat. Ferner sind sowohl Luftzuführungsrohr *8* als auch Abzugsrohr *3* mit Hähnen (*7*, *5*) versehen. Man nitriert bei offenen Hähnen (*7*, *5*), indem man 50 g Glyzerin zu 384 g Mischsäure fließen

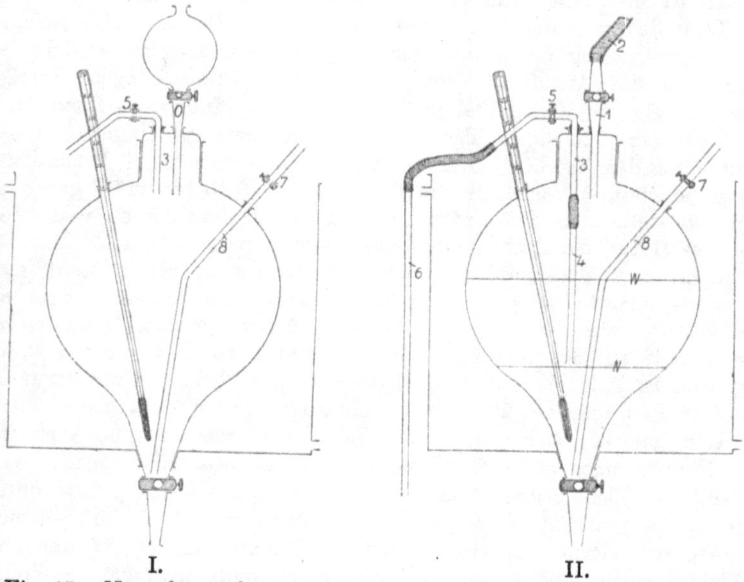

I. II.

Fig. 15. Novaks verbesserter Schlegelscher Probenitrier-Apparat.

läßt. Ist die Nitrierung und die Ausscheidung des gebildeten Nitroglyzerins zu Ende, so wird letzteres nach Ablassen der Abfallmischsäuren und Abstellung der äußeren Kühlung im Nitriergefäße zurückbehalten. Nun wird der Glyzerintrichter *O* abgenommen und an dessen Stelle das mit Hahn versehene Zuflußrohr *1* (Fig. 15, II) aufgesetzt. Das Gasabzugsrohr *3* wird ebenfalls herausgenommen und daran mittels Kautschukverbindung einerseits das Glasrohr *4*, andererseits das Glasrohr *6* befestigt; letztere Glasröhren — Weite der Röhren ungefähr wie bei Gasabzugsrohr *3* — haben die Aufgabe, als Heber zum Abhebern der oberhalb des Nitroglyzerins nach der Waschung sich ansammelnden Waschflüssigkeit zu wirken. Glasrohr *4* hat eine Länge von etwa 12 bis 15 cm und wird derart mittels eines Kautschukschlauches mit *3* verbunden, daß das untere Ende etwas über das Niveau des Nitroglyzerins N zu stehen kommt, was ein für allemal durch Ausprobieren ermittelt wird. In dem Apparat nach II wird nun bei geschlossenen Hähnen *5* und *7* mit dem Waschen begonnen, indem man aus den die Waschflüssigkeit enthaltenden Vorratsflaschen (es kann hierzu auch ein etwa 300 bis 400 ccm fassender gewöhnlicher Glastrichter dienen, der jedesmal mit der eben zum Waschen nötigen Flüssigkeit gefüllt wird) mittels der Kautschukverbindung *2* und Öffnen des Hahnes *1* die nötige Flüssigkeitsmenge in das Nitriergefäß einfließen läßt. Ist dies geschehen, so wird die Verbindung *2* mit den Vorratsflaschen abgestellt und *1* mit der ins Freie führenden Gasableitung verbunden. Während nun Hahn *5* noch geschlossen bleibt, läßt man, nach dem Öffnen von 7, durch einen Luftstrom die Waschung fünf Minuten lang vor sich gehen, worauf man den Hahn 7 wieder schließt und das Ganze der Ruhe überläßt. Nach kurzer Zeit hat sich sämtliches Nitroglyzerin am Boden des Gefäßes gesammelt. Hierauf wird nach Abstellung der Verbindung mit der Gasableitung durch das Zuflußrohr *1* mittels eines Gummiballens ein geringer Druck auf die im Nitriergefäße enthaltene Flüssigkeit erzeugt, wodurch beim Öffnen des Hahnes *5* die Waschflüssigkeit W, welche sich oberhalb des Nitroglyzerins N befindet, durch die als Heber wirkende Rohrleitung *4, 3, 5, 6* aus dem Nitriergefäße entfernt wird. Ein unter *6* aufgestelltes Gefäß dient zur Aufnahme der Waschflüssigkeit. Zur Ausführung der übrigen Waschungen wird in gleicher Weise vorgegangen, indem nach dem Schließen von *5* und *7* neue Waschflüssigkeit in das Nitriergefäß eingelassen, dann die Verbindung zwischen *1* und der Gasableitung hergestellt, gewaschen und abgehebert wird. — Zur Bestimmung der erhaltenen Kubikzentimeter Nitroglyzerin wird dieses nach vollendeten Waschungen in ein graduiertes Meßgefäß abgelassen.

Das versuchsweise dargestellte Nitroglyzerin muß natürlich zerstört werden. Zu diesem Zwecke gießt man dasselbe in dünnem Strahl über eine auf einer Eisenplatte ruhende Schicht Sägemehl in der Weise aus, daß lokale Ansammlungen nicht stattfinden; die Masse läßt sich nun mit einem Streichholz leicht entzünden und brennt rasch und gefahrlos ab.

Die folgenden Tabellen[1] enthalten die spezifischen Gewichte wässeriger Lösungen chemisch reinen Glyzerins nach den Bestimmungen von Lenz, Strohmer, Gerlach und Nicol. Die Reinheit des von Lenz untersuchten chemisch reinen Glyzerins war durch die Elementaranalyse festgelegt worden. Strohmer benutzte kristallisiertes Glyzerin, das durch wiederholtes Pressen zwischen Filtrierpapier von Wasser befreit worden war. Gerlach stellte sein konzentriertes Glyzerin durch Eindampfen von „chemisch reinem Glyzerin“ vom spez. Gew. 1·220 her, indem er es erhitzte, bis es eine Temperatur von 290° erreichte, worauf es einen konstanten Siedepunkt zeigte.

[1] Aus dem Werke von Lewkowitsch entnommen.

Spezifische Gewichte wässeriger Lösungen chemisch reinen Glyzerins.

Glyzerin Prozent	Lenz Spez. Gew. bei 12—14 °C (Wasser von 12·5° = 1)	Strohmer Spez. Gew. bei 17·5° (Wasser von 17·5° = 1)	Gerlach Spez. Gew. bei 15° (Wasser von 15° = 1)	Gerlach Spez. Gew. bei 20° (Wasser von 20° = 1)	Nicol Spez. Gew. bei 20° (Wasser von 20° = 1)
100	1·2691	1·262	1·2653	1·2620	1·26348
99	1·2664	1·259	1·2628	1·2594	1·26091
98	1·2637	1·257	1·2602	1·2568	1·25832
97	1·2610	1·254	1·2577	1·2542	1·25572
96	1·2584	1·252	1·2552	1·2516	1·25312
95	1·2557	1·249	1·2526	1·2490	1·25052
94	1·2531	1·246	1·2501	1·2464	1·24790
93	1·2504	1·244	1·2476	1·2438	1·24526
92	1·2478	1·241	1·2451	1·2412	1·24259
91	1·2451	1·239	1·2425	1·2386	1·23990
90	1·2425	1·236	1·2400	1·2360	1·23720
89	1·2398	1·233	1·2373	1·2333	1·23449
88	1·2372	1·231	1·2346	1·2306	1·23178
87	1·2345	1·228	1·2319	1·2279	1·22907
86	1·2318	1·226	1·2292	1·2252	1·22636
85	1·2292	1·223	1 2265	1·2225	1·22365
84	1·2265	1·220	1·2238	1·2198	1·22094
83	1·2238	1·218	1·2211	1·2171	1·21823
82	1·2212	1·215	1·2184	1·2144	1·21552
81	1·2185	1·213	1·2157	1·2117	1·21281
80	1·2159	1·210	1·2130	1·2090	1·21010
79	1·2122	1·207	1·2102	1·2063	1·20739
78	1·2106	1·204	1·2074	1·2036	1·20468
77	1·2079	1·202	1·2046	1·2009	1·20197
76	1·2042	1·199	1·2018	1·1982	1·19925
75	1·2016	1·196	1·1990	1·1955	1·19653
74	1·1999	1·193	1·1962	1·1928	1·19381
73	1·1973	1·190	1·1934	1·1901	1·19109
72	1·1945	1·188	1·1906	1·1874	1·18837
71	1·1918	1·185	1·1878	1·1847	1·18565
70	1·1889	1·182	1·1850	1·1820	1·18293
69	1·1858	1·179	—	—	1·18020
68	1·1826	1·176	—	—	1·17747
67	1·1795	1·173	—	—	1·17474
66	1·1764	1·170	—	—	1·17201
65	1·1733	1·167	1·1711	1·1685	1·16928
64	1·1702	1·163	—	—	1·16654
63	1·1671	1·160	—	—	1·16380

Glyzerin Prozent	Lenz Spez. Gew. bei 12—14° C (Wasser von 12·5° = 1)	Strohmer Spez. Gew. bei 17·5° (Wasser von 17·5° = 1)	Gerlach Spez. Gew. bei 15° (Wasser von 15° = 1)	Gerlach Spez. Gew. bei 20° (Wasser von 20° = 1)	Nicol Spez. Gew. bei 20° (Wasser von 20° = 1)
62	1·1640	1·157	—	—	1·16107
61	1·1610	1·154	—	—	1·15834
60	1·1582	1·151	1·5070	1·1550	1·15561
59	1·1556	1·149	—	—	1·15288
58	1·1530	1·146	—	—	1·15015
57	1·1505	1·144	—	—	1·14742
56	1·1480	1·142	—	—	1·14469
55	1·1455	1·140	1·1430	1·1415	1·14196
54	1·1430	1·137	—	—	1·13923
53	1·1403	1·135	—	—	1·13650
52	1·1375	1·133	—	—	1·13377
51	1·1348	1·130	—	—	1·13104
50	1·1320	1·128	1·1290	1·1280	1·12831
45	1·1183	—	1·1155	1·1145	1·11469
40	1·1045	—	1·1020	1·1010	1·10118
35	1·0907	—	1·0885	1·0875	1·08786
30	1·0771	—	1·0750	1·0740	1·07469
25	1·0635	—	1·0620	1·0610	1·06166
20	1·0498	—	1·0490	1·0480	1·04884
15	1·0374	—	—	—	1·03622
10	1·0245	—	1·0245	1·0235	1·02391
5	1·0123	—	—	—	1·01184
0	1·0000	—	1·0000	1·0000	1·0000

B. Die Mischsäuren.

Das Glyzerin wird nach der Gleichung

$$C_3H_5\begin{cases}OH\\OH\\OH\end{cases} + 3\,NO_2\cdot OH = C_3H_5\begin{cases}O\cdot NO_2\\O\cdot NO_2\\O\cdot NO_2\end{cases} + 3\,H_2O$$

in den Dreifach-Salpetersäureester, das Glyzerintrinitrat, auch Trinitroglyzerin oder kurz Nitroglyzerin genannt, übergeführt. Nach der Reaktionsgleichung ergeben 92 Teile Glyzerin mit 189 Tln. Salpetersäuremonohydrat eine Ausbeute von 227 Tln. Nitroglyzerin, bzw. 100 Tle. Glyzerin + 205·4 Tle. HNO_3 = 246·7 Tle. Nitroglyzerin. Man muß jedoch einen Überschuß an Salpetersäure verwenden, damit nicht an der einen oder andern Stelle des Nitriergemisches ein Manko auftritt. Gewöhnlich verwendet man auf

1 Tl. Glyzerin 2·5 Tle. Salpetersäuremonohydrat, bzw. 2·72 Tle. einer konzentrierten Salpetersäure von 92 Prozent Gehalt an Monohydrat. — Zur Bindung des bei der Esterifizierung entstehenden Wassers setzt man konzentrierte Schwefelsäure von 96 bis 98 Prozent, möglichst mit 98 Prozent Monohydrat, zu. Auf 1 Tl. Glyzerin nimmt man gewöhnlich 4·6 Tle. H_2SO_4, also 4·7 Tle. 98prozentiger Schwefelsäure. Die Ausbeute an Nitroglyzerin bleibt nicht unerheblich hinter der theoretischen von 2·46 kg für 1 kg Glyzerin zurück und schwankt zwischen 2·12 und 2·17; normal beträgt sie 2·15 kg.

Die Mischsäuren werden in Kesseln (Säureaufguß) angesetzt, die meist einem Tagesbedarf entsprechen (Fig. 16), und werden

Fig. 16. Anlage zur Herstellung von Mischsäuren.

von da nach ihrer Abkühlung (mittels Kühlbottichnetz in der Säurestation) mittels Druckluft in ein Reservoir befördert, welches derart auf einem Holzgestell ruht, daß sein Niveau zum mindesten 2 bis $2^1/_2$ m höher als die Nitrierungswerkstätte zu liegen kommt, oder man drückt direkt Mischsäure aus der Säurestation in den Nitrierapparat. In der Nitrierstätte befindet sich ein zweites, bleiernes, kleiner gehaltenes Gefäß, welches mit dem ersten mittels Rohrleitung und Sperrhahn verbunden ist. Sein Fassungsraum ist derart bemessen, daß die bis zur angebrachten Marke eingelassene Menge des Säuregemisches zu einer Operation ausreicht; es dient gewissermaßen als Vorratsgefäß und gestattet, gleich nachdem die Nitration zu Ende und der Nitrierapparat entleert wurde, eine neue Menge frischer Mischsäure für die darauf folgende Operation einfließen zu lassen. Der Tagesbedarf an Mischsäuren ergibt sich, wenn man im Maximum sechzehn Operationen pro Tag zugrunde legt, je nach der Größe der Charge, die 100, aber auch 200, 220 und 250 kg Glyzerin betragen kann. In Amerika nitriert man sogar Chargen von 400 kg Glyzerin.

Die Zentralstelle Neubabelsberg hat gefunden (englisches Patent 2776 [1906]), daß es vorteilhaft ist, zur Nitrierung von Glyzerin an Stelle von frisch bereiteter Nitriersäure die Abfallsäure einer vorhergegangenen Glyzerinnitrierung zu verwenden, welche durch Zusatz von frischer Säure wieder auf ihre ursprüngliche Zusammensetzung gebracht ist. Bei Anwendung einer derartig wiederbelebten Säure erhielt die Zentralstelle bei der Nitrierung des Glyzerins eine wesentlich höhere Ausbeute an Nitroglyzerin, als bei Benutzung eines frisch bereiteten Nitriergemisches mit dem gleichen Prozentgehalt an Schwefelsäure, Salpetersäure und Wasser. Während z. B. 100 Tle. Glyzerin bei der Nitrierung mittels 900 g eines aus 60 Prozent H_2SO_4, 30 Prozent HNO_3 und 10 Prozent H_2O bestehenden Nitriergemisches 201 g reines Nitroglyzerin lieferten, wurden bei Anwendung von 900 g wiederbelebter Abfallsäure von der gleichen Zusammensetzung unter sonst gleichen Arbeitsbedingungen aus 100 g Glyzerin 228 g reines Nitroglyzerin erhalten. Ähnliche Resultate wurden auch mit zwei- und dreimal wiederbelebter Mischsäure und zwar auch solcher mit höherem Wassergehalt (15 und 20 Prozent) erhalten, was den weiteren Vorteil bedingt, daß die Nitrierung ruhiger und gefahrloser verläuft. — Nathan, Thomson, Rintoul und Scott verwenden (nach französischem Patent 366593) eine Mischung von rauchender Salpetersäure mit Nordhäuser Schwefelsäure. Auf 10 Tle. Glyzerin nehmen dieselben ein Gemisch aus 28 Tln. rauchender Salpetersäure und 34 Tln. Nordhäuser Schwefelsäure mit etwa 20 Prozent SO_3-Gehalt; hierbei ist also die Salpetersäuremenge im Verhältnis zur Schwefelsäure größer als früher; dagegen ist die Gesamtsäuremenge gegenüber dem Glyzerin kleiner. Die Ausbeute an Nitroglyzerin soll hierbei 230 Prozent betragen.

C. Die Nitrierung.

In der Nitrierwerkstätte (Nitrierstation) befindet sich der Nitrierapparat und darüber der Glyzerinbehälter.[1] Letzterer ist ein entsprechend starkes Druckgefäß aus Eisenblech, innen verzinnt, das die genau abgewogene oder (bei konstanter Temperatur) abgemessene, für eine Operation ausreichende Glyzerinmenge zu fassen imstande ist. Man gibt diesem Gefäß gewöhnlich nachfolgende Anordnung (Fig. 17). Das Glyzerin wird

[1] In manchen Fabriken wird das Glyzerin in der Säurestation in ein Gefäß hineinfiltriert und von dort durch ein Glyzerin-Montejus nach der Nitrierstation gedrückt.

durch den Trichter *a* — der zur Zurückhaltung eventuell hinzugekommener Verunreinigungen, wie Holzteilchen, Fasern usw., ein Sieb *b* enthält — in das Druckgefäß *A* eingelassen; in *d* befindet sich ein mit Hahn und Ventil versehenes Rohr, um in das gefüllte Gefäß nach Schließung der Ein- und Ablaßhähne *c* und *f* komprimierte Luft einzulassen. Die einfache Vorrichtung *e* ermöglicht, den jeweiligen Stand des Glyzerins im Druckgefäß zu ersehen. — Die Temperatur des einfließenden Glyzerins muß innerhalb festgesetzter Grenzen bleiben; sie darf nicht zu niedrig sein, um das Glyzerin nicht dickflüssig und schwer verteilbar zu machen, andererseits nicht zu hoch, um nicht zur Erwärmung des Nitriergemisches beizutragen; die beste Temperatur des Glyzerins ist 20 bis 25° C. — Bei großen Apparaten wird auch das Glyzerin mittels eines Injektors am Boden des Nitrierapparates eingeführt und dort mittels Preßluft rasch in der Flüssigkeit verteilt. Dieses Verfahren hat den Vorteil, eine direkte Nitrierung zu bewerkstelligen und gleichzeitig gefährliche lokale Wärmeansammlungen zu vermeiden; das Glyzerin muß aber hierbei eine etwas höhere Temperatur haben, damit es nicht zu dickflüssig in den Apparat eintritt.

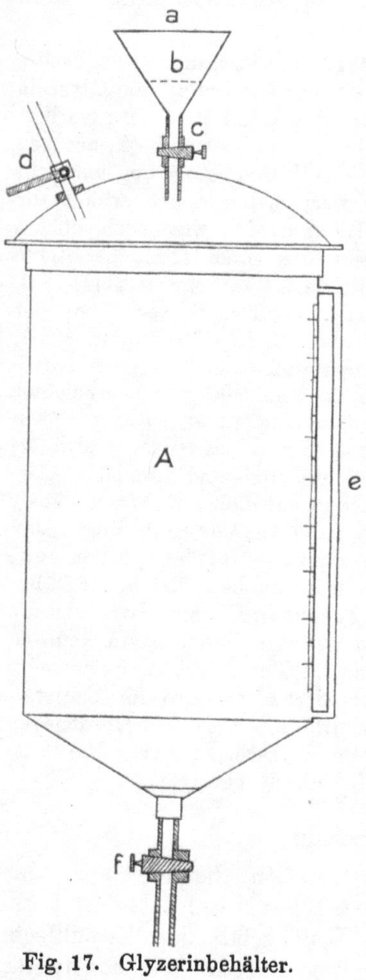

Fig. 17. Glyzerinbehälter.

Bei der Nitrierung ist die Einhaltung bestimmter Temperaturgrenzen (zwischen +10° und +26°) von großer Bedeutung. Die obere Grenze von 26° C darf n i e überschritten werden. Da nun beim Zufügen des Glyzerins zum Säuregemisch Wärme frei wird und dadurch die Temperatur in zunehmendem Grade steigt, so ist — um einer Zersetzung des im Nitrierapparate bereits gebildeten Nitroglyzerins vorzubeugen — es notwendig zu kühlen. Ferner sind Rührvorrichtungen angezeigt, um lokale Wärmeansammlungen im Nitrierapparate hintanzuhalten. Zur Kühlung des Nitriergemisches verwendet man[1] zwei Schlangen aus starkem Bleirohr von ca. 1·25 Zoll lichtem Durchmesser, welche vom Boden bis zum oberen Rande des Nitrierbottichs sich erstrecken. Diese beiden Schlangen sind getrennt voneinander angeordnet und bildet jede ein eigenes Kühlsystem, welches von kaltem Wasser zur Abkühlung durchströmt wird. Sollte eine Schlange ihre Wirksamkeit versagen, bzw. repariert werden müssen, so tritt die andere Schlange in Arbeit. Zum Rühren wurden anfänglich runde, durchlöcherte, mit Blei überzogene Eisenplatten von zwei Fuß Durchmesser verwendet, deren Zentren in einem kleinen Abstande voneinander horizontal an einer vertikalen Eisenstange befestigt waren. Die Platten bewegten sich vermittelst einer Zugvorrichtung, welche am oberen Ende der Eisenstange angebracht war, im Bottich langsam auf und nieder. Diese Bewegung der Rührvorrichtung, welche mit einem über Rollen gehenden Seile verbunden war, wurde durch drei Arbeiter bewirkt, welche, 30 bis 40 Fuß vom Apparate entfernt, hinter einem starken Walle geschützt standen.

G. M. Mowbray in North Adams in Massachusetts benutzte im Jahre 1868 zuerst kalte und getrocknete Preßluft zum Rühren des Nitriergemisches, welche von einer eisernen Hauptleitung durch 16 Zoll lange und $^1/_4$ Zoll weite Glasröhren in das Gemisch eingeführt wurde. Ähnliche Methoden sind dann in den D.R.P. 6208 und 8463 (Kurtz), sowie 29130 (Schroeder) beschrieben worden. Jetzt ist die Anwendung von komprimierter Luft zum Mischen des Glyzerins mit der Nitriersäure allgemein üblich.

Die Nitrierapparate unterscheiden sich in den verschiedenen Betrieben in einigen unbedeutenden Einzelheiten oder in ihren Dimensionen, stimmen jedoch im Prinzip überein und lassen eine direkte Nitrierung des Glyzerins zu. Nachfolgend beschriebener Nitrierapparat ist in der Praxis fast allgemein eingeführt (Fig. 18):

Ein bleierner Bottich *d* von 1 cm Wandstärke, dessen innerer Durchmesser je nach der in einer Operation zur Nitrierung gelangenden Menge Glyzerin (58 bis 116 kg) ungefähr 60 bzw. 120 cm groß ist und dessen Höhe 1·3 bzw. 2·6 m beträgt, ist zur Erleichterung des Nitroglyzerinabflusses unten kegelförmig abgeschlossen und mit einem weiten Entleerungsrohr *f* versehen, woran sich ein großer, aus Steinzeug gefertigter Entleerungshahn *g* (Bohrung 50 mm) dicht anschließt. Der auf Träger *a* ruhende Apparat ist vollständig in einen hölzernen

---

[1] Capitaine, Dinglers polyt. Journ. 1872, S. 37. — Scheiding, Zeitschr. angew. Chemie 1890, S. 609.

Bottich *c*, eingeschlossen, welcher den Bleibottich in Form eines Kühlmantels umgibt. In den Zwischenraum wird während der Dauer der Nitrierung durch *s'* Kühlwasser eingelassen, das bei *s* wieder austritt. Der ebenfalls aus Blei konisch geformte Apparatendeckel *e* schließt dicht an und wird bei *r* mittels einer plastischen Kittmasse hermetisch geschlossen, um das Entweichen gesundheitsschädlicher Gase zu verhindern. Der Deckel trägt am Scheitel einen Trichter *o* für die Einführung des Glyzerins, welches aus dem Druckgefäß durch Rohr *l* zugeführt wird. Außerdem sind im Deckel zwei Thermometer *m* derart angebracht, daß der eine die Temperatur der oberen Schichten der Nitrierflüssigkeit, der andere diejenige der am Boden befindlichen genau angibt. Drei bleierne Rohre *n* gestatten, Misch- und Kühlluft in das Innere zu drücken und erhalten die ganze Masse während der Nitrierung in einer wallenden Bewegung.[1] Überdies befinden sich am Deckel drei, in der Figur nicht ersichtliche Glaslaternen, welche jederzeit die Überwachung der Operation ermöglichen; ferner eine Öffnung *h* zum Entweichen der Gase. An *h* schließt sich zunächst ein breites Glasrohr *i* und weiterhin ein Kamin *k* aus Steinzeug an. Das Rohr *i* sowie die Glaslaternen gestatten eine Kontrolle der entweichenden Gase, so daß man sich über

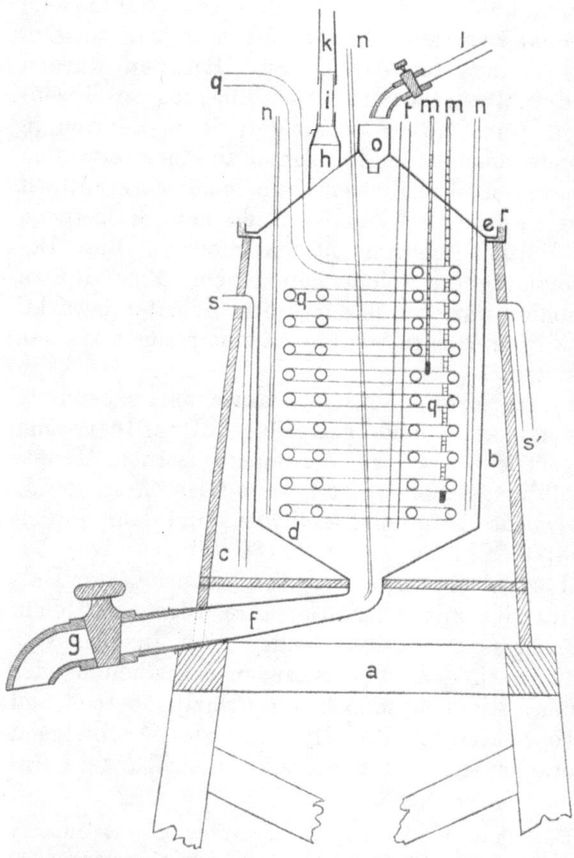

Fig. 18. Schnitt durch den Nitrierapparat.

[1] Manche Fabriken haben doppelte Luftrührung (Haupt- und Nebenrührung); letztere soll die lokalen Zersetzungen hintanhalten.

den Verlauf des Prozesses stets Rechenschaft verschaffen kann. Mittels des Rohres *t*, das zum mindesten einen inneren Durchmesser von 5 cm hat, tritt das Säuregemisch in den Apparat ein. Durch die bleiernen, konzentrisch geordneten Kühlschlangen *q* zirkuliert kaltes Wasser und kühlt das Innere gleichmäßig ab. Die Nitrierung wird nun folgendermaßen ausgeführt: Aus dem Säurereservoir werden die abgemessenen Mischsäuren durch Rohr *t* in den Nitrierapparat eingelassen (oder gedrückt). Man beginnt dann sofort mit der Luftrührung und der Wasserkühlung und kühlt so lange, bis das Säuregemisch auf eine Temperatur von etwa 15° C herabgesunken ist. Die zum Rühren gebrauchte Druckluft muß mittels eines Regulators von drei auf eine Atmosphäre gebracht und während der ganzen Operation auf dieser Höhe gehalten werden. Man läßt nun durch Öffnen des Hahnes im Rohre *l* das Glyzerin in dünnem Strahle in den Apparat einfließen und regelt den Zulauf so, daß ein rasches Aufsteigen der Temperatur im Nitrierapparate vermieden wird. Die Temperatur soll 30° C nicht überschreiten. Eine Toleranz von höchstens 2° C ist im äußersten Falle noch zulässig. Die Dicke des einfließenden Strahles Glyzerin hängt von der jeweiligen Temperatur des Gemisches ab. Die Nitrierung bringt stets eine Temperaturerhöhung mit sich, welcher man eben durch Abkühlung und Rührung entgegenarbeitet. Die beiden an dem Deckel angebrachten Thermometer *m* zeigen die Temperatur der Mischung am Boden und in den oberen Schichten der Flüssigkeit an, während ein drittes Thermometer die Temperatur des aus den Kühlschlangen austretenden Wassers angibt. Letzteres nimmt während des Durchlaufes durch den Apparat eine Temperatur an, die gewöhnlich um 2 bis 3° C höher ist als die Eintrittstemperatur. Sollte eine höhere Temperatursteigerung als die maximal zulässige (30°) eintreten, so muß man die Operation unterbrechen. Ist die ganze Glyzerinmenge in den Apparat hineingeflossen, so setzt man Kühlen und Rühren noch 10 bis 15 Minuten fort, bis der Inhalt eine Temperatur von etwa 15° C angenommen hat; dann ist die Operation zu Ende. Bei einer Temperatur des Kühlwassers von 8 bis 9° C dauert die Nitrierung 18 bis 20 Minuten, so daß in einem Vormittag etwa 6 Operationen vorgenommen werden können; hat das Kühlwasser eine Temperatur von 15 bis 18° C, so dauert eine Nitrieroperation 30 bis 40 Minuten.

Gemäß der Gleichung:

$$C_3H_8O_3 + 3\,HNO_3 = 3\,H_2O + C_3H_5(O \cdot NO_2)_3,$$

berechnen sich theoretisch auf 92 Gewichtsteile Glyzerin 227 Gewichtsteile Nitroglyzerin, bzw. auf 100:246·7. — In der Praxis verhält es sich jedoch nicht so. Mit fortschreitender Nitrierung nimmt nämlich die Salpetersäure beständig ab, bis sie zuletzt in so geringer Menge vorhanden ist, daß sie einen Teil des Glyzerins gar nicht zu nitrieren vermag; letzterer löst sich in der Schwefelsäure auf. Würde man den Zusatz an Glyzerin um diesen in Verlust geratenden Teil vermindern, so würde man zwar in der Praxis einen größeren Ertrag an Nitroglyzerin erzielen, dagegen würde eine größere Menge Salpetersäure unausgenützt verloren gehen. Wie man in den einzelnen Fällen vorgehen und welchen der beiden Stoffe man im Überschuß anwenden soll, wird sich nach der jeweiligen Preislage des Glyzerins und der Salpetersäure richten. Weitere Verluste rühren von der Bildung niederer Nitrierungsprodukte des Glyzerins (Mono- und Dinitroglyzerin) her, welche in den Säuren löslich sind und mit diesen abgezogen werden. — Im Mittel erhält man bei richtig durchgeführter Operation einen Nitroglyzerinertrag von 215 Prozent des angewandten Glyzerins. Im Sommer ist die Ausbeute etwas niedriger, im Winter dagegen etwas höher; niemals sollte sie aber unter 200 Prozent sinken. Aus diesen Schwankungen der Ausbeute mit der Temperatur ersieht man, welch' außerordentlich wichtiger Faktor für die Erzielung eines günstigen Resultates die Kühlwassertemperatur ist.

Der Nitrierungsprozeß ist die gefährlichste und empfindlichste Operation bei der Nitroglyzerinerzeugung, und es muß demselben die größte Aufmerksamkeit gewidmet werden. Man muß bedenken, daß bei dem Esterifizierungsprozeß — d. h. der Reaktion zwischen Säuregemisch und Glyzerin — Wärme frei wird, welche, falls sie zu hoch steigen würde, eine Explosion des Nitroglyzerins herbeiführen kann. Um diese Gefahr hintanzuhalten, muß vor allem folgendes beachtet werden: 1. Langsamer und stetig kontrollierter Zufluß des Glyzerins; 2. entsprechend starke Abkühlung des Gemisches durch Kühlwasser und Luft; 3. beständiges Umrühren des Nitriergemisches zur Vermeidung lokaler Wärmeansammlungen; 4. genaueste Kontrolle der Thermometer; 5. beständige Kontrolle der sich entwickelnden Gase und Dämpfe. — Wenn man für strenge Beobachtung dieser Punkte sorgt, so geht die Operation leicht und ohne Gefahr vor sich. Der den Nitrierprozeß leitende Arbeiter muß stets sein Augenmerk auf die Thermometer und auf die im Apparate eventuell sich bildenden und durch den Kamin *i* entweichenden Dämpfe gerichtet haben. Sollte die Temperatur über 28° steigen, so muß man der Druckluft vollen Zutritt geben. Sollte dies nichts nützen und die sich entwickelnden Gase noch immer mit rotbrauner Farbe durch den Kamin *i* entweichen, so muß man die Operation unterbrechen und den Apparat entleeren, um einer etwaigen Explosionsgefahr vorzubeugen. Diesem Zwecke dient folgende Einrichtung: der große Entleerungshahn des Nitrierapparates — und was wir von diesem sagen, gilt überhaupt für alle Nitroglyzerin-Ablaßhähne, welche bei den später zu beschreibenden Apparaten vorkommen — ist im allgemeinen mit mindestens zwei Rohrleitungen in Verbindung. Während die betreffende Operation, in diesem Falle also die Nitrierung, im Gang ist, steht der geschlossene Ablaßhahn in Verbindung mit der Rohrleitung, die zu einem Notbehälter (Sicherheitsbottich, Bassin) führt. Nach vollendeter Operation wird hingegen die Verbindung mit der Leitung, welche zum nächstfolgenden Apparate führt, hergestellt. Soll wegen drohender Gefahr die Operation zum Stehen gebracht und der Apparat entleert werden, so braucht bloß der Hahn geöffnet zu werden[1] und das Nitroglyzerin fließt in den Notbehälter, wo es unschädlich gemacht wird. Dieses Not-(Sicherheits-)bassin ist eine in nächster Nähe außerhalb der Werkstatt befindliche, gewöhnlich im Boden ausgehobene Grube, die mit Steinzeug oder Zement ausgefüttert ist und welche einen etwa 8 bis 10mal größeren Fassungsraum als der Nitrierapparat besitzt; sie ist stets bis zu $^2/_3$ mit frischem Wasser gefüllt. Durch einen Deckel werden Verunreinigungen abgehalten. Im Winter muß das Wasser auf irgendwelche Weise vor dem Gefrieren geschützt werden. An der tiefsten Stelle des schräg ablaufenden Bodens befindet sich sodann ein Ablaufrohr mit Hahn, um für die Entleerung und Reinigung des Bassins sorgen zu können. Infolge der, der Nitroglyzerinmenge gegenüber großen Wassermenge erleidet erstere in diesem Behälter eine solche Verteilung und Abkühlung, daß eine Explosionsgefahr abgewendet wird. Um dies leichter bewerkstelligen zu können, ist der Notbehälter auch mit einer Druckluftrührung versehen. Damit der Notbehälter im Notfalle wirklich seinem Zwecke entsprechen kann muß die Zuleitung und der am Nitrierungsapparat angebrachte Entleerungshahn solche Dimensionen haben, daß das Nitroglyzerin in möglichst kurzer Zeit in das Notbassin abgelassen werden kann. Früher baute man den Notbehälter in die Nitrierungswerkstätte selbst und direkt unterhalb des Nitrierapparates ein. Durch das plötzliche Einlassen der ganzen im Apparate enthaltenen Flüssigkeitsmasse wurde aber die Gefahr vergrößert, und man griff daher zu der jetzt allgemein gebrauchten Form der Verlegung des Sicherheitsbehälters, die infolge der Rohrleitung nur ein allmähliches Entleeren des Nitrierapparates gestattet und überdies den Vorteil bietet, den Nitrierraum von gesundheitsschädlichen Gasen frei zu halten. — Leider gewähren auch die Notbehälter nicht immer die vollste

[1] Der Arbeiter selbst bringt sich durch den tunnelartigen Ausgang durch den das Gebäude umgebenden Schutzwall in Sicherheit, bzw. vollführt alle ferneren, ihm durch spezielle Sicherheitsvorschriften vorgezeichneten Maßregeln.

Sicherheit. Manchmal tritt die Zersetzung des im Nitrierapparat befindlichen Gemisches so plötzlich ein und verbreitet sich mit einer solchen Geschwindigkeit, daß der beaufsichtigende Arbeiter gar nicht zur Entleerung des Apparates gelangen kann. Übrigens darf das Ablassen in den Notbehälter nur in den dringendsten Fällen gestattet sein, da außer dem dabei stattfindenden Materialverlust die gänzliche Entfernung des Nitroglyzerins aus dem Notbassin große Schwierigkeiten mit sich bringt.

Der Nutzen der Sicherheitsbottiche wird — nach Lesser[1] — nur dann gesichert sein, wenn die Möglichkeit gegeben ist, die Hähne von einem Unterstande außerhalb der Umwallung aus umzustellen. Es ist kaum zu verlangen, daß ein Arbeiter, der die Explosion einer benachbarten Hütte hört oder an dem Aufsteigen roter Dämpfe bemerkt, daß seinem eigenen Apparat die Gefahr der Explosion droht, zunächst noch einen oder gar mehrere Hähne umstellt und erst dann die Flucht ergreift. Deshalb ist in den meisten Fabriken die Einrichtung getroffen, daß der Hahn *g* (Fig. 18) von einem Unterstand aus mittels Druckluft umgestellt werden kann. Die übliche Konstruktion ist die, daß neben jeden Hahn ein Zylinder (Kompressor) gelegt wird, in dem ein Kolben von der Druckluft vorgeschoben wird; dieser stellt mittels Hebel und Ketten den Hahn um. Alle derartigen Hähne in einer Sprengölfabrik sind an dieselbe Druckluftleitung angeschlossen, von der auch die Abzweigungen in die Apparate und Sicherheitsbottiche geführt sind. Läßt man also, was in der Regel von mehreren Seiten aus möglich ist, Druckluft in diese Leitung ein, so werden gleichzeitig sämtliche Hähne umgestellt; das Öl fließt in die Sicherheitsbottiche, und in diesen und in sämtlichen Apparaten tritt gleichzeitig eine verstärkte Luftrührung ein. Gewöhnlich bringt man an einer Abzweigung auch noch eine Signalpfeife für die beim Apparate notwendige Signalgebung an. — Lesser hält die Anordnung der Zylinder für verbesserungsbedürftig. Wenn die Druckleitung auch noch so sorgfältig — möglichst unterirdisch — verlegt wird, so wird doch kaum volle Sicherheit zu erreichen sein, daß sie nicht bei einer Explosion einer der Hütten, z. B. einer Mischhütte, beschädigt wird; dann aber wird die Wirkung ausbleiben. Lesser hält es für richtiger, den Zylinder ständig unter Druck zu halten, so daß die Verschiebung des Kolbens eintritt, sobald die Leitung geöffnet wird oder abreißt; in diesem Falle tritt die Wirkung selbsttätig ein.

Eine solche Einrichtung stellt Fig. 19 dar; es ist der Zylinder einer Karpenterbremse ohne die Konstruktionsteile, welche nur für die Bremsung der Eisenbahnfahrzüge Bedeutung haben. Eine Spiralfeder drückt den Kolben nach links gegen den Dichtungsring *a*. Die Druckluft tritt bei *c* ein und durch den feinen Schlitz *b b* auch hinter den Kolben. Reißt die Druckleitung ab, oder wird irgendwo in derselben ein Hahn geöffnet, so entleert sich die linke Seite des Zylinders, Aus der

[1] Zeitschr. Schieß-Sprengstoffwesen II, S. 48.

rechten Seite kann aber die Druckluft durch den schmalen Schlitz nicht so schnell entweichen; sie verschiebt daher den Kolben nach rechts, wobei die Dichtung nunmehr durch die Stopfbüchse stattfindet. Zum Wiederanstellen wird auch die linke Seite durch den Hahn *d* entleert. — Die Rührluft muß bei dieser Einrichtung den Apparaten durch eine besondere Leitung zugeführt werden. Man würde etwa Vierwegehähne anlegen, so daß gleichzeitig die Zylinder mit der Außenluft, die Rührleitung mit der Druckluft in Verbindung gesetzt werden. Dabei bleibt noch immer die Gefahr des Versagens der Luftrührung bei Leitungsbruch bestehen. Man hat dieser Möglichkeit auf zwei verschiedenen Wegen zu begegnen gesucht, und zwar einmal dadurch, daß man in der Nähe der Nitrierhäuser und des Waschhauses einen größeren Druckluftkessel — gewissermaßen wie das Gegenreservoir bei Wasserleitungen — einschaltet, dann zweitens durch Anbringen einer mit flüssiger Kohlensäure gefüllten Flasche. Die erstere Maßregel verspricht einen Erfolg, wenn auch nur für begrenzte Zeit. Der Nutzen der letztgenannten Maßregel wird dagegen ziemlich allgemein bezweifelt. Öffnet man das Ventil einer Kohlensäureflasche schnell — und das wird im Falle der Gefahr fast stets geschehen —, so friert es sehr leicht ein; dies trifft für die handelsübliche, meistens nicht vollkommen trockene Kohlensäure fast immer zu. Lesser will daher ein anderes indifferentes Gas mit tieferliegendem Gefrierpunkt — etwa Stickstoff — wählen. Der Gefahr, daß die Flasche im Augenblicke des Bedarfs gerade leer sein könnte, begegnet man durch häufigeres Nachwiegen. Manche stellen die Flasche deshalb auch dauernd auf die Wage.

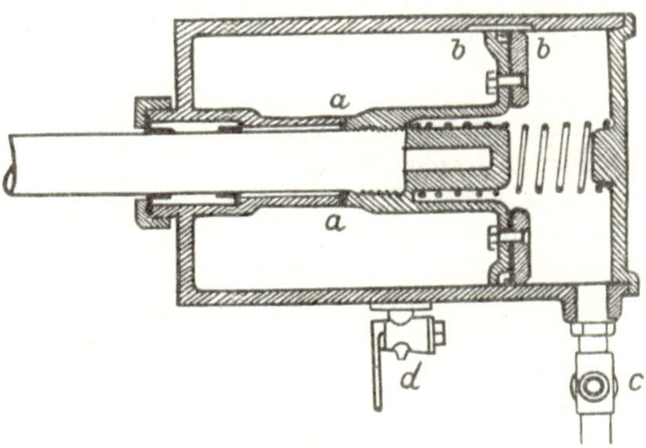

Fig. 19. Druckluftzylinder nach Lesser.

Um im Falle der Explosionsgefahr den weiteren Glyzerinzufluß absperren zu können, hat man vereinzelt auch diesen Hahn mit dem Kolben eines Druckluftzylinders verbunden. Zweckmäßiger dürfte es sein, wenn der Hahn durch eine Feder selbsttätig geschlossen wird, sowie der Arbeiter die Hand davon nimmt. Ein Versagen ist nicht zu befürchten, da ein Lahmwerden der Feder bei dem täglichen Gebrauche sofort bemerkt werden müßte; diese Einrichtung ist übrigens auch bereits hinreichend erprobt worden.

Um Explosionsgefahrmöglichkeiten auszuschließen, ist es weiter notwendig, die größte Sorgfalt auf die Instandhaltung der Apparate zu verwenden. Wir haben gesehen, daß der Nitrierapparat vollständig aus Blei konstruiert ist. Die Säuren üben auf die Wände des Gefäßes und auf die Kühlschlangen eine nachteilige Wirkung aus, indem sie die Bleiplatten mit der Zeit durchfressen. Anfangs bildet sich eine schützende Schicht von Bleisulfat, allein diese wird mit der Zeit porös und springt ab. Die Folge davon ist außer einer Verunreinigung des Nitroglyzerins, daß neue Teile der Bleiplatten von der Schwefelsäure angegriffen werden. Dauert dieser Vorgang einige Zeit hindurch, so kann es vorkommen, daß, während die Nitrierung im Gange ist, das Kühlwasser an der beschädigten Stelle in den Apparat eintritt. Die Folge davon wäre eine augenblickliche Zersetzung der Nitriermasse, hervorgerufen durch die hohe Temperatur, welche beim Zusammentreffen von Wasser und Säuregemisch erzeugt wird. Deshalb ist es nötig, täglich den Apparat gründlich zu reinigen und zu prüfen. Am einfachsten geschieht dies, indem man Kühlmantel und Kühlschlangen über Nacht unter Druckwasser läßt. Ist an einer Stelle ein Schaden eingetreten, so gibt sich dies bis am nächsten Morgen durch das an der tiefsten Stelle des Apparates angesammelte Wasser leicht zu erkennen. Um die notwendigen Reparaturen und Reinigungen vornehmen zu können, muß der Apparat überdies derart konstruiert sein, daß er leicht in seine einzelnen Bestandteile zerlegt werden kann.

In manchen Fabriken sind Unfälle vorgekommen, weil der Entleerungshahn nicht gut funktionierte. Es ist daher ratsam, ihn stets mit Vaselin gut geschmiert zu halten. Dies gilt überhaupt für alle Hähne, welche mit Nitroglyzerin in Berührung kommen. Um das Eindringen fremder Stoffe (namentlich organischer Körper, Fette usw., die leicht eine Explosion hervorrufen könnten) in den Apparat zu verhindern, ist es zweckmäßig, oberhalb des Gasentbindungsrohres *k* eine Haube oder ähnliche Vorrichtung anzubringen.

Nach Beendigung der Operation kann es vorkommen, daß noch einzelne Glyzerintropfen in den im Nitriergefäße verbliebenen Säurerest tropfen, so daß sich daraus noch nachträglich etwas Nitroglyzerin bildet und dieses sich zersetzen kann; die Gefahr ist jedoch verhältnismäßig unbedeutend. Lesser erwähnt einen Fall, bei dem lediglich die zur Abdeckung des Apparates dienenden Glasscheiben zerstört wurden. Da aber schließlich jede Entzündung von Nitroglyzerin als Einleitung einer größeren Explosion gefährlich werden kann, hat man die Einrichtung getroffen, daß die Mündungen des Glyzerin-Einflußrohres nach der Beendigung des Zuflusses umgelegt werden, so daß etwa noch abtropfendes Glyzerin nicht mehr in die Säure fällt.

Die aus dem Kamin *k* (Fig. 18) entweichenden Gase bestehen zum größten Teile aus nitrosen Dämpfen. Früher, als man diese Gase als unnütz verloren gab, sammelten sich dieselben infolge ihrer spezifischen Schwere am Boden an und übten eine nachteilige Wirkung auf die Vegetation aus; heute werden diese Gase in Kondensationstürme, wie z. B. in Rohrmannsche Plattentürme geleitet, wo solche nach der Gleichung $N_2O_4 + O + H_2O = 2\,HNO_3$ wieder in Salpetersäure übergeführt werden.

Der Vollständigkeit halber seien hier noch einige ältere, heute kaum mehr benutzte Herstellungsverfahren für Nitroglyzerin beschrieben.

Das Verfahren von Champion und Pellet besteht im wesentlichen darin, daß Glyzerin durch Salpetersäure–Schwefelsäure fast augenblicklich in Nitroglyzerin umgesetzt wird. Man läßt sowohl das Glyzerin als auch die Säuremischung in einem Strahle von bestimmter Dicke in das Innere eines gläsernen, von außen mit Kühlwasser abgekühlten Schlangenrohres einfließen. Die Ausbeute ist aber wegen der ungenügenden Rührung und Mischung eine sehr niedrige. Diese Methode war 1870/71 in dem belagerten Paris in Anwendung.

Boutmy und Faucher schlugen 1872 ein Verfahren zur Nitroglyzeringewinnung vor, das sich auf den zweiten der Berthelotschen thermochemischen Grundsätze stützt. Dieser Grundsatz der Äquivalenz zwischen Wärme und chemischer Umwandlung besagt: „Wenn ein System einfacher oder zusammengesetzter Körper unter bestimmten Verhältnissen gegeben ist und dasselbe physikalische oder chemische Änderungen erfährt, welche das System in einen neuen Zustand überführen, ohne daß dabei äußere mechanische Wirkungen vollbracht werden, so hängt die bei diesen Änderungen erzeugte oder absorbierte Wärmemenge einzig von dem Anfangs- und dem Endzustande des Systems ab, ist jedoch immer dieselbe, welches auch die Art und die Folge der Zwischenzustände sein mag.“ (Sur la force des matières explosives d'après la thermochimie. 3. Aufl. Bd. I. S. 176.)

Diesem Prinzipe folgend, verteilen Boutmy und Faucher die im Laufe der Nitration frei werdende Wärmemenge auf zwei Phasen. Sie bereiten zuerst eine Mischung aus Glyzerin und Schwefelsäure einerseits, eine Mischung von Salpetersäure und Schwefelsäure andererseits. Durch Zusammenbringen dieser beiden Mischungen stellen sie sodann das Nitroglyzerin her, wobei die Temperatur niemals 22 ° C überschreiten darf.

Im folgenden geben wir eine kurze Beschreibung des Verfahrens, wie es in der französischen Staatspulverfabrik zu Vonges bis 1882 betrieben wurde: In einem gußeisernen Behälter, welcher auswendig durch Kühlwasser abgekühlt werden konnte und mit einer mechanischen Rührvorrichtung versehen war, wurden 100 kg Glyzerin mit 320 kg Schwefelsäure von 66 ° Bé gemischt. Nach Beendigung dieser Operation wurde die Mischung in Säureballons eingefüllt, wo man dieselbe bis zum nächsten Morgen abkühlen ließ. Andererseits wurde in Steinzeugbehältern eine Mischung aus gleichen Gewichtsteilen (je 280 kg) Schwefelsäure von 66 ° Bé und Salpetersäure von 48 ° Bé hergestellt. Gewöhnlich des Abends schritt man sodann zur Nitroglyzerinbereitung, und ließ in große, auf den Kopf gestellte Glasglocken zuerst die Glyzerinschwefelsäuremischung und hierauf die Mischsäure einlaufen. Die chemische Reaktion stellte sich bald ein, wobei die Temperatur des Gemisches bis auf höchstens 22 ° C stieg. Das Nitroglyzerin ging in Form öliger Tropfen an die Oberfläche der Flüssigkeit und sammelte sich dort allmählich zu einer von der Säuremischung scharf getrennten Flüssigkeitsschicht an. Man ließ über Nacht stehen, und am nächsten Morgen konnte man das Nitroglyzerin durch Ablassen der Säure mittels eines am Boden angebrachten Hahnes gewinnen. Man arbeitete so mit einem Ertrage von 200 bis 205 Prozent des angewandten Glyzerins. Die Reaktionsgefäße waren mit Bleideckel verschlossen, welche mit einem Gasentbindungsrohr für die untersalpetersauren Dämpfe versehen waren, und konnten sich bei Druck im Gefäß automatisch öffnen. Sie besaßen im übrigen alle jene Vorrichtungen, die zur Vermeidung von Explosionen heute zweckdienlich noch verwendet werden. Der Vorteil der niederen Reaktionstemperatur bei diesem Verfahren wurde aber durch bedeutende Nachteile wieder aufgewogen, und zwar vor allem durch jenen der langen Berührungsdauer zwischen Nitroglyzerin und Säuren. Wie wir später näher ausführen werden, erleidet das mit Säuren behaftete unreine Nitroglyzerin sehr leicht eine spontane Zersetzung, die selbst zur Explosion führen kann. Tatsächlich kamen zu Pembrey, wo die „Explosives Comp. Ltd." die Herstellung von Nitroglyzerin nach dem Boutmy-Faucher-Verfahren betrieb, am 11. und 17. November 1882 zwei Explosionen vor. Die Methode wurde deshalb wieder in der Praxis fallen gelassen.

Über das Verfahren von A. E. Rudberg in Stockholm sei Nachstehendes erwähnt: Das Säuregemisch kommt nach vollständigem Erkalten in das Gefäß *1* (Fig. 20); das Gefäß *2* enthält Glyzerin, Gefäß *3* wird mit kaltem Wasser gefüllt. Durch die mit den Hähnen *a* und *b* versehenen Abflußrohre *A* und *B* kommunizieren die Gefäße *1* und *2* mit einem Kasten *C*, welcher entweder pendelartig aufgehängt ist oder auf Rädern ruht, so daß demselben mit einer Lenkstange und einer Kurbel, wie aus den punktierten Linien ersichtlich, eine kontinuierliche, hin- und hergehende Bewegung erteilt werden kann. In dem Trichterrohr des Kastens *C* ist ein Thermometer angebracht, an welchem die durch die Reaktionen erzeugte Temperatur abgelesen werden kann. Das im Gefäße *3* befindliche Wasser fließt durch das mit Hahn *m* versehene Rohr *g* in einen mit Blei ausgefütterten, mit treppenartig verteilten Fächern versehenen und von einem Holztrog wasserdicht umschlossenen Kanal *D*. Man beginnt die Operation damit, daß man zuerst den Kanal *D* durch Öffnen des Hahnes *m* mit Wasser umgibt; hierauf läßt man langsam das Säuregemisch in den Trichter *C* fließen

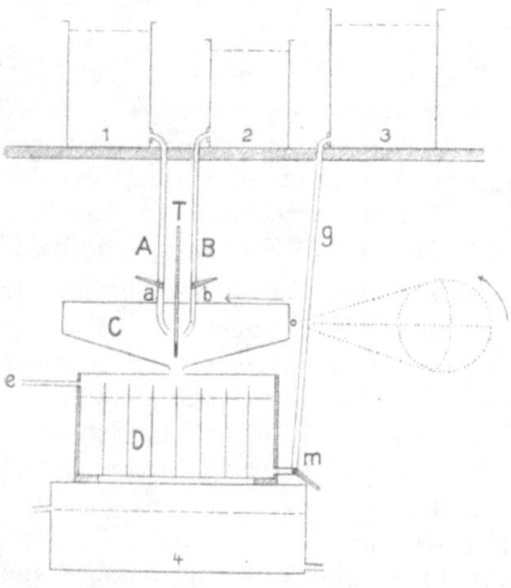

Fig. 20. Herstellungsverfahren für Nitroglyzerin nach Rudberg.

und setzt diesen dabei in oszillierende Bewegung, so daß sein Rohr sich abwechselnd über den verschiedenen Fächern des Kanals *D* befindet. Sobald die Säure aus allen diesen Fächern gleichzeitig herauszurinnen beginnt, läßt man Glyzerin hinzufließen und mit der Säure sich mischen. Die Reaktion zwischen Glyzerin und Salpetersäure tritt sofort ein. Sie ist beendigt, sobald das Gemisch den durch Wasserzufluß stets kalt zu haltenden Kanal *D* passiert hat. Nunmehr läßt man das erhaltene Gemisch in den Behälter *4* abfließen, welcher mit Wasser gefüllt ist. Das Nitroglyzerin scheidet sich als schwere Flüssigkeit am Boden aus und wird wie gewöhnlich sorgfältig ausgewaschen. Die Temperatur steigt im Rudbergschen Apparat nie über 30° C.

Mowbrays Verfahren.[1] — Mowbray sah zuerst die große Wichtigkeit der Verwendung chemisch reinen Glyzerins und der Reinigung des Nitroglyzerins von anhaftenden Säuren ein und erzielte daher zuerst ein reineres und daher ungefährlicheres Produkt. Er arbeitet in einem Nitrierhaus von 150 Fuß Länge, in welchem sich neun hölzerne Tröge und in diesen 116 Steinzeugkrüge befinden. In jeden Krug werden 17 Pfund des Säuregemisches gegossen, die Tröge selbst mit eiskaltem Wasser oder einem Gemisch von Eis und Salz bis zu 4 Zoll vom Rande der Säuregefäße gefüllt. Auf Brettern oberhalb der Tröge befinden sich Glasgefäße, und zwar je eines zu einem Steinzeugtopf. In jedem Gefäße sind 2 Pfund reines Glyzerin vorhanden, welch letzteres mittels Heber und Gummischlauch tropfenweise in das zugehörige Säuregemisch eingeführt wird. Unterhalb der Bretter, auf welchen die Glyzerintöpfe stehen, geht eine eiserne Röhre von $2^1/_2$ Zoll Durchmesser entlang, durch welche kalte und trockene Luft strömt, die während der Nitrierung durch 16 Zoll lange und $^1/_4$ Zoll weite Glasröhren in das Gemisch eingeführt wird, wodurch Säure und Glyzerin innig durcheinander gemischt, die Flüssigkeit abgekühlt und von salpetriger Säure befreit wird. Das so erhaltene Nitroglyzerin ist nach dem Waschen usw. rein und vollkommen farblos. Die vorgeschilderte Darstellung ist jedoch zu umständlich befunden worden und daher nicht mehr im Gebrauche.

Verfahren von Kurtz in Köln. — Nach D.R.P. 6208 wird das durch eine Brause fein verteilte Glyzerin von unten her in den Mischsäurebehälter eingeführt, während durch komprimierte Luft eine energische Mischung und gleichzeitige Abkühlung erzielt wird, Das sich bildende Nitroglyzerin setzt sich oben ab und fließt von dort stetig in ein anderes Gefäß über, wo es mit Wasser behandelt und durch Überlaufrohre in eine Reihe von Waschgefäßen geleitet wird. Die Zuführung des Glyzerins, des Wassers und der Säure wird durch komprimierte Luft bewirkt.

Nach dem D.R.P. 8463 stellt Kurtz durch Mischen von Glyzerin und Luft eine Emulsion her, die er in das nitrierende Säuregemisch einführt. Zur Bereitung der Emulsion wird ein Injektor verwendet, der

---

[1] Dinglers polyt. Journ. 1869, S. 172.

mit komprimierter kalter Luft betrieben wird. Kalte Luft kann auch zu jeder Zeit in das Mischgefäß eingeführt werden, um die Temperatur bei der Nitrierung zu regulieren. Die sich aus der Nitrierungsflüssigkeit zu verschiedenen Zeiten abscheidenden Nitroglyzerinschichten werden getrennt abgehoben und mit Wasser und Lauge gewaschen.

Schillings D.R.P. 17568 betrifft einen Trichter, welcher den Zufluß des Glyzerins zum Säuregemisch regulieren soll. Nach dem D.R.P. 29130 wird das zu nitrierende Glyzerin aus einem hochstehenden, verschließbaren Gefäß mittels komprimierter kalter Luft durch eine Glasröhre in das Nitriergefäß gedrückt, wobei die Einrichtung derart getroffen ist, daß auch gleichzeitig Luft in das Abflußrohr des Glyzerins geblasen wird. Auf diese Weise wird der Glyzerinstrahl sehr fein zerteilt von unten durch die Nitriersäure getrieben und eine innige und volllständige Vermischung beider Stoffe erzielt.

D.R.P. 11141 von Engels beschreibt eine in sieben Wagen transportable Nitroglyzerinfabrik. Hierbei besteht der Nitrierapparat aus einem zu einem Drittel offenen Zylinder, welcher vermittelst zweier an den beiden Kopfenden durch Winkeleisen befestigter hohler Achsenstücke gedreht wird. Durch die Achsenstücke und den Zylinder ist eine feste, nicht rotierende, ebenfalls hohle Achse gelegt, welche dazu dient, von der einen Seite zuerst die Nitriersäure und später das Glyzerin in den Zylinder einzuführen und an der anderen Seite das Gemisch, nachdem dasselbe durch die an der inneren Peripherie des Zylinders angebrachten Schaufeln in die festliegende hohle Achse eingeschöpft worden ist, in den Dekantierkasten ausfließen zu lassen. Der Zylinder besteht aus zwei zusammengeschraubten Hälften und liegt teilweise im Wasser, welches sich in einem offenen eisernen Gefäß befindet und zum Abkühlen des Gemisches dient.

Einzelheiten der früheren Patente, wie namentlich die Anwendung von komprimierter Luft zum Mischen des Glyzerins mit der Nitriersäure haben sich bewährt und sind, wie früher geschildert, noch in Gebrauch.

Bei dem neueren Verfahren von Nathan, Thomson und Rintoul (engl. Patent 15983 [1901] und 3020 [1903]), auf welches wir später noch zurückkommen werden, erfolgt der Einlaß der Mischsäure in den Nitrierapparat nicht von oben her, sondern durch ein an der tiefsten Stelle des Bodens angebrachtes Rohr.

Es bliebe nun noch Einiges über die Rührvorrichtungen zu erwähnen übrig.

In manchen Fabriken läßt man die zum Rühren verwendete Luft mit einem Drucke von 4 Atmosphären in den Apparat eintreten. Anderwärts wird mit 2 Atmosphären, in einigen Fabriken — wie wir gesehen haben — auch mit 1 Atmosphäre gearbeitet. Es ist besser, mit geringerem Drucke zu rühren, und nur im Bedarfsfalle — bei größeren Wärmeansammlungen — den Druck zu erhöhen. — Früher verwendete man zum Rühren durchwegs mechanische Rührvorrichtungen in Form gußeiserner, bleiüberzogener Schrauben, welche neuerdings

J. G. Blomen wieder vorgeschlagen hat. Es kann nämlich bei der Rührung mit komprimierter Luft der Luftzutritt in den Apparat eine Zeitlang unterbrochen werden, sei es durch die Beschädigung oder Verstopfung der den Nitrierapparat mit der Kompressionsluftpumpe verbindenden Rohrleitung, sei es durch die Beschädigung der Kompressionspumpe selbst; hierbei schlägt sich in der Leitung Feuchtigkeit aus der Luft nieder und wird durch den ersten Kolbenstoß der Pumpe auf einmal in den Apparat gedrückt. Es ist leicht einzusehen, welch' nachteilige Folgen ein solcher Eintritt des Kondenswassers in die Säuremischung mit sich bringen kann. Diesem Übelstande kann aber durch Anwendung trockener komprimierter Luft (engl. Patent 1416 [1905]) abgeholfen werden. Danach verwenden Hesketh und Willcox zum Mischen der Nitriersäure, sowie zum Rühren einen Strom komprimierter und getrockneter Luft, der mit Hilfe einer Kältemaschine vorher auf eine niedrige Temperatur gebracht wurde.

Robert Evers verwendet nach einem Patente vom 21. Dezember 1902 (D.R.P. 183183) keine Preßluft, weil mit der austretenden Luft ein Teil der Säure entweicht, also vor der Reaktion verloren geht; er bewirkt vielmehr die innige Vermischung der Komponenten durch eine Düse, welche durch die unter Druck gesetzte Mischsäure betrieben wird. Ist die Spannung und Temperatur der Flüssigkeiten, die Größe der Düse u. dgl. auf eine bestimmte Leistung des Apparates eingestellt, so wird bei gleichbleibendem Zustand beider Komponenten das Produkt nach der Zusammensetzung und Menge, sowie die Arbeitsweise des Apparates stets die gleiche sein. Es wird also eine stets gleichbleibende Nitrierung erzielt. Das Ergebnis des Verfahrens hängt sonach nicht allein von der Geschicklichkeit und Aufmerksamkeit des Arbeiters ab. Während des gleichzeitigen Eintrittes der Komponenten in abgestimmten Mengen findet die Bildung des Nitroglyzerins statt, und es kann daher im ununterbrochenen Betriebe gearbeitet werden.

Fig. 21 zeigt einen solchen Nitrierapparat, während Fig. 22 ein Bild der Streudüse gibt. — Der Nitrierapparat besitzt die bekannte Einrichtung und besteht aus dem Bleigefäß *a* mit der Haube *b*, an welcher das Abzugsrohr *c* und die Düse *i* angeordnet sind. Der Boden des Apparates ist abgeschrägt, um ein gutes Auslaufen der Flüssigkeit zu ermöglichen. Die Komponenten werden in den Apparat durch eine Düse gebracht, durch welche die unter Spannung gesetzte Nitriersäure das Glyzerin ansaugen und zerstäuben kann. Die Düse selbst ist aus Ton oder Porzellan oder dgl. hergestellt und besteht aus dem Körper *i*, in welchen das Einsatzstück *g* so eingesetzt ist, daß dessen Innenraum durch einen Flansch in zwei Kammern geteilt wird. Die obere Kammer ist ein freier Raum, in welchem sich die einlaufende Flüssigkeit, das Glyzerin, verbreiten kann. Die untere

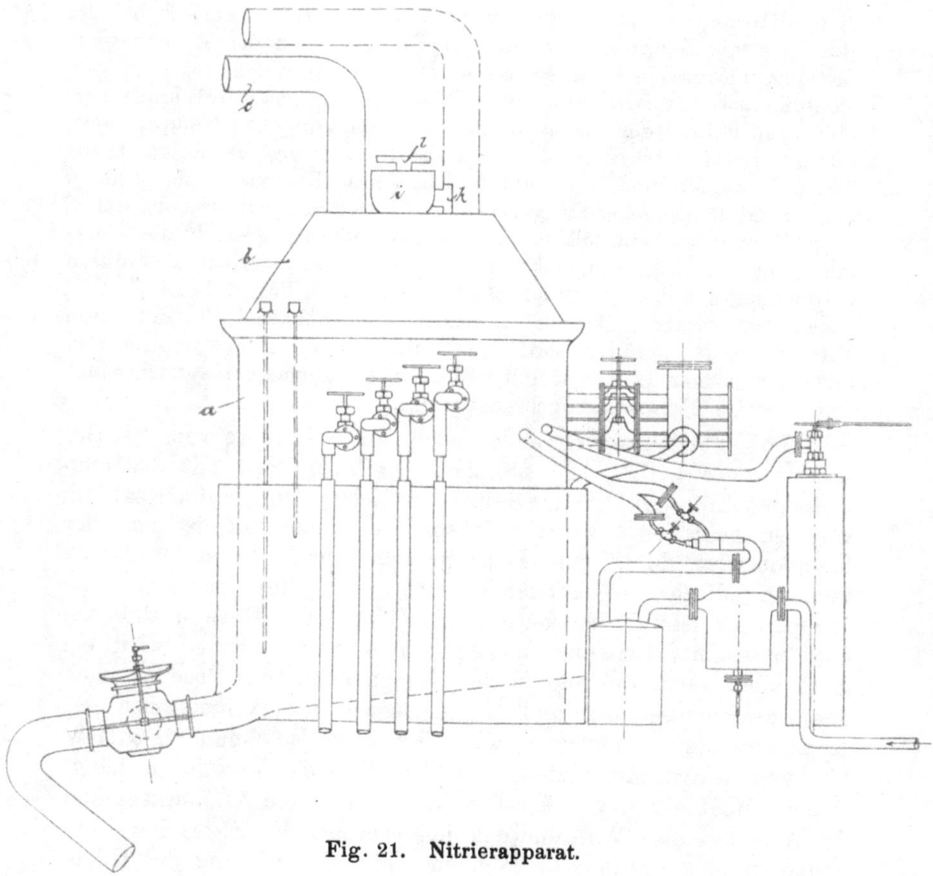

Fig. 21. **Nitrierapparat.**

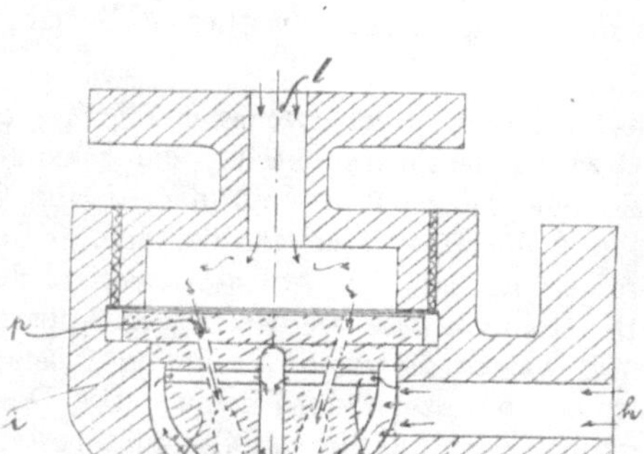

Fig. 22. **Streudüse.**

Kammer füllt das Einsatzstück *g* so weit aus, daß nur ein schmaler Raum bleibt, der mit dem Zuflußrohr *h* in Verbindung steht. Das Einsatzstück enthält zwei Gruppen von Bohrungen *p* und *m*, von denen die Gruppe *p* mit der oberen Kaumer, in die das Zuleitungsrohr *l* mündet, die andere Gruppe *m* mit dem Rohr *h* in Verbindung steht. Das Rohr *h* dient für den Zufluß der Nitriersäure und das Rohr *l* für den Zufluß des Glyzerins. Die horizontalen Kanäle vereinigen sich in dem zentralen senkrechten Kanal *n*. Der Zwischenraum zwischen Düsenwand und Einsatzstück steht mit den Kanälen *m* in Verbindung und diese münden durch die Öffnungen *o* in das Nitriergefäß. Die Kanäle *p* durchziehen das Einsatzstück *g*, münden aber in die obere Kammer und unten gleichfalls in das Nitriergefäß. Die durch das Rohr *h* zuströmende Nitriersäure umspült das Einsatzstück *g*, dringt in die Kanäle *m* und strömt durch die Öffnungen *n*, *o* aus. Das Glyzerin fließt durch das Rohr *l* zu, verbreitet sich in der oberen Kammer und fließt durch die Kanäle *p* unten aus. Die Austrittsöffnungen sind so gestellt, daß die Säurestrahlen auf die Strahlen des Glyzerins treffen und diese zerstäuben.

Fig. 23 bis 25 zeigen einen Nitrierraum, wie solcher von Ingenieur J. L. C. Eckelt in Berlin gebaut wird. *A* ist der Nitrierapparat aus

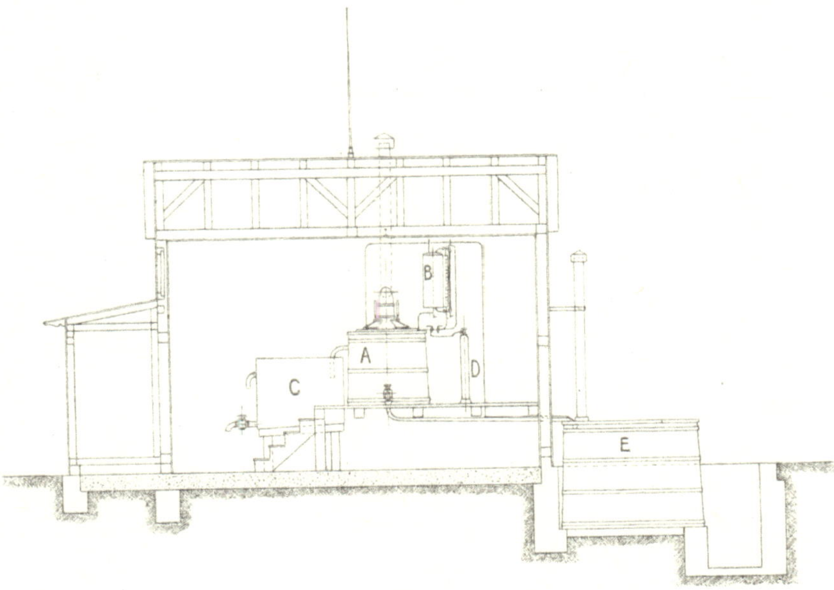

Fig. 23. Nitrierraum (nach Eckelt).

starkem Blei in einem Holzgefäß mit Deckel, Beobachtungsfenstern, Thermometer und Gasabzug; *B* ist der Glyzerinbehälter mit Niveaustandsanzeiger und Skala; *D* ist eine Flasche mit flüssiger Kohlensäure, welche in besonderen Fällen als Sicherheitskühlung angewandt wird; *C* ist ein Sammelbehälter für Nitroglyzerin. Eckelt vermeidet die Ansammlung von viel Nitroglyzerin im Nitrierapparat, indem er noch während der Nitrierung einen Teil des gebildeten Nitroglyzerins in den Behälter *C* übertreten läßt, der mit Wasser gefüllt ist und einen Wasserzulauf hat, Von da wird das Nitroglyzerin durch Tonkrüge nach dem Separator (Abscheider) gebracht, in welchen nach beendigter Nitrierung der übrige Inhalt des Nitrierapparates (Nitroglyzerin und Mischsäuren) übergeleitet wird. *E* ist der Sicherheitsbottich.

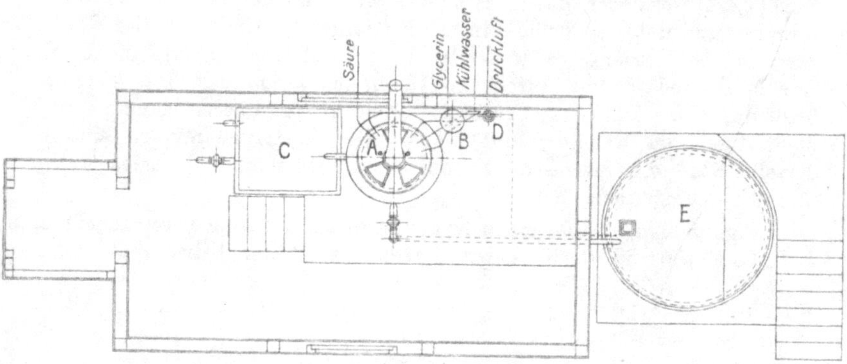

Fig. 24. Nitrierraum (nach Eckelt).

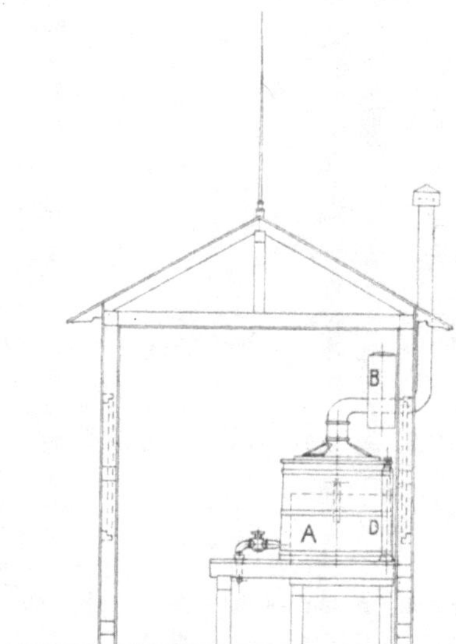

Fig. 25. Nitrierraum (nach Eckelt).

Das Nitrieren und Scheiden wird in vielen Fabriken in demselben Raume, dem Nitrierhause, aber nicht gleichzeitig, vorgenommen. Mit dem Nitrieren einer neuen Charge darf nicht früher begonnen werden, bevor die vorhergehende den Scheidetrichter verlassen hat. Diese Vorschrift hat ihren guten Grund, denn es ist vorgekommen, daß man nach einer Explosion im Separator das Nitriergefäß noch mit Nitroglyzerin gefüllt, umgestürzt, aber unversehrt vorgefunden hat. Die Beseitigung des Nitroglyzerins ist dann, wie man es auch anfangen mag, stets gefährlich. Nach einer neueren polizeilichen Bestimmung ist es gestattet, schon vor der Beendigung der Scheidung, das Nitriergefäß wieder mit Mischsäure zu füllen, wenn für dieses und den Separator je ein besonderer Sicherheitsbottich vorhanden ist.

D. Die Scheidung.

Hierunter versteht man die Trennung des Nitroglyzerins von den Säuren. Ist die Nitrierung beendet, so verbindet man das bisher mit dem Notbehälter in Verbindung gestandene Rohr *f* (Fig. 18) des Nitrierapparates mit dem Abscheider oder Separator und läßt durch Öffnen des Entleerungshahnes *g* das Gemisch von Nitroglyzerin und Säure in diesen Behälter einfließen. Der Separator kann im Nitrierungsraum selbst oder, was vorzuziehen ist, in einem eigenen, etwas tiefer liegenden Schuppen untergebracht werden.

Figur 26 bis 28 zeigt einen Scheideraum nach J. L. C. Eckelt.

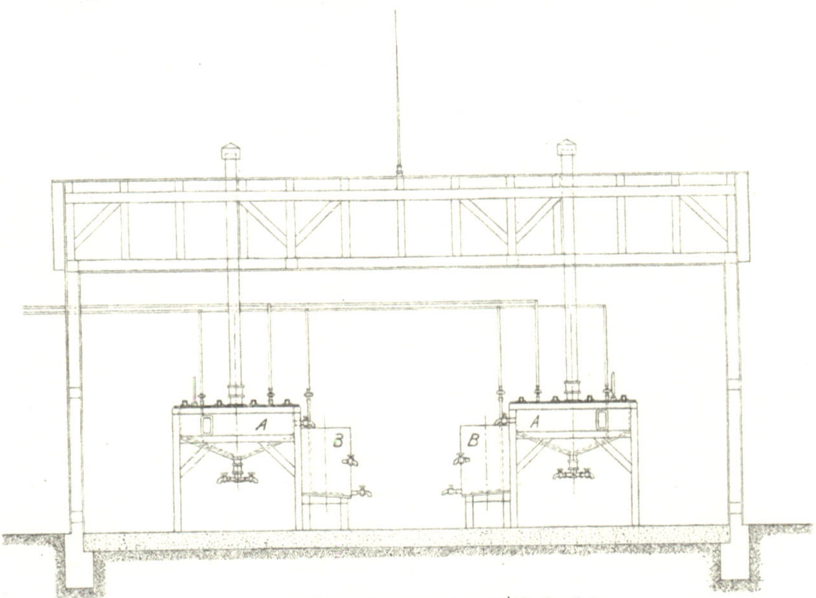

Fig. 26. Scheideraum (nach Eckelt).

Darin sind *AA* Scheideapparate, *BB* Vorwaschgefäße, *C* ein Sicherheitsbottich. Der Separator *A* (Fig. 29) ist ein bleiernes Gefäß

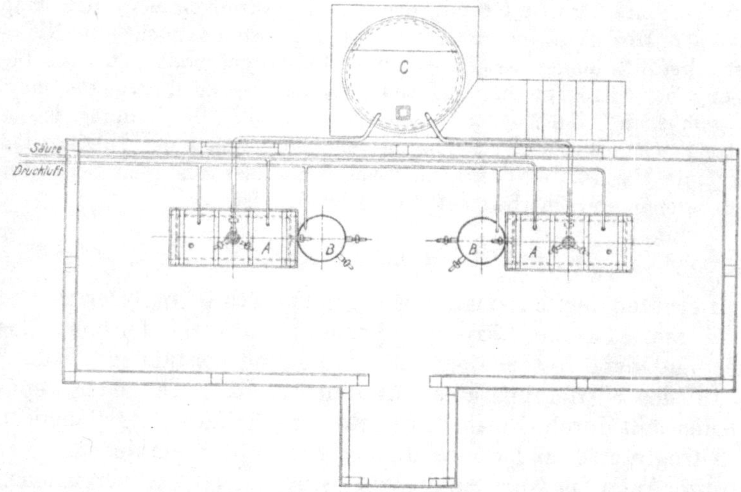

Fig. 27. Scheideraum (nach (Eckelt).

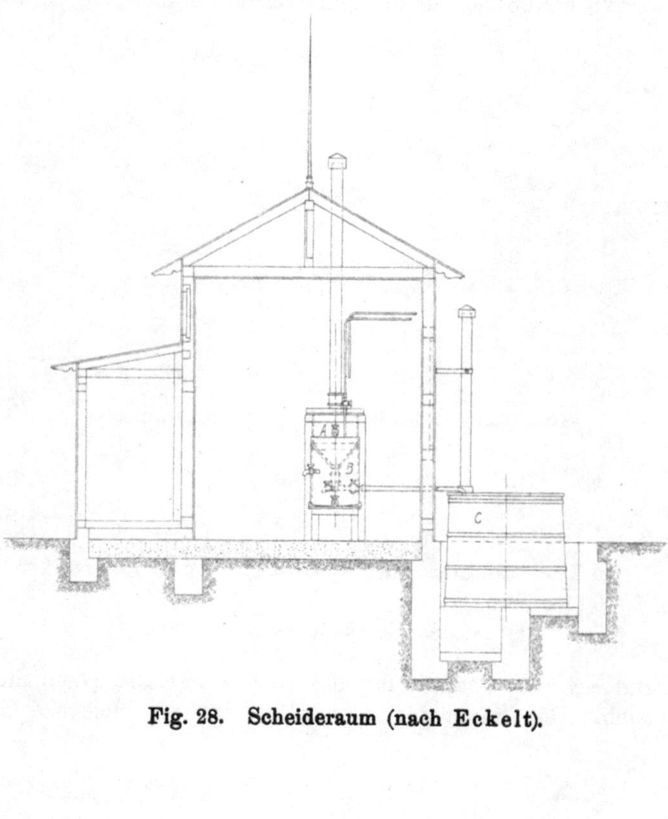

Fig. 28. Scheideraum (nach Eckelt).

von 0·5 bis 1 cm Wandstärke, 1 bis 2 m Höhe und (je nach der Größe des Nitrierapparates) von 60 bis 120 cm Durchmesser; er ist gewöhnlich von quadratischem Durchschnitt (in manchen Fabriken wird wegen der leichteren Konstruktion die zylindrische Form vorgezogen) und mittels eines dicht anschließenden Holzmantels *b* versteift. Ein kegelförmig nach abwärts gerichteter Boden *c* endigt an der tiefsten Stelle in eine mit zwei bis drei

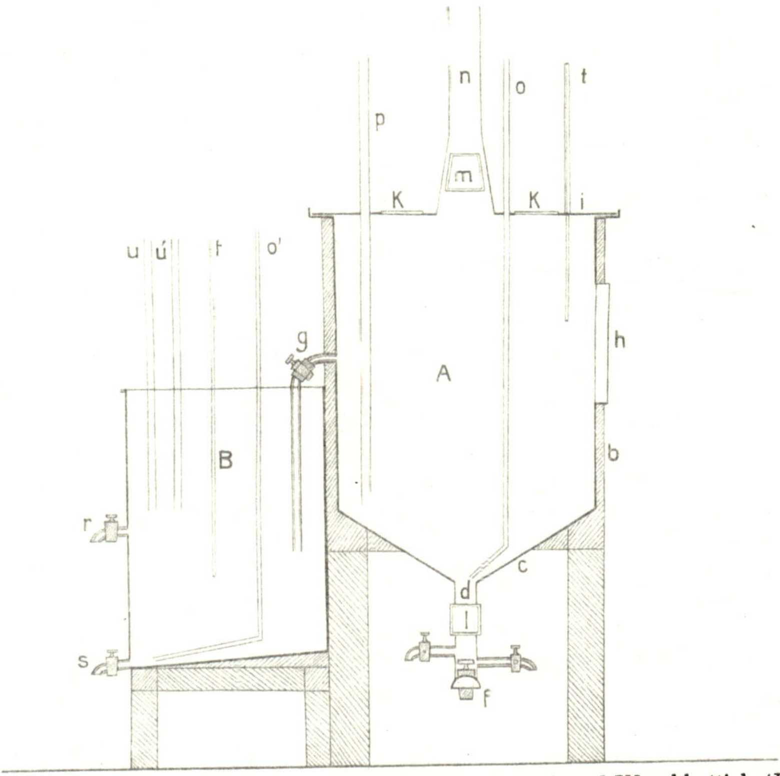

Fig. 29. Schnitt durch den Abscheider (Separator) *A* und Waschbottich (*B*).

Hähnen versehene Rohrleitung *d*, welche mit einer Laterne *l* zur Überwachung der abfließenden Masse versehen ist. Der größere (*f*) der drei Hähne steht mit der zum Notbehälter *C* führenden Leitung in Verbindung, und dient zur eventuellen Entleerung des Abscheiders bei drohender Gefahr. Die übrigen (1 bis 2) Hähne dienen zum Ablassen der Säuren. Ein weiterer Hahn *g*, der zum Ablassen des Nitroglyzerins dient, ist am Mantel ungefähr in der Höhe, wo sich gewöhnlich die Grenzschicht zwischen Sprengöl und

Säuren befindet, angebracht. Etwa in gleicher Höhe befindet sich am Mantel eine Glaslaterne *h*, welche das Fortschreiten der Scheidung überprüfen lassen soll. Der Separator ist mit einem Blei- oder mit einem Glasdeckel *i* verschlossen. Im ersteren Falle ist eine Laterne *k* eingesetzt, um die Operation überwachen zu können. Im Deckel befindet sich ein bis etwa zur Mitte der Nitroglyzerinschicht reichendes Thermometer *t* und ein mit Schutzhaube und Laterne *m* versehenes Gasabzugsrohr *n*. Auch bringt man in dem Separator für alle Fälle ein Druckluftrohr *o* an, um gegebenen Falles durch Luftrührung dem Steigen der Temperatur entgegenzuwirken. Die eingepreßte Luft tritt durch *p* wieder aus.

Die Scheidung geht nun folgendermaßen vor sich: Nach beendigter Nitrierung befindet sich im Nitrierapparate außer dem Nitroglyzerin noch ein Gemisch, bestehend aus der angewendeten Menge Schwefelsäure, ungefähr 8 bis 10 Prozent Salpetersäure und dem bei der chemischen Reaktion gebildeten Wasser. Während nun das Nitroglyzerin eine Dichte von 1·6 hat, besitzen die Abfallsäuren ein spezifisches Gewicht von 1·7. Läßt man aus dem Nitrierapparat die Flüssigkeitsmasse in den Separator abfließen, so erfolgt innerhalb einer halben bis einer ganzen Stunde die Trennung des zunächst in Form einer Emulsion in den Säuren befindlichen Nitroglyzerins und der Abfallsäuren infolge der Verschiedenheit ihrer spezifischen Gewichte. Je besser das verwendete Glyzerin war und bei je niedrigerer Temperatur die Nitrierung vorgenommen wurde, um so rascher wird die Scheidung vor sich gehen. Das Nitroglyzerin scheidet sich an der Oberfläche ab; es soll eine ganz scharfe Trennungslinie zwischen den trüben Abfallsäuren und dem klaren Nitroglyzerin auftreten. Das Vorhandensein von Verunreinigungen im Glyzerin oder von Bleisulfat in den Säuren verzögert die Scheidung. Auch bei der Scheidung ist eine Explosionsgefahr nicht ausgeschlossen. Die Temperatur darf niemals 25° übersteigen,[1] und muß daher auf das Thermometer, sowie auf die Farbe der entweichenden Gase die größte Aufmerksamkeit gerichtet werden. Scheint Gefahr im Anzuge, so wird vorerst mittels Druckluft gerührt, eventuell die ganze Masse in den Notbebälter entleert. Auch wenn die Scheidung zu lange dauern und nach $1^1/_2$ Stunden noch nicht beendigt sein sollte, zieht man es vor, die ganze Ladung in den Not-

[1] Zweckmäßig befinden sich im Separator noch ein paar elektrische Thermometer, die ein außerhalb des Walles befindliches Läutewerk in Bewegung setzen, sobald der Quecksilberfaden eine festgesetzte höchste Temperatur erreicht.

behälter abzulassen, da infolge des langen Kontaktes zwischen Nitroglyzerin und Säuren sehr leicht eine Zersetzung des letzteren eintreten könnte. Ist die Scheidung des Nitroglyzerins normal verlaufen, so läßt man dasselbe durch Öffnen des am Mantel des Apparates angebrachten Hahnes *g* in den Vorwaschbottich *B* (Fig. 29) einfließen, wo das Sprengöl der ersten Waschung unterworfen wird.

Der Vorwaschbottich *B* soll das schon geschiedene saure Nitroglyzerin zunächst in viel Wasser verteilen, um dadurch einer noch in diesem Stadium möglichen Zersetzung vorzubeugen, wozu abermals eine Umrührung mittels Druckluft erforderlich ist. Es ist nicht nötig, daß der Vorwäscher die ganze Menge des Nitroglyzerins auf einmal faßt; der Arbeiter kann es vielmehr so einrichten, daß der Zufluß von Wasser und von saurem Nitroglyzerin aus dem Separator nur in dem Maße stattfindet, wie dasselbe — nach dieser vorläufigen rohen Durchrührung — mit dem sauren Waschwasser nach dem Waschhause abläuft. Das kleine Gefäß darf natürlich nicht überlaufen; auch darf bei der Umrührung mit komprimierter Luft kein saures Nitroglyzerin über die Wandung verspritzt werden. Nach Entfernung des Nitroglyzerins aus dem Separator wird letzterer durch Öffnen der am Boden des Gefäßes angebrachten Hähne entleert. Vermittelst des obersten der Hähne läßt man die Abfallsäuren zu einem Schuppen fließen, wo sie in einer zweiten Scheidung, der sogenannten Nachscheidung möglichst vollständig von noch anhaftendem Sprengöl befreit werden. Ist der größte Teil der Säuren abgelassen, so beobachtet man durch die am Ablaßrohre *d* angebrachte Laterne *l* die Farbe der ablaufenden Flüssigkeit. Sobald letztere schmutzig und trübe durchläuft, sperrt man den Hahn ab und läßt durch den niedriger angebrachten Hahn den Säurerest in Guttapercheeimer abfließen. In manchen Fabriken werden diese, zum größten Teil aus niedrigen Nitrierprodukten und Verunreinigungen bestehenden Reste dem Nitroglyzerin im Wasserbottiche *B* zugegeben; in andern Betrieben werden solche durch Eingießen in große Behälter mit Wasser unschädlich gemacht.

Neuerdings wurden zur Beschleunigung der Abscheidung des Nitroglyzerins zwei Patente genommen.

Das D.R.P. 171106 von Robert Möller in Hamburg besagt, daß, durch Zusatz geeigneter Mittel in bestimmten Mengen, die Abscheidung des Nitroglyzerins sich beschleunigen läßt und dadurch gleichzeitig eine glatte und scharfe Scheidung erzielt werden kann. Als solche Zusatzmittel werden besonders Paraffin, Vaseline, hochmolekulare Fettsäuren und Fettsäureester empfohlen. Diese Substanzen können entweder dem Glyzerin oder dem Säuregemisch vor Beginn des Nitrierprozesses oder aber während der Nitrieroperation oder auch erst nach völliger Beendigung derselben, d. h. nachdem das Glyzerin dem Säuregemisch zugeführt und die Bildung des Nitroglyzerins stattgefunden hat, zugesetzt werden. Beispielsweise verfährt man wie folgt: Nachdem die Nitriersäure (35·5 Prozent Salpetersäure, 60·5 Prozent Schwefelsäure, 4 Prozent Wasser) in den Nitrierapparat eingelassen ist, setzt man den Rührapparat in Bewegung und fügt nunmehr Paraffinöl oder Vaseline [und zwar 0·5 bis 2 pro Mille vom Gewicht des Glyzerins] zu und beginnt dann mit der Zuführung des Glyzerins. Der Nitrierprozeß geht ohne Störung vor sich und die Scheidung des Nitroglyzerins von dem Säuregemisch ist in sehr kurzer Zeit, nach Angabe der Patentschrift in einem Drittel der sonst üblichen Dauer, beendet. Nach erfolgter Scheidung wird das Nitroglyzerin wie üblich gereinigt, wobei das Zusatzmittel weggespült wird. In dem D.R.P. 181489 der The Eastern Dynamite Company in Wilmington wird hingewiesen, daß gelatinöse, gallertartige Flüssigkeiten emulgierte Teilchen lange schwebend erhalten. es wurde gefunden, daß speziell gallertartige Silikate, bzw. Kieselsäure auch in sehr geringen Mengen, wie solche in den Säuren und im Glyzerin leicht vorkommen, die Ausscheidung des Nitroglyzerins, d. h. die Zeitdauer, welche das Nitroglyzerin zum Übergang aus der Emulsionsform in diejenige einer reinen Flüssigkeit braucht, verlangsamen. Nach der Patentschrift werden daher dem Reaktionsgemisch Substanzen zugesetzt, welche das gallertartige Silikat in eine solche Form überzuführen imstande sind, daß die Beimischungen ihre emulgierende Wirkung verlieren. Als solche Zusätze werden Fluornatrium, überhaupt Fluorverbindungen empfohlen, welche mit der Kieselsäure Siliciumfluorid $SiFl_4$) ergeben. Von Fluornatrium soll ein Zusatz von 0·001 Prozent zum Glyzerin vor dessen Eingabe in das Nitriergefäß und ein nachträglicher gleich großer Zusatz zum Reaktionsgemisch genügen. Das amerikanische Patent auf diese Neuerung 804817 lautet auf Charles L. Reese.

In früherer Zeit, als man an die Verwertung der Abfallsäuren nicht dachte, verwandte man auch die sog. direkte Scheidung, indem man das ganze aus den Nitrierapparaten kommende Nitriergemisch in Wasser einlaufen ließ, wobei sich das Nitroglyzerin am Boden absetzte. Dieses Verfahren ist heute aus wirtschaftlichen wie hygienischen Rücksichten gänzlich verlassen worden.

E. Die Reinigung.

Die Reinigung des Nitroglyzerins umfaßt folgende Operationen: die erste und die zweite Waschung, die Filtration und die Entwässerung.

Die erste Waschung erfolgt in dem Vorwäscher *B* (Fig. 27), wohin das Sprengöl aus dem Abscheider durch Hahn *g* abgelassen wurde. Dieser Waschbottich ist ein aus Bleiblech gefertigtes zylindrisches Gefäß von kleineren Dimensionen als der Separator selbst. Ein schräg ablaufender, mit Hahn *s* (Fig. 29) versehener Boden gestattet das Nitroglyzerin abzuziehen; der höher angebrachte Hahn *r* dient zum Ablassen der Waschwässer. Hahn *s* ist während der Reinigung in Verbindung mit dem Notbehälter. Das Nitroglyzerin findet beim Einfließen in den Waschbottich schon eine entsprechende Menge kalten Wassers vor. Infolge der spezifischen Schwere sinkt das Nitroglyzerin zu Boden, wird aber durch den bei *o'* eintretenden Luftstrom verteilt und mit dem Waschwasser in innige Berührung gebracht. Nach Ablassen des ersten Waschwassers durch *r* gibt man 4 bis 5mal frisches Waschwasser zu und zwar allmählich. Zum Schlusse wäscht man unter Zusatz von etwas Sodalösung. Die, durch einen Thermometer *t* beobachtete Temperatur soll beim Waschen einerseits nie unter 12° C sinken, da sonst die an den Wänden des Gefäßes befindlichen Nitroglyzerinteilchen gefrieren und zu Explosionen Veranlassung geben könnten, andrerseits muß man vermeiden, daß die Reaktion zwischen der mitgerissenen Säure und dem Waschwasser niemals eine Temperaturerhöhung über 25° C bewirkt. Zur Einhaltung dieser Temperaturgrenzen sind am Apparate zwei Zuleitungsrohre u und u_1 angebracht, welche Wasser von 25 bis 30°, bzw. 12 bis 15° zuführen können. Der Zusatz von Sodalösung zum Schlusse der Waschung hat den Zweck, die Befreiung des Nitroglyzerins von den anhaftenden Säuren durch Neutralisierung derselben möglichst zu erreichen.

Nach Entfernung der letzten Waschwässer kommt das vorgewaschene Sprengöl dann zur sorgfältigen Waschung in ein anderes Gebäude.

Fig. 30 bis 32 zeigen — nach Eckelt — einen Wasch- und Filtrierraum. *AA* sind Waschgefäße aus starkem Blei bzw. Holz mit Bleiverkleidung, in welchen das Nitroglyzerin mit Wasser und Druckluft gewaschen wird. *B* (Fig. 31) ist wieder ein Sicherheitsbehälter, der zugleich als Absatzbehälter für mitgerissene Partikelchen von Nitroglyzerin dient, indem das Waschwasser durch den Bottich geleitet wird. *C* ist ein weiteres Wasser-reservoir; *D* ein Filter für das gewaschene und mit Sodalauge neutralisierte Nitroglyzerin.

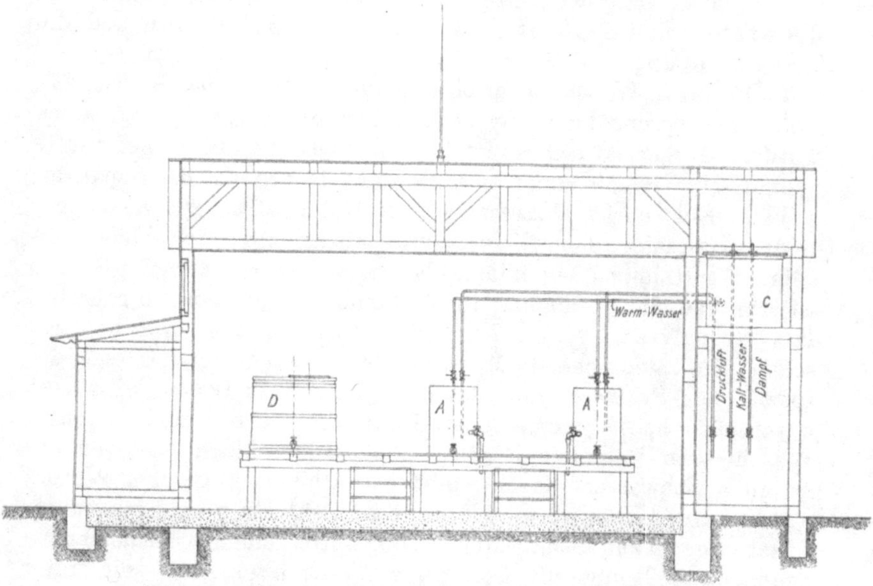

Fig. 30. Wasch- und Filtrierraum (nach Eckelt).

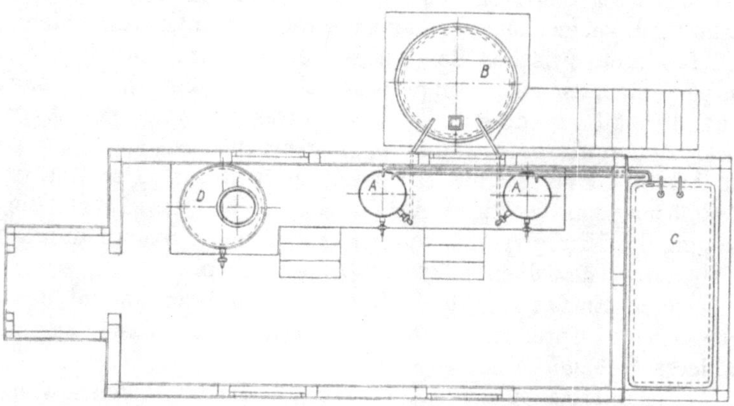

Fig. 31. Wasch- und Filtrierraum (nach Eckelt).

In den Waschbottichen ist an der tiefsten Stelle des schräg ablaufenden Bodens ein Hahn zum Ablassen des Nitroglyzerins angebracht; ein zweiter, darüber befindlicher Hahn dient zum Abziehen der Waschwässer. Die Bottiche werden zuerst mit der entsprechenden Menge kalten oder lauwarmen Wassers angefüllt, hierauf das Nitroglyzerin eingelassen und mittels komprimierter Luft gerührt. Nach etwa 15 bis 30 Minuten wird das Rühren eingestellt, durch den oberen Hahn das verbrauchte Waschwasser

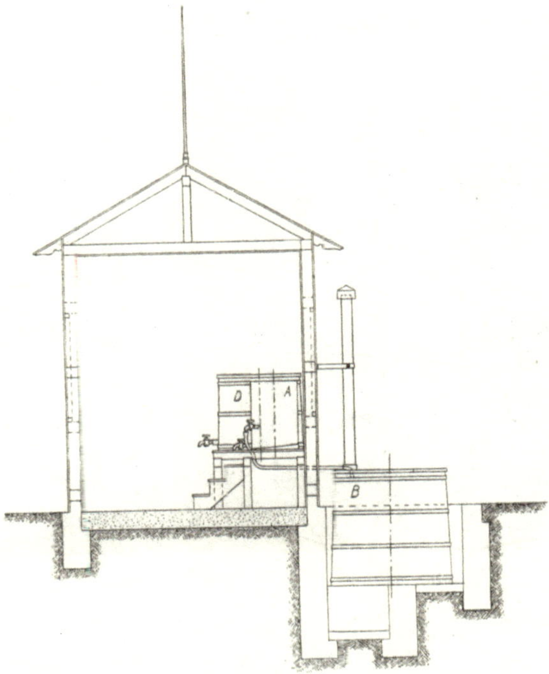

Fig. 32. Wasch- und Filtrierraum (nach Eckelt).

entfernt und durch das Zulaufrohr allmählich neues Wasser eingelassen. Diese Operation wird so oft (gewöhnlich 3 bis 4 mal) wiederholt, bis eine Probe des Nitroglyzerins, mit Lackmuspapier geprüft, eine neutrale Reaktion zeigt.

In den Staaten, in welchen das Nitroglyzerin einer strengen Wärmeprobe unterzogen wird, genügt die Waschung mittels Wasser nicht, sondern es muß noch Sodalauge in Anwendung kommen. Es wird dann so lange mit Wasser nachgewaschen, bis die Abwässer keine alkalische Reaktion mehr zeigen.

In Waltham Abbey wird die Waschung so geregelt, daß zuerst mit Sodalösung und dann mit Wasser gewaschen wird, bis im fertigen Nitroglyzerin nicht mehr als 0·01 Prozent Alkali vorhanden sind. Allgemeine Regeln für die Waschung lassen sich nicht aufstellen, dieselbe regelt sich nach der Probe, die das

Endprodukt zu bestehen hat. So wird in einigen Fabriken, in denen besonders hohe Anforderungen an das Nitroglyzerin gestellt werden, mit lauwarmem Wasser von etwa 50° C gewaschen. Bei dieser Temperatur verflüchtigt sich aber schon etwas Nitroglyzerin, und dessen Dämpfe sind sehr unangenehm, so daß man nicht gern so warmes Waschwasser anwendet.

Fig. 33. Innere Ansicht des Waschhauses.

Nachstehend sei ein Beispiel angeführt, d. i. die Nitroglyzerinwaschung in der kgl. Pulverfabrik Waltham-Abbey (nach Daniel) Zuerst läßt man in den Waschbottich eine Sodalösung bis zu einer Höhe von etwa 10 cm einfließen, hierauf werden 340 kg des zu reinigenden Nitroglyzerins und dann abermals 10 cm Sodalösung hinzugefügt; schließlich gibt man Wasser bis zur Füllung des Bottichs zu, wodurch man eine Sodalösung von 2·68 Prozent Soda bekommt. Nach $^1/_4$ Stunde wird das Waschwasser abgelassen, und 5 ccm einer Lösung von 1.91 Prozent Soda zugegeben. Nach $^1/_4$ Stunde wird die Lösung wieder erneuert, worauf man die Flüssigkeit $^3/_4$ Stunden lang sich in dem Bottich absetzen läßt. Zum Schluß wäscht man $^1/_4$ Stunde lang mit einer 0·38prozentigen Lösung.[1]

Die Waschwässer werden nun durch eine eigenartige Vorrichtung entfernt, welche es ermöglicht, verschieden große Mengen

[1] In einigen Fabriken wäscht man zehnmal, prüft dann auf Reinheit, worauf das Nitroglyzerin in die Ölkästen abgelassen, bzw. zu den Filterkästen aufgedrückt wird.

Nitroglyzerin nach Belieben zu bearbeiten. Ein hoher in Holz eingefaßter Bleibottich *A* (Fig. 34) von gewöhnlicher Konstruktion trägt einen schiefen Boden *c*, einen Nitroglyzerin-Ablaßhahn *d*, und eine Rührvorrichtung *h*. Der Hahn *e* steht mittels des Schlauches *f* mit dem Trichter *g* in Verbindung, der aus dünnem Messingblech

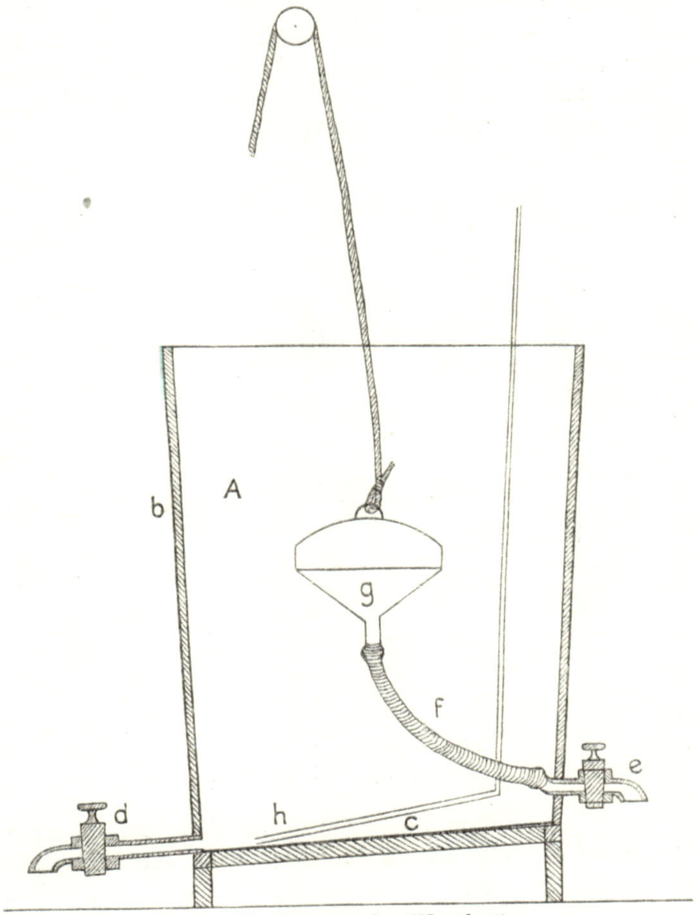

Fig. 34. Entfernung der Waschwässer.

hergestellt ist und durch ein Gegengewicht stets nach aufwärts gezogen wird. Will man die Waschwässer entfernen, so wird durch einen geringen Zug an einer Rolle der Trichter zum Sinken gebracht und der Hahn *e* geöffnet.

Das im Bottich zurückbleibende Nitroglyzerin enthält stets schleimige Bestandteile, Sodaschlamm, schwefelsaures Blei u. dgl. m., und muß daher der Filtration unterworfen werden. Letzteres geschieht, indem man das Sprengöl direkt aus dem Waschbottich über flanellbespannte Rahmen laufen läßt. In manchen Fabriken wendet man zwei übereinander gestellte Rahmen an, zwischen welchen sich trockenes Kochsalz befindet, um das Nitroglyzerin gleichzeitig zu entwässern. Nach mehrmaligem Gebrauch wird das Kochsalz entfernt, aufgelöst und das daran anhaftende Nitroglyzerin wieder gewonnen. Auch gibt man kleine gebrochene Glasstücke auf das Filter, um die schleimigen Bestandteile zurückzuhalten und so das Filter weniger rasch sich verstopfen zu lassen. Es ist jedoch

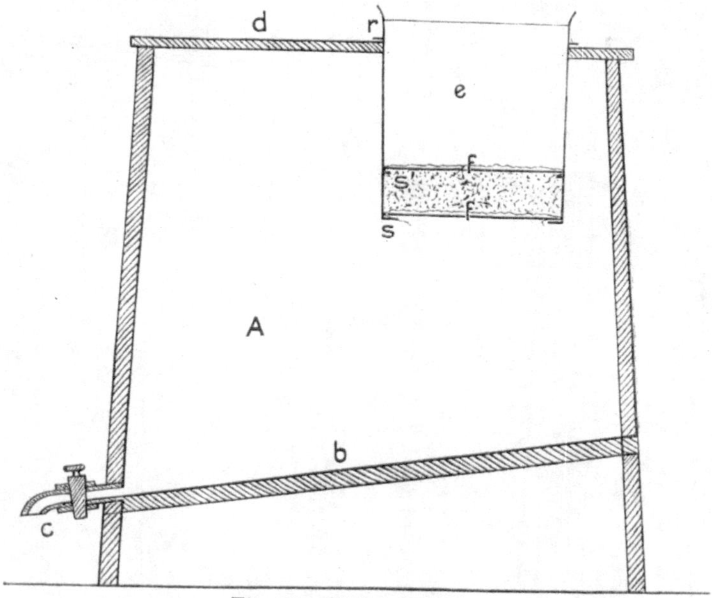

Fig. 35. Filtrierapparat.

immer nötig, die Filter zeitweise zu reinigen und zu erneuern. Fig. 35 zeigt eine gebräuchliche Form des Filtrierapparates Ein hölzerner, innen mit Blei ausgekleideter Bottich *A* mit schräg ablaufendem Boden *b* hat an der tiefsten Stelle den Nitroglyzerin-Ablaßhahn *c*. Der mit Blei überzogene Deckel *d* besitzt eine Öffnung, in welche ein mit Handgriff versehener Bleizylinder *e* paßt; letzterer legt sich mit dem Rande *r* an den Deckel an und kann mittels der Handgriffe aus der Öffnung herausgehoben werden. Auf den unteren Rand *s* und den etwas höher angebrachten Ring s_1 legen sich die mit Drahtgewebe überspannten Filterrahmen *f*, worauf die Filtertücher zu liegen kommen. Der

Zwischenraum zwischen den beiden Filtern wird durch eine Kochsalzschicht ausgefüllt. Das Nitroglyzerin wird in *e* eingegossen und fließt bei *c* rein heraus. Es ist allerdings noch etwas wasserhaltig, besonders wenn es nicht durch Kochsalz getrocknet wurde. Um das Endprodukt vollständig wasserfrei zu haben, wird das aus dem Filtrierraume abfließende Nitroglyzerin ein bis zwei Tage in großen Bleibehältern stehen gelassen, wobei das suspendierte Wasser an die Oberfläche geht und entfernt werden kann. Vorteilhaft ist es, den dazu dienenden Raum auf 25 bis 30° zu erwärmen.

Das in dieser Weise hergestellte Nitroglyzerin ist eine ölige, klare, schwach gelb gefärbte Flüssigkeit, welche in Eimern aus Guttapercha oder Holz mit innerer Bleiverkleidung an die weiteren Verarbeitungsstätten transportiert wird. Andere Metalle, wie Gußeisen usw. dürfen hierzu nicht verwendet werden. — Was die Waschwässer betrifft, so werden solche von mitgerissenem Nitroglyzerin in einer besonderen Werkstatt in eigenen Überlaufvorrichtungen befreit. Letztere sind 4 bis 5 m lange viereckige Behälter aus Blei, die durch Zwischenwände aus gleichem Material in eine Anzahl Abteilungen geteilt sind (Fig. 36).

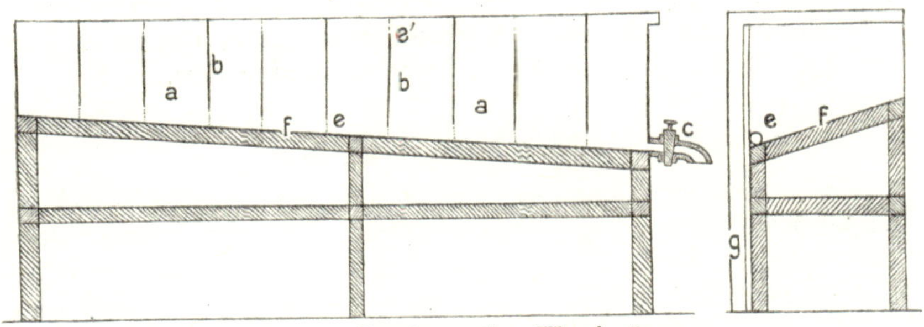

Fig. 36. Reinigung der Waschwässer.

Die Querwände tragen abwechselnd oben und unten Löcher, durch welche die Verbindungen zwischen den einzelnen Abteilungen gebildet werden. Auf dem Schlangenwege nun, den das Wasser macht, setzen sich die spezifisch schwereren Nitroglyzerinteilchen an den Boden der Abteilungen an, und fließen dann längs des schräglaufenden Bodens gegen den Ablaßhahn zu, wo das Sprengöl von Zeit zu Zeit abgelassen und dann im Filterhaus weiter gereinigt wird, während die nitroglyzerinfreien Abwässer in einen eigenen Ablaufkanal abfließen. Es ist ratsam, dem Boden des Apparates eine doppelte Neigung, der Länge wie der Breite nach, zu geben, um das Abfließen des Nitroglyzerins leichter zu gestalten.

Ebenso ist der Instandhaltung des Apparates, der durch die sauren Waschwässer angegriffen wird, eine große Sorgfalt zu widmen.

Lesser führt hinsichtlich der Reinigung noch folgendes aus: In dem Waschhause stehen in der Regel zwei Apparate nebeneinander, in welchen je zwei Chargen vereinigt gewaschen werden können. Allerdings sind meistens nicht beide Apparate gleichzeitig im Betriebe; es kann aber in der Praxis wohl vorkommen, daß das gereinigte Nitroglyzerin den einen Apparat noch nicht verlassen hat, während der zweite schon beschickt worden ist. Da in manchen Fabriken die Chargen bis zu 500 kg Sprengöl betragen, kommen dadurch schon 2000 kg im Waschhause zusammen. Neben den Apparaten und etwas tiefer stehen dann die mit Filtriertüchern bedeckten Gefäße zur Aufnahme des gereinigten Sprengöls, und es kommt vor, daß auch in diesem noch erhebliche Mengen solchen Öls, die nicht sofort weiterverarbeitet werden können, vorübergehend lagern. Zudem müssen oft noch nicht unbedeutende Mengen Sprengöl in den Mischhütten aufbewahrt werden. Lesser bezeichnet es daher als durchaus zweckmäßig, wenn in den einzelnen Fabriken, zwischen dem Waschhaus und den Mischhütten zur Dynamitherstellung, ein besonderes Filterhaus eingeschaltet wird, in dem das Öl aufbewahrt wird und das nur zu gelegentlicher Revision und zum Umstellen der Hähne von einzelnen Arbeitern betreten werden darf.

F. Die Nachscheidung.

Die aus dem Separator ablaufenden Abfallsäuren bestehen zu 60 bis 70 Prozent aus Schwefelsäure, zu 8 bis 10 Prozent aus Salpetersäure, 20 bis 25 Prozent aus Wasser, dann enthalten solche Säuren noch Trinitroglyzerin, sowie die niedrigeren Nitrierungsstufen des Glyzerins (Glyzerindinitrat und Glyzerinmononitrat) neben unverändertem Glyzerin. Das Trinitroglyzerin der Abfallsäuren muß gewonnen werden, und zwar einmal zur Erhöhung der Ausbeute und dann, weil für die weitere Verarbeitung der Abfallsäuren das Nitroglyzerin aus demselben entfernt sein muß. Deshalb wird die sog. Nachscheidung vorgenommen.

Ein hierzu dienender Apparat ist in Fig. 37 abgebildet. Es ist dies ein großer, etwa 2000 kg Säure fassender Holzbottich *A* mit schräg ablaufendem Boden und einem konischen bleiernen Deckel *b*. An der Spitze des Kegels ist ein etwa 10 cm im Durchmesser breites und 30 cm hohes Glasrohr *c*, das am untern Teile einen Glashahn *e* trägt. An das Glasrohr schließt sich oben ein für die Ableitung der Gase dienendes Rohr *d*, welches zum Schutze gegen Verunreinigungen mit einer Haube versehen ist. Die Flüssigkeit im Behälter wird durch Kühlschlangen *q* (oder mittels eines Kühlmantels) innerhalb bestimmter Temperaturgrenzen gehalten. Zwei Thermometer, ein Druckluftzuleitungsrohr und ein an der tiefsten Stelle des Bodens angebrachter Entleerungshahn *f*, der während der Operation des Nachscheidens mit einem großen Notbehälter in Verbindung steht,

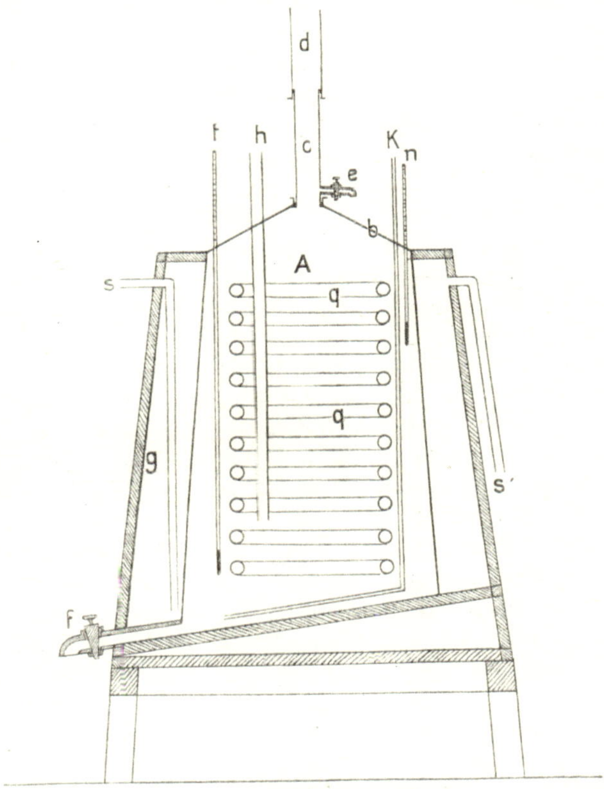

Fig. 37. Nachscheideapparat.

nach der Operation aber zu den Säurevorratsgefäßen führt, vervollständigen die Apparatur des Nachscheiders.

Das Nachscheiden selbst wird ausgeführt, indem man den Apparat bis ungefähr zur Mitte des am Deckel angebrachten Glasrohres mit den Abfallsäuren anfüllt. Nach einigen Stunden ruhigen Stehenlassens steigt das Nitroglyzerin in Form von Tröpfchen an die Oberfläche und sammelt sich hier an. Durch Öffnen des Hahnes *e* (Fig. 37) wird der abgeschiedene Teil in einen Guttaperchaeimer abgelassen, sofort in ein bereitstehendes Gefäß mit Wasser gegossen, gewaschen und zur weiteren Reinigung in das Filtrierhaus gebracht. Man läßt nunmehr in den Nachscheider neue Abfallsäure zufließen, und zwar so lange, bis das ursprüngliche Niveau wieder erreicht ist. In der gleichen Weise verfährt man während mehrerer Tage wiederholt, wobei man durch öfteres Abziehen des Nitroglyzerins einer Ansammlung größerer Nitroglyzerinmengen vorbeugt. Innerhalb 10 bis 14 Tagen ist die im Nachscheider befindliche Säuremenge vollständig frei von Sprengöl. Sie wird dann durch den Entleerungshahn in die Säurevorratsgefäße abgelassen und von hier zur weiteren Verarbeitung befördert.

Bei der Nachscheidung ist die Anwesenheit von geringen Mengen Nitroglyzerin gegenüber großen Mengen Säure und Wasser nicht ungefährlich. Es können Zersetzungen mit einer nachfolgenden Explosion eintreten. Der Beginn solcher Zersetzungen ist an der Temperaturerhöhung und an der rotbraunen Farbe der entweichenden Gase erkennbar; man muß daher auf das Thermometer und auf das am Deckel angebrachte Glasrohr ein stetes Augenmerk richten.

Lokale Wärmeansammlungen werden durch Wasserzirkulation in den Kühlröhren *q* (Fig. 37) und eventuell durch das Einleiten komprimierter Luft bei *k* verhindert. Im Notfalle muß der Inhalt des Nachscheiders in ein Notbassin abgelassen werden. Der Apparat ist öfters zu untersuchen, da Beschädigungen an den Kühlschlangen, welche von dem Angriff der Säuren herrühren, sehr nachteilige Folgen haben können. Sollte während der Nachscheidung selbst ein Kühlrohr leck werden, so muß man das Kühlwasser sofort einstellen und der Druckluft vollen Einlaß geben. Ein Arbeiter muß die Apparate beständig, bei Tag und Nacht, überwachen. Nebenstehende Fig. 38 zeigt die Nachscheidungsapparate im Betriebe.

Nach L e s s e r findet man hinsichtlich der N a c h s c h e i d u n g s a n l a g e n erhebliche Unterschiede, und zwar namentlich in bezug auf die Größe. In einzelnen Fabriken vermag die Nachscheidung nur die vierfache Tagesmenge aufzunehmen, während man doch meistens die Abfallsäure 10 bis 14 Tage in der Nachscheidung behält. (Bei den modernen Denitrierapparaten scheint es auf eine vollständige Ausscheidung des Sprengöls nicht so genau anzukommen.) L e s s e r unterscheidet in der Einrichtung der Nachscheidung zwei verschiedene Anordnungen. Entweder ist ein hölzernes Podest vorhanden, von dem aus der Arbeiter die Hähne und Ausflußöffnungen erreichen kann, oder die Gefäße sind frei aufgestellt, so daß man sie jederzeit vollständig besichtigen kann.

Holz, welches beim Ausfließen der Säure in Brand geraten könnte, wird bis auf leichte, neben den Apparaten aufgestellte Tritte vermieden.[1]

In der englischen Regierungs-Pulverfabrik zu Waltham-Abbey wurde neuerdings von dem Direktor, Oberstleutnant Sir F. L. Nathan, von dem Betriebsführer J. M. Thomson und dem Chemiker W. Rintoul ein Verfahren ausgearbeitet und in den englischen Patenten 15983 (1901) und 3020 (1903) beschrieben, wonach die Weiterbildung und Abscheidung von gelöstem oder mechanisch

Fig. 38. Nachscheidungsapparate im Betriebe.

gebundenem Nitroglyzerin in der Abfallsäure aufgehoben und dadurch, neben anderen Vorteilen, die Nachscheidung ganz vermieden werden soll.[2] Es hat sich nämlich herausgestellt, daß, wenn man nach der in gewöhnlicher Weise vorgenommenen Nitrierung des Glyzerins und nach der Entfernung des gebildeten Nitroglyzerins eine kleine Menge Wasser zu dem zurückbleibenden Säuregemisch (der Abfallsäure) setzt, in letzterer auch dann keine weitere Bildung und Abscheidung von Nitroglyzerin erfolgt, wenn man die Säure längere Zeit bei niedriger Temperatur hält Die

[1] Manchmal besteht die Nachscheidung aus zwei Anlagen I und II; die Säure läuft zuerst in ein Sammelgefäß, wird durch Montejus in den oberen Verteilungskasten gedrückt, läuft dann in die Nachscheidebatterien der Abteilung I und von hier durch Ablauf und Montejus in Abteilung II, von da in die Denitrierung.

[2] Vgl. G. Lunge, Zeitschr. Schieß- u. Sprengstoffwesen I, S. 393.

hinzuzugebende Menge Wasser ist hierbei so gering, daß weder die Abscheidung der Abfallsäure, noch ihre Wiederkonzentration dadurch berührt werden. Man kann daher die Abfallsäure ohne Nachscheidung in beliebigen Behältern und ohne die sonst erforderliche fortwährende Aufsicht aufbewahren. Nachstehende Abbildung des Apparates gibt dessen Aufriß und Horizontalschnitt (Fig. 39).

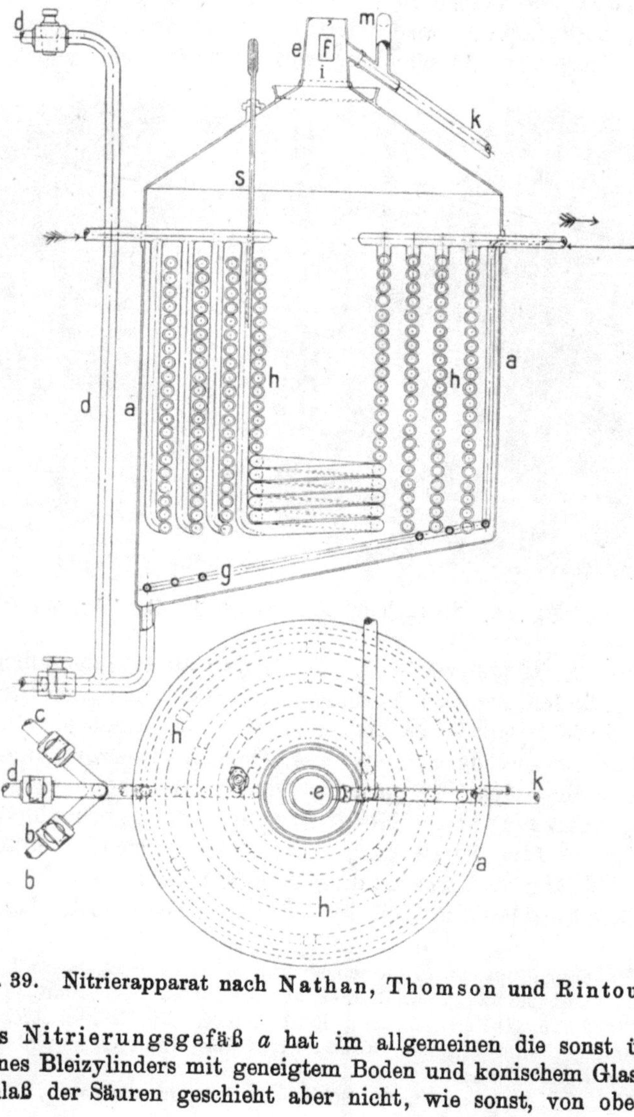

Fig. 39. Nitrierapparat nach Nathan, Thomson und Rintoul.

Das Nitrierungsgefäß *a* hat im allgemeinen die sonst übliche Form eines Bleizylinders mit geneigtem Boden und konischem Glasdache. Der Einlaß der Säuren geschieht aber nicht, wie sonst, von oben her, sondern durch ein an der tiefsten Stelle des Bodens angebrachtes Rohr, das drei Abzweigungen besitzt. Die eine davon *b*, führt zum Denitrierungsgefäß oder zum Druckkessel für Abfallsäure, die zweite *c* zu dem Ersäufungsbottich (Notbassin), die dritte *d* steigt in die Höhe und teilt sich dort in zwei Arme, von denen einer nach dem Vorratsbehälter für Mischsäure, der andere nach dem Behälter für Abfallsäure führt. Das Säurerohr ist 30 cm tiefer als die tiefste Stelle des Bodens geführt, um es unmöglich zu machen, daß während des Umrührens etwas Nitroglyzerin in das aufsteigende Rohr gerät. Auf dem schrägen Boden des Gefäßes *a* liegt eine mit vielen Löchern versehene Schlange *g* zum Einblasen von Luft. Im zylindrischen Raume des Gefäßes befinden sich, wie gewöhnlich, mehrere Kühlwasserschlangen *hh*. Über dem konischen Dache befindet sich ein Bleizylinder *e* mit Fenster *f* und mit seitlichem Auslaß angebracht; dieser mündet in ein Bleirohr *k*, das zu dem Vorwaschgefäße für Nitroglyzerin führt. Aus dem Rohre *k* steigt ein Rohr *m* auf, durch welches die Dämpfe abziehen. *s* ist ein Thermometer, dessen Gefäß in das Gemisch im Innern von *a* eintaucht. Zur Ausführung einer Nitrierung läßt man die Mischsäure durch *d* einfließen, dann Glyzerin zutreten und bewirkt durch Einblasen von Luft durch die Schlange *g* die nötige Mischung unter Kühlung mittels der Schlangen *hk*. — Wenn die Nitrierung beendigt und die Temperatur etwas gefallen ist, stellt man die Luft in *g* und das Wasser in *h* ab und läßt das Gemisch im Nitrierapparat selbst — es ist also kein Separator[1] vorhanden — zur Ruhe und Scheidung kommen, wobei die Temperatur jedoch nicht unter 15° C fallen soll. Nun läßt man die Abfallsäure der früheren Operationen langsam durch *d* von unten her in *a* eintreten, so daß sie eine Schicht unterhalb des Reaktionsgemisches bildet und letzteres im Nitriergefäß allmählich gehoben wird. Das Nitroglyzerin kommt dann in dem Zylinder *e* zum Vorschein und läuft durch *k* nach dem Vorwaschgefäße ab, wo es, wie gewöhnlich, sofort in Wasser aufgenommen und einer alkalischen Waschung unterzogen wird. Der Zulauf der Verdrängungssäure muß so langsam geschehen, daß das klare Nitroglyzerin, frei von suspendierter Säure, in dem Maße abfließt, wie die Scheidung erfolgt. Schließlich bemerkt man bei *f* eine scharfe Trennungslinie zwischen der Säure und dem Nitroglyzerin und man stellt dann den Zufluß der Säure durch *d* ab. Nun läßt man,

[1] Man könnte auch das bisherige Verfahren insofern beibehalten, daß man das Gemisch von Nitroglyzerin und Abfallsäure ohne vorherige Scheidung in einen Separator laufen läßt und dort, nach der Entfernung des Nitroglyzerins, zu den Abfallsäuren die zwei Prozent Wasser zusetzt, wodurch die Nachscheidung überflüssig wird; allein beim Ablassen von Nitroglyzerin und Abfallsäure in den Separator durch einen Tonhahn besteht eine Quelle von Gefahren darin, daß zwischen dem Hahnküken und dem Hahngefäß beim Drehen des ersteren Reibung vorhanden ist, besonders wenn fremde Substanzen dazwischen kommen; auch wird beim Schließen des Hahnes ungereinigtes Nitroglyzerin in demselben zurückbleiben. Hierin liegen Explosionsmöglichkeiten.

um bei dem späteren Umrühren ein Überspritzen zu verhüten, ein wenig von der Abfallsäure unten ablaufen, stellt den Luftstrom durch *g* wieder an und setzt langsam ein wenig Wasser im Betrage von 2 Prozent des Gewichts der Abfallsäure zu, welches sich infolge der Luftrührung sofort mit der Säure mischt. Während dieses Zusetzens von Wasser wird fortwährend durch den Luftstrom umgerührt, aber nicht abgekühlt. Die Temperatur steigt gewöhnlich um etwa 3 °C für jedes Prozent Wasser, das zugesetzt wird. Nach Beendigung des Zusatzes bläst man noch kurze Zeit Luft ein, bis die Temperatur anfängt zu sinken; dann wird die Luft abgestellt und durch *d* so viel ältere Abfallsäure von unten zugeführt, daß das Niveau wieder bis zu dem oberen Ablauf steigt. Man wartet noch eine kurze Zeit, damit das an dem Gefäße *a* und den Kühlschlangen *h* adhärierende Nitroglyzerin in die Höhe steigt und durch *k* ablaufen kann. Hierauf kann man die nun vollständig nitroglyzerinfreie Abfallsäure durch *b* nach dem dafür bestimmten Behälter abfließen lassen, wovon man dann so viel in den höheren, mit *d* kommunizierenden Behälter hebt, als man bei einer späteren Operation zur Verdrängung des Nitroglyzerins aus *a* braucht. Den Rest der Abfallsäure kann man, ohne jede Nachscheidung, in beliebigen Vorratsbehältern und ohne weitere Aufsicht aufbewahren, um sie dann zu denitrieren.

In Waltham-Abbey gibt es jetzt kein Nachscheidungsgebäude mehr, und das neue Verfahren hat sich ohne Schwierigkeiten und ohne Nachteile gegenüber dem sonst üblichen Verfahren gezeigt. Die neue Methode ist gefahrloser, weil das immerhin bedenkliche Durchlaufen von Nitroglyzerin durch Tonhähne ganz fortfällt. Eine weitere Verminderung von Explosionsgefahr wird durch die Entfernung des Nitroglyzerins unmittelbar nach seiner Trennung von der Säure, durch die Kühlung während der Scheidung und Nachscheidung, durch weniger häufiges Hin- und Herlaufen des Nitroglyzerins und der Abfallsäure bewirkt, was besonders dann unangenehm ist, wenn man diese Flüssigkeiten aus einem Gebäude in ein anderes durch Rinnen weiterleiten muß. Statt Nitriergefäß, Scheidegefäß, Sicherheitsgefäß und 16 Nachscheidebottichen braucht man bei dem neuen Verfahren nur zwei Nitriergefäße. Damit kann man täglich je fünf Chargen zu 453 kg Glyzerin nitrieren. Bei dem gewöhnlichen Verfahren braucht man, um das Nitroglyzerin durch natürliches Gefälle von einer Stelle zur anderen laufen zu lassen, einen Niveauunterschied von 6,7 m von dem Deckel des Nitrierapparates bis zu dem Ablauf für das fertige Nitroglyzerin, bei dem neuen Verfahren nur 3,6 m.

Nachstehende Fig. 40 zeigt im Maßstabe 1 : 96 die Vertikalanordnung der verschiedenen Apparate für die vorbeschriebene Methode der Erzeugung und den dafür nötigen Fall der Leitungsverbindung.

Die Ausbeute an Nitroglyzerin soll um etwa 5 Prozent größer sein als bei dem älteren Verfahren und 220 Prozent des Glyzeringewichtes betragen. Dies erklärt sich daraus, daß während der Scheidung und Nachscheidung die Temperatur niedriger als bisher ist und daher weniger Nitroglyzerin in der Abfallsäure gelöst bleibt; ferner, daß das abgeschiedene Nitroglyzerin sofort entfernt und gewaschen wird, also der weiteren Wirkung der Säuren nicht mehr ausgesetzt ist, und endlich, daß, infolge der geringeren Zahl von Gefäßen beim Auswaschen derselben, weniger Nitroglyzerin mit den Waschwässern fortgeht.

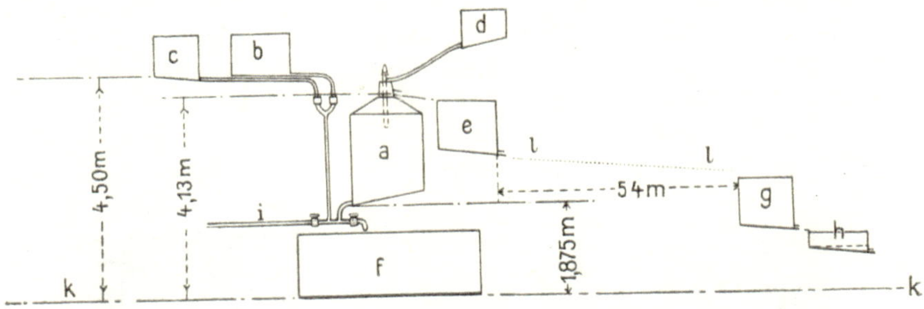

Fig. 40.

a ist das Nitriergefäß, *b* Behälter für Nitriersäure, *c* für Verdrängungssäure, *d* für Glyzerin, *e* Vorwascher, *f* Notbassin, *g* Endwascher, *h* Filter, *i* Ablauf für Abfallsäure, *l—l* eine 54 m lange Rinne mit Fall 1:120, *k k* Fußboden.

Novak und Escales (deutsche Patentanmeldung E. 11632 vom 10. April 1906) vermeiden die lange Nachscheidung beim gewöhnlichen Verfahren in der Weise, daß dieselben die Abfallmischsäuren ganz kurze Zeit mit dem elektrischen Strom behandeln, wobei das Nitroglyzerin sofort an die Oberfläche geht und isoliert werden kann. Die Abfallsäuren sind dann ganz frei von Nitroglyzerin und können als solche denitriert werden.

G. Die Denitrierung und Regenerierung der Mischsäuren.

Nachdem die Abfallsäuren von den letzten Spuren Nitroglyzerin befreit sind, werden dieselben durch die sog. Denitrierung in der Weise in ihre Bestandteile — Schwefelsäure und Salpetersäure — zerlegt, daß jede Säure für sich in möglichst reinem Zustande rückgewonnen wird.

Bei den Denitrieranlagen der Deutschen Steinzeugwarenfabrik in Friedrichsfeld (Preis einer kompletten Anlage ca. Mk. 2600) wird die Misch(-Abfall-)säure in einem Turm zersetzt, welcher von unten durch Dampf erhitzt wird, wobei die nach dem Gegenstromprinzip von oben herabrieselnde Säure mit dem Dampf in höchst innige Berührung gebracht wird. Die flüssig bleibende Schwefelsäure fließt unten aus dem Turme ab, während die gasförmige Salpetersäure oben entweicht und in der anschließenden Kondensationsbatterie wieder kondensiert wird.

Der Denitrierturm kann aus Eisen mit einer starken Auskleidung aus säurefesten Steinen sein. Gewöhnlich nimmt man einen Zylinder aus Volvic-Lava oder säurefestem Sandstein. Oben auf dem Turme befindet sich eine Verteilungsschale, in welche durch ein Sicherheitstrichterrohr die Mischsäure einläuft, ohne daß dem Gase der Austritt gestattet wäre. Als Füllmaterial finden zweckmäßig die Guttmann-Kugeln Anwendung, bei denen die Denitrierung sehr vollkommen vor sich geht, indem die Säure wegen den inneren Becken nur langsam nach abwärts gelangt, sonach Zeit hat, die Salpetersäure abzustoßen. Der dünne Scherben der Kugeln läßt eine sehr schnelle Erhitzung zu. Zwischen Deni-

Fig. 41. Denitrierungsanlage.

trierturm und der Salpetersäure-Kondensationsanlage ist zweckmäßig ein Saug- und Blasapparat eingeschaltet. Die Kondensationsbatterie selbst besteht zunächst aus einem Luftröhrenkühler, an welchen sich Tourills mit Aufsatzröhren anschließen. Die Röhrenkühlung bedingt eine energische Abkühlung und Kondensation der Gase. Am Schlusse der Tourillbatterie ist zur Kondensation — auch der letzten Spuren von salpetersauren Gasen — ein Kondensationsturm, der von oben mit Wasser berieselt wird, mit mäßigem Zulauf, damit die abfließende Salpetersäure genügend konzentriert ist. Neuerdings verwendet man zwei oder vier Kugeltürme gewöhnlicher Größe (3 m Höhe, 70 cm Durchmesser), welche mit kleinen kontinuierlichen Montejus von einem

Turm zum andern gespeist werden. Mit zwei Türmen kann man 8- bis 10000 kg, mit vier Türmen 16000 kg Abfallsäure in 24 Stunden denitrieren.

Die entfallende Schwefelsäure hat eine Stärke von 56° Bé, die resultierende Salpetersäure hat 38 bis 40° Bé; durch wiederholtes Zirkulieren kann dieselbe auf volle 40° Bé gebracht werden.

Ein Patent von Robert Evers in Förde (D.R.P. 182216) betrifft ein Denitrierverfahren, wonach ein Gemisch von atmosphärischer Luft und Dampf an einer oder mehreren Stellen des Denitrierturmes in möglichst hoch erhitztem Zustande eingeführt wird. Zur Ausführung dieses Verfahrens werden Reaktionstürme verwendet, welche nicht vollständig mit Füllkörpern ausgesetzt, sondern durch zwischengelegte durchbrochene Böden in Kammern geteilt werden, die abwechselnd mit Füllkörpern ausgesetzt werden oder hohl sind, wobei in letzterem noch Mischapparate nach D.R.P. 145743 angeordnet werden. Die von oben durchfließende und zu denitrierende Säure wird durch die Füllkörper verteilt, fällt durch den durchlochten Boden der Kammer in die zweite darunter liegende, wo sie durch den Mischapparat mit den von unten aufsteigenden Gasen und dem Gemisch aus Dampf und Luft in innige Berührung gebracht wird.[1] Mit einer solchen Eversschen Denitrieranlage, in der weder maschinelle Einrichtungen, noch automatische Montejus u. dergl. eingebaut sind, und die von einem Arbeiter bedient wird, werden in 24 Stunden 20- bis 22000 kg Mischsäure denitriert.

Die Salpetersäure wird bei sehr guter Ausbeute zu $^1/_5$ als Säure von 36° Bé und zu $^4/_5$ als Säure von 40° Bé wiedergewonnen. Sie enthält bis höchstens 0·3 Prozent Untersalpetersäure und geringe Spuren von Schwefelsäure. Die Schwefelsäure hat 60° Bé, ist voll ständig wasserhell und klar, sowie frei von Salpetersäure. Der Kohlenverbrauch beträgt pro 1000 kg Mischsäure ca. 30 kg; der Koksverbrauch zum Erhitzen der Luft ca. 14 kg. Der Verschleiß der Apparate ist sehr gering.

Nach einem neueren Patent der Salpetersäure-Industrie-Gesellschaft in Gelsenkirchen (D.R.P. 180587) wird die Abfallsäure in der Weise elektrolysiert, daß man dieselbe als Anodenflüssigkeit verwendet, während man als Kathodenflüssigkeit verdünnte Salpetersäure nimmt. Hierbei wird also die Abfallsäure nicht denitriert, sondern durch Aufnahme von Stickoxyden, die

[1] Siehe auch Bd. II, S. 110 bis 113. — Zeitschr. Schieß- u. Sprengstoffwesen II, S. 144.

sich an der Kathode bilden und dann in der Anodenflüssigkeit mit dem verdünnenden Wasser Salpetersäure liefern, in der Weise regeneriert, daß man eine Mischsäure erhält, welche ganz oder größtenteils der Konzentration der ursprünglich verwendeten Säure entspricht.

H. Die Fabrikanlage.

Bei der Anordnung der Räumlichkeiten einer Nitroglyzerinfabrik sind im allgemeinen alle jene Vorsichtsmaßregeln zu beachten, welche für Explosivstofffabriken überhaupt in Betracht kommen. Es liegt hier insofern ein besonderer Fall vor, als es sich sowohl bei den Ausgangsmaterialien wie bei dem Endprodukte um Flüssigkeiten handelt. Um letztere ohne besonderen Kraftverbrauch, lediglich mit Ausnutzung der Schwerkraft durch Rohrleitungen von einem Ort zum andern zu schaffen, wählt man zur Anlage der Fabrik gern die Lehne eines Bergabhanges oder sonst ein in schiefer Ebene liegendes Terrain.

Die einzelnen Operationen, wie die Nitrierung, Scheidung usw., ließ man früher zur Raumersparung in einem und demselben Gebäude durchführen; später kam man aber zur Einsicht, daß die Verschiedenheit der vorzunehmenden Operationen eine Störung verursacht, und gegenwärtig wird allgemein so gearbeitet, daß nur Operationen einer und derselben Art in demselben Raume ausgeführt werden. Durch die Arbeitsteilung und durch die Einheitlichkeit der in einem Raume stattfindenden Arbeit kann die Leistungsfähigkeit solcher Fabriken bedeutend vergrößert werden; auch bleibt die bei einer Operation stattfindende Zersetzung bzw. Explosion örtlich isoliert. Deshalb werden die einzelnen Werkstätten durch Wälle getrennt, welch' letztere noch höher als die zwischen denselben errichteten Gebäude sind. Die Wälle werden oben mit einer Schichte guter Erde bedeckt und mit Gras besät, um zu verhindern, daß durch Wind und Sturm Sandkörner in die Fabriksräumlichkeiten hineingeweht werden; an heißen Sommertagen werden die Wälle überdies mit Wasser besprengt.

Die Reihenfolge der Gebäude ist die, daß an der obersten Stelle der Raum für die Säurereservoirs und der Glyzerinwärmeapparat etabliert wird, woran sich, mit dem Nitrierhaus beginnend, die übrigen Gebäude nach der Reihenfolge der Operationen anschließen. Die Neigung der angebauten schiefen Ebene soll zum mindesten 1 Prozent betragen, wobei der Niveauunterschied zwischen der obersten und untersten Werkstätte (Gebäudeanlage) sich nach der Anzahl der vorzunehmenden Operationen richtet.

Die Zahl der für die eigentliche Fabrikation notwendigen Objekte und Räumlichkeiten ist keine bestimmte und richtet sich nach der Höhe der Produktion. In einem Nitrierhause vereinigt man nicht mehr als 3 bis 4 Nitrierapparate. Hat die Fabrik eine große Tagesproduktion an Nitroglyzerin zu liefern, so wird man mehrere Nitrierhäuser aufstellen und dementsprechend auch die Räume für die andern Operationen vermehren.

Die Gebäude, in welchen eine Explosionsgefahr nicht besteht, also die Lagerhäuser für die Salpetersäure, Schwefelsäure, Mischsäure, für das Glyzerin, ferner die Maschinenhäuser, Reparaturwerkstätten, Heizzentralen usw., sind aus solidem Material (Stein oder Beton) zu errichten und nicht durch Wälle zu schützen. Dagegen sind die Räume, in welchen das Nitroglyzerin hergestellt, verarbeitet oder gelagert wird, aus Bretterwänden oder auch aus Korksteinen zu fertigen, welche innen mit Teer, außen mit Kalk oder mit hellen wetterbeständigen Ölfarben angestrichen werden. Die Dächer dieser Werkstätten sind ebenfalls sehr leicht zu halten, um im Falle einer Explosion keinen großen Widerstand zu bieten. Gut eignen sich präparierte, weiß angestrichene Pappen. Die Verwendung von Holzbauten für die Fabrikationsräume ist stellenweise sogar behördlich vorgeschrieben. Allerdings haben diese Bauten den Nachteil, daß sie durch in der Nähe stattfindende Explosionen allzuleicht eingedrückt werden, wobei häufig die Türen durch Trümmer versperrt und die Arbeiter an der Flucht behindert werden. Nach Lesser sollte man daher stets auf eine besonders sorgfältige Zimmerarbeit halten. Größere eiserne Laschen und Anker könnten bei einer eventuellen Explosion als Geschosse wirken und sind daher zu vermeiden. Dagegen läßt sich die Baukonstruktion dadurch verstärken, daß man neben die mit recht tiefem Versatz und starken Zapfen versehenen Wandstreben, oben und unten gut befestigte Drahtbündel legt und mit einem Wirbel fest zusammendreht. Auch die Böden der Arbeitsräume erheischen große Sorgfalt. Um die Apparate bringt man zweckmäßig einen Bleibelag mit 1 cm hohem Rande oder ein Bleigefäß an, um durch Spritzen oder Leckwerden der Apparatur entfallendes Sprengöl aufzunehmen. Im übrigen nimmt man für die Böden glattgehobeltes, gut anschließendes Holz, event. auch Linoleumbelag. Zum Entfernen von Nitroglyzerinspritzern hält man stets Eimer mit Wasser und Schwämmen bereit, welch' letztere immer im Wasser sein müssen, damit nicht aufgesaugte Nitroglyzerintropfen im Schwamme selbst eine Explosion verursachen können. In sehr sandiger Gegend kann man auch die Böden mit Sand bestreuen und die obersten Schichten, welche die Nitroglyzerintropfen absorbieren, jeweilig entfernen und durch frischen Sand ersetzen; letzterer muß aber an Ort und Stelle kostenlos zu haben sein. — Alle Räume einer Nitroglyzerinfabrik werden von einer Zentralstelle aus mit Leitungen für Licht, Heizung, Dampf und Druckluft versehen, auch muß jeder Arbeitsraum eine gut funktionierende Ventilation besitzen, da die Nitroglyzerindämpfe, in größerer Menge eingeatmet, nachteilige Folgen für die Gesundheit der Arbeiter verursachen können.

Der Transport ungereinigten Sprengöls vom Nitrierhause zum Waschhause geschieht durch Rohrleitungen. Damit letztere nicht durch Temperaturwechsel, Gefrieren, Belichtung usw. leiden, errichtet man eigene, durch die Wälle hindurchlaufende Verbindungsgänge, die durch Dampf stets warm gehalten und von einem Arbeiter zur Reinigung begangen werden sollen. In diesen Gängen liegen dann offene Leitungsrinnen. Auch auf Trägern ruhende Leitungskanäle werden angewandt, auf welchen Bleirinnen liegen, welche durch dicht anschließende, aber abnehmbare Bleideckel geschützt sind. Die Rinnen haben die Form eines **V** oder eines Halbkreises; ihre Wandstärke beträgt etwa 5 mm für Nitroglyzerin und 10 mm für Abfallsäure; zum Schutze gegen das Gefrieren im Winter werden sie mit einer Warmwasserleitung versehen. Nach dem Durchgange des Nitroglyzerins spült man die Leitungen stets mit Wasser nach, um dieselben von anhaftenden Öltropfen zu reinigen und so die Gefahr der Übertragung einer Explosion von einer Hütte auf die andere nur auf jene kurze Zeit zu beschränken, während welcher das Öl fließt.

Bei gereinigtem Sprengöl sind die Ansichten hinsichtlich dessen Fortleitung verschieden. Meistens schafft man auch dieses durch Rohrleitungen fort und benutzt sogar da, wo das nötige Gefälle fehlt, besondere Hebevorrichtungen (mit Druckluft betriebene Montejus). Andere halten es aus Furcht vor Übertragung von Explosionen durch die Rohrleitungen für besser, das Öl in Kannen aus Hartgummi transportieren zu lassen. Es ist allerdings nicht selten schon vorgekommen, daß eine Explosion in einer Werkstätte sich durch die Röhrenleitung nach einem andern Arbeitsraume fortpflanzte. Man unterbricht daher zweckmäßig die Rohre an einzelnen Stellen durch Schlauchverbindungen von etwa 1 m Länge, die nach Durchfließen des Nitroglyzerins wieder abgehängt werden. Natürlich wird dadurch nur jene Hütte geschützt, in deren Umwallung die Unterbrechung liegt.

Nachstehend geben wir die allgemeine Anordnung einer

Nitroglyzerinanlage nach J. L. C. Eckelt (Fig. 42). Die einzelnen Gebäude sind mit einem Gefälle von 7 bis 8 cm auf einen

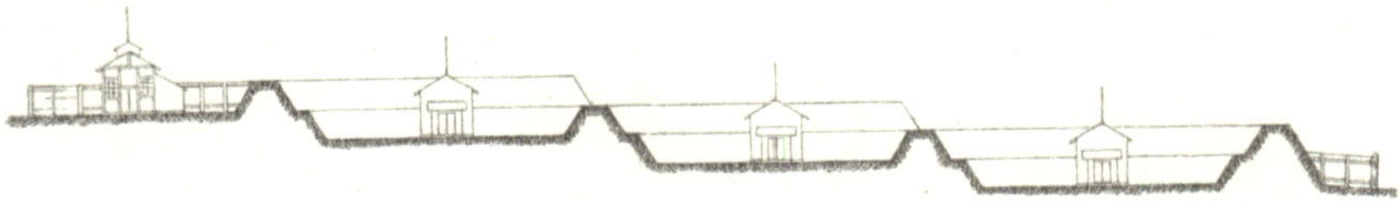

Fig. 42. Nitroglyzerinanlage.

Meter angelegt. Das links außerhalb der Wälle befindliche Gebäude enthält das Glyzerin und die Säuren.

I. Gesetzliche Vorschriften.[1]

Nachstehend seien mitgeteilt:

1. Besondere Unfallverhütungsvorschriften für Nitroglyzerin-Sprengstoffabriken.
2. Bestimmungen über die Errichtung und den Betrieb von Anlagen zur Herstellung von nitroglyzerinhaltigen Sprengstoffen.
3. Vorschriften über Blitzschutzvorrichtungen.

1. Besondere Unfallverhütungsvorschriften für Nitroglyzerinsprengstoffabriken

(vom 18. Oktober 1891 und 19. Juni 1903).

a) Vorschriften für Arbeitgeber.

I. Allgemeine Bestimmungen.

§ 1. Bei der Herstellung und Verpackung der Sprengstoffe dürfen jugendliche Arbeiter nicht angestellt werden; es sind nur nüchterne und zuverlässige Leute zu beschäftigen.

§ 2. Fremden Personen soll der Zutritt nur unter besonderer Erlaubnis und in der Regel nur unter zuverlässiger Begleitung gestattet sein.

§ 3. Das Fabrikgrundstück, auf welchem die Sprengstoffe hergestellt werden, muß mit einer geeigneten Umzäunung umgeben sein, welche das unbeabsichtigte Betreten möglichst verhindert; das unbefugte Betreten ist auch durch Warnungstafeln an den Zugängen zu verbieten.

§ 4. Die Gebäude, in denen Nitroglyzerin oder Nitroglyzerinpräparate hergestellt und verarbeitet werden, müssen einzeln mit einem Erdwall umgeben sein. Magazine, in denen Nitroglyzerinsprengstoffe auf den Fabriken gelagert werden, müssen entweder vollständig mit

[1] Ein Teil nachstehender Vorschriften bezieht sich nicht auf die Nitroglyzerinerzeugung, sondern auf die Verarbeitung des Sprengöls zu Dynamiten; doch seien die Vorschriften im Zusammenhang wiedergegeben.

einer dicken Erdschicht bedeckt oder mit Wällen umgeben sein. Die Wälle müssen die Dachtraufe der eingeschlossenen Gebäude um mindestens 1 m überragen. Die Gänge durch die Wälle dürfen nicht in der Schußlinie nach Verkehrswegen oder nahen Gebäuden angelegt sein.

§ 5. Die Vorplätze der von den Schutzwällen eingeschlossenen Gebäude und die Gänge durch die Wälle müssen so hergestellt sein, daß sie sich leicht rein halten lassen. Fußwege und Treppen innerhalb der Fabrik, auf denen Sprengstoffe transportiert werden, sind im Winter schneefrei zu halten und bei Glatteis zu bestreuen.

§ 6. Die Gebäude, in denen Nitroglyzerin oder Nitroglyzerinpräparate hergestellt oder verarbeitet werden, müssen in leichtem Material ausgeführt sein.

§ 7. Das Holzwerk der Gebäude mit Explosionsgefahr muß tunlichst durch Wasserglas oder sonstigen geeigneten Mitteln gegen die Einwirkung von Feuer möglichst widerstandsfähig gemacht werden.

§ 8. Die der Sonnenseite zu belegenen Fensterscheiben der Gebäude mit Explosivgefahr müssen geblendet sein. Sämtliche Fensterscheiben dieser, sowie auch in der Nähe gelegener Gebäude sind innen mit Drahtnetzen zu versehen.

§ 9. Die Türen der Gebäude mit Explosivgefahr sollen nach außen aufschlagen.

§ 10. Vorhandene Blitzableiter müssen stets in gutem Zustande gehalten und jährlich mindestens einmal durch Sachverständige geprüft werden; die Prüfung hat sich sowohl auf die oberirdische wie auf die Erdleitung zu erstrecken.

§ 11. In Nitroglyzerinsprengstofffabriken muß die größte Ordnung und Reinlichkeit herrschen.

§ 12. Die künstliche Beleuchtung von Betriebsabteilungen mit Explosivgefahr darf nur mittels zuverlässig isolierter Lampen (Kerzen) bewirkt werden. Jede Ablagerung von explosiblem Staub an der Lichtquelle muß verhütet werden. Bei elektrischer Beleuchtung muß eine Erhitzung der Leitungsdrähte und jede Funkenerzeugung ausgeschlossen sein; die Beleuchtungsanlage ist von Zeit zu Zeit auf ihre Feuersicherheit sachverständig zu untersuchen. Die Besorgung der Lampen und Laternen ist bestimmten Arbeitern zu übertragen.

§ 13. Die Beheizung der Räume muß durch Dampf- oder Wasserheizung bewirkt werden.

§ 14. Verschüttetes Nitroglyzerin ist sofort mittels Schwamm, Gur, oder in anderer geeigneter Weise aufzunehmen. Wo dies bei durchlässigem Boden nicht möglich ist, muß die durchtränkte Stelle vorsichtig aufgenommen und an ungefährlichem Orte nach Anweisung eines Beamten oder Meisters unschädlich gemacht werden. Der Filterschlamm ist sorgfältig auszuwaschen und an ungefährlicher Stelle aufzubewahren. Die angesammelten Mengen sind von Zeit zu Zeit durch Verbrennung oder in Erdlöchern unter Anwendung starker Initialladung von Dynamit und unter Aufsicht eines Beamten oder Meisters unschädlich zu machen.

§ 15. Filterschlamm, sowie verunreinigtes Nitroglyzerin und Nitroglyzerinpräparate durch Versenken in fließendes Wasser oder Vergraben in die Erde unschädlich machen zu wollen, ist verboten.

§ 16. Bei der Herstellung von Nitroglyzerinsprengstoffen müssen die Arbeiter durch geeignete Vorrichtungen möglichst gegen das Einatmen der sich dabei entwickelnden schädlichen Gase geschützt werden.

§ 17. Auf den Säurelagerplätzen sind Kübel mit Wasser vorrätig zu halten, damit bei Verbrennungen durch Säure die Arbeiter die Brandwunden sogleich mit großen Mengen Wasser auswaschen können.

§ 18. Metallgefäße und Leitungen, die mit Nitroglyzerin in Berührung gekommen sind, dürfen nicht durch Löten oder Hämmern ausgebessert werden. Ausgenommen sind diejenigen Gefäße und Leitungen, in denen Nitroglyzerin*abfallsäure* enthalten war. Diese dürfen nach sorgfältiger Reinigung ausgebessert werden. Metallgegenstände, die mit Nitroglyzerin in Berührung waren, dürfen erst eingeschmolzen werden, wenn sie unter Beobachtung der nötigen Vorsichtsmaßregeln mit hellem Feuer gründlich abgebrannt sind und man sich vergewissert hat, daß kein Nitroglyzerin mehr am Gegenstand haftet. Holz darf da, wo Nitroglyzerin an demselben haftet, mit Werkzeugen nicht bearbeitet werden. Bei Abbrucharbeiten ist die unvermeidliche Anwendung von Werkzeugen erst nach möglichst sorgfältiger Reinigung der abzubrechenden Gegenstände und unter Beobachtung der nötigen Vorsichtsmaßregeln (§ 22) gestattet. Unbrauchbar gewordene Gegenstände irgend welcher Art, die mit Nitroglyzerinpräparaten in Berührung gewesen sind, müssen durch Sprengung oder Verbrennung vernichtet oder, wenn dieses nicht angängig ist, vor weiterer Aufbewahrung durch Abbrennen über offenem, hellem Feuer vollständig unschädlich gemacht werden.

§ 19. Gefrorenes Nitroglyzerin, oder solches Nitroglyzerin enthaltende Präparate, Gefäße, Rohrleitungen und Hähne dürfen nur in erwärmten umwallten Räumen oder mittels warmen Wassers aufgetaut werden, und zwar nur unter Aufsicht eines Beamten oder Meisters.

§ 20. In den Räumen, in denen Nitroglyzerin hergestellt und verarbeitet wird, darf die Temperatur nicht unter $+ 10^{0}$ C sinken. Der auf den Heizkörpern in diesen Räumen sich ablagernde Staub ist gründlich zu entfernen.

§ 21. Während eines sich über dem Betriebsorte entladenden Gewitters ist die Arbeit in den Patronen-, Meng-, Pack- und Trockenräumen, und wenn möglich auch im Nitrierraume zu unterbrechen.

§ 22. Bei zeitweiligen Umänderungs- oder Ausbesserungsarbeiten mit Explosionsgefahr ist nicht nur die Zahl der beschäftigten Arbeiter auf die durchaus notwendige zu beschränken, sondern auch der Verkehr und der Aufenthalt anderer Arbeiter in der Nähe zu verbieten.

II. Bestimmungen für besondere Abteilungen.

§ 23. Bevor das Glyzerin in die Nitriergefäße einfließt, muß es ein Sieb passieren, damit etwaige grobe Verunreinigungen ausgeschieden werden.

§ 24. Sämtliche Aufsaugestoffe und Zumischpulver bei der Dynamitfabrikation sind vor ihrer Verwendung durch möglichst feine Siebe zu geben. Alle fertigen, nicht gelatinierten Nitroglyzerinpräparate sind vor ihrer Verarbeitung in Patronenmaschinen zur Ausscheidung etwa noch darin vorhandener Fremdkörper aufs sorgfältigste durchzusieben. Die zur Gelatinierung von Nitroglyzerin bestimmte Kollodiumwolle ist in feuchtem Zustande durch möglichst feine Siebe durchzureiben.

§ 25. Nitriergefäße und Scheidetrichter (Abscheider) müssen eine Einrichtung haben, um bei drohender Gefahr den ganzen Inhalt in kürzester Frist in geeignet aufgestellte, mit Wasser gefüllte Sicherheitsbottiche ablassen zu können.

§ 26. Nitriergefäße und Scheidetrichter sind mit Thermometern zu versehen.

§ 27. Da, wo die Kegel der Tonhähne an Behältern oder in Leitungen der Gefahr ausgesetzt sind, herauszufliegen, sollen sie durch geeignete Vorrichtungen daran verhindert werden.

b) Vorschriften für die Arbeiter.

I. Allgemeine Bestimmungen.

§ 28. Soweit das Rauchen überhaupt gestattet ist, darf es nur in den von den Betriebsleitern angewiesenen Räumen geschehen, woselbst sich auch eine Gelegenheit zur Aufbewahrung der Rauchgeräte befindet; andere Rauchgeräte als die dort aufzubewahrenden, sowie Feuerzeug darf überhaupt nicht mit zur Fabrik gebracht werden.

§ 29. Das Einnehmen der Mahlzeiten in den Räumen mit Explosionsgefahr, mit Ausnahme im Nitrierungs-, Wasch- und Nachscheideraum ist verboten.

§ 30. Die Arbeiter dürfen Räume mit Explosionsgefahr, in denen sie nicht zu arbeiten haben, ohne besondere Erlaubnis nicht betreten.

§ 31. Die Räume, in welchen an Sprengstoffen gearbeitet wird, sind stets sorgfältig rein zu halten; namentlich sind auch die Heizkörper stets frei von Staub zu halten.

§ 32. Verschüttetes Nitroglyzerin ist sofort mit Schwämmen, Gur u. dergl. aufzunehmen. Verunreinigtes Nitroglyzerin, sowie auch andere verunreinigte Nitroglyzerinpräparate sind nach Anweisung und unter Aufsicht des Meisters oder Betriebsführers unschädlich zu machen.

§ 33. Gefäße, Apparate, Leitungen und Geräte, an denen Nitroglyzerin haftet, dürfen nicht mit Werkzeugen bearbeitet, gestoßen oder geworfen werden. Eingeschmolzen dürfen sie erst werden, nachdem das anhaftende Nitroglyzerin über lebhaftem Feuer nach Angabe des Meisters oder Betriebsleiters zerstört ist. Holz und Holzteile, die mit Nitroglyzerin in Berührung gekommen sind, dürfen ebenfalls nicht mit Werkzeugen bearbeitet, gestoßen oder geworfen werden. Das Verbrennen darf nur unter Aufsicht eines Meisters oder Betriebsleiters erfolgen.

§ 34. Gefrorenes Nitroglyzerin, oder solche Nitroglyzerinpräparate, oder Gefäße, Hähne und Leitungen mit gefrorenem Nitroglyzerin dürfen nur nach Anweisung eines Meisters oder Betriebsleiters aufgetaut und bearbeitet werden.

§ 35. In den Räumen, in denen Nitroglyzerin hergestellt und verarbeitet wird, darf die Temperatur nicht unter + 10° C sinken. Der auf den Heizkörpern in diesen Räumen sich ablagernde Staub ist gründlich zu entfernen.

§ 36. Während eines Gewitters, welches sich über dem Betriebsort entladet, darf sich niemand in den Räumen, in denen Sprengstoff verarbeitet wird, aufhalten. Ausgenommen ist der Aufenthalt in der Nitroglyzerinfabrik, wenn die Arbeit darin nicht unterbrochen werden kann.

§ 37. Hähne aus Ton, Metall, Hartgummi und anderem Material, welche mit Nitroglyzerin oder nitroglyzerinhaltigen Säuren in Berührung kommen, müssen sorgfältig in geeigneter Weise geschmiert werden, und haben sich die Arbeiter stets über deren leichte Gangbarkeit zu vergewissern. Namentlich hat dies stets vor Beginn der Arbeit zu geschehen.

§ 38. Den Patronenarbeitern ist strenge untersagt, Justierungen an ihren Maschinen selbst vorzunehmen, an denselben zu hämmern oder zu schlagen. Justierungen dürfen nur durch den damit beauftragten Meister ausgeführt werden. Das Auswechseln der Hülsen, wenn die Patronenmaschine auf andere Patronendurchmesser eingestellt werden soll, darf ebenfalls nur von dem betreffenden Meister vorgenommen und die Patronenmaschine erst dann von dem Arbeiter benutzt werden, nachdem sich der Meister persönlich von dem ordnungsmäßigen Gange der Maschine überzeugt hat.

§ 39. Es ist darauf zu achten, daß ein Verstäuben der Kollodiumwolle in den Trockenhäusern möglichst vermieden wird. Jedenfalls ist Sorge zu tragen, daß der entwickelte Staub von den Wandungen und Hordengestellen durch Abwischen mit feuchten Schwämmen und Tüchern gründlich entfernt wird. Die Darrhorden dürfen auf ihren Unterlagen nicht geschoben werden. Überhaupt ist jede Reibung bei trockener Kollodiumwolle zu vermeiden.

2. Bestimmungen über die Errichtung und den Betrieb von Anlagen zur Herstellung von nitroglyzerinhaltigen Sprengstoffen

vom 10. Oktober 1893.

1. Vorschriften über bauliche Anlagen.

§ 1. Die Fabrikation von Nitroglyzerinsprengstoffen hat in räumlich getrennten Abteilungen zu erfolgen, welche so anzuordnen sind, daß

a) die Sprengölfabrik,

b) die Räume zur Verarbeitung des Sprengöls zu Sprengstoffen,

c) die Räume zur Patronierung und Verpackung der Sprengstoffe 80 m Abstand voneinander haben und

d) die ungefährlichen Fabrikanlagen von den Gebäuden der Abteilungen a), b), c) mindestens je 250 m entfernt liegen,

e) die Magazine von den Gebäuden der Abteilungen a), b), c) und d) mindestens je 250 m und unter sich bei einem Fassungsraume von 2500 kg je 100 m, bei dem größtzulässigen Fassungsraume von 5000 kg Sprengstoff je 150 m voneinander entfernt liegen.

§ 2. Jeder Punkt der Fabrikationsabteilungen a) bis d) muß

1. mindestens 500 m von etwaigen, dem Unternehmer gehörigen, nicht zu Wohnzwecken benutzten Gebäuden oder Anlagen, sowie von wenig benutzten Straßen und Wegen untergeordneter Bedeutung,

2. mindestens 1000 m[1] von bewohnten Gebäuden und Betriebsanlagen aller Art, Eisenbahnen, öffentlichen Land- und Wasserstraßen, sowie stark benutzten Wegen entfernt liegen.

§ 3. Das Fabrikgrundstück, auf welchem Nitroglyzerinsprengstoffe hergestellt werden sollen, muß im ganzen Umfange mit einer starken, $2^1/_4$ m hohen Umzäunung umgeben sein, welche ein unbeabsichtigtes Betreten des Grundstückes ausschließt und ein Übersteigen nach Möglichkeit erschwert. Alle Baulichkeiten der Fabrik müssen von dieser Umzäunung 5 m entfernt bleiben. An allen Zugängen und Zufahrtstraßen zu dem Fabrikterrain sind Warnungstafeln deutlich sichtbar anzubringen.

§ 4. Sämtliche, Sprengstoffe enthaltenden Gebäude sind mit berasten Erdwällen von 1 m Kronbreite und mindestens einfacher Böschungsanlage, 1 m höher als der First der Gebäude zu umgeben. Der Fuß der Dämme muß wenigstens 1 m von dem Gebäudesockel entfernt sein. Die Umwallungen sind so anzulegen, daß Vorüber-

---

[1] Der Abstand von 1000 m muß selbstverständlich auch von der Fabrik bei etwaiger Errichtung von Arbeiter- oder Beamtenwohnhäusern gewahrt werden, da seine Verminderung nicht nur die Gefahr für die Arbeiter und Beamten selbst, sondern auch für diejenigen erhöht, welche aus geschäftlicher oder anderer Veranlassung die Wohnungen aufsuchen müssen. Andererseits ist es für den Betrieb dringend erwünscht, daß Beamte der Fabrik nahe genug wohnen, um bei unvorhergesehenen Zwischenfällen ungesäumt eingreifen und die Aufsicht über den Verkehr in der Fabrik auch von der Wohnung aus wahrnehmen zu können. Nach eingeholten gutachtlichen Äußerungen mehrerer Regierungspräsidenten scheinen die Fabriken den letzteren Gesichtspunkten besonderen Wert beizulegen und die Entfernung von 1000 m vielfach als zu weit anzusehen. Auch die befragten Regierungspräsidenten selbst erkennen das Wohnen von Beamten auf den Werken oder in unmittelbarer Nähe als ein Bedürfnis an und empfehlen den vorgeschriebenen Abstand für die Wohnungen einzelner Betriebsbeamten zu ermäßigen. Mit Rücksicht hierauf und auf die mit den Sprengversuchen mit Dynamitmagazinen auf dem Schießplatz in Kummersdorf gemachten günstigen Erfahrungen über die Flugweite von Sprengstücken und die unmittelbare Luftwirkung von Explosionen ermächtigt eine Ministerialverfügung vom 19. November 1900, bei Anlagen zur Herstellung nitroglyzerinhaltiger Sprengstoffe Wohnungen von Betriebsbeamten in Entfernungen bis zu 600 m von den mit a) bis d) bezeichneten Fabrikanlagen ohne weiteres zuzulassen, sowie in besonderen Fällen, z. B. bei gedeckter Lage der zu errichtenden Wohnung für Betriebsbeamte oder anderen günstigen Umständen, ausnahmsweise auch geringere Entfernungen zu gestatten.

gehende in jedem Falle gegen direkte Schußwirkung gedeckt sind. Unterbrechungen der Wälle, wie Tunnel und Kanäle, sind zu gleichem Zwecke in gebrochener oder gekrümmter Linie anzulegen, die Kanäle an den Ausgängen zu beiden Seiten mit starken Eichenholztüren gegen Schußwirkung zu sichern. Neben jedem Tunnel ist in der Außenseite des Walles eine gegen herabfallende Trümmer gesicherte Deckung anzubringen. Von dieser Deckung aus müssen die Sicherheitsvorrichtungen in Wirksamkeit zu bringen sein.

§ 5. Gebäude, in denen Sprengstoffe hergestellt werden, müssen möglichst leicht in Holz konstruiert und mit Dachpappe gedeckt sein. Die Dächer sind weiß, die Wände ebenso oder hell zu streichen. Tür- und Fensterbeschläge sind aus Messing herzustellen. Das Holzwerk muß mit Wasserglas oder sonstigen geeigneten Mitteln gegen die Einwirkung von Feuer widerstandsfähig gemacht werden. Die Innenwände sind glattzuhobeln und die Fugen zu dichten. Der Fußboden ist durch eine 20 cm hohe Schüttung von Sand oder Kieselgur auf Dielenbelag oder aus Holz, Blei mit Gummibelag herzustellen. Die letzteren dürfen jedoch keine Risse haben. Die oberste Schicht der Sand- oder Kieselgurschüttung ist alle 8 Tage zu entfernen und neu zu ersetzen. Bühnen, Plattformen, Treppen usw., deren Holzteile mit Nitroglyzerin im Laufe der Zeit durchtränkt werden können, müssen einen Bleibelag erhalten. Im Kollodiumwolle-Trockenhaus ist der Fußboden mit Blei, Linoleum oder leinenen Läufern zu belegen. In den Magazinen dagegen kann der Fußboden aus Dielen ohne Bleibelag hergestellt werden. — Sämtliche Gebäude sind gut verschließbar zu machen. Zur Herstellung von Fundamenten ist die Verwendung von Ziegelsteinen oder Beton erlaubt. Alle Schornsteine unter 20 m Höhe sind mit Funkenfängern zu versehen.

§ 6. Alle Räume der Gebäude, in welchen Sprengstoffe hergestellt werden, müssen durch Warmwasser oder Dampf heizbar sein.

§ 7. Die künstliche Beleuchtung solcher Gebäude, sofern sie nicht durch elektrische Glühlichter bewirkt wird, darf nur von außen durch wohlverschlossene, hell leuchtende Laternen, welche vor verschlossenem Fenster aufgehängt werden, geschehen. Als Leuchtstoffe dürfen leicht flüchtige und leicht entzündliche Brennstoffe nicht verwendet werden. Jede Ablagerung von explosiblem Staub an der Lichtquelle muß verhütet werden. Bei elektrischer Beleuchtung muß eine schädliche Erwärmung der Leitungsdrähte und jede Funkenerzeugung ausgeschlossen sein. Elektrische Glühlichter im Innern der Gebäude des gefährlichen Betriebes müssen doppelte starke Verglasung haben. Die Anlage ist nach jedem stärkeren Gewitter, mindestens aber halbjährlich einmal auf ihre Feuersicherheit sachverständig zu untersuchen.

§ 8. Die Fenster von Gebäuden, in denen Sprengstoffe hergestellt werden, sind nach der Sonnenseite zu blenden, so daß direkte Sonnenstrahlen nicht in das Innere der Gebäude dringen können. Die Türen sollen nach außen aufgeschlagen und so angelegt sein, daß sie auf kürzestem Wege zur nächsten Deckung führen.

§ 9. Die Leitungen für Säuren und Sprengöl, sowie für saures Wasser können aus Ton, Steingut oder Blei sein. Sie müssen so gelegt sein, daß sie jederzeit ohne Anwendung künstlicher Beleuchtung auf Dichtigkeit und Sauberkeit untersucht werden können. Ungleichmäßiges Gefälle, tote Punkte sind zu vermeiden. Das Eindringen von Fremdkörpern und der Einfluß der Witterung bei offenen Leitungen sind fernzuhalten.

§ 10. Die Gebäude, in welchen Sprengstoffe hergestellt und aufbewahrt werden, sind durch eine hinreichende Anzahl Blitzableiter gegen Blitzgefahr zu schützen. Der Winkel des angenommenen Schutzkegels soll nicht mehr als 45^0 gegen die Vertikale betragen. Die Erdleitung muß mit dem Grundwasser zweifellos in gut leitender Verbindung stehen. Alle größeren Metallmassen der Leitungen, Maschinen und Apparate, welche sich in der Nähe der Blitzableiter befinden, sind mit dem Blitzableiter oder mit dem Grundwasser direkt in leitende Verbindung zu bringen.

§ 11. Die Magazine sind entweder aus Ziegelstein- oder aus Betonmauerwerk von mindestens $1^1/_2$ Stein Wandstärke herzustellen und mit doppelter Verdachung zu versehen, deren Zwischenraum von mindestens 50 cm Höhe mit einem geeigneten Material, wie z. B. Torf, ausgefüllt sein muß. Es sind Doppeltüren anzubringen, welche mit besonders starken Schlössern verschließbar sein müssen. Die Sprengstoffkisten müssen so aufgestellt werden, daß die Luft zwischen ihnen durchstreicht. Für den Eintritt frischer Luft ist durch Ventilationseinrichtung dergestalt zu sorgen, daß das Eindringen von Regen oder Schnee verhindert wird. Der Fußboden muß aus Holz bestehen. Die Wände des Magazins sind glatt zu putzen. Die Magazine sind in gleicher Weise zu umwallen, wie die Gebäude, in denen Sprengstoffe hergestellt werden.

§ 12. In der Nähe des Fabrikeinganges ist ein Gebäude zu errichten, welches Räume zum Wechseln der Kleider, zum Waschen und zum Aufenthalt während der Arbeitspausen enthält. Diese müssen so angeordnet sein, daß sie eine Kontrolle der Arbeiter beim Betreten und Verlassen der Fabrik und eine Durchsuchung ermöglichen. Die Räume dürfen nicht durch Öfen, sondern nur durch Dampf- oder Warmwasserheizung geheizt werden.

II. Vorschriften für den Betrieb.

§ 13. Nitroglyzerinsprengstoffe dürfen nur unter der Aufsicht eines Betriebsleiters hergestellt werden, der Zeugnisse über die erforderlichen chemischen Kenntnisse und über eine wenigstens einjährige Beschäftigung in einer Fabrik nitroglyzerinhaltiger Sprengstoffe besitzt.

§ 14. Bei Herstellung und Verpackung der Sprengstoffe dürfen jugendliche Arbeiter nicht angestellt werden. Es sind nur nüchterne und zuverlässige Leute zu beschäftigen.

§ 15. Fremden Personen soll der Zutritt nur mit besonderer Erlaubnis und nach Eintragung ihres Namens in ein zu diesem Zwecke geführtes Register und in zuverlässiger Begleitung gestattet sein.

§ 16. Die Sprengstoffarbeiter haben vor Beginn der Arbeit besondere Anzüge ohne Taschen anzuziehen und vor dem Verlassen der Fabrik unter Aufsicht wieder abzulegen. In der Fabrik darf keine Fußbekleidung, die mit Eisen beschlagen ist, getragen werden. Für gute Aufbewahrung der eigenen Kleider der Sprengstoffarbeiter ist Sorge zu tragen.

§ 17. Soweit das Rauchen überhaupt gestattet ist, darf es nur in den von dem Betriebsleiter angewiesenen Räumen geschehen. Für Feuerzeug hat die Fabrik Sorge zu tragen. Arbeiter dürfen Feuerzeug überhaupt nicht mit zur Fabrik bringen. Den Sprengstoffarbeitern ist das Rauchen, solange sie die Arbeitskleidung tragen, verboten.

§ 18. Das Einnehmen von Mahlzeiten in den Räumen mit Explosionsgefahr, mit Ausnahme des Nitrier-, Wasch- und Nachscheideraumes, ist verboten.

§ 19. Die Arbeiter dürfen Räume mit Explosionsgefahr, in denen sie nicht zu arbeiten haben, ohne Erlaubnis nicht betreten.

§ 20. Durch sorgfältige Reinhaltung des Inneren der Räume und durch peinlichste Ordnung und Aufsicht ist dafür Sorge zu tragen, daß ein Verschütten von Nitroglyzerin- und Sprengstoffgemischen nicht unbemerkt bleiben kann. Verschüttetes Nitroglyzerin ist sofort mit Schwämmen oder Gur aufzunehmen. Wenn dasselbe vom Boden aufgesaugt ist, so ist das durchtränkte Stück sorgfältig zu beseitigen. Verunreinigtes Nitroglyzerin oder Nitroglyzerinmischungen sind nach Anweisung und unter Aufsicht eines Beamten oder Meisters unschädlich zu machen.

§ 21. Der Filterschlamm ist sorgfältig neutral zu waschen und an ungefährlicher Stelle aufzubewahren. Saurer Schlamm und saures Öl dürfen überhaupt nicht aufbewahrt werden. Die angesammelten Mengen Schlamm sind von Zeit zu Zeit durch Verbrennung oder in Erdlöchern durch starke Initialladungen von Dynamit unter Aufsicht eines Beamten oder Meisters unschädlich zu machen. Filterschlamm, sowie verunreinigtes Nitroglyzerin und Nitroglyzerinpräparate in fließendes Wasser zu versenken oder in die Erde zu vergraben ist verboten.

§ 22. Bei der Herstellung von Nitroglyzerinsprengstoffen müssen die Arbeiter durch geeignete Vorrichtungen möglichst gegen das Einatmen der sich dabei entwickelnden schädlichen Gase geschützt sein.

§ 23. Auf den Säurelagerplätzen sind Kübel mit Wasser vorrätig zu halten, damit bei Verbrennungen durch Säure die Arbeiter die Brandwunden sogleich mit großen Mengen Wasser auswaschen können.

§ 24. Metallgefäße und Leitungen, die mit Nitroglyzerin in Berührung gekommen sind, dürfen nicht durch Löten oder Hämmern ausgebessert werden, noch mit Werkzeugen bearbeitet, gestoßen oder geworfen werden. Ausgenommen sind diejenigen Gefäße und Leitungen, in denen Nitroglyzerinabfallsäure enthalten war; diese dürfen nach sorgfältiger Reinigung ausgebessert werden. Eingeschmolzen dürfen Metallgegenstände, die mit Nitroglyzerin in Berührung waren, erst werden, nachdem sie unter Beobachtung der nötigen Vorsichtsmaßregeln mit hellem Feuer gründlich abgebrannt sind und man sich vergewissert hat, daß kein Nitroglyzerin mehr am Gegenstand haftet. Holz darf da, wo Nitroglyzerin an demselben haftet, mit Werkzeugen nicht bearbeitet werden. Bei Abbruchsarbeiten ist die unvermeidliche Anwendung von Werkzeugen nach möglichst sorgfältiger Reinigung der abzubrechenden Gegenstände und unter Beobachtung der nötigen Vorsichtsmaßregeln gestattet. Unbrauchbar gewordene Gegenstände irgend welcher Art, die mit Nitroglyzerinpräparaten in Berührung gewesen sind, müssen durch Sprengung oder Verbrennung vernichtet, oder, wenn dieses nicht angängig ist, vor weiterer Aufbewahrung durch Abbrennen über offenem hellen Feuer vollständig unschädlich gemacht werden.

§ 25. Gefrorenes Nitroglyzerin oder Nitroglyzerin enthaltende Präparate und solche enthaltende Gefäße, Rohrleitungen und Hähne dürfen nur in erwärmten umwallten Räumen oder mittels warmen Wassers aufgetaut werden, und zwar nur unter Aufsicht eines Beamten oder Meisters.

§ 26. In den Räumen, in denen Nitroglyzerin hergestellt und verarbeitet wird, darf die Temperatur nicht unter $+12^0$ C. sinken. Der auf den Heizkörpern in diesen Räumen sich ablagernde Staub ist gründlich zu entfernen.

§ 27. Während eines sich über dem Betriebsort entladenden Gewitters ist die Arbeit in den Patronen-, Meng-, Pack- und Trockenräumen und wenn möglich auch im Nitrierraum zu unterbrechen.

§ 28. Bei zeitweiligen Umänderungs- oder Ausbesserungsarbeiten mit Explosionsgefahr ist nicht nur die Zahl der beschäftigten Arbeiter auf die durchaus notwendige zu beschränken, sondern auch der Verkehr und der Aufenthalt anderer Arbeiter in der Nähe zu verbieten.

§ 29. Nitroglyzerinhaltige Schwämme oder Filtertücher müssen, wenn sie nicht gebraucht werden, unter Wasser oder dünner Sodalösung aufbewahrt werden.

§ 30. Hähne aus Ton, Metall, Hartgummi oder anderem Material, welche mit Nitroglyzerin oder nitroglyzerinhaltigen Säuren in Berührung kommen, müssen sorgfältig in geeigneter Weise geschmiert werden und haben sich die Arbeiter stets über die leichte Gangbarkeit zu vergewissern. Namentlich hat dies auch stets vor Beginn der Arbeit zu geschehen. Da, wo die Kegel der Tonhähne an Behältern oder in Leitungen der Gefahr ausgesetzt sind, herauszufliegen, sollen sie durch geeignete Vorrichtungen daran verhindert werden.

§ 31. Den Patronenarbeitern ist streng untersagt, das Einstellen ihrer Maschinen selbst vorzunehmen, an denselben zu hämmern oder zu schlagen. Das Einstellen darf nur durch den damit beauftragten Meister ausgeführt werden. Das Auswechseln der Hülsen, wenn die Patronenmaschine auf andere Patronendurchmesser eingestellt werden soll, darf ebenfalls nur von dem betreffenden Meister vorgenommen und die Patronenmaschine erst dann von dem Arbeiter benutzt werden, nachdem sich der Meister persönlich von dem ordnungsmäßigen Gang der Maschine überzeugt hat. Werkzeuge, welche zum Einstellen von Maschinen oder zur Reinigung derselben dienen, dürfen niemals innerhalb der Gebäude aufbewahrt werden. Mit Schmieröl getränkte Putzlappen oder Putzwolle sind außerhalb der Gebäude in besonderen Blechkästen unterzubringen.

§ 32. Es ist darauf zu achten, daß ein Verstäuben von Kollodiumwolle in den Trockenhäusern für dieselbe möglichst vermieden wird. Jedenfalls ist Sorge zu tragen, daß der entwickelte Staub von den Wandungen und Hordengestellen durch Abwischen mit feuchten Schwämmen oder Tüchern gründlich entfernt wird. Die Darrhorden dürfen auf ihren Unterlagen nicht geschoben werden. Überhaupt ist jede Reibung bei trockener Kollodiumwolle zu vermeiden. Das Betreten des Kollodiumwolltrockenhauses ist nur mit Filzschuhen gestattet.

§ 33. Bevor das Glyzerin in die Nitriergefäße einfließt, muß es ein Sieb durchlaufen, damit etwaige grobe Verunreinigungen ausgeschieden werden.

§ 34. Sämtliche Aufsaugestoffe und Zumischpulver bei der Dynamitfabrikation sind vor ihrer Verwendung durch möglichst feine Siebe zu geben. Alle fertigen, nicht gelatinierten Nitroglyzerinpräparate sind vor ihrer Verarbeitung in Patronenmaschinen aufs sorgfältigste durchzusieben zur Ausscheidung etwa noch darin vorhandener Fremdkörper. Die zur Gelatinierung von Nitroglyzerin bestimmte Kollodiumwolle ist in feuchtem Zustande durch möglichst feine Siebe durchzureiben.

§ 35. Nitriergefäße und Scheidetrichter müssen eine Einrichtung haben, um bei drohender Gefahr den ganzen Inhalt in kürzester Frist in geeignet aufgestellte, mit Wasser gefüllte Sicherheitsbottiche ablassen zu können. Nitriergefäße und Scheidetrichter sind mit Thermometern zu versehen.

§ 36. Der Transport von Sprengöl darf nur in leicht verschlossenen Gefäßen aus Guttapercha erfolgen.

§ 37. Die Wartung und Anbringung der Beleuchtungsvorrichtungen ist einem besonderen Arbeiter zu übertragen.

§ 38. Die Vorplätze der von den Schutzwällen eingeschlossenen Gebäude und die Gänge durch die Wälle müssen gut rein gehalten werden. Fußwege und Treppen innerhalb der Fabrik, auf denen Sprengstoffe transportiert werden, sind im Winter schneefrei zu halten und bei Glatteis zu bestreuen.

§ 39. Im Nitrierhaus darf sich nicht mehr als 500 kg Nitroglyzerin auf einmal befinden. Bevor die Ladung den Scheidetrichter verlassen hat, darf mit der Füllung des Nitrierapparates für eine neue Operation nicht begonnen werden, es sei denn, daß ein Zusammenfließen des Scheidetrichters und des Nitrierapparates unmöglich gemacht ist, z. B. dadurch, daß zwei Sicherheitsbottiche angebracht sind, von denen der eine nur mit dem Scheidetrichter, der andere nur mit dem Sicherheitsapparat verbunden ist.[1] — In den Patronenbuden darf sich nicht mehr als 50 kg, in den Packhäusern nicht mehr als 500 kg

[1] Neufassung dieses Passus durch Verfügungen vom 15. Februar 1906 und 23. November 1906.

Sprengstoff befinden. Am Eingang jeden Raumes ist eine dauerhafte Tafel anzubringen, auf welcher die Art des Sprengstoffes, die zulässige Menge desselben und die zulässige Zahl der Arbeiter angegeben ist.

§ 40. Die Blitzableiter sind nach jedem stärkeren Gewitter, mindestens aber halbjährlich einmal, durch Messung der Widerstände der Erd- und der Metalleitung auf die Zuverlässigkeit des Anschlusses des Leiters an das Grundwasser oder einen mit diesem zweifellos in sicherer Verbindung stehenden guten elektrischen Leiter zu untersuchen. Ergibt sich ein größerer Gesamtwiderstand als 80 Ohm, so ist die Ursache zu ermitteln und event. durch Verlegung der Leitung Abhilfe zu schaffen. Über die Ergebnisse der Untersuchung sind Aufzeichnungen zu machen. Ein Meßapparat ist auf der Fabrik bereit zu halten und mit dessen Handhabung ein Beamter vertraut zu machen.

§ 41. Zu Ausbesserungsarbeiten dürfen nicht mehr Arbeiter, als zu diesem Zwecke unbedingt nötig sind, zugezogen werden. Die Arbeit darf erst beginnen, nachdem aller Sprengstoff entfernt und Maschinen, Arbeitstische, Geräte und Apparate sorgfältig gereinigt sind.

§ 42. Die Aufsicht über die ordnungsmäßige Verwendung des gefertigten Sprengstoffes ist in der Weise zu führen, daß die Mengung der abgewogenen Quantitäten in der Verausgabung an die Patronenhütten sorgfältig verwogen und gebucht werden. Desgleichen sind im Packhaus die aus den Patronenhäusern empfangenen Patronen zu wägen und zu buchen, und schließlich ist der Eingang und der augenblickliche Inhalt der Magazine durch in diesen aufgehängte und doppelt geführte Lagerverzeichnisse nach Gewicht und bei unverschlossenen einzelnen Schachteln nach Gewicht und Patronenzahl jederzeit ersichtlich zu machen. Die Ergebnisse sämtlicher Stationen sind in einem Buche bei Arbeitsschluß zusammenzustellen.

§ 43. Alle Räume der Nitroglyzerinsprengstofffabrik sind außerhalb der Arbeitszeit stets verschlossen zu halten.

3. Anleitung zu Vorschriften über Blitzschutzvorrichtungen für Pulver- und Sprengstofffabriken, sowie für Pulver- und Sprengstoffmagazine.[1 2]

A. Vorschriften für Gebäude, die mit besonderen Erdschutzwällen oder Erdschutzwänden zu umgeben sind.

1. Vorbemerkung.

Dem Blitzschutz dienen:

a) Der äußere Teil der Blitzableiteranlage, welcher einen einschlagenden Blitz aufzufangen und dadurch vom Gebäude fernzuhalten hat.

---

[1] Verordnung des preußischen Ministers für Handel und Gewerbe vom 13. November 1906.

[2] Die Vorschriften unter A sind auf Betriebsverhältnisse zugeschnitten, wie sie in Anlagen zur Herstellung von Nitroglyzerinsprengstoffgemischen üblich sind. Das Vorhandensein erheblicher Metallmassen und namentlich

b) Der innere Teil der Blitzableiteranlage, welcher unmittelbar an den Gebäuden anzubringen ist und die Bestimmung hat, einen vom äußeren System nicht genügend aufgefangenen und abgeleiteten Blitz oder eine Teilentladung aufzunehmen, unschädlich abzuleiten und insbesondere das Innere des Gebäudes von elektrischen Spannungen freizuhalten.

c) Maßregeln für die Rohr- und elektrischen Leitungen, welche die Einführung höherer elektrischer Spannungen in das Innere der Gebäude vermeiden sollen.

d) Maßregeln in bezug auf die metallenen Gegenstände im Innern der Gebäude, um dort Entladungen, hervorgerufen durch Spannungen zwischen einzelnen Gegenständen, zu vermeiden.

2. Äußerer Teil der Blitzableiteranlage.

Der äußere Teil wird dadurch gebildet, daß etwa 2 m über dem höchsten Punkt des Gebäudes ein wagerechtes Netz aus Drahtseilen, Drähten oder Bändern (verzinktes Eisen oder Kupfer) von etwa 10 bis 15 qmm Querschnitt mit einer Maschenweite von 1 m ausgespannt wird. Diese Leitungen werden, etwa zu vier oder fünf zusammengefaßt, an eisernen Stangen aufgehängt, die auf der Krone der Umschließungswälle befestigt werden. Eine ebensolche Leitung verbindet die oberen Enden der Stangen untereinander.

Zwischen den Stangen ist in der Wallkrone eine leitende Verbindung vermittelst eines fingerstarken Blei- oder Kupferdrahts herzustellen, welcher in eine Schüttung von Nußkoks (etwa 20 cm im Quadrat) eingelegt wird.

Weiter sind von den Stangen auf der äußeren Seite des Walles Leitungen zu der Erdleitung zu führen, welche zunächst in einer äußeren Ringleitung am Fuße des Walles besteht. Auch diese Leitung ist in eine Koksschüttung einzulegen, welche in einem Graben von 50 cm Tiefe, 20 cm hoch und 30 cm breit auszulegen ist. In der Mitte dieser Schüttung liegt die metallische Ringleitung. Wenn verschiedene Gebäude durch gemeinsame Wälle getrennt sind, so ist die äußere Ringleitung nur am Fuße des Umfassungswalles anzubringen.

Sind Grundwasser führende Erdschichten leicht zu erreichen, so

---

langgestreckter, vielfach parallel verlaufender Metallröhren und -leitungen, wie sie sich im Nitroglyzerinsprengstoffbetriebe nicht wohl vermeiden lassen, ist als besonders gefahrbringend erachtet, weil bei einer Blitzwirkung der Sprengstoff unter Umständen durch Induktionsfunken zur Detonation kommen kann. Zur Abwehr dieser Gefahr ist das doppelte Drahtnetz vorgeschrieben, dessen Anbringung den für Nitroglyzerinwerke vorgeschriebenen baulichen Maßnahmen angepaßt ist.

Für Fabriken von Schwarzpulver und gelatiniertem rauchschwachem Pulver, sowie für Pulver- und Sprengstoffmagazine werden dagegen im allgemeinen die unter B vorgeschriebenen Maßregeln genügen. (Verordnung vom 1. Juni 1907.)

müssen mindestens zwei der Ableitungen, die zu der äußeren Ringleitung führen, bis zu jenen Schichten verlängert und in großflächige Berührung mit denselben gebracht werden. Wo dieses nicht leicht auszuführen ist, sind an Stelle dieser Weiterführung 10 m lange Drähte, etwa vier an der Zahl, strahlförmig, etwa 50 cm unter der Oberfläche zu verlegen.

Ferner sind die zu dem zu schützenden Gebäude führenden Rohrleitungen mit Ausnahme derjenigen, welche Nitroglyzerin enthalten, sowie etwa vorhandene Schienenleitungen und andere benachbarte Rohrleitungen mit dieser äußeren Ringleitung zu verbinden. Es empfiehlt sich, in dem Graben der äußeren Ringleitung altes Eisen oder anderes Altmetall einzulegen.

Der Schutzwall ist mit Gras zu bepflanzen.

3. Innerer Teil der Blitzableiteranlage.

Der innere Teil besteht aus einem Drahtnetz von 2 mm starkem verzinktem Eisendraht mit 10 cm weiten Maschen, welches auf dem Dache verlegt wird.

Von diesem inneren Netze gehen Querleitungen in Abständen von 3 m nach einer Ringleitung in der inneren Böschung und von dieser Leitung Abzweigungen nach der Koksschüttung am Fuße des inneren Walles.

Das innere Drahtnetz kann bei kleineren Gebäuden fehlen, welche keine größeren Metallmassen enthalten, wie Patronenhütten und Packhäuser.

Fangstangen sind auf den Gebäuden nicht anzubringen. Schornsteine oder Dunstaufsätze sind mit der Dachleitung zu verbinden. Bestehen dieselben aus nicht metallischem Material, so sind um ihre höchsten Spitzen Blechbänder zu legen, die mit der Dachleitung verbunden werden. Metallkappen können an Stelle dieser Bleche treten.

4. Rohr- und elektrische Leitungen.

Alle in das Haus einführende Rohrleitungen sind möglichst unter der Bodenoberfläche zu verlegen.

Die elektrischen Leitungen dürfen nicht über die Wallkrone geführt werden. Es empfiehlt sich, sie als unterirdische Kabelleitungen anzuordnen, welche an der Außenwand des Gebäudes aufsteigen und dort mittels Steckkontakte mit der in das Innere des Gebäudes führenden Leitung verbunden werden können. Die elektrischen Leitungen sind vor dem Steckkontakte mit einem Starkstromblitzableiter versehen.

Bei Lösung des Kontaktes muß zwischen dem Ende der Kabelleitung und der in das Innere des Gebäudes führenden Leitung ein Abstand von mindestens 1 m hergestellt werden können.

Drahtzüge dürfen nicht in die Gebäude führen.

Die Leitungen im Innern des Gebäudes sind durch Bleikabel herzustellen, oder durch Gummiaderleitungen, welche in starkwandigen Rohren zu führen sind.

5. Einrichtungen im Innern des Gebäudes.

Die Verwendung von Treibriemen ist möglichst zu vermeiden.

Elektrische Motoren dürfen nur voll eingekapselt benutzt werden. Die Verwendung von Drehstrommotoren, die ohne funkensprühende Bürsten arbeiten, verdient den Vorzug.

Die metallenen Gefäße müssen mit dem oberen Rande mindestens 1 m weit von der Decke entfernt sein; sie sind untereinander durch angelötete Bleistreifen zu verbinden, wenn sie eine geringere Entfernung als 10 cm voneinander haben.

Mit dem inneren Drahtnetz sind diese metallenen Gegenstände nicht zu verbinden; auch ist keine besondere Verbindung mit der Erde herzustellen; andererseits sind aber auch besondere Isolierungsmaßnahmen für diese Gegenstände nicht zu treffen. Solche Metallgefäße, in welchen Nichtleiter bewegt werden, wie Poliertrommeln für Pulver und andere Sprengstoffe, müssen dagegen für sich, d. h. ohne Anschluß an das vorhandene Schutznetz geerdet werden.

Sämtliche Rohrleitungen sind an den Eintrittsstellen in das Gebäude, insbesondere auch in der Nähe des Bleibodens möglichst durch Rohrstücke aus nicht leitendem Material (Ton, Porzellan, Gummi) von mindestens 50 cm Länge zu unterbrechen. Auch an den Einmündungsstellen dieser Rohrleitungen in die Gefäße im Innern des Gebäudes sind solche isolierende Stücke von 10 cm Länge anzubringen.

6. Prüfung der Blitzschutzvorrichtungen.

Es genügt eine einmalige jährliche gründliche Besichtigung der Blitzschutzanlagen durch einen hierzu geeigneten Sachverständigen — am besten Anfangs März.

In Zeiträumen von fünf zu fünf Jahren muß an verschiedenen Stellen die Erdleitung und die Verbindung der inneren Leitung mit den Ableitungen bloßgelegt werden, um die Güte dieser Leitungen und Verbindungen zu untersuchen, sowie eine galvanische Messung des Erdübergangwiderstandes auszuführen.

In Anlagen zur Herstellung von nitroglyzerinhaltigen Sprengstoffen sind, soweit es die Betriebsrücksichten gestatten, beim Nahen eines Gewitters die äußeren Sprengöl- und Säureleitungen zu entleeren.

B. Vorschriften für Gebäude, die nicht mit besonderen Erdschutzwällen oder Erdschutzwänden umgeben zu werden brauchen.

7. Auffangvorrichtungen und Gebäudeleitungen.

Alle voraussichtlichen Einschlagstellen des Blitzes (Firstkanten, bei Dachneigungen von weniger als 45° auch die Giebel- und Traufkanten, Schornsteine, Dunstabzugsrohre, Türmchen, stehende Dachfenster und sonstige die Dachfläche überragende Gebäudeteile) sind durch Auffangleitungen oder andere an den gefährdeten Stellen angebrachte Auffangvorrichtungen zu schützen. Derartige Stellen bedürfen, wenn sie bereits mit Metall überdeckt sind, keiner besonderen Schutzvorrichtungen (vgl. unten Ziffer 9 Abs. 2), sind aber an das allgemeine Ableitungssystem anzuschließen.

Von den Enden der Firstkanten und dazwischen in Abständen von höchstens 5 m, sowie von allen die Dachflächen überragenden Gebäudeteilen sind Gebäudeleitungen auf dem zulässig kürzesten Weg und unter tunlichster Vermeidung schärferer Krümmungen zur Erde zu führen.

Sofern Auffangstangen verwendet werden, sind sie in den Kreuzungspunkten des Leitungsnetzes, in den Firstkanten und bei Dachneigungen von weniger als 45° auch in den Traufkanten, sowie auf den die Dachfläche überragenden, nicht schon anderweitig geschützten Gebäudeteilen zu errichten. Ihre Höhe ist zweckmäßigerweise auf etwa 1 m zu beschränken. Die Stangen sind nach Möglichkeit so einzurichten, daß sie das Dach nicht durchdringen; läßt sich dies nicht vermeiden, so dürfen sie höchstens 20 cm in das Innere hineinragen.

Sämtliche Auffangvorrichtungen und Leitungen müssen so unter sich und mit der Erdleitung verbunden sein, daß ein einschlagender Blitz sich von der Einschlagstelle aus über das ganze Leitungsnetz ausbreiten kann.

8. Erdleitungen.

Die Erdleitungen bestehen aus langgestreckten, strahlenförmig unter der Erdoberfläche verlegten metallischen Bändern, Drähten oder Drahtnetzen, oder aus haltbaren metallenen großflächigen Platten, die in das Grundwasser, in fließendes Wasser oder in ständig feuchtes Erdreich zu legen sind. Sofern es die örtlichen Verhältnisse erlauben, sind die Gebäude statt dessen mit einer ringsherum laufenden metallischen Leitung zu umgeben, welche 30 bis 50 cm unter der Erdoberfläche zu verlegen ist. Diese Ringleitungen sind einerseits mit sämtlichen Gebäudeleitungen, andererseits mit vorhandenen unterirdischen Rohrleitungen und außerdem, wo es möglich ist, durch besondere Zuleitungen mit fließendem Wasser oder Grundwasser in großflächige Verbindung zu bringen. Solcher Verbindungsleitungen zu vorüberführenden Rohrleitungen und zum Grundwasser sind stets mehrere anzulegen und auf den Umfang der Ringleitung zu verteilen. In Ermangelung von Rohrleitungen oder dauernd feuchten Stellen sind von diesen Leitungen etwa 10 m lange Leiter in Abständen von etwa 10 m oder mehrere strahlenförmige Ausläufer mit einer Länge von je etwa 5 m abzuzweigen.

Die in geringer Tiefe verlegte Erdleitung kann durch eine Koksschüttung oder Einlage von Alteisen verbessert werden (vgl. oben Ziffer 2, Abs. 2 und 5).

Wo angängig, sind die Erdleitungen benachbarter Gebäude unter sich zu verbinden.

9. Anschluß von Metallmassen.

Alle größeren Metallteile der äußeren Hausfläche (Dachrinnen, Abfallrohre, eiserne Türen, Beleuchtungskästen u. dgl.) sind an die

Blitzableitung anzuschließen, kleinere Metallteile nur dann, wenn sie sich nahe der Leitung befinden.

Insoweit die metallenen Gebäudeteile den oben gestellten Anforderungen an Auffangvorrichtungen und Gebäudeleitungen entsprechen (Wellblechdächer, Dachrinnen, Abfallrohre usw.) sind besondere Auffangvorrichtungen und Gebäudeleitungen entbehrlich.

Die in die Gebäude hineinragenden unteren Enden von Auffangstangen, die Auffang- und Gebäudeleitungen, sowie deren Befestigungsmittel sind möglichst weit, mindestens aber 1 m entfernt von inneren Metallmassen anzubringen. Ist dies nicht durchzuführen (z. B. bei eisernen Dachkonstruktionen), so müssen diese Metallmassen doppelseitig an den Blitzableiter angeschlossen werden, und es ist streng zu vermeiden, Sprengstoffe mit ihnen in Berührung zu bringen.

Im übrigen finden bezüglich der inneren Metallgegenstände, Rohrleitungen und elektrischen Leitungen die Vorschriften unter Ziffer 4 und 5 sinngemäße Anwendung.

10. Besondere Blitzschutzvorrichtungen.

Die Sicherheit wird erhöht, wenn außer den oben beschriebenen, an den Gebäuden selbst angebrachten Blitzableitern neben dem zu schützenden Gebäude auf freistehenden, das Gebäude überragenden Masten besondere Auffangvorrichtungen mit Ableitungen und guten, mit jenen der Gebäude zusammenhängenden Erdleitungen angebracht werden. Für kleinere Gebäude, welche Explosivstoffe, aber keine größeren Metallmassen enthalten, genügen als Schutz freistehende Maste mit Auffangvorrichtung und Erdleitung, wenn die Maste die Gebäude um das Maß ihres wagrechten Abstands vom Gebäude überragen.

Bäume, deren Zweige näher als 5 m an Gebäude heranreichen, sind mit einer etwa in der Mitte der Krone beginnenden und an die Erdleitung des Gebäudes anzuschließenden Blitzableitung zu versehen. Außerdem sind da, wo die Zweige in größere Nähe des Gebäudes kommen, diesen gegenüber Auffangvorrichtungen mit den erforderlichen Gebäude- und Erdleitungen anzuordnen.

11. Ausführung der Blitzableiter und besondere Vorsichtsmaßregeln.

Als Material für Blitzableiter ist Kupfer oder Eisen (verzinktes Eisen) zu wählen. Zu natürlichen Gebäudeleitungen (Dachrinnen, Abfallröhren u. dgl.) kann auch Zink, zu Erdleitungen außerdem Blei verwendet werden. Verzweigte Leitungen aus Eisen sollen nicht unter 50 qmm, unverzweigte nicht unter 100 qmm stark sein. Für Kupfer ist die Hälfte dieser Querschnitte ausreichend. Zink ist mindestens vom ein- und einhalbfachen, Blei vom dreifachen Querschnitt des Eisens zu wählen. Der Leiter soll nach Form und Befestigung sturmsicher sein. Leitungsverbindungen und Anschlüsse sind dauerhaft, fest, dicht und möglichst großflächig herzustellen. Nicht geschweißte oder gelötete Verbindungsstellen sollen metallische Berührungsflächen von nicht unter 10 qcm erhalten.

Die Gebäudeleitungen können auf den Dach- und Wandflächen aufliegend angeordnet werden; auf weicher Dachung aber (z. B. bei Dächern aus Asphaltpappe), sind sie in einem Abstande von mindestens 10 cm von der Dachfläche zu führen. Die Leitungen brauchen nicht isoliert zu werden.

Metallene Schutzbekleidungen der Leitungen sind mit diesen an beiden Enden metallisch zu verbinden.

Soweit keine praktischen Gründe entgegenstehen, ist großflächigen band- und blechförmigen, in größeren Längen hergestellten Leitern der Vorzug vor Drähten zu geben.

Bei der Aufstapelung von Pulver und Sprengstoffen in Magazinen ist die unmittelbare Berührung der Verpackungsgefäße mit Metallteilen zu vermeiden.

12. Vorschriften für Gebäude ohne gefährlichen Inhalt.

Für diejenigen Gebäude, welche weder Explosivstoffe noch größere Mengen anderer leicht entzündlicher Stoffe enthalten, genügen Blitzableiter nach den für gewöhnliche Gebäude geltenden Grundsätzen (vgl. Leitsätze über den Schutz der Gebäude gegen den Blitz, aufgestellt vom Elektrotechnischen Verein in Wien, Elektrotechnische Zeitschrift 1901, S. 390).

13. Prüfung der Blitzschutzvorrichtungen.

Alljährlich, am besten im Frühling, und nach jedem starken Gewitter ist eine gründliche Besichtigung der Blitzableiteranlage und mindestens alle fünf Jahre eine genaue sachverständige Untersuchung, verbunden mit galvanischer Messung des Erdübergangswiderstandes erforderlich.

Dritter Abschnitt.

Die Eigenschaften des Glyzerintrinitrates.

a) Physikalische Eigenschaften.

Das Nitroglyzerin ist eine durchsichtig-klare, ölartige Flüssigkeit, welche nur in reinem Zustande ganz farblos, in dem fabrikmäßig hergestellten Produkte jedoch hellgelb bis gelblich-braun ist; es besitzt einen anfangs süßlichen, später brennenden Geschmack. Das spezifische Gewicht des Nitroglyzerins beträgt 1·60 (nach Beckerhinn 1·599). Beim Gefrieren zieht sich Nitroglyzerin um $^{10}/_{121}$ seines Volumens zusammen und hat dann ein spezifisches Gewicht von 1·735. — Nitroglyzerin ist nicht hygroskopisch, d. h. es nimmt auch in feuchtem Raume kein Wasser auf. Die Löslichkeit im Wasser ist nur sehr gering; beim

Schütteln in reichlich überschüssigem Wasser werden in einer Stunde nur 0·2 Prozent Sprengöl gelöst. Nach Haeussermann ist das Nitroglyzerin wenn auch schwer, so doch vollständig mit Wasserdampf flüchtig. Bei der Destillation im Wasserdampfstrom gehen mit 1 l Wasser etwa 8 g Nitroglyzerin über. Auf der Flüchtigkeit mit Wasserdämpfen beruht es auch, daß Nitroglyzerin sich rasch der feuchten Zimmerluft mitteilt.

A. H. Elliot (School of mines Quarterly, Vol. IV, S. 15) hat die folgende Lösungstabelle angegeben, wobei die Versuche in der Wärme durch Einstecken eines Probierglases in kochendes Wasser ausgeführt wurden.

Lösungsmittel	kalt	warm
Wasser	unlöslich	ein wenig löslich
Absoluter Alkohol	löslich	löslich
93 prozentiger Alkohol	"	"
80 prozentiger "	langsam löslich	"
50 prozentiger "	unlöslich	ein wenig löslich
Äther	löslich	löslich
Essigäther	"	"
Aceton	"	"
Glyzerin	unlöslich	unlöslich
Chloroform	löslich	löslich
Eisessig	"	"
Methylalkohol	"	"
Amylalkohol	"	"
Benzol	"	"
Toluol	"	"
Nitrobenzol	"	"
Karbolsäure	"	"
Schwefelkohlenstoff	unlöslich	teilweise angegriffen
Terpentin	"	löslich
Mineralfett (Vaseline)	"	unlöslich
Petroleumnaphta (71 bis 76° Bé)	"	"
Astralöl	"	"
Olivenöl	löslich	löslich
Stearinöl	"	"
Natronlauge (1 : 10)	unlöslich	unlöslich
Ammoniak (spez. Gew. 0·98)	"	unlöslich, ein wenig angegriffen
Konz. Schwefelsäure	löslich	löslich
Salpetersäure (1·4)	langsam löslich	"
Salzsäure (1·2)	unlösl., langsam zersetzt	langsam löslich

Die spezifische Wärme und die Erstarrungswärme des Nitroglyzerins sind von S. Nauckhoff[1] bestimmt worden. Der Mittelwert der spezifischen Wärme bei flüssigem Nitroglyzerin (C_1) wurde mit 0·356, bei festem Nitroglyzerin (C_2) mit 0·315 kal. gefunden. Eine Bestimmung der Erstarrungswärme des Nitroglyzerins ergab bei einer mittleren Temperatur von $+ 1^0$ den Wert $W_{1^0} = 22{\cdot}56$ kal. und bei $1{\cdot}5^0$ den Wert $W_{1{\cdot}5^0} = 22{\cdot}74$ kal. Aus dem ersteren Wert berechnet sich nach der Formel:

$$W_{12{\cdot}3^0} = W_{1^0} + 11{\cdot}3\,(C_1 - C_2) = 22{\cdot}56 + 11{\cdot}3\,(0{\cdot}356 - 0{\cdot}315)$$

für $W_{12{\cdot}3^0}$ der Betrag von 23·02 kal. Aus dem zweiten Wert berechnet sich der entsprechende Betrag von 23·18 kal.; im Mittel also für $12{\cdot}3^0$ $W = 23{\cdot}1$ kal.[2] Diese Werte wurden im Quecksilberkalorimeter gefunden, während im Nernstschen Wasserkalorimeter ein Mittelwert von 24·8 kal. erhalten wurde. Eine Bestimmung der latenten Schmelzwärme (Erstarrungswärme) des Nitroglyzerins in dem von der Temperatur der Umgebung vollständig unabhängigen Bunsenschen Eiskalorimeter steht noch aus. — Kennt man den Gefrierpunkt und die latente Schmelzwärme eines Stoffes, der als Lösungsmittel wirken kann (in diesem Falle also des Nitroglyzerins), so kann man nach dem Gesetze von Raoult die Gefrierpunktserniedrigung Δ berechnen, die m g eines Stoffes mit dem Molekulargewicht M in 100 g Nitroglyzerin aufgelöst, in diesem hervorrufen; denn es ist:

$$\Delta = E \frac{m}{M},$$

worin E eine für das Nitroglyzerin charakteristische Konstante bedeutet, welche nach van't Hoff berechnet werden kann, mit:

$$E = \frac{R\,T^2}{100\,W}.$$

Hierin bedeutet R die Gaskonstante (in kal. = 1·99), $T (= 273 + t)$ die absolute Schmelztemperatur des Lösungsmittels und W seine latente Schmelzwärme. Obige Formel kann also geschrieben werden:

$$E = \frac{0{\cdot}01991 \cdot (273 + t)^2}{W},$$

oder ungefähr

$$= 0{\cdot}2 \frac{(273 + t)^2}{W}.$$

Das ergibt (bei $W = 23{\cdot}1$ kal. und beim Schmelzpunkt $+ 12{\cdot}3^0$):

[1] Zeitschr. angew. Chemie 1905.

[2] Nauckhoff berechnet für F.P. = $12{\cdot}3^0$; tatsächlich liegt der Schmelzpunkt nach Kast um etwa 1 Grad höher.

$$E = 0{\cdot}02 \frac{(273 + 12{\cdot}3)^2}{23{\cdot}1},$$

oder

$$E = 70{\cdot}5,$$

demnach

$$\varDelta = 70{\cdot}5 \frac{m}{M}.$$

Gefrier- und Schmelzpunkt. Das Glyzerin besitzt in hohem Maße die Eigenschaft der Unterkühlung, d. h. es bleibt oft weit unter seinem Gefrierpunkt noch flüssig, gefriert dann aber sofort, wenn ein noch so kleines Nitroglyzerinkriställchen hineingeworfen wird. Nach Tammann kommen für die Unterkühlungsfähigkeit einer Flüssigkeit in Betracht: das spontane Kristallisationsvermögen, welches durch die Zahl der spontan entstehenden Kristallisationszentren in der Gewichtseinheit der unterkühlten Flüssigkeit pro Zeiteinheit bei gegebener Temperatur gemessen wird, und die lineare Kristallisationsgeschwindigkeit, d. h. die Strecke, um die sich in der Zeiteinheit die Grenze zwischen dem Kristallisierten und der Flüssigkeit fortbewegt. Das spontane Kristallisationsvermögen des Nitroglyzerins ist nicht bekannt, muß aber sehr gering sein, wozu zweifelsohne die verhältnismäßig große Viskosität beiträgt. Die Kristallisationsgeschwindigkeit wurde von S. Nauckhoff[1] bei verschiedenen Temperaturen ($+5^{\circ}$, $\pm 0^{\circ}$, -5°, -17°) gemessen und als sehr klein gefunden (0·145, 0·183, 0·267, 0·125 mm pro Minute).

Wegen der Unterkühlungserscheinung kann man die Gefriertemperatur des Nitroglyzerins nicht durch jene Temperatur bestimmen, bei welcher die Kristallisation beginnt. Man kann sie jedoch nach Nauckhoff in der Weise direkt bestimmen, daß man die höchste Temperatur beobachtet, die ein in gefrierendes Nitroglyzerin hineingesetztes Thermometer zeigt. Das Nitroglyzerin befindet sich hierbei in einem mit Thermometer und Rührer versehenen Rohre (z. B. in einem Apparat, wie er sonst zu Molekulargewichtsbestimmungen verwendet wird) und wird durch Eintauchen des Rohres in Eiswasser unterkühlt. Beim Einführen eines Impfkriställchens fängt das Nitroglyzerin zu gefrieren an. Das Rohr wird jetzt in ein größeres Rohr eingesetzt, damit der so entstandene Luftmantel gegen zu schnelle Wärmeabgabe schützt. Man setzt den Apparat dann in ein Wasserbad, dessen Temperatur etwas niedriger ist als die Gefriertemperatur des Nitroglyzerins. Während des Gefrierens muß man die Masse umrühren, damit

[1] Zeitschr. angew. Chemie 1905, S. 16.

nur fein verteiltes Eis sich bildet. Die Temperatur steigt anfangs schnell und nachher langsamer, bis sie schließlich bei der wirklichen Gefriertemperatur des Nitroglyzerins konstant bleibt. Nauckhoff ermittelte auf diese Weise die Gefriertemperatur für reines Nitroglyzerin zu $+12 \cdot 3^0$ (Mittel aus drei Versuchen), für technisches Nitroglyzerin zu $+10 \cdot 5^0$.

Einfacher als vorher ist es, die Schmelztemperatur gefrorenen Nitroglyzerins zu ermitteln, wozu sich Nauckhoff nebenstehenden Apparates (Fig. 43) bediente.

Ein Glasröhrchen *a*, unten zu einer dünnwandigen Pipette mit 1 mm Spitze ausgeblasen, wurde zum Teil mit unterkühltem Nitroglyzerin gefüllt, welches durch ein Impfkriställchen zum Gefrieren gebracht wurde. Das Röhrchen wurde alsdann an einem empfindlichen Thermometer *b* befestigt, und zwar mit der Spitze dicht neben der Thermometerkugel. Das Ganze wurde hierauf in einen Becher *c* mit Wasser hineingesetzt, dessen Temperatur sich etwas unterhalb der Schmelztemperatur des Nitroglyzerins befand (z. B. $+10$ bis $+11^0$). Damit das Wasser nicht zu schnell Wärme aus der umgebenden Luft aufnehmen konnte, wurde das Becherglas durch einen zweiten, etwas größeren Becher *d* geschützt. Bei dieser Anordnung steigt die Temperatur des Wassers passend schnell, wenn man bei gewöhnlicher Zimmertemperatur arbeitet. Das Wasser wurde mit Hilfe des Rührers *e* in ständiger Bewegung gehalten und jene Temperatur beobachtet, bei welcher das erste Tröpflein Nitroglyzerin sich an der Spitze der Pipette zeigte. Um das geschmolzene Nitroglyzerin gleich bei der Entstehung herauszudrücken und das gefrorene Nitroglyzerin in enger Berührung mit den Wandungen des Gefäßes zu halten, wurde das Röhrchen mit Wasser gefüllt.

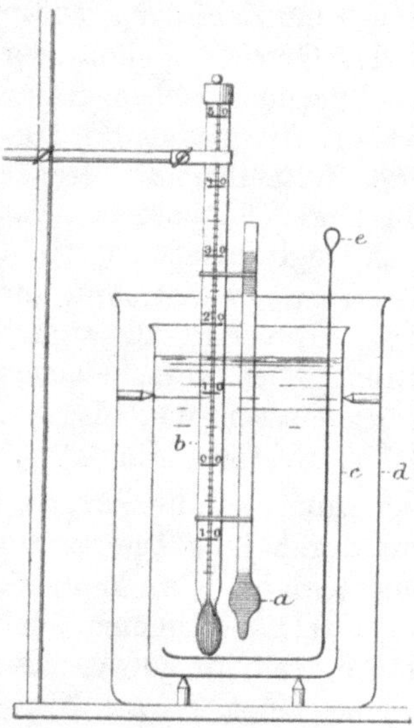

Fig. 43. Nauckhoffscher Apparat zur Schmelzpunktbestimmung.

In dieser Weise ermittelte Nauckhoff die Schmelztemperatur des chemisch reinen Nitroglyzerins zu $+12^0$ bis $+12 \cdot 4^0$, und diejenige des technischen Nitroglyzerins (bei mehreren Proben regelmäßig) zu $+10 \cdot 4^0$ bis $+10 \cdot 5^0$. Nauckhoff beobachtete auch, daß das Nitroglyzerin außer dem festen, kristallisierten Zustande auch noch einen festen, amorphen, glasartigen Zustand annehmen kann.

H. Kast[1] bediente sich zur Bestimmung des Gefrier- oder Erstarrungspunktes, sowie des Schmelzpunktes eines ähnlichen Apparates (Fig. 44), wobei im ersteren Falle eine Kältemischung, im zweiten entsprechend temperiertes Wasser angewandt wurde.

Zur Bestimmung des Gefrierpunktes befanden sich 15 ccm Nitroglyzerin in einem weiten, mit Thermometer *t* und mechanisch betätigtem Rührer *r* versehenen Reagensglas *a*, das zur Erzielung einer isolierenden Luftschicht von einem zweiten ähnlichen Reagensglas *b* umgeben und in diesem durch zwei Gummiringe *g* festgehalten war. Beide Reagensgläser waren in einen weithalsigen, zur Aufnahme der Kältemischung bestimmten Erlenmeyerkolben *c* eingesetzt, der seinerseits in ein mit einem Holzdeckel bedecktes leeres Batterieglas *e* eingehängt war. Nachdem das Nitroglyzerin genügend (um ca. 8° unterhalb des Erstarrungspunktes) abgekühlt war, wurde ein Impfkristall zugesetzt und unter fortwährendem Rühren das Thermometer beobachtet; der höchst erreichbare Punkt des Thermometers wurde als Erstarrungspunkt angenommen. — Die Gewinnung des zur Impfung nötigen festen Nitroglyzerins bereitete anfangs einige Schwierigkeiten, doch konnten diese späterhin leicht dadurch behoben werden, daß man ein erbsengroßes Stück Gurdynamit in einem Reagensglas mit Hilfe einer Kältemischung zum Erstarren brachte und

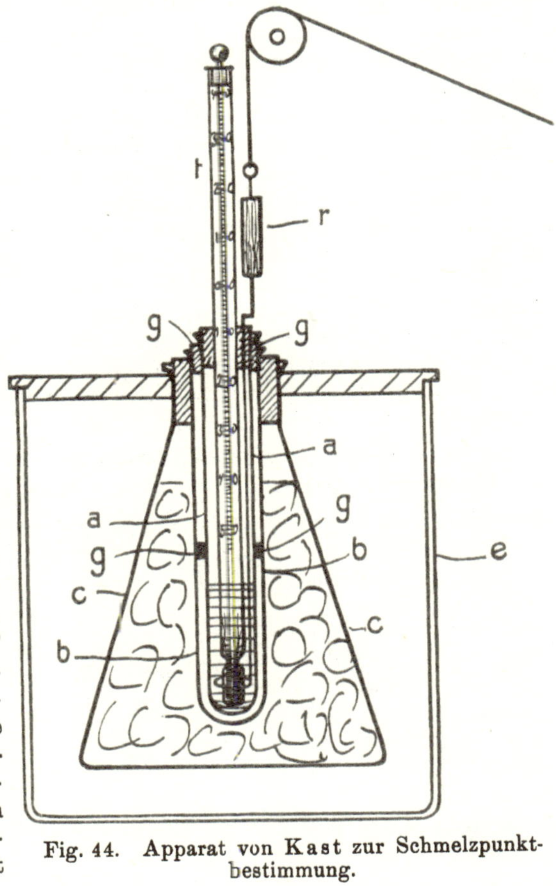

Fig. 44. Apparat von Kast zur Schmelzpunktbestimmung.

[1] Zeitschr. Schieß-Sprengstoffwesen I, S. 225.

einen Kristall davon auf eine kleine Menge abgekühlten Nitroglyzerins überimpfte. Der Erstarrungspunkt hat sich bei den einzelnen Versuchen von der Schnelligkeit abhängig gezeigt, mit der die Kristallisation eingeleitet wurde und vor sich ging, was sich nur sehr schwer gleichmäßig gestalten läßt. Für eine scharfe Bestimmung müßte die Temperatur des Kältebades möglichst nahe am Erstarrungspunkt liegen; doch nimmt dann die Bestimmung zu lange Zeit in Anspruch. In jedem Falle muß ziemlich rasch gerührt werden, um ein Ansetzen größerer Kristalle an Glaswandung und Thermometer zu vermeiden, die ein Festhängen des Rührers und damit eine vorzeitige Unterbrechung der Rührung zur Folge haben.

Zur Bestimmung des Schmelzpunktes wurde statt der Kältemischung entsprechend temperiertes Wasser in den Apparat gebracht. Als Schmelzpunkt wurde dann der Temperaturpunkt angenommen, bei dem die erstarrte Masse anfing, durchsichtig zu werden, so daß das Thermometergefäß wieder von außen sichtbar wurde. Dieser Punkt fällt genau mit dem Punkte zusammen, bei dem das Thermometer anfängt schneller zu steigen, nachdem es vorher innerhalb ganz weniger Zehntelgrade längere Zeit konstant geblieben war. Der Schmelzpunkt liegt je nach der Reinheit des Nitroglyzerins mehr oder weniger weit über dem Erstarrungspunkt; er läßt sich ziemlich scharf festlegen, so daß die einzelnen Werte auf 1 bis 2 Zehntelgrade miteinander überein stimmen.

Kast fand nun, daß dem Nitroglyzerin zwei Erstarrungs- bzw. Schmelzpunkte zukommen, und zwar folgende:

Nitroglyzerin-sorte	Aussehen	Stickstoff-gehalt	Erstarrungspunkt		Schmelzpunkt	
			I.	II.	I.	II.
Chemisch reines	fast wasserhell	18·50 Proz.	2·1°	13·2°	2·8°	13·5°
Technisches aus Gurdynamit Nr. I	gelblich	18·48 Proz.	2·2°	13·1°	2·8°	13·5°
Technisches aus Gurdynamit Nr. II	gelblich	18·46 Proz.	1·9°	12·3°	2·5°	13·1°

Das niedriger schmelzende Nitroglyzerin erwies sich als ein labileres Produkt und ließ sich durch Berührung mit einem höher schmelzenden Kristall in das höher schmelzende stabile vollständig umwandeln; es liegt hier also eine monotrope Allotropie vor. Die beiden allotropen Modifikationen können aus flüssigem Nitroglyzerin erhalten werden, je nachdem man Kristalle von der stabilen oder labilen Form aussät.

Über die Art und Weise der freiwilligen Bildung des labilen und stabilen Produktes ohne Aussaat von Kristallen stellte Kast folgendes fest: Nitroglyzerin ist im Reagensglas in kleinen Mengen nur äußerst schwer zum Erstarren zu bringen. Bei sehr starker Abkühlung in Kohlensäure und Äther nimmt es einen amorphen festen Zustand an, der durch Erwärmen auf unterhalb des eigentlichen Erstarrungspunktes liegende Temperaturen wieder in den dünnflüssigen Zustand übergeht. In größeren Mengen (25 bis 100 g) geht die Erstarrung leichter von statten. Nitroglyzerin, das einmal erstarrt war, gefriert leichter als das nicht erstarrt gewesene. Bei sehr starker Unterkühlung bildet sich die labilere Form leichter als die stabile. Die labile Form läßt sich schon äußerlich durch ihr glasigeres Aussehen von der stabileren Form unterscheiden, besser aber daran, daß sie in einem 6 bis 8° warmen Wasserbad schnell zum Schmelzen zu bringen ist.

b) Chemische Eigenschaften.

Behandelt man Nitroglyzerin mit reduzierenden Mitteln (wie z. B. Zinn und Salzsäure), so wird Glyzerin regeneriert. Bei Einwirkung von fixen Alkalien bildet sich einerseits Glyzerin, andererseits salpetersaures Alkali. Danach ist Nitroglyzerin als ein Ester aufzufassen, d. h. als eine durch Kondensation zustande gekommene Verbindung eines Alkohols (Glyzerin) und einer Säure (Salpetersäure). Die rationelle Formel ist daher:

$$\begin{array}{l} CH_2\cdot O\cdot NO_2 \\ | \\ CH\ \cdot O\cdot NO_2 \\ | \\ CH_2\cdot O\cdot NO_2 \,; \end{array}$$

wonach also die Nitro-(NO_2)-Gruppen durch Vermittelung eines Sauerstoff-(O)-Atomes an Kohlenstoff gebunden sind. Die richtige Bezeichnung für das gewöhnliche Sprengöl ist sonach Glyzerintrinitrat oder dreifach Salpetersäureester des Glyzerins.[1]

Bei der Behandlung des Nitroglyzerins mit alkoholischem Kali bilden sich (nach Hess und Schwab) salpetersaures und salpetrigsaures Kali. Der Alkohol und vielleicht auch ein Teil des Glyzerins wird durch den Sauerstoff der Nitrogruppen zu

---

[1] Bei den Nitrokörpern (z. B. Nitromethan, Nitrobenzol, Trinitrophenol) ist die Nitrogruppe direkt, d. h. ohne Brücken-Sauerstoffatom an Kohlenstoff gebunden. Durch reduzierende Mittel werden die Nitroverbindungen in Amidoverbindungen übergeführt. Die übliche Bezeichnung Nitroglyzerin oder Trinitroglyzerin ist daher falsch, denn das Sprengöl ist kein Nitrokörper, sondern ein Nitrat.

Essigsäure, Ameisensäure und einem braunen, sich ausscheidenden Körper (Aldehydharz) oxydiert. Nach Hay (Monit. Scient. **15**, 424) erfolgt die Verseifung mit Alkali nach dem Schema:

$$C_3H_5(ONO_2)_3 + 5KOH = KNO_3 + 2KNO_2 + CH_3COOK + HCOOK;$$

doch stimmt diese Reaktionsgleichung mit den Tatsachen nicht überein, da noch Ammoniak und andere Produkte bei der Verseifung auftreten. Haeussermann hat beobachtet, daß beim Behandeln des Sprengöls mit Essigsäure und Zink der Stickstoff sich als Ammoniak abspaltet.

Nitroglyzerin löst sich mit größter Leichtigkeit — wohl unter ganzer oder teilweiser Umsetzung zu Glyzerinschwefelsäure und Salpetersäure — in konzentrierter Schwefelsäure.

c) Physiologische Wirkungen.

Das Nitroglyzerin gehört zu den organischen Giftstoffen. Seine Wirkung auf den menschlichen Organismus macht sich oft in den minimalsten Dosen schon bemerkbar. Für viele, die für solche Einwirkung besonders disponiert sind, genügt das Betreten der Räume, in denen Nitroglyzerin verarbeitet wird und das Einatmen des verflüchtigten Sprengöls, um einen mehrstündigen Kopfschmerz und ein Druckgefühl in der Stirn und im Hinterkopf hervorzurufen. Innerlich genommen (bzw. bei Berührung mit der Zunge), rufen schon sehr geringe Mengen von Nitroglyzerin ein eigentümliches Gefühl von Kratzen im Schlund, eine vermehrte Speichelabsonderung und nach wenigen Minuten einen dumpfen drückenden Kopfschmerz mit dem Gefühl von Klopfen in der Stirn oder in den Schläfen, sowie die Empfindung von Ziehen in den Kaumuskeln hervor, dann Übelkeit, Anwandlung von Ohnmacht und Bewußtlosigkeit. Nach einigen Minuten kehrt das Bewußtsein zurück; die starke Eingenommenheit des Kopfes hält einige Stunden an. Eine besondere Gefahr liegt darin, daß das Nitroglyzerin schnell durch die unversehrte Haut eindringt und Vergiftungserscheinungen hervorruft, indem es wahrscheinlich im tierischen Körper eine Zersetzung unter Stickoxydbildung erleidet. Bei den meisten Arbeitern der Dynamitfabriken tritt jedoch in kurzer Zeit eine Gewöhnung an und Abstumpfung gegen die Einwirkungen des Nitroglyzerins ein. Ein Aussetzen der Arbeit von ein bis zwei Wochen macht eine neue Gewöhnung nötig. Vereinzelte Arbeiter können sich niemals an das Nitroglyzerin gewöhnen und müssen daher die Arbeit einstellen. Bei heftigem Kopfschmerz — insbesondere im Hinterhaupt — werden als Gegenmittel kalte Umschläge auf den Kopf und in den Nacken, frische Luft, auch das Trinken von schwarzem Kaffee, Einnehmen von Antipyrin, Morphiumacetat (nach ärztlicher Vorschrift) empfohlen; vor Spirituosen wird gewarnt. Die Arbeiter sind streng anzuhalten, nach der Arbeit in einem besonderen Raume ihre Oberkleider völlig zu wechseln, vor dem Essen sich Hände und Gesicht sorgfältig zu waschen und besonders die Nägel zu reinigen; der Mund soll vor dem Essen ausgespült werden. Die Arbeiter, welche die Mengung des Nitroglyzerins mit Kieselgur und das Durchsieben dieses Gemenges, sowie ähnliche Operationen vornehmen, sind anzuhalten, bei diesen Manipulationen leichte Gummihandschuhe zu tragen.

Die in der Luft, im Wasser, in der Erde, Dünger, Holz usw. am häufigsten vorkommenden Bakterien sind (nach Malenkovic) nicht imstande, Nitroglyzerin irgendwie zu verändern. Nitroglyzerin ist — im Gegensatz zu den meisten Estern des Glyzerins — für derlei Pilze nicht nur kein Nährstoff, sondern ein Gift.

d) Chemische Untersuchung.

1. Feuchtigkeit. Eine gewogene Menge Nitroglyzerin wird in einem Exsikkator über Chlorcalcium getrocknet und wieder gewogen.

2. Neutralität. Das Nitroglyzerin darf keine freie Säure enthalten; bei saurer Reaktion ist dasselbe noch weiter zu waschen. Das Sprengöl darf aber auch nicht alkalisch reagieren, da sonst eine Täuschung möglich ist. Wird nämlich die etwa vorhandene überschüssige Soda ausgewaschen, so kann das Nitroglyzerin immer noch Spuren von Säure zeigen, welche der Einwirkung der Soda sich entzogen haben, oder von der Zersetzung des Nitroglyzerins durch die Soda herrühren. Man übergießt deshalb die Nitroglyzerinprobe mit destilliertem Wasser, schüttelt sie kräftig durch, trennt im Scheidetrichter und prüft das Waschwasser auf eine alkalische Reaktion mit Kongorot oder Methylorange.

3. Stickstoffbestimmung. Der Stickstoff wird gewöhnlich als Stickoxyd volumetrisch bestimmt, und zwar entweder a) durch Zersetzung mit metallischem Quecksilber und Schwefelsäure, oder b) durch Reduktion mit Eisenoxydulsalz und Salzsäure, bzw. Schwefelsäure. Oder aber man verseift das Nitroglyzerin mit Alkali und führt die hierbei entstehenden Stickstoffverbindungen entweder sämtlich in Salpetersäure über, welche volumetrisch oder gewichtsanalytisch bestimmt werden kann (c) oder in Ammoniak, das titrimetrisch bestimmt wird (d).

a) Zersetzung durch Quecksilber und Schwefelsäure. Allgemein wurde diese Nitrometermethode zuerst von G. Lunge[1] angegeben. Auf Nitroglyzerin wurde die Methode ungefähr gleichzeitig von F. Hess und von W. Hempel angewandt. Lunge selbst beschrieb die Stickstoffbestimmung von Nitroglyzerin mittels Nitrometer in Dinglers polyt. Journ. Bd. 245, S. 171.

α) Verfahren von Hess.[2]

Man füllt zuerst durch einen bei *a* (Fig. 45) einzusetzenden Glastrichter das Rohr *ab* des Apparates mit Quecksilber, während der Glashahn *h* so gestellt ist, daß seine diametrale Bohrung die Kommunikation zwischen dem Innern des Rohres *cd* und dem Aufsatze *A* herstellt, die Luft über dem Quecksilber also durch jene Bohrung entweichen kann. Es gelingt, nachdem die in *ab* noch enthaltenen Luftblasen durch Drücken des Gummischlauches *bd* beseitigt worden sind, bei einiger Übung ganz leicht, das Steigrohr *cd* durch allmähliches Tieferstellen mitsamt der Bohrung des Hahnes eben vollauf zu füllen und hierauf den Hahn zu schließen. Um einen vollkommen gasdichten Verschluß zu erzielen, wird der Hahn vor dem Versuche mit reiner Vaseline gut geschmiert. — Ist das Rohr *cd* und die diametrale Hahnbohrung mit Quecksilber gefüllt, so ist der Apparat zum Versuch vorbereitet. Man löst nun eine gewogene Menge (etwa 0·12 g) Nitroglyzerin in der 40- bis 60 fachen Menge konzentrierter Schwefelsäure, was schon bei gewöhnlicher Temperatur binnen wenigen Minuten gelingt. Eine Erwärmung beschleunigt wohl erheblich die Lösung, ist aber wegen der dabei zuweilen eintretenden vorzeitigen Entbindung von Stickoxyd nicht ratsam. Die Lösung wird nun in den Aufsatzbecher *A* gegossen und, nachdem das Rohr *cd* mit diesem ent-

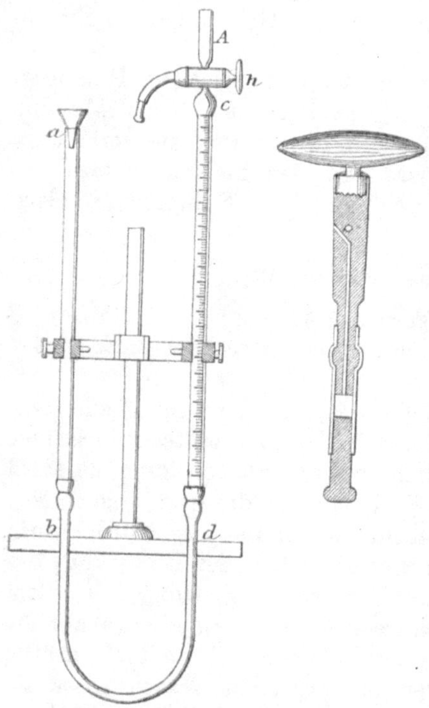

Fig. 45. Stickstoffbestimmung im Nitrometer nach Hess.

[1] Lunge, Ber. deutsch. chem. Ges. XI, 436.
[2] Mitteil. Art.- u. Geniewesen 1881. Notizen S. 137.

sprechend gehoben worden ist, durch vorsichtiges Öffnen des Hahnes nach *c d* überführt. Das Probegläschen, in welchem die Lösung dargestellt worden ist, wird nochmals mit der gleichen Menge konzentrierter Schwefelsäure durch Schütteln ausgewaschen, wobei man den das Gläschen schließenden Daumen durch paraffiniertes Zigarettenpapier schützt. Die Waschsäure wird gleichfalls nach *A* gebracht und von hier aus gleichfalls nach *c d* abgelassen. Das Mitreißen von Luftblasen ist sorgfältig zu vermeiden. Man sperrt den Hahn, sobald sich noch ein Tropfen der Flüssigkeit oberhalb der Hahnbohrung befindet. Zum Schlusse wird die Schale noch mit einer geringen Menge wenig verdünnter Schwefelsäure (etwa 2 Tle. Säure, 1 Tl. Wasser, die Mischung gut abgekühlt) unter den genannten Vorsichten nachgespült und der Hahn nach Ablassen dieses Restes gegen *c d* so gestellt, daß die axiale Bohrung mit *A* kommuniziert. Der freie Teil des durchbohrten Hahnkörpers wurde schon früher mit einem Stückchen Gummischlauch und mit einem Glasstäbchen verschlossen. Sind zur Herstellung der Originallösung etwa 3 ccm, ebensoviel zum Ausschütteln des Probegläschens und die gleiche Menge zum Nachspülen des Bechers *A* verwendet worden, so hat man etwa 9 bis 10 ccm Flüssigkeit im Meßrohre, welches Quantum dem Zwecke der Analyse am besten entspricht. Das Einleiten der Gasentbindung durch wiederholtes Neigen und Aufrichten des Meßrohres und das Zuendeführen derselben durch kräftiges, einige Minuten währendes Schütteln, erfolgt wie bei der Untersuchung der Nitrose. Zur Ausgleichung des Druckes beachte man, daß die mit Quecksilbersulfat beladene konzentrierte Schwefelsäure ein spezifisches Gewicht hat, welches sich zu jenem des Quecksilbers ungefähr wie 1 : 6·5 verhält. Man mißt also die Schwefelsäureschicht und dividiert deren Betrag durch 6·5, um die Höhe der gleich stark gegendrückenden Quecksilbersäule zu finden. Der Druckausgleich ist erst nach etwa einer halben Stunde, also nach erfolgtem Temperaturausgleiche zu bewirken und sind erst dann alle nötigen Ablesungen zu machen. Die Resultate fallen um eine sehr geringe Größe zu niedrig aus, wenn man das Ausspülen des Aufsatzes *A* mit konz. Schwefelsäure bewirkt. Das Anwenden einer im obigen Verhältnisse verdünnten Säure bewirkt aber eine sehr vollständige Durchspülung und gibt scharf richtige Resultate. Es wurden erhalten: bei der Nachspülung mit konz. Schwefelsäure: 18·2 Prozent; bei der Nachspülung mit verdünnter Schwefelsäure: 18·4 Prozent (berechnet: 18·5 Prozent).

β) Verfahren von W. Hempel.

Hempel[1] fand, daß man beim Nitrometer die Quecksilberkuppen nicht genügend deutlich sieht und die großen Quecksilbermassen sich durch die Reaktion so stark erwärmen, daß man wenigstens eine Stunde warten muß, ehe man eine Ablesung machen darf. Hempel hat daher nachstehend beschriebenen

[1] Zeitschr. analyt. Chemie **20**, 82 und **26**, 312.

Apparat[1] (Fig. 46) angegeben, bei welchem die Entwicklung und Messung des Stickstoffes in getrennten Räumen vorgenommen wird.

Als Entwicklungsgefäß dient ein etwa 5 cm weites, 9 cm langes zylindrisches Glas *c*, welches nach oben in eine Kapillarröhre ausläuft, nach unten aber flaschenhalsförmig zusammengezogen ist. Oben bei *i* ist der Entwickler durch einen Glashahn geschlossen, unten seitlich ist ein Glasrohr *x* angesetzt. Das Entwicklungsgefäß wird durch den gebogenen eisernen Halter *f* getragen. Den unteren Verschluß bildet ein doppelt durchbohrter Gummistopfen, dessen Abrutschen während der Arbeit infolge der Last des Quecksilbers durch eine einfache Sicherheitsvorrichtung *n* (aus einem gebogenen Draht, einem Bügel und zwei Schrauben bestehend) verhindert wird. In der einen Bohrung des Stopfens steckt ein kurzes Glasrohr *l*, welches durch den dünnen Gummischlauch *m* mit dem Kugelgefäß *e* verbunden ist, welch letzteres durch Klemme *g* getragen wird und nach Bedürfnis durch Glashahn *o* abgeschlossen werden kann. Die zweite Bohrung dient zur Aufnahme eines Glasstabes *q*, welcher an seinem oberen Ende in ein unten geschlossenes Glasgefäß *k* übergeht. — Als **Meßgefäß** dient eine Glasbürette *a*, *b*. Zur Analyse wägt man zunächst das Nitroglyzerin in das Röhrchen *k*, wobei man letzteres mittels eines Platindrahtes an die Wage hängt; dann füllt man die Kugel *e* — bei geschlossenem Hahn *o* — vollständig mit Quecksilber, steckt das Röhrchen *k* mit dem Sprengöl in den Gummistopfen und setzt den Entwickler zusammen, ohne jedoch solchen mit der Glasbürette zu verbinden. Durch Öffnen der Hähne *o* und *i* und entsprechendes Heben der Kugel *e* wird dann das Entwicklungsgefäß *c* vollständig mit Quecksilber gefüllt und sodann der Hahn *i* geschlossen. Gießt man hierauf in den Rohransatz *x* die zur Zersetzung nötige Schwefelsäure, so kann man leicht durch Senken der Kugel *e*

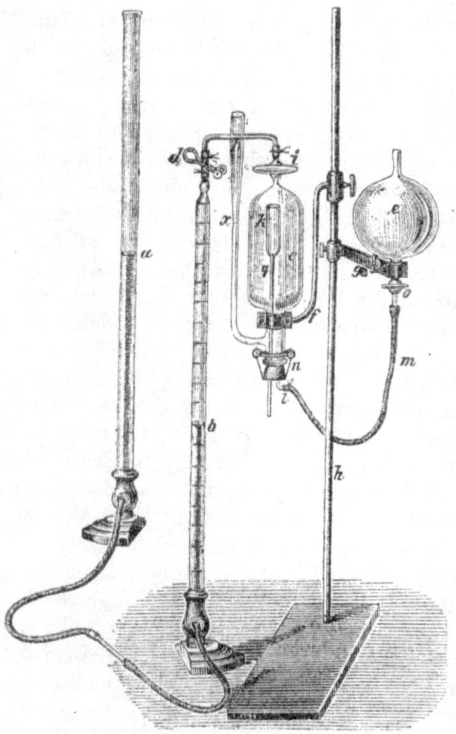

Fig. 46. Apparat von Hempel zur Stickstoffbestimmung.

[1] Zu beziehen von Ephraim Greiner in Stützerbach.

dieselbe in das Entwicklungsgefäß einsaugen. Durch Schließen des Hahnes *o* kann man jeden Augenblick das nötige Einströmen der Schwefelsäure unterbrechen und so mit der größten Leichtigkeit den Übertritt von Luft vermeiden. Man stellt hierauf in dem Apparat durch Heben der Kugel *e* und Öffnen des Hahnes *o* den Atmosphärendruck her und schüttelt so lange, bis bei geschlossenem Hahn *o* nach erneutem Schütteln in *x* kein Steigen des Quecksilbers mehr zu beobachten ist. Bleibt zwischen zwei Schütteloperationen der Quecksilberspiegel bei geschlossenem Hahne *o* in *x* in gleicher Höhe stehen, so ist die Reaktion beendet. Röhrchen *k* ist nur so groß zu wählen, daß das Sprengöl gerade darin Platz hat. Ist die Gasentwicklung beendet, so verbindet man die mit Quecksilber gefüllte und vorher mit ganz wenig Wasser befeuchtete Bürette mit dem Entwicklungsgefäß und führt das Stickoxyd durch Öffnen der Hähne *o*, *i* und *d* und Heben der Kugel *e* in die Bürette über. Unter Berücksichtigung der Tension des Wasserdampfes wird dann das Gasvolumen in bekannter Weise gemessen und berechnet. Die Bürette soll man an einem Ort von gleichmäßiger Temperatur aufbewahren und nur zum Überfüllen das Entwicklungsgefäß neben die Bürette stellen, dabei Erwärmen der Bürette durch die Hände vermeiden. Man kann sodann in längstens 10 Minuten ablesen und in einer Stunde zwei Analysen machen. Die Ablesungen sind vollständig scharf, da in die Glasbüretten keine Schwefelsäure kommen darf.

b) Durch Reduktion mit Eisenoxydulsalz und Säure.

α) Verfahren von Hess: Kochen mit Ferrosulfat in schwefelsaurer Lösung.

Filipp Hess[1] hat auf Grund der von Champion und Pellet (Compt. rend. 83, 707) früher angegebenen Methode der Stickstoffbestimmung in der Nitrozellulose durch Kochen mit Eisenchlorür und Salzsäure (und Messen als Stickoxyd) eine analoge Methode für die flüssigen Salpetersäureester ausgearbeitet.

Hess benutzt nachstehenden Apparat (Fig. 47).

Zu Beginn der Analyse werden in einem etwa 150 bis 200 ccm haltenden Erlenmeyer-Kölbchen *K* etwa 20 bis 25 g kristallisiertes Eisenvitriol in ca. 100 ccm destillierten Wassers gelöst und zu der Flüssigkeit einige reine Platinschnitzel gegeben, um das Stoßen beim Einkochen zu verhindern. Nunmehr wird mit dem von den beiden Röhren r_1 und r_2 durchsetzten Kautschukpfropf das Kölbchen verschlossen, das Rohr r_1 durch entsprechende Stellung des diametral gebohrten, mit reiner Vaseline geschmierten Glashahnes *h* gesperrt, r_2 aber durch Lüften des Quetschhahnes *q* an dem Gummischlauchstück *s* geöffnet. Nachdem durch anhaltendes Kochen alle Luft aus dem Kölbchen vertrieben worden, wird die Wanne *w* mit gut ausgekochter Ätznatronlauge gefüllt, das winklig abgebogene freie Ende des Rohres r_2

[1] Mitteil. Art.- u. Geniewesen 1888. Notizen S. 139.

unter die Laugenoberfläche getaucht und hierauf, nach Entfernung des Gasbrenners unter dem Kölbchen, der Quetschhahn q geschlossen. Man füllt sofort das Meßrohr R mit der Natronlauge und setzt es über die Öffnung von r_2 in die pneumatische Wanne w ein, worauf es passend fixiert wird. — Die in einem kleinen Probegläschen unterdessen bereit gehaltene, genau abgewogene Menge des Nitroglyzerins (0·12 bis 0·16 g) wird nun in ca. 5 bis 6 ccm konzentrierter Schwefelsäure gelöst und die Lösung in die Aufgußschale von r_1 gegossen. Der an den Wänden des Probegläschens haftende Rest der Substanz wird mit etwa 2 bis 3 ccm Schwefelsäure geschüttelt (Schutz des Daumens durch paraffiniertes Papier) und bereitgestellt. Man zieht nunmehr durch vorsichtiges Öffnen des Hahnes h die saure Lösung des Esters in das Kölbchen ab, wobei das Eindringen von Luftblasen sorgfältig zu vermeiden ist, spült zuerst mit der Waschsäure aus dem Probe-

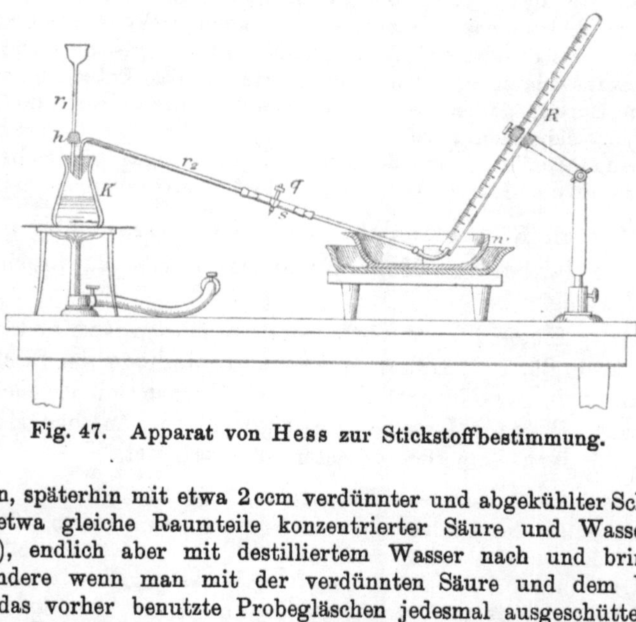

Fig. 47. Apparat von Hess zur Stickstoffbestimmung.

gläschen, späterhin mit etwa 2 ccm verdünnter und abgekühlter Schwefelsäure (etwa gleiche Raumteile konzentrierter Säure und Wasser enthaltend), endlich aber mit destilliertem Wasser nach und bringt so, insbesondere wenn man mit der verdünnten Säure und dem Wasser zuerst das vorher benutzte Probegläschen jedesmal ausgeschüttelt hat, die ganze Estermenge quantitativ in das Kölbchen. Das Eintragen der sauren Lösung muß langsam und partieweise erfolgen, damit sich der Inhalt des Kölbchens nicht zu sehr erhitze. Man wendet schließlich soviel Wasser zum Nachfüllen an, daß in dem Kölbchen etwa 80 ccm Flüssigkeit resultieren. Nachdem man durch Anwärmen einen minimalen Überdruck erzielt hat, wird q vorsichtig geöffnet und das gebildete Stickoxyd mit dem Wasserdampf nach R übergetrieben. Im Anfang sammelt sich nur jene Gasmenge an, welche sich durch die Berührung der konzentrierten Säurelösung mit der Eisenvitriollösung sofort hat bilden können; die übrige Menge des Stickoxyds wird erst bei der Konzentration des Kolbeninhalts durch das Einkochen sukzessive gebildet und ein kleiner Rest davon bleibt sogar in der Flüssigkeit noch zurück, wenn diese schon so konzentriert wurde, daß sie zu stoßen beginnt. Man sperrt in diesem Momente r_2 durch q, entfernt den Brenner und läßt in K neuerdings ein Vakuum entstehen, in welchem sofort der noch absorbierte Rest des Stickoxyds entbunden wird. Nachdem man wieder eine entsprechende Menge destillierten Wassers (etwa 20 bis 25 ccm) in das Kölbchen eingesaugt hat, wird weiter destilliert, wobei der letzte Rest des Stickoxyds mit der größten Leichtigkeit nach R getrieben und der Prozeß beendet wird, sobald das Gasvolum in dem Meßrohre nicht mehr zunimmt. Hess erhielt nach dieser Methode Zahlen, die 18·52, 18·42, 18·55 Prozent Stickstoff (theoretisch 18·50 Prozent) entsprechen.

β) Verfahren von Wolff, Zersetzen mit Eisenchlorür und Salzsäure im Kohlensäurestrom.

C. H. Wolff[1] verwendet zum Vertreiben der atmosphärischen Luft aus dem Reaktionsgefäße vor der Zersetzung durch Ferrosalz, anstatt des Wasserdampfes einen Strom von Kohlensäure und vermeidet dadurch die mit der Behandlung von Überdruckapparaten verbundene Unbequemlichkeit.

In einen kleinen, etwa 50 ccm fassenden Zersetzungskolben kommt die gewogene Menge Nitroglyzerin, dann je 5 ccm vorher aufgekochte und wieder erkaltete konzentrierte Eisenchlorürlösung und Salzsäure; hierauf wird der Kolben geschlossen und aus einem Entwicklungsapparate Kohlensäure zur Vertreibung der Luft durch den Kolben geleitet. Werden die Gasblasen, nachdem das Gasableitungsrohr unter die Meßröhre geschoben ist, von der in dieser enthaltenen 20prozentigen Natronlauge vollkommen absorbiert, so schließt man den Hahn des Kohlensäureentwicklers und erwärmt den Kolben durch eine kleine Gasflamme ganz allmählich, worauf die Zersetzung des Nitroglyzerins unter Entbindung von Stickoxyd vor sich geht. Ist die Zersetzung beendet, so erhitzt man stärker und kocht endlich bis auf wenige Kubikzentimeter ein. Schließlich führt man durch Einleiten von Kohlensäure die letzten Spuren Stickoxyd in die Meßröhre über.

c) Man kann den Stickstoff des Nitroglyzerins auch in Salpetersäure überführen und letztere titrimetrisch oder gewichtsanalytisch (mit Nitron) bestimmen. Hampe[2] zerlegt das Nitroglyzerin mittels konzentrierter Schwefelsäure und Quecksilber, führt die gebildeten Stickstoff-Sauerstoffverbindungen mittels Sauerstoff und Wasserstoffsuperoxyd in Salpetersäure über, und bestimmt letztere durch Titrieren mit Natronlauge. — Einfacher ist es

[1] Repertorium der analyt. Chemie 1881, Nr. 13.
[2] Zeitschr. Berg-, Hütten- u. Salinenwesen Bd. 31.

wohl, das Nitroglyzerin durch Alkali in ein Gemenge von salpetersaurem und salpetrigsaurem Salz überzuführen, sodann mittels Wasserstoffsuperoxyd zu Nitrat zu oxydieren und hierauf die Salpetersäure mittels Nitron gewichtsanalytisch zu bestimmen.[1]

Es sei noch auf eine Broschüre von Dr. Paul Schellbach: „Über die Methoden, den Stickstoffgehalt in Nitroverbindungen zu bestimmen", hingewiesen (Berlin 1884, R. Gaertners Verlag).

d) Silberrad, Phillips und Merrimann (Journ. Soc. Chem. Ind. **25**, 628) verseifen das Nitroglyzerin durch sechsstündiges Erhitzen mit Natronlauge (Wasserbad, guter Rückflußkühler); von den Verseifungsprodukten wird ein aliquoter Teil in einen Rundkolben gegeben, hier mit zwei Teilen gepulvertem Zink und einem Teil reduzierten Eisen in 40prozentiger Natronlauge zu Ammoniak reduziert, das übergehende Ammoniak in $\frac{N}{10}$ Säure aufgefangen und die überschüssige Säure zurücktitriert. Die Autoren erhielten 18·39 Prozent, 18·46 Prozent, 18·53 Prozent N (statt 18·50 Prozent).

4. Stabilität. Bei Beurteilung eines Sprengstoffes spielt die Beständigkeit desselben bei einwirkender Hitze eine wichtige Rolle, da von ihr immer ein Rückschluß auf die Reinheit des fraglichen Präparates gezogen werden kann. Die Salpetersäureester, die Schießwolle und das Nitroglyzerin, zeigen speziell die Tendenz, neben der chemisch gebundenen Salpetersäure noch einen Teil der beim Nitrierungsprozeß im Überschuß vorhandenen Säuren mechanisch aufzunehmen und außerordentlich gut festzuhalten, so daß es selbst durch anhaltendes Waschen mit Alkalien nur schwer gelingt, die letzten Reste dieser freien Säure zu entfernen. Schießwolle ist oft durch ein tagelanges Digerieren mit verdünntem Ammoniak nicht säurefrei zu bekommen. Auch das Nitroglyzerin mit warmer Sodalösung durch einen eingeblasenen kräftigen Luftstrom auf das innigste vermengt, enthält nach dem Auswaschen der Soda noch immer Spuren von Säure. Daß diese anhaftende Säure allmählich den Zusammenhang der Moleküle lockert und schließlich eine vollständige, in der Regel von Explosion begleitete Auflösung herbeiführt, beweisen häufig beobachtete freiwillige Zersetzungen von Nitroglyzerin und Schießbaumwolle, welche nicht selten zu traurigen Unglücksfällen Veranlassung gegeben haben und die stets auf unreine Produkte zurückzuführen sind.

Ein Kriterium für die Reinheit bietet die Beständigkeit bei einer

---

[1] Cf. Bd. II, S. 218. — Zeitschr. Schieß-Sprengstoffwesen I, 232.

gewissen Temperaturerhöhung. Erhitzt man z. B. chemisch reines Nitroglyzerin auf 70 bis 75° C, so ist nach halb- bis einstündiger Versuchsdauer eine Veränderung desselben nicht wahrzunehmen. Anders gestaltet sich jedoch die Sache, wenn das Präparat noch etwas Säure enthält. Die bei 86° C siedende Salpetersäure wird bei obiger Temperatur schon teilweise verdampfen und sich allmählich zersetzen. Schwefelsäure, wenn solche dem Nitroglyzerin von seiner Bereitung her noch anhaftet, wird zwar bei 70 bis 75° C nicht gasförmig, spaltet aber aus dem Glyzerintrinitrat ein äquivalentes Quantum Salpetersäure unter Bildung von Glyzerinschwefelsäure ab. Diese zerfällt leicht in Glyzerin und Schwefelsäure, welch letztere dann den Zersetzungsprozeß von neuem einleitet. Infolge dieser Bildung und des Wiederzerfalles von Glyzerinschwefelsäure vermag eine geringe Menge Schwefelsäure aus Nitroglyzerin schon große Quantitäten Salpetersäure abzuscheiden. — Die abdunstende Salpetersäure erleidet unter den gegebenen Verhältnissen weitere Zersetzungen; einerseits zerfällt sie schon durch das Erwärmen teilweise in Stickstoffdioxyd, salpetrige Säure, Sauerstoff und Wasser, andererseits bilden sich aus ihr durch die Einwirkung der Schwefelsäure, welche in mangelhaft gewaschenem Sprengöl immer vorhanden ist, salpetrige Säure, Wasser und Sauerstoff. Weiterhin wird das infolge der Denitrierung durch die Schwefelsäure regenerierte Glyzerin bei der vorliegenden Temperatur und bei Gegenwart des gebildeten Wassers reduzierend auf die Salpetersäuredämpfe einwirken und ebenfalls einen Impuls zur Entstehung von salpetriger Säure geben. — Tatsächlich entweicht beim Erwärmen von Nitroglyzerin, welches Salpetersäure oder Schwefelsäure oder beide Säuren gleichzeitig enthält, stets salpetrige Säure, auf welche man in der Jodkaliumstärke ein äußerst empfindliches Reagens besitzt. Man kann also die geringsten Spuren anhaftender freier Säure entdecken, wenn man das Nitroglyzerin im Wasserbade längere Zeit erwärmt und die entweichenden Dämpfe mit einem befeuchteten Jodkaliumstärkepapier prüft. Da täglich eine größere Anzahl von Proben dieser Untersuchung unterworfen werden, so richtet man sich zweckmäßig folgende Apparate und Lösungen her:

1. einen Kessel aus 1 mm starkem Kupferblech, von ca. 20 cm Höhe und 20 cm Durchmesser, der bis etwa 2 cm unter den Rand mit Wasser gefüllt ist. Der Kessel ist mit einem gleichfalls aus Kupferblech hergestellten Deckel verschlossen, dessen übergreifender Rand ein Verschieben oder Herabgleiten unmöglich macht, und der 15 bis 20 kreisförmige Öffnungen von 20 mm Durchmesser hat. Eine derselben wird mit einem durchbohrten Kork

verschlossen, in welchem ein Celsiusthermometer steckt, das mit seiner Kugel ca. 10 cm tief in das Wasser eintauchen muß; durch die übrigen Öffnungen des Deckels, deren jede unten mit drei federnden Blechstreifen versehen ist, werden Reagensgläschen mit den Proben in das Wasser geschoben. 2. Reagensgläschen von 16 mm Durchmesser und 14 bis 15 cm Höhe. Man verschließt dieselben durch konische Korkstopfen, auf deren oberer ebenen Fläche Marken zur Unterscheidung der Proben angebracht sind. 3. Eine Partie ꞅ-förmig gekrümmter, etwa 9 cm langer Platindrähte, bestimmt zum Einhängen der Reagenspapierstreifen in die Probiergläschen. Der Papierstreifen wird an den untern Teil des Drahtes angehakt, in das Röhrchen eingeführt und durch Aufsetzen des Korkes so fixiert, daß der Papierstreifen zwischen Nitroglyzerin und Kork frei in der Röhre hängt. 4. Jodkaliumstärkepapier. Nach einer Vorschrift von Oberst Majendie soll man 2·7 g weiße, mit kaltem Wasser gewaschene Stärke zu 248·5 g destilliertem Wasser geben, umrühren, zum Sieden erhitzen und 10 Minuten im gelinden Kochen erhalten; ferner 0·9 g aus Alkohol umkristallisiertes Jodkalium ebenfalls in 248·5 g Wasser lösen und beide Lösungen innig mischen. Inzwischen hat man sich Streifen aus weißem, mit Wasser gewaschenen Filtrierpapier geschnitten, welche mindestens 10 Sekunden in der Lösung gelassen, sodann herausgezogen und in einem säure- und staubfreien Raum getrocknet werden. Das trockene Papier schneidet man dann in kleine Streifchen von 10 mm Breite und 30 mm Länge und bewahrt letztere in wohlverstopften Flaschen aus dunklem Glase auf, da sie namentlich in feuchtem Zustande ziemlich lichtempfindlich sind. Es ist deshalb auch nicht rätlich, an Stelle des kupfernen Kessels ein Glasgefäß zu benutzen, da letzteres den Lichtstrahlen den Durchgang gestatten würde. 5. Glyzerinlösung, hergestellt aus 0·5 Tln. reinem Glyzerin + 0·5 Wasser (oder auch 0·4 : 0·6). Feuchtes Jodkaliumstärkepapier ist ungleich reaktionsempfindlicher als trockenes. Das Befeuchten mit Wasser wäre wegen des Verdunstens zwecklos. Man verwendet daher eine 50- oder 40prozentige Glyzerinlösung. Zur Aufbewahrung der Lösung empfiehlt sich ein Glasfläschchen, durch dessen durchbohrten Kork ein feiner Haarpinsel gesteckt ist; mit diesem trägt man die Flüssigkeit auf die obere Hälfte des Papiers auf, bzw. macht auf das letztere in halber Höhe einen Strich.

Die Stabilitätsprobe muß in einem absolut säurefreien Raum ausgeführt werden. Man erhitzt das Wasser des Kessels über einer bequem zu regulierenden Flamme, z. B. einem Petroleumofen (mit dem man sehr leicht eine konstante Hitze erzielt) auf 83° C (180° Fahrenheit)[1] und reguliert die Flamme derart, daß größere Temperaturschwankungen nicht mehr möglich sind. Inzwischen hat man ca. 3·2 g (= 2 ccm) des zu testenden Nitroglyzerins so in ein Probeglas eingewogen, daß die Seiten der Röhre nicht beschmutzt werden. In Fabrikslaboratorien wägt man nicht ab, sondern bedient sich einer Pipette, welche bis zu einer Marke obige Menge faßt und deren Inhalt man auf den Boden des Probierglases tropfen läßt. Beim Arbeiten mit der Pipette muß man sich natürlich sehr hüten, Nitroglyzerin in den Mund zu bekommen. Das Reagenspapier darf nicht mit den Händen berührt werden, weil die geringste Unreinlichkeit das Papier beeinflußt. Man bringt ein Streifchen mittels einer Pinzette auf einen großen flachen Korkstopfen, sticht mit einer zweiten Pinzette ein kleines Loch in das Papier und führt den Platindraht durch, führt sodann den Draht und das Papier in das Probeglas ein und befestigt dieselben durch Aufsetzen des Korkes. Die Gläser mit den Proben werden dann unter Notierung der Zeit in ein Wasserbad eingesetzt, und zwar so tief, daß sich die zu prüfende Substanz in gleicher Höhe mit der Thermometerkugel befindet. Während man nun die Temperatur des Bades durch genaue Regulierung der Flamme immer möglichst konstant hält, nimmt man von Zeit zu Zeit die Gläschen heraus und betrachtet die Papiere. Die Probe ist beendigt, wenn die schwachbraune Linie, welche nach einiger Zeit an der Scheidelinie zwischen dem trockenen und dem feuchten Teile des Papiers erscheint, in der Farbe der braunen Linie des „Normalfarbepapiers" gleich ist. Das zu prüfende Nitroglyzerin gilt nicht als genügend rein, wenn die zur Erzeugung der Normalfarbe nötige Zeit nicht mindestens 15 Minuten beträgt. Gewöhnlich beträgt dieselbe mehr, so daß die Probe nach einer halben bis einer Stunde abgebrochen werden kann, ohne daß bis dahin die Braunfärbung eingetreten ist.

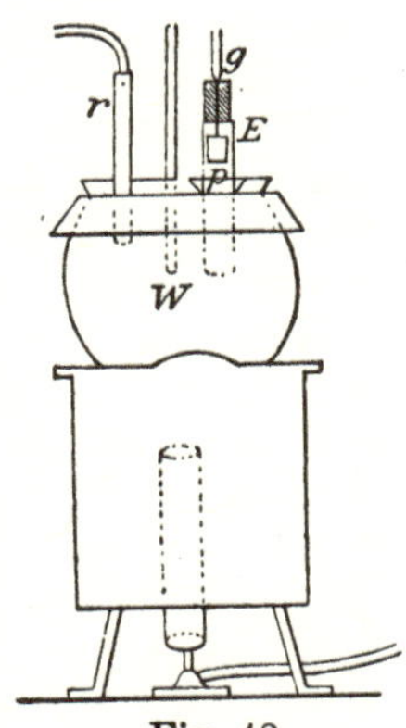

Fig. 48.
W Wasserbad, *E* Reagensglas mit Glasstab *g* und Probepapier *p*.

Diese Methode rührt von Abel her, der sich des in Fig. 48 dargestellten Apparates bediente.

Es ist nicht zu verkennen, daß diese Probe allein für die Beurteilung der chemischen Stabilität nicht maßgebend sein kann,

[1] Für andere als kriegstechnische Zwecke genügt Erhitzen auf 72° C (160° F).

weil es sich weniger darum handelt, ob früher oder später eine erste Spur von Zersetzung auftritt unter gewissen Bedingungen,[1] als darum, ob die so eingeleitete Zersetzung überhaupt fortschreitet und ob das Fortschreiten langsam oder rasch erfolgt, also ob die im letzten Falle progressiv sich ansammelnde Wärme endlich zu einer stürmischen Zersetzung, oder zu einer Explosion in kürzerer oder längerer Zeit führen kann.

Hess hat daher (M. A. G. 1879, S. 349) eine Methode ausgearbeitet, welche gestattet, den Zersetzungsverlauf in einzelnen Stadien genau zu verfolgen.

Von dem zu untersuchenden Explosivstoffe wird ein bestimmtes, gewogenes Quantum (ca. 0·5 g) in einem Porzellanschiffchen möglichst gleichmäßig ausgebreitet und mit diesem in eine Glasröhre *R* geschoben, welche sich in einem, durch Gasbrenner *B* und Thermoregulator *T* stets bei gleicher Temperatur erhaltenen Luftbade befindet, d. i. einem aus Schwarzblech angefertigten Kasten, der oben noch Thermometer *C* enthält. Die Röhre *R* ist von der Austrittsstelle *m* an verengt, bei *n* knieförmig nach abwärts gebogen und bei *p* wieder (auf eine Länge von 5 cm) erweitert (Fig. 49).

Während der Explosivstoff auf eine gewisse höhere Temperatur gebracht und für die Versuchdauer kontinuierlich bei derselben erhalten wird, läßt man über ihn einen langsamen Strom atmosphärischer Luft hinziehen, welche durch den Aspirator *A* angesaugt, beim Passieren des Kölbchens *a* mittels Jodkaliumstärkelösung von Ozon und nitrosen Gasen, beim Durchgange durch das mit Ätzkalistücken gefüllte Glasrohr *b* von Kohlensäure und anderen noch nicht absorbierten flüchtigen Säuren und endlich bei Passierung des U-förmigen Rohres *c* von jeder Spur von Feuchtigkeit befreit wird. Die so gereinigte und getrocknete Luft ist sehr geeignet, von dem Augenblick des Beginnes der Zersetzung an, alle flüchtigen Zersetzungsprodukte, unter welchen bekanntlich die zuerst auftretenden Sauerstoffverbindungen des Stickstoffs durch ihr Verhalten gegen Jodmetalle so gut charakterisiert sind, aufzunehmen und wird, mit ihnen beladen, vor ihrem Eintritt in den Aspirator durch das Kölbchen *k*, welches Jodzinkstärkelösung enthält, und durch den größeren Kolben *l*, in welchem eine weitere mit Wasser verdünnte Menge dieser Lösung sich befindet, geführt. In *k* befinden sich 30 ccm Lösung, welche durch Herstellung einer dünnen Stärkeflüssigkeit und Eintragen von 20 g Jodzink pro Liter zu bereiten und für Beschickung des Kolbens *l* noch mit dem vierfachen Volumen Wasser zu verdünnen ist. Die charakteristischen Zersetzungsreaktionen

---

[1] Durch ganz geringen Zusatz von Quecksilberchlorid werden die Stickoxyde zurückgehalten und so die Prüfung illusorisch gemacht. In den englischen Kolonien werden neuerdings Dynamite mit Quecksilbergehalt nicht eingelassen. Die Prüfung auf Quecksilber erfolgt spektralanalytisch nach Dupré oder chemisch nach Hargreaves (Soc. Chem. Ind. 1907, S. 813).

spielen sich insgesamt im Innern des Kölbchens *k* ab, während der Inhalt des Kolbens *l* nur dazu dient, einen etwa zu rasch werdenden Verlauf der Zersetzung durch Bläuung der in ihm enthaltenen Flüssigkeit erkennen zu lassen. Zur Regulierung der Gleichförmigkeit des

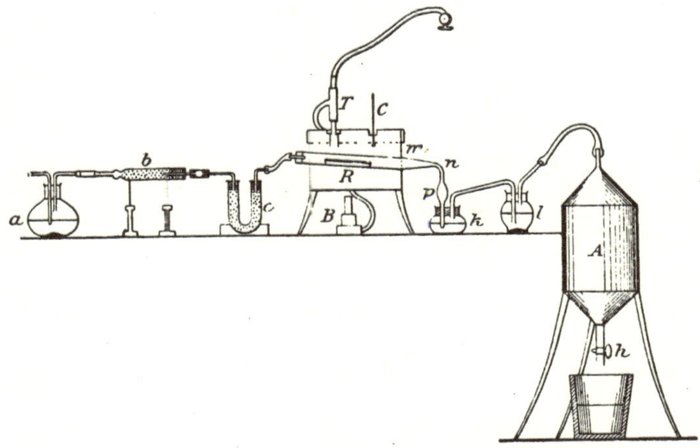

Fig. 49. Apparat von Hess zur Stabilitätsprüfung.

Luftstromes kann die Anzahl der Luftblasen festgestellt werden, welche die Flüssigkeit in *k* in einer Minute zu passieren haben. Durch Regulierung mit dem Abflußhahn *h* des Aspirators *A* läßt sich die gewünschte Stärke, bzw. Geschwindigkeit des Luftstromes jederzeit erzielen. — Hess regulierte derart, daß binnen 6 Stunden 10 Liter Luft den Apparat passierten.

Die ersten Zeichen einer Zersetzung können in dem Auftreten eines blauen oder violetten Ringes erblickt werden, welcher sich in der Nähe des unter die Flüssigkeitsoberfläche in *k* tauchenden Rohrendes allmählich ansetzt. Man kann den Moment der Wahrnehmung der ersten Spur jenes farbigen Ansatzes als das erste Stadium, den Moment, wo der Ring sich vollkommen geschlossen hat und deutlich sichtbar geworden ist, als ein zweites Stadium, den Augenblick, in welchem eine erste Spur von Färbung der Flüssigkeit in *k* bemerkbar wird, als ein drittes, jenen Zeitpunkt, in welchem die Färbung deutlich auftritt, bzw. in welchem sie so stark ist, daß die Flüssigkeit ihre Durchsichtigkeit in Schichten von etwa 5 cm Dicke verliert, als ein viertes, event. fünftes Stadium der Zersetzung ansehen, und kann endlich die Exponierung selbst so lange fortsetzen, bis eine Entzündung oder Explosion des Präparates eintritt. Für praktische Zwecke dürfte es hinreichen, die Beobachtung nicht weiter als bis zur deutlichen Färbung der 30 ccm messenden Flüssigkeit in *k* fortzusetzen, weil man damit schon einen guten Einblick in das Tempo des Zersetzungsvorgangs bekommt. Eine weitere Ausdehnung der Versuche nimmt nicht nur zu viel Zeit in Anspruch, sondern gefährdet jedesmal auch den ganzen Apparat oder mindestens das Thermometer und den Thermoregulator.

Hess hat mit Nitroglyzerin folgende Resultate erhalten:

	Zeit in Minuten, vom Beginn der Exponierung an			
	bis zum Erscheinen der ersten Spur eines Ansatzes	bis zum Deutlichwerden und der Vollendung eines blauen Ringes	bis zum Eintritt einer Spur von Färbung der Flüssigkeit	bis zur deutlichen Färbung der Flüssigkeit
Nitroglyzerin I bei 70°	238	676	1096	1816
	215	598	1002	1738
Nitroglyzerin II bei 70°	180	412	660	840
	183	436	nicht fortgesetzt	
Nitroglyzerin bei 100°	5	6	7	9
	5	6	8	10

Auf der von Hess angegebenen Prüfungsmethode beruhend, haben später Dr. Weeren und Dr. Schellbach Stabilitätsapparate angegeben, worüber Hess in den Mitteil. Art. u. Geniewesen 1884, S. 202 Näheres mitgeteilt hat.

Dr. Weeren verwendet als Wärmebad kochende Flüssigkeiten von verschiedenem Siedepunkt (Aceton, SP. 56°; Äthylalkohol, SP. 78°; Wasser, SP. 100°) und bringt einen Rückflußkühler *R* an, so daß die Dämpfe immer wieder kondensiert nach dem Bad zurückgelangen. Der Apparat (Fig. 50) besteht aus einem weißblechernen Siedegefäß *A*, welches einen aufgelöteten Deckel mit acht zylindrischen Einsatzhülsen *hh* besitzt, wovon eine zur Aufnahme eines Thermoregulators dient, während die übrigen sieben für die Reagensröhren mit den Sprengstoffproben bestimmt sind. Der das Siedegefäß und den Brenner umschließende, bis zum Deckel *T* reichende eisenblecherne Mantel *M* bewirkt die Zuführung der nötigen Luft bei Vermeidung jedes überflüssigen Zuges und jeder schädlichen Abkühlung.

Die, die Sprengstoffproben enthaltenden Zersetzungsgläser sind in den kupfernen Einsatzhülsen *h* von nebenstehender Einrichtung (Fig. 51) eingebracht.

Der untere Teil der Gläser *g* ist sehr verengt und dient zur Aufnahme der Proben. Es soll hierdurch die möglichst rasche Annahme der Badtemperatur durch den Explosivstoff begünstigt werden. Der Zwischenraum zwischen *h* und *g* ist mit Wasser gefüllt, um so ein gewisses Wärmereservoir zu erhalten, welches gegen Temperaturschwankungen schützt. Durch das unten etwas aufgebogene Rohr *u* wird vollkommen gereinigte, trockene Luft über den Explosivstoff geführt, während die mit den eventuell auftretenden Zersetzungsgasen beladene Luft in das U-förmige Rohr L und zu einem gemeinsamen Aspirator gesaugt wird. Das Rohr L ist mit Asbest beschickt, welches mit Jodkaliumstärkekleister getränkt wurde, um die auftretenden nitrosen Säuren anzuzeigen.

Dr. Schellbach benutzt einen Apparat, welcher aus einem durch ein Wasserbad mit konstanter Temperatur geheizten, nach außen zu durch Kieselgurschichten isolierten Luftbade besteht, in welchem die Röhren mit den Sprengstoffproben in kurzen Einsatzzylindern hängen.

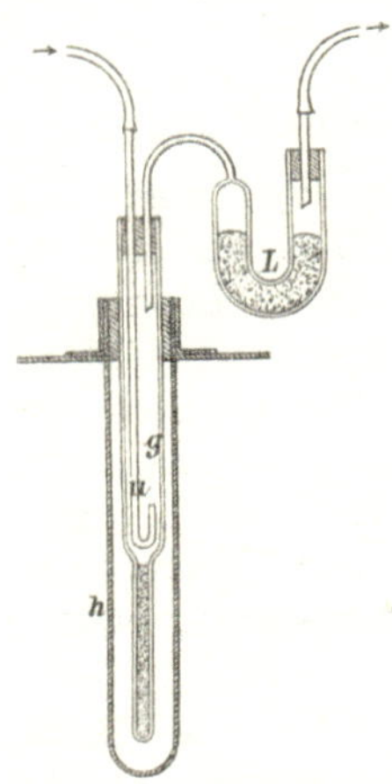

Fig. 51. Zersetzungsglas von Weeren.

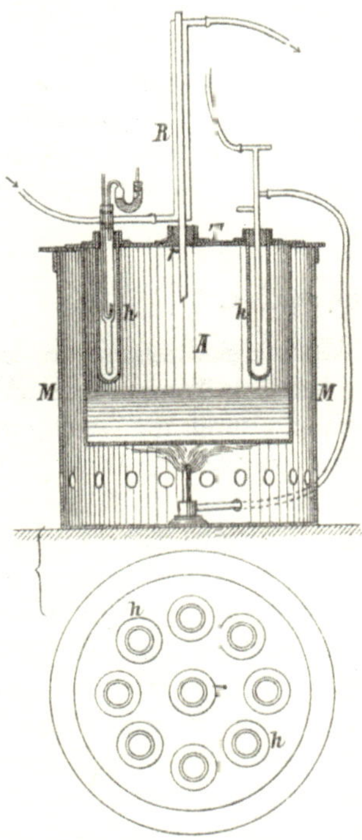

Fig. 50. Apparat von Weeren.

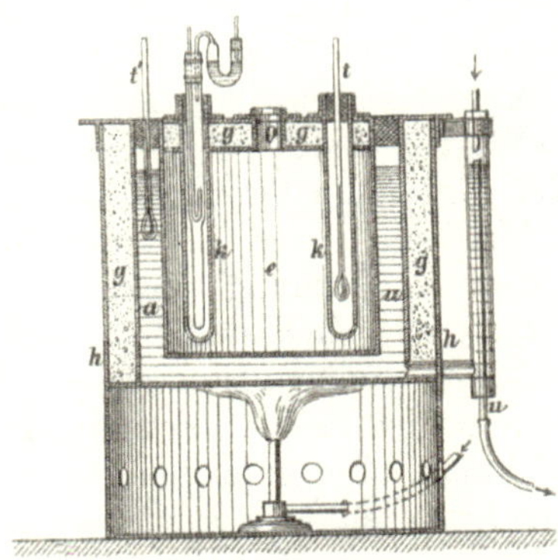

Fig. 52. Apparat von Schellbach.

a a (Fig. 52) ist das Wasserbad mit konstantem Niveau (mit Überflußrohr *u*), *g g* sind die isolierenden Gurschichten, zwischen Blechwände (auch zwischen jene des Deckels) eingefüllt. Im Wasserbad ist das Luftbad *e*, in welchem die kupfernen Einsatzhülsen *k k* hängen. In letzteren sind wieder, in Pfropfen gefaßt, die Zersetzungsröhren mit den zu prüfenden Substanzen vorhanden. Der Zwischenraum zwischen Hülsen und Zersetzungsröhren wird mit Wasser ausgefüllt. In einer der Hülsen befindet sich ein Thermometer, in einer zweiten ein Thermoregulator, die übrigen Hülsen enthalten Sprengstoffproben. Bei *o* kann event. Rückflußkühler eingesetzt werden. — Für die Untersuchung bei 100° verwendet Schellbach statt des Wasserluftbades ein nach außen zu mit Kieselgurschichten isoliertes Paraffinbad mit ähnlichen Einsätzen wie beim Luftbad. Die Glasröhren sind hier in die Kupferhülsen durch Ringe aus Asbestpappe eingepaßt.

Die Einrichtung der Zersetzungsröhren und ihrer Vorlagen ist dieselbe wie bei dem Apparate von Weeren.

Man kann auch das Studium der Zersetzungserscheinungen in geschlossenen Reagensgläsern vornehmen, indem man in letztere blaue Lakmuspapierstreifchen und Ozonpapierstreifchen (mäßig befeuchtet) einführt. Es ergeben sich dann etwa die folgenden, deutlich voneinander zu unterscheidenden Zersetzungsstadien: Rötung des blauen Lakmuspapiers — Bläuung des Ozonpapiers — Angriff des Korkes durch nitrose Säuren — Auftreten der gelben Dämpfe der Untersalpetersäure, deren Menge dann sogar kolorimetrisch geschätzt werden kann.

e) Entzündung bzw. Detonation.

1. Selbstentzündung. Wie bei der Schießbaumwolle hat man auch beim Sprengöl außer der durch erhöhte Temperatur oder gewaltigen Druck erfolgenden explosiven Zersetzung ein langsames Zerfallen des Sprengöles unter Gasentwicklung beobachtet; doch kommt diese freiwillige Zersetzung nur bei unreinem Produkte vor. Insbesondere scheint die Gegenwart geringer Mengen Salpetersäure oder Untersalpetersäure die langsame, spontane Zersetzung zu begünstigen. Das in Zersetzung begriffene Nitroglyzerin färbt sich unter Bildung von salpetriger Säure, Stickoxydul, Kohlensäure grün; nach und nach scheiden sich Oxalsäurekristalle aus, und nach einigen Monaten ist das Nitroglyzerin in eine sulzige, gallertartige Masse, bestehend aus Oxalsäure, Wasser, Ammoniak usw. übergegangen. Bei gewöhnlicher Temperatur ist die Zersetzung eine langsame und — besonders bei offenen Gefäßen und kleineren Mengen Sprengöl — nicht gerade gefährliche. Durch Rühren mittels einer Rührvorrichtung oder mittels komprimierter Luft kann die entstehende Wärme abgeführt werden, und die Zersetzung erfolgt unter reichlicher Entwicklung von nitrosen Dämpfen ohne Explosionserscheinungen. Findet jedoch die Selbstzersetzung in Gefäßen statt, welche den Gasen keinen oder nur einen verhältnismäßig geringen Abzug gewähren, dann tritt infolge der Ansammlung von Wärme schließlich eine Explosion ein.

2. Entzündung durch mechanische Einwirkungen. Nitroglyzerin ist sehr empfindlich gegen Schlag und Stoß. Es detoniert leicht durch Schlag von Eisen auf Eisen oder von Eisen auf harten Stein; Schlag von Kupfer auf Kupfer oder Holz auf Holz ist weniger wirksam. — Werden auf einem Amboß einige Tropfen Sprengöl durch einen kräftigen Hammerschlag getroffen, so detonieren nur die direkt getroffenen Teile, auf die benachbarten setzt sich die Explosion nicht fort, es sei denn, daß die Masse eingehüllt oder wenigstens bedeckt ist.

Zur Prüfung eines Sprengstoffes auf seine Empfindlichkeit gegen Stoß usw. sind — nach Will[1] — sehr mannigfaltige Methoden in Anwendung gekommen. Man prüft das Verhalten des Explosivstoffes:

a) durch Aufschlagen mit einem Hammer, wobei durch die Wahl wechselnd harter Unterlagen eine Abstufung der Bedingung möglich ist. b) Man reibt den Explosivstoff in einer rauhen Porzellanschale mit einem harten Stempel oder zwischen rauhen Flächen, wie mit Sand oder Glaspapier überzogenen Brettern. c) Dupré in London benutzt den gleitenden Stoß eines harten Holzstabes auf dem Holz- oder Steinboden, — ein Verfahren, das als eine Kombination von Stoß und Reibung betrachtet werden kann. d) Man läßt den Explosivstoff mit oder ohne Umhüllung von verschiedenen Fallhöhen auf harte Unterlagen fallen. e) Die zu prüfende Substanz wird mit einem Gewehr beschossen, wobei die Entfernung des Gewehres, bzw. Geschwindigkeit des Geschosses, die Dicke der durchschossenen Schicht und andere Bedingungen variiert werden können (Beschußprobe). f) Die verbreitetste und am meisten zur Aufstellung von Tabellen der relativen Empfindlichkeit von Sprengstoffen benutzte Methode ist die sog. Fallhammermethode, bei welcher ermittelt wird, welche Fallhöhe für einen Hammer von bestimmtem Gewicht erforderlich ist, um den Sprengstoff zur Detonation zu bringen. g) Verhalten gegen eine Knallquecksilbersprengkapsel. Eine Hülse wird mit der zu prüfenden Substanz gefüllt, in die Mitte derselben wird eine Sprengkapsel eingeführt und letztere entzündet. Je nach der Stärke (0·3 bis 3·0 g Ladung) der zur Auslösung der Explosion erforderlichen Sprengkapsel beurteilt man den Empfindlichkeitsgrad des Explosivstoffes. Anstatt den Explosivstoff freiliegend zu prüfen, kann man ihn auch in einen Bleizylinder einschließen. Unter letzterer Bedingung zeigen sich Substanzen noch als explosibel, die an freier Luft keine explosive Zersetzung mehr erfahren.

Mit dem Gewehr beschossen, explodiert Nitroglyzerin bei einer Entfernung von 150 m. — Betreffs der Versuche mit der Fallhammermethode sei auf die Arbeit von Prof. Dr. F. Lenze[2] hingewiesen.

---

[1] Zeitschr. Schieß-Sprengstoffwesen I, S. 210.

[2] Zeitschr. Schieß-Sprengstoffwesen I, S. 287.

Lenze verwendet zur Ausschaltung von Fehlerquellen, die aus wechselnder Bodenbeschaffenheit usw. resultieren, einen feststehenden Fallhammer. Auf einem festem, gemauerten Fundament ruht ein massiver, viereckiger Eisenklotz mit gehärtetem Amboß. Die Gleitschienen, zwischen welchen sich das Fallgewicht bewegt, sind durch eiserne Stützen festgehalten, welche in die Zimmerwand eingefügt sind. Die Vorrichtung zum Festhalten des Fallgewichts ist auf einer besonderen, an den Stützen der Gleitschiene mitbefestigten Schiene beweglich, auf welch letzterer auch die zum Ablesen der Fallhöhe bestimmte verstellbare Skala angebracht ist. Als Fallgewichte kommen 2, 5, 10 und 20 kg-Gewichte zur Anwendung. — Zur Prüfung des Sprengstoffes hat Dr. H. Kast sich nebenstehenden Apparat (Fig. 53) schützen lassen (D.R.G.M. 281 313): Der Teil A, der auf dem festruhenden großen Amboß F aufgelegt ist, dient zum Festhalten des eigentlichen Prüfungsapparates; letzterer besteht aus dem kleinen Amboß B, dem darüber befindlichen Schlagbolzen C und dem Führungsring D, welcher den Amboß und Schlagring enganliegend umschließt. Die Schlagflächen von Amboß und Schlagbolzen passen genau aufeinander und sind $^1/_2$ qcm groß; zwischen beiden befindet sich die Sprengstoffprobe E.

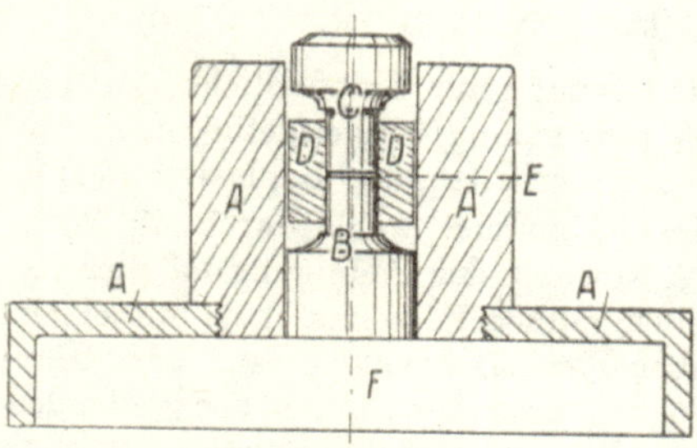

Fig. 53. Apparat von Kast.

Will prüfte trockenes Trinitroglyzerin mit einem Fallhammer von 2 kg bei auf die Probe aufgesetztem Stempel und fand, daß eine Detonation bei 4 cm Fallhöhe eintrat. H. Kast erhielt mit seinem, oben angegebenen Prüfungsapparat mit dem 2 kg-Gewicht eine Detonation bei 4 cm Fallhöhe, mit dem 10 kg-Gewicht bei 2 cm Fallhöhe. Blochmann erhielt eine Detonation mit einem Hammergewicht von 250 g bei 5 cm Fallhöhe, mit einem Hammer von 100 g bei 10 cm.[1] — Gody gibt an, daß 65 mg Trinitroglyzerin von 16° durch ein Fallgewicht von 450 g aus 45 cm Fallhöhe detonierten, dagegen 65 mg Trinitroglyzerin von 94° schon bei 22 cm Fallhöhe durch 450 g Gewicht explodierten, woraus die größere Empfindlichkeit des erwärmten Nitroglyzerins hervorgeht.

Mit Rücksicht auf seine sehr große Empfindlichkeit ist das Nitroglyzerin als solches, und auch in Lösungen, durch die Polizeiverordnung vom 14. September 1905 als nicht transportfähig bezeichnet und vom Verkehr ausgeschlossen worden.

[1] Brunswig gibt an: bei Fallhammer von 250 g explodierte das Sprengöl bei weniger als 5 cm, bei Fallhammer von 100 g bei 5 bis 10 cm Fallhöhe.

Über die Empfindlichkeit gefrorenen Nitroglyzerins sei folgendes bemerkt: Schon Nobel[1] hat darauf aufmerksam gemacht, daß gefrorenes Nitroglyzerin unempfindlicher gegen Stoß und Schlag ist wie flüssiges. Dasselbe haben die Versuche von Mowbray[2] gelehrt, welcher infolge dieser Erkenntnis das Nitroglyzerin stets in gefrorenem Zustande beförderte und bei seinen umfangreichen Transporten viele Jahre lang angeblich keinerlei Unfall erfuhr. W. Cronquist[3] fand in Übereinstimmung mit vorstehendem, daß Nitroglyzerin

bei 30° . . . . . . 0·6 bis 0·7 mkg,
bei 15° . . . . . . 0·8 mkg,
bei 0° (ganz gefroren) 1·0 bis 1·5 mkg

Stoßarbeit zur Detonationseinleitung bedurfte. Bei 10 bis 12° kam ein teilweise flüssiges, teilweise noch hartes Material unter 0·3 bis 0·4 mkg zur Detonation. Eine Aufklärung über die Empfindlichkeit dieses Gemenges erblickt Cronquist in der Gegenwart der sehr harten Nitroglyzerinkristalle, welche beim Stoß auf den flüssigen Teil des Nitroglyzerins dieselbe Wirkung ausübten, wie Sand oder Eisenpartikelchen. — Auch Beckerhinn[4] fand die theoretisch zu erwartende geringere Empfindlichkeit des gefrorenen Nitroglyzerins gegenüber dem flüssigen durch Versuche bestätigt, indem er nachwies, daß eine für die Detonation flüssigen Sprengöls noch ausreichende Sprengkapsel, denselben Sprengstoff in gefrorenem Zustande nicht mehr zur Explosion brachte, und daß mit einem Fallgewicht von 2·13 kg bei einer Stoßfläche von 7 qmm die Explosionsgrenze für flüssiges Nitroglyzerin bei einer Fallhöhe von 0·78 m, für gefrorenes hingegen bei einer Fallhöhe von 2·13 m lag. Er fand also, daß eine Stoßarbeit von 1·66 mkg für flüssiges und von 4·53 mkg für festes Nitroglyzerin zur Detonation erforderlich ist. — Hess[5] hat aus seinen zahlreichen Versuchen über die Explosionsfähigkeit gefrorener Sprengstoffe ebenfalls die Überzeugung gewonnen, daß Sprengöl überhaupt in gefrorenem Zustande gegen mechanische Einwirkungen sich indifferenter verhalte als das flüssige Produkt. Will[6] hat Versuche mit einem Fallhammer von 1 kg angestellt, und zwar bei Anwendung von etwa drei Tropfen (0·1 g) gefrorenen Nitroglyzerins, das auf etwa −20° abgekühlt war. Hierfür war eine Fallhöhe von

[1] Wagners Jahresbericht 1869, S. 260.
[2] Dinglers polyt. Journ. 1869, S. 172.
[3] Österr. Berg- u. Hüttenmänn. Zeitschr. 1894, S. 221.
[4] Wagners Jahresber. 1876, S. 486.
[5] Mitteil. Art. u. Geniewesen 1876, S. 213.
[6] Zeitschr. Berg-, Hütten- u. Salinenwesen 1905, S. 26.

38 bis 40 cm notwendig, während für flüssiges Nitroglyzerin von 15° eine Fallhöhe von 10 cm zur Detonationseinleitung genügte. Nach Bredig ist es nicht ausgeschlossen, daß die Selbstentzündung bzw. Explosion bei gefrorenem oder halbgefrorenem Trinitroglyzerin auf der spontanen Entstehung elektrischer Leitungen beruht.

3. Entzündung durch hohe Temperatur oder Flamme. Das Nitroglyzerin ist bei gewöhnlicher Temperatur wenig flüchtig, mehr bei 50°. Bei plötzlicher Erhitzung auf 180° explodiert es. Bei gewöhnlicher Temperatur ist das Nitroglyzerin durch die Berührung mit brennenden oder glühenden Körpern nicht zur Explosion, selbst schwer zur Entzündung zu bringen. Entzündet brennt es ruhig ab. Einige Tropfen Nitroglyzerin auf ein Platinblech gegossen, lassen sich mit Hilfe einer Bunsenflamme nur langsam entzünden; erst nach 20 bis 30 Sekunden fängt die Masse Feuer und verbrennt mit schwacher, grünlich-fahler Flamme ohne Geräusch. Meist weicht ein Teil des Öles aus oder bleibt unverbrannt zurück und läßt sich erst durch weiteres Erwärmen zur Entflammung bringen. H. Biltz deutet diesen Vorgang wie folgt: Durch die Flamme werden die dieser zunächst liegenden Moleküle zur Zerlegung gebracht. Bei der Schwierigkeit, die Zerlegung weiter zu verbreiten, werden die benachbarten Moleküle erst viel später und die weiter entfernten durch diese erst noch später entzündet, und die Zerlegung verbreitet sich also langsam durch die Masse. Hierdurch erklärt sich, daß das dichte Nitroglyzerin nur langsam verbrennt. Wenn durch länger dauernde Erwärmung an einer Stelle oder durch die Erhitzung einer größeren Menge bereits eine leichte Zersetzung und dadurch eine Tendenz zur Trennung der verbundenen Atome vorhanden ist, so kann eine weitere geringe Erhitzung an dem Zersetzungsorte, hervorgebracht durch direkte Wärmemitteilung oder durch starken Stoß, die partielle Detonation und damit die Explosion großer Mengen von Sprengöl hervorrufen. Eine Detonation tritt um so leichter ein, je mehr das Sprengöl eingeschlossen ist, je mehr also die Verbrennungsgase am Entweichen behindert sind und unter Druck geraten. Dann hat ein Erhitzen auf 180° oder darüber unfehlbar eine Explosion zur Folge.

Oskar Hagen hat vergleichende Versuche angestellt, indem derselbe einmal einen Tropfen Sprengöl in einem Reagensgläschen einer innerhalb 10 Minuten von 140 auf 200° C steigenden Erhitzung aussetzte, das andere Mal einen Tropfen während einer Minute von 177 auf 187° C erhitzt. Zur Ausführung der Versuche diente ein kleines Paraffinbad, worin — durch Klammern oder sonstwie festgehalten — sich ein Thermometer (bis zur halben Höhe des Paraffins) befindet und in das man im gewünschten Moment das Reagensglas so einschiebt daß dessen unteres Ende sich mit der Quecksilberkugel des Thermometers in gleicher Höhe befindet; nach erfolgter Detonation liest man sofort die Temperatur des Bades ab. — Nitroglyzerin erleidet schon bei ca. 150° C eine allmählich weiterschreitende partielle Zersetzung; beim ersten Versuche füllte sich daher, bei 150° C anfangend, das Reagensglas nach und nach mit salpetrigen Dämpfen, der Tropfen verschwand, aber eine Explosion trat nicht ein. — Beim zweiten Versuche erfolgte Explosion und zwar wurde in zehnmaliger Wiederholung die Explosionstemperatur im Mittel zu 183·7° C bestimmt.

Victor Meyer pflegte in seinen Vorlesungen folgenden Versuch zu zeigen: Einige Tropfen Nitroglyzerin wurden in ein dünnwandiges Kapillarrohr aufgesaugt und dieses Röhrchen in eine Flamme gebracht; es erfolgt eine lebhafte Explosion, aber jedesmal explodierte nur ein Teil des Sprengöls, trotzdem der aufgesaugte Tropfen im Röhrchen eine zusammenhängende, durch Luftbläschen nicht unterbrochene Masse bildete. Bringt man dann den Rest des Kapillarrohres noch einmal in die Flamme, so erfolgt stets eine zweite Explosion. Danach vermag also die Explosion des einen durch die Flamme erwärmten und zur brisanten Zersetzung gebrachten Teiles des Nitroglyzerins nicht die übrige Masse zur Explosion zu bringen. Nitroglyzerin ist also ein schlechter Leiter der eigenen Explosion.

4. Initialzündung. Ganz anders liegen die Verhältnisse, wenn das Sprengöl durch Initialzündung zur Explosion gebracht wird, d. h. dadurch, daß eine geringe Menge eines andern, durch Stoß oder Entzündung leicht zur momentanen Explosion zu bringenden, hochbrisanten Sprengstoffes innerhalb oder dicht neben der Masse des Sprengöls entzündet wird. Als Initialstoff eignet sich am besten Knallquecksilber. Durch die plötzliche Erschütterung infolge des Initialstoßes werden sämtliche Moleküle des Sprengöls gleichzeitig getroffen und zur Zerlegung veranlaßt.

Wie in der Einleitung schon geschildert, hat Nobel in seinen englischen Patenten Nr. 1813 (1864) und Nr. 1345 (1867) zuerst die Herbeiführung der Detonation des Nitroglyzerins durch Knallquecksilber-Sprengkapseln angegeben. Nach Berthelot wird durch die kinetische Energie des Detonatorstoßes, die sich in Wärme verwandelt, die Temperatur einer, wenn auch kleinen Menge Nitroglyzerins gleich zu Anfang so gesteigert, daß die „kritische Verbrennungsgeschwindigkeit“ (Threlfall) überschritten wird. Die Detonation pflanzt sich wellenförmig fort, indem die Explosionswelle inmitten der sich umwandelnden Materie fast momentan einen gewissen Zustand herstellt, charakterisiert durch die Bildung einer regelmäßigen Oberfläche, auf welcher sich die Umwandlung vollzieht und welche Orte gleichen Druckes und gleicher Temperatur darstellt. Sie tritt bei stark erhöhtem Druck gegen die Nachbarteile auf, wobei die Umwandlung der regellosen Bewegung in die geordnete offenbar den abnorm hohen Drücken zuzuschreiben ist. Diese enorm hohen Drucke aber werden durch den Initialimpuls von außerordentlicher Geschwindigkeit unter augenblicklicher Entfaltung der gesamten Reaktionswärme lokal erzeugt und veranlassen durch den Gasstoß in regelmäßig wiederkehrender, kontinuierlicher Folge von Schicht zu Schicht, chemische und damit auch teilweise thermische und mechanische Wirkungen mit wachsender Geschwindigkeit. Der Anfangsdruck der Primärexplosion muß sehr hoch sein, damit die Explosionswelle sofort einsetzt Zur Erzeugung des hohen Druckes ist eine große Ladedichte des Detonators Grundbedingung. Berthelot betrachtet also die Wirkung des Detonators lediglich als eine mechanische Stoßwirkung. Dieser Auffassung schließt sich neuerdings L. Wöhler[1] an, der auch andere hochexplosive Stoffe als zur Initialzündung geeignet erkannte, insbesondere Silberazid, Perchloratotrimerkuraldehyd und Chloratotrimerkuraldehyd, und welcher direkt nachweist, daß die Initialwirkung proportional der Stoßwirkung auf der freien Bleiplatte ist.

Andererseits hat Sir F. Abel wieder die Hypothese aufgestellt, daß die bei der Explosion des Knallquecksilbers entstehenden Explosionswellen synchronisch auf das Sprengöl wirken und so dessen Detonation hervorrufen. Die Abelsche Hypothese war bisher vielfach angenommen worden, und wir hatten solche noch in der Einleitung (S. 15) angeführt. Nach der Arbeit von L. Wöhler (mit O. Matter) muß aber der Abelsche Vibrationssynchronismus zugunsten der Berthelotschen mechanischen Stoßwirkung aufgegeben werden.

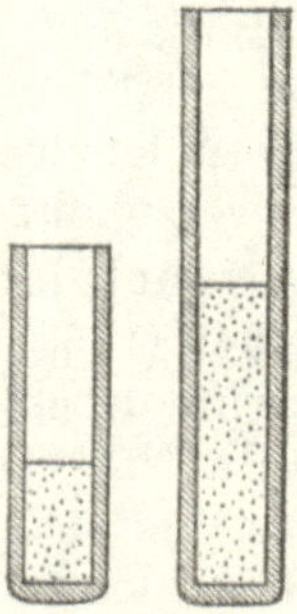

Fig. 54.

Die Sprengkapseln (Fig. 54) sind zylindrische, an dem einen Ende geschlossene Kupferhülsen, deren lichte Weite, von 5 bis 8 mm wechselnd, dem üblichen Durchmesser der Zündschnüre entspricht. Die Kapseln sind teilweise (bis zu $^2/_3$) mit einem innigen Gemisch von 85 Prozent Knallquecksilber und 15 Prozent Kaliumchlorat gefüllt. Dieser „Knallsatz" wird mit 250 kg pro 1 qcm auf eine Ladedichte von 2·8 komprimiert. Das Satzgemisch läßt sich mit Gummilösung wegen seiner Knet- und Formbarkeit in den Sieb- und Füllmaschinen viel besser verarbeiten als reine Knallqueck-

[1] Zeitschr. Schieß-Sprengstoffwesen II, S. 269.

silberkristalle; andererseits hat der Knallsatz trotz der größeren Arbeitsfähigkeit infolge der Komplikation chemischer Wechselwirkung der Komponenten und seiner kleineren Ladedichte eine geringere Wirkung als reines Knallquecksilber (also ohne Kaliumchlorat), so daß z. B. die französische Regierung für amtliche Versuche sich des reinen Knallquecksilbers für die Initialzündung bedient.

Die gewöhnlichen Sprengkapseln werden handelsüblich in zehn verschiedenen Größen mit entsprechend wechselndem Inhalt gebraucht und mit den Nummern 1 bis 10 bezeichnet. Die Knallsatzfüllung beträgt 0·3, 0·4, 0·54, 0·65, 0·8, 1·0, 1·5, 2·0, 2·5 und bei der stärksten Sprengkapsel, Nr. 10, 3·0 g.

Neuerdings verwendet man bei den Sprengkapseln weniger Knallsalz und gibt dafür in die Sprengkapsel einen sogenannten „Zwischenzünder", wie Pikrinsäure, Trinitrotoluol usw.

Die Zündung der Sprengkapsel erfolgt entweder durch eine eingeklemmte Zündschnur, welche direkt den Knallsatz zur Explosion bringt, oder mittels elektrischer Zünder, wobei aber in den Sprengkapseln nebst dem Knallsatze noch eine geringe Menge eines — durch Glüh- oder Funkenzünder leicht entflammbaren — Zündsatzes vorhanden sein muß, dessen Abbrennen erst die Explosion des Knallsatzes herbeiführt.

Es ist sehr wichtig, daß die Sprengkapseln normales Initiierungsvermögen besitzen und auch richtig in das zu detonierende Nitroglyzerin eingeführt werden; sonst kann die Detonation ausbleiben, oder es findet nur ein Auskochen des Sprengöls statt, d. i. ein bloßes Abbrennen, das nicht nur durch die verschiedene Schnelligkeit des chemischen Zerfalles und durch die fehlende Sprengwirkung, sondern auch durch die Art der Zersetzung sich von der Detonation unterscheidet, indem hiebei nicht die Detonationsgase, sondern die Verbrennungsgase, also hauptsächlich die wegen ihrer Giftigkeit höchst gefährlichen Verbindungen Stickoxyd und Kohlenoxyd auftreten. — Bei richtiger Detonation zerfällt das Nitroglyzerin nach der folgenden Gleichung:

$$4\,C_3H_5(ONO_2)_3 = 12\,CO_2 + 10\,H_2O + 6\,N_2 + O_2,$$

also in ganz ungefährliche Gase.

5. Detonationsgeschwindigkeit. Die Schnelligkeit der chemischen Zersetzung oder, mechanisch ausgedrückt, die Schnelligkeit der Gasdruckentwicklung eines detonierenden Sprengstoffes nennt man seine „Detonationsgeschwindigkeit", die in erster Linie für die Stoßwirkung der Sprengmittel von größter Wichtig-

keit ist. — Berthelot und Vieille[1] füllten Nitroglyzerin in Röhren (aus Blei, Zinn oder Britanniametall) von 3, 4 oder 6 mm innerem Durchmesser und einer Länge von 30 bis 200 m, an deren einem Ende die Sprengkapsel angebracht wird; außerdem gehen quer durch den Strang zwei dünne Kupferdrähte, welche in einem genau bemessenen Abstand voneinander angebracht sind. Das Ganze wird zweckmäßig in den Erdboden vergraben, da bei der Explosion das ganze Metallrohr in Stücke geht. Ist durch die Entzündung der Sprengkapsel die Detonation am einen Ende eingeleitet, so wird durch die von hier aus einsetzende Explosionswelle zunächst der eine und dann der zweite Kupferdraht zerstört. Die beiden Kupferdrähte hatten je einen elektrischen Stromkreis geschlossen, und man mißt nun mittels empfindlicher Instrumente die Zeit, welche zwischen den beiden Drahtunterbrechungen verstreicht. Dann ergibt eine einfache Umrechnung die auf eine Sekunde bezogene Fortpflanzungsgeschwindigkeit. Zum Messen der Detonationsgeschwindigkeit verwandte Berthelot elektromagnetische Chronographen von Le Boulengé und von Schulz-Depret. Er fand beim Messen der Detonationsgeschwindigkeit von Nitroglyzerin in Bleiröhren von 3 mm innerem Durchmesser die Werte von 1133, 1486, 1210 und 1457 m, im Mittel 1132 m per Sekunde. — Abel[2] fand in einem dünnwandigen Bleirohr von 30 mm Durchmesser eine Detonationsgeschwindigkeit von 1525 m per Sekunde. Mettegang[3] verwandte rein elektrische, auf dem Prinzip des Funkeninduktors von Siemens und Martin de Brettes beruhende Chronographen, und fand für Nitroglyzerin in eisernen, $1^1/_2$ m tief eingegrabenen Röhren von 30 mm Durchmesser die Werte: 2098, 1978 und 2059, also im Mittel 2045 m per Sekunde. — Neuere Arbeiten über Detonationsgeschwindigkeiten wurden von Dautriche (Compt. rend. **143**, 641 und **144**, 1030) in Zinkröhren von 12 bis 20 mm innerem Durchmesser und 50 cm wirksamer Länge ausgeführt, und auch die Änderung der Detonationsgeschwindigkeit mit der Dichte studiert.

Jedenfalls ist die Detonationsgeschwindigkeit abhängig von der Art der Initiierung und von dem Drucke, bzw. von der Ladedichte.

6. Fernwirkung. Vieille hatte gefunden, das die Explosionswelle mit wachsendem Abstande vom Explosionsherde ab-

---

[1] Mém. Poudr. Salp. IV, 7 (1891). — Cf. Ann. Chim. Phys. 1885 u. 1891.
[2] Phil. Transact. **156**, 269; **157**, 181.
[3] Internat. Kongreßbericht 1903, II, S. 322.

nimmt. — In den Jahren 1896 bis 1899 wurden auf dem Schießplatz Cummersdorf folgende Untersuchungen angestellt:[1]

a) Die Ermittelung der Fortpflanzungsgeschwindigkeit der Explosionswirkung, gemessen mittels Luftstoßanzeigern; das sind elektrische Kontakte, welche durch den Ausschlag einer von einem Luftstoß getroffenen Metallmembran geöffnet oder geschlossen werden. Danach betrug die Fortpflanzungsgeschwindigkeit des Nitroglyzerins in der Nähe des Explosionsherdes bis zu 800 m pro Sekunde; sie nimmt — in Übereinstimmung mit den von den Federkraftmessern (siehe c) erhaltenen Aufzeichnungen — schnell ab und nähert sich mit zunehmender Entfernung der Schallfortpflanzungsgeschwindigkeit (340 m).

Ferner wurden Versuche mit aufgestellten Glasscheiben angestellt. Je weiter die Scheiben vom Explosionsherd entfernt waren, um so höher war der Prozentsatz der Bruchstücke, die nach dem Explosionsherd zu gefallen waren, bis schließlich alle Splitter in diese Richtung fielen. Während also in der näheren Umgebung sowohl positiv gerichtete Kräfte auftreten, welche die Körper vom Explosionsherde weg bewegen, als auch entgegengesetzt gerichtete, welche die Körper zum Explosionsherde hin bewegen, ist in weiterer Entfernung vom Explosionsherde lediglich die letztere, gewissermaßen hinsaugende Wirkung zu beobachten.

b) Die Ermittelung des Verlaufes der Verdichtung der Luft und die Größe dieser Verdichtung an verschiedenen Stellen des Explosionsherdes. Es handelt sich hier um Wellenbewegungen. Die Verdichtungen sind nicht wie beim Schall unendlich klein, sondern meßbar. Nach Prof. Wolff findet die Explosion eines Sprengstoffes stets unter einem sehr hohen Druck im Explosionsherde statt, welcher infolge der rapiden Gasentwicklung mehrere Tausend Atmosphären beträgt. In dieser plötzlichen Gleichgewichtsstörung hat die Wellenbewegung ihren Ursprung. Durch die Explosionsgase wird an ihrer Oberfläche eine erhebliche Luftverdichtung mit unmittelbar darauf folgender Luftverdünnung erzeugt, die sich nach den Gesetzen der longitudinalen Wellenbewegung fortpflanzen. Die Explosionsgase selbst werden dabei nur bis in eine geringe Entfernung vom Explosionsherde fortgeschleudert. Die Verdichtung und Verdünnung der Luft aber überträgt sich von Schicht zu Schicht der umgebenden Luft mit der (mit Hilfe eines Luftstoßanzeigers gemessenen) Geschwindigkeit. Überall zerfällt das erschütterte Gebiet — die Explosionsschallwelle — in zwei nach entgegengesetzten Richtungen fortschreitende Wellenzüge. Mit der Explosionswelle sind daher zwei in entgegengesetztem Sinne wirkende Kräfte verbunden, wie dies auch aus dem Verhalten der Fensterscheiben zu erkennen war. Im Verlaufe der Bewegung ändert sich die Wellenform. Der vordere Teil der Welle wird allmählich steiler, und damit die positiv gerichtete Kraftwirkung geringer, während der hintere Teil der Welle allmählich flacher, und damit die negative Kraftwirkung allmählich größer wird, bis, von einer

[1] Sitzungsber. Ver. Bef. Gew.fleiß 1900, S. 45.

gewissen Entfernung an, nur noch die indirekten Wirkungen auftreten. Es entspricht dies bei den Versuchen der Stelle, wo die Glassplitter nur noch nach dem Magazin zu geworfen waren. — Ein Strömen der Luft vom Explosionsherd nach ferner gelegenen Punkten, und umgekehrt, findet nicht statt.

c) Die Bestimmung der Energie, welche in verschiedenen Entfernungen vom Explosionsherd von bestimmten Körpern aufgenommen wird; hierzu wurden zwei verschiedene Methoden angewandt. Einmal wurden auf aufgestellten Pfählen auf besonderen Unterlagen Kugeln von verschiedenen Stoffen und von verschiedenen Größen sehr empfindlich aufgelegt, welche durch die Explosionswirkung herabgeworfen werden sollten. Aus ihrer Fallhöhe, Wurfweite und Masse konnte die von ihnen aufgenommene Energie berechnet werden. Zum zweiten wurden besonders konstruierte Federkraftmesser verwendet, bei denen der Explosionsstoß von Stempeln bekannten Querschnitts aufgefangen wurde. Die Stempel wirkten auf vorher geaichte Federn, deren Verkürzung sodann registriert wurde. Aus der Federverkürzung wurde die von diesen Instrumenten registrierte Energie berechnet.

Es hat sich ergeben, daß die Umgebung des Explosionsherdes durch die von der Luft übertragene Energie relativ wenig gefährdet ist, und daß die Energie, wenn auch in der Nähe des Sprengherdes sehr groß, mit wachsender Entfernung sehr schnell abnimmt und schon in der Entfernung von 200 m praktisch gleich Null zu setzen ist.

d) Endlich wurde noch (von Dr. Hecker) die Bodenerschütterung studiert. Danach durchlaufen die Erschütterungswellen den Erdboden in ähnlicher Weise wie die Explosionsschallwellen die Luft; dagegen scheint eine Abnahme der Fortpflanzungsgeschwindigkeit der Erschütterungswellen nicht einzutreten, vielmehr die Geschwindigkeit annähernd konstant 250 m zu betragen.

Neuerdings hat die französische Sprengstoffkommission eingehende Untersuchungen über Explosionsfernwirkungen angestellt,[1] nach welchen die Fernwirkungsgrenzen ungefähr proportional den Quadratwurzeln aus den Sprengstoffmengen sind.

f) Die Explosions- bzw. Verbrennungsprodukte.

Trinitroglyzerin enthält genügend Sauerstoff, um bei der explosiven Zersetzung des Moleküls die Elemente Kohlenstoff und Wasserstoff vollständig in Kohlensäure und Wasser nach der Gleichung:

$$4[C_3H_5N_3O_9] = 12CO_2 + 10H_2O + 6N_2 + O_2$$

überzuführen. Es entstehen bei der regulären Explosion 58·2 Pro-

[1] Mémorial Poudr. Salpêtre XIII. — Zeitschr. Schieß-Sprengstoffwesen II.

zent Kohlensäure, 19·8 Prozent Wasserdampf, 18·5 Prozent Stickstoff und 3·5 Prozent Sauerstoff.

Das Volumen der Gase läßt sich nach dem Gesetz von Avogadro berechnen. Danach nehmen die Moleküle aller Gase bei gleicher Temperatur und gleichem Druck ein gleiches Volumen ein; die Gasvolumina verhalten sich wie die Zahlen der erhaltenen Moleküle. Das in Gramm ausgedrückte Molekulargewicht irgend eines Gases nimmt bei 0° und 760 mm einen Raum von 22·32 l, bei t^0 einen Raum von 22·32 $[1 + \alpha t]$[1] ein. Da nun aus vier Molekülen Nitroglyzerin (4 × 227 = 908 g) sich 29 gasförmige Moleküle bilden, so berechnet sich das aus einem Kilogramm entstehende Gasvolumen (für 0° und 760 mm) zu $\frac{29 \times 22 \cdot 32}{908} = 712$ l, wovon nach obiger Zusammensetzung 414·3 l Kohlensäure, 141 l Wasserdampf, 131·7 l Stickstoff und 25 l Sauerstoff sind. — Berücksichtigt man nur die permanenten Gase (also H_2O flüssig), so erhält man aus 4 Molekülen Nitroglyzerin nur 19 Gasmoleküle, also aus einem Kilogramm Nitroglyzerin $\frac{19 \times 22 \cdot 32}{908} = 467$ l Gase, bestehend zu 63·2 Prozent aus Kohlensäure, 31·5 Prozent aus Stickstoff und 5·3 Prozent aus Sauerstoff. — Sarrau und Vieille erhielten beim experimentellen Versuch in der kalorimetrischen Bombe 465 l permanente Gase (auf 0° und 760 mm reduziert), also eine ganz nahekommende Zahl.

Es ist für die Sprengarbeiten, insbesondere im Bergbaue, von größter Bedeutung, daß die Explosionsgase (Nachschwaden) frei von giftigen Bestandteilen (Kohlenoxyd, nitrosen Gasen) sind. Solche Gase treten auf, wenn das Nitroglyzerin nicht detoniert, sondern abbrennt (auskocht). Nach Sarrau und Vieille bestehen die Verbrennungsgase des Sprengöls aus: 35·9 Prozent CO, 12·8 Prozent CO_2, 48·2 Prozent NO, 1·3 Prozent N_2, 1·6 Prozent H_2 und 0·2 Prozent CH_4. Ein Kilogramm Nitroglyzerin liefert danach 162 l CO, 58 l CO_2, 218 l NO, 6 l N_2, 7 l H_2 und 1 l CH_4.

Dieses Auskochen kann stattfinden, wenn die Initiierung eine ungenügende ist; eventuell kann das Nitroglyzerin erst ins Kochen geraten und dann erst bei zunehmendem Gasdruck explodieren.

Spezifisches Gasvolumen. Der Raum, welchen die von 1 g eines explosiblen Systems erzeugten Gase bei 0° und 760 mm einnehmen, ist ein, im allgemeinen nur von der Zusammensetzung

---

[1] Also bei 15° gilt die Zahl $22 \cdot 32 (1 + \frac{1}{273} \cdot 15) = 23 \cdot 55$.

der Explosionsgase abhängiges, und daher für Explosivstoffe charakteristisches Merkmal, das man auch als spezifisches Gasvolumen bezeichnet. Man kann dasselbe mit Hilfe geeigneter Gasometer ermitteln,[1] nachdem man den Explosionsvorgang in einer Bombe vollzogen hat. — Über den Einfluß der Sprengkapsel hierbei sei auf eine Arbeit der Dynamit-Aktiengesellschaft vorm. Nobel verwiesen.[2]

g) Die Wärmeentwicklung.

Die bei der Explosion freiwerdende Wärme, welche sowohl berechnet als auch gemessen werden kann, bildet die Grundlage für den Gasdruck und für die Arbeitsleistung.

Die bei einer Änderung des chemischen Zustandes eines Systems freiwerdende Wärme ist gleich dem Überschuß der Bildungswärmen des Endzustandes über die Bildungswärme des Anfangszustandes. Bezeichnet man mit Q_1 bzw. Q_2 die durch die Bildung der Körper aus ihren Elementen freiwerdenden Wärmemengen des Anfangs- bzw. Endzustandes, so gilt die Gleichung:

$$Q = Q_2 - Q_1 .$$

Für das Molekül Nitroglyzerin berechnet sich nach der Reaktionsgleichung:

$$4[C_3H_5N_3O_9] = 12CO_2 + 10H_2O + 6N_2 + O_2$$

bei Einsetzen der bezüglichen Bildungswärmen, und zwar in Wärmeeinheiten (Kalorien) gemessen:

$$\begin{aligned} Q &= (12 \times 94{\cdot}31) + (10 \times 58{\cdot}3) - (4 \times 98{\cdot}9) \\ &= (1131{\cdot}7 + 583) - 395{\cdot}6 \\ &= 1319 \text{ kal.,} \end{aligned}$$

bzw. für ein Molekül $\frac{1319}{4} = 329{\cdot}7$ kal. Diese Zahl gilt bei Annahme konstanten Druckes, also für $Q_{m.p}$. Bei der Explosion trifft aber diese Annahme nicht zu, vielmehr müssen wir auf konstantes Volumen umrechnen, weil das anfängliche Volumen der Gase annähernd dem Volumen des Sprengstoffes entspricht. Die bei gleichbleibendem Volumen freiwerdende Wärmemenge ist aber etwas größer als jene bei der Zersetzung an freier Luft und bei konstantem Druck, weil die an freier Luft entwickelten Gase

---

[1] Sarrau u. Vieille, Mém. Poudr. Salp. II, 134.

[2] Zeitschr. Schieß-Sprengstoffwesen II, S. 281.

beim Verdrängen der Luft Arbeit verrichten, sonach die Wärme verzehren.

Da $Q_v = Q_p + 0{\cdot}57\,n$, wobei n die Zahl der gasförmigen Moleküle bedeutet, ist für das Nitroglyzerin:

$$Q_{m\cdot v} = Q_{m\cdot p} + 0{\cdot}57 \times \frac{29}{4},$$

woraus sich die aus einem Molekül Nitroglyzerin bei konstantem Volumen entwickelte Wärmemenge auf 333·7 kal. berechnet.

Wenn nun aus einem Molekül (227 g) Nitroglyzerin eine Wärmemenge von 333·7 kal. frei wird, so ergibt sich für 1 kg eine Explosionswärme von 1470 kal., oder $Q_{k\cdot v} = 1470$ kal.

Berthelot gibt folgende Zahlen an, und zwar für

für $$Q_{m\cdot p} = 331{\cdot}1, \quad Q_{m\cdot v} = 335{\cdot}6 \text{ kal.}$$

Danach berechnet sich $Q_{k\cdot v} = 1478$ kal.

Vorstehende Zahlen gelten unter der Annahme, daß das gebildete Wasser als Dampf vorhanden ist; denn durch Kondensation dieses Dampfes zu flüssigem Wasser wird weitere Wärme frei, bzw. die Bildungswärme des flüssigen Wassers ist größer als die des Wasserdampfes. Die erste Gleichung lautet dann:

$$Q = (12 \times 94{\cdot}31) + (10 \times 69) - (4 \times 98{\cdot}9).$$

Daraus ergibt sich $Q_{m\cdot p}(H_2O \text{ flüssig}) = 356{\cdot}5$ kal.,

und $$Q_{m\cdot v}(H_2O \text{ flüssig}) = 360{\cdot}6 \text{ kal.}$$
$$Q_{k\cdot v}(H_2O \text{ flüssig}) = 1589 \text{ kal.}$$

Sarrau und Vieille erhielten beim Messen in der kalorimetrischen Bombe (für $Q_{k\cdot v}$) 1600 kal., — also eine der Berechnung ganz nahekommende Zahl.

Das Explosionskalorimeter dient allgemein zur Messung der Wärmetönung eines Explosionsvorganges. Man vollzieht die Explosion in einer kleinen Bombe, welche mit elektrischer Zündung versehen ist. Unter Berücksichtigung des Wasserwertes des Apparates wird aus der Temperatursteigerung des Wasserkalorimeters sodaun die bei der Explosion freigewordene Wärmemenge bestimmt.

h) Der Gasdruck (Explosionsdruck).

Die Gase, welche durch die explosive Auslösung eines Sprengstoffes frei werden, stoßen auf die ihnen Widerstand bietende Umschließung, bzw. Unterlage, wobei eine mehr oder weniger schnell sich vollziehende Drucksteigerung eintritt. Der hierbei auftretende Maximaldruck kann entweder berechnet oder gemessen werden.

I. Berechnung. Hierzu ist erforderlich:

1. die Kenntnis der theoretischen Flammen-, oder Explosionstemperatur t, d. h. derjenigen Temperatur, bis zu welcher die Explosionsprodukte durch die bei der Umwandlung entwickelte Wärme erhitzt werden können. Diese Berechnung ist mit Berücksichtigung der Wärmekapazität der Gase möglich. Die Explosionstemperatur ergibt sich, wenn man die freiwerdende Explosionswärme $Q_{m.v}$ durch die mittlere spezifische Wärme der Explosionsgase dividiert. Die spezifischen Wärmen der Gase sind von der Temperatur abhängig; Nach Mallard und Le Chatelier gelten folgende Werte:

für Kohlensäure : $6{\cdot}26 + 0{\cdot}0037\, t$,
für Wasserdampf: $5{\cdot}61 + 0{\cdot}0033\, t$,
für Stickstoff : $4{\cdot}80 + 0{\cdot}0006\, t$,
für Sauerstoff : $4{\cdot}80 + 0{\cdot}0006\, t$.

Für die Gleichung:

$$4\,C_3H_5N_3O_9 = 12\,CO_2 + 10\,H_2O + 6\,N_2 + O_2,$$

ergibt sich die spezifische Wärme der Explosionsgase C, wenn man die spezifischen Wärmen c_1, c_2, c_3, c_4 der einzelnen Gase berechnet:

$$\begin{array}{lcl}
c_1 \text{ (für } 12\,CO_2) & = & 12 \times 6{\cdot}26 \text{ plus } 12 \times 0{\cdot}0037\, t \\
c_2 \text{ (für } 10\,H_2O) & = & 10 \times 5{\cdot}61 \text{ plus } 10 \times 0{\cdot}0033\, t \\
c_3 \text{ (für } 6\,N_2) & = & 6 \times 4{\cdot}80 \text{ plus } 6 \times 0{\cdot}0006\, t \\
c_4 \text{ (für } O_2) & = & 1 \times 4{\cdot}80 \text{ plus } 1 \times 0{\cdot}0006\, t \\
\hline
C & = & 164{\cdot}82 \text{ plus } 0{\cdot}0816\, t.
\end{array}$$

Da

$$t = \frac{Q}{C} \quad \text{oder} \quad Q = C \cdot t$$

ist, so ergibt sich:

$$Q = 164{\cdot}82\, t + 0{\cdot}0816\, t^2,$$

oder

$$0{\cdot}0816\, t^2 + 164{\cdot}82\, t - Q = 0;$$

daher

$$t = \frac{-\,164{\cdot}82 + \sqrt{164{\cdot}82^2 + 4 \times 0{\cdot}0816\, Q}}{2 \times 0{\cdot}0816}.$$

Hieraus berechnet sich — nach Heise — eine Explosionstemperatur von 3158° C. — Gody gibt für dieselbe 3153° an. —

Auzenat berechnet 3469°, v. Wuich[1] dagegen nur 3005° C. Den Berechnungen der französischen Schlagwetterkommission wird die Explosionstemperatur des Nitroglyzerins mit 3200° C, dagegen die des Ammonsalpeters mit 1130° C zugrunde gelegt.

In Wirklichkeit sind die Explosionstemperaturen wohl niedriger, als aus der thermochemischen Rechnung hervorgeht, welch letzterer man den idealen Grenzfall einer ohne Wärmeverlust verlaufenden exothermen Reaktion zugrunde legen muß. Eine direkte Messung der Temperatur ist bis jetzt noch nicht gelungen.

2. Das Explosionsvolumen.

Aus dem Gasvolumen v_0 bei 0° und 760 mm läßt sich bei der Kenntnis der Explosionstemperatur das Volumen $v_{t \cdot k}$ berechnen, welches die Explosionsgase bei der Explosionstemperatur t (unter Annahme konstanten Druckes) einnehmen. Nach dem Gay-Lussacschen Gesetze ist nämlich $v_{t \cdot k} = \frac{v_0 (273 + t)}{273}$.

3. Berechnung des Gasdruckes P.

Aus dem Verhältnis des Explosionsvolumens v_t zu dem Volumen v_0 der ursprünglichen Substanz ergibt sich der Gasdruck P, welchen die Explosionsgase ausüben. Die Größe dieses Gasdruckes ist eine für jeden Sprengstoff charakteristische Größe und wird nach Berthelot „spezifischer Druck" genannt und gewöhnlich mit f bezeichnet. Die Berechnung von f, d. h. des Druckes, der von 1 kg (Gewichtseinheit) Sprengstoff bei der Explosionstemperatur t in einem Liter (Raumeinheit) — also bei der Ladedichte 1 — ausgeübt wird, erfolgt auf Grund des Mariotteschen Gesetzes, wonach die Volumina umgekehrt proportional den Drücken sind.

Bezeichnet: $v_{0 \cdot k}$ das Volumen der von 1 kg Sprengstoff bei 0° und 760 mm gelieferten Explosionsgase, $v_{t \cdot k}$ das Volumen derselben Gasmenge bei der Explosionstemperatur t und 760 mm, p_0 den atmosphärischen Druck (1·033 kg auf 1 qcm), so verhält sich nach dem Gesetz von Mariotte:

$$f : p_0 = v_{t \cdot k} : 1 \cdot 033, \quad \text{oder} \quad f = 1 \cdot 033 \cdot v_{t \cdot k},$$

wenn für v_0 als Raumeinheit 1 angenommen wird. Setzen wir in letztere Gleichung den unter 2. berechneten Wert des Explosionsvolumens, so ergibt sich

$$f = \frac{1 \cdot 033 \cdot v_{0 \cdot k} (273 + t)}{273}.$$

Danach berechnet sich für Nitroglyzerin ein spezifischer Druck von 9281 kg.

[1] Mitteil. Art.- u. Geniewesen 1891. S. 67.

Einfluß vom Covolumen. Unter Covolumen α versteht man den nicht mehr zu verkleinernden Inhalt der Gasmoleküle selbst, etwa $^1/_{1000}$ desjenigen Volumens, der von der betreffenden Gasmenge bei 0° und 760 mm eingenommen wird $\left(\alpha = \frac{1}{1000} v_0\right)$. Danach steht den Sprengstoffgasen nicht der ganze Raum V zur Verfügung, in welchem die Explosion vor sich geht, sondern nur um ein um das Covolumen verminderter Raum $(V - \alpha)$; durch diese Raumverminderung wird der Gasdruck erhöht.

Ladedichte. Der wirkliche Maximalgasdruck ist hauptsächlich von der Ladedichte abhängig, d. h. von dem Verhältnis vom Ladungsgewicht in Gramm zum Verbrennungsraum in Kubikzentimetern. Diesen Quotienten bezeichnet man mit Δ.

$$P = f \cdot \Delta.$$

Unter Berücksichtigung des Covolumens ist dann

$$P = \frac{f \cdot \Delta}{1 - \alpha \cdot \Delta}.$$

Will[1] gibt folgende Zusammenstellung nach Sarraus Berechnungen für verschiedene Ladedichten:

Explosionsdruck bei wechselnden Ladedichten.

Ladedichte Δ	Druck in Kilogramm pro Quadratzentimeter						
	Schwarzpulver	Schießwollpulver	Schießwolle	Nitroglyzerin	Pikrinsäure	Ammonnitrat	Knallquecksilber
0·1	336	858	1 061	1 098	983	542	468
0·2	708	2 026	2 343	2 351	2 174	1 217	966
0·3	1 123	3 275	3 921	3 847	3 650	2 077	1 501
0·4	1 587		5 912	5 640	5 523	3 211	2 072
0·5	2 112		8 502	7 829	7 982	4 779	2 686
0·6	2 708		12 000	10 560	11 350	7 082	3 347
0·7	3 393		17 020	14 060	16 240	10 800	4 062
0·8	4 201		24 810	21 520	24 030	17 870	4 952
0·9	5 126		38 500	25 270	38 310	36 250	5 683
1·0	6 236		—	35 010	—	∞	6 602
1·2	9 255		∞	—	∞		8 726
1·4	14 130			∞			11 320
1·6	29 340						14 560
1·8	—						18 790
2·0	∞						24 350
2·4							43 970
3·2							∞

[1] Zeitschr. Elektrochemie 1906, S. 563.

II. Die Messung des Gasdruckes.

Dieselbe erfolgt in sog. Stauchapparaten (crusher gauge), welche von Sir Andrew Noble angegeben worden sind. Der Explosivstoff befindet sich in einer Höhlung eines Stahlzylinders, dessen oberer Verschluß eine Schraube bildet, durch welche die elektrische Zündung geht. Den unteren Abschluß des Hohlraumes (in welchem die Explosion vor sich geht) bildet ein Stahlstempel, welcher bei der Explosion seine Bewegung gegen einen Kupferzylinder richtet, denselben gegen ein festes Widerlager preßt und ihn, da er aus verhältnismäßig weichem Metall besteht, je nach der Größe des Druckes zusammenstaucht.

Einen unmittelbaren Gasdruckmesser hat C. E. Bichel konstruiert (D.R.P. 109187). Es ist dies ein Verfahren zum Messen der Explosionskraft und Brisanz von Explosivstoffen mittels Aufzeichnens von Diagrammen durch Indikatorwirkung, welches dadurch gekennzeichnet wird, daß die auf den Indikator einwirkende Explosion einer abgemessenen Menge des zu untersuchenden Explosivstoffes im luftverdünnten oder luftleeren Raum ohne oder in Anwesenheit eines indifferenten Gases vorgenommen wird.

i) Die Stoßwirkung.

Die durch die Ausdehnung der Gase infolge der außerordentlichen Wärme entstehende Druckwirkung ist nicht der einzige Effekt des Nitroglyzerins; es ist auch dessen Stoßwirkung zu berücksichtigen, worauf zuerst C. E. Bichel[1] hingewiesen hat. Während die Druckwirkung ein statischer, in Kilogramm pro Quadratzentimeter ausdrückbarer Vorgang ist, stellt sich die Stoßwirkung als ein dynamischer Vorgang dar, der in Sekunden-Kilogramm ausgedrückt wird. Das Maß für die Stoßwirkung ist die lebendige Energie, welche den Zersetzungsprodukten mitgeteilt wird und die durch die Formel $\frac{m \cdot v^2}{2}$ wiedergegeben werden kann, worin m die Masse der Zersetzungsprodukte des Sprengstoffes und v die Detonationsgeschwindigkeit bedeutet.

k) Die Arbeitsleistung.

1. Theoretische Arbeitsleistung. Als relatives Maß für die mechanische Arbeitsleistung eines Explosivstoffes wurde von Berthelot das Produkt aus spezifischem Gasvolumen und

[1] In „Glückauf“, Jahrg. 1905, Nr. 15. — Siehe auch Bichel-Larsen, New Methods of testing Explosives.

Temperatursteigerung ($V_0 \cdot t$) vorgeschlagen. Da $V_0 t = \frac{V_0 Q}{c}$ ist, und c, sofern es sich um Explosionsgase von annähernd gleicher spezifischer Wärme handelt, außer Betracht bleiben kann, so ergibt sich $V_0 Q$ als das sogenannte „charakteristische Produkt" eines Sprengstoffes. Doch hat man damit keinen zuverlässigen Wertmesser.

Brunswig gibt folgende tabellarische Übersicht über die Größe dieses Produktes:

Explosivstoff	Spezif. Volumen, in Litern (bezogen auf 1 kg u. H_2O-Dampf)	Berechnete Explosionstemperatur Grad C	Charakterist. Produkt	
			$v_0 Q$	Wertverhältnis, Sprenggelatine = 100 gesetzt
Sprenggelatine (93 : 7)	710	3540	1 164 000	100
Nitroglyzerin . . .	712	3470	1 125 000	97
Nitromannit	723	3430	1 099 000	95
Dynamit (75 Prozent Nitroglyzerin)	628	3160	810 000	70
Nitroglyzerinpulver (40 Prozent Nitroglyzerin)	840	2900	1 084 000	93
Schießwolle (13 Prozent Stickstoff) . . .	859	2710	945 000	81
Schießwollpulver . . .	830	2400	747 000	64
Kollodiumwolle (12 Prozent N) . . .	974	1940	711 000	61
Ammonsalpetersprengstoff (Ammonsalpeter + 10 Prozent Nitronaphtalin)	925	2120	860 000	74
Pikrinsäure	877	2430	710 000	61
Schwarzpulver	285	2770	195 000	17
Ammonsalpeter	937	2120	590 000	50
Knallquecksilber . . .	314	3530	129 000	11

Ein anderes, häufiger benutztes Maß für die theoretische Arbeitsleistung (oder den Energie-Inhalt) eines Sprengstoffes erhält man, wenn man die bei der Explosion freiwerdende Wärmemenge Q mit 425 (dem mechanischen Wärmeäquivalent) multipliziert. Man bekommt so die mechanische Arbeitsleistung in Meterkilogrammen. Hierfür ergibt sich folgende Tabelle:[1]

[1] Will, Zeitschr. f. Elektrochemie 1906, S. 560. — Brunswig, Die Explosivstoffe. S. 15.

Explosivstoff	Explosionswärme in Kalorien, bezogen auf 1 kg, konstantes Volumen und H_2O flüssig	Arbeitsleistung in m·kg	Wertverhältnis, Sprenggelatine = 100 gesetzt
Sprengelatine (7 Prozent Kollodiumwolle)	1640	700 000	100
Nitroglyzerin	1580	670 000	96
Nitromannit	1520	645 000	92
Dynamit (75 Prozent Nitroglyzerin)	1290	550 000	79
Nitroglyzerinpulver (40 Prozent Nitroglyzerin)	1290	550 000	79
Schießwolle (13 Prozent Stickstoff)	1100	465 000	66
Schießwollpulver	900	380 000	54
Kollodiumwolle (12 Proz. Stickstoff)	730	310 000	44
Ammonsalpetersprengstoff (Ammonsalpeter + 10 Prozent Nitronaphtalin)	930	385 000	58
Pikrinsäure	810	345 000	49
Schwarzpulver	685	290 000	41
Ammonsalpeter	630	265 000	38
Knallquecksilber	410	175 000	25

Auch diese angeführten Werte sagen nichts über die Geschwindigkeit, mit welcher sich der Explosionsprozeß vollzieht. Der zeitliche Verlauf des Prozesses ist aber für die tatsächliche Wirkung naturgemäß von größter Bedeutung, da bei raschem Explosionsverlauf größere Anfangsdrucke auftreten. Besonders zu berücksichtigen ist, daß für einen und denselben brisanten Sprengstoff, z. B. für das Nitroglyzerin, die Detonationsgeschwindigkeit eine sehr wechselnde sein kann, und zwar je nach dem Initialimpuls, der physikalischen Beschaffenheit usw.

2. Praktische Arbeitsleistung oder Sprengwirkung. Um einen Maßstab für die Sprengwirkung eines Explosivkörpers zu haben, bedient man sich verschiedener empirischer Methoden:

a) Trauzlsche Bleiblockprobe — von J. Trauzl im Anschlusse an Versuche von Beckerhinn[1] in die Sprengtechnik eingeführt.

[1] Mitteil. Gegenst. Art.- u. Geniewesen 8, S. 71. Wird auch als „Schlagprobe" bezeichnet.

Hierfür sind vom V. Internationalen Kongreß für angewandte Chemie in Berlin folgende Normalien vereinbart worden:

α) Abmessung des Apparates. Der Apparat besteht aus einem Bleizylinder von 200 mm Höhe und 200 mm Durchmesser. In der Achse des Zylinders befindet sich eine 125 mm tiefe und 25 mm weite Ausbohrung, welche zur Aufnahme des Sprengstoffes bestimmt ist. Das für die Zylinder verwendete Blei soll möglichst reines raffiniertes Weichblei sein und die für eine Versuchsreihe bestimmten Zylinder sollen ein und derselben Schmelze entstammen. Fig. 55 zeigt den Bleizylinder, Fig. 56 eine zweckmäßige Form zum Gießen derselben. Zur Erwärmung des Gießstutzens ist ein glühend gemachter Ring um den Stutzen zu legen.

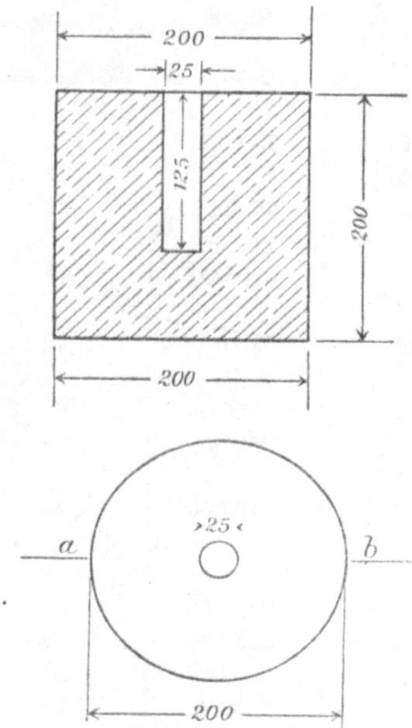

Fig. 55. Bleizylinder.

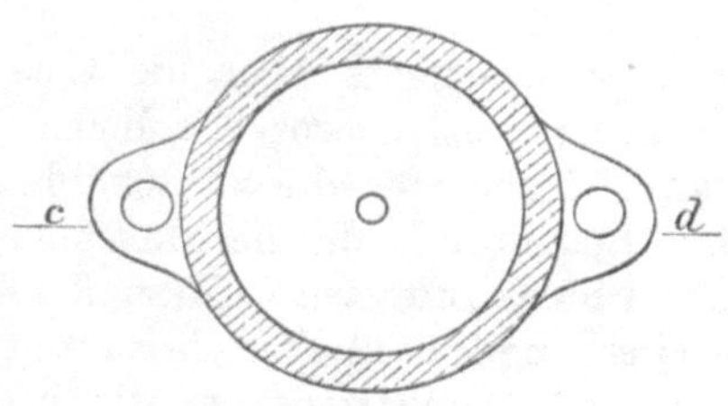

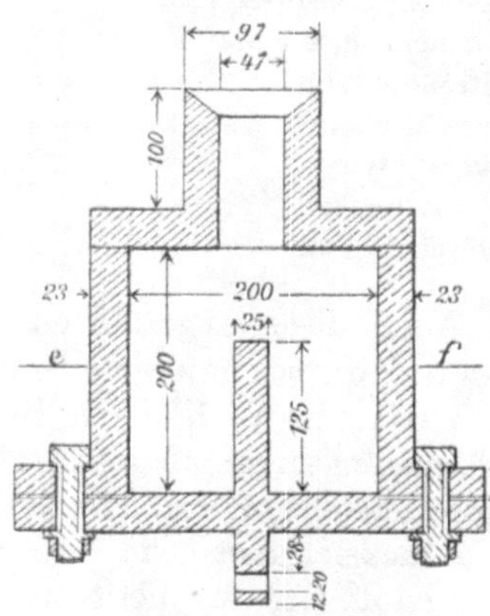

Fig. 56. Gießform.

β) Beschreibung des Verfahrens. Zu den Versuchen sind Bleizylinder zu verwenden, welche genügend lange gestanden haben, um eine gleichmäßige Temperatur von 15 bis 20° C durchweg mit Sicherheit zu erhalten. Eine Menge von 10 g des zu prüfenden Sprengstoffes wird abgewogen und in Zinnfolie von 80 bis 100 g·qcm nach nebenstehender Abmessung zu einer Patrone von 25 mm Durchmesser geformt (Fig. 57). Als Initialzündung wird in die Mitte des Sprengstoffes eine Sprengkapsel mit 2 g Ladung mit ausschließlich elektrischer Zündung eingesetzt. Die Patrone wird in das Bohrloch mit

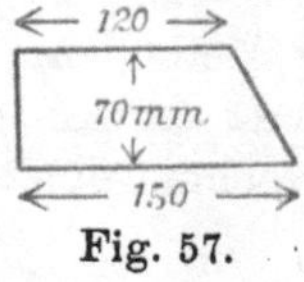

Fig. 57.

Hilfe eines Holzstäbchens bis auf den Grund des Bohrlochs hinuntergeführt und sanft angedrückt, während die Zünddrähte in der Mitte des Bohrlochs gehalten werden. Zum Besatz dient scharf getrockneter Quarzsand, welcher durch ein Sieb von 0·35 mm Drahtstärke und 144 Maschen pro Quadratzentimeter durchläuft. Diesen Sand läßt man gleichmäßig einlaufen, bis der Hohlraum vollständig gefüllt ist und streicht den etwaigen Sandüberschuß von der Oberfläche ab. Der so fertig vorbereitete Schuß wird elektrisch abgetan. Nach dem Abfeuern des Schusses wird der Bleiblock umgestülpt und dann werden mit der Bürste etwaige Rückstände entfernt. Die danach bis zur vollkommenen Füllung von dem gebildeten Hohlraum aufgenommene Anzahl Kubikzentimeter Wasser (nach Abzug der Ausbohrung des Zylinders) geben das Maß für die Wirkung des Sprengstoffes.

γ) Bewertung der Messung. 1. Bleizylindermessungen können nur Anspruch auf zuverlässige Vergleichsresultate machen, wenn sie für ein und dieselbe Art von brisanten Sprengstoffen angewendet werden. Bei größeren Unterschieden in der Geschwindigkeit der Druckwirkung verschiedener Sprengstoffe ist ein Vergleich der Ergebnisse nicht mehr zulässig. 2. Die Angaben über die Wirkung von Sprengstoffen sind stets aus mindestens drei Versuchsergebnissen zu entnehmen. 3. Die Zuverlässigkeit der Messung wird wesentlich beeinflußt: a) durch die Gleichmäßigkeit der Temperatur des Bleies zur Zeit der Messung; als solche wird 15 bis 20° C normal angeschrieben; b) von der Gleichmäßigkeit des Besatzmaterials; c) von der Gleichmäßigkeit der Messung. — Die nach dieser Methode ermittelten Werte decken sich auch nicht immer mit den bei Gesteinssprengungen erzielten Resultaten. Die Ausbauchungszahlen geben nur insoweit einen brauchbaren Anhalt für das Verhältnis der Sprengstoffwirkung, als es sich um eine analoge Auswertung handelt. Rascher detonierende Sprengstoffe werden gegenüber langsameren, also z. B. Dynamit gegenüber Schwarzpulver, zu günstig beurteilt.

Will gibt nachfolgende Tabelle über die im Trauzlschen Bleiblock — mit je 10 g Explosivstoff — gefundenen Werte:

Sprengstoff	Ausbauchung in Kubikzentimetern brutto
Nitroglyzerin	563
Schießwolle (gepreßt, N = 13·18 Prozent	420
Pikrinsäure	365
Donarit	385
Sprenggelatine	590
Knallquecksilber	213
Schießwollpulver	183
Würfelpulver	368
Schwarzpulver (Hirschmarke Nr. 4)	112

Brunswig gibt folgende Zusammenstellung:

Explosivstoff	Ausbauchung im Bleiblock in Kubikzentimetern[1]	Wertverhältnis[2]	
		nach der Ausbauchung	nach der vorhandenen Energie
Nitromannit	650	125	136
Nitroglyzerin	600	115	120
Sprenggelatine (8 Prozent Kollodiumwolle)	520	100	100
Schießwolle (13 Prozent N)	420	81	123
Gelatinedynamit (60 Proz. Nitroglyzerin)	410	79	132
Gurdynamit (75 Prozent Nitroglyzerin)	350	67	85
Kollodiumwolle (12 Prozent N)	250	48	108
Pikrinsäure	300	58	118
Ammonsalpetersprengstoff	300	58	95
Nitroglyzerinpulver (40 Prozent Nitroglyzerin)	150	29	37
Schießwollpulver	150	29	54
Knallquecksilber	150	29	116
Schwarzpulver	30	6	15

b) Die Stauchprobe. Zwei Bleizylinder von 20 oder 30 mm Höhe und 31 bzw. 40 mm Durchmesser werden aufeinandergestellt. Darüber kommt ein Stahlplättchen von 3·13 mm Dicke und darauf der Sprengstoff. Letzterer (ca. 100 g) ist zunächst von einer Papierhülle und dann von einem Messinggewebe umgeben. Auf den Sprengstoff wird ein Pappdeckel mit einem zentralen Loch für eine 2 g-Sprengkapsel mit Zündschnur oder Leitungsdraht gelegt. Der untere Bleizylinder dient nur als weiche Unterlage für den oberen Zylinder, der durch die Explosion mehr oder weniger deformiert (gestaucht) wird. Die Stauchung bildet ein Maß für die Explosionskraft eines detonierenden Sprengstoffes, der frei aufliegend wirken soll (Brisanzprobe). Der untere Zylinder ist in einer kleinen Vertiefung einer breiten gußeisernen Unterlage angebracht. Der ganze Aufbau ist überdies durch Befestigungsdrähte mit der Unterlage verbunden.

[1] Nach Abzug von 61 ccm für den ursprünglichen Hohlraum, sowie 17 ccm für die 2 g-Sprengkapsel.

[2] Sprenggelatine = 100 gesetzt. Ferner ist die Voraussetzung gemacht, daß von je 100 vorhandener Energie bei Sprenggelatine durch die Ausbauchung 100 nachgewiesen werden.

c) Das ballistische Pendel. Dasselbe wird in mehreren Ausführungen zur Ermittelung der Kraftleistung von Sprengstoffen benützt. Ein auf der englischen Versuchsstrecke zu Woolwich gebrauchter Apparat besteht[1] aus: einem Mörser von 5 t Gewicht und 13 Zoll Kaliber, der in einem eisernen Rahmen an einem Balken aufgehängt ist und wie ein Pendel ausschlagen kann. Um die Kraft eines Sprengstoffes zu messen, wird nun eine besondere Kanone mit einer bestimmten Sprengstoffmenge geladen und mit einem genau abgewogenen Lattenbesatz verdämmt. Die Kanone wird sodann auf eine bestimmte Entfernung der Mündung des Mörsers gegenüber aufgestellt und abgefeuert. Der nun erfolgte größte Ausschlag des Mörsers kann an einem sich zusammenschiebenden Maßstabe abgelesen werden. Bei dieser Versuchsmethode kann man verhältnismäßig große Ladungen anwenden (z. B. 100 g). Man erhält regelmäßige Ergebnisse, und kann alle Arten von Sprengstoffen unmittelbar miteinander vergleichen.

d) Die Wurfprobe (Mörserprobe). Aus einem Mörser wird unter einem Winkel von 45° ein zylindrisches oder kugelförmiges Geschoß (ersteres für weniger brisante, letzteres für brisante Sprengstoffe), welches 15 bis 17 kg schwer ist und aus massivem Eisen besteht, mit 10 g Explosivstoff hinausgeschleudert. Die Wurfweite (in Metern) gibt ein Maß für die Kraft des Explosivstoffes.

e) Die Balkenprobe. Ein Balken aus weichem Holz von 22 × 30 cm Querschnitt und 1·5 m Länge wird 80 cm über dem Erdboden auf die hohe Kante und auf einen Meter freiliegend, angewendet. Die Sprengladung wird auf der Mitte des Balkens zur Detonation gebracht.[2]

Über Sprengstoffmessungen siehe noch: die Referate von Brunswig und Bichel, den Kongreßbericht 1903, Bd. II, S. 286 und S. 292; Bichel, Glückauf 1904, Hft. 35 und 1905, Hft. 15; Will, Zeitschr. f. Elektrochemie 1906, S. 558; Bichel, Untersuchungsmethoden für Sprengstoffe, Berlin 1902; Brunswig, Die Explosivstoffe, Leipzig 1907.

[1] Nach Heise, Sprengstoffe usw., S. 38.

[2] Näheres in Technischer Unterricht für die k. u. k. Eisenbahntruppe, 6. Teil, Sprengarbeiten, S. 66.

Vierter Abschnitt.

Das Glyzerindinitrat
(Dinitroglyzerin, basisches Nitroglyzerin).

1. Herstellung.

Das von Dr. Anton Mikolajczak in seiner Patentanmeldung vom 15. August 1903 angegebene Darstellungsverfahren ist schon auf Seite 40 mitgeteilt.

In der Fabrik Rummenohl bei Hagen, welche die Castroper Sicherheitssprengstoff-Aktiengesellschaft errichtet hat, um nach dem Mikolajczakschen Verfahren Dinitroglyzerin herzustellen, wird nach neueren Mitteilungen[1] in folgender Weise gearbeitet:

Die Herstellung verläuft in verschiedenen Abschnitten, die man als Nitrierung, Neutralisation, Scheidung, Waschung und Laugenverarbeitung trennen kann. — Für die Nitrierung läßt man das Glyzerin im langsamen Strahle unter ständiger Umrührung mit Luft in Salpetersäure einfließen, wobei sich das Gemisch bis zu einem gewissen Grade erwärmt und rote Dämpfe entweichen. Nachdem sämtliches Öl eingeflossen ist, erfolgt eine etwa zweistündige Nachnitrierung, um möglichst das ganze Öl in Dinitroglyzerin überzuführen. Danach haben wir ein Gemisch, das aus Dinitroglyzerin einerseits und der Säure andererseits besteht, in dem aber die beiden Flüssigkeiten gleichmäßig durcheinandergemengt erscheinen; es kommt nun darauf an, die beiden Flüssigkeiten voneinander zu trennen; dies kann erst geschehen, nachdem die Säure neutralisiert oder abgestumpft ist. Zu diesem Zweck bringt man Kalkspat in das Gemisch, das man gleichzeitig verdünnt; nunmehr bildet sich Kalksalpeter, der sich in Wasser löst; da das Dinitroglyzerin leichter ist als die wässerige Kalksalpeterlösung, steigt es nach oben. In der Scheidung zapft man das Dinitroglyzerin von der Lauge ab, so daß man für die weitere Verarbeitung es von nun an mit zwei Flüssigkeiten zu tun hat. — Waschung des Diöls. Das Dinitroglyzerin enthält zunächst noch Überreste der Säure und viel Wasser, durch Zusatz von Soda wird zunächst die Säure vollständig entfernt; zur Herausschaffung des Wassers wird das Öl durch eine besondere Behandlung getrocknet und schließlich als ein gelbrotes Öl vom spez. Gew. 1·5 erhalten. — Laugenverarbeitung. Die als Nebenprodukt sich ergebende Kalksalpeterlauge wird durch Behandlung mit Ammonsulfat in Ammonsalpeter und Kalksulfat (Gips) übergeführt, wovon der erstere für Sprengstoffbereitung, der Gips als künstliches Düngemittel Verwendung findet.

---

[1] Heise, Der Bergbau, 1907, Heft 35.

Nach dem D.R.P. 181385[1] der Zentralstelle für wissenschaftlich-technische Untersuchungen in Neubabelsberg ist bei der Darstellung von Dinitrat folgendes zu beachten: Die Zusammensetzung des Säuregemisches sowie dessen Menge im Verhältnis zur angewandten Menge Glyzerin werden zweckmäßig so gewählt, daß bei dem allmählichen Zusammenbringen beider Agenzien nur geringe Abscheidung von Öl stattfindet; die Bildung eines unlöslichen Öls (Trinitroglyzerin) muß möglichst vermieden werden, wenn es sich darum handelt, die Bildung von Dinitroglyzerin zu begünstigen. — Folgende Arbeitsweisen werden empfohlen:

Beispiel 1. 10 g Glyzerin werden in 500 g einer Mischsäure von der Zusammensetzung $10\,\%\,H_2O + 22{\cdot}5\,\%\,HNO_3 + 67{\cdot}5\,\%\,H_2SO_4$ bei 18 bis 20° C unter Umrühren einfließen gelassen; eine ölige Abscheidung tritt hierbei nicht oder nur in sehr geringem Maße ein; sie besteht in letzterem Falle ausschließlich aus Trinitroglyzerin. Man trennt dieses Öl in üblicher Weise ab und verdünnt die Säure, in welcher sich das gesamte gebildete Dinitroglyzerin befindet, mit Wasser; zweckmäßig verwendet man auf 1 Volumen dieser Säure 10 Volumen Wasser, indem bei solcher Verdünnung eine Einwirkung der Säure auf das Extraktionsmittel vermieden wird. Das mit dem Dinitroglyzerin beladene Extraktionsmittel (Äther usw.) wird zunächst neutralisiert; es hinterläßt nach dem Abdestillieren eine ölige Flüssigkeit, welche in der Regel noch Spuren von Trinitroglyzerin enthält. Man löst behufs weiterer Reinigung dieses Produkt in Wasser, wobei etwa vorhandenes Trinitroglyzerin ungelöst zurückbleibt; man extrahiert dann die wässerige Lösung zum zweiten Male, destilliert das Extraktionsmittel ab und trocknet das zurückbleibende Dinitroglyzerin. Man kann auch in der Weise verfahren, daß man die saure Lösung des Dinitroglyzerins neutralisiert, von eventuell ausgeschiedenem Sulfat abpreßt und die nunmehr neutrale Flüssigkeit extrahiert und im Vakuum destilliert. Die erhaltenen Ausbeuten betragen über 60 Prozent der Theorie.

Die Zusammensetzung der Mischsäuren kann auch folgende sein:

Beispiel 2. 100 g Glyzerin, 400 g Mischsäure von der Zusammensetzung: $8\,\%\,H_2O + 30{\cdot}7\,\%\,HNO_3 + 61{\cdot}3\,\%\,H_2SO_4$.

Beispiel 3. 100 g Glyzerin, 700 g Mischsäure von der Zusammensetzung: $12\,\%\,H_2O + 17{\cdot}6\,\%\,HNO_3 + 70{\cdot}4\,\%\,H_2SO_4$.

Nach dem D.R.P. 175751 der Zentralstelle Neubabelsberg läßt sich Dinitroglyzerin aus Trinitroglyzerin gewinnen, wenn man letzteres mit Schwefelsäure behandelt, die so

---

[1] Französ. Patent 352486 der Dynamit-Akt.-Ges. vorm. Alfred Nobel & Cie.

erhaltene saure Lösung mit Wasser verdünnt und aus dieser Lösung das Dinitroglyzerin mit den üblichen Hilfsmitteln extrahiert.

Die Auflösung des Trinitroglyzerins in der Schwefelsäure wird von einem chemischen Vorgang begleitet, dessen wesentliches Merkmal darin besteht, daß das Glyzerintrinitrat zu Glyzerindinitrat abgebaut wird; die sich vollziehende Auflösung des Trinitroglyzerins in der Schwefelsäure ist also kein rein physikalischer Prozeß in dem Sinne, wie Zucker von Wasser gelöst wird, sondern es findet gleichzeitig eine chemische Umwandlung statt, bei welcher das Trinitroglyzerin verschwindet, da es in der Schwefelsäure als solches nicht existenzfähig ist. Daß dieser Vorgang tatsächlich Platz greift, erkennt man unter anderm daran, daß die mit Wasser stark verdünnte schwefelsaure Lösung kein Öl abscheidet, was der Fall sein würde, wenn sie das in verdünnten Säuren unlösliche Trinitroglyzerin noch enthielte. Auch die chemische Analyse weist nach, daß in der wässerigen Schwefelsäurelösung, die nach der vorliegenden Erfindung mit Lösungsmitteln behandelt wird, kein Trinitroglyzerin vorhanden ist, sondern Dinitroglyzerin. Eine Trennung von Trinitroglyzerin vom Dinitroglyzerin kommt demnach bei dem vorliegenden Verfahren nicht in Frage, sondern es handelt sich darum, das in der verdünnten schwefelsauren Lösung enthaltene Dinitroglyzerin aus dieser Lösung zu isolieren. — Als zweckmäßige Arbeitsweise wird folgende angegeben: 100 g Trinitroglyzerin werden mit 1000 g Schwefelsäure von 70 Prozent H_2SO_4 geschüttelt, bis eine klare oder nahezu klare Lösung entstanden ist. Der Prozeß geht glatt, ohne sichtbare Zersetzungserscheinung (Bildung von roten Dämpfen) vor sich. Etwa ungelöst gebliebenes Trinitroglyzerin wird abgeschöpft und die klare Lösung hierauf unter den üblichen Vorsichtsmaßregeln, wie Vermeidung von Temperatursteigerung, in 4 bis 5 Liter Wasser gegossen. Man extrahiert mit Äther, neutralisiert und erhält nach dem Abdestillieren des Äthers reines Dinitroglyzerin. Man kann auch (statt mit Äther) mit Chloroform, Benzol, Benzin extrahieren.

Nach einer Patentanmeldung der Aktiengesellschaft Dynamit Nobel in Wien vom 28. Oktober 1905 trägt man zur Erzeugung von Glyzerindinitrat verdünntes Glyzerin in Salpetersäure von ungefähr 48° Bé bei Temperaturen unter 25° C ein, läßt das entstandene Gemisch sofort in Wasser laufen und scheidet nach erfolgter Neutralisation das gebildete Öl ab.

Escales und Novak (deutsche Patentanmeldung vom 10. November 1906) stellen durch Vermischen von 1 Teil Glyzerin mit etwas über 2 Tln. Schwefelsäure Glyzerindischwefelsäure her; letztere wird nicht isoliert, sondern durch Behandeln mit Salpetersäure in Glyzerindinitrat übergeführt.

Eine zweckmäßige Arbeitsweise ist beispielsweise folgende: 92 g Glyzerin vom spez. Gewicht 1·26 werden mit etwa 200 g Schwefelsäure (1·84) zusammengebracht, durchgemischt und dann auf eine Temperatur von 15 bis 20° C abkühlen gelassen; hierauf werden ca. 150 g Salpetersäure (1·48 spez. Gew.) zugesetzt und bei dieser Nitration Temperatursteigerungen über 30° C hinaus vermieden; nach beendigter Nitrierung kühlt man auf ca. 20° ab und überläßt dann das Gemisch so lange sich selbst, bis die Temperatur ohne oder auch mit langsamer äußerer Wärmezufuhr auf 30 bis 35° gestiegen ist; hierauf rührt man das Gemisch in das zwei- bis dreifache Volumen Wasser. Zum Schluß wird mit Äther oder einem andern Lösungsmittel extrahiert.

Für die Praxis empfiehlt sich vielfach die Herstellung eines Gemenges von Di- und Trinitroglyzerin; auch hierfür sind mehrere Verfahren in der Patentliteratur angegeben.

Mikolajczak[1] beschreibt ein Verfahren zur Herstellung von Glyzerindinitrat in Mischung mit Glyzerintrinitrat, dadurch gekennzeichnet, daß man entweder eine Lösung von Glyzerin in Salpetersäure länger als fünf Stunden einer Nachnitrierung unterwirft und das gebildete Sprengöl durch Neutralisation der Säure abscheidet oder eine Lösung von Glyzerin in Salpetersäure oder in Salpeterschwefelsäure mit Salpeterschwefelsäure oder mit Schwefelsäure allein zwecks Abscheidung des Sprengöls behandelt.

Um ein Dinitroglyzerin mit geringem, etwa bis 20 Prozent ansteigendem Gehalt an Glyzerintrinitrat herzustellen, genügt es, eine Lösung von Glyzerin in starker Salpetersäure etwa 12 Stunden an einem mäßig warmen Orte einer langsamen Nachnitrierung zu unterziehen und darauf das Öl durch Neutralisation der Säure abzuscheiden. Schneller und ökonomischer gewinnt man aber derartige Gemische von Dinitroglyzerin mit beliebigem Gehalt an Trinitroglyzerin unter gemeinsamer Anwendung von Salpetersäure und Schwefelsäure. Um z. B. Dinitroglyzerin mit etwa 33 Prozent Glyzerintrinitrat zu gewinnen, arbeitet man wie nachstehend angegeben: Etwa 100 Gewichtsteile Glyzerin vom spez. Gew. 1·261 bis 1·262 werden unter Umrühren und guter Kühlung in etwa 90 Teilen starker, von Untersalpetersäure möglichst freier Salpetersäure, deren spezifisches Gewicht tunlichst nicht unter 1·5 liegt, gelöst. In diese Lösung, deren Temperatur man möglichst bei + 10° bis + 15° C hält, wird ein ebenfalls gekühltes Gemisch von 160 Teilen einer Schwefelsäure von ca. 64° Bé (= 1·795 spez. Gew.) unter stetem Umrühren langsam eingetragen. Das durch den Säurezusatz ausgeschiedene Öl wird darauf in bekannter Weise im Scheidetrichter von der Säure getrennt. Da das Dinitroglyzerin in Wasser erheblich leichter löslich ist als das bekannte Trinitroglyzerin, so ist

[1] Französ. Patent 349078; deutsche Patentanmeldung M 24611 vom 18. Dez. 1903; engl. Patent 27706 (1904); amerik. Patent 830909.

es bei dem nun folgenden Entsäuern und Waschen des Öls zur Vermeidung von Verlusten ratsam, mit dem Waschwasser sowie mit der eventuell noch verwendeten Soda- oder andern alkalischen Lauge recht sparsam zu sein; dies wird erreicht, wenn man die einzelnen Waschwässer gut abklären läßt. Das gewaschene Öl wird, eventuell durch Zuhilfenahme unschädlicher, wasserentziehender Mittel, getrocknet; es ist trocken, wenn es sich in Benzol klar löst. — Die im Scheidetrichter vom erhaltenen Öl entnommene Säure wird nun gekühlt, unter Rühren mit etwa 120 Teilen 66prozentiger Schwefelsäure versetzt und das Gemisch dann zwecks weiterer Scheidung der Ruhe überlassen, wobei Glyzerintrinitrat zur Abscheidung gelangt, welches in üblicher Weise gewaschen und entsäuert wird. Die Abfallsäure wird der üblichen Nachscheidung unterworfen und dann denitriert. — Ändert man in dem oben beschriebenen Verfahren die Konzentration oder auch die Menge der Schwefelsäure, so erhält man ein Produkt mit mehr oder weniger hohem Gehalt an Trinitroglyzerin, so z. B. erhält man ein Gemenge von gleichen Teilen Tri- und Dinitrat, wenn man 225 Teile der 64prozentigen Schwefelsäure statt obiger 180 Teile anwendet. — Das Glyzerin kann man auch erst mit der ganzen Menge Salpetersäure vermischen, einer Nachnitrierung unterziehen und zum Schluß durch Schwefelsäurezusatz das Öl zur Abscheidung bringen. — In allen diesen Fällen resultiert ein Produkt mit bedeutendem Gehalt an Glyzerintrinitrat; auch hat auf den glatten Verlauf und den Prozentsatz an Trinitrat die Konzentration des Glyzerins ebenfalls einen mitbestimmenden Einfluß.

Escales und Novak (deutsche Patentanmeldung vom 12. September 1906) gehen aus von der Glyzerindischwefelsäure; letztere wird erhalten, indem man 100 g Glyzerin (spez. Gew. 1·26) und 440 g Schwefelsäure (spez. Gew. 1·84) zusammengießt und von selbst erkalten läßt, dann 120 g lufttrockenen Kalk zufügt, abfiltriert und das Filtrat eindampft.

Die Glyzerindischwefelsäure (vom spez. Gew. 1·5) wird entweder mit einem Gemisch von Salpetersäure und Schwefelsäure oder besser mit Salpetersäure (spez. Gew. 1·52) allein nitriert (Verfahren wie bei der Herstellung von Trinitroglyzerin, Temperatur nicht über 30° C). Nach der Nitrierung wird die überschüssige Schwefel- und Salpetersäure mit Kalk neutralisiert und aus dem Filtrat das Sprengöl mit Äther ausgezogen. Das gelbbraune Öl bleibt nach dem Verdunsten des Äthers zurück.

2. Eigenschaften des Glyzerindinitrates.

Während im gewöhnlichen (Tri-)Nitroglyzerin $C_3H_5(ONO_2)_3$ sämtliche drei Hydroxylgruppen des Glyzerins durch Salpetersäure esterifiziert sind, bleibt die Esterifizierung beim Dinitroglyzerin auf zwei Hydroxylgruppen beschränkt, die dritte Hydroxylgruppe ist intakt; die chemische Zusammensetzung ist daher

$C_3H_5OH(ONO_2)_2$.[1] Die Bezeichnung basisches Nitroglyzerin dürfte am zweckentsprechendsten sein. Das Dinitroglyzerin oder basische Nitroglyzerin ist nach Mikolajczak völlig gefahrlos herzustellen; selbst bei absichtlich eingeleiteten Zersetzungen erfolgte keine Explosion.

Dinitroglyzerin ist ein farbloses oder schwach gelbliches geruchloses Öl vom spez. Gew. 1·47 bei 15°. Bei 15 mm Druck siedet es konstant bei 146° C. Es erstarrt zu einer glasigen Masse erst bei unter — 30° C liegenden Temperaturen. In Wasser von 15° C löst es sich etwa im Verhältnis von 1 : 20, noch leichter (etwa 1 : 5) in verdünnten Säuren. Dinitroglyzerin schmeckt brennend und hat auf die Kopfnerven eine ähnliche giftige Einwirkung wie Trinitroglyzerin. Gegen höhere Temperaturen ist es unempfindlicher als Trinitroglyzerin; es brennt, durch Feuer zur Entzündung gebracht, ruhig und ohne Detonation ab; auch gegen mechanische Einwirkungen (Stoß oder Schlag) ist es weniger empfindlich als das Trinitrat; nach Will detoniert trockenes Trinitrat unter einem Fallhammer von 2 kg bei einer Fallhöhe von 4 cm, trockenes Dinitrat bei 7 cm Fallhöhe.

Mikolajczak bezeichnet das Dinitrat als durchaus stabile Verbindung. Bei der Explosion im Trauzlschen Bleiblock erzeugen (nach Will)

7·5 g Dinitroglyzerin }
2·5 g Kieselgur } eine Ausbauchung von 290 ccm,

7·5 g Trinitroglyzerin }
2·5 g Kieselgur } eine Ausbauchung von 345 ccm.

Dinitroglyzerin ist ein ebenso gutes Lösungs- bzw. Gelatinierungsmittel für die verschiedensten Körper, z. B. Nitrozellulose, Nitrostärke usw.; Kollodiumwolle wird sogar schon in der Kälte vollkommen gelatiniert. — Das Dinitrat löst bzw. mischt sich in jedem Verhältnis mit Trinitrat und drückt den Gefrierpunkt des letzteren wesentlich herab; Gemenge von 50 Prozent Di- und 50 Prozent Trinitrat behalten bei — 20° und tiefer noch ihren flüssigen Zustand bei, Mischungen von 30 Prozent Di- und 70 Prozent Trinitrat erstarren bei — 12° C.

Blochmann[2] gibt die nachstehend abgedruckte Zusammenstellung:

---

[1] Theoretisch sind zwei verschiedene Dinitrate möglich, nämlich:

$$CH_2ONO_2—CHOH—CH_2ONO_2$$

und

$$CH_2ONO_2—CHONO_2—CH_2OH.$$

[2] In „Der Bergbau“ 1905 Nr. 48.

1	2	3	4	5	6	7
	Dichte bei 15° C	Beständigkeitsprobe (Test) mit Jodzinkstärkepapier im Ölbade von 70° C	Deflagration. Eine Patrone von 100 g gelatinierter Substanz verbrennt nach Entflammung	Verpuffungstemperatur bei allmählicher Erhitzung	Explosionsübertragung. Eine Patrone von 100 g gelatinierter Substanz entzündet eine Nachbarpatrone bis zu	Wasserlöslichkeit. Beim Schütteln in reichlich überschüssigem Wasser werden aufgenommen in einer Stunde
Glyzerindinitrat	1·51	nach 8 Minuten kräftige Schwärzung	lebhaft mit heller Flamme	167°	5 cm	5·5%
Glyzerintrinitrat	1·60	unverändert während 20 Minuten	lebhaft mit heller, zischender Flamme.	180°	25 cm	0·2%

	8		9	10			11		12		
	Hygroskopizität. Es wird aufgenommen von Wasser in der feuchten Kammer		Wärmemenge, die von 1 kg entwickelt wird in Kalorien	Detonationsgeschwindigkeit. Substanz			Ausbauchung im Bleiblock		Fallhammer-Versuch. Explosion tritt ein bei einem Fallhammergewicht von … bei einer Fallhöhe von		
	a) in 1 Tag	b) in 7 Tagen		flüssig	gelatiniert	mit 25% Gur	gelatiniert	mit 25% Gur	100 g	250 g	500 g
Dinitrat	3·3%	11%	942	1525	3320	4290	330	270	15	10	5
Trinitrat	0%	0%	1550	1525	7000	6820	420	370	10	5	5

Im Dinitroglyzerin läßt sich die noch vorhandene Hydroxylgruppe esterifizieren, so erhält man mit Acetylchlorid, Benzoylchlorid u. a. entsprechende Ester, z. B. $C_3H_5(ONO_2)_2 \cdot (O \cdot CH_3 \cdot CO)$ Acetyl-Dinitroglyzerin; diese Ester besitzen ein hohes Gelatinierungsvermögen gegenüber nitrierter Zellulose, nitrierter Stärke, Nitroglyzerin usw.; sie sind nicht hygroskopisch, sind unlöslich in Wasser, aber leicht löslich in Äther, Alkohol, Aceton; sie können in der Fabrikation von rauchlosem Pulver, Zelluloid usw. Verwendung finden.

Fünfter Abschnitt.

Gemischte Glyzerinester.

Am Schlusse des vorigen Abschnittes wurde erwähnt, daß man das Glyzerindinitrat $C_3H_5(ONO_2)_2OH$ noch weiter esterifizieren kann, z. B. zu $C_3H_5(ONO_2)_2(OCH_3CO)$ Dinitromonoacetylglyzerin; gewöhnlich geht man aber zur Herstellung solcher gemischten Ester nicht von einem partiell mit Salpetersäure esterifizierten Glyzerin aus, sondern von einem Glyzerin, dessen eine oder auch zwei Hydroxylgruppen durch Salzsäure oder auch Essigsäure oder Ameisensäure esterifiziert sind und läßt dann auf diese Chlorhydrine bzw. Acetine oder Formine zur vollständigen Esterifizierung Salpetersäure (+ Schwefelsäure) einwirken.

A. Dinitromonochlorhydrin (Monochlordinitroglyzerin) $C_3H_5Cl(ONO_2)_2$.

a) Das Ausgangsmaterial ist Chlorhydrin (Monochlorhydrin) $C_3H_5 \cdot Cl(OH)_2$, also ein Glyzerin, in dem eine Hydroxylgruppe (OH) durch Chlor ersetzt ist, bzw. der Mono-Salzsäure-Ester des Glyzerins.

Nach dem D.R.P. 180668 der Deutschen Sprengstoff-Aktiengesellschaft läßt sich Chlorhydrin gewinnen, wenn man Glyzerin mit gewöhnlicher wässeriger Salzsäure (spez. Gew. 1·185) im Autoklaven während 15 Stunden auf 120° erhitzt; der durch die wässerige Salzsäure eingeführte Wasserzusatz verhindert vollkommen die Bildung von Dichlorhydrin ($C_3H_5Cl_2OH$), während andererseits der Druck von etwa einer Atmosphäre genügt, um die Chlorierung in gewünschtem Sinne in sehr guter Ausbeute durchzuführen. — Nach dem Abtreiben des Wassers und der überschüssigen Salzsäure verbleibt ein Gemenge von etwa 75 Prozent Monochlorhydrin und 25 Prozent unverändertem Glyzerin, aus welchem das Monochlorhydrin durch fraktionierte Destillation im Vakuum gewonnen werden kann. In der Praxis nitriert man das Gemenge und erhält dann ein Gemisch von Dinitro-chlorhydrin und Trinitroglyzerin.

Beispiel: 100 kg Dynamitglyzerin werden bei gewöhnlicher Temperatur mit 150 kg wässeriger Salzsäure, spez. Gew. 1·180 bis

1·190, gemischt und dann während 15 Stunden im Autoklaven auf 120° unter 1 Atm. Druck erhitzt; wird das hierdurch erhaltene Chlorierungsgut der fraktionierten Destillation im Vakuum (12 bis 15 mm Druck) unterworfen, so entweicht zuerst das Wasser und zugleich mit diesem die unverbrauchte Säure; hierauf destilliert das Monochlorhydrin zwischen 130 und 150° C und zum Schlusse zwischen 165 und 180° das unveränderte Glyzerin; bei Verwendung zu Sprengstoffzwecken kann diese letzte Destillation unterbleiben.

Nach dem französischen Patent 370224 der Deutschen Sprengstoff-Aktiengesellschaft wird Monochlorhydrin erhalten, wenn man Glyzerin bei gewöhnlicher Temperatur unter kräftigem Rühren mit der berechneten Menge Chlorschwefel vermischt und die Temperatur dann so regelt, daß die Reaktion sich bei 40 bis 50° C vollzieht. Es werden auf diese Weise 80 bis 90 Prozent des angewendeten Glyzerins direkt in Monochlorhydrin übergeführt; der Rest besteht aus unverändertem Glyzerin. Das während der Reaktion gebildete Wasser wird durch Erhitzen im Vakuum bei 60 bis 70° entfernt. Die Trennung des Monochlorhydrins von dem Glyzerin kann durch Destillation im Vakuum bewirkt werden, zur Nitrierung wird jedoch gewöhnlich das Gemisch verwendet.

Nach dem französischen Patent 352750 der Westfälisch-Anhaltischen Sprengstoff-Aktiengesellschaft wird α-Monochlorhydrin $CH_2Cl—CHOH—CH_2OH$ erhalten, wenn man Salzsäure in Glyzerin leitet, das auf 70 bis 100° erwärmt ist (nebenbei bildet sich etwas β-Chlorhydrin $CH_2OH—CH \cdot Cl—CH_2OH$); nach beendigter Einwirkung destilliert man im Vakuum, wobei das Chlorhydrin zwischen 135 und 165° übergeht.

b) Herstellung von Dinitromonochlorhydrin. Nach F. Roewer[1] läßt sich das Monochlorhydrin in der gleichen Weise wie Glyzerin durch ein Gemisch von Salpetersäure und Schwefelsäure nitrieren; das gebildete Dinitromonochlorhydrin scheidet sich nach der Nitrierung bei dem Stehen der Reaktionsmasse scharf und schnell von dem Säuregemisch ab, kann leicht getrennt und dann durch Waschen mit Wasser oder leicht alkalischen Wässern ohne alle Schwierigkeit stabilisiert werden; es erfüllt nicht nur die Vorschriften des englischen Jodkaliumstärketest, sondern ist viel beständiger, so daß die Färbung des Papiers selbst nach der dreifachen Zeit nicht auftritt. Das Dinitromonochlorhydrin (Monochlordinitroglyzerin) stellt eine schwach gelbliche, leicht bewegliche Flüssigkeit von schwach aromatischem Geruch dar, die in organischen Lösungsmitteln, wie Äther, Alkohol, Aceton, Chloroform usw., löslich, dagegen in Wasser und Säuren unlöslich ist; das spezifische Gewicht beträgt 1·5408 bei 15° C. — Beim

[1] Zeitschr. Schieß-Sprengstoffwesen I, S. 229.

Erhitzen beginnt es bei ca. 180° gelbliche Dämpfe auszustoßen und bei ca. 190° zu sieden und abzudestillieren, ohne daß Detonation oder Verpuffung eintritt; der Siedepunkt bei gewöhnlichem Atmosphärendruck liegt bei 190 bis 193° C, Zersetzungserscheinungen treten beim Destillieren nur in geringem Maße (gelbliche Dämpfe) auf; bei vermindertem Druck läßt es sich völlig unzersetzt destillieren; unter einem Druck von 15 mm geht es bei 121 bis 123° C als ein fast farbloses Öl über. — Besonders bemerkenswert ist die große Unempfindlichkeit des Dinitromonochlorhydrins gegen Stoß, Schlag und Reibung; während unter einem 2 kg-Fallhammer Trinitroglyzerin bei einer Fallhöhe von 3 bis 5 cm, Dinitroglyzerin bei 5 bis 7 cm Fallhöhe detoniert, ist das Dinitromonochlorhydrin selbst bei einer Fallhöhe von 2 m noch nicht zur Detonation zu bringen; auch bei Anwendung schwererer Fallhämmer (bis zu 20 kg) detonierte es nicht,[1] ist also gegen Stoß, Schlag und Reibung als besonders unempfindlich zu betrachten; durch Zumischung zum Trinitroglyzerin setzt es die Empfindlichkeit des letzteren erheblich herab. — Mit einer Knallquecksilbersprengkapsel initiiert detoniert das Dinitromonochlorhydrin regelmäßig und vollständig; die Wirkung im Trauzlschen Bleiblock ist ungefähr die gleiche wie beim Trinitrat. — Temperaturerniedrigung bis auf — 25° bis — 30° C brachte das Dinitromonochlorhydrin nicht zum Erstarren, bzw. Kristallisieren. Das Produkt ist nicht hygroskopisch; die völlige Unlöslichkeit in Wasser und Säuren machen dasselbe nicht nur für die Verwendung von Sprengstoffen besonders geeignet, sondern bieten auch für die fabrikatorische Herstellung große Vorteile, da sich das Öl nach beendigter Nitrierung glatt ohne jegliche Manipulation von der Nitriersäure abscheiden läßt und den nachfolgenden Waschprozeß zu einem äußerst einfachen und leichten gestaltet. Das Dinitromonochlorhydrin löst, was für Sprengstoffzwecke sehr wichtig ist, Nitrozellulose auf und bildet mit derselben eine plastische, nicht abtropfende Gelatine, verhält sich in dieser Beziehung also genau wie Trinitroglyzerin. — Die wichtigste Eigenschaft des Dinitromonochlorhydrins ist aber das außerordentlich große Lösungsvermögen für Trinitroglyzerin, das so groß ist, daß selbst bei verhältnismäßig sehr niedrigen Temperaturen selbst eine partielle Entmischung nicht stattfindet. Schon bei einem Zusatz von 5 bis 10 Prozent Dinitromonochlorhydrin zu Nitroglyzerin wird eine beträchtliche Herabsetzung des Gefrier-

---

[1] Nach franz. Patent 352750 detoniert Trinitroglyzerin bei 15 bis 20 cm, dagegen Dinitromonochlorhydrin bei 80 bis 85 cm Fallhöhe.

punktes des Nitroglyzerins bzw. der damit hergestellten Sprengstoffe erreicht; mit einem Zusatz von ca. 20 Prozent Dinitromonochlorhydrin erzielt man für die in Deutschland in Betracht kommenden Wintertemperaturen schon ungefrierbare Nitroglyzerinsprengstoffe; in kälteren Ländern wird man den Zusatz eventuell etwas erhöhen müssen. — Nach dem D.R.P. 183400 der Deutschen Sprengstoff-Aktiengesellschaft werden dem Nitroglyzerin, welches zu Sprengstoffen Verwendung findet, 5 bis 20 Prozent Monochlordinitroglyzerin zugesetzt, wodurch es gelingt, je nach der Menge des Zusatzes die Gefrierbarkeit der Sprengstoffe ganz aufzuheben oder doch erheblich herabzusetzen, ohne daß die Brisanz darunter leidet. Nitroglyzerin mit einem Zusatz von 20 Prozent Monochlordinitroglyzerin wurde z. B. in einer Schale auf ein Kältegemisch bei einer Temperatur von etwa — 13° C gestellt und mit einem Nitroglyzerinkristall geimpft; nach sechsstündigem Aufbewahren in dem Kältegemisch war keine Vergrößerung des Impfkristalles wahrnehmbar, während reines Nitroglyzerin unter gleichen Umständen sehr rasch erstarrte. Bei der Herstellung von nicht gelatinierten Sprengstoffen führt das Monochlordinitroglyzerin keine Unbequemlichkeiten mit sich, während es bei der Darstellung gelatinierter Sprengstoffe insofern förderlich wirkt, als die Gelatinierfähigkeit mit Kollodiumwolle erhöht wird. — Von einem Nachteile des Dinitromonochlorhydrins kann man insofern sprechen, als es bei der Detonation freie Salzsäure bildet; für die Absättigung der letzteren, die unter Tag Belästigungen der Arbeiter hervorrufen könnte, muß natürlich gesorgt werden und geschieht dies am bequemsten dadurch, daß man dem Sprengstoff Alkalinitrate zusetzt; das bei der Reaktion sich bildende Natriumkarbonat neutralisiert dann die Salzsäure unter Bildung von Chlornatrium; man kann auch Metalle hinzusetzen, dann werden die betreffenden Metallchloride gebildet; bekanntlich wird durch Zusatz von Chlornatrium und anderen Chloriden die Wettersicherheit der Sprengstoffe erhöht.

In der Praxis erzeugt man das Gemisch von Trinitroglyzerin und Dinitromonochlorhydrin nicht in der Weise, daß man zunächst das eine und andere Sprengöl getrennt herstellt, sondern man nitriert gleich ein Gemisch von Glyzerin und Monochlorhydrin in solchem Verhältnis, daß bei nachfolgender Nitrierung des Gemisches ein Sprengöl von der gewünschten Zusammensetzung erhalten wird.

Das Dinitrochlorhydrin läßt sich nach D.R.P. 74253 durch Behandeln mit pikrinsaurem Kali in alkoholischer Lösung bei 70 bis 80° in Triphenoldinitroglyzerin $C_3H_5[OC_6H_2(NO_2)_3](O \cdot NO_2)_2$ überführen.

B. Mononitrodichlorhydrin.

Man geht aus von Dichlorhydrin $C_3H_5Cl_2OH$ und führt solches durch Nitrieren in Nitrodichlorhydrin $C_3H_5(NO_2)Cl_2$ über.

Nach dem englischen Patent 17891 (1906) wird dem Trinitroglyzerin eine Mischung von Dinitromonochlorhydrin und Nitrodichlorhydrin zugesetzt, wodurch nicht nur die Gefrierbarkeit derselben, sondern auch ihre Empfindlichkeit gegen Schlag und Stoß bedeutend herabgesetzt werden soll; die Mischung aus Dinitromonochlorhydrin und Nitrodichlorhydrin kann entweder durch Nitrieren einer Mischung von Chlorhydrin und Dichlorhydrin oder durch direktes Mischen beider Komponenten hergestellt werden.

C. Nitroacetine und Nitroformine.

Dr. Vender[1] fand, daß die Nitrierung von basischen Acetinen [$C_3H_5(OH)_2(OCH_3CO)$ Monoacetin; $C_3H_5OH(O\cdot CH_3CO)_2$ Biacetin] mit gewöhnlicher Salpeterschwefelsäure, wie solche zur Herstellung von Trinitroglyzerin verwendet wird, zu Trinitroglyzerin mit nur wenig Nitroacetin führt und überhaupt schlechte Ausbeute an Nitraten liefert; nur bei Anwendung von reiner Salpetersäure mit mehr als 65 Prozent HNO_3 oder von Salpeter-Schwefelsäure-Mischungen, welche mehr Salpetersäure als Schwefelsäure enthalten, bekam Vender die reinen Nitroacetine.

Man erhält z. B. Dinitroacetin $C_3H_5(ONO_2)_2(OCH_3CO)$ in einer Ausbeute von 95 Prozent der theoretischen, wenn man 40 Teile Monoacetin allmählich in eine Mischung aus 100 Teilen Salpetersäure von 1·513 und 25 Teilen Oleum mit 25 Prozent SO_3-Gehalt einträgt und dabei derart abkühlt, daß die Temperatur niemals über 25° C steigt; nach beendigter Nitrierung gießt man in Wasser und wäscht zum Schluß das erhaltene Produkt zuerst mit kalter, dann mit 70° C warmer verdünnter Sodalösung. — Das Dinitroacetin ist ein blaßgelbes Öl vom spez. Gew. 1·45 bei 15° C, das in Wasser, Benzol, Schwefelkohlenstoff unlöslich, in Salpetersäure, Äthyl- und Methylalkohol, Aceton, Äther und Nitroglyzerin leicht löslich ist; im Nitrometer wurde sein Stickstoffgehalt zu 12·5 Prozent N bestimmt. Durch Schlag mit dem Hammer explodiert es nicht, leicht aber mit der Sprengkapsel; im Trauzlschen Bleizylinder ergeben 10 g eine Ausbauchung von 450 ccm. — Das Dinitroacetin besitzt ein so großes Lösungsvermögen für Nitrozellulosen, daß es leicht schon in der Kälte Schießbaumwolle mit 13·4 Prozent N gelatiniert; die so erhaltene Gelatine und die daraus hergestellten hornartigen Sprengstoffe und Pulver sind ganz homogen; sie können bei Temperaturen bis zu —20° lange mit Nitroglyzerinkristallen in Berührung bleiben, ohne selbst zu erstarren.

[1] Zeitschr. Schieß-Sprengstoffwesen II, S. 21.

Dinitroformin $C_3H_5(ONO_2)_2(O\cdot CHO)$ wurde von Vender in ähnlicher Weise wie Dinitroacetin erhalten. Ein Gemisch von Glyzerin mit der Hälfte seines Gemisches wasserfreier Oxalsäure wird zuerst auf 100°, dann 20 Stunden lang auf 140 bis 150° erwärmt und hierauf mit Salpeterschwefelsäure nitriert; das mit verdünnter Sodalösung gewaschene Produkt ist ein Gemisch von 70 Prozent Glyzerintrinitrat und 30 Prozent Dinitroformin und kann direkt zur Herstellung schwer gefrierbarer Sprengstoffe Verwendung finden.

Nach Vender sind Dinitroacetin und Dinitroformin Sprengöle von sehr niedrigem Erstarrungspunkt; im Verhältnis von 10 bis 30 Prozent dem Trinitroglyzerin beigefügt, ergeben sie Explosivstoffe, deren Erstarrungspunkt (in Berührung mit Nitroglyzerinkristallen) bis zu —20° heruntergeht. Dinitroformin und Dinitroacetin entwickeln beinahe die gleiche Sprengkraft wie Trinitroglyzerin; sie sind viel weniger empfindlich als letzteres beim Stoß und Schlag, explodieren aber schon leicht bei Anwendung schwacher Sprengkapseln an freier Luft; gegen Wärme sind sie viel beständiger als Trinitroglyzerin, so kann man Dinitroacetin leicht destillieren.

Sechster Abschnitt.

Nitrate von polymerisiertem Glyzerin.

1. Nach dem D.R.P. 58957 (vom 17. August 1890) von Dr. Alfred Wohl wird Glyzerin durch Erhitzen mit konzentrierter Schwefelsäure auf 130 bis 160° polymerisiert; je nach der verwendeten Säuremenge und der Dauer des Erhitzens ist die Anhydridbildung weiter vorgeschritten; ein Teil des Glyzerins ist dann nach der Gleichung

$$2\,C_3H_5(OH)_3 = H_2O + \begin{matrix} C_3H_5(OH)_2 \\ C_3H_5(OH)_2 \end{matrix}\!\!>\!O$$

in Diglyzerin (Glyzeryläther des Glyzerins) umgewandelt; das erhaltene Gemisch[1] von Glyzerin und Diglyzerin wird dann nach dem Erkalten nitriert.

Will[2] hat dieses Verfahren nacharbeiten lassen; es ist aber nicht gelungen, beim Erhitzen von Glyzerin mit 0·5 bis 5 Prozent Schwefelsäure ein Produkt zu erhalten, welches sich zu einem

---

[1] Wohl setzt eventuell noch Isoamylalkohol und andere Alkohole zu, das resultierende Gemenge enthält dann neben Glyzerin und Diglyzerin noch Alkylglyzerinäther.

[2] Zeitschr. Schieß-Sprengstoffwesen I, S. 231.

brauchbaren Sprengöl hätte nitrieren lassen. Die Reaktion ergab nicht nur Gemenge von Glyzerin mit Polyglyzerinen, bzw. deren Sulfosäuren, sondern noch andersartige Nebenprodukte, welche bewirkten, daß bei der Nitrierung braune, nicht zu reinigende Öle entstanden.

2. Will und Stöhrer[1] haben Glyzerin durch einfaches Erhitzen von Glyzerin (ohne Säurezusatz) polymerisiert; zweckmäßig erwies sich ein 7- bis 8stündiges Erhitzen auf 290 bis 295° C. Wenn dafür Sorge getragen wird, daß nur das abgespaltene Wasser abdestilliert, die höher siedenden flüchtigen Teile aber wieder zu dem Reaktionsgemisch zurückfließen, so bilden sich aus dem Glyzerin bis zu 60 Prozent Diglyzerine und je nach der Erhitzung 4 bis 6 Prozent Tri-, bzw. Polyglyzerine; die Isolierung der polymerisierten Glyzerine kann am besten durch fraktionierte Destillation bei 8 bis 10 mm Druck bewirkt werden; hierbei destilliert das Glyzerin bei 160 bis 220°, das polymerisierte Glyzerin bei 220 bis 270° über; durch mehrfach wiederholte Vakuumdestillation kann man das reine Diglyzerin gewinnen. Das Diglyzerin stellt eine wasserhelle, sehr zähe, süßschmeckende, in Wasser leicht lösliche Flüssigkeit dar, die bei 8 mm Druck bei 240 bis 250° C unzersetzt destilliert; das spezifische Gewicht beträgt 1·33, die Viskosität ist elfmal so groß als die des Glyzerins.

Das Diglyzerin läßt sich leicht nitrieren in ähnlicher Weise wie Glyzerin selbst; man erhält ein ziemlich zähflüssiges, wasserunlösliches Öl, das Tetranitrodiglyzerin $C_6H_{10}N_4O_{13}$, oder

$$\begin{matrix} C_3H_5(ONO_2)_2 \diagdown \\ \rangle O\,. \\ C_3H_5(ONO_2)_2 \diagup \end{matrix}$$

Das Tetranitrodiglyzerin (Diglyzerintetranitrat) verhält sich dem gewöhnlichen Trinitroglyzerin ähnlich; es ist in organischen Lösungsmitteln, wie Äther, Alkohol usw., leicht löslich, detoniert leicht durch Stoß oder mit Hilfe einer Initialzündung wie Knallquecksilber, zeigt (in Mischung mit Kieselgur) bei der Detonation fast die gleiche Sprengwirkung wie das gewöhnliche Trinitroglyzerin, ist aber im allgemeinen weniger empfindlich als dieses. Besonders bemerkenswert ist die Eigenschaft des Tetranitrodiglyzerins, auch bei sehr hohen Kältegraden flüssig oder wenigstens zähe zu bleiben; auch Gemenge von Trinitroglyzerin mit 20 bis 25 Prozent Tetranitrodiglyzerin sind bei den gewöhnlichen Wintertemperaturen nicht gefroren. — In der Praxis wird man das, durch 6- bis 7stündiges Erhitzen von Glyzerin auf 295° er-

[1] Zeitschr. Schieß-Sprengstoffwesen I. S. 231.

haltene Produkt durch frischen Zusatz von unpolymerisiertem Glyzerin verdünnen und dieses Gemenge von 75 bis 80 Prozent Glyzerin mit 10 bis 25 Prozent polymerisiertem Glyzerin nitrieren; die hierbei entstehenden Nitrate geben praktisch ungefrierbare Dynamite.

3. Lourenzo[1] vermischte zur Herstellung von Diglyzerin gleiche Teile Glyzerin mit einem durch Zusatz von 33 Prozent Wasser verdünnten, mit gasförmiger Salzsäure gesättigten und auf 100° erwärmten Glyzerin; dieses Gemenge wird in einem Ölbade am Rückflußkühler 12 bis 15 Stunden lang auf 130° C erwärmt und daraus durch fraktionierte Destillation Diglyzerin (in schlechter Ausbeute) gewonnen. Eine Nitrierung der erhaltenen Produkte wurde weder von Lourenzo noch von Will, der die Lourenzoschen Versuche wiederholte, durchgeführt.

Escales und Novak haben das Lourenzosche Verfahren abgeändert und die entstehenden Körper durch Nitrierung in Sprengöle übergeführt.[2]

Ein Teil Glyzerin wird mit $^1/_6$ bis $^1/_5$ Gewichtsteilen Wasser oder einer wässerigen Salzsäurelösung, welche $^1/_5$ des Glyzeringewichtes nicht übersteigt, versetzt und hierauf durch die Flüssigkeit bei etwa 100° ein Strom Salzsäure während einiger Stunden hindurchgeleitet; der Flüssigkeit wird dann die gleiche Menge reines Glyzerin zugefügt und das so erhaltene Produkt am Rückflußkühler etwa 20 bis 24 Stunden hindurch einer Temperatur von etwa 100° C ausgesetzt. — Statt im Anfang Dynamitglyzerin vom spez. Gew. 1·262 mit Wasser zu verdünnen, kann man auch verdünntes Glyzerin mit gewünschtem Wassergehalt anwenden. — Statt dem mit Salzsäure behandelten Glyzerin die ungefähr gleiche Menge reines Glyzerin zuzufügen, genügen auch geringere Glyzerinzusätze oder man kann ohne weiteren Glyzerinzusatz zur Kondensation schreiten. — Nach der Kondensation kann man die letzten Reste freier Salzsäure, die bei der darauf folgenden Nitrierung störend wirken könnten, durch Erhitzen auf 150 bis 160° vertreiben. — Man kann auch gewöhnliches Dynamitglyzerin ohne jede Verdünnung bei 100° mit gasförmiger Salzsäure sättigen und dann bei 150° kondensieren.

Bei der Kondensation des Glyzerins mit sich selbst und mit der Salzsäure entsteht ein Produkt, das neben unverändertem Glyzerin folgende Verbindungen enthält: Monochlorhydrin, Dichlorhydrin, Diglyzerin, Chlorhydrine des Diglyzerins, Triglyzerin, Chlorhydrine des Triglyzerins. — Dieses Gemisch wird nun der Nitrierung unterworfen, wobei neben dem Trinitroglyzerin auch die Nitrate der übrigen obengenannten Verbindungen gebildet werden, von denen besonders die verschiedenen Nitrochlorhydrine

[1] Lieb. Ann. **119**, 218; Compt. rend. 1861, 359.

[2] Deutsche Patentanmeldung vom 12. Mai 1906 und Zusatzanmeldungen.

dem nitroglyzerinhaltigen Gemische einen niedrigen Gefrierpunkt verleihen. Je nach der längeren oder kürzeren Einwirkungsdauer des Salzsäurestromes auf das Glyzerin und je nach der Dauer der Kondensation erhält man bei der darauf folgenden Nitrierung Sprengöle von verschieden niedrigem Gefrierpunkt.

Siebenter Abschnitt.

Mischdynamite.[1]
(Dynamite im engeren Sinne.)

I. Mit chemisch unwirksamer Basis (Gurdynamit und ähnliche).

Wie schon in dem historischen Überblick erwähnt, hat Alfred Nobel im Jahre 1866 aus 75 Prozent Nitroglyzerin und

[1] Man versteht unter Dynamiten im weiteren Sinne körnige oder plastische Produkte, die als wesentlichen Bestandteil ein Nitrat des Glyzerins enthalten in Gemenge mit Stoffen, welche das Glyzerinnitrat aufsaugen und möglichst so festhalten, daß weder durch Wärme oder Kälte, Luftfeuchtigkeit oder mäßigen Druck ein Ausscheiden des Sprengöls stattfindet. — Wir teilen die Dynamite in folgende Unterklassen:

1. Dynamite (im engeren Sinne) oder Mischdynamite; hierbei wird Trinitroglyzerin direkt mit porösen Stoffen gemischt, die entweder chemisch unwirksam sind (wie Kieselgur) oder wirksam (wie sog. Zumischpulver aus Holzmehl und Nitraten).
2. Sprenggelatine und Gelatinedynamite; hierbei wird das Trinitroglyzerin zunächst durch Kollodiumwolle (oder ähnlich wirkende Stoffe) gelatiniert.
3. Wettersichere Dynamite; dieselben sollen gegen schlagende Wetter und Kohlenstaub sicher sein und enthalten daher einen geringeren Prozentsatz an Nitroglyzerin; Fabrikation kann im übrigen nach 1. (direkte Mischung) oder nach 2. (vorherige Gelatinierung des Sprengöls) erfolgen.
4. Schwer gefrierbare Dynamite; Fabrikation entweder auf Basis von Trinitroglyzerin unter entsprechenden Zusätzen, oder aber auf Basis von Dinitroglyzerin, Dinitromonochlorhydrin u. a.
5. Als Anhang werden Ammonsalpetersprengstoffe mit Zusatz von 4 bis 12 Prozent Nitroglyzerin besprochen.

25 Prozent Kieselgur eine knetbare Masse, das Gurdynamit, hergestellt und darauf in England, Schweden usw. Patente genommen. Das schwedische Patent (vom 19. September 1867) lautet in der Übersetzung wie folgt:

„Meine Erfindung bezweckt hauptsächlich, die Eigenschaften des Nitroglyzerins so zu verändern, daß es unempfindlich gegen Stoß und Feuersgefahr wird; auch wollte ich ihm eine transportablere Form geben, als es die flüssige ist. Ich erreiche dies dadurch, daß ich Nitroglyzerin in den Hohlräumen poröser, nicht explosiver Materien aufsaugen lasse, z. B. von poröser Kieselsäure, Papier, Papiermasse, Holzlumpen, Ziegelmehl, Kohle, trockenem Ton, Gips und anderen Stoffen, die nicht chemisch auf Nitroglyzerin einwirken. Die durch solche Absorption gewonnene, je nach der Menge des absorbierten Nitroglyzerins mehr oder weniger trockene Materie nenne ich Dynamit oder Nobel-Pulver. Ist die absorbierende Materie staubförmig, so kann damit ein Pulver hergestellt werden, welches entweder direkt in Bohrlöcher geladen oder in Patronen gefüllt werden kann. Dynamit, besonders mit nur soviel Nitroglyzerin, daß die Masse ein trockenes Aussehen hat, besitzt ganz andere Eigenschaften als das flüssige Nitroglyzerin; ein mit solchem Dynamit gefülltes Gefäß kann ohne Gefahr heftigen Stößen ausgesetzt, ebenso gefahrlos direkt über Feuer verbrannt werden: es explodiert dabei nicht. Wenn man es luftdicht (oder beinahe luftdicht) in einen geschlossenen Raum bringt (wie z. B. in ein Gefäß aus Eisenblech oder in ein Bohrloch in hartem Gestein), so kann man das Dynamit durch direktes Anzünden mit einer Zündschnur zur Explosion mit sehr vehementer Wirkung bringen. In mehr oder weniger geklüftetem Gestein oder auch im offenen Raum wird Dynamit durch Sprengkapseln zur Detonation gebracht; die Sprengkapsel muß fest an das Ende der Zündschnur angepreßt, bzw. zugedrückt oder geklemmt werden, wodurch die Explosionskraft und die Tension der entwickelten Gase verstärkt werden. — Die Vorteile des Dynamits sind folgende: 1. Die umständliche und teure Verpackung des Nitroglyzerins in Flaschen fällt weg, weil Dynamit in Tonnen, Kisten usw. verpackt werden kann; 2. der Transport und die Lagerung sind ganz ungefährlich, weil Dynamit weder durch Schlag, noch Feuer explodiert; 3. es verschwinden diejenigen Unglücksfälle, bei denen flüssiges Nitroglyzerin in Risse oder Spalten im Gestein eindringt und dann durch die Bohrapparate zur Detonation gebracht wird; 4. man kann Gesteinsspalten oder Risse mit Dynamit laden, was mit flüssigem Nitroglyzerin nicht möglich war; 5. man kann harten, festen Besatz anwenden, wodurch die Wirkung erhöht wird."

Die Gur oder Kieselgur wird in der Lüneburger Heide (in der Nähe von Unterlüß), ferner in Österreich, Schottland, Norwegen usw. gewonnen; sie bildet eine in trockenem Zustande leicht zerstäubbare, mehlartige Masse von rein weißer bis schmutziggrauer und grüner Farbe, je nach Reinheit. Die Gur besteht aus den Kieselpanzern einer Algengattung (der Diatomeen), welche eine Unzahl kleiner Zellen bilden, die eine sehr bedeutende Festigkeit besitzen und trotz jahrtausendelanger Lagerung sich noch in ganz wohlerhaltenem Zustande befinden. Diese Kieselerde hat ein sehr bedeutendes Flüssigkeitsaufsaugevermögen; dabei besitzen die einzelnen Teilchen eine sehr große Widerstandsfähigkeit gegen Druck und Stoß, so daß sie ihre Form auch während langen Transportes beibehalten; die Kieselerderöhrchen bilden gewissermaßen kleine Verpackungsgefäße des Sprengöls, in denen dasselbe durch Kapillarität festgehalten wird. Die chemische Analyse einer guten, lufttrockenen Gur ergab (nach Sanford): 94·3 Prozent Kieselsäure, 2·1 Prozent Magnesia, 1·3 Prozent Eisenoxyd und Tonerde, 0·4 Prozent organische Stoffe und 1·9 Prozent Feuchtigkeit. Zur Entfernung der beiden letzteren Bestandteile wird die Gur bei Rotglut calciniert. Dies geschieht entweder in offenen Flammöfen oder besser in Muffelöfen, welche zwei oder vier übereinander angeordnete Etagen besitzen, in denen die Infusorienerde allmählich von der obersten nach der untersten befördert wird; die Flamme streicht am Boden der untersten Etage, geht dann über das Gewölbe derselben zum Boden der zweiten Etage usw. — Die ausgeglühte Gur kommt in eiserne Gefäße, in welchen man sie erkalten läßt; hierauf werden die mehr oder weniger zusammengebackenen Klumpen auf einem Walzwerk zu feinem Pulver vermahlen (eventuell auch durch Handwalzen zerdrückt) und zum Schluß durchgesiebt; das so erhaltene feine Pulver wird in dichte Säcke eingefüllt und dann noch am gleichen Tage auf Dynamit verarbeitet, da die Gur sonst trotz bester Verpackung zu viel Feuchtigkeit aufnehmen würde. Eine Analyse einer gut calcinierten wasserfreien Gur ergab (nach Hagen): 96·34 Prozent SiO_2, 1·5 Prozent Al_2O_3, 0·5 Prozent Fe_2O_3 und 1·64 Prozent CaO. — Man bringt zur weiteren Verarbeitung entweder die abgewogene Menge der calcinierten Gur zum Nitroglyzerin-Vorratshause und mischt dort oberflächlich durch,. worauf man die Masse zur weiteren Durcharbeitung nach dem eigentlichen Mischhause transportiert; oder aber man bringt die Gur (in Säcken) und das Sprengöl (in Kautschuk- oder lackierten Holzeimern in speziellen Transportwagen, bei denen Verschütten möglichst vermieden und jeder Eimer in ein Fach gestellt wird) jedes für sich nach dem Mischhause und gibt die Bestandteile erst dort zusammen. Das Durchmischen der Gur mit dem Nitroglyzerin erfolgt in flachen Holzkästen, worauf die Arbeiter die Masse tüchtig mit den Händen durchkneten. Man hat versucht, den Arbeitern für diese Hantierung Gummihandschuhe vorzuschreiben, da das Sprengöl durch die Haut eindringt und infolge seiner giftigen Eigenschaften nachteilig auf den Organismus einwirkt; allein den Leuten sind die Handschuhe unbequem, auch haben sie nur mit der unbedeckten Hand die richtige Empfindung für das gleichmäßige Durcharbeiten der Masse. Neuerdings werden übrigens auch Maschinen zum Mischen verwendet (von Werner & Pfleiderer in Stuttgart, Karl Seemann in Berlin, Richard Lehmann in Dresden). Früher fabrizierte man Gurdynamite mit 75 Prozent, 50 Prozent und 30 Prozent Nitroglyzerin; jetzt wird nur noch die erste Sorte (75 Prozent Sprengöl) hergestellt und gewöhnlich als Dynamit Nr. 1 bezeichnet.[1] Nach Scheiding ist eine Beimengung von Schwerspat nicht als Verschlechterung oder gar Verfälschung zu betrachten, da er bei guter Kieselgur notwendig ist, um dem Dynamit die zur vorteilhaften Sprengwirkung notwendige Weichheit zu geben. Zur Neutralisierung von Säure, die sich während der Aufbewahrung entwickeln könnte, wird vielfach eine geringe Menge einfach- oder doppeltkohlensaures Natron, kohlensaure Magnesia oder Kreide zugefügt; in England ist die Zusammensetzung gewöhnlich: 73·8 Prozent Nitroglyzerin, 25·4 Prozent calcinierte Kieselgur, 0·8 Prozent calcinierte Soda. Außerdem setzt man in vielen Fabriken etwa $^1/_4$ Prozent gebrannten Ocker hinzu, um eine gleichmäßige, von den verschiedenen Gursorten, sowie den Zufälligkeiten des Glühens unabhängige Farbe zu erzielen. Nach dem Durchmischen wird die Masse zur Erzielung größter Gleichmäßigkeit und Zurückhaltung von eventuell vorhandenen größeren Kieselkörnern durch Drahtsiebe gerieben. Das fertige Dynamit soll weder zu trocken noch zu fett sein, etwa wie frische Gartenerde oder Brotkrume aussehen. Außer der Infusorienerde benutzt man auch andere Kieselerde zur Dynamitfabrikation, so in Frankreich den in der Auvergne vorkommenden Randanit, d. i. natürliche Kieselerde aus verwittertem Feldspat. Auch auf chemischem Wege, z. B. durch Zersetzung von Siliciumfluorid mit Wasser, hergestellte amorphe Kieselsäure ist (nach Berthelot) gut verwendbar. — Nobel selbst hat eine Reihe von Aufsaugestoffen angegeben; öfters benutzte man gesinterten Kalk, calcinierten Ton, kohlensaure Magnesia (in Amerika noch in Gebrauch), Asche von Bogheadkohle (1870 im belagerten Paris angewandt); neuerdings wird Meerschaum (wasserhaltiges Magnesiasilikat), das in Neu-Mexiko in größeren Mengen vorhanden

[1] In Österreich und Frankreich ist die Zusammensetzung gewöhnlich: 70 Prozent Nitroglyzerin, 30 Prozent Kieselgur.

sein soll, als Aufsaugemittel vorgeschlagen, da es dem Nitroglyzerin ein Minimum an Explosivkraft entziehe. — Homogenität und Stabilität des Gemenges sind eine Hauptsache; das Nitroglyzerin muß von der als Basis funktionierenden Substanz völlig aufgesogen werden, das Gemenge muß gleichheitlich bleiben; insbesondere dürfen keine chemischen Veränderungen stattfinden, auch keine Ausschwitzungen von Sprengöl, beides auch nicht bei Temperaturveränderungen oder Erschütterungen beim Transport; andernfalls würden sich wieder die beim reinen Nitroglyzerin bemerkten Übelstände und Gefahren ergeben. — Die fertige Dynamitmasse wird, um solche in Bohrlöcher laden zu können, in Form zylindrischer Patronen gebracht, welche einen Durchmesser von 18, 20, 23, 25, 28 und 30 mm haben und 10 cm lang sind; außerdem fertigt man kleine Patronen von $2^1/_2$ cm Länge, sog. Zündpatronen, in welche die Sprengkapsel kommt; zur Umhüllung der Sprengstoffmasse dienen Hülsen aus paraffiniertem Papier, wie man solches in der Fabrik selbst herstellen kann, indem man eine endlose Rolle Papier durch ein Gemisch aus 20 Teilen Paraffin, 60 Tln. Harz und 30 Tln. Talg laufen läßt; oder man verwendet Pergamentpapier; mit Lieferung von Patronenpapieren befaßt sich speziell die Firma C. Rob. Lohmann in Westhofen (Westfalen); die Form des Patronenpapieres bildet ein schräg abgeschnittenes Viereck, welches auf einer Seite um etwa 3 cm kürzer ist als auf der anderen, wodurch ein besserer Verschluß der Patronen gesichert ist.

Capitaine gibt folgende Beschreibung einer Patroniermaschine: Ein Quantum von etwa 5 kg Dynamit befindet sich in einem Leinwandbehälter, der unten offen ist und sich dort an ein trichterförmiges Messingstück anschließt; in letzteres reicht ein Kolben, welcher von oben in den Leinwandsack eintritt und durch einen Hebel auf- und abbewegt werden kann. Bei der höchsten Stellung des in den Trichter reichenden Kolbens bleibt die Mündung des Trichters offen, so daß Dynamit eintreten kann, welcher beim Niedergang des Kolbens in den Trichter und den damit verbundenen rohrförmigen Ansatz gepreßt wird und in Gestalt eines festen Zylinders von Dynamit unten austritt. Um das fortwährende Nachrücken des Dynamits beim Auf- und Niedergehen des Kolbens zu bewirken, ist der obere Rand des Leinwandsackes mit dem Hebel des Kolbens in Verbindung, der ihn also auf- und abschüttelt, und außerdem befinden sich an den Seiten des Leinwandsackes Holzklappen, welche ebenfalls mit dem Hebel in Verbindung stehen und den Sack hin- und herschütteln. Die unten am Trichter angeschraubte Röhre hat im Lichten den Durchmesser der Dynamitpatrone; ist durch die Bewegungen des Kolbenhebels diese Röhre ganz gefüllt, so wird ein entsprechendes Blatt Pergamentpapier herumgewickelt und der Zylinder aus Pergamentpapier unter der Mündung der Röhre umgeschlagen, bzw. geschlossen. Bei weiteren Bewegungen des Kolbenhebels schiebt sich unten ein Zylinder aus Dynamit vor, welcher die Hülse aus Pergamentpapier mitnimmt. Der Zylinder wird abgebrochen, wenn er die genügende Länge erreicht hat; das Patronenpapier wird dann auch oben umgeschlagen und die Patrone ist fertig. — Engels hat im Jahre 1879 ein Patent (D.R.P. 6180) auf einen „Apparat zur Anfertigung von Patronen aus Nitroglyzerinpräparaten" genommen. Hierbei ist die Ladestange mittels eines Scharniers mit einer Exzenterstange verbunden. An der Kolbenstange befindet sich ein Kreuz von vier Messingstäben, auf welchen ein Messingring befestigt ist. An demselben befindet sich ein Beutel, der mit dem unteren Teile in den oberen Ring der Stopfbüchse vermittelst eines Ringes von Guttapercha angepreßt ist; dieser Beutel dient zum Füllen mit dem Nitroglyzerinpräparate, von welchem die Patronen gefertigt werden sollen. Durch das Aufgehen der Kolbenstange wird der Beutel gespannt und entleert seinen Inhalt in die Stopf- oder Fallbüchse, welcher Inhalt dann beim Niedergang der Kolbenstange in die Füllröhre eingepreßt und zur Patrone geformt wird. — Eine ähnliche Maschine zeigt beifolgende Fig. 58; man erhält aus der Dynamitmasse eine Wurst, welche durch Hebeldruck in die von dem Arbeiter untergehaltene Papierhülse gebracht wird, worauf man letztere auch oben mit der Hand schließt.

Fig. 58. Patroniermaschine für Dynamit.

Im Gegensatz zu vorstehenden intermittierenden Pressen hat Oskar Guttmann[1] eine kontinuierliche Presse angegeben, bei welcher man eine endlose Wurst erzeugt, dann in Abständen von 10 cm abbricht und in Papier wickelt. — N. Ceipek

[1] Schieß- und Sprengmittel, S. 149.

(D.R.P. 117111 und 140758) verläßt das Prinzip der Stopf- bzw. Wurstmaschine und benutzt die Zentrifugalkraft; das Dynamit (gleichgültig in welcher Form) wird in den „Füllraum" gegeben, welcher mit Gummiplatten an den Seitenwänden belegt ist, und läuft, sobald die Zentrifugalkraft zu wirken beginnt, durch trichterförmige Auslaufröhren in die Papierhülsen hinein.

Betreffs Verpackung der Dynamitpatronen gelten in Deutschland folgende Eisenbahn-Versendungsvorschriften:

Zu den Patronen darf kein gefettetes oder geöltes, wohl aber paraffiniertes Papier verwendet werden; die Patronen sind durch eine feste Umhüllung von Papier in Pakete zu vereinigen und in den Paketen mittels Wellpappe so zu verpacken, daß sie schichtweise in ihrer Lage festgehalten werden (für das Ausland gilt letztere Bestimmung der deutschen Eisenbahnen nicht). Die Pakete sind in hölzerne, haltbare und dem Gewicht des Inhalts entsprechend starke Kisten oder Tonnen, deren Fugen so gedichtet sind, daß ein Ausstreuen nicht stattfinden kann und die nicht mit eisernen Reifen oder Bändern versehen sind, so fest einzusetzen, daß sie sich nicht gegeneinander verschieben können. Statt der hölzernen Kisten oder Tonnen können auch aus mehrfachen Lagen sehr starken und steifen gefirnisten Pappdeckels gefertigte Fässer (sog. amerikanische Fässer) verwendet werden. Der Verschluß der Kisten darf nicht mittels eiserner Nägel erfolgen. Auch werden solche Patronen nur in den ursprünglichen Behältern und nur in der Originalverpackung zum Eisenbahntransporte zugelassen. — Die zur Verpackung dienenden Kisten sind an zwei gegenüberliegenden Schmalseiten mit zuverlässigen Handgriffen oder Handleisten zu versehen; bei Fässern und Tonnen sind solche Handgriffe nicht erforderlich, wenn durch tief eingelassene Böden und Deckel eine feste Handhabe gegeben ist. Das Bruttogewicht der Behälter darf 35 kg nicht übersteigen. Die Behälter müssen je nach ihrem Inhalt mit der deutlichen, gedruckten oder schablonierten Aufschrift „Dynamitpatronen" usw., sowie mit der Bezeichnung des Ursprungsortes (Fabrikmarke) versehen sein.

Pappschachteln liefert die Firma Himmelmann & Co. in Fröndenberg an der Ruhr. — Die Pakete enthalten meist $2^1/_2$ kg Dynamit, zehn Pakete werden in eine Kiste (Inhalt gewöhnlich 25 kg) verpackt.

In Österreich gelten für militärische Verwendungszwecke folgende Vorschriften:[1] Als Hülle wird bei kleinen Ladungen Pergamentpapier, Leinwand oder Blech, bei größeren Ladungen Blech oder Holz angewendet; dort, wo die Hülle wasserdicht sein soll, verwendet man fast ausschließlich blecherne Gefäße. Wenn genügend Zeit und Material vorhanden ist, so werden die Ladungen laboriert, d. h. das lose Dynamit wird in vorbereitete Hüllen von entsprechender Form derart eingepreßt, daß es die Dichte von 1·4 erhält. Dynamitladungen bis zu 30 kg werden gewöhnlich in einem Teile, größere Ladungen in

[1] Technischer Unterricht, Tl. 6, S. 81.

Teilen zu 16 kg laboriert; die Form der Teilladungen richtet sich nach jener der Gesamtladung. Das Laborieren des Dynamits soll bei mäßiger Wärme (12 bis 18° C) in rasch ventilierbaren Lokalen vorgenommen werden; in warmer Jahreszeit ist das Laborieren im Freien an trockenen, schattigen Orten zulässig; unmittelbare Berührung der Haut ist beim Laborieren zu vermeiden. Jeder Mann enthält die entsprechende Dynamitmenge in einer Holzschüssel, bringt sodann mit dem Holzlöffel eine 2 bis 3 cm hohe Schicht des lockeren Dynamits in die Ladungshülle ein und drückt solche mit einem Laborierstock derart zusammen, daß das Dynamit an der Oberfläche noch trocken erscheint, d. h. daß das Nitroglyzerin noch nicht austrete. Dieses Verfahren wird fortgesetzt, bis die Hülle gefüllt ist, sodann der Deckel aufgebracht, überhaupt die Hülle geschlossen. An jenen Stellen, wo die Zündung erfolgen soll, muß, wenn dies nicht schon in der Form der Ladungshülle geschehen ist, der Raum für die Zündpatrone oder Sprengkapsel ausgespart werden; für erstere geschieht dies durch Einstellen des Einsatzzylinders. Hölzerne Kisten, in denen Dynamit laboriert wird, sollen womöglich immer mit Pergamentpapier bekleidet werden — eine Vorsicht, die bei Blechgefäßen nur dann geboten erscheint, wenn die laborierte Munition längere Zeit deponiert bleiben soll. Die Befestigung der Deckel solcher hölzernen Gefäße soll nur mittels Holznägeln erfolgen. Bei geringen Querschnittsausmaßen der Ladungen kann das Laborieren derselben in Papier- oder Leinwandhüllen ohne weiteres vorgenommen werden. Verstreutes Dynamit muß sorgfältigst aufgelesen und im Freien verbrannt werden. Fettgewordene Laborierrequisiten oder Tische werden mit lauwarmem Seifenwasser sorgfältig gereinigt.

Eigenschaften des Gurdynamits. a) Physikalische Eigenschaften. Das Gurdynamit ist eine gelbe bis braune (bzw. wenn mit Ocker gefärbt, eine rote), geruchlose, trockene, plastische Masse von 1·45 bis 1·6 spez. Gewicht. Während der Herstellung des Dynamits läßt sich eine auffallende Kontraktion des Materials beobachten; das Sprengöl nimmt weniger Raum ein, als die vorher in der Kieselerde befindliche Luft. — Das Gurdynamit fühlt sich etwas fettig an, soll jedoch keine nennenswerten Ausscheidungen von Nitroglyzerin erfolgen lassen; insbesondere ist es für die längere Lagerung, sowie für den Transport nach warmen Klimaten wichtig, daß auch bei mäßiger Wärme (bis 30° C) kein „Fetten" erfolgt, das Nitroglyzerin also nicht ausschwitzt, sondern dauernd aufgesaugt erhalten bleibt. — Das Dynamit ist an sich so gut wie nicht hygroskopisch, d. h. es zieht aus feuchter Luft fast kein Wasser an; bei direkter Berührung von flüssigem Wasser mit Dynamit hat aber ersteres die Eigenschaft, sich allmählich der Kieselerde zu bemächtigen und das Sprengöl zu verdrängen, bzw. zur Ausscheidung in flüssiger Form zu zwingen; dieser Prozeß geht langsam, aber sicher vor sich, so daß jedes durchnäßte Dynamit gefährlich wird. In nassen Bohrlöchern kann unter Umständen das ausgetretene Sprengöl in Klüften und Spalten so weit fortsickern, daß es später von der Explosion der Ladung nicht mehr gefaßt wird; wenn nun beim Weiterarbeiten ein Bohrer auf derartiges Nitroglyzerin stößt, sind unvermutete Explosionen nicht ausgeschlossen. Andererseits kann man aus Gurdynamit rasch Nitroglyzerin — für Versuche, Analyse usw. — erhalten, indem man in die Spitze eines Glastrichters einen Pfropfen von Glaswolle legt und darüber loses Dynamit ziemlich dicht eindrückt; auf das Dynamit schüttet man sodann destilliertes Wasser und läßt das Ganze, nachdem man ein Becherglas unter den Trichter gestellt hat, einige Zeit ruhig stehen; nach etwa einer halben Stunde hat das Wasser begonnen, das Nitroglyzerin aus dem Dynamit zu verdrängen; das Sprengöl fließt in das Becherglas ab, und zwar — durch die Kieselgur filtriert — vollständig wasserhell und rein. — Das Dynamit gefriert leicht, worauf später noch zurückzukommen ist; hierbei verwandelt sich das Dynamit in eine harte Masse, wobei die äußeren Flächen der Patronen weißlich werden, da das Nitroglyzerin sich zusammenzieht; die Patrone selbst dehnt sich dadurch etwas aus, da ja die lufthaltige Gur mehr Raum einnimmt als die sprengölhaltige. — Das Dynamit ist giftig und erzeugt, mit der Haut längere Zeit in Verbindung gebracht oder in kleinen Mengen innerlich eingenommen, Kopfweh und Übelkeit; der Genuß von größeren Mengen kann selbst den Tod herbeiführen. In Wasser ist Dynamit noch in einer Verdünnung von 1 : 800 gesundheitsschädlich. — Sind Teile der Haut zufällig mit Dynamit berührt, so sind dieselben sogleich mit verdünnter, warmer Kalilauge und dann mit reinem Wasser zu waschen. Bei beginnenden Vergiftungserscheinungen sind anzuwenden: Eisumschläge und Übergießungen des Kopfes mit kaltem Wasser; Einnehmen von starkem schwarzen kalten Kaffee; reizende Klystiere; Blutegel an den Schläfen und Zitzenfortsätzen; Brech- und Abführmittel; essigsaures Morphium (unter ärztlicher Aufsicht).

b) Chemische Untersuchung.[1] α) Qualitativ. Man nimmt etwas fein verteiltes Dynamit und behandelt es mit wasserfreiem Äther; hierdurch werden das Sprengöl selbst, sowie etwa vorhandenes Paraffin, Schwefel und Harz aufgelöst; der Äther wird bei 30° auf dem Wasserbad verdunstet; das zurückbleibende Öl wird wie folgt auf Nitroglyzeringehalt geprüft: Ein Tropfen mit einem Stückchen Fließpapier aufgesaugt, auf einen Amboß gelegt, muß durch Schlag explodieren; ein Tropfen in eine mit Salzsäure versetzte Lösung von Eisenvitriol

[1] Für Gurdynamit und andere Mischdynamite. Nach Hess, Mitteil. Gegenst. Art.- u. Geniewesen 1881, S. 15.

gebracht, soll beim Erwärmen Stickoxydreaktion ergeben; ein Tropfen in eine mit sehr verdünnter Schwefelsäure angesäuerte und mit wenig Zinkspänen versetzte Lösung von Jodkaliumstärkekleister gebracht, färbt die Lösung blau; ein Tropfen in Alkohol gelöst und mit einer Lösung von Schwefelammon in Alkohol versetzt, scheidet zunächst Polysulfide, dann Schwefel ab. Wenn der ölige Rückstand offenbar gleichmäßig ist, sein spez. Gewicht etwa 1·6 beträgt und keinen besonderen Geruch zeigt, so kann man annehmen, daß er nur aus Nitroglyzerin bestehe. — Sind mehr als Spuren von Schwefel, Paraffin oder Harz vorhanden, so scheiden sich dieselben beim Abdunsten des Äthers aus; zur Prüfung preßt man die ausgeschiedenen Stoffe zwischen Filtrierpapier ab. Der Schwefel scheidet sich kristallinisch ab und ist daran, sowie an dem Geruche und seiner Flamme beim Entzünden zu erkennen; beim Behandeln mit kaltem Alkohol bleibt das Paraffin zurück; Harz läßt sich durch Kochen mit Sodalösung verseifen und aus der Seife durch Fällen mit Salzsäure wieder isolieren. Sind alle drei Stoffe gleichzeitig im Dynamit vorhanden, so dekantiert man zuerst das Nitroglyzerin und preßt den Rückstand zwischen Filtrierpapier sorgfältig ab; sodann scheidet man durch Kochen mit Sodalösung zuerst das Harz ab, wäscht den Rückstand mit Wasser und trocknet ihn. Einen Teil desselben behandelt man mit Königswasser, um etwa vorhandenen Schwefel in Schwefelsäure zu verwandeln und in Form von Bariumsulfat nachzuweisen; einen andern Teil kocht man mit Schwefelammonlösung, wobei sich der Schwefel unter Bildung von Ammonpolysulfid löst, das Paraffin aber nach dem Erkalten als Kruste auf der Flüssigkeit schwimmt und sodann mit Wasser gewaschen, getrocknet und weiter geprüft werden kann. Der Rückstand von der Extraktion des Sprengmittels mit Äther wird zunächst mit heißem destillierten Wasser ausgezogen, wobei die Nitrate, Chlorate und wasserlöslichen Karbonate in Lösung gehen und nachgewiesen werden können. — Den unlöslichen Rückstand prüft man zunächst mikroskopisch, wobei man Kieselgur, Holzmehl und Holzkohle durch Struktur und Färbung erkennt. Wenn man den Rückstand verascht, so findet man neben der Holz- oder Kohlenasche die etwa sonst noch vorhandenen Mineralsubstanzen. Schießwolle im Rückstande erkennt man bei Prüfung unter dem Mikroskop im polarisierten Licht, sowie beim Kochen mit Eisenvitriol und Salzsäure (NO-Reaktion).

β) Quantitativ. Sind in dem Dynamit keine anderen ätherlöslichen Stoffe vorhanden als Sprengöl, so wird letzteres aus einer abgewogenen, über Chlorcalcium im Exsikkator getrockneten Menge Dynamit, entweder in einem Soxhletschen Extraktionsapparate, der nur Glasverbindungen und einen besonders gut wirksamen Kühler besitzt, oder aber in einem bedeckten Trichter, in welchem man das Dynamit anf ein getrocknetes und gewogenes Leinenfilter legt und durch häufiges Aufgießen von Äther auslaugt, mittels Äther extrahiert. Der ätherische Auszug wird in einem kleinen, zuvor gewogenen Becherglase gesammelt und auf einem Wasserbad bei sehr gelinder Temperatur durch Abdunsten vom Äther befreit. Es ist zu beachten, daß schon bei 40 bis 50° sich Nitroglyzerin selbst nicht unbedeutend verflüchtigt. Während des Abdunstens beginnt sich die bis dahin klare Flüssigkeit infolge der teilweisen Ausscheidung von Nitroglyzerin aus dem Äther milchig zu trüben; man beobachtet dann das Eindunsten so lange, bis die Trübung wieder verschwindet und entfernt hierauf sofort das Becherglas vom Wasserbade. Zur Entfernung der letzten Spuren von Äther, sowie von Feuchtigkeit wird im Exsikkator über Chlorcalcium getrocknet und dann gewogen. — Falls in dem Dynamit noch Paraffin, Harz, Schvefel, oder dergl. anwesend waren, wird der vom Äther befreite Auszug nach dem Trocknen gewogen und in Sodalösung auf dem Wasserbade erwärmt. Hierbei geht das Harz in Lösung und kann durch Dekantieren und Nachwaschen mit destilliertem Wasser von dem Reste getrennt werden. In der Lösung fällt man das Harz durch Salzsäure, sammelt es auf einem bei 100° getrockneten und gewogenen Filter, wäscht, trocknet und wägt. — In dem Rückstand von der vorigen Operation nimmt man das Nitroglyzerin mit hochprozentigem Alkohol auf, dekantiert und spült das zurückbleibende Gemenge von Paraffin und Schwefel mit starkem Alkohol ab, trocknet und wägt es. Um den Schwefel von dem Paraffin zu trennen, erwärmt man das Gemenge mit einer wässerigen Lösung von Schwefelammonium, läßt erkalten, durchsticht die Paraffinschicht, dekantiert, wäscht mit Wasser nach, trocknet und wägt das Paraffin. Die Menge des Nitroglyzerins und des Schwefels wird aus den Differenzen gefunden. — Der Rückstand aus der Extraktion, sofern er nur aus feuerbeständigen Stoffen besteht, wird im trocknen Luftstrom bei 60° getrocknet und gewogen, sodann eingeäschert und nach dem Erkalten wieder gewogen, um aus einer etwaigen Differenz zu erfahren, ob kleine Mengen von organischen Stoffen in dem Rückstande enthalten waren. Sind andere Bestandteile vorhanden, so wird der Rückstand zuerst auf einem Filter getrocknet und gewogen, sodann mit heißem destillierten Wasser behandelt, die Lauge eingedampft, bei 120° getrocknet und der Rückstand gewogen. Sind Karbonate vorhanden, so wird der Auszug, falls er keine chlorsauren Salze enthält, wieder mit Wasser aufgenommen, mit Salzsäure neutralisiert, auf dem Wasserbade eingedampft, bei 120° getrocknet und abermals gewogen. Hierdurch werden die Karbonate in Nitrate verwandelt, ohne etwaige organische Extraktivstoffe zu verändern, und aus der Differenz der beiden zuletzt ermittelten Gewichte berechnet man die Menge der vorhandenen Kohlensäure. Die trockene Masse wird hierauf geglüht, nach dem Erkalten mit Salpetersäure befeuchtet, von der freien Salpetersäure befreit und wieder geglüht, endlich nach dem Erkalten gewogen. Man hat dann alle durch Wasser extrahierten Salze als Nitrate, die organischen Extraktivstoffe aber zerstört; die Differenz der beiden letzten Wägungen gibt sonach den Gehalt an organischen Extraktivstoffen. — Sind in dem wässerigen Extrakte auch chlorsaure Salze enthalten, so muß man in demselben durch Fällung mit salpetersaurem Kalk die Kohlensäure als Calciumkarbonat, in einem Teile nach Eindampfen und Glühen die Chlorsäure in

Form von Chlorsilber bestimmen; in einem andern Teile des Extraktes ermittelt man die Menge der Salpetersäure durch Überführung derselben in Ammoniak. In dem Rückstande von der Extraktion mit Wasser können nur Holzkohle oder ähnliche organische Stoffe, sowie unlösliche Saugstoffe enthalten sein. Man beseitigt die organischen Stoffe durch Einäschern und wägt den Rest nach der Abkühlung, wodurch man das Gewicht der unlöslichen mineralischen Stoffe enthält.

γ) Stabilitätsprüfung. Man testet nicht das Dynamit selbst, sondern scheidet zunächst das Nitroglyzerin aus, um letzteres zu prüfen. Im Dynamit ist das Sprengöl auf einer sehr großen Oberfläche in sehr feiner Schicht verteilt und zeigt ein ganz anderes Verhalten als außer Kontakt mit der Gur, es findet ein viel leichteres und schnelleres Abdunsten der Säure statt, veranlaßt durch die große Oberfläche und die zwischen den Partikelchen beim Erwärmen zirkulierende Luft, sowie die scharfen Ränder der zahllosen mikroskopischen Röhrchen der Gur. O. Hagen hat 500 g Sprengöl mit 25 ccm Wasser geschüttelt, in denen ein Tropfen konz. Schwefelsäure aufgelöst war, dann im Scheidetrichter getrennt. Im Sprengöl selbst war die geringe Säurespur nicht nachweisbar, bei 80° C zeigte sich beim Testen auch nach 65 Minuten noch keine Reaktion; dagegen gab Gurdynamit, aus diesem Sprengöl hergestellt, bei 80° getestet schon nach drei Minuten leicht erkennbare braune Ränder auf dem Prüfungspapier.

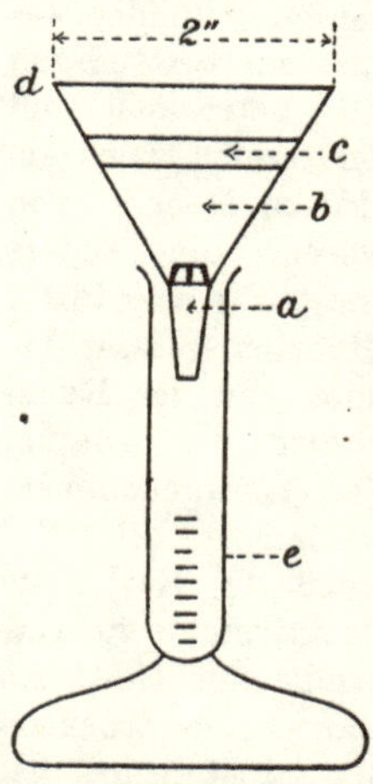

Fig. 59. Abscheidung von Nitroglyzerin aus Dynamit behufs Stabilitätsprüfung.

Nach der englischen Prüfungsvorschrift für Dynamit müssen Nitroglyzerinpräparate, aus welchen das Nitroglyzerin in der unten beschriebenen Weise extrahiert werden kann, folgenden Test bestehen; diese Prüfung jedoch, obwohl sie zurzeit als die wichtigste angesehen wird, um die Reinheit des Nitroglyzerins zu prüfen, ist nur eine von mehreren, welchen ein gegebenes Muster einer Nitroglyzerinmischung genügen muß, um deren Übereinstimmung mit der Definition in der „Authorised List" festzustellen. Erforderlich ist ein Trichter *d* (Fig. 59) von zwei Zoll[1] Durchmesser und ein in Grains eingeteilter Meßzylinder *e*. Ungefähr 300 bis 400 Grains (20 bis 25 g) fein verteilten Dynamits *b* werden in den Trichter gegeben, welcher vorher mit etwas frisch geglühtem Asbest *a* leicht verstopft wird. Die Oberfläche des Dynamits wird mit Hilfe einer flachköpfigen Glasstange oder eines Stöpsels glatt gemacht und darüber etwas rein gewaschene und getrock-

[1] Ein Zoll (inch) = 2·54 cm; ein Grain = 0·064799 g.

nete Kieselgur *c* etwa $^1/_8$ Zoll hoch ausgebreitet; sodann wird aus einer Waschflasche vorsichtig destilliertes Wasser auf die Gur getropft, und sobald der erste Teil aufgesaugt ist, wird mehr hinzugefügt. Das wird wiederholt, bis genügend Nitroglyzerin in dem graduierten Meßgefäß unterhalb aufgefangen wurde. Sollte mit dem Sprengöl etwas Wasser durchgegangen sein, so wird es mit einem Stück Löschpapier entfernt und das Nitroglyzerin, wenn nötig, durch ein trockenes Papierfilter filtriert. — Zur Ausführung der Probe wird ein Wasserbad von 160° Fahrenheit (71° C), bzw. für kriegstechnische Zwecke von 180° F (82° C) verwandt, in welches ein Thermometer $2^3/_4$ Zoll tief eintaucht; etwa 50 Grains (3·24 g) Nitroglyzerin werden in ein Reagenzglas eingewogen. Das zu prüfende Nitroglyzerin wird nicht als vollständig gereinigt angesehen, wenn die zur Erzeugung der Braunfärbung auf dem mit Glyzerinwasser halb befeuchteten Jodkaliumstärkepapier erforderliche Zeit nicht mindestens 15 Minuten beträgt.

Diese Art der Ausführung ist für Fabrikslaboratorien, wo es sich um die tägliche Untersuchung von 20 bis 25 Proben handeln kann, etwas zu kompliziert und zeitraubend; Oskar Hagen[1] hat daher folgendes Verfahren vorgeschlagen:

In einem Reagenzglasgestell bereitet man so viel Probegläschen mit aufgesetzten Trichterröhrchen vor, als Dynamitpatronen zur Untersuchung vorliegen. Die Reagenzgläschen haben eine Höhe von 14 bis 15 cm bei 16 mm Durchmesser; zu jedem gehört ein konischer Korkstopfen, auf dessen oberer ebener Fläche Marken zur Unterscheidung der Proben angebracht sind. Die Trichterröhrchen haben nebenstehende Form (Fig. 60), eine Gesamtlänge von etwa 8 cm (der Hals *a* ist etwa 1·5 cm lang), eine Weite von 17 bis 18 mm, der Hals ist 8 mm weit; letzterer wird mit einem erbsengroßen Stopfen von reinem Fließpapier locker verschlossen. Die Dynamitpatronen (gefrorene müssen aufgetaut werden) werden der Reihe nach auf einer Glasplatte mit einem breiten zugeschärften Spachtel aus Holz möglichst fein geschnitten und zerdrückt und dann wird mit der zerkleinerten Masse einer jeden Patrone je ein Trichterröhrchen beschickt. Das Festdrücken des Dynamits in den Trichterröhrchen erfordert einige Übung; drückt man zu stark, so verstopft sich das Röhrchen und verhindert das Durchsickern des Wassers; drückt man zu schwach, so läuft Wasser und Nitroglyzerin gleichzeitig in das untergestellte Probiergläschen und man ist genötigt, die Probe von neuem anzusetzen. Nachdem man unter Beobachtung dieser Regeln alle Trichterröhrchen bis zu etwa $^4/_5$ ihrer Länge geladen hat, füllt man sie bis zum Rande mit destilliertem Wasser von 90° C;

Fig. 60. Trichterröhrchen.

[1] Repert. analyt. Chem. 1886, S. 1.

das heiße Wasser bewirkt eine schnellere Filtration als kaltes. Das Niedergehen der Wasserschicht kann man in dem hellgefärbten Dynamit sehr gut beobachten, da sie eine scharf markierte dunkle Zone bildet. — Wenn sich ungefähr 2 ccm klares, wasserfreies Sprengöl im Probegläschen angesammelt haben, entfernt man das Trichterröhrchen. Bei richtigem Manipulieren muß die Filtration sämtlicher Proben nach 30 bis 40 Minuten beendet sein. Es werden dann die Papiere eingehangen, die Stopfen aufgesetzt und die Gläschen ins Wasserbad gebracht. Die Patronen sind numeriert, desgleichen die Korke der Probierröhrchen. Bei dem jetzt folgenden Erwärmen ruft ein gut gewaschenes Nitroglyzerin auch bei 80° C nach Ablauf einer Stunde noch keine Farbenerscheinung auf dem Papiere hervor. Die Reaktion, wenn eine solche auftritt, macht sich immer zuerst an der Grenze zwischen dem feuchten und dem trockenen Teile des Papiers bemerkbar. Bei Gegenwart geringer Spuren von Säure zeigt sich daselbst eine schwache braune Linie, die bei längerer Einwirkung der sauren Dämpfe oder bei größeren Säuremengen breiter und intensiver braun wird und schließlich in Blau übergeht.

c) Entzündung, bzw. Detonation. — α) Selbstentzündung. Dynamit aus vollständig gewaschenem, keine freie Säure enthaltenden Nitroglyzerin hergestellt, ist an sich haltbar; Berührung mit Eisen und andere Einflüsse können eine minimale Abspaltung von Säure bewirken, die weitergehend zu spontanen Explosionen führen kann. In Bergwerken usw. dürfen nitroglyzerinhaltige Sprengstoffe, welche sich zu zersetzen beginnen (was durch stechenden Geruch oder Entwicklung rotbrauner Dämpfe zu erkennen ist), nicht verausgabt werden. — β) Entzündung durch mechanische Einwirkung. Dynamit benötigt zur Detonation einen viel heftigeren Schlag als Nitroglyzerin. Schlag von Holz auf Holz vermag Dynamit nicht zur Explosion zu bringen, wohl aber Schlag von Eisen auf Eisen oder von Eisen auf Stein. Schlägt man auf Dynamit mit einem Hammer, so detoniert nur die direkt getroffene Partie, die umgebenden Teile werden einfach weggeschleudert. Auf Grund dieses Umstandes können die Wirkungen vom Einfachen bis zum Doppelten schwanken, vorausgesetzt, daß das Dynamit nicht in eine widerstandsfähige und völlig ausgefüllte Packung eingeschlossen wird. Dynamit ist gegen Schlag und Stoß um so empfindlicher, je mehr Sprengöl es enthält und je mehr sich die Temperatur der Zersetzungstemperatur nähert. Nach Wills Versuchen mit Fallhammer von 2 kg Gewicht detonierte trockenes Nitroglyzerin bei 4 cm Fallhöhe, plastisches Gurdynamit bei 7 cm Fallhöhe. Dynamit detoniert durch direkten Schuß aus 50 m Entfernung und darüber. — γ) Entzündung durch Erwärmen. In gelinder

Wärme zeigt Dynamit keine Veränderung (außer geringer Verflüchtigung des Sprengöls); man kann Gurdynamit selbst eine Stunde lang auf 100° erwärmen; bei einer andauernden Temperatur von + 60° zersetzt sich das Dynamit sehr langsam. Bei rascher Erhitzung (innerhalb einer Minute von 177 bis 187°) zeigt (nach O. Hagen) Gurdynamit (aus 75 Prozent Sprengöl und 25 Prozent calcinierter Gur) eine mittlere Explosionstemperatur von 182·3° C, englisches Gurdynamit (aus 73·8 Prozent Sprengöl, 25·4 Prozent Gur und 0·8 Prozent calcinierter Soda) eine Explosionstemperatur von 184·7° C. — Loses oder in einer Papierhülle befindliches Dynamit brennt ruhig ab, wenn man es mittels Flamme oder Glut entzündet oder in ein offenes Feuer wirft; bei großen konzentrierten Quantitäten tritt unter solchen Umständen Explosionsgefahr ein. Befindet sich jedoch das zur Entzündung gelangende Dynamit in einer Blechbüchse oder sonst irgend einem festen und geschlossenen Gefäße, so explodiert es. — Bolley, Kundt und Pestalozzi haben im Jahre 1869 in Dinglers polyt. Journal ein ausführliches Gutachten über die Einwirkung von Stoß, Licht, höherer Temperatur und Elektrizität abgegeben, worauf verwiesen sei. — δ) Entzündung durch Initialimpuls. Plastisches, nicht gefrorenes Dynamit wird durch Sprengkapsel Nr. 3 (Füllung 0·54 g eines Gemisches von 85 Prozent Knallquecksilber und 15 Prozent chlorsaurem Kali) zur vollständigen Detonation gebracht. Die Detonationsgeschwindigkeit beträgt nach C. E. Bichel[1] 6818 m in der Sekunde. Eine Patrone von 30 mm Durchmesser überträgt die Detonation auf eine andere Patrone auf eine Entfernung von 310 mm. Die von 100 g Sprengstoff erzeugte Stichflamme hat eine Länge von 228 mm und eine Dauer von 8·31 Tausendstel Sekunden. Es zünden schon 5 g Gurdynamit ein Luftgasgemisch von 7 Prozent Grubengas und aufgewirbeltem Kohlenstaub. — ε) Die Explosionsprodukte eines Gurdynamits mit chemisch unwirksamer Basis sind die des Nitroglyzerins. Bei vollkommener Detonation entstehen dieselben also nach der Gleichung:

$$4[C_3H_5N_3O_9] = 12CO_2 + 10H_2O + 6N_2 + O_2.$$

Nach Bichel ist die größte, für Gurdynamit zu erreichende Ladedichte: 1·58. Ein Kilogramm Sprengstoff nimmt einen Raum ein von 0·633 l und läßt für die vergasenden Bestandteile einen Raum übrig von 0·524 l. Ein Kilogramm Gurdynamit bildet im Moment der Detonation 536 l Gase und Dämpfe im Gewicht von

[1] „Untersuchungsmethoden für Sprengstoffe." Berlin 1902, W. Ernst & Sohn. — Aufsatz über „Sprengwirkungen" in Glückauf 1905.

0·75 kg; ein Liter wiegt also 1·33 g. Bichel teilt folgendes Versuchsergebnis mit: Gewicht der Ladung (mit Umhüllung und Zündung): 106 g 75prozentiges Gurdynamit; die Sprengkammer enthielt nach der Detonation: 39·97 g feste und flüssige Rückstände, 60·53 g abgekühlte Gase unter Druck; letztere nahmen einen Raum ein von 37·21 l.

Einen Gegensatz zur Detonation bildet das Abbrennen oder sog. Auskochen, das in der Praxis ziemlich häufig bei allen nitroglyzerinhaltigen Sprengstoffen beobachtet wird. Hierbei findet nicht eine innere Zersetzung des Nitroglyzerinmoleküls statt, sondern eine Verbrennung unter Mitwirkung des atmosphärischen Sauerstoffes, wobei sich besonders Kohlenoxyd, Stickoxyd und Stickstoffdioxyd, also giftige Gase bilden. Jacoby und His[1] haben einen Fall aus der Praxis und seine Folgen ausführlich beschrieben. Tatsächlich bemerkt man bei allen auskochenden Sprengschüssen, daß aus dem Bohrloche große Mengen gelbroten Qualms hervorbrodeln, die sich schon nach ihrem Aussehen als Oxydverbindungen des Stickstoffs kennzeichnen und die bei regelrechter Detonation fehlen. Nach Wappler[2] sind die wichtigsten Ursachen für das unbeabsichtigte Auskochen der Sprengladungen: zu schwache Sprengkapseln oder Zündungen ohne Sprengkapseln; schlechtes Einsetzen der Zündschnur mit der Kapsel in die Ladung, so daß letztere vor der Explosion der Kapsel entzündet wird; Nichtaneinanderstoßen der einzelnen Sprengpatronen und die Verwendung gefrorenen Dynamits. Auskochen und Explosion der Sprengladung können in einem und demselben Bohrloche stattfinden, so daß die Ladung zum Teil abbrennt und zum Teil explodiert. Häufig wird (nach Heise) der Sprengstoff zunächst ins Kochen geraten und erst nachträglich entweder als Folge des unter dem Besatze sich entwickelnden Gasdruckes oder mittels der verspätet explodierenden Sprengkapsel zur Explosion kommen. In anderen Fällen wird der vorderste Teil der Ladung ordnungsmäßig explodieren, während die hinteren Patronen, die vielleicht durch einen Bohrmehlpfropfen abgesondert lagen, zu spät und zu schwach gezündet werden und nachträglich langsam abbrennen. — H. Walker (D.R.P. 185363) hat als Mittel, um solche Dynamitverbrennungsgase unschädlich zu machen, die Anwendung von wasserdichten Patronen aus Kaliumpermanganat (mit Zusatz von etwas Salmiak und Kaliumchlorat) vorgeschlagen; für je fünf

---

[1] Zeitschr. Schieß-Sprengstoffwesen 1907, S. 261. — Siehe auch Heise, „Auskochende Sprengschüsse und ihre Gefahren" in Glückauf 1898, S. 146.

[2] Jahrbuch Berg- u. Hüttenwesen im Königr. Sachsen 1887, S. 31.

Dynamitpatronen wird eine solche Oxydationspatrone angewandt, welche eine große Menge Sauerstoff liefern soll. — ζ) Die Wärmeentwicklung beträgt 1170 (1153) große Kalorien von einem Kilogramm 75prozentigen Gurdynamit. Die höchste Temperatur des Sprengstoffes bei der Zersetzung beträgt 2999° C. — η) Der Gasdruck P im Moment der Detonation im eigenen Volumen unter Berücksichtigung des Raumes der nicht vergasenden Bestandteile beträgt (nach Bichel): $1055\left(1+\frac{2999}{273}\right) = 12644$ kg/qcm; die Zahl 1055 kg/qcm stellt den Druck der Gase von 1 kg Sprengstoff im eigenen Volumen dar. In der 15 l-Kammer des Bichelschen Gasdruckmessers wurde als Druck einer Patrone von 100 g Gurdynamit gemessen: 48·2 kg/qcm. — ϑ) Stoßkraft. Die lebendige Energie $\frac{m v^2}{2}$ beträgt (nach Bichel) für 75prozentiges Gurdynamit: $\frac{1 \times 6818^2}{2 \times 9 \cdot 81} = 2369272$ sek./kg/m. — ι) Arbeitsleistung. Im Trauzlschen Bleiblock (Durchmesser und Höhe 20 cm) wird von 10 g Gurdynamit nach Bichel eine Ausbauchung von 520 ccm erzielt; Brunswig gibt 350 ccm an. — Dynamit ist weniger brisant als flüssiges Nitroglyzerin, weil die entwickelte Wärme sich auf die Zersetzungsprodukte und den indifferenten Träger verteilt; somit ist auch die Explosionstemperatur weniger hoch und der Anfangsdruck niedriger. Wasserfreie Kieselsäure und Tonerde haben bei konstantem Volumen ungefähr die gleiche spezifische Wärme (0·19) wie die gasförmigen Zersetzungsprodukte des Nitroglyzerins. Eine Beimengung von 25 Prozent Kieselgur wird (bei der Detonation im völlig geschlossenen Raum) also Temperatur und Anfangsdruck um $^1/_4$ erniedrigen. Für das gleiche Gewicht Nitroglyzerin ergibt sich also eine Verminderung der brisanten Eigenschaften proportional zur angewandten Menge indifferenten Trägers. Auch die Übertragung der Entzündung von einem kleinen Teil der Masse auf die benachbarten Teile ist durch die indifferente Beimengung erschwert.

d) Gefrorenes Gurdynamit. Über das Gefrieren des Gurdynamits hat die Königl. Bergwerksdirektion Saarbrücken im Jahre 1905 eingehende Versuche angestellt. Das Dynamit war in 35 mm-Patronen, welche teils einzeln ausgelegt, teils in kleinen Kisten mit Originalverpackung in einen Gefrierapparat von bestimmter Temperatur gebracht wurden. Dieser Apparat bestand aus drei Kästen, einem äußersten Holzkasten, der mit Isoliermasse (Holzwolle und Sägemehl) gefüllt war, einem mittleren eisernen Kasten zur Aufnahme des zur Erzeugung der gewünschten

Temperatur erforderlichen Wassers oder einer Kältemischung und eines inneren aus Eisenblech hergestellten, mit Holzdeckel und Filzunterlagen dicht abgeschlossenen Kastens zur Aufnahme der Sprengstoffe.

Folgende Resultate wurden erhalten:

Temperatur	a) Einzeln ausgelegte Patronen.		b) In 2 Kisten mit Originalverpackung.	
	Beginn des Gefrierens	Vollständig gefroren	Beginn des Gefrierens	Vollständig gefroren
	nach Stunden		nach Stunden	
0 bis + 2° C	3 bis 4	7 bis 8	8 bis 10	18 bis 24
+ 7 bis + 8°	etwa 18	24	24	48 bis 50
+ 10·5 bis + 11°	nach 11 Tagen war noch nichts gefroren			

Bei + 7 bis + 8° C gefriert Gurdynamit wesentlich rascher als die gelatinösen nitroglyzerinhaltigen Sprengstoffe. In Holzkisten erfolgt (durch die isolierende Wirkung des Holzes) das Gefrieren bedeutend langsamer als in frei ausliegenden Patronen. — Bei − 2° bis ± 0° C war Gurdynamit in gewöhnlichen Pappschachteln im Freien nach 4 bis 5 Stunden gefroren.

Gleichzeitig mit den Gefrierversuchen wurden Beobachtungen betreffend Auftauens der Sprengstoffe und Zersetzung angestellt. Die Auftauversuche wurden in einem unterirdischen Magazin von + 14 bis 15° Lufttemperatur vorgenommen. In einzelnen Patronen taute gefrorenes Gurdynamit in 10 bis 15 Stunden wieder auf, in Kisten mit Originalverpackung erst in etwa 60 Stunden. Versuche betr. Zersetzung gefrorenen Dynamits wurden in dem Gefrierapparat bei + 10,5 bis 11° ausgeführt. Bei einer Lagerzeit von 11 Tagen konnte weder an den freiliegenden noch an den in Kisten aufbewahrten Patronen eine Veränderung wahrgenommen werden.

Im allgemeinen wurde aus den betr. Versuchen entnommen, daß nitroglyzerinhaltige Sprengstoffe bei Temperaturen bis + 8° C gefrieren und bei Temperaturen unter + 11° C nicht auftauen. In der Praxis muß man — bei oberirdischen Lagern — daher 6 Monate im Jahr mit gefrorenem Dynamit rechnen.

In kleinen Mengen gefriert Gurdynamit (nach Kast) viel leichter als flüssiges Nitroglyzerin.

Über die Empfindlichkeit des gefrorenen Dynamits sind

von verschiedener Seite[1] Versuche angestellt worden. Nach Will wurde bei Fallhammerversuchen mit dem 1 kg-Gewicht weiches Material bei 12 bis 15 cm zur Detonation gebracht, während gefrorenes einer Fallhöhe von 110 bis 120 cm bedurfte.

Für ein 2 kg-Fallgewicht gibt Will eine Fallhöhe von 7 cm bei plastischem und 20 cm bei gefrorenem Gurdynamit an. Beim Beschuß aus dem Militärgewehr detonierte das auf Holzunterlage in Patronen sehr wechselnder Länge angewendete Gurdynamit in plastischem Zustande jedesmal, in gefrorenem dagegen nicht. In der Regel durchdringt das Geschoß infolge der Sprödigkeit des Materials die hartgefrorene Patrone nicht vollständig, sondern wird nach dem Zerspringen der Patrone vorzeitig abgelenkt. — Versuche, ob bei (zehnmal) wiederholtem Auftauen und Wiedergefrierenlassen die Empfindlichkeit gegen Stoß und Schlag sich erhöht, führten — im Gegensatz zu den Resultaten von Majendie und Dupré — zum Ergebnis, daß ein Wachsen der Empfindlichkeit nicht wahrzunehmen sei.

Will faßt seine Versuchsergebnisse folgendermaßen zusammen: 1. Gurdynamit ist in gefrorenem Zustande für alle Prüfungsarbeiten erheblich unempfindlicher als in plastischem Zustande. 2. Eine Anreicherung der Stoßenergie durch geeignete Wahl der Form der zu prüfenden Körper ließ sich nicht feststellen, weil das Material auch in gefrorenem Zustande vor der Explosion zur Zertrümmerung kam. 3. Wiederholtes Gefrierenlassen und Wiederauftauen führte bei den Versuchen nicht zu der Entstehung eines Materials von größerer Empfindlichkeit.

Auch bei den Versuchen der Bergwerksdirektion Saarbrücken erwies sich Gurdynamit in gefrorener Form unempfindlicher als in plastischer.

Dagegen kommt General Ph. Hess auf Grund seiner Beobachtungen zu dem Urteil, daß Dynamit halbgefroren, also im Übergangszustande, empfindlicher und gefährlicher sein kann. Möglicherweise führen (nach G. Bredig) elektrische Ladungen zu Explosionen. Das einfache Zerbrechen oder Zerschneiden

---

[1] Dinglers polyt. Journal 1865, Bd. 178, S. 411. — Mowbray in Dinglers polyt. Journ. 1869. Bd. 192, S. 172. — Hess in Mitteil. Gegenst. Art.- u. Geniewesen 1876, S. 213. — Dupré in Annal Report Insp. Explos. 1879 u. 1889. — Cronquist in Berg- u. Hüttenmänn. Ztg. 1894, S. 221. — Der Bergbau 1903, Heft 18. — Will und Bergwerksdirektion Saarbrücken in Zeitschr. Berg-, Hütten- u. Salinenwesen 1905. (Sonderabdruck bei W. Ernst & Sohn in Berlin.)

gefrorener (oder teilweise gefrorener) Patronen hat häufig deren Explosion veranlaßt. Das Verhalten gefrorenen Dynamits beim Transport und beim Laden ist unberechenbar und muß auf Grund der praktischen Erfahrungen als höchst gefährlich bezeichnet werden. Dazu kommt, daß bei der Benutzung gefrorenen Dynamits ganze oder teilweise Schußversager auftreten. Die völligen Versager müssen beseitigt werden, was gefährlich ist; bei den teilweisen Versagern bleiben Sprengstoffreste im Felsen oder Haufwerk und bilden dort eine dauernde Gefahrenquelle, besonders wenn durch warme Witterung der Sprengstoff wieder weich wird. — In England kamen im Jahre 1901 bei der Verwendung nitroglyzerinhaltiger Sprengstoffe 86 Unglücksfälle vor beim Besetzen, beim Anbohren nicht explodierter Ladungen und bei der gewaltsamen Berührung von Sprengstoffen im Geröll. Hiervon entfielen auf die Monate: Dezember Januar, Februar, März und April: 8, 17, 25, 10 und 9 Unfälle; auf die Monate: Mai, Juni, Juli, August, September, Oktober und November: 6, 3, 1, 0, 2, 1 und 4 Unfälle. Der Einfluß der kälteren Jahreszeit ist hierbei unverkennbar.

Gefrorenes Dynamit soll demnach unter keinen Umständen verwendet, sondern muß unbedingt vor dem Laden[1] aufgetaut werden. Trotzdem ist es kaum ganz zu vermeiden, daß der Arbeiter unter Umständen gefrorene Patronen in die Hand bekommt. In den einzelnen Patronenpaketen ist häufig die äußere Patronenlage weich, während sich in der Mitte des Pakets noch ganz oder teilweise gefrorene Patronen befinden.

Eine vorbeugende Maßregel ist die, daß sprengölhaltige Sprengstoffe nur in Magazinen aufbewahrt werden, in denen die Temperatur nicht unter $+8^0$ C sinkt. Die nötige Warmhaltung des oberirdischen Magazins geschieht durch eine Warmwasserleitung (Temperatur des Wassers nicht über 60^0 C) oder durch Pferdedünger, bzw. baut man unterirdische Magazine, in denen es nicht so kalt wird.

Das Auftauen des gefrorenen Dynamits ist zeitraubend, umständlich und setzt besondere Vorrichtungen voraus, die nicht überall vorhanden sein können. Übrigens ist gerade der Übergang vom festen Zustand zum weichen besonders gefährlich und kommen beim Auftauen alljährlich Unglücksfälle vor. In England traten (in der Zeit 1875 bis 1902) beim Auftauen nitro-

[1] Auch das Brechen und Schneiden gefrorenen Dynamits, überhaupt das Bearbeiten desselben mit festen Körpern, ist zu unterlassen.

glyzerinhaltiger Sprengstoffe 98 Unfälle ein, wobei 71 Personen getötet und 112 verletzt wurden. Jedenfalls muß man beim Auftauen die größte Vorsicht walten lassen; das gefrorene Dynamit soll zu diesem Zwecke einer mäßigen, 60° C keinesfalls übersteigenden und gleichmäßig wirkenden Erwärmung ausgesetzt werden; in keinem Falle dürfen Patronen an die Flamme eines Lichtes, in die Nähe von offenem Feuer, von Öfen oder Herden, von Dampfkesseln oder Dampfheizungen oder überhaupt an Stellen gebracht werden, die wärmer sind, als die Hand verträgt. Das Auftauen gefrorenen Dynamits soll nur unter Leitung eines Aufsehers in besonders gelegenen Räumen in angemessener Entfernung von der Betriebsstelle erfolgen. Zum Auftauen selbst sind die vielfach verwendeten, mehr oder weniger langen, dem Patronendurchmesser entsprechenden Blechröhren, welche in warmes Wasser gestellt werden, nicht zu empfehlen, da sich ihr Inneres der Beobachtung entzieht und schwer zu reinigen ist. Zweckmäßig sind wasserdichte Blechgefäße, welche in einem größeren, mit warmem Wasser gefüllten Behälter hineingesetzt oder von warmem Wasser umspült werden. Es ist darauf zu achten, daß der für die Aufnahme des Sprengstoffes bestimmte Einsatz trocken ist und frei von Krusten bleibt; nötigenfalls ist derselbe mit warmer Sodalauge oder einer Lösung von 2 Teilen Ätznatron und 2 Teilen Alkohol in 96 Teilen Wasser zu säubern. — Der sog. Nobelsche Topf (Fig. 61) ist ein doppeltes Zinkblechgefäß, in welchem warmes Wasser von 50 bis 60° C die Auftauung besorgt; das äußere Gefäß sowie der Deckel sind durch Wärmeschutzmittel gegen Abkühlung gesichert. — In den letzten Jahren wurden auch sog. Dynamit-Thermophore in den Handel gebracht, die von der „Deutschen Thermophor-Aktiengesellschaft“ zu Andernach a. Rh. hergestellt werden. Die Wirkung der Thermophore beruht darauf, daß erwärmtes und geschmolzenes Natriumacetat langsam unter Wärmeabgabe auskristallisiert. Der Apparat kann, nachdem die im Mantel untergebrachte Wärmemasse durch kochendes Wasser zum Schmelzen gebracht ist und so eine bedeutende Wärmemenge aufgenommen hat, längere Zeit für Auftauzwecke benutzt werden und ist für alle Orte geeignet, an denen die regelmäßige Zufuhr warmen Wassers Schwierigkeiten macht. Vorgenannte Gesellschaft liefert zwei Typen von Dynamit-Thermophoren: eine in Form von länglichen, mehr oder

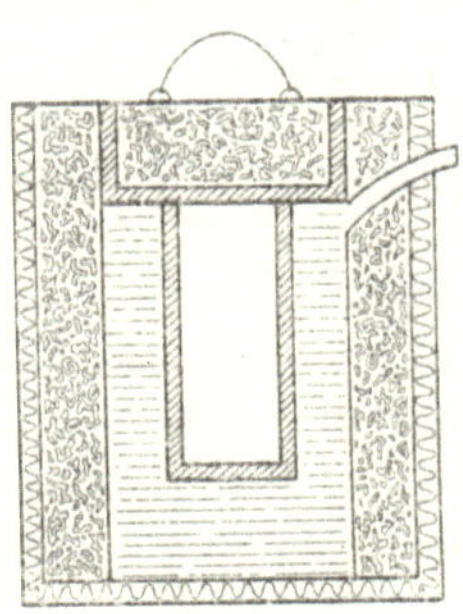

Fig. 61.
Nobelscher Topf.

weniger flachen Kästen[1] mit Holzhülle und Tragvorrichtung und eine andere in Form von runden Kesseln[2] und Tragegriff.[3]

e) Anwendung des Dynamits. Über die Gebrauchsweise und Verwendung des Dynamits für Bergbau, Steinbrüche, Tunnels, Eisensprengungen usw. siehe Trauzl, „Explosive Nitrilverbindungen, insbesondere Dynamit und Schießwolle, deren Eigenschaften und Verwendung in der Sprengtechnik", Wien 1870, Kommissionsverlag von Carl Gerolds Sohn; Joh. Lauer, Spreng- und Zündversuche mit Dynamit und komprimierter Schießbaumwolle, Wien 1872, L. W. Seidel & Sohn; Heise, Sprengstoffe und Zündung der Sprengschüsse, Berlin 1904, Julius Springer; Oskar Guttmann, Handbuch der Sprengarbeit, Braunschweig 1906, Friedr. Vieweg & Sohn; Denker, Unfallverhütung bei Sprengarbeiten in Steinbrüchen, Berlin 1907, C. Heymanns Verlag; Technischer Unterricht für die k. und k. Eisenbahntruppe, Hft. 6, Sprengarbeiten, Wien 1900. — Die Verwendung von Gurdynamit ist seit Erfindung der gelatinierten Sprengstoffe in starker Abnahme begriffen und in Deutschland nur noch sehr gering.

f) Vernichtung von Dynamit (nach Heise). Hierzu darf unter keiner Bedingung Wasser genommen werden, da solches Nitroglyzerin in Freiheit setzt, wodurch unter Umständen nachträglich Unheil angerichtet werden kann. Kleinere Mengen Dynamit kann man brockenweise in offenes Feuer schieben oder man bringt die Patronen einzeln mittels Sprengkapseln zur Explosion. Eine größere Anzahl Dynamitpatronen legt man — nach Entfernung des Patronenpapiers — mit ihren Enden aneinander und zündet die erste Patrone durch ein Stückchen Zündschnur (ohne Kapsel) oder mittels darübergelegten Papieres an; dann zieht man sich in angemessene Entfernung zurück, da der Eintritt einer plötzlichen Explosion der Masse nicht unmöglich ist. Die Patronensäule ist übrigens so zu legen und anzuzünden, daß etwaiger Wind die Flamme vom Sprengstoffe wegtreibt, um ein zu lebhaftes Feuer zu verhindern. Gefrorenes Dynamit ist besonders vorsichtig zu behandeln, da bei ihm die Verbrennung leicht in Explosion übergehen kann; es darf nicht gebrochen werden.

---

[1] Der kleinste Apparat dieser „Dynamitauftaukasten mit verschließbarem Holzkasten und Tragriemen" ist für ein $2^1/_2$ kg-Paket berechnet und kostet M. 35.—.

[2] Die Kessel haben eine Größe von 5 bis 100 l; der Preis schwankt dementsprechend von M. 22.— bis M. 130.—.

[3] Über Dynamit-Thermophore siehe auch: Österr. Zeitschr. Berg- u. Hüttenwesen **49**, Heft 17, sowie Mitteil. Gegenst. Art.- u. Geniewesen 1901, Heft 10.

II. Mit chemisch wirksamer Basis.

a) Gurdynamit und ähnliche Sprengpräparate enthalten in dem Aufsaugestoff, der Kieselgur (Ton, Magnesiasalz usw.), einen Bestandteil, der chemisch unwirksam ist und sogar bei der Explosion des Sprengöls, statt Wärme zu erzeugen, solche absorbiert, also die Sprengwirkung herabsetzt. Man versuchte daher, die Kieselgur ganz oder teilweise durch schwarzpulverähnliche Mischungen zu ersetzen, was übrigens Nobel schon zu Beginn seiner Versuche getan hatte. So entstand das Coloniapulver, eine Mischung von 30 bis 35 Prozent Nitroglyzerin und 65 bis 70 Prozent Schwarzpulver. Nobel nahm 1869 Patente auf Sprengpräparate aus 20 Teilen Sprengöl, 68 bis 70 Tln. Bariumnitrat und 10 bis 12 Tln. Kohle oder Harz; Gebr. Krebs & Cie. in Deutz fabrizierten einen Sprengstoff Lithofracteur, aus 55 Prozent Nitroglyzerin, Kieselgur, Salpeter, Schwefel und Kohle bestehend. W. B. Brains Sprengpulver war ein Gemisch von 40 bis 78 Prozent Sprengöl mit einem hauptsächlich aus chlorsaurem Kali bestehenden Chloratpulver.

b) Baron Trützscher-Falkenstein verwandte Holzfaser als Aufsaugestoff; sein Gemisch aus Nitroglyzerin und Holzsubstanz nannte er Lignose und stellte solches fabrikmäßig her. — Der im Jahre 1871 auf einer Reise in Nordamerika ermordete preußische Artillerieleutnant Dittmar erfand das Dualin, ein Gemisch von Nitroglyzerin mit Sägespänen (oder Holzzeug der Papierfabriken), die vorher mit einem Gemisch von Salpeter-Schwefelsäure nitriert oder auch nur mit einer Lösung von Kalisalpeter getränkt wurden. Auch das Sebastin (von Beckmann in Schweden) war im wesentlichen ein Gemisch von Nitroglyzerin mit Kohle und Nitrozellulose. Die Bestrebungen, Dynamite mit Zellulose oder Nitrozellulose als Basis herzustellen, wurden besonders intensiv in Österreich gefördert. In diesem Lande (wie übrigens auch in Frankreich und Rußland) hatte man im Jahre 1869 das Gurdynamit, nachdem solches sich zwei Jahre in der Zivilsprengtechnik bewährt hatte, auch als Kriegssprengmittel benutzt, während man in Preußen und England an der komprimierten Schießbaumwolle festhielt. Nachdem die Eigenschaft der Schießwolle entdeckt war, selbst bei recht beträchtlichem Wassergehalt noch explodieren zu können, wenn nur ein hinreichend starker Initialimpuls vorhanden ist; nachdem ferner die große Ungefährlichkeit der nassen Schießwolle gegen mechanische Einflüsse, Feuer und gegen aus der Nähe abgefeuerte Gewehrgeschosse einerseits, das ungünstige Verhalten des Gurdynamits andererseits gegen Wasser (wodurch Nitroglyzerin zur Abscheidung gebracht wird) und gegen mäßige Wärme (wobei ein ähnlicher Vorgang, bzw. Fetten erfolgt), sonach seine Empfindlichkeit gegen Gewehrgeschosse erkannt war, bemühte man sich im österreichischen technischen Militärkomitee, mit Nitroglyzerin bessere Präparate als das Gurdynamit herzustellen, auch unter möglichster Vermeidung des Übelstandes, den die Kieselgur oder ähnliche anorganische Stoffe mit Rücksicht auf ihre Unverbrennlichkeit und Unwirksamkeit mit sich brachten. Der österreichische Genieoffizier J. Trauzl stellte daher ein Zellulosedynamit her, ein Gemenge von 70 bis 75 Prozent Nitroglyzerin mit fein verteiltem Holzfaserstoff (aus gemahlenem, harzfreiem, mit Sodalösung behandeltem oder aus fast bis zur Verkohlung unter Luftabschluß erhitztem und hiernach zerriebenem Holz). Gegen Wasser zeigte das Zellulosedynamit eine viel höhere Widerstandsfähigkeit als das Gurdynamit; dagegen blieben Bemühungen, durch Zusatz von 15 bis 20 Prozent Wasser Unempfindlichkeit gegen mechanische Impulse herbeizuführen, ohne Erfolg, da ein solches wasserhaltiges Zellulosedynamit schon bei geringem Drucke Nitroglyzerin austreten läßt. Dagegen konnte Trauzl aus 75 Teilen Sprengöl, 23 Tln. Schießwolle und 2 Tln. Kohle ein Schießwolledynamit herstellen, das bei viertägigem Liegen im Wasser 15 Prozent von letzterem aufnahm und auch dann noch durch einen starken Detonator leicht zur Explosion gebracht werden konnte. Leider ließ sich Schießwolledynamit im großen Maßstabe nur schwer erzeugen, wegen der Eigentümlichkeit der Adhäsionsverhältnisse von Schießbaumwolle und Nitroglyzerin und wegen der großen Gefährlichkeit des Mischprozesses; die österreichische Kriegsverwaltung hatte jedoch eine Zeitlang für einen ganz speziellen Zweck, nämlich zur sicheren Einleitung der vollen Explosion gefrorenen Gurdynamits, Schießwolledynamit adoptiert. Es sei hier auch erwähnt, daß Siersch und Roth in der Nobelschen Dynamitfabrik in Preßburg später aus 60 Prozent Nitroglyzerin und 40 Prozent nitrierter Hydrozellulose (durch Behandeln von Baumwolle mit verdünnter Schwefelsäure erhält man nach Girard ein feines, weißes, als Hydrozellulose bezeichnetes Pulver, das dann nitriert wurde) ein äußerst kräftiges Sprengmittel herstellten, das gleichfalls als Zündmittel für gewisse Zwecke verwandt wurde.

c) Wichtiger als die beiden vorbeschriebenen Gruppen (Nitroglyzerin mit Schwarzpulver, Nitroglyzerin mit Zellulose oder Nitrozellulosen) ist eine dritte Gruppe, bei welcher Nitroglyzerin mit Holzmehl und einem Nitrat gemischt wird. Diese Mischdynamite sind in Österreich, Frankreich und besonders in den

Vereinigten Staaten noch viel in Gebrauch. In letzterem Lande stellt man hauptsächlich diese nicht gelatinierten Mischdynamite her, die als straight dynamite bezeichnet werden; sie enthalten durchschnittlich 40 Prozent Sprengöl, etwa 12 Prozent Holzmehl als Aufsaugestoff, dann ca. 46 Prozent Natronsalpeter, etwa $^1/_2$ bis 1 Prozent Calcium- oder Magnesiumkarbonat, der Rest ist Feuchtigkeit. — In Frankreich fabriziert die Société Générale: Dynamit Nr. 0, bestehend aus 70 Prozent Nitroglyzerin + 30 Prozent Holzmehl, Dynamit Nr. 2 (35 Prozent Nitroglyzerin, 52 Prozent Natronsalper, 13 Prozent Holz- oder Getreidemehl) und Dynamit Nr. 3 (22 Prozent Nitroglyzerin, 66 Prozent Natronsalpeter, 12 Prozent Kohle); die Société française erzeugt neben Dynamit Nr. 0 (74 Prozent Nitroglyzerin, 26 Prozent Holzmehl) ein Dynamit Nr. 2 (48 Prozent Nitroglyzerin, 39 Prozent Kalisalpeter und 13 Prozent Holzmehl) sowie Dynamit Nr. 3 (25 Prozent Nitroglyzerin, 63 Prozent Kalisalpeter und 12 Prozent Kohle). Weitere französische Mischdynamite sind: Dynamit Nr. 2: 48 Prozent Nitroglyzerin, 39 Prozent Kalisalpeter, 13 Prozent Holzmehl; Dynamit Nr. 2E (Export): 40 Prozent Nitroglyzerin, 43 Prozent Kalisalpeter, 17 Prozent Holzmehl; Dynamit Nr. 6: 39·5 Prozent Nitroglyzerin, 43 Prozent Natronsalpeter, 17 Prozent Holzmehl, 0·3 Prozent Soda, 0·2 Prozent Ocker; Dynamit Nr. 7: 29 Prozent Nitroglyzerin, 50·35 Prozent Natronsalpeter, 11 Prozent Holzmehl, 0·5 Prozent Soda, 0·15 Prozent Ocker, 9 Prozent Getreidemehl. — In Österreich werden hergestellt: Rhexit II, bestehend aus 50 Prozent Sprengöl, 6 Prozent Holzmehl und 44 Prozent Saugstoff (aus 74 Teilen Natronsalpeter, 25 Tln. Holzmehl und 1 Tl. Soda bestehend); Rhexit III (35 Prozent Sprengöl, 15 Prozent Holzmehl, 50 Prozent Saugstoff); Rhexit IV (24 Prozent Nitroglyzerin, 76 Prozent Holzmehl und Saugstoff); Rhexit V (15 Prozent Nitroglyzerin, 85 Prozent Holzmehl und Saugstoff); außerdem Dynamit II B, bestehend aus 25 Prozent Nitroglyzerin und 75 Prozent eines Saugstoffes, der aus 70 Teilen Natronsalpeter, 1 Tl. Soda, 15 Tln. Holzkohle und 14 Tln. Schwefel zusammengesetzt ist; endlich Dynamit III, enthaltend 15 Prozent Nitroglyzerin und 85 Prozent Saugstoff (wie bei Dynamit II B). Die österreichischen ärarealischen „Stopfdynamite" haben demnach folgende Zusammensetztung: Dynamit II B enthält 25 Prozent Nitroglyzerin, 52·5 Prozent Natronsalpeter, 11·25 Prozent Weißerlenpulverkohle, 10·5 Prozent Schwefel, 0·75 Prozent Soda; Farbe: schwarz; Ausbauchung im Trauzl: 700 bis 750 ccm (einschließlich 160 ccm Laderaum). Dynamit III enthält 15 Prozent Nitroglyzerin, 59·5 Prozent Natronsalpeter,

12·75 Prozent Weißerlenpulverkohle, 11·9 Prozent Schwefel, 0·85 Prozent Soda; als Zündpatrone hierzu wird Dynamit II verwendet; die Ausbauchung im Trauzl beträgt 450 bis 550 ccm; die Farbe von Dynamit III ist schwarz. Der Sprengstoff Meganit einer ungarischen Fabrik besteht aus 60 Prozent Sprengöl, 10 Prozent nitriertem Holz, 10 Prozent nitriertem Steinnußmehl, 20 Prozent Natronsalpeter. — Die Patronierung der Mischdynamite mit aktiver Basis erfolgt in Paraffinpapierhülsen gewöhnlich in 20- und 23 mm-Patronen, doch kommen auch die Kaliber 18, 25, 28, 30, 32, 35, 40, 45 und 60 mm vor. Die Sprengpatronen wiegen etwa 80 g, die Zündpatronen ca. 30 g; manchmal werden auch kleine Sprengpatronen im Gewicht von ca. 50 g angefertigt. In Österreich erfolgt die Verpackung der Patronen in Pappkartons aus 0·6 bis 0·7 mm starkem Pappendeckel, die nach Verschluß noch in geschmolzenes Paraffin getaucht werden. Die für 2·5 kg Sprengstoff berechneten Kartons sind 205 mm lang, 140 mm breit und 90 mm hoch. Zehn Kartons werden in zwei Lagen in Kistchen (475 : 220 : 295 mm) eingelegt und letztere mit verzinnten Stiften zugenagelt.

Diese Mischdynamite, durch einfaches Zusammenmischen von Nitroglyzerin mit Zumischpulver (hauptsächlich Holzmehl und Salpeter) erhalten, sind also in Fabrikation und Zusammensetzung dem Gurdynamit ähnlich, nur enthalten sie statt der chemisch unwirksamen Kieselgur das verbrennliche, Gase entwickelnde und daher wirksame Zumischpulver; andererseits ist ihre Zusammensetzung eine ganz analoge wie die der später zu beschreibenden Gelatinedynamite; bei letzteren ist jedoch das Sprengöl durch etwas aufgelöste Kollodiumwolle zähflüssig gemacht (gelatiniert) und vermag daher das Zumischpulver viel besser festzuhalten, während bei den nicht gelatinierten Mischdynamiten das Nitroglyzerin leicht ausschwitzt, der Sprengstoff auch durch Wasser leicht verdorben wird.

Die Mischdynamite mit aktiver Basis sind lockere, etwas fettige Pulver, auf welchen sich auch beim Drücken keine Öltropfen zeigen dürfen; an Papier dürfen durch Druck höchstens geringfügige Fettspuren abgegeben werden. Das zur Umhüllung dienende Paraffinpapier darf an der Außenseite gar keine, an der Innenseite nur sehr geringe Fettspuren zeigen, auch dann, wenn die Patronen wiederholt nacheinander gefroren waren und wieder aufgetaut wurden. Auch an den Verschlußstellen dürfen die Patronen Sprengstoff nicht austreten lassen oder mit solchem äußerlich verunreinigt sein. Diese Dynamite sollen nicht länger als zwölf Monate — vom Zeitpunkt ihrer Erzeugung ab — lagern.

Es ist zweckmäßig, durch blaue Lakmusstreifen, sowie Geruch zeitweilig zu prüfen, ob sich saure Gase entwickeln.

d) Eine vierte Gruppe, und zwar besonders starke Mischdynamite erhält man durch Anwendung eines Gemisches von Nitroglyzerin und Ammonsalpeter. — Am 31. Mai 1867 hatten die Schweden J. H. Norrbin und Joh. Ohlsson in ihrem Vaterlande ein Patent genommen auf einen neuen Sprengstoff Ammoniakkrut, ein Gemenge von Ammonsalpeter mit Kohle, Sägespänen, Kohlenwasserstoffen oder Nitrokohlenwasserstoffen; kurz darauf — am 19. Juni 1867 — nahm E. A. Björkman ein schwedisches Patent auf ein durch Pulver, Zündsatz oder Elektrizität zur Explosion zu bringendes Gemenge von 100 Teilen Ammonsalpeter, 12 Tln. Sägespänen, 25 Tln. Nitroglyzerin und 1 Tl. Benzol; oder von 200 Tln. Ammonsalpeter, 19 Tln. Kohle, 35 Tln. Nitroglyzerin und 1 Tl. Kreosotöl; der Sprengstoff erhielt den Namen Seranin.

Über Mischdynamite mit Ammonnitrat als Basis sagt Berthelot folgendes: Diese Präparate sind sehr interessant infolge ihrer großen Energie, welch letztere vom Nitroglyzerin und dem Ammonsalpeter herrührt; sie können als dritten Bestandteil einen brennbaren Körper enthalten oder nicht; letzterer (Kohle, Zellulose usw.) soll einerseits das Aufsaugevermögen verbessern, andererseits den vom Nitroglyzerin und dem Ammonsalpeter gelieferten überschüssigen Sauerstoff ausnützen. Die jeweiligen Mengen der drei Bestandteile (Ammonsalpeter, Nitroglyzerin und brennbare Substanz) können sehr verschieden sein, selbst wenn man eine totale Verbrennung anstrebt. Als brennbare Substanz wollen wir Kohle nehmen und solche der Einfachheit halber als reinen Kohlenstoff betrachten. — Alle Systeme, welche der Bedingung einer vollständigen Verbrennung entsprechen, beziehen sich auf folgende Formeln:

$$x(C_3H_5N_3O_9 + {}^1/_4 C) + y(NH_4NO_3 + {}^1/_2 C),$$

dann $$C_3H_5N_3O_9 = 3CO_2 + 2{\cdot}5H_2O + 1{\cdot}5N_2 + 0{\cdot}5O,$$

bzw. $$NH_4NO_3 = N_2 + 2H_2O + O,$$

somit brauche ich für ein Molekül Nitroglyzerin ${}^1/_4$ C, für ein Molekül Ammonsalpeter aber ${}^1/_2$ C, um den freiwerdenden Sauerstoff in Kohlensäure überzuführen; es entstehen dann $(3{\cdot}25\,x + 0{\cdot}5\,y)\,CO_2 + (2{\cdot}5\,x + 2\,y)\,H_2O + (1{\cdot}5\,x + 1\,y)\,N_2$; diese Gase wiegen in Grammen: $230\,x + 86\,y$; die entwickelte Wärme beträgt (für H_2O dampfförmig): $325{\cdot}7\,x + 79{\cdot}2\,y$; oder — für ein Kilogramm berechnet — $\frac{1000}{230\,x + 86\,y}(325{\cdot}7\,x + 79{\cdot}2\,y)$; das Gasvolumen beträgt: $(7{\cdot}25\,x + 4{\cdot}5\,y)\,22{\cdot}32\,\mathrm{l}\,(1 + \alpha t)\frac{0{\cdot}760}{H}$.

Beispiel: Es sei $x = 1$, $y = 16$; prozentuale Zusammensetzung: 14·1 Prozent Nitroglyzerin, 76·6 Prozent Ammonsalpeter, 6·3 Prozent

Kohle. Das Gewicht der Gase beträgt dann 1606 g; die entwickelte Wärme 1593 Kal. (H_2O Dampf), bzw. 1938 Kal. (H_2O flüssig), oder für 1 kg: 992 Kal. (H_2O Dampf), bzw. 1207 Kal. (H_2O flüssig); das reduzierte Gasvolumen = 1769 l (H_2O Dampf), bzw. 642 l (H_2O flüssig), oder für 1 kg: 1101 l (H_2O Dampf), bzw. 400 l (H_2O flüssig); der Gasdruck (H_2O flüssig) $= \frac{400}{n - 0{\cdot}39}$ Atmosphären.

In Frankreich wird ein Ammondynamit Nr. 1 hergestellt aus 40 Prozent Nitroglyzerin, 45 Prozent Ammonsalpeter, 5 Prozent Natronsalpeter und 10 Prozent Holz- oder Getreidemehl. — Dynamite Nr. 2 à l'ammoniaque hat die Zusammensetzung: 20 Prozent Nitroglyzerin, 75 Prozent Ammonsalpeter, 5 Prozent Holzmehl. — Ammondynamit Nr. 2 b besteht aus 22 Prozent Nitroglyzerin, 75 Prozent Ammonsalpeter und 3 Prozent Holzkohle. Im allgemeinen sind jedoch Mischungen aus nicht gelatiniertem Sprengöl und Ammonsalpeter zu empfindlich gegen Feuchtigkeit.

Zum Schlusse des siebenten Abschnittes geben wir die Einteilung der Mischdynamite nach Berthelot:[1]

I. Dynamite mit unwirksamer Basis (Nitroglyzerin mit Kieselgur, Tonerde, Magnesiakarbonat usw.).

II. Dynamite mit wirksamer Basis.

1. Dynamite mit einfach verbrennlichen Zusätzen; hierbei wird dem reinen oder dem mit Kieselgur usw. vermengten Nitroglyzerin nur so viel Kohle, Holzmehl oder Schwefel zugesetzt, als dem bei der Detonation des Nitroglyzerins entstehenden überschüssigen Sauerstoffe entspricht.
2. Dynamite mit gemischter Basis, wobei im Interesse einer besseren Absorption mehr brennbare Substanz zugesetzt wird, was natürlich auf die Art der Zersetzung des Nitroglyzerins von Einfluß ist.
3. Dynamite mit gleichzeitig wirksamer aktiver Basis; darunter sind Mischungen von Nitroglyzerin mit einem explosiven Körper (wie Ammoniumnitrat, Kaliumchlorat) verstanden, der gleichzeitig detoniert, ohne daß die Elemente des einen Bestandteils bei der Zersetzung des andern chemisch mitwirken.
4. Dynamite mit explosiver, verbrennlicher Basis, wobei man als Zusatz zum Nitroglyzerin ein an sich explosives Präparat (Schießbaumwolle, nitrierter Holzstoff, Schwarzpulver) verwendet, das aber zu seiner vollständigen Verbrennung nicht genügend Sauerstoff enthält.

[1] Sur la force des matières explosives.

Achter Abschnitt.

Sprenggelatine und Gelatinedynamite.

Eine bahnbrechende Neuerung gegenüber den Mischdynamiten bedeutete die von Alfred Nobel im Jahre 1875 gemachte Erfindung,[1] das Nitroglyzerin dadurch zu gelatinieren, daß man in mäßiger Wärme einige Prozente Kollodiumwolle im Sprengöl auflöst.

Das schwedische Patent hat nachstehenden Wortlaut:

Wie bekannt, hat sich das Nitroglyzerin in flüssiger Form als allzu gefährlich für industrielle Zwecke erwiesen. Infolge dieser Gefährlichkeit habe ich das Dynamit, d. i. Nitroglyzerin in höchst porösen Stoffen absorbiert, erfunden; allein Dynamit besitzt nur $^2/_3$ der Kraft des Nitroglyzerins und ist empfindlich gegen Berührung oder Druck von Wasser, weil dadurch das flüssige Sprengöl aus dem Dynamit herausgedrängt wird. Deshalb habe ich mich bemüht, dem Nitroglyzerin auf andere Weise eine feste Form zu geben; ich erreiche dies durch einen Gelatinierungsprozeß; letzterer wird so ausgeführt, daß ich in Nitroglyzerin, welches auf dem Wasserbade gelinde erwärmt wird, Nitrozellulose, und zwar solche, die zur Kollodiumbereitung verwendet wird, auflöse. Die explosive Flüssigkeit wird dadurch mehr oder weniger dickflüssig, und erreicht, nachdem sie 6 bis 7 Prozent ihres Gewichts nitrierter Pflanzenfaser aufgenommen hat, eine gummi- oder gelatineartige Konsistenz, welche sich besonders gut zu industriellen Zwecken eignet. Ich beschränke die Lösung jedoch nicht auf den angeführten Prozentsatz, weil für verschiedene Zwecke verschiedene Härtegrade des Explosivmittels erforderlich sind und der Härtegrad bedingt wird durch die relative Menge gelöster nitrierter Pflanzenfaser. Bei der Gelatinierung des Nitroglyzerins muß beachtet werden: 1. daß diese Flüssigkeit keine Verunreinigungen enthält, wodurch ihre Fähigkeit, in der Wärme nitrierte Zellulose zu lösen, unvorteilhaft beeinflußt wird; 2. daß nur leicht lösliche Nitrozellulose angewandt wird; 3. daß die Auflösung der nitrierten Zellulose, besonders wenn dieselbe sehr zusammenhängt, dadurch erleichtert wird, daß man die Masse umarbeitet und knetet.

Das gelatinierte Nitroglyzerin läßt sich mit Leichtigkeit zu Patronen pressen, auch kann man ihm eine andere Form geben. — Für gewisse, besonders militärische Zwecke, ist es von Bedeutung, daß man dem Nitroglyzerin indifferente oder wenig explosive Stoffe beifügt, welche die Fähigkeit besitzen, das Sprengöl und die zur Gelatinierung dienende Nitrozellulose zu lösen. Solche Stoffe sind: Acetin (Glyzerin-Essigsäureester), Biacetin, Triacetin, Methylacetat, Äthylacetat, Essigsäure, Aceton,

[1] Englisches Patent 4179 (1875), schwedisches Patent vom 8. Juli 1876, deutsches Patent 4829; siehe Seite 31.

Nitrobenzol, Dinitrobenzol, Methylnitrat, Äthylnitrat u. a. Diese Stoffe haben die Fähigkeit, den Gelatinierungsprozeß zu erleichtern; ferner vermindern sie die Empfindlichkeit des Nitroglyzerins gegen Stoß, sowie seine Detonationsgeschwindigkeit; auch setzen sie den Gefrierpunkt des Nitroglyzerins herab. Die am wenigsten flüchtigen Stoffe, wie Triacetin, Nitrobenzol und Dinitrobenzol, sind vorzuziehen, weil sie nicht verdunsten, so daß im Laufe der Zeit ihre Wirkung nicht durch Verdunsten verloren geht. — Die Menge der zugesetzten Stoffe hängt von dem Verwendungszwecke ab. Will man bloß den Gelatinierungsprozeß erleichtern, so genügen wenige Prozent, ja sogar schon ein halbes Prozent vom Gewicht des angewandten Nitroglyzerins. Will man dagegen die Empfindlichkeit des Nitroglyzerins gegen Stoß oder seine Explosionsgeschwindigkeit vermeiden, um es als Sprengladung in Bomben oder als Treibmittel in Schießwaffen zu verwenden, so muß man mehr zusetzen, und zwar je nach Bedarf. Dasselbe ist der Fall, wenn man den Gefrierpunkt des Nitroglyzerins heruntersetzen will; hierzu eignen sich am besten Methylnitrat, Äthylnitrat, Nitrobenzol, Acetin, Biacetin und Triacetin. — Ein Zusatz der genannten Stoffe erhöht den relativen Gehalt des gelatinierten Nitroglyzerins an Kohlenstoff und Wasserstoff und vermindert dessen Sauerstoffgehalt. Das dadurch enstehende Mißverhältnis kann man ausgleichen, indem man Natronsalpeter, Kalisalpeter, chlorsaures Kali oder andere sauerstoffreiche Stoffe in fein pulverisierter Form und in solcher Menge einknetet, die — nach der chemischen Formel der Stoffe berechnet — nötig ist, um im Augenblick der Explosion allen Wasserstoff zu Wasserdampf und alle Kohle zu Kohlensäure zu verbrennen. — Da es nicht möglich ist, alle Mischungen anzugeben, wozu obengenannte Verhältnisse führen können, so begnüge ich mich mit der Aufstellung von vier charakteristischen Typen:

I. Nitroglyzerin, gelatiniert durch Auflösen von 7 Prozent nitrierter Zellulose — oder mehr oder weniger, je nach dem angestrebten Härtegrade des Gelatinierungsproduktes.

II. Sub I genannte Mischung mit Zusatz von $^1/_2$ Prozent bis 30 Prozent Acetin, Biacetin, Triacetin, Nitrobenzol oder einem andern der oben angegebenen Stoffe. Die weite Grenze zwischen $^1/_2$ und 30 Prozent erklärt sich dadurch, daß Explosivstoffe für einige Zwecke mit Leichtigkeit detonieren müssen, während in anderen Fällen eine trägere Explosion gewünscht wird.

III. Sub II genannte Mischungen, denen man durch Einkneten so große Mengen Salpeter oder andere sauerstoffreiche Stoffe ähnlicher Zusammensetzung beifügt, als erforderlich ist, um allen Kohlenstoff zu Kohlensäure und allen Wasserstoff zu Wasser zu verbrennen.

IV. Sub I und II genannte Mischungen, denen man durch Einmischen oder Einkneten billige Explosivstoffe beifügt, oder solche Mischungen, die auf Kosten ihres eigenen Sauerstoffgehalts abbrennen können. Derartige Mischungen sind: Gewöhnliches

Pulver sowie Mischungen von salpetersauren oder chlorsauren Salzen mit Kohle, Schwefel, Zucker, Stärke, Sägespänen, Harzen, Fetten usw.; ferner alle organischen nitrierten Stoffe mit oder ohne Zusatz von Salpeter oder ähnlichen Stoffen in einem zur vollständigen Verbrennung erforderlichen Verhältnis, mit einem Wort: jede bis dato bekannte explosive Mischung, die mit dem gelatinierten Nitroglyzerin mechanisch vereinigt werden kann.

Solche Einmischungen sind hauptsächlich von Nutzen, weil die verminderte Kraftansammlung durch billigeren Herstellungspreis ausgeglichen wird. In der Praxis nimmt man gewöhnlich Mischungen aus 35 Gewichtsteilen Natronsalpeter (oder 100 Teile Kalisalpeter oder 200 Ammoniaksalpeter oder 100 chlorsaures Kali) mit 15 bis 30 Gewichtsteilen Kohle (15 Teile für vollständige Verbrennung zu Kohlensäure, 30 Teile für Verbrennung zu Kohlenoxyd) oder entsprechende, mittels der chemischen Formeln leicht zu berechnende Mengen anderer organischer Stoffe. Nachstehend gebe ich zum besseren Verständnis einige für praktische Zwecke geeignete Mischungsbeispiele:

A) 93 Gewichtsteile Nitroglyzerin, gelatiniert mit
7 „ löslichem Pyroxylin.

B) 91 Gewichtsteile Nitroglyzerin und
2 „ Triacetin (oder Biacetin, Acetin, Nitrobenzol, Dinitrobenzol, Essigäther oder analoger Stoff),
7 „ lösliches Pyroxylin.
Das Ganze gelatiniert.

C) 82 Gewichtsteile Nitroglyzerin
10 „ Methylnitrat
8 „ lösliches Pyroxylin
} gelatiniert.

Diese Mischung (C) soll wegen der leichten Flüchtigkeit des Methylnitrats unter Wasser aufbewahrt werden; sie besitzt den Vorzug, daß das Nitroglyzerin auch bei sehr niedriger Temperatur nicht gefriert.

D) 82 Gewichtsteile Nitroglyzerin,
10 „ Nitrobenzol (oder Dinitrobenzol, Triacetin, Biacetin, Acetin, Essigäther oder analoge Stoffe) gelatiniert mit
8 „ löslichem Pyroxylin.

E) 80 Gewichtsteile der Mischung D),
20 „ Natronsalpeter,
innig gemischt.

F) 30 Gewichtsteile von Mischung A), B), C) oder D),
70 „ gewöhnliches Schwarzpulver oder ähnliche Stoffe,
innig gemischt.

G) 30 Gewichtsteile von Mischung A), B), C) oder D),
59 „ Natronsalpeter (oder dieselbe Menge eines ähnlichen sauerstoffreichen Körpers),
11 „ Tierkohle (oder andere brennbare Substanz).

Die Mischungen A), B), C) und D) eignen sich besonders für Sprengungen in hartem Gestein, die Mischungen F) und G) für lockeres Gestein; die übrigen sind vorgesehen für solche Fälle, wo die Empfindlichkeit des Nitroglyzerins gegen Stoß, sowie seine Detonationsgeschwindigkeit gemäßigt werden soll.

Außer Nitroglyzerin gibt es noch andere explosive Flüssigkeiten, die in ähnlicher Weise gelatiniert werden können; in erster Linie nenne ich das Methylnitrat, als an und für sich am besten geeignet, da es wegen der Leichtlöslichkeit von Pyroxylin in ihm, sowie wegen der großen Kraftkonzentration bald nach dem Nitroglyzerin in Betracht kommt; dagegen erschwert die große Flüchtigkeit des Methylnitrats dessen praktische Verwendbarkeit.

Außer Nitrozellulose können andererseits auch noch andere Stoffe die Fähigkeit besitzen, das Nitroglyzerin zu gelatinieren; deshalb betone ich nochmals, daß der springende Punkt meiner Erfindung in der Idee liegt, durch Gelatinierung dem flüssigen Nitroglyzerin eine feste Konsistenz zu geben.

Das gelatinierte Nitroglyzerin kann in Bohrlöchern verwendet werden — mit passender Vorladung — und durch einfache Zündschnur zur Explosion gebracht werden; es entwickelt dabei keine schädlichen Gase wie das Dynamit. — Im allgemeinen ist aber doch die für Nitroglyzerinpräparate gebräuchliche Sprengkapselzündung vorzuziehen.

Wenn gelatiniertes Nitroglyzerin gefriert, so explodiert es bei Sprengkapselzündung leichter als gefrorenes Dynamit; doch ist beim gefrorenen gelatinierten Nitroglyzerin die Zündung durch Zündpatronen von Pulver, ungefrorenem Dynamit oder ungefrorenem gelatiniertem Nitroglyzerin vorzuziehen.

Hat man das Nitroglyzerin unter Zusatz größerer Mengen Acetin, Nitro- oder Dinitrobenzol gelatiniert, so ist es ziemlich schwer entzündbar und erfordert außer einer besonderen Zündpatrone auch noch einen geschlossenen Raum mit starken Wänden, wie z. B. eine Bombe, um zur vollen Kraftentfaltung zu kommen.

Das gelatinierte Nitroglyzerin hat als hauptsächlichen Vorzug den in die Wage zu legen, daß es um beinahe 50 Prozent stärker ist als Dynamit mit 75 Prozent Nitroglyzeringehalt; ferner ist die explosive Flüssigkeit nicht nur mechanisch gebunden wie beim Dynamit und kommt es daher nicht vor, daß das Sprengöl durch Druck oder Berührung mit Wasser ausgeschieden wird.

Die gelatinierten Nitroglyzerinsprengstoffe scheidet man in zwei Gruppen. Bei der ersten wird das Sprengöl durch eine relativ größere Menge (7 bis 10 Prozent) Kollodiumwolle in eine zähe, elastische Masse, die Sprenggelatine, übergeführt, welch letztere direkt als Sprengstoff verwendet wird; bei der zweiten Gruppe stellt man zunächst durch Auflösen von erheblich weniger Kollodiumwolle eine dünnflüssige, mehr sirupartige Masse, das sog. gelatinierte Öl her, woraus dann durch Vermischen mit Zumischpulver die Gelatinedynamite (bzw. wenn das Zumischpulver hauptsächlich aus Ammonsalpeter besteht, die Ammongelatinedynamite) erzeugt werden.

Sowohl für Sprenggelatine als Gelatinedynamite bildet also die Kollodiumwolle ein wichtiges Ausgangsmaterial. Die als Kollodiumwolle bezeichneten Nitrozellulosen sind kein einheitlicher Körper, sondern ein Gemisch verschiedener Nietrierungsstufen. Für die hier in Betracht kommende Fabrikation sind von wesentlicher Bedeutung: Löslichkeit, Viskosität, Bindungsfähigkeit, Stickstoffgehalt.

Löslichkeit (in Ätheralkohol). Früher glaubte man, daß zwischen Löslichkeit und Stickstoffgehalt ein direkter Zusammenhang bestehe und daß man einerseits nicht über eine Enneanitrozellulose $C_{24}H_{31}O_{11}(NO_3)_9$ mit 11·96 Prozent Stickstoff hinaus, andererseits nicht unter eine Oktonitrozellulose $C_{24}H_{32}O_{12}(NO_3)_8$ mit 11·11 Prozent Stickstoff heruntergehen könne, wenn das Produkt löslich sein solle. Nach neueren Untersuchungen wird die Löslichkeit auch von anderen Faktoren als dem Stickstoffgehalt bedingt, insbesondere ist die Art der Herstellung von Einfluß. Es gelang Lunge[1] und seinen Schülern, lösliche Dekanitrozellulose $C_{24}H_{30}O_{11}(NO_3)_{10}$ mit 12·75 Prozent Stickstoff und Heptanitrozellulose $C_{24}H_{33}O_{11}(NO_3)_7$ mit 10·18 Prozent Stickstoff herzustellen; im allgemeinen liegt jedoch der Bereich der Kollodiumwollen zwischen 12·5 und 11 Prozent N. In einer neueren Arbeit teilt G. Lunge[2] mit, daß man in Ätheralkohol lösliche Nitrozellulosen erhält, wenn man ganz trockene Baumwolle mit einem Gemisch aus gleichen Teilen Salpetersäure und Schwefelsäure bei Gegenwart von 17 bis 18 Prozent (weitere Grenzen 15·5 bis 19 Prozent) Wasser nitriert; mit steigender Darstellungstemperatur nimmt die Löslichkeit zu; entsprechend ist die Zeitdauer der Nitrierung einzuschränken (bei 20° wurde acht Stunden, bei 40° zwei Stunden, bei 60° nur $^1/_4$ bis $^1/_2$ Stunde nitriert. — Nach Oskar Guttmann[3] ist es allgemein üblich, zum Nitrieren der Baumwolle gleiche Teile Salpetersäure von 75 Prozent Monohydrat und Schwefelsäure von 96 Prozent Monohydrat zu nehmen und bei einer Temperatur von 40° zwischen 1 und $1^1/_2$ Stunden lang zu nitrieren. Das Verhältnis von Baumwolle zu Säuregemisch beträgt meist 1 zu 25 (Grenze 1 zu 30); man erhält im Großbetriebe selbst bei nur 14 Prozent Wasser eine ausgezeichnet lösliche Nitrozellulose.[4] — Nach Ver-

---

[1] Siehe Band II, Seite 167.

[2] Zeitschr. angew. Chemie 1906, S. 2051.

[3] Zeitschr. angew. Chemie 1907, S. 262.

[4] Zur Löslichkeitsbestimmung in Ätheralkohol (1 Vol. absol. Alkohol + 2 Vol. absol. Äther) werden 2·5 g Nitrozellulose und 250 ccm Ätheralkohol in einem eingeteilten 250 ccm-Zylinder 1 bis 12 Stunden lang geschüttelt; nach der Lösung und dem Absetzen des Ungelösten wird das Volumen der Flüssigkeit an der Teilung des Zylinders abgelesen, je 50 ccm

suchen von O. Silberrad[1] besteht aber durchaus kein Parallelismus zwischen der Löslichkeit von Kollodiumwollen in Ätheralkohol und derjenigen in Nitroglyzerin; für letztere scheint der Wassergehalt des Nitriergemisches nicht von Einfluß zu sein.

Viskosität. Die im Nitroglyzerin aufgelöste Kollodiumwolle wirkt um so besser, je dickflüssiger sie das Nitroglyzerin macht. Lunge hat (mit Suter) die Viskositätsverhältnisse näher untersucht[2] und gelangte zu folgenden Schlüssen: die Viskosität der Ätheralkohol-Lösungen von Kollodiumwollen ist eine direkte Funktion der Konzentration der Lösungen, ist aber auch bei gleicher Konzentration eine sehr verschiedene, je nach der Art der Herstellung der Produkte; sie steht in keiner direkten Beziehung zum Stickstoffgehalt der Kollodiumwolle, doch tritt ihr Maximum beim höchsten Stickstoffgehalte ein; sie sinkt mit dem Steigen der Nitrierungstemperatur; sie sinkt ebenso mit der Dauer der Berührung des Produktes mit der Nitriersäure und kann dadurch in den weitesten Grenzen variiert werden; endlich sinkt sie mit steigendem Wassergehalt der Nitriersäuren. Die geringsten Viskositäten erzielt man bei gleichbleibender Konzentration der Nitriersäuren und daher gleichbleibendem Stickstoffgehalt der Kollodiumwolle durch Anwendung einer höheren Nitrierungstemperatur und bei konzentrierten Säuren durch Verlängerung der Nitrierungszeit; die höchsten Viskositäten erzielt man durch die wasserärmeren Nitriergemische bei kürzerer Dauer der Operation. Kollodiumlösungen verlieren in kurzer Zeit bedeutend an Viskosität, wenn sie auch nur sehr geringe Mengen von Säuren enthalten. — Lunge nimmt es als sehr wahrscheinlich an, daß die Viskosität der Lösungen von Kollodiumwolle in Nitroglyzerin durchaus parallel derjenigen von Lösungen in Ätheralkohol geht.

Bindefähigkeit. Die Kollodiumwolle soll das Sprengöl dauernd zu einer homogenen Masse binden. In der Praxis prüft man wie folgt: 2·5 g gut gepülpte Kollodiumwolle werden nach Trocknung langsam

---

in gewogene Bechergläser abgehebert und darin auf einem Dampfofen zur Trockne gebracht, unter vorherigem Zusatz von ein wenig Wasser, was die Bildung eines pulverigen Rückstandes und dadurch besseres Austrocknen bewirkt; es wird dann bei 50° zur Trockne und zur Gewichtskonstanz gebracht. Nach $^1/_4$stündigem Stehen im Wägezimmer, unter Bedeckung mit einem Uhrglase, wobei das Produkt noch keine merkliche Menge Wasser anzieht, wird rasch gewogen.

[1] Zeitschr. angew. Chemie 1906, S. 2051.

[2] Zeitschr. angew. Chemie 1906, S. 2055. — Zur Bestimmung diente das Viskosimeter von Cochius, ein mit Stöpseln versehener Glaszylinder, worin durch einen Glashahn eine Trennung in einen größeren, mit der zu untersuchenden Flüssigkeit gefüllten und in einen kleineren, etwa 3 ccm großen Raum, der mit Luft gefüllt ist, herbeigeführt wird; durch Öffnen des Hahnes läßt man eine Luftblase emporsteigen und hat in der Zeit, die zwischen dem Passieren zweier Marken durch die Luftblase verstreicht, ein Maß für die Viskosität der Flüssigkeit; auf die Temperaturkonstanz ist bei den Messungen sorgfältig zu achten.

in 40 ccm Nitroglyzerin eingetragen, so daß letzteres 3·76 Prozent Nitrozellulose enthält; das Gemisch wird in einem Kupferzylinder gut durchgerührt und 10 Minuten stehen gelassen; nach Ablauf dieser Zeit fügt man noch 1 ccm eines Gemisches von drei Teilen Methylalkohol und einem Teil Aceton hinzu, stellt den Becher in warmes Wasser (70 bis 75°) und rührt ungefähr fünf Minuten lang mit einem Hornspachtel fleißig durch; es soll dann aus der ursprünglich dünnflüssigen eine zähe Masse geworden sein. Nach weiteren 20 Minuten hebt man den Becher aus dem Wasser und läßt abkühlen; in etwa einer halben Stunde muß sich die Gelatine mit dem Spachtel vom Boden aufnehmen lassen, ohne den Zusammenhang zu verlieren und ohne Spuren von Nitroglyzerin am Boden zurückzulassen.

Stickstoffgehalt. Da die Kollodiumwolle ein aktiver Bestandteil der Sprengstoffe sein soll, wird ein so hoher Stickstoffgehalt angestrebt, wie unbeschadet guter Löslichkeit, Viskosität und Bindefähigkeit zu erreichen ist. Vielfach angewandt wird Kollodiumwolle mit 11·8 bis 11·9 Prozent N; jedenfalls soll der Stickstoffgehalt mindestens 11 Prozent betragen. Die Kollodiumwolle muß von guter Stabilität sein und wird nach dieser Richtung hin stets geprüft.

Die Kollodiumwolle soll möglichst wenig Beimengungen von unlöslicher Schießbaumwolle einerseits, von nicht nitrierter Baumwolle andererseits enthalten; der Gehalt an letzterer soll jedenfalls 0·5 Prozent nicht übersteigen. Sanford teilt die Analyse einer Kollodiumwolle mit, die sehr gute Gelatine lieferte und die — bei einem durchschnittlichen Stickstoffgehalt von 11·64 Prozent — 99·118 Prozent lösliche Nitrozellulose, 0·642 Prozent unlösliche Schießbaumwolle und 0·240 Prozent nicht nitrierte Zellulose enthält. — Die Kollodiumwolle soll keinen Sand oder andere Fremdkörper enthalten und nicht mehr als 0·25 Prozent Asche geben.

Die Kollodiumwolle wird nach ihrer Herstellung im Holländer zermahlen (gepülpt) und in feuchtem Zustande (gewöhnlich mit 20 bis 35 Prozent Wasser) in verzinkten Holzkisten gelagert. Die zur Herstellung der Sprenggelatine und Gelatinedynamite dienende Kollodiumwolle muß aber, ebenso wie die anderen Ausgangsstoffe, ganz trocken sein, da sonst der Gelatinierungsprozeß schwierig vor sich geht und der fertige Sprengstoff Nitroglyzerin ausschwitzt. — Das Trocknen der gepülpten Wolle ist eine wichtige und nicht ungefährliche Operation; es erfolgt in eigenen, aus Holz gebauten und von Wällen umgebenen Trockenhäusern. Die Kollodiumwolle wird in Schichten von 5 cm Höhe auf Hürden gelagert, deren Böden ein Gewebe aus Kupfer- oder Bronzedrähten bildet, worauf zunächst Tücher liegen; die Hürden müssen in leitender Verbindung mit der Erde stehen, da sich beim Trocknen Elektrizität ansammelt. Die Erwärmung des in mehrere Abteilungen geteilten Trockenhauses erfolgt durch Einblasen erwärmter Luft mittels eines außerhalb aufgestellten Ventilators; die Temperatur im Innern soll 40° C nicht übersteigen und wird stets durch ein Thermometer kontrolliert. Zur Vermeidung von Wärmeverlusten hat das Haus Doppelwände mit Zwischenraum, der durch Asche ausgefüllt ist; das Dach ist mit Filz belegt; der Raum muß gute Ventilation besitzen. Innerhalb desselben befindet sich eine Warmwasserheizung mit möglichst wenig hervortretenden Heizröhren, damit sich daselbst kein Staub von Kollodiumwolle ansetzt und erhitzt, wodurch Explosionen entstehen könnten. Boden und Fenstersimse müssen täglich von Kollodiumstaub befreit werden; der Boden ist zweckmäßig mit Linoleum zu belegen.

Den Fortschritt der Trocknung kann man durch Wasserbestimmungen verfolgen; zunächst nimmt man aus der Mitte mehrerer Kisten der feuchten Kollodiumwolle Proben von zusammen etwa einem Kilogramm und bestimmt den Wassergehalt durch einstündiges Erhitzen auf 100° im Trockenschrank; nachdem die ganze Menge Kollodiumwolle 48 Stunden im Trockenhaus war, wird eine neue Probe genommen, und so weiter, bis der gewünschte minimale Feuchtigkeitsgrad von 0·25 bis 0·50 Prozent erreicht ist.

Die Entleerung der Trockenstuben soll erst erfolgen, wenn das Innere derselben sich auf die Außentemperatur abgekühlt hat; beim Wegnehmen der Horden von den Gestellen soll jede Reibung vermieden werden. Jede Möglichkeit der Anhäufung von trockenem, explosivem Nitrozellulosestaub ist auszuschließen. — In dem Trockenhause befindet sich ein Raum zum Sieben der trockenen Kollodiumwolle; hierbei ist besondere Vorsicht nötig, da trockene Nitrozellulose bei Reibung sehr leicht elektrische Eigenschaften annimmt, die zu Selbstentzündungen führen; die Siebvorrichtung muß aus einem schwer oxydierbaren Metallgewebe (Bronze) hergestellt und mit der Erde leitend verbunden werden. Das Sieben der trockenen Nitrozellulose darf nur durch Rütteln der Siebe, nicht durch Hindurchdrücken des (übrigens auf möglichst kleine Mengen beschränkten) Siebgutes durch das Metallgewebe bewirkt werden. Der damit beschäftigte Arbeiter befindet sich in einem durch eine hinreichend starke Mauer von dem Siebraum getrennten Gelaß und bedient eine, durch eine sehr kleine Öffnung der Trennungsmauer geführte Zugeinrichtung. Jegliche Reibung ist bei der ganzen Anlage bis an die Grenze des Möglichen zu vermeiden. Die trockene Kollodiumwolle ist hygroskopisch; sie muß daher vor Luftzutritt geschützt und schnellstmöglich in wasserdichte Behälter aus Zink oder Kautschuk verpackt werden.

I. Sprenggelatine.

Die Sprenggelatine besteht aus 90 bis 93 Prozent Nitroglyzerin und 7 bis 10 Prozent Kollodiumwolle, welche unter Erwärmen und Umrühren zu einer homogenen, durchsichtigen und elastischen Masse vereinigt sind. Das Verhältnis der beiden Bestandteile variiert etwas in den verschiedenen Ländern; in Österreich und Deutschland hat man 93 : 7, in Frankreich 92 : 8, in England 90 bis 91 : 10 bis 9. Theoretisch die beste Mischung wäre 92·71 : 7·29 (vgl. S. 241). Das Vermischen des Sprengöls mit der Kollodiumwolle erfolgt im Gelatinierhause, woselbst eine Anzahl größerer, meist rechteckiger Gefäße aus Kupfer oder Blei aufgestellt sind, welche doppelte Wände besitzen, so daß Zwischenräume vorhanden sind, durch welche warmes Wasser von 60 bis 80° fließt. Man kann auf diese Weise in den inneren Behältern Temperaturen von 45 bis 50°, bei welchen die Gelatinierung vor sich geht, erzeugen, eventuell aber auch das warme Wasser durch kaltes ersetzen, falls Explosionsgefahr vorhanden sein sollte. Der Warmwasserbehälter ist gewöhnlich außerhalb des Gelatinierhauses aufgestellt und wird automatisch gespeist; von da geht dann das nötige Heizwasser mit bestimmter Temperatur durch die verschiedenen Gelatinierapparate. — Das Sprengöl wird in Guttaperchaflaschen, die Kollodiumwolle in wasserdichten Behältern zum Gelatinierhause gebracht. Man gibt entweder die berechneten Mengen der beiden Bestandteile bei gewöhnlicher Temperatur in die Behälter (zunächst die Kollodiumwolle, worauf man das Nitroglyzerin gießt), mischt durch und erhitzt dann; oder man gießt zunächst nur Sprengöl in die Behälter, erhitzt dieses auf 45 bis 50° und gibt dann die Kollodiumwolle zu, worauf man mit einer hölzernen Schaufel umrührt, bis die Masse gründlich durchgemischt ist. Das Umrühren wird im Laufe der nächsten zwei Stunden von Zeit zu Zeit wiederholt. Dann wird die Masse, ähnlich wie Brotteig, mit den Händen durchgeknetet, bis dieselbe eine gleichförmige Beschaffenheit angenommen hat; nach dem Erkalten resultiert die zähflüssige Sprenggelatine.

Statt die Gelatinierung durch Durchkneten mittels der Hände vorzunehmen, kann dies auch maschinell geschehen. Diese Knetmaschinen sind ähnlich denen, welche die Bäcker bei Herstellung des Brotteiges benutzen. Werner & Pfleiderer in Cannstatt bauen eine Maschine, Typ Nito (Fig. 62); bei derselben bewegen sich zwei Misch- und Knetschaufeln in einem gemeinsamen, unten halbkreisförmig ausgebauten Mischtrog, der aus Bronze von besonderer Legierung hergestellt ist; an den Mischtrog ist außen ein Mantel angelötet, durch welchen warmes Wasser (nötigenfalls Kühlwasser) durchgelassen werden kann. Das Gestell der Maschine ist möglichst leicht aus Schmiedeeisen gebaut, der Antrieb kann nach Bedarf gewählt werden, und zwar entweder

Fig. 62. Knetmaschine von Werner & Pfleiderer.

durch den für Vor- und Rückwärtsgang sowie plötzlichen Stillstand der Schaufeln eingerichteten Reversierapparat, oder mittels Ketten, so daß der eigentliche Antrieb entfernt vom Mischwerke liegt. Bei der Konstruktion dieser Maschine ist darauf Rücksicht genommen, daß schädliche Reibungen vermieden werden und daß die Maschine behufs leichter Reinigung gut auseinandernehmbar ist. Die Knetschaufeln bewegen sich verschieden schnell und können sowohl zueinander als auseinander laufen.

Auch Karl Seemann in Berlin sowie Richard Lehmann in Dresden bauen Knetmaschinen ähnlicher Konstruktion.

George Mc Roberts[1] hat folgende Knetmaschine beschrieben

[1] Journ. Society Chemical Industry 1890.

(Fig. 63 u. 64), welche in der Nobelschen Fabrik in Ardeer in Gebrauch ist.

Die Maschine besteht aus einem starken Gestelle *a* aus Eichenholz, auf welchem ein falscher Boden *b* mit Hilfe von zwei Schrauben-

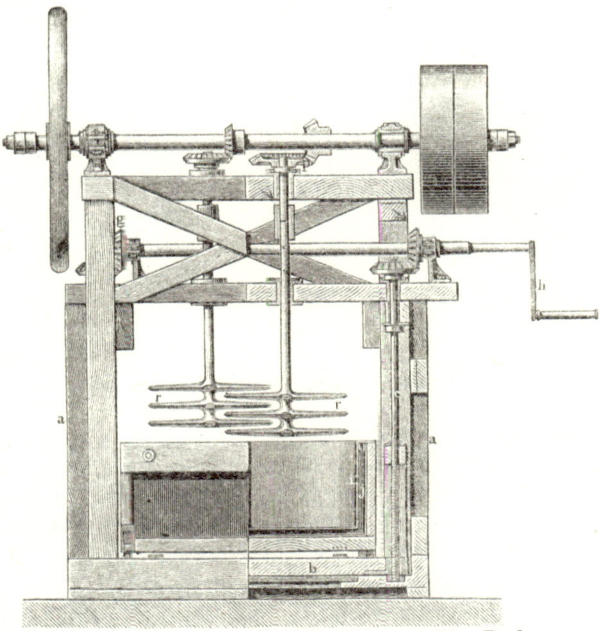

Fig. 63. Knetmaschine nach George Mc Roberts.

wellen *c* höher oder tiefer gestellt werden kann; letzteres geschieht durch diesen an der Kurbel *h*. Auf den falschen Boden kommt eine aus Kupfer gefertigte, auf vier Rädern laufende Wasserpfanne *i* mit Wassermantel *j*, welcher durch einen Kautschukschlauch mit einer Warmwasserleitung verbunden werden kann. Die Rührflügel *r* sind so gestellt, daß die Finger der beiden Flügel ineinandergreifen, wie aus Fig. 64 ersichtlich. Die Arbeit erfolgt in der Weise, daß der Wagen mit der doppelten Pfanne auf den falschen Boden geschoben, die Verbindung mit der Warmwasserleitung hergestellt und dann Pfanne *i* durch Drehung der Handkurbel in die Höhe gehoben wird, bis die Rührflügel eintauchen, worauf man letztere in Bewegung setzt.

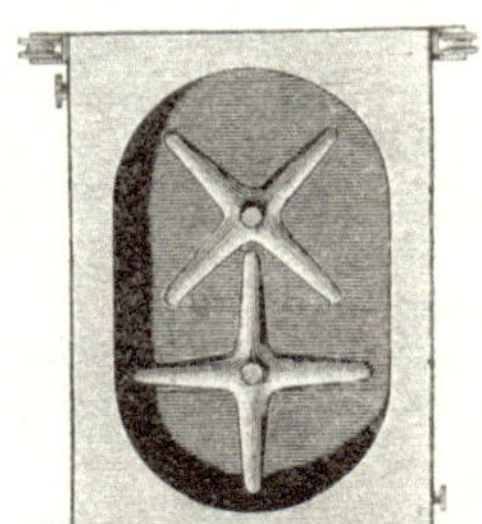

Fig. 64. Rührflügel der Robertsschen Knetmaschine.

Die fertige Sprenggelatine wird in Holzkisten nach den Patronierbuden gebracht. Die Patronierung der gelatinösen

Sprengstoffe kann nicht in Stopfmaschinen erfolgen, sie geschieht gewöhnlich mittels Schraubenpressen.

Mc Roberts beschreibt eine Maschine (Fig. 65), aus einem trichterförmigen Gehäuse *a* mit Einfüllgosse *b* bestehend, an welches ein dem Durchmesser der Patrone entsprechendes Mundstück *c* angeschraubt ist. In dem Gehäuse bewegt sich, von zwei außerhalb desselben angebrachten

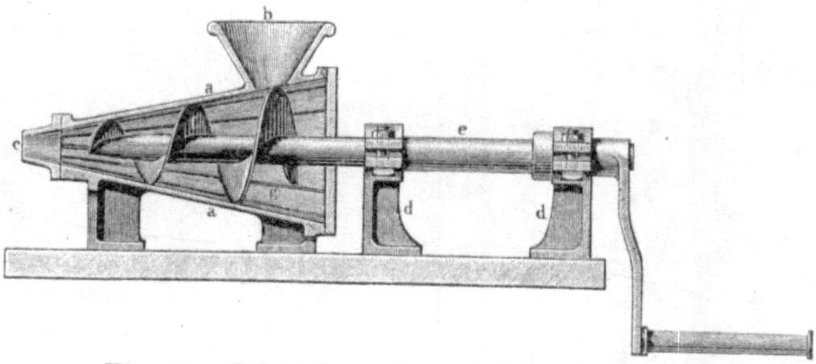

Fig. 65. Schraubenpresse nach Mc Roberts.

Lagern *d d* getragen, eine Welle *e* mit Schraube *f*, welche die durch die Einfüllgosse kommende Masse allmählich gegen das Mundstück zudrückt und daselbst in Form einer Wurst herausbringt. In dem Innern des Gehäuses sind Nuten *g* angebracht, welche verhindern, daß die Masse sich mit der Schraube einfach umdrehe.

Eine ähnliche Maschine (Fig. 66), jedoch mit zylindrischem Gehäuse, wird von O. Guttmann beschrieben. Die Welle *f* mit der Schraube *g*

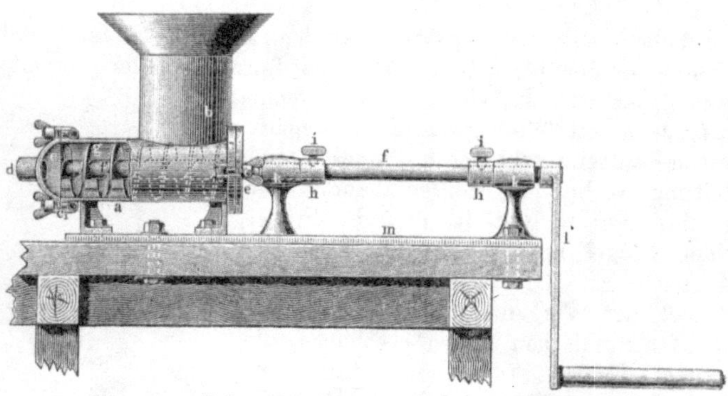

Fig. 66. Schraubenpresse nach O. Guttmann.

ist in zwei Lagern *k* und dem Deckel *e* durch die aufgeschobene Kurbel *l* drehbar; sie wird durch Stellringe *h* in ihrer Lage gehalten. Gewöhnlich haben diese Maschinen, welche auf einer Grundplatte *m* und damit auf einem Tisch montiert sind, einen mit zwei und mehr

Mundstücken *d* versehenen Ansatz *c*, so daß gleichzeitig mehrere Würste die Presse verlassen.[1]

Diese Schraubenpatroniermaschinen können zu Explosionen Anlaß geben, wenn in dem zu patronierenden Sprengstoff Fremdkörper enthalten sind, wodurch eine Reibung entsteht. Norbert Ceipek (D.R.P. 117111) verwendet daher Zentrifugalmaschinen (Fig. 67), bei denen keine Reibung möglich ist.

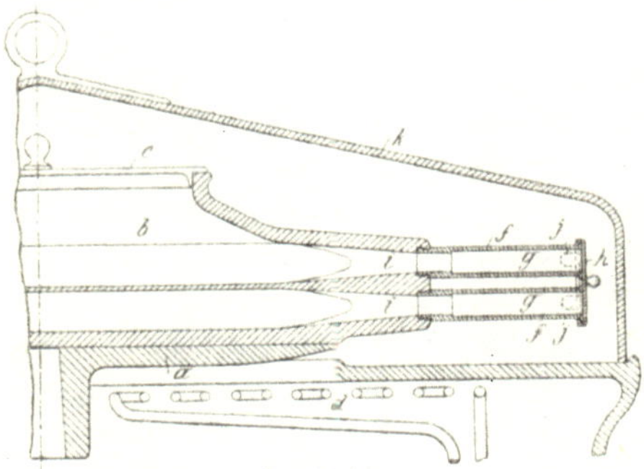

Fig 67a.

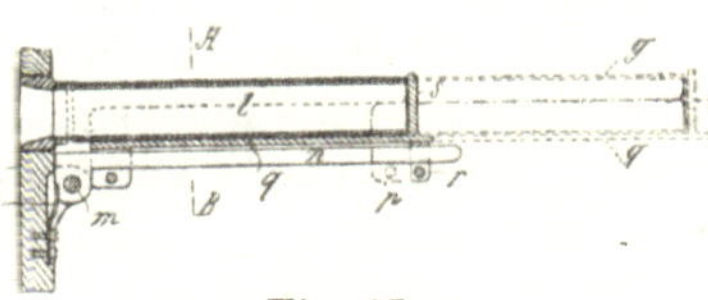

Fig. 67c.

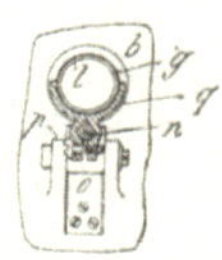

Fig. 67d.

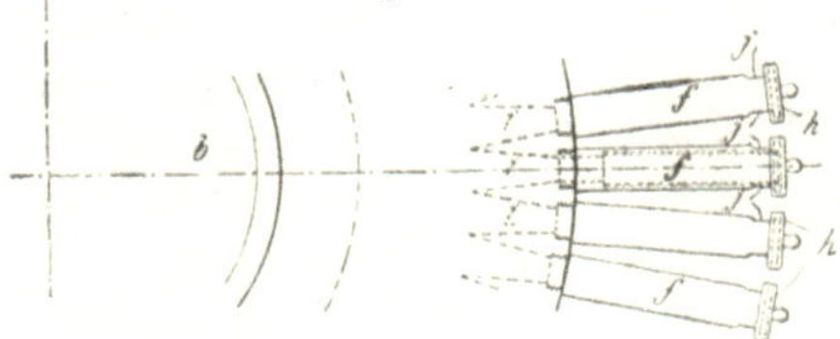

Fig. 67b.

Fig. 67. Zentrifugalmaschine nach Norbert Ceipek.

Die Einrichtung ist gekennzeichnet durch eine Zentrifuge, deren Korb an seinem Umfange Röhren oder Mundstücke besitzt, mit welchen die zu füllenden Patronen lösbar verbunden werden, bzw. auf oder in welchen dieselben verschiebbar angeordnet sind, wobei im ersteren Fall die Dichte der Füllung durch die gewählte Umdrehungszahl der Zentrifuge allein, im letzteren Fall durch diese Umdrehungszahl und einen der Verschiebung der Hüllen bei der Füllung entgegenwirkenden Widerstand festgesetzt werden kann. Fig. 67a veranschaulicht den senkrechten Schnitt eines Teiles einer derartigen Zentrifuge nebst den Füllrohren (*a* Teller, *b* Korb, *c* Deckel der Zentrifuge; Dampfrohr *d* ermöglicht die Erwärmung; *i* kegelförmige Korböffnungen, *g* Hülsen, *f* Füllrohre, *j* Ausschnitte zum Herausziehen der Hülsen; *k* Sicherheitsglocken aus Hartgummi. — Fig. 67b gibt die Anordnung der Füllrohre im Grund-

[1] Eine neuere Maschine ist von George P. Jones angegeben (amerik. Patent 869307).

riß. — Fig. 67c zeigt einen senkrechten, Fig. 67d einen Querschnitt (nach *AB*) einer Einrichtung zum Füllen von Hüllen, bei welcher sich die Hülle über dem mit der Zentrifuge verbundenen Mundstück vorschiebt.

Während bei der Ceipekschen Maschine der Sprengstoff in leere Hülsen läuft, werden die aus den Schraubenmaschinen kommenden Würste durch ein der Länge der Patrone entsprechendes Bronzemesser mit zwei Schneiden geteilt, in Pergament- oder Paraffinpapier eingewickelt und in üblicher Weise weiter verpackt.

Die Deutsche Sprengstoff-Aktiengesellschaft hat im Jahre 1877 sich ein Verfahren schützen lassen (D.R.P. 42452), wonach die Erwärmung des Nitroglyzerins beim Gelatinieren vermieden wird, indem man zunächst bis zu 10 Prozent Pikrinsäure im Sprengöl auflöst; die fein gemahlene Kollodiumwolle löst sich dann schon beim Durcharbeiten bei gewöhnlicher Temperatur auf. Da die Gegenwart von Säure in der Sprenggelatine verboten ist und auch das Gelatinieren ohne Wärmezufuhr länger dauert, hat das Verfahren keine praktische Anwendung gefunden.

Von größerer Bedeutung ist ein Zusatz von Kampfer. Nach dem D.R.P. 5528 (vom 2. Juli 1878) der Dynamit-Aktiengesellschaft Nobel löst sich Kampfer (auch Kampfene, wie Terpentinöl) in Nitroglyzerin und setzt dessen explosive Eigenschaften herab, macht also den herzustellenden Sprengstoff unempfindlicher. Die Größe des Zusatzes schwankt je nach dem gewünschten Maße der Herabminderung der Explosibilität zwischen 0 und 10 Prozent, kann aber ausnahmsweise — wenn hohe Unempfindlichkeit gefordert wird — 10 bis 30 Prozent betragen.

Diese Verwendung des Kampfers beruht auf Versuchen von Trauzl, welche derselbe in der Nobelschen Dynamitfabrik in Zamky durchgeführt hat, und worüber Hess[1] ausführlich berichtete. Für militärische Zwecke erzeugte man von 1878 bis 1892 in Österreich eine Kriegs-Sprenggelatine, bestehend aus 96 Teilen einer aus 90 Prozent Nitroglyzerin und 10 Prozent Kollodiumwolle zusammengesetzten Sprenggelatine und 4 Teilen Kampfer.

Solche unempfindliche Sprenggelatine kann man sich im Laboratorium wie folgt herstellen.

Man zerschneidet feuchte Kollodiumwolle (man prüft zunächst, indem man etwas Wolle anzuzünden versucht), indem man ein Päckchen Wolle in die linke Hand nimmt und kleine Stückchen abschneidet,

---

[1] Mitteil. Gegenst. Art.- u. Geniewesen 1878, S. 217.

welche auf ein ausgebreitetes schwarzes Glanzpapier fallen; das Zerschnittene nimmt man dann in die Hand und schneidet es kreuz und quer noch weiter, um ein möglichst feines Präparat zu erhalten. Vor dem Gelatinieren wird dann die Kollodiumwolle bei 40° im Trockenschranke getrocknet; beim Anzünden einer Probe mit dem Streichholz muß diese Wolle rasch verbrennen. — Man hat sich unterdessen in einem Becherglas 92 g trockenes Nitroglyzerin abgewogen und bei 50 bis 60° im Wasserbad 5 g Kampfer darin gelöst; dazu gibt man dann 3 g getrocknete Kollodiumwolle, welche in einer Glasschale abgewogen wurden. Man stellt nun das Becherglas auf eine Porzellanplatte, die auf einem Dreifuß sich in einer Emailwanne befindet, welche letztere warmes Wasser enthält, das durch ein unter der Wanne befindliches Flämmchen zunächst auf 50°, dann auf 50 bis 60° C gehalten wird. Man tränkt die Kollodiumwolle mittels eines Hornspachtels in das Nitroglyzerin ein und läßt im warmen Wasser stehen, bis vollständige Lösung eingetreten ist und sich eine homogene Masse gebildet hat, was 2 bis 3 Stunden dauert; von Zeit zu Zeit nimmt man das Becherglas aus dem Wasserbad in die Hand und rührt mit dem Spachtel gründlich durch. Wenn die Sprenggelatine so zäh geworden ist, daß man sie aus dem Becherglas nehmen kann, ohne daß die Gelatine ihren Zusammenhang verliert, dann ist das Produkt fertig; man läßt nun kalt werden, wobei die Masse härter wird und nimmt die Sprenggelatine dann aus dem Glase heraus.

Eine Vorstellung von dem wechselseitigen Zustande der Bestandteile (Nitroglyzerin und Nitrozellulose) in der Sprenggelatine kann man sich (nach H. Brunswig) verschaffen, indem man auf dem Wasserbad 0·2 g Agar-Agar in 7·8 g Glyzerin auflöst, gut durchrührt und erkalten läßt; man erhält eine gelatinöse, in der Wärme fadenziehende, in der Kälte elastische Masse, deren äußeres Aussehen vollkommen dem der Sprenggelatine gleicht und die wahrscheinlich auch beide Komponenten in der Art gebunden zeigt, welche in der Sprenggelatine vorliegt.

Eigenschaften der Sprenggelatine.

Sprenggelatine ist eine gummiartige, dehnbare, zähe, plastische, durchscheinende, blaßgelbe Masse vom spez. Gew. von ca. 1·6. Sprenggelatine ist in physikalischer Beziehung bedeutend stabiler als Mischdynamite, denn selbst ein sehr starker Druck (1 t pro Quadratzentimeter) ist nicht imstande, eine Auspressung von Sprengöl aus der Masse herbeizuführen. Ebensowenig vermag Wasser das Nitroglyzerin aus der Gelatine zu verdrängen. Die Sprenggelatine nimmt im Wasser nach einiger Zeit an der Oberfläche ein milchiges Aussehen an und trübt sich je nach der Dauer der Einwirkung bis auf eine gewisse Tiefe. Man kann jedoch Sprenggelatine längere Zeit unter Wasser aufbewahren, ohne daß eine nennenswerte Gewichtsveränderung zu konstatieren ist; jedenfalls wird die Sprengwirkung nicht beeinträchtigt und man verwendet daher die Sprenggelatine vorteilhaft in nassen Gruben oder bei Sprengungen unter Wasser.

Das Gefrieren des Nitroglyzerins erfolgt in der Sprenggelatine viel schwerer als im Gurdynamit, das Auftauen hingegen leichter und verhältnismäßig sehr rasch, ohne daß hierbei — wie beim Auftauen des Gurdynamits — eine teilweise Durchfettung oder ein teilweises Austreten von Nitroglyzerin zu beobachten wäre. Wenn das Nitroglyzerin einer Sprenggelatine erstarrt ist, so bildet das Präparat eine feste, kandiszuckerartige Masse; der Sprengstoff hat seine Biegsamkeit und Elastizität verloren und ist dann empfindlicher gegen Stoß als in weichem Zustande. Über das Gefrieren der Sprenggelatine hat die Bergwerksdirektion Saarbrücken folgende Angaben gemacht: Bei Versuchen im Freien bei -2^{0} bis 0^{0} gefror Sprenggelatine (in 30 mm-Patronen) in gewöhnlichen Pappschachteln nach 5 bis 6 Stunden; bei $+0^{0}$ bis $+2^{0}$ begannen einzelne Patronen nach 4 bis 5 Stunden zu gefrieren und waren nach 10 bis 12 Stunden vollständig gefroren. In Kisten mit Originalverpackung begann bei dieser Temperatur das Gefrieren nach 20 bis 24 Stunden und war nach 48 bis 60 Stunden vollständig. — Bei $+7^{0}$ bis $+8^{0}$ waren einzeln ausgelegte Patronen nach etwa 90 bis 120 Stunden außen mit einer dünnen festen Kruste überzogen, die innere Masse war jedoch noch weich; in Kisten waren die Patronen nach 120 Stunden Lagerzeit mit einer sehr dünnen Kruste überzogen. — Bei $+10{\cdot}5^{0}$ bis $+11^{0}$ war nach 11 Tagen noch nichts gefroren.

Gegen Stoß, Schlag und Reibung ist Sprenggelatine unempfindlicher als Gurdynamit.

Bezüglich der Empfindlichkeit der Sprenggelatine kommt Will zu folgenden Ergebnissen: 1. Sprenggelatine ist in jeder Form und in jedem Zustand empfindlicher als gefrorenes Gurdynamit, aber unempfindlicher wie plastisches, nicht gefrorenes Gurdynamit. Die Detonation mit 2 kg-Fallhammer trat ein:

bei plastischem Gurdynamit	: bei 7 cm	Fallhöhe,
bei plastischer Sprenggelatine	: bei 12 cm	„ ,
bei gefrorener Sprenggelatine	: bei 12 bis 15 cm	„ ,
bei plastischem Gelatinedynamit	: bei 17 cm	„ ,
bei gefrorenem Gurdynamit	: bei 20 cm	„ .

Zieht man nur die Beschußergebnisse in Betracht, so zeigt sich kein Unterschied in der Empfindlichkeit zwischen hartgefrorener Sprenggelatine und plastischem Gurdynamit. — 2. Der Empfindlichkeitsunterschied zwischen gefrorener und plastischer Sprenggelatine ist wesentlich geringer als zwischen gefrorenem und plastischem Gurdynamit. —

3. Hartgefrorene Sprenggelatine verhält sich unverkennbar empfindlicher als plastische nur bei der Beschußprobe; die Fallhammerprobe führt eher zur entgegengesetzten Beurteilung. — 4. Eine wesentliche Erhöhung der Empfindlichkeit durch wiederholtes Gefrieren und Wiederauftauenlassen konnte nicht nachgewiesen werden.

Nach den Versuchen der Bergwerksdirektion Saarbrücken zeigt ein Vergleich der Fallhammerversuche mit Gurdynamit, Sprenggelatine und Gelatinedynamit, daß — unter denselben Bedingungen — plastisches Gurdynamit am empfindlichsten und gefrorenes Gelatinedynamit am unempfindlichsten ist, Sprenggelatine und Gelatinedynamit in plastischer Form dem gefrorenen Gurdynamit ungefähr gleich sind, Gelatinedynamit sogar noch etwas empfindlicher als letzteres ist. Gefrorene Sprenggelatine steht in bezug auf Widerstandsfähigkeit zwischen gefrorenem Gurdynamit und gefrorenem Gelatinedynamit.

Nach Hess sind die Ergebnisse von Beschießungsversuchen bei gefrorener Sprenggelatine unter sonst gleichen Bedingungen von der Dicke der beschossenen Schicht abhängig. In 2 bis 4 cm dicken, zwischen Holzbrettchen eingepreßten Kuchen blieb die Sprenggelatine schußsicher, während eine größere, mit dem Sprengmittel gefüllte Kiste — bei welcher die Kugel einen mehr als zehnfachen Weg in der Sprengmasse zurückzulegen hatte — bei dem ersten Schusse vollständig in Explosion aufging. Ferner sagt Hess: Man kann zugeben, daß im allgemeinen gefrorenes Dynamit schwerer als ungefrorenes zur Explosion zu bringen ist; es liegt trotzdem kein Widerspruch darin, daß unter gewissen Umständen örtliche, mechanische Einwirkungen (Schlag oder Stoß) den gefrorenen Sprengstoff leichter entzünden als den ungefrorenen. Ist der Sprengstoff plastisch, so weichen seine einzelnen Teilchen leicht aus; ist er dagegen infolge Gefrierens starr und unnachgiebig, so kann die durch Stoß, Schlag oder Reibung entstehende Wärme an einzelnen Punkten der Masse sich bis zu dem Grade steigern, daß der Sprengstoff trotz seiner verminderten Empfindlichkeit leicht zur Explosion gelangt. Die Verhältnisse in der Praxis sind so außerordentlich verschieden, daß ein und derselbe Stoff unter anscheinend äußerst ähnlichen Umständen sich ganz verschieden benehmen kann. Im Sinne der Gebrauchsbedingungen und nach den Erfahrungen der großen Praxis sind demnach gefrorene Dynamite und Sprenggelatine aller Art entschieden gefährlicher als die weichen Sprengmittel.

Auch gegen Wärme ist Sprenggelatine beständiger als Gurdynamit. Hess konnte Sprenggelatine 8 Tage auf 45° C erhitzen, ohne daß das Präparat in nennenswerter Weise fettete. Gegen länger andauernde Erhitzung bis auf 70° erwies sich die Sprenggelatine als sehr widerstandsfähig. Die Explosion erfolgt nach Hess bei 204°, wenn man von 60° ab langsam weiter erhitzt; bei raschem Erhitzen bei 240° C. Nach O. Hagen liegt die Explosionstemperatur der Sprenggelatine bei 183·9° C. — Bei öfterem, starkem Temperaturwechsel scheidet die Sprenggelatine manchmal Sprengöl in geringen Quantitäten aus; auf diese Ausschwitzungen, welche die relative Ungefährlichkeit des Sprengstoffes herabsetzen, ist zu achten und sind die betreffenden Patronen vor allen anderen schleunigst und mit großer Vorsicht zu verbrauchen.

Der Initialstoß, der zur Detonationseinleitung bei der Sprenggelatine nötig ist, muß erheblich größer sein als bei Gurdynamit; man verwendet Knallquecksilber-Sprengkapseln mit mindestens 0·8 g Füllung (Nr. 5) oder aber man setzt auf die Sprenggelatine eine Zündpatrone von Gur- oder Gelatinedynamit, welche schon mit Sprengkapsel Nr. 3 (Füllung 0·54 g) zur Detonation gebracht wird und solche dann auf die Sprenggelatine überträgt.

In England muß die Sprenggelatine folgende Verflüssigungsprobe bestehen: Von der zu prüfenden Patrone wird ein Zylinder abgeschnitten, dessen Länge ungefähr gleich seinem Durchmesser ist und dessen Enden scharf abgeschnitten sind. Der Zylinder wird ohne Umhüllung auf die Stirnseite auf eine flache Oberfläche gelegt und durch eine durch seine Mitte vertikal hindurchgehende Stecknadel festgehalten; in diesem Zustand wird der Zylinder während 144 Stunden (sechs Tage und sechs Nächte) einer Temperatur von $29^4/_9$ bis $32^2/_9$ ° C (85 bis 90 ° Fahrenheit) ausgesetzt; während dieser Zeit soll der Zylinder in Höhe um nicht mehr als ein Viertel der ursprünglichen sich verringern und die obere abgeschnittene Fläche soll ihre Geradheit und die Schärfe ihrer Ränder beibehalten.

Probe auf Neigung zum Ausschwitzen. Von der Masse der Sprenggelatine soll keine Substanz sich ausscheiden, welche von geringerer Konsistenz ist als die Gesamtheit des übriggebliebenen Teils des Materials, unter welchen Bedingungen immer bei der Einlagerung, Transport oder Gebrauch, oder wenn das Material dreimal hintereinander abwechselndem Frieren und Auftauen unterworfen wird, oder wenn es der vorhin beschriebenen Verflüssigungsprobe unterworfen wird.

Zur Stabilitätsprobe werden nach englischer Vorschrift 3·24 g Sprenggelatine mit 6·48 g Talkpulver gründlich gemischt, indem man die zwei Materialien in einem hölzernen Mörser mit einem hölzernen Pistill sorgfältig verarbeitet. (Das Talkpulver muß vorher mit destilliertem Wasser gewaschen, in einem Wasserbade getrocknet und dann unter einer Glasglocke so lange feuchter Luft ausgesetzt werden, bis es ungefähr 0·5 Prozent Feuchtigkeit aufgenommen hat; in diesem Zustande wird es in verschlossener Flasche aufbewahrt.) Die Gelatine-Talkmischung wird allmählich in ein Reagensrohr eingeführt, indem man dabei leicht auf den Tisch klopft, während man sukzessive zugibt; schließlich soll das Reagensrohr bis zu $1^3/_4$ Zoll seiner Höhe angefüllt sein. Man prüft dann bei 72 ° C (160 ° F), wobei es mindestens zehn Minuten dauern muß, bis das Probepapier die Färbung des Normalpapieres annimmt.

Detonation der Sprenggelatine.

Die Zersetzungsgleichung der Kollodiumwolle ist:

$$C_{24}H_{32}N_8O_{36} = 6\,CO_2 + 18\,CO + 6\,H_2O + 10\,H_2 + 4\,N_2;$$

zur Überführung des Kohlenoxyds in Kohlensäure und des Wasserstoffs in Wasser fehlen 28 Atome Sauerstoff. Bei dem explosiven Zerfall des Nitroglyzerins nach der Gleichung:

$$2\,C_3H_5N_3O_9 = 6\,CO_2 + 5\,H_2O + 3\,N_2 + O$$

wird andererseits überschüssiger Sauerstoff frei, und zwar erübrigt sich aus zwei Molekülen Nitroglyzerin ein verfügbares freies Atom Sauerstoff. Aus der rationellen Gleichung:

$$56\,C_3H_5N_3O_9 + C_{24}H_{32}N_8O_{36} = 192\,CO_2 + 156\,H_2O + 88\,N_2$$

berechnen sich als theoretisch entsprechendes Mengenverhältnis: 56 × 227 = 12712 g Nitroglyzerin, 1008 g Kollodiumwolle; also die Relation 92·71 Prozent zu 7·29 Prozent.

Gody bestimmte danach folgende Werte:

$m = 13720$; $Q_{mp} = 21038$ kal.; $Q_{mv} = 21275$ kal.;
$Q_{kp} = 1533$ kal.; $Q_{k \cdot v} = 1551$ kal.; $V_m = 9731 \cdot 5$ Liter;
$V_k = 710$ Liter; $t = 3213^{\circ}$ C; $f = 9396$ kg;
$\alpha = 0 \cdot 710$; $A = 659175$ kg/m.

Für eine Sprenggelatine 92:8 gibt Gody folgende Gleichung:

$$51\,C_3H_5N_3O_9 + C_{24}H_{32}N_8O_{36} = 174 \cdot 5\,CO_2 + 2 \cdot 5\,CO + 143 \cdot 5\,H_2O + 80 \cdot 5\,N_2.$$

Heise gibt für eine Sprenggelatine von der Zusammensetzung 93 : 7 folgende Gleichung:

$$61 \cdot 6\,C_3H_5N_3O_9 + C_{24}H_{31}N_9O_{38} = 209\,CO_2 + 170\,H_2O + 2\,O_2 + 97\,N_2,$$

und nachstehende Werte:

$L = 1 \cdot 4$ bis $1 \cdot 5$; $t = 3203^{\circ}$ C; $f = 9332$ kg;
$V_0 = 708$ Liter; $Q = 1535$ kal.; $A = 652375$ m/kg.

Bichel gibt für Gurdynamit, Sprenggelatine und Gelatinedynamit folgende Daten (in Glückauf 1904):

	Normal-ausbauchung im Bleiblock in ccm	Menge der entwickelten Kalorien pro 1 kg Sprengstoff	Schwadenanalyse nach Gewichtsprozenten	Aus der Kalorien- und Schwadenanalyse errechnete Explosionstemperatur
Gurdynamit (75:25)	433	1153	43·7 CO_2; 2·6 O; 13·9 N; 14·8 H_2O; 25 SiO_2	2999°
Sprenggelatine	620	1550	61·2 CO_2; 0·4 O; 18·1 N; 20·3 H_2O	3216°
Gelatinedynamit 63·5 Nitroglyzerin, 1·5 Kollodiumwolle. 27 Natronsalpeter, 8 Holzmehl	482	1321	45·9 CO_2; 16·9 N; 20·5 H_2O; 16·7 Na_2CO_3	2758°

Die Explosionstemperatur ist nach der Formel $t = \frac{Q}{a + b\,t}$ oder $Q = a\,t + b\,t^2$ ermittelt; danach berechnet sich für 100 g Sprenggelatine:

$$155 = t\,(6{\cdot}26 \times 1{\cdot}4 + 5{\cdot}61 \times 1{\cdot}13 + 4{\cdot}8 \times 0{\cdot}66) + t^2(0{\cdot}0037 \times 1{\cdot}4 + 0{\cdot}0033 \times 1{\cdot}13 + 0{\cdot}0006 \times 0{\cdot}66),$$

und daraus $t = 3216^{\circ}$ C.

C. E. Bichel[1] hat zuerst den Explosionsvorgang aller brisanten Sprengstoffe in zwei Phasen zerlegt, einen dynamischen und einen statischen Vorgang.

Von dem Augenblick an, wo durch die Sprengkapsel die Umsetzung des Sprengstoffes eingeleitet wird, bis zu dem Zeitpunkte, wo auch die letzte Patrone der Sprengstoffladung zersetzt ist, verstreicht eine gewisse Zeit, die als Detonationszeit bezeichnet wird und welche von der dem betreffenden Sprengstoffe eigenen Detonationsgeschwindigkeit abhängig ist. Die heißen Zerfallgase und -dämpfe, sowie sonstigen Zersetzungsprodukte haben ein enormes Raumbedürfnis, sie werden gegen die Bohrlochwandungen geschleudert, und zwar mit einer lebendigen Energie, deren Größe durch die Formel $\frac{m\,v^2}{2}$ wiedergegeben wird. Hierin ist m die Masse der Zersetzungsprodukte des Sprengstoffes und v die Detonationsgeschwindigkeit. Diese lebendige Energie ist das Maß der Stoßwirkung, welche die Sprengstoffschwaden ausüben.

Für Sprenggelatine (92 : 8) gibt Bichel die Detonationsgeschwindigkeit mit 7700 m in der Sekunde an und berechnet daraus

[1] Glückauf 1905, Heft 15. — Broschüre: Methoden und Apparate zur Prüfung von Sprengstoffen, Hamburg 1907.

die lebendige Energie (Stoßkraft) nach $\frac{m v^2}{2}$ (worin m = Gewicht des Sprengstoffes dividiert durch 9·81) zu

$$\frac{1 \times 7700^2}{9 \cdot 81 \times 2} = 3\,021\,916 \text{ sek/kg/m.}$$

Im Vergleich damit hat Schwarzpulver, im geschlossenen Raume mit Sprengkapsel detoniert, nur eine Geschwindigkeit von 300 m in der Sekunde und entwickelt danach eine Stoßkraft von

$$\frac{1 \times 300^2}{9 \cdot 81 \times 2} = 4587 \text{ sek/kg/m;}$$

Gurdynamit (75 : 25) hat bei einer Detonationsgeschwindigkeit von 6818 m eine Stoßkraft von

$$\frac{1 \times 6818^2}{9 \cdot 81 \times 2} = 2\,369\,272 \text{ sek/kg/m,}$$

und das später zu besprechende Gelatinedynamit (63·5 Prozent Nitroglyzerin, 1·5 Prozent Kollodiumwolle, 27 Prozent Natronsalpeter und 8 Prozent Holzmehl) bei einer Detonationsgeschwindigkeit von 7000 m in der Sekunde eine Stoßkraft von

$$\frac{1 \times 7000^2}{9 \cdot 81 \times 2} = 2\,497\,452 \text{ sek/kg/m.}$$

Nach Bichel ist die von der Masse der Zersetzungsprodukte mit der Detonationsgeschwindigkeit geleistete dynamische Stoßarbeit das am meisten charakteristische Merkmal eines Sprengstoffes, vor allem ein Maßstab für die Zertrümmerung der Umgebung.

Aus vorstehendem ergibt sich, daß Sprenggelatine ein außerordentlich brisantes Sprengmittel und daher zur Bewältigung sehr fester, zäher Widerstände besonders geeignet ist. Die Sprenggelatine mit ihrem hohen spezifischen Gewicht gestattet die Anwendung eines geringen Durchmessers und führt damit zur Ersparung von Bohrkosten, weil die große Detonationsgeschwindigkeit schon bei einem geringen Patronendurchmesser erreicht wird. Hat man aber ein weiches Gesteinsmaterial, so würden die Bohrlochwände durch die Stoßkraft der Schwaden zertrümmert, das Bohrloch erweitert und so ein schädlicher Raum geschaffen, und zwar ehe der Druck zur Wirkung gelangt; in weichem Material würde sich also Sprenggelatine „totschlagen", wie der Bergmann sagt. Auch in härterem Gestein kann Sprenggelatine dann nicht zur Verwendung gelangen, wenn es nicht auf die Zertrümmerung, sondern auf Bewegung und Gewinnung der Massen ankommt. — Nachstehend geben wir der Übersicht halber die von C. E. Bichel für die Stoßkraft der verschiedenen Sprengmittel gefundenen Werte.

Stoßkraft verschiedener Sprengstoffe nach C. E. Bichel.

Sprengstoff	Zusammensetzung	Ladedichte	Detonationsgeschwindigkeit in m/sek.	Stoßkraft in sek/kg/m
Schwarzpulver . .	75 Kalisalpeter 13 Kohle 12 Schwefel	1·04	300	4 578
Kohlencarbonit . .	25 Nitroglyzerin 34 Kalisalpeter 38·5 Mehl 1 Holzmehl 1 Barytsalpeter 0·5 Soda	1·42	2700	371 559
Ammoncarbonit . .	82 Ammonsalpeter 10 Kalisalpeter 4 gel. Sprengöl 4 Mehl	1·19	3094	487 912
Donarit	80 Ammonsalpeter 12 Trinitrotoluol 4 gel. Sprengöl 4 Mehl	1·31	4137	872 312
Schießbaumwolle .	$C_{24}H_{30}(NO_3)_{10}O_{10}$	1·25	6383	2 076 589
Gurdynamit . . .	75 Nitroglyzerin 25 Kieselgur	1·58	6818	2 369 272
Gelatinedynamit . .	63·5 Nitroglyzerin 1·5 Kollod.-Wolle 27 Natronsalpeter 8 Holzmehl	1·67	7000	2 497 452
Trinitrotoluol . . .	$C_6H_2(NO_2)_3CH_3$	1·55	7618	2 957 896
Sprenggelatine . .	92 Nitroglyzerin 8 Kollodiumwolle	1·63	7700	3 021 916
Pikrinsäure . . .	$C_6H_2(NO_2)_3OH$	1·55	8183	3 412 920

Im Gegensatz zur dynamischen Stoßwirkung betrachtet Bichel den Explosionsdruck als einen statischen Vorgang, der im Gipfelpunkt der größten Umsetzung, also am Schluß der ersten Phase der Explosion auftritt. Theoretisch muß im Augenblick der höchsten Erwärmung und Spannung (Maximal-Gasdruck) ein Ruhepunkt vorhanden sein, worauf dann langsame Abkühlung der Gase erfolgt. Die Messung des höchsten Druckes am Ende der ersten und bei Beginn der zweiten Phase — der Abkühlung der Explosionsprodukte — setzt ein widerstandsfähiges Gefäß voraus, dessen Wände nicht nachgeben. Der Gasdruck drückt sich in Kilogramm auf 1 qcm der im Bohrloch zur Verfügung stehenden Oberfläche aus und ist als statisch anzusehen; er wird nur von den durch die Wärme ausgedehnten, bereits infolge des geringen zur Verfügung stehenden Explosionsraumes hochgespannten Gasen und Dämpfen der Zersetzungsprodukte ausgeübt.

Was den zeitlichen Zusammenhang der Stoß- und Druckwirkung angeht, so besteht (nach Bichel) wohl kein Zweifel, daß sich schon gleichzeitig mit der Einleitung der ersten Umsetzung der Sprengstoffpartikelchen bereits Stoßwirkungen und Drucke bilden; beide Erscheinungen sind daher in der Zeitfolge nur insofern auseinanderzuhalten, als der größte Druck im Bohrloch erst eintreten kann, nachdem die vollkommene Umsetzung des Sprengstoffes stattgefunden hat, die damit verbundene Stoßwirkung der Gase und Dämpfe also bereits eingetreten sein muß. — Mit zunehmender Stoßwirkung nimmt auch die Druckwirkung der Sprengstoffe zu, jedoch scheint eine bestimmte Relation zwischen diesen beiden Größen nicht zu bestehen.

Die vorstehend genannten Sprengstoffe entwickeln nach C. E. Bichel folgende Drucke:

	Druck P im Moment der Detonation im eigenen Volumen unter Berücksichtigung des Raumes der nicht vergasenden Bestandteile in kg/qcm	Der Druck von 100 g in der 15 Liter-Kammer des Bichelschen Druckmessers	
		umgerechnet kg/qcm	gemessen kg/qm
Schwarzpulver . .	$409\left(1+\frac{2537}{273}\right) = 4209$	20·27	18·60
Kohlencarbonit .	$1402\left(1+\frac{1561}{273}\right) = 9418$	38·17	31·00
Ammoncarbonit .	$1186\left(1+\frac{1648}{273}\right) = 8345$	44·97	42·25
Donarit	$1285\left(1+\frac{2066}{273}\right) = 11009$	55·99	48·70
Schießbaumwolle .	$1145\left(1+\frac{2380}{273}\right) = 11127$	59·36	53·48
Gurdynamit . . .	$1055\left(1+\frac{2999}{273}\right) = 12644$	44·16	48·20
Gelatinedynamit .	$1229\left(1+\frac{2758}{273}\right) = 13645$	48·40	55·40
Trinitrotoluol . .	$1400\left(1+\frac{2142}{273}\right) = 12384$	51·78	48·10
Sprenggelatine . .	$1393\left(1+\frac{3216}{273}\right) = 17803$	72·87	70·40
Pikrinsäure . . .	$1298\left(1+\frac{2498}{273}\right) = 13175$	53·67	51·84

Für Sprenggelatine (92 : 8) macht C. E. Bichel in „Glückauf“ 1905 noch folgende Angaben: Größte erreichbare Ladedichte:

1·63; ein Kilo Sprengstoff nimmt einen Raum ein von 0·614 Liter; ein Kilo Sprengstoff bildet im Moment der Detonation 828 Liter Gase oder Dämpfe, die 1 kg wiegen.

Kriegs-Sprenggelatine[1] aus 96 Prozent einer aus 90 Teilen Nitroglyzerin und 10 Teilen löslicher Nitrozellulose bestehenden Sprenggelatine und 4 Prozent Kampfer zusammengesetzt. Das Präparat stellt eine gelatineartige, elastische, durchscheinende, blaßgelb gefärbte Masse (Dichte = 1·6) etwa von der Konsistenz einer sehr steifen Sülze dar, welche sich leicht biegen, mit dem Messer schneiden und sehr stark drücken läßt, ohne auch nur die geringsten Mengen von Nitroglyzerin austreten zu lassen oder irgendein Fettwerden zu zeigen. Auch bei Temperaturen zwischen 50 und 60° C erweicht das Präparat wohl in geringerem Grade, fettet aber trotzdem noch immer nicht oder doch bei weitem nicht so wie manche Gurdynamite. Bei zweimonatlichem Erhitzen (täglich 7 Stunden lang) auf 40 bis 45° tritt keine Zersetzung, wohl aber ein Gewichtsverlust von 7·7 Prozent durch Verflüchtigung ein. Beim Erhitzen auf höhere Temperatur explodiert Kriegs-Sprenggelatine mit 4 Prozent Kampfer selbst bei 300 bis 330° C nicht, sondern sprüht ab oder verbrennt einfach. Bei einem Gehalt von 10 Prozent Kampfer kann Kriegs-Sprenggelatine durch langsames Erwärmen gar nicht mehr zur Explosion gebracht werden, sondern es findet eine langsame Zersetzung, ein Absprühen statt. Bei raschem Erhitzen tritt Explosion ein, jedoch liegt die Explosiontemperatur dann sehr hoch. — Gegen Stoß und Schlag ist Sprenggelatine als elastische Masse an sich schon ziemlich unempfindlich; in erhöhtem Maße wird die Unempfindlichkeit durch den Kampferzusatz bewirkt, so daß auch mit Detonator nur schwierig eine Explosion herbeigeführt werden kann. Kriegs-Sprenggelatine mit 4 Prozent Kampfer wird weder durch Sprengkapseln mit 2 g Knallquecksilber, noch durch Zündpatronen aus komprimierter Schießwolle, noch durch Patronen von Schießwolledynamit (75 Prozent Nitroglyzerin + 25 Prozent Schießwolle) zur Explosion gebracht. Dagegen erreicht man Detonation mittels besonders starken Zündpatronen, bestehend aus 60 Prozent Nitroglyzerin und 40 Prozent Nitrohydrozellulose. Letzteres Gemenge stellt eine zarte, weiße, seifig anzufühlende, durchaus gleichförmige Substanz dar, welche außerordentlich brisant ist.

Kriegs-Sprenggelatine ist gegen Wasser sehr unempfindlich; an der äußersten Schicht geht etwas Sprengöl und Kampfer in

---

[1] Nach Hess, Mitteil. Gegenst. Art.- u. Geniewesen 1878, S. 217.

das Wasser, aus der zurückbleibenden Nitrozellulose bildet sich ein Kollodiumhäutchen, welches die Innenmasse vor weiteren Angriffen des Wassers in einem ziemlich hohen Grade schützt. — Eine Ozonisierung der Luft, welche der Zersetzung der Sprenggelatine Vorschub leisten würde, wird durch den Kampfergehalt nicht herbeigeführt. — Die Empfindlichkeit der Kriegs-Sprenggelatine wurde durch Versuche ermittelt, bei denen der Sprengstoff sowohl im weichen als im gefrorenen Zustand unter Anwendung verschiedenartiger Hinterlage (Holz und Eisen) aus 25 m Distanz beschossen wurde. Hierbei ergaben sich folgende Resultate: Weiche Sprenggelatine auch mit nur 1 Prozent Kampfer ist selbst unter sehr extremen Verhältnissen, nämlich bei Eisenhinterlage aus einer Entfernung von 25 m senkrecht beschossen, nahezu vollkommen schußsicher. Weiche Kriegs-Sprenggelatine mit mehr als 1 Prozent Kampfer kann selbst nach oft wiederholten Schüssen aus 25 m Distanz nicht mehr zur Explosion gebracht werden, sobald Holzhinterlage angeordnet wird. Gefrorene Sprenggelatine ist bei Holzhinterlage nicht schußsicher bei 1 Prozent Kampfer, schußsicher bei 2 Prozent; bei Eisenhinterlage ist sie auch bei 4 Prozent Kampfer nicht mehr schußsicher. Vergleichsversuch mit weicher Sprenggelatine ohne Kampferzusatz ergab auch bei Holzhinterlage volle Explosion. — Sprengversuche: Bei der Balkenschlagprobe erwies sich Kriegs-Sprenggelatine mit 4 Prozent Kampfer etwa um 25 Prozent stärker als Gurdynamit, ebenso bei Eisensprengungen; bei letzteren wurden als normale Durchschlagsladungen ermittelt: für 13 mm-Platten 100 g, für 26 mm-Platten 160 g, für 40 mm-Platten 190 g. — Die Kriegs-Sprenggelatine, welche auf Grund der Versuche von Siersch, Roth, Trauzl und Hess in die österreichische Armee eingeführt worden war, wurde etwa im Jahre 1892 in Österreich als Kriegssprengmittel zugunsten des Ecrasits wieder außer Gebrauch gesetzt.

Außer der gewöhnlichen Sprenggelatine (93 : 7 oder 92 : 8) wird auch eine schwächere, sog. Bergwerkssprenggelatine hergestellt, welche weniger Nitroglyzerin und Kollodiumwolle, dafür Beimengungen von Holzmehl, Zellulose und Holzkohle enthält; z. B. 70 bis 80 Teile eines aus 95 : 5 hergestellten gelatinierten Öles und 20 Teile Zusatzstoffe; in England nennt man solche schwächere Sprenggelatine Gelatinedynamit Nr. 1.

II. Gelatinedynamite.

Die eigentlichen Gelatinedynamite sind Mischungen von gelatiniertem Sprengöl mit einem salpeterhaltigen Zumischpulver; hierfür hat man in Deutschland allgemein die Bezeichnung Gelatinedynamit eingeführt, in England bezeichnet man diese Sprengstoffe mit Gelatinedynamit Nr. 2 oder Gelignit. Eine häufige Zusammensetzung des Gelatinedynamits ist

a) 65 Teile gelatiniertes Öl,
b) 35 Teile Zumischpulver.

Das gelatinierte Öl besteht seinerseits aus $96^2/_{13}$ Prozent Nitroglyzerin und $3^{11}/_{13}$ Prozent Kollodiumwolle, das Zumischpulver aus 75 Prozent Natron- oder Kalisalpeter, 24 Prozent Holzmehl, 1 Prozent Soda; daraus ergibt sich die Zusammensetzung des ganzen Sprengstoffes wie folgt:

62·5	Prozent	Nitroglyzerin,
2·5	„	Kollodiumwolle,
26·25	„	Natron(oder Kali-)salpeter,
8·4	„	Holzmehl,
0·35	„	Soda.

Zur Herstellung wird zunächst im Gelatinierhause die Kollodiumwolle in Sprengöl aufgelöst, in ähnlicher Weise wie bei Erzeugung der Sprenggelatine; nur kommt hier ein geringerer Prozentsatz Kollodiumwolle in Anwendung. Das dickflüssige, gelatinierte Nitroglyzerin wird in verschlossenen Behältern durch die Tunnels nach dem Menghause gebracht, in welchem die Knetmaschinen aufgestellt sind; letztere werden durch Motoren, die außerhalb des Menghauses in einem eigenen Schuppen sich befinden, in Bewegung gesetzt. Ferner wird das, im sog. ungefährlichen Teile der Fabrik, zusammengesetzte Zumischpulver[1] nach

[1] Das nötige Holzmehl wird in Holzschleifereien erzeugt; Holzblöcke aus Fichten- oder Tannenholz werden durch Gegengewichte gegen vertikale oder horizontale Schleifsteine gepreßt, wobei Wasser fortwährend auf den Stein fließt; die erhaltene Pülpe wird gemahlen, durch Knotenfänger gereinigt, entwässert und getrocknet, worauf sie — besonders aus Fabriken in Norwegen und Österreich-Ungarn — als Holzmehl von verschiedener Feinheit in den Handel kommt. Vor Verarbeitung zu Zumischpulver für Dynamite wird das lufttrockene, gewöhnlich noch 12 Prozent Feuchtigkeit und harzige Stoffe enthaltende Holzmehl gut getrocknet und leicht geröstet; hierbei soll sich jedoch keine Essigsäure bilden, da letztere auf die Stabilität und jedenfalls auf die Stabilitätsprobe Einfluß hätte. Das Holzmehl soll verschiedenen Anforderungen entsprechen; es soll so fein sein, daß es ein Messingsieb von 6 Maschen auf den Quadratzentimeter leicht passiert; beim Verbrennen eines Gemisches von 1 Teil Holzmehl mit 3 Teilen Kalisalpeter in einem leicht bedeckten Tiegel soll der Rückstand

dem Menghause gebracht und dann werden gelatiniertes Sprengöl und Zumischpulver in den Knetmaschinen sorgfältig durcheinandergearbeitet; eine Werner-Pfleiderer-Maschine knetet und mischt 100 kg Gelatinedynamit in 15 bis 20 Minuten inklusive Entleerung des Troges. Das fertige Gelatinedynamit wird dann den Patronierbuden zugeführt und daselbst ebenso wie Sprenggelatine zu Patronen verarbeitet. Da Gelatinedynamit, besonders solches mit hygroskopischen Salpeterarten, gegen Feuchtigkeit nicht unempfindlich ist, so sind Umhüllungen aus paraffiniertem Papier oder sonstigem wasserdichten Material nötig.

Für die Verpackung gelten in Österreich folgende Vorschriften: Die Patronen kommen zu 1 kg in Kartons von 135 mm Länge, 95 mm Breite und 65 mm Höhe; 20 solcher Kartons werden in Kistchen (20 kg Inhalt) von 375 mm Länge, 210 mm Breite und 285 mm Höhe verpackt. — Oder die Patronen kommen zu 1·25 kg in Kartons von 138 mm Länge, 110 mm Breite und 65 mm Höhe; 20 solcher Kartons werden in Kistchen (25 kg Inhalt) von 361 mm Länge, 242 mm Breite und 285 mm Höhe verpackt. — Oder endlich die Patronen kommen zu 2 kg in Kartons von 180 mm Länge, 135 mm Breite und 65 mm Höhe; 10 solcher Kartons werden in Kistchen (20 kg Inhalt) von 375 : 210 : 285 verpackt.

Herstellung von Gelatinedynamit im Laboratorium. Nachdem man sich im Laboratorium Sprengöl hergestellt, dasselbe gereinigt, getrocknet und getestet hat, wägt man das Becherglas mit dem Nitroglyzerin auf der Handwage, gießt das Sprengöl in eine Porzellanschale und wägt das Becherglas leer zurück. Angenommen 130·8 minus 39·8 g ergibt 91 g zu verarbeitendes Nitroglyzerin. — Da wir ein Gelatinedynamit von der Zusammensetzung 62·5 Prozent Nitroglyzerin, 2·5 Prozent Kollodiumwolle und 35 Prozent Zumischpulver herstellen wollen, so brauchen wir für unsere 91 g Nitroglyzerin (nach der Gleichung $62 \cdot 5 : 2 \cdot 5 = 91 : x$) 3·6 g Kollodiumwolle. Letztere wird wie bei Sprenggelatine vorbereitet, trocken in einer Glasschale abgewogen, dann dem Nitroglyzerin in der Porzellanschale hinzugefügt und durch Untertauchen mittels Hornspachtel ganz mit dem Sprengöl benetzt, worauf man das Gemenge eine Zeitlang ruhig stehen läßt, während der man das Zumischpulver abwägt. Man stellt dann die Porzellanschale auf einen Dreifuß in eine Blechwanne und gießt in letztere vorsichtig Wasser von 50° C, welche Temperatur durch ein unter der Wanne befindliches Flämmchen konstant gehalten wird (Kon-

---

nicht mehr als 10 Prozent betragen; in einer bleiernen oder eisernen Rinne am einen Ende angezündet, soll das Holzmehl möglichst rasch abbrennen.

Manchmal verwendet man auch Roggenmehl, das von konstanterer Zusammensetzung und auch feiner ist, aber kein so gutes Aufsaugevermögen besitzt als Holzmehl.

trolle mit Thermometer). Bei 50° C soll das Gemisch von Sprengöl und Kollodiumwolle gelatinieren; man kann diesen Prozeß durch Hinzufügen eines Kubikzentimeters eines Gemenges von 3 Teilen Methylalkohol und 1 Teil Aceton erleichtern. Das Gemisch in der Porzellanschale wird (immer bei 50° C) mit einem Hornspachtel bis zur dünnflüssigen, gelatinösen Konsistenz umgerührt, was etwa eine halbe Stunde dauert; die Zeit wird durch die Beschaffenheit der Kollodiumwolle beeinflußt. Zweckmäßig arbeiten beim Gelatinieren zwei Mann zusammen; der eine hält die Porzellanschale auf dem Dreifuß und kontrolliert das Thermometer, der andere rührt mit dem Spachtel; letzterer muß von Horn sein, auch zum Patronieren des Dynamits darf man nur einen Hornspachtel verwenden. — Schon vorher hat man sich in einer Glasschale das Zumischpulver[1] abgewogen, wovon wir nach der Gleichung $62 \cdot 5 : 35 = 91 : x$ für unsere 91 g Sprengöl 50·9 g benötigen. Sobald das Gemisch von Nitroglyzerin und Kollodiumwolle in der Schale durch das Erwärmen auf 50° C und Umrühren sirupös geworden ist, trägt man das Zumischpulver ein. Man mischt dann zunächst mit dem Hornspachtel durch, hierauf knetet man die Masse wie einen Backteig; zunächst läßt man die Masse in der Schale liegen und drückt mit der flachen Hand (Ringe vorher ausziehen!) darauf; dann nimmt man die Masse in die Hand[2] und knutscht solche bis zur Gleichmäßigkeit durch. Schließlich nimmt man die Porzellanschale aus dem Wasserbad und legt die Teigkugel hinein. — Zum Patronieren des Gelatinedynamits legt man die Teigkugel auf eine runde Glasplatte und teilt sie mit dem Hornspachtel in kleine Stückchen; letztere bringt man in Patronenhülsen aus Papier (Pergamentpapier) und drückt sie jeweils mit dem Patronenholz fest; ist die Hülse zu groß, so darf man das Papier nicht mit der Schere abschneiden, überhaupt darf man kein Metall an das Nitroglyzerin bringen, da sonst Explosion erfolgt. — Die vom Verarbeiten und Patronieren zurückbleibenden kleinen Reste Dynamit nimmt man in etwas Aceton auf, bringt die Lösung in eine Porzellanschale, gibt Zumischpulver zu, rührt um, bringt die Masse auf Ton und brennt solche dann im Freien ab.

Die Zusammensetzung des Gelatinedynamits entspricht nicht immer der oben angegebenen (62·5 Prozent Nitroglyzerin, 2·5 Prozent Kollodiumwolle, 35 Prozent Zumischpulver); in Österreich wird unter der Bezeichnung Dynamit I ein Gelatinedynamit hergestellt aus 65·5 Prozent Nitroglyzerin, 2·1 Prozent Kollodiumwolle, 7·41 Prozent Holzmehl, 24·05 Prozent Natronsalpeter, 0·78 Prozent Totenkopf, 0·26 Prozent Soda; die Farbe dieses

[1] Ein aus 75 Teilen Natronsalpeter, 24 Tln. Holzmehl und 1 Tl. Soda bestehendes Zumischpulver kann man in einer Dose im Laboratorium vorrätig halten.

[2] Die Hände wäscht man sich dann mit einer Mischung von 3 Teilen Methylalkohol und 1 Tl. Aceton. — Gewöhnlich stellen sich abends Kopfschmerzen ein, gegen die man kalte Umschläge anwendet.

Dynamit I ist braunrot, Ausbauchung im Trauzl 1450 bis 1550 ccm (einschließlich 160 ccm ursprünglicher Laderaum). Ferner werden in Österreich noch zwei geringere Gelatinedynamite angefertigt; Dynamit II enthält 46 Prozent Nitroglyzerin, 1·25 Prozent Kollodiumwolle, 12·03 Prozent Roggenmehl, 39·03 Prozent Natronsalpeter, 1·27 Prozent Totenkopf, 0·42 Prozent Soda; Farbe: braunrot; Ausbauchung: 1050 bis 1150 ccm. Dynamit II A besteht aus 38 Prozent Nitroglyzerin, 1 Prozent Kollodiumwolle, 1·5 Prozent Weißerlenpulverkohle, 6 Prozent Bergkreide, 13 Prozent Roggenmehl, 40 Prozent Natronsalpeter, 0.5 Prozent Soda; Farbe: schwarz; Ausbauchung: 800 bis 850 ccm. — In Frankreich ist die Variation in der Zusammensetzung der Gelatinedynamite ziemlich groß; nachstehend seien einige angegeben:

Französische Gelatinedynamite.

	Gomme B	Gomme B′	Gomme J	Gomme G	Gomme B″	Gomme M D	Gélat. Dyn. Mª	Gomme C	Gomme D	Gélatiné	Gélatiné 1 B
Nitroglyzerin	86	85	84	83	82	74	74	70	69·5	67	64
Kollodiumwolle	5	5	5	5	6	6	4	4	5·5	3	3
Kalisalpeter	4	8	9	10	9	15·5	11	16	24·75	20	—
Natronsalpeter	—	—	—	—	—	—	—	—	—	—	24
Holzmehl	5	4	2	2	3	4·5	10·5	} 10	0·25	10	8
Getreidemehl	—	—	—	—	—	—	—		—	—	—
Magnesia	—	—	—	—	—	—	0·5	—	—	—	1

	Gélignite	Gélignite	Dynamite No. 4	Gélignite	Dynamite gélatiné 1	Gélatiné	Dynamite gélatiné 2a	Gomme E	Dynamite No. 5	Dynamite gélatiné 2b	Dynamite gélatiné 2c
Nitroglyzerin	60	60	59	57·9	57·5	57	50	49	48	45	43
Kollodiumwolle	3	6	1·5	2·1	2·5	3	1·5	2	1	2	2
Kalisalpeter	26·6	26·6	—	—	32	34	42	—	—	42	41
Natronsalpeter	—	—	25	28·7	—	—	—	36	36·3	—	—
Holzmehl	10	10·4	14	} 11·3	8	} 6	6·5	10	14	10	14
Getreidemehl	—	—	—		—		—	3	—	—	—
Magnesia oder Soda	0·4	—	0·35	—	—	—	—	—	0·45	—	—
Ocker	—	—	0·15	—	—	—	—	—	0·25	—	—

Nachstehend die Zusammensetzung einiger belgischer Gelatinedynamite, die als Forcite in den Handel kommen:

	Forcite extra	Forcite supérieure	Super Forcite	Forcite No. 1	Forcite No. 1 P	Forcite No. 2	Forcite No. 2 P
Nitroglyzerin	74	64	64	49	49	36	36
Kollodiumwolle . . .	6	3	3	2	2	3	2
Natronsalpeter . . .	—	24	—	36	—	35	—
Kalisalpeter	14	—	23	—	37	—	46
Holzmehl	5·5	8	9	13	11	11	—
Getreidemehl	—	—	—	—	—	14	15
Magnesia	1	1	1	—	1	1	1

Im allgemeinen kann man die aus gelatiniertem Nitroglyzerin und natron- oder kalisalpeterhaltigem Zumischpulver hergestellten Gelatinedynamite in drei Unterabteilungen gliedern:

α) mit bis 50 Prozent Nitroglyzerin,
β) mit 50 bis 65 Prozent Nitroglyzerin,
γ) mit über 65 Prozent Nitroglyzerin.

Der Zusatz von Kollodiumwolle variiert; bei den billigeren Sorten nimmt man 3 bis 4 Prozent, bei den besseren 5 bis 6 Prozent, auf das Gewicht des Sprengöls bezogen. Bei α) wird gewöhnlich Natronsalpeter verwandt, bei γ) der teurere, aber weniger hygroskopische Kalisalpeter, für β) teils Natron-, teils Kalisalpeter.

Die Gelatinedynamite mit mindestens 55 bis 60 Prozent Sprengöl, höherem Prozentsatz von Kollodiumwolle und mit Kalisalpeter im Zumischpulver bezeichnet man auch als Gelignite.

Eigenschaften. Die Gelatinedynamite sind in ungefrorenem Zustande plastische, pastöse Massen. Gegen Feuchtigkeit sollen dieselben widerstandsfähig sein; man läßt zur Probe die Dynamitpatronen zwei Monate lang in einer mit feuchten Sägespänen gefüllten Kiste lagern, wobei kein Ausscheiden von Sprengöl erfolgen soll. — Bei dreimal wiederholtem Gefrierenlassen und Wiederauftauen soll kein Nitroglyzerin ausschwitzen. — Das Verhalten gegen Wärme prüft man, indem man die Patronen 24 Stunden lang (Tag und Nacht) in einem Thermoregulator bei 40° (falls für Export bestimmt bei 50°) erhitzt, wobei das Patronenpapier nicht fettig werden soll; bei 30° C soll auch bei länger fortgesetztem Erwärmen (während 8 Tagen und Nächten) kein Nitroglyzerin ausschwitzen. — Zwischen den Bestandteilen des Gelatinedynamits darf keine chemische Reaktion stattfinden, bei welcher sich Gase entwickeln könnten.

Empfindlichkeit gegen Stoß und Schlag. Plastisches Gelatinedynamit detoniert nach Will durch ein 2 kg-Fallgewicht bei 17 cm Fallhöhe. — Lenze erhielt folgende Resultate (mit zwei verschiedenen Apparaten α und β) bei je fünf Versuchen:

a) Mit 2 kg-Fallgewicht. Bei 5 cm Fallhöhe α) in vier Fällen keine Detonation, in einem Falle sehr starke Detonation; β) in drei Fällen keine Detonation, in einem Falle schwache, in einem Falle starke Detonation. — Bei 10 cm Fallhöhe α) in zwei Fällen schwache, in zwei Fällen starke, in einem Falle sehr starke Detonation; β) in einem Falle keine, in drei Fällen schwache, in einem Falle sehr starke Detonation. — Bei 15 cm Fallhöhe α) in vier Fällen starke, in einem Falle sehr starke Detonation; β) in zwei Fällen starke, in drei Fällen sehr starke Detonation.

b) Mit 5 kg-Fallgewicht. Bei 2 cm Fallhöhe α) und β) in fünf Fällen keine Detonation. — Bei 4 cm Fallhöhe α) in vier Fällen keine, in einem Falle schwache Detonation; β) in einem Falle keine, in zwei Fällen schwache, in einem Falle starke, in einem Falle sehr starke Detonation. — Bei 6 cm Fallhöhe α) in einem Falle schwache, in zwei Fällen starke, in zwei Fällen sehr starke Detonation; β) in zwei Fällen schwache, in einem Falle starke, in zwei Fällen sehr starke Detonation. — Bei 8 cm Fallhöhe α) in zwei Fällen schwache, in zwei Fällen starke, in einem Falle sehr starke Detonation; β) in einem Falle starke, in vier Fällen sehr starke Detonation. — Bei 10 cm Fallhöhe α) und β) in fünf Fällen sehr starke Detonation.

c) Mit 10 kg-Fallgewicht. Bei 1 cm Fallhöhe α) in fünf Fällen keine Detonation; β) in vier Fällen keine, in einem Falle sehr starke Detonation. — Bei 2 cm Fallhöhe α) in drei Fällen keine, in einem Falle starke, in einem Falle sehr starke Detonation; β) in drei Fällen keine, in zwei Fällen schwache Detonation. — Bei 3 cm Fallhöhe α) in zwei Fällen schwache, in zwei Fällen starke, in einem Falle sehr starke Detonation; β) in einem Falle keine, in einem Falle schwache, in zwei Fällen starke und in einem Falle sehr starke Detonation. — Bei 4 cm Fallhöhe α) in drei Fällen starke, in zwei Fällen sehr starke Detonation; β) in einem Falle schwache, in drei Fällen starke, in einem Falle sehr starke Detonation. — Bei 5 cm Fallhöhe α) in einem Falle starke, in vier Fällen sehr starke Detonation; β) in fünf Fällen sehr starke Detonation.

d) Mit 20 kg-Fallgewicht. Bei 1 cm Fallhöhe α) in vier Fällen keine, in einem Falle starke Detonation; β) in drei Fällen keine, in einem Falle starke, in einem Falle sehr starke Detonation. — Bei 2 cm Fallhöhe α) in drei Fällen starke, in zwei Fällen sehr starke Detonation; β) in zwei Fällen starke, in drei Fällen sehr starke Detonation.

Will weist darauf hin, daß die, durch die hygroskopische Beschaffenheit des Holzmehls verursachten Schwankungen im Flüssigkeitsgehalt die Empfindlichkeit des Gelatinedynamits gegen Stoß und Schlag variieren; z. B. erforderte (bei einem Fallgewicht von 1 kg) eine trockene Patrone eine Fallhöhe von 25 cm, eine an feuchter Luft aufbewahrte dagegen eine Fallhöhe von 130 bis 140 cm.

Bei Gefrierversuchen mit Gelatinedynamit erhielt die Bergwerksdirektion Saarbrücken folgende Resultate:

Sprengstoff	Temperatur im Gefrierraum in Celsius-Graden	Einzeln ausgelegte Patronen		In Kisten mit Originalverpackung	
		Beginn des Gefrierens	vollständig gefroren	Beginn des Gefrierens	vollständig gefroren
		nach Stunden		nach Stunden	
Gelatinedynamit in 35 mm-Patronen, frisch	0 bis + 1°	4 bis 5	6 bis 7	—	—
Desgleichen	1 bis + 1·5°	5 bis 6	7 bis 9	—	—
Desgleichen	1 bis + 2°	4 bis 5	8 bis 9	12 bis 15	40 bis 48
Gelatinedynamit in 35 mm-Patronen, zum zweitenmal gefroren	0 bis + 1°	2 bis 3	4 bis 5	—	—
Desgleichen	+ 1°	3 bis 4	5 bis 6	—	—
Desgleichen	+ 1 bis + 2°	3 bis 4	5 bis 6	12 bis 15	24 bis 30
Gelatinedynamit in 35 mm-Patronen, mehrere Male gefroren	0°	$1^1/_2$ bis 2	4	6 bis 7	20 bis 24
Desgleichen	0 bis + 2°	3 bis 4	5 bis 6	9 bis 10	18 bis 20
Gelatinedynamit in 35 mm-Patronen, frisch	+ 7 bis + 8°	48 bis 50	70 bis 72	etwa 80	Nach 120 Stunden waren noch einzelne weiche Stellen an den Patronen wahrzunehmen.
Gelatinedynamit in 35 mm- u. 23 mm-Patronen	+ 10·5 bis + 11°	Nach 11 Tagen war noch nichts gefroren			
Gelatinedynamit in 23 mm-Patronen	− 2 bis 0°	Im Freien in gewöhnlichen Pappschachteln in 3 Stunden gefroren			
Gelatinedynamit in 35 mm-Patronen	− 2 bis 0°	Im Freien in gewöhnlichen Pappschachteln in 4 bis 5 Stunden gefroren			

Bei den Auftauversuchen ergab sich folgendes: Im unterirdischen Magazin bei 14 bis 15° taute gefrorenes Gelatinedynamit in einzeln ausgelegten Patronen in 8 bis 10 Stunden, in Kisten mit Originalverpackung in 54 bis 60 Stunden auf.

Was die Empfindlichkeit des gefrorenen im Vergleich zu der des plastischen Gelatinedynamits anlangt, so detonierte bei den Saarbrücker Versuchen bei 50 kg Fallgewicht plastisches Gelatinedynamit bei 70, gefrorenes bei 120 cm Fallhöhe; auch bei 15 kg Fallgewicht zeigte das plastische Gelatinedynamit größere Empfindlichkeit als das gefrorene. — Bei Beschußproben aus einer Jagdbüchse — 9·3 mm Bleigeschoß, 3·5 g Schwarzpulverladung — aus 14 m Entfernung explodierten gefrorenes wie plastisches Gelatinedynamit, jedoch war die Detonation des gefrorenen Dynamits bedeutend schwächer, auch fanden sich bei gefrorenem Dynamit zuweilen abgesplitterte Sprengstoffteile. Das plastische Dynamit hatte bei der Explosion das Eisenblech, gegen welches die Patronen angelehnt waren, durchschlagen; beim gefrorenen waren in dieser Hinsicht keine Einwirkungen zu bemerken. — Gegen Eintreiben von Nägeln mit dem Fallgewicht in die Patronen verhielt sich das gefrorene Gelatinedynamit unempfindlich; die Patrone wurde in Stücke zersplittert.

Qualitative Untersuchung von Sprenggelatine und Gelatinedynamit (nach Hess).[1] Man schneidet aus der Mitte der Sprengstoffpatrone eine Scheibe heraus und zerteilt letztere mittels eines hornenen oder hölzernen Messers möglichst fein in kleine Würfel; letztere übergießt man in einem kleinen Kölbchen mit einem Gemenge aus zwei Teilen wasserfreiem Äther und einem Teil wasserfreiem Alkohol; hierbei gehen Nitroglyzerin und Kollodiumwolle in Lösung (ebenso event. vorhandene Beimengungen von Kampfer, Harz, Paraffin, Schwefel). Aus der Lösnng wird die Kollodiumwolle durch überschüssiges Chloroform gefällt und nach Dekantieren zwischen Filtrierpapier abgepreßt; man charakterisiert die Kollodiumwolle durch ihre Entzündlichkeit, an der Explodierbarkeit durch Schlagen zwischen Hammer und Amboß, an dem Verhalten gegen Schwefelnatriumlösung (die beim Kochen Kollodiumwolle auflöst) und gegen Salzsäure und Eisenvitriol, wodurch beim Kochen Stickoxyd entwickelt wird. — Die von der Kollodiumwolle dekantierte Flüssigkeit wird zunächst auf 30° erwärmt, wobei die flüchtigen Lösungsmittel zum größten Teil, sodann auf 80°, wobei letztere ganz entfernt werden. Den Rückstand prüft man in gleicher Weise, wie dies bei den Mischdynamiten geschieht.

Quantitative Untersuchung. Zur Feuchtigkeitsbestimmung zerteilt man ein Muster mit einem Hornspachtel in kleine Stückchen und läßt solche 5 bis 6 Tage über Chlorcalcium im Exsikkator stehen. — Zur Nitroglyzerin- und Kollodiumwollebestimmung übergießt man 5 g des fein verteilten gelatinösen Explosivstoffes in einem Erlenmeyerkölbchen mit 200 ccm Ätheralkohol, schüttelt einige Stunden durch und läßt dann über Nacht stehen. Die Lösung versetzt man mit einem Überschusse von Chloroform, das zurückbleibende Gemenge filtriert man durch ein getrocknetes und gewogenes Leinenfilter; das Filtrat wird auf dem Wasserbad bei etwa 30° von Äther-Alkohol befreit und ergibt den Gehalt an Kollodiumwolle, nachdem event. vorhandener Kampfer durch Schütteln mit Schwefelkohlenstoff entfernt ist.

Dr. Scheiding[2] schlägt vor, die Sprenggelatine zuerst mit Äther allein zu behandeln, wodurch bloß das Nitroglyzerin entfernt wird.

---

[1] Mitteil. Gegenst. Art.- u. Geniewesen 1881.

[2] Zeitschr. angew. Chemie 1890, S. 614.

Hierauf zieht er den Rückstand mit kochendem Wasser aus, aus dem Rückstand durch kalten Essigäther die Kollodiumwolle. — Ist Gehalt an Schießwolle zu bestimmen, so extrahiert er zuerst mit Äther-Alkohol (2 : 1) und dann mit Essigäther.

Die explosive Zersetzung des Gelatinedynamits verläuft (nach Heise) folgendermaßen:

$$82{\cdot}6\,C_3H_5N_3O_9 + 0{\cdot}7\,C_{24}H_{31}N_9O_{38} + 91{\cdot}4\,NaNO_3 + 16{\cdot}2\,C_6H_{10}O_5 + Na_2CO_3 = 316\,CO_2 + 298\,H_2O + 29\,O_2 + 172\,N_2 + 47\,Na_2CO_3.$$

$$L = 1{\cdot}5; \quad t = 2984^0\,C; \quad Q = 1267\text{ Kal.}$$

$$f = 7476\text{ kg}; \quad V_0 = 606\text{ l}; \quad A = 538475.$$

Der feste Rückstand (Rauch) beträgt 166 g von 1000 g Sprengstoff.

Die Dynamit-Aktiengesellschaft vorm. Nobel gibt für Gelatinedynamit mit 65 Prozent gelatiniertem Öl (62·5 Prozent Nitroglyzerin, 2·5 Prozent Kollodiumwolle) folgende Daten: Explosionstemperatur 2960° C; Gasvolumen bei der Explosion 720 l; Wärmeentwicklung 1242 Kal. (H_2O Dampf) bzw. 1393 Kal. (H_2O flüssig); Ausbauchung von 10 g Sprengstoff im Trauzl: 432 ccm.

C. E. Bichel macht über ein aus 63·5 Prozent Nitroglyzerin, 1·5 Prozent Kollodiumwolle, 27 Prozent Natronsalpeter und 8 Prozent Holzmehl hergestelltes Gelatinedynamit folgende Angaben: Dichte 1·67; 1 kg Sprengstoff nimmt einen Raum ein von 0·599 l und entwickelt bei der Explosion 1321 große Kalorien; die Gase von 1 kg Sprengstoff nehmen einen Raum ein von 633 l und wiegen 0·83 kg. Die höchste Explosionstemperatur beträgt 2758° C, die Detonationsgeschwindigkeit 7000 m in der Sekunde, die Stoßkraft 2497452 sek./kg/m, der Druck 13645 kg/qcm.

Ammongelatinedynamite. Durch Kombination von gelatiniertem Sprengöl mit Ammonsalpeter werden besonders kräftige Gelatinedynamite erhalten. In Österreich wird unter der Bezeichnung Dynamit 0 ein Ammongelatinedynamit folgender Zusammensetzung hergestellt: 50 Prozent Nitroglyzerin, 2·25 bis 2·5 Prozent Kollodiumwolle, 2·375 Prozent Roggenmehl, 44·65 Prozent Ammonsalpeter, 0·475 Prozent Kienruß; Farbe: schwarz; Ausbauchung von 20 g im Trauzl: 1600 bis 1700 ccm, einschließlich 160 ccm ursprünglicher Laderaum.

Der belgische Sprengstoff Forcite extra besteht aus 64 Prozent Nitroglyzerin, 3·5 Prozent Kollodiumwolle, 6·5 Prozent trockenes Holzmehl, 25 Prozent Ammonsalpeter, 1 Prozent Magnesia.

III. Abgeänderte Gelatinierungsverfahren.

Bei der Gelatinierung des Nitroglyzerins durch Kollodiumwolle sind verschiedene Neuerungen angewandt worden; Zusätze von bis zu 10 Prozent Pikrinsäure (D.R.P. 42452) und von Kampfer (D.R.P. 5528) wurden früher schon erwähnt. Abel und Dewar ließen sich durch D.R.P. 53294 einen Zusatz von Tannin schützen. — Callenberg (D.R.P. 108402) löst die Kollodiumwolle zuerst in Terpentinöl auf und gelatiniert dann. Beispielsweise wird zu 4 Gewichtsteilen Terpentinöl 1 Teil Kollodiumwolle gegeben, das Gemisch auf dem Wasserbade bei 40° C erwärmt und demselben 30 Gewichtsteile Nitroglyzerin hinzugefügt, worauf man die Temperatur auf 75 bis 80° C steigen läßt. Die Masse gelatiniert dann schnell und gleichmäßig. Mit dieser Gelatine zusammen werden sodann 40 Teile Kalisalpeter, 24 Teile Bittersalz und 1 Teil Soda, welche zuvor in einer Kugelmühle gemengt wurden, eingeknetet; die fertige Masse wird mit Transportschnecke patroniert. — Schachtebeck (D.R.P. 172651) will den mit großen Gefahren verbundenen Trockenprozeß der Kollodiumwolle überflüssig machen, indem derselbe durch Leim, Dextrin oder Stärke der nassen Kollodiumwolle die Feuchtigkeit entzieht. Wird feuchte Kollodiumwolle mit trockenem Leimpulver vermischt, so nimmt der Leim in etwa 24 Stunden alle Feuchtigkeit der Nitrozellulose auf; da nun das für die Gelatinierung mit Glyzerinnitraten hinderliche Wasser aus der Nitrozellulosefaser entfernt ist, so zeigt dieselbe die gleiche Gelatinierfähigkeit wie die vorher getrocknete Nitrozellulose und kann in derselben Weise wie letztere zu Sprengstoffen verarbeitet werden; bei einem Wassergehalt der Wolle von 30 bis 40 Prozent muß die Menge des zuzusetzenden Leimpulvers mindestens gleich dem Trockengewicht der Wolle sein. Beispiele: I. 60·25 Prozent Nitroglyzerin, 2·5 Prozent Kollodiumwolle mit 35 Prozent Wasser, 3 Prozent Leim, 7 Prozent Holzmehl, 1 Prozent Mehl, 24 Prozent Natronsalpeter, 3 Prozent Ammonsalpeter. II. 63·1 Prozent Nitroglyzerin, 2·7 Prozent Kollodiumwolle mit 36 Prozent Wasser, 1 Prozent Leim, 9 Prozent Holzmehl, 25 Prozent Natronsalpeter. Die erhaltene Gelatine wird mit den bekannten Zumischpulvern versetzt, durchgeknetet und wie üblich patroniert.

Andere Erfinder haben sich die Aufgabe gestellt, andere Substanzen als Kollodiumwolle zum Gelatinieren des Sprengöls zu verwenden. Lewin nahm im Jahre 1881 ein Patent (D.R.P. 15073) auf Herstellung eines gallertartigen Nitroglyzerins mittels Baumwolle und Dextrin. Danach wird sorgfältig gereinigte und getrocknete Baumwolle mit 5 Teilen Dextrin unter Beigabe von etwas Ammoniumacetat in einem geschlossenen Kessel bei sechs Atmosphären Spannung gekocht; die erhaltene Gallerte, bis 7 Prozent in Nitroglyzerin gelöst, bildet mit demselben eine Masse, welche kein Sprengöl entweichen läßt. Zur Herstellung des Sprengstoffes Forcit (in seiner ursprünglichen Zusammensetzung) wurden 76 Teile gallertartigen Nitroglyzerins mit 15 Teilen Salpeter und 9 Teilen Sägemehl gemischt. — Goldenberg, Giromont & Cie. (D.R.P. 110621) stellten Dynamit aus Nitroglyzerin und Factis her, kautschukähnlichen Stoffen, die chemisch als Triglyzerinester geschwefelter Fettsäuren aufzufassen sind und die bei der Einwirkung von Chlorschwefel auf fette Öle, wie z. B. Baumwollsaatöl, Rüböl usw., unter Salzsäureabspaltung resultieren. — Bielefeldt (D.R.P. 93351) gelatiniert durch Eintragen von Chlorschwefel (SCl_2) in Nitroglyzerin, wobei der Wärmeentwicklung wegen gekühlt werden muß; man erhält eine schnell erstarrende, bis hornartig harte Gelatine. Ähnlich wirken — nach D.R.P. 95390 — auch andere Chlorschwefelverbindungen. — Hermann (D.R.P. 176072) stellt durch Kondensation von Anilin mit Formaldehyd bei Gegenwart von Nitroglyzerin ein Produkt her, worin das gebildete Anhydroformaldehydanilin $C_6H_5NCH_2$ das Sprengöl festhält; die Masse ist in der Wärme weich, beim Abkühlen tritt nach und nach Erstarren bis zur zähen Beschaffenheit ein; durch Zusatz von Nitraten und Chloraten werden Sprengstoffe erhalten, welche gegen mechanische Einwirkung unempfindlich sind. — Bichel (D.R.P. 180685) verwendet zum Gelatinieren von Nitroglyzerin eine Lösung von kolloiden Stoffen (z. B. Leim, Gelatine oder dergl.) in hierzu geeigneten Flüssigkeiten von höherem Siedepunkt als Wasser, z. B. in Glyzerin, worin Leim unter stetem Umrühren in der Wärme gelöst wird. Die nach dem Erkalten resultierende Glyzerin-Leimgelatine vermag beim Erwärmen unter Umrühren je nach der Konsistenz bis zur fünffachen Menge Nitroglyzerin aufzunehmen und festzuhalten; man erhält eine zähe, seidenglänzende Gelatine, welche in jeder Beziehung dasselbe äußere Verhalten zeigt, wie die aus Kollodiumwolle und Nitroglyzerin hergestellten Gelatinen und welche sich in derselben Weise sowohl als Sprenggelatine wie zur Herstellung von Gelatinedynamiten und anderen plastischen Sprengstoffen verwenden läßt. Beispiel: 63 Prozent Nitroglyzerin, 11·5 Prozent Leimglyzerin (im Verhältnis 1 : 7), 19·3 Prozent Natronsalpeter und 6·2 Prozent Holzmehl. — Bichel verfährt auch so, daß derselbe in Sprenggelatine und Gelatinedynamiten einen Teil der Kollodiumwolle durch Leimgelatine ersetzt, wobei durch Ausnützung des überschüssigen Sauerstoffes des Nitroglyzerins eine größere Sprengkraft erzielt und ein Teil der teuren Kollodiumwolle durch die billigere Leimgelatine ersetzt wird. 93 Prozent Nitroglyzerin + 7 Prozent Kollodiumwolle geben durchschnittlich 565 ccm Ausbauchung im Trauzl; 93 Prozent Nitroglyzerin, 6 Prozent Kollodiumwolle + 1 Prozent Leimglyzeringelatine: 595 ccm; 93 Prozent Nitroglyzerin, 5 Prozent Kollodiumwolle, 2 Prozent Leimglyzeringelatine: 620 ccm; 93 Prozent Nitroglyzerin, 4 Prozent Kollodiumwolle, 3 Prozent Leimglyzeringelatine: 610 ccm; 93 Prozent Nitroglyzerin, 3 Prozent Kollodiumwolle, 4 Prozent Leimglyzeringelatine: 590 ccm; 93 Prozent Nitroglyzerin, 2 Prozent Kollodiumwolle, 5 Prozent Leimglyzeringelatine: 585 ccm.

Neunter Abschnitt.

Wettersichere Nitroglyzerinsprengstoffe.

Die Sprengarbeit in den Kohlengruben führte zahlreiche Unglücksfälle herbei, welche zu einem hohen Prozentsatze auf die Entzündung von schlagenden Wettern durch Explosivstoffe zurückzuführen waren;[1] man begann daher vor etwa 30 Jahren in verschiedenen Staaten der Frage näher zu treten, ob es möglich sei, durch Anwendung Wetter nicht zündender Sprengstoffe die Gefahren zu beseitigen oder wenigstens zu verringern.[2] Die französischen Forscher Mallard und Le Chatelier[3] untersuchten zunächst die Entzündlichkeit von Grubengas-Luftgemischen; die Explosion ist am kräftigsten, wenn der Methangehalt etwa $9^1/_2$ Prozent beträgt, d. h. wenn der Sauerstoffgehalt der Luft gerade zur völligen Verbrennung des Methans ausreicht; die selbsttätige Fortpflanzung der Explosion der Schlagwettergemische hört auf, wenn der Methangehalt unter 5 Prozent sinkt oder über 14 Prozent steigt; doch sind auch dann die Gemische nicht ungefährlich.

---

[1] Bei einer Schlagwetterexplosion entsteht zunächst durch die plötzliche Volumvermehrung bei der Explosion ein heftiger Schlag, dessen mechanische Wirkungen hinreichen, alles Lebende zu vernichten und fürchterliche Zerstörungen zu verursachen. Durch die große Explosionswärme tritt ferner die Gefahr des Verbrennens ein. Weiterhin entsteht durch Zusammenziehung der Gase und Kondensation der Dämpfe ein gefährlicher Rückschlag. Endlich sind die Nachschwaden infolge ihres Mangels an Sauerstoff gefährlich und vernichten oft mehr Bergleute als die eigentliche Explosion.

[2] Vgl. Haton de la Goupillière, Bericht der französischen Schlagwetterkommission. Annales des mines 1880. — Haslacher, Hauptbericht der preußischen Schlagwetterkommission 1887. — Bericht der französischen Kommission. Annales des mines 1888. — Schlußbericht der österreichischen Schlagwetterkommission. Wien 1891.

[3] Recherches experimentales et théoriques sur la combustion des mélanges gazeux explosifs. Annales des mines 1883.

Zur Feststellung der Entzündungstemperatur, d. h. derjenigen Temperatur, deren Erreichung notwendig ist, damit die explosive Verbrennung des Methans mit dem Sauerstoff der Luft vor sich geht, ließen Mallard und Le Chatelier das Gasgemisch in einen röhrenförmigen Behälter einströmen, der vorher auf eine bestimmte Temperatur gebracht war. Durch eine größere Anzahl von Versuchen mit teils zündenden, teils nicht zündenden Temperaturen der Versuchsröhre kamen die genannten Forscher zu einer Entzündungstemperatur von 650° C. — Hierbei ist aber eine gewisse Verzögerung der Entzündung zu konstatieren, d. h. wenn man das Gasgemisch auf 650° C erhitzt, so dauert es bis zu 10 Sekunden, bis die Explosion eintritt; bei höherer Temperatur verringert sich die Verzögerung, bei 1000° ist sie kaum mehr schätzbar. Von Einfluß ist auch der Gasdruck; durch höheren Druck zusammengepreßte Gase sind schneller entzündlich als Gase, die infolge verminderten Druckes verdünnt sind. — Die französische Kommission ging nun von der Ansicht aus, daß die Entzündung der schlagenden Wetter durch die Flammentemperatur des Schusses verursacht werde; diese Flammentemperatur läßt sich aus der Zusammensetzung des Sprengstoffes rechnerisch feststellen; sie darf an sich wesentlich höher liegen als 650°, da durch Ausdehnung und Arbeitsleistung der Explosionsgase sofort starke Abkühlung eintritt; auf Grund von praktischen Versuchen kam man in Frankreich dazu, die höchste Flammentemperatur für wettersichere Sprengstoffe auf 2200° zu fixieren; später wurde dieselbe auf 1500° für Kohlenflöze und auf 1900° für Nebengestein fixiert.[1] Die Temperatur wird berechnet aus der Zersetzungsgleichung des explodierenden Sprengstoffes unter Zugrundelegung einer theoretisch angenommenen Zersetzung in bestimmte Explosionsprodukte, ohne Rücksichtnahme auf den Einfluß der Initiierung, auf die Dichte des Sprengstoffes, auf die Festigkeit der Einschließung usw. Außerdem wird von dem Sprengstoff verlangt, daß keine brennbaren Gase, wie Wasserstoff, Kohlenoxyd und kein fester Kohlenstoff bei den Nachschwaden vorhanden sein sollen. — Da Ammonsalpeter die niedrige Flammentemperatur von 1130° hat, so empfahl man in Frankreich Nitroglyzerin oder Nitrozellulosen mit Ammonsalpeter zu vermengen, um Sprengstoffe von relativ niedriger Flammentemperatur zu erhalten.

In anderen Ländern begnügte man sich — im Gegensatz zur

---

[1] Reglementation des explosifs à employer dans les mines à grisou et dans les mines poussiéreuses dont les poussières sont inflammables. Paris, 1er Août 1890.

französischen Bergverwaltung — nicht damit, einfach die rechnungsmäßigen Explosionstemperaturen als Maßstab der Sicherheit der Explosivstoffe festzusetzen. Man gründete Versuchsanstalten, die sog. Versuchsstrecken, um über die tatsächliche Schlagwettersicherheit der verschiedenen Sprengstoffe durch praktische Schießversuche eine vergleichsweise Übersicht zu bekommen. Hierbei wurde zunächst festgestellt, daß von einer wirklichen Sicherheit der Sprengstoffe überhaupt nicht die Rede sein kann und daß sämtliche Sprengstoffe die Schlagwetter zünden, wenn entsprechend große Ladungen zur Explosion gelangen; Winckhaus[1] hat die Methode der Beurteilung der Sprengstoffe nach der Ladegröße, also der Gewichtsmenge, welche mindestens vorhanden sein muß, damit Zündung eintritt, zuerst experimentell durchgeführt; Watteyne[2] hat hierfür das Wort „Grenzladung" (charge limite) festgesetzt. Heise[3] fand, daß Explosionstemperaturen und Sicherheit der Sprengstoffe durchaus nicht immer im umgekehrten Verhältnis stehen und daß für die Schußsicherheit auch noch andere Bedingungen mitsprechen; insbesondere wies er auf den Einfluß der Detonationsgeschwindigkeit hin, wodurch verschieden große Verdichtungswärme der Gase erzeugt wird. General Hess[4] hat die Wirkung der mechanischen Stoßarbeit der Explosionsgase dem Auge durch photographische Aufnahme wahrnehmbar gemacht. Watteyne und Denoël[5] wiesen auf den Einfluß der Dichte des Sprengstoffes hin.

In der Preßburger Fabrik der Dynamitgesellschaft Nobel hat Siersch festgestellt, daß die Flammenerscheinung, welche bei der Explosion einer Sprengstoffpatrone auftritt, in derartigem Parallelismus zu der Wettersicherheit des Sprengstoffes steht, daß sie als Maß derselben gelten kann; eine Sprengstoffpatrone wird frei aufgehängt und in etwa 2·3 m Entfernung wird der nachts abgetane Schuß photographiert; man fand dabei,[6] daß diejenigen Sprengstoffe, welche große Flammenbilder geben, geringe Schlagwettersicherheit zeigen, umgekehrt schlagwettersichere Sprengstoffe kleine Flammenbilder geben.

Von besonderer Bedeutung sind die Versuche, welche C. E. Bichel (größtenteils in Gemeinschaft mit Mettegang) an-

---

[1] Glückauf 1895/96.
[2] Kongreßbericht 1903, Bd. II, S. 312.
[3] Glückauf 1898/99.
[4] Mitteil. Gegenst. Art.- u. Geniewesen 1900.
[5] Bull. Soc. Ind. Min. 1900.
[6] Österr. Zeitschr. Berg- u. Hüttenwesen 1896. — Zeitschr. Schieß-Sprengstoffwesen 1907, S. 141.

gestellt hat.[1] Bichel folgerte daraus, daß man Sicherheitssprengstoffe mit mehr als 30 Prozent Nitroglyzerin nicht herstellen könne, daß die Schlagwettersicherheit in einem festen Verhältnis zur Wirkungsgröße steht und bei Verstärkung der letzteren die Sicherheit abnimmt; er stellte sich die Aufgabe, aus gegebenem Rohstoff durch Versuche ein günstiges Verhältnis nach beiden Richtungen, stärkste Wirkung und größte Sicherheit, zu ermitteln. Er fand, daß bei Sicherheitssprengstoffen die Detonationsgeschwindigkeit, Höchsttemperatur der Zersetzungsprodukte, die Flammenlänge und Flammendauer bei gegebenem Druck möglichst klein sein müssen und daß keine dieser Erscheinungen eine gewisse Grenze überschreiten darf, weil ein Ausgleich durch überwiegend günstigen Einfluß der übrigen Erscheinungen nicht stattfindet. Bichel verglich insbesondere das Verhältnis von Detonationsgeschwindigkeit und Flammendauer und führte für dasselbe die Bezeichnung Nachflammverhältnis ein. Detonationsgeschwindigkeit und Flammendauer sind deshalb nicht identisch, weil auch nach dem explosiven Zerfall noch chemische Umwandlungen vor sich gehen, die von Feuerscheinungen begleitet sind. (Eine ähnliche Erscheinung liegt beim Mündungsfeuer der rauchlosen Pulver vor.) Man hat das für die Schlagwettersicherheit ausschlaggebende Nachflammverhältnis für alle Sprengstoffe festgestellt und als zulässiges Maximum für Sprengungen im Kohlenbergbau 1 : 15 angenommen. Je kleiner das Verhältnis ist, um so besser; so beträgt dasselbe z. B. bei Ammoncarbonit nur 1 : 8, d. h. die Flamme erscheint nur achtmal so lange, als die Detonation an Zeit gebraucht; demgegenüber hat Schwarzpulver ein Nachflammverhältnis von 1 : 330, Sprenggelatine von 1 : 883.

Zusammenfassend könnte man sagen: „Während den Versuchsstrecken die Aufgabe zufiel, die höchste Sprengstoffladung festzustellen, mit welcher ein Sprengstoff in bezug auf Zündung von Schlagwettern und Kohlenstaub noch sicher ist, so befaßt sich die Untersuchung des Herrn C. E. Bichel und Dr. Mettegang mit der Frage, welche Eigenschaften der Sprengstoffe einen Einfluß auf die Zündung von Schlagwettern besitzen. Es war dazu nötig, zunächst diese Eigenschaften festzustellen und in ihrer Größe zu messen, wozu wiederum die Konstruktion zahlreicher Apparate erforderlich war. Alsdann wurden durch tabellarische Zusammenstellungen der gewonnenen Resultate Schlüsse auf den Einfluß der verschiedenen Vorgänge bei der Explosion von Sprengstoffen gezogen. Im allgemeinen kann man das Resultat dahin zusammenfassen:

---

[1] Untersuchungsmethoden für Sprengstoffe. Berlin 1902, W. Ernst & Sohn; Glückauf 1904, Heft 35; Broschüre Methoden und Apparate zur Prüfung von Sprengstoffen. 1907.

1. daß die Explosionstemperatur und die Detonationsgeschwindigkeit bei Sprengstoffen hauptsächlich in Frage kommen, wenn es sich um Zündung von Schlagwettern handelt und daß die Flammenlänge und Flammendauer eines Sprengstoffes von wesentlichem Einflusse auf die Zündung sind;

2. daß aber keiner der vorgenannten Faktoren allein maßgebend ist, sondern daß vielmehr für die Ungefährlichkeit der Sprengstoffe eine Beschränkung dieser Faktoren auf ein bestimmtes Mindestmaß erforderlich ist, weil sonst die Zündungsgrenze überschritten wird."

Meßapparate. Der von Bichel angegebene und benutzte Apparat zur Messung der Detonationsgeschwindigkeit, sowie sein Druckmesser sind näher beschrieben in der von der Sprengstoff-Aktiengesellschaft Carbonit herausgegebenen Broschüre: Methoden und Apparate zur Prüfung von Sprengstoffen, worauf verwiesen sei. Die Messung der Flammenlänge und Flammendauer wird nach Bichel bei Nacht auf photographischem Wege vorgenommen. Der Sprengstoff wird hierbei aus einem Schießmörser verschossen, einem aufrechtstehenden Stahlblock mit einer Einbohrung von 55 mm Durchmesser und 500 mm Tiefe, der etwa 6 m vom photographischen Apparat entfernt steht. Letzterer besteht aus einem Holzkasten, welcher vorn als Objektiv eine Quarzlinse trägt, da Quarz auch die ultravioletten Strahlen durchläßt; in dem Apparat befindet sich eine in einem Bügel in Spitzenschrauben laufende Trommel, auf welche der lichtempfindliche Film gespannt wird. Die Trommel wird durch einen Elektromotor vermittelst einer Zahnradübertragung angetrieben; sie hat einen Umfang von 50 cm und kann bis 40 Touren pro Sekunde machen, legt an Umfang also im Maximum einen Weg von 20 m pro Sekunde zurück; die Feststellung der Tourenzahl erfolgt durch ein Vibrationstachometer; zwischen der Quarzlinse und der Trommel, dicht vor der letzteren, ist ein gebogener Schirm mit einem Schlitz in axialer Richtung der Trommel befestigt. — Zur Ausführung der Versuche wird in der Dunkelkammer bei stark gedämpftem rotem Licht ein Film gespannt und an den zusammenstoßenden Rändern mit einem Streifen gummierter Leinwand zusammengehalten. In den Schießmörser wird eine Sprengpatrone gesteckt und letztere, sobald die Trommel die gewünschte Umdrehungsgeschwindigkeit hat, auf elektrischem Wege abgefeuert. Bei stillstehender Trommel würde die Länge des Bildes der Flammenlänge, die Breite des Bildes der Spaltbreite entsprechen. Bei schnellaufender Trommel verzerrt sich das Bild nach der Breite; die Breitenausdehnung des Bildes bezogen auf die Umdrehungsgeschwindigkeit der Trommel gibt die Flammendauer in $^1/_{1000}$ Sekunden an.

Bichel gibt folgendes Schema für eine Sprengstoffuntersuchung:

1. Name des Sprengstoffes.
2. Zusammensetzung des Sprengstoffes in Prozenten.
3. Detonationsgeschwindigkeit in Metern pro Sekunde.

4. Druck von 100 g in der 15 Liter-Kammer (nach Ausschaltung der Oberfläche) in Kilogramm pro Quadratzentimeter.
5. Anzahl der von 1 kg Sprengstoff entwickelten Kalorien.
6. Berechnete Detonationstemperatur in Grad Celsius.
7. Dauer der Stichflamme von 100 g Sprengstoff in $^1/_{1000}$ Sekunden.
8. Länge der Stichflamme von 100 g Sprengstoff.
9. Gewichtsanalyse der Explosionsprodukte.
10. Menge der Explosionsprodukte von 1 kg Sprengstoff bei 15° C und 760 mm Atmosphärendruck; die gas- und dampfförmigen Produkte in Litern, die festen Bestandteile in Grammen.
11. Bleiblockausbauchung, netto normal, nach Abzug des Bohrloches in Kubikzentimetern.
12. Empfindlichkeit gegen Stoß und Schlag. Mit Fallgewichten von 100, 250, 500, 1000, 2000 und 5000 g wird festgestellt, bei welcher Fallhöhe Explosion erfolgt.

Kohlenstaubexplosionen. In neuerer Zeit hat man auch den Explosionen in Bergwerken, welche durch Entzündung fein verteilten Kohlenstaubes herbeigeführt werden, größere Aufmerksamkeit geschenkt. Kohlenstaub ist um so gefährlicher, je feiner derselbe ist, je leichter derselbe also von der Luft getragen wird; ferner spielt der Gasgehalt der Kohle eine wichtige Rolle; Staubsorten mit etwa 22 bis 35 Prozent Gasgehalt sind am leichtesten entzündlich, während die Staubsorten mit einem darunter- und darüberliegenden Gasgehalte weniger gefährlich sind. Das Zustandekommen einer Kohlenstaubexplosion ist so zu erklären, daß durch die bei einer Schlagwetterexplosion oder durch einen auspfeifenden Schuß entstandene Hitze der aufgewirbelte Kohlenstaub entgast wird, so daß ein explosibles Gemenge entsteht, das durch die ursprüngliche Explosionsflamme oder den Feuerstrahl eines Lochpfeifers entzündet wird. In den Gruben sucht man zunächst der Explosionsgefahr durch Befeuchtung vorzubeugen; es sind vielfach eigene Spritzmeister angestellt, welche die Verantwortung dafür tragen, daß morgens vor dem Schichtbeginn sämtliche Strecken naß sind und kein Kohlenstaub vorhanden ist; durch das Befeuchten wird der Staub niedergeschlagen. Immerhin muß stets mit der Möglichkeit des Vorhandenseins von Kohlenstaub gerechnet und dafür gesorgt werden, daß solcher nicht durch Sprengschüsse entzündet wird. Kohlenstaub-Luftgemische werden durch das Hinzukommen geringer, an sich nicht entzündlicher Schlagwettermengen zufolge Vergrößerung der Schußflamme leichter entzündlich. Solche Schlagwettergemische, die einen Methangehalt von 5 bis 14 Prozent besitzen und an sich leicht entzündlich sind, werden durch Beimengung von Kohlenstaub nicht wesentlich beeinflußt. Neuere Versuche von Beyling[1] haben ergeben, daß Sprengstoffe, die gegenüber Schlagwettern sicher sind, beim Schießen aus engen (40 mm) Bohrlöchern in der Versuchsstrecke Kohlenstaub zünden; es ist dies besonders dann der Fall, wenn die Nachschwaden des Sprengstoffes Kohlenoxyd und Wasserstoff enthalten, die mit einer so hohen Temperatur aus dem engen Bohrloch herauskommen, daß eine Entzündung der erwähnten brennbaren Gase mit dem Sauerstoff der Luft erfolgt; durch diese explosionsartige Aufflammung vor dem Bohrloch kann dann eine Kohlenstaubexplosion zustande kommen. Ist kein Kohlenstaub, dagegen ein 8- bis 9 prozentiges Schlagwettergemisch vorhanden, so finden die heißen brennbaren Gase vor dem Bohrloch keine reine Luft, sondern schon ein explosibles Gasgemisch vor. Wo die Gase zusammentreffen, entsteht daher ein Gemisch von Luft, Grubengas, Kohlenoxyd und Wasserstoff, das überreich an Gas, dagegen zu arm an Sauerstoff und deshalb nicht mehr entzündlich ist; infolgedessen tritt eine Schlagwetterexplosion nicht ein.

Versuchsstrecken.[2] Wenn auch die Bestimmung aller einzelnen Faktoren unstreitig das beste Bild von der Natur und dem Wert eines Sprengstoffes in jeder Hinscht gibt, so steht dieser Untersuchungsmethode doch entgegen, daß sie hohe Anforderungen an die apparativen Einrichtungen und Schulung im Gebrauch stellt. Es wird daher der Hauptwert auf die Prüfung der Sicherheitssprengstoffe in den Versuchsstrecken gelegt, wobei die zu prüfenden Sprengstoffe in ein Gemisch von Schlagwettern und aufgewirbelten Kohlenstaub hinein abgeschossen werden. Es handelt sich also um ein Verfahren, welches sich an die Verhältnisse der praktischen Verwendung der Sprengstoffe anlehnt. Das Resultat wird zahlenmäßig so ausgedrückt, daß angegeben wird, welche Menge eines Sprengstoffes zur Detonation gebracht werden kann, ohne das Schlagwettergemisch zu zünden.

In den Gruben bieten gegenüber schlagenden Wettern und Kohlenstaub diejenigen Schüsse die meiste Gefahr, welche nicht reißen, welche also die bei der Detonation der Sprengladung entwickelte Wärme nicht in Arbeit umsetzen, sondern mit der hohen Temperatur der Sprengstoffgase aus dem Bohrloche auspfeifen (Lochpfeifer). In der Versuchsstrecke werden diese ungünstigen Verhältnisse nachgebildet, indem man die Schüsse aus einem starkwandigen, etwas geneigt liegenden, in den

---

[1] Glückauf 1907, S. 1142; Bestätigung dieser Versuchresultate bleibt abzuwarten.

[2] Vgl. Eschweiler, Internationaler Kongreßbericht, Bd. II, S. 307. — Beyling, Glückauf 1903, Nr. 19; 1907, Nr. 36/37. — Bichel, Zeitschr. Schieß-Sprengstoffwesen 1907, S. 169.

starken Mauerabschluß der Strecke eingebauten Stahlmörser in ein explosibles Schlagwetter- und Kohlenstaubgemisch hinein abtut. Die Sprengstoffpatronen werden in einem einheitlichen Durchmesser von 35 mm zur Prüfung herangezogen; das Bohrloch des Mörsers hat eine Weite von 55 mm, eine Tiefe von 500 bis 600 mm; die Patronen werden lose hintereinander in das Mörserbohrloch geladen, so daß die zuerst eingeführte auf der Bohrlochsohle aufsitzt; die oberste Patrone ist stets die Zündpatrone, in der sich die Sprengkapsel befindet. Die mit jedem Sprengstoff vorzunehmenden Versuche werden mit einer mittelstarken Ladung, z. B. 300 g, begonnen; erfolgt dabei keine Zündung der Schlagwetter, so wird die Ladungsmenge von Schuß zu Schuß um 50 g erhöht, andernfalls wird sie um dieselbe Menge herabgesetzt, bis die Grenze der Sicherheit erreicht ist; als solche wird diejenige höchste Ladungsmenge angesehen, bei welcher der Sprengstoff unter den angegebenen Bedingungen in fünf Schüssen keine Explosion verursacht. Die Versuchsstrecke wird so vorbereitet, daß die — vorher durch starkes Packpapier gut abgedichtete — Explosionskammer ein 8 bis 8·5 Prozent Grubengas enthaltendes, also hochexplosibles Gasgemisch enthält; nach Beendigung der Gaszuführung werden in der Explosionskammer zwei Liter feingemahlener Fettkohlenstaub aufgewirbelt. Die Schüsse werden ohne Besatz abgetan, während in der Grube jeder Schuß mit gutem Besatz versehen sein muß. Die Versuchsbedingungen sind also der Praxis gegenüber absichtlich erschwert, da sonst allzu große Ladungen geschossen werden müßten. Dagegen sind sie dadurch, daß die Schüsse aus einem Stahlmörser abgetan werden, dessen Wandungen einen Teil der bei der Detonation entstehenden Wärme aufnehmen, sowie durch die Weite des Mörserbohrloches wiederum erleichtert. Letzteres würde beim Schießen mit freiliegenden Patronen wegfallen, doch hat dieses Verfahren den Nachteil, daß nicht alle Sprengstoffe an freier Luft glatt und vollständig explodieren. — Die deutschen Versuchsstrecken befinden sich in Gelsenkirchen, Neunkirchen, Aachen, Zwickau und Beuthen in O/S. (letztere nur für Kohlenstaub); eine österreichische in Mährisch-Ostrau, eine vorzüglich eingerichtete belgische Strecke in Frameries.[1]

Die Versuchsergebnisse können nicht unmittelbar auf die Praxis übertragen werden; sie sollen vielmehr in erster Linie ein vergleichendes Bild davon geben, wie sich die Sprengstoffe hinsichtlich ihrer Sicherheit zueinander verhalten.

Die wettersicheren Nitroglyzerinsprengstoffe[2] kann man einteilen in

a) Grisoutine, c) Karbonite,
b) Grisoutite, d) wettersichere Gelatinedynamite.

[1] Watteyne u. Stassart, Annales des mines de Belgique. Tome X. — Zeitschr. Schieß-Sprengstoffwesen I, 135.

[2] Eine große Anzahl wettersicherer Sprengstoffe wird ohne Anwendung von Nitroglyzerin auf der Basis von Ammonsalpeter hergestellt; in Frankreich heißen solche Grisounite.

a) Grisoutine. Diese entstanden infolge Anregung der französischen Schlagwetterkommission, durch Zusatz von Ammonsalpeter die Flammentemperatur der Nitroglyzerinsprengstoffe herabzusetzen; für Mischungen von Gurdynamit (75:25) und Ammonnitrat werden folgende Zahlen angegeben:

Gurdynamit	Ammonsalpeter	t	f	α	P
0	100	1130°	5180	0·976	5080
20	80	1468°	6208	0·944	5940
50	50	2090°	7740	0·865	6550
100	0	2940°	8490	0·710	6580

Die in Frankreich meist angewandten Grisoutine sind: 12prozentige Grisoutine (mit 12 Prozent gelatiniertem Sprengöl und der Zusammensetzung: 11·75 Prozent Nitroglyzerin, 0·25 Prozent Kollodiumwolle, 88 Prozent Ammonsalpeter; Explosionstemperatur 1432° C); 20prozentige Grisoutine (19·6 Prozent Nitroglyzerin, 0·4 Prozent Kollodiumwolle, 80 Prozent Ammonsalpeter); 30prozentige Grisoutine (29·4 Prozent Nitroglyzerin, 0·6 Prozent Kollodiumwolle, 70 Prozent Ammonsalpeter); dann sog. Gomme de sûreté mit 25 Prozent Nitroglyzerin, 1 Prozent Kollodiumwolle, 64 Prozent Ammonsalpeter und 10 Prozent Kali- oder Natronsalpeter. — Diesen französischen Grisoutinen sehr ähnlich sind die neuerdings in Deutschland viel fabrizierten Gelatinekarbonite (wettersichere Ammongelatinedynamite), von denen später die Rede sein wird.

b) Grisoutite. Bei den früheren Versuchen, die Temperatur der Explosionsgase abzukühlen, hatte man auch die sog. Settlesche Wasserpatrone verwendet, bei welcher die Dynamitpatrone in eine zweite Hülse gesteckt und der Zwischenraum mit Wasser ausgefüllt war (D.R.P. 38003). Man versuchte ferner als einen die Flamme löschenden Besatz solche Salze anzuwenden, welche chemisch gebundenes Wasser enthalten. Die Salze (wie kristallisierte Soda, Glaubersalz, Magnesiasulfat) sollten infolge der Erhitzung ihr Kristallwasser abgeben und so einerseits durch Absorption von Wärme die Explosionsgase abkühlen, andererseits durch Vermittelung des verdampfenden Kristallwassers die absorbierte Wärme in ausnutzbare Energieform umwandeln.[1]

[1] Nach dem D.R.P. 22006 wird als Besatz eine Masse aus 90 Prozent kristallisierter Soda, 7 Prozent Kreide, 2 Prozent Mangansuperoxyd und 1 Prozent Seife verwandt. Nach dem D.R.P. 103731 werden vor der Ladung im Bohrloch Salzkörper angebracht, die der Länge nach mit einem oder mehreren Kanälen durchbohrt sind; die Flamme und die gasförmigen Ex-

Von dem Gedanken, kristallwasserhaltige Salze als Besatz anzuwenden, kam man dazu, solche Salze dem Sprengstoffe selbst zuzumischen, und erhielt so die Wetterdynamite. Außer kristallwasserhaltigen Salzen hat man dann auch Salze angewandt, welche sich unter Gasentwicklung zersetzen, wie Bikarbonate, Oxalate u. a.

Das früher in Deutschland hergestellte Wetterdynamit enthielt 52 Prozent Sprengöl, 13 Prozent Kieselgur und 35 Prozent kristallisierte Soda. Zwei englische Wetterdynamite hatten folgende Zusammensetzung: I. 40 Prozent Gurdynamit, 45 Prozent Ammonoxalat, 15 Prozent Natronsalpeter; II. 31 bis 34 Prozent Nitroglyzerin, 11 bis 14 Prozent Kieselgur, 47 bis 51 Prozent Magnesiasulfat und 4 bis 6 Prozent Kalisalpeter.

In Belgien wird noch viel fabriziert: Grisoutit mit 44 Prozent Sprengöl, 44 Prozent Magnesiasulfat ($MgSO_4 + 7\,H_2O$), 12 Prozent Zellulose; Dynamite antigrisouteuse mit 44 Prozent Sprengöl, 44 Prozent Natriumsulfat ($Na_2SO_2 + 10\,H_2O$), 12 Prozent Holzmehl; ersteres ist sicher bis zu 300 g, letzteres bis 650 g.

c) Karbonite. Die Karbonite wurden von C. E. Bichel in die Sprengtechnik eingeführt und stellen Gemenge von 25 bis 30 Prozent Sprengöl mit 25 bis 40 Prozent Roggenmehl und mit ebensoviel Kali- oder Natronsalpeter dar; manchmal finden sich Zusätze von anderen Salzen.[1] Diese Sprengstoffe sind als schwache Mischdynamite zu charakterisieren. Zur Herstellung der Karbonite werden zunächst Salpeter und Mehl nach voraufgegangener Trocknung und feinster Vermahlung miteinander gemischt; die weitere Verarbeitung erfolgt in besonderen Mischmaschinen, wobei in das durch Flügel umgerührte Pulver in feinem Strahle Nitroglyzerin einfließt.

Die Karbonite (nach Brotteig riechende graue Masse) gefrieren in der Kälte; Zündung der Karbonite mit Sprengkapsel 5 oder 6. Infolge der relativ großen Menge Kohlehydrat (Mehl) kann nicht aller Kohlenstoff zu Kohlensäure verbrennen, die Nachschwaden enthalten vielmehr nicht unerhebliche Mengen Kohlenoxyd und sind in der Regel brennbar. — Karbonite besitzen hohe Schlagwettersicherheit.

Bichel (Glückauf 1904, S. 1043) gibt nachfolgende Daten:

plosionsprodukte können alsdann in die Bohrungen eintreten, auf das Salz einwirken und ihre Wärme der ganzen Längsoberfläche des Salzes mitteilen; aus letzterem wird das Kristallwasser in Freiheit gesetzt, der entwickelte Dampf trägt zur effektiven Wirkung der Ladung gleichfalls bei.

[1] D.R.P. 97 852 schützt den teilweisen Ersatz des Salpeters durch Chromate, Bichromate oder Permanganate.

	Zusammensetzung	Normalausbauchung im Bleiblock in ccm	Menge der entwickelten Kalorien pro kg Sprengstoff in Kal.	Schwadenanalyse nach Gewichtsprozenten	Flammenlänge von 100 g Sprengstoff in cm	Flammendauer von 100 g Sprengstoff in $^1/_{1000}$ Sek.	Detonationszeit von 100 g in $^1/_{1000}$ Sek.	Detonationsgeschwindigkeit per Sekunde in m	Verhältnis von Detonationszeit zur Flammendauer	Errechnete Temperatur aus den Kal. u. Schwadenanalysen	Grenzgewicht des Sprengstoffs, welches Schlagwetter noch nicht zündet in g
Kohlenkarbonit	25 Nitroglyzerin 34 Kalisalpeter 1 Barytsalpeter 38·5 Mehl 1 Lohmehl 0·5 Soda	213	506	34·4 CO_2 21·1 CO 2·7 H 13·8 N 5·0 H_2O 22·0 K_2CO_3	41	0·31	0·036	2700	1:8,7	1561°	1100
Karbonit . .	25 Nitroglyzerin 30·5 Kalisalpeter 4 Barytsalpeter 40 Lohmehl 0·5 Soda	235	576	32·1 CO_2 20·5 CO 0·9 H 0·8 CH_4 9·7 N 9·6 H_2O 22 K_2CO_3 3 BaO 1·4 Na_2CO_3	40	0·33	0·053	2443	1:6,5	1874°	1100
Karbonit I .	25 Nitroglyzerin 30·5 Natronsalpeter 39·5 Mehl 5 Kaliumbichromat	240	536	31·05 CO_2 19·25 CO 1·0 H 1·95 CH_4 11·54 N 12·3 H_2O 18·7 Na_2CO_3 1·65 K_2CO_3 2·56 Cr_2O_3	45	0·47	0·030	3042	1:15	1666°	1000
Karbonit II .	30 Nitroglyzerin 24·5 Natronsalpeter 40·5 Mehl 5 Kaliumbichromat	258	602	32·22 CO_2 20·25 CO 1·0 H 1·95 CH_4 11·54 N 12·3 H_2O 18·7 Na_2CO_3 1·65 K_2CO_3 2·56 Cr_2O_3	48	0·53	0·038	2472	1:14	1639°	900

Die Dynamit-Aktiengesellschaft vorm. Nobel & Cie. gibt folgende Zusammenstellung:[1]

	Kalorien pro Gramm H_2O flüssig	Kalorien pro Gramm H_2O Dampf	Explosions-temperatur	Gasvolumen bei der Explosion	10 g geben Ausbauchung von	Ausbauchung im Verhältnis zum Gelat.-Dynamit	Sicher bis zu Gramm Ladung
Gelatinedynamit mit 65 Proz. gelat. Öl	1393	1242	2960°	720·0	432	100·0	—
Kohlenkarbonit	633	579	1773°	465·0	185	42·8	1000
Karbonit I	685	598	1933°	560·6	195	45·1	1000
Karbonit II	665	—	—	—	205	47·4	850
Nobels Wetterdynamit I	705	613	1877°	587·8	200	46·3	900
Nobels Wetterdynamit II	755	688	2003°	616·0	220	50·9	800

Nobels Wetterdynamit I hat die Zusammensetzung: 30 Prozent Nitroglyzerin, 31 Prozent Natronsalpeter, 36 Prozent Kohlehydrate, 2 Prozent Naphtalin, 1 Prozent Alaun;

Nobels Wetterdynamit II besteht aus 25 Prozent Nitroglyzerin, 1 Prozent vegetabilischem Öl, 32 Prozent Natronsalpeter, 37 Prozent Kohlehydraten, 5 Prozent Alaun.

In Belgien werden unter den Bezeichnungen: Colinite antigrisouteuse, Forcite antigrisouteuse, Minite, Sécurophore III Sprengstoffe hergestellt, welche genau die Zusammensetzung des Kohlenkarbonits haben.

In England werden eine ganze Reihe Sprengstoffe nach dem Typus des Karbonits fabriziert, wie nachfolgende Übersicht zeigt.

	Britonit	Cambrit	Karbonit	Nobel-Karbonit	Clydit	Kolax
Nitroglyzerin	27—25	27—25	27—25	27—25	27—23	26—24
Kalisalpeter	34—31	32—28	36—30 (Kalisalpeter und Barytsalpeter)	32—28	—	27—25
Barytsalpeter	—	4·5—3·25		4·5—3·5	36—29·5	6—4
Holzmehl	43—49	42—36	42—39	42—39	41·5—35·5	32—29
Soda	0·5	0·5 (Soda und Calciumkarbonat)	0·5	0·5	0·5	—
Calciumkarbonat	—					—
Geschwefeltes Benzol	0·5	0·5	0·5	0·5	0·5	—
Stärke	—	—	—	—	—	10—8

[1] Untersuchung von Sicherheitssprengstoffen in Zeitschrift für Schieß- und Sprengstoffwesen 1906.

	Kynit	Kynit cond.	Pitit	Tutol	Victorit
Nitroglyzerin . . .	27—25	26—24	27—25	26—24	27—25
Kalisalpeter . . .	—	—	—	34·5—32	—
Barytsalpeter . . .	36—40	34·5—31·5	35—31	3—1	36—32
Holzmehl	42—39	7—5	43—40	38—35	41·5—38·5
Soda	—	—	} 0·5	0·5	} 0·5
Calciumkarbonat . .	0·5	0·5		—	
Geschwefeltes Benzol	—	—	—	—	0·5
Stärke	—	32·5—36	—	—	—

d) Wenn man bei den Karboniten statt des flüssigen Nitroglyzerins gelatiniertes Sprengöl anwendet, so erhält man Gelatinekarbonite oder wettersichere Gelatinedynamite. In England werden z. B. folgende Sprengstoffe fabriziert:

	Karbonit extra	Phönix-Pulver	Haylit No. 1	Oaklit No. 1
Nitroglyzerin . . .	36—34	31—28	27—25	26—24
Nitrozellulose . . .	0·5—0·1	1	1·5—0·5	1·5—0·5
Kalisalpeter	27—24	34—30	21—19	35·5—32·5
Barytsalpeter . . .	5—3	—	21—19	—
Holzmehl	35—31	37—33	14—12	36·5—33·5
Gelat. Kieselsäure . .	—	—	8—6	—
Ammonoxalat . . .	—	—	12—10	—
Soda	—	—	—	—
Magnesiakarbonat .	—	—	—	0·5

In Deutschland wendet man da, wo gelatiniertes Sprengöl gebraucht wird, statt des Kali- oder Natronsalpeters den wirksameren Ammonsalpeter an und stellt also wettersichere Ammongelatinedynamite her. Hierher gehören Gelatinekarbonit der Karbonitfabrik, bestehend aus 25·3 Prozent Sprengöl, 0·7 Prozent Kollodiumwolle, 6·9 Prozent Glyzerinleimgelatine, 25·6 Prozent Chlornatrium und 45·5 Prozent Ammonsalpeter. Ausbauchung im Bleiblock 317 ccm, Wettersicherheit 500 g. — Der Sprengstoff hat das hohe spezifische Gewicht von 1·6, so daß eine Ladedichte von 1·3 bis 1·4 mindestens erreichbar sein wird; der Sprengstoff wird blau gefärbt geliefert, ist weich und plastisch und läßt sich gut in das Bohrloch einpressen. — Hierbei ist zur Erhöhung der Sicherheit ein starker Zusatz von Chlornatrium angewandt; ein ähnlicher Sprengstoff (bestehend aus 25 Prozent Nitroglyzerin, 0·6 Prozent Kollodiumwolle, 6·8 Prozent

Leimglyzeringelatine [Leim:Glyzerin = 1:3·5], 24 Prozent Natronsalpeter, 43·6 Prozent Ammonsalpeter) ist nur bis zu 300 g sicher; ersetzt man in letzterer Mischung wiederum 15 Prozent Ammonsalpeter durch 15 Prozent Chlorammonium (nach D.R.P. 175391), so erhöht sich die Wettersicherheit auf 400 g.

Die Dynamitgesellschaft Nobel hat sich die Aufgabe gestellt, den Karboniten (und ähnlichen schwächeren Nitroglyzerinsprengstoffen mit 30 bis 40 Prozent Sprengöl) eine Plastizität zu geben, welche durch die 2 bis 3 Prozent (vom Gewicht des Nitroglyzerins) Kollodiumwolle (im ganzen etwa 0·7 Prozent Kollodiumwolle) nicht zu erzielen ist. Gelatinedynamite mit 65 Prozent gelatiniertem Öl sind vollständig plastisch und gelatinös; dagegen sind die Karbonite krümelig und bröckelig und schmiegen sich daher beim Gebrauch nicht so gut an die Bohrlochwandungen an.

Nach dem D.R.P. 182030 werden nun (an Stelle der bisher üblichen wasserunlöslichen Kohlenstoffträger) ganz oder teilweise in Wasser lösliche amorphe Kohlehydrate (wie Stärke, Gummiarten, Dextrin) zur Nitroglyzerin-Kollodiumwolle-Gelatine zugesetzt, und zwar beim Beginn des Gelatinierprozesses, wobei die erwähnten Kohlehydrate sich mit der Gelatine verbinden und sie „verlängern", ohne deren Plastizität zu beeinträchtigen. Es werden folgende Mischungsbeispiele gegeben:

I. 32 Prozent Nitroglyzerin, 0·7 Prozent Kollodiumwolle, 15·5 Prozent Dextrin, 1 Prozent vegetabilisches Öl, 35·8 Prozent Ammonsalpeter, 3 Prozent Ammonoxalat, 2 Prozent Holzmehl, 2 Prozent Chlornatrium, 8 Prozent Alaun.

II. 28 Prozent Nitroglyzerin, 0·7 Prozent Kollodiumwolle, 8·5 Prozent vegetabilisches Öl, 11 bis 12 Prozent Dextrin, 1·5 bis 2·5 Prozent Holzmehl, 39·7 Prozent Ammonsalpeter und 17·6 Prozent Chlornatrium.

III. 28 Prozent Nitroglyzerin, 0·7 Prozent Kollodiumwolle, 0·5 Prozent vegetabilisches Öl, 6·5 Prozent Dextrin, 0·5 Prozent Holzmehl, 45 Prozent Ammonsalpeter, 19·3 Prozent Kochsalz.

Die sub II genannte Mischung kommt als Nobelit auf den Markt; der Sprengstoff gibt 946 Kalorien (H_2O flüssig), bzw. 768 Kalorien (H_2O Dampf); die Explosionstemperatur beträgt 2068° C, das Gasvolumen bei der Explosion 635 Liter, 10 g Sprengstoff geben im Trauzl 280 ccm Ausbauchung (gegen 432 ccm von 65 prozentigem Gelatinedynamit); Nobelit ist sicher bis zu 550 g Ladung.

Die Klasse der wettersicheren Ammongelatinedynamite spielt gegenwärtig in Deutschland eine wesentliche Rolle; alle

Dynamitfabriken, welche Sicherheitssprengstoffe in den Handel bringen, stellen mindestens je einen derartigen Sprengstoff her; denn auf dieser Basis lassen sich sehr kräftige Sprengstoffe aufbauen und man ist der Ansicht, daß letztere sich auch verhältnismäßig wettersicher gestalten lassen, besonders wenn diese Sprengstoffe einen größeren Prozentsatz von Chlornatrium, Chlorkalium oder Chlorammonium enthalten; deshalb werden sie von den Steinkohlenbergwerken zurzeit sehr bevorzugt; es seien daher außer Gelatinekarbonit und Nobelit noch folgende erwähnt:

Wettersicheres Gelatinedynamit I der Westfälisch-Anhaltischen Sprengstoff-Aktiengesellschaft mit folgender Zusammensetzung: 40 Prozent Nitroglyzerin, 1 Prozent Kollodiumwolle, 27 Prozent Ammonsalpeter, 4 Prozent Kalisalpeter, 12·5 Prozent fettsaures Salz, 10 Prozent Roggenmehl, 3·5 Prozent flüssiger Kohlenwasserstoff und 2 Prozent Holzmehl; ähnliche Sprengstoffe mit der Bezeichnung Ia, Ib, II, III und IV werden von der gleichen Firma in den Handel gebracht. — Die Siegener Dynamitfabrik erzeugt ein Sicherheits-Gallertedynamit von der Zusammensetzung: 32·25 Prozent Nitroglyzerin, 1·25 Prozent Kollodiumwolle, 1·05 Prozent Leim, 1·05 Prozent Dextrin, 4·3 Prozent Glyzerin, 3·2 Prozent Wasser, 22·6 Prozent Ammonsalpeter, 10·8 Prozent Natronsalpeter, 18 Prozent Mehl, 5·5 Prozent Chlorkalium; die gleiche Firma liefert Fördit, bestehend aus 25·5 Prozent Nitroglyzerin, 1·5 Prozent Kollodiumwolle, 5 Prozent Nitrotoluol, 4 Prozent Dextrin, 3 Prozent Glyzerin, 37 Prozent Ammonsalpeter, 24 Prozent Chlorkalium. Bei den wettersicheren Gelatinedynamiten wird die größere Sicherheit hauptsächlich durch relativ große Beimengungen von Chlornatrium, Chlorkalium oder Chlorammonium erzielt.

Ein in Belgien gebrauchter Sprengstoff Securophor II hat folgende Zusammensetzung: 36·36 Prozent Nitroglyzerin, 0·91 Prozent Nitrozellulose, 24·55 Prozent Ammonsalpeter, 3·64 Prozent Kalisalpeter, 11·36 Prozent sebacinsaures Salz, 9·09 Prozent Roggenmehl, 1·82 Prozent Holzmehl, 3·18 Prozent flüssiger Kohlenwasserstoff, 9·09 Prozent Chlornatrium. Dieser Sprengstoff ist wettersicher bis zu 250 g.

Sicherheits-Sprengstoffe in England.[1] Seit dem Jahre 1896 besteht in England eine „Permitted List" und seit dem Jahre 1900 eine „Spezial List" von Sprengstoffen, welche auf Grund einer Prüfung in Woolwich aufgestellt werden. Das dort angenommene System ist von dem kontinentalen grundsätzlich verschieden. Während das letztere unbesetzte Schüsse in Betracht zieht, hat man in Eng-

[1] Bichel, Zeitschr. Schieß-Sprengstoffwesen II, S. 170.

land nur besetzte Schüsse untersucht; man nahm dort an, daß zuverlässig darauf gerechnet werden könne, daß nur gutbesetzte Schüsse zum Abschießen gelangen und daß daher unbesetzte Schüsse nicht berücksichtigt zu werden brauchten. Der englische Test besteht darin, daß man besetzte Schüsse aus einem Mörser in eine mit 15 Prozent Leuchtgas und 85 Prozent Luft gefüllte Kammer einer Versuchsstrecke von 72 cm Durchmesser und hinreichender Länge hineinfeuert, ohne daß Zündung erfolgen darf. Der Unterschied gegen das kontinentale System liegt also: 1. in dem viel geringeren Querschnitt der Strecke, welcher ein Ausweichen des Zündgemisches gegenüber den Explosionsgasen des Sprengstoffes schwieriger macht; 2. in der vergrößerten Empfindlichkeit des Zündgemisches von 15 Prozent Leuchtgas; in einem solchen Gemisch müssen alle bekannten Sicherheitssprengstoffe schon bei geringen Mengen Zündung herbeiführen, wenn ihre Explosionsgase damit in Berührung kommen; 3. in der Anbringung des Besatzes, welcher die Explosionsgase abkühlt und von der Berührung mit dem Zündstoff getrennt hält; 4. in der Unmöglichkeit der Feststellung einer Grenzladung, welcher Begriff bei diesem Test überhaupt keinen Sinn hat.

Nach der englischen Vorschrift wird verlangt, daß von 20 Schüssen mit Mengen, welche einen bestimmten Ausschlag des ballistischen Pendels geben, bei einem Besatz von 12 bzw. 9 Zoll kein Schuß eine Zündung ergeben darf; dabei muß stets volle Detonation der Schüsse eingetreten sein. Kohlenstaub wird in der Strecke nicht berücksichtigt.

Eine große Anzahl von Nitroglyzerinsprengstoffen, welche auf dem Kontinent nicht als sicher gelten, stehen daher auf der englischen Liste; es sind dies (außer den früher schon erwähnten Karboniten) folgende:

	Albionit	Rippit	Geloxit	Saxonit
Nitroglyzerin . . .	72—67·5	62·5—59·5	64—54	62—42·5
Nitrozellulose . .	6—4·25	4·5—3·5	5—4	5—2·5
Kalisalpeter . . .	9—7	20—18	22—13	27·5—16
Holzmehl	2·75—1·75	5·5—3·5	7—4	8—3·5
Kreide	0·5	—	—	0·5
Castoröl	—	1·5—0·5	—	—
Ammonoxalat . .	16—14	11—9	15—12	27—9

	Stowit	Celtit	Arkit	Frakturit
Nitroglyzerin . . .	61—58	59—56	54—51	53·5—51·5
Nitrozellulose . .	5—4·5	3·5—2	4—3	4—3
Kalisalpeter . . .	20—18	21—17	23—21	25—21
Holzmehl	7—6	9—8	8—6	7—5
Kreide	—	—	0·5	—
Castoröl	—	—	—	—
Ammonoxalat . .	13—11	13—11	16—14	16—14

Cornuailles-Pulver mit 57 bis 54 Prozent Nitroglyzerin, 4 bis 3 Prozent Nitrozellulose, 20 bis 17 Prozent Kalisalpeter, 7 bis 5 Prozent Holzmehl, 18 bis 16 Prozent Magnesiasulfat.

Cliffit mit 48 bis 45 Prozent Nitroglyzerin, 3·5 bis 2·5 Prozent Nitrozellulose und 45 bis 41 Prozent Stärke.

	Russelit	Coronit (Permitit)	Dragonit	Normanit
Nitroglyzerin	42—40	40—38	37—34	34·5—32·5
Nitrozellulose	2·75—1·75	1·3—0·8	3—2	2—1
Kalisalpeter	26—24	5—3	46—43	46·5—42·5
Ammonsalpeter	—	28—23	—	—
Ammonoxalat	24—22	—	—	12—10
Holzmehl	5—3	4—2	} 13·5—11	9—7
Holzkohle	—	—		2—1
Getreidemehl	—	11—8	—	—
Aluminiumstearat	—	14—11	—	—
Flüss. Kohlenwasserstoff	—	4—2	—	—
Vaselin	—	—	6·5	—
Calciumkarbonat	0·5	—	—	—

Zehnter Abschnitt.

Schwer gefrierbare Nitroglyzerinsprengstoffe.

Abgesehen von dem Umstande, daß gefrorene Nitroglyzerinsprengstoffe schlechtere Sprengwirkung und schädlichere Nachschwaden ergeben, ist mit denselben immer eine gewisse Gefahr verbunden, sowohl bei der Sprengarbeit selbst, als beim Transport, Auspacken usw., wobei als das Gefährlichste eine Mischung aus gefrorenem und nicht gefrorenem Nitroglyzerin angesehen wird. Auch das Auftauen ist eine recht gefährliche Manipulation, bei der z. B. in den Jahren 1875 bis 1902 in England 98 Unfälle eingetreten sind, wobei 71 Personen getötet und 112 verletzt wurden. — Man hat sich daher seit Einführung des Nitroglyzerins in die Sprengtechnik bemüht, nitroglyzerinhaltige Sprengstoffe mit möglichst niedriger Gefriertemperatur herzustellen. In seinem schwedischen Patent vom 30. April 1866 schlug A. E. Rudberg vor, dem fertig gewaschenen Sprengöl zur Herabsetzung seines Gefrierpunktes Benzol, Nitrobenzol oder einen anderen passenden Stoff beizumischen. — Alfred Nobel, der anfangs geglaubt hatte, durch sorgfältiges Trocknen das Nitroglyzerin schwer gefrierbar machen zu können, empfiehlt in seinem bekannten Patent vom

Jahre 1875 (Sprenggelatine) den Zusatz von Methyl- und Äthylnitrat, Nitrobenzol, Acetin, Biacetin und Triacetin als Mittel, um den Gefrierpunkt zu erniedrigen. — Mowbray erwähnt in seinem Buche „Nitroglycerin as applied in the Hoosac tunnel“ (Newyork 1874) eine Mischung von 30 Teilen Nitroglyzerin und 10 Teilen Nitrotoluol als unempfindlich gegen Schlag und schwer gefrierbar. — A. W. Wahlenberg und K. J. Sundström nahmen am 13. April 1877 ein schwedisches Patent auf Zusatz von 2 bis 10 Prozent Orthonitrotoluol, wodurch der Gefrierpunkt des Sprengöls auf -20^{0} sinke. — Andere Vorschläge, von Amark, Liebert u. a., wurden im historischen Überblick erwähnt. — Sigurd Nauckhoff[1] kommt auf Grund einer größeren physikalisch-chemischen Untersuchung zu dem Ergebnis, daß als Gefrierpunktserniedrigungsmittel nur Stoffe in Betracht kommen, die sich in Nitroglyzerin lösen und den Sprengstoff nicht allzusehr abschwächen, auch nicht so leicht sich verflüchtigen, daß der Sprengstoff bei längerer Aufbewahrung etwas davon verliert; der Zusatz soll möglichst selbst ein Lösungsmittel für die Nitrozellulose sein, jedenfalls der Gelatinierung der letzteren nicht entgegenwirken; ferner darf die Stabilität des Sprengstoffes nicht darunter leiden. Nauckhoff empfiehlt gleichfalls die Nitroverbindungen der Benzol-Kohlenwasserstoffe, besonders das Nitrobenzol wegen seines niedrigen Molekulargewichtes. — In der Praxis werden insbesondere Zusätze von Nitrobenzol und ortho-Nitrotoluol häufig angewandt. — Die Sprengstoffwerke Dr. R. Nahnsen & Cie. in Hamburg stellen ein sog. Gummidynamit her (spez. Gew. 1·49) aus gelatiniertem Nitroglyzerin, dem einige Prozente Nitrobenzol beigemischt sind, und Ammonsalpeter. — In Österreich werden fabriziert:

Dynamit I schwerfrierbar, bestehend aus 55 Prozent Nitroglyzerin, 2 Prozent Kollodiumwolle, 10 Prozent Nitrotoluol, 8 Prozent Holzmehl, 24 Prozent Natronsalpeter, 0·5 Prozent Totenkopf, 0·5 Prozent Soda; Farbe braunrot; 20 g Sprengstoff geben im Trauzl eine Ausbauchung von 1350 bis 1450 ccm (einschließlich 160 ccm ursprünglichen Laderaums).

Dynamit II schwerfrierbar, bestehend aus 38·5 Prozent Nitroglyzerin, 1·5 Prozent Kollodiumwolle, 8 Prozent Nitrotoluol, 0·52 Prozent Kienruß, 4·16 Prozent Holzmehl, 3·12 Prozent Roggenmehl, 43·68 Prozent Natronsalpeter, 0·52 Prozent Totenkopf; Farbe: schwarz; Ausbauchung von 20 g: 1100 bis 1250 ccm. — Diese schwerfrierbaren Dynamite dürfen bei -5^{0} noch nicht fest werden.

[1] Zeitschr. angew. Chemie 1905, S. 11 u. 53.

Das ungefrierbare Nobelit (Sicherheitssprengstoff) der Dynamit-Aktiengesellschaft vorm. Nobel & Cie. in Hamburg besteht aus 28·05 Prozent Sprengöl, 1·2 Prozent Kollodiumwolle, 4·95 Prozent Nitrotoluol, 0·3 Prozent Holzmehl, 43·9 Prozent Ammonsalpeter und 21·6 Prozent Kochsalz. — Ein ähnlicher Sprengstoff, der bei -10^0 flüssig bleiben soll, wird von Blochmann erwähnt; Zusammensetzung: 28 Prozent Trinitroglyzerin, 12 Prozent Mononitrotoluol, 1·5 Prozent Kollodiumwolle, 1 Prozent Holzmehl und 57·5 Prozent Ammonsalpeter.

A. Leroux[1] empfahl den Zusatz von festen Nitrotoluolen, insbesondere von Dinitrotoluol und Trinitrotoluol; eine Beimengung von 10 Prozent soll den Gefrierpunkt des Sprengöls bis auf -25^0 herunterdrücken. Der Sprengstoff Salit besteht aus 11·77 Prozent Trinitroglyzerin, 0·54 Prozent Kollodiumwolle,. 8·46 Prozent Dinitrotoluol, 53·63 Prozent Ammonsalpeter, 2·52 Prozent Dextrin und 23·08 Prozent Kochsalz.

Im Dezember 1902 fand auf der Zeche Gneisenau bei Dortmund eine Explosion von gefrorenem Dynamit statt, die größeren Schaden anrichtete und Veranlassung gab, sich mit der Herstellung schwer gefrierbarer Dynamite neuerdings besonders intensiv zu beschäftigen. Am 15. August 1903 wurde das Mikolajczaksche Patent auf Herstellung und Verwendung von Glyzerindinitrat eingereicht, und seitdem gebraucht die Sprengstoffindustrie neben dem leicht gefrierbaren Trinitroglyzerin auch andere Glyzerinnitrate von niedrigem Erstarrungspunkt als Basis von Dynamiten.

1. Anwendung von Glyzerindinitrat (Dinitroglyzerin, Diöl). Mikolajczak gibt folgende Beispiele:

a) Gurdynamite. 45 Prozent Dinitroglyzerin, 30 Prozent Trinitroglyzerin, 2 Prozent Kreide, 23 Prozent Kieselgur. — 41 Prozent Diöl, 34 Prozent Triöl, 1 Prozent Kreide, 24 Prozent Gur. — 12·5 Prozent Diöl, 62·5 Prozent Triöl, 1 Prozent Kreide, 24 Prozent Gur. — 17 Prozent Diöl, 58 Prozent Triöl, 2 Prozent Kreide, 23 Prozent Gur. — b) Sprenggelatine. 14 Prozent Diöl, 78 Prozent Triöl, 8 Prozent Kollodiumwolle. — c) Gelatinedynamite. 61 Prozent Diöl, 1·8 Prozent Kollodiumwolle, 30 Prozent Kalisalpeter, 7·2 Prozent Holzmehl. — 38·4 Prozent Diöl, 25·6 Prozent Triöl, 1·7 Prozent Kollodiumwolle, 27 Prozent Natronsalpeter, 7·3 Prozent Holzmehl. — 40 Prozent Diöl, 1·2 Prozent Kollodiumwolle, 8·3 Prozent Holzmehl, 50·5 Prozent Kalisalpeter. — d) Ammongelatinedynamite. 40 Prozent Diöl, 1·2 Prozent

[1] Kongreßbericht Rom 1906, Bd. II, S. 576. — Vgl. englische Patente 14627 und 25797 vom Jahre 1903; in letzterem wird ein Gemenge von $^4/_5$ Dinitrotoluol und $^1/_5$ Trinitrotoluol empfohlen.

Kollodiumwolle, 4·8 Prozent Curcumamehl, 54 Prozent Ammonsalpeter. — 40 Prozent Diöl, 1·2 Prozent Kollodiumwolle, 7·2 Prozent Holzmehl, 23·6 Prozent Ammonsalpeter, 28 Prozent Kalisalpeter. — 30 Prozent Diöl, 1 Prozent Kollodiumwolle, 6 Prozent Stärke, 2 Prozent Ferrocyankalium, 24 Prozent Natronsalpeter und 37 Prozent Ammonsalpeter.

Die Castroper Sicherheitssprengstoff-Aktiengesellschaft, welche auf Grund der Mikolajczakschen Patente eine Fabrik in Rummenohl errichtet hat, fabriziert folgende Sicherheitssprengstoffe:

Tremonit S I, bestehend aus 35 Prozent Diöl, 1 Prozent Kollodiumwolle, 1·7 Prozent Holzmehl, 7·4 Prozent Natronoxalat, 6 Prozent Salmiak, 8 Prozent Kochsalz, 40·9 Prozent Ammonsalpeter. Ausbauchung von 10 g im Trauzl: 337 ccm; Wettersicherheit: 700 g.

Tremonit S II, bestehend aus 33 Prozent Dinitroglyzerin, 1 Prozent Kollodiumwolle, 12 Prozent Erbsenmehl, 2·5 Prozent Trinitrotoluol, 25 Prozent Kochsalz und 26·5 Prozent Ammonsalpeter.

Es ist leicht verständlich, daß bei sonst gleicher Zusammensetzung das Diöl als nur zweifach nitriertes (bzw. durch Salpetersäure esterifiziertes) Glyzerin sprengtechnisch weniger leistet als das Trinitrat; im Trauzl gibt ein 75prozentiges Gurdynamit bei Trinitroglyzerin als Basis eine Ausbauchung von 345 ccm, bei Dinitrat eine solche von 290 ccm; doch läßt sich dieser Nachteil durch geeignete Zusammensetzung der Sprengstoffe ausgleichen. — Besonders zweckmäßig ist es, Mischungen von Di- und Trinitrat zu verwenden; ein Gemenge von $^3/_5$ Di- und $^2/_5$ Triöl bleibt auch bei der stärksten Winterkälte flüssig. Die Zersetzung des Diöls erfolgt nach der Gleichung:

$$2C_3H_5OH(ONO_2)_2 = 6CO_2 + 2H_2O + 4H_2 + 2N_2;$$

hier ist also nicht genügend Sauerstoff vorhanden, um den freiwerdenden Wasserstoff zu Wasser zu verbrennen; dagegen entsteht bekanntlich beim explosiven Zerfall des Trinitrates freier Sauerstoff im Überschuß, so daß Gemische von Di- und Triöl den größten Effekt geben. — Wenn trotzdem z. B. in Rummenohl Sprengstoffe auf Basis von Dinitrat allein fabriziert werden, so liegt der Grund hierfür wohl darin, daß für Herstellung von Diöl und reinen Diölsprengstoffen die Konzessionsbedingungen leichtere sind.

Die Hygroskopizität des Dinitroglyzerins scheint sich in der Praxis nicht unangenehm fühlbar zu machen; nach Volpert[1] ist

[1] Zeitschr. Schieß-Sprengstoffwesen I, S. 167.

ein mäßiger Wassergehalt der Dinitroglyzerinsprengstoffe auf die Haltbarkeit und praktische Wirksamkeit derselben nicht von schädigendem Einfluß. Es wurden in gelatinösen, Ammonsalpeter enthaltenden Dinitroglyzerinsprengstoffen das eine Mal dem Öl absichtlich wenige Prozente Wasser zugesetzt, das andere Mal nicht; auch im ersteren Falle blieben die Sprengstoffe nach monatelanger Lagerung gut; bei Sprengversuchen in der Grube zeigte sich kein Unterschied zwischen den wasserfreien Dinitroglyzerinsprengstoffen und den anderen. Nach dem gleichen Autor eignen sich Glyzerindinitratsprengstoffe auch zu Sprengungen unter Wasser.

2. Verwendung von Dinitromonochlorhydrin.

Hierüber hat F. Roewer[1] ausführliche Mitteilungen gemacht. Danach wird schon bei einem Zusatz von 5 bis 10 Prozent Dinitromonochlorhydrin zu Nitroglyzerin eine beträchtliche Herabsetzung des Gefrierpunktes des Nitroglyzerins bzw. der damit hergestellten Sprengstoffe erreicht. Mit einem Zusatz von ca. 20 Prozent Dinitromonochlorhydrin erzielt man für die in Deutschland in Betracht kommenden Wintertemperaturen schon ungefrierbare Nitroglyzerinsprengstoffe; in kälteren Ländern wird man den Zusatz eventuell etwas erhöhen müssen. Es wurden Gefrierversuche vorgenommen mit verschiedenen Nitroglyzerinsprengstoffen (wie Gurdynamit, Sprenggelatine, Gelatinedynamit), die aus Sprengöl hergestellt waren, welches 80 Prozent Trinitroglyzerin und 20 Prozent Dinitromonochlorhydrin enthielt. Patronen solcher Sprengstoffmischungen wurden in den üblichen Durchmessern bei Frostperioden von sechs bis acht Tagen, während welcher die Temperatur zwischen $+1^0$ und -12^0 schwankte, ohne jeglichen Schutz ins Freie gelegt, wobei keine der Patronen gefror, während die gleichzeitig zur Kontrolle ausgelegten gewöhnlichen Trinitroglyzerinsprengstoffe sämtlich gefroren. Auch mit Kältemischungen wurden viele Versuche in der Weise vorgenommen, daß man die Patronen in geschlossenen Metallbehältern in ein konstantes Kältegemisch von -15^0 bis -18^0 derart einbettete, daß die Behälter allseitig von der Kältemischung umgeben waren; den Metallbehälter ließ man 14 Tage ohne Unterbrechung in dem Kältegemisch stehen; hierbei zeigte sich allerdings, daß bei einem der Versuche einmal eine Patrone mit 20 Prozent Dinitromonochlorhydrinzusatz zum Teil erstarrt war, während alle anderen plastisch geblieben waren; dagegen war bei Patronen mit 25 Prozent Zusatz von Dinitromonochlorhydrin keine einzige gefroren.

---

[1] Zeitschr. Schieß-Sprengstoffwesen I, S. 228.

Versuche im Trauzl ergaben folgende Resultate:

	Gurdynamit	Sprenggelatine	Gelignite
	Ausbauchung	Ausbauchung	Ausbauchung
a) Aus Trinitroglyzerin gefertigt	300 ccm	555 ccm	395 ccm
b) Aus Trinitroglyzerin + 20 Proz. Zusatz Dinitromonochlorhydrin gefertigt	301 ccm	541 ccm	384 ccm

Im ballistischen Pendel wurden folgende Resultate erhalten:

	Gurdynamit	Sprenggelatine	Gelignite
a) Aus Trinitroglyzerin gefertigt	74·024 kgm	111·391 kgm	90·816 kgm
b) Aus Trinitroglyzerin + 20 Proz. Dinitromonochlorhydrin-Zusatz gefertigt	75·916 kgm	111·391 kgm	88·451 kgm

Folgende rechnerische Daten werden mitgeteilt:

	Wärmemenge bei Detonation pro 1 kg Sprengstoff entwickelt	Explosionstemperatur	Gasmenge pro 1 kg Sprengstoff bei der Explosion
a) 65 prozentiges Gelatinedynamit von der Zusammensetzung: 63 Proz. Trinitroglyzerin 2 „ Kollodiumwolle 26 „ Natronsalpeter 9 „ Zellulose	1244 Kalorien	2939° C	7167·7 Liter
b) 65 prozentiges Gelatinedynamit von der Zusammensetzung: 50·4 Proz. Trinitroglyzerin 2·0 „ Kollodiumwolle 12·6 „ Dinitromonochlorhydrin 26·6 „ Natronsalpeter 9·0 „ Zellulose	1278 Kalorien	2835° C	6872·3 Liter

Das Dinitromonochlorhydrin hat den Nachteil, bei der Detonation freie Salzsäure zu entwickeln; da solche unter Tag Belästigungen der Arbeiter hervorrufen könnte, so muß für die Absättigung der Säure gesorgt werden. Man setzt daher dem Sprengstoff entweder Alkalinitrate zu, dann neutralisiert das sich bei der Detonation bildende Natriumkarbonat die Salzsäure unter Bildung von Chlornatrium; oder man fügt Metalle zu, dann werden die betreffenden Metallchloride gebildet. Durch die Entstehung von Chlornatrium bzw. Metallchlorid wird die Schlagwettersicherheit der Sprengstoffe erhöht.

In der Praxis erzeugt man das Gemisch von Trinitroglyzerin und Dinitromonochlorhydrin in der Weise, daß man ein Gemisch von Glyzerin und Monochlorhydrin nitriert, und zwar in solchem Verhältnis, daß ein Sprengöl von der gewünschten Zusammensetzung erhalten wird. Die Nitrierung verläuft schneller als bei reinem Glyzerin, da die freiwerdende Wärmemenge geringer ist.

3. Verwendung von nitrierten Polyglyzerinen.

Nach Will bleibt Tetranitroglyzerin auch bei sehr hohen Kältegraden flüssig oder wenigstens zähe, ebenso Gemenge von Tetranitrodiglyzerin mit Trinitroglyzerin, so daß ein verhältnismäßig geringer Prozentgehalt eines Glyzerins, 20 bis 25 Prozent Diglyzerin, genügt, um ein Gefrieren des daraus beim Nitrieren entstehenden Produktes bei in Betracht kommenden Wintertemperaturen zu verhindern. Will schlägt also vor, Glyzerin zunächst durch Erhitzen auf 295° zu polymerisieren, hierauf mit frischem Glyzerin auf etwa 20 bis 25 Prozent Diglyzeringehalt zu verdünnen und dann wie üblich zu nitrieren. Ein mit einem solchen Produkt hergestellter 75prozentiger Gurdynamit gab die gleiche Bleiblockausbauchung wie aus reinem Trinitroglyzerin hergestellter, war aber auch bei andauernder Abkühlung auf Temperaturen von —15 bis —20° nicht zum Erstarren zu bringen.

Nach dem amerikanischen Patent 855595 wird Glyzerin durch längeres Kochen am Rückflußkühler zum Teil in Diglyzerin übergeführt und das erhaltene Gemisch allmählich bei 10 bis 15° in eine Mischung von 58 Teilen Schwefelsäure, 29 Tln. Salpetersäure und 13 Tln. Wasser einfließen gelassen. Das Produkt, ein aus Trinitroglyzerin und Tetranitrodiglyzerin bestehendes Sprengöl, das infolge des Gehalts an letzterem auch bei —15° bis —20° nicht gefriert, dient als Ausgangsmaterial für Dynamite.

In dem amerikanischen Patent 852142 werden folgende Zusammensetzungen angegeben:

Schwer gefrierbare Mischdynamite. a) 25 Prozent Trinitroglyzerin, 15 Prozent Tetranitrodiglyzerin, 50 Prozent Natronsalpeter, 10 Prozent Holzmehl. b) 15 Prozent Trinitroglyzerin, 15 Prozent Tetranitrodiglyzerin, 3 Prozent Schwefel, 2 Prozent Harz, 55 Prozent Natronsalpeter, 10 Prozent Holzmehl.

Schwer gefrierbares Gelatinedynamit. 20 Prozent Trinitroglyzerin, 10 Prozent Tetranitrodiglyzerin, 10 Prozent Kollodiumwolle, 27 Prozent Ammoniumnitrat, 30 Prozent Natriumnitrat.

4. Verwendung von gemischten Glyzerinestern.

Vender[1] setzt 10 bis 30 Prozent Dinitroformin oder Dinitroacetin dem Trinitroglyzerin zu und erhält so Dynamite, deren Erstarrungspunkt (in Berührung mit Nitroglyzerinkristallen) bis zu -20^{0} C heruntergeht; auch die nicht nitrierten Acetine kann man benutzen (vgl. französisches Patent 372267).

Elfter Abschnitt.

Ammonsalpeter-Sprengstoffe mit geringem Nitroglyzerinzusatz.

In neuerer Zeit haben die Ammonsalpeter-Sprengstoffe, welche der Hauptsache nach aus Ammonnitrat und Kohle oder Kohlenstoffträgern bestehen, eine außerordentliche Bedeutung erlangt; es sei an die Favier-Sprengstoffe, an Dahmenit, Roburit u. a. erinnert, welche kein Sprengöl enthalten. Ein Nachteil der reinen Ammonsalpeter-Sprengstoffe liegt in ihrer nicht immer vollständigen Detonation; man hat sich daher bemüht, durch Hinzufügung einer geringen Menge Nitroglyzerin die Ammonite empfindlicher zu machen.

So besteht der Sprengstoff Astralit aus 84·5 Prozent Ammonsalpeter, 1 Prozent Holzkohle, 7 Prozent Trinitrotoluol, 2·5 Prozent Paraffinöl, 1 Prozent Holzmehl und 4 Prozent Nitroglyzerin; Wetterastralit aus 74·5 Prozent Ammonsalpeter, 1 Prozent Holzkohle, 7 Prozent Trinitrotoluol, 2·5 Prozent Paraffinöl, 1 Prozent Holzmehl, 4 Prozent Nitroglyzerin und 10 Prozent Kochsalz. Thunderite enthält 92 Prozent Ammonsalpeter, 4 Prozent Mehl bzw. Stärke und 4 Prozent Trinitrotoluol.

Bei anderen Sprengstoffen wird das Sprengöl in gelatinierter Form angewandt, etwa 3·8 Prozent Trinitroglyzerin + 0·2 Prozent Kollodiumwolle.

[1] Zeitschr. Schieß-Sprengstoffwesen II, S. 21 u. 195.

So besteht Donarit aus 80 Prozent Ammonsalpeter, 12 Prozent Trinitrotoluol, 4 Prozent Mehl, 3·8 Prozent Nitroglyzerin, 0·2 Prozent Kollodiumwolle. Ammonkarbonit enthält 82 Prozent Ammonsalpeter, 10 Prozent Kalisalpeter, 4 Prozent Mehl oder Stärke, 3·8 Prozent Sprengöl, 0·2 Prozent Kollodiumwolle. — Ammonkarbonit I besteht aus 80·3 Prozent Ammonsalpeter, 5 Prozent Kalisalpeter, 6 Prozent Kohlenstaub, 4·5 Prozent Mehl bzw. Stärke, 4 Prozent Sprengöl, 0·2 Prozent Kollodiumwolle.

Durch diesen verhältnismäßig geringen Gehalt von etwa 4 Prozent Trinitroglyzerin oder gelatiniertem Trinitroglyzerin wird sichere und vollständige Detonation der Ammonsalpeter-Sprengstoffe herbeigeführt.

Über die Fabrikation wird folgendes mitgeteilt:

Zur Herstellung des Donarits werden die Materialien: feingepulverter Ammoniaksalpeter, Trinitrotoluol und Mehl auf tellerförmige, durch Dampf auf 80 bis 90° C erwärmte Mischpfannen gebracht und zur Verkleisterung des Mehles Wasser zugesetzt. Durch ein mit Schaufeln und Walzen versehenes Rührwerk wird die Mischung bewirkt und diese Bearbeitung fortgesetzt, bis ein völlig trockenes Pulver resultiert; dem in dieser Weise erhaltenen Pulver wird das Nitroglyzerin in einer besonderen Mischmaschine beigemengt; das Nitroglyzerin fließt in feinen Strahlen in den Mischkasten, in welchem durch eine Schaufelwelle das Pulver in fortwährender Bewegung gehalten wird. Die Aufsaugung des Nitroglyzerins und die gleichmäßige Durchmischung zur homogenen Masse erfolgen in vollkommener Weise. Der fertige Sprengstoff stellt ein wenig gefärbtes, beim Zusammendrücken etwas plastisches Pulver dar. Die Patronierung geschieht durch leichtes Einpressen des Pulvers in Papierhülsen; zum Schutze gegen Feuchtigkeit werden die Patronen mit einer Ceresinmischung überzogen.

Die Herstellung des Ammonkarbonits, der sich von Donarit durch Fehlen des Trinitrotoluols unterscheidet, erfolgt in sonst analoger Weise; der Sprengstoff wird in gewöhnliche Papierhülsen lose eingepreßt; zum Schutz gegen Feuchtigkeit sind die Patronen noch mit einer zweiten Papierhülle umgeben, welche mit einer Mischung aus Ceresin und Harz getränkt ist.

Über Donarit, Ammonkarbonit und Ammonkarbonit I gibt Bichel[1] nachstehende Daten:

---

[1] Glückauf 1904, S. 1043.

	Normalausbauchung im Bleiblock in ccm	Menge der entwickelten Kalorien pro 1 kg Sprengstoff	Schwadenanalyse nach Gewichtsprozenten	Flammenlänge von 100 g Sprengstoff in cm	Flammendauer von 100 g Sprengstoff in $^1/_{1000}$ Sekunden	Detonationszeit von 100 g Sprengstoff in $^1/_{1000}$ Sekunden	Detonationsgeschwindigkeit pro Sekunde in m	Verhältnis der Detonationszeit zur Flammendauer	Errechnete Temperaturen aus Kalorien und Schwadenanalysen	Grenzgewicht des Sprengstoffes, welches Schlagwetter noch nicht entzündet, in g
Donarit	450	836	29·7 CO_2 0·6 CO 35·8 N 33·9 H_2O	69	0·4	0·026	4137	1 : 15	2066°	130 (nicht wettersicher)
Ammonkarbonit . . .	260	609	12·3 CO_2 31·7 N 10·4 O 38·3 H_2O 7·3 K_2CO_3	51	0·28	0·038	3094	1 : 7·4	1648°	500 } Sicherheitssprengstoffe
Ammonkarbonit I . .	355	890	22·81 CO_2 29·16 N 1·71 O 39·83 H_2O 6·49 K_2CO_3	56	0·32	0·040	3195	1 : 8	2078°	300 } Sicherheitssprengstoffe

Über Astralit, Wetterastralit und Donarit hat die Dynamit-Aktiengesellschaft vorm. Alfred Nobel & Cie. in einer größeren Arbeit: „Untersuchung von Sicherheitssprengstoffen" (Zeitschr. Schieß-Sprengstoffwesen 1906) nähere Mitteilung gemacht.

In Frankreich werden folgende ähnliche Sprengstoffe hergestellt: Grisoutine A (mit 5 Prozent gelatiniertem Öl), bestehend aus 90·45 Prozent Ammonsalpeter, 4·85 Prozent Nitroglyzerin, 0·15 Prozent Kollodiumwolle, 4·55 Prozent Harz. — Grisoutine B (mit 6 Prozent gelatiniertem Öl), bestehend aus 94 Prozent Ammonsalpeter, 5·875 Prozent Nitroglyzerin und 0·125 Prozent Kollodiumwolle. — Dynamite de sûreté (mit 10 Prozent gelatiniertem Öl), bestehend aus 70·2 Prozent Ammonsalpeter, 9·9 Prozent Nitroglyzerin, 0·1 Prozent Kollodiumwolle und 19·8 Prozent Ammoncresilat.

Englische Sprengstoffe, die auf der List of permitted Explosives stehen und in diesen Abschnitt gehören, sind:

Abbcit und Monobel Powder (78 bis 82 Teile Ammoniumnitrat. 9 bis 11 Tle. Nitroglyzerin, 8 bis 10 Tle. Holzmehl, 0·5 bis 2·5 Tle. Feuchtigkeit);

Excellit (80 bis 84 Teile Ammoniumnitrat, 7 bis 9 Tle. Nitroglyzerin, 0·5 bis 1·5 Tle. Kollodiumwolle, 2·5 bis 3·5 Tle. Dinitrotoluol, 3·5 bis 4·5 Tle. Holzmehl, 0·5 bis 1·5 Tle. Castoröl, 0 bis 2 Tle. Feuchtigkeit).

Zwölfter Abschnitt.

Sprengstofflager.

In Preußen sind die Grundsätze als vorbildlich hingestellt worden, welche in der von dem Regierungspräsidenten zu Wiesbaden am 2. April 1902 erlassenen Anweisung enthalten sind und die nachstehend wiedergegeben werden:

Genehmigung zur Lagerung von Sprengstoffen.

Für die Lagerung selbst der kleinsten Mengen von Sprengstoffen ist eine besondere polizeiliche Erlaubnis notwendig. Für Schießpulver, Sprengsalpeter, brennbaren Salpeter, Feuerwerkskörper und Zündplättchen sind Ausnahmen insoweit zugelassen, als für die Lagerung kleiner Mengen bis zu gewissen Grenzen keine Genehmigung notwendig ist.

Für die Sprengstofflager, die unter Aufsicht der Bergbehörden stehen, sind diese Behörden, für alle übrigen Lager — einschließlich der Handelsniederlagen — die Polizeibehörden nach Maßgabe der Ministerialverordnung vom 11. September 1884 zur Erteilung der Genehmigung zuständig.

Für alle derartigen Genehmigungen sind die nachstehenden Bestimmungen zugrunde zu legen. Nur bei Niederlagen von geringem Umfange bis höchstens zu 5 kg, die nur vorübergehend für kurze Zeit benutzt werden — z. B. bei Brunnenarbeiten, Kanalisationsarbeiten, Ausschachtungen für Häuser usw. —, kann von einzelnen Vorschriften sowie von der Anlegung eines besonderen Aufbewahrungsraumes abgesehen werden, wenn in anderer Weise für genügende Sicherheit gegen Diebstahl und Schutz der Umgebung gesorgt wird. In solchen Fällen kann es z. B. genügen, vorzuschreiben, daß der Sprengstoff in einer hölzernen, starken und gut verschließbaren Kiste aufzubewahren ist, und daß allabendlich die nicht verbrauchten Sprengstoffreste in dieser Kiste an einem sicheren Ort in nicht bewohnten Räumen unterzubringen sind.

Die Verfügung ist aber auch in solchen Fällen schriftlich zu erlassen und ein entsprechender Vermerk in den Erlaubnisschein aufzunehmen.

I. Verbrauchslager an den Arbeitsstätten, welche höchstens 50 kg Sprengpulver oder 50 kg Sprengstoffe enthalten.

a) Lage.

Die Lager müssen von Wohnstätten, Eisenbahnen, öffentlichen Wegen und Landstraßen mindestens 100 m entfernt sein, sofern nicht die besonderen örtlichen Verhältnisse eine geringere Entfernung rechtfertigen. Von den Arbeitsstätten (Steinbrüchen) oder von sonstigen Plätzen, an denen Menschen sich regelmäßig aufhalten, müssen die Lager mindestens 50 m entfernt sein, soweit nicht durch die örtlichen Verhältnisse oder durch Errichtung von first-hohen Dämmen mit mindestens einfacher Böschung und einem Meter Kronenbreite ein ausreichender Schutz gegen etwaige Sprengwirkung erreicht werden kann. Direkte Schußlinien nach den Arbeitsplätzen müssen unbedingt — erforderlichenfalls durch Einrichtung von Schutzdämmen — vermieden werden. An den Zugängen zu den Arbeitsplätzen (Steinbrüchen) sowie innerhalb solcher Steinbrüche, welche noch betrieben werden, dürfen Lager nicht errichtet werden.

b) Bauart.

1. Die Lager sind in festem Gestein als einbruchsichere Nischen einzubauen oder massiv mit Wandstärke von etwa $1^1/_2$ Stein aufzuführen und mit Erdanschüttung zu umgeben. Die Ausführung aus Holzwerk wird provisorisch, jedoch nur mit kräftiger innerer und äußerer Verschalung zuzulassen sein.

2. Beim Nischenbau muß das Gestein über der Nische genügende Stärke haben und auch vor dem Türrahmen so weit vorstehen, daß letztere fest vermauert oder mit dem Gestein fest verankert werden kann.

3. Alle Magazine sind in besonders sorgfältiger Weise gegen Diebstahl zu sichern; solche Magazine, welche nicht unter ständiger Aufsicht stehen oder bei denen nicht in anderer zuverlässiger Weise für Sicherheit gegen Diebstahl gesorgt ist, müssen mit einem mindestens 2·25 m hohen Zaun von eingerammten, starken, dicht aneinander stehenden Pallisaden ohne äußere Querlatten, von starken, oben spitzen Eisenstäben, von Drahtgeflecht oder mit einer glatten, oben mit Glasscherben versehenen Steinmauer umgeben werden. Die Einfriedigung wird zweckmäßig oben auf den Wall gesetzt, mit Stacheldraht gesichert und mit einer verschließbaren Tür versehen.

4. Der Lagerraum muß genügend groß sein, um ein gefahrloses Hantieren mit den Sprengstoffen zu ermöglichen.

Die Zufuhrwege sind in ordnungsmäßigem Zustande zu erhalten.

5. Die Wände sind innen glatt in Zement zu verputzen oder mit glatter, hölzerner Innenverschalung zu versehen und mit heller Ölfarbe zu streichen.

6. Der Fußboden ist aus hohlliegenden, dichtgefugten Brettern herzustellen, in denen die Nägel zu versenken und zu verkitten sind; der Fußboden ist ferner mit starken Haardecken (Pferdedecken, Wolldecken) zu belegen.

7. Der Verschluß soll durch zwei hintereinander liegende, nach außen aufschlagende, starke, einbruchsichere Türen mit starken Beschlägen und Schlössern gebildet werden. Die Türbeschläge und Schwellen sind so einzurichten, daß gefährliche Reibung von Eisen auf Stein oder Eisen ausgeschlossen ist, erforderlichenfalls sind die reibenden Teile aus Messing herzustellen oder in geeigneter Weise mit Zink, Messing, Kupfer, Holz zu verkleiden. Die Schlüssel zu eisernen Schlössern sind aus Messing herzustellen.

Der Türrahmen oder die Angeln sind im Gestein oder im Mauerwerk fest zu verankern und zu vermauern. Das Mauerwerk oder das gewachsene Gestein (Türwangen) muß wenigstens 25 cm (1 Stein) vor der Tür vorstehen.

8. Das etwaige Dach der Lager ist gegen Einbruch kräftig zu bauen und bei hölzerner Bauart zweckmäßig mit Asphaltpappe oder präpariertem Segeltuch zu belegen. (Die vielfach übliche weitere Belegung der Dachfläche mit Steinen ist unzweckmäßig und würde nur die Wirkung etwaiger Explosionen auf die Umgebung vergrößern.)

9. Ventilationsöffnungen sind fest zu vergittern, innen mit Drahtgaze zu verschließen und so anzubringen, daß Regen nicht hineingelangen kann.

10. Jedes Lager ist mit einem Blitzableiter zu versehen, sofern nicht die Anlage eines solchen nach dem Urteile von Sachverständigen unmöglich oder zwecklos ist. Die Auffangestange ist auf dem Wall, nicht auf dem Lagerhause selbst, anzubringen und muß eine dementsprechende Höhe haben.

Die Leitungsdrähte sollen aus Kupfer oder Bronze bestehen.

Der Blitzableiter ist ständig in guter Ordnung zu halten und jährlich sachgemäß zu revidieren. Diese Revisionen sind in ein besonderes im Lager aufzubewahrendes Buch einzutragen und von dem betreffenden Revisor, der ausreichende Sachkunde besitzen muß, zu unterschreiben.

c) Benutzung.

1. Pulver und Dynamit dürfen nicht zusammen gelagert werden, sondern sind in getrennten Lagern unterzubringen.

Pulver ist am besten in einer gut verschlossenen Kanne von Zinkblech (nicht von Eisenblech oder Weißblech) aufzubewahren. Der Fußboden des Pulverlagerraums ist mit einer Haardecke (Pferdedecke, Wolldecke) zu belegen, die ab und zu auszuklopfen und von verstreutem Pulver sorgfältig zu reinigen ist. Auch außen vor der Tür darf kein Pulver oder Pulverstaub liegen. Dynamit und sonstige nitroglyzerinhaltige Sprengstoffe sind in einer starken und dichten, gegen Feuchtigkeit schützenden Holzkiste oder Zinkblechtrommel und nie offen aufzubewahren.

2. Zündhütchen (Sprengkapseln) und sonstige Zündstoffe sind nicht in demselben Behälter mit Dynamit, sondern nur getrennt für sich in einer besonderen, starken und dichten, verschlossenen Holzkiste unterzubringen.

Auch können Zündhütchen in einer derartigen Kiste in einem sonstigen unbewohnten Raum oder im Vorraume des Lagers aufbewahrt werden.

3. Im Lager darf nur Sprengstoff von der in der Genehmigung angegebenen Art und Menge aufbewahrt werden.

Pulvermagazine dürfen nur mit Filzschuhen betreten werden. Verstreuter Sprengstoff, Pulver usw. sind sofort zu beseitigen. Für größte Ordnung und Sauberkeit muß gesorgt werden, alle leeren Kisten, Hüllen usw. sind sogleich zu entfernen. Das Anzünden von Licht und Feuer und das Rauchen sind im Lagerraume strengstens zu untersagen. Sofern in der kalten Jahreszeit mit Dynamit gesprengt wird, ist ein Auftaukasten von Zinkblech zu beschaffen, Das Auftauen muß mittels warmen Wassers von nicht über 60 Grad Celsius geschehen.

In jedem Sprengstoffmagazine müssen stets geeignete Reinigungsgeräte — Haarbesen, Handfeger und Müllschippe — vorhanden sein, in Pulvermagazinen außerdem einige Paar Filzschuhe.

Die Lager sind stets unter Verschluß zu halten derart, daß sie von Unbefugten ohne Anwendung von Gewalt nicht geöffnet werden können.

Die Werkzeuge zum Öffnen der Packgefäße (Kisten und Tonnen) sowie zum Abmessen des Pulvers müssen aus Kupfer, Messing, Bronze, Zink, Holz sein.

4. Über den Empfang und die Ausgabe der unter das Reichsgesetz vom 9. Juni 1884 (Dynamitgesetz) fallenden Sprengstoffe hat der Verwalter des Magazins (Aufseher, Schießmeister usw.) ein Buch zu führen, welches den Zeitpunkt des Empfanges und der Verausgabung

und die Menge der Stoffe (Dynamitpatronen, Zündhütchen) nach Zahl oder Gewicht (bei Kisten auch deren Firma und Nummer) angibt. Auch ist der Name des Empfängers anzugeben, wenn der Verwalter die Sprengstoffe nicht persönlich verwendet.

II. Verbrauchslager, welche mehr als 50 kg Sprengpulver oder Sprengstoffe enthalten.

a) Lage.

Die Entfernung des Lagers von Wohnstätten oder zum Aufenthalte von Menschen dienenden Gebäuden, Arbeitsstätten, Verkehrswegen und Eisenbahnen richtet sich nach den besonderen Umständen des Einzelfalles.

Bei freier, ungedeckter Lage der in Betracht kommenden Punkte sind folgende Mindestentfernungen zu fordern:

150 m für Lager, welche 51 bis 250 kg,
250 m für Lager, welche 250 bis 1000 kg,
500 m für Lager, welche 1000 und mehr kg

an Sprengstoffen enthalten.

Diese Entfernungen können unter besonderen günstigen örtlichen Verhältnissen, z. B. Deckung durch Wald oder Berge, entsprechend verringert werden. Zweckmäßig geschieht die Anlage eines Lagers in verlassenen Steinbrüchen, in tief eingeschnittenen Tälern oder mitten in einem Walde.

Im übrigen finden die unter Ia angegebenen Vorschriften auch für die größeren Lager Anwendung.

b) Bauart.

Außer den unter Ib angegebenen Bestimmungen sind noch nachstehende zu beachten:

1. Sprengstofflager mit größeren Vorräten müssen außerdem bequeme, auch während des Winters sicher gangbare Zufuhrwege erhalten und geräumig genug sein, um die Sprengstoffe leicht und sicher ein- und ausbringen zu können. Läßt sich das Lager nicht in festem Gestein anlegen oder massiv in gewachsenes Erdreich eingraben, so wird es zweckmäßig in den Wandungen massiv, am besten aus Bimssandstein oder Kiesbeton, hergestellt werden. Im besonderen werden Lager für brisante Sprengstoffe vorteilhaft mit massiven Wänden und gewölbter Decke aus Kiesbeton so herzustellen sein, daß das Kappengewölbe allmählich in die nach unten stärker werdenden Seitenwände übergeht. Die geringste Stärke des Gewölbes und der Wände soll 38 cm betragen und die Korngröße des Kieses 20 mm nicht übersteigen.

Lager für Schwarzpulver sind entweder mit massiven Wänden und gewölbter Decke aus Bimssandstein (Schwemmsteinen) herzustellen oder mit leichtem, hölzernem Dache zu versehen. Wände und Decken sind innen glatt zu verputzen.

2. Die Fußböden der Sprengpulverlager müssen aus hohlliegender, dicht gefugter und mit versenkter Nagelung verlegter Holzdielung her-

gestellt und in ganzer Fläche mit Linoleum oder ähnlichen leicht zu reinigenden Stoffen belegt werden. Fußböden in Sprengstofflagern können auch aus glattem Zementbeton hergestellt werden, müssen dann aber in ganzer Fläche mit Linoleum belegt werden.

3. Als Verschluß der Lager sind zwei hintereinander liegende, nach außen aufschlagende, wetterfeste und einbruchsichere Türen von mindestens 1·6 m Höhe und 0·7 m Breite mit kräftigen Schlössern und Beschlägen anzubringen. In Schwarzpulverlagern sind die inneren Türen zweckmäßig aus Holz zu fertigen und sämtliche Türbeschläge so einzurichten, daß eine Reibung von Eisen auf Eisen vermieden wird.

Die Türen sind weiterhin so anzulegen, daß der Einfall direkten Sonnenlichtes in das Lager verhütet wird. Für größere Lager ist zu demselben Zweck ein Vorraum zwischen den beiden Türen von mindestens 1 m Tiefe anzulegen, welcher zweckmäßig zugleich zum Öffnen der Packgefäße benutzt wird.

4. Von der Umwallung des Lagers wird nur in ganz seltenen Fällen abgesehen werden können, wenn die natürlichen Bodenverhältnisse dies rechtfertigen. In allen anderen Fällen ist eine vollständige Umwallung notwendig. Die Wälle müssen einfache bis $1^1/_2$fache Böschung bei einer Kronenbreite von 1 m haben und mindestens bis zur Höhe der Dachfirst des Lagers reichen. Der Zugang zum Lager durch diesen Wall (Wallgang) ist in gebrochener Linie anzulegen, um keine direkten Schußkanäle zu erhalten.

Die Wälle müssen 1 m vom Gebäude entfernt stehen und gut begrast sein. Der Raum zwischen Wall und Gebäude ist von Gras und brennbaren Stoffen freizuhalten.

Die Lager sind gemäß den Vorschriften unter I b. 3 gegen Diebstahl zu sichern.

c) Benutzung.

Außer den bereits unter I gegebenen Bestimmungen sind noch nachstehende zu beachten:

1. Die Sprengstoffkisten müssen so aufgestellt werden, daß die Luft zwischen ihnen durchstreicht; dieselben dürfen im Lager nicht unmittelbar aufeinander gestapelt werden; nötigenfalls sind Latten zwischenzulegen. Fässer sind so festzulegen, daß sie nicht rollen.

2. Lager für nitroglyzerinhaltige Sprengstoffe sind mit einem Thermometer zu versehen, die Temperatur im Aufbewahrungsraume soll nicht unter $+8^0$ C sinken und nicht über $+30^0$ C steigen. Geschieht dies doch, so ist in geeigneter Weise für Regelung der Temperatur zu sorgen.

3. Falls eine Beleuchtung unbedingt notwendig wird, so hat dieselbe nur durch Sicherheitslampen zu erfolgen.

Über die Errichtung von Magazinen für brisante Sprengstoffe sagt eine preußische Ministerialverfügung vom 6. Februar 1900 folgendes:

Bei der Errichtung von Magazinen für brisante Sprengstoffe wird von den genehmigenden Behörden mit Recht daran festgehalten, daß die Bauart der Magazine für den Fall einer Explosion möglichst große Sicherheit der Umgebung gegen Sprengstücke gewährleisten soll. Für Magazine über Tag pflegt daher die Forderung aufgestellt zu werden, daß sie möglichst leicht oder wenigstens mit leichter Bedachung herzustellen sind. Gegen diese Bauart werden seit einiger Zeit Bedenken geltend gemacht, deren Berechtigung bis zu einem gewissen Grade anzuerkennen ist. Es muß u. a. zugegeben werden, daß die meistverbreitete Ausführung der Sprengstoffmagazine in Holzwerk nur geringen Schutz gegen äußere Gefahren, vor allem Blitz- und Feuersgefahr gewährt, und daß außerdem ebensowohl diese Art der Bauausführung wie die zur Sicherung der Umwohner meist gewählte isolierte Lage der Magazine die Entwendung von Sprengstoffen erleichtert. Von beteiligter Seite wurde daher darauf angetragen, für brisante Sprengstoffe Magazine aus Kiesbeton mit gewölbter Decke zuzulassen, denen neben ihrer Sicherheit gegen äußere Einflüsse vor allem nachgerühmt wurde, daß sie die Nachbarschaft nicht stärker gefährdeten, als leicht gebaute Magazine, da der Beton bei Explosionen in ungefährliche Bruchstücke zerfalle. Gleichzeitig wurde angeregt, entsprechende Sprengversuche auszuführen. Dieser Anregung zufolge haben unter Beteiligung der Militärverwaltung und der vereinigten Sprengstofffabriken vergleichende Sprengversuche zwischen Magazinen aus leichten Baustoffen (Hartgipsdielen, Zementplatten, leichte Monierkonstruktion, ohne Verwendung von Holz) und zwei solchen aus Kiesbeton auf dem Militärschießplatze in Kunnersdorf stattgefunden. Von letzteren enthielt das eine dieselbe Menge Sprengstoff wie die leicht gebauten Magazine, nämlich 1500 kg Gelatinedynamit, während es bei der Sprengung des zweiten Kiesbeton-Magazins darauf ankam, festzustellen, ob auch verhältnismäßig geringe Mengen dieses Sprengstoffes genügen würden, das Gefüge des Kiesbetons derart zu lockern, daß die Streuung größerer Sprengstücke vermieden würde. Es kamen daher bei diesem Versuche nur 500 kg Gelatinedynamit zur Anwendung. Die Bauart der Kiesbeton-Magazine war die eines Kappengewölbes von 2 m Spannweite bei 0·5 m Stärke im Scheitel, welches allmählich in die als Widerlager ausgebildeten Seitenwände überging, deren Stärke nach der Sohle zu bis auf 1·25 m zunahm. Senkrechte Endwände in dem gleichen Stampfbeton wie das Gewölbe und von 0·5 m Stärke schlossen das letztere beiderseits ab. In einer dieser Endwände befand sich der Zugang, der bei dem ersten Magazin zunächst in einen von dem Hauptmagazin getrennten Vorraum führte; letzterer kam bei dem zweiten Magazin in Wegfall. Die Zugangstüren waren bei dem ersten Sprengversuch aus starkem armierten Stahlblech, in Falzen dicht schließend, bei dem zweiten Versuch aus Holz mit Blechverkleidung hergestellt. In 2 m Entfernung war vor dem Eingange zu den Magazinen bei beiden Sprengversuchen ein Erdwall aufgeschüttet worden, um Sprengstücke, etwa von den Türen herrührend, aufzufangen.

Die bei der Sprengung der Kiesbeton-Magazine gewonnenen Erfahrungen reichen zwar nicht hin, um über alle in Betracht kommenden Fragen sicheren Aufschluß zu geben, jedoch darf mindestens als festgestellt erachtet werden, daß die Befürchtung, es werde bei der Explosion solcher Magazine die Umgebung der Sprengstelle durch Schleuderstücke in höherem Grade und auf weitere Entfernungen gefährdet, als dies bei den leicht gebauten Magazinen beobachtet worden ist, nicht zutreffend ist. Durch die Erschütterung der Explosion wird anscheinend ein Zerfall des gebundenen Zements herbeigeführt, mindestens aber der feste Zusammenhang so gelockert, daß nur verhältnismäßig kleine Stücke, die nicht einmal die größten Abmessungen der bei den vorausgegangenen Sprengungen leichter Magazine aufgefundenen erreichten, weggeschleudert wurden. Bei der Sprengung mit 1500 kg Dynamit waren die verbleibenden Schleuderstücke zudem so mürbe, daß sie mit der Hand zerdrückt werden konnten. Nur die bei dem ersten Versuch angewendeten eisernen Türen haben weiterfliegende Stücke geliefert, während die durch Blech verstärkte Holztür ziemlich vollständig zerstört wurde. Ferner scheinen die größeren Schleuderstücke der ersten Sprengung wesentlich aus dem Vorraum zum Magazin zu stammen, der von der Explosionsstätte am weitesten entfernt lag.

Es erscheint nach den Versuchen erwiesen, daß durch die Lagerung brisanter Sprengstoffe in einem aus Kiesbeton massiv und einbruchssicher hergestellten Magazin im Explosionsfalle die Umgebung durch Sprengstücke nicht stärker gefährdet wird, als dies bei der Lagerung in leicht gebauten Magazinen der Fall ist, und daß Magazine aus Kiesbeton einer über das jetzt übliche Maß hinausgehenden Schutzzone nicht bedürfen. Dabei ist vorausgesetzt, daß zu dem Beton Kies von einer 20 mm nicht übersteigenden Korngröße verwendet wird, daß die Verschlußtüren nicht durchweg aus starkem Eisen oder Stahl, sondern aus Holz mit Blechverkleidung bestehen, daß zum Auffangen von Schleuderstücken, die durch wagerecht verlaufende direkte Stoßwirkungen weggeschleudert werden, Wälle in den üblichen Abmessungen in möglichster Nähe um das Magazin aufgeschüttet und Vorräume, soweit es sich nicht um Ausgabemagazine handelt, tunlichst vermieden werden.

Auf Grund dieser Ergebnisse liegt kein Bedenken mehr vor, an Stelle leicht gebauter Magazine für brisante Sprengstoffe in der Folge solche aus Kiesbeton zuzulassen, sofern die vorerwähnten Voraussetzungen erfüllt werden. Unter Umständen möchte sogar solchen Magazinen der Vorzug vor den leichtgebauten zu geben sein.

Feuchtinger[1] gibt auf Grund der österreichischen Vorschriften nachfolgende Beschreibung von obertägigen und unterirdischen Magazinen:

[1] Spreng- und Zündmittelmagazine. Wien 1907.

a) Obertägiges Dynamitmagazin für Einlagerung von 25 bzw. 50 kg Dynamit. — Das Magazin ist als ein einfacher verschalter Holzriegelbau von ca. 1·6 m Länge, 1·35 m Breite und im Mittel 1·8 m Höhe ausgeführt, besitzt in ca. 70 cm Höhe über dem Terrain zwei außen stark beschlagene und gut absperrbare Türen (die einen Zwischenraum von ca. 20 cm Tiefe einschließen), hinter demselben einen 50 cm tiefen Manipulationsraum (nicht betretbar) und die eigentliche Einlagerungsnische (Dynamitdepotraum), die mit einer kleinen absperrbaren Lattentür gegen den genannten Vorraum abgegrenzt ist. Die Abmessungen der Nische entsprechen dem jeweilig begehrten Einlagerungsquantum von 25 bzw. 50 kg. — Die Originalkisten mit Dynamit ruhen auf gefalzten, 8 cm starken Kanthölzern und werden zwecks Entnahme der Dynamitpatronen in den Manipulationsraum vorgeschoben. Letzterer dient auch zur Aufnahme eines Thermometers und Vormerktafel, auf welcher das jeweilig eingelagerte Quantum ersichtlich zu machen ist. Die Entlüftung der Nische geschieht durch eine mit Sieben verschlossene Luftzuführung von außen, welche, um ein Einwerfen von Gegenständen usw. in das Magazindepot zu vermeiden, auf dem Wege zu den Außentüren (unterhalb derselben in der Holzverkleidung angelegte, erste vergitterte Luftzuführungsöffnung), dem Magazinszwischenboden (zweite vergitterte Öffnung) und der Lattentür der Nische zweimal rechtwinklig gebrochen erscheint. Die Seiten- und Rückwände des Magazins sind gegen das Eindringen von Erdfeuchtigkeit außen mit Dachpappe verkleidet; der ganze Holzbau ist mit Ausnahme der Stirnseite (Tür) durch eine 1 m hohe Überschüttung von steinfreier Erde gedeckt, deren Böschungen je nach ihrer Anlage berast, besämt oder durch Holzverschalungen gesichert werden. Die Abhaltung und Ableitung von Niederschlagswässern wird zweckmäßig durch Anlage von Sandschüttungen, Gräben bzw. Drainagen im Bereich des Magazins zu erzielen sein.

b) Unterirdische Sprengmittelmagazine. In der Regel sollen diese Magazine nach der Luftlinie mindestens 100 m von den in Betrieb stehenden Schächten, Füllorten und Belegorten entfernt sein. Bezüglich der in Betrieb stehenden Fahr- und Förderstrecken sowie der obertägigen Objekte sind bei einer Einlagerung bis maximal 100 kg Dynamit mindestens 100 m, bei mehr als 100 kg bis höchstens 250 kg mindestens 150 m und bei einer Einlagerung von mehr als 250 kg bis 500 kg mindestens 200 m Entfernung der Verbrauchsmagazine einzuhalten, wobei jedoch Erleichterungen zugestanden werden können. Die Zündmittelmagazine sind stets getrennt von den Sprengmittelverbrauchsmagazinen und ebenfalls so anzulegen, daß im Falle einer Explosion eine Rückwirkung ausgeschlossen erscheint. Ferner darf nur eine der Maximaleinlagerung im Verbrauchsmagazin entsprechende Menge des Zündmaterials in den Zündmittelmagazinen aufbewahrt werden. Die Verbrauchsmagazine sind in auf die Zugangsstrecke senkrecht stehende Umbruchsstrecken herzustellen, damit der Anprall der Gase im Falle einer Explosion voll gegen die gegenüberliegende Gesteinswand und nicht etwa gegen eine Fahr- oder Förderstrecke oder einen Schacht stattfinde. Die Magazins(Einlagerungs-)nische ist durch eine hölzerne, mittels Kunstschloß versperrbare Lattentüre (in versetzten Angeln) abzuschließen. Der eigentliche Magazinsraum ist mit einer eisernen Gittertür (gelochte Eisenblechtür) in versetzten Angeln mittels Kunstschloß abzusperren, da durch massive Türen die Spannung der Gase im Falle der Explosion erheblich vermehrt würde. Die Größe der Magazinsnische soll dem Sprengstoffquantum entsprechen. In den Zugangsstrecken ist in einer Minimalentfernung von 18 bis 20 m vom Verbrauchsmagazin eine zweite mittels Kunstschloß absperrbare (eisenbeschlagene, gelochte) Tür in versetzten Angeln anzubringen, an welcher die üblichen Warnungszeichen (Tafeln) ersichtlich zu machen sind. Die Magazine müssen mit zwei Zugängen versehen sein, wenn die Verausgabe der Sprengmittel von mehr als zwei Personen erfolgt. Die Verabfolgung oder Einlagerung der Sprengmittel muß stets zu einer Zeit geschehen, wo keine Mannschaftsfahrung stattfindet; die Einlagerung darf nur in Originalverpackung (Kisten) erfolgen. Die Magazine sind derart zu situieren, daß in der Regel in denselben eine möglichst konstante Temperatur, nicht unter 8 bis 9° C herrscht. Besondere Verhältnisse, namentlich rasche Steigerung der Temperatur, sind sofort durch das mit der Ausgabe des Sprengmittels betraute Organ der Werksleitung anzuzeigen. Die Wetterführung ist so anzulegen, daß im Falle einer Explosion die austretenden Gase nicht über Abbauräume, welche im Betriebe stehen, streichen können. Der Magazinsraum (Nische) ist durch einen entsprechend dimensionierten Kanal zu bewettern, die Öffnungen desselben sind gegen die Sohle und die First des Magazinsvorraumes durch feine Drahtsiebe zu verwahren. In die zur Wetterführung aus dem Magazinsvorraume in die Zugangsstrecke zum Magazin angelegten Schlitze sind solide eiserne Gitter einzubauen, welche den Zutritt zum Vorraum verwehren. Im Magazinsraume ist ein Thermometer aufzuhängen, welches bei jedesmaliger Dynamitentnahme abzulesen ist. Die Temperaturablesungen sowie der Dynamitbestand sind auf der im Magazinsvorraume anzubringenden Tafel zu notieren. Der Magazinsvorraum ist mit einem Lehmanstrich zu versehen, auf welchem eine Zwilchplache aufzulegen ist; in diesem Raume ist ein Manipulationstisch aufzustellen. In der Zugangsstrecke zum Magazinsvorraum sind eine Sicherheitslampe und ein Paar Filzschuhe bereitzustellen. Die Schlüssel zu sämtlichen Türen des Magazins dürfen nur in den Händen der mit der Dynamitausgabe betrauten Personen sich befinden und sind Reserveschlüssel in der Betriebskanzlei sicher zu verwahren. Im Umkreise von 100 m vom Magazine dürfen während der Dauer der Benützung keine Abbaue, Schächte, Fahr- und Förderstrecken, sowie Hauptwetterstrecken neu angelegt werden. Die Einbringung des Dynamits in den Schacht und der Transport desselben zum Magazin hat nur nach vorheriger Benachrichtigung des Maschinenwärters und des Anschlägers am Füllorte zu erfolgen. Während der Förderung des Dynamits im Schachte sind die Schachtverschlüsse auf der Hängebank und am Tagkranze geschlossen zu halten und durch eine verläßliche Person zu überwachen.

Eine Beschreibung eines unterirdischen Sprengstofflagers (nebst Zeichnung) ist auch von W. Serlo mitgeteilt (Zeitschrift Glückauf 1906, S. 1684).

Dreizehnter Abschnitt.

Wirtschaftliche Entwicklung.

In Deutschland entstanden alsbald nach Erfindung des Dynamits große Unternehmungen, welche sich gegenseitig hart befehdeten; im Jahre 1880 jedoch gab das in Frankreich gegründete Glyzerinsyndikat, welches die Preise für Dynamitglyzerin bis Mk. 250.— pro 100 kg in die Höhe trieb, Veranlassung zu einer Verständigung zunächst behufs gemeinsamen Vorgehens im Glyzerineinkauf; daran schloß sich eine Preiskonvention für Dynamit, die zwischen

der Dynamit-Aktiengesellschaft vorm. Alfred Nobel & Co. in Hamburg,

der Kölner Dynamitfabrik in Küppersteg,

der Rheinischen Dynamitfabrik in Opladen

und den Ver. Rhein.-Westfäl. Pulverfabriken in Köln,

welch letztere den größten Teil der Aktien der Rheinischen Dynamitfabrik erworben hatte, abgeschlossen wurde.

Aber schon im Jahre 1882 mußte sich diese Konvention wegen der in diesem Jahre auftretenden scharfen Konkurrenz der Sächsischen Dynamitfabrik Freiberg (welche 1884 mit der Dresdener Dynamitfabrik fusioniert wurde) und der Deutschen Sprengstoff-Aktiengesellschaft in Hamburg auflösen.

Drei Jahre später, nämlich 1885, schritt man daher zur Gründung eines neuen Verbandes, nämlich der Deutschen Union. An letzterer sind beteiligt:

die Dynamit-Aktiengesellschaft in Hamburg,

die Rheinische Dynamitfabrik in Opladen,

die Deutsche Sprengstoff-Aktiengesellschaft in Hamburg,

die Dresdener Dynamitfabrik in Dresden.

Der bilanzmäßige Gewinn dieser vier Gesellschaften wird jährlich zu einer einzigen Summe vereinigt und prozentual an die einzelnen Gesellschaften verteilt.

Auf dem Weltmarkte trafen besonders die Dynamit-Aktiengesellschaft in Hamburg und die Nobels Explosives Comp. Ltd. in Glasgow als die bedeutendsten Konkurrenten hart zusammen. Es wurde darum 1884 eine internationale Konvention zunächst auf 5 Jahre geschlossen, welche für die einzelnen Exportmärkte die Preise regelte; bald jedoch ließen gemeinschaftliche Interessen eine nähere Vereinigung für wünschenswert erachten. Hierbei ergab sich nun die Schwierigkeit, daß nach der Rechtsprechung in Großbritannien Syndikatsverträge unter gewissen Voraussetzungen nicht anerkannt werden; übrigens hielt man auch eine Kartellorganisation für eine straffe Regelung des Dynamitgeschäfts nicht für geeignet und dauerhaft genug. Man fand daher Ende des Jahres 1886 die neue Organisation des Trust, eine zentralisierte Zusammenfassung gleichartiger Unternehmungen für einheitliche Leitung und erhöhten gleichmäßigen Gewinn, bei welcher die Aktien verschiedener Gesellschaften gegen Aktien einer zu gründenden Gesellschaft umgetauscht werden. Der Dynamit-Aktiengesellschaft in Hamburg schlossen sich die anderen in der Union vereinigten Firmen an. Die Hauptaktionäre der fünf Gesellschaften schlossen einen Vertrag, in welchem sie sich verpflichteten, ihre sämtlichen Dynamitaktien einer noch zu gründenden Gesellschaft zu einer festgesetzten Bewertung abzutreten; den übrigen Aktionären wurde der Beitritt unter gleichen Bedingungen gesichert. Er wurden gewährt:

Für jede volleingezahlte Aktie von	der Aktiengesellschaft	£ des eingezahlten Kapitals der Trust-Comp.
£ 10.—	Nobels Expl.-Comp. in Glasgow	£ 25.—
ℳ 500.—	Dynamit-Akt.-Ges. in Hamburg	„ 47. 7.76
„ 600.—	Rhein. Dynamitfabrik, Opladen	„ 106. 5.—
„ 500.—	Deutsche Sprengst.-Akt.-Ges., Hamburg	„ 70.—.—
„ 500.—	Dresdener Dynamitfabrik, Dresden	„ 58.18. 2

Im gleichen Jahre erwarb die Trust-Company sämtliche Aktien von weiteren fünf kleineren ausländischen Dynamitunternehmungen,

der South Wales Explosives Comp., Ltd. in London,
der Alliance Explosives Company, Ltd. in London,
der Sociedad Nacional Mexicana de la Dynamite Nobel in Mexiko,
der Sociedade Nacional Brazileira de la Dynamite Nobel in Rio de Janeiro,
und der Sociedad Anonima para el Comercio de los Explosives en las Costas de la Pacificio in Bilbao.

Um die Aktien jener zehn Gesellschaften zu erwerben, wurde ein Aktienkapital von zwei Millionen Pfd. Sterl. (ca 40 Millionen Mark) in 200000 Aktien zu 10 Pfd. Sterl. aufgebracht. In späteren Jahren fanden wiederholt Emissionen von Trustaktien statt zur Erwerbung von Aktien verschiedener Explosivstoffgesellschaften, z. B. der Standard Explosives Company of New York (seither wieder verkauft) und zum Erwerb von 10000 Aktien der Australian Explosives and Chemical-Comp. — Durch Beschluß der Generalversammlung vom 26. Mai 1898 wurde das Kapital um eine Million Pfd. Sterl., anfangs 1902 um eine halbe Million Pfd. Sterl. und Ende 1907 abermals um eine halbe Million Pfd. Sterl. erhöht, besteht also jetzt aus vier Millionen Pfd. Sterl. (80 Millionen Mark).

An der Spitze der Dynamite-Trust-Company steht der „Board of directors" (gebildet von 10 bis 14 Deutschen und Engländern), welcher alle Rechte aus den in den Besitz der Trustgesellschaft übergegangenen Aktien ausüben kann. — Den früheren Besitzern der erworbenen Aktien wurden „Anteilscheine" (Certificates) ausgehändigt, welche zu einer bestimmten Anzahl von Trustaktien berechtigten, oder Inhaberaktien.

Jeglicher Jahresgewinn, welcher von den Untergesellschaften erzielt wird, fließt naturgemäß der Trust-Company als Aktionärin zu, wird dort in üblicher Weise verrechnet und gleichmäßig unter die Zertifikatinhaber (Registered Shares), bzw. die Aktieninhaber (Warrants to bearer) verteilt. — Der Wortlaut des Memorandum of Association of The Nobel-Dynamite-Trust-Company, Limited, findet sich in Dr. Gustav Martin, Geschichtliche Entwicklung der Kartellbildung in der deutschen Sprengstoffindustrie. Inaug.-Dissert. Heidelberg 1903. — Der Trust stipulierte folgende Verpflichtungen der Händler und Vertreter:

I. a) Händler und Vertreter dürfen ohne vorher einzuholende ausdrückliche Genehmigung der von ihnen vertretenen, liefernden Fabriksfirma Sprengstoffe nur an diejenigen Kunden und/oder für diejenigen Verbrauchsstellen auf Lieferungsabschluß offerieren und/oder verkaufen, für welche ihnen diese Genehmigung abseiten der liefernden Fabriksfirma generell erteilt worden ist. Diese generell erteilte Erlaubnis erstreckt sich für die unter diesen Kunden befindlichen Unternehmer so weit, als dieselben Arbeiten in dem seitens der Fabriksfirma dem Händler und/oder Vertreter überwiesenen Verkaufsrevier ausführen.

b) Ist solche Genehmigung generell für einen Kunden erteilt, so bezieht sich dieselbe jedoch nicht auf etwaige neue, von diesem Kunden eröffnete Verbrauchsstellen. Als neue Verbrauchsstellen im Sinne dieser Bestimmungen werden alle solche Neuanlagen angesehen, für welche ein anderer Auslieferungsort als der bisherige vorgeschrieben wird.

c) Die generell erteilte Befugnis, an einen Kunden zu liefern, erlischt, wenn ein solcher Kunde während zweier aufeinander folgender Jahre kein Gurdynamit, Gelatinedynamit oder Sprenggelatine bezogen hat.

d) Es ist den Händlern und/oder Vertretern nicht untersagt, an kleine Kunden, welche nicht auf der Liste der ihnen generell von der Fabriksfirma zur Belieferung überwiesenen Kunden stehen, freihändige Verkäufe ohne Tätigung eines Lieferungsabschlusses zu machen. Die Händler und/oder Vertreter verpflichten sich indessen für solche Verkäufe zur strikten Innehaltung der ihnen jeweils von der liefernden Fabriksfirma bekannt gegebenen Kleinhandelspreise und Bedingungen, sowie ferner, daß sie derartige freihändige Verkäufe nur innerhalb des ihnen von der Fabriksfirma überwiesenen Verkaufsreviers ausführen.

II. a) Die Händler und Vertreter sind verpflichtet, die ihnen jeweilig aufgegebenen Minimalpreise bei Offerten sowohl als auch bei Abschlüssen auf das strengste einzuhalten. Es ist auch die Einräumung jeglicher direkten und/oder indirekten Begünstigungen an Kunden bei Feststellung des Preises untersagt. Als sosche Begünstigungen sind beispielsweise anzusehen: 1. das Zurücknehmen von leeren Dynamitkisten; 2. Verknüpfen eines Dynamitabschlusses mit anderen Geschäften, durch welche dem Dynamitkäufer ein Vorteil zugewendet wird; 3. die Vergütung von Fracht und Fuhrlohn über die bestehenden Sätze hinaus, sowie die Bezahlung von Lagergeld an Konsumenten; 4. bei Schutzofferten an die geschützte Kundschaft einer anderen Fabriksfirma oder eines anderen Händlers und/oder Vertreters dürfen keine günstigeren Anlieferungsbedingungen offeriert werden, als wie die zuständige Fabriksfirma, Händler und/oder Vertreter sie offerieren; 5. die Gewährung einer Baissegarantie ist verboten, es sei denn, daß der Händler oder Vertreter von seiner Fabriksfirma diesbezüglich eine besondere Ausnahmeinstruktion erhalten hat.

b) Falls ein Händler und/oder Vertreter auf eine abgegebene Schutzofferte hin den Zuschlag seitens des Kunden erhält, so hat er für die auf solche Abschlüsse gemachten Lieferungen den Schutzaufschlag im Abschlußpreis unverkürzt seiner Fabriksfirma auszuzahlen. Es steht den Händlern und/oder Vertretern auch keine Provision auf diese Schutzaufschläge im Abschlußpreis zu.

c) Wegen der abzugebenden Schutzofferte haben die Händler und/oder Vertreter unter allen Umständen vorher die Instruktion ihrer Fabriksfirma einzuholen und dieselbe bei Abgabe der Schutzofferte genau zu befolgen. Die Händler und/oder Vertreter sind verpflichtet, ihre Fabriksfirma gleichzeitig mit der Abgabe einer Schutzofferte hiervon unverzüglich zu benachrichtigen.

d) Händler und/oder Vertreter dürfen bei der Ausschreibung von Submissionen Offerten nur dann abgeben, wenn ihnen seitens ihrer Fabriksfirma dazu ausdrücklich die Genehmigung erteilt worden ist. In diesem Falle sind die Händler und/oder Vertreter unter allen Umständen verpflichtet, für die abzugebende Offerte die empfangene Instruktion der Fabriksfirma genau zu befolgen.

III. Die den Händlern und/oder Vertretern von ihrer Fabriksfirma aufgegebenen Minimalpreise für Lieferungsabschlüsse verstehen sich franko Verbrauchsstelle bei Kisten von 25 kg Nettoinhalt, gleich 10 Pakete à $2^1/_2$ kg. Für Packung von Paketen von 1 kg ist ein Preisaufschlag von Mk. 3.— per 100 kg zu fordern. Wird seitens der Kunden die Lieferung in Kisten von weniger als 25 kg Inhalt verlangt, so haben die Händler und/oder Vertreter den ihnen von der Fabriksfirma aufgegebenen Preisaufschlag bei ihren Offerten und bei der Fakturierung der Lieferung einzuhalten. Die Händler und Vertreter sind verpflichtet, diese Preisaufschläge mit der Fabriksfirma abzurechnen.

IV. a) Als Zahlungsbedingung für die Tätigung von Lieferungsabschlüssen und die Abgabe von Offerten gilt ohne Ausnahme: „Zahlung netto ohne Abzug bis zum 25. des der Lieferung folgenden Monats."

b) Auch auf die Kleinhandelspreise bei freihändigen Verkäufen darf weder Rabatt noch Skonto gewährt werden.

c) Maßgebend für die Festsetzung des den Kunden zu berechnenden Preises ist der Ort des Verbrauches, nicht aber der Wohnort des Kunden.

d) Die Abgabe von Offerten für Lieferungsabschlüsse und die Tätigung solcher Abschlüsse darf ohne ausdrückliche besondere Genehmigung der liefernden Fabriksfirma nur für eine Lieferungsdauer von 12 vollen Monaten erfolgen.

V. Händler und/oder Vertreter dürfen ohne ausdrückliche Genehmigung ihrer Fabriksfirma Gurdynamit, Gelatinedynamit und Sprenggelatine weder von einer anderen Fabriksfirma kaufen, noch einer solchen offerieren oder verkaufen.

VI. Verbraucher von Sprengstoffen oder in deren Dienst stehende Personen dürfen weder Händler noch Vertreter sein, und sind auch nicht berechtigt, von den gekauften bzw. angelieferten Sprengstoffen an andere Verbraucher abzugeben. Die Händler und/oder Vertreter sind verpflichtet, ihren Kunden die strengste Innehaltung dieser Bestimmung aufzuerlegen.

VII. a) Jede wissentliche oder fahrlässige Verletzung aller dieser Bestimmungen mittels Offerte zieht eine Konventionalstrafe von eintausend Mark nach sich. Wird auf Grund solcher Offerten ein Abschluß getätigt, so ist außerdem für jedes auf den Abschluß gelieferte Quantum Sprengstoffe eine Konventionalstrafe von achtzig Mark per 100 kg zugunsten der durch den Händler und/oder Vertreter vertretenen Fabriksfirma verwirkt.

b) Jeder Händler und/oder Vertreter ist für alle Handlungen seiner Vertreter sowie etwaiger Unterhändler in gleicher Weise verantwortlich wie für seine eigenen Handlungen.

c) Abgesehen von der Forderung der Konventionalstrafe ist die von den Händlern und/oder Vertretern vertretene Fabriksfirma bei einer Verletzung dieser Bedingungen außerdem befugt, falls sie dies in ihrem Interesse erachtet, jegliche Lieferung auf einen gegen die vorstehenden Bedingungen verstoßenden Vertrag für die Zukunft zu verweigern und jede weitere Geschäftsverbindung mit dem Händler und/oder Vertreter abzubrechen.

Folgende Bedingungen für den Verkauf von Nitroglyzerinsprengstoffen sind stipuliert:

1. Konsumenten oder in deren Dienst stehende Personen dürfen weder Händler noch Vertreter von Nitroglyzerinsprengstoffen sein. Nitroglyzerinsprengstoffe, welche zum eigenen Gebrauch gekauft bzw. angeliefert sind, dürfen an andere Konsumenten nicht abgegeben werden. Als solche andere Konsumenten gelten auch die im Betriebe des Käufers für ihre eigene Rechnung arbeitenden Unternehmer.

2. Die Verwendung der gekauften bzw. angelieferten Sprengstoffe an anderen als den namhaft gemachten Verbrauchsstellen ist ausdrücklich untersagt.

3. Die liefernde Fabriksfirma ist nicht verpflichtet, während der letzten zwei Monate des Vertragsjahres bzw. der Vertragsdauer ein größeres Quantum anzuliefern, als während der vorhergegangenen Vertragszeit für zwei Monate im Durchschnitt bezogen worden ist.

4. Zuwiderhandlungen gegen die Vertragsbedingungen seitens des Käufers hebt jeden Anspruch auf Weiterlieferung auf; die liefernde Fabriksfirma ist dann berechtigt, die Geschäftsverbindung aufzuheben.

In einem angegliederten Verhältnis zum deutsch-englischen Dynamit-Trust steht die Sprengstoff-Aktiengesellschaft Karbonit in Hamburg (Fabrik in Schlebusch bei Köln), welche am 12. August 1890 von Christian Emil Bichel gegründet wurde. Diese — mit einem Kapital von 1600000 Mark arbeitende — Gesellschaft überweist nach Ablauf jeden Geschäftsjahres ihr gesamtes Geschäftsergebnis (ohne Abschreibungen) der Nobel-Gesellschaft; dagegen erhält die Karbonitgesellschaft: a) eine jährliche Vergütung von 5 Prozent von ihren Anlagewerten an Immobilien und Mobilien, sowie 2 Prozent vom Buchwert ihrer Patente und Konzessionen; b) eine Gewinnquote von $^3/_4$ des Prozentsatzes der Jahresdividende der Nobel-Dynamite-Trust Company sowie c) die für Reservefonds- und Aufsichtsrats-Tantièmen erforderlichen Summen. Dieser Vertrag gilt bis Ende des Jahres 1925, nach dieser Zeit führt die Karbonitgesellschaft entweder die Geschäfte auf eigene Rechnung fort oder übergibt ihre Aktiven und Passiven an die Nobel-Gesellschaft zu einem Preise, welcher auf Grund der Jahre 1918 bis 1922 bei einer 6prozentigen Verzinsung der Quote b) sich ergibt.

Folgende deutsche Fabriken sind unabhängig vom Trust: 1. die Sprengstoffwerke Dr. R. Nahnsen & Cie. in Hamburg, Fabriken in Dömitz und Anzhausen, Glyzerinanlage in Neuwied; 2. die Oberschlesische Aktiengesellschaft für Fabrikation von Lignose, Schießwollfabrik für Armee und Marine in Kruppamühle in Oberschlesien; 3. die Sprengstoffgesellschaft Hoppecke in Hamburg; 4. die Westfälisch-Anhaltische Sprengstoff-Aktiengesellschaft in Berlin mit Fabrik in Haltern und 5. die Castroper Sicherheitssprengstoff-Aktiengesellschaft mit Fabrik in Rummenohl.

In Großbritannien befindet sich die Fabrik der Nobels Explosives Company, Ltd., in Ardeer. Die Firma Kynoch Limited hat Dynamitfabriken in Kynochtown und in Arklow; die Fabrik von British Explosives Syndicate, Ltd., befindet sich in Pitsea; die der National Explosives Company, Ltd., in Upton Towans; die von Curtis & Harvey in Cliffe; die der Cotton Porder Company bei Faversham; die der Explosives and Chemical Products in Bramble Island; der New Explosives Company, Limited, in Stowmarket. — In Österreich besteht Monopol, die Herstellung der Nitroglyzerinsprengstoffe ist der Aktiengesellschaft Dynamit Nobel übertragen, welche Fabriken in Zamky bei Prag und in Preßburg hat. — In Belgien bestehen selbständige Dynamitfabriken in Matagne-la-Grande, in Baelen-Wezel und in Arendonck. — In Frankreich besteht im allgemeinen ein Monopol für Explosivstoffe; jedoch wurde für Nitroglyzerinsprengstoffe eine Ausnahme gemacht, indem die Fabrikation derselben durch Gesetz vom 8. März 1875 der Privatindustrie überlassen wurde. Die Société Génerale de Dynamite hat Fabriken in Paulilles, in Ablon und in La Rachée; die Société française de explosifs hat ihre Fabrik in Cugny; die Société anonyme d'Explosifs et Produit chimiques in St. Martin de Crau Die ersteren beiden Gesellschaften gehören zum sog. lateinischen Nobel-Trust, der seine Fabriken außer in Italien (Avigliana) noch in der Schweiz, in Spanien und in Mexiko hat und von der Société centrale de Dynamite in Paris geleitet wird.

Zu Ende des Jahres 1907 wurde eine freie Vereinigung sämtlicher Dynamitfabriken geschlossen unter dem Namen High Explosives Association, und zu dem Zwecke, die sehr gedrückten Preise für alle brisanten Sprengstoffe um 20 Prozent zu erhöhen.

In den Vereinigten Staaten von Nordamerika wurden im Jahre 1902 aus 16983918 Pfund Glyzerin und 108227320 Pfund Mischsäure insgesamt 35482947 Pfund Nitroglyzerin in 22 Etablissements (hauptsächlich in Ohio, dann in Pennsylvanien und Indiana) erzeugt; hiervon wurden 3618692 Pfund auf den Markt gebracht (Wert 783299 Dollars); die übrigen 31661806 Pfund wurden auf Dynamite verarbeitet, wozu noch 20090 Tonnen Natronsalpeter, 9934360 Pfund Holzwolle, 82558 Pfund Nitrozellulose und 483975 Pfund Ammonsalpeter gebraucht wurden; durchschnittlich enthielten die Dynamite 40 Prozent Nitroglyzerin. Ein solches 40prozentiges straight dynamite enthielt, einer Analyse zufolge, 39·8 Prozent Nitroglyzerin, 46·1 Prozent Natronsalpeter, 11·5 Prozent Holzwolle, 0·7 Prozent Calciumkarbonat, 1·9 Prozent Wasser. — An der Herstellung von Dynamit beteiligten sich 31 Etablissements in 8 Staaten, besonders in Kalifornien, New-Jersey, Missouri, Pennsylvanien, Michigan, Ohio. — Die Fabrikation von Dynamit in den Vereinigten Staaten betrug im Jahre 1890: 30626738 Pfund im Werte von 4253032 Dollars; im Jahre 1900: 85846456 Pfund im Werte von 8247223 Dollars.

Vierzehnter Abschnitt.

Gesetzliche und polizeiliche Bestimmungen.

I. Gesetz gegen den verbrecherischen und gemeingefährlichen Gebrauch von Sprengstoffen, vom 9. Juni 1884.

§ 1. Die Herstellung, der Vertrieb und der Besitz von Sprengstoffen sowie die Einführung derselben aus dem Auslande ist unbeschadet der bestehenden sonstigen Beschränkungen nur mit polizeilicher Genehmigung zulässig.

Wer sich mit der Herstellung oder dem Vertriebe von Sprengstoffen befaßt, hat ein Register zu führen, aus welchem die Mengen der hergestellten, aus dem Auslande eingeführten oder sonst zum Zweck des Vertriebes angeschafften Sprengstoffe, sowie die Bezugsquellen und der Verbleib derselben ersichtlich sein müssen. Dieses Register ist der zuständigen Behörde auf Erfordern jederzeit vorzulegen.

Auf Sprengstoffe, welche vorzugsweise als Schießmittel gebraucht werden, finden, vorbehaltlich abweichender landesrechtlicher Vorschriften, die Bestimmungen des ersten und des zweiten Absatzes keine Anwendung. Die Bezeichnung dieser Stoffe erfolgt durch Beschluß des Bundesrats.

Insoweit Sprengstoffe zum eigenen Gebrauch durch Reichs- oder Landesbehörden von der zuständigen Verwaltung hergestellt, besessen, eingeführt oder vertrieben werden, bleiben die Vorschriften des ersten und zweiten Absatzes ebenfalls ausgeschlossen.

§ 2. Die Zentralbehörden der Bundesstaaten erlassen die zur Ausführung der Vorschriften in dem § 1 Abs. 1 und 2, sowie in dem § 15 erforderlichen näheren Anordnungen und bestimmen die Behörden, welche über die Gesuche um Gestattung der Herstellung, des Vertriebes, des Besitzes und der Einführung von Sprengstoffen Entscheidung zu treffen haben.

§ 3. Gegen die versagende Verfügung ist nur die Beschwerde an die Aufsichtsbehörde innerhalb vierzehn Tagen zulässig. Dieselbe hat keine aufschiebende Wirkung.

§ 4. Die Erteilung der nach § 1 Abs. 1 erforderlichen Erlaubnis erfolgt in widerruflicher Weise. Wegen der Beschwerde gegen die Zurücknahme gilt die Vorschrift des § 3 des gegenwärtigen Gesetzes.

§ 5. Wer vorsätzlich durch Anwendung von Sprengstoffen Gefahr für das Eigentum, die Gesundheit oder das Leben eines anderen herbeiführt, wird mit Zuchthaus bestraft.

Ist durch die Handlung eine schwere Körperverletzung verursacht worden, so tritt Zuchthausstrafe nicht unter fünf Jahren, und wenn der Tod eines Menschen verursacht worden ist, Zuchthausstrafe nicht unter zehn Jahren oder lebenslängliche Zuchthausstrafe ein.

Ist durch die Handlung der Tod eines Menschen herbeigeführt worden und hat der Täter einen solchen Erfolg voraussehen können, so ist auf Todesstrafe zu erkennen.

§ 6. Haben mehrere die Ausführung einer oder mehrerer nach § 5 zu ahndender strafbarer Handlungen verabredet oder sich zur fortgesetzten Begehung derartiger, wenn auch im einzelnen noch nicht bestimmter Handlungen verbunden, so werden dieselben, auch ohne daß der Entschluß der Verübung des Verbrechens durch Handlungen, welche einen Anfang der Ausführung enthalten, betätigt worden ist, mit Zuchthaus nicht unter fünf Jahren bestraft.

§ 7. Wer Sprengstoffe herstellt, anschafft, bestellt, oder in seinem Besitze hat, in der Absicht, durch Anwendung derselben Gefahr für das Eigentum, die Gesundheit oder das Leben eines anderen entweder selbst herbeizuführen oder andere Personen zur Begehung dieses Verbrechens in den Stand zu setzen, wird mit Zuchthaus bis zu zehn Jahren bestraft.

Der gleichen Strafe verfällt, wer Sprengstoffe, wissend, daß dieselben zur Begehung eines in dem § 5 vorgesehenen Verbrechens bestimmt sind, an andere Personen überläßt.

§ 8. Wer Sprengstoffe herstellt, anschafft, bestellt, wissentlich in seinem Besitze hat oder an andere Personen überläßt unter Umständen, welche nicht erweisen, daß dies zu einem erlaubten Zweck geschieht, wird mit Zuchthausstrafe bis zu fünf Jahren oder mit Gefängnis nicht unter einem Jahre bestraft. Diese Bestimmung findet auf die gemäß § 1 Abs. 3 vom Bundesrat bezeichneten Stoffe nicht Anwendung.

§ 9. Wer der Vorschrift in dem ersten Absatz des § 1 zuwider es unternimmt, ohne polizeiliche Ermächtigung Sprengstoffe herzustellen, vom Auslande einzuführen, feilzuhalten, zu verkaufen oder sonst an andere zu überlassen, oder wer im Besitze derartiger Stoffe betroffen wird, ohne polizeiliche Erlaubnis hierzu nachweisen zu können, ist mit Gefängnis von drei Monaten bis zu zwei Jahren zu bestrafen.

Gleicher Strafe verfällt, wer die Vorschriften des § 1 Abs. 2, die von den Zentralbehörden in Gemäßheit des § 2 getroffenen Anordnungen oder die bereits bestehenden oder noch zu erlassenden sonstigen polizeilichen Bestimmungen über den Verkehr mit Sprengstoffen, auf welche § 1 Abs. 1 Anwendung finden, übertritt.

§ 10. Wer öffentlich vor einer Menschenmenge oder wer durch Verbreitung oder öffentlichen Anschlag oder öffentliche Ausstellung von Schriften oder anderen Darstellungen, oder wer in Schriften oder anderen Darstellungen zur Begehung einer der in den §§ 5 und 6 bezeichneten strafbaren Handlungen oder zur Teilnahme an denselben auffordert, wird mit Zuchthaus bestraft.

Gleiche Strafe trifft denjenigen, welcher auf die vorbezeichnete Weise zur Begehung der im Abs. 1 gedachten strafbaren Handlungen insbesondere dadurch anreizt oder verleitet, daß er dieselben anpreist oder als etwas Rühmliches darstellt.

§ 11. In den Fällen der §§ 5, 6, 7, 8 und 10 kann auf Zulässigkeit von Polizeiaufsicht erkannt werden. In den Fällen der §§ 5, 6, 7, 8 und in dem Falle einer Anwendung der Strafvorschriften des § 9 ist auf Einziehung der zur Zubereitung der Sprengstoffe gebrauchten oder bestimmten Gegenstände, sowie der im Besitze des Verurteilten vorgefundenen Vorräte von Sprengstoffen zu erkennen, ohne Unterschied, ob dieselben dem Verurteilten gehören oder nicht.

§ 12. Die Bestimmungen im § 4 Abs. 2 Nr. 1 des Strafgesetzbuchs für das Deutsche Reich finden auch auf die in den § 5, 6, 7, 8 und 10 dieses Gesetzes vorgesehenen Verbrechen Anwendung.

§ 13. Der in dem § 139 des Strafgesetzbuchs für das Deutsche Reich angedrohten Strafe verfällt, wer von dem Vorhaben eines im § 5 vorgesehenen Verbrechens oder von einer im § 6 vorgesehenen Verabredung oder von dem Tatbestande eines im § 7 des gegenwärtigen

Gesetzes unter Strafe gestellten Verbrechens in glaubhafter Weise Kenntnis erhält und es unterläßt, der durch das Verbrechen bedrohten Person oder der Behörde rechtzeitig Anzeige zu machen.

§ 14. Die §§ 1, 2, 3, 4, 9 dieses Gesetzes treten drei Monate nach dessen Verkündigung, die übrigen Bestimmungen desselben mit dem Tage der Verkündigung in Kraft.

§ 15. Auf Personen, welche bei dem Inkrafttreten der §§ 1, 2, 3, 4, 9 dieses Gesetzes sich bereits im Besitze von Sprengstoffen befinden oder sich bis zu diesem Tage gewerbsmäßig mit der Herstellung oder mit dem Vertriebe von Sprengstoffen beschäftigt haben, finden die Vorschriften des § 9 Abs. 1 erst zwei Wochen nach dem Inkrafttreten der gedachten Paragraphen und wenn seitens dieser Personen innerhalb dieser Frist ein Gesuch um Erteilung der nach § 1 Abs. 1 erforderlichen polizeilichen Genehmigung bei der zuständigen Behörde eingereicht worden ist, erst eine Woche nach Behändigung des ablehnenden Bescheides letzter Instanz (§ 3) Anwendung.

---

2. Ausführungsverordnung zu I. vom II. September 1884.

Auf Grund des § 2 des Gesetzes gegen den verbrecherischen und gemeingefährlichen Gebrauch von Sprengstoffen vom 9. Juni 1884 wird nachstehendes bestimmt:

1. Über Gesuche um Gestattung der Herstellung, des Vertriebes, des Besitzes sowie der Einführung von Sprengstoffen aus dem Auslande haben die Landräte, in Städten von mehr als 10 000 Einwohnern die Ortspolizeibehörden, in erster Instanz Entscheidung zu treffen. In der Provinz Hannover entscheiden hierüber bis zum Inkrafttreten des Landesverwaltungs- und des Zuständigkeitsgesetes die Amtshauptleute, in den Städten, auf welche die hannoversche revidierte Städteordnung vom 24. August 1858 Anwendung findet, die Magistrate, nach dem Inkrafttreten der gedachten Gesetze dagegen die Landräte und in den vorgenannten Städten mit Ausnahme der in § 27 Abs. 2 der Kreisordnung vom 6. Mai 1884 bezeichneten Städte die Magistrate.

Zuständig ist diejenige Behörde, in deren Bezirk der die Genehmigung Nachsuchende wohnt.

Aufsichtsbehörden im Sinne des qu. Gesetzes sind in den Provinzen Ostpreußen, Westpreußen, Brandenburg, Pommern, Schlesien, Sachsen, sowie in Hohenzollern der Regierungspräsident, für den Stadtkreis Berlin der Oberpräsident, für die übrigen Landesteile die Regierungen (Landdrosteien).

2. In den Gesuchen um Gestattung der Herstellung, des Besitzes und der Einführung von Sprengstoffen aus dem Auslande sind die Zwecke, zu welchen diese Stoffe dem Gesuchsteller dienen sollen, anzugeben.

Die Behörde entscheidet über das Gesuch nach freiem Ermessen. Über die Gründe zur Versagung der Genehmigung ist dieselbe nur der Aufsichtsbehörde Auskunft zu geben verpflichtet.

Solchen Personen, welche bei dem Inkrafttreten der §§ 1, 2, 3, 4, 9 des Gesetzes die Herstellung von Sprengstoffen auf Grund einer gemäß § 16 der Gewerbeordnung erteilten Erlaubnis, oder den Vertrieb von Sprengstoffen als stehendes Gewerbe betrieben haben, ist die Genehmigung nur dann zu versagen, wenn gegen dieselben Tatsachen vorliegen, welche ihre Unzuverlässigkeit dartun. Eine solche Unzuverlässigkeit ist in der Regel anzunehmen, wenn sich dieselben eine Versendung von Sprengstoffen unter falscher Deklaration oder einer sonstigen wissentlichen oder auf grober Fahrlässigkeit beruhenden Übertretung der über die Lagerung, die Aufbewahrung und die Versendung von Sprengstoffen erlassenen Vorschriften schuldig gemacht haben.

Die Erlaubnis zur Herstellung, zum Vertriebe und zur Einführung von Sprengstoffen aus dem Auslande schließt die Erlaubnis zum Besitze von Sprengstoffen in sich.

Die Erlaubnisscheine sind mit dem Amtssiegel oder dem amtlichen Stempel der ausfertigenden Behörde zu versehen.

3. Der Vertrieb von Sprengstoffen darf nur an solche Personen erfolgen, welche im Besitze einer der im § 1 Abs. 1 des Gesetzes gedachten Genehmigungen sind.

3. Für das nach § 1 Abs. 2 des Gesetzes zu führende Register ist das nachstehende Schema in Anwendung zu bringen.

I. Lagerregister.

Laufende Nr.	Bezeichnung der Person, welche die Eintragung bewirkt hat.	Tag und Stunde der Aufnahme von Sprengstoffen in das Lager.	Name des Sprengstoffes	Verpackung (Gefäß usw.).	Quantität nach Gewicht, Maß, Anzahl der Patronen usw.	Genaue Angabe der Bezugsquelle (eigene Herstellung eventuell Fabrik, Name, Stand, Wohnung und Legitimation des Verkäufers oder sonstigen Abgebers).	Tag und Stunde der polizeilichen Revision.	Revisionsbefund.	Unterschrift des revidierenden Beamten.	Bemerkungen.

II. Abgangsregister.

Laufende Nr.	Name derjenigen Person, welche den Verkauf oder sonstigen Abgang, sowie die Eintragung bewirkt hat.	Tag und Stunde des Abganges.	Nahme, Stand und Wohnung des Abnehmers.	Datum des Erlaubnisscheines und Bezeichnung der Behörde, welche denselben ausgestellt hat.	Bezeichnung des Stoffes.	Quantität (Gewicht, Maß, Anzahl der Patronen).	Verpackung.	Tag und Stunde der polizeilichen Revision.	Revisionsbefund.	Unterschrift des revidierenden Beamten.	Bemerkungen.

5. Die nach einem Orte des Inlandes bestimmten Sendungen von Sprengstoffen aus dem Auslande werden nur unter der Bedingung eingelassen, daß der den Adressaten zur Einführung von Sprengstoffen aus dem Auslande ermächtigende Erlaubnisschein den Begleitpapieren der Sendung beigefügt wird.

6. Erfolgt die Zurücknahme einer gemäß § 1 Abs. 1 des Gesetzes erteilten Genehmigung, so ist der Erlaubnisschein an die Behörde zurückzureichen.

Die Zurücknahme ist ferner durch den Deutschen Reichs- und Preußischen Staatsanzeiger bekannt zu machen.

3. Ministerialverfügung vom 14. April 1904. Anstellungsbedingungen und Dienstanweisung für Führer von Sprengstoff- und Pulverfabriken.

§ 1. Ein Führer von Sprengstoff- oder Pulvertransporten hat stets dessen eingedenk zu sein, daß eine Sprengstoff- oder Pulverladung für ihn selbst, für seine Mitmenschen und deren Eigentum eine Gefahr in sich birgt. Er hat sich deshalb der größten Nüchternheit zu befleißigen und mit Überlegung und Ruhe diejenigen Vorsichtsmaßregeln anzuwenden, welche in diesen Anstellungsbedingungen und in den angehefteten polizeilichen Vorschriften enthalten sind. Sollten Fälle vorkommen, die in den genannten Vorschriften nicht enthalten sind, so hat der Transportführer sich bei der nächsten Polizeibehörde zu melden und durch deren Vermittlung bei der absendenden Fabrik telegraphisch anzufragen und weitere Anordnungen abzuwarten.

§ 2. Der Transportführer hat sich von der richtigen Übernahme der ihm überlieferten Sprengstoffe respektive Pulvergefäße zu überzeugen und ist für die richtige Ablieferung an die auf der Frachtbescheinigung angegebenen Ablieferungsstellen verantwortlich.

§ 3. Von dem Reichsgesetz vom 9. Juni 1884 und von der Polizeiverordnung vom 19. Oktober 1893, welche diesen Anstellungsbedingungen angefügt sind, hat der Transportführer eingehende Kenntnis zu nehmen und sich deren Inhalt, soweit er sich auf Landtransporte bezieht, ganz zu eigen zu machen, besonders wird auf § 9 des ersteren Gesetzes und §§ 4 bis 19 inklusive der Polizeiverordnung aufmerksam gemacht.

§ 4. Ganz besondere Vorsicht hat der Transportführer beim Überschreiten von Eisenbahnübergängen, sowohl bei bewachten als auch unbewachten, anzuwenden und insbesondere folgendes zu beachten:

Sobald sich der Transportführer einem Eisenbahnübergange nähert, hat er sich durch den Augenschein zu überzeugen, ob ein Zug naht. Ist dies nicht der Fall, so hat er den Eisenbahnübergang sofort zu überschreiten. Ist der Eisenbahnübergang nicht ohne weiteres übersichtlich und der Transportführer nicht in der Lage, das Eisenbahnterrain zu beiden Seiten genügend weit zu übersehen, so hat er Halt zu machen und sich erst volle Überzeugung zu verschaffen, daß von keiner Seite ein Zug in Annäherung begriffen ist. Besonders unübersichtliche, unbewachte Eisenbahnübergänge dürfen nur passiert werden, nachdem ein aus der letzten Ortschaft mitgenommener Begleiter dem Transportführer durch Zeichen mitgeteilt hat, daß ein Überschreiten der Geleise ohne Gefahr möglich ist. Der Transportführer hat sich, falls er seinen Weg zum ersten Male macht, bei Beginn der Reise nach solchen unübersichtlichen, unbewachten Übergängen zu erkundigen.

§ 5. Die Transportführer haben ein von ihnen unterschriebenes Exemplar dieser Anstellungsbedingungen stets bei sich zu führen und auf Verlangen der Behörde vorzuzeigen.

§ 6. Die Transportführer, welche gegen diese Bestimmungen verstoßen, werden beim ersten Male von ihren Arbeitgebern in von diesen zu bestimmende Geldstrafen genommen und im Wiederholungsfalle entlassen.

---

4. Ministerialverfügung vom 22. September 1902.

In dieser Verfügung des preußischen Ministers für Handel und Gewerbe wird folgende Anweisung für Ausstellung von Erlaubnisscheinen zum Besitz von Sprengstoffen empfohlen, welche unter dem 2. April 1902 von dem Regierungspräsidenten in Wiesbaden aufgestellt worden war:

I. Erlaubnisschein für Betriebe unter ortspolizeilicher Aufsicht.

1. Im allgemeinen sind Erlaubnisscheine zum Besitze von Sprengstoffen nicht mehr Personen auszustellen als es der Betrieb oder die Umstände durchaus erfordern. Bei kleinen Betrieben ist nur dem Besitzer oder dem Aufseher (Bruchmeister, Vorarbeiter) ein Schein auszustellen; in größeren Betrieben kann neben dem verantwortlichen Betriebsleiter (Besitzer oder dem Aufseher) auch der Vertreter des letzteren oder ein besonderer Schießmeister einen Erlaubnisschein erhalten.

2. Die Ausstellung des Erlaubnisscheins darf erst erfolgen, nachdem die Ortspolizeibehörde sich darüber geäußert hat, daß der Betreffende

a) zuverlässig ist,
b) eine genügende Kenntnis in der Behandlung und Verwendung von Sprengstoffen (Dynamit, Roburit usw.) und der hierüber bestehenden gesetzlichen Vorschriften hat, (im allgemeinen wird der Nachweis einer längeren Beschäftigung mit Sprengstoffen genügen,)
c) über einen vorschriftsmäßigen Aufbewahrungsraum für die betreffenden Sprengstoffe verfügt, oder daß in dem Betriebe, für den der Schein ausgestellt werden soll, ein solches Sprengstoffmagazin vorhanden ist.

Das Vorhandensein der Voraussetzung unter b) und c) ist durch eine Bescheinigung des zuständigen Gewerbe-Aufsichtsbeamten nachzuweisen.

3. Der Schein muß den Namen und Wohnort des Inhabers enthalten, sowie einen Vermerk, daß der Inhaber einen Sprengstoff bestimmter Art (z. B. Dynamit, Roburit, Sicherheits-Sprengpulver usw.) nebst zugehörigen Sprengkapseln empfangen, für einen bestimmten Zweck, in einem bestimmten, namhaft zu machenden Betriebe (z. B. Steinbruch X. X.) verwenden und in einem dazu gehörigen Magazin aufbewahren darf. Die Abgabe von Sprengstoffen an andere Personen, auch an solche, die im Besitze von Dynamitscheinen sind, ist ausdrücklich zu untersagen; dieses Verbot bezieht sich nicht auf die Abgabe an Beamte oder Arbeiter desselben Betriebes zur sofortigen Verwendung, vorausgesetzt, daß der Empfänger im Besitz eines Erlaubnisscheines ist.

4. Auch für regelmäßige Betriebe sind die Scheine an die in Position 1 bezeichneten Personen höchstens auf die Dauer eines Kalenderjahres auszustellen, nach dessen Ablauf sie unter Beachtung der Vorschriften zu 2. einer besonderen Erneuerung bedürfen.

Die Verlängerung hat so rechtzeitig zu erfolgen, daß möglichst keine Störung im Betrieb eintritt. Für vorübergehende Betriebe sind die Scheine nur für bestimmt anzugebende kurze Fristen (Wochen, Monate) auszustellen.

5. Unter Berücksichtigung der vorstehenden Vorschriften ist nachstehender Entwurf zu einem Erlaubnisscheine zum Besitz und zur Verwendung von Sprengstoffen aufgestellt, dessen Verwendung als Vordruck den zuständigen Behörden empfohlen wird.

Erlaubnisschein.

Dem . . . . . (Steinbruchbesitzer, Bruchmeister, Stellvertreter des Aufsehers, Schießmeister usw.) zu . . . . . wird hierdurch die im § 1 des Gesetzes gegen den verbrecherischen und gemeingefährlichen Gebrauch von Sprengstoffen vom 9. Juni 1884 vorgeschriebene polizeiliche Erlaubnis erteilt, ... (Bezeichnung des Sprengstoffs) nebst zugehörigen Sprengkapseln bis zur Höchstmenge von . . . . . kg, zu empfangen, in dem . . . . . (Bezeichnung des Betriebs z. B. Steinbruch des N. N.) zum . . . . . (Zweck der Verwendung z. B. Brunnenmachen, Ausschachten) zu verwenden und in dem durch Verfügung der Polizeibehörde genehmigten Magazine zu . . . . . aufzubewahren.

Diese Erlaubnis wird unter dem Vorbehalte des jederzeitigen Widerrufs auf . . . . . (Jahre, Monate, Wochen) erteilt.

Es ist verboten, Dynamit an irgend jemand käuflich oder leihweise zu überlassen, selbst an solche Personen, welchen die vorgeschriebene polizeiliche Genehmigung zum Besitze von Sprengstoffen erteilt worden ist.

Dieses Verbot bezieht sich nicht auf die Abgabe an Beamte und Arbeiter desselben Betriebes zur sofortigen Verwendung, vorausgesetzt, daß der Empfänger im Besitz eines Erlaubnisscheines ist.

Es wird die größte Sorgfalt in der Behandlung und Aufbewahrung des Sprengstoffs zur Pflicht gemacht und darauf hingewiesen, daß jede Übertretung der Bestimmungen durch das Reichsgesetz vom 9. Juni 1884 mit schwerer Freiheitsstrafe bedroht ist.

Die Arbeiter und sonstigen Untergebenen sind vor jeder Aneignung des Sprengstoffs zu warnen, da dessen Besitz ohne die polizeiliche Genehmigung auch in Ermangelung jeder bösen Absicht mit Gefängnis von mindestens 3 Monaten bestraft werden muß.

Dem Inhaber des Scheins wird hierbei die Verpflichtung auferlegt, daß nach § 27 der Polizeiverordnung vom 19. Oktober 1893 (Amtsbl. S. 437) vorgeschriebene Buch für Verbrauchsmagazin zu führen und es der Ortspolizeibehörde sowie den Gewerbeaufsichtsbeamten auf Erfordern jederzeit vorzulegen.

(L. S.) (Unterschrift.)

Wird ein Betrieb eingestellt, ändert der Inhaber seine Stellung oder treten Verhältnisse ein, welche die Einziehung des Erlaubnisscheins notwendig machen, so hat die Ortspolizeibehörde hiervon dem Landrate sofort Mitteilung zu machen und den Schein vom Inhaber einzufordern.

II. Erlaubnisscheine für Betriebe unter bergpolizeilicher Aufsicht.

1. Die Ausstellung des Scheins darf erst nach Benehmen mit dem zuständigen Bergrevierbeamten über den unter I 2. erwähnten Punkte erfolgen.

2. Der Erlaubnisschein hat sich jeder Bestimmung über die Menge des aufzubewahrenden Sprengstoffes und den Ort der Aufbewahrung zu enthalten, da hierfür lediglich die Bergrevierbeamten zuständig sind.

3. Der Schein kann auf besonderes Verlangen des Bergrevierbeamten auf mehrere Jahre ausgestellt werden; die Erlaubnis zum Besitz und zur Verwendung der Sprengstoffe ist auch auf die Beamten und Arbeiter des betreffenden Bergwerks auszudehnen, soweit sie von ihren Vorgesetzten zur Verwendung von Sprengstoffen Anweisung haben.

4. Nach Benehmen mit dem Königlichen Oberbergamte zu Bonn wird für die Erlaubnisscheine, welche für die unter bergpolizeilicher Aufsicht stehenden Betriebe auszustellen sind, nachstehendes Muster empfohlen:

Erlaubnisschein.

Dem . . . . . (Bergwerksbesitzer, Repräsentanten, Betriebsführer) zu . . . . . wird hierdurch die im § 1 des Gesetzes gegen den verbrecherischen und gemeingefährlichen Gebrauch von Sprengstoffen vom 9. Juni 1884 vorgeschriebene polizeiliche Erlaubnis zum Empfange von . . . . . (Bezeichnung des Sprengstoffes) nebst zugehörigen Sprengkapseln, zu dessen Aufbewahrung in einem dazu gehörigen Magazin und zu dessen Verwendung im Betriebe des Bergwerks ..... bei ....., vorbehaltlich jederzeitigen Widerrufs auf ... Jahre erteilt.

Diese Erlaubnis erstreckt sich innerhalb des Betriebs des vorgenannten Bergwerks auch auf die dem ..... unterstellten Beamten und Arbeiter, insoweit sie von ihren Vorgesetzten zur Verwendung von Sprengstoffen Anweisung haben.

Die Abgabe von ..... (Bezeichnung des Sprengstoffes) und Sprengkapseln an andere, wenn auch mit Erlaubnisschein versehene Personen ist untersagt.

(L. S.) (Unterschrift.)

5. Von jeder Ausstellung und von jeder Entziehung eines Erlaubnisscheines ist unverzüglich dem Königlichen Revierbeamten eine Mitteilung zu machen.

6. Die Königlichen Revierbeamten werden den Landräten und den Ortspolizeibehörden eine Mitteilung zukommen lassen, sobald ein Betrieb eingestellt wird, der Inhaber des Erlaubnisscheins seine Stellung ändert oder aufgibt, oder Verhältnisse eintreten, welche die Entziehung des Scheins notwendig machen. In diesen Fällen ist der Erlaubnisschein von dem Inhaber einzuziehen.

---

5. Polizeiverordnung, betr. den Verkehr mit Sprengstoffen, vom 14. September 1905.

§ 1. Die nachstehenden Bestimmungen begreifen: 1. die Versendung von Sprengstoffen auf Land- und Wasserwegen — mit Ausnahme des Eisenbahn- und Postverkehrs und des unter militärischer Begleitung stattfindenden Verkehrs von Sprengstoffen und Munitionsgegenständen der Militär- und Marineverwaltung sowie der Versendung von Sprengstoffen in Kauffahrteischiffen —;

2. den Handel mit Sprengstoffen;

3. die Aufbewahrung und Verausgabung von Sprengstoffen innerhalb des Betriebs von Bergwerken, Steinbrüchen, Bauten und gewerblichen Anlagen;

4. die Lagerung von Sprengstoffen — mit Ausnahme der Lagerung in Niederlagen oder Magazinen der Militär- und Marineverwaltung —.

Zu den Sprengstoffen im Sinne dieser Bestimmungen gehören nicht: a) die in dem Heere und in der Marine vorgeschriebenen, nicht sprengkräftigen Zündungen; b) die für Feuerwaffen bestimmten Zündhütchen und Zündspiegel, die für Handfeuerwaffen bestimmten Metallpatronen und alle Jagdpatronen, c) Zündschnüre.

I. Allgemeine Bestimmungen.

§ 2. Zum Verkehr im Sinne des § 1 Ziffer 1 bis 3 sind zugelassen:

1. Pulver — Sprengsalpeter — brennbarer Salpeter — (ein sehr inniges Gemisch aus neutral reagierenden Salpeterarten und Kohle oder

Stoffen, deren wesentliche Bestandteile Kohlenstoff, Wasserstoff und Sauerstoff sind, mit oder ohne Schwefel);

2. folgende Nitroglyzerin enthaltende Präparate: a) Dynamit I (ein bei mittlerer Temperatur plastisches, nicht abtropfbares Gemisch von Nitroglyzerin mit pulverförmigen, an sich nicht sprengkräftigen und nicht selbstentzündlichen Stoffen), b) Dynamit II und III (Kohlendynamit, ein Gemisch von Nitroglyzerin mit schießpulverähnlichen Gemengen), c) Sprenggelatine (ein bei mittlerer Temperatur zähelastisches Gemisch, bestehend aus Nitroglyzerin, welches durch Nitrozellulose gelatiniert ist, mit oder ohne kohlensauren Alkalien [bzw. alkalischen Erden] oder neutral reagierenden Salpeterarten), d) Rohmasse für rauchloses Pulver, bestehend aus einem innigen Gemenge von Nitroglyzerin und feuchter Nitrozellulose, dessen Wassergehalt mindestens 30 Prozent und dessen Nitroglyzeringehalt höchstens 28 Prozent beträgt, e) Gelatinedynamit (ein bei mittlerer Temperatur plastisches Gemisch, bestehend aus Nitroglyzerin, welches durch Nitrozellulose gelatiniert ist, und Holzmehl, Salpeter und kohlensauren Alkalien [bzw. alkalischen Erden]), f) Karbonit (ein Gemisch von Nitroglyzerin mit schießpulverähnlichen Gemengen und mit flüssigen, an sich nicht sprengkräftigen oder nicht selbstentzündlichen Stoffen);

3. Nitrozellulose (lockere mit mindestens 20 Prozent Wassergehalt und gepreßte, nicht gelatinierte), insbesondere Schießbaumwolle und Kollodiumwolle sowie Gemische von Nitrozellulose mit neutral reagierenden Salpeterarten;

4. Feuerwerkskörper, sofern sie nicht pikrinsaure Salze enthalten, geladene Geschosse, Geschützpatronen, Kartuschen, Petarden, sprengkräftige Zündungen, welche zum Entzünden von Ladungen dienen (z. B. Sprengkapseln), Zündplättchen (amorcés);

5. alle jeweilig zur Versendung auf den Eisenbahnen zugelassenen Sprengstoffe.

Zu Versuchszwecken kann die Versendung neuer, hier nicht aufgeführter Sprengstoffe auf bestimmten Wegen sowie die Aufbewahrung und Verausgabung derselben von der Landespolizeibehörde gestattet werden.

§ 3. Vom Verkehr im Sinne des § 1 Ziffer 1 und 3 sind ausgeschlossen die nicht nach § 2 zugelassenen Sprengstoffe, insbesondere:

1. Nitroglyzerin als solches und in Lösungen;

2. Knallgold, trocken in fester oder Pulverform, Knallquecksilber, Knallsilber und die damit dargestellten Präparate;

3. Nitrozuckerarten, Nitrostärkearten und die damit hergestellten Gemische;

4. Gemische, welche Nitroglyzerin abtropfen lassen;

5. Sprengstoffe, welche entweder: a) bei einer Temperatur bis zu + 40° C zur Selbstzersetzung neigen, oder b) welche enthalten: aa) chlorsaure Salze (mit Ausnahme der Sprengkapseln und Zündplättchen [§ 2 Nr. 4]), oder bb) pikrinsaure Salze, oder cc) Phosphor (mit Ausnahme der Zündplättchen [§ 2 Nr. 4]) oder dd) Schwefelkupfer;

6. Sprengstoffe in Patronenhülsen, sofern diese äußerlich mit Nitroglyzerin (Ziffer 1) oder mit anderer Sprengflüssigkeit benetzt oder äußerlich mit festen Sprengstoffen behaftet sind;

7. Sprengpräparate, bei welchen die einzelnen an und für sich nicht sprengkräftigen Bestandteile in einem geschlossenen Behälter durch leicht brechbare Scheidewände oder Hahnvorrichtungen so lange getrennt gehalten werden, bis die Explosion, durch Zertrümmerung, Verschiebung der Scheidewände oder Öffnen der Hahnvorrichtungen veranlaßt, stattfinden soll.

§ 4. Wer Sprengstoffe in Mengen von mehr als 35 kg Bruttogewicht versendet, muß unter Angabe der Bestimmungsorte der Ortspolizeibehörde des Versendungsortes den Frachtschein zur Visierung vorlegen. Der Empfang der Sendung ist vom Empfänger auf dem dem Frachtscheine beigefügten Lieferscheine zu bescheinigen. Die bescheinigten Lieferscheine sind der Ortspolizeibehörde des Versendungsortes jederzeit auf Verlangen vorzulegen.

§ 5. Wer an der Versendung von solchen Sprengstoffen, welche den Vorschriften des Reichsgesetzes vom 9. Juni 1884 gegen den verbrecherischen und gemeingefährlichen Gebrauch von Sprengstoffen (R.G.Bl. S. 61) unterliegen, in der Weise teilnimmt, daß er dabei in den Besitz von Sprengstoffen gelangt (Spediteur, Transportführer, Transportbegleiter), muß den vorgeschriebenen Erlaubnisschein zum Besitz von Sprengstoffen oder beglaubigte Abschrift desselben während der Dauer seines Besitzes stets bei sich führen und auf Verlangen vorzeigen.

§ 6. Für die Versendung auf Land- und Wasserwegen sind Sprengstoffe in hölzerne, haltbare und dem Gewichte des Inhalts entsprechend starke Kisten oder Tonnen, deren Fugen so gedichtet sind, daß ein Ausstreuen nicht stattfinden kann, und welche nicht mit eisernen Reifen oder Bändern versehen sind, fest zu verpacken. Statt der hölzernen Kisten oder Tonnen können auch aus mehrfachen Lagen sehr starken und steifen, gefirnißten Pappdeckels gefertigte Fässer (sogen. amerikanische Fässer) verwendet werden. Die zum Transporte von Pulver, Sprengsalpeter und brennbarem Salpeter (§ 2 Ziffer 1) verwendeten Behälter dürfen keine eisernen Nägel, Schrauben oder sonstige eiserne Befestigungsmittel haben.

Pulver, Sprengsalpeter, brennbarer Salpeter (§ 2 Ziffer 1) und das aus gelatinierter Nitrozellulose mit oder ohne Salpeter hergestellte Pulver (§ 2 Ziffer 3) darf in metallene Behälter, ausgenommen solche von Eisen, verpackt werden. Vor der Verpackung in Tonnen oder Kisten müssen diese Stoffe entweder in Pakete (Blechbehälter) bis zu höchstens $2^1/_2$ kg Gewicht verpackt oder in dichte, aus haltbaren Stoffen gefertigte Säcke, Mehlpulver in Säcke aus Leder oder dichtem Kautschukstoff geschüttet werden.

Die im § 2 Ziffer 2 aufgeführten Sprengstoffe dürfen ebenso wie die nach § 2 Ziffer 5 zugelassenen Sprengstoffe, soweit die Versendung der letzteren auf Eisenbahnen nur in Patronenform erfolgen darf, nur in Patronen, nicht auch in loser Masse versendet werden. Diese Patronen sowie Patronen aus gepreßter Schießbaumwolle mit oder ohne Paraffinüberzug (§ 2 Ziffer 3) sind durch eine Umhüllung von Papier in Pakete zu vereinigen. Die Patronen sind in den Paketen und diese in den sie umschließenden Behältern fest zu verpacken. Bei nitroglyzerinhaltigen Sprengstoffen sind die Patronen in den Paketen mittels Wellpappe so zu verpacken, daß die Patronen schichtweise in ihrer Lage festgehalten werden, und die Pakete in die sie umschließenden Behälter so fest einzusetzen, daß sie sich nicht gegeneinander verschieben können. Für die Ausfuhr bestimmte Sprengstoffe werden von der Vorschrift der Benutzung von Wellpappe bei der Verpackung nicht betroffen.

Gepreßte Schießwollkörper mit mindestens 15 Prozent Wassergehalt dürfen auch in dichtschließende Blechbüchsen oder Pappschachteln verpackt werden.

Für die Versendung der Nitrozellulose mit mindestens 20 Prozent Wassergehalt ist feste Verpackung in starkwandige, luftdichte Behälter erforderlich.

Rohmasse für rauchloses Pulver (§ 2 Ziffer 2d) darf lose verpackt werden. Sie muß jedoch vor der Verpackung in einer Tonne oder Kiste (Absatz 1) in einem Beutel aus Kautschukstoff dicht verschnürt werden.

Sprengstoffe jeder Art, einschließlich der geladenen Geschosse, dürfen nicht mit Zündungen oder Zündschnüren versehen sein. Auf Gewehr- und Geschützpatronen findet diese Bestimmung keine Anwendung, doch dürfen die geladenen Geschosse von Geschützpatronen Zündungen nicht tragen. Geladene Geschosse und die geladenen Geschosse von Geschützpatronen müssen einen sicheren Abschluß der Sprengladung besitzen. Es ist untersagt, Zündungen, Zündschnüre oder Patronen für Feuerwaffen mit anderen Sprengstoffen in dieselben Behälter zu verpacken.

Die zur Verpackung von Sprengstoffen dienenden Behälter müssen je nach ihrem Inhalte mit der Aufschrift: Pulver, Sprengsalpeter, brennbare Salpeter, Pulver aus Nitrozellulose und Salpeter, geladene Geschosse, Geschützpatronen, Kartuschen, Petarden, Feuerwerkskörper, Zündungen, Dynamitpatronen, Kohlendynamitpatronen, Sprenggelatinepatronen, Gelatinedynamitpatronen, Karbonitpatronen, Schießbaumwolle usw. versehen sein. Außerdem müssen dieselben mit der Firma oder der Marke der Fabrik, aus welcher die Sprengstoffe herrühren, bezeichnet sein, oder eine von der Zentralbehörde gebilligte und öffentlich bekannt gemachte Bezeichnung der Fabrik tragen. Die zur Verpackung von nitroglyzerinhaltigen Sprengstoffen dienenden Kisten sind an zwei gegenüberliegenden Schmalseiten mit zuverlässigen Handgriffen oder Handleisten zu versehen; bei Fässern und Tonnen sind solche Handgriffe nur insoweit erforderlich, als nicht durch tief eingelassene Böden und Deckel eine feste Handhabe gegeben ist. Für die Ausfuhr in das Ausland bestimmte Behälter werden hiervon nicht betroffen.

Das Bruttogewicht der Versendungsstücke darf bei Pulver, Sprengsalpeter, brennbarem Salpeter (§ 2 Ziffer 1), bei Schießbaumwolle (§ 2

Ziffer 3), bei Kartuschen, Petarden, Feuerwerkskörpern oder Zündungen (§ 2 Ziffer 4) 90 kg, bei sonstigen Sprengstoffen 35 kg nicht übersteigen. Auf prismatisches Geschützpulver in Kartuschen finden diese Gewichtsbestimmungen keine Anwendung. Für Versendungsstücke von geladenen Geschossen und Geschützpatronen darf das Höchstgewicht 150 kg nicht übersteigen. Für Behälter mit einem Geschoß oder mit einer Geschützpatrone kommt diese Gewichtsgrenze in Wegfall.

Die für den Eisenbahnverkehr jeweilig vorgeschriebene Verpackung genügt auch für die Versendung auf Land- und Wasserwegen.

II. Besondere Bestimmungen für den Landverkehr.

§ 7. Die Beförderung von Sprengstoffen auf Fuhrwerken, welche Personen befördern, ist verboten.

Eine Ausnahme findet nur statt, wenn in dringenden Fällen allgemeiner Gefahr, z. B. bei Eisstopfungen, die nötigen Sprengbüchsen und das zu deren Füllung erforderliche Material unter zuverlässiger Begleitung in kürzester Frist nach dem Bestimmungsorte geschafft werden soll.

§ 8. Bei dem Verpacken und dem Verladen sowie bei dem Abladen und Auspacken darf Feuer oder offenes Licht nicht gehalten, Tabak nicht geraucht werden.

Das Verladen und Abladen hat unter sorgfältiger Vermeidung von Erschütterungen zu erfolgen. Die Versendungsstücke dürfen deshalb nie gerollt oder abgeworfen werden. Das Verladen nitroglyzerinhaltiger Sprengstoffe auf Fuhrwerke und das Abladen von solchen darf nur an Rampen oder gleichwertigen Einrichtungen unter Benutzung von weichen Unterlagen stattfinden. Das Auf- und Abladen darf nur von zuverlässigen, unterrichteten Personen und unter Aufsicht erfolgen.

Soll das Verladen oder Abladen ausnahmsweise nicht vor der Fabrik oder dem Lagerraum oder innerhalb dieser Räume geschehen, so ist hierzu die Genehmigung der Ortspolizeibehörde einzuholen.

§ 9. Die Versendungsstücke müssen auf dem Fuhrwerke so fest verpackt werden, daß sie gegen Scheuern, Rütteln, Stoßen, Umkanten und Herabfallen aus ihrer Lage gesichert sind, insbesondere dürfen Tonnen nicht aufrecht gestellt, müssen vielmehr gelegt und durch Holzunterlagen unter Haar- oder Strohdecken gegen jede rollende Bewegung gesichert werden.

§ 10. Sprengstoffe dürfen nicht mit Zündhütchen, Zündpräparaten oder sonstigen leichtentzündlichen oder selbstentzündlichen Gegenständen zusammen verladen werden.

Die im § 2 und 3 aufgeführten Stoffe dürfen nicht mit Pulver, Sprengsalpeter, brennbarem Salpeter (§ 2 Ziffer 1), Kartuschen, Petarden, Feuerwerkskörpern, Zündungen (§ 2 Ziffer 4) oder mit Patronen für Feuerwaffen zusammen verladen werden.

§ 11. Zur Beförderung von Sprengstoffen dienende Fuhrwerke müssen so dicht schließende Wagenkasten besitzen, daß die Sprengstoffe nicht verstreut werden können. Sind die Wagenkasten oben offen, so müssen sie mit einem dichtschließenden, feuersicheren Plantuche (z. B. imprägnierte Leinwand) überspannt sein.

Auch die Vorder- und Hinterseite der Fuhrwerke sind mit demselben Materiale zu schließen.

Zum Sperren der Räder dürfen nur hölzerne Radschuhe angewendet werden; bei Eisbahn ist eine eiserne Sperrvorrichtung (Krätzer) gestattet, sofern sie ganz vom Radschuhe bedeckt ist.

Die Fuhrwerke müssen als Warnungszeichen eine von weitem erkennbare, stets ausgespannt gehaltene schwarze Flagge mit einem weißen P führen.

Beim Verladen der Sprengstoffe auf Fuhrwerke und beim Abladen von solchen müssen die Zugtiere ausgespannt sein.

§ 12. Fuhrwerke, welche Sprengstoffe führen, dürfen niemals ohne Bewachung bleiben

Auf denselben darf Feuer oder offenes Licht nicht gehalten, Tabak nicht geraucht werden. Auch in der Nähe der Fuhrwerke ist das Anzünden von Feuer oder Licht sowie das Tabakrauchen verboten.

§ 13. Fuhrwerke, welche Sprengstoffe führen, dürfen nur im Schritt fahren und von Fuhrwerken sowie von Reitern nur im Schritt passiert werden.

Besteht ein Transport aus mehreren Fuhrwerken, so müssen diese während der Fahrt eine Entfernung von mindestens 50 m untereinander innehalten.

§ 14. Bei jedem Aufenthalt von mehr als einer halben Stunde ist eine Entfernung von mindestens 300 m von Fabriken, Werkstätten und bewohnten Gebäuden einzuhalten.

Die Ortspolizeibehörde darf, falls eine geeignete Haltestelle in solcher Entfernung nicht zu finden ist, gestatten, daß eine Haltestelle in einer geringeren, wenn aber nicht ein anderer Schutz geboten ist, mindestens 200 m betragenden Entfernung von Fabriken, Werkstätten und bewohnten Gebäuden gewählt wird.

Bei einem Aufenthalte von mehr als einer halben Stunde in der Nähe von Ortschaften ist überdies der Ortspolizeibehörde tunlichst schleunig Anzeige zu erstatten; die Ortspolizeibehörde hat darauf die ihr notwendig erscheinenden Vorsichtsmaßregeln zu treffen.

§ 15. Fuhrwerke, welche Sprengstoffe führen, müssen von Eisenbahnzügen oder geheizten Lokomotiven, Dampfwalzen, Dampfpflügen und ähnlichen Maschinen möglichst weit entfernt bleiben,

Neben der Eisenbahn herlaufende Wege sowie Wege, auf welchen Dampfstraßenbahnen liegen, dürfen nur dann von solchen Fuhrwerken befahren werden, wenn der Bestimmungsort von Frachtfuhrwerk auf einem anderen gut fahrbaren Wege nicht zu erreichen ist.

§ 16. Der Transport durch zusammenhängend gebaute Ortschaften ist nur gestattet, wenn diese nicht von Frachtfuhrwerk auf gut fahrbaren Wegen umfahren werden können. Ist die Durchfahrt unvermeidlich, so hat der Transportführer der Ortspolizeibehörde Anzeige zu erstatten und deren Bestimmungen vor der Einfahrt in den Ort abzuwarten. Die Ortspolizeibehörde hat den zu nehmenden Straßenzug zu bestimmen und von anderen Fahrzeugen möglichst frei zu halten, auch Sorge zu tragen, daß die Durchfahrt ohne unnötigen Aufenthalt und mit Vermeidung besonderer Gefahren erfolgt.

§ 17. Werden zur Beförderung von Sprengstoffen Fuhrwerke verwendet, welche mit festen, dicht schließenden und feuersicher hergestellten, während des Transports unter Verschluß gehaltenen Wagenkasten versehen sind, so finden hinsichtlich der Beförderung solcher Transporte nur die Vorschriften im § 11 Absatz 3 und 4, § 12, § 13 Absatz 1 und § 14 Anwendung, und zwar die des § 14 mit der Maßgabe, daß die regelmäßig einzuhaltende Entfernung 200 m beträgt.

§ 18. Gerät eine Sprengstoffsendung unterwegs in einen Zustand, daß der weitere Versand bedenklich erscheint, so hat die Ortspolizeibehörde, welcher von dem Transportführer tunlichst schleunig Anzeige zu erstatten ist, die zur gefahrlosen weiteren Behandlung der Sendung nötigen Anordnungen zu treffen, und zwar je nach den Umständen unter Zuziehung eines auf ihre Aufforderung von dem Absender zu entsendenden Sachverständigen.

Ist Gefahr im Verzuge, so erfolgt die Vernichtung der Sprengstoffe durch die Polizeibehörde auf Kosten des Absenders ohne vorherige Benachrichtigung desselben, wenn möglich nach der Angabe und unter Aufsicht eines Sachverständigen.

§ 19. Werden Sprengstoffe in Mengen von nicht mehr als 35 kg Bruttogewicht versendet, so finden auf dergleichen Sendungen von den Vorschriften dieses Abschnitts nur die §§ 7 bis 10 Anwendung.

III. Besondere Bestimmungen für den Wasserverkehr.

§ 20. Auf Dampfschiffen, welche Personen befördern, dürfen Sprengstoffe nicht transportiert, an Schießpulver oder Feuerwerkskörpern jedoch darf soviel mitgeführt werden, als zur Abgabe von Signalen notwendig ist.

Die im § 7 enthaltene Ausnahmebestimmung findet auch hier Anwendung.

Fähren, welche Fuhrwerk mit Sprengstoffen übersetzen, dürfen nicht andere Fuhrwerke oder Personen befördern.

§ 21. Die §§ 7 bis 10, 11 Absatz 4, 12 Absatz 1, 13 Absatz 2, 14, 18 und 19 finden für den Schiffsverkehr sinngemäße Anwendung.

Werden zur Beförderung von Sprengstoffen eiserne oder stählerne Schiffe verwendet, welche mit dichtschließenden und feuersicher hergestellten, während des Transports unter Verschluß gehaltenen Laderäumen versehen sind, so finden von den im Absatz 1 angezogenen Vorschriften nur die §§ 8, 11 Absatz 4, 12, Absatz 1, 14, 18 und 19 sinngemäße Anwendung, und zwar die des § 14 mit der Maßgabe, daß die regelmäßig einzuhaltende Entfernung 200 m beträgt.

Zur Versendung auf Schiffen sind Patronen der im § 2 Ziffer 2 aufgeführten Stoffe außerdem mit einer das Eindringen von Wasser oder Feuchtigkeit verhindernden Umhüllung (z. B. mit Gummilösung verklebten Gummibeutel) zu versehen. Auf den Transport auf Fähren findet dies keine Anwendung.

Das Ein- und Ausladen darf nur an einer von der Ortspolizeibehörde dazu angewiesenen Stelle, welche mindestens 300 m von bewohnten Gebäuden entfernt sein muß, erfolgen. Mit unserer Genehmigung kann auch in geringerer Entfernung von bewohnten Gebäuden eine Stelle angewiesen werden, sofern diese Gebäude durch Erdwälle oder in anderer Weise gegen die Wirkungen einer auf der Ladestelle eintretenden Explosion genügend gesichert sind.

Die Ladestelle darf während ihrer Benutzung dem Publikum nicht zugänglich sein und ist, wenn ausnahmsweise das Aus- oder Einladen bei Dunkelheit stattfindet, mit fest- und hochstehenden Laternen zu erleuchten. Die mit Sprengstoffen gefüllten Behälter dürfen nicht eher auf die Ladestelle gebracht oder zugelassen werden, bis die Verladung beginnen soll.

§ 22. Die Sprengstoffe müssen auf dem Schiffe in einem abgeschlossenen Raum, welcher bei Dampfschiffen möglichst weit von den Kesselräumen entfernt ist, unter Deck fest verstaut werden. Bei Verladung in offenen Booten müssen letztere mit einem dichtschließenden, feuersicheren Plantuche (z. B. imprägnierte Leinwand) überspannt sein.

Weder in den so benutzten, noch in den unmittelbar daranstoßenden Räumen dürfen Zündhütchen und Zündschnüre verpackt sein.

Leichtentzündliche oder selbstentzündliche Stoffe, zu welchen Steinkohlen und Koks nicht gerechnet werden, sind von der gleichzeitigen Beförderung überhaupt ausgeschlossen.

§ 22. Sind zu öffnende Brücken oder Schleusen zu passieren, so hat der Transportführer dem Brücken- oder Schleusenwärter Anzeige zu erstatten und vor der Durchfahrt dessen Bestimmungen abzuwarten. Der Brücken- oder Schleusenwärter hat Sorge zu tragen, daß die Durchfahrt ohne unnötigen Aufenthalt und mit Vermeidung besonderer Gefahren erfolgt.

Das Anlegen darf nur an Orten geschehen, welche während des Aufenthalts dem Publikum nicht zugänglich sind.

Die Ortspolizeibehörde ist stets vorher in Kenntnis zu setzen und hat Vorschriften über Ort und Zeit zu geben und Vorsichtsmaßregeln im einzelnen zu treffen.

IV. Bestimmungen über den Handel mit Sprengstoffen sowie über deren Aufbewahrung und Verausgabung.

§ 24. Wer Sprengstoffe feilhalten will, muß davon der Ortspolizeibehörde Anzeige machen. Wer Sprengstoffe feilhalten will, welche den Vorschriften des Reichsgesetzes vom 9. Juni 1884 unterliegen, bedarf dazu der polizeilichen Erlaubnis gemäß § 1 dieses Gesetzes.

Sprengpatronen dürfen von den Fabriken und Händlern und ihren Beauftragten nicht einzeln und lose, sondern nur in den nach § 6 dafür vorgesehenen Behältern oder kleineren dichtschließenden Originalverpackungen der Fabrikationsstätte von $^1/_4$, $^1/_2$, 1 und $2^1/_2$ kg abgegeben werden. Diese Behälter und Originalverpackungen müssen mit der Jahreszahl der Abgabe aus der Fabrikationsstätte und mit einer durch das Jahr der Abgabe fortlaufenden Nummer versehen sein. Dieselbe Zahl und Nummer müssen auch an jeder in den Behälter verpackten Sprengpatrone angebracht sein. Die Angabe der Jahreszahl und Nummer auf den Behältern und Sprengpatronen darf auch in chiffrierter Form erfolgen, welche vor der Anwendung uns zur Genehmigung vorzulegen ist. Außerdem muß an jeder Sprengpatrone der Name des Sprengstoffs sowie die Firma oder Marke der Fabrik oder eine von uns gebilligte und öffentlich bekannt gemachte Bezeichnung der Fabrik angebracht sein. Die von der Zentralbehörde des Bundesstaats, in dem eine Fabrik betrieben wird, dieser Fabrik erteilte Genehmigung ihrer Nummernchiffern und Billigung ihrer Fabrikbezeichnung hat für den Verkehr mit Erzeugnissen dieser Fabrik im ganzen Reiche Geltung.

In dem gemäß § 1 Absatz 2 des Reichsgesetzes vom 9. Juni 1884 zu führenden Register sind Jahreszahl und Nummer der gekauften und abgegebenen Sprengpatronen zu vermerken.

§ 25. Wer sich mit der Anfertigung oder dem Verkaufe von Sprengstoffen befaßt, welche dem Reichsgesetze vom 9. Juni 1884 nicht unterliegen, ist verpflichtet, über alle An- und Verkäufe dieser Stoffe in Mengen von mehr als 1 kg ein Buch zu führen, welches den Namen der Verkäufer und der Abnehmer, den Zeitpunkt des Ankaufs und der Abgabe, die Mengen der gekauften und abgegebenen Stoffe sowie bei Sprengpatronen deren Jahreszahl und Nummer angibt. Dieses Buch ist auf Verlangen der Polizeibehörde zur Einsicht vorzulegen. Hinsichtlich der Buchführung greifen im übrigen die auf Grund des Reichsgesetzes vom 9. Juni 1884 erlassenen Vorschriften Platz.

§ 26. Die Abgabe von Sprengstoffen an Personen, von welchen ein Mißbrauch zu befürchten ist, insbesondere an Personen unter 16 Jahren, ist verboten. Dies gilt insbesondere auch von solchen Feuerwerkskörpern, mit deren Verwendung eine erhebliche Gefahr für Personen oder Eigentum verbunden ist (Kanonenschläge, Frösche, Schwärmer u. dergl). Dagegen findet diese Vorschrift keine Anwendung auf Spielwaren, welche ganz geringe Mengen von Sprengstoffen enthalten. Zündplättchen (Amorces), welche mehr als 7,5 g Sprengmischung (Knallsatz) auf 1000 Plättchen enthalten, dürfen als Spielwaren nicht in den Verkehr gebracht werden.

Die Abgabe von Sprengstoffen, welche den Vorschriften des Reichsgesetzes vom 9. Juni 1884 unterliegen, darf seitens der Fabriken und Händler und ihrer Beauftragten nur an solche Personen erfolgen, welche nach den gemäß § 2 dieses Gesetzes erlassenen Anordnungen zum Besitze von Sprengstoffen berechtigt sind. Bei Staatswerken, welche besonderer Erlaubnis zum Besitze von Sprengstoffen nicht bedürfen, kann die Abgabe an solche Personen erfolgen, welche von der Verwaltung des Werkes zu der Annahme ausdrücklich ermächtigt sind.

§ 27. Die Verausgabung von Sprengstoffen, welche den Vorschriften des Reichsgesetzes vom 9. Juni 1884 unterliegen, an die in Bergwerken, Steinbrüchen, Bauten und gewerblichen Anlagen beschäftigten Bergleute, Arbeiter usw. darf nur von denjenigen Betriebsleitern, Beamten oder Aufsehern bewirkt werden, welche nach den gemäß § 2 dieses Gesetzes erlassenen Anordnungen zum Besitze von Sprengstoffen berechtigt sind. Diese Personen sind verpflichtet, über die Verausgabung ein Buch zu führen, welches den Namen der Empfänger, den Zeitpunkt der Verausgabung, die Menge der verausgabten Stoffe sowie bei Sprengpatronen deren Jahreszahl und Nummer angibt. Bei Staatswerken, welche besonderer Erlaubnis zum Besitze von Sprengstoffen nicht bedürfen, kann die Verausgabung von solchen Personen bewirkt werden, welche von der Verwaltung des Werkes zu der Verausgabung ausdrücklich ermächtigt sind.

Die Leiter der Bergwerke, Steinbrüche, Bauten und gewerblichen Anlagen sind verpflichtet, Maßregeln zu treffen, welche eine Verwendung der zum Verbrauch im Betriebe verausgabten Sprengstoffe durch die Bergleute, Arbeiter usw. zu anderen Zwecken tunlichst ausschließen.

V. Bestimmungen über die Lagerung von Sprengstoffen.

§ 28. Geraten Sprengstoffe auf ihrem Lager in einen Zustand, daß die weitere Lagerung bedenklich erscheint, so finden die Vorschriften des § 18 entsprechende Anwendung.

§ 29. Wer mit Pulver, Sprengsalpeter, brennbarem Salpeter (§ 2 Ziffer 1), Feuerwerkskörpern oder Zündplättchen — Amorces — (§ 2 Ziffer 4) oder solchen Patronen für Handfeuerwaffen, welche nicht unter § 1 Absatz 5b fallen, Handel treibt, darf:

1. im Kaufladen nicht mehr als $2^1/_2$ kg,
2. im Hause außerdem nicht mehr als 10 kg vorrätig halten.

Auf Nachweis eines besonderen Bedürfnisses kann die Erhöhung des Vorrats unter 2 zeitweilig bis auf 15 kg gestattet werden.

Die Aufbewahrung muß in einem auf dem Dachboden (Speicher) belegenen, mit keinem Schornsteinrohr in Verbindung stehenden abgesonderten Raume erfolgen, welcher beständig unter Verschluß gehalten und mit Licht nicht betreten wird. Die Behälter müssen den Bestimmungen im § 6 Absatz 1 und 2 entsprechen und mit stets festgeschlossenen Deckeln versehen sein.

§ 30. Personen, welche nicht unter die Bestimmung des § 29 fallen, bedürfen für die Aufbewahrung von mehr als $2^1/_2$ kg der daselbst genannten Sprengstoffe der polizeilichen Erlaubnis.

§ 31. Größere als die im § 29 angegebenen Mengen dieser Sprengstoffe sind außerhalb der Ortschaften in besonderen Magazinen aufzubewahren, von deren Sicherheit die Polizeibehörde sich überzeugt hat. Die Magazine müssen sich, wenn sie über Tage liegen, im Wirkungsbereiche sachgemäß ausgeführter und unter Aufsicht stehender Blitzableiter befinden.

Handelt es sich um Magazine, welche zu einem der Aufsicht der Bergbehörde unterstehenden Werke gehören, so hat die Polizeibehörde die Prüfung in Gemeinschaft mit der Bergbehörde vorzunehmen.

Es kann angeordnet werden, daß die Schlüssel zu diesen Magazinen in den Händen der Behörde bleiben.

§ 32. Die Aufbewahrung der im § 29 genannten Sprengstoffe an der Herstellungsstätte sowie an der Verbrauchsstätte unterliegt den im § 33 gegebenen Vorschriften.

§ 33. Die im § 2 aufgeführten Sprengstoffe dürfen — abgesehen von den im § 29 vorgesehenen Ausnahmen — nur an der Herstellungsstätte oder an denjenigen Orten, wo sie innerhalb eines Betriebs zur unmittelbaren Verwendung gelangen, oder in besonderen Magazinen gelagert werden.

Für die Lagerung an der Herstellungsstätte sind in Ermangelung besonderer, bei Genehmigung der Anlage gemäß § 16 der Gewerbeordnung vorgeschriebener Bedingungen die Weisungen der Ortspolizeibehörde zu beachten.

Die Niederlagen an der Verbrauchsstätte sowie die besonderen Magazine bedürfen der polizeilichen Genehmigung und sind nach den von der Polizeibehörde zu erteilenden Vorschriften einzurichten.

Für solche Niederlagen oder Magazine, welche zu einem der Aufsicht der Bergbehörde unterstehenden Werke gehören, tritt diese an die Stelle der Polizeibehörde.

Es kann angeordnet werden, daß die Schlüssel zu den Niederlagen oder Magazinen in den Händen der Behörde bleiben.

§ 34. Andere als die im § 2 anfgeführten, insbesondere die im § 3 genannten Sprengstoffe dürfen nur an der Herstellungsstätte gelagert werden.

Zu Versuchszwecken kann die Lagerung neuer Sprengstoffe an anderen Orten von der Landespolizeibehörde gestattet werden.

VI. Strafbestimmungen.

§ 35. Zuwiderhandlungen gegen vorstehende Vorschriften werden nach § 367 Nr. 5 des Strafgesetzbuchs bestraft, sofern nicht härtere Strafen nach dem Reichsgesetze vom 9. Juni 1884 verwirkt werden.

Schlußbestimmungen.

§ 36. Weitergehende bergpolizeiliche Vorschriften und Anordnungen über die Verwendung von Sprengstoffen beim Bergbau werden durch die vorstehenden Bestimmungen nicht berührt. Auch bleiben die internationalen Verabredungen über den Verkehr mit Sprengstoffen unberührt.

§ 37. Diese Polizeiverordnung tritt mit dem 1. Oktober 1905 in Kraft, mit welchem Tage die Polizeiverordnungen der Minister des Innern und für Handel und Gewerbe vom 19. Oktober 1893 und 29. Juni 1898 unwirksam werden.

Literatur.

J. Trauzl, Explosive Nitrilverbindungen, insbesondere Dynamit und Schießbaumwolle. Wien 1870.

Dr. W. F. Gintl, Die Zündwaren und Explosivstoffe. (Ausstellungsbericht.) Wien 1873.

Dr. E. von Meyer, Die Explosivkörper und die Feuerwerkerei. Braunschweig 1874.

G. Nordenström och A. W. Cronquist, Om nitroglycerinhaltiga Sprängämnen. Stockholm 1880.

M. Berthelot, Sur la force des matières explosives d'après la thermochimie. Paris 1883.

Dr. Paul Schellbach, Über die Methoden, den Stickstoffgehalt in Nitroverbindungen zu bestimmen. Berlin 1884.

Das Wesen und die Behandlung von brisanten Sprengstoffen. Berlin 1888.

Cundill-Désortiaux, Dictionnaire des Explosifs. Paris 1893.

Dr. C. Haeussermann, Sprengstoffe und Zündwaren. Stuttgart 1894.

Dr. F. Böckmann, Die explosiven Stoffe. Wien 1895.

Oskar Guttmann, Die Industrie der Explosivstoffe. Braunschweig 1895.

Aktiengesellschaft Dynamit Nobel, Das Dynamit und seine kulturhistorische und technische Bedeutung. Wien 1896.

J. Daniel (Sanford), Explosifs nitrés. Paris 1898.

Technischer Unterricht für die k. und k. Eisenbahntruppen. 6. Teil. Sprengarbeiten. Wien 1900.

Oskar Guttmann, Schieß- und Sprengmittel. Braunschweig 1900.

Dr. J. Daniel, Dictionnaire des matières explosives. Paris 1902.

C. E. Bichel, Untersuchungsmethoden für Sprengstoffe. Berlin 1902.

Vorschrift über die Deponierung, Konservierung, den Umsatz und Transport der Spreng- und Zündmittel des k. und k. Heeres. Wien 1903.

Dr. Gustav Martin, Geschichtliche Entwicklung der Kartellbildung in der deutschen Sprengstoffindustrie. Heidelberg 1903.

Bericht über den V. Internationalen Kongreß für angewandte Chemie. Berlin 1904.

Wilhelm Denker, Die bergmännischen Sprengarbeiten im Lichte der Unfallstatistik. Gummersbach 1904.

L. R. Auzenat, Notions sur les explosifs brisants. Paris.

F. Heise, Sprengstoffe und Zündung der Sprengschüsse. Berlin 1904.

Zentralstelle Neubabelsberg und Bergwerksdirektion Saarbrücken, Versuche zur Prüfung der Empfindlichkeit gefrorener und halbgefrorener Nitroglyzerinsprengstoffe gegenüber plastischen. Berlin 1905.

Bruno Zschokke, Sprengmittel und Sprengarbeit beim Bau des Simplontunnels. Zürich 1905.

Hanns v. Jüptner, Lehrbuch der chemischen Technologie der Energien. Band II. Explosivstoffe und Verbrennungsmotoren. Leipzig und Wien 1906.

Oskar Guttmann, Handbuch der Sprengarbeit. Braunschweig 1906.

André Dejean et Pierre Le Play, Code des Explosifs. Arras 1906.

Léon Gody, Traité théorique et pratique des matières explosives. Namur 1907.

A. Cooper-Key and J. H. Thomson, A Primer of Explosives. London 1905.

Rudolf Feuchtinger, Spreng- und Zündmittelmagazine. Wien 1907.

Dr. H. Brunswig, Die Explosivstoffe; Einführung in die Chemie der explosiven Vorgänge. Wien 1907.

Atti del VI Congresso internazionale de chimica applicata. Roma 1907.

Dinglers polytechnisches Journal.

Berichte der deutschen chemischen Gesellschaft.

Zeitschrift für angewandte Chemie.

Journal of the Society of chemical Industry.

Mémorial des Poudres et Salpêtres.

Mitteilungen über Gegenstände des Artillerie- und Geniewesens.

Zeitschrift für das gesamte Schieß- und Sprengstoffwesen.

Zeitschrift für Berg-, Hütten- und Salinenwesen im preußischen Staate.

„Glückauf", Berg- und hüttenmännische Zeitschrift.

„Der Bergbau", Bergtechnische Wochenschrift.

Annales des mines.

Annales des mines de Belgique.

Annual Reports of His Majesty's Inspectors of Explosives.

Patente.[1]

[1] Register bearbeitet von Dr. Paul Keim.

Autorenregister.[1]

[1] Bearbeitet von Dr. Paul Keim.

Sachregister.[1]

[1] Bearbeitet von Dr. Paul Keim.

Druck von Metzger & Wittig in Leipzig.

www.ingramcontent.com/pod-product-compliance
Lightning Source LLC
LaVergne TN
LVHW042229300926
849161LV00003B/310
* 9 7 8 3 1 1 2 4 3 2 1 9 8 *